MERRILL
BIOLOGY
The Dynamics of Life

Authors

Alton L. Biggs
Donald S. Emmeluth, Ed.D.
Chris L. Gentry
Rachel I. Hays, Ph.D.
Linda Lundgren
Francesca Mollura, Ph.D.

MERRILL
Publishing Company
Columbus, Ohio

A MERRILL BIOLOGY PROGRAM

Biology: The Dynamics of Life, *Student Edition*
Biology: The Dynamics of Life, *Teacher Edition*
Biology: The Dynamics of Life, *Teacher Resource Package*
Biology: The Dynamics of Life, *Transparency Package*
Biology: The Dynamics of Life, *Laboratory Manual, Student Edition*
Biology: The Dynamics of Life, *Laboratory Manual, Teacher Edition*
Biology: The Dynamics of Life, *Test Bank Software*

CONTENT CONSULTANTS

Marie A. DiBerardino, Ph.D.
Professor of Physiology
Department of Physiology and
Biochemistry
The Medical College of
Pennsylvania
Philadelphia, PA

Jerry Downhower, Ph.D.
Professor of Zoology
Department of Zoology
The Ohio State University
Columbus, OH

James A. Gavan, Ph.D.
*Professor Emeritus of
Anthropology*
Department of Anthropology
University of Missouri–Columbia
Columbia, MO

Robert P. Gendron, Ph.D.
Assistant Professor of Biology
Indiana University of
Pennsylvania
Indiana, PA

Donald Kaufman, Ph.D.
Associate Professor of Zoology
Department of Zoology
Miami University
Oxford, OH

Lois A. Pfiester, Ph.D.
Professor of Botany
Department of Botany and
Microbiology
University of Oklahoma
Norman, OK

Richard D. Storey, Ph.D.
Associate Professor of Biology
Department of Biology
Colorado College
Colorado Springs, CO

Susan E. Verhoek, Ph.D.
Professor of Biology
Department of Biology
Lebanon Valley College
Annville, PA

E. Peter Volpe, Ph.D.
Professor of Genetics
Department of Basic Medical
Sciences
School of Medicine
Mercer University
Macon, GA

READING CONSULTANT

Barbara S. Pettegrew, Ph.D.
*Director of Reading/Study Center
Assistant Professor of Education*
Otterbein College
Westerville, OH

REVIEWERS

Maxine A. Claar
Graham High School
Graham, NC

Frank M. Curl
Brazosport High School
Freeport, TX

Rebecca Holt
Lake Highlands High School
Dallas, TX

Susan S. Hutchinson
Benicia High School
Benicia, CA

Mary Loretta Loykasek
Burleson High School
Burleson, TX

Dianne P. Reavis
Southwest Independent High
School
San Antonio, TX

Joe Doyle Reed, Jr.
Big Spring High School
Big Spring, TX

Richard L. Reger
Santa Ana High School
Santa Ana, CA

James C. W. Roberts
Ecorse High School
Ecorse, MI

Timothy Sampson
Weslaco High School
Weslaco, TX

William M. Selenke, Ph.D.
Cincinnati, OH

Joanne Smith
Thornton High School
Denver, CO

Thomas P. Talbot
Skyline High School
Salt Lake City, UT

Sue G. Vantrease
Wichita Falls High School
Wichita Falls, TX

Gary C. Vermillion
Thomas Jefferson High School
Dallas, TX

Gary J. Vitta
West Orange High School
West Orange, NJ

Project Editor: Angela E. Priestley, Ph.D.; **Editors:** Linda Biggs Thornhill, Ellen Powers Geisler, Robert Davisson, Linda K. Blumenthal, Jane Marn Magni; **Production Editor:** Joy E. Dickerson; **Editorial Assistants:** Meg Bishop, Peg MacPherson; **Designer:** Terry D. Anderson; **Production Buyer:** Mark Bourgea; **Project Artist:** David L. Gossell; **Artist:** April Clark; **Illustrators:** David Dennis, Rebecca Dodson, Thomas Gagliano, 158 St. Design Group, Intergraphics, H. K. Portfolio, Tom Kennedy, Steve Botts, Laurie O'Keefe, Publishers Graphics, Jim Shough, Charles Passarelli, Kirchoff/Wohlberg, Ruth Krabach, Illustrated Alaskan Moose Studios, Tim Jobst; **Photo Editor:** Mark Burnett; **Photo Researchers:** Sam Dudgeon, Sheila Norman

ISBN 0-675-06508-9

Published by

Merrill Publishing Company

Columbus, Ohio 43216

9 10 11 12 13 14 15 RRW/MC 00 99 98 97 96 95 94

Alton Biggs is Biology Instructor and Science Department Chairperson at Allen High School, Allen, Texas. Mr. Biggs received his B.S. in Natural Sciences and an M.S. in Biology from East Texas State University. He was a Resident in Science and Technology at Oak Ridge National Laboratory in 1986. Among the teaching awards he has received are Texas Outstanding Biology Teacher in 1982, Presidential Science Teacher Award Finalist in 1986, and Texas Teacher of the Year Finalist in 1988. Mr. Biggs has led several naturalist excursions abroad and is the founding president of TABT.

Donald Emmeluth is Professor of Science at Fulton-Montgomery Community College, Johnstown, NY. He received a B.S. in Biology from Wagner College, an M.S. in Education from S.U.N.Y., Plattsburgh, an Ed.S. in Curriculum and Instruction, and an Ed.D. in Microbiology and Science Education from Florida Atlantic University. Dr. Emmeluth is a past president of NABT, recipient of the Chancellor's Award for Excellence in Teaching, and is listed in Who's Who in American Education 1988, 1989, 1990, Men of Achievement, and Outstanding Educators of America. He is active in many national, state, and local science and teacher organizations.

Chris Gentry is Biology Instructor and doctoral student in the Physiology Department, University of Nevada School of Medicine, Reno, Nevada. Previously she taught high school biology at Boise High School, Boise, Idaho. She received a B.S. in Biology from Boise State University and an M.S. in Microbiology from Washington State University. Ms. Gentry received the Presidential Award for Excellence in Science Teaching in 1986, the NABT Biology Award in 1987, and the Sigma Xi Distinguished Science Teaching Award in 1987.

Rachel Hays, presently a substitute science and math teacher in Loveland, Colorado, is a former Instructor at the junior high and college levels in Colorado and California. Dr. Hays received a B.S. in Biology from San Diego State University, an M.S. in Botany from the University of California, Davis, and a Ph.D. in Botany from the University of California, Davis.

Linda Lundgren is Biology Instructor at Bear Creek High School, Lakewood, Colorado. Mrs. Lundgren received a B.A. in Journalism and Zoology from the University of Massachusetts and an M.S. in Zoology from the Ohio State University. She has been awarded several grants for research in many areas of biology, including wildlife biology, mountain and desert ecology, animal behavior, microbiology, and entomology. Mrs. Lundgren has also been awarded grants to develop new curriculum materials for a variety of science classes. She has also served in the community as a park ranger, wildlife refuge manager, and environmental consultant.

Francesca Mollura is Assistant to the Science Coordinator of the Kansas City Schools, Kansas City, Missouri. She has taught at the high school and college levels for 24 years. Dr. Mollura received a B.S. in Chemistry from Le Moyne College, Syracuse, NY, an M.S. in Biology from Boston College, Chestnut Hill, MA, an M.S. in Physiology and a Ph.D. in Science Education from Cornell University, Ithaca, NY. She is active in many education associations and was the recipient of the Edison Foundation Citation for Distinguished Service in Science Education

The Author Team

BIOLABS

Have you ever seen an animal capture and eat its prey using tentacles that surround its mouth? You may do this in one of the 36 **Biolabs** provided in your textbook. In another **Biolab,** you may recreate some of the events in the origin of life on Earth. In other **Biolabs** you test the effects of pollution and excess nutrients on tiny water organisms. **Biolabs** let you *do* biology as you use your knowledge to predict the outcome of biological events.

TABLE of CONTENTS

THINKING CRITICALLY

Do you think fish drink water? Why would they need to? How can fish survive in salty seawater? In **Thinking Critically** features, you can apply your knowledge to solve biological problems and puzzles. What happened millions of years ago that produced coal deposits all over the world? Why isn't coal being made today—or is it? How does the addition of starch to plastic make the plastic biodegradable? These are some of the problems you can solve in **Thinking Critically.**

DEVELOPING A VIEWPOINT

Today it is possible to make completely new kinds of organisms in the laboratory. Should this be done? Should an organism's "inventor" be able to obtain a patent on the organism? This is an example of an issue in which science and society interact as people line up on both sides of the debate. **Developing a Viewpoint** features discuss real cases and present questions to help you form your *own* opinion about a current topic of debate in biology. Should a person's genetic code be used as evidence in a criminal trial? Should people be prevented from cutting down forests to provide farmland? These and many other issues involving ethics, ecology, health, pollution, and conservation are presented in **Developing a Viewpoint** features.

BIOTECHNOLOGY

What do biologists do with new information about living things? A fungus that causes diseases in some plants produces a chemical that gives us delicious seedless grapes. Learning to put that chemical to practical use is one example of biotechnology. Your textbook's **Biotechnology** features show examples of biological knowledge at work. In **Biotechnology,** you learn how bacteria help rid coal of acid-producing sulfur or how understanding the way we experience pain helps scientists develop powerful new pain killers.

CAREER CHOICES

What will you do with everything you learn in your biology course? Maybe you'll begin thinking about a career in a field involving biology. **Career Choices** are designed to give you some examples of career paths you might follow. With a college degree, you might become an immunologist who works to understand disease and finds ways to prevent it. Or, you could be a wildlife biologist working to discover how Earth's wild organisms live in balance with their surroundings.

With a high school diploma plus additional training you could enter the field of floriculture, in which you grow and sell plants and cut flowers, or become a forestry technician who scouts the forest for evidence of disease and selects trees for harvest.

APPENDICES

SKILL HANDBOOK

GLOSSARY-INDEX

814

Why are *you* taking biology?

"A lot of my friends signed up for it."   **"It might be fun."**   "I like science."

"I don't know."

"I have to take more science to graduate."   **"I had to take *something* third period."**

"I like the teacher."

TAKE THE BIOLOGY CHALLENGE

Why *should* you take biology? What can you expect to get out of it? What's so special about biology? What is the Biology Challenge?

You'll learn in Chapter 1 of ***BIOLOGY: THE DYNAMICS OF LIFE*** that biology is the study of life. You'll learn in this course that the daily lives of all organisms—from one-celled amoebas to giant redwood trees—are filled with challenges. All organisms must survive, adjust to surroundings, and reproduce. Biology is a study of how evolution operates as a mechanism that—over time—uniquely equips each species as it meets the challenges of living.

The ways in which living things have evolved are as numerous as the number of species on Earth— estimated in the millions. Through your study of biology, you will come to appreciate the wonderful diversity of species on Earth and the way each species fits into the dynamic pattern of life on our planet.

When you think of life, you probably think of growth, development, movement, and change. But, an equally important aspect of life is about staying the same. Even while responding to a dynamic, changing environment, the conditions within an organism must stay in balance. Maintaining a balance in the face of changing conditions is called homeostasis. In humans, a common example of homeostasis is sweating. When your body begins to overheat, you begin to sweat. Sweating helps to cool you down. When your body cools off, you stop sweating. Sweating is just one way your body maintains a constant temperature of 37°C.

Evolution and homeostasis are two of the key concepts you'll learn about when you take on the Biology Challenge. You'll learn how change and staying the same are reflected in the ability of all living things to meet the basic challenges of living.

Coast redwoods

Amoebas

Bios (life) + logos (the study of) = CHALLENGE

Biology is a challenge to biologists—the scientists who have chosen the study of life as a profession. Every day, new species are discovered and named, new information about life becomes available, the technology to study life improves, and new ideas are formed. Biologists are driven by a desire to contribute to knowledge of the natural world, by a wish to solve ecology and health problems, and by plain old curiosity.

Biology is a challenge to citizens. The separation of science and society becomes less clear every day. How will we use the knowledge, technology, and ideas coming from the field of biology? What will we do with new capabilities to manipulate genetic material or to alter habitats? You, as a citizen, will have to make decisions about biology. With knowledge from this course, you will be able to examine the issues and make informed choices.

Biology is a challenge to students to learn and teachers to teach. It's not the hardest subject in the world, but it will require study, preparation, and thought. If you undertake the Biology Challenge, your reward will be more than a good grade on your report card. Your reward will be a deeper knowledge of our planet and the life it shelters.

You'll also gain useful skills from **BIOLOGY: THE DYNAMICS OF LIFE.** For example, you'll learn to examine problems scientifically by observing, hypothesizing, experimenting, analyzing data, and drawing conclusions. This scientific approach to problem solving is an important part of studying biology that you'll be able to use in solving all sorts of problems—not just in biology class. You'll use it again and again as you meet challenges in your own life—at school, at work, in your family, and in your community.

You already have most of the tools you need to meet the Biology Challenge. You can already read, write, discuss, debate, and ask questions. This book, **BIOLOGY: THE DYNAMICS OF LIFE,** is yet another tool. Your challenge is to use these tools to learn biology to the best of your ability. It's that simple.

Seattle skyline

xiv

Mountain lion

Biology can be fun!

What do you and an octopus have in common? How is a saguaro cactus like a city? Why are calico cats almost always female? How do the feet of a caribou keep from freezing? How does a slice of pizza become energy you can use? Why are baby diapers controversial?

These questions (and many more) are answered in **BIOLOGY: THE DYNAMICS OF LIFE.** Biology is not all hard work—it can be fun, too. As you work through this book, you'll find answers to *your* questions about the natural world, as well as new questions to ask. Biology is, after all, the study of your world and *you.* What could be more interesting?

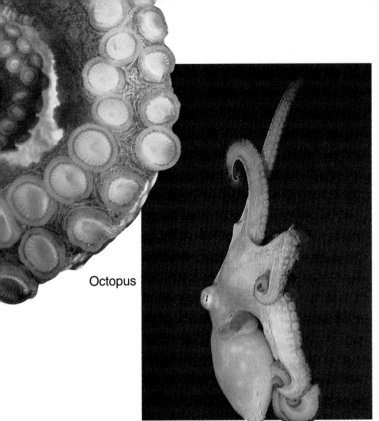

Octopus

Saguaro cactus

We'd like to hear from you . . .

The authors and editors of **BIOLOGY: THE DYNAMICS OF LIFE** have worked hard to give you a textbook that helps, not hinders, your study of biology. You'll find lots of features in this book that clarify, illustrate, simplify, highlight, and extend the basic ideas, and help make sense of hard concepts. That was our challenge.

How did we do? Please let us know by writing to the address below. Tell us what you like and don't like about this book. But, most of all, let us know how you're coming along in your efforts to meet the Biology Challenge.

Write to: Executive Editor, Science
Merrill Publishing Company
936 Eastwind Drive
Westerville, OH 43081

LIFE

What is life?
It is the flash of a firefly in the night.
It is the breath of a buffalo in the wintertime.
It is the little shadow which runs across the grass
    and loses itself in the sunset.

Crowfoot

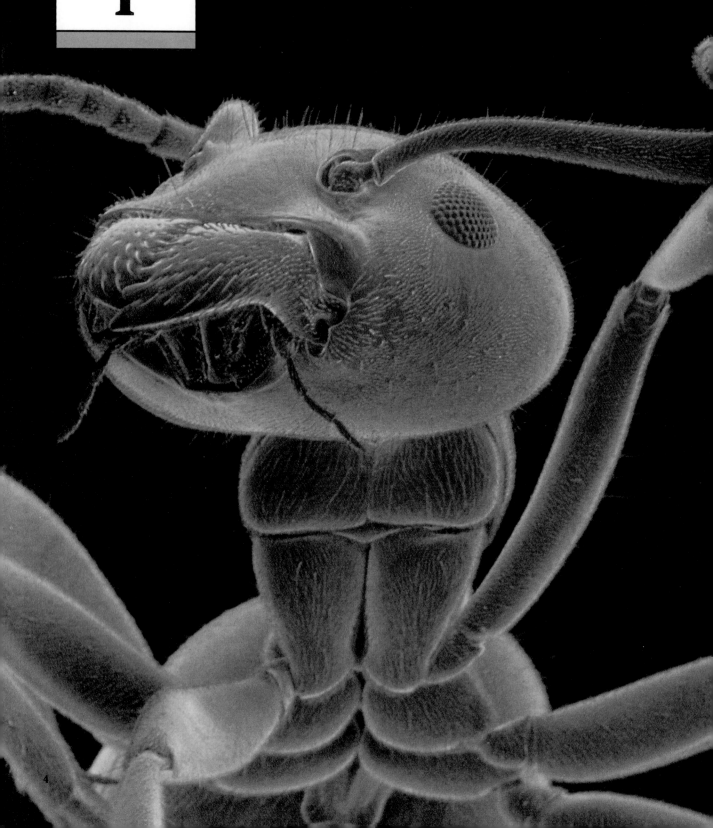

BIOLOGY: THE SCIENCE OF LIFE

How would you describe scientists? Are they strange or careless in their appearance? Are they a lot more intelligent than other people? Do they spend all of their days and nights working in laboratories and wearing white coats? This is the mental image of scientists that many students hold. Before you label scientists as weird, you should find out something about them.

Where would you go to find scientists at work? Whom would you ask to get information about scientists and their work? When you learn how scientists think and act, you may find that you need only to look in a mirror to find a scientist.

SCIENCE IN OUR LIVES

Are scientists really different from other people? Like you, scientists are curious about the world around them. They want to make the world a better place to live. As you will see, anyone who is curious enough to learn how the world works and who takes a logical approach to solving problems is entitled to be called a scientist.

Objectives:
- describe a scientist.
- distinguish between science and technology.
- list four limitations on science.

1:1 Science and Technology

Scientists spend much of their time asking questions. To answer these questions, they conduct experiments, make observations, and collect information. The information gathered becomes part of a body of knowledge about our world. This body of knowledge makes up one part of what is called science. However, science also is a method of thinking and acting that leads to a greater understanding of nature. Thus, science is both information about nature and a process of finding answers and seeking explanations.

Every day you use many products of technology. **Technology** is the practical application of science. Your television set, your toothbrush, a computer, and the microscopes in your classroom are examples of practical applications of science. Society uses the products of its technology to improve the standard of living for its members. New technology depends on information supplied by

science:
scire (L) to know

technology:
techne (GK) skill, art
logos (GK) study of

An ant as seen under a scanning electron microscope

scientists. In turn, scientists depend on the new equipment and materials developed by technology. For example, science has provided knowledge about the action of viruses in causing diseases. This knowledge has led to the development of new drugs that fight viruses. These drugs are then used as tools in experiments to learn more about viruses and disease.

Curiosity is the main characteristic of scientists. They enjoy finding out what things are, what they are made of, and how they are related to other things in nature. Scientists also like to learn how events in nature happen. Most scientists believe that curiosity does not have to be aimed at particular problems of society. Instead, they tend to believe that any new knowledge about nature is important. If the knowledge has a practical application that can benefit society, then so much the better. On the other hand, society usually considers problems involving the life and health of its citizens important. Most modern science is funded by society through governments. Therefore, money and equipment for scientific research is directed toward society's most important problems. It is up to informed citizens to decide what those problems are.

There is nothing good or bad about scientific knowledge. However, the technology that people develop from that knowledge can be helpful or harmful—sometimes both. Many of the products of technology make our lives better. Discoveries in medicine, nutrition, and agriculture help people to live longer. New medical equipment and drugs provide better diagnosis and treatment of diseases and injuries. But with these advances have come new problems. As people live longer, the world's population increases. Resources are used up more rapidly. Waste products, pollutants, and toxic materials accumulate. Solving these problems has become a new part of the science agenda.

FIGURE 1–1.

Increased yields and quality of food crops have resulted from new agricultural technology. This technology is a result of scientific discoveries in biology.

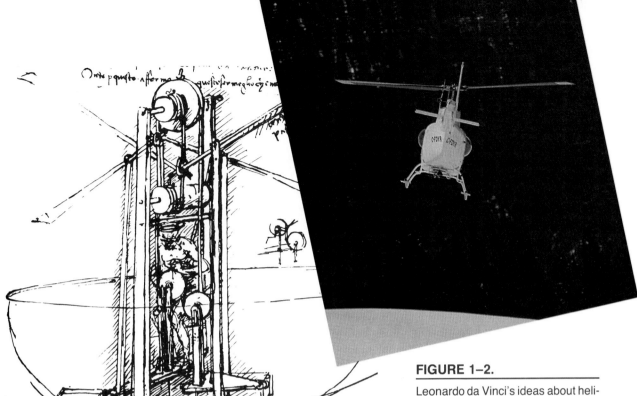

FIGURE 1–2.

Leonardo da Vinci's ideas about helicopters could not be developed in his time. Today's technology makes many kinds of aircraft possible.

1:2 Limitations of Science

Science and technology have been responsible for many remarkable achievements. Landing on the moon and sending probes to explore the sun and planets are examples. Producing powerful yet inexpensive portable computers is another. Because of achievements like these, people sometimes have unrealistic expectations of science and technology.

There are limitations on what scientists and engineers can do. Leonardo da Vinci (1452–1519) drew detailed designs for airplanes and helicopters. However, he lived in a time when no one knew how to make the necessary parts or what materials to use. In short, scientists and engineers can't do something if the needed equipment, skills, or materials don't exist. This limitation is often overcome with time. After 400 years, gasoline engines and strong, lightweight materials made airplanes and helicopters possible. Further advances led to rockets, satellites, and space travel.

Answers to scientific questions are often based on measurements. The quality of measurements is limited by the equipment used. As equipment becomes more precise, so do our measurements. As the measurements become more precise, our understanding of nature often changes. At one time, pesticides and other toxic substances were detectable only in fairly large quantities. Today, instruments can measure quantities of substances in parts per billion parts of air or water. As a result, the questions science must answer have changed. It used to be enough simply to determine whether a toxic substance was present or not. Now the question science must answer is, "How much toxic substance is too much?"

NoteWorthy

During the Middle Ages in England, length was measured by a model foot stored in St. Paul's Cathedral. One rod, a surveyor's measure, was taken to be the total length of the left feet of the first sixteen men coming out of church on a certain Sunday.

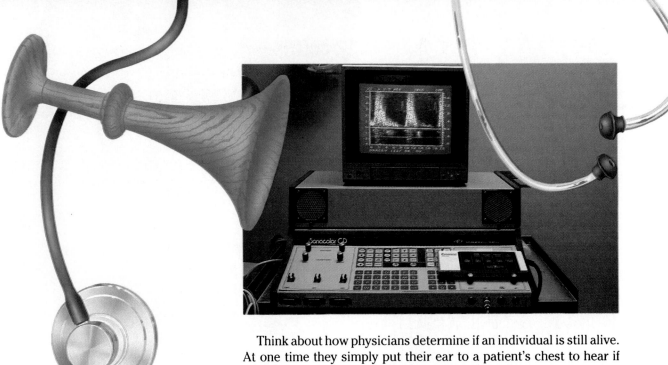

FIGURE 1–3.

The first stethoscopes were an improvement over the technique of putting an ear to the patient's chest. Even the best modern stethoscope cannot reveal all the information that electronic monitors can show.

Think about how physicians determine if an individual is still alive. At one time they simply put their ear to a patient's chest to hear if the patient's heart was still beating. Today, devices can monitor the patient's heartbeat, brain activity, and other bodily functions. As a result, the line between life and death is not so clear. Heart function may continue, even when no brain activity is detectable. This brings science and technology face to face with ethical and moral questions that formerly remained outside science.

Even when knowledge and equipment is available, other factors may limit scientific research. Money may be lacking because of a society's economic problems. Or, a society's ideas of which problems are important may change. Political factors may prevent or limit a scientific research project. For a time there were no communication satellites in space, even though the technology for building and launching them was known. The satellites were launched only after countries agreed not to use them for spying.

REVIEW

1. What is science?
2. How do science and technology differ?
3. What factors limit science and technology?
4. **SKILL REVIEW:** Two people, one a scientist and one a nonscientist, pass a pond each day. They notice that the goldfish are near the surface on cloudy days but are near the bottom on clear days. Suggest ways that their thoughts and attitudes about this observation might differ. For more help, refer to Reading Science in the Skill Handbook, pages 798 to 799.
5. **USING CONCEPTS:** Suppose a new drug has shown evidence that it can reduce the rate of coronary heart disease in rats. What factors might affect a proposal to test the drug on the entire adult population of a city of 100 000?

BIOLAB

Solving a Scientific Problem

Problem: How does gibberellic acid affect plant growth?

Materials

plant seedlings (10)
planting tray
soil
gibberellic acid
   solution

distilled water
droppers (2)
masking tape
marker
metric ruler

Procedures

1. Before beginning, scan Sections 1:3 through 1:6 to see what is known about gibberellic acid's effect on plants. Be sure you understand what a hypothesis is.
2. Copy the data table.
3. Make a **hypothesis** stating how the gibberellic acid will affect growth of plants.
4. Select 10 plants. All plants should be of the same kind. Plants should have been growing in soil for about two weeks.
5. Place plants, soil and all, into a planting tray.
6. Using masking tape and a marker, label the plant positions 1 through 10.
7. Measure each of the plants in centimeters from the seed leaves to the tip of the shoot. Ask your teacher if you are not sure where to measure. Record your measurements in the data table.
8. To plants 1 through 5, apply one drop of gibberellic acid solution to the tip of each shoot.
9. Use a clean dropper and apply one drop of distilled water to the tip of each plant numbered 6 through 10.
10. Water the root systems of all the plants with equal amounts of tap water. Do not get water on the leaves and stems of the plants.
11. Place the tray of plants in a location that gets some sunlight each day. Turn the tray each day and water if soil is drying out. Do not overwater.
12. At one week intervals, repeat steps 5 through 8. Straighten the plant to measure the length of the shoot. Be careful not to crush or damage the tip of the shoot.

Data and Observations

Length of Shoot (cm)										
Interval	1	2	3	4	5	6	7	8	9	10
Start										
Week 1										
Week 2										
Week 3										

Questions and Conclusion

1. Identify the dependent and independent variables in the experiment.
2. Did your results support or oppose your **hypothesis**? How did your results compare to those of other groups in the class?
3. What was the purpose of plants 6 through 10? Why was distilled water applied to these plants instead of just applying nothing?
4. Why was it important that all the plants be treated and measured in the same way?
5. Suggest ways to change the problem statement of this experiment to make it better defined.
6. Using the data gathered by the entire class, could you state a scientific theory about the effects of gibberellic acid? Explain your answer.

Conclusion: What effects of gibberellic acid on plant growth did you observe?

FIGURE 1–4.

Some maple leaves change from green to shades of red and yellow. This change attracts many tourists in some parts of the country. Changes such as this sparked some of the earliest questions about events in nature.

Objectives:

- list the steps in scientific problem solving.
- describe the characteristics of a controlled experiment.
- explain the difference between a hypothesis and a theory.

What is the first step in solving a scientific problem?

SCIENTIFIC PROBLEM SOLVING

Wondering about how things happen is part of human nature. In temperate climates, the leaves of some trees change color and fall to the ground in autumn. Perhaps you wonder what produces the color change and why the leaves fall. Most scientists agree that there is no single method for solving problems. There are probably as many methods as there are problems and people to solve them. One characteristic of scientific problem solving is the logical and organized approach that is taken. You might be surprised to find that you often use a scientific approach in solving your own problems.

1:3 Defining the Problem

A scientist must be specific about the problem to be solved. The first step in solving a problem involves defining and confining the problem. For example, what are the effects of radiation on the life functions of bacteria? At first, this may sound like a good scientific problem. However, there are many kinds of bacteria and many types of radiation. A scientist must define the kind of bacteria and the kind of radiation to be tested. Thus, the starting point is a very specific question that can be answered by observing and experimenting.

Let's examine a real problem that was solved by a scientific approach. In the late 1920s, Japanese rice farmers noticed that some of their rice plants were growing very tall and thin. Those rice plants drooped and fell over, making them impossible to harvest. The farmers called this problem "foolish seedling" disease. Scientists began an investigation. The specific question they asked was, "What causes some rice plants to grow tall and thin?"

The next step in scientific problem solving is to collect information on the problem. Scientists read the scientific literature and talk with other scientists. By doing this, scientists find out what is known about the problem. They may even find that the problem has already been solved. With computers, scientists can gather information from all over the world. The Japanese scientists who studied rice plants had no computers. They searched through scientific journals, but it appeared that no one had ever studied the problem of the drooping rice plants. However, they learned all they could about normal growth of rice plants. The scientists began to examine many rice plants. They found that a fungus was growing on the tall, drooping plants. Healthy rice plants had no fungus. Finally, the scientists were ready to begin their experimentation.

1:4 Making and Testing a Hypothesis

After gathering information on a problem, a scientist suggests a hypothesis. A **hypothesis** is a possible solution to a problem based on all the currently known facts. A hypothesis must be testable and should predict what will happen when it is tested. The scientists hypothesized that when the fungus was present on a rice plant, the plant would grow abnormally. They also hypothesized that the fungus produced a chemical substance that would cause a rice plant to grow too tall and thin to support itself.

NoteWorthy

Louis Pasteur was a French scientist who discovered that many diseases are spread by bacteria. He hypothesized that if he injected an animal with disease-causing microbes that are first weakened in the laboratory, the animal would develop resistance to the disease. In 1881, he tested his hypothesis by injecting weakened anthrax bacteria into sheep. The sheep became resistant to the disease.

FIGURE 1–5.

Both radish plants shown here are the same age. The one on the left is a normal plant. The radish on the right has been treated with the same chemical that affected the diseased rice plants.

a

b

FIGURE 1–6.

Scientists found they could grow the "foolish seedling" fungus in flasks on an artificial medium (a). A fungus closely related to the rice disease fungus causes other plant diseases such as corn ear rot (b).

What are dependent and independent variables?

Having made a hypothesis, scientists test it by doing experiments. An **experiment** is a procedure that tests a hypothesis by the process of collecting information under controlled conditions. In a controlled experiment, two groups are compared. Except for the condition being tested, all conditions are kept identical for the experimental groups. The condition being tested is called the **independent variable.** An independent variable might be the amount of a chemical the experimenter applies to plants in each group. During the experiment, the scientists observe or measure a single factor in both groups, called the **dependent variable.** This could be the growth rate of the plants in each group. The independent variable is present in differing degrees in the experimental groups. The group of plants that receives no chemical is a control group. Scientists compare the effects produced by the independent variable to this group.

In the Japanese scientists' experiment, they transferred some of the fungus from diseased plants to healthy plants. The healthy plants became infected and began to grow tall and thin. Next they experimented to test the hypothesis that the fungus produced a chemical that could cause abnormal growth. The scientists grew the fungus in flasks. In the flasks they placed an artificial food source called a nutrient medium. The scientists assumed that any chemical produced by the fungus would accumulate in the nutrient medium. After growing the fungus, they separated it from the nutrient medium. When a few drops of the medium in which the fungus had grown were placed on the tips of healthy rice plants, they began to grow tall and thin. These plants were the experimental group. Other rice plants were treated with some of the medium that had no fungus grown in it. These plants continued to grow normally. This group of rice plants was the control group. The independent variable was whether or not fungus had grown in the nutrient medium. The dependent variable was the growth of the plants.

1:5 Making and Recording Observations

During the course of an experiment, scientists collect and record data. Data are not only measurements. Data also include every kind of observation made during an experiment. Large amounts of data are necessary to ensure that a hypothesis is adequately tested. This usually means that an experiment must be repeated several times.

Scientists must keep careful records while doing experiments so that both they and other scientists can repeat and test their work. The records must include how the experiment was set up, how it was carried out, what equipment was used, how long the experiment was run, and the results of the experiment. Such records may include graphs, charts, data tables, diagrams, photographs, and written observations.

The Japanese scientists took many photographs of the rice plants before, during, and after their experiments. They carefully measured and recorded the growth of the plants. Their work was published, but communication with other scientists was interrupted during World War II. In 1950, their work was rediscovered by scientists in the United States and England. Other scientists were able to repeat the experiments and confirm the research because the Japanese scientists had made such an accurate recording of their work.

NoteWorthy

Scientific information increases by 13 percent every year. At this rate, it doubles every 5.5 years, and the rate is increasing. At present, almost 7000 scientific articles are written each day.

FIGURE 1–7.

Scientists must make and record observations carefully, but sometimes the laboratory is outdoors in the field.

FOOLISH SEEDLINGS TO DELICIOUS FRUIT

Fifty years ago, the discovery of gibberellic acid provided an explanation for tall, spindly rice plants. In fact, scientists soon discovered that gibberellins were natural growth-control substances in many plants. Soon, people began to think of possible technological applications for the chemical. Today, people who grow flowers and plants use gibberellins to alter the natural growth habits of plants.

One use of gibberellins is in the production of large seedless grapes. Seedless grapes occur in nature, but they are small compared to seeded grapes. The size of a grape depends on the number of cells that are produced during its development. Gibberellin controls cell development and, therefore, grape size. However, gibberellin is produced in the grape seed. Seedless grapes begin life with a seed, but that seed does not develop. With no seed to produce gibberellin, the grape produces no new cells. To produce the large, seedless grapes that you see in the store, grape farmers spray them with gibberellin while they are still on the vine.

Gibberellins applied to celery produce tall stalks. Gibberellin use has increased sugarcane yields and produced plump blueberries and tangelos. Gibberellins have improved the ability of some grasses to withstand cold and are used to suppress a viral disease in cherries.

Gibberellins, which caused rice to grow tall and weak, caused vines to produce these grapes.

1:6 Drawing Conclusions

After data are collected and recorded, they must be organized and analyzed. Graphs and tables help scientists understand the results of an experiment. If the results support the hypothesis, the scientist can accept the hypothesis. If the data do not support the hypothesis, it must be rejected. Scientists then do two things. First they go back and see if there was an error in their experimental procedure. Was the problem defined correctly? Did the experiment test what it was designed to test? Keep in mind that an experiment is never "wrong." All experiments yield valuable information. If there were no errors, scientists use the experimental results to propose a new hypothesis that fits the data.

If the results of several experiments support the hypothesis, you might think that the work is finished. However, for a hypothesis to be useful, it must stand repeated testing. Other scientists should be able to repeat the experiment using the same materials and conditions and get the same results. To accomplish this, the scientists submit a report of the research to other scientists, usually by publishing an article in a scientific journal. In addition, they may report their findings at a scientific meeting.

When a hypothesis has undergone a large number of tests and has not been disproved, it becomes an accepted explanation called a **theory**. A **theory** is a scientific explanation in which there is a high degree of confidence. Because theories have been tested many times,

NoteWorthy

Barbara McClintock, an American scientist, conducted research in genetics using corn plants. Her work showed that genes, which control the traits of organisms, could change position on chromosomes. Other geneticists did not believe her conclusions. She continued her work for over 40 years, however, testing her hypotheses and developing theories. Eventually, her ideas were accepted by other scientists, and, in 1983, Barbara McClintock won the Nobel Prize.

they are difficult to disprove. However, theories can usually be improved upon. A good theory is testable and will provide a framework for further investigations. Exceptions to theories form the basis for new observations and questions. It has been said that every answer leads to more questions. Thus, scientists continue to ask questions and seek answers about our natural world.

Although the term *scientific law* sounds impressive, it is simply a description of a repeated event in nature. That water flows downhill is a law. Theories are explanations of laws. In the case of water running downhill, theories of gravitation and the molecular structure of water explain it. With the rice seedlings, the observation that plants infected with a certain fungus always grow tall and fall over is a simple law. In your study of genetics in Chapter 9, you will learn about Mendel's laws that can predict hereditary characteristics. These laws are explained by theories that deal with translation of the hereditary code.

The Japanese scientists in our tale of the drooping rice plants concluded that the fungus on the diseased plants produced a chemical that caused the abnormal growth of the rice plants. Later experiments isolated this substance. It was named gibberellic acid after the *Gibberella* fungus that produces it. The discovery of gibberellic acid led to many other questions. Does it cause other effects in rice plants? Is this chemical produced only by this fungus? Does gibberellic acid affect plants other than rice? How does it increase stem length? Over 60 different compounds, chemically related to gibberellic acid, have since been identified. We now know that these compounds occur not only in fungi but also occur naturally in many plants. As you will learn in Chapter 18, they are very important growth-control substances in plants.

NoteWorthy

Gibberellic acid has many uses in agriculture today. It helps prevent aging of orange rinds. Gibberellic acid is sprayed on the oranges while they are still on the tree. This allows oranges to be stored on the tree and extends their marketing period.

FIGURE 1–8.

There is no one way to solve scientific problems. This chart shows a method scientists commonly follow.

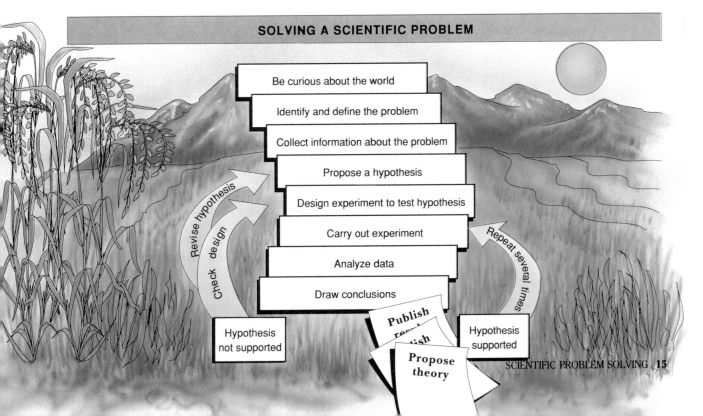

SOLVING A SCIENTIFIC PROBLEM

Be curious about the world

Identify and define the problem

Collect information about the problem

Propose a hypothesis

Design experiment to test hypothesis

Carry out experiment

Analyze data

Draw conclusions

Revise hypothesis

Check design

Repeat several times

Hypothesis not supported

Hypothesis supported

Publish results

Propose theory

6. Outline the procedures that scientists use most often in solving problems.
7. What is the purpose of a hypothesis in a scientific investigation?
8. What are the relationships among hypotheses, theories, and laws?
9. **SKILL REVIEW:** Suppose you wanted to determine the effects of hard water and the presence of iron compounds in the soil on the germination and growth of tomato seedlings. How would you experiment to determine the effects of these factors? Reread Section 1:4 carefully. For more help, refer to Designing an Experiment in the Skill Handbook, pages 802 to 803.
10. **USING CONCEPTS:** What conclusions could have been drawn if the medium in which fungus had been grown had not affected the growth of the rice plants?

THE SCIENCE OF BIOLOGY

Objectives:
- determine the meaning of a scientific term using knowledge of Greek and Latin roots.
- list the levels of organization of a multicellular organism.
- explain why organisms require a supply of energy and matter.
- differentiate among reproduction, growth, and development.
- describe an adaptation and give an example.
- describe homeostasis and give an example.

biology:
bios (GK) life
logos (GK) study of

Most people feel confident that they can tell the difference between living and nonliving things. But living things have some characteristics that are also found in nonliving things. So, how do you tell the difference? Usually, you look at the structure of the thing and observe its activities. You decide whether it's alive based on how it looks and how it acts. You consider all of its characteristics together.

1:7 Biology as a Science

This textbook is about the science of biology. **Biology** is the organized study of living things. Biology includes the study of all aspects of life. People often divide science into different categories—biology, chemistry, physics, earth science. Biology serves to unify all these areas of study. Living things are composed of the same chemical building blocks as nonliving things. Physical principles involving energy, force, and motion apply to all objects, including living objects. Life evolved on Earth and has been greatly affected by Earth's changes. As you see, the boundaries between these sciences are not at all clear. As you enjoy your study of biology, perhaps you will want to learn more about chemistry, physics, and earth science. Remember, a scientist is driven by curiosity about *all* things.

In your study of biology, you will learn many new words. Some may seem complicated. However, many words in science are based on a small number of root words, prefixes, and suffixes drawn from Greek and Latin. If you learn the meanings of some of these word parts, you will be surprised how easy it is to learn the meanings of new words that use the same parts.

The makeup of many science words is given in the margins throughout this book. The word is presented, followed by its breakdown into Latin (L) or Greek (GK) parts. In the margin on page 16, you have just seen how the word biology comes from the Greek word *bios,* life, and *logos,* the study of something. Suppose you have learned that chemistry is the science of matter. Then you see the word *biochemistry.* If you assume that biochemistry is the science of matter that makes up living things, you would be right. A microscope is a device that allows us to see *(skopein)* things that are very small *(mikros).* What do you suppose microbiologists do? If you answered that they study very small living things, you are right again.

Take a moment now and flip through the book and note this feature in the margin. Can you find words that use the same roots? In Appendix B on pages 786 to 789 you will find a list of Greek and Latin roots along with some examples of how biological terms are built from these roots. Breaking words down this way will help you to understand them and to learn new words easily.

FIGURE 1–9.

That an object is living is not always obvious at first. These plants are called lithops from Greek *lithos,* meaning stone.

1:8 Levels of Organization

Organism is the term scientists use to describe an entire and independent living thing. Bacteria, birds, snails, trees, and mushrooms are all examples of organisms. The basic living unit of structure of an organism is the **cell.** Bacteria are examples of organisms that consist of a single cell. A single-celled organism is called a **unicellular organism.** All of the processes of life are carried out within that single cell. Larger organisms consist of many cells. An organism consisting of more than one cell is a **multicellular organism.** Trees, octopuses, and humans may consist of trillions of cells.

uni-, multi-:
  uni (L) one
  multi (L) many

FIGURE 1–10.

Unicellular organisms (a) perform all life functions within one cell. Multicellular organisms, such as birds or a rhinoceros, (b) have many cells.

a

b

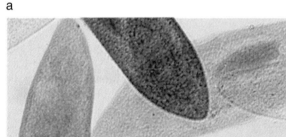

In many ways, a cell is like a factory. Materials are brought into the factory, and the factory constructs the products it needs. Some materials are used to construct the factory's own machinery or to build an entire new factory. Other materials are used as sources of energy to keep the factory going. The cell's activities follow a program that is stored within the cell. The program is the cell's genetic information. This information provides the instructions to build the machinery a cell needs to carry out its activities.

To understand living organisms, you need to understand what they are made of and how they are organized. Like all objects, living things are made of matter. **Matter** is anything that takes up space. Put another way, matter is the "stuff" that makes up everything in the universe. What is *not* matter? Light, radiant heat, and ideas are not matter. Atoms are the basic building blocks of all matter. Chemicals that make up cells are composed of several kinds of atoms. These atoms are almost always chemically combined with one another. In Chapter 3, you will learn more about atoms and how they combine to form life substances. Neither atoms nor the chemicals they form are living things.

The main characteristic that distinguishes living matter from nonliving matter is organization. Cells have been described as bags of organized chemicals. In all but the simplest cells, some chemicals

a

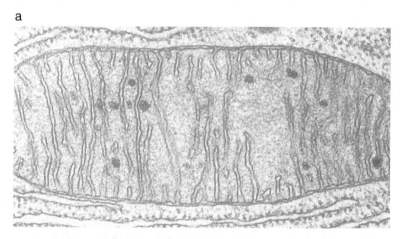

b

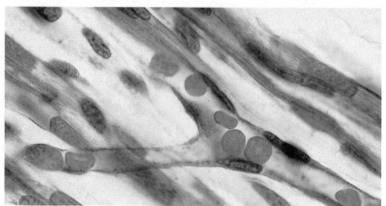

FIGURE 1–11.

An organelle, such as this mitochondrion (a), is a cell structure made up of organized molecules. Organelles perform a single function for a cell. In organs, tissues work together to perform a single function. For example blood must bring food and oxygen to muscle cells (b) and remove waste so that the muscle can continue to contract and do work.

LEVELS OF ORGANIZATION

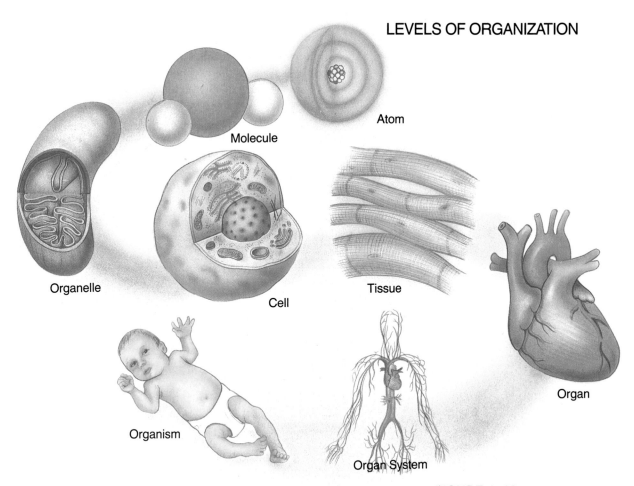

Organelle

Molecule

Atom

Cell

Tissue

Organ

Organism

Organ System

FIGURE 1–12.

A multicellular organism has many levels of organization, from atom and molecule through organ system. The organism can live only if balance and coordination is maintained through all these levels.

are arranged in tiny structures called organelles. An **organelle** is a cell structure that performs a specific function. Some organelles produce other chemicals needed by the cell. Other organelles provide energy for cell activities. Still other organelles move and store materials. Because an organelle does not perform all life functions, it is not considered to be living.

Most multicellular organisms are organized in ways that make life functions most efficient for the whole organism. Their individual cells are specialized and can no longer carry out all life functions. Your muscle and nerve cells are both human cells, but are quite different in form and function. A **tissue** is a group of similar cells organized to carry out a specific function. The outer layer of your skin is one kind of tissue. Its function is to cover and protect the inner layers of the skin. Many plants have tissues whose function is to move water and dissolved substances between leaves and roots.

An **organ** is a group of tissues combined to form a structural unit that performs a specific function. Muscles, eyes, roots, and leaves are examples of organs. Cooperation between organs makes life functions even more efficient. An **organ system** is a group of organs that work together to carry out life functions. Your nervous system and a flower are examples of organ systems.

organelle:
  organon (GK) tool, implement
  ella (GK) small

1:9 Growth and Reproduction

All living organisms, whether unicellular or multicellular, require energy and matter. Energy is the ability to do work. Thus, energy is needed to carry out an organism's activities. In living organisms, food is the fuel that supplies energy. In cells, food is broken down and the energy is released. The organism can then use this energy to carry out all of its functions. An organism's most important activity is maintaining its organization. Living organisms must have a continuous supply of energy or they will die. Even when an organism is resting, it is doing work. A sleeping lion must breathe and its heart must beat. Life processes must be carried out.

Building new cell parts requires both energy and matter. Some needed chemicals come from the breakdown of old parts. Others must be taken into the cell from outside. Cells are constantly making new materials and breaking down old ones. Releasing energy, storing energy, building new chemicals, and breaking down old ones all involve chemical changes. **Metabolism** is all the chemical changes that take place in an organism.

If an organism builds new parts faster than old ones wear out, the organism will grow. **Growth** results in an increase in the amount of living material and the formation of new structures. Different parts of organisms may grow at different rates. The entire organism increases in size as the individual parts grow.

Unicellular organisms may change very little during their lives. However, as multicellular organisms grow, their structure and appearance often change. Humans begin as a single cell. That cell

FIGURE 1–13.

One characteristic of living organisms is growth. Growth results from an increase in living material. A growing organism must have a source of matter and energy. Metabolism includes all the chemical changes that result in growth.

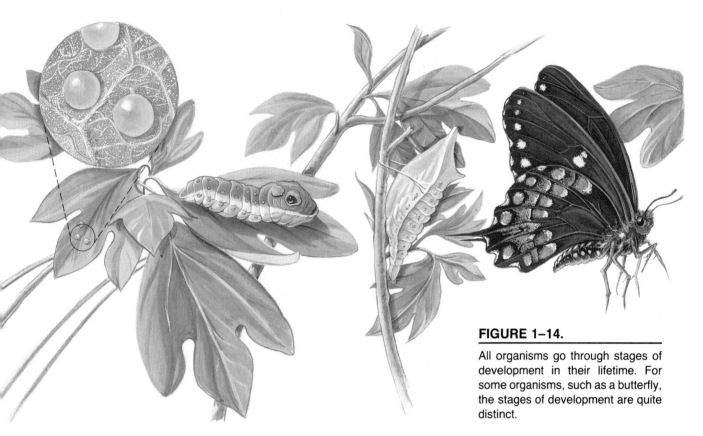

FIGURE 1–14.

All organisms go through stages of development in their lifetime. For some organisms, such as a butterfly, the stages of development are quite distinct.

makes new materials and forms new cells. Groups of cells begin to carry out specific functions. For example, heart muscle cells beat rhythmically while certain eye cells sense light. The shape and appearance of an organism change as it ages and matures. All of the changes that take place during the life of an organism are known as its **development.** At times in your life, you develop rapidly. At other times, little change occurs for many years.

Organisms don't live forever. Instead, they die. For life to continue, organisms must replace themselves. The process by which an organism produces more of its own kind is called **reproduction.** Unicellular organisms, such as bacteria, may simply divide into two new cells. For multicellular organisms, the process is not so simple. Most produce specialized cells which must join to begin the growth of a new organism. An organism reproduces according to the directions in its genetic information. Humans produce humans, not fish. Maple trees produce new maple trees, not pine trees. The process of reproduction ensures that the same kind of organism will survive even after an individual has died.

reproduction:
 re (L) again
 production (L) to bring forth

1:10 Responding to Change

Organisms must interact with their internal and external environment. The external environment includes air, water, weather, temperature, and many other factors. It also includes all the other organisms in the area. The internal environment of an organism includes its temperature and the quantities of water, nutrients, and dissolved minerals inside its body.

Environmental conditions change constantly. Sometimes the change is gradual, as in a slow increase or decrease in the temperature of Earth's atmosphere over many years. At other times the change may be sudden, as with a volcanic eruption or a hurricane. To survive, a group of organisms must have characteristics that allow it to adjust to the changes. Any variation in an individual or group of organisms that makes it better able to cope with its environment is called an **adaptation.** Some adaptations are responses to short-term environmental changes. A bison may respond to an especially cold winter by growing an unusually thick coat of hair. This thick coat is not passed on to the bison's offspring. However, the *ability* to grow a thick coat in response to cold weather is a long-term adaptation. It is passed on to offspring and is a result of evolution, as you will learn when you study Chapter 10.

Any condition to which an organism can react is called a **stimulus** (*pl.* stimuli). Humans and other complex organisms have sense organs that help them to detect different stimuli. The reaction of an organism to a stimulus is called a **response.** When you feel hungry, you respond by getting something to eat. When you find yourself in a dangerous situation, you may respond by moving away from the danger.

The ability to respond to external or internal changes helps an organism maintain a steady internal environment. The regulation of an organism's internal environment to maintain conditions suitable for life is known as **homeostasis.** Homeostasis helps to keep the cells of an organism operating within normal limits. It provides a way of maintaining a balance between internal and external conditions.

FIGURE 1–15.

All organisms are adapted to their surroundings. This species of katydid (a) has camouflage to protect it from predators. Bison (b) have the ability to grow long, thick hair for winter protection.

b

a

FIGURE 1–16.

Even during hibernation, a bear's body maintains homeostasis. Scientists are only beginning to understand its adaptations for maintaining internal balance.

If you are running in a race, your muscles are working hard. They need extra food and oxygen and are producing waste products at a rapid rate. Fortunately, your body responds to maintain homeostasis. Your heart and lungs must respond to these demands by working harder than usual. Large amounts of heat are produced by muscle activity. If your body were unable to get rid of the heat, your temperature would rise and your cells would be destroyed. You sweat and the evaporation of the sweat helps cool your body and maintains its internal temperature. This example happens to be one that applies to humans. All organisms have abilities to maintain chemical and energy balances. In biology, you will learn about many of those abilities as you study the great variety of life on Earth.

homeostasis:
homoios (GK) alike, same
stasis (GK) standing, staying

REVIEW

11. What would happen to a runner who couldn't sweat?
12. Why must organisms take in matter and energy continuously?
13. Distinguish between long-term and short-term adaptations and give an example of each.
14. **SKILL REVIEW:** List the levels of organization in a complex multicellular organism, beginning with the smallest particle of matter. For more help, refer to Reading Science in the Skill Handbook, pages 798 to 799.
15. **USING CONCEPTS:** Differentiate among growth, development, and reproduction.

CHAPTER REVIEW

SUMMARY

1. Science is both knowledge and a process of seeking explanations. Technology is applied science. Science is limited by technology, money, and societal considerations. **1:1, 1:2**
2. Scientists first define a problem, then gather information related to the problem. **1:3**
3. Based on information, a hypothesis is proposed and tested by controlled experiments. **1:4**
4. Scientists carefully experiment, collect data, draw conclusions, and report results. **1:5, 1:6**
5. A theory is a well-tested hypothesis but remains subject to change. **1:6**
6. Biology is the study of living things. **1:7**
7. Organisms are whole living things and are made up of cells. Multicellular organisms are arranged into tissues, organs, and organ systems. **1:8**
8. Organisms need a continuous supply of matter and energy to grow, develop, and reproduce. **1:9**
9. Adaptations allow organisms to respond to changes, thus maintaining homeostasis. **1:10**

LANGUAGE OF BIOLOGY

adaptation	multicellular
biology	organism
cell	organ
dependent variable	organelle
development	organism
experiment	organ system
growth	reproduction
homeostasis	response
hypothesis	stimulus
independent	technology
variable	theory
matter	tissue
metabolism	unicellular organism

Choose the word or phrase from the list above that completes the sentence.

1. ___ is applied science.
2. The science of living things is ___.
3. A(n) ___ is a cell structure that performs a specific function.
4. A possible solution to a problem or answer to a question is called a(n) ___.
5. The condition being tested in a controlled experiment is the ___.
6. Organisms make more organisms by ___.
7. A(n) ___ is composed of many cells.
8. The regulation of an organism's internal environment is known as ___.
9. Cells operating together to carry out a specific function make up a(n) ___.
10. An increase in the amount of living material in an organism is called ___.

REVIEWING CONCEPTS

Choose the word or phrase that completes the sentence or answers the question.

11. The factor that scientists measure in a controlled experiment is the ___.
    a. independent variable
    b. dependent variable
    c. control
    d. hypothesis
12. A ___ is a scientific explanation that has been thoroughly tested by many experiments.
    a. hypothesis   c. law
    b. theory   d. statement
13. A(n) ___ is the smallest unit of life.
    a. cell   c. molecule
    b. atom   d. organelle
14. A reaction to a stimulus is called a(n) ___.
    a. adaptation   c. response
    b. environment   d. evolution
15. All scientists are ___.
    a. highly intelligent   c. biologists
    b. curious   d. strange

16. ___ supplies energy for a cell's activities.
   a. Heat   c. Food
   b. Water   d. Oxygen

17. Changes that occur during an organism's life are its ___.
   a. growth   c. development
   b. reproduction   d. metabolism

18. The prefix *geo-* refers to Earth. The study of Earth is ___.
   a. geometry   c. geology
   b. geochemistry   d. geobiology

19. The design of a new kind of airplane engine is an example of ___.
   a. science   c. technology
   b. knowledge   d. scientific research

20. A procedure that tests a hypothesis is a(n) ___.
   a. theory   c. variable
   b. experiment   d. control.

UNDERSTANDING CONCEPTS

Answer the following questions using complete sentences.

21. How are science, technology, and society related?

22. How do unicellular and multicellular organisms differ? How are they alike?

23. What can be done if a proposed solution to a question does not work?

24. Why must a scientific problem be carefully defined?

25. How are organs and organelles alike? How are they different?

26. How does a cell use matter and energy?

27. List five major activities of living things.

28. What may happen to a bison that is unable to grow a thick coat of hair in cold weather?

29. Why do scientists collect information on a problem before beginning experimentation?

30. List four limitations on science.

APPLYING CONCEPTS

Answer the following questions using complete sentences.

31. Suggest reasons that scientists considered the "foolish seedling" rice disease a significant scientific problem worth investigating.

32. Why are all hypotheses uncertain?

33. What is the relationship between metabolism and homeostasis?

34. Explain how reproduction, growth, and development are related.

35. Why are more complex structures necessary for the survival of complex multicellular organisms?

EXTENSIONS

1. Design a controlled experiment to determine which color of light will cause a bean plant to grow fastest.

2. Make a list of scientific discoveries that have been of great benefit to society. Include the names of the scientists in your list.

3. Research the various definitions of life and death. Write a report discussing the various definitions and describing the problems with each definition.

READINGS

Crick, Francis. "Lessons from Biology." *Natural History,* Nov. 1988, pp. 32–39.

Gould, S. J. "The Chain of Reason vs. the Chain of Thumbs." *Natural History,* July 1989, pp. 12–21.

Wiesner, Jerome B. "On Science Advice to the President." *Scientific American,* Jan. 1989, pp. 34–39.

Chapter 2

DIVERSITY

D id you ever collect insects, baseball cards, or cassette tapes? As your collection grew, you probably attempted to organize it to help you identify groups of similar items. Earth is home to countless organisms. This rich diversity of living things also has been organized in a way that can be useful to everyone. In this chapter, you will begin to learn about the variety of living things on our planet, how organisms have changed over time, and how they are classified into a system to show relationships.

Praying mantis

LIFE ON EARTH

Ever since Nicolas Copernicus (1473–1543) explained that Earth is not the center of the universe, science fiction writers have created other populated worlds in stories. Today, scientists know that the existence of life seems unlikely elsewhere within our solar system. Mercury, the planet nearest to the sun, is far too hot to support life. The surface temperature on Venus, next in distance from the sun, could melt lead. The third planet from the sun is Earth, home to all life as we know it. Mars, the fourth planet, is the only other planet besides Earth known to contain organic matter. The sun's rays may never penetrate the dense gaseous atmospheres of Jupiter and Saturn, the fifth and sixth planets. The outer planets, Uranus, Neptune, and Pluto, are very cold. Our solar system is inhospitable to life— except for the single oasis of Earth.

Objectives:
- sequence the events in Earth's history that led to the origin of organisms and list the major periods of extinction.
- explain the importance of populations in the evolution of species.
- explain the difference between relative and absolute dating of fossils.

2:1 Early Earth

Life on Earth exists in the biosphere. The **biosphere** is the portion of Earth that supports life. It extends from the deepest parts of the ocean to several kilometers up in the atmosphere. The early atmosphere of Earth would have been toxic to most forms of life that exist today. The patterns of land, sea, and atmosphere on Earth were different in the past.

FIGURE 2–1.

Each organism affects and is affected by other organisms in all of Earth's ecosystems. Clockwise from bottom left is a lizard in the desert, mice in a woodland, a butterfly on a thistle, a kingfisher by a stream, and an otter by the seashore.

When did life on Earth begin?

Four billion years ago, Earth's atmosphere is thought to have consisted of water vapor, nitrogen, methane, ammonia, carbon dioxide, and hydrogen. There was no ozone layer to protect Earth's surface from the sun's damaging ultraviolet radiation. Free oxygen began to form by the release of oxygen from the water vapor. At about the same period in Earth's history, life began.

Early life forms probably lived five to ten meters below the surface of the oceans where the ocean water provided a shield from the deadly ultraviolet radiation. There are organisms today that still live in a dark and watery environment. The first life forms were probably consumers. A **consumer** is an organism that obtains its energy from eating other organisms. Some early consumers then changed and obtained their energy by chemosynthesis. **Chemosynthesis** is a chemical process in which the energy from reactions between inorganic molecules is used by organisms to synthesize food.

As the supply of nutrients was used up about three billion years ago, photosynthesis evolved. **Photosynthesis** is the chemical process that uses light, carbon dioxide, and water to synthesize food and produce oxygen. Life forms that used photosynthesis were the first producers. A **producer** is an organism that makes its own food. As more oxygen was released into the atmosphere by producers, the ozone layer formed around the planet. Earth's first organisms were probably like bacteria of today.

Multicellular organisms eventually evolved from the earlier unicellular life forms. After millions of years, the biosphere became a complex system with a great diversity of life. Different organisms became adapted to different environments, resulting in a type of homeostasis in ecosystems. An **ecosystem** is a system on Earth that results from interaction of all the organisms in one area with their environment. What are some interactions between organism and environment shown in Figure 2–1? You will study more about ecosystems in Unit 9.

evolution:
evolutus (L) rolled out

2:2 Variations and Adaptation

Organisms are grouped into species (*pl.* species). A **species** is a group of organisms whose members look alike and successfully mate among themselves. All the organisms of one species that live in the same area make a **population.** All species show variations within populations. Notice in Figure 2–2 how roses differ from one variety to another. All living things have natural variations. Some variations allow organisms to survive in changing environments. Organisms that are adapted to a particular environment will survive. As more and more organisms with particular adaptations survive and reproduce, the population changes and a new species evolves. **Evolution** is a gradual genetic change in a population of organisms. Changes in populations usually occur over many generations. Viewed over the entire history of life, several generations is not a very long time. You will study more about the processes of evolution in Unit 3.

What is a population?

FIGURE 2–2.

All the different varieties of garden roses belong to the genus *Rosa.* The enormous variety has been developed from just a few species.

GEOLOGIC TIME SCALE

ERA	PERIOD	MILLON YEARS AGO	MAJOR EVOLUTIONARY EVENTS	MAJOR EXTINCTIONS
Cenozoic	Quaternary	24	Humans evolve	
Cenozoic	Tertiary	65	First placental mammals	 Large mammals
Mesozoic	Cretaceous	144	Flowering plants dominant	 Dinosaurs
Mesozoic	Jurassic	213	First birds First mammals First flowering plants	Ammonoids
Mesozoic	Triassic	248	First dinosaurs	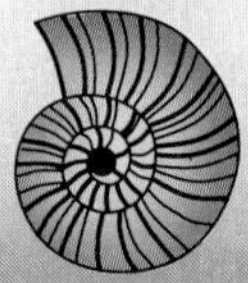
Paleozoic	Permian	286	Conifers dominant	
Paleozoic	Carboniferous	320 / 360	First reptiles Great coal deposits form First seed plants	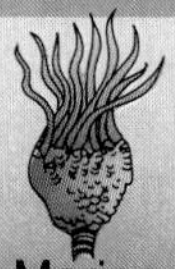 Marine invertebrates
Paleozoic	Devonian	408	First amphibians First land plants First jawed fishes	Trilobites
Paleozoic	Silurian	438	Algae dominant First vertebrates	
Paleozoic	Ordovician	505	Simple invertebrates	
Paleozoic	Cambrian	590		
Precambrian		3500	Life diversifies Eukaryotes Prokaryotes Life evolves	

FIGURE 2–3.

The history of life on Earth can be read in the Geologic Time Scale. Major periods of evolution and extinction are obvious in Earth's rock layers.

2:3 The Fossil Record

Life has existed on Earth for most of Earth's history. Evidence of this life comes from fossils. A **fossil** is the remains or traces of an organism that are preserved in Earth's crust. Fossils are bones or impressions, such as the imprint of a leaf.

The ages of fossils were first estimated by their relative positions in layers of rock. While excavating for a canal, William Smith (1769–1839), a surveyor, observed that fossils occurred in layers. He noticed that fossils of one layer were different from those of another layer. Because rock layers are formed in sequence, it was known that the oldest rocks form the lower layers and the youngest rocks are on the top. Therefore, Smith reasoned that fossils in the lower rock layers are older than those in the upper layers. This method of dating fossils is now called relative dating.

A fossil's age can now be determined by absolute dating from the presence of naturally occurring radioactive atoms. Many radioactive forms of elements decay to form more stable elements. For example, carbon 14 is an unstable form of carbon that is taken in by organisms along with stable forms of carbon. When an organism dies, carbon 14 continues to decay. The longer an organism has been dead, the less carbon 14 its fossil will contain. Carbon-14 dating is reliable for fossils up to 50 000 years old. For older fossils, other radioactive elements are necessary for absolute dating. Scientists have used both relative and absolute dating methods to reconstruct Earth's history in a geologic time scale as shown in Figure 2–3.

It is clear from the fossil record that millions of species have undergone extinction. **Extinction** is the condition in which all members of a species die. Figure 2–3 shows five major periods of extinction: at the end of the Cambrian; after the Devonian; after the Permian; after the Jurassic; and at the end of the Cretaceous. Notice from Figure 2–3 that life first evolved around 3.5 billion years ago. Simple animals made their appearance about 570 million years ago, and the first land plants appeared about 430 million years ago. Modern humans did not appear until 100 000 years ago.

FIGURE 2–4.

Nearly two billion years are represented in the exposed rocks of the Grand Canyon, from the rims dated as paleozoic to the precambrian rocks of the deep inner gorge.

NoteWorthy

Half of the carbon 14 in an organism decays in 5730 years. If an organism contained 2 g of carbon 14 at death, after 5730 years the fossil would contain 1 g of carbon 14. After another 5730 years, the fossil would contain 0.5 g, and so on.

REVIEW

1. In geologic history, what are three major periods of extinction?
2. What is the difference between chemosynthesis and photosynthesis?
3. How is carbon 14 useful in dating fossils?
4. **SKILL REVIEW:** Sequence the major groups of fossils as seen in the fossil record from the Permian to the Cretaceous periods. For more help, refer to Reading Science in the Skill Handbook, pages 798 to 799.
5. **USING CONCEPTS:** Explain how a consumer, such as a bird, and a producer, such as an oak tree, might be important in maintaining a balance in an ecosystem.

DEVELOPING A VIEWPOINT

ENDANGERED SPECIES

Perhaps one in four of the world's plant and animal species might be considered endangered or threatened. This means that these species are in danger of becoming extinct in the near future.

Some people are not concerned about endangered species. They say that extinction is a natural response to the competition among species and the changes that take place in habitats. Some think that this process should not be interfered with. Others blame human activities such as habitat destruction for the threat to many species. Their view is that far more species are extinct or are in danger of becoming extinct due to pressures from a rapidly increasing human population than would be if the process were due to natural causes alone.

BACKGROUND

Many of Earth's species are affected by human activity. Forests are cut down to make land avail-able for farming. The trees are cut for paper, building products, and firewood. Plant and animal species are used for food. Long-term considerations such as the preservation of these species or their habitats are sometimes ignored by people. There is an increasing need to feed the rising populations of people in the world. This has resulted in the destruction of natural habitats and the extinction of many plants and animals that lived in those habitats. The present rate of extinction of species may be reduced by educational programs and the use of proper land management.

CASE STUDIES

1. The Endangered Species Act 19 requires the development and implementation of plans to aid all species that are listed as endangered or threatened. The Act attempts to prohibit projects that would destroy the habitats of endangered wildlife. Each project proposal must describe the possible effects the project would have on all wildlife, even those species not listed as endangered in that area.

2. Today, zoos are involved in breeding endangered animals. In the history of zoos, there has been an interest in showing rare and unusual animals. For example, there are several giant pandas in captivity. Breeding giant pandas has proved to be a major problem for most zoos because the giant panda's natural environment is difficult to copy. However, giant pandas attract huge crowds and therefore bring in funds for other zoo research. Another unusual animal that zoos are breeding is the white tiger. Some people think that zoos should not breed white tigers because they would not survive in the wild. White tigers also attract large crowds to the zoos.

3. Some species are disappearing so fast that methods have been developed for saving them. Botanic gardens and seed banks save endangered plant species. Animals may be placed in wildlife preserves. Another is to reintroduce captive-born

Hawaiian *Hibiscus* is an endangered plant.

animals into these preserves where the numbers are low. In the case of the Florida panther, a related species may be introduced to help reestablish the natural population.

4. Large animals are in greater danger of becoming extinct than small animals because large animals have smaller populations. Large animals are often hunted by poachers for skins, tusks, and horns. These large animals are protected in wildlife sanctuaries but the profits for poachers are so high they are willing to take risks.

5. Today, humans are very successful in competing for food and space against many other animals. Some people reason that if species became extinct due to human activities, this extinction is natural and should not be prevented.

6. Botanists believe that about 700 plant species native to the United States will become extinct by the year 2000. Some of these exist only in gardens or in wilderness areas. Many wildflowers such as ginseng are becoming rare because of over collecting. The roots of these wildflowers are valued for having medicinal properties. In addition, about 3000 species of plants are at risk of extinction, mostly due to habitat loss as a result of agriculture or the spread of cities.

DEVELOPING YOUR VIEWPOINT

1. Is the Endangered Species Act fair to humans?
2. Should all rare animals be bred in captivity?
3. How does our dependence on plants and animals affect endangered species?
4. Should people wear fur or leather clothing?
5. Should collecting of animals and wildflowers be controlled?
6. Should people pay taxes to preserve endangered or threatened species?

SUGGESTED READINGS

1. Drew, Lisa. "Are We Loving the Panda to Death?" *National Wildlife,* Dec.–Jan. 1989, pp. 14–17.
2. Ferraro, Jerry L. "Starting Over." *National Wildlife,* Feb.–Mar. 1989, pp. 18–21.
3. Mlott, Christine. "The Science of Saving Endangered Species." *Bioscience,* Feb. 1989, pp. 68–70.

African elephants are hunted for their ivory tusks.

FIGURE 2–5.

Most people organize their kitchens to make it easy to find items such as pans, glassware, and different types of food. This organizing is called classifying.

CLASSIFICATION

If you look closely at the world around you, you will notice many kinds of organisms. New species are discovered almost daily. Most new species are found in less-explored areas like tropical forests and oceans, but occasionally they are discovered in well-populated ecosystems such as those in the United States. The key to understanding the enormous number of species is to organize them. Recall how useful it was for you to organize your own collection of seashells, baseball cards, or cassette tapes.

2:4 Taxonomy

Classification is the grouping of objects for practical purposes. If you examine your kitchen, you may find that the items stored in each cabinet are classified into plates, glassware, cups, and pans like those shown in Figure 2–5. People have always classified things. Early peoples learned to distinguish between edible plants and poisonous ones from noticing the effects of eating the plants. Taxonomy developed from these very early experiments. **Taxonomy** is the science of the classification of organisms. The purpose of taxonomy is to use information from many different sources in order to classify organisms. Depending on the purpose of the classification, the method of taxonomy used to group organisms will vary.

All members of a species are definitely related. But what are the characteristics used by scientists to recognize relationships among species? Taxonomists recognize relationships by comparisons of all available characteristics of each species.

Objectives:
- describe the methods and purpose of taxonomy.
- explain the importance of the taxonomic contributions made by Linnaeus.
- list the categories in the taxonomic hierarchy.
- distinguish between prokaryotes and eukaryotes.
- explain the purpose of a phylogenetic classification.

taxonomy:
taxo (GK) to arrange
nomy (GK) ordered knowledge

Aristotle (384–322 B.C.), a close observer of nature, was one of the earliest taxonomists. He classified living things into two groups: plants and animals. He grouped plants into herbs, shrubs, and trees. He grouped animals into those that live on land, those that live in the air, and those that live in water. This artificial system of classification does not show relationships among organisms. For example, birds live on land, in water, and in the air. Aristotle listed only about 500 species of organisms. Today, biologists estimate that there are at least 5 million species of organisms on Earth. Yet, only 1.5 million have been named.

One goal of modern taxonomy is to produce a system of natural classification. "Natural" implies a classification based on evolutionary relationships. In a natural classification system, closely related organisms have more characteristics in common than those less related. For example, ceramic cups and drinking glasses may have similar functions, but ceramic cups have more properties in common with ceramic plates than with glassware. For the same reasons, to identify one kind of animal it might not be useful to know that it has wings. Bees and birds have wings but they are not closely related. A grouping of animals with wings, as shown in Figure 2–6, is an artificial classification. The more characteristics that are compared among species, the more natural the classification will be.

What is a natural classification?

2:5 Nomenclature

A Swedish botanist, Carolus Linnaeus (luh NAY us) (1707–1778), developed a method of taxonomy that is still used today. Linnaeus selected characteristics that led to more natural groupings of species. He identified each species by two names, one for the species and one for the genus (*pl.* genera). A **genus** is a group of similar species. The process of naming objects is known as nomenclature.

FIGURE 2–6.

An insect, a bird, and a bat are each animals and they each have wings. However, they have so many other characteristics that are not alike that this classification is very artificial.

FIGURE 2–7.

All species in the plant family Malvaceae have five petals, many fused stamens, and one pistil with five stigmas.

FIGURE 2–8.

The scientific names of *Aix sponsa* (a) *Anas platyrhynchos* (b), and *Aix galericulata* (c) are useful in communicating species relationships.

The system of naming devised by Linnaeus that provides each organism with a genus name followed by a species name is **binomial nomenclature.** For example, *Juglans nigra* is the scientific name for a black walnut tree. The name of a species always includes a genus name, which begins with a capital letter, and a species name, which follows with a lowercase letter. Scientific names of species are printed in italics or written with an underline.

In practice, binomial nomenclature is similar to the system used in a telephone book to distinguish names such as *Rivas, Jose* from *Rivas, Jon.* For example, the binomial for the wood duck is *Aix sponsa,* and for the mandarin duck is *Aix galericulata.* The Mallard duck is *Anas platyrhynchos.* These three birds, as shown in Figure 2–8, are all commonly called ducks, along with many other waterfowl. From the genus name of the mandarin duck, which lives in Eastern Asia, we know that it is more closely related to the wood duck than to the mallard duck, both of North America. Clearly, the common names of ducks do not explain relationships. Another important advantage of binomial nomenclature is that the Latin name is used by all scientists, no matter what their native language. Scientists in the United States, Japan, Norway, India, or any other country use the same language for names of organisms.

In taxonomy, organisms are grouped into a series of categories, each one larger than the previous one, as shown in Figure 2–9. The categories fit together like nested boxes. You already know that similar species are grouped together into the larger category of genus. The next larger box, or category, is family. A **family** is a group of related genera. If you know a genus belongs to a particular family, you immediately know many things about it. For example, the flower in Figure 2–7 looks like an *Hibiscus,* an okra, or a cotton flower and so all three plants are classified in the same plant family.

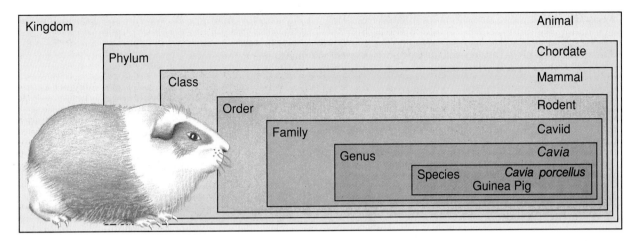

Kingdom							Animal
Phylum							Chordate
	Class						Mammal
		Order					Rodent
			Family				Caviid
				Genus			*Cavia*
					Species		*Cavia porcellus* Guinea Pig

The remaining categories are order, class, phylum or division, and kingdom. An **order** is a group of related families. A **class** is a group of related orders. A **phylum** (*pl.* phyla) or **division** is a group of related classes, and a **kingdom** is a group of related phyla or divisions. Generally, plant groups are called divisions, and groups of other organisms are called phyla.

Before 1850, all life was classified into one of two kingdoms—animal or plant. New systems of classification have since been developed, even one that included as many as 13 kingdoms. Today, the five kingdom system is the one in common use and the one used in this textbook.

Ernst Haeckel (1834–1919), a German biologist, placed unicellular organisms into Kingdom Protista. He later separated the bacteria because he recognized the importance of their lack of a nucleus. The presence or absence of a nucleus in a cell distinguishes two major types of cellular organization. A **prokaryote** is an organism with cells that lack structures surrounded by membranes. Prokaryotes do not have a nucleus. A **eukaryote** is an organism that has cells with membrane-bound structures. Examine the differences between a prokaryote cell and a eukaryote cell in Figure 2–10.

2:6 Classification and Phylogeny

As biologists in the 20th century tried to develop a more natural classification, they looked carefully for characteristics to indicate relationships. They also compared modern-day life forms with fossils of similar forms. As scientists studied organisms from this new point of view, a phylogenetic classification scheme began to develop. **Phylogeny** is the evolutionary history of species. A model of this new system of classification looks like a branching tree with all the modern day species at the tips of the branches. Identify the five kingdoms in the model of a phylogenetic classification shown in Figure 2–11. Notice that the "trunk" of the tree represents the pathway of life's evolution within the geologic time scale.

FIGURE 2–9.

Any organism can be classified into each of the taxonomic categories. Each species has only one scientific name.

FIGURE 2–10.

A prokaryote (a) has no nucleus. All bacteria are prokaryotes. Other organisms are eukaryotes (b), such as this protist cell, and have a nucleus as well as many other cell parts surrounded by membranes.

a

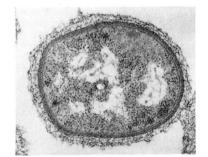

b

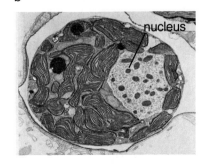

nucleus

FIGURE 2–11.

The five kingdoms of life are moneran, protist, fungus, plant, and animal. The radiation of phyla on the geologic time scale shows their relationships.

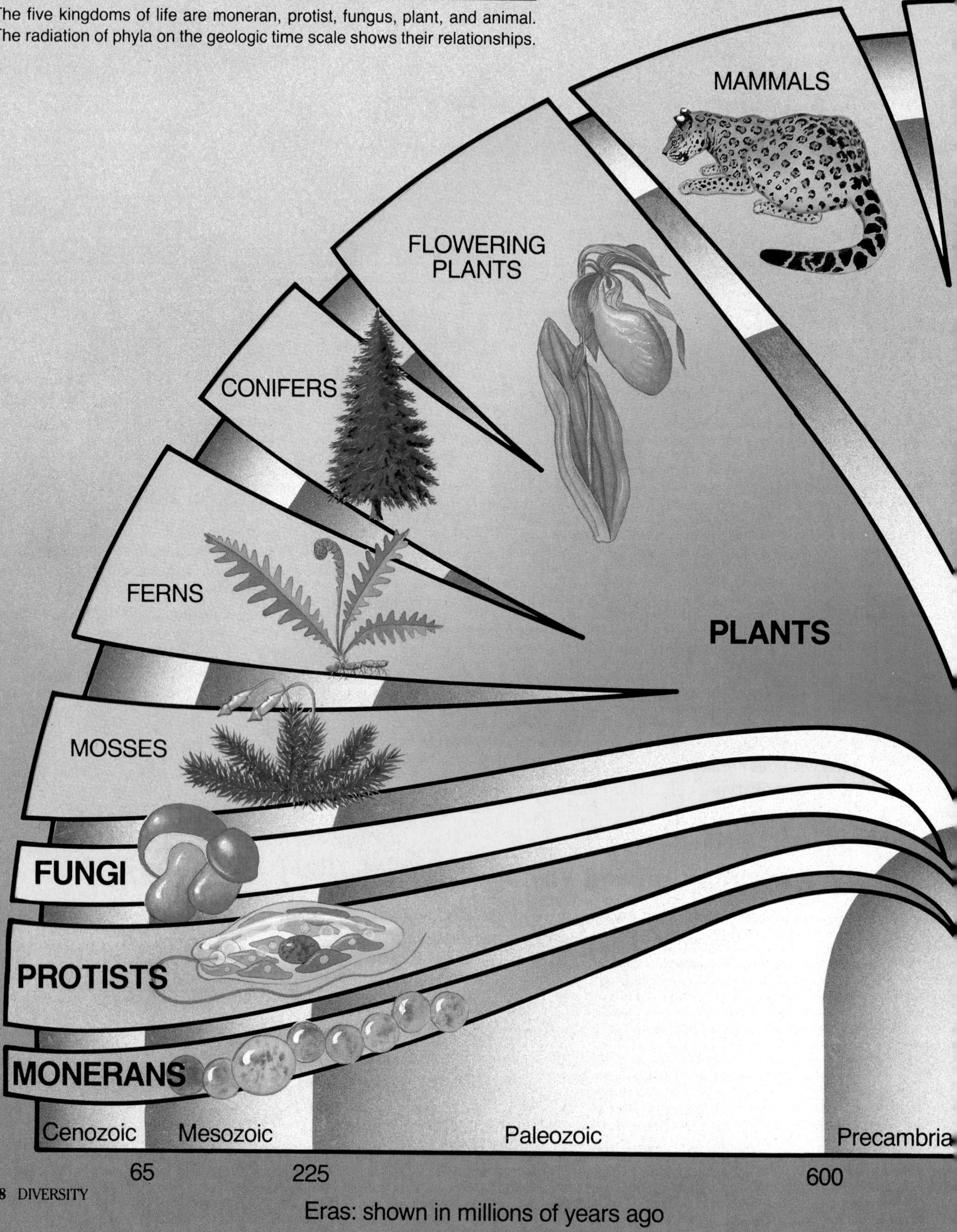

MAMMALS

FLOWERING PLANTS

CONIFERS

FERNS

MOSSES

PLANTS

FUNGI

PROTISTS

MONERANS

| Cenozoic | Mesozoic | Paleozoic | Precambria |

65   225   600

Eras: shown in millions of years ago

LIFE'S FIVE KINGDOMS

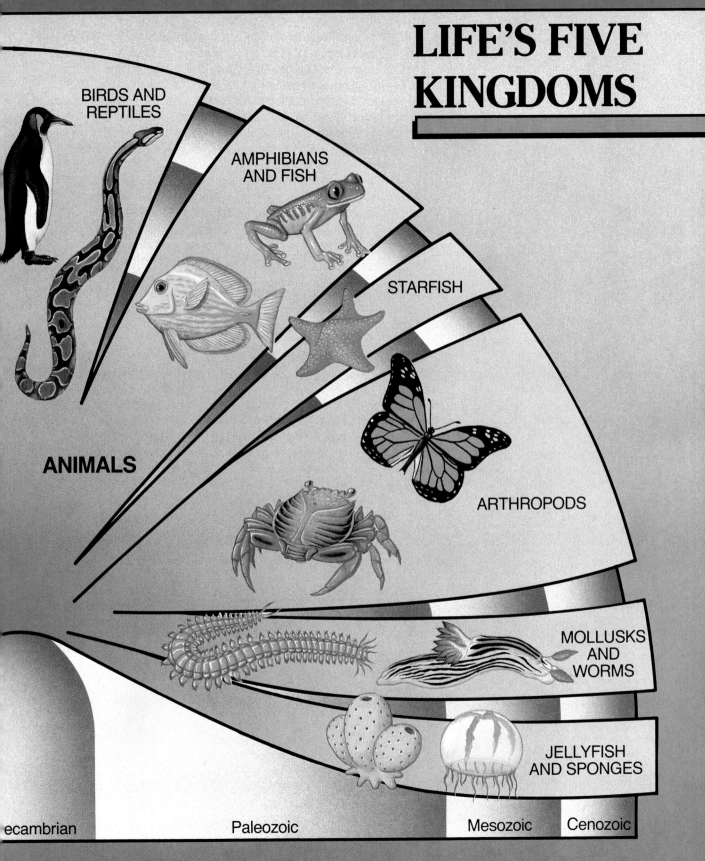

BIRDS AND REPTILES

AMPHIBIANS AND FISH

STARFISH

ANIMALS

ARTHROPODS

MOLLUSKS AND WORMS

JELLYFISH AND SPONGES

ecambrian   Paleozoic   Mesozoic   Cenozoic

Numbers of petals help in the classification of flowers.

NoteWorthy

The species with the most characteristics in common with *Homo sapiens*, the human species, is the chimpanzee.

Biologists reasoned that as organisms adapted and populations changed, new species formed. This evolution of species is represented in Figure 2–11 by branching into the five kingdoms from a common origin. Groups joined closer together on the tree share many characteristics; groups that are far apart are very different and therefore probably not as closely related. As you study the groups of organisms presented in this textbook, you will learn not only about individual taxonomic groups, but also about their phylogenetic relationships as represented in Figure 2–11.

The fan shape of the model in Figure 2–11 indicates that life originated about 4 billion years ago. The outermost layer of the model represents present time. Within each kingdom, there are representative examples of present-day organisms. Notice that some groups, such as mammals, evolved relatively late in the history of life. In general, the later in time two groups of organisms became distinct, the more alike and the more closely related they seem to be. For example, flowering plants and fish have been distinct groups for a much longer time in history than have reptiles and fish. From a comparison of all their characteristics, fish are obviously much more related to reptiles than to flowering plants.

Many kinds of data are compared to determine relationships among organisms. Taxonomists compare external appearances, internal structures, stages in development, and chemical makeup. For example, the nesting and breeding behaviors of birds have been used to infer species relationships. Human evolution has been studied by comparing the fossil remains of other primate genera. The number of petals in a flower is used to group a plant into a particular family. Cell structures are important in showing relationships within kingdoms.

As you study the taxonomic groups in this textbook, refer back to Figure 2–11 regularly as a reminder that each group of organisms is in some way related to all the others.

REVIEW

6. What is the purpose of taxonomy?
7. Name the taxonomic categories in order from kingdom to species.
8. What kinds of data are used to classify organisms?
9. **SKILL REVIEW:** Use Figure 2–11 to sequence the five kingdoms and their subcategories of related organisms in the order of their times of origin. For more help, refer to Reading Science in the Skill Handbook, pages 798 to 799.
10. **USING CONCEPTS:** Why is a phylogenetic classification more natural than one based on characteristics such as usefulness in medicine, or shapes, sizes, and colors of body structures alone?

BIOLAB

Classifying

2

Problem: Are closely related species more similar than less closely related species?

Materials
specimens of three species A, B, and C
dissecting microscope
forceps
petri dishes (3)

Procedures
1. Make a table like the one shown.
2. In the left column of the table list the characteristics of your specimens as instructed by your teacher.
3. Examine the specimens of your three species and make a **hypothesis** as to their relationships.
4. Examine each species for each characteristic you listed in your table. Record "yes" if the character is present. Record "no" if the character is not present.
5. Summarize your data in the last three columns in the following way. If the two species being considered both have the same answer, record a score of one. If the two species have different answers, record a score of zero.
6. Total each of the last three columns and compare the sums. The more similar the two species being compared are, the higher the total will be.

Questions and Conclusion
1. Which two species showed the greatest similarity?
2. What would a total of zero between two species indicate?
3. How is this activity useful in classifying organisms?
4. Was your **hypothesis** shown to be correct? Explain.

Conclusion: Are closely related species more similar than less closely related species?

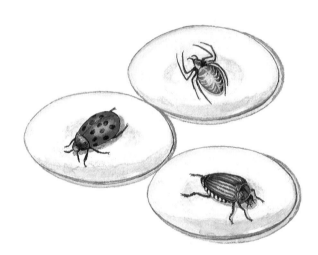

Data and Observations

Characteristic	Species			Scores		
	A	**B**	**C**	**A-B**	**A-C**	**B-C**
chewing mouthparts						
6 legs						
wings						
antennae						
			Total Score			

LIFE'S FIVE KINGDOMS

Objectives:
- compare the five kingdoms of organisms.
- distinguish the Kingdoms Monera, Protista, Fungi, Plantae, and Animalia.

What are flagella?

NoteWorthy

All prokaryotes and some protists are collectively referred to as microorganisms. Sometimes the word *microbes* is used instead to include viruses.

This textbook presents the five kingdoms of life organized in a phylogenetic classification. The following sections describe the major characteristics of each kingdom. In general, the five kingdoms can be distinguished by cellular structures and functions. You will notice that every category of organisms in this textbook is based on a combination of characteristics. Some species are difficult to classify because they have characteristics of more than one category. These species are classified into the group with which they share the most characteristics.

The five kingdoms can be distinguished by their methods of obtaining food for their energy needs, by their cellular structures, and by the chemical makeup of their cells.

2:7 Monerans

Kingdom Monera is distinct from the other four kingdoms by having only prokaryotes. They first appear in the fossil record dated at 3.5 billion years. More than 10 000 species of monerans are named and described. Bacteria and cyanobacteria are monerans. A **moneran** is unicellular and a prokaryote. Monerans do not have a nucleus. Many monerans have a cell wall and flagella. **Flagella** are threadlike structures that project out from a cell's surface and are used in movement. Although organisms in other kingdoms have cells with flagella, moneran flagella have a simpler structure, as shown in Figure 2–12.

Species of bacteria are often recognized by differences in their metabolism. Some bacteria obtain energy by chemosynthesis. Others, including cyanobacteria, use photosynthesis.

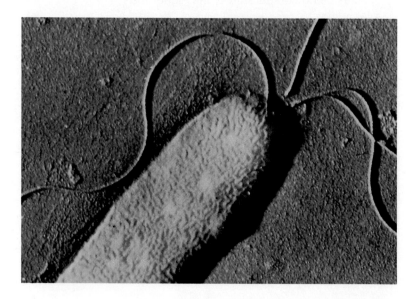

FIGURE 2–12.

The flagella of bacteria consist of a single fiber with no complex internal structures.

A SIX KINGDOM CLASSIFICATION?

The majority of monerans share a similar cell chemistry. However, one group of bacteria, the archaebacteria, is very different from the others. Some of their cell structures are composed of different chemicals, and their proteins and genetic material contain important differences.

The archaebacteria include three groups of organisms that live in extreme environments that can't be tolerated by most other organisms: very salty environments, hot acid sulfur springs, and other anaerobic conditions. They cannot tolerate oxygen and die when exposed to air.

The early atmosphere of Earth is thought to have been rich in carbon dioxide and hydrogen. Extreme conditions such as hot acid springs and salt ponds existed on early Earth. Because archaebacteria are adapted to living under such conditions, they are thought to have been among the first organisms on Earth.

Archaebacteria are presently classified in the Kingdom Monera with other bacteria. Some biologists have suggested that they be placed in a separate kingdom, Archaebacteria, meaning "ancient bacteria." Their view is that these organisms are as different from other monerans as prokaryotes are from eukaryotes. Other biologists are of the opinion that the differences are not great enough to justify a sixth kingdom. They are concerned that if the classification system becomes too subdivided, it will cease to be useful. All classification systems are created by humans. The value of a classification system is to help us learn about life on Earth. What are some of the advantages and disadvantages of recognizing the archaebacteria as a sixth kingdom?

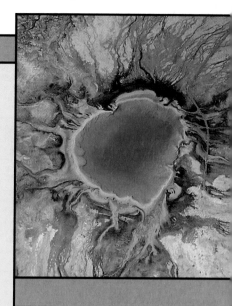

Bacteria live in the alkaline hot springs of Yellowstone National Park.

2:8 Protists

Kingdom Protista is recognized by a combination of different characteristics—some plantlike, some animal-like, and some funguslike. A **protist** is a simple eukaryote that lacks complex organ systems and lives in or near water. Protists are either producers or consumers. Some protists have rigid cell walls and some have flagella with complex inner structures or other means for movement. The number of protist species ranges from 90 000 to 200 000.

The first protist eukaryotes appear in the fossil record dated at one billion years. Most protists are unicellular organisms, but the seaweeds are multicellular. Animal-like protists include amoebas, plantlike protists include seaweeds, and funguslike protists include slime molds. The protist kingdom is the least uniform in its members of all the five kingdoms.

What are the three types of protists?

2:9 Fungi

How do fungi obtain their food?

Until recently, species of fungi were classified as plants. A **fungus** is a unicellular or multicellular eukaryote that obtains food by absorption. Fungi are consumers. They can't move about from place to place. No species has flagella, but they all have cell walls. The chemical makeup of the cell walls is like that in the outer body covering of insects. Most fungi are multicellular.

There are now more than 100 000 named species of fungi. When fungi first appear in the fossil record, dated around 400 million years, they are associated with plants. Some biologists have suggested that these ancient associations were important for survival of plants on land. Even today, fungi live in association with the roots of plants and provide the plants with nutrients.

2:10 Plants

Organisms in the plant kingdom are multicellular eukaryotes. Most plants are producers. Few plant cells have flagella. Plants have cell walls and are usually green.

The plant kingdom contains very large and long-lived species. The ancestors of plants were probably like green algae of the protist kingdom. Because plant tissues do not form fossils as easily as bones of animals, the oldest plant fossils to be discovered are only 400 million years old. Half a million species of plants have been described. Flowering plants and conifers are the best known of plant species. They are important for providing Earth with oxygen. As you know, oxygen is not only important to the life processes in organisms, but also to the formation of Earth's protective ozone layer.

NoteWorthy

Wolffia is the smallest plant at less than 0.1 mm across. The California redwood is the largest plant at over 100 m tall.

FIGURE 2–13.

A fungus (a) and a plant (b) share the characteristic of not moving from place to place to obtain food. However, they have very different cell structures.

a

b

2:11 Animals

Animals are the organisms with the most complex body structures. All organisms in the animal kingdom are multicellular and eukaryotic. Animals are consumers. There are more than one million species of animals. Animals often have complex nervous systems and can move from place to place. The cells of most animals are organized into tissues, organs, and organ systems. Some animals, such as some worms, are microscopic; others, such as whales, are the largest of all organisms. Figure 2–14 shows a very limited selection of animals. Animals first appear in the fossil record dated at 700 million years.

FIGURE 2–14.

The great diversity of animal species reflects their ability to adapt and is also a result of their evolution over 700 million years.

REVIEW

11. Describe the five kingdoms of life based on methods that organisms use to obtain food.
12. How do monerans differ from the other four kingdoms?
13. Describe the five kingdoms by their cell structures.
14. **SKILL REVIEW:** Make a table that compares characteristics of members of each of the five kingdoms. For more help, refer to Organizing Information in the Skill Handbook, pages 810 to 813.
15. **USING CONCEPTS:** If the present system of classification were divided into more kingdoms, which of the present kingdoms do you think would be divided? Explain your reasons.

CHAPTER REVIEW

SUMMARY

1. Life on Earth began around four billion years ago. The first organisms were probably consumers. **2:1**
2. Variation among organisms allows for evolution. Fossils are dated by relative and absolute dating techniques. **2:2, 2:3**
3. One goal of taxonomy is to make a natural classification. **2:4**
4. Taxonomic categories include species, genus, family, order, class, phylum or division, and kingdom. Organisms are either prokaryotes or eukaryotes and are classified into five kingdoms to indicate phylogeny. **2:5, 2:6**
5. Monerans are unicellular, prokaryotes, and have cell walls and flagella. Protists are unicellular or multicellular, eukaryotes, and many have flagella. Fungi are eukaryotes, have no flagella, and absorb food. **2:7, 2:8, 2:9**
6. Plants are multicellular, eukaryotes, and have cell walls. Most plants make their own food. Animals are multicellular, eukaryotes, and have no cell walls. Animals are consumers. **2:10, 2:11**

LANGUAGE OF BIOLOGY

binomial nomenclature	fungus
biosphere	genus
chemosynthesis	kingdom
class	moneran
classification	order
consumer	photosynthesis
division	phylogeny
ecosystem	phylum
eukaryote	population
evolution	producer
extinction	prokaryote
family	protist
flagella	species
fossil	taxonomy

Choose the word or phrase from the list above that completes the sentence.

1. Any structure originating from an organism and preserved in Earth's crust is a(n) ____.
2. The evolutionary history of species is ____.
3. ____ is a genetic change in a population of organisms.
4. ____ is the science of classifying organisms.
5. A red, brown, or green alga is a ____.
6. ____ is the two part naming system of classification.
7. Many monerans have ____ for movement.
8. A(n) ____ is an organism with no cellular membrane-bound structures.
9. ____ is the use of light to make food.
10. Bacteria are in the ____ kingdom.

REVIEWING CONCEPTS

Choose the word or phrase that completes the sentence or answers the question.

11. A class does NOT include ____.
    - a. phyla and divisions
    - b. families
    - c. genera and species
    - d. orders
12. ____ is the grouping of organisms.
    - a. Evolution
    - b. Classification
    - c. Taxonomy
    - d. Phylogeny
13. The flagella of ____ are simpler in structure than those in all other groups.
    - a. animals
    - b. protists
    - c. plants
    - d. monerans
14. A nucleus is present in the cells of ____.
    - a. monerans
    - b. bacteria
    - c. prokaryotes
    - d. eukaryotes
15. Eukaryotes that absorb their food are ____.
    - a. plants
    - b. fungi
    - c. animals
    - d. cyanobacteria
16. Binomial nomenclature names ____.
    - a. classes
    - b. kingdoms
    - c. species
    - d. phyla

17. Protists differ from fungi in having ____.
    a. nuclei   c. cell walls
    b. flagella   d. membranes
18. In the fossil record ____ are the oldest known organisms.
    a. animals   c. protists
    b. bacteria   d. fungi
19. A geologic time scale can show when species ____.
    a. became fossilized
    b. became extinct
    c. changed ecosystems
    d. evolved
20. ____ uses light for food production.
    a. Respiration   c. Classification
    b. Chemosynthesis d. Photosynthesis

UNDERSTANDING CONCEPTS

Answer the following questions using complete sentences.

21. If two fungi are in the same class, what other categories must they also share?
22. Why is the job of classifying all living things on Earth not completed?
23. What types of information are useful for identifying relationships among species?
24. How are algae different from other protists?
25. Why is the eukaryotic feature not a defining characteristic for fungi?
26. Why do evolutionary changes occur only in populations rather than in individuals?
27. If two families are not in the same order, what other taxa could they not share?
28. How could the time of origin of a kingdom be established?
29. The species name of a moneran is *circinalis.* This moneran belongs to the same genus as *Anabaena flos-aquae.* Write the scientific name of the first species.
30. How is the relative age of a fossil determined?

APPLYING CONCEPTS

Answer the following questions using complete sentences.

31. How does natural variation in a population of organisms affect the evolution of a species?
32. Why were the first life forms on Earth consumers and not producers?
33. Explain why the early systems of classification are not used today.
34. An organism is unicellular, is a producer, has a rigid cell wall, a nucleus, and a flagellum. To what kingdom does it belong?
35. You have four organisms. Organism A has wings, six legs, and antennae. Organism B has wings, two legs, and large ears. Organism C has no wings, four legs, and large ears. Organism D has wings, two legs, and no ears. Classify these four organisms to show which are more closely related.

EXTENSIONS

1. Research the major groups of organisms that show mass extinctions in the fossil record. Prepare a chart to present to the class.
2. Prepare diagrams of organisms under each of the five kingdoms as presented in Figure 2–11.
3. Select one organism and prepare a poster that shows its classification using each taxonomic category.

READINGS

Gore, Rick. "Extinctions." *National Geographic,* June 1989, pp. 662–699.

Lewin, Roger. *Thread of Life.* Washington, DC: Smithsonian Books, 1982.

Sagan, D. and L. Margulis. "Bacterial Bedfellows." *Natural History,* Mar. 1987, pp. 26–33.

CELLS

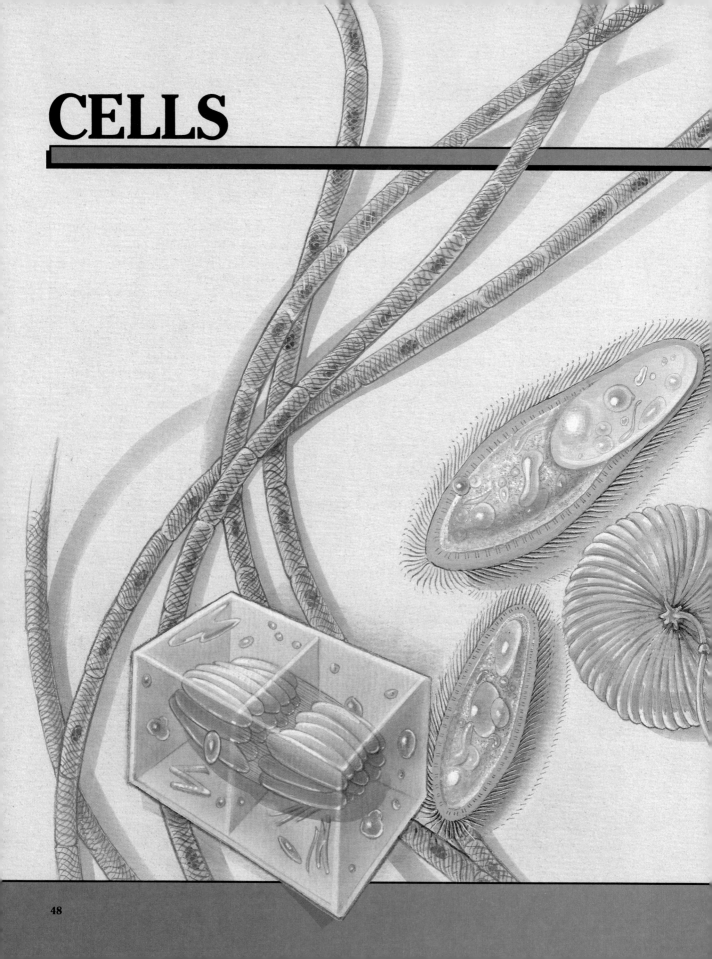

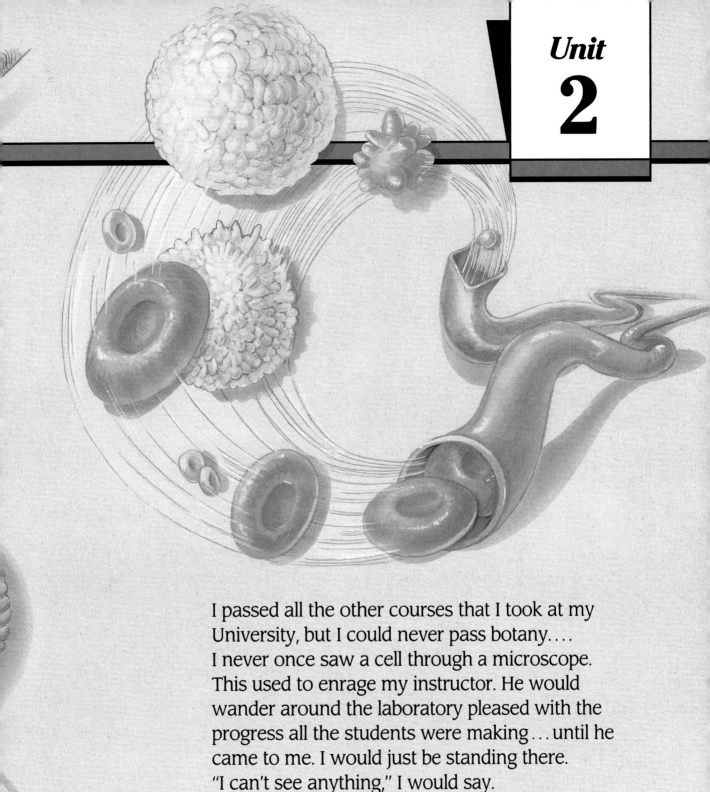

I passed all the other courses that I took at my University, but I could never pass botany....
I never once saw a cell through a microscope. This used to enrage my instructor. He would wander around the laboratory pleased with the progress all the students were making...until he came to me. I would just be standing there. "I can't see anything," I would say.

James Thurber
My Life and Hard Times

SIMPLE CHEMISTRY

S uppose you wanted to describe a rose plant. You could easily see that it had roots, stems, leaves, and flowers. With a light microscope, you could see various kinds of cells. Smaller parts inside cells would be barely visible. Until about 100 years ago, no one could describe an organism in any more detail. People believed that life processes were guided by a mysterious vital force that humans could never understand.

Today, biologists know that chemicals in living things act in the same way as chemicals in the nonliving world. New types of microscopes can show atoms and molecules. Now, to describe a rose, you begin with atoms and molecules. You could say that molecules of geraniol make up part of the rose's fragrance. To describe how an organism lives, you begin with chemical changes and energy.

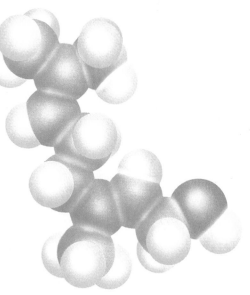

Geraniol molecule

MATTER AND LIVING THINGS

Much of our understanding of organisms is based on a knowledge of matter and energy. The structure of living organisms can be understood in terms of the structures of the chemicals that make up the organisms. Life processes can be understood in terms of the chemical changes that occur in organisms.

3:1 Atoms and Elements

Atoms are the basic building blocks of all matter. An **atom** is the smallest particle of an element that has the characteristics of that element. An element is a substance that can't be broken down into simpler substances. Each element is made of only one kind of atom. Carbon and iron are elements that occur in organisms. Carbon is composed only of carbon atoms and iron is composed only of iron atoms. To make writing formulas for chemical substances easier, scientists use a symbol having one or two letters for each element. For example, the symbol C represents the element carbon, and Fe stands for iron. Table 3–1 lists several elements that are found in living organisms, along with their symbols.

Objectives:
- describe the structure of an atom.
- interpret the formulas of chemical compounds.
- relate the formation of chemical bonds to the stability of atoms.
- distinguish between ionic and covalent bonds.
- interpret equations for chemical reactions.
- characterize three types of mixtures—solutions, suspensions, and colloids.
- relate the polarity of water to its ability to dissolve substances.
- compare water solutions of acids and bases.

The flower of a wild rose

Table 3–1.

ELEMENTS THAT MAKE UP LIVING THINGS					
Element	Symbol	Percent by Mass in Human Body	Element	Symbol	Percent by Mass in Human Body
Oxygen	O	65.0	Iron	Fe	trace
Carbon	C	18.5	Iodine	I	trace
Hydrogen	H	9.5	Copper	Cu	trace
Nitrogen	N	3.3	Manganese	Mn	trace
Calcium	Ca	1.5	Molybdenum	Mo	trace
Phosphorus	P	1.0	Cobalt	Co	trace
Potassium	K	0.4	Boron	B	trace
Sulfur	S	0.3	Zinc	Zn	trace
Sodium	Na	0.2	Fluorine	F	trace
Chlorine	Cl	0.2	Selenium	Se	trace
Magnesium	Mg	0.1	Chromium	Cr	trace

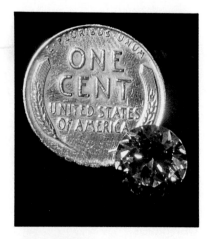

FIGURE 3–1.

Copper is an element. It is made of only copper atoms. The diamond is pure carbon and consists of only carbon atoms.

Where are electrons located in an atom?

There are 92 elements that occur naturally on Earth. About 25 of the 92 are essential to life. Four of these—carbon (C), oxygen (O), hydrogen (H), and nitrogen (N)—make up more than 95 percent of living matter. Other elements are needed in small but significant quantities. These elements include calcium (Ca), phosphorus (P), potassium (K), sulfur (S), sodium (Na), chlorine (Cl), and magnesium (Mg). Magnesium is essential in photosynthesis and other processes involving energy transfer.

Elements that are required by organisms in very small amounts are called trace elements. Iron (Fe) is needed by many animals to make hemoglobin, one of the components of blood. Iodine (I) is involved in controlling the rate of life processes and growth of the human body. Trace elements, such as copper (Cu), zinc (Zn), and cobalt (Co), are needed by all organisms to maintain good health. The most common elements of organisms are listed in Table 3–1.

The center of an atom is called the **nucleus** (*pl.* nuclei). It is made up of particles called protons and neutrons packed tightly together. Protons are positively charged particles and neutrons are particles that have no charge. Protons are represented by the symbol p^+ and neutrons by n^0. The atomic nucleus is positive because of the presence of the protons. Electrons are negatively charged particles that move rapidly about the nucleus in a region called an electron cloud. Electrons stay in the electron cloud because the positive nucleus and the negative electrons attract each other. Electrons are represented by the symbol e^-.

Electrons move about in certain regions within the electron cloud. These regions within the cloud are known as energy levels. The first energy level, the one closest to the nucleus, can hold two electrons. The next level can hold eight, and the third can hold eighteen. For example, an atom of oxygen has eight electrons. Two are in the first energy level and six are in the second. The number and arrangement of electrons in the energy level of an atom determine the chemical characteristics of that element.

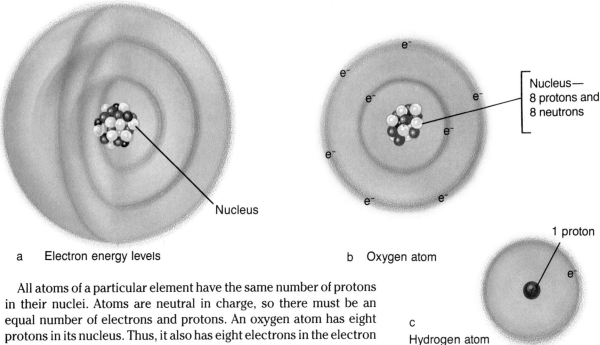

a   Electron energy levels

b   Oxygen atom

Nucleus—
8 protons and
8 neutrons

1 proton

c
Hydrogen atom

All atoms of a particular element have the same number of protons in their nuclei. Atoms are neutral in charge, so there must be an equal number of electrons and protons. An oxygen atom has eight protons in its nucleus. Thus, it also has eight electrons in the electron cloud. As a result, an oxygen atom is neutral. A sodium atom has eleven protons and eleven electrons. Hydrogen, the simplest atom, has just one electron and one proton.

Although all atoms of an element have the same number of protons, they can differ in the number of neutrons they contain. Two atoms of the same element that have different numbers of neutrons are called **isotopes** of that element. Most carbon atoms have six neutrons. However, some have eight neutrons instead. The nuclei of some isotopes are unstable and break down. When nuclei break down, they give off detectable radiation. Thus, the unstable isotope is said to be radioactive. Because they can be detected, radioactive isotopes have many useful applications in biology. They are used to locate and treat cancer cells. Scientists use isotopes to trace the reactions of substances in living organisms.

FIGURE 3–2.

An atom has a nucleus and electrons in cloudlike energy levels (a). An oxygen atom (b) is neutral because it has 8 protons and 8 electrons. Hydrogen (c) is the simplest atom.

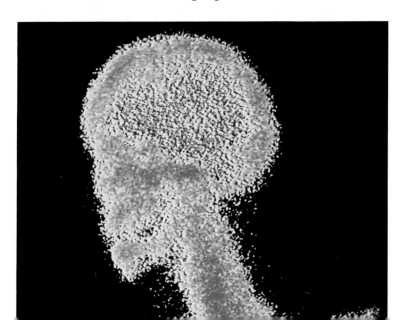

FIGURE 3–3.

Some radioactive isotopes can be taken into the body by mouth or by injections. Powerful instruments detect radiation from locations where the isotope collects in the body. The image of a human head and neck was produced by radioactive isotopes inside the body.

MATTER AND LIVING THINGS **53**

FIGURE 3–4.

The compound, sodium chloride, is ordinary table salt. It resembles neither the metallic element, sodium, nor the gaseous element, chlorine.

3:2 Molecules and Compounds

Although living organisms contain many different elements, these elements are seldom found alone. Instead, they are combined with other elements to form substances called compounds. A **compound** is a substance that is formed when atoms of different elements combine chemically. Water (H_2O) is a compound that is made of atoms of the elements hydrogen and oxygen chemically combined. Table sugar ($C_{12}H_{22}O_{11}$) contains atoms of carbon, hydrogen, and oxygen. The properties of a compound are different from those of the elements that formed it. For example, the element sodium (Na) is a gray-white metal that reacts violently with water. Chlorine (Cl) is a poisonous, yellow-green gas. When sodium and chlorine are placed together, they combine chemically. One atom of sodium combines with one atom of chlorine to form sodium chloride. Sodium chloride (NaCl) is also called table salt. Table salt consists of white crystals that no longer resemble either sodium or chlorine.

But how and why do atoms combine? Atoms combine with each other in such a way that their outer energy levels become stable. Most atoms are stable when the outer level has eight electrons. Hydrogen, though, has one electron in an energy level that can hold only two electrons. Thus, hydrogen becomes stable when its energy level contains two electrons.

One way that atoms can become stable is by sharing electrons with other atoms. When hydrogen combines with other atoms, it must gain one electron to become stable. Two hydrogen atoms can combine with each other by sharing their electrons. The two shared electrons move about in the energy levels of both atoms, Figure 3–5. The two shared electrons stabilize both atoms. The attraction of both nuclei for the shared electrons holds the atoms together.

How is a compound formed?

When are most atoms stable?

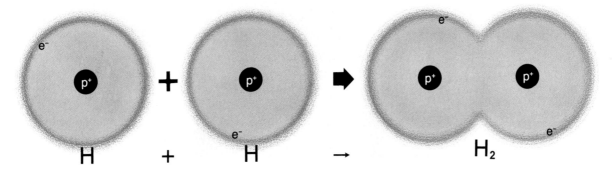

The forces that hold chemically combined atoms together are called chemical bonds. When two atoms share electrons, the force that holds them together is called a **covalent bond.** Most substances in living organisms have covalent bonds. A particle in which atoms are bonded by the sharing of electrons in covalent bonds is called a **molecule.** A molecule of hydrogen is represented by the chemical formula H_2. The subscript 2 tells you that two atoms of hydrogen make up one molecule of hydrogen. Several other elements occur as two-atom molecules. Some of these are oxygen (O_2), nitrogen (N_2), and chlorine (Cl_2).

An atom will combine to share as many electrons as are needed to become stable. Recall that eight electrons in the outer energy level make most atoms stable. A carbon atom has four electrons in its outer energy level. Therefore, a carbon atom can become stable by sharing to get four more electrons. Notice in Figure 3–6 how this sharing makes the atoms in methane (CH_4) stable.

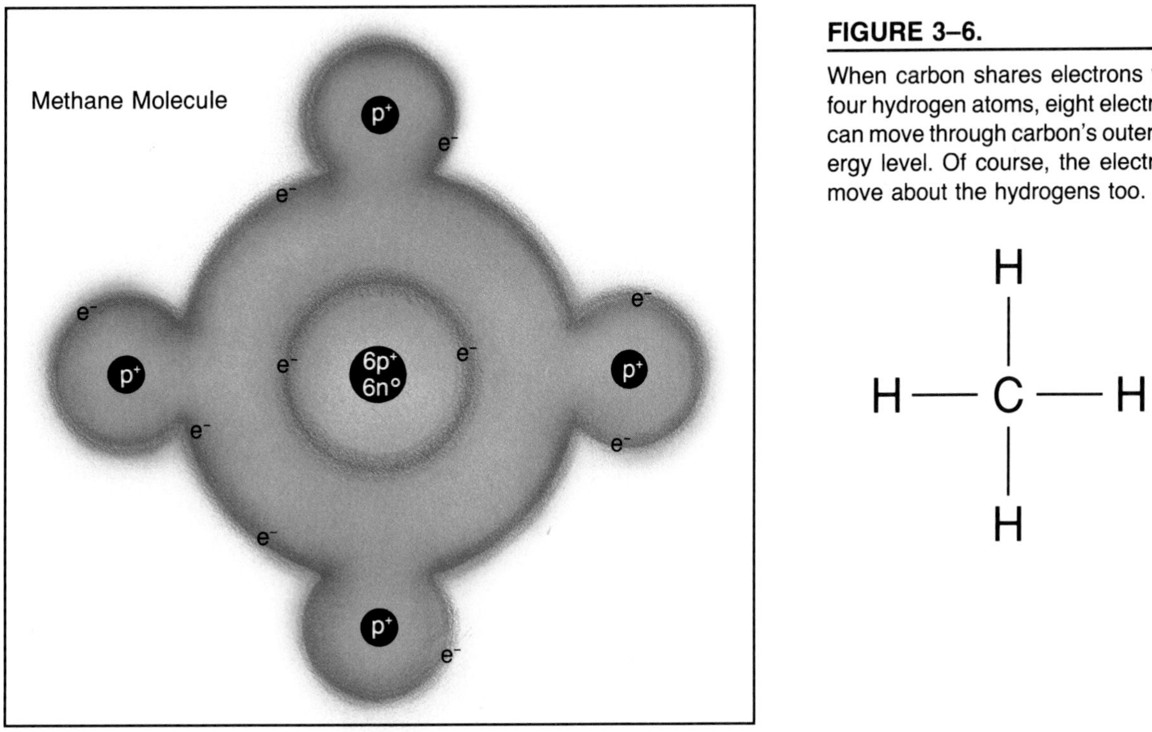

FIGURE 3–5.

Hydrogen atoms become stable when they share electrons in a covalent bond, thus forming a molecule.

What is a molecule?

Methane Molecule

FIGURE 3–6.

When carbon shares electrons with four hydrogen atoms, eight electrons can move through carbon's outer energy level. Of course, the electrons move about the hydrogens too.

FIGURE 3–7.

In this photograph, electrons are being transferred from sodium atoms to chlorine atoms to form the compound, sodium chloride.

What force causes ionic bonding?

FIGURE 3–8.

When sodium and chlorine react, they become charged ions and attract each other. This attraction is an ionic bond.

3:3 Ions and Ionic Bonds

Sometimes atoms combine with each other by gaining or losing electrons in their outer energy levels. Follow this process in Figure 3–8. A sodium atom contains eleven electrons—two in the first energy level, eight in the second, and one in the third. Chlorine atoms have seventeen electrons, with the outer level holding seven of these. Chlorine needs one more electron to be stable. When sodium and chlorine combine, the sodium atom loses its one outer electron and the chlorine gains it. Thus, chlorine now is stable with eight electrons in its outer level. Sodium has lost the electron that was in its third energy level. The second level is now sodium's outer level. It has eight electrons and therefore is stable.

Recall that a sodium atom contains eleven protons and eleven electrons and is neutral in charge. When a sodium atom loses one electron, it then has eleven protons and ten electrons. By losing an electron, the sodium atom is left with one more positive charge than negative charge. An atom that has become charged by gaining or losing electrons is called an **ion.** The sodium atom has become a sodium ion with a single positive charge. It is represented by the symbol Na^+. The chlorine atom gains one electron, becoming an ion with a single negative charge. The chloride ion is represented by Cl^-. Note that a the negative ion of an element has a different name from the element. The name of the ion ends in *-ide.*

A different type of chemical bond holds ions together. Because sodium ions and chloride ions have opposite charges, they attract each other. The attractive force between two ions of opposite charge is known as an **ionic bond.** The compound formed when sodium and chlorine react to form ions is known as sodium chloride. It is represented by the chemical formula NaCl. Compounds held together by ionic bonds are called ionic compounds.

Although ionic compounds are less abundant in organisms than covalent molecules, they are very important in biological processes. Sodium and potassium ions are required for the transmission of nerve impulses. Calcium ions are necessary for muscle contraction. Plant roots absorb needed minerals in the form of ions.

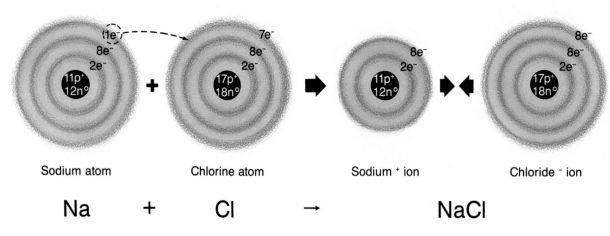

| Sodium atom | Chlorine atom | Sodium $^+$ ion | Chloride $^-$ ion |

Na + Cl → NaCl

3:4 Chemical Reactions

The making and breaking of chemical bonds occur during chemical reactions. Whenever chemical reactions occur, substances change into different substances. Elements and compounds that undergo chemical reactions are called reactants. The substances that are produced are called products. In the formation of sodium chloride, sodium and chlorine are reactants. Ionic sodium chloride is the product. A chemical reaction can be expressed as an equation, using formulas and symbols to represent the reactants and products.

Methane (CH_4) is the main component of natural gas. Oxygen makes up 21 percent of air. Suppose methane burns in air. The reaction can be represented by the following equation.

$$CH_4 + 2O_2 \rightarrow CO_2 + 2H_2O$$

This equation is read: one molecule of methane plus 2 molecules of oxygen yields one molecule of carbon dioxide plus two molecules of water. The subscript numbers in the formulas indicate the number of atoms of each element in a molecule of the substance. The number before each chemical formula indicates the number of molecules of that substance involved in the reaction. In chemical formulas and equations, the lack of a number means that one atom or molecule is present. Notice in Figure 3–9 that there is one carbon atom, four hydrogen atoms, and four oxygen atoms on each side of the equation. Equations must always be written so that they are balanced. A balanced equation has equal numbers of each kind of atom on either side of the equation. Writing a balanced equation simply reflects the fact that chemical reactions only rearrange the atoms that were present in reactants. Atoms are never created or destroyed in chemical reactions.

What are reactants and products in a chemical reaction?

Why are chemical equations written in a balanced form?

FIGURE 3–9.

Notice that the atoms involved in the burning of methane are only rearranged into different molecules.

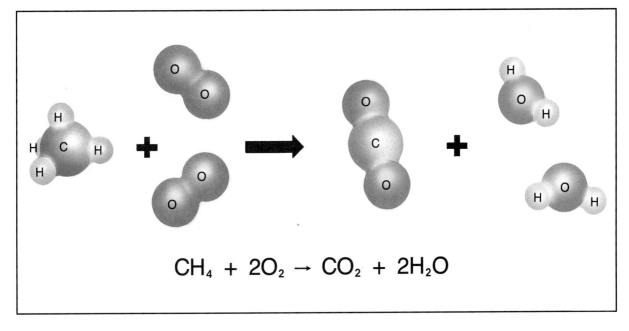

$$CH_4 + 2O_2 \rightarrow CO_2 + 2H_2O$$

3:5 Mixtures

When elements combine to form a compound, they no longer have their original properties. You learned in Section 3:2 that the properties of sodium chloride resemble neither those of sodium nor those of chlorine. But what happens if substances are just mixed together and do not combine chemically? A **mixture** is a combination of substances in which the individual components retain their own properties. For example, you can stir sand and table salt together. Neither one changes.

The components of a mixture can be separated from each other because they are not combined chemically. Components can be separated by some method that takes advantage of the differences in their properties. For example, salt dissolves in water while sand does not. So, if you stirred a sand-salt mixture in water, the salt would dissolve. Then you could filter the mixture to recover the sand. Evaporating the water would recover the solid salt.

The three most important kinds of mixtures in living organisms are solutions, suspensions, and colloids. A **solution** is a mixture in which one or more substances is distributed evenly in another substance. Sugar will dissolve in water to form a solution. The sugar molecules mix evenly throughout the water molecules. The substance being dissolved, the sugar, is called the solute. The substance in which the solute is dissolved, the water, is called the solvent. Neither the sugar nor the water changes chemically. They can be recovered by evaporating the water. The sugar does not evaporate and is left behind.

Many important substances in living organisms, such as sugars and mineral ions, are dissolved in water. The concentration of a solution is a measure of the amount of solute dissolved in the solvent. Organisms cannot live unless concentrations of dissolved substances stay within a very narrow range. Thus, processes of homeostasis move molecules and ions to keep dissolved substances in correct concentration.

What is a mixture?

What is a solution?

What is meant by the concentration of a solution? How do processes of homeostasis maintain correct solution concentration?

FIGURE 3–10.

As this compound is mixed with water, its ions become mixed completely among water molecules. The ions will never settle, nor can they be filtered out. These are the characteristics of a solution.

FIGURE 3–11.

Gelatin forms a colloid when mixed with water. When it is warm it is a liquid sol. After cooling it becomes a gel which holds its shape.

A **suspension** is a mixture in which particles of materials are temporarily mixed together. In addition, the particles are much larger than single molecules or ions. A suspension will separate if left standing. When sand and water are stirred together, the sand is suspended for a short time but will settle out. Suspensions can also be separated by filtering. Because the particles are much larger than molecules, you can see them. Therefore, suspensions appear cloudy. Blood is a suspension. If a test tube of blood is prevented from clotting and is left undisturbed, the blood cells will settle out.

A **colloid** is a mixture in which the particles are larger than those in a solution but smaller than those in a suspension. The particles cannot be filtered out, nor will they settle out over time. Colloids exist in two states; sol and gel. A sol is liquid, and gels are jelly-like. When gelatin dessert is mixed with hot water, it forms a sol colloid. As it cools, it changes from a sol to a gel. Much of the material inside a cell is a colloid.

colloid:
kolla (GK) glue
eidos (GK) form, like

3:6 Water

Water is one of the most important compounds in organisms. It makes up 70 to 95 percent of most organisms. The water molecule is composed of two atoms of hydrogen linked by covalent bonds to one atom of oxygen, Figure 3–12a. Each hydrogen atom has one electron. The oxygen atom has six electrons in its outer energy level. To become stable, each hydrogen must have two electrons and oxygen must have eight electrons in its outer energy level. The hydrogen atoms share electrons with the oxygen. This gives each atom the electrons it needs to be stable. Notice that one oxygen atom and two hydrogen atoms are enough to form a stable molecule. For this reason, the water molecule has the formula H_2O.

NoteWorthy

A colloid can be distinguished from a solution by the fact that the colloid scatters a beam of light shined through it. Try this with gelatin dessert and a flashlight. You can see the beam of a spotlight in the air because water droplets in air form a colloid.

FIGURE 3–12.

Electrons are shared unequally in the bonds of water (a). As a result, the water molecule is polar (b).

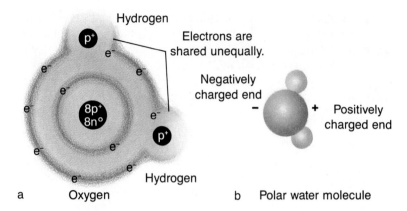

Hydrogen

Electrons are shared unequally.

Negatively charged end

− + Positively charged end

a   Oxygen

b   Polar water molecule

Hydrogen

Sometimes when atoms form covalent bonds, they do not share electrons equally. In a water molecule, the oxygen atom has a stronger attraction for the shared electrons than the hydrogen atoms. As a result, the electrons spend more time near the oxygen atom than they do near the hydrogen atom. Thus, the electron-rich oxygen has a slight negative charge. The electron-deficient hydrogen atoms have a slight positive charge. Notice that a water molecule has a bent shape, Figure 3–12b. The hydrogens are on one side and the oxygen protrudes on the other side. A **polar molecule** is a molecule with an unequal distribution of charge. Because of its shape and the unequal sharing of electrons, a water molecule is polar. Each molecule has a positive end and a negative end.

Water molecules are polar. Therefore, they attract other polar molecules. Because of this attraction, water dissolves many polar substances. Polar molecules such as alcohol and sugar will dissolve in water. Water molecules also attract ions in ionic compounds. If the attraction is strong enough to pull the ions away from each other, the ionic compound will dissolve in water, Figure 3–13. For instance, the ions of compounds such as salt and baking soda separate and dissolve when placed in water.

What makes water molecules polar? Why does water dissolve many substances?

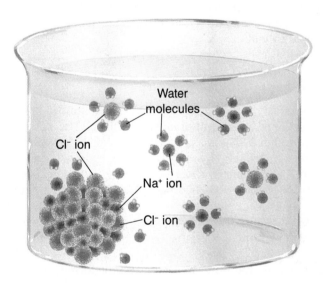

Water molecules

Cl⁻ ion

Na⁺ ion

Cl⁻ ion

FIGURE 3–13.

Polar water molecules are attracted to the ions of a salt crystal. This attraction pulls the ions into solution.

Polar water molecules also attract each other. Positively charged hydrogen atoms attract negatively charged oxygen atoms. This attraction of opposite charges forms weak bonds called hydrogen bonds between water molecules. In fact, hydrogen bonds can form between a bonded hydrogen and any electron-rich atom. Hydrogen bonds are weak compared to covalent or ionic bonds. However, they are vitally important in living organisms. Hydrogen bonds hold proteins in the correct shape and help keep DNA together.

Water's polarity causes it to be attracted to polar molecules or ions of solid surfaces. This attraction causes water to move up very thin tubes such as those in plant stems. This effect helps the leaves of plants obtain water from the soil.

3:7 Acids and Bases

Most water molecules exist in the form of H_2O. However, a small fraction of water molecules break down to form positively charged hydrogen ions (H^+) and negatively charged hydroxide ions (OH^-). Excess hydrogen ions cause a water solution to be acidic. Excess hydroxide ions cause it to be basic. Since there are equal numbers of these two ions in pure water, it is said to be neutral.

If hydrogen chloride (HCl) is added to water, hydrogen ions (H^+) and chloride ions (Cl^-) are formed. A substance that forms hydrogen ions in water is called an **acid.** Hydrogen chloride in solution is called hydrochloric acid. Hydrochloric acid is formed in your stomach, where it aids in digestion of food.

If sodium hydroxide (NaOH) is dissolved in water, it forms sodium ions (Na^+) and hydroxide ions (OH^-). A substance that forms hydroxide ions in water is called a **base.**

The pH scale is used to measure how acidic or basic a solution is. The pH scale as shown in Figure 3–14 has a range from 0 to 14. As the pH of a solution becomes lower, the concentration of hydrogen ions becomes greater. A solution with a pH below 7 is acidic. As pH becomes higher, the concentration of hydroxide ions in solution becomes greater. A solution with a pH above 7 is basic. At pH 7, there are equal numbers of hydrogen and hydroxide ions in solution. A pH of 7 is neutral. Pure water has a pH of 7.

Why is pure water neither acidic nor basic?

FIGURE 3–14.

This scale shows the pH of some common materials.

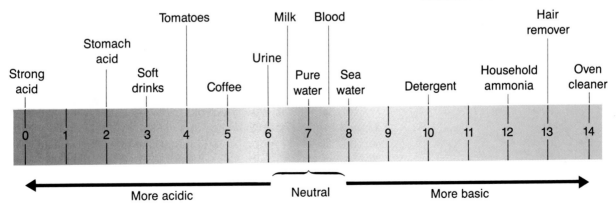

1. Why do atoms combine chemically with other atoms?
2. How does the formation of an ionic bond differ from the formation of a covalent bond?
3. A water solution of a substance has a pH of 2. What can you say about the proportion of hydrogen and hydroxide ions in solution?
4. **SKILL REVIEW:** Study the diagram in Figure 3–13, which shows the process of an ionic compound dissolving in water. In your own words, describe the process in a step-by-step fashion. Tell what the water molecules are doing and why. Describe what is happening to the salt ions and why. Describe the nature of the mixture after the compound dissolves. For more help, refer to Reading Science in the Skill Handbook, pages 798 to 799.
5. **USING CONCEPTS:** List the number and kinds of atoms present in each of the following compounds. All of these compounds can be found in living organisms.
   a. ammonia (NH_3)
   b. phosphoric acid (H_3PO_4)
   c. acetic acid ($C_2H_4O_2$)
   d. ribose sugar ($C_5H_{10}O_5$)
   e. hydrogen sulfide (H_2S)

LIFE SUBSTANCES

Most of the mass of an organism that is not water consists of carbon-based compounds. Most compounds that contain carbon are organic compounds. The first carbon compounds that scientists studied came from living organisms. Because of this, they were called organic compounds. Scientists once believed that organic compounds could be made only by a mysterious vital force present in living things. Today, organic compounds are made every day in chemical plants. A whole range of items—from plastic dishpans to prescription drugs—are made of organic compounds. Organic compounds that are made by living things generally are called biomolecules.

Objectives:
- explain why organic compounds exist in such large variety.
- describe the structure of a polymer and tell how polymers are formed and broken down.
- describe carbohydrates and give examples and uses of three carbohydrates that are polymers.
- describe the structure and functions of lipids in organisms.
- describe the structure and functions of proteins in organisms.
- describe the structure and function of nucleic acids.

3:8 The Role of Carbon in Living Things

A carbon atom has four electrons in its outer energy level. It needs a total of eight electrons in the outer energy level to be stable. Thus, carbon can form four covalent bonds at one time. Carbon can bond with other carbon atoms as well as with other elements. When carbon atoms bond to each other, they form straight chains, branched chains, or rings. Thus, a huge number of carbon structures are possible. These carbon structures form the skeletons of many of the compounds found in functioning cells. These compounds can range from simple molecules having one or two carbon atoms to macromolecules. Macromolecules are very large molecules containing many thousands of atoms.

When two carbon atoms bond, they can share one electron each and form a single covalent bond. They can also share two or three electrons. When each atom shares two electrons, a double bond is formed. When each shares three electrons, a triple bond is formed. A double bond is represented as $\diagup C{=}C\diagdown$. A triple bond is shown as $-C{\equiv}C-$. Carbon skeletons thus vary in bonding as well as in arrangement of the atoms.

Because so much variety is possible in organic structures, compounds with the same formula can differ in structure. Compounds that have the same simple formula but different three-dimensional structures are called **isomers.** Isomers have different chemical and physical properties. Only their chemical formulas are the same. Glucose and fructose are two sugars, both with the formula $C_6H_{12}O_6$, yet they differ in molecular structure, Figure 3–15. Glucose and fructose are isomers. Scientists use structural formulas such as those in Figure 3–15 to represent organic molecules. Structural formulas, along with chemical names, make it clear which compound a scientist is talking about.

Carbon compounds vary greatly in both size and shape. Learning how smaller compounds combine to form macromolecules will aid you in understanding how these molecules work in a living cell. Cells make these macromolecules by bonding small molecules to form chains called polymers. A **polymer** is a very large molecule consisting of repeated linked units. Each of the subunits that acts as a building block of the polymer is called a **monomer.**

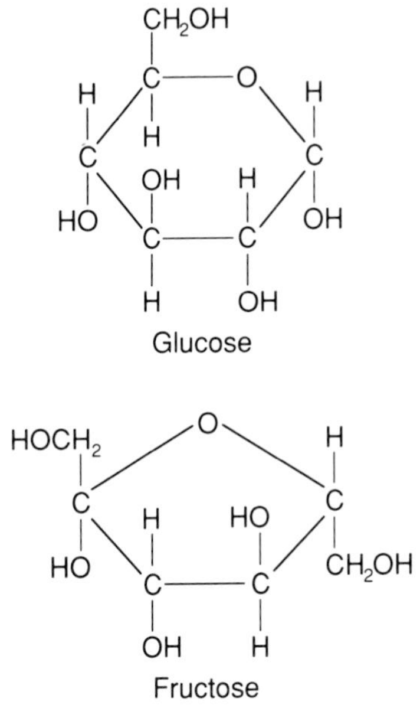

FIGURE 3–15.

To prove to yourself that glucose and fructose are isomers, count the number of each kind of atom in each molecule.

polymer:
poly (GK) many
meros (GK) part

FIGURE 3–16.

Spider silk is an example of a polymer produced by an organism. It is so strong that scientists hope to learn how to manufacture it.

FIGURE 3–17.

In living things, most polymers form by condensation reactions among monomers.

HO – Monomer – OH

HO – Monomer – OH   HO – Monomer – O-

HO – Monomer – OH

HO – Monomer – OH   Condensation

HO – Monomer – OH

HO – Monomer – OH

→ H_2O

Polymer chain

Different polymers are made up of different kinds of monomers. However, in living things, the chemical reactions that make and break polymers are generally the same. When monomers join, one loses a hydrogen ion (H^+) and the other a hydroxide ion (OH^-) to form water. A covalent bond forms between the two atoms that lost the hydrogen ion and the hydroxide ion. Thus, the monomers link and one molecule of water is produced, as shown in Figure 3–17. Condensation is the process by which two molecules are linked by the removal of a water molecule between them.

Polymers are broken down by the process of hydrolysis. This process takes place when you digest food. Hydrolysis is the breaking apart of a molecule by the addition of water. Bonds between the monomer subunits in a polymer are broken by the addition of water molecules. A hydrogen ion from water attaches to one side of a bond between monomers and the hydroxide ion is added to the other. This process continues until the polymer is reduced to its monomers. Thus, hydrolysis is the reverse of condensation.

What is condensation?

hydrolysis:
hydro (GK) water
lysis (GK) to split, loosen

FIGURE 3–18.

Corn starch can be changed by hydrolysis into corn syrup and other useful products. Likewise, proteins from soybeans can be hydrolyzed to make soy sauce.

Glucose + Fructose → Sucrose + H_2O

FIGURE 3–19.

Sucrose is produced by a condensation reaction between glucose and fructose.

3:9 Carbohydrates

A **carbohydrate** is an organic compound composed of carbon, hydrogen, and oxygen, with two hydrogen atoms for every oxygen atom. Starch, sugars, and cellulose are common carbohydrates. The simplest type of carbohydrate is a simple sugar, called a **monosaccharide.** Monosaccharides are the monomers of which all carbohydrates are composed. Glucose and fructose, sugars found in many fruits and in honey, are two common monosaccharides.

Two monosaccharides can link together to form a **disaccharide,** a two-sugar carbohydrate. If glucose and fructose combine in a condensation reaction, a molecule of sucrose is formed. Sucrose is known as table sugar and is also the major form of sugar transported in plants. Two glucose molecules form maltose, malt sugar.

The largest carbohydrate molecules are polysaccharides. A **polysaccharide** is a polymer composed of many simple sugar monomers. Some polysaccharides contain thousands of sugar units. Plants store food in the form of starch, a polymer of glucose. Animals store some food as glycogen, another glucose polymer. Suppose your body needs energy quickly. The glycogen stored in your liver and muscles is quickly broken down into glucose by hydrolysis. The glucose releases energy when broken down in cells. Some polysaccharides are used for structural material rather than for storage of energy. Cellulose is another glucose polymer that forms the cell walls of plants and gives plants structural support.

Starch polymer

FIGURE 3–20.

Humans and other organisms get energy from foods containing starch, a polymer of glucose sugar monomers.

Unsaturated lipids (oils) are more common in organisms whose cells must withstand cold. Oils stay liquid at lower temperatures. Fish oils and oils from plants that grow in colder regions typically are unsaturated. Conversely, saturated fats are common in warm-blooded animals and in tropical plants. In these organisms, cells do not get cold enough for the fat to solidify.

3:10 Lipids

Lipids are organic compounds made by cells mainly for long-term energy storage. Like carbohydrates, lipids are composed of carbon, hydrogen, and oxygen. However, lipids have a greater proportion of hydrogen atoms than carbohydrates. Lipids that contain only single bonds are referred to as saturated. Saturated lipids are usually solid at room temperature and are classified as fats. Animals store lipids as fats. Lipids with double bonds are called unsaturated. Unsaturated lipids are usually liquids and are called oils. Plants usually store lipids as oils. Lipids are often part of the food stored in seeds. Lipids are a necessary part of cell membranes and are used to make hormones.

The most common type of lipid consists of three fatty acids bonded to a molecule of glycerol, Figure 3–21. Glycerol is a three-carbon molecule that serves as a backbone for the lipid molecule. Attached to the glycerol by condensation are three fatty acids. Because of this three-chain structure, these lipids are called triglycerides. There are many different fatty acids, but all have a long chain of carbon and hydrogen atoms. Fatty acids vary in the number of carbons in the chain as well as in the position and number of double bonds.

Fats, oils, and waxes are all lipids. Because the long carbon-hydrogen chains of lipids are not polar, water molecules are not attracted to them. Therefore, lipids do not dissolve in water. Because of this property, lipids are valuable to some organisms as a protective coating. Sea birds and other aquatic animals such as sea otters have a thin layer of oil to prevent water from matting down their feathers or fur. If their feathers or fur become waterlogged, they cannot stay afloat and will drown. Many plants have a waxy lipid coating that helps protect the cells beneath from drying out.

FIGURE 3–21.

The most common type of lipid consists of three fatty acids bonded to a glycerol unit. The fatty acid chains may be saturated or unsaturated.

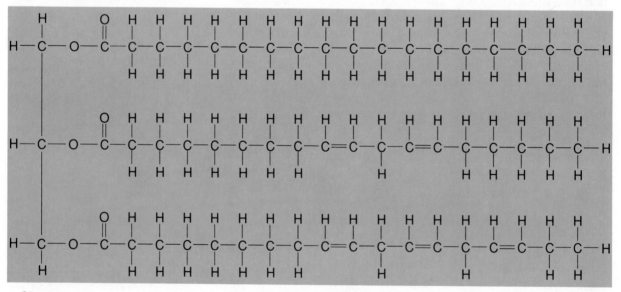

Glycerol
unit

Fatty acid chains

FIGURE 3–22.

Water birds spread natural oils through their feathers so that the feathers will shed water and stay dry.

Lipids are used by cells for energy storage. When energy is needed, lipids are broken down to smaller molecules that can provide energy for cellular activities. Because lipids yield a large amount of energy per gram, they are very high-energy nutrients.

3:11 Proteins

A **protein** is a large, complex polymer composed of carbon, hydrogen, oxygen, and nitrogen. Some proteins also contain sulfur. The monomers that link together to form proteins are called **amino acids.** There are 20 common amino acids. Each amino acid contains a central carbon atom, to which are attached a carboxyl group (—COOH), a hydrogen atom, and an amino group (—NH$_2$), as shown in Figure 3–23. Also attached to the central carbon atom is a group that makes each amino acid different. Condensation reactions bond amino acids together. The amino group of one amino acid reacts with the carboxyl group of another amino acid. The covalent bond formed between amino acids is called a **peptide bond.** Amino acids bond together to form a long chain called a **polypeptide.** A polypeptide chain can contain hundreds of amino acids.

Proteins are composed of one or more polypeptide chains. Most proteins are made of the same 20 amino acids. However, the order in which the amino acids are arranged in the chains determines the kind of protein that is formed. Hydrogen bonding and other attractive forces between the amino acids in the polypeptide chains cause the chains to be folded and bent. The folded chains form a three-dimensional structure that is unique to each protein.

What is the monomer of proteins?

FIGURE 3–23.

Condensation between two amino acids produces a peptide bond. Proteins consist of many amino acids linked by peptide bonds.

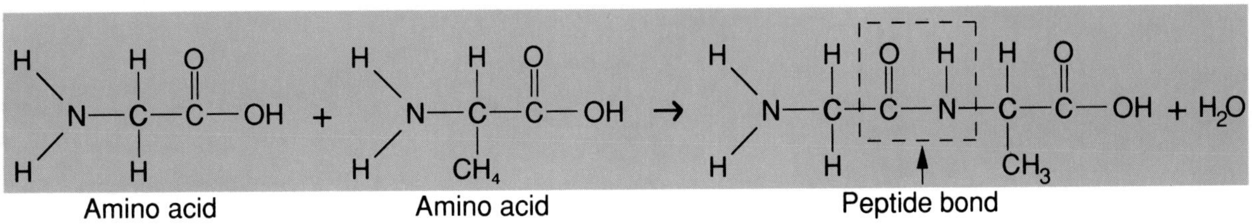

Amino acid + Amino acid → Peptide bond + H$_2$O

FIGURE 3–24.

This model of an actual protein shows that protein chains are folded into a compact shape.

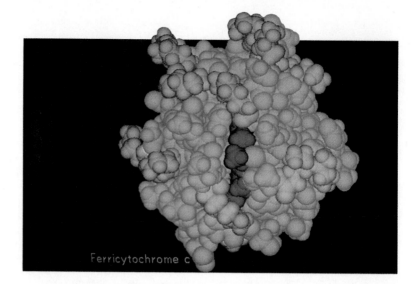

Ferricytochrome c

Of all the molecules in living things, proteins are the most variable in structure. This explains why they can perform so many different functions. Hair, skin, and spider webs are made of protein. Hemoglobin, the red component of blood, is a complex protein. Proteins can even yield energy when other food supplies are used up.

Some proteins act to speed up chemical reactions in cells. An **enzyme** is a protein that speeds up the rate of a chemical reaction without being permanently affected by that reaction. In fact, enzymes cause reactions that would not otherwise take place at all. Enzymes carry out nearly all life processes. They digest food, make needed molecules, transfer substances through membranes, release energy, and generally, make life possible. Each enzyme acts on a specific molecule or set of molecules called substrates. The enzyme enables the substrates to undergo a chemical reaction to form new substances, and the enzyme is released unchanged. Each substrate fits into an area of the enzyme called the active site. This fitting together has been compared to a lock and key. However, scientists know that enzymes and substrates usually change shape to fit together in a process called induced fit.

What is an enzyme?

FIGURE 3–25.

Enzymes fit together with specific substrates and enable them to undergo reaction.

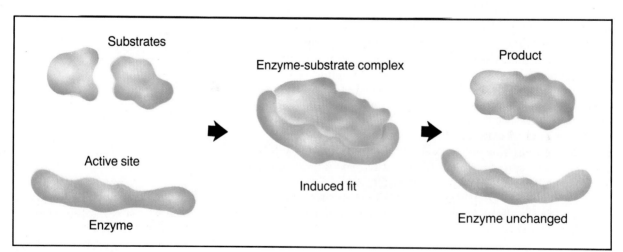

Substrates

Enzyme-substrate complex

Product

Active site

Induced fit

Enzyme

Enzyme unchanged

PROTEINS MADE TO ORDER

Engineers should be able to design and construct proteins the same as any other structure. How does protein engineering work? One way is by finding ways to produce existing proteins in large quantities. Recall that genetic information in a cell's nucleus forms a code for making protein. Scientists can splice the code for a certain human protein into bacteria. By growing large quantities of the bacteria, the protein can be manufactured outside the human body. This method has allowed scientists to mass-produce both human growth hormone and human insulin. Another engineered protein, tissue plasminogen activator, dissolves blood clots in heart attack patients. Scientists have also produced a protein that binds with the AIDS virus, which may block the virus from infecting cells.

In another type of protein engineering, scientists plan to improve existing proteins and eventually to invent some new ones. One technique allows scientists to modify the genetic code in order to replace one or more amino acids in the protein molecule. This slight change may give the protein a completely different function. One company has engineered lipase, an enzyme that breaks down fat. They plan on using a fungus to produce lipase for use in laundry detergents.

One of the processes in the production of human insulin

3:12 Nucleic Acids

A **nucleic acid** is a large and complex macromolecule that stores information in the form of a code. A nucleic acid may consist of hundreds of thousands of atoms of carbon, hydrogen, oxygen, nitrogen, and phosphorus. The monomers that link together to form nucleic acids are called **nucleotides**. Each nucleotide is formed from a nitrogen base bonded to a ribose or deoxyribose sugar molecule which is bonded to a phosphate group as shown in Figure 3–26. The nucleotide polymer in some nucleic acids forms a long, spiral-shaped molecule.

Nucleic acids form a code that contains the instructions a cell uses to form the thousands of compounds needed in life processes. Two important nucleic acids are deoxyribonucleic acid (DNA) and ribonucleic acid (RNA). **DNA** is the "master copy" of an organism's information code. In eukaryotes, DNA is found in the nucleus. In the nucleus, DNA is copied in the form of RNA. The RNA code moves out of the nucleus and into the cell's cytoplasm. Here the code is read, and protein molecules are made according to its pattern. The DNA code also passes an organism's instructions from generation to generation. Thus, it is called the genetic code.

Because it forms the genetic code, the order in which nucleotides bond in DNA is critical to the life of an organism. Small changes in the order of nucleotides can cause a changed enzyme to be formed.

FIGURE 3–26.

Nucleotides like this one are the monomers of nucleic acids.

FIGURE 3–27.

This computer image of DNA shows its spiral-shaped structure.

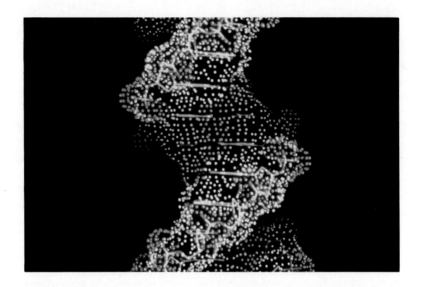

This can cause changes in the form of an organism or in its life processes. Sometimes the changed organism cannot survive. However, some changes can help the organism survive better than others of its species. Such changes, over time, result in the evolution of new characteristics and perhaps new species.

REVIEW

6. List three functions of lipids in organisms.
7. Describe the process by which most polymers in living things are formed from monomers.
8. If there are only 20 different amino acids commonly found in organisms, why is it possible to have thousands of different proteins?
9. **SKILL REVIEW:** Make a table comparing carbohydrates, lipids, proteins, and nucleic acids. List these four types of biomolecules in the left column. In the next three columns, list the components of each type, the functions of each in organisms, and list all the examples for each given in the chapter. For more help, refer to Organizing Information in the Skill Handbook, pages 810 to 813.
10. **USING CONCEPTS:** Look at the following two organic structural formulas. Write simple formulas for each. Are the compounds the same or different? Explain.

BIOLAB

Enzyme Action

3

Problem: What fruits contain enzymes that act on protein?

Materials

paper cups (4)
stirring rod
hot plate
pot holders
wax paper
refrigerator
ice

package gelatin dessert (1)
1000-mL beakers (2)
100-mL graduated cylinder
fresh pineapple
canned chunk pineapple
grapes or orange sections
knife

Procedures

1. Copy the data table.
2. Number paper cups 1 through 4.
3. Measure 350 mL water and pour into a beaker. Bring to a boil on a hot plate. **CAUTION:** *Use extreme caution when handling and pouring hot liquids.*
4. Select 3 chunks of canned pineapple. Cut 3 chunks of fresh pineapple the same size as the canned chunks. Cut 3 grapes in half or choose three orange slices. Set these aside on wax paper.
5. Measure 225 mL of cold water and pour into a second beaker. Add enough ice to fill the beaker to 650 mL.
6. When the water is boiling, add all the gelatin and stir until completely dissolved. Remove the beaker from the hot plate.

7. Add the cold water and ice cubes to the gelatin. Stir until slightly thickened.
8. Pour 100 mL gelatin into each paper cup.
9. When the gelatin is slightly thickened (about 6–8 minutes), add the following to each cup. Make sure fruits are submerged.
   Cup 1—nothing
   Cup 2—canned pineapple chunks
   Cup 3—fresh pineapple chunks
   Cup 4—grape halves or orange slices
10. Set the cups in the refrigerator. Check the consistency of the gelatin every 5 minutes. Record observations in the data table.

Questions and Conclusion

1. Gelatin is a protein. Bromelin is a protein-digesting enzyme found in pineapple. What evidence of enzyme action did you observe in this activity?
2. What was the purpose of cup 1?
3. Find out about the process of canning pineapple. What factor would you suppose has the greatest effect on enzyme action?
4. People who must handle raw pineapple over long periods of time wear gloves. Why do you think this is advisable?
5. Meat tenderizers contain enzymes such as bromelin or papain, a similar enzyme from papaya. Suggest how these products work.

Conclusion: Based on this activity, what can you conclude about which fruits have enzymes that act on protein?

Data and Observations

Cup and Contents	Time in Minutes					
	5	10	15	20	25	30
1. Gelatin only						
2. Gelatin + canned pineapple						
3. Gelatin + fresh pineapple						
4. Gelatin + other fruit						

CHAPTER REVIEW

SUMMARY

1. Atoms contain a positive nucleus surrounded by negative electrons. **3:1**
2. Atoms share or transfer electrons in order to have stable outer energy levels. **3:2, 3:3**
3. When chemical reactions occur, reactants change into new substances called products. **3:4**
4. In mixtures, substances do not combine chemically. **3:5**
5. Water's polarity gives water the ability to dissolve a wide variety of substances. **3:6**
6. In water solution, acids produce H^+ ions, while bases produce OH^- ions. **3:7**
7. Carbon atoms can bond to form straight chains, branched chains, and rings. **3:8**
8. Carbohydrates include starch, cellulose, and glycogen, polymers of simple sugars. **3:9**
9. Lipids include fats, oils, and waxes. Lipids are used for long-term energy storage. **3:10**
10. Enzymes are proteins that speed up the rate of chemical reactions in organisms. **3:11**
11. Nucleic acids are polymers that make up the information code for an organism. **3:12**

LANGUAGE OF BIOLOGY

acid	isomers
amino acids	isotopes
atom	lipids
base	mixture
carbohydrate	molecule
colloid	monomer
compound	monosaccharide
covalent bond	nucleic acid
disaccharide	nucleotides
DNA	nucleus
enzyme	peptide bond
ion	polar molecule
ionic bond	polymer

polypeptide   solution
polysaccharide   suspension
protein

Choose the word or phrase from the list above that completes the sentence.

1. When two atoms of different elements combine chemically, they form a(n) ____.
2. Particles having positive and neutral charges are found in the ____ of an atom.
3. A compound that forms hydrogen ions when dissolved in water is a(n) ____.
4. A(n) ____ is a macromolecule that stores information.
5. A(n) ____ between atoms is formed when electrons are shared.
6. An atom that has become charged by the gain or loss of electrons is called a(n) ____.
7. A(n) ____ is a molecule with an unequal distribution of electrons.
8. A(n) ____ is a protein that speeds up the rate of a chemical reaction.
9. ____ may be fats, oils, or waxes.
10. A(n) ____ is a polymer consisting of a chain of amino acids.

REVIEWING CONCEPTS

Choose the word or phrase that completes the sentence or answers the question.

11. In the reaction $4Fe + 3O_2 \rightarrow 2Fe_2O_3$, the substance Fe_2O_3 is a(n) ____.
    a. product   c. element
    b. mixture   d. reactant
12. You would expect two isotopes of oxygen to differ in the number of ____ each contains.
    a. electrons   c. neutrons
    b. protons   d. ions
13. Which of the following is a carbohydrate?
    a. carbon   c. enzyme
    b. glycogen   d. oil

14. Ions bond because of the attraction of ___.
    a. polar molecules   c. hydrogen atoms
    b. shared electrons   d. opposite charges

15. Which of the following contains nitrogen?
    a. carbon   c. lipids
    b. enzymes   d. cellulose

16. A ___ is a mixture in which substances are uniformly distributed.
    a. suspension   c. solution
    b. compound   d. solvent

17. Isomers differ in ___.
    a. elements   c. neutrons
    b. simple formula   d. structure

18. Water dissolves many different substances because its molecules are ___.
    a. ionic   c. bonded
    b. polar   d. polymers

19. A solution of pH 12 has excess ___ ions.
    a. acid   c. hydrogen
    b. neutral   d. hydroxide

20. ___ is a polysaccharide.
    a. Starch   c. Wax
    b. A simple sugar   d. Nucleic acid

UNDERSTANDING CONCEPTS

Answer the following questions using complete sentences.

21. What is the charge on an atom that has lost two electrons in a reaction? Explain.
22. Why is the oxygen in a water molecule slightly more negative than the hydrogens?
23. If three amino acids link by condensation, how many molecules of water would form?
24. Why are foods with a large proportion of starch considered to be good energy sources?
25. Since proteins are made of polypeptide chains, how can you account for their blob-shaped structure?
26. Why don't lipids dissolve in water?

27. What element would you expect to find in molecules of most acids?
28. How do elements and compounds differ?
29. What is the function of an enzyme?
30. Why is DNA so important to organisms?

APPLYING CONCEPTS

Answer the following questions using complete sentences.

31. A magnesium atom has 12 electrons. When it reacts, it usually loses two electrons. How does this make magnesium more stable?
32. Suggest reasons why diet and exercise can help people lose fat.
33. What is the purpose of the large amount of starch found in the seeds of many plants?
34. Heating a white substance produces a vapor and black material. Was the substance an element or a compound? Explain.
35. Digestion of food cannot occur without sufficient water. Explain why this is so.

EXTENSIONS

1. Research the use of radioactive isotopes in medical diagnosis and biological research.
2. Create and display structural models of some of the organic molecules in this chapter.
3. Research the functions of proteins such as keratin, actin, myosin, insulin, and collagen.

READINGS

Atkins, P.W. *Molecules.* New York: Scientific American Library, 1987.

Peterson, Ivars. "A Biological Antifreeze." *Science News,* Nov. 22, 1986, pp. 330–332.

Scientific American, Oct. 1985. The entire issue deals with the molecules of life.

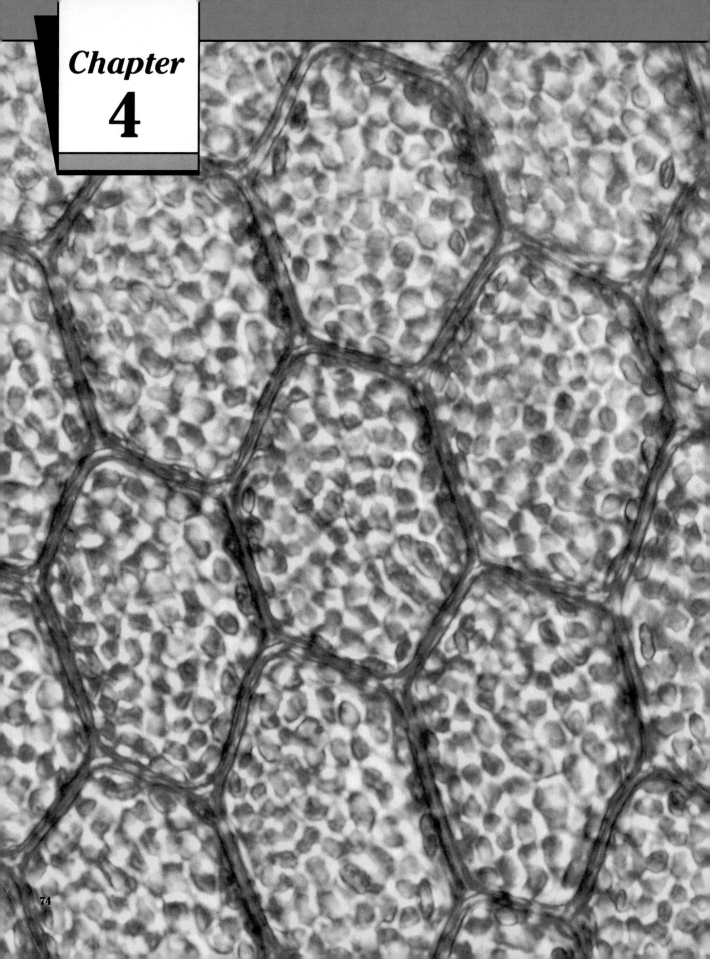

A VIEW OF THE CELL

I magine a miniature factory where all the activities necessary to life are carried out. A central office governs the factory's operations and keeps the factory's records and plans. A power plant provides the energy for all the processes in the factory. Raw materials needed by the factory enter the receiving department. Products are made in the manufacturing area, then stored in the warehousing area. Finally, products are sent out by the shipping department. There is a waste recycling system. A tight security system surrounds the factory, ensuring safety from trespassers.

What is this factory? It is a living cell. Most cells are so small that you can't see them without a microscope. Yet, despite its tiny size, the cell carries out the many functions of life.

THE CELLULAR BASIS OF LIFE

From the smallest bacterium to the largest whale, all living things are made up of cells. Whether an organism is an alga of only one cell or a giant redwood with millions of cells, cells carry out its life functions. The amazing internal organization of the cell enables it to function with the precision of a well-run factory.

4:1 The Cell Theory

In 1665, an English scientist, Robert Hooke (1635–1703), used a microscope to examine very thin slices of cork. He observed that the cork was not solid. Instead, it was composed of tiny, hollow boxes that Hooke called cells. Today, we know that the structures Hooke saw were only the walls of dead cells. Hooke's observations were important not because he made them, but because he published them. In Hooke's time, modern science was just beginning. Scientists were starting to form societies in which they could report, discuss, and publish their work. Hooke's publication of his drawings and descriptions led other scientists of the time to look for evidence of cells.

Objectives:
- relate advances in microscope technology to discoveries about cells and cell structure.
- describe the operation of a compound light microscope and an electron microscope.
- state the main ideas of the cell theory.

NoteWorthy

Hooke named cells after their resemblance to small rooms in monasteries, which were called *cellulae.*

Cells of plant leaf

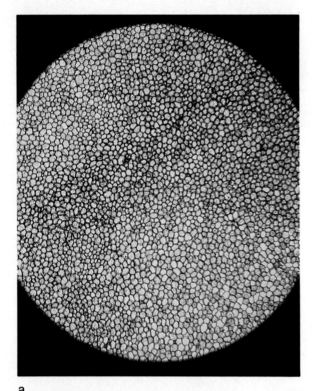

lens

a

b

FIGURE 4–1.

Hooke thought cork cells (a) looked like little boxes. Van Leeuwenhoek's microscopes (b) had only one lens.

microscope:
mikros (GK) small
skopein (GK) to look

Hooke was able to make his discoveries only because of advances in precision lensmaking. A lens is a curved piece of transparent material such as glass or plastic. A lens bends light rays as they pass through it. A magnifying glass is a lens you have probably used. An expert Dutch lensmaker, Anton van Leeuwenhoek (LAY vun hook) (1632–1723), made many improvements in microscopes. With his microscopes, Leeuwenhoek reported his discovery of many organisms invisible to the unaided eye. Leeuwenhoek's microscopes were simple microscopes, consisting of only one magnifying lens. Even so, they were the best microscopes of their time.

Other scientists began to experiment with compound microscopes. In a compound microscope, one lens forms an enlarged image of the object. A second lens further magnifies the image formed by the first lens. A **compound light microscope** has two or more lenses to magnify an object and uses light to make the object visible. Trace the path of light rays through a compound microscope in Figure 4–2. With improved microscopes, people were able to see not only cells but even smaller structures within cells.

During the next 200 years, microscopes were greatly improved. By the 1830s, two German scientists, Matthias Schleiden and Theodor Schwann, were able to view many different organisms and draw some important conclusions. Schleiden observed plants with a microscope and concluded that all plants are composed of cells and depend on cells to function. Schwann made similar observations about animals. Based on their work, Schleiden and Schwann proposed that cells are the basic units of structure and function of all living things. This idea formed the basis of the cell theory.

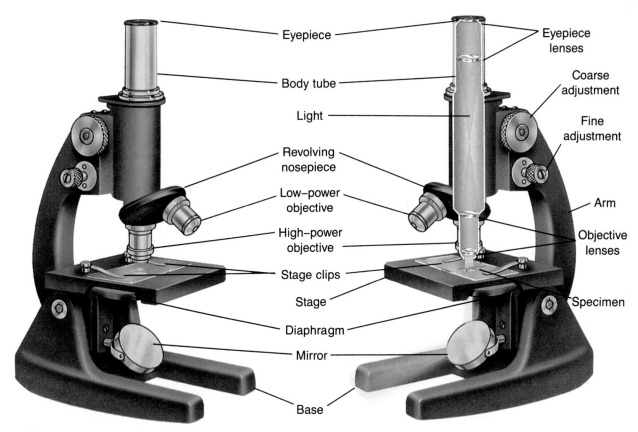

Eyepiece
Body tube
Light
Revolving nosepiece
Low–power objective
High–power objective
Stage clips
Stage
Diaphragm
Mirror
Base

Eyepiece lenses
Coarse adjustment
Fine adjustment
Arm
Objective lenses
Specimen

The cell theory was further expanded in 1855 by the work of another German scientist, Rudolf Virchow. Virchow concluded that all cells come from other living cells.

The **cell theory** is made up of three main ideas:

1. All organisms are composed of one or more cells.
2. The cell is the basic unit of organization of organisms.
3. All cells come from pre-existing cells.

4:2 How Scientists Study Cells

The invention and development of the light microscope enabled scientists to discover and study cells. In the last fifty years, scientists have been using microscopes more powerful than light microscopes to observe cells. This is possible because a beam of electrons, rather than light, is used to illuminate the objects being studied. An **electron microscope** passes electrons over or through an object to form a magnified image of the object. Electrons can form a clear image at much higher levels of magnification. A **transmission electron microscope** (TEM) aims a beam of electrons through the object being viewed. A **scanning electron microscope** (SEM) moves the electron beam over the surface of an object. Instead of glass lenses, electron microscopes use electromagnets to focus and magnify the image. The image is formed on a screen similar to a television. Photographic film may be inserted in place of the screen to produce a permanent image. Compare these two types of electron microscopes in Figure 4–3.

FIGURE 4–2.

You may use a compound microscope like this one. Notice there is more than one lens.

NoteWorthy

The magnification of light microscopes is limited to about 2500 times. Beyond this, image quality becomes poor because light waves are scattered by the lenses.

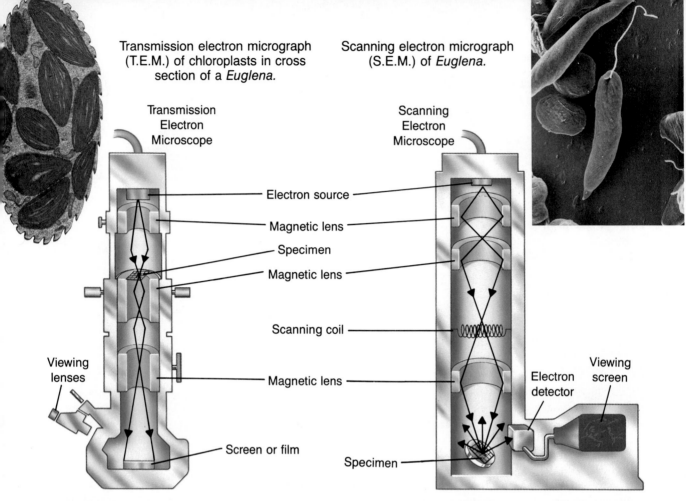

Transmission electron micrograph (T.E.M.) of chloroplasts in cross section of a *Euglena*.

Scanning electron micrograph (S.E.M.) of *Euglena*.

Transmission Electron Microscope

Scanning Electron Microscope

Electron source

Magnetic lens

Specimen

Magnetic lens

Scanning coil

Viewing lenses

Magnetic lens

Electron detector

Viewing screen

Screen or film

Specimen

FIGURE 4–3.

The transmission electron microscope can show fine detail but the scanning electron microscope image shows surface texture and gives a three-dimensional effect.

Using electron microscopes, biologists have been able to view more details of cell structure. The ultrastructure is the more detailed structure of the cell. Ultrastructure includes not only internal structure, but also surface structure of the cell. From this more exact view of the cell, scientists have learned where cell structures are located and how they function together.

REVIEW

1. What was the importance of the work of Hooke and van Leeuwenhoek to the understanding of organisms?
2. State the three main ideas of the cell theory.
3. Compare the way images are formed in light microscopes and electron microscopes.
4. **SKILL REVIEW:** A compound light microscope has objective lenses that magnify 6, 40, and 95 times. What magnifications are available if an eyepiece that magnifies 15 times is used? For more help, refer to Using a Microscope in the Skill Handbook, pages 804 to 805.
5. **USING CONCEPTS:** Explain how scientists' understanding of cells depended on developments in lensmaking and new kinds of microscopes.

CELL ORGANIZATION

Both cells and factories vary greatly in size and shape. If you stood outside a factory and looked at it, how much could you tell about what went on inside? You could probably see what raw materials were delivered and what products were shipped out. You might even be able to figure out some of the processes that turned raw materials into products. But only by actually seeing inside could you be sure how all the machines, conveyors, and controls actually worked. In the sections that follow, you will see inside the cell to learn about its machinery and organization.

4:3 Control and Boundaries

The organelle that acts as a control center in a eukaryotic cell is the **nucleus.** The nucleus is surrounded by a nuclear membrane and controls most cellular activities. This control is possible because the nucleus contains the nucleic acid, DNA. DNA forms the genetic code, which makes up the set of master plans for building cell proteins, including enzymes. In Chapter 7 you will see how the cell makes proteins according to this code. Copies of the DNA code are passed on to make new cells that are identical to the original cell. Except when the nucleus is dividing, its DNA is wound around protein molecules forming tangles of long strands. These DNA tangles are called **chromatin.** Also within the nucleus is the **nucleolus**, a structure that produces the RNA for production of cell particles called ribosomes. You will learn the function of ribosomes in Section 4:4.

Objectives:
- describe the structure and function of the parts of typical cells.
- explain the advantages of highly folded membranes in cells.

What is the function of DNA?

FIGURE 4–4.

Note that the nucleus has pores in its outer membrane. Information passes to the cytoplasm through these pores.

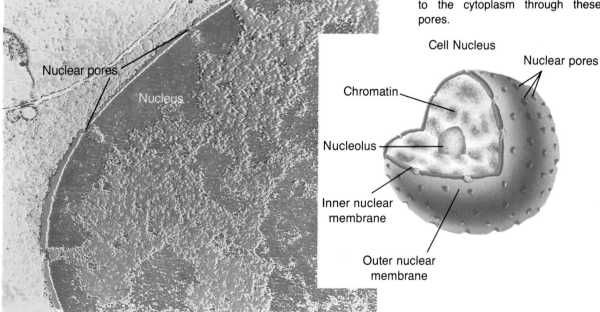

Nuclear pores

Nucleus

Cell Nucleus

Nuclear pores

Chromatin

Nucleolus

Inner nuclear membrane

Outer nuclear membrane

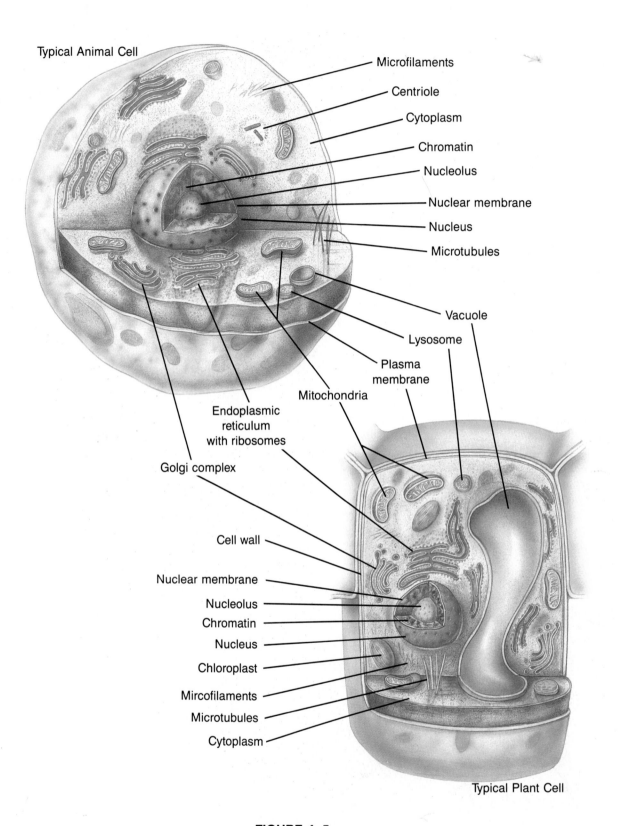

Typical Animal Cell

Microfilaments

Centriole

Cytoplasm

Chromatin

Nucleolus

Nuclear membrane

Nucleus

Microtubules

Vacuole

Lysosome

Plasma
membrane

Mitochondria

Endoplasmic
reticulum
with ribosomes

Golgi complex

Cell wall

Nuclear membrane

Nucleolus

Chromatin

Nucleus

Chloroplast

Mircofilaments

Microtubules

Cytoplasm

Typical Plant Cell

FIGURE 4–5.

Structure of a typical animal cell and a typical plant cell.

FIGURE 4–6.

Very high magnification shows that the plasma membrane is made of two layers of molecules.

The structure that serves as a boundary between a cell and its external environment is the **plasma membrane.** The plasma membrane controls the movement of materials that enter and leave the cell. The plasma membrane allows useful materials such as oxygen and nutrients to enter, and waste products such as excess water to leave. Thus, the plasma membrane helps maintain homeostasis within the cell. In Chapter 5, you will learn more about the plasma membrane.

The cells of plants, fungi, some monerans, and some protists have cell walls. Animal cells do not. A **cell wall** is a rigid structure that surrounds the plasma membrane. The cell wall is much thicker than the plasma membrane. The cell walls of different organisms contain different substances. Plant cell walls contain cellulose. **Cellulose** is a polysaccharide made up of chains of bonded glucose sugar units. Cellulose molecules form interconnecting fibers. The fibers are interwoven in a strong network that protects a plant cell and gives the plant support. Chitin is another polysaccharide composed of different sugar units. Chitin makes up the cell walls of fungi.

NoteWorthy

Chitin occurs not only in the cell walls of fungi but also in the outer skeleton or "shell" of insects and animals such as spiders and shrimp.

a

b

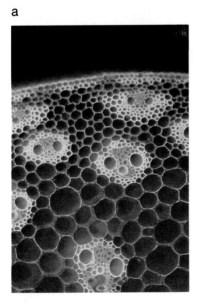

FIGURE 4–7.

Plant cells are bounded by rigid cell walls (a). These walls are made of interwoven fibers of cellulose (b).

4:4 Storage and Assembly

The material that fills the cell and contains the organelles is called the **cytoplasm.** The cytoplasm is the material in which the organelles of the cell are suspended. At times, the cytoplasm may be as thin as water. At other times it may be thick like gelatin.

Suppose you took all the tissues from an ordinary box of facial tissue and spread them out. How much surface area could you cover with the tissues? Probably several square meters. Yet, all this surface area was packed into a small box. Many cell processes take place on the surface of membranes. Eukaryotic cells contain a highly folded system of membranes. This system provides a large membrane surface area. Therefore, cell processes can be more efficient. Most of the membrane system is the endoplasmic reticulum, abbreviated ER. The **endoplasmic reticulum** is a folded membrane that forms a network of interconnected compartments. The ER connects the nuclear membrane with the plasma membrane and is involved in the assembly and transport of proteins.

Some of the ER has ribosomes attached. **Ribosomes** are small structures on which proteins are made. Parts of the ER that have ribosomes attached are referred to as rough ER. Where there are no ribosomes, the ER is called smooth ER. In the cell factory, the ER is like the factory floor with its conveyor system for moving products. The ribosomes are like the production machines.

Packets of proteins made by ribosomes on the ER sometimes pass to the Golgi (GAWL jee) complex. The **Golgi complex** is an organelle that packages and ships proteins made by the cell. It is composed of a series of closely stacked, flattened sacs. The Golgi complex can be thought of as the warehouse and shipping area of the cell factory. It resembles smooth ER in appearance. The proteins packaged by the Golgi complex move either out of the cell or to another part of the cell.

How do cells provide large membrane surface areas?

FIGURE 4–8.

Folds of endoplasmic reticulum fill a large portion of many cells. Ribosomes on the ER manufacture protein.

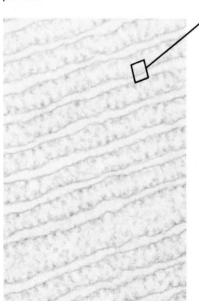

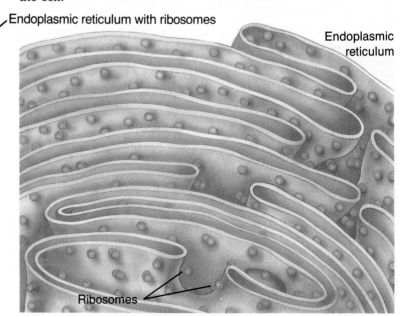

Endoplasmic reticulum with ribosomes

Endoplasmic reticulum

Ribosomes

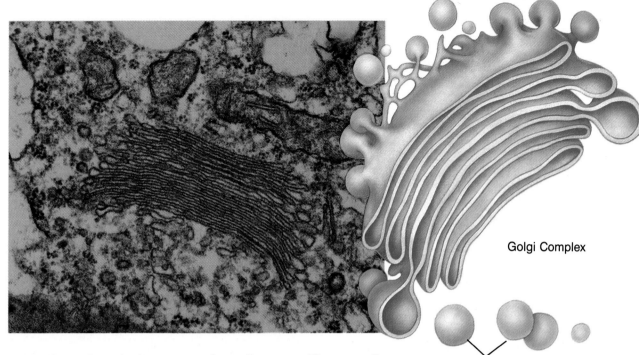

Golgi Complex

Sacs of protein moving out

FIGURE 4–9.

Sacs of proteins pinch off and move away at the edge of the Golgi complex.

All efficient factories have a way of recycling waste. The organelle that carries out this function in the cell is the lysosome (LI suh sohm). The **lysosome** is a round organelle that contains digestive enzymes. The lysosome digests excess or worn-out cell parts, food particles, and invading viruses or bacteria. Sometimes lysosomes digest the cells that contain them. When a tadpole develops into a frog, lysosomes digest the cells of the tadpole's tail. The molecules produced by digestion are used to build new and different cells.

Like factories, cells also have areas for temporary storage of materials. In cells, these spaces are called vacuoles (VAK yuh wohlz). A **vacuole** is a sac of fluid surrounded by a membrane. Vacuoles often store food, enzymes, and other materials needed by a cell. Some vacuoles store waste products. In some protists, a specialized vacuole collects excess water and pumps it out of the cell. A plant cell has a single large vacuole that stores water and other substances.

NoteWorthy

Because it can digest the cell it is in, the lysosome has been called the "suicide bag."

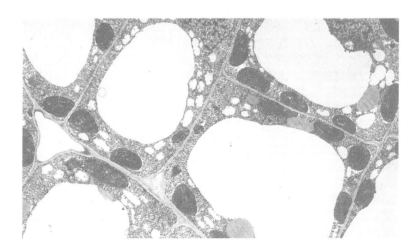

FIGURE 4–10.

Typical plant cells have very large vacuoles containing water and dissolved substances. These vacuoles also cause pressure inside plant cells. When the vacuoles lose water, the plant wilts.

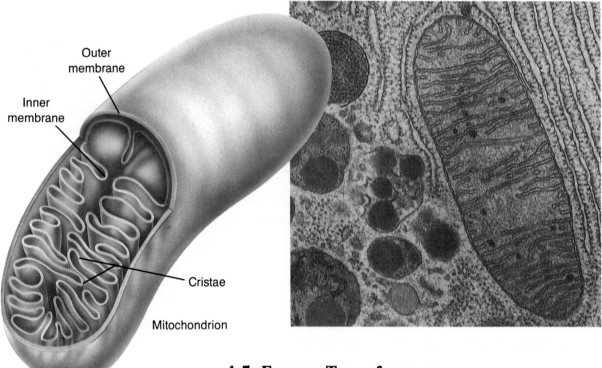

Outer membrane

Inner membrane

Cristae

Mitochondrion

FIGURE 4–11.

Mitochondria contain enzymes needed to release energy from food molecules.

FIGURE 4–12.

In chloroplasts, light changes to chemical energy on folded stacks of membranes.

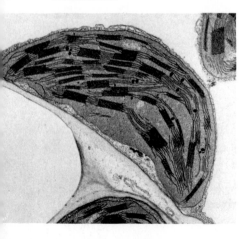

4:5 Energy Transformers

Factories need energy in order to run. Many factories have power plants that burn fuel to release energy. They transform the energy stored in fuel into energy useful to the factory. Two organelles serve as energy transformers in cells. One of these organelles is the mitochondrion (mite uh KAHN dree un) (*pl.* mitochondria). **Mitochondria** are organelles in which food molecules are broken down to release energy. This energy is then used to produce other molecules that can release energy easily. The cell uses these molecules to furnish energy for cell reactions. You will learn more about cell energy processes in Chapter 6.

A mitochondrion has an outer membrane and a highly folded inner membrane. The inner membrane forms long, narrow folds called cristae. Much of the energy-releasing process takes place on the inner membrane. As with the ER, the folds of the inner membrane provide more surface area in a small space.

Not many factories have a device that can transform light directly into usable energy. However, cells of green plants and some protists have organelles that can do just that. **Chloroplasts** convert light energy into chemical energy and store that energy in food molecules. These foods include sugars and starches. The chloroplast is a type of **plastid** (PLAS tud), an organelle that contains pigments. Plastids are named according to their color or the pigment that they contain. The chloroplast contains the green pigment chlorophyll, which gives plant leaves and stems their green color. It is chlorophyll that captures light energy and starts the conversion process. In Chapter 6, you will learn more about the structure of chloroplasts and how they convert light into chemical energy.

4:6 The Cytoskeleton

You have seen how knowledge of cell structure has followed advances in microscope technology. Not many years ago, scientists thought organelles just floated in cytoplasm. Now, scientists have discovered that cells have a support structure called the cytoskeleton.

The **cytoskeleton** is a network of thin, hollow tubes and small fibers that provides support for organelles and helps maintain cell shape. Microtubules and microfilaments make up most of the cytoskeleton. **Microtubules** are thin, hollow cylinders made of protein. **Microfilaments** are thin protein fibers.

Microtubules have functions other than maintaining the shape of cells. They form tracks along which small organelles move. They also may provide channels for the movement of substances in cells. Microfilaments are made of a protein found in muscle cells. Contraction of microfilaments is responsible for many cell movements. Both microfilaments and microtubules have important functions in cell division as you will see in Chapter 7.

4:7 Cilia and Flagella

Some cells have structures for movement. These structures are cilia (SIHL ee uh) and flagella (fluh JEL uh). **Cilia** are short, hairlike projections of the plasma membrane. **Flagella** (*sing.* flagellum) are longer, whiplike projections of the plasma membrane. Cilia are much more numerous than flagella. There are usually only one or two flagella per cell.

Cilia and flagella are visible on the exterior of cells. In eukaryotic cells, cilia and flagella are composed of microtubules arranged in a ring of nine pairs surrounding a tenth pair. Both cilia and flagella move when the microtubules slide past one another. Cilia move in a beating motion. Flagella propel cells by lashing back and forth. In

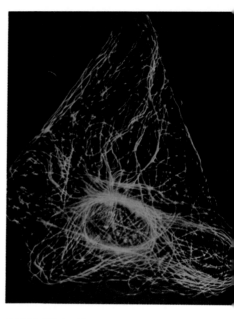

FIGURE 4–13.

This cell was treated to show its cytoskeleton.

flagellum:
flagellum (L) whip

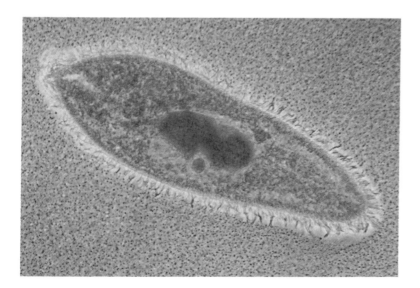

FIGURE 4–14.

This paramecium is a protist that moves about by beating its cilia.

What is a function of cilia in stationary cells in the windpipe?

unicellular organisms, cilia and flagella are the major means of moving about. In multicellular organisms such as humans, cilia are found in certain organs, such as in the lining of the windpipe. These cells do not move about. Instead, their beating cilia move mucus along the surface of a passage. Sperm cells of plants and animals move by means of flagella.

REVIEW

6. What is the advantage of highly folded membranes to a cell?
7. What are the functions of the plasma membrane and ribosomes?
8. What is the function of the nucleus in a cell?
9. **SKILL REVIEW:** Suppose you are viewing cells with an electron microscope. Some cells have large numbers of mitochondria having many internal folds. Other cells have few mitochondria with few internal folds. What could you conclude about the functions of these two types of cells? For more help, refer to Observing and Inferring in the Skill Handbook, page 809.
10. **USING CONCEPTS:** Compare the functions of mitochondria and chloroplasts. Why are they referred to in the text as energy transformers rather than energy producers or energy generators?

Acetabularia

THINKING CRITICALLY

WHO'S IN CONTROL?

At one time, there was a great scientific debate over the question of what controlled the cell. Some scientists thought that the cytoplasm contained some undiscovered material that controlled the cell. Others argued for the nucleus as the cell controller. To answer the question, scientists experimented with a unicellular green alga, *Acetabularia*. This organism consists of a wide base that contains the nucleus, a long, thin stalk, and a wide cap. In one experiment, the stalk and cap of an organism were removed from the base. The removed stalk and cap died, but the base grew a new stalk and cap and became whole again. In a second experiment, the stalk of a different species of *Acetabularia* was attached to the base of the original species. As before, a new cap grew at the top of the stalk. When scientists examined the organism, they found that the cap was not of the same species as the stalk, but was of the same species as the base. If you were the scientist who conducted these experiments, what conclusions would you draw? Explain your reasoning. The experiments were repeated many times using several combinations of bases, stems and caps. Why do you think this was done?

BIOLAB

Comparing Cells

Problem: What cell structures can be seen with a light microscope?

Materials

microscope
slides and coverslips
medicine droppers
scalpel
forceps

flat toothpick
Elodea plant
potato
methylene blue stain
iodine stain

Procedures

Elodea leaf

1. Copy the data table.
2. Using a medicine dropper, place a drop of water in the center of a slide. Using forceps, remove a leaf from the tip of an *Elodea* sprig and place it in the drop of water on your slide. Add a coverslip.
3. With low power, look for a thin area of the leaf where you can see the cells most clearly. Change to high power and locate a single cell. Observe carefully for a minute.
4. Record your observations in the data table. Draw the cell and label structures you see.

Human epithelial cells

5. Using a medicine dropper place a drop of methylene blue on a slide. *Gently* scrape the inside lining of your cheek with the flat edge of a toothpick. Mix the material on the toothpick in the drop of stain. Immediately dispose of the toothpick in the wastebasket. **CAUTION:** *Do not reuse toothpicks.* Add a coverslip to the slide.
6. View under low power, moving the slide to center a single cell in the field. Change to high power and observe the cell carefully. Repeat step 4.

Potato cells

7. Using a medicine dropper place one drop of iodine on a slide. **CAUTION:** *Iodine is poisonous. Avoid contact with skin and clothing.* Carefully use a scalpel to cut a paper-thin slice of potato. Add a coverslip.
8. Focus on low power first and then on high power. Iodine and starch react to produce a blue-black color. Repeat step 4.

Data and Observations

Cell type	Structures observed	Other observations
Elodea		
Human epithelial		
Potato		

Questions and Conclusion

1. What structures did you observe only in *Elodea*? What is their function?
2. What structure did you observe in both the potato and *Elodea* cells but not in the human cells? What is its function?
3. Methylene blue and iodine are two examples of many stains used when observing cells with the light microscope. What was the function of these stains? Why are stains necessary in cell observation?
4. Compare the shape of the potato and *Elodea* cells to the shape of the cheek cells. What accounts for the difference?
5. What evidence of starch did you see in the potato cells? Potato cells store starch in small cell structures called amyloplasts. What is the function of the stored starch?

Conclusion: What structures were visible in all the cells? What differences were seen between the plant and animal cells?

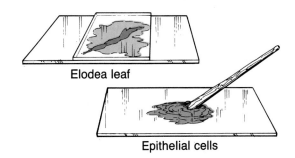

Elodea leaf

Epithelial cells

CHAPTER REVIEW

SUMMARY

1. The development of the microscope enabled scientists to propose the cell theory. According to the cell theory, all organisms are composed of cells, the cell is the basic unit of structure and function in organisms, and all cells come from other cells. **4:1**
2. Using electron microscopes, scientists have studied more detailed cell structure. **4:2**
3. The nucleus is the control center of eukaryotic cells. Cells are enclosed by a plasma membrane. Many cells have cell walls that provide support and protection. **4:3**
4. Proteins are made on ribosomes, which are attached to the highly folded endoplasmic reticulum which provides a large surface area for cell processes. **4:4**
5. Mitochondria break down food molecules to release energy. Chloroplasts convert light energy into chemical energy. **4:5**
6. The cytoskeleton helps maintain cell shape and is responsible for movement of cells and structures within cells. **4:6**
7. Cilia and flagella are structures made of microtubules and allow cells to move or move materials past the cell surface. **4:7**

LANGUAGE OF BIOLOGY

cell theory	endoplasmic reticulum
cellulose	flagella
cell wall	Golgi complex
chloroplasts	lysosome
chromatin	microfilaments
cilia	microtubules
compound light	mitochondria
microscope	nucleolus
cytoplasm	nucleus
cytoskeleton	plasma membrane
electron microscope	plastid

ribosomes	transmission electron
scanning electron	microscope
microscope	vacuole

Choose the word or phrase from the list above that completes the sentence.

1. Food molecules are broken down to release energy in the ___.
2. ___ convert light into chemical energy.
3. A(n) ___ passes electrons through an object to produce a magnified image.
4. The ___ is the control center of a cell.
5. The ___ serves as a boundary between a cell and its external environment.
6. ___ are organelles where proteins are made.
7. The ___ packages and ships proteins.
8. The ___ recycles cell waste.
9. A(n) ___ uses light to magnify objects.
10. ___ are short, hairlike projections that enable cellular movement.

REVIEWING CONCEPTS

Choose the word or phrase that completes the sentence or answers the question.

11. When Hooke saw tiny boxlike structures in cork slices, he called them ___.
    a. organelles   c. molecules
    b. cells   d. lenses
12. The highest magnification of a cell is possible with a(n) ___.
    a. electron microscope   c. light microscope
    b. simple microscope   d. glass lens
13. The network of folded membranes within a eukaryotic cell is the ___.
    a. endoplasmic reticulum
    b. cytoskeleton
    c. plasma membrane
    d. nucleus
14. Plant cell walls are composed mainly of ___.
    a. starch   c. cellulose
    b. chlorophyll   d. plasma membrane

15. A round organelle that contains digestive enzymes is a ___.

a. ribosome   c. vacuole
b. nucleus   d. lysosome

16. A ___ is an organelle that contains pigments.

a. ribosome   c. mitochondrion
b. plastid   d. flagellum

17. The work of Schleiden and Schwann led to the idea that all ___ are made of cells.

a. organelles   c. solids
b. nuclei   d. organisms

18. Many cell processes take place on the surface of ___.

a. chloroplasts   c. cytoplasm
b. membranes   d. cell walls

19. The cell organelle that produces ribosomes is the ___.

a. plasma membrane   c. nucleolus
b. chromatin   d. Golgi complex

20. Endoplasmic reticulum with ribosomes attached is called ___.

a. smooth ER   c. cytoskeleton
b. rough ER   d. mitochondria

UNDERSTANDING CONCEPTS

Answer the following questions using complete sentences.

21. How does the nucleus control a cell?
22. What is the importance of the plasma membrane to cell function?
23. Compare cell walls in plants and fungi.
24. What might occur if cells had no lysosomes?
25. What functions do plant cell walls perform?
26. How are cilia and the cytoskeleton related?
27. How do compound light microscopes differ from those used by van Leeuwenhoek?
28. Why are cilia and flagella especially important in unicellular organisms?

29. Why are folded membranes in cells more effective than non-folded membranes?
30. How do SEMs and TEMs differ in operation?

APPLYING CONCEPTS

Answer the following questions using complete sentences.

31. Why did it take almost 200 years for the cell theory to be developed?
32. Sometimes, packets of proteins collected by the Golgi complex merge with a lysosome. Suggest reasons for this activity.
33. Why did Schleiden and Schwann conclude that cells are the basic units of all life?
34. Why must plant cells have both mitochondria and chloroplasts?
35. You find a new microorganism in some ocean water. Applying the cell theory, what can you say for certain about this organism?

EXTENSIONS

1. Make a timeline showing the discovery of cell organelles and the scientists involved.
2. Research the operation of the scanning tunneling electron microscope.
3. Construct labeled models of typical cells using common materials. Include a prokaryotic cell.

READINGS

Allen, R. "The Microtubule as an Intracellular Engine." *Scientific American,* Feb. 1987, pp. 42–49.

deDuve, Christian. *A Guided Tour of the Living Cell* (2 Volumes). New York: Scientific American Library, 1984.

Kluger, Jeffrey. "A Dream Come True." *Discover,* Jan. 1989, p. 56.

Chapter 5

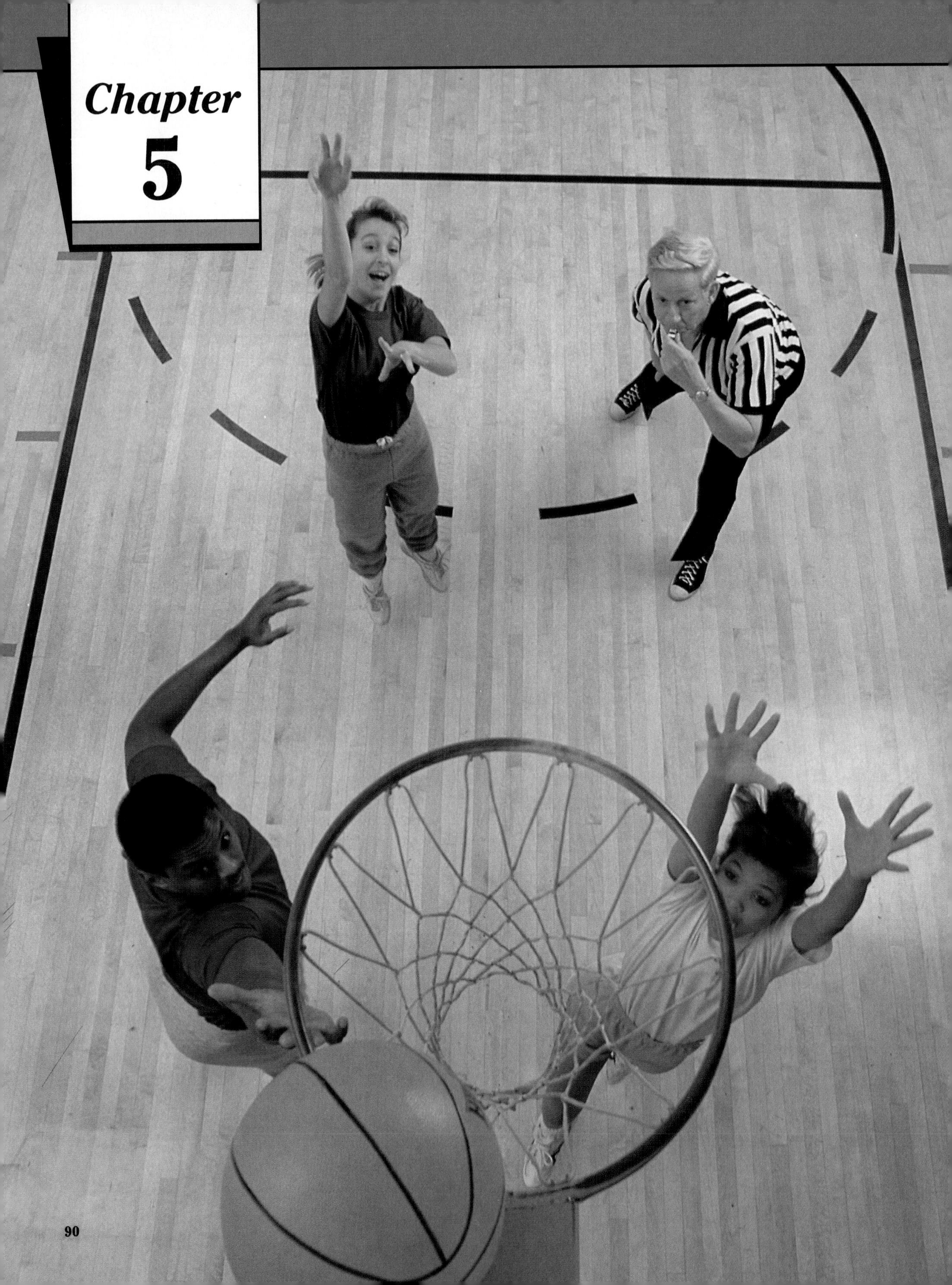

HOMEOSTASIS AND THE PLASMA MEMBRANE

O n the basketball court, players respond quickly to sudden changes in the position of every other player. Every time a new play is called, the team must remain organized and react as a group to the new strategy. If the team doesn't, it loses the game. Like a basketball team, cells react to changes in their environment. In order to survive, cells must adjust quickly to each of the changes. If cells do not, they die.

Volvox colonies

THE PLASMA MEMBRANE

An efficient factory must take in needed materials in the right amounts. A factory that makes shoes is not likely to need a truckload of frozen peas. Shoe production will stop if the factory runs out of thread, no matter how much leather, canvas, and rubber it has on hand. A factory must also ship out waste materials and finished products readily. Otherwise, they will accumulate and force the factory to stop. At the same time, though, the factory must keep its raw materials, plans, tools, and machinery inside. Therefore, a factory must control what leaves as well as what comes in. It must keep a balance of materials to operate at peak efficiency.

Living cells also maintain a balance by controlling materials that enter and leave. Some materials must be brought into the cell, while others must be kept out. Conversely, some materials must be removed from the cell, while others are kept in. Without this ability, the cell cannot maintain homeostasis and will die. The plasma membrane controls the passage of materials in and out of a cell.

Objectives:
- describe the general function of a cell's plasma membrane.
- tell what is meant by selective permeability.
- describe the fluid mosaic model of the plasma membrane and list the kinds of molecules that make up the membrane.

5:1 Maintaining a Balance

To stay alive, each cell in a unicellular or multicellular organism must maintain homeostasis. This means that a cell must maintain a stable internal environment even though the external environment may change. Changes in a cell's external environment usually involve changes in concentrations of materials. Sometimes it's easy for a cell to keep its internal concentrations of various substances constant. As wastes build up, they move easily out of the cell. However,

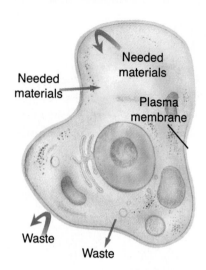

FIGURE 5–1.

A cell must remove waste and keep other waste from entering. Likewise, it must take in and keep needed materials while maintaining a balance with its surroundings.

permeable:
per (L) through
meare (L) to glide

depending on conditions outside the cell, waste substances can build up inside. How the plasma membrane responds to changing conditions will determine if a cell will survive.

Concentrations of dissolved substances, food materials, and waste substances change constantly both inside and outside of a cell. To maintain homeostasis, each cell's plasma membrane must be selective as to what is allowed to enter and leave the cell. The proper balance for a cell depends on the organism and the type of cell. The membrane of a cell in the root of a fir tree might allow passage of substances that could not cross the membrane of a cell in a turtle's lung. Differences in selectivity also allow cells to carry on different activities within the same organism. For example, only nerve cells in the human body may respond to a certain chemical even though the chemical is present in the bloodstream and all cells in the body are exposed to it. The membranes of the nerve cells accept the chemical, while the membranes of other cells reject it.

The property of a membrane that allows some materials to pass through while rejecting others is known as **selective permeability.** The structure and properties of a plasma membrane show how it can be selective and maintain cell homeostasis.

5:2 Structure of the Plasma Membrane

Scientists have known for 70 years that the plasma membrane is a two-layered structure called a bilayer. More recently, powerful electron microscopes have revealed the two-layered structure as shown in Figure 5–2. Each layer is made up of a sheet of lipid molecules, with protein molecules embedded in the lipid layers. Some of these proteins extend all the way through the bilayer. Others are located either on the inner or the outer layer of the membrane. As you will see, these proteins aid in the movement of materials through the membrane.

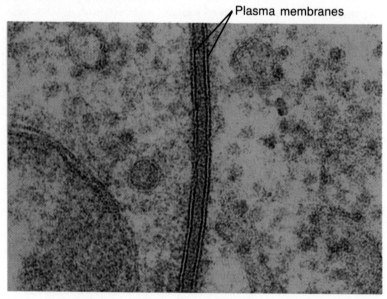

FIGURE 5–2.

The transmission electron microscope is an excellent tool for showing cell structure. The two cells shown here side by side illustrate clearly that each is bounded by a plasma membrane made of two layers.

The lipids that make up the plasma membrane differ from triglyceride lipids made by cells for long-term energy storage. Those lipids, as discussed in Chapter 3, consist of three fatty acids bonded to a glycerol group. Most of the lipids that make up the layers in plasma membranes have two fatty acids attached to glycerol instead of three. In place of a third fatty acid, a lipid in a plasma membrane has a phosphate group and thus is called a **phospholipid.** The phosphate group is soluble in water because it is polar and therefore is attracted to water molecules. The fatty acid chains are not soluble in water because they are nonpolar. As you can see in Figure 5–3, phospholipids have polar, water-soluble heads attached to long nonpolar, insoluble tails.

Cells have a watery environment both inside and out. Because water attracts the phosphate ends of phospholipids, they form double layers with the water-soluble phosphate ends toward the outside of each layer. The nonpolar tails lie on the inside of the bilayer. Note the sandwich-like bilayer of a plasma membrane in Figure 5–3.

Notice also in Figure 5–3 that the phospholipid molecules are not chemically bonded to one another. They are free to move sideways within the layer. Some of the proteins are also free to move, like icebergs floating in a sea of phospholipids. Thus, the bilayer can be considered to be a fluid, a material that flows. This description of a plasma membrane as a structure made up of many similar molecules that are free to flow among one another is called the **fluid mosaic model.** Some cell organelles are also enclosed by membranes that have the fluid mosaic structure. The kinds and arrangements of proteins and lipids vary from one membrane to another and give each type of membrane specific permeability properties.

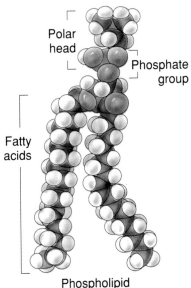

Polar head

Phosphate group

Fatty acids

Phospholipid molecule

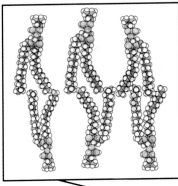

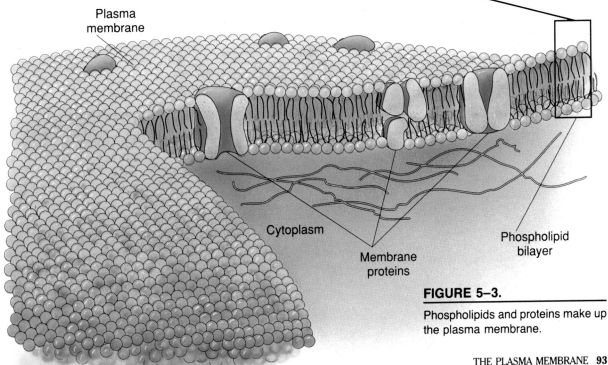

Plasma membrane

Cytoplasm

Membrane proteins

Phospholipid bilayer

FIGURE 5–3.

Phospholipids and proteins make up the plasma membrane.

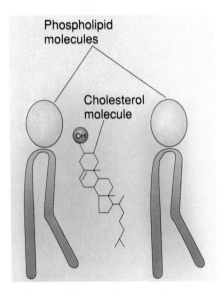

FIGURE 5–4.

Cholesterol stabilizes the plasma membranes of eukaryotic cells. Arctic caribou have adaptations to keep cell membranes fluid in freezing temperatures.

In many eukaryotes, especially animals, cholesterol is an important part of the plasma membrane. Fatty acid chains are flexible, but the cholesterol structure is rigid. The presence of cholesterol molecules makes the fluid mosaic more stable. In addition, the cholesterol helps keep the fatty acid tails of the phospholipids free and separate. Cells grown experimentally without cholesterol do not hold together because the plasma membrane is so weak.

In caribou, an arctic animal, the membranes of cells near the animal's hoofs have phospholipids with many unsaturated fatty acids. Unsaturated fatty acids remain liquid at low temperatures. Thus, the cell membrane remains fluid. The cell membranes of the rest of the caribou's body have more saturated lipids. The unsaturated lipids allow the caribou's feet and legs to drop to almost 0°C in the arctic winters and still maintain cell membrane function.

REVIEW

1. What is the main function of the plasma membrane?
2. Describe the structure of the plasma membrane. Why is it referred to as a fluid mosaic structure?
3. Tell what is meant by selective permeability. Explain why selective permeability is necessary for homeostasis within a cell.
4. **SKILL REVIEW:** Look up the word *mosaic* in a dictionary. Explain why this word is applied to the structure of a plasma membrane. For more help, refer to Reading Science in the Skill Handbook, pages 798 to 799.
5. **USING CONCEPTS:** Suggest a reason that the molecules of the plasma membrane tend to stay together.

CELLULAR TRANSPORT

From your study of chemistry in Chapter 3, you learned that the electrons of atoms are constantly moving about the nucleus. In fact, all particles of matter are in constant motion. The atoms, ions, and molecules that make up all materials are moving. Their movements are limited by the distances between particles. It makes no difference whether a material is solid, liquid, or gas. Its particles are in constant motion in a totally random fashion. This random movement helps explain how materials enter or leave cells by crossing the plasma membrane.

5:3 Diffusion

In 1827, Robert Brown (1773–1858), a Scottish scientist, used a microscope to observe tiny particles suspended in water. He noticed that the particles moved constantly in little jerks as if being struck by invisible objects. This motion is called Brownian motion. Today, we know that Brown was observing evidence of the random motion of molecules. These were the invisible objects that were moving the tiny visible particles.

All objects in motion have energy of motion, called **kinetic energy.** A moving particle of matter moves in a straight line until it collides with another particle. After the collision, both particles rebound. The particles will move off in straight lines until the next collision. Imagine a room full of Ping-Pong balls, all in constant motion, colliding with each other with no loss in energy. Particles of matter move in the same way.

Most substances in and around a cell are in water solution. Recall from Chapter 3 that a water solution is a mixture in which the ions or molecules of a solute are distributed evenly among water molecules. When a solute is placed in water, all the particles, both

Objectives:
- describe the process of diffusion and dynamic equilibrium.
- describe the process of osmosis and its importance in living things.
- predict the direction of diffusion of a dissolved substance, given concentration information.
- describe three mechanisms of passive transport.
- describe active transport and tell why it is a necessary process for living things.
- explain how cells move large particles into and out of cells.
- explain why cell size is limited.

FIGURE 5–5.

The fish in this school have kinetic energy. Like particles of matter, all moving objects have kinetic energy.

kinetic:
kinein (GK) to move

Water molecules

FIGURE 5–6.

Random movement of water molecules and dissolved particles causes them to diffuse until they become evenly distributed.

FIGURE 5–7.

In dynamic equilibrium, there is motion, but no net change.

Material moving into cell $=$ Material moving out of cell

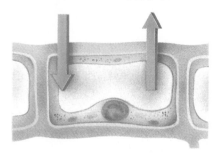

water and solute, move randomly, colliding with each other. These random collisions tend to scatter particles of solute and solvent until they are evenly mixed. One way of observing this effect is to drop a tablet of colored dye into a beaker of water. As the tablet dissolves, the dye molecules and water molecules move randomly. At first, most of the dissolved dye is found around the dissolving tablet. The moving dye molecules collide with moving water molecules and with each other, causing the dye to spread out. Keep in mind that the movement of individual particles is random. However, the overall effect is the movement of dye molecules from an area of higher concentration (near the tablet) to an area of lower concentration (throughout the water). **Diffusion** is the net movement of particles from an area of higher concentration to an area of lower concentration. Diffusion occurs because of the random movement of particles.

Eventually, the dye molecules become evenly distributed throughout the molecules of water in the beaker. After this point, the molecules continue to move randomly and collide with one another. However, there will be no change in concentration. This condition in which there is continuous movement but no overall change is called **dynamic equilibrium.** The word *dynamic* refers to movement or change, while *equilibrium* refers to balance. Maintaining a dynamic equilibrium is one of the characteristics of homeostasis.

Obviously, diffusion cannot occur unless a substance is in higher concentration in one region than it is in another. The difference in concentration of a substance across space is called a **concentration gradient.** Ions or molecules naturally move from an area of higher concentration to an area of lower concentration. They are said to move with a gradient. If no other processes interfere, diffusion will continue until there is no concentration gradient. At this point, equilibrium occurs. Many biological processes require moving ions or molecules of a substance against a concentration gradient, from low to high concentration. This process requires work.

Many kinds of molecules and ions can diffuse across artificial membranes, such as thin sheets of plastic, by passing between the molecules that make up the membrane. A rubber balloon filled with helium slowly deflates because the helium atoms diffuse through the rubber membrane. Recall, however, that plasma membranes are selectively permeable. Only water, oxygen, nitrogen, carbon dioxide, and a few other small molecules can diffuse freely across plasma membranes. Most ions and polar molecules can't diffuse directly through a phospholipid bilayer. As you will see, cells have specific ways to allow needed molecules, such as sugars, to enter.

5:4 Osmosis

Water molecules are in constant motion, so they diffuse just like any other molecules. **Osmosis** is the diffusion of water molecules through a membrane from an area of higher water concentration to one of lower water concentration. A strong solution of sugar has a lower concentration of water than a weaker sugar solution. Compare the two solutions in Figure 5–8. If these two solutions were placed in direct contact, water would diffuse in one direction, while sugar would diffuse in the other. What would happen if a membrane that allowed only water to pass through separated the two solutions? Osmosis would occur as water molecules diffused across the membrane toward the more concentrated sugar solution. The result would be a buildup of water on one side of the membrane. As you can see, a cell will lose or gain water by osmosis if it is placed in an environment in which the water concentration is different from that of the cell contents.

FIGURE 5–8.

Osmosis transfers water across a selectively permeable membrane when one side has a higher concentration of a dissolved material that cannot pass through the membrane.

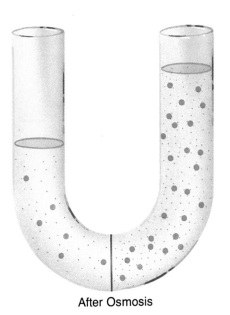

Before Osmosis   Selectively permeable membrane

Water Molecule   ● Sugar Molecule

After Osmosis

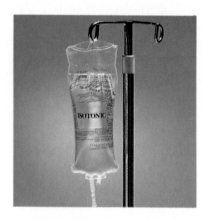

FIGURE 5–9.

Solutions to be injected into the body are usually isotonic with the blood or cell contents.

iso-, hypo-, hyper-:
  isos (GK) equal
  hypo (GK) under
  hyper (GK) over

What is a hypertonic solution?

What is plasmolysis?

All cells, whether in multicellular or unicellular organisms, are surrounded by water solutions. An **isotonic solution** is a solution in which the concentration of dissolved substances is the same as the concentration inside the cell. This also means that the concentration of water is the same as in the cell. Water molecules still move into and out of the cell at random, but there is no net movement of water. A cell placed in an isotonic solution is in dynamic equilibrium. If you have ever looked at bottles of medicine prepared for injection you may have seen the word *isotonic* written on the label. Solutions injected into the body must be isotonic so that cells are not damaged by the loss or gain of water.

A **hypotonic solution** is a solution in which the concentration of dissolved substances is lower than the concentration inside the cell. Thus, the concentration of water is higher than inside the cell. If a cell is placed in a hypotonic solution, osmosis will occur, and water will move through the plasma membrane into the cell. As water diffuses into the cell, the cell swells and its internal pressure increases. Plant cells have strong cell walls that can resist the internal pressure. The pressure that builds in a plant cell as a result of osmosis is called **turgor** (TUR gur) **pressure**. Plant cells have normal turgor pressure in isotonic solutions. Turgor pressure causes the cytoplasm and the plasma membrane to press outward against the cell wall, making the cell rigid. This rigidity supports plants that are not woody and gives them shape.

Animal cells do not have cell walls. An animal cell in a hypotonic solution will also swell and may burst. Many organisms that lack cell walls are adapted to live in hypotonic solutions, such as fresh water. These organisms have evolved mechanisms to keep cells from bursting and to maintain homeostasis. One mechanism is to continually excrete excess water from cells. Some protists contain organelles called **contractile vacuoles** that collect excess water and then contract, squeezing the water out of the cell. Other organisms, such as fish, have evolved a closed body structure in which isotonic solutions are maintained.

A **hypertonic solution** is a solution in which the concentration of dissolved substances is higher than the concentration inside the cell. As a result, the concentration of water is lower than inside the cell. If a cell is placed in a hypertonic solution, osmosis will occur and water will move out of the cell. Animal cells placed in a hypertonic solution will shrivel up because of the decreased pressure in the cells. Cookbooks generally suggest that you not add too much salt to meat before cooking. The salt causes a strong hypertonic solution to form on the meat's surface. The result is meat that is dry and tough. If a plant cell is placed in a hypertonic environment, it will lose water, mainly from its central vacuole. The plasma membrane and cytoplasm will shrink away from the cell wall as shown in Figure 5–10. This loss of water resulting in a drop in turgor pressure is called **plasmolysis.** Plasmolysis causes a plant to wilt. Wilting can be reversed by putting the plant into a hypotonic solution. Vegetables in grocery stores lose water to the air and wilt. Store workers often spray vegetables with water to restore their crispness.

EFFECTS OF SOLUTION CONCENTRATIONS ON CELLS

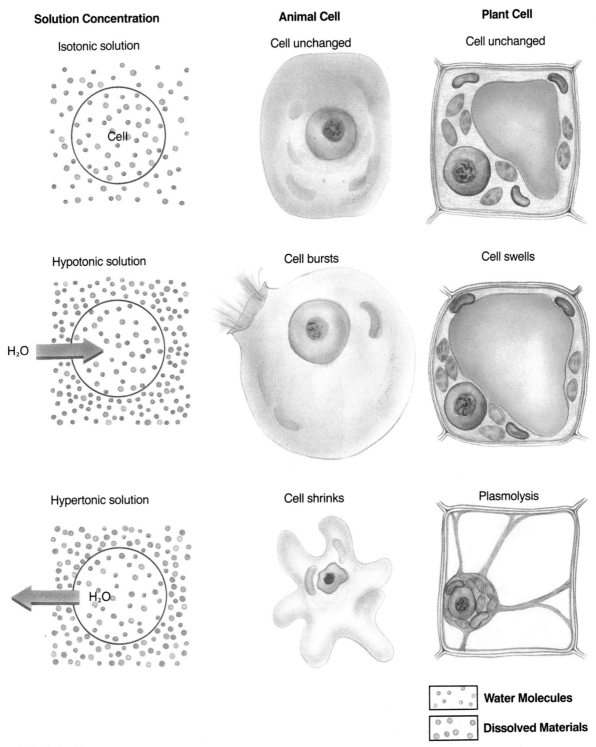

Solution Concentration	Animal Cell	Plant Cell
Isotonic solution	Cell unchanged	Cell unchanged
Hypotonic solution	Cell bursts	Cell swells
Hypertonic solution	Cell shrinks	Plasmolysis

Cell

H₂O

H₂O

Water Molecules

Dissolved Materials

FIGURE 5–10.

As a result of osmosis, cells respond differently in isotonic, hypotonic, and hypertonic solutions.

BIOLAB

Selective Permeability

5

Problem: Will starch, iodine, and water molecules cross a thin polyethylene membrane?

Materials

250-mL beaker (2)   starch solution
small plastic bag (2)   iodine solution
twist ties (2)   masking tape
graduated cylinder   plastic funnel

Procedures

1. Copy the data table. Using tape, label the beakers A and B.
2. Using the graduated cylinder, carefully pour 80 mL of starch solution into a plastic bag. Leave some air space. Seal the bag tightly with a twist tie.
3. In Beaker A, place 40 mL of water. Add 40 mL of iodine solution to the water. **CAUTION:** *Iodine is poisonous. Avoid contact with skin and clothing.* Swirl the beaker gently to mix the solutions.
4. Carefully place the bag containing starch into beaker A. Observe for several minutes and record your observations in the data table.
5. Into the second bag, pour 40 mL of water and 40 mL of iodine solution and seal.
6. Into beaker B, pour 80 mL of starch solution.
7. Carefully place the bag containing iodine into beaker B. Record your observations in the data table.
8. Write a **hypothesis** regarding the movement of starch, iodine, and water molecules in the two beakers and bags.
9. Allow the two beakers to stand overnight.
10. The next day, record your observations.
11. Remove the bag from beaker A and dry the outside with paper towels. Unseal the bag carefully. Use the funnel and pour the bag's contents into the graduated cylinder. Record the volume of the bag's contents. Discard the solution and bag. Wash and dry the cylinder.
12. Measure and record the volume of the remaining contents of beaker A.
13. Repeat steps 11 and 12 with beaker B.

Data and Observations

	At Start		After 24 Hours	
	Color	Volume	Color	Volume
Bag A				
Beaker A				
Bag B				
Beaker B				

Questions and Conclusion

1. Which way did iodine molecules move through the membrane? Explain how you know this.
2. Did starch molecules pass through the membranes? Explain how you know this.
3. In which direction did water move in beaker A? Beaker B? Explain how you know this.
4. What can you infer from this experiment about movement of large molecules through a thin polyethylene membrane?
5. Do your data support your **hypothesis**?
6. Can you call the membrane in this experiment selectively permeable? Explain your answer.

Conclusion: Of the molecules tested, which diffused through a polyethylene membrane?

5:5 Passive Transport

Because particles are in constant, random motion, diffusion takes place without additional energy input from the cell. The net movement of substances across plasma membranes without additional energy is called **passive transport.** However, only a few substances are able to pass through a phospholipid bilayer by diffusion. Water, of course, is the most common. Passive transport of other substances occurs in different ways. In Section 5:2, you learned that there are many different kinds of proteins embedded in the lipid bilayer of the plasma membrane. **Transport proteins** allow needed substances or waste materials to move through the plasma membrane.

The diffusion of materials across a plasma membrane by transport proteins is called **facilitated diffusion.** The transport proteins facilitate or help substances cross the membrane by providing convenient openings for them to pass through. Facilitated diffusion is a type of passive transport because no energy is expended by the cell. Movement of materials is the same as in any other diffusion. Random motion of particles brings them into contact with the transport proteins. Also, particles move from high to low concentrations. Diffusion of ions involves another factor. Because ions have an electrical charge, they diffuse toward a region of opposite charge.

Some transport proteins simply provide tube-like water channels through which small dissolved particles can diffuse. Most of these dissolved materials are substances that would not ordinarily diffuse through the lipid bilayer. Other kinds of transport proteins are called carrier proteins because they seem to "pick up" ions and molecules and move them through the plasma membrane. Most of these carriers have specific shapes and transport only one or two kinds of ions or molecules. For example, the carrier protein that transports glucose cannot transport other simple sugars.

NoteWorthy

Cystic fibrosis, a lung disease, may be caused by a failure in the cell membrane to transport the chloride ion. The channels through which chloride ions enter and leave the cells become blocked and inhibit normal cell function.

FIGURE 5–11.

Passive transport may involve diffusion directly through the bilayer or facilitated diffusion using transport proteins.

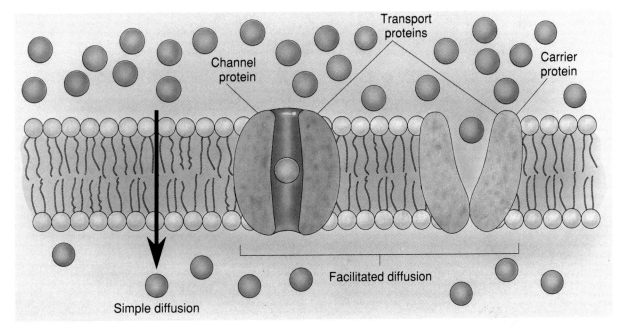

Transport proteins

Channel protein

Carrier protein

Facilitated diffusion

Simple diffusion

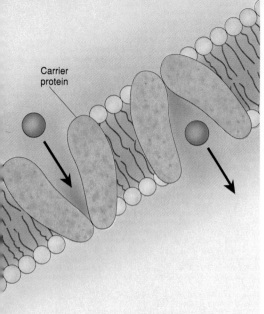

Carrier protein

FIGURE 5–12.

In facilitated diffusion, carrier proteins change shape to allow molecules to cross plasma membranes.

Recall that glucose is a major source of energy for cells. Glucose is transported into cells by facilitated diffusion. The use of carrier proteins increases the rate of transport, so that cells can respond quickly to changes in environment. When the demand for energy inside a cell is high, glucose can be allowed to diffuse rapidly into the cell by facilitated diffusion. If glucose builds up in the cell, it is transported out quickly by the same method. Under normal conditions, glucose diffuses very slowly across the plasma membrane.

The way carrier proteins work is not well understood. Experiments indicate that the binding of the molecule or ion to be transported causes the carrier protein to change its shape, opening a temporary channel. The molecule or ion passes into or out of the cell through this opening and the carrier then returns to its original shape. In some cases, transport proteins have "gates" that open and close depending on the concentration of the substance being transported. Others are affected by chemical substances that cause them to open and close their channels.

5:6 Active Transport

Cells often require nutrients, such as minerals, that are scarce in the environment. If the concentration of a substance outside a cell were lower than the concentration inside, you would expect the cell to lose that substance rather than gain it. Such a situation would be harmful to the cell. Some cells are adapted to move materials from areas of low concentration to areas of higher concentration. Transport of materials against a gradient requires energy and is called **active transport.** Root tip cells of plants concentrate ions of minerals from soil by active transport. Thus, active transport helps maintain homeostasis in plant cells by gathering and conserving much-needed minerals such as potassium, molybdenum, and magnesium. Saltwater fish remove excess salt from their bodies by active transport through their gills. Kidney cells sort needed materials from waste materials by active transport.

FIGURE 5–13.

Plant roots conserve minerals by active transport, while saltwater fish use active transport to get rid of salt.

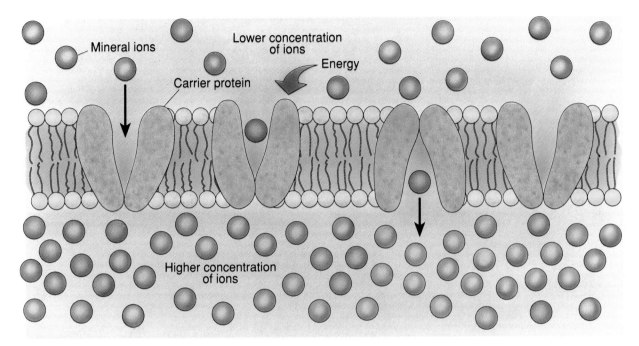

Mineral ions

Lower concentration
of ions

Energy

Carrier protein

Higher concentration
of ions

FIGURE 5–14.

In active transport, energy from ATP is used to modify the shape of a carrier protein. This change can move an ion or molecule through the membrane from low to higher concentration.

In active transport, a carrier protein first binds with a particle of the substance to be transported. Another location on the carrier protein binds to a molecule that provides chemical energy. As energy is transferred to the carrier, it changes shape and moves the particle into or out of the cell. Thus, the molecule or ion can be moved against a gradient. This type of active transport mechanism is sometimes referred to as an ionic or molecular pump. This is because it acts somewhat like a water pump, which uses energy to move water from a lower level to a higher level.

5:7 Transport of Large Particles

The transport processes discussed so far involve the movement of small molecules and ions across the plasma membrane. Some cells can take in large molecules, groups of molecules, or even whole cells. **Endocytosis** is a process in which a cell surrounds and takes in material from its environment. This material does not pass through the membrane. Instead, it is engulfed and enclosed by a portion of the membrane and cytoplasm. That portion of the membrane then breaks away, and the resulting vacuole with its contents moves to the inside of the cell. The membrane and its contents form a small sac that is not really a portion of the cell's cytoplasm. Once inside the cell, the membrane surrounding the vacuole may burst, releasing its contents into the cytoplasm. If the vacuole contains material to be digested, it joins with a lysosome. Recall from Chapter 4 that a lysosome contains digestive enzymes. The enzymes digest the contents of the vacuole. The products of digestion diffuse or are transported through the vacuole's membrane into the cell's cytoplasm. Follow this process of endocytosis in Figure 5–15.

endo-, exo-:
    endon (GK) within
    exo (GK) out
phago-, pino-:
    phagein (GK) to eat
    piein (GK) to drink

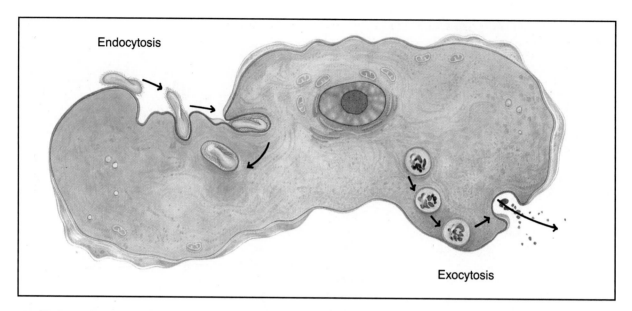

FIGURE 5–15.

Endocytosis can involve either phagocytosis or pinocytosis. Sacs of cell products or wastes are released to the surroundings by exocytosis.

Biologists distinguish two types of endocytosis on the basis of the kind of material taken in. **Phagocytosis** is the movement of large particles of solid food or whole cells into the cell. White blood cells can engulf and digest bacterial cells and other large particles that invade the body. Some unicellular organisms, such as amoebas, use phagocytosis to ingest food as shown in Figure 5–16. **Pinocytosis** is a form of endocytosis that involves the transport of liquid droplets or small particles. The droplets may contain nutrients in solution or large molecules in suspension.

Exocytosis is the reverse of endocytosis. Cells use exocytosis to move waste particles from the interior to the outside environment. They also use this method to secrete sacs of molecules such as hormones. Recall the function of the Golgi complex in Chapter 4. Exocytosis also is shown in Figure 5–15. Because endocytosis and exocytosis require energy to move cytoplasm, they can also be classified as active transport.

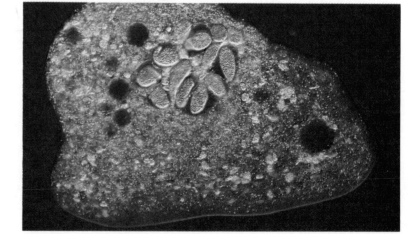

FIGURE 5–16.

Some protists, such as this amoeba, can dine on rather large organisms by phagocytosis. Note the cluster of vacuoles containing smaller green protists that the amoeba has captured.

Many cells produce proteins for export into the surroundings. Some of these proteins leave the cell as they are produced. The first chain of amino acids formed is inserted through the plasma membrane. It then attaches to the outside of the membrane. As the remainder of the amino acid chain is produced, it passes through the phospholipid bilayer like thread being pulled through cloth. Only as these proteins leave the cell are they modified into finished, active proteins. For example, some digestive enzymes are produced by cells that line the inside of the digestive tract. These enzymes become active and carry out their digestive functions only after reaching the inside of the tract. Other proteins pass through the endoplasmic reticulum as they are produced and are stored in vacuoles until needed. Often, the Golgi complex is involved in collecting, sorting, and shipping these proteins. Insulin is an example of a protein produced and stored in this way. Certain cells of the pancreas produce insulin. When released into the bloodstream, it affects the plasma membranes of other body cells, causing them to take in and store glucose.

How do proteins pass through plasma membranes?

THINKING CRITICALLY

LIKE A FISH IN WATER

Did you ever wonder if fish drink water? Fish that live in fresh water don't drink water because they live in a hypotonic environment. The concentration of water is greater outside than inside the fish. Therefore, freshwater fish are gaining water continuously through osmosis into the cells. Why don't the fish swell up and burst? Freshwater fish have evolved an efficient excretory mechanism for getting rid of excess water. They produce large amounts of dilute urine. However, they also lose salt in the urine and have to replace the lost salt to maintain homeostasis. To gain salt, freshwater fish actively transport it from their surroundings into gill cells.

Saltwater fish face the opposite problem. A saltwater fish lives in a hypertonic environment and continuously loses water from its body cells through osmosis. Therefore, saltwater fish drink water to replace the lost liquid. However, when saltwater fish drink salt water, they gain an excess of salt. They remove this salt through active transport across the gills and through the production of small amounts of urine with a high salt concentration. This action helps get rid of salt, but conserves water. Sharks, an ancient group of fish, have solved the problem of living in a hypertonic environment in a different way. Sharks produce urine but retain it in their bloodstream. How would this mechanism help sharks maintain a concentration balance with the environment?

Humans swim in fresh water, which is hypotonic to our blood and cells. We also swim in salt water, which is hypertonic to our blood and cells. What adaptations or mechanisms prevent us from swelling or shriveling up by osmosis in such situations?

This freshwater fish is adapted to overcome the effects of osmosis.

5:8 Cell Size

In Chapter 4, you learned that it was more than 200 years after the first microscopes were made until scientists concluded that all organisms were made of cells. Scientists are still learning the details of cell structure and function. Why do you suppose it has taken so long to learn about the cell structure of living things? The main reason is quite simple. Cells are very small. Ordinary cells are barely visible to the unaided eye. Why do you suppose that cells do not grow to very large sizes? In order to survive, a cell must take in nutrients, such as amino acids, sugar, and oxygen. Wastes such as carbon dioxide, ammonia, and excess water must be removed. You have just studied that the cell must move materials in and out across its plasma membrane. This fact limits the size to which cells can grow.

Picture a cube-shaped cell one millimeter on a side. Each surface of this cube has an area of 1 mm $\times$ 1 mm or 1 square millimeter (1 mm^2). Recall that the area of a rectangular surface equals the length multiplied by the width. Since a cube has six sides, the total surface area of the cell is 6 mm^2. The volume of a cube is equal to the length times the width times the height. Therefore the volume of the cell is 1 mm $\times$ 1 mm $\times$ 1 mm or 1 cubic millimeter (1 mm^3). All the materials to be transported in or out of this cell having a volume of 1 mm^3 must pass through a membrane with a surface area of 6 mm^2.

If this cell grows until it is two millimeters in each dimension, each surface will have an area of 2 mm $\times$ 2 mm or 4 mm^2. The total surface area of the cell's 6 sides will be 24 mm^2. The surface area of the cell has grown from 6 to 24 mm^2, a fourfold increase. Its new volume is now 2 mm $\times$ 2 mm $\times$ 2 mm or 8 mm^3. Its previous volume

FIGURE 5–17.

As a cell grows, its volume increases more than its surface area.

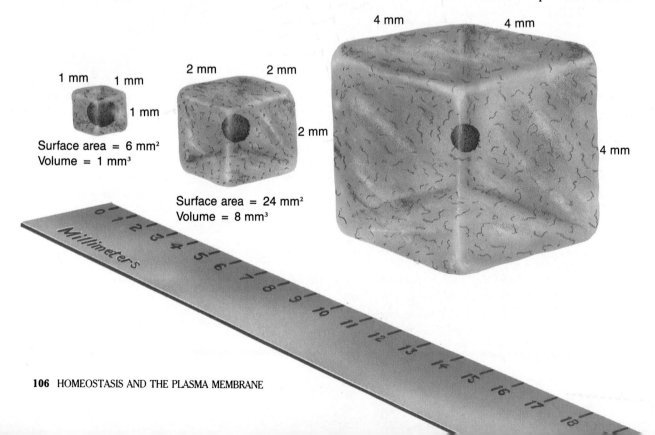

1 mm 1 mm

1 mm

Surface area = 6 mm²
Volume = 1 mm³

2 mm 2 mm

2 mm

Surface area = 24 mm²
Volume = 8 mm³

4 mm 4 mm

4 mm

4 mm

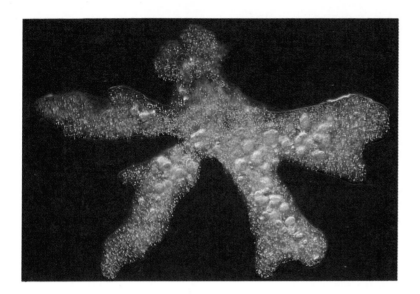

FIGURE 5–18.

Some organisms that have very large cells also have several nuclei per cell. Some scientists believe this adaptation allows the cell to manage and control a large volume. This giant amoeba, *Pelomyxa,* has several nuclei, which are not clearly visible in this photo.

was 1 mm³, so its volume is eight times greater than before. This larger cell will need eight times more nutrients and must get rid of eight times as much waste. Eight times as much material will have to pass through a surface membrane that is only four times as large as before. Try calculating what would happen if the cell's dimensions doubled again, to 4 mm on a side.

You can see that as a cell grows larger and larger, its volume increases much faster than its surface area. Soon, a cell would grow to a size where it could not pass enough material through its plasma membrane to stay alive. Homeostasis would be disrupted. The cell either would starve because of a lack of nutrients or would poison itself because of a buildup of wastes. As cells grow, then, either of two things happens. One is that the cell stops growing before it becomes too large. The other is that the cell divides, forming two smaller cells. You will learn more about cell division in Chapter 7.

NoteWorthy

Some scientists believe that another factor limiting cell size is that the nucleus can exert control only over a limited volume of cell contents. Some very large cells have several nuclei.

REVIEW

6. What is diffusion? How do osmosis and diffusion differ?
7. What factors affect the diffusion of a dissolved substance through a membrane?
8. How do active transport and facilitated diffusion differ? How are they alike? How does active transport help maintain homeostasis?
9. **SKILL REVIEW:** Kinetic energy of molecules increases with an increase in temperature. What effect do you think an increase in temperature has on diffusion? For more help, refer to Observing and Inferring in the Skill Handbook, page 809.
10. **USING CONCEPTS:** Cells in the human body constantly use oxygen during metabolism. Blood contains oxygen. Why does oxygen move into the cells from the bloodstream?

CHAPTER REVIEW

1. The plasma membrane controls what enters and leaves a cell. **5:1**
2. The plasma membrane is a phospholipid bilayer with embedded protein molecules. **5:2**
3. Particles of matter are in constant motion and diffuse from high to low concentration. **5:3**
4. Osmosis is the diffusion of water through a membrane and depends on the concentrations of solutes on both sides of the membrane. **5:4**
5. Facilitated diffusion is made possible by transport proteins in the plasma membrane. **5:5**
6. Active transport uses energy and can move materials against a concentration gradient. **5:6**
7. Large particles may enter a cell by endocytosis and leave by exocytosis. **5:7**
8. Cell size is limited by the amount of material that can cross the plasma membrane. **5:8**

LANGUAGE OF BIOLOGY

active transport	isotonic solution
concentration gradient	kinetic energy
contractile vacuoles	osmosis
diffusion	passive transport
dynamic equilibrium	phagocytosis
endocytosis	phospholipid
exocytosis	pinocytosis
facilitated diffusion	plasmolysis
fluid mosaic model	selective permeability
hypertonic solution	transport proteins
hypotonic solution	turgor pressure

Choose the word or phrase from the list above that completes the sentence.

1. The ____ describes the structure of a plasma membrane.
2. All objects in motion have ____.
3. Plasma membranes have ____ because they let some substances in and reject others.

4. Plants will wilt when there is a decrease in ____ inside their cells.
5. The proteins embedded in the plasma membrane serve as ____.
6. The movement of particles from an area of high to low concentration is known as ____.
7. Amoebas ingest large particles of food by ____.
8. A solution that has the same concentration of dissolved materials as the contents of a cell it surrounds is said to be a(n) ____.
9. Cells secrete hormones by ____.
10. Movement of substances using an energy source and proteins is known as ____.

REVIEWING CONCEPTS

Choose the word or phrase that completes the sentence or answers the question.

11. The concentration of water in a(n) ____ solution is lower than that inside the cell.
    a. hypotonic   c. hypertonic
    b. isotonic   d. equilibrium
12. Cell size is limited by the cell's ____.
    a. turgor pressure   c. equilibrium
    b. surface area   d. flexibility
13. An increase in ____ pressure is caused by the movement of water into a plant cell.
    a. turgor   c. transport
    b. diffusion   d. molecular
14. Plasma membranes maintain homeostasis by being selectively ____ to substances.
    a. isotonic   c. permeable
    b. osmotic   d. polar
15. The plasma membrane is a bilayer that consists mainly of ____ molecules.
    a. carbohydrate   c. protein
    b. phospholipid   d. DNA
16. In diffusion, particles move toward areas of ____ concentration.
    a. higher   c. the same
    b. lower   d. water

17. ___ is a substance that diffuses rapidly through the bilayer of the plasma membrane.
    a. Oxygen   c. Sodium chloride
    b. Protein   d. Sugar
18. When dynamic equilibrium occurs, ions and molecules no longer change ___.
    a. concentration   c. motion
    b. position   d. energy
19. ___ is a substance that crosses the plasma membrane by facilitated diffusion.
    a. Oxygen   c. Water
    b. Carbon dioxide   d. Glucose
20. Some cells take in liquid droplets by ___.
    a. exocytosis   c. diffusion
    b. pinocytosis   d. passive transport

UNDERSTANDING CONCEPTS

Answer the following questions using complete sentences.

21. Describe the molecules that make up the plasma membrane and their arrangement.
22. Describe three mechanisms of passive transport.
23. How do cholesterol and unsaturated lipids function in plasma membranes?
24. Describe how dissolved particles are moved across a plasma membrane from lower to higher concentration.
25. What is the relationship between a cell's surface area and its volume as the cell grows? How does this limit cell size?
26. How does an amoeba ingest food particles?
27. What easily crosses the lipid bilayer?
28. Under what conditions does diffusion occur? Describe how diffusion takes place.
29. Why must a cell regulate the substances that enter and leave?
30. Explain how active transport operates. Why is an active transport mechanism is often described as a pump?

APPLYING CONCEPTS

Answer the following questions using complete sentences.

31. How would you expect the number of mitochondria in a cell to relate to the amount of active transport it carries out? Explain.
32. Explain why drinking ocean water would be dangerous to humans. Hint: The body must excrete salt in solution with a lot of water.
33. How does the structure of the plasma membrane allow materials to move both ways?
34. When an amoeba from the sea is placed in fresh water, it forms a contractile vacuole. Explain how this is an adaptation for survival.
35. A stalk of celery becomes limp and rubbery in salt water. Describe how this occurs.

EXTENSIONS

1. Write a report on the functions of sodium-potassium pumps in the human body. Include a discussion of recent research on the causes of cystic fibrosis.
2. Put raisins in warm water for several minutes. Explain any changes in terms of diffusion.
3. Research the use of salt and sugar in the preservation of food such as in pickling, salt curing, and making jellies and jams.

READINGS

Bretscher, M. "The Molecules of the Cell Membrane." *Scientific American,* Oct. 1985, pp. 100–108.

Karasov, W.H., and J.M. Diamond. "Interplay Between Physiology and Ecology in Digestion." *BioScience,* Oct. 1988, pp. 602–611.

Levitan, Irwin B., "The Basic Defect in Cystic Fibrosis." *Science,* June 23, 1989, p. 1423.

ENERGY IN A CELL

Running free in the sun is fun for both horses and humans. Running takes energy, but neither horse nor human can get its running energy straight from the sun. Both must stop and eat from time to time. The horse may choose some tender grass, or perhaps stretch its neck across a fence for a bite of a farmer's wheat crop. The human may eat a sandwich on bread made from wheat. In either case, the animal is taking in food that its cells can break down to release energy. But where does wheat get energy? From the sun, or, like the animal, from food? Actually, both answers are right. As the horse runs, it breathes deeper and faster to take in more oxygen. You will learn how oxygen and food energy are connected.

Wheat

ATP: ENERGY IN A MOLECULE

Gasoline is a fuel that provides energy to run a car. Likewise, food molecules are the fuel of living cells. After filling a car's tank with gas, you wouldn't think of trying to make the car run by dropping a lighted match into the tank. Instead, gas must be delivered to the engine at a carefully measured rate. In this way, energy is released from the fuel in a useful, controlled process. Likewise, mechanisms have evolved that allow living organisms to release energy from food in a controlled way. The energy released is used to make new molecules that serve as temporary energy carriers. The most important of these molecules is ATP.

6:1 Capturing Cell Energy

Life processes constantly move and rearrange atoms, ions, and molecules. Work is done whenever anything is moved. **Energy** is the ability to do work, so living cells need a steady supply of energy. Your muscle cells need energy to contract when you exercise. Energy is used to move ions and molecules across membranes in your nerves and kidneys. Your cells use energy even when you are asleep. Your heart muscle continues to pump blood. New molecules are made for growth and repair.

Objectives:
- explain why organisms need a way of storing energy.
- describe how energy is stored in ATP.
- list four cell activities that require energy from ATP.

How are energy and work related?

FIGURE 6–1.

This ant is doing work by moving a large object. For a small organism, it needs a lot of energy from food molecules.

Cell reactions can release energy whenever food molecules are available. However, a cell can't always use all the energy immediately. A chemical mechanism has evolved that balances energy supply and demand. As energy is released from food, it is used to form energy-storage molecules. As energy is needed, energy-storage molecules are broken down, and the stored energy is released. **Adenosine triphosphate,** or ATP, is a molecule that stores energy in a usable form in cells. Without a constant and abundant source of ATP, cells die.

Look at the structure of ATP in Figure 6–3. Notice that the molecule contains adenine, a sugar called ribose, and three phosphate groups bonded in a row. The two phosphate-phosphate bonds are represented by wavy lines. When phosphate-phosphate bonds form, energy is stored. Cells store energy by bonding a third phosphate group to adenosine diphosphate to form ATP. **Adenosine diphosphate,** or ADP, contains adenine, ribose, and two phosphate groups. When the phosphate group breaks off of an ATP molecule, the result is ADP, a phosphate group, and energy. ADP is available again to store energy by forming ATP.

What is the function of ATP?
How does ATP release energy?

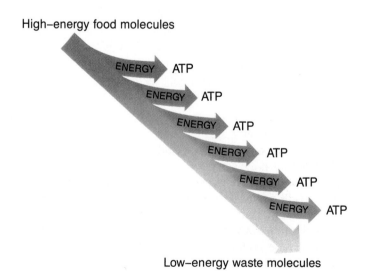

FIGURE 6–2.

When food molecules are available, they are broken down in several steps, and their energy is stored in ATP.

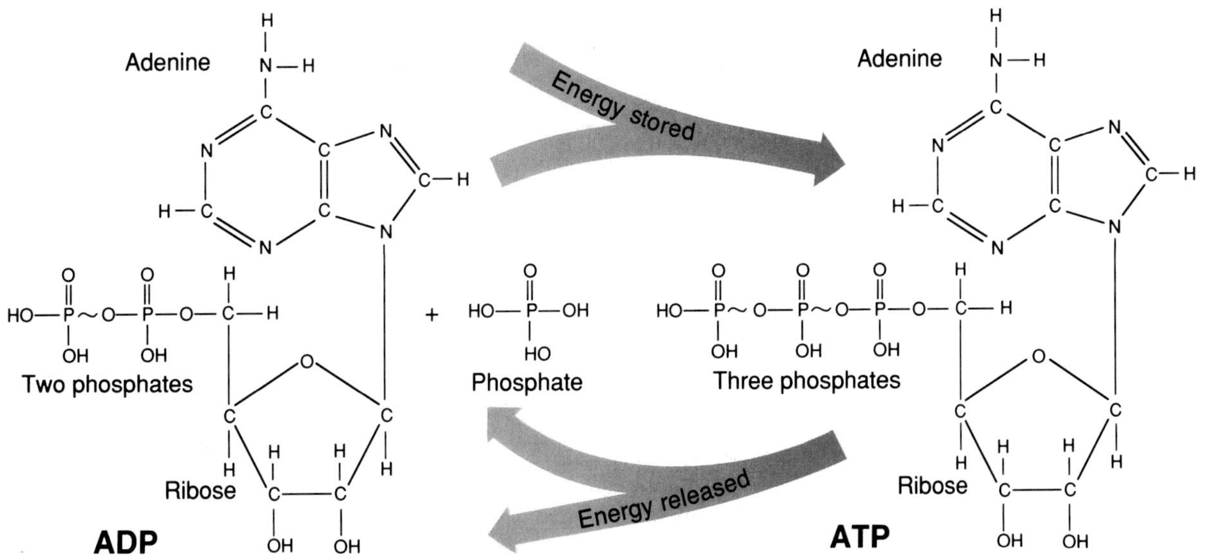

The diagram shows the ADP-ATP cycle. On the left is ADP, on the right is ATP, with "Energy stored" arrow pointing right and "Energy released" arrow pointing left.

ADP (left structure): Adenine, Two phosphates, Ribose

$$HO-P\sim O-P-O-C-H$$ with OH groups, Two phosphates, Ribose with OH OH

+ Phosphate: $HO-P-OH$ with O and HO

ATP (right structure): Adenine, Three phosphates, Ribose

Energy stored →

← Energy released

Within a cell, formation of ATP from ADP and phosphate occurs over and over, storing energy each time. Likewise, ATP breaks down repeatedly to release energy, ADP, and phosphate. The conversion reactions of ADP and ATP are shown by the following equation. The symbol P_i represents an inorganic phosphate group.

$$\underset{\text{Lower energy}}{ADP} + P_i + energy \rightleftarrows \underset{\text{Higher energy}}{ATP}$$

This process is a cycle, as shown in Figure 6–3. It is estimated that a resting adult human processes more than 40 kg of ATP each day.

6:2 Uses of Cell Energy

Cells use energy to maintain homeostasis. Kidneys use energy to move molecules and ions in order to keep the blood chemically balanced. Some protists use energy to expel excess water from their cytoplasm. While you are reading this page, your cells are using energy to build many kinds of molecules. Some of these molecules are used to build membranes or cell organelles. Others are enzymes that carry out reactions. All of these processes use the energy released from the breakdown of ATP to ADP.

Active transport uses energy from ATP to move molecules and ions across membranes. Kidney cells use active transport during excretion. Active transport keeps nerve cells ready to transmit impulses. Movement of organelles and cells themselves uses energy from ATP. Cell structures must move during cell reproduction. Of course muscle cells move, but so do white blood cells and cells that have cilia or flagella.

Chemical changes always involve energy. Suppose energy could simply be moved from one chemical bond to another without any change. Then, organisms would never need additional food molecules for energy. However, some energy is always converted to forms that cells can no longer use. The most common form is heat. Evolution has produced some organisms that make use of this

FIGURE 6–3.

Cell energy is stored and released in the ADP-ATP cycle.

FIGURE 6–4.

This hummingbird's cells must convert a large amount of ATP to ADP just to hover in the air. A steady supply of rich food is critical to its survival.

a

b

FIGURE 6–5.

Warm-blooded animals use "waste" heat to maintain a constant body temperature. (a) In some organisms, energy from ATP is used to produce light (b).

"waste" heat. These organisms are warm-blooded animals and include humans. Using heat, we maintain a warm body temperature that is ideal for most cell activities. With mechanisms of homeostasis to control body temperature, warm-blooded animals can be active in many different climates.

Fireflies and many deep-sea creatures are among organisms that give off light. About 80 percent of deep sea fish produce light. The production of light by organisms is called bioluminescence (bi oh lew muh NES unts). The light results from a chemical reaction that is powered by the breakdown of ATP. This light-producing reaction is used in the lab to test for the presence of ATP.

REVIEW

1. How does ATP store energy?
2. Why must there be a mechanism for storing energy given off during the breakdown of food molecules?
3. Energy is the ability to do work. List four ways in which work is done within organisms.
4. **SKILL REVIEW:** When animals shiver in the cold, muscles move almost uncontrollably. Suggest how shivering helps an animal survive in the cold. For more help, refer to Observing and Inferring in the Skill Handbook, page 809.
5. **USING CONCEPTS:** List all the ways you can think of that an eagle might use energy from the breakdown of ATP.

GETTING ENERGY TO MAKE ATP

Cells break down ATP to obtain energy for cell processes. As ATP is used, it must be replenished. The energy to build more ATP comes from food. It takes energy to break down food molecules. However, cells get more energy from the food than they use to break it down. Different processes yield different amounts of energy.

6:3 Respiration

When scientists talk about food molecules in cells, they don't mean fried chicken or broccoli. Molecules of glucose and other 6-carbon sugars are the major source of energy for many organisms. Cells break down glucose through a series of chemical reactions. The stored energy of the sugar is used in forming ATP from ADP and phosphate. The energy from the sugar is now stored in a form that is readily usable by cells—ATP.

Respiration is the process by which food molecules are broken down to release energy. Respiration can occur with or without oxygen. **Aerobic** (uh ROH bihk) **processes** require oxygen in order to take place. **Anaerobic processes** occur in the absence of oxygen. In many cells, both anaerobic and aerobic processes take place during respiration. The anaerobic processes are simple and yield energy quickly. However, as you will see, the energy payoff is much greater when molecules are broken down aerobically.

6:4 Glycolysis and Fermentation

When glucose starts to break down, it is changed into two molecules of a compound called PGAL (phosphoglyceraldehyde), a 3-carbon molecule. The PGAL molecules are then changed to pyruvic acid molecules, which also contain three carbon atoms each. The anaerobic process of splitting glucose and forming two molecules of pyruvic acid is called **glycolysis** (gli KAHL uh sus). Notice in Figure 6–6 that glycolysis uses the energy from two molecules of ATP. However, four ATP molecules are formed using the energy released by glycolysis. Thus, in glycolysis, the energy payoff for the breakdown of one molecule of glucose is only two molecules of ATP.

anaerobic:
an (GK) without
aeros (GK) air

FIGURE 6–6.

Glycolysis uses two ATPs in the breakdown of glucose. However, the formation of pyruvic acid forms four ATPs.

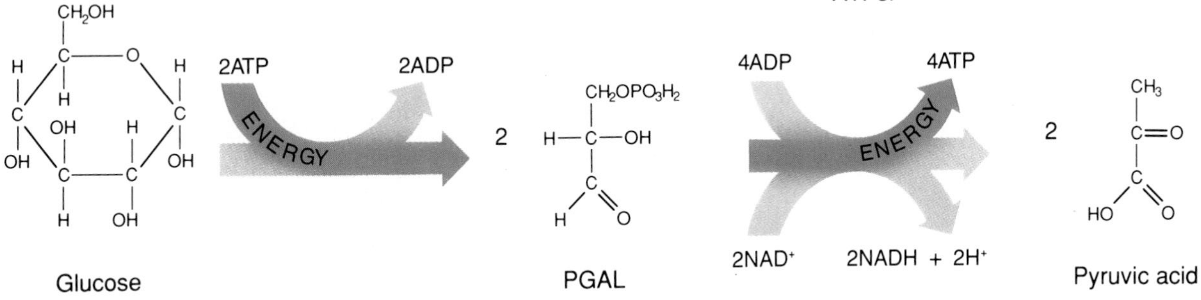

Glucose → 2ATP → 2ADP → ENERGY → 2 PGAL → 4ADP → 4ATP → ENERGY → 2 Pyruvic acid

2NAD⁺ → 2NADH + 2H⁺

$$CH_3$$
$$|$$
$$C=O$$
$$|$$
$$C$$
$$HO \quad O$$

Pyruvic acid

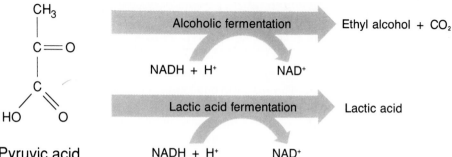

Alcoholic fermentation → Ethyl alcohol + CO_2

$NADH + H^+$ NAD^+

Lactic acid fermentation → Lactic acid

$NADH + H^+$ NAD^+

FIGURE 6–7.

Without oxygen, organisms can regain NAD^+ in two ways—alcoholic fermentation or lactic acid fermentation.

What is the importance of fermentation?

FIGURE 6–8.

Both photographs show organisms carrying out fermentation. The runner's leg muscles (a) are producing lactic acid. The yeast cells in rising dough (b) are producing alcohol and CO_2.

Glycolysis also produces hydrogen ions and electrons. These combine with organic carrier ions called NAD^+ (nicotinamide adenine dinucleotide) to form $NADH + H^+$. The compound NAD is one of a class of small organic molecules called coenzymes. Coenzymes act as carriers in many biological reactions. Many coenzymes are made from vitamins. For instance, NAD is derived from niacin.

Pyruvic acid from glycolysis can be changed further without oxygen. This process is called fermentation. No additional ATP is formed by fermentation. However, fermentation regenerates NAD^+ ions that are needed for glycolysis to continue. In fermentation, pyruvic acid changes to ethyl alcohol and carbon dioxide or to lactic acid.

When ethyl alcohol and carbon dioxide are end products, the fermentation is called **alcoholic fermentation.** Many bacteria and fungi such as yeast carry out alcoholic fermentation. The following reaction shows the process. Notice that NAD^+ is produced.

pyruvic acid $\rightarrow$ ethyl alcohol + carbon dioxide
$NADH + H^+$ NAD^+

In industry, ethyl alcohol is produced when yeast ferments sugar from grain, fruit, and other organic materials. Ethyl alcohol used as a gasoline additive is produced this way. Maybe you have made pizza at home and have added yeast to the dough. The carbon dioxide given off during alcoholic fermentation is trapped as bubbles in the dough, and causes it to rise. The ethyl alcohol produced evaporates during baking and gives the dough an extra "push."

a

b

When lactic acid is formed as an end product of fermentation, the process is called **lactic acid fermentation.** Lactic acid fermentation occurs in some bacteria, plants, and in most animals. Some bacteria cause milk to sour when they break down lactose sugar in the milk to lactic acid. Fermentation of milk produces yogurt and some kinds of cheese. This conversion of simple sugars to lactic acid also is used to make soy sauce, sourdough bread, and chocolate. The following reaction shows the overall process of lactic acid fermentation.

$$\text{pyruvic acid} \longrightarrow \text{lactic acid}$$
$$\text{NADH} + \text{H}^+ \qquad \text{NAD}^+$$

When you move a muscle, respiration in muscle cells speeds up. First, glycolysis converts glucose to pyruvic acid. You know that when you exercise, you breathe faster and more deeply. If your exercise is strenuous, oxygen cannot get to the cells fast enough. If not enough oxygen is available, lactic acid fermentation will occur. As a result, lactic acid begins to build up in your muscles. Lactic acid makes your muscles begin to ache during strenuous exercise, and the pain may cause you to stop exercising. After you stop, you continue breathing rapidly for a while. You feel out of breath because your body has built up an oxygen debt. Your body needs oxygen to break down the lactic acid remaining from fermentation.

Glycolysis and fermentation take place in the cytoplasm of cells. If oxygen is present, different reactions follow glycolysis. These reactions yield more energy and take place in the mitochondria.

6:5 Aerobic Respiration

In most cells, if oxygen is present, glucose is broken down in a different way. The process begins with glycolysis, giving a net yield of two molecules of ATP for each molecule of glucose broken down. Glycolysis is anaerobic. However, if enough oxygen is present, fermentation doesn't occur. Instead, oxygen is used to break down pyruvic acid further, producing more energy to make additional ATP. These reactions take place in a mitochondrion, the powerhouse of the cell. Respiration that uses oxygen is referred to as aerobic respiration.

Aerobic respiration has four main parts. The first part involves the reactions of glycolysis, which you have just studied. The remaining three parts take place in the mitochondrion. The second part includes reactions that change pyruvic acid as shown in Figure 6–9. Pyruvic acid, a 3-carbon compound, is changed to acetic acid, a 2-carbon compound. The third carbon atom forms carbon dioxide, CO_2. Acetic acid is combined with a substance called coenzyme A to form a compound called acetyl-CoA.

The third part of aerobic respiration is the **citric acid cycle,** Figure 6–10. This cycle of chemical reactions produces more ATP and releases additional electrons. The electrons are picked up by the carriers NAD^+ and FAD, which is similar to NAD^+. In the citric acid cycle, acetyl-CoA combines with a 4-carbon molecule to form a 6-carbon molecule, citric acid. In the figure, locate the reactions

Cell respiration should not be confused with breathing. Breathing is the mechanical process by which some animals take air into their bodies and expel waste gases.

FIGURE 6–9.

Pyruvic acid changes to acetic acid by losing a CO_2 molecule. It then forms acetyl-CoA before entering the citric acid cycle.

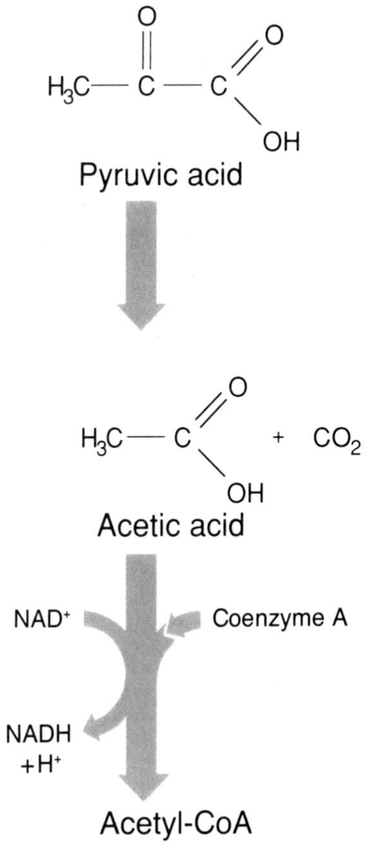

Pyruvic acid

Acetic acid

Acetyl-CoA

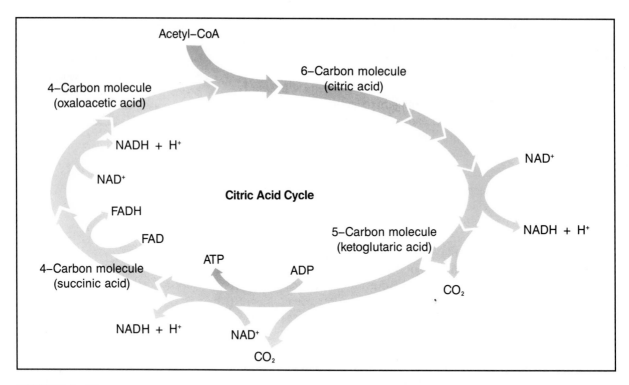

Acetyl–CoA

6–Carbon molecule
(citric acid)

4–Carbon molecule
(oxaloacetic acid)

NADH + H⁺

NAD⁺

NAD⁺

Citric Acid Cycle

FADH

FAD

NADH + H⁺

5–Carbon molecule
(ketoglutaric acid)

4–Carbon molecule
(succinic acid)

ATP

ADP

CO₂

NADH + H⁺

NAD⁺

CO₂

FIGURE 6–10.

In one turn of the citric acid cycle, a 2-carbon acetyl unit is changed to two carbon dioxide molecules, hydrogen, and electrons.

NoteWorthy

To learn more about the citric acid cycle and the chemical structures involved, turn to Appendix C, Biochemistry, on pages 790 to 793.

What is the function of oxygen in aerobic respiration?

in which citric acid is changed to a 5-carbon molecule and then to a 4-carbon molecule. Notice that a carbon dioxide molecule is given off in each of these reactions. This loss of two CO_2 molecules produces a 4-carbon molecule that reacts to regenerate the original 4-carbon substance. Thus, a new 4-carbon molecule is available to combine with each new acetyl-CoA that enters the cycle.

In both glycolysis and the citric acid cycle, some energy is trapped in the ATP formed. However, more important than the formation of ATP, these sets of reactions also release electrons. The fourth part of aerobic respiration is called the electron transport chain, Figure 6–11. The **electron transport chain** is a series of substances along which electrons are transferred, releasing energy. Carrier molecules bring electrons from the reactions of both glycolysis and the citric acid cycle to the electron transport chain. The molecules of the electron transport chain are located on the inner membranes of mitochondria.

At the electron transport chain, the carrier molecules give up electrons that pass through a series of reactions. Figure 6–11 also shows that electrons at the top of the chain have high energy. As electrons pass down the chain, the energy given off is captured in molecules of ATP. Notice where ATP molecules are produced as a result of electrons passing down the chain.

The final electron acceptor in the chain is oxygen. This is why the process is aerobic. The reactions of the electron transport chain cannot take place in the absence of oxygen. If the final electron acceptor, oxygen, is used up, the chain becomes jammed. It is somewhat like a parking lot with a blocked exit. If the first car can't exit, the cars behind can't get out either. Also, just as additional cars

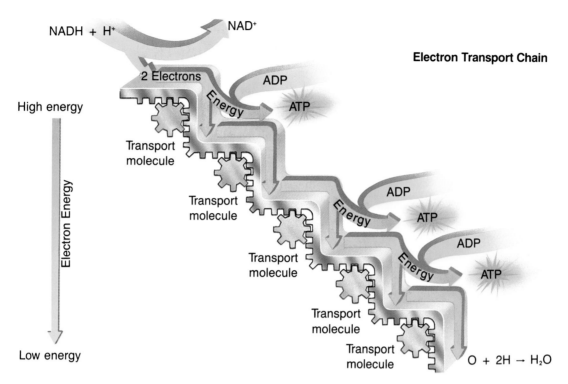

NADH + H⁺ → NAD⁺

Electron Transport Chain

High energy

Electron Energy

2 Electrons

Energy

ADP

ATP

Transport molecule

Transport molecule

Energy

ADP

ATP

Transport molecule

Energy

ADP

ATP

Transport molecule

Transport molecule

Low energy

$O + 2H \rightarrow H_2O$

FIGURE 6–11.

The transport molecules in the electron transport chain are proteins.

can't enter, neither can electrons. These blocked reactions force cells to carry out anaerobic processes that produce ethyl alcohol or lactic acid through fermentation reactions.

When oxygen accepts electrons, it combines with two hydrogen ions to form a molecule of water, H_2O. The water vapor and carbon dioxide that you exhale are produced by aerobic respiration. The following shows the aerobic breakdown of a glucose molecule.

$$C_6H_{12}O_6 + 6O_2 + 38ADP + 38P_i \rightarrow 6H_2O + 6CO_2 + 38ATP$$

When no oxygen is available, only 2 ATP are produced by glycolysis and fermentation. However, with oxygen, enough energy is released to form as many as 38 ATP molecules.

NoteWorthy

Depending on the organism and conditions, fewer than 38 molecules of ATP may be produced from one glucose molecule.

REVIEW

6. Compare the ATP yields of glycolysis and aerobic respiration.
7. How do alcoholic and lactic acid fermentation differ?
8. How is most of the ATP from aerobic respiration produced?
9. **SKILL REVIEW:** Use sections 6:4 and 6:5 to summarize what happens to each of the six carbon atoms in a molecule of glucose during aerobic respiration. For more help, refer to Reading Science in the Skill Handbook, pages 798 to 799.
10. **USING CONCEPTS:** Compare the energy-producing processes in a jogger's leg muscles to those of a sprinter's leg muscles. Which is likely to build up more lactic acid? Which runner is more likely to be out of breath after running? Explain.

Objectives:

- describe the function of chlorophyll and other pigments.
- write the chemical equation for photosynthesis and name each substance.
- describe the light reactions.
- describe the events of the Calvin cycle.
- list two alternate methods of CO_2 fixation.
- relate photosynthesis and respiration.

chlorophyll:
chloros (GK) pale green
phyllon (GK) leaf

FIGURE 6–12.

Out of all the colors in the visible spectrum, chlorophyll reflects green and some yellow. It absorbs all others.

The sandwich, soup, or salad you had for lunch contained carbohydrates that are changed to glucose in your body. In your cells, respiration breaks down the glucose to release energy and form ATP. Think about organisms such as green plants. They, too, must break down sugars to form ATP. However, they don't take in these sugars as food. Instead, they trap energy from sunlight in the process of photosynthesis. They then use this trapped energy to build carbohydrates for food.

6:6 Green Plants and Sunlight

Suppose you spot a rainbow in the sky after a rain shower. What colors does it include? A rainbow forms when white light from the sun is separated into its colors by water droplets. A rainbow is actually a visible spectrum showing the range of colors contained in light from the sun. The visible colors of sunlight's spectrum range from red through orange, yellow, green, blue, indigo, and violet.

Sunlight is the natural energy source for photosynthesis. Energy from sunlight is trapped by pigments and used to form sugars from carbon dioxide and water. Energy can then be released by breaking down these sugars. Different pigments have different colors because they reflect different colors of light. **Chlorophyll** is a green pigment that traps energy from sunlight. Chlorophyll appears green because it reflects green and yellow light. Chlorophyll absorbs other colors of light.

Chlorophyll is the main pigment that traps light in a chloroplast. Other pigments are found in the same layers that hold chlorophyll in a chloroplast. These pigments trap energy from colors of light that chlorophyll does not absorb well. One class of these pigments

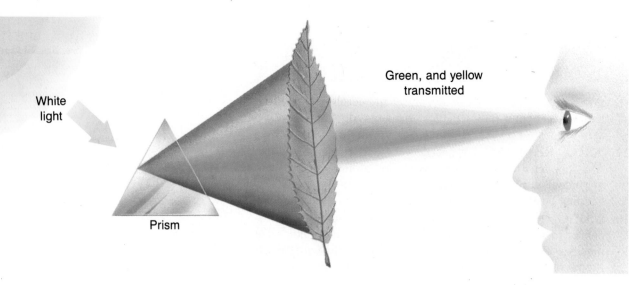

White light

Prism

Green, and yellow transmitted

is the carotenoids. The carotenoids reflect red and yellow light. They give color to carrots, tomatoes, and some fruits. Other pigments that function in photosynthesis reflect purple or blue light. You can see the colors of these pigments in places where the leaves of trees lose their chlorophyll in the autumn.

In plant cells, light energy is trapped in chloroplasts, Figure 6–14. A chloroplast has two surrounding membranes and two main inner parts. One part is a series of membranes called **thylakoid** (THI luh koyd) **membranes** within which energy from sunlight is trapped by chlorophyll. The thylakoid membranes may be arranged in stacks of membranous sacs called **grana.** A second part of the chloroplast, the **stroma,** is the material that surrounds the grana.

Trapping the energy of the sun in the chloroplasts is the first stage of photosynthesis. Recall that photosynthesis converts light energy into stored chemical energy by making carbohydrates. Water and carbon dioxide are raw materials. Chlorophyll traps light energy but is not permanently changed. The general reaction for photosynthesis follows.

$$6CO_2 + 6H_2O + \text{light energy} \xrightarrow{\text{chlorophyll}} C_6H_{12}O_6 + 6O_2$$

FIGURE 6–13.

Leaves contain pigments other than chlorophyll. These pigments are easy to see in autumn.

FIGURE 6–14.

Like a mitochondrion, a chloroplast has a large surface area arranged inside a small space. The chloroplast is surrounded by a second outer membrane not shown in this diagram.

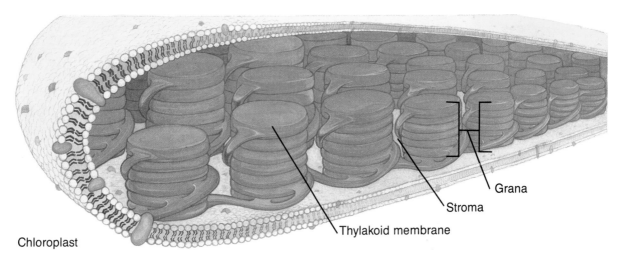

Chloroplast

Thylakoid membrane

Stroma

Grana

The general reaction of photosynthesis, just like the general reaction for aerobic respiration, is simple. It represents the sum of many chemical reactions that take place when simple sugars are formed. Many enzymes are involved in the process.

Photosynthesis is divided into two main groups of reactions. These are the light reactions and the Calvin cycle. **Light reactions** are the reactions in which light excites electrons and water splits into hydrogen and oxygen. The light reactions are the *photo* part of photosynthesis. The **Calvin cycle** is the series of reactions that forms simple sugars using carbon dioxide and hydrogen from water. The Calvin cycle is the *synthesis* part of photosynthesis.

What are the light reactions of photosynthesis? What takes place in the Calvin cycle?

6:7 Light Reactions

When light strikes chlorophyll, electrons within the chlorophyll molecule absorb energy and become "excited." Excited electrons leave the chlorophyll molecule and pass down an electron transport chain. This chain is located in the thylakoids. As electrons pass down the chain, their extra energy is stored in the bonds of ATP. This ATP is used in the Calvin cycle.

Notice in the general equation for photosynthesis that water is one of the reactants. In the light reactions, water splits into hydrogen and oxygen. The splitting of water during photosynthesis is called **photolysis** (foh TAHL uh sus). Photolysis accomplishes two things. First, it frees hydrogen, which is picked up by $NADP^+$ ions to form $NADPH + H^+$. Like NAD^+, $NADP^+$ picks up electrons and hydrogen ions. The $NADPH + H^+$ carries hydrogen to the Calvin cycle. Second, photolysis provides electrons that replace those lost from chlorophyll. Oxygen is given off as a waste product.

FIGURE 6–15.

In photosynthesis, the light reactions work like a factory that furnishes energy and some raw materials to the Calvin cycle.

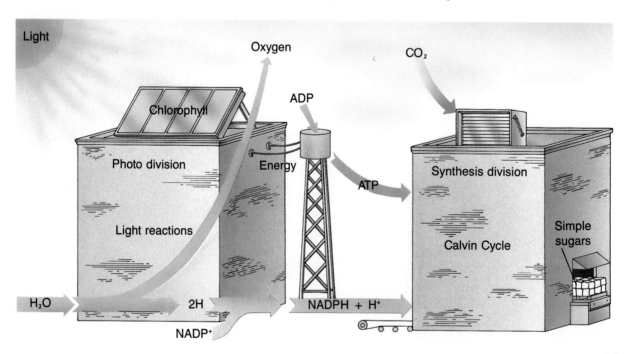

The light reactions of photosynthesis are quite complex and the process is still under study. Remember, many reactions and enzymes are involved. The important parts of the light reactions are summarized in Figure 6–15. Chlorophyll traps energy, which is used in a chain of reactions to form ATP. Water is split into oxygen, which is released as a gas, and hydrogen, which combines with $NADP^+$ to form $NADPH + H^+$. The light reactions provide ATP and $NADPH + H^+$ for the Calvin cycle reactions.

Where does the oxygen given off during photosynthesis come from?

6:8 The Calvin Cycle

In the Calvin cycle, an enzyme adds, or fixes, the carbon of carbon dioxide to a 5-carbon molecule. For this reason, the process is sometimes called carbon fixation. As you will see in Chapter 33, carbon fixation is vital to life on Earth. Figure 6–16 shows some of the reactions of the Calvin cycle.

The Calvin cycle reactions take place in the stroma of the chloroplasts. The overall effect of the Calvin cycle is that carbon dioxide combines with hydrogen to form carbohydrates such as sugars, starch, and cellulose. Carbon dioxide enters the leaves and stems of green plants through hundreds of small openings.

Besides carbon dioxide, ATP is needed to provide energy for Calvin cycle reactions. Also, hydrogen from the splitting of water is used in the reactions. Notice that because the reactions occur in a cycle, the 5-carbon molecules are always being produced. Therefore, molecules to combine with carbon dioxide are always available so long as the light reactions occur.

NoteWorthy

To learn more about the Calvin cycle and the chemical structures involved, turn to Appendix C, Biochemistry, on pages 790 to 793.

FIGURE 6–16.

The direct products of the Calvin cycle are 3-carbon sugars. However, these sugars almost immediately react. Among the products formed are starch, cellulose, and more complex sugars.

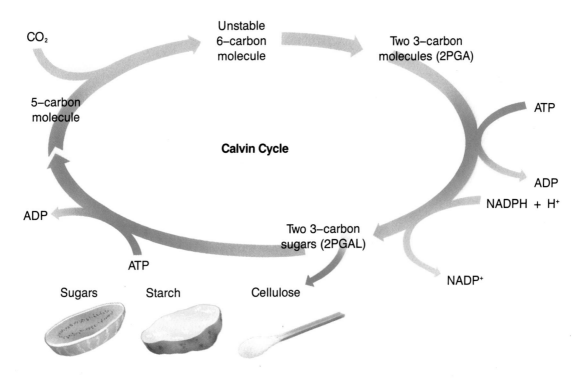

When carbon dioxide combines with the 5-carbon molecule, the 6-carbon molecule that forms splits immediately into two 3-carbon molecules. For this reason, the Calvin cycle is sometimes called the C-3 cycle. Plants that can fix carbon only in the Calvin cycle are called C-3 plants. The two 3-carbon molecules formed are phosphoglyceric acid (PGA) molecules. These molecules are converted into two 3-carbon sugars, PGAL, using the hydrogens of $NADPH + H^+$ and energy from ATP. Some of these sugars leave the cycle and are used to form other sugars, starch, or other complex carbohydrates that can later be used by the plant in respiration.

6:9 Alternate Forms of Photosynthesis

A more efficient way of trapping CO_2 has evolved in some tropical grasses, including corn, crabgrass, and sugarcane. These plants have cells that contain 3-carbon molecules with a strong attraction for CO_2. When CO_2 bonds to these 3-carbon molecules, 4-carbon molecules of malic acid are formed. Malic acid molecules move to the cells in which the Calvin cycle is taking place. Thus, the 4-carbon molecule acts as a specialized delivery system to get CO_2 molecules to the Calvin cycle. As a result, the Calvin cycle can operate at high efficiency. Plants that have this mechanism are called C-4 plants because carbon is fixed as a 4-carbon molecule.

Another specialized method for trapping CO_2 is called crassulacean acid metabolism or CAM for short. CAM is found in desert plants, such as cactus, which are adapted for hot, dry conditions. CAM plants take in CO_2 at night and store it as malic acid. In the daytime, the CO_2 is already inside the plant, available for use in the Calvin cycle. With CAM, the desert plants do not have to open their pores during the heat of the day in order to take in CO_2. This adaptation helps prevent water loss.

Why is corn called a C-4 plant? How does CAM help desert plants prevent water loss?

FIGURE 6–17.

The efficient C-4 photosynthesis system of corn (a) makes it a valuable food producer for humans. A cactus (b) conserves water by CAM.

a

b

BIOLAB *Photosynthesis* 6

Problem: How does light intensity affect the rate of photosynthesis?

Materials
test tube
weak sodium
  bicarbonate solution
bright light

sprig of *Elodea*
magnifying glass
400-mL beaker
stopwatch or clock

Procedures
1. Copy the data table.
2. Fill the test tube and beaker with sodium bicarbonate solution.
3. Place a freshly-cut sprig of *Elodea* into the test tube. Make sure the cut end of the *Elodea* is downward in the tube. Do not push the sprig more than halfway into the tube.
4. Seal the mouth of the test tube with your thumb and turn the test tube upside down. Try not to trap an air bubble under your thumb.
5. Place the mouth of the test tube under the surface of the solution in the beaker. Remove your thumb from the opening of the tube. Lower the test tube into the beaker so that the test tube leans against the side of the beaker.
6. Place your setup in the dark for five minutes or shield it from light with a piece of black construction paper.
7. Make a **hypothesis** about how the rate of photosynthesis in *Elodea* will change in response to light intensity.
8. Expose the setup to normal room light. Count the number of bubbles produced by the *Elodea* in the test tube for five minutes. You may need to use a magnifying glass. Observe where the bubbles emerge from the *Elodea.* Record your number in the data table.
9. Lower the lights in the room and count the bubbles again for five minutes. Record this number in the data table.
10. Turn on the lights in the classroom. Shine a bright light on the tube and count the bubbles again for five minutes. Record this number in the data table.

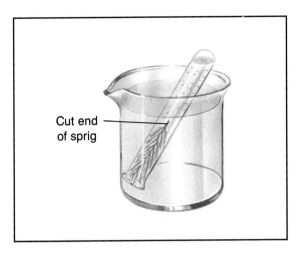

Cut end of sprig

Data and Observations

Trial	Light Conditions	Number of Bubbles in Five Minutes
1		
2		
3		

Questions and Conclusion
1. When was the number of bubbles produced the greatest? the least?
2. From where did the bubbles emerge?
3. Explain how counting bubbles measures the rate of photosynthesis.
4. What was the purpose of placing the test tube in a beaker of solution?
5. How might you prove that the bubbles were oxygen?
6. Did your results support your **hypothesis?** Explain why they did or did not.
7. Suggest a way of testing the effect of light color on photosynthesis.
Conclusion: How does light intensity affect the rate of photosynthesis?

6:10 Comparing Photosynthesis and Aerobic Respiration

In what ways are photosynthesis and aerobic respiration alike? How are they opposite?

Both photosynthesis and aerobic respiration are complex sets of reactions that are alike in several ways. Both require enzymes, both occur in specific organelles, and both involve the movement of electrons in transport chains.

In many ways, photosynthesis is the opposite of aerobic respiration. The end products of photosynthesis are the starting materials of respiration. In photosynthesis, starch or sugars are formed and oxygen is released as a waste product. Using oxygen, aerobic respiration breaks down sugars. Carbon dioxide and water are given off as wastes. So, the end products of aerobic respiration are the starting materials of photosynthesis. Compare the reactions in Figure 6–18.

Also notice in Figure 6–18 another difference between the two reactions. In photosynthesis, energy from sunlight is converted to chemical energy in the bonds of carbohydrate molecules. In respiration, chemical energy from the bonds of carbohydrate molecules is released and stored in readily usable form as ATP. It is important to remember that organisms of all five kingdoms must have food molecules. The big difference is in how they get these molecules. Photosynthetic organisms such as plants, algae, and cyanobacteria make their own. All others must take them in.

FIGURE 6–18.

The products of photosynthesis are the starting materials for aerobic respiration.

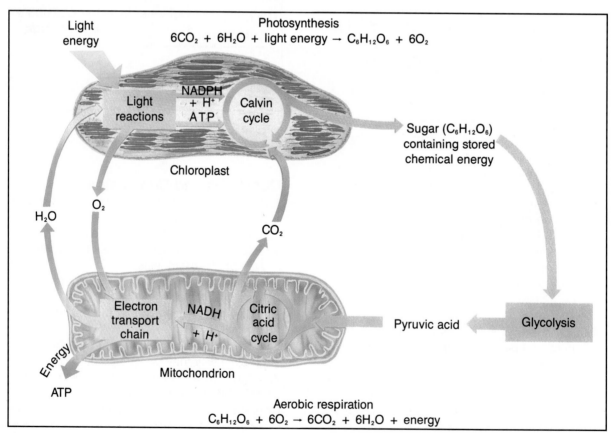

Photosynthesis
$6CO_2 + 6H_2O + \text{light energy} \rightarrow C_6H_{12}O_6 + 6O_2$

Aerobic respiration
$C_6H_{12}O_6 + 6O_2 \rightarrow 6CO_2 + 6H_2O + \text{energy}$

11. What are the main events of the light reactions?
12. What happens in the Calvin cycle?
13. Discuss two ways in which photosynthesis is different from aerobic respiration.
14. **SKILL REVIEW:** Design an experiment that would compare photosynthesis in red, green, and blue light. What would you use as a control? For more help, refer to Designing an Experiment in the Skill Handbook, pages 802 to 803.
15. **USING CONCEPTS:** In the general equation for photosynthesis, why is chlorophyll written over the arrow rather than on the left side of the equation?

THINKING CRITICALLY

A LONG, HOT SUMMER

During most of Earth's 4.6-billion year history, carbon dioxide has been a component of the atmosphere. Scientists believe the level of CO_2 was much higher in Earth's early atmosphere than it is today. When light from the sun strikes Earth's surface, it is reflected back as radiant heat. Carbon dioxide absorbs radiant heat and becomes warmer. This is one reason that Earth's early atmosphere was much warmer than it is today. When the process of photosynthesis evolved, CO_2 levels began to drop. Because less heat was absorbed, the atmosphere cooled. As a result, the polar ice caps increased in size as more ocean water froze. This freezing caused the sea levels to drop and expose more land surface.

Even today, CO_2 enters the atmosphere from several sources. Inorganic sources include volcanoes and the erosion of rocks composed of carbonate compounds. Organic sources include respiration by living things, forest fires, and burning fossil fuels (coal, oil, and natural gas). Most of these sources can't be controlled by humans. However, scientists estimate that more than five billion metric tons of CO_2 are released each year from burning fossil fuels. This burning is a direct result of human activity.

In 1958, the average CO_2 level was 312 parts per million parts of air. By 1980, the average was more than 340 parts per million and has increased each year. Some scientists predict that by the year 2050 the amount of CO_2 will double, producing disastrous effects. Why would atmospheric CO_2 levels drop with the evolution of photosynthesis? What "disastrous effects" might scientists predict as a result of a buildup of CO_2 in the atmosphere? Earth's early atmosphere contained almost no free oxygen. Suggest a reason for the increase in atmospheric oxygen.

Earth's atmosphere allows heat to escape back into space.

CHAPTER REVIEW

SUMMARY

1. ATP is the molecule that receives energy released in cell reactions. Energy from ATP may be used to make large molecules, allow cell movement, drive active transport, and make electrical and light energy. **6:1, 6:2**
2. Respiration is the process in which cells break down molecules to release energy. **6:3**
3. Energy can be released anaerobically by glycolysis followed by fermentation. **6:4**
4. Aerobic respiration takes place in mitochondria, uses oxygen, and yields many more ATP than anaerobic processes. **6:5**
5. Photosynthesis is the process by which plants use energy from light to make their own food. Photosynthesis consists of light reactions and a set of reactions in which carbohydrates are made. **6:6**
6. The light reactions use light to produce ATP and result in the splitting of water. **6:7**
7. The Calvin cycle reactions make carbohydrates using CO_2 along with ATP and hydrogen from the light reactions. **6:8**
8. Some plants have specialized methods for fixing carbon dioxide. **6:9**
9. The end products of photosynthesis are the starting products for respiration. **6:10**

LANGUAGE OF BIOLOGY

adenosine diphosphate
adenosine triphosphate
aerobic processes
alcoholic fermentation
anaerobic processes
Calvin cycle
chlorophyll
citric acid cycle
electron transport
   chain
energy
glycolysis
grana
lactic acid
   fermentation
light reactions
photolysis
respiration
stroma
thylakoid membranes

Choose the word or phrase from the list above that completes the sentence.

1. ____ is an important molecule that stores energy in a usable form in cells.
2. The process by which food molecules are broken down to release energy is called ____.
3. ____ require oxygen in order to take place.
4. The end product of ____ is ethyl alcohol.
5. The end product of ____ is lactic acid.
6. A(n) ____ is a series of substances along which electrons are transferred, releasing energy.
7. ____ is a green pigment that traps energy from sunlight.
8. Energy is trapped by chlorophyll molecules located in the ____.
9. The material in the chloroplast that surrounds the grana is the ____.
10. During the ____, light excites electrons and water is split.

REVIEWING CONCEPTS

Choose the word or phrase that completes the sentence or answers the question.

11. Green plants are able to trap ____ energy.
    a. heat   c. animal
    b. light   d. chemical
12. When cells break down glucose by aerobic respiration, ____ is formed.
    a. ADP   c. oxygen
    b. sugar   d. carbon dioxide
13. Chlorophyll appears green because it ____ green light.
    a. reflects   c. refracts
    b. absorbs   d. produces
14. Oxygen is given off as a waste product during the part of photosynthesis called ____.
    a. respiration
    b. photolysis
    c. electron transport
    d. the Calvin cycle

15. Energy is stored when a(n) ____ is added to ADP.

   a. sugar
   c. ATP
   b. carotenoid
   d. phosphate

16. ____ takes place in the stroma of chloroplasts.

   a. Glycolysis
   c. Light trapping
   b. Fermentation
   d. The Calvin cycle

17. An adaptation that helps desert plants prevent water loss is ____.

   a. C-4 delivery
   c. NADP
   b. CAM
   d. NADPH

18. The most common waste energy is ____.

   a. water
   c. light
   b. heat
   d. work

19. Plants and animals release energy by breaking down sugar molecules in the ____.

   a. nucleus
   c. chloroplasts
   b. cell membrane
   d. mitochondria

20. ____ produces the most ATP.

   a. Aerobic respiration
   b. Alcoholic fermentation
   c. Lactic acid fermentation
   d. Glycolysis

UNDERSTANDING CONCEPTS

Answer the following questions using complete sentences.

21. Why do living organisms require phosphorus?
22. What three substances must be supplied to the Calvin cycle? What are their sources?
23. What happens to the products of photosynthesis in plants?
24. Why is it important for plants to have a constant supply of water?
25. How do aerobic and anaerobic processes differ?
26. What is the function of coenzymes? How are coenzymes related to vitamins?
27. What is the source of heat in the human body?
28. What is oxygen debt? Explain how it develops.

29. If four ATPs are produced by glycolysis, why is the net yield only two ATPs?
30. What is the purpose of oxygen in aerobic respiration?

APPLYING CONCEPTS

Answer the following questions using complete sentences.

31. Why would human muscle cells contain many more mitochondria than skin cells?
32. Why do we say that aerobic respiration and photosynthesis are opposite processes?
33. Predict what would happen to Earth's atmosphere if photosynthesis suddenly stopped.
34. A person tells you that plants "live off light energy instead of food." What could you say to help the person's understanding?
35. What happens to the sunlight that strikes a leaf but is not trapped by photosynthesis?

EXTENSIONS

1. Design an experiment to show that dough rises because carbon dioxide is produced by yeast.
2. How can you show that respiration occurs in germinating peas or beans even though they do not photosynthesize?
3. Research the work of Melvin Calvin or Hans Krebs and write a report.

READINGS

Goldsworthy, Andrew. "How Purple Was My Valley." *Discover,* Nov. 1987, pp. 14–15.

Pennesi, E. "The Making of Biosphere II." *Science Year 1989,* pp. 142–153. Chicago: World Book, 1988.

Youvan, Douglas C. and Barry L. Marrs. "Molecular Mechanisms of Photosynthesis." *Scientific American,* June 1987, pp. 42–48.

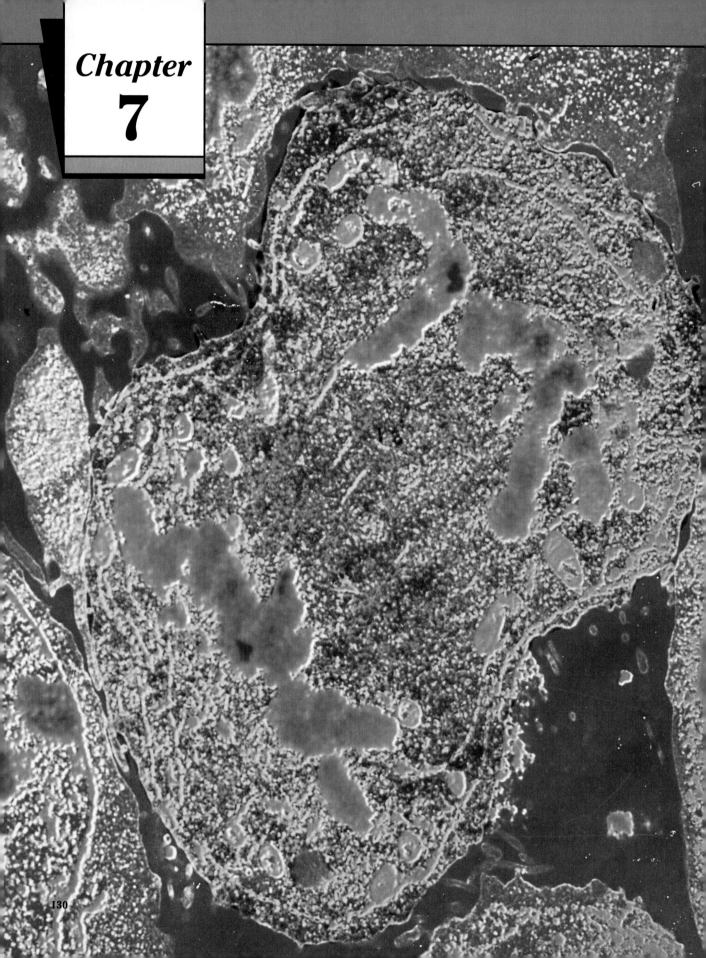

FROM ONE CELL TO TWO

D o you like to work puzzles? The puzzle of how cells reproduce, keep their identity, and make new substances is fairly well understood, but a number of parts are still unsolved. Scientists over many years have been trying to put together all the pieces. The nucleic acids, DNA and RNA, are the pieces involved in maintaining genetic continuity from generation to generation. The way these pieces fit together helps to explain how cells reproduce. At left, you see a cell reproducing by dividing into two identical cells.

DNA: THE SOLUTION TO HEREDITY

In Chapter 3, you studied the main groups of biomolecules that are found in all living organisms. These groups are carbohydrates, lipids, proteins, and nucleic acids. One of the nucleic acids is DNA, deoxyribonucleic acid. DNA is present in all organisms of every kingdom, but is different in each individual. As you will see, it is the molecular structure of DNA that makes each individual unique.

Objectives:
- describe the function, composition, and structure of DNA.
- list the contributions of Watson, Crick, and Franklin to the determination of DNA's structure.
- describe the process of replication of DNA and state the value of DNA replication to organisms.

7:1 Structure and Function of DNA

Besides curiosity, another characteristic of many scientists is a competitive spirit and a desire to be first with a new discovery. In modern times, it is not often that scientists make major discoveries from just a few experiments of their own. Most often, they study the conclusions of many related experiments, including their own, and propose an overall theory. Famous scientists are often those who are best at putting together many findings into one general idea.

By the 1950s, scientists knew that DNA formed the genetic code, which determined the hereditary characteristics of organisms. They also knew that DNA was a very large polymer made up of monomers called nucleotides. Each DNA nucleotide consists of a phosphate group, the sugar deoxyribose, and a nitrogen base. The only difference among the four nucleotides of DNA is in their nitrogen bases. The four **nitrogen bases** of DNA are the organic ring structures,

Animal cells dividing

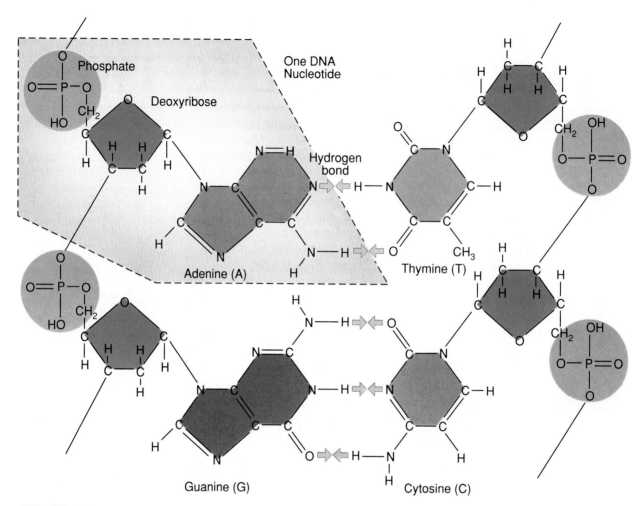

FIGURE 7–1.

DNA consists of chains of four nucleotides that differ only in their nitrogen bases. These are always paired adenine to thymine and guanine to cytosine.

NoteWorthy

When DNA was first found to hold the genetic code, many scientists thought the proteins associated with DNA were responsible. It was hard to imagine only four nucleotides forming a code for complex protein molecules.

adenine, guanine, cytosine, and thymine. Notice in Figure 7–1 that only the nitrogen bases of the nucleotides vary. In addition, scientists knew that the amounts of adenine and thymine nucleotides were equal. Likewise, the amounts of guanine and cytosine nucleotides were equal.

With the facts available, the time was right for someone to figure out the structure of DNA. Knowing the structure of DNA would help scientists answer three puzzling questions. How could a complex genetic code be made up of only four nucleotides? How was the code copied to pass on to new cells and to produce new offspring? How did the DNA code determine the structure of proteins and thus control the cell? Answering these questions would help scientists finally understand such things as evolutionary relationships among organisms and the nature of hereditary diseases. So, the race was on to propose an accepted structure for DNA.

One way of determining the structure of a substance is by X-ray diffraction. In this method, a beam of X rays is passed through a pure crystal of the substance. The X rays are deflected in patterns depending on the positions of the atoms that make up the crystal. In England, Rosalind Franklin carried out X-ray diffraction on very pure fibers of DNA. The patterns on her X-ray film showed that the phosphate of one nucleotide was linked to the sugar of the next, forming a continuous chain. The angles of these bonds cause the chain to have the shape of a helix, which is a spiral shape. Each turn of the helix consists of ten nucleotides.

At Cambridge University in England, James Watson, an American biologist, and Francis Crick, a British physicist, studied the available information on DNA. In 1953, they built a model that fit all the observations. The Watson-Crick model of DNA has two DNA strands. The phosphate-sugar chain forms a backbone for each strand. The nitrogen bases of each strand pair with the nitrogen bases of the other strand by hydrogen bonding. Adenine (A) always pairs with thymine (T), and guanine (G) always pairs with cytosine (C). This explained why these pairs of nucleotides always occur in equal quantities.

Because there are two strands in a spiral, the shape of DNA is described as a **double helix**. The DNA double helix is sometimes compared to a twisted ladder. The sides of the ladder are the sugar-phosphate backbones. The rungs are the pairs of nitrogen bases. Notice the base pairing in the structure of DNA in Figure 7–2. It is the order of these bases that makes up the genetic code. Differences in that order give individuality to each living organism. Differences in the order are slight among individuals of the same species. Differences in base order become progressively greater as organisms become further separated in phylogeny. When a cell divides, DNA preserves this individuality by passing exact copies of itself to each new cell.

helix:
helix (GK) spiral

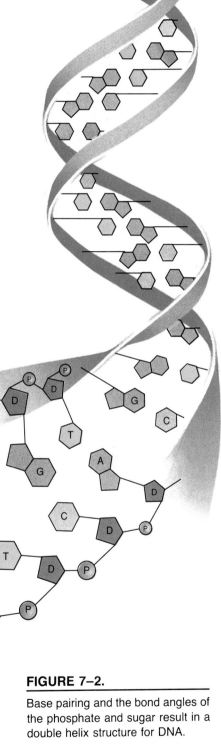

Key

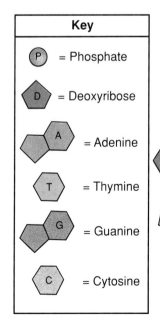

P	= Phosphate
D	= Deoxyribose
A	= Adenine
T	= Thymine
G	= Guanine
C	= Cytosine

FIGURE 7–2.

Base pairing and the bond angles of the phosphate and sugar result in a double helix structure for DNA.

7:2 Replication of DNA

The pairing of nitrogen bases in DNA is the key feature that allows DNA to be copied. The process by which a DNA molecule is copied is called **replication.** When a DNA molecule replicates, enzymes "unzip" the two strands along the paired bases. Each strand then serves as a pattern along which a new strand can form. Follow the diagram of the replication process in Figure 7–3.

replication:
re (L) again
plicare (L) to fold

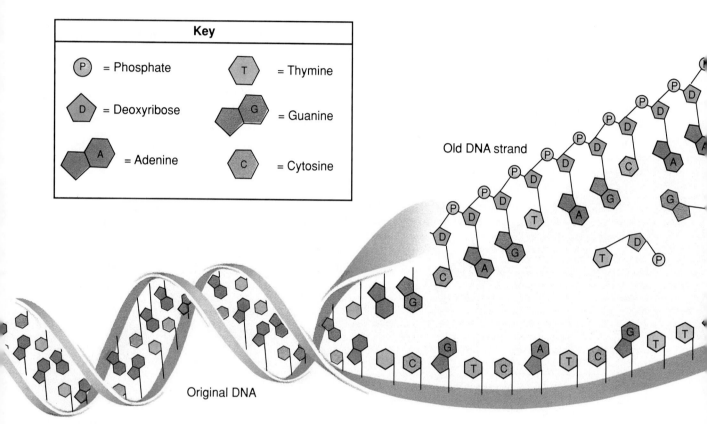

Key

(P) = Phosphate   (T) = Thymine

(D) = Deoxyribose   (G) = Guanine

(A) = Adenine   (C) = Cytosine

Old DNA strand

Original DNA

FIGURE 7–3.

The ability of DNA to replicate is one of the most important features of life. Notice that replication is possible and accurate because of base pairing.

1. Enzymes break the hydrogen bonds between the nitrogen base pairs, causing the two nucleotide chains to separate. The nitrogen bases are now exposed on both DNA chains.
2. Each chain serves as a pattern for the formation of a new nucleotide chain. Free nucleotides present in the nucleus pair with bases exposed on the chains. Adenine (A) pairs only with thymine (T), and cytosine (C) pairs only with guanine (G).
3. As base pairs bond, another enzyme links the phosphate of each new nucleotide to the sugar of the previous one.
4. The pairing and bonding continue until each of the original two DNA chains has a new paired chain. Thus, two new molecules of DNA form in double helix shapes.

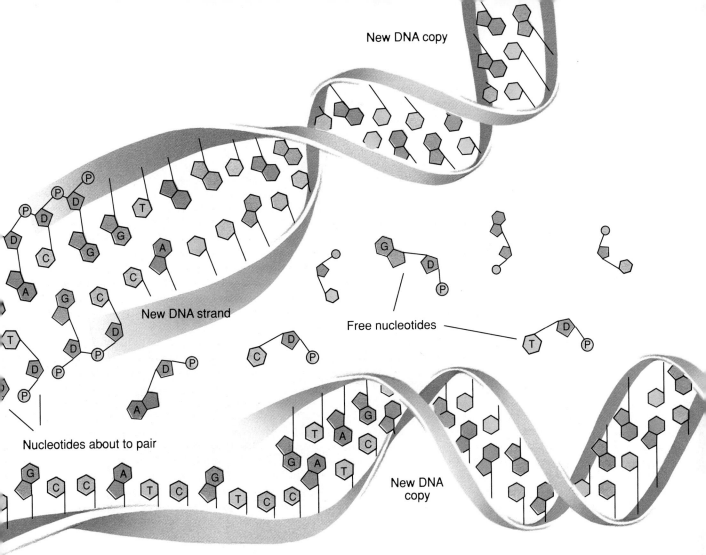

New DNA copy

New DNA strand

Free nucleotides

Nucleotides about to pair

New DNA copy

The result of replication is two molecules of DNA, each identical to the original molecule. Both have exactly the same order of bases. In ordinary cell division, two sets of the organism's genetic code are now ready to pass, one to each new cell. The discovery of this process answered the question of how DNA was able to pass genetic information to new cells and to offspring.

What is the result of DNA replication?

REVIEW

1. Describe the general structure of DNA.
2. What is the function of DNA?
3. What feature of DNA enables it to be replicated?
4. **SKILL REVIEW:** Write the sequence of bases in a replicating DNA molecule if one strand has the following base sequence: ATCCGG. For more help, refer to Reading Science in the Skill Handbook, pages 798 to 799.
5. **USING CONCEPTS:** DNA has been described as the maker of individuality. Explain the meaning of this statement.

Objectives:

- describe how DNA makes up the genetic code.
- list ways in which RNA and DNA differ.
- list the three types of RNA and their functions.
- describe how the DNA code is transcribed into RNA.
- describe how the RNA code is translated into protein.

In Chapters 3 through 6, you learned that proteins vary greatly both in structure and function. Some proteins build cell structures. For example, the cytoskeleton is composed mainly of protein. In multicellular organisms, proteins produced by some cells cause changes in other cells. Enzyme proteins carry out the chemical reactions of cells. Enzyme reactions store or release energy and make or break up other molecules. Proteins help control the movement of materials through plasma membranes. You can say that an organism's proteins determine what it is and how it functions. Because DNA forms the code for making proteins, it is DNA that makes up the "master plan" for an organism—the genetic code. You have seen how that code can be copied, but how is it translated?

FIGURE 7–4.

DNA is the master plan for an organism. Its ability to replicate makes it possible for offspring to inherit the characteristics of their parents.

7:3 The DNA Code

What property of a DNA molecule enables it to store the information needed for the synthesis of all the proteins in a cell? Recall that proteins are polymers made up of 20 different amino acids. A functional protein must have its amino acids in the correct order. Scientists now know that the sequence of nitrogen bases in DNA acts as a chemical code for the sequence of amino acids in proteins.

The English language contains many thousands of words. However, all the words can be formed from an alphabet of 26 letters simply by rearranging the letters. The four nitrogen bases of DNA—A, T, C, and G—make up the "genetic alphabet." Each unit of the

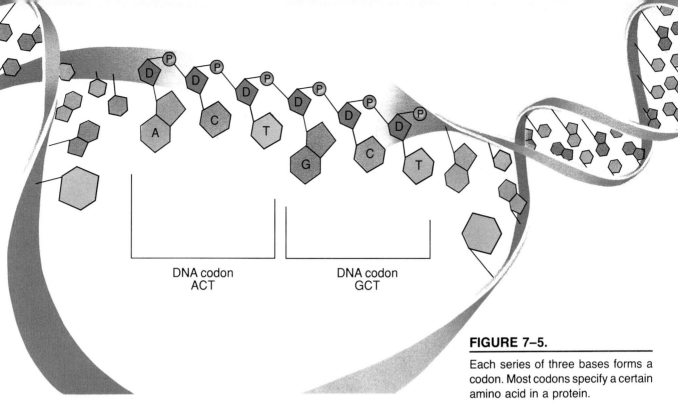

DNA codon
ACT

DNA codon
GCT

FIGURE 7–5.

Each series of three bases forms a codon. Most codons specify a certain amino acid in a protein.

codon:
  codex (L) tablet for writing

genetic code is a sequence of three bases called a **codon**. Most codons specify a certain amino acid in a protein. For example, the DNA codon CCA specifies the amino acid glycine. There are 64 different possible combinations of the four different nitrogen bases taken three at a time. Recall from Chapter 3 that there are only 20 common amino acids in proteins. Therefore, some amino acids can be specified by one of several different codons. Thus, a DNA strand of several hundred codons, using only four nucleotides, can form the code for a complex protein. One codon is a start code that begins the production of a protein chain. Three codons are stop codes that specify the end of a protein chain. As you will learn, the DNA code is not used directly to make proteins.

7:4 Structure and Function of RNA

After architects draw plans for a house, they do not take the original drawings to the building site. Instead they make several blueprint copies for builders to use. The original drawings are kept safe back at the office. In a similar way, the genetic code is copied for use at the site of protein synthesis, the ribosome. This copy is in the form of molecules of RNA, ribonucleic acid.

Like DNA, RNA is a nucleic acid made of bonded nucleotides. However, there are some important differences between the molecules. DNA contains the sugar deoxyribose, but RNA contains ribose, a slightly different sugar. Instead of the base thymine, RNA contains the nitrogen base uracil (U). Uracil pairs with adenine, just as thymine does in DNA. Thus, RNA contains the four bases adenine, uracil, cytosine, and guanine. Whereas a DNA molecule takes the shape of a double helix, RNA molecules are single-stranded.

FIGURE 7–6.

Like a blueprint, mRNA is the plan from which a protein is constructed.

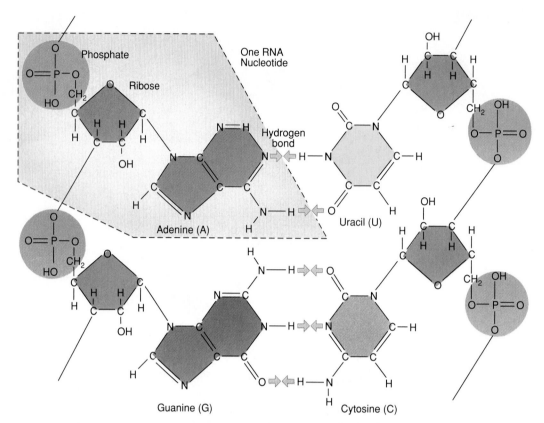

FIGURE 7–7.

RNA differs from DNA in the structure of the sugar and the presence of the base uracil instead of thymine.

There are three main kinds of RNA found in organisms. **Messenger RNA,** known as mRNA, is the RNA copy of the DNA code for the sequence of amino acids in a particular protein chain. It is mRNA that transfers the genetic code from DNA in the nucleus to the ribosomes in the cytoplasm. **Transfer RNA,** known as tRNA, transfers amino acids to the ribosomes for addition to the protein chain. Finally, **ribosomal RNA,** known as rRNA, makes up part of the ribosomes. The exact function of rRNA is not completely known.

7:5 Transcription: DNA to RNA

To make proteins, a copy of the correct code must be brought to the ribosomes. Follow the steps of the process in Figure 7–8. As in DNA replication, an enzyme unzips a portion of the DNA double helix. RNA nucleotides pair with the exposed DNA bases and are bonded together in a chain. **Transcription** is construction of RNA along portions of the DNA molecule. All three types of RNA are made by transcription from DNA. Some portions of DNA molecules are codes strictly for the production of tRNA and rRNA. Other portions of DNA produce mRNA, which carries the code for specific protein chains. Each DNA codon produces a corresponding RNA codon. For example, the DNA codon for glycine, CCA, would become GGU in mRNA. In prokaryotic cells, ribosomes attach to mRNA as soon as it separates from DNA. In eukaryotic cells, the mRNA copy moves out of the nucleus to the ribosomes in the cytoplasm.

NoteWorthy

In discussing the genetic code, scientists usually refer to the nitrogen bases instead of whole nucleotides.

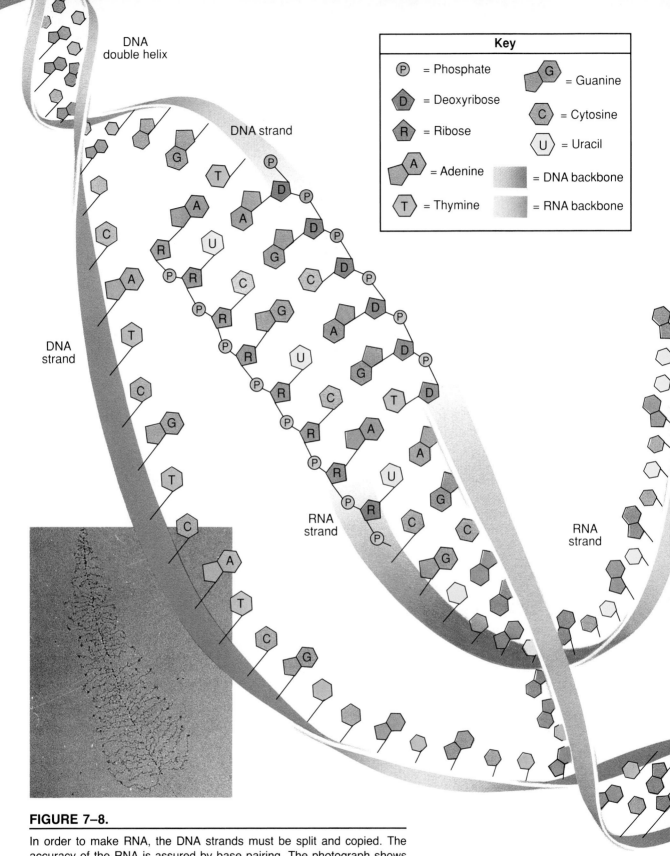

DNA double helix

DNA strand

DNA strand

RNA strand

RNA strand

Key	
P = Phosphate	G = Guanine
D = Deoxyribose	C = Cytosine
R = Ribose	U = Uracil
A = Adenine	= DNA backbone
T = Thymine	= RNA backbone

FIGURE 7–8.

In order to make RNA, the DNA strands must be split and copied. The accuracy of the RNA is assured by base pairing. The photograph shows many RNA molecules being produced from the same section of DNA.

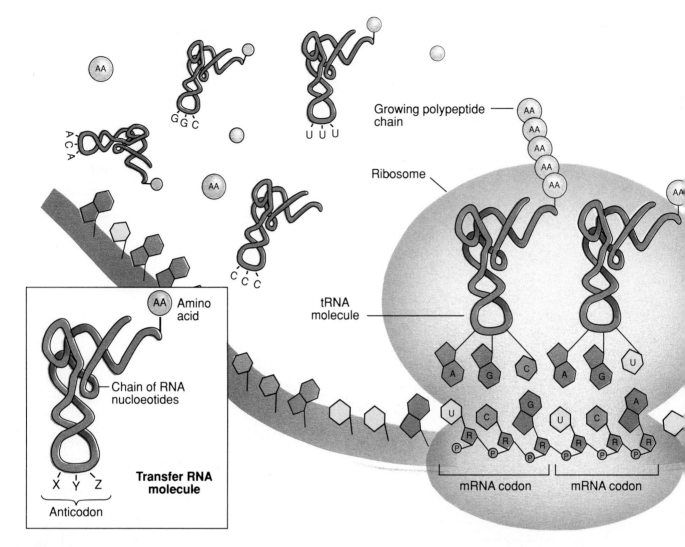

Growing polypeptide chain

Ribosome

tRNA molecule

mRNA codon   mRNA codon

AA Amino acid

Chain of RNA nucloeotides

Transfer RNA molecule

X Y Z

Anticodon

FIGURE 7–9.

Protein is made when the mRNA code is translated. Each mRNA codon pairs with the anticodon of tRNA carrying an amino acid. Enzymes then form peptide bonds between the amino acids.

What is the function of tRNA?

7:6 Translation: RNA to Protein

When mRNA binds to a ribosome, the production of a protein chain can begin. **Translation** is the process in which the mRNA code is read and converted into a specific amino acid sequence in a protein chain. Transfer RNA begins bringing amino acids to the ribosome according to each successive codon of the mRNA. All tRNAs have the same general three-looped shape. Each tRNA also has a triplet of nitrogen bases, called an **anticodon**, that will pair with a corresponding codon triplet. In the cytoplasm, an enzyme attaches the proper amino acid to each tRNA according to the anticodon it carries. During protein production, each tRNA anticodon pairs with the corresponding mRNA codon. As the mRNA codons are read, tRNA molecules carrying their amino acids, bind to the mRNA at the ribosome, anticodon to codon. This process lines up each new amino

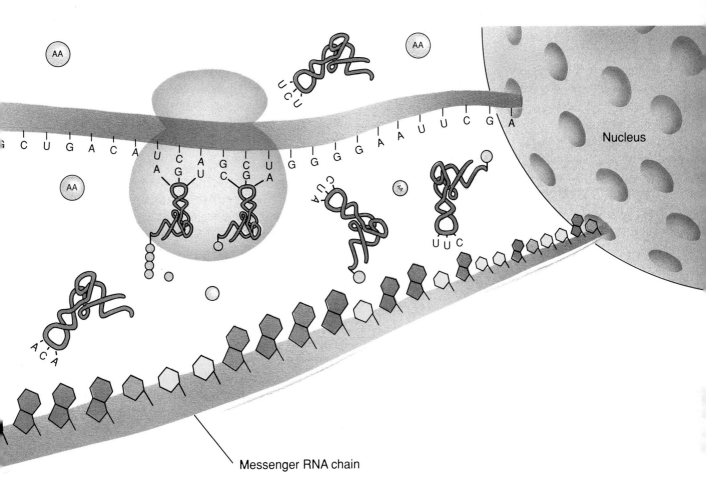

Messenger RNA chain

acid with the last. An enzyme attaches the amino acids together by forming a peptide bond between them. Once amino acids are linked, the tRNA is released and returns to the cytoplasm and picks up another amino acid. The translation process continues until a complete polypeptide chain is formed. After all chains are made, they link to form a functional protein.

REVIEW

6. What is the function of mRNA? How is mRNA formed?
7. In what ways do the chemical structures of DNA and RNA differ?
8. What is the function of tRNA?
9. **SKILL REVIEW:** If a codon on an mRNA molecule reads AUC, what would the tRNA anticodon read? For more help, refer to Reading Science in the Skill Handbook, pages 798 to 799.
10. **USING CONCEPTS:** How is the sequence of bases in an anticodon related to the original sequence of bases in the DNA molecule?

DEVELOPING A VIEWPOINT

PATENTING ORGANISMS

A patent is a claim that is made for the ownership of an invention or a process. A government grants a license that gives the patent owner rights to control the making and selling of the patented object or process. Can you patent a living organism or products of living organisms? Is it all right to patent a plant? What about a bacterium or hormones from tissues taken from someone during surgery?

BACKGROUND

An organism that already exists in nature cannot be patented. But suppose genes from one species of plant are placed in another kind of plant. By law, this plant can be patented if it is useful to humans.

In April, 1988, the United States Patent and Trademark Office granted Harvard University the first patent for a transgenic animal. A transgenic animal has one or more genes from another kind of animal. In this case, a human gene was placed in a mouse, making the mouse a transgenic animal.

Engineered tomato

CASE STUDIES

1. The research at Harvard University that produced the transgenic mouse was funded by a corporation. Therefore, this company owns the commercial rights to the results of this research. The transgenic mice are now being bred and offered for sale for research. These patented mice have a genetic tendency to develop certain tumors. The patent that was issued covers all transgenic non-human mammals engineered with the human genes that cause tumors. Since there are about 40 known genes that cause tumors, the company can now own other transgenic mammals that it develops for cancer research.

2. Farm organizations and animal rights groups oppose the development and subsequent patenting of transgenic animals. The farm organizations believe that the present distribution of genes in farm animals should be known before transgenic animals are developed. Religious leaders have expressed concerns about the moral and social issues in regard to developing new animals by transgenic means.

3. In 1973, a convention of European nations agreed to prohibit patents on transgenic organisms in the European Economic Community. Now economic leaders are beginning to recognize that patents for transgenic organisms may be necessary for the growth of the biotechnology industries in Europe. A European commission is now working to establish a legal framework for patenting transgenic organisms.

4. A group of companies has been studying human genes to map the genes that are on specific chromosomes. Some people think the companies withhold the information they acquire in order to make a profit. The Human Genome Initiative, sponsored by the National Institutes of Health and the Department of Energy, would like to use the information that the companies have acquired. However, the companies have spent large amounts of time and money developing the information and techniques. These companies can prosper and continue only if they are guaranteed ownership rights through copyrights and patents. Some researchers think that the scientific tradition of sharing information should be followed.

5. Tissues that people pay to have removed, such as an appendix or a tumor, are sometimes used by researchers to make products such as unusual proteins or scarce human hormones. The products, cells, or processes are then patented. However, who owns the tissues after they are removed, and who should profit from them? Hormones and cancer drugs have been produced from such tissues. In 1987, about 350 companies produced about $600 million worth of products from human tissues. Now, however, lawsuits over the ownership of the removed tissues is slowing the research. A spokesperson for the industry states that only 1 in 10 000 tissue samples may have commercial value. Their argument against paying for the tissues is that the tissues are worthless without the skills of the researchers.

DEVELOPING YOUR VIEWPOINT

1. Why would transgenic mice be useful to the researchers who buy them?
2. Should the concerns of farm organizations, animal rights groups, and religious leaders be taken into account before transgenic animals are developed and patented?
3. What are the main arguments for and against patenting of transgenic organisms and human tissue products?
4. What do you think could be accomplished if researchers could map the human genome?

5. Suppose a hormone or cancer drug is produced from tissues taken from your body. Do you think you are entitled to profit from the sales of that material?
6. Discuss whether or not all scientific information should be freely available to all scientists. Is there any instance when this information should not be freely available?

SUGGESTED READINGS

1. Barinaga, Marcia. "Making Transgenic Mice: Is It Really That Easy?" *Science,* Aug. 11, 1989, pp. 590–591
2. Dickson, David. "Europe Tries to Untangle Laws on Patenting Life." *Science,* Feb. 24, 1989, pp. 1002–1003.
3. Pimentel, D., *et al.* "Benefits and Risks of Genetic Engineering in Agriculture." *BioScience,* Oct. 1989, pp. 606–614.
4. Schwartz, John and Susan E. Katz. "Selling a Pound of Flesh." *Newsweek,* Apr. 20, 1987, p. 55.
5. Stone, Judith. "Cells for Sale." *Discover,* Aug. 1988, pp. 32–39.
6. "Transgenic Tomatoes." *BioScience,* May 1988, p. 320.
7. Wright, Karen. "Playing Demigod." *Scientific American,* May 1989, pp. 30–31.

Experimental mice

Biochemist

Cytotechnologist

Developmental Biologist

How do cells metabolize? What processes are responsible for memory and learning? What chemical signals let cells "know" when to stop dividing? These are only a few of the topics that interest biochemists. Biochemistry is the study of the chemistry of living things. It includes the substances that compose them and how those substances react in life processes. Biochemical research has found that many of the basic chemical structures and processes of living systems are shared by all life forms. Most biochemists work in research and development. Basic biochemical research discovers the unknown, whereas applied research (development) takes the conclusions of basic research and uses them to develop practical applications.

A **biochemist** is a scientist who investigates the chemical composition and processes of living organisms. As a biochemist, you might do independent research to unravel the complex chemical reactions that occur during cell metabolism. As an applied biochemical researcher, you might work to determine the biochemical causes for aging, genetic disorders, or obesity. Some biochemists in the pharmaceutical industry do research to learn how the chemicals of the nervous system are related to pain, depression, anxiety, or diseases such as schizophrenia and Alzheimer's disease. Other pharmaceutical biochemists develop drugs to treat or prevent such disorders.

A **cytotechnologist** is a biologist who specializes in the preparation and analysis of cells. As a hospital cytotechnologist, you might receive samples of human tissue for study. You would operate equipment to prepare and mount human tissue samples for analysis. You might study the sections to determine whether some cells are diseased or abnormal in some way. Also, you might run tests to see if cells have been affected by certain physical and chemical reactions. Your work as a hospital cytotechnologist would be an integral part of the diagnosis and treatment of patients by physicians and other members of the medical team. Some cytotechnologists work for independent medical technology laboratories to which samples of tissues and body fluids are sent for analysis. Veterinary hospitals employ cytotechnologists for the same reasons as hospitals that treat human patients. Plants, of course, have diseases too. As a plant cytotechnologist, you might work in a government laboratory studying crop plants for evidence of disease. If disease is found, you may prepare plant tissues for diagnosis.

A **developmental biologist** might describe the sequence of the stages of development in an organism. Developmental biologists also study the biochemical interactions among cells and tissues. As a research developmental biologist, you might analyze the changes in proteins that are synthesized by developing cells. The main questions you would want to answer involve the nature of the changes that occur during development and reasons for those changes. Some developmental biologists study the biochemical causes for birth defects and inherited diseases.

CELL REPRODUCTION

Recall from Chapter 5 that cells do not continue to grow larger and larger. Instead, the cell either stops growing or divides into two cells. Scientists still do not know all the factors that determine when and if a cell will divide. The ability of a cell to form new cells like itself is one of the basic characteristics of living things. According to the cell theory, all organisms are composed of cells, and all cells come from pre-existing cells. Therefore, cell reproduction is necessary for life to continue.

Objectives:
- describe cell reproduction in prokaryotes.
- explain why and how reproduction of eukaryotic and prokaryotic cells differs.
- describe and identify each stage of the cell cycle.
- tell what is accomplished by mitosis.

7:7 Types of Cell Division

Cell reproduction in prokaryotic cells is relatively simple. Prokaryotic cells such as bacteria have only one large circular DNA molecule. Before cell division, this DNA replicates to form two sets of genetic code. Prokaryotes reproduce by a process called binary fission. During **binary fission**, the cell pinches apart into two new cells with each cell having its own copy of the DNA code. Other unicellular organisms, such as protists, often reproduce by a type of binary fission. Follow the process of binary fission as shown in Figure 7–10.

binary fission:
binarius (L) pair
fissus (L) a split

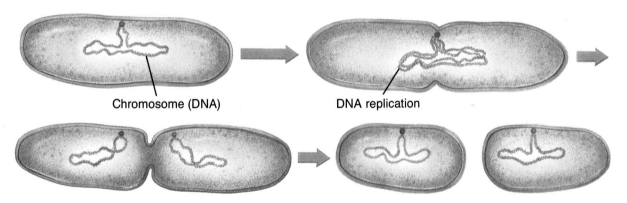

Chromosome (DNA) DNA replication

FIGURE 7–10.

Prokaryotes reproduce by binary fission. Each new cell receives a copy of the DNA code.

Cell reproduction in eukaryotes is more complicated than in prokaryotes for two main reasons. First, recall from Chapter 4 that the DNA of eukaryotic cells is inside a membrane-bound nucleus. Second, most eukaryotic organisms have several very large DNA molecules. Each DNA molecule with its associated proteins is called a **chromosome**. Human cells, for instance, have 46 chromosomes. In eukaryotes, a mechanism has evolved that ensures the genetic code remains complete and organized during cell reproduction. This mechanism is called mitosis. **Mitosis** is the division of the nucleus into two nuclei containing identical DNA. Actual cell division takes place only as the highly organized process of mitosis finishes. Mitosis results in the distribution of a complete set of genetic code into each new cell.

mitosis:
mitos (GK) thread

7:8 The Cell Cycle

In actively dividing eukaryotic cells, the **cell cycle** is the sequence of events that occurs from the end of one division to the end of the next division. During most of the time of the cycle, the cell is in interphase. During **interphase**, the cell grows, produces new organelles, and replicates its chromosomes, which form loose tangles of chromatin. Only powerful electron microscopes can show chromosome strands during interphase. Following interphase, mitosis begins. Four stages of mitosis are recognized: prophase, metaphase, anaphase, and telophase. However, mitosis is a continuous process in which each stage merges into the next.

Prophase: In early **prophase**, the chromosomes coil very tightly, becoming short and thick. At this point, chromosomes form a visible jumble near the center of the cell when viewed under a light microscope. Recall that the chromosomes are replicated during interphase. The two identical copies of each chromosome are called **sister chromatids.** These sister chromatids are held together at a specific region called the **centromere.** The nucleolus and nuclear membrane disassemble during prophase. In most eukaryotes, other than plants, two centrioles appear next to the disappearing nuclear membrane. **Centrioles** are bundles of microtubules organized like cilia. They are not present in plant cells. As microtubules form around the centrioles, the centrioles begin to move to opposite ends of the cell. In middle prophase, the microtubules extend to form spindle fibers. **Spindle fibers** are protein microtubules that extend from centriole to centriole across the cell. The ends of the spindle are called poles.

INTERPHASE

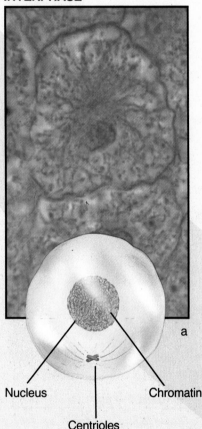

Nucleus

Centrioles

Chromatin

a

PROPHASE

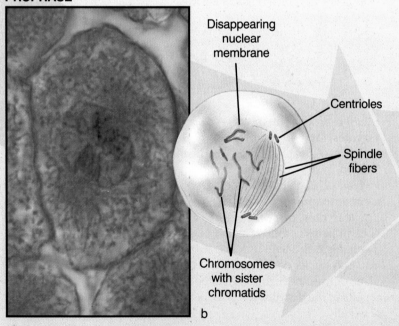

Disappearing nuclear membrane

Centrioles

Spindle fibers

Chromosomes with sister chromatids

b

FIGURE 7–11.

Identify the characteristics of each stage in the cell cycle of an animal cell: interphase (a), prophase (b), metaphase (c), anaphase (d), and telophase (e).

Metaphase: During early **metaphase**, the network of spindle fibers is fully formed and the sister chromatids become attached to the spindle fibers. Each chromatid has a spot on the centromere that attaches the chromatid to spindle fibers. The sister chromatids line up in the middle of the cell, still attached to the spindle fibers. The middle of the cell where chromatids align is called the cell's equator. At this point, chromatids are most condensed and distinct. Under the microscope, metaphase may be identified by the tight line of sister chromatids across the equator of the cell.

Anaphase: As **anaphase** begins, the centromeres divide, and sister chromatids separate from one another. Remember that each pair of chromatids are exact copies of one chromosome. The action of the spindle fibers pulls the pairs apart. One chromatid of each pair then moves toward the each pole of the cell. As a result, a complete set of chromosomes moves toward each end of the cell. Scientists are still trying to determine the mechanism by which this movement occurs. With a microscope, anaphase is distinguished by the two distinct rows of chromosomes with a space between them.

Telophase: The last stage of mitosis is **telophase**. The chromosomes arrive at opposite ends of the cell and the spindle fibers disassemble. A new nuclear membrane forms around each set of chromosomes. The chromosomes uncoil and revert back to a mass of tangled chromatin. A nucleolus re-forms in each new nucleus. The cell begins to make new RNA and the production of protein resumes. Each nucleus now contains a complete set of the genetic code and mitosis is finished. Notice in Figure 7–11, however, that cell division is not yet complete.

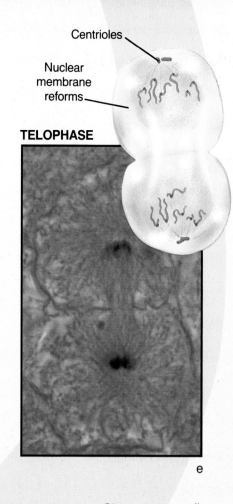

Centrioles

Nuclear membrane reforms

TELOPHASE

e

METAPHASE

ANAPHASE

Chromosomes meet at equator

Centromere

Sister chromatids

Chromosomes pull apart at centromere

Spindle fibers

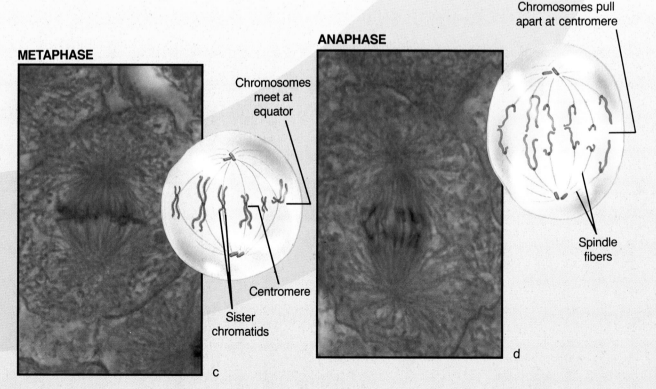

c

d

FIGURE 7–12.

This diagram of the cell cycle is typical for some actively dividing cells of mammals. Note that the largest portion of time is spent in interphase.

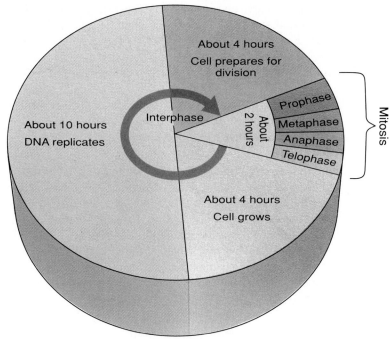

About 4 hours
Cell prepares for division

Prophase
Metaphase
Anaphase
Telophase

Mitosis

Interphase

About 2 hours

About 10 hours
DNA replicates

About 4 hours
Cell grows

A 20-Hour Cell Cycle

How does a plant cell divide after mitosis?

NoteWorthy

Some bacteria divide every 20 minutes. At this rate, one cell would become 5 trillion billion cells in a day.

The last part of the cell cycle is division of the cytoplasm to form two separate cells. This division usually begins during late mitosis. In animal cells, microfilaments pinch the cell membrane together until two new cells are formed. Each new cell receives one nucleus and about half of the cell contents, including organelles, membranes, and cytoplasm. Because plant cells have a rigid cell wall, they cannot pinch apart. Instead, a membrane called a cell plate forms, dividing the cell in two. Each new cell then forms its own cell wall.

As cells grow, new mitochondria and chloroplasts are necessary. These organelles reproduce on their own because they contain their own genetic code. Most have DNA molecules similar to those found in prokaryotes. As you will see in Chapter 11, this provides strong evidence for the way life has evolved.

REVIEW

11. Describe the process by which prokaryotic cells divide.
12. What are sister chromatids?
13. In terms of the genetic code, what is accomplished by mitosis?
14. **SKILL REVIEW:** Sequence and outline the steps of the cell cycle. For more help, refer to Organizing Information in the Skill Handbook, pages 810 to 813.
15. **USING CONCEPTS:** At one time, interphase was referred to as the resting phase of mitosis. Why do you think this description is no longer used?

BIOLAB

Observing the Cell Cycle

Problem: What features identify the stages of the cell cycle?

Materials
microscope
prepared slide of mitosis in animal cells

Procedures
1. Copy the data table. Have extra paper available for drawing.
2. Place a slide on the microscope stage.
3. Focus with low power to locate the specimen and to scan for a region of cells that seem to be in various stages of cell division.
4. Switch to high power and find a distinct cell in one of the stages of the cell cycle. Don't search for cells in the order of stages. Just try to find the best cell in each stage. Try to view several cells at each stage.
5. Record the characteristics of that stage in the data table. Be sure to record the positions of objects as well as their appearance. Draw the stage and label its structures.
6. Find a cell at another stage and repeat step 5. If you find a clear example of a stage, share your view with other groups.

Questions and Conclusion
1. When are chromosomes first visible?
2. What are the main features of telophase?

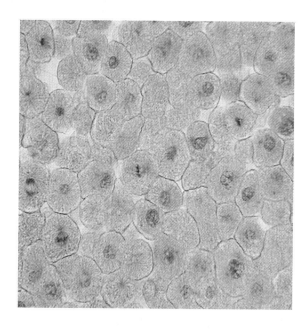

3. Did each stage have the same appearance in all the examples you observed? Explain.
4. Which stage was most numerous on the slide? How can you explain this observation?
5. What is happening in anaphase that makes it appear different from metaphase?

Conclusion: Summarize the features that distinguish each phase of the cell cycle.

Data and Observations

Appearance of Dividing Cell					
Stage	**Nucleus**	**Chromosomes**	**Centrioles**	**Spindle**	**Cell membrane**
Interphase					
Prophase					
Metaphase					
Anaphase					
Telophase					
Division of cytoplasm					

CHAPTER REVIEW

SUMMARY

1. The double helix structure of DNA results from pairing of the nitrogen bases. **7:1**
2. DNA replicates by base pairing, giving two exact copies of the DNA molecule and thus, the genetic code of an organism. **7:2**
3. A sequence of three nitrogen bases forms the code for a particular amino acid. **7:3**
4. Each kind of RNA, messenger, transfer, and ribosomal, has a unique function. **7:4**
5. The DNA code is transcribed to mRNA which carries DNA's message to the ribosomes. **7:5**
6. Protein is made when the mRNA code is translated. Each mRNA codon pairs with the anticodon of tRNA carrying an amino acid. **7:6**
7. Prokaryotes divide by binary fission. Eukaryotic cell division begins with mitosis. **7:7**
8. The cell cycle includes all the events between one division and the next. **7:8**
9. Mitosis consists of four phases: prophase, metaphase, anaphase, and telophase. **7:8**

LANGUAGE OF BIOLOGY

anaphase
anticodon
binary fission
cell cycle
centrioles
centromere
chromosome
codon
double helix
interphase
messenger RNA
metaphase
mitosis
nitrogen bases
prophase
replication
ribosomal RNA
sister chromatids
spindle fibers
telophase
transcription
transfer RNA
translation

Choose the word or phrase from the list above that completes the sentence.

1. Prokaryotes reproduce by ____.
2. The shape of a DNA molecule is a(n) ____.
3. Most of a cell's lifetime is spent in the part of the cell cycle called ____.
4. At the phase of mitosis called ____, the chromosomes line up at the middle of the cell.
5. The nuclear membrane is re-formed during the phase of mitosis called ____.
6. The region of the chromosome that attaches to the spindle fibers is the ____.
7. A sequence of three bases is called a(n) ____.
8. The synthesis of mRNA along a portion of the DNA molecule is called ____.
9. ____ converts the mRNA message to a specific amino acid sequence at a ribosome.
10. During protein synthesis, the codon on mRNA links with the ____ on tRNA.

REVIEWING CONCEPTS

Choose the word or phrase that completes the sentence or answers the question.

11. ____ are the monomers that make up DNA.
    a. Nucleic acids
    b. Peptides
    c. Amino acids
    d. Nucleotides
12. The helix shape of DNA was discovered by ____.
    a. comparing nucleotides
    b. X-ray diffraction
    c. using enzymes
    d. counting bases
13. The strands of the DNA double helix are held together by pairing of ____.
    a. sugars
    b. nitrogen bases
    c. phosphates
    d. nucleotides
14. The process of ____ copies the DNA of a cell.
    a. mitosis
    b. transcription
    c. replication
    d. translation
15. Division of the nucleus occurs during ____.
    a. mitosis
    b. binary fission
    c. interphase
    d. replication
16. Prokaryotic cells reproduce by ____.
    a. centrioles
    b. binary fission
    c. nuclear division
    d. mitosis

17. During prophase of mitosis, microtubules begin to form a structure called a ___.
    a. chromatid   c. centriole
    b. cell wall   d. spindle
18. The nitrogen base ___ is not present in RNA.
    a. thymine   c. cytosine
    b. adenine   d. uracil
19. RNA copies of the genetic information carried by DNA are made by ___.
    a. transcription   c. translation
    b. tRNA   d. mitosis
20. A ___ is not found in plant cells.
    a. cell wall   c. nucleus
    b. centromere   d. centriole

UNDERSTANDING CONCEPTS

Answer the following questions using complete sentences.

21. Why is DNA able to make an organism unique?
22. What was Franklin's evidence that led Watson and Crick to propose their structure for DNA? How did the model account for the occurrence of certain nucleotides in equal amounts in DNA?
23. Suppose the DNA sequence ATTGACGTC is transcribed to mRNA. What will be the mRNA base sequence? What three tRNA base sequences will pair with the mRNA?
24. What binds the nitrogen base pairs together in the DNA molecule?
25. How does replication result in two exact copies of a DNA molecule?
26. What is the function of the spindle fibers during cell division?
27. Explain how the correct amino acids are brought to the site where protein is made.
28. What causes chromosomes to separate in anaphase? What does anaphase accomplish?
29. As viewed under the microscope, what features characterize each phase of mitosis?
30. Describe the process of DNA transcription.

APPLYING CONCEPTS

Answer the following questions using complete sentences.

31. Suggest what might happen if an extra nucleotide became inserted in a DNA molecule?
32. In what ways does cell reproduction in prokaryotes and eukaryotes differ?
33. Why is it difficult to view chromosomes during interphase?
34. Scientists are mapping the entire DNA code for humans. Suggest possible benefits and risks of this project.
35. In eukaryotes, why must mRNA pass out of the nucleus before protein can be made?

EXTENSIONS

1. Report on the research that led up to the Watson-Crick model for DNA. Include the work of Griffith, Chargaff, Wilkins, and Pauling.
2. Create a poster summarizing the processes discussed in this chapter. Begin with the structure of DNA, branching to replication and cell division in one direction. Branch to transcription and protein production in the other direction.
3. Create a model of DNA using common materials. Plastic clothespins of four different colors make good models of base pairing.

READINGS

Avise, John C., "Nature's Family Archives." *Natural History,* Mar. 1989, pp. 24–27.
Radman, Miroslav and R. Wagner. "The High Fidelity of DNA Duplication." *Scientific American,* Aug 1988, pp. 40–46.
Watson, James D. *The Double Helix.* New York: Atheneum, 1968.

GENETICS
and EVOLUTION

There would seem to be only one commandment for living things: Survive! And the forms and species and units and groups are armed for survival, fanged for survival, timid for it, fierce for it, clever for it, poisonous for it, intelligent for it. This commandment decrees the death and destruction of myriads of individuals for the survival of the whole. Life has one final end, to be alive; and all the tricks and mechanisms, all the successes and all the failures, are aimed at that end.

John Steinbeck
The Log from the Sea of Cortez

GENES AND CHROMOSOMES

You have learned that mitosis leads to the formation of two identical cells, resulting in growth and repair of the organism. However, in order for a species to survive, organisms must reproduce. Unlike body cells, reproductive cells are not usually identical. They provide the variation that is so important to the survival of a species. The walruses in the photo may all look alike, but each one is slightly variable. Differences can more easily be observed between parent and offspring as shown here in the scarlet tanager. In this chapter, you will be presented with a model that explains how the genetic information in the cell is rearranged for sexual reproduction.

Scarlet tanager

CHROMOSOMES AND MEIOSIS

Most of the complex organisms reproduce sexually. Sexual reproduction ensures that genetic information is passed from one generation to the next. In the process, this information is shuffled, causing the wide range of variation you see in species. Imagine what it would be like if all the plants were the same, all the animals looked alike, and you couldn't tell your own parents from those of your friends. The next sections will explain the cellular and molecular mechanism of sexual reproduction.

8:1 Chromosome Structure and Number

In Chapter 7, you learned that when a body cell divides, so do its chromosomes. Recall that chromosomes are threadlike structures inside the nucleus. In cells that are not dividing, the chromosomes are stretched out into long, thin strands and are virtually invisible. A chromosome is made up of genes. A **gene** is a segment of DNA that helps to control a particular hereditary trait such as leaf length or eye color. Like beads on a necklace, the genes are strung together to form chromosomes. The activity of genes is greatest when the cell is not dividing.

Objectives:
- explain how chromosome number and structure are important to classification.
- distinguish between haploid and diploid cells.
- describe and sequence the stages of meiosis.

What is a gene?

Walruses

Table 8–1.

CHROMOSOME NUMBERS OF SOME COMMON ORGANISMS		
Organism	**Body Cell (2n)**	**Gamete (n)**
Monerans		
Bacteria	1	—
Plants		
Carrot	18	9
Garden Pea	14	7
Corn	20	10
Tobacco	48	24
Animals		
Earthworm	36	18
Fruit Fly	8	4
Bullfrog	26	13
Goldfish	94	47
Chicken	78	39
Dog	78	39
Chimpanzee	48	24
Human	46	23

FIGURE 8–1.

Homologous chromosomes are often easy to identify by their similar structures.

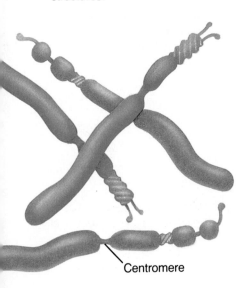

Centromere

The shape and number of chromosomes can be used to identify species just as any other characteristic such as flower color in plants or beak shape in birds is used. Each species has its own chromosome number. Table 8–1 shows the characteristic numbers of chromosomes for some species. Also, notice in Figure 8–1 that different chromosomes have characteristic shapes. Each species has a unique set of chromosomes.

Note that the number of chromosomes does not reflect the complexity or relatedness of organisms. For example, Table 8–1 shows that the chimpanzee and the tobacco plant have the same number of chromosomes, but, clearly, these organisms aren't closely related.

In all sexually reproducing organisms, each body cell contains two sets of chromosomes. Each chromosome of a set matches one from the other set. In other words, the chromosomes occur in pairs. The members of each chromosome pair are called **homologous chromosomes.** Each pair of homologous chromosomes is distinct in appearance from all other pairs in the cell.

A cell that contains two sets of chromosomes is called **diploid.** A diploid cell is indicated as 2n. The basic number of homologous pairs of chromosomes for the species is n. Thus, in human body cells, the diploid number of chromosomes (2n) is 46, or 23 homologous pairs. Match the pairs of chromosomes in Figure 8–1.

When an organism reproduces sexually, the number of chromosomes found in a body cell is halved during the production of gametes. A **gamete** is a sex cell. The female gamete is an **egg.** The male gamete is a **sperm.** Egg and sperm are both haploid. A **haploid** cell is one that contains one set of chromosomes. A haploid cell is indicated as n. Human gametes have a haploid chromosome number (n) of 23. Gametes are formed only from cells in sex organs.

8:2 Meiosis

Gametes are produced by meiosis. **Meiosis** is the process of cell division that results in the formation of gametes. Meiosis has stages similar to those of mitosis: interphase, prophase, metaphase, anaphase, and telophase. However, the result of meiosis is the reduction of the chromosome number by half. Recall from Chapter 7 that chromosomes become duplicated into sister chromatids before a mitotic cell division. This duplication of chromosomes also occurs in the homologous chromosomes before cell division by meiosis. So what happens to chromosomes when a cell divides to form gametes? What are the differences between mitosis and meiosis? Chromosomes are easily studied because as a cell prepares to divide, the chromosomes begin to contract. The strands coil and shorten, becoming progressively tighter. The chromosomes can then be seen with the aid of a light microscope.

Meiosis occurs in the cells of reproductive organs. Figure 8–3 shows a simplified diagram of the process of meiosis in a reproductive cell with just two pairs of homologous chromosomes. In Figure 8–3, notice that meiosis consists of two divisions of the nucleus. In the first division, the chromosomes of each homologous pair separate and move into two new cells. The first division is often known as the reduction division, because the chromosome number is reduced by half to the haploid condition. In the second division, the sister chromatids of each chromosome separate when their centromeres break apart. The result is four sex cells, each having the haploid number of chromosomes.

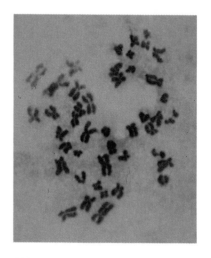

FIGURE 8–2.

The structure and number of chromosomes in a human body cell show up clearly when stained with a purple dye.

How many cell divisions are there in meiosis?

a   Reduction Division

A diploid cell

Two haploid cells

1

2

Two pairs of homologous chromosomes

One chromosome of each pair in each cell

b   Second Division

3

4

The centromeres divide

Four haploid gametes

FIGURE 8–3.

The reduction division of meiosis (a) results in a halving of chromosome number. The second division of meiosis (b) results in four sex cells.

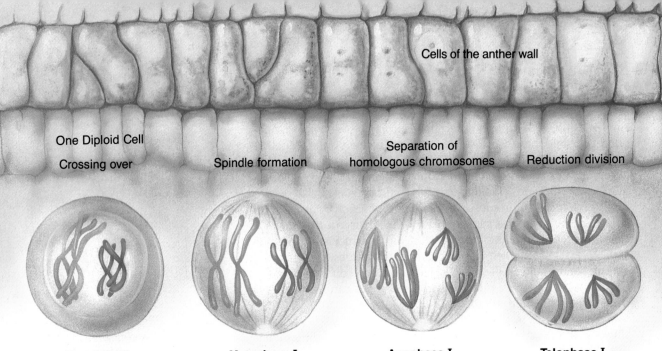

Cells of the anther wall

One Diploid Cell

Crossing over

Spindle formation

Separation of
homologous chromosomes

Reduction division

Prophase I **Metaphase I** **Anaphase I** **Telophase I**

FIGURE 8–4.

Two pairs of homologous chromosomes are shown here to illustrate
meiosis in the formation of pollen
grains that carry the male gametes
of seed plants.

Follow the stages of meiosis in pollen mother cells of a flower
as shown in Figure 8–4 as you read about the movements of the
chromosomes. In prophase I of meiosis, chromosomes shorten, coil,
and contract. The nuclear membrane dissolves and disappears. During this time, the chromatids of each pair of homologous chromosomes wind around each other, and pieces of chromosomes from
homologous pairs of sister chromatids are exchanged. This exchange
of genetic material is called **crossing over.**

The homologous chromosomes line up at the equator of the pollen
mother cell. This stage is called metaphase I. Metaphase I is very
different from metaphase of mitosis. Note that, unlike mitosis with
single chromosomes, pairs of chromosomes are at the equator. Also,
the genetic information is reorganized. However, like mitosis, the
centromeres of each chromosome with its sister chromatids are
attached to the spindle fibers.

The next stage is anaphase I. Once all of the homologous pairs of
chromosomes are aligned, one chromosome of each pair begins to
move to each pole of the cell. Notice that the centromeres do not
divide as they do in mitosis. The sister chromatids remain connected
to one another. Anaphase I is the stage when the chromosome
number is reduced by half. If there is any abnormality in the chromosomes, it will often be noticed at anaphase I. Entire chromosomes
may fail to separate properly. Organisms produced from these cells
may have genetic disorders or may even die.

During telophase I, the cell cytoplasm begins to divide. In some
female sex cells, including the eggs of humans, there may not be an
equal division of the cytoplasm. The cell that receives the larger
amount of cytoplasm becomes the functional egg. The cells that do
not develop are called polar bodies. These polar bodies contain little
cytoplasm and disintegrate. The cytoplasm of male sex cells, shown
here in pollen tissue, divides evenly.

prophase:
 pro (GK) before
metaphase:
 meta (GK) following
anaphase:
 ana (L) away
telophase:
 telo (GK) end
 phase (GK) stage

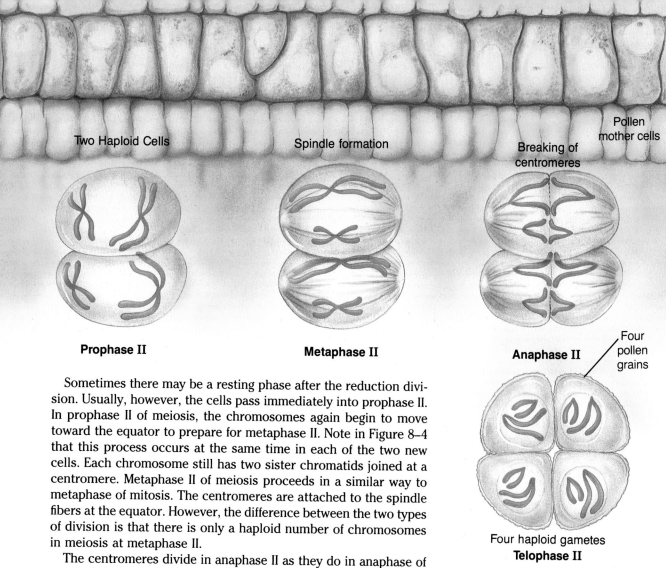

Prophase II

Metaphase II

Two Haploid Cells

Spindle formation

Breaking of centromeres

Pollen mother cells

Anaphase II

Four pollen grains

Four haploid gametes
Telophase II

Sometimes there may be a resting phase after the reduction division. Usually, however, the cells pass immediately into prophase II. In prophase II of meiosis, the chromosomes again begin to move toward the equator to prepare for metaphase II. Note in Figure 8–4 that this process occurs at the same time in each of the two new cells. Each chromosome still has two sister chromatids joined at a centromere. Metaphase II of meiosis proceeds in a similar way to metaphase of mitosis. The centromeres are attached to the spindle fibers at the equator. However, the difference between the two types of division is that there is only a haploid number of chromosomes in meiosis at metaphase II.

The centromeres divide in anaphase II as they do in anaphase of mitosis. The sister chromatids are pulled apart toward opposite poles of the cells. During telophase II, at the end of meiosis, the gametes are formed. Each of these new cells contains the haploid number of chromosomes. In humans, four sperm or one egg are produced from each meiotic division.

How is anaphase II of meiosis similar to anaphase of mitosis?

REVIEW

1. How is chromosome number useful in classification?
2. In which stage of meiosis does the cell become haploid?
3. How does a pair of homologous chromosomes differ from sister chromatids?
4. **SKILL REVIEW:** Sequence the stages of meiosis and compare this with the stages of mitosis. For more help, refer to Reading Science in the Skill Handbook, pages 798 to 799.
5. **USING CONCEPTS:** How does meiosis help a species survive?

Objectives:

- distinguish between genotype and phenotype.
- compare the genotypes of males and females.
- explain how crossing over results in genetic recombination.
- describe how linkage groups can be used in chromosome mapping.
- distinguish between structural and regulatory genes.

In 1903, when Walter Sutton was a young research student at Columbia University, he proposed that genetic traits are determined by the chromosomes. He hypothesized that the information for each trait was carried on pairs of genes because this would correspond to the pairs of chromosomes observed during meiosis. In 1909, Thomas Hunt Morgan located the first gene on a chromosome of a fruit fly. In these next sections, you will learn how a knowledge of genes is important to an understanding of inheritance.

8:3 Sex Chromosomes

Since the discovery of the gene, many lengthy breeding programs involving plants and insects have revealed the mechanisms of inheritance. At the same time, it has become obvious that each organism has a unique genotype. The **genotype** is an organism's genetic makeup. The genotype determines the traits that an organism will have when the chromosomes of a sperm combine with the chromosomes of an egg at fertilization. **Fertilization** is the fusion of a male and a female gamete. Fertilization restores the diploid condition. The genes from each parent determine an organism's genotype. In contrast, the physical appearance of an organism is its phenotype. The **phenotype** is an organism's outward appearance. Outward appearance of an organism is often influenced by environmental factors. For example, a rabbit with a white coat in winter but a brown coat in summer is showing two phenotypes. The genotype of the rabbit does not change.

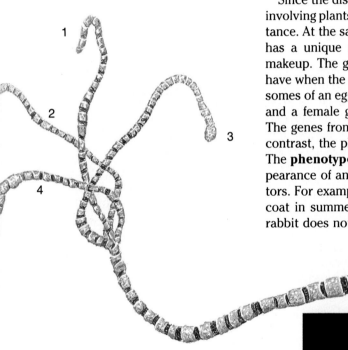

The DNA helix

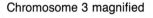

Chromosome 3 magnified

FIGURE 8–5.

A fruit fly gamete has four chromosomes. Since Thomas Hunt Morgan discovered that genes of a fruit fly are on its chromosomes, we now know exactly where some of the genes are located.

FIGURE 8–6.

The black and yellow coat color of a tortoiseshell cat occurs only in females. Because males have only one X chromosome, their coat colors would always be only either yellow and white or black and white.

NoteWorthy

In animals other than humans, the male genotype may be XO and the female XY. The location of the genes that control sex determination have not yet been identified.

FIGURE 8–7.

Sorrel is a common weed that has both male and female plants.

Female plant

Recall from Table 8–1 that the diploid number of chromosomes in humans is 46. Each of your parents contributed 23 chromosomes to your genotype. One pair of your chromosomes are known as sex chromosomes. **Sex chromosomes** carry genes that determine the sex of an individual. They are usually indicated by an X or a Y. In humans and many other organisms, the female chromosome is designated X. All females have a pair of X chromosomes, one inherited from the father and one inherited from the mother. The genotype of a female is, therefore, XX. Males have one X chromosome that they inherit from their mother, and a Y chromosome that they inherit from their father. A male genotype is, therefore, designated as XY. In some birds and amphibians, the genotypes are reversed. The male is XX and the female is XY.

In humans and many other species, it is the male gamete that determines the sex of an offspring. If the male's sperm that fertilizes the egg contains an X chromosome, a female offspring results. If the male's sperm contains a Y chromosome, a male offspring results. Since the male's sperm has an equal chance of having either the X or the Y chromosome, it would be expected that equal numbers of the sexes would be produced. However, the Y chromosome is smaller and has a slightly lower mass than the X chromosome. This results in a slight advantage for Y-bearing sperm in the race to each egg. In fact, in humans, between 102 and 106 males are born for every 100 females.

Most species of plants have both male and female sex organs on a single plant. A few groups of plants, however, such as the willow, ginkgo, and stinging nettle families, have plants that are either male or female. Unlike animals, plants rarely have separate sex chromosomes. The genes that determine sex are located on other chromosomes. One widespread weed that has distinct X and Y chromosomes is shown in Figure 8–7.

8:4 Genetic Recombination

All of the genes in a particular chromosome can be thought of as being linked to each other. Genes that are usually inherited together are called a **linkage group.** The number of linkage groups is equal to the haploid number of chromosomes. The fruit fly has four linkage groups. Humans have 23 linkage groups.

Recall that crossing over occurs during prophase I of meiosis. Crossing over allows exchange of genes between linkage groups on homologous chromosomes. Genes that are very close together are less likely to be separated by crossing over. Those genes at greater distances on each chromatid have a greater chance of being inherited separately. They do not appear to be linked in the offspring. The areas of a chromatid that break are exchanged with matching areas on a chromatid of its homologous chromosome. This exchange of genetic material results in **genetic recombination.** Genetic recombination results in more variations in the offspring. As you have learned, variation in individuals gives the species a better chance of surviving in a changing environment.

Rearrangement of the genes between homologous chromosomes may produce more advantageous combinations of genes than were previously available. Because of this process, and the random distribution of chromosomes during meiosis, it is almost impossible for two identical organisms to result from sexual reproduction.

Why is variation important to a species?

8:5 Chromosome Mapping

Scientists can now determine the location of each gene in a chromosome by the traits each controls. Crossing over is a useful tool for this chromosome mapping. The frequency with which linked genes cross over is measured. Recall that the further apart two genes are on a chromosome, the greater the chance or frequency of their crossing over onto the homologous chromosome.

FIGURE 8–8.

In prophase I, homologous chromosomes (a) come together and duplicate (b). Aa, Bb, Cc, Dd, and Ee represent five matching pairs of genes. After crossing over (c) the pairs of genes are recombined (d).

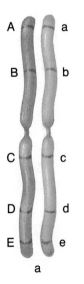

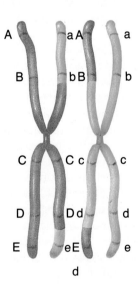

FIGURE 8–9.

In order to map the genes of chromosomes, first the nitrogen bases are broken along the DNA chain. An electric field is used to move the different lengths of DNA through a gel. The resulting bands reveal the order of bases in the original DNA chain.

Whether a gene has crossed over to its partner chromosome or not is determined by an examination of traits in the offspring. The frequency of crossing over of genes is used to indicate the distance from one gene to another. If the frequency is determined for all the known genes in an organism, a chromosome map can be made. A **chromosome map** is a model that shows the location of all the known genes in a chromosome.

Damaged chromosomes also are useful in mapping genes. Chromosomes can be damaged by chemicals or radiation. This damage may result in the loss of a part of a chromosome. This deletion of a piece of chromosome can often be detected during the stages of meiosis. By relating the missing part of a chromosome with missing enzymes or traits from the organism, it is possible to map and identify certain genes.

Chromosome maps have been made for fruit flies and a few other organisms. Thousands of genes have already been mapped for human chromosomes. This research has been slow because chromosome-damaging experiments can't be carried out on humans. Scientists have only been able to look at human chromosomes damaged as a result of exposure to chemicals and radiation in everyday life or to naturally damaged chromosomes.

New and harmless methods using cells cultured in the laboratory have been developed to map the genes in human chromosomes, as shown in Figure 8–9. When human chromosome mapping is complete, there will be a greater chance of curing human genetic disorders.

NoteWorthy

Dr. James Watson, Nobel Laureate and joint discoverer of the molecular appearance of DNA, is the director of the Human Genome Initiative project in the United States. The project goal is to determine the positions of all genes on human chromosomes.

How many human genes have been mapped?

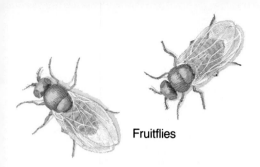

Fruitflies

8:6 Gene Expression

You have learned that genes control traits. The appearance of a trait is an expression of a gene or group of genes. Several traits of humans are disorders caused by the absence of certain enzymes. For example some people lack the enzyme lactase, which is important in the digestion of milk. These people cannot drink milk without having a physical reaction. Recall that enzymes are important proteins in the metabolism of cells. In 1941, two American geneticists, George Beadle and Edward Tatum, discovered this connection between genes and enzymes. The two scientists damaged the genes of a common bread mold with X rays and found that each damaged gene resulted in a missing enzyme in the new growths of molds. This damage was obvious from the phenotypes of the new strains. Therefore, Beadle and Tatum concluded that genes control the production of enzymes. They hypothesized that each enzyme was an expression of just one gene. This became known as the one-gene-one-enzyme hypothesis.

Later it was discovered that DNA forms the genes and carries the genetic information for the production of proteins. You studied in Chapter 3 that proteins are made of polypeptides. A gene that controls the production of polypeptide chains and proteins is a **structural gene.** For example, the production of the protein myosin that makes up the muscle tissue in your body is controlled by a structural gene. A single polypeptide chain may fold upon itself to form a protein or it may join with other polypeptide chains to produce enzymes and other cellular proteins. These differences are determined by structural genes.

It has been found that some genes regulate the expression of other genes. A **regulatory gene** is a gene responsible for turning structural genes on and off. Because all cells in the organism have the same set of genes, you might wonder why muscle cells, for example, look different from brain cells. The differences are caused by the action of regulatory genes. An example of how regulatory genes work can be seen in the formation of human hemoglobin molecules. Different hemoglobins are made during different stages of human development. The embryonic, fetal, and adult globin genes function only during the proper developmental stages. They are switched off by regulatory genes when they are not needed.

A **modifier gene** is a kind of regulatory gene that changes the expression of other genes. An interesting example of a modifier gene is the prune killer gene in fruit flies. Prune is one variation of eye color in fruit flies. Flies with the prune killer gene and any other of its possible eye colors will survive. Flies with prune color eyes and no prune killer gene also will survive. However, a fly with the prune eye color gene and the prune killer gene will die. The prune killer gene affects only flies that have prune colored eyes. Other modifier genes include those that affect seasonal changes in an animal's coat color due to different temperatures.

Several human genetic disorders are only switched on at a certain stage of life by modifier genes. Huntington disease is a genetic disor-

FIGURE 8–10.

A fruit fly's eye color is useful for interpreting its genotype.

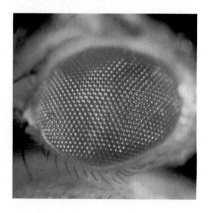

der causing a gradual degeneration of nervous tissues. It appears in individuals between 30 and 50 years of age. People who have ancestors who suffered from this genetic disorder can now be tested to determine if they carry this lethal gene.

REVIEW

6. How do structural and regulatory genes control the production of muscle cells?
7. What is the sex chromosome genotype of a female? Of a male?
8. During crossing over, which structures break and join to cause genetic recombination?
9. **SKILL REVIEW:** Using a dictionary, make a list of all the words that begin with the prefixes *geno-* or *pheno-* and give their meanings. For more help, refer to Reading Science in the Skill Handbook, pages 798 to 799.
10. **USING CONCEPTS:** If there was no crossing over between homologous chromosomes, how would variation in a population be affected?

BIOTECHNOLOGY

SCANNING TUNNELING MICROSCOPES

Most biological molecules are too small to be seen with the light microscope, and the electron beam of electron microscopes often damages their structures. The scanning tunneling microscope (STM) produces three-dimensional images of atoms and molecules without the use of destructive electron beams.

Since the STM was developed in 1981, it has made a dramatic impact on the understanding of surface structures of molecules. It can magnify molecules several billion times.

The microscope works by using a procedure called electron tunneling. A sample must conduct electrons if it is to be imaged with the STM. The samples are coated with metals and the scanning tunneling microscope detects electrons "tunneling" or jumping from the surface of the specimen. An electrically conductive, needlelike probe, usually made of tungsten, scans the surface billionths of a millimeter above the sample. It follows the sample's surface outline by maintaining a constant distance from the surface. The probe is attached to a computer that projects a three-dimensional image onto a fluorescent screen.

A team of scientists in California recently used the STM to obtain the first direct image of DNA. These new images show the three-dimensional structure of DNA and provide support for theories that DNA exists in several helical variations.

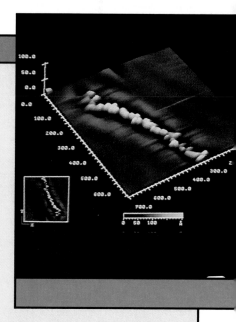

STM image of a DNA molecule

- list causes of mutations.
- distinguish between a point mutation and a frameshift mutation in genes.
- distinguish between inversions, translocations, and deletions in chromosomes.
- describe the causes and effects of polyploidy.

NoteWorthy

Information in DNA can be thought of as messages in a four-letter language. A mutation is equivalent to a misprint in a line of type; "time to think" might become "time to thank." One letter is equivalent to a single base. An average gene has 1200 base pairs.

Recall that chromosomes are made up of strands of DNA. DNA is a very stable organic molecule. During the lifetime of an organism, its DNA is duplicated millions of times. Most of the time, duplication occurs accurately and the new DNA molecule is identical to the original strand. Occasionally, though, a mistake occurs and the DNA molecule is changed. How do these changes affect the organism?

8:7 Gene Mutations

You have studied how variations in species are a product of genetic recombination. Sometimes, the information in the genetic code changes by mutation. A **mutation** is a permanent change in the genetic material of a cell. Mutations usually affect individual genes. These mutations provide the variations that are the basis of changes in a population and, eventually, a species.

Mutations are often caused by mutagens. A **mutagen** is a substance or condition that causes or increases the rate of mutation. Some viruses and very high temperatures are mutagens. Other mutagens include chemicals such as industrial chemicals, pesticides, cigarette smoke, and some food additives.

Radiation is a well known mutagen. X rays and gamma rays contain large amounts of energy. The energy from these forms of radiation is strong enough to damage DNA, possibly resulting in bone marrow cancers and leukemia. Large amounts of ultraviolet light from the sun cause premature aging of the skin and an increase in the number of skin cancers.

FIGURE 8–11.

The clean air in high altitudes allows more damaging ultraviolet rays—possible mutagens—to penetrate the atmosphere. Mountain climbers have to protect themselves from high levels of ultraviolet rays that may cause skin cancer.

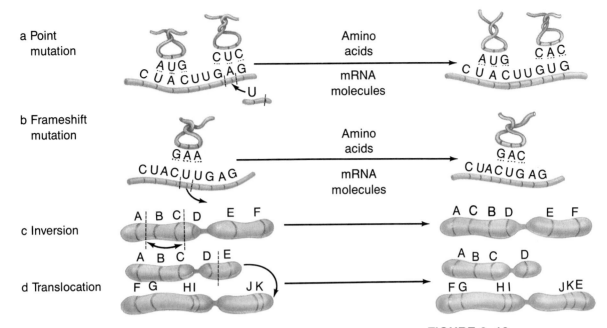

a Point mutation

b Frameshift mutation

c Inversion

d Translocation

FIGURE 8–12.

Mutations occur in codons of genes in a point mutation (a) and a frameshift mutation (b). Mutations in chromosomes include inversions (c) and translocations (d).

In order to understand how mutation occurs in genes, recall how nitrogen bases are arranged in DNA and RNA. You learned in Chapter 7 that a sequence of three nitrogen bases called a codon, such as GAG, codes for a specific amino acid. The incorrect substitution of a single base in a codon of a gene, as shown in Figure 8–12, is called a **point mutation.** For example, a mutation such as GAG to GUG is a point mutation that causes the wrong amino acid to be coded and results in a different protein. Some base substitutions may cause genetic disorders such as sickle cell anemia. People who have this blood disorder often die young.

Insertion or deletion of a nitrogen base produces a type of gene mutation known as a **frameshift mutation.** This type of mutation causes a shift of the genetic code. All amino acids in the protein chain beyond the point at which the mutation occurred will be affected. Frameshift mutations are generally more damaging than base substitutions because they change many more amino acids. Distinguish the two types of gene mutation in Figure 8–12.

8:8 Chromosome Rearrangements

Just as genes may be changed, so may chromosomes. Altered or damaged chromosomes can have effects ranging from unnoticeable to lethal. One kind of chromosomal change involves rearrangement of the chromosomal material. A chromosome **inversion** occurs when a part of a chromosome is broken and becomes reinserted backwards. No genetic information is lost, but the cell may still be affected if the relative positions of the genes are important in producing a necessary protein. A **translocation** occurs if the broken piece of chromosome attaches to a chromosome of a different homologous pair. In plants, translocation often results in sterility.

FIGURE 8–13.

The coast redwood of California, *Sequoia sempervirens,* is a hexaploid with 2n = 66. This means that it is a polyploid with six times the basic number of chromosomes.

monosomy:
  mono (GK) single
  soma (GK) body

A chromosome **deletion** occurs when a part of a chromosome breaks off and is lost to the offspring. Deletions may include a part of a gene, a single gene, or a group of genes. The more genes deleted, the greater the adverse effect in the offspring.

Sometimes changes occur when chromosomes fail to follow their usual sequence of events during meiosis. The chromatids or homologous chromosomes might fail to separate. This type of chromosome abnormality is called **nondisjunction.** Two kinds of gametes are formed as a result of nondisjunction. One has an extra chromosome and the other is missing a chromosome. If the gamete that is missing a chromosome fuses with a normal gamete, the resulting zygote contains only one chromosome of the pair. This condition is called **monosomy.** Monosomy is usually lethal because a great deal of genetic material is lost.

Chromosome duplication occurs when the gamete that contains the extra chromosome fuses with a normal gamete. The resulting zygote contains three copies, rather than the usual two, of that chromosome. This condition is called **trisomy.** One of the best studied examples of trisomy is Down syndrome in humans, in which there is an extra copy of chromosome number 21.

In some instances, entire sets of chromosomes may be duplicated. This is called **polyploidy.** Polyploidy occurs if the nucleus does not undergo the second division of meiosis. The most common forms of polyploids are tetraploids that have four sets of the haploid number (4n) of chromosomes. Polyploidy is rare and usually lethal in animals, but is fairly common in plants. Polyploid plants are important agriculturally because they may be larger and healthier than the normal diploid varieties. Polyploid strawberries, as well as other fruits and flowers, are grown commercially.

If a diploid gamete is fertilized by a normal haploid gamete, the resulting offspring has three complete sets of chromosomes instead of two. This individual is referred to as 3n, or triploid. Triploid plants such as bananas are often sterile. The abnormal number of chromosomes will not separate properly to form functional gametes in meiosis. Triploid bananas can't produce seeds. They must be reproduced by using cuttings from existing plant stock.

REVIEW

11. What are three examples of mutagens?
12. What is the difference between an inversion and a translocation?
13. Describe the cause of a frameshift mutation.
14. **SKILL REVIEW:** Classify the following mutations as chromosome or gene mutations: point mutation, nondisjunction, frameshift mutation, translocation, trisomy. For more help, refer to Organizing Information in the Skill Handbook, pages 810 to 813.
15. **USING CONCEPTS:** Why is monosomy usually more harmful to an organism than trisomy or polyploidy?

BIOLAB

Genetic Variations

8

Problem: What are some genetic variations in fruit flies?

Materials
dissecting microscope or hand lens
camel's-hair brush
petri dish halves
anesthetizing apparatus
fruit-fly cultures *(Drosophila melanogaster)*:

wild type	white eye
vestigial wings	prune eye
curled wings	brown eye
crossveinless	eyeless

Procedures
1. Make a table like the one shown.
2. Variations in fruit flies are due to genetic or chromosomal mutations. Observe the characteristics of each fruit-fly culture.
3. Anesthetize the fruit flies in each culture using the anesthetizing apparatus as directed by your teacher.
4. Place a few flies in the petri dish and observe them with the microscope. The flies will remain sleepy for about 50 minutes.
5. Record your observations for each type of fly in your data table.

6. After recording your observations of each culture of fruit fly, return the flies to their proper container. Be sure to put each type of fly back with its own type.

Questions and Conclusion
1. What color eyes did the wild type of *Drosophila* have?
2. What differences did you note in the eye color of the different types of fruit flies?
3. What kind of wings did the wild type of *Drosophila* have?
4. What differences did you note in the wings among the types of fruit flies?
5. From your observations of *Drosophila,* make a **hypothesis** about why gene mutations can be detrimental to an organism.

Conclusion: What are some genetic variations in fruit flies?

Data and Observations

Fly Culture	Description
wild type	
vestigial wings	
curled wings	
crossveinless	
white eye	
prune eye	
brown eye	
eyeless	

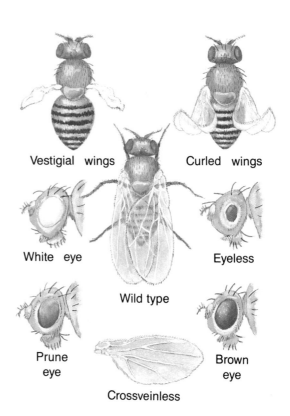

Vestigial wings   Curled wings

White eye   Eyeless

Wild type

Prune eye   Brown eye

Crossveinless

CHAPTER REVIEW

SUMMARY

1. Genes are strung together to form chromosomes. Each species has a basic number (n) of homologous pairs of chromosomes. **8:1**
2. Meiosis produces gametes with the haploid number (n) of chromosomes. **8:2**
3. Genotype is an organism's genetic makeup; its appearance is its phenotype. An individual's sex is controlled by sex chromosomes. **8:3**
4. Crossing over during meiosis results in genetic recombination. Genes on a chromosome form linkage groups. **8:4**
5. Chromosome maps can be made from studies of crossing over. **8:5**
6. Each structural gene codes for a specific polypeptide chain. Regulatory genes control structural genes. **8:6**
7. Gene mutations result from substitution, insertion, or deletion of bases in the DNA of genes. Mutagens increase the rate of mutations. **8:7**
8. Chromosome deletion, translocation, and inversion are chromosome mutations. **8:8**

LANGUAGE OF BIOLOGY

chromosome map	inversion
crossing over	linkage group
deletion	meiosis
diploid	modifier gene
egg	monosomy
fertilization	mutagen
frameshift mutation	mutation
gamete	nondisjunction
gene	phenotype
genetic recombination	point mutation
genotype	polyploidy
haploid	regulatory gene
homologous	sex chromosomes
chromosomes	sperm

structural gene   trisomy
translocation

Choose the word or phrase from the list above that completes the sentence.

1. A sex cell is also known as a(n) ____.
2. A(n) ____ cell has half the normal body cell's number of chromosomes.
3. ____ results in gametes having more or less than the 2n number of chromosomes.
4. Down syndrome may result from a type of chromosome abnormality called ____.
5. ____ often results in larger and healthier than normal plants.
6. Chromosome number is reduced by one half during ____.
7. ____ come together during prophase of meiosis.
8. A(n) ____ is caused by the insertion or deletion of nitrogen bases.
9. A(n) ____ is one that controls the production of polypeptide chains.
10. The rearranging of genetic material as a result of crossing over is ____.

REVIEWING CONCEPTS

Choose the word or phrase that completes the sentence or answers the question.

11. Polyploidy produces ____ organisms.
    a. 1n   b. 2n   c. 4n   d. no
12. The part of a chromosome that holds sister chromatids together is the ____.
    a. homologue   c. spindle
    b. centromere   d. gene
13. The stage in which homologous chromosomes line up along the cell's equator is ____.
    a. prophase I   c. anaphase I
    b. metaphase I   d. telophase I
14. ____ turn other genes on and off.
    a. regulatory genes   c. prune killer genes
    b. structural genes   d. mutagens

8

15. A(n) ____ is a mutation that does not involve loss of genetic material in the offspring.
    a. translocation   c. deletion
    b. frameshift   d. inversion
       mutation

16. A ____ increases the rate of mutation.
    a. mutagen   c. trisomy
    b. diploid   d. monosomy

17. An example of a mutagen is ____.
    a. cigarette smoke   c. ultraviolet rays
    b. X rays   d. all of these

18. Sickle cell anemia is an example of a trait caused by a ____.
    a. point mutation   c. deletion
    b. frameshift   d. translocation
       mutation

19. Crossing over occurs during ____.
    a. mitosis   c. polyploidy
    b. meiosis   d. all of these

20. A point mutation is a(n) ____ of a single nitrogen base.
    a. deletion   c. inversion
    b. substitution   d. insertion

UNDERSTANDING CONCEPTS

Answer the following questions using complete sentences.

21. If two plants have the same chromosome number but different chromosome shapes, are they the same or different species?
22. What is meant by gene expression?
23. Describe two kinds of gene mutations.
24. When do chromosomes contract so that they can be seen during meiosis?
25. Why are chromosomes difficult to observe during interphase?
26. In humans, which sex is always associated with the Y chromosome?
27. Why are chromosome deletions generally harmful to organisms?

28. Compare metaphase and anaphase of mitosis with metaphase II and anaphase II of meiosis.
29. Compare anaphase I and II in meiosis.
30. Why can't mitosis produce gametes?

APPLYING CONCEPTS

Answer the following questions using complete sentences.

31. How does meiosis benefit organisms during periods of change in the environment?
32. Why do body cells of all plants and animals have an even number of chromosomes?
33. Why does a chromosome abnormality have a much greater effect on an organism than a gene mutation?
34. Propose an experiment to determine the distance between two genes on a chromosome.
35. Which mutation causes more damage: an insertion between the first and second nitrogen bases or a deletion of the ninth nitrogen base?

EXTENSIONS

1. Make a poster that compares the stages of mitosis and meiosis.
2. Research a particular human genetic disorder.
3. Examine seed packages to find out which plants are polyploid. Compare their traits.

READINGS

Brownlee, Shannon. "The Lords of the Flies." *Discover,* Apr. 1987, pp. 26–40.

Finnell, Rebecca B. "Daughters or Sons." *Natural History,* Apr. 1988, pp. 63–82.

Murray, Andrew W., and Jack Szostak. "Artificial Chromosomes." *Scientific American,* Nov. 1987, pp. 62–68.

PATTERNS OF HEREDITY

Look at the large photograph. Does everyone have the same hair color? Is everyone the same height and weight? You, your classmates, and every person in the photograph are all different, because most physical traits in the cell are inherited. Physical traits are an expression of genes on the chromosomes as shown here. Even the composition of the chemicals in your body is determined by your genes. In this chapter, you will study how genes are inherited and their effects on the organisms that carry them.

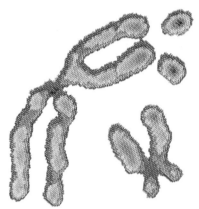

Human chromosomes

MENDEL'S LAWS OF HEREDITY

In Chapter 8, you learned how to distinguish between the genotype and the phenotype of an organism. When genes are passed on from one generation to another, the offspring inherit half their genes from each parent. The phenotypes of the offspring may or may not reflect their genotypes.

One of the first scientific studies of inheritance was carried out in the mid-1800s by Gregor Mendel, an Austrian monk. Although Mendel wrote many scientific papers presenting his findings to other scientists, his discoveries were overlooked for 40 years. The following sections will describe and explain the discoveries and conclusions made by Mendel.

9:1 The Work of Mendel

One of Gregor Mendel's responsibilities in the monastery was to take care of its garden. He noticed how plants showed variations from generation to generation. He became interested in breeding plants and in how traits are inherited. The passing on of traits from parents to offspring is called **heredity.** The branch of biology that deals with the study of heredity is called **genetics.** The traits of an organism are the characteristics studied in genetics. Mendel decided to carry out some simple experiments comparing the traits of garden

Objectives:
- state and explain Mendel's laws of heredity.
- distinguish between inbreeding and outbreeding.
- explain the difference between dominant and recessive traits.
- distinguish between homozygous and heterozygous traits.
- use a Punnett square to find the possible offspring of a genetic cross.
- compare a monohybrid cross with a dihybrid cross.

FIGURE 9–1.

The flower of a garden pea has five petals. Two petals are fused to form the keel that surrounds the pistil, two petals are wings, and one large petal on the outside is called the standard.

allele:
  allelon (GK) of each other

pea plants. At the time, nothing was known about chromosomes, genes, or about the events of meiosis. However, Mendel did know that seed production usually requires the transfer of pollen from one plant to another.

Mendel chose the garden pea for his experiments because these plants were easy to raise and they produced large numbers of offspring in a short time. The structure of the flower of a pea plant as shown in Figure 9–1 prevents pollen of other flowers from entering. As a result, pea plants are naturally self fertilizing. In other words, the gametes that unite are produced by a single parent plant. By transferring pollen from one flower to another, Mendel could control which plants were being mated. He had observed that garden peas have many traits with only two different phenotypes. Recall from Chapter 8 that the phenotype is the outward appearance of an organism. Mendel noticed that seeds of garden pea plants have two phenotypes for color: they are either yellow or green. Also he observed that the seeds have either a round or a wrinkled seed coat. Fortunately for Mendel, traits that have only two phenotypes are controlled by one pair of alleles (uh LEELZ). An **allele** is the genetic factor that controls one form of expression of a gene. For example, in pea plants, there are two alleles for seed color: one that controls a yellow seed color and one that results in a green seed color. Notice in Figure 9–2 how round versus wrinkled seed coat is also controlled by one pair of alleles. Mendel's choice of characters was fortunate because it is now known that many traits are controlled by more than one allele pair. Inheritance of traits that are controlled by one pair of alleles is, therefore, called simple Mendelian inheritance.

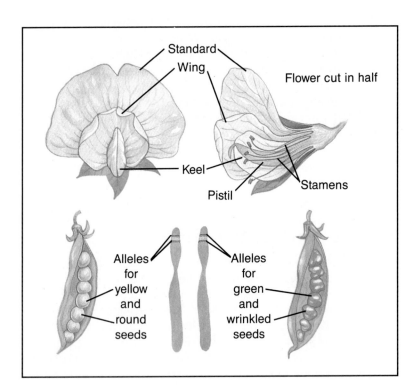

FIGURE 9–2.

Many traits in garden peas are controlled by one pair of alleles.

9:2 Laws of Dominance and Segregation

Mendel began his experiments by choosing pea plants that bred true for a particular trait generation after generation. In other words, the offspring resembled the parents in every generation. This type of hereditary pattern results from inbreeding. **Inbreeding** is fertilization of gametes that are from the same parent or from closely related parents. When offspring are produced by inbreeding over many generations, a pure line of traits is produced. You know that in pea plants, inbreeding often occurs naturally. Mendel recognized and used a pure line of pea plants for each of several different traits of which five are shown in Table 9–1. For each trait there were two clearly different phenotypes.

In his first series of experiments, Mendel used outbreeding to cross two separate pure lines for one trait. **Outbreeding** is fertilization of gametes from unrelated parents. For example, he crossed plants that had green seeds with plants that had yellow seeds. He crossed tall plants with short plants. He used each one of the contrasting pairs of traits in his crossing experiments. Mendel called the offspring of the crosses of these parent plants the first filial, or F_1 **generation.** The phenotypes of the F_1 generation were always the same as those of one of the pure parent lines. These offspring, however, were no longer of a pure line.

Table 9–1.

MENDEL'S CONTRASTING TRAITS OF PEA PLANTS		
Trait	**Phenotype A**	**Phenotype B**
seed shape	round	wrinkled
seed color	yellow	green
flower color	violet and purple	white
stem length	tall	short
flower position	axial	terminal

When Mendel observed the phenotypes of the F₁ generation, he found that for each of the traits under study, all the plants showed only one of the two different phenotypes. For example, when tall plants and short plants were crossed, all the offspring were tall. When the parents had green seeds and yellow seeds, all the offspring had yellow seeds. Thus, it appeared that for each cross, one of the two different phenotypes of the trait never appeared in the F₁ offspring and the other form always appeared.

Mendel continued his experiments by inbreeding each plant of the F₁ generation. He fertilized a flower with its own pollen. This inbreeding of plants produced offspring in a second filial or **F₂ generation.** For each trait studied, the form that did not appear in the F₁ generation reappeared in some members of the F₂ generation. For example, some of the F₂ plants had green seeds and some plants were short. Mendel called an observable trait of the F₁ generation a **dominant trait.** When only the dominant trait appears in the offspring of a cross between two pure lines for different traits, this is known as Mendel's **law of dominance.** Mendel called a trait that was hidden in the F₁ generation but reappeared in the F₂ generation a **recessive trait.**

What is Mendel's law of dominance?

From careful analysis of large numbers of offspring, Mendel saw, as shown in Figure 9–3, that in the F₂ generation, the ratio of dominant to recessive traits was always 3:1; that is, three-fourths of the offspring showed the dominant trait, and one-fourth showed the recessive trait. Mendel hypothesized that members of the F₁ generation had received what he called "factors" from both members of the parent generation. Otherwise, the recessive trait could not reappear in members of the F₂ generation. Furthermore, Mendel realized that

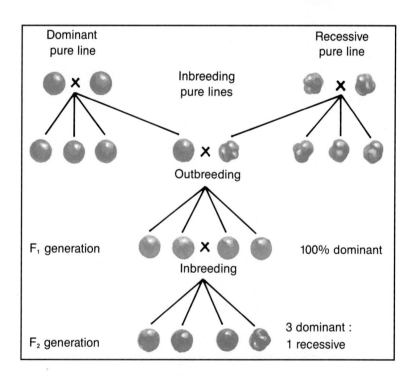

FIGURE 9–3.

The breeding of garden peas led Mendel to his law of dominance. The recessive trait is masked in the F₁ generation but shows up again in the F₂ generation.

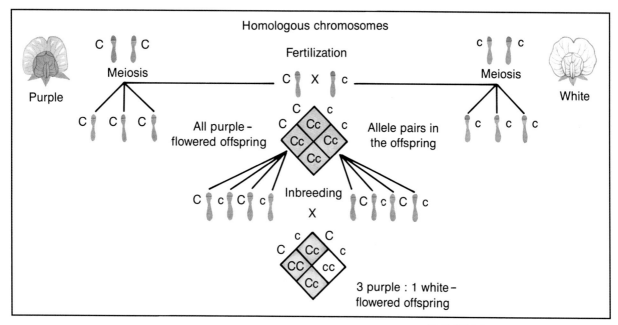

these factors had to separate from one another at some point during the reproductive process, or all members of the F_2 generation would have the same phenotypes as in the F_1 generation. Can you recognize any similarity between the inheritance of traits in Mendel's peas and the movement of chromosomes during meiosis? Use Figure 9–4 to follow the movement of alleles that control the flower color in pea plants from the parents to the F_2 generation.

Mendel determined that each trait is controlled by a pair of factors, which we now know to be alleles. Mendel's **law of segregation** states that during reproduction, the two factors that control each trait segregate, or, in other words, separate and move to different gametes, and one factor from each pair is passed to the offspring. Remember that Mendel knew nothing about genes or chromosomes, or about the separation of pairs of chromosomes during meiosis, as you know from your studies in Chapter 8 and as you can see in Figure 9–4. What Mendel called the "segregation of factors" is related to the separation of homologous pairs of chromosomes and their alleles during meiosis.

9:3 Alleles and the Genotype

When two gametes fuse during fertilization, homologous chromosomes come together again in the zygote. A **zygote** is the single cell that results from fertilization. Zygotes have the diploid number of chromosomes. Each allele is paired with a corresponding allele on its homologous chromosome. Each chromosome of an homologous pair has the same code for a trait but the expression of that code may be different. The different phenotypes of offspring are caused by different combinations of alleles.

FIGURE 9–4.

The gametes produced by the parent plants are either all dominant or all recessive. The offspring in the F_1 generation all inherited the purple flowers. The white flowers reappeared in 25 percent of the F_2 generation.

What is Mendel's law of segregation?

zygote:
  zygotos (GK) yolk

a

b

FIGURE 9–5.

Different breeds of poultry show differences in phenotype.

You have seen from Mendel's experiments that two phenotypes are controlled by one pair of alleles. When both alleles on homologous chromosomes have the same expression, such as for short plant height, the organism is said to be **homozygous** for that trait. The homozygous condition for short plant height can be represented as tt. For tall plant height the homozygous condition is written as TT. A dominant allele is represented by a capital letter, while the recessive allele is always represented by the lowercase form of the same letter. Because short plant height is a recessive trait, the organism would be homozygous recessive. A homozygous recessive trait is always written with two lowercase letters that are matching, as in tt. If the alleles were both dominant, then the organism would be homozygous dominant, or TT. If the two homologous chromosomes have different alleles for a trait, the organism is said to be **heterozygous** for that trait. This condition for plant height would be written Tt.

Recall from Chapter 8 that the genotype is the actual genetic makeup as inherited from the parents. In working out problems in genetics, genotypes are represented by upper and lowercase letters as explained for plant height. For example, in seed color where yellow seeds are dominant over green, the homozygous dominant trait would be shown to have a genotype of YY. The seeds with YY genotype show a yellow phenotype. The homozygous recessive trait would be shown as yy. The seeds with yy genotype would show a green phenotype. The heterozygous form would be Yy. The seeds with Yy genotype would show a yellow phenotype because yellow is dominant over green.

homozygous:
   homo (GK) same
   zygotos (GK) yolk

heterozygous:
   hetero (GK) the other of two
   zygotos (GK) yolk

9:4 Punnett Squares

The heredity of characteristics in a population of organisms can be predicted using a Punnett (PUN ut) square. A **Punnett square** is a useful device for predicting the possible offspring of crosses between different genotypes. The Punnett square in Figure 9–6 shows a cross between pure line tall pea plants (TT) and pure line short pea plants (tt). A cross such as this that involves only one trait with two phenotypes is called a **monohybrid cross.**

The first step in making a Punnett square is to determine the kinds of gametes that can be produced by meiosis in each parent. Remember that gametes are haploid. Notice in Figure 9–6 that when homologous chromosomes separate during meiosis, one allele of each gene goes into separate gametes. In pure tall and pure short pea plants, both parents are homozygous. Therefore, all gametes produced by the tall parent will contain the allele for tallness (T). All gametes produced by the true-breeding short parent will contain the allele for shortness (t).

The gametes produced by one parent are shown to one side of the Punnett square in Figure 9–6a. The gametes of the other parent are shown at the other side of the square. Each box in the square is then filled in with the letters from both directions similar to a multiplication table. When filling in the boxes, it is common practice to write a capital letter before a lowercase letter.

This Punnett square shows why the F_1 generation in Mendel's crosses of pure lines all showed the dominant phenotype. The next Punnett square in Figure 9–6b shows what happened when the F_1 generation was allowed to inbreed. Notice that each parent produced two kinds of gametes.

What is a monohybrid cross?

FIGURE 9–6.

Punnett squares are useful for predicting ratios of offspring from crosses between parents with known dominant and recessive traits.

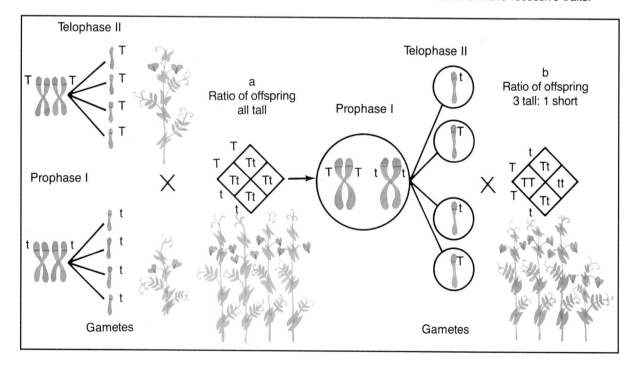

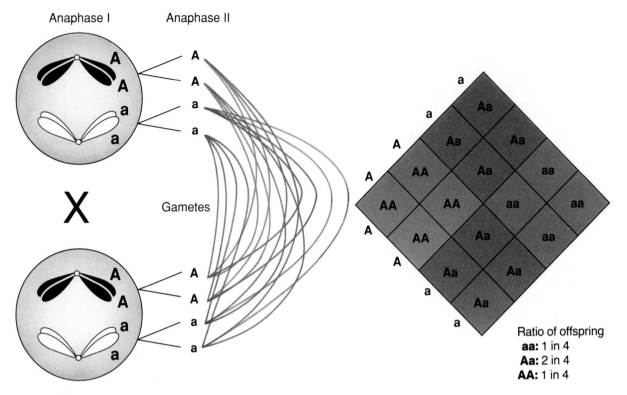

Gametes

Ratio of offspring
aa: 1 in 4
Aa: 2 in 4
AA: 1 in 4

FIGURE 9–7.

All the possible combinations between two heterozygotes are shown
more clearly by including all the gametes in a Punnett square.

What is probability?

9:5 Probability

Probability is the branch of mathematics that predicts the occurrence of chance events. The Punnett square in Figure 9–6b shows
the offspring of the inbreeding F_2 generation. You can see that the
probability that an individual will be homozygous recessive (tt) is
one in four.

When you toss a coin, the probability that it will land heads up is
one in two, or 50 percent. There is an equal probability that it will
land tails up. By the same laws of chance, when you roll a die, the
probability that a six will be on top is one in six. Any event involving
chance must be repeated many times before the data for the possible
outcomes can be considered valid. For example, if you toss a coin
five times, you might get four heads and one tail. If you toss it twenty
times, you might get twelve tails and eight heads. But if you toss it
two thousand times, your results probably will be very close to half
heads, half tails.

When Mendel carried out his experiments with pea plants, he
counted hundreds, and in some cases, thousands of offspring for
each of the traits he studied. If he had counted only a few offspring
for each trait, the results might have been so mixed that he could
not have explained them, and his conclusions might not have led to
our present-day understanding of heredity.

In a genetic cross, the combinations of alleles found in the offspring are determined by chance because crossing over during meiosis is random, and chromosomes are passed to gametes independently of one another. In a heterozygote, Aa, the homologous

chromosomes separate during anaphase I in meiosis and each gamete formed receives either A or a. When gametes from two heterozygotes for Aa combine at fertilization, it is purely a matter of chance whether the resulting offspring is AA, Aa, or aa. All the possible combinations are shown in Figure 9–7.

9:6 The Law of Independent Assortment

Once Mendel had determined the pattern of inheritance for each of the traits in pea plants, he became interested in discovering whether such traits are inherited independently of one another, or whether they are passed on together from one generation to the next. For example, is a yellow seed always inherited along with tall height and purple flowers, or are all these traits independent of one another?

Mendel again began his experiments with pure line plants, but each of these plants was homozygous for two traits instead of only one. A cross involving two different traits is called a **dihybrid cross.** A dihybrid cross is performed between two individuals that differ in two characteristics. For example, Mendel crossed plants pure for two dominant traits with plants pure for two recessive traits. In one cross, the dominant traits were round and yellow seeds (RRYY) and the recessive traits were wrinkled and green seeds (rryy). As might be expected from Mendel's study of dominance, all the F_1 plants were dominant in phenotype for both traits. Look at the Punnett square for this cross in Figure 9–8. Are the offspring homozygous dominant or heterozygous for both traits? Will these plants have the dominant or the recessive phenotype? Mendel next allowed the plants of the F_1 generation to undergo self-pollination. Can you determine the different kinds of gametes that can be produced by these plants?

What is a dihybrid cross?

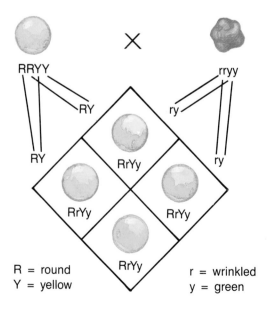

R = round
Y = yellow

r = wrinkled
y = green

FIGURE 9–8.

A dihybrid cross results in all heterozygous offspring with the dominant traits masking the recessive traits in the F_1 generation.

Table 9–2.

MENDEL'S DIHYBRID CROSS YYRR × yyrr F$_2$ GENERATION				
Phenotypes	yellow round	yellow wrinkled	green round	green wrinkled
Probable ratio	9	3	3	1
Mendel's results	315	101	108	32
Experimental ratio	9.1	2.9	3.1	0.9

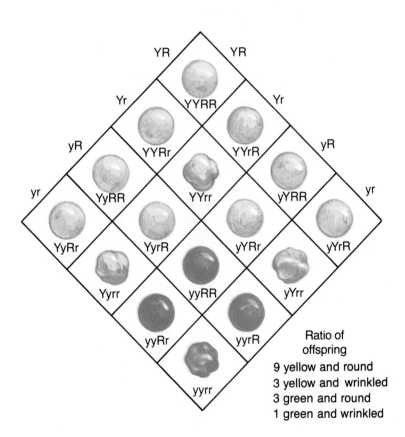

Ratio of offspring
9 yellow and round
3 yellow and wrinkled
3 green and round
1 green and wrinkled

FIGURE 9–9.

In the F$_2$ generation of a dihybrid cross, it becomes obvious that the traits are inherited independently.

Table 9–2 shows Mendel's actual results for this dihybrid cross. He found that in the F$_2$ generation, some plants showed both dominant traits, some showed both recessive traits, and some showed one dominant and one recessive trait. The Punnett square in Figure 9–9 shows the genotypes of the F$_2$ generation. This 9:3:3:1 ratio of phenotypes is typical of a dihybrid cross involving parents that are heterozygous for two different traits.

Because some offspring had one dominant and one recessive trait, a combination not found in the F$_1$ generation, Mendel concluded that the factors for the two traits separated and then recombined independently of each other. This finding led to what is now known as

a

b

Mendel's law of independent assortment. The **law of independent assortment** states that the inheritance of alleles for one trait is not affected by the inheritance of alleles for a different trait if the genes for the traits are located on separate chromosomes. Mendel was able to develop this law only because he had selected traits that happened to be on separate chromosomes. If he had chosen traits that were on the same chromosome, they might have been inherited together. In fact, most traits of organisms are linked by being on the same chromosomes. Mendel's work provided scientists with information that was fundamental to our present-day understanding of genetics and evolution.

FIGURE 9–10.

The understanding of inheritance as genes passed on from parents to offspring (a) began with the breeding experiments carried out by Gregor Mendel (b).

REVIEW

1. How does a dihybrid cross show that alleles are inherited separately?
2. List two pairs of different alleles found in garden pea plants and give the genotype and phenotype for each.
3. How do Punnett squares and probability help in the study of heredity?
4. **SKILL REVIEW:** Using a Punnett square, estimate the ratio of offspring in the F_2 generation from the cross between two pure line rabbits that have the following traits. One rabbit has floppy ears and long fur. Both traits are dominant. The other rabbit has straight ears and short fur. For more help, refer to Measuring in SI in the Skill Handbook, pages 806 to 808.
5. **USING CONCEPTS:** Draw a Punnett square for the cross AaBb × AaBb to show all possible genotypes.

BIOLAB

A Dihybrid Cross

9

Problem: What ratio can be expected from a dihybrid cross between heterozygous individuals?

Materials

genetic corn on the cob
graph paper

Procedures

1. Make a table similar to the one shown.
2. Make a **hypothesis** using information from Mendel's three laws about what ratio of phenotypes to expect when corn plants heterozygous for two traits are crossed.
3. Observe your ear of corn and carefully record a description of each phenotype of corn kernels.
4. Make a diagram of a 10 × 10 kernel area of your ear of corn on a piece of graph paper.
5. Count each phenotype one at a time and record these in your data table.
6. Combine your data with those of your classmates and record these in your data table.
7. Calculate and record the ratios of each phenotype.

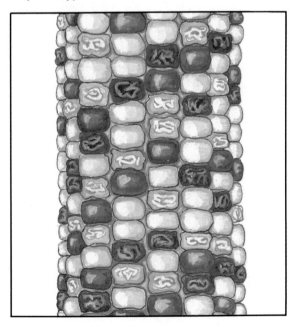

Data and Observations

Phenotypes	1	2	3	4
Description				
Numbers present				
Class results				
Ratios				

Questions and Conclusion

1. Draw a Punnett square to show the predicted ratio of your four phenotypes from a dihybrid cross.
2. What phenotype did most kernels have? Why?
3. What phenotype did the fewest kernels have? Why?
4. Were your results similar to those of your classmates? Why do you think they were or were not?
5. What ratio did you observe? Which of Mendel's crosses gave similar ratios?
6. How do each of Mendel's laws apply to the phenotypes inherited in this activity?
7. Why would you expect the combined results of your class to be closer to Mendel's predicted ratio of 9:3:3:1 than any single member's results?
8. How many pairs of alleles were necessary to produce the results you observed?
9. Was your **hypothesis** correct? Explain.

Conclusion: What ratio of phenotypes can be expected from a dihybrid cross between heterozygous individuals?

Not all traits follow simple Mendelian inheritance. In some organisms, there are traits in which the phenotypes of offspring are different from those of either parent. In other cases, more than one pair of alleles or genes controls the inheritance of particular traits. Some traits are controlled by a single allele.

9:7 Incomplete Dominance

When a homozygous red-flowered sweet pea plant is crossed with a homozygous white-flowered sweet pea plant, all the offspring have pink flowers, as shown in Figure 9–11. Neither the color for red nor white flowers is a dominant trait. Instead, the alleles for both flower colors are expressed in the phenotype at the same time. Thus, flower color in sweet pea plants is said to show **incomplete dominance,** which is when two alleles produce three phenotypes instead of two. Neither one nor the other allele of a pair is completely dominant. In humans, hair type is inherited by incomplete dominance. If one parent has straight hair and the other parent has curly hair, the offspring can have straight hair, curly hair, or wavy hair. Wavy hair is the result of a mixing of expression between the two completely dominant alleles for straight and curly hair.

The Punnett square in Figure 9–11 shows a cross between red-flowered and white-flowered sweet pea plants. Note that the segregation of alleles is the same as in the more common pattern of dominance. However, because the alleles are equally dominant, all pink flowers result in the F_1 generation. When pink-flowered F_1 plants are inbred, the offspring in the F_2 generation show a 1:2:1 phenotypic ratio of red to pink to white flowers. This result supports Mendel's law of independent assortment.

Objectives:
- explain and give an example of incomplete dominance.
- discuss the importance of multiple alleles in the inheritance of human blood type.
- define sex-linked genes.
- explain how polygenic inheritance differs from Mendelian inheritance.

What is incomplete dominance?

FIGURE 9–11.

When two alleles are equally dominant, the offspring of the F_1 generation appear to have an intermediate trait, such as in these pink sweet pea flowers.

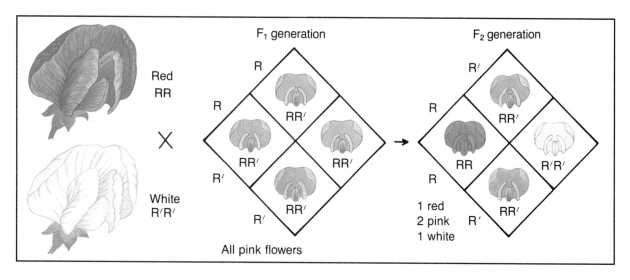

Red
RR

×

White
R′R′

F_1 generation

R
R
RR′
RR′
RR′
R′
RR′
R′

All pink flowers

F_2 generation

R′
R
RR′
RR
R′R′
R
RR′
R′

1 red
2 pink
1 white

FIGURE 9–12.

Multiple alleles control coat color in rabbits. Fully-colored is dominant to both albino and himalayan, which when crossed produce only himalayan offspring, indicating that himalayan is dominant to the albino condition.

9:8 Multiple Alleles

Some traits have more than one pair of alleles. Traits controlled by several alleles are said to have **multiple alleles.** In rabbits, one gene that controls coat color has multiple alleles: C is the allele for black coat; c^h is for the white body with black points called a himalayan; and c is for a white coat. An enzyme that activates the production of pigment is controlled by the C allele. This enzyme is lacking in cc rabbits. In $c^h c^h$ rabbits, the enzyme only works in cooler regions of the body, resulting in the himalayan pattern as shown in Figure 9–12. The allele C is dominant to c^h and c, and c^h is dominant to c.

The inheritance of ABO blood groups in humans involves equal dominance, often called codominance, of two alleles and a recessive third allele. Blood type is determined by the presence of antigens in the blood. The presence or absence of these proteins is determined by three alleles, I^A, I^B, and i. The I^A allele produces type A blood with A antigens. The I^B allele produces type B blood with B antigens. The i allele produces type O blood with no antigens. I^A and I^B are the codominant alleles, while i is recessive to both I^A and I^B.

A person with the genotype $I^A I^B$ has type AB blood, with both A and B antigens. A person with the genotype $I^A i$ or genotype $I^A I^A$ has

Table 9–3.

HUMAN BLOOD GROUPS		
Genotypes	Antigens	Phenotype
$I^A I^A$ or $I^A i$	A	A
$I^B I^B$ or $I^B i$	B	B
$I^A I^B$	A and B	AB
ii	none	O

type A blood with A antigens. A person with the genotype $I^B i$, or genotype $I^B I^B$ has type B blood with B antigens. Only people with the genotype ii have type O blood with neither the A nor B antigens. Therefore, there are four possible phenotypes from three alleles in the population: A, B, AB, and O as shown in Table 9–3.

9:9 Sex-Linked Inheritance

You studied in Chapter 8 how sex in animals is controlled by the sex chromosomes X and Y. Genes that are located on the sex chromosomes are called **sex-linked genes.** Sex-linked genes, and the traits they control, are usually associated with one particular sex and are inherited with the sex chromosome. Most known sex-linked genes are located on the X chromosome, but a few have been found on the Y chromosome. Hemophilia is a relatively rare sex-linked trait that affects blood-clotting. The gene that controls this trait is recessive and located on the X chromosome. A female must carry this trait on both of her X chromosomes to be a hemophiliac. However, since males have only one X chromosome, which is inherited from their mother, they will be hemophiliacs if that chromosome carries the trait. There is no dominant allele on the Y chromosome to hide the effects of the recessive hemophilia allele. Therefore, males have a greater chance of hemophilia than females.

Another recessive sex-linked condition in humans is red-green color blindness. Follow the pattern of inheritance of two crosses involving color blindness in Figure 9–13. Notice how the daughters all have the recessive gene for this trait. Use Figure 9–14 to check your own phenotype for color blindness.

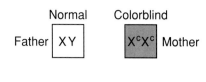

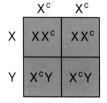

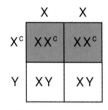

all daughters are carriers
all sons are colorblind

all daughters are carriers
all sons are normal

FIGURE 9–13.

Two possible inheritance patterns for color blindness are shown in these Punnett squares. Practice making Punnett squares by showing other inheritance patterns of this sex-linked gene.

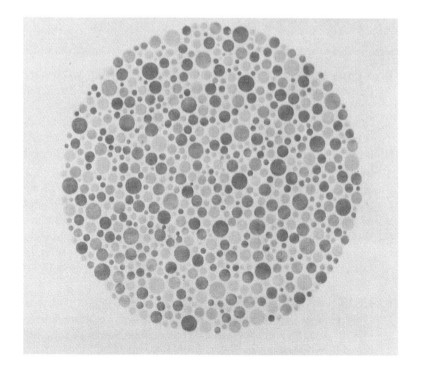

FIGURE 9–14.

Human color vision depends on genes that produce three kinds of light-absorbing molecules in the retina. Each molecule is sensitive to either red, green, or blue colors. To color-blind people, the green seventy-four in this standard test appears gray.

FIGURE 9–15.

Different amounts of pigment in the skin depend on the ratio of dominant to recessive alleles inherited.

9:10 Polygenic Inheritance

You are now aware that some traits are determined by one gene with a single pair of alleles and others are controlled by multiple alleles. However, a very large number of traits are determined by several genes. **Polygenic inheritance** is inheritance of a trait that is controlled by two or more genes. The genes may be on the same or on different chromosomes. In polygenic inheritance, each dominant gene contributes a small, but equal, increment to the trait being expressed. The result is a blending effect. Many traits such as stem length, hand width, and skin color range from one form through many variations to another form. The effects of polygenic alleles blend together and are expressed as the completely recessive form through to the completely dominant form.

REVIEW

6. A cross between a pure line animal with black fur and a pure line animal with white fur yields offspring with gray fur. What kind of inheritance is involved?

7. How does the inheritance of human blood groups differ from simple Mendelian inheritance?

8. If four children with the same two parents have four different hair colors, what type of inheritance is being shown?

9. **SKILL REVIEW:** Design an experiment that would prove the type of inheritance for feather color in chickens. You want to know if your black, white, and blue-feathered chickens are showing simple Mendelian inheritance, incomplete dominance, or are controlled by multiple alleles. For more help, refer to Designing an Experiment in the Skill Handbook, pages 802 to 803.

10. **USING CONCEPTS:** Queen Victoria of England had nine children. One of four sons had hemophilia and two of five daughters carried the recessive gene. What was the actual probability of each child inheriting this sex-linked gene?

INHERITANCE OF CYSTIC FIBROSIS

Cystic fibrosis is the most common genetic disorder that is inherited by whites in the United States. The disease results in the accumulation of excessive mucus in the respiratory tract. Cystic fibrosis patients also lose large amounts of salt from their bodies, resulting in very salty sweat. For many years, salty sweat was used as a diagnosis of this disease.

A test has recently been developed that determines which people are at risk of having a child with cystic fibrosis. The test is based on the discovery that skin cells from carriers of the cystic fibrosis gene, when grown in the laboratory, do not transport sodium ions as well as skin cells from healthy people.

Scientists studied sodium transport in the skin cells of cystic fibrosis patients, their parents, and their healthy siblings. The scientists discovered that the cells of the cystic fibrosis patients, their parents, and most of the healthy sisters and brothers showed poor sodium transport. Since they knew that both parents had to be carriers of the disease, they concluded that the offspring with the skin cell symptoms must also be carriers. There is a fifty percent chance of any offspring being a carrier. Given this information, determine how cystic fibrosis is inherited. Make a Punnett square to help you.

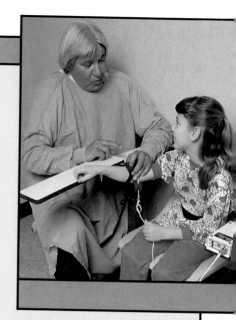

The "sweat test" for cystic fibrosis

APPLIED GENETICS

Probably the greatest benefit of genetics to humans will eventually be in the curing of genetic diseases. However, humans have been using genetics to raise and breed plants and animals for thousands of years. Organisms with preferred traits have been crossed in hopes of producing offspring with these traits. As a result of this artificial selection, most of the food you eat and the animals you take in as pets have been changed to suit the needs of humans.

9:11 Pedigrees

You have already studied the genetic inheritance of hemophilia. This and many other human genetic disorders can have serious consequences for those affected. A famous case of the transmission of hemophilia is that of some royal families in Europe. All could be traced back to Queen Victoria of England. By understanding Mendel's laws and applying technology, genetic disorders such as this may one day be predicted, detected, and even cured.

Objectives:
- explain the usefulness of a pedigree.
- explain the purpose of a testcross.
- describe how selective breeding has led to the development of plant crops and animal breeds.
- explain how genetic engineering results in recombinant DNA.

pedigree:
pedis (L) foot
grus (GK) crane

One method of predicting the probability of offspring inheriting a genetic disorder is by studying a pedigree. A **pedigree** is a record of an organism's ancestry. The pedigree shown in Figure 9–16 lists the individuals of related organisms that include albinos. As you can see, albinism has been observed in a variety of animals. It also occurs in humans. Other human disorders that are caused by the homozygous recessive condition include cystic fibrosis, hemophilia, Tay-Sach's disease, and sickle cell anemia.

The probability of the offspring having a particular allele can be predicted from a pedigree. Many breeds of livestock, crops, garden flowers, and pets are controlled with the aid of pedigrees.

9:12 The Testcross

There are many traits in plants and animals that breeders would prefer not to introduce into their lines of plant and animal breeds. In many cases unfavorable traits such as hemophilia are controlled by recessive alleles. For example, dwarfism is a recessive condition in which Alaskan malamute dogs lack cartilage in their front legs. A dwarf malamute has a very short life span. Dogs that carry the recessive allele appear normal. A **carrier** is an organism that doesn't show symptoms of a disorder, but carries the recessive allele that may be inherited by its offspring.

FIGURE 9–16.

The complete absence of pigment from skin, hair, and eyes called albinism is a condition inherited by several species. As the pedigree shows, organisms that are albinos can have normal parents, but both must have been carriers of the recessive allele.

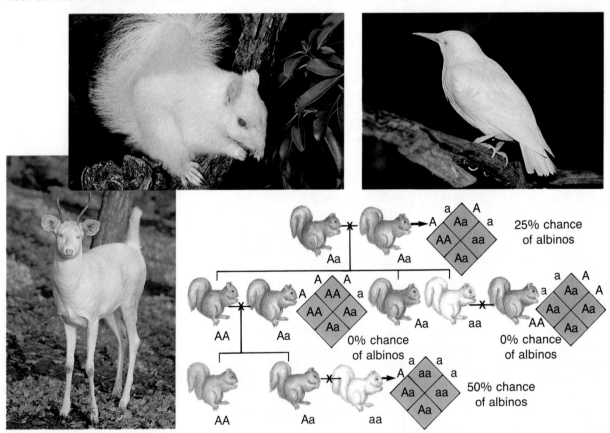

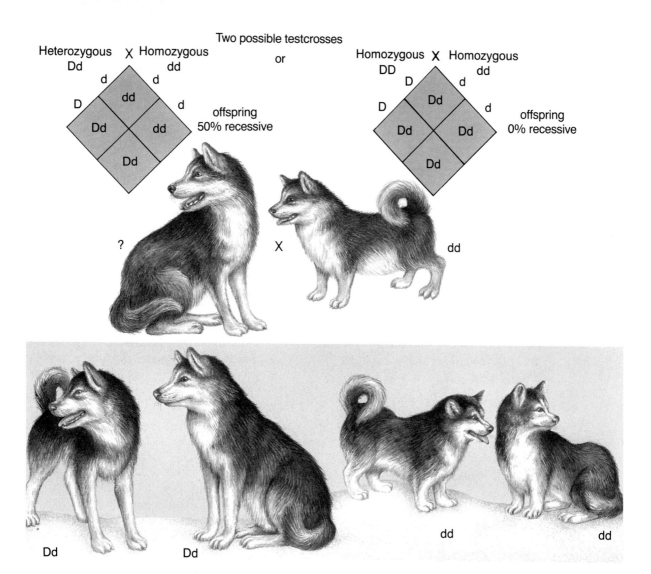

Two possible testcrosses

Heterozygous X Homozygous
Dd   dd

offspring 50% recessive

or

Homozygous X Homozygous
DD   dd

offspring 0% recessive

? X dd

Dd   Dd   dd   dd

How can it be determined whether an organism that shows a dominant trait, such as a normal Alaskan malamute, is a carrier? Obviously, a carrier such as this will be heterozygous for the undesirable condition. You can find out if an organism is homozygous or heterozygous by using a testcross. A **testcross** is a cross between two organisms, one of which has the homozygous recessive phenotype, in order to determine the genotype of the other organism. You know that if the recessive condition appears in the phenotype then it must be homozygous. If any of the offspring of this cross show the recessive trait, the organism being tested is proved to be heterozygous, as shown in Figure 9–17. If the test organism were homozygous dominant for the trait, all of the offspring would be heterozygous and would have the phenotype of the dominant condition. All the offspring of this testcross would then become carriers of the recessive trait. The only way of showing that an Alaskan malamute is a carrier of the recessive dwarf allele is by using a testcross with a malamute that has the dwarf phenotype.

FIGURE 9–17.

From the Punnett squares, what can you determine about the genotype of the unknown Alaskan malamute parent?

What is a testcross?

DEVELOPING A VIEWPOINT

GENETIC TESTING

People have tested plants and animals for valuable traits since the beginning of civilization. These tests involved extensive breeding programs and observations of phenotypes. Today, scientists still test crops and livestock but use modern technology to examine genotypes. Because of this technology, it is now possible to test the genotypes of humans. Many people feel that only good can come from this work, but others raise questions about it. Some ask if such work should take place at all. Others feel that there must be strict guidelines for work done on humans. What are some of the different ways in which human DNA is being tested?

BACKGROUND

One of the tests being used today was developed in England by a scientist named Alec Jeffreys. It is referred to as DNA fingerprinting. The DNA from the cells of a person or other organism can be analyzed and positively identified as belonging to that person or organism. The cells used are from samples of hair, blood, skin, or even reproductive cells.

Other tests include those for tracing genetic diseases within families, finding the genes that cause genetic diseases, trying to neutralize them, and trying to cure cancer by means of inserting therapeutic genes.

CASE STUDIES

1. DNA fingerprinting has now been used in forensic medicine for the solution and prosecution of crimes. If blood, sperm, or any other human cells are left at the scene of a crime, the DNA in the cells can be analyzed and compared with some DNA taken from the suspect's blood. If they match, this information and the testimony of a scientist can be used to help convict a rapist or murderer. DNA fingerprinting has been called the greatest boon to forensic medicine since the discovery of the unique nature of fingerprints.

2. Genetically altered tumor-fighting cells are now being given to terminal cancer patients. The first trial was in May, 1989. Many scientists believe that this trial marked the beginning of a new era of biomedical research in which scientists give therapeutic genes to patients with genetic diseases. The cells now being given to cancer patients will not cure them because their cancers are too far advanced. But the tumors may be reduced in some patients. The trials might lead to gene therapy that would provide the body with an ability to rid itself of cancer.

3. All the genetic diseases that people can get eventually may be understood as a result of a project of decoding and mapping the entire human genotype. This project is expected to take as long as 15 years and cost about $3 billion. There are an estimated 1×10^5 human genes that have to be decoded and mapped for human DNA.

4. A kind of "backward genetics" is now being used to combat cancers and viruses. The strategy is to disable a piece of the genetic code by using an opposite, or complementary, piece of code. This strategy works because the opposite codes cancel each other out. Scientists manipulate the cell's own DNA to produce the complementary molecules. They do this by taking duplicates of some of the cell's DNA and altering it. Then they return the altered DNA to the cell nucleus where the altered DNA becomes a part of the cell's regular DNA.

5. Danny, a boy born in the United Kingdom, had emigrated to Africa to be with his father. He later decided to join his mother, brother, and two sisters in England. Immigration authorities suspected that the boy returning was not Danny. Standard blood tests of the boy and his mother showed a high probability that they were related but they could not be used to prove they were mother and son. The boy could have been a nephew. He was refused entry into the U.K. Later, genetic testing proved that the boy was in fact Danny. Danny's father was not available for testing so the DNA of the boy and his brothers and sisters were compared. The probability of two unrelated people sharing a single DNA marker is 0.26. Danny shared 25 markers with his siblings. The probability of being unrelated and sharing 25 markers is 0.26^{25} or in scientific notation 2×10^{-15}. Thus, it was evident that the boy was in fact Danny, and he was permitted entry into the U.K.

6. Mary was adopted when she was three days old. When Mary was six years old, her adoptive parents told her that she was an adopted child. Now that Mary is married and expecting a baby, she feels she wants to know who her birth parents are. She has reason to suspect that her birth mother is a distant cousin of her adoptive mother. Mary has read about DNA fingerprinting and wants to have the cousin and herself tested.

DNA fingerprinting techniques and the equipment needed to carry out these tests are costly, but can serve a real function. In recent years much publicity has been given to tracing missing children. DNA tests have been used to help convict people involved in kidnapping children. Hair samples or skin cells of longtime kidnapped children were found to match those of parents who had reported their children missing.

DEVELOPING YOUR VIEWPOINT

1. Should DNA fingerprinting be used to test all suspects of violent crimes?
2. Is it ethical to ask terminal cancer patients to volunteer for genetic testing?
3. Should the United States be spending so much time and money on mapping the human chromosomes?
4. What might happen to an undesirable piece of the genetic code when the cell that has had altered DNA duplicates itself?
5. Discuss the value of genetic testing for identification purposes.

SUGGESTED READINGS

1. Jaret, Peter. "Genes: the Hidden Health Predictors." *Family Circle,* June 27, 1989, pp. 80–84, 126–127.
2. Jaroff, Leon. "The Gene Hunt." *Time,* Mar. 20, 1989, pp. 62–67.
3. Lewis, Ricki. "DNA Fingerprints: Witness for the Prosecution." *Discover,* June 1988, pp.

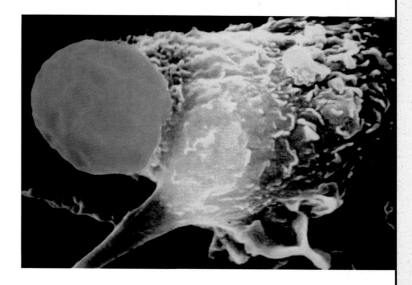

A cell (yellow) is genetically altered to fight a tumor (orange).

Examples of animal hybrids are ligers (lion and tiger), and mules (horse and donkey).

9:13 Plant and Animal Breeding

In the past two decades, selective breeding of plant crops has increased their value as food for humans. For example, one variety of apple tree that produces many apples is crossed with another variety that is resistant to disease, resulting in offspring that produce many apples and a tree that is resistant to disease. This is also true for many cereal crops, such as rice and corn. Almost all the corn grown in the United States is hybrid corn. A **hybrid** is the result of a cross between closely related species of organisms. The hybrid corn is larger and more disease resistant than other varieties. Many garden flowers have been developed by artificial selection. For example, rose breeders regularly develop new varieties of roses. These new varieties are not new species. The different varieties belong to the same species and, therefore, can be crossed easily.

Animals are also selected artificially by breeders. Farmers and ranchers selectively breed chickens, turkeys, and other kinds of fowl, as well as horses, cattle, sheep, pigs, and goats to concentrate desirable traits. Livestock might be bred for increased egg production, milk production, or more meat.

People also selectively breed dogs, cats, and horses as a hobby. Dog breeds first were artificially selected for characteristics that allowed them to perform different kinds of work for humans. For example, English sheep dogs were bred for the ability to herd sheep, and greyhounds were bred for the ability to hunt. Many animals have also been bred for sports or as companions for humans.

FIGURE 9–18.

Dogs were probably the first animals to be domesticated. Breeds include sporting dogs, hounds, terriers, working dogs, herding dogs, toy dogs, and non-sporting dogs. All dogs are color-blind, but all have a sense of hearing superior to that of humans.

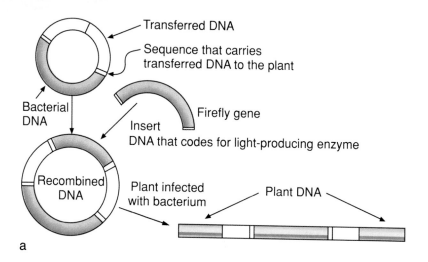

- Transferred DNA
- Sequence that carries transferred DNA to the plant

Bacterial DNA

Firefly gene

Insert
DNA that codes for light-producing enzyme

Recombined DNA

Plant infected with bacterium

Plant DNA

a

b

9:14 Genetic Engineering

Scientists can now move genes from one organism to another in a process called **genetic engineering.** The altered genetic material is called **recombinant DNA.** Selected genes are cut from a chromosome and spliced into another chromosome of a different cell. **Gene splicing** is the cutting of DNA by enzymes and insertion of a piece of foreign DNA.

One spectacular example of genetic engineering was when the gene that causes the light in a firefly was spliced into plant cells. The plant cells containing the gene glowed in the dark. The techniques developed in this 1987 experiment, as shown in Figure 9–19, have since been useful in treating human disorders. The gene that directs the production of human insulin was introduced into a type of bacterium that then produced human insulin for use by diabetics. When the bacteria containing the introduced genes divide, their offspring receive copies of the human genes, and the offspring can also produce insulin. This technique has dramatically increased the supply of this and other vital substances.

FIGURE 9–19.

A section of DNA that codes for light production in fireflies was inserted into a circular piece of bacterial genetic material (a). The recombined DNA was injected into a tobacco plant that glowed in the dark when watered with a substrate for the light-producing enzyme.

REVIEW

11. How is recombinant DNA produced?
12. How are new varieties of plants and animals developed?
13. How is a pedigree useful in preventing human disorders?
14. **SKILL REVIEW:** Make a hypothesis about what would happen to the appearance of corn if humans stopped producing hybrids. For more help, refer to Designing an Experiment in the Skill Handbook, pages 802 to 803.
15. **USING CONCEPTS:** An animal breeder has a guinea pig with black fur, a dominant trait to brown fur. How can you determine if the animal is homozygous or heterozygous for the trait? Draw Punnett squares to illustrate your answer.

CHAPTER REVIEW

SUMMARY

1. Traits are controlled by pairs of alleles. The law of dominance states that the dominant trait is the only one to appear in the F_1 generation in a cross between two pure lines. The law of segregation states that alleles are inherited separately. **9:1, 9:2**
2. The homozygous condition is when two alleles have the same expression. The heterozygous condition has two forms of an allele. **9:3**
3. A monohybrid cross involves one trait. A Punnett square shows the probability of inheriting a trait. **9:4, 9:5**
4. The law of independent assortment states that traits are inherited separately. A dihybrid cross involves two traits. **9:6**
5. In incomplete dominance, the trait of the heterozygote is a third phenotype. Some traits are controlled by multiple alleles. **9:7, 9:8**
6. Some traits are sex-linked. Polygenic inheritance involves the control of a trait by two or more pairs of alleles. **9:9, 9:10**
7. A pedigree is used to trace a genetic trait. A testcross is used to determine the genotype of an organism. **9:11, 9:12**
8. Plant and animal breeding has resulted in improved crops, livestock, and pets. **9:13**
9. DNA is recombined artificially by the process of genetic engineering. **9:14**

LANGUAGE OF BIOLOGY

allele
carrier
dihybrid cross
dominant trait
F_1 generation
F_2 generation
gene splicing
genetic engineering
genetics

heredity
heterozygous
homozygous
hybrid
inbreeding
incomplete dominance
law of dominance
law of independent
   assortment

law of segregation
monohybrid cross
multiple alleles
outbreeding
pedigree
polygenic inheritance
probability

Punnett square
recessive trait
recombinant DNA
sex-linked genes
testcross
zygote

Choose the word or phrase from the list above that completes the sentence.

1. Color blindness is controlled by ____.
2. The ____ states that alleles separate during the formation of gametes.
3. ____ is the passing on of traits.
4. Traits controlled by more than two pairs of alleles have ____.
5. An organism that has two matching alleles for a trait is ____.
6. ____ results in three phenotypes from one pair of alleles.
7. Altering of genetic material is called ____.
8. A(n) ____ controls one phenotype of a trait.
9. A cross that results in two phenotypes of one allele pair is a(n) ____.
10. ____ produces zygotes from unrelated parents.

REVIEWING CONCEPTS

Choose the word or phrase that completes the sentence or answers the question.

11. In a cross between heterozygotes Aa × Aa, the offspring will be ____ homozygous.
    a. all   c. ¼
    b. ½   d. ¾
12. A(n) ____ allele is one that produces a trait even in a heterozygous condition.
    a. multiple   c. recessive
    b. dominant   d. incomplete
13. ____ control incomplete dominance.
    a. Two alleles   c. Sex-linkages
    b. Multiple alleles   d. Polygenes

14. ____ dominance refers to only one of two alleles expressed in the F$_1$ generation.
    a. The law of   c. Incomplete
    b. Independent   d. Genetic

15. The ratio predicted by a dihybrid cross between heterozygous parents is ____.
    a. 3:1   c. 1:2:1
    b. 9:6:1   d. 9:3:3:1

16. A trait with both forms of a gene is ____.
    a. dominant   c. recessive
    b. homozygous   d. heterozygous

17. Transfer of genes between different organisms is called ____.
    a. inbreeding   c. genetic
                           engineering
    b. dominance   d. segregation

18. Polygenic inheritance does NOT affect ____.
    a. skin color   c. hemophilia
    b. stem length   d. hand width

19. A poodle and a greyhound are ____.
    a. varieties   c. species
    b. breeds   d. families

20. What is the ratio of phenotypes from a cross between two heterozygotes Aa?
    a. 3:1   c. 1:2:1
    b. 9:6:1   d. 9:3:3:1

UNDERSTANDING CONCEPTS

Answer the following questions using complete sentences.

21. What is the kind of inheritance that causes a range in height of people?
22. What are the possible blood types of the children of two people with type AB blood?
23. Describe how recombinant DNA is made.
24. Distinguish between inbreeding and outbreeding.
25. Compare incompletely dominant alleles with simple Mendelian inheritance.
26. Summarize the purpose of a testcross.

27. Compare polygenic inheritance and inheritance of multiple alleles.
28. Contrast phenotypes and genotypes in incomplete dominance.
29. Why does incomplete dominance prove Mendel's law of independent assortment?
30. How is a Punnett square useful?

APPLYING CONCEPTS

Answer the following questions using complete sentences.

31. Why is inbreeding a disadvantage?
32. How is a new flower variety developed?
33. Why can an individual carry only two alleles for a given gene?
34. Heterozygous cattle (RR′) are called roan, a combination of red and white. Is it possible to produce a line of cattle that produces no other colors except roan? Why or why not?
35. Is it possible for a man with type B blood and a woman with type A blood to produce a child with type O blood? Why or why not?

EXTENSIONS

1. Research the rhesus alleles in humans and how this condition is controlled.
2. Construct a pedigree showing the presence or absence of a specific trait in your family.
3. Research a human genetic disorder.

READINGS

Albrech, Pere. "Possible Dogs." *Natural History,* Dec. 1986, pp. 4–8.
Montgomery, Geoffrey. "Seeing With the Brain." *Discover,* Dec. 1988, p. 52.

Chapter 10

EVOLUTION: CHANGE THROUGH TIME

H ave organisms changed since they first appeared on Earth? Are living things changing now? People once believed that living things didn't change through time. Today, evolution is accepted because of much evidence from observation and experimentation. We now know that present-day organisms such as the Great Blue Heron have evolved from other life forms of the past such as the dinosaurs. The mechanisms of evolution are still operating today. In this chapter, you will examine these mechanisms and some of the evidence for evolution. You will begin to see why evolution has been called the most important concept of biology.

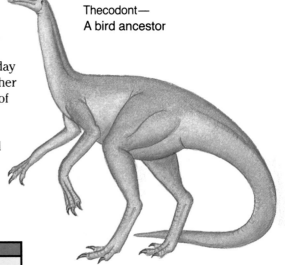

Thecodont—
A bird ancestor

EVIDENCE OF EVOLUTION

There have been enormous changes in living things since they first appeared on Earth about 3.5 billion years ago. Recall from Chapter 2 that evolution is a genetic change in a population of organisms. Evolution can result in the production of new species from existing species. There are several kinds of evidence that show that changes have taken place in species over time. By studying this evidence, scientists infer relationships among organisms and piece together a history of living things.

10:1 Fossils and Evolution

You have probably seen fossil dinosaur bones in a natural history museum. You may even have found a fossil of a leaf, or a shell in a rock. A fossil is formed when an organism, or part of one, is preserved before it can decay. Most fossils are found in sedimentary rocks. Organisms that became fossils in these rocks were buried in layers of mud or sand. As the layers of sediment built up, the lower layers became compressed and hardened. Eventually, sedimentary rock such as sandstone, limestone, or shale formed.

Objectives:
- describe the four kinds of fossils and state how fossils provide evidence of evolution.
- compare homologous, vestigial, and analogous structures.
- state how embryos are used to show relationships among vertebrates.
- describe how RNA and DNA are used to interpret evolutionary relationships.

Great blue heron

FIGURE 10–1.

A replica of a famous person is made in a way similar to the formation of a cast fossil.

NoteWorthy

Ages of fossils dated over 50 000 years have been estimated by the use of radioactive isotopes such as uranium 235, uranium 238, thorium 232, rubidium 87, or potassium 40. Uranium and thorium isotopes decay to form radioactive lead. Rubidium 87 becomes strontium 87, and potassium 40 decays to argon 40.

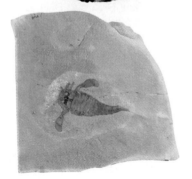

Fossils are one of four kinds: imprint, mold, cast, or petrified. As the soft parts of a buried organism break down, they may leave an imprint in the mud similar to a pattern made by a rubber stamp. Leaves and bird feathers are often found as imprint fossils. Animal tracks or holes left by the decay of an organism's hard parts such as shells or bones may leave deeper depressions in the mud on hardening. This kind of fossil is called a mold. You may have seen a plastic model of a famous sports or rock star. Plastic models are made in a way as shown in Figure 10–1, similar to that of some fossils. After the parts of an organism decompose leaving a mold, the mold sometimes becomes filled with other materials, such as minerals, that harden and form a cast fossil. This is similar to the way the plastic hardens inside the plaster cast of the famous figure. Ammonoids and trilobites are typical cast fossils. Dissolved minerals sometimes replace the hard parts of organisms, forming petrified fossils. Petrified tree trunks, shells, bones, and teeth are common fossils.

Recall from Chapter 2 that the position a fossil occupies in layers of rock is used to determine the fossil's relative age. The relative age of a fossil is its relationship, younger or older, to other fossils. From fossil evidence, it appears that the kinds of species on Earth have changed over time. Fossils found in older rock layers are, in general, simpler in structure than the fossils found in more recent layers. More recent fossils are in many cases intermediate in structure between present-day organisms and more ancient fossils. From this, scientists can infer that simple organisms were more common during the early history of Earth and that these living things evolved or changed into more complex organisms over time.

The fossil record shows that throughout history there have been many periods of great species diversity. But, it also shows that just before these periods, there existed just a few of these species. For example, most of the animal phyla originated in Late Precambrian and Early Cambrian time, over 500 million years ago. Likewise, most of the modern orders of mammals evolved in the Cenozoic, about 60 million years ago. From these observations, scientists have inferred that many different species evolved from a single ancestor. The evolutionary history of many, including humans, has been interpreted by comparing structures and dates of fossils.

Studying evolution from the fossil record is similar to trying to read and understand a book that is missing some of its pages because the fossil record is incomplete. Fossils of many intermediate forms of life have not been found. However, sufficient evidence gathered from fossils has convinced scientists that evolution has taken place.

When did most animal phyla originate?

10:2 Structures and Evolution

The study of structures of different organisms has provided evidence of evolution. In different species, structures that are similar and are derived from the same body parts are called **homologous structures.** Figure 10–2 shows the bone structure of the front flippers and rear flippers of the walrus, the sea lion, and the seal, all members of the family Pinnipedia. The similarities in the bone structures indicate that the three species had a common ancestor. In some cases, such as in the forelimbs of a human, a bat, and a whale, it is also obvious that the structures are homologous, but the relationships among these species are less close than those of the pinnipeds. The shorter the time span since the groups diverged from their common ancestor, the more similar they appear.

FIGURE 10–2.

The flipper bones of pinnipeds all have long first digits in the front flippers and a similar elongation of first and fifth digits of the rear flippers, even though walruses, sea lions, and seals use their flippers in different ways.

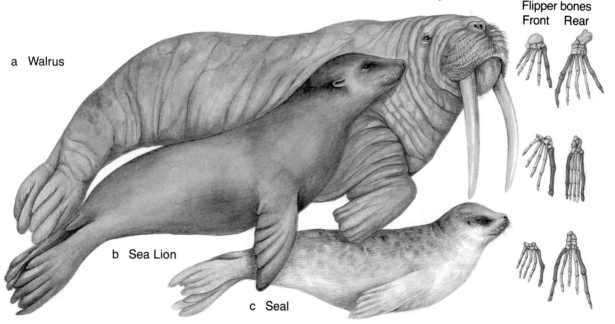

Flipper bones
Front   Rear

a Walrus

b Sea Lion

c Seal

a

b

FIGURE 10–3.

The honey locust thorn (a) and the cactus spine (b) both function to protect the plant from consumers. The two structures are, however, derived from two separate plant organs; a stem and a leaf, and are, therefore, analogous.

FIGURE 10–4.

All vertebrate embryos have a tail and gill slits in the early stages of development.

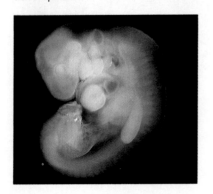

Other body parts that provide evidence of evolution are **vestigial structures,** which are body parts that are reduced in size and appear to serve no function. A vestigial structure is thought to be the remnant of a structure that was once functional in an ancestor. For example, certain blind fish that live in caves where there is no light have small vestigial eyes. Since there is no adaptive advantage in the evolution of a useless organ, the eyes have probably become sightless over years of disuse. The ancestors of the blind cave fish probably had eyes with sight.

Body parts that are similar in function but have different structures are **analogous structures.** These body parts don't always indicate evolutionary relationships. The thorn of a honey locust and the spine of a cactus both protect the plants from grazing animals. However, they are modifications of two completely different plant structures. A honey locust thorn is a modified stem. The cactus spine is a very reduced leaf. Analogous structures are produced when unrelated organisms become adapted to similar environments.

10:3 Development and Evolution

The fossil record indicates that aquatic, gill-breathing vertebrates preceded air-breathing land forms, and comparisons of embryos of different classes of vertebrates support this view of evolutionary change. An **embryo** is an organism in its earliest stages of development. In the early stages of embryo development of reptiles, birds, and mammals, a tail and gill slits can be observed. As you know, fish use gills to breathe under water. Fish embryos retain these structures; reptile, bird, and mammal embryos lose them as their development continues. In the human embryo, a tail is visible up to the sixth week of development. In humans, the tail disappears, but in fish, reptiles, and birds the tail is retained into maturity.

10:4 DNA and Evolution

The most recent evidence to support evolution has come from comparisons of RNA and DNA. Recall from Chapter 3 that all living things contain these nucleic acids in their cells.

The study of DNA or RNA sequences in different species reveals relationships that are probably more reliable than those shown by studies of major body structures. This is because DNA and RNA molecules change at a steady rate, whereas changes in body structures are affected more by the environment and so occur at irregular intervals. Ribosomal RNA has been found to be particularly useful because of its basic similarity of structure among all organisms. Small differences in nucleotide base sequences make it possible to construct phylogenetic trees of all organisms. This type of research has been carried out since the 1970s, and the relationships among many taxonomic groups such as the birds shown in Figure 10–5 have been revealed. The technique of sequencing involves separating the nucleotide bases and comparing the types of bases from different species. Using this technique, Chinese giant pandas were found to be closely related to bears, but Chinese red pandas were shown to be more closely related to raccoons than to bears.

Genetic comparisons have also been made using proteins and DNA from mitochondria. For example, cytochrome c is a protein found in mitochondria of all eukaryotes. The cytochrome c gene in humans and monkeys differs by only one nucleotide; in humans and turtles, however, the difference is 19 nucleotides. Because it's obvious that humans have far more characteristics in common with monkeys than with turtles, this information confirms that organisms that share closer evolutionary relationships have fewer differences in nucleotide sequences.

NoteWorthy

The first automated DNA-sequencing machine was developed in 1986 at the California Institute of Technology. The machine can read up to 8000 nucleotide bases a day.

FIGURE 10–5.

Comparisons of DNA sequences among several orders of large birds have been used to construct a phylogenetic tree. DNA sequences were more similar between storks and New World vultures than with any other group. Flamingos had the least number of DNA sequences in common with any other group.

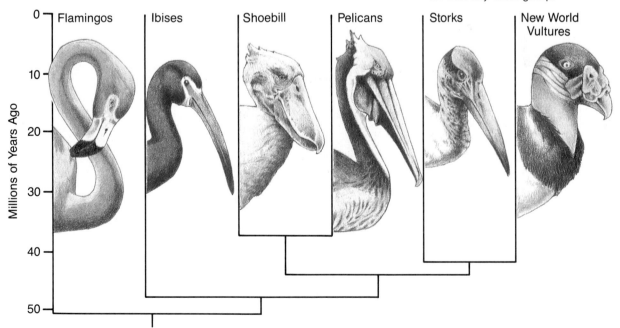

1. Give an example of each of the four kinds of fossils.
2. What are two structures in embryos that indicate relationships between classes of vertebrates?
3. How do homologous and analogous structures differ?
4. **SKILL REVIEW:** What can you infer if two species that appear different have similar RNA sequences? For more help, refer to Observing and Inferring in the Skill Handbook, page 809.
5. **USING CONCEPTS:** The DNA code is basically the same in all organisms. For example, a bacterium is able to use the information from human genes to make proteins when the human genes are inserted into it using genetic engineering techniques. What does this fact suggest about evolution?

THE HISTORY OF EVOLUTION

Objectives:

- describe Lamarck's hypothesis of evolution.
- explain how Darwin developed his theory of natural selection.
- summarize the theory of evolution by natural selection.
- compare Lamarck's and Darwin's explanations for the evolution of the giraffe's neck.
- give an example of a structural, physiological, or behavioral adaptation.
- compare gradualism and punctuated equilibrium.

At one time, most people believed that species could not change, that there was a fixed number of species, and that each species had a given set of traits that remained with it forever. Some scientists who studied organisms in great detail began to question this idea because of the evidence they saw for evolution. They began to form the view that living things change over long periods of time. Two scientists, Jean Lamarck and Charles Darwin, led the way in the search for the mechanisms that caused these changes. Because of subsequent studies by the world's scientists, it is now known that organisms throughout Earth's history have not remained constant but are constantly changing.

FIGURE 10–6.

The works of Jean Baptiste de Lamarck (left) and Charles Robert Darwin (right) have been a valuable source of ideas on the mechanisms of evolution for over 100 years.

10:5 Jean Baptiste de Lamarck

Jean Baptiste de Lamarck (1744–1829) was a French scientist who, in 1809, proposed a hypothesis to explain the enormous variation in animals that he had observed. Lamarck believed that body changes that developed during an organism's lifetime, called **acquired characteristics,** could be passed on to the offspring. As an example, Lamarck used his hypothesis to explain how the giraffe developed its long neck. According to Lamarck's hypothesis, the original population of giraffes had short necks. As they ate all the grass and leaves from the lower branches of trees, they stretched their necks in an attempt to reach the higher branches where there was a supply of young, tender leaves. Over their lifetimes, they stretched their necks longer and longer. Giraffe offspring inherited the longer necks acquired by their parents. Each new generation acquired longer necks until all giraffes permanently had very long necks.

Recall from Chapter 1 that a hypothesis must be tested many times before it is accepted as a theory. Suppose you removed one half the petals from each flower in a population of flowering plants. Would plants in the next generation have only half a set of petals? Suppose you kept up the experiment generation after generation. If Lamarck's hypothesis were correct, you would be able to produce a strain of flowers with only half the usual number of petals. An example more similar to that described by Lamarck for giraffes might be in the attempts in the past of some women to have a small waist size. No matter how much women strived to develop a small waist by dieting or surgery for the removal of their lower ribs, the results were never inherited by daughters or granddaughters. After collecting large amounts of data on the inheritance of acquired characteristics, scientists rejected Lamarck's hypothesis of changes in species due to the effects of the environment.

10:6 Charles Darwin

Charles Darwin (1809–1882) wasn't sure he would ever find his purpose in life. Darwin tried to become a doctor like his father, but the sight of illness was too unpleasant for him. He then studied to be a clergyman, but lost interest. One of Darwin's teachers suggested that he might be interested in being a ship's naturalist. Darwin accepted that position on a voyage of exploration around the world. At 22, he was responsible for recording all the plants and animals observed on a trip to South America aboard *H.M.S. Beagle.*

The voyage Darwin took on *H.M.S. Beagle* lasted five years. During the trip, he collected previously unknown fossils, plants, and animals. He noted the variety in the living things he observed. He found fossils of marine organisms on mountains and realized that the mountains must have been under the ocean at one time. He asked himself questions and made hypotheses about the origin and adaptations of species, and on how species might have become so diverse. Darwin returned home to England in 1836. For the next twenty-two years he studied his collections, thought about his observations, and collected enormous amounts of data from further studies.

Darwin was very interested in breeding pigeons for racing, a common hobby at that time. From his observations of the effects of artificial selection on characteristics in pigeons, he began to realize how changes might occur in natural populations. He also studied breeds of dogs, varieties of flowers, and breeds of farm animals. He even studied variations in humans.

FIGURE 10–7.

Darwin discovered that breeds of pigeons vary much more than do most families of wild birds.

Darwin noted that no two individuals in a population are exactly alike. Organisms vary in size, color, and many other traits. He began to understand that it is variation, rather than acquired characteristics, that is passed on to offspring. Gradually, Darwin began to form his now well-known theory of natural selection. **Natural selection** is a mechanism for change in populations that occurs when individuals with the most favorable variations for a particular environment survive and pass these traits on to offspring. Darwin concluded from his studies that organisms that don't successfully compete for resources are less likely to survive in that environment. Organisms that survive can pass on their traits to the next generation. Each new generation would be largely made up of offspring from individuals that are the most adapted.

The theory of evolution by natural selection can be summarized in four statements.

1. Variations exist within populations.
2. Some variations are more advantageous for survival and reproduction than others.
3. Organisms produce more offspring than can survive.
4. Over time, offspring of survivors will make up a larger proportion of the population.

How would Darwin's hypothesis explain the long necks of giraffes? Suppose the original population of giraffes had neck lengths ranging from short to long. While grass was plentiful, a longer neck would be of no advantage to an individual. If grass became scarce, however, giraffes with longer necks would be able to reach a new food supply, the leaves of trees. Many individuals with short necks would be unable to compete and would die of starvation. More longer-necked giraffes would survive the competition for food and reproduce. The genes that control the longer necks would be passed on to their offspring. In the next generation, the percentage of longer-necked giraffes would be greater. As shorter-necked individuals died young, and longer-necked individuals survived and reproduced, the average neck length of giraffes would increase with each succeeding generation until giraffes as a species had long necks. As long as the environment remained the same, the longer-necked giraffes would survive because they were best adapted to these conditions.

Darwin planned to write six large books to explain his ideas. After he began writing, he received a short manuscript from Alfred Russel Wallace, another English naturalist working in Indonesia, a region with high species diversity. Independently, Wallace had come to the same conclusions as Darwin. Their ideas were presented together to the Linnean Society of London in 1858. However, since Darwin contributed so much more evidence to support the mechanism of evolution, his name is usually associated with natural selection. The publication of Darwin's book *On the Origin of Species By Means of Natural Selection,* in 1859, changed the course of studies in biology forever.

Giraffe evolution

BIOLAB

Species Variations

Problem: How much do traits vary within populations?

Materials
pinto beans (25)
metric ruler
graph paper

Procedures
1. Make a table that is similar to the one shown.
2. **Hypothesize** the shapes of graphs that show variations in small populations, such as in 25 beans and a class of students.
3. Measure the length of each of the beans to the nearest millimeter. Record the number of beans for each length.
4. Determine the number of darker splotches on each of the beans. Record the number of beans for each number of spots.
5. Measure to the nearest centimeter the length of the right ears of 25 of your classmates from the bottom of the earlobe to the top of the ear. Record the number of students for each length.
6. Measure to the nearest centimeter the span of the right hand of 25 of your classmates. Record the number of students for each length.
7. Make four line graphs—one for each trait.

Questions and Conclusion
1. What other variations might you measure in bean seeds?
2. Was your **hypothesis** supported? Explain.
3. How do the shapes of your three graphs compare?
4. Which trait showed the greatest amount of variation?
5. If you planted all the bean seeds and harvested the beans of the next generation, will the amount of variation be greater, smaller, or about the same? Why?
6. What are some possible sources of error?
7. How are variations in traits important to evolution?

Conclusion: How much do traits vary within populations?

Data and Observations

Traits	Length or Number of Each Trait											
	1 ...	6	7	8	9	10	11	12	13	14	15	... 25
Bean length (mm)												
Spots (Number)												
Ear length (cm)												
Hand span length (cm)												

10:7 Adaptations and Natural Selection

The evolution of new species is seldom observed because the changes usually require many generations. However, scientists have observed many examples of the natural selection of adaptations. One of the best-studied examples involves the peppered moth in England. During the 1800s, there were two kinds of peppered moths—a common light-colored variety and a rarer dark-colored variety. These moths rested during the day on light-colored tree trunks. In 1850, almost all the moths were light in color. Then, during a rapid expansion of industry around that time, the air became full of smoke and soot. This extreme pollution of the air turned the trunks of trees black. By the end of the century, most of the peppered moth population in England was dark colored. The light-colored individuals had become rare. By careful observation over many years, scientists have been able to explain how this happened.

FIGURE 10–8.

Which of the peppered moths is easier to see? How is camouflage important to the ptarmigan on the left and the peppered moths above?

In 1950, scientists performed an experiment to determine if natural selection had caused the dark variety of moths to become more numerous. They observed light and dark moths in both industrial and rural areas. The experiment showed that birds ate more dark moths in rural areas where the trees were light-colored and more light moths in industrial areas where the trees were dark-colored. Through natural selection, populations of peppered moths had become adapted to living in industrial areas. The experiment showed that organisms whose color provides better camouflage are more likely to survive and reproduce. **Camouflage** is a protective adaptation that allows an organism to blend into its surroundings.

What is camouflage?

FIGURE 10–9.

The peacock has a most obvious behavioral adaptation for attracting mates.

mimicry:
mimos (GK) a mime

Scientists have identified three kinds of adaptations: structural, physiological, and behavioral. Structural adaptations involve a change in the structure of body parts. For example, **mimicry** is a structural adaptation that provides an organism protection by its copying the appearance of another species. Monarch butterflies have a bitter taste and are avoided by birds. If a bird eats a monarch butterfly, it will get sick and learn to avoid them in the future. Viceroy butterflies, which look and act like monarchs, are not bitter tasting; however they are also avoided by birds. By appearing to be monarchs, they survive. Examine the luna moth as shown in Figure 10–10. Why might the bright color and pattern on the luna moth's wings help it survive?

Physiological adaptations involve changes in an organism's metabolic processes. Penicillin was called a wonder drug 50 years ago, when it was first introduced. It killed all kinds of bacteria. Over time, mutant strains of bacteria, with adaptations that protect them from antibiotics such as penicillin, have evolved. Some strains of bacteria produce an enzyme that inactivates penicillin; others have cell walls that block the penicillin molecule from entering. As new antibiotics are introduced, new strains of bacteria evolve that are resistant to each drug.

Behavioral adaptations are inherited behavior patterns that allow an organism to survive in an environment. Over time, many animals have evolved special courtship behaviors that allow them to recognize and attract members of the opposite sex of their own species. Such adaptations result in reproductive success.

FIGURE 10–10.

The moon shapes on this luna moth's wings help to distract a hungry bird. *Luna* is Latin for "the moon."

MIMICRY IN PLANTS

The flowers of many orchids are shaped like their insect pollinators. Some have scents that mimic the smells of the females of the pollinating insect species. A male is attracted to the flower as if it were its mate. The male then attempts to mate with the flower, mistaking the smell and shape with that of a female insect. During "mating" the pollen grains become attached to the male's back. Orchid flowers usually have their pollen grains in masses called pollinia that are different shapes for different species of orchids. The shape of each pollinia fits perfectly the shape of the insect pollinator's body. The male then flies away, and later may attempt to mate with another flower of the same species. A mechanism in the second flower ensures that the pollinia becomes detached from the male insect's back and is placed in the exact spot to allow for fertilization of hundreds of ovules in the ovary. How could the process of natural selection be used to explain these intricate relationships between species? What might happen to these orchids if their insect pollinators became extinct?

A bee orchid

10:8 The Rate of Evolution

What is the rate of evolution? Darwin believed that evolution occurs very slowly. This view of evolution describes **gradualism,** the gradual change of species over time. If evolution is gradual, there should be evidence of many intermediate forms of all species in the fossil record. Scientists have found remains of some of these intermediate forms, but the fossil record also shows that most species remain largely the same for hundreds of thousands of years. Then, suddenly, in a span of 50 000 years or less, a new species is formed. This steplike pattern of evolution in the fossil record is called **punctuated equilibrium.**

gradualism:
  gradus (L) a step
punctuated:
  punctus (L) a point

REVIEW

6. Describe one example of natural selection as observed in nature.
7. Why isn't Lamarck's hypothesis of evolution accepted today?
8. List and describe the four major points of Darwin's theory.
9. **SKILL REVIEW:** Design an experiment to test an insect's resistance to a pesticide. For more help, refer to Designing an Experiment in the Skill Handbook, pages 802 to 803.
10. **USING CONCEPTS:** England passed a series of clean air acts in the 1960s. Predict what would have happened to the relative numbers of dark and light peppered moths following the enforcement of these air pollution controls.

For over 100 years, Darwin's theory has continued to be the best explanation for the mechanism of evolution. However, as information about genes and genetics accumulated, the theory of natural selection was modified. The modern understanding of evolution is based on Darwin's theory, but now includes principles of genes and genetics.

10:9 Genetic Equilibrium

Natural selection acts only upon the phenotype of an organism. For example, if the allele for brown color is recessive it will only show up in the phenotype when it's in the homozygous recessive condition. If brown color happens to be a useful adaptation, natural selection can't affect it unless it shows up in an individual. When it does, this brown-colored individual will have a better chance of surviving and also of reproducing. In the same way, harmful traits that are controlled by recessive alleles take a long time to disappear from a population. The recessive allele remains hidden in the heterozygote. Since natural selection acts only on the phenotype, variability is maintained in the population. You have studied how useful this was to the peppered moth.

Evolution occurs when there is a change in the genetic makeup of a population. All the genes in a population make up a **gene pool.** Within a population, a trait may be controlled by one or several alleles. The proportion of each allele in the gene pool is the **allele frequency.** For example, in a population of leopards there are two alleles for coat color; the allele for spotted coat is dominant to the allele for black coat. Recall from Chapter 9, that in a monohybrid cross the ratio of offspring in the F_2 generation is 3:1. Therefore, in a population of 1000, 750 leopards have spotted coats and 250 have black coats. As you can see in Figure 10–12, the allele frequencies are 50 percent for each allele. If the allele frequencies in a population remain the same from one generation to the next, that population is in **genetic equilibrium.** If the allele frequencies change, the genetic equilibrium is altered and evolution has taken place.

10:10 Changes in Genetic Equilibrium

What are the mechanisms that cause changes in genetic equilibrium? In other words, what are the mechanisms of evolution? Recall from Chapter 8 that mutations are changes in the genetic material of an organism. Mutation in a population is one mechanism of evolution. Most mutations have minor effects, such as changing the color of the scales of a butterfly's wing, but they provide the variation that can be acted upon by natural selection. Mutations occur constantly as chance events, causing changes in the gene pool. These changes

Objectives:
- list three mechanisms that alter allele frequency in a gene pool.
- compare the three types of natural selection that act on the gene pool.
- describe how isolating mechanisms cause speciation.
- distinguish between convergent evolution, divergent evolution, and adaptive radiation.

What is a gene pool?

FIGURE 10–11.

Genes that control the colors of the scales on a butterfly's wing are expressed in its phenotype.

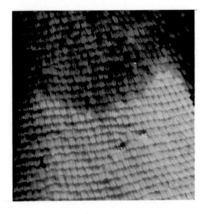

are difficult to detect because many mutations are recessive and are seldom expressed in the phenotype of individuals. Eventually, though, a recessive mutation may appear in the phenotype and natural selection can act upon it, and if the mutation is harmful, the individual may die. The mutation is then removed from the gene pool. Mutation provides the only new genetic material in a species. All other mechanisms of evolution merely shuffle the genetic material that is already present.

Another mechanism of evolution is genetic drift. **Genetic drift** is the change in allele frequencies of a population as a result of chance processes. For example, if a small population of sunflowers has only a few individuals with the allele for hairless stems, that allele could be removed from the gene pool if all those hairless-stemmed plants accidentally die. The chances of genetic drift in larger populations are less. For example, in a population the size of a football field the hairless sunflowers might be scattered throughout the field. The chances are less that all of these rare plants will accidentally die if a tractor should pass through the population. In a population the size of your kitchen, there's a much greater chance that all the rare plants will be affected by such an event. Chance is also involved in genetic recombinations during crossing over in meiosis. Chance determines which eggs hatch when several thousands are laid. All of these random processes cause genetic drift in a population.

Genetic equilibrium may also be disrupted by gene flow. **Gene flow** is the movement of genes in and out of the gene pool. When an organism leaves the population, its genes leave the gene pool. Genes are added to the pool when an organism enters a population. Gene flow in a population results in evolution.

FIGURE 10–12.

The spotted leopard may be heterozygous (Ss) for coat color or homozygous (SS). The black leopard is homozygous recessive (ss). The allele frequency, as shown in the Punnett square, is 50 percent for both S and s alleles.

NoteWorthy

Small populations of such endangered species as the California condor, the cheetah, and the Houston toad may accumulate disadvantageous traits because of genetic drift.

Natural selection acts on changes in the gene pool and maintains a species or forms new species. Three types of natural selection have been identified: stabilizing, directional, and disruptive. **Stabilizing selection** is a kind of natural selection that favors the average individuals of a population. For example, in a large population of grass plants, the range of length of grass blades is 8 cm to 28 cm. Most of the grass blades are around 18 cm high. The shorter grass blades are at a disadvantage because they are shaded and therefore don't trap as much sunlight as the taller grass blades. The tall grass blades are at a disadvantage because they are the first plants to be eaten by grazing animals such as rabbits and sheep. The average height plants are therefore favored by this mechanism of stabilizing selection as shown in Figure 10–13a.

Directional selection is a kind of natural selection that produces a regular change of a population in one direction. For example, if you have an infection, your body contains a population of bacteria, some of which may be resistant to penicillin. If you begin taking penicillin, the non-resistant bacteria will die. The resistant individuals will survive and continue to reproduce. Gradually, the frequency of bacteria with the allele controlling penicillin resistance will increase in the bacteria's gene pool. The allele for penicillin sensitivity may eventually disappear from the population as shown in Figure 10–13b.

Disruptive selection is a kind of natural selection that results in two separate populations that have distinct characteristics. For example, in an area where there has been a rapid change in the environment a population may be fragmented. When a volcano

disruptive:
dis (L) apart
rumpere (L) to break

FIGURE 10–13.

The distribution of species is affected by three types of natural selection as shown on these three graphs.

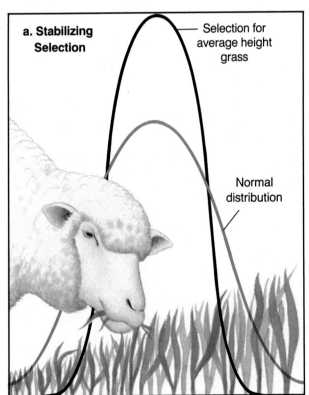

a. Stabilizing Selection

Selection for average height grass

Normal distribution

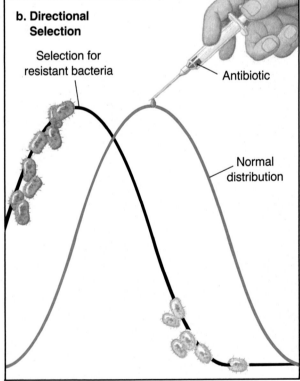

b. Directional Selection

Selection for resistant bacteria

Antibiotic

Normal distribution

erupts or when a valley is flooded, one large population of plants or animals, such as lizards, may be split up into several small populations that can no longer interbreed, as shown in Figure 10–13c. Different environmental conditions in the isolated populations will cause natural selection to have different effects in each population.

Mutation, genetic drift, and gene flow occur in all populations at all times. Natural selection acts on these changes in the gene pool to form stable, new, or separate populations.

10:11 Speciation

Natural selection doesn't necessarily result in **speciation,** the formation of new species. For speciation to occur, a permanent barrier to breeding between members of the same species must occur, causing groups to become genetically isolated. There are two kinds of genetic isolation: geographic and reproductive.

Geographic isolation occurs if a physical barrier separates a population into groups. Barriers may be rivers, mountain ranges, or oceans. Such barriers exist on islands such as the Hawaiian and Galapagos islands. Darwin recognized 13 distinct species of finches on the Galapagos Islands that were different from the finches on the nearest mainland of Central and South America. The finches on each island were similar but because of certain distinct traits they formed unique species. The water between each of the islands and the mainland acted as a barrier and allowed speciation to occur. Within individual islands, volcanoes are barriers. Species of animals may be isolated within the valleys caused by lava flows. They are not able to cross the high ridges into neighboring valleys to breed with related populations. Given enough time, all separated populations will tend to develop genetic isolation and become separate species.

What are three kinds of geographic barriers?

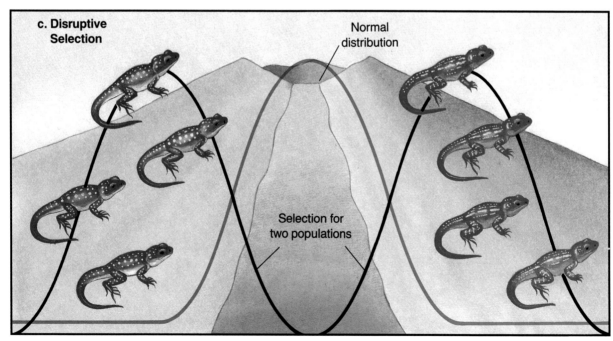

c. Disruptive Selection

Normal distribution

Selection for two populations

Reproductive isolation occurs when formerly interbreeding groups of organisms are prevented from producing fertile offspring. There are many different types of reproductive isolation. One type of reproductive isolation is seasonal. If one group of lizards, for example, normally mates in April and another group mates in June, these two groups are reproductively isolated. Many related plant species are reproductively isolated because they have different flowering times. Another type of reproductive isolation is polyploidy. Many species of plants arose by polyploidy. If a polyploid strawberry plant is fertilized by sperm from the diploid parent population, the hybrid will be sterile because the extra set of chromosomes can't segregate normally during meiosis. This hybrid sterility ensures the genetic equilibrium of the polyploid population. A population of polyploids can be produced in only a few generations. This is an example of rapid speciation. Reproductive isolation may eventually lead to the formation of new species. The greater the difference in environment between the parent population and the isolated population, and the smaller the two populations, as on islands, the more rapidly speciation occurs.

10:12 Patterns of Evolution

The Galapagos finches all evolved from a common ancestral species that probably arrived one time from the mainland. Such an evolutionary pattern, where related species become less alike, is called **divergent evolution.** Divergent evolution occurs as species are formed. At first, the new species are similar to the ancestral species. As time goes on, however, the new species each become

Galapagos Islands

Warbler finch

Woodpecker finch

Large cactus finch

Small tree finch

Large ground finch

Small ground finch

FIGURE 10–14.

Darwin's finches illustrate adaptive radiation that has resulted in different shapes and sizes of beaks that suit different feeding habits.

adapted to their new environments and become less and less alike. These island bird species all have different adaptations that suit each island. Figure 10–14 shows some of these adaptations. These finches are a result of **adaptive radiation,** the process by which members of species adapt to a variety of environmental conditions and radiate out into several separate species through divergent evolution followed by isolation.

What is adaptive radiation?

The process by which unrelated taxonomic groups become more similar is called **convergent evolution.** This pattern of evolution is shown when two groups of unrelated species adapt to the same kind of environment. Cacti that grow in the American desert and euphorbs that grow in African deserts have developed the same kinds of adaptations to dry, desert conditions. Fleshy stems are adaptations for water storage, and spines are adaptations for protection and for reduction of water loss. These examples of convergent evolution show how the environment has an important selective effect on the evolution of a species.

FIGURE 10–15.

Two animals, such as a hummingbird and a hummingbird moth, that look alike but are classified in different phyla are the result of convergent evolution.

REVIEW

11. Describe two mechanisms that alter allele frequency in a gene pool.
12. Compare convergent and divergent evolution.
13. Give two examples of how isolation can result in speciation.
14. **SKILL REVIEW:** Make three graphs that show the effects of stabilizing, directional, and disruptive selection on a population. For more help, refer to Organizing Information in the Skill Handbook, pages 810 to 813.
15. **USING CONCEPTS:** Two different species of squirrels live on opposite sides of the Grand Canyon. They are obviously closely related. Describe a mechanism for the evolution of these two species.

CHAPTER REVIEW

SUMMARY

1. There are four kinds of fossils. The fossil record provides evidence of evolution. **10:1**
2. Homologous, vestigial, and analogous structures indicate species relationships. **10:2**
3. Comparative embryology shows relationships among vertebrates. Related species have similar RNA and DNA sequences. **10:3, 10:4**
4. Lamarck explained evolution as the inheritance of acquired characteristics. Darwin developed a theory of natural selection based on the gradual accumulation of inherited traits. **10:5, 10:6**
5. Structural, physiological, and behavioral are three main types of adaptations. **10:7**
6. Gradualism and punctuated equilibrium are two different rates of evolution. **10:8**
7. Genetic equilibrium is altered by mutation, genetic drift, and gene flow. Stabilizing, directional, and disruptive selection are three types of natural selection. **10:9, 10:10**
8. Speciation results from the permanent isolation of groups of a population. **10:11**
9. Divergence, convergence, and adaptive radiation are three patterns of evolution. **10:12**

LANGUAGE OF BIOLOGY

acquired
  characteristics
adaptive radiation
allele frequency
analogous structures
camouflage
convergent evolution
directional selection
disruptive selection
divergent evolution
embryo
gene flow
gene pool

genetic drift
genetic equilibrium
geographic isolation
gradualism
homologous structures
mimicry
natural selection
punctuated equilibrium
reproductive isolation
speciation
stabilizing selection
vestigial structures

Choose the word or phrase from the list above that completes the sentence.

1. _____ involves the movement of individuals into or out of a population.
2. _____ has occurred when two unrelated species have similar adaptations.
3. The natural process by which adaptations are maintained in a population is _____.
4. Evolution of several species from a single common ancestor is _____.
5. _____ were functional in an ancestor, but appear to have no present function.
6. A type of adaptation that hides an individual in its surroundings is _____.
7. A change in the allele frequency of a population by chance events is called _____.
8. An early stage of an organism's development is a(n) _____.
9. _____ are attained during a lifetime.
10. The formation of new species is called _____.

REVIEWING CONCEPTS

Choose the word or phrase that completes the sentence or answers the question.

11. _____ structures have similar appearances and are derived from the same body parts.
    a. Analogous   c. Vestigial
    b. Homologous   d. None of these
12. A type of adaptation that offers protection to an organism by imitation is _____.
    a. camouflage   c. mimicry
    b. genetic drift   d. acquired
13. _____ is a slow and steady pattern of evolution.
    a. Speciation
    b. Gradualism
    c. Genetic drift
    d. Punctuated equilibrium
14. A _____ contains all the alleles in a population.
    a. genetic   c. gene frequency
       equilibrium
    b. genetic drift   d. gene pool

15. The presence of ____ in vertebrate embryos provides evidence for evolution.

   a. limbs   c. a tail

   b. lungs   d. an exoskeleton

16. Giraffes evolved long necks by ____.

   a. stretching   c. natural selection

   b. stabilization   d. isolation

17. Adaptive radiation occurs when separated groups of a species adapt to new ____.

   a. traits   c. camouflage

   b. environments   d. convergence

18. Ribosomal ____ is similar in all organisms.

   a. proteins   c. DNA

   b. RNA   d. cytochrome *c*

19. A(n) ____ fossil is formed when the hard parts of an organism are filled in with minerals.

   a. petrified   c. mold

   b. imprint   d. cast

20. Polyploidy results in ____ isolation.

   a. adaptive   c. geographic

   b. stabilizing   d. reproductive

UNDERSTANDING CONCEPTS

Answer the following questions using complete sentences.

21. Compare three methods of natural selection.

22. Outline two kinds of evidence Darwin used to support his theory.

23. Why does genetic drift have a greater effect on small than large populations?

24. Summarize the theory of natural selection.

25. How does geographic isolation cause speciation?

26. How did Darwin explain the long necks of giraffes?

27. Explain why the wings of bats and butterflies are examples of convergent evolution.

28. What is punctuated equilibrium?

29. Compare camouflage and mimicry.

30. How can mutations affect the gene pool?

APPLYING CONCEPTS

Answer the following questions using complete sentences.

31. In a population of snails, the shells are a mix of three patterns. In a sample of fossils of the same species, the number of patterns is fifteen. Explain how selection might have caused this change.

32. If a population of palm trees were planted on a mountain in the Rockies, would you expect them to evolve into a new species? Explain.

33. Many poisonous plants and animals have striking patterns of red and black colors. How and why might this similarity have evolved?

34. Humans and chimpanzees share 98.8 percent of their DNA sequences. Humans and gorillas share 98.6 percent. What are the relationships among these three primates?

35. In a population, flower color is represented by two alleles. The population consists of 10 *BB* flowers, 20 *Bb* flowers, and 10 *bb* flowers. What are the allele frequencies?

EXTENSIONS

1. Make models of homologous structures and label the parts to show which are similar.

2. Make a collection of fossils, identify each one, and describe where and when it was found.

READINGS

Gould, Stephen Jay. "A Tale of Three Pictures." *Natural History,* May 1988, pp. 14–21.

Plage, Mary, and Dieter Plage. "Galapagos Wildlife Under Pressure." *National Geographic,* Jan. 1988, pp. 122–145.

Chapter 11

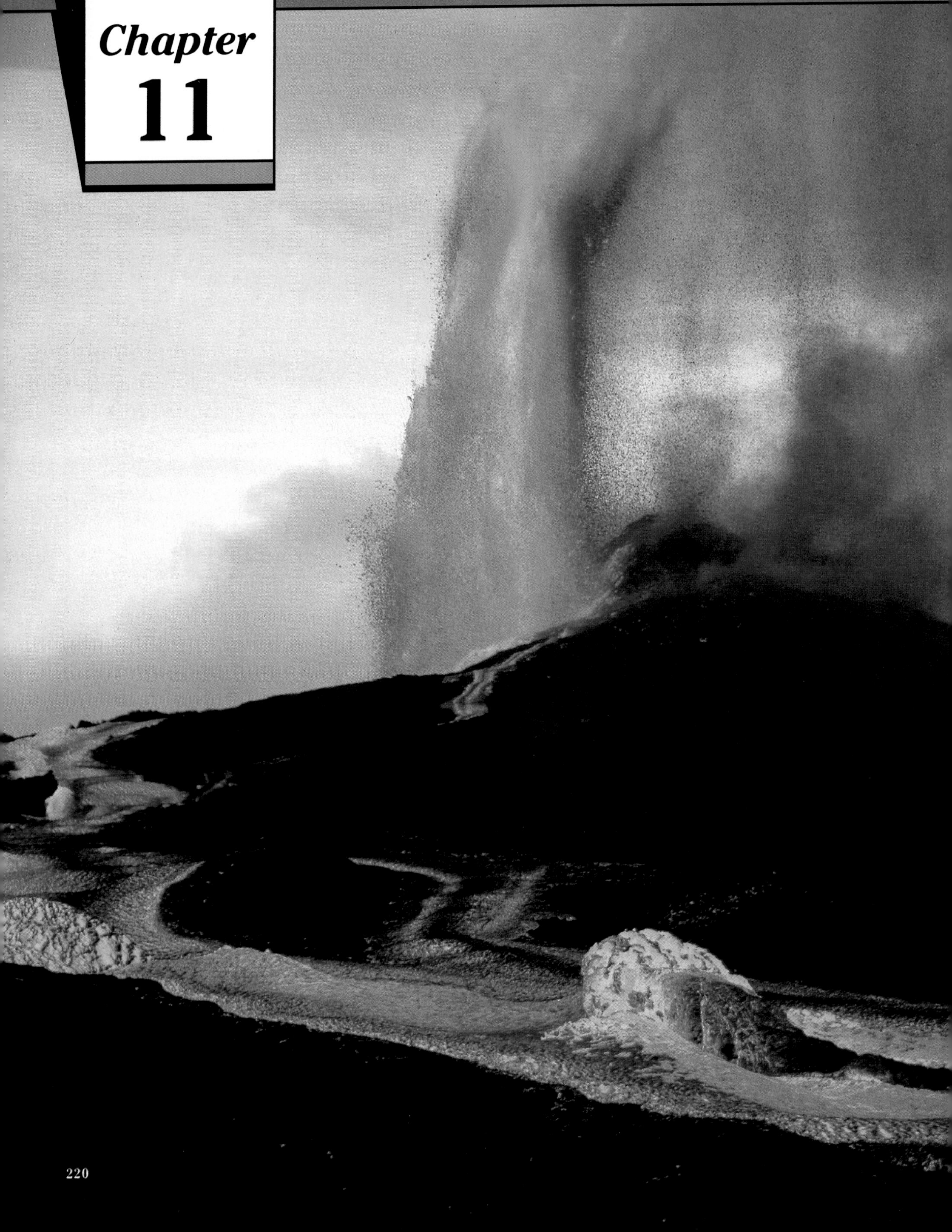

THE HISTORY OF LIFE

H ow did life on Earth begin? Do present-day life-forms
resemble life-forms of long ago, such as the ancient
trilobite on this page? In this chapter, you will explore
the scientific evidence that helps answer these questions. Some of
the early beliefs about how life began may surprise you. Today,
life's origins are explained in terms of biological, chemical, and
geological processes. You will find that the answers to how life on
Earth began are incomplete. As with many important questions,
one answer gives rise to many other questions.

Trilobite fossil

ORIGINS

When you look up at the stars at night, you might assume that the
light you see is being made as you see it. In fact, some of the light
from the most distant stars has traveled through space for millions
of years before reaching your eyes. The distance light travels from
the stars to Earth supplies us with clues about the age of the universe
and the age of Earth. It is difficult for the human mind to grasp a
time span covering billions of years. However, scientists have a great
deal of evidence that Earth formed four to five billion years ago.

In this section you will study hypotheses about the formation of
Earth. You also will study some of the early ideas about how life
originated on Earth.

Objectives:
- describe the atmosphere on Earth
  before life evolved.
- explain plate tectonics and how it
  accounts for the locations of continents and oceans today.
- relate the idea of spontaneous
  generation.
- describe experimental evidence
  that disproved spontaneous generation in favor of biogenesis.

11:1 The Origin of Earth

Hypotheses that account for the formation of Earth describe the
young planet as an inhospitable place. Volcanoes spewed out poisonous gases. Lava lakes, kept hot by the molten interior of Earth, dotted
the landscape. Earth was much too hot for life to exist. About 3.8 to
3.9 billion years ago, Earth had cooled enough for water vapor to
condense. Imagine the first violent rains falling to Earth to form its
oceans. Although Earth became cooler, most places on Earth still
weren't suitable places for life forms to inhabit.

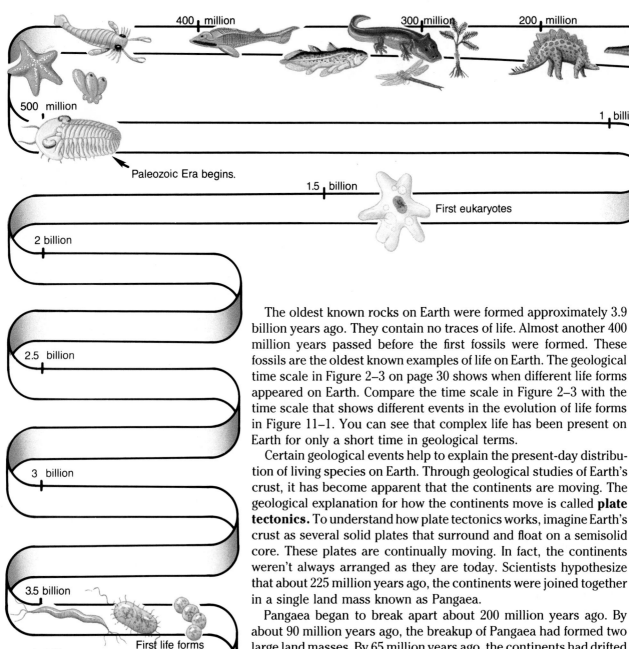

400 million

300 million

200 million

500 million

1 billion

Paleozoic Era begins.

1.5 billion

First eukaryotes

2 billion

2.5 billion

3 billion

3.5 billion

4 billion years ago

First life forms

FIGURE 11–1.

The first life appeared on Earth about 3.5 billion years ago. Another three billion years passed before the enormous array of life forms seen in the fossil record and on Earth today evolved.

The oldest known rocks on Earth were formed approximately 3.9 billion years ago. They contain no traces of life. Almost another 400 million years passed before the first fossils were formed. These fossils are the oldest known examples of life on Earth. The geological time scale in Figure 2–3 on page 30 shows when different life forms appeared on Earth. Compare the time scale in Figure 2–3 with the time scale that shows different events in the evolution of life forms in Figure 11–1. You can see that complex life has been present on Earth for only a short time in geological terms.

Certain geological events help to explain the present-day distribution of living species on Earth. Through geological studies of Earth's crust, it has become apparent that the continents are moving. The geological explanation for how the continents move is called **plate tectonics.** To understand how plate tectonics works, imagine Earth's crust as several solid plates that surround and float on a semisolid core. These plates are continually moving. In fact, the continents weren't always arranged as they are today. Scientists hypothesize that about 225 million years ago, the continents were joined together in a single land mass known as Pangaea.

Pangaea began to break apart about 200 million years ago. By about 90 million years ago, the breakup of Pangaea had formed two large land masses. By 65 million years ago, the continents had drifted far enough apart that they were in the shapes we recognize today. During the Eocene Epoch, about 55 million years ago, the continents reached the approximate locations that you see on a globe today.

Evidence from plate tectonics indicates that the continents and other plates are still moving. The San Andreas fault in California is a line where two plates are sliding past each other. Continental mountain ranges build up where continents run into one another through plate movement. Examples of such mountainous areas include the Alps and the Himalayas. Oceanic mountain chains are also a product of plate tectonics. If you look at a map, you can see that island chains like Hawaii appear to be made of smaller and smaller

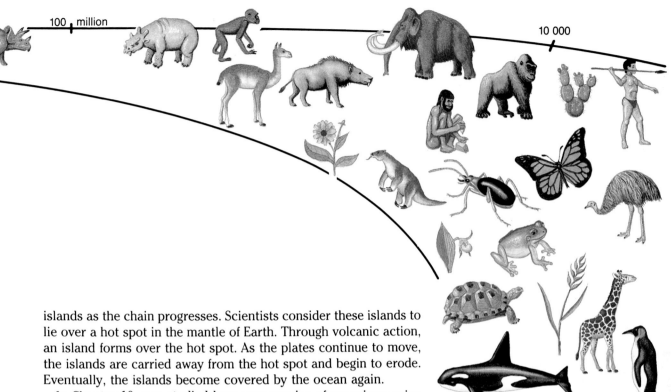

islands as the chain progresses. Scientists consider these islands to lie over a hot spot in the mantle of Earth. Through volcanic action, an island forms over the hot spot. As the plates continue to move, the islands are carried away from the hot spot and begin to erode. Eventually, the islands become covered by the ocean again.

In Chapter 10, you studied how new species of organisms arise when geographic isolation occurs. Plate tectonics is one mechanism that causes geographic isolation. As land masses break away and separate, populations of plants and animals become isolated. Over periods of time, these isolated populations adapt to changing environments and new species may arise.

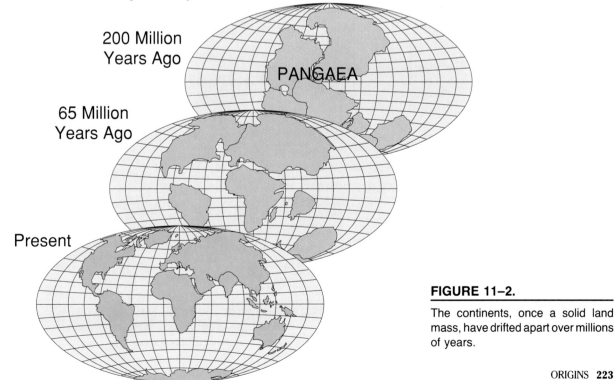

FIGURE 11–2.

The continents, once a solid land mass, have drifted apart over millions of years.

11:2 The Origin of Life: Early Ideas

Now that you have studied the conditions that existed when Earth was a young planet, you are probably wondering where life came from. This question has concerned people for thousands of years. People once believed that life could arise from inanimate materials, an idea known as **spontaneous generation.** Several observations led people to believe in spontaneous generation. Bacteria seemed to form directly from dust in the air. Tadpoles appeared to develop from mud at the bottoms of ponds. Rotting meat apparently gave rise to maggots. In the early 17th century, a Belgian physician devised a recipe for obtaining mice from wheat kernels. He claimed to have produced mice by wrapping wheat germ in a dirty shirt that provided a "generating principle," present in human sweat.

Francesco Redi, an Italian physician, was the first scientist to use experimental evidence gained from a rigorously followed scientific method to disprove spontaneous generation. In 1668, he described a series of experiments that demonstrated that the little white maggots found in rotting meat were actually fly larvae. In developing his hypothesis about the origin of these larvae, Redi first observed that maggots became flies and that flies were always found near decaying meat. Perhaps, he hypothesized, flies laid eggs that hatched into maggots that turned into flies. Follow the steps of Redi's experiment in Figure 11–3. Redi's experiments convinced people that larger animals, animals that could be seen by the unaided eye, needed parents and did not arise spontaneously. But microbes were a different matter. People speculated that microbes were too small to have parents. Therefore, most people refused to totally give up the idea of spontaneous generation.

Describe Francesco Redi's experiment.

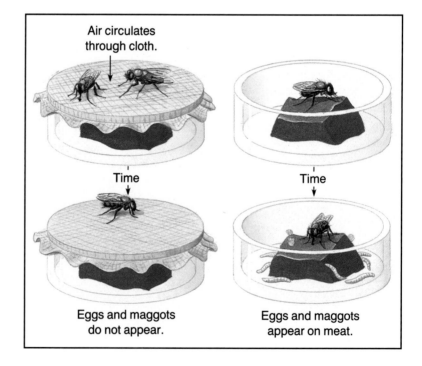

Air circulates through cloth.

Time

Time

Eggs and maggots do not appear.

Eggs and maggots appear on meat.

FIGURE 11–3.

Redi's experiments showed that maggots did not spontaneously generate in meat.

FIGURE 11–4.

Spallanzani's experiments convinced some scientists that spontaneous generation did not occur.

Broth is boiled.

Flask is sealed.

No growth of microbes.

In the 1700s, an English scientist named John Needham tried to show that bacteria could arise spontaneously in flasks of broth. He boiled meat broth for several minutes, then sealed the flasks loosely with cork stoppers. After several days, he examined the broth and found that bacteria were growing in it. He concluded that the bacteria arose from the broth.

About 25 years later, in 1765, an Italian biologist named Lazzaro Spallanzani challenged Needham's work. Spallanzani demonstrated that Needham had not boiled the broth long enough to kill all the bacteria it contained. He also maintained that Needham had not closed the flasks tightly enough. Look at Spallanzani's experimental setup in Figure 11–4. Spallanzani's work convinced a few scientists that spontaneous generation did not occur in microbes. However, some people charged that Spallanzani killed the "vital force," a mysterious property of air that allowed life to begin, when he boiled the broth. When Spallanzani sealed the container, they argued, he kept out this "vital force."

People once thought that frogs arose from the muck at the bottom of ponds.

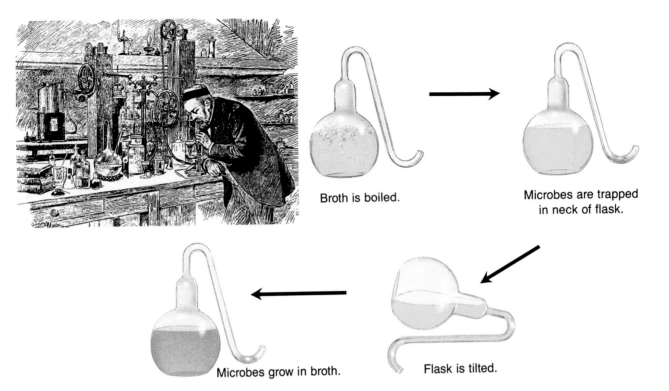

Broth is boiled.

Microbes are trapped in neck of flask.

Flask is tilted.

Microbes grow in broth.

FIGURE 11–5.

Pasteur's swan-necked flasks prevented microbes from entering the broth but allowed air to circulate. The photo shows some of the equipment Pasteur used.

The idea of spontaneous generation was finally disproved by Louis Pasteur in 1864. Pasteur did not believe in "vital forces." He thought that all cells came from other cells. Microbes must be in the air, he hypothesized. Pasteur made flasks with the necks bent to resemble the necks of swans, Figure 11–5. Air could get to the broth in the flask, but dust particles would settle in the curves of the neck. If a "vital force" existed, it would be able to get to the liquid. No microbes developed in these specially designed flasks. When Pasteur poured liquid into the neck and then tilted the flask so that the liquid entered the main flask, bacteria grew. Thus, he proved that the microbes in the flasks came from microbes carried on dust particles in the air, not from the air itself. Pasteur laid to rest the controversy surrounding spontaneous generation. In doing so, he provided support for **biogenesis,** the theory that life comes only from other life.

REVIEW

1. What was the atmosphere on Earth like before life appeared?
2. How does plate tectonics affect speciation?
3. Why is Louis Pasteur credited with disproving spontaneous generation?
4. **SKILL REVIEW:** What portion of a pie graph would represent the time period from the breakup of Pangaea to the present? For more help, refer to Organizing Information in the Skill Handbook, pages 810 to 813.
5. **USING CONCEPTS:** Why have no fossils dating back to Earth's origins been found?

THE ORIGIN OF LIFE ON EARTH

The concept of biogenesis has been accepted by biologists for over 100 years. However, biogenesis does not answer one of the most basic questions. Where did the first living thing come from? In this section you will study a model for the origin of life on Earth.

11:3 The Origin of Life: Modern Ideas

You have seen that the Earth of several billion years ago was very different from today's Earth. The atmosphere had no free oxygen as it does today. Instead, the air was probably made of water vapor, hydrogen, methane, and ammonia. These gases were also dissolved in the oceans, just as the gases of today's atmosphere are. In addition, the early oceans contained many other elements and simple compounds. In the 1930s, Alexander Oparin, a Soviet scientist, proposed that life began in these early oceans. He suggested that energy from ultraviolet radiation and lightning could produce chemical reactions in the air. Such reactions would form simple organic compounds such as amino acids and nitrogen bases, the building blocks of nucleic acids. Rain would carry these molecules into the oceans, where a kind of "primordial soup," a mixture containing all the ingredients necessary for life, would form. Oparin suggested that these molecules reacted with each other and, over very long periods of time, formed the complex molecules found in living things.

Objectives:
- state Oparin's hypothesis and list the evidence that supports it.
- describe the evolution of prokaryotes and compare early prokaryotes with living prokaryotes.
- describe the evidence that supports the symbiosis hypothesis.

FIGURE 11–6.

Using the setup shown in this illustration, Miller and Urey were able to synthesize several kinds of organic compounds.

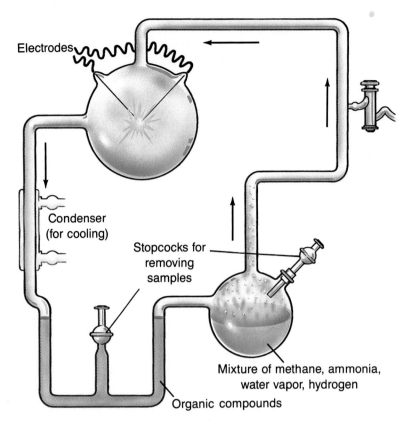

Electrodes

Condenser (for cooling)

Stopcocks for removing samples

Mixture of methane, ammonia, water vapor, hydrogen

Organic compounds

This chemical evolution that Oparin hypothesized still didn't explain how life originated. The complex molecules of living things are enclosed in membranes to form cells. Oparin realized that this enclosure or encapsulation would have had to occur before life could arise. He also knew that membrane-enclosed units couldn't be called "life" unless they could grow, metabolize, and reproduce.

In 1953, Oparin's hypothesis was tested by Stanley Miller and Harold Urey, two American scientists. Miller and Urey placed a mixture of gases into a flask containing water. These gases were in the proportions believed present in the primitive atmosphere of Earth. As you can see in Figure 11–6, the flask was subjected to electrical sparks that simulated lightning. Miller and Urey also repeatedly heated and cooled the mixture, simulating changes in daily temperatures. After a week of such treatment, they analyzed the chemicals in the flask. They found amino acids, sugars, and other organic compounds just as Oparin had predicted.

Since Miller and Urey's experiments, scientists have produced conditions leading to the formation of several other molecules found in living things. They have shown that amino acids will link together to form polypeptide chains when heated in the absence of oxygen. Nucleic acids and ATP also have been formed. Other experiments have shown that proteins can clump together to form spherical structures called microspheres. Microspheres resemble cells, but they don't contain nucleic acids or enzymes. They may represent an early stage in the development of life.

BIOLAB *Microspheres* **11**

Problem: How are microspheres produced?

Materials

microscope
microscope slide
coverslip
50-mL graduated
  cylinder
50-mL Erlenmeyer
  flask (2)
500-mL beaker
1% NaCl solution
  (5 mL)
aspartic acid (0.5 g)
glutamic acid (0.5 g)
glycine (0.5 g)

hot plate
ring stand
ring stand clamp
tongs
watch
stirring rod
pipette
apron
oven mits (2)
goggles

Procedures

1. Pour 250 mL of water into the beaker.
2. Place the beaker on the hot plate.
   CAUTION: *Use care when working with the hot plate.*
3. Clamp one of the flasks to the ring stand.
4. Add 0.5 g each of aspartic acid, glutamic acid, and glycine to the flask. Use the stirring rod to mix these amino acids thoroughly.
5. When the water in the beaker begins to boil, carefully loosen the clamp and lower the flask into the water. Tighten the clamp.
6. Heat the amino acids for 20 minutes.
7. Measure and pour 5 mL of the 1% NaCl solution into the second flask. Place this second flask on the hot plate.
8. When the NaCl solution begins to boil, use tongs to remove the second flask from the hot plate. Slowly add the NaCl solution to the amino acids. Turn off the hot plate.
9. Loosen the clamp on the ring stand and raise the flask containing the amino acid solution out of the beaker. **CAUTION:** *Use care when handling hot objects. Be sure to wear oven mits.* Allow the contents of the flask to cool for 10 minutes.
10. Make a wet mount using one drop of the mixture and observe under low power. Diagram a microsphere.

11. Switch to high power to examine the microspheres. Diagram a microsphere under high power.
12. After you have finished observing the microspheres, clean and return all equipment to its proper place. **CAUTION:** *Be sure the hot plate has cooled sufficiently before putting it away.*

Data and Observations

Diagram	
Low power	
High power	

Questions and Conclusion

1. How does the method you used to generate microspheres compare with the conditions present on primitive Earth?
2. How do microspheres resemble cells? How are they different?
3. What features of living things do microspheres exhibit?
4. Compare your experimental setup with that of Stanley Miller.

Conclusion: How can microspheres be produced in the lab?

FIGURE 11–7.

This step-by-step series of events is one explanation for how cells formed.

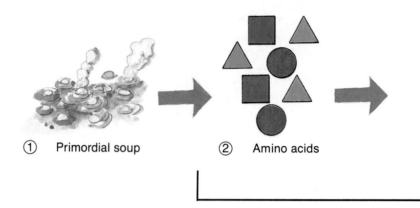

① Primordial soup   ② Amino acids

You have seen how chemicals necessary for life may have formed, but how did these chemicals combine to form the first cells? American scientist Sidney Fox and his colleagues have proposed a step-by-step series of events to explain how cells formed. Study these steps in Figure 11–7. According to Fox, Miller and Urey's experiment reached step 2. In further experiments, Fox has been able to produce protocells (step 4). A **protocell** is a large, ordered molecule that has some activities associated with life. Protocells simulate cell division and energy metabolism.

Although protocells have been produced experimentally, attempts to synthesize cells containing nucleic acids have failed. One obstacle to the synthesis of living cells in the laboratory is the lack of time. Scientists propose that it may have taken a billion years for the first cell to develop.

How do Fox's results compare to those of Miller and Urey?

11:4 The Origin of Prokaryotes

The first cells on Earth were most likely prokaryotic, having no membranes surrounding their nuclear material. A membrane could have arisen through mutation and been retained through natural selection. These first cells would have been anaerobic, since the early atmosphere contained no oxygen. They also would have been heterotrophs, organisms that use the organic compounds in their environment for food. Autotrophs, organisms that produce their own food, couldn't have survived in the atmosphere of primitive Earth. Autotrophs require carbon dioxide, not present in the primitive atmosphere, and specific organelles to carry out photosynthesis.

The first organisms to appear in the fossil record lived about 3.5 billion years ago. These fossil remains are called microfossils. A **microfossil** is a microscopic fossil that is either spherical in shape or a filament composed of short rods. Microfossils probably were not the first living cells, but descendants of them. The oldest known microfossil is an **archaebacterium,** a cell that resembles a very simple bacterium. Archaebacteria are adapted to life in very hostile

archaebacteria:
  archaios (GK) ancient
  bakteron (GK) little staff

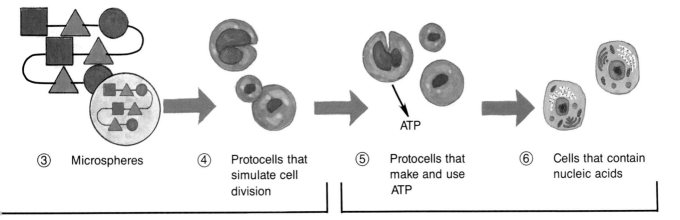

③ Microspheres   ④ Protocells that simulate cell division   ⑤ Protocells that make and use ATP   ⑥ Cells that contain nucleic acids

Presently accomplished   Modeled in experiments

environments. Archaebacteria live in salt ponds, acid waters, or hot sulfur springs. These environments are similar to the ones that are proposed to have been on Earth when life first began.

The next type of prokaryote to evolve probably had the ability to carry on photosynthesis. Photosynthetic prokaryotes would have had an advantage over heterotrophs because of their ability to manufacture food from carbon dioxide and water when organic nutrients become scarce. The cell structure and organization of early microfossils indicate that they were indeed photosynthetic organisms. Photosynthetic organisms produce oxygen, which would have changed the composition of the early atmosphere over time. Organisms adapted to using atmospheric oxygen in aerobic respiration would have evolved. There are indications in the fossil record that major changes in the atmosphere led to the development of different and more complex microorganisms about 2.8 billion years ago.

FIGURE 11–8.

The oldest microfossils are archaebacteria, organisms that are adapted to especially hot, salty, or acidic environments such as found in this hot spring in Yellowstone National Park.

11:5 The Origin of Eukaryotes

The first eukaryotes appeared 1.5 billion years ago. Although scientists do not know exactly how eukaryotes evolved, they speculate that eukaryotes evolved from prokaryotes. Heterotrophic and autotrophic bacteria, both prokaryotes, may have developed symbiotic associations with each other. **Symbiosis** is a close relationship between organisms, often with mutual benefit. In a symbiotic relationship, protection, food, or energy are shared. The **symbiosis hypothesis** suggests that ancestral plant and animal cells may have evolved as a result of symbiotic relationships between large anaerobic prokaryotes and aerobic bacterial cells, Figure 11–9. Over time, the prokaryote hosts and aerobic bacteria lost their ability to live apart. The aerobic bacteria came to function as mitochondria inside their prokaryote hosts. Both the host cells and the bacterial cells continued to divide and grow. When the host divided, some of the bacteria were distributed to each daughter cell. Later, spiral-shaped bacteria may have joined in other symbiotic relationships with the host cell to form flagella and cilia. The resulting cells probably resembled protists in some ways.

Biologists have found similarities between organelles and some prokaryotes that provide evidence for the symbiosis hypothesis. For example, mitochondria resemble bacteria in many ways. Mitochondria and bacteria can reproduce themselves, have similar nucleic

What is the symbiosis hypothesis?

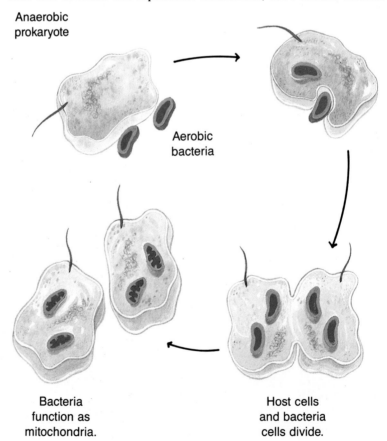

Anaerobic prokaryote

Aerobic bacteria

Bacteria function as mitochondria.

Host cells and bacteria cells divide.

FIGURE 11–9.

The symbiosis hypothesis states that eukaryotes evolved as a result of symbiotic relationships between large, prokaryotic cells and smaller bacterial cells.

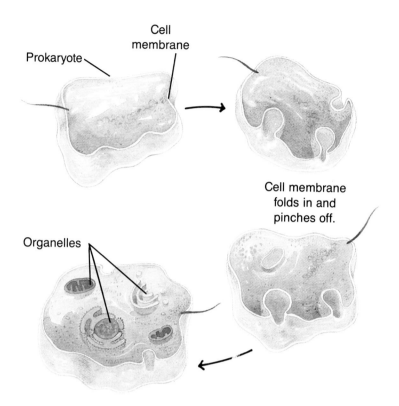

Prokaryote

Cell membrane

Cell membrane folds in and pinches off.

Organelles

FIGURE 11–10.

One hypothesis for the evolution of eukaryotes states that organelles were formed by the folding in of the cell membrane.

acids, are about the same size and shape, and carry on protein synthesis in their ribosomes. Chloroplasts and cyanobacteria also share important characteristics, the most important of which is the ability to carry on photosynthesis.

Another hypothesis to explain the formation of eukaryotes suggests that they evolved directly from prokaryotes. Organelles were formed by the infolding and pinching off of portions of the cell membrane, Figure 11–10. The double membranes of mitochondria and chloroplasts are thought to have arisen in this manner.

REVIEW

6. What was the "primordial soup" and how was it formed?
7. What evidence is there to support the symbiosis hypothesis?
8. Why do scientists think the first living cells were anaerobic, heterotrophic organisms?
9. **SKILL REVIEW:** Make a time line to show the evolution of life from the earliest forms of life to complex eukaryotes. For more help, refer to Reading Science in the Skill Handbook, pages 798 to 799.
10. **USING CONCEPTS:** Why is Oparin's hypothesis so difficult to prove?

THE ORIGIN OF HUMANS

Have you ever put together a jigsaw puzzle? How many pieces did you have to put together before you could recognize the picture? Anthropologists, scientists who study human origins, must piece together human evolution based on the discovery of a few fossil remains. Therefore, it has been difficult to determine the sequence of events leading to the appearance of modern humans. Many scientific fields have provided information to help assemble the few available puzzle pieces into a recognizable picture of human evolution.

11:6 Primates

Humans, monkeys, and apes belong to an order of mammals called the **primates.** Primates share several characteristics that have led scientists to suggest that all primates evolved from a common ancestor. Notice in Figure 11–11 that the evolution of primates that are alive today began about 40 million years ago. Humans and apes are thought to have evolved from a more recent common ancestor and are, therefore, more closely related to each other than to monkeys.

Compare the relatedness of humans and apes with that of humans and monkeys.

All primates share certain characteristics. They have a highly developed sense of vision. Their eyes face forward, allowing them

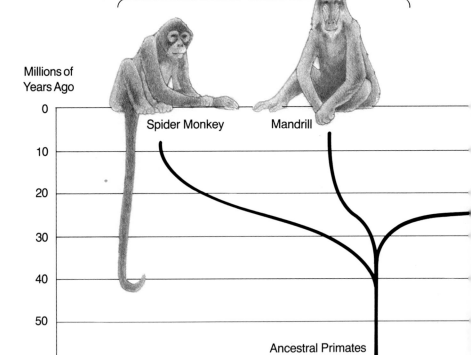

FIGURE 11–11.

Present-day primate groups began to evolve about 40 million years ago from ancestral primates that probably resembled the tarsier (left photo), a primitive primate. Primates share certain characteristics, including eyes that face forward, rotating forelimbs, and opposable thumbs.

to see objects in three dimensions. This type of vision is known as stereo vision. The eyes of most other animals are located on opposite sides of their heads. This feature allows them to see in two different directions simultaneously. Primates have more complex brains than any other animal group. Brain complexity has enabled primates to adapt to a wide variety of environments.

All primates have flexible shoulders and rotating forelimbs. In tree-dwelling primates, these characteristics allow them to swing easily from branch to branch. Most primates have an opposable thumb, allowing them to cross the tip of the thumb over the palm of the hand to touch each of the other four fingers. This adaptation allows primates to grasp things easily. To illustrate the importance of an opposable thumb, tape your thumb to your hand. Pick up your pencil and try to write your name. Imagine how difficult your life would be if you did not have an opposable thumb!

In Chapter 10, you studied that homologous structures provide evidence of common ancestry. The structures of the thumbs, fore-limbs, brain, and eyes all provide evidence that humans and other primates evolved from a common ancestor.

More recent evidence for primate ancestry comes from biochemical studies. For instance, the amino acid sequence for hemoglobin is identical in humans and chimpanzees. Also, studies of nucleotide sequences in the DNA of humans, gorillas, and chimpanzees show remarkable similarities. This evidence suggests a common ancestor for humans and the African apes.

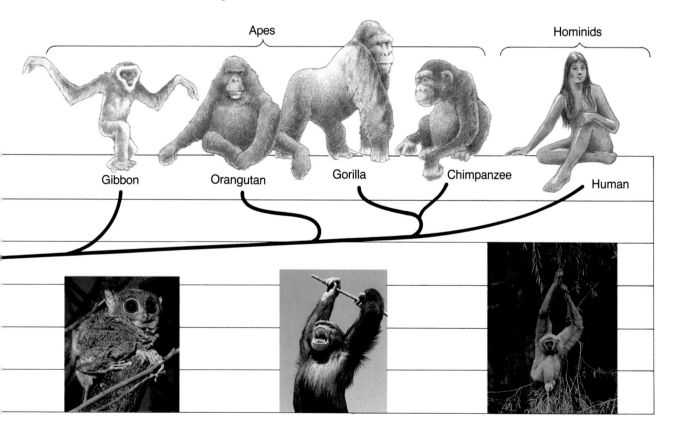

Apes

Hominids

Gibbon   Orangutan   Gorilla   Chimpanzee   Human

11:7 Human Ancestors

In 1924, Raymond Dart, a South African scientist, discovered an unusual skull in Africa. It had a small, ape-like brain cavity, but its teeth and jaw were distinctly humanlike. The opening in the skull, where the spinal column is connected, was on the bottom. This feature indicated that the head was supported by the spinal column and that the organism probably walked upright. Organisms with the ability to walk upright on their hind limbs are **bipedal.** Dart named his discovery ***Australopithecus,*** or "southern ape." Radioactive dating later showed the skull to be two to three million years old.

Since 1924, many fossils of *Australopithecus* have been found in Africa. These human ancestors, along with many others that have been discovered, are known as hominids. A **hominid** is a humanlike, bipedal primate. In 1974, an almost complete skeleton of a small *Australopithecus* female was discovered by Donald Johanson, an American anthropologist, and his colleagues. The fossil was estimated to be 2.9 to 3.4 million years old and was named Lucy by its discoverers. Lucy had a small brain like an ape, yet walked upright like a human, thus ending the debate on whether large brain size or bipedalism evolved first. Many anthropologists today consider humans to have evolved in Africa from ancestors similar to Lucy.

About 40 years after the discovery of *Australopithecus,* in East Africa, anthropologists Louis and Mary Leakey and their son Richard discovered a hominid fossil that created much excitement in the scientific community. This fossil was more similar in form to present-day humans than was *Australopithecus.* It was bipedal but had a larger brain than *Australopithecus.* The Leakeys named this hominid ***Homo habilis,*** the "handy human" because they found simple stone tools near the fossil. *Homo habilis* was dated 1.5 to 2 million years old and was the first hominid known to use tools.

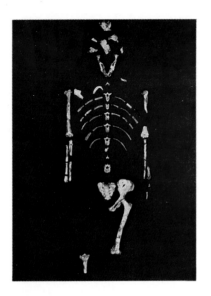

FIGURE 11–12.

The remains of Lucy, a member of the genus *Australopithecus,* are estimated to be 2.9 to 3.4 million years old.

FIGURE 11–13.

Although facial features and height differ among hominid forms, all have an upright stance.

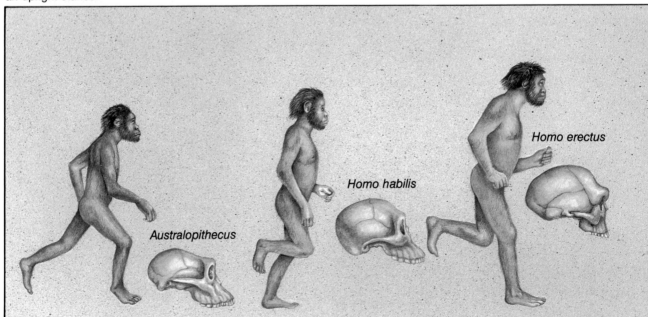

Australopithecus

Homo habilis

Homo erectus

Another important fossil discovery was named **Homo erectus,** "upright human." This hominid lived about 1.5 million years ago. Fossils of *Homo erectus* have been found in Africa, Europe, China, and the island of Java. Most anthropologists agree that *Homo erectus* originated in Africa and migrated to Asia and then to Europe. This group of hominids used well-made stone tools for hunting, and they ate meat and plants. Traces of charred bones indicate that *H. erectus* built fires for cooking and probably also for warmth and protection against predators.

Homo erectus looked somewhat like modern humans. Members of this species had a thick skull, a low forehead, large ridges of bone above the eyes, and a very small chin. The brain size of *Homo erectus* was midway between that of *H. habilis* and modern humans.

11:8 Modern Humans

The fossil record shows that hominids of our own species, **Homo sapiens,** the "wise human," first appeared in Europe about 125 000 years ago. Scientists, however, propose that *H. sapiens* also evolved in Africa. The brain size of early *H. sapiens* was about equal to that of modern humans. There were two main types of early *H. sapiens.* Fossils of the Neanderthal group, the earlier of the two, have been found in Europe and Asia. **Neanderthals** were hominids with short heavy bodies, thick massive bones, small chins, and large brow ridges. Fossils of leg bones indicate that these early humans were about 1.5 m tall. Neanderthals were hunters who killed mammoths, bears, and other large animals with well-made stone tools. These people lived in groups in caves and stone shelters. They buried their dead, sometimes including small ritual objects in the graves. Neanderthals are not a direct ancestor to modern humans.

NoteWorthy

The first recorded human signatures were found in the Lascaux caves of France, where Neanderthals and Cro-Magnons lived. The signatures were formed by the individual placing his or her hand against the wall and blowing pigment around the hand to form a negative image.

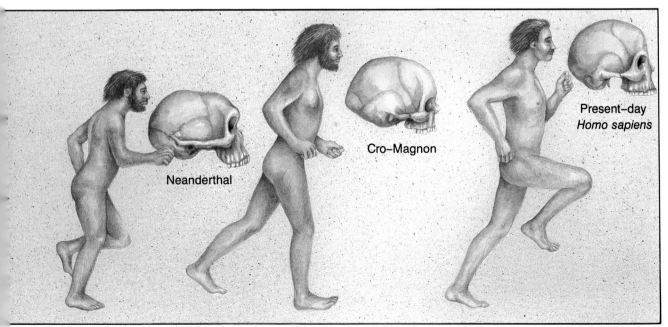

Neanderthal

Cro–Magnon

Present–day
Homo sapiens

FIGURE 11–14.

These spectacular paintings were discovered at the Tassilin-Ajjer Plateau in Algeria. Scientists have been unable to date the paintings.

The second type of early *H. sapiens* was the **Cro-Magnon.** Cro-Magnons looked very much like modern humans. Fossils of Cro-Magnons have been found in Europe, Asia, and Australia. Cro-Magnons had high foreheads, prominent chins, and lacked brow ridges. They stood about 1.8 m tall. They first appeared about 35 000 years ago and are thought to be the direct ancestors of modern humans. Neanderthals and Cro-Magnons lived in the same area and at the same time. Then, the Neanderthals disappeared, probably because they could not compete with Cro-Magnons.

The Cro-Magnons lived in caves and made elaborate stone, wood, and bone tools. They decorated their caves with paintings and stone sculptures. They were very much like people of today. Humans have remained almost unchanged for the past 35 000 years.

REVIEW

11. What evidence is there for a common ancestor for humans and other primates?
12. What is the evolutionary significance of *Australopithecus?*
13. What were the Cro-Magnons?
14. **SKILL REVIEW:** Make a time line sequencing the evolution of hominids during the past 3 million years. For more help, refer to Reading Science in the Skill Handbook, pages 798 to 799.
15. **USING CONCEPTS:** How was an opposable thumb important in the evolution of humans?

CAREER CHOICES

We know that humans are members of the primate order of mammals, an order that evolved about 65 million years ago. *Homo habilis* was a primate believed to be the most recent ancestor of *H. sapiens*, modern humans. But how do we gain information on the evolutionary histories of humans and other organisms? Geneticists, paleontologists, and anthropologists are just a few of the life scientists who study the evolution of organisms.

Microbial geneticists are scientists who study how genes, structures that are composed of DNA, control cellular activity. Many microbial geneticists work for genetic engineering companies. As a microbial geneticist, you might isolate a microorganism and engineer it to perform a certain function, such as breaking down a pollutant or producing an antibiotic. Genetic engineering scientists also inject foreign genes into various microorganisms and observe the results. Microbial geneticists might be involved in conducting studies of amino acid sequences or DNA base sequences of different strains of bacteria. Some microbial geneticists use comparative biochemistry to determine why certain substances made by different life forms have the same functions.

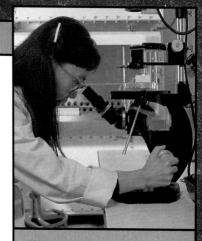
Microbial geneticist

How are dinosaurs related to birds? A **paleontologist** is a life scientist who studies fossils, the remains of plants and animals preserved in Earth's rocks. As a vertebrate paleontologist, you might study evolutionary trends in dinosaurs and try to shed light on why these creatures became extinct 65 million years ago. Although paleontologists are often pictured working with large bones or shells, many of these scientists work with microfossils. Microfossils provide much of the data on plant and animal evolutionary trends that have occurred throughout Earth's four-billion-year history. To gain an understanding of the ancient plant and animal life in an area, a paleontologist might take core samples from a lake bed. These samples would then be analyzed in a lab to determine the ages of the samples and other characteristics, such as chemical makeup. Core samples tell what kinds of aquatic organisms lived in an area, or they may give clues to the age of a lake.

Paleontologist

When did humans first appear on Earth? **Anthropologists** study the evolution of humans. As a physical anthropologist, you might study variations among different populations and species of primates. Your research might involve studying the relationships between diet and growth patterns and disease patterns among humans. A cultural anthropologist might be concerned with human social behavior. As a cultural anthropologist, you might search for similarities and differences between different cultures that provide clues to "human nature." Your work could involve studying different tribes of Indians or different cultures throughout the world.

Anthropologist

CHAPTER REVIEW

SUMMARY

1. The oldest known fossils are 3.5 billion years old. The distribution of organisms on Earth is best explained by plate tectonics. **11:1**
2. Spontaneous generation, the idea that life arose from inanimate materials, was disproved by Redi, Spallanzani, and Pasteur. **11:2**
3. Oparin's hypothesis suggests that life on Earth may have arisen through chemical evolution in a primitive environment consisting of a primordial soup that contained all the ingredients necessary for life. **11:3**
4. Prokaryotes were probably the first cell types. **11:4**
5. The symbiosis hypothesis suggests that the first eukaryotic cells may have evolved from the symbiotic association between several kinds of prokaryotic cells. **11:5**
6. Present-day primates began to evolve approximately 40 million years ago. **11:6**
7. *Australopithecus* was a hominid that lived approximately 3 million years ago and may be an ancestor to humans. **11:7**
8. Neanderthals and Cro-Magnons were two groups of early *Homo sapiens* that exhibited characteristics similar to those of present-day humans. **11:8**

LANGUAGE OF BIOLOGY

archaebacterium
Australopithecus
biogenesis
bipedal
Cro-Magnon
hominid
Homo erectus
Homo habilis
Homo sapiens
microfossil

Neanderthals
plate tectonics
primates
protocell
spontaneous
  generation
symbiosis
symbiosis
  hypothesis

Choose the word or phrase from the list above that completes the sentence.

1. A close relationship between organisms that is usually beneficial is called ____.
2. Humans and apes are part of an order of mammals called the ____.
3. The appearance of life from inanimate materials is known as ____.
4. A large ordered molecule that has some activities associated with life is a(n) ____.
5. The continents and oceans came to be located where they are today by ____.
6. A(n) ____ is a fossil that was a descendant of the first living cell.
7. ____ is a hominid that looks very much like present-day humans.
8. ____ is the idea that all life comes from other life.
9. An animal that walks upright is ____.
10. ____ are *H. sapiens* but are not considered a direct ancestor to modern humans.

REVIEWING CONCEPTS

Choose the word or phrase that completes the sentence or answers the question.

11. The earliest *Homo sapiens* were ____.
    a. Lucy
    b. Neanderthals
    c. Cro-Magnons
    d. *Australopithecus*
12. The oldest known rocks on Earth were formed ____ years ago.
    a. 3.9 million
    b. 3.9 billion
    c. 5 billion
    d. 400 million
13. According to ____, the continents float on a semiliquid core.
    a. biogenesis
    b. Pangaea
    c. plate tectonics
    d. chemical evolution
14. The idea that life arises only from other life is the theory of ____.
    a. evolution
    b. biogenesis
    c. symbiosis
    d. protocells

15. Oparin suggested that the energy needed to produce life came from ____.
    a. lightning
    b. chemical reactions
    c. primordial soup
    d. clay and water

16. ____ have been produced synthetically.
    a. Cells
    b. Archaebacteria
    c. Protocells
    d. Microfossils

17. The oldest microfossils are ____.
    a. protocells
    b. microspheres
    c. mitochondria
    d. archaebacteria

18. Scientists hypothesize that eukaryotes evolved from ____.
    a. microspheres
    b. chloroplasts
    c. prokaryotes
    d. mitochondria

19. ____ are primates.
    a. Apes
    b. Cro-Magnons
    c. Neanderthals
    d. All of the above

20. Lucy was ____.
    a. a Cro-Magnon
    b. bipedal
    c. an ape
    d. a Neanderthal

UNDERSTANDING CONCEPTS

Answer the following questions using complete sentences.

21. How do island chains form?
22. Compare the theories of spontaneous generation and biogenesis.
23. What procedures did Miller and Urey follow to test Oparin's hypothesis?
24. What is the relationship between microspheres and the first cells?
25. Describe the first prokaryotes.
26. What is the probable sequence of events in eukaryote evolution?
27. What characteristics do all primates share?
28. What characteristic of a fossil skull indicates that the animal was bipedal?
29. What are hominids?
30. How was Neanderthal different from modern *Homo sapiens?*

APPLYING CONCEPTS

Answer the following questions using complete sentences.

31. Why was Louis Pasteur's experiment more convincing than Redi's or Spallanzani's?
32. Why are front-facing eyes an important adaptive advantage in human evolution?
33. Why would you expect mountain ranges to form in straight lines?
34. Which kingdom of living things was the first to evolve?
35. Explain why you think that synthetic life may or may never be formed in the laboratory.

EXTENSIONS

1. Prepare a report on the recent findings of anthropologists that suggest how early humans may have lived.
2. Visit a zoo. Collect information on the behavior of a particular primate, such as a gorilla. Decide which behaviors you believe are parallel to those in humans.
3. Make a collection of fossils. Do library research to find out their relative ages. Suggest what Earth may have been like when the organisms were alive.

READINGS

Garrett, Wilbur E. "Where Did We Come From?" *National Geographic,* Oct. 1988, pp. 434–438.

Leakey, Richard and Alan Walker. *"Homo erectus Unearthed." National Geographic,* Nov. 1985, pp. 624–629.

Rigaud, Jeane-Philippe. "Art Treasures from the Ice Age Lascaux Cave." *National Geographic,* Oct. 1988, pp. 440–499.

MICROBIOLOGY

Where the telescope ends, the microscope begins.
Which of the two has the grander view?

Victor Hugo
Les Miserables

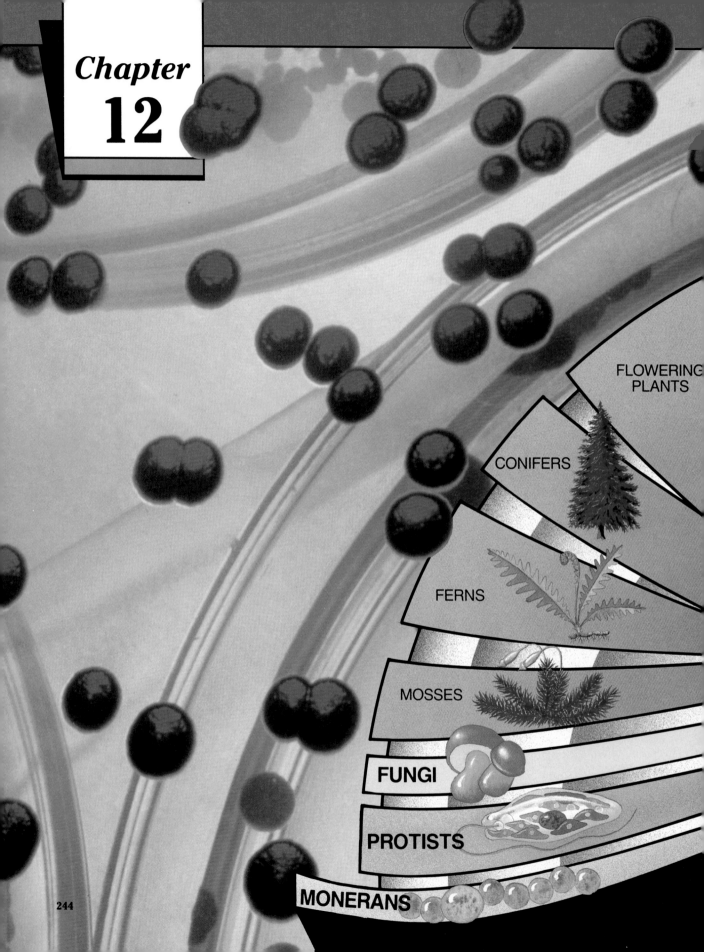

FLOWERING
PLANTS

CONIFERS

FERNS

MOSSES

FUNGI

PROTISTS

MONERANS

VIRUSES AND MONERANS

I t is estimated that millions of people of all ages have colds
each year. The common cold is caused by particles called
viruses. Viruses are smaller than the smallest known cell.
You know from the reports of research on AIDS that viruses
cause many diseases other than colds.

It is hard to believe that so much discomfort is caused by
something so small. When you have a cold you may also have
complications such as a strep throat or an ear infection. These
are diseases caused by bacteria in the Kingdom Monera. Bacteria
grow everywhere, even on a pinpoint. In the laboratory, bacteria
grow in colonies, such as those in the petri dish to the left. In
this chapter, you will learn about both viruses and monerans.

Bacteria on a pinpoint

VIRUSES

If people were the size of viruses, you and everyone else in the
United States would fit on the end of two pencil erasers with room
left over for future generations. Viruses are visible only with the help
of an electron microscope. They are not living organisms. Viruses
appear to be a bridge between living and nonliving things.

12:1 The Nature of Viruses

In Chapter 1, you learned that living things have some very specific
properties that set them apart as being alive. Living things move,
feed, and respond. They are made up of cells, grow, and reproduce.
Viruses, on the other hand, are complex submicroscopic organic
particles that have almost none of the life characteristics listed
above. It is almost easier to describe a virus by what it isn't. They
are not cells. They carry out no life functions on their own. Many
viruses can be crystallized and stored for years in this state, yet still
cause disease when placed in contact with living cells. Viruses do
replicate themselves, but only after they have invaded a living cell.
Viruses are parasites. They disrupt the lives of the cells they invade.
Viruses are found in air, water, and soil. They enter the body through
the skin, by way of food and drink, and by being inhaled.

Objectives:
- describe the parts of a virus.
- describe three characteristics used to classify viruses.
- distinguish between the lytic and lysogenic cycles of viruses.
- describe ways in which the body is defended from viral attack.
- describe the origin and history of viruses.

Bacterial colonies on agar in a petri dish

A virus is a particle made up of a nucleic acid core and a protein coat called a capsid. All living cells contain both DNA and RNA. In contrast, the core of a virus is made up of either DNA or RNA, but not both. Therefore, there are DNA viruses and RNA viruses. Human polio virus contains RNA as its nucleic acid. Human smallpox virus contains DNA. The nucleic acids in viruses are organized into genes. The smallest viruses have ten or fewer genes. Large viruses have as many as 500 genes. Cells in your body, by contrast, have thousands of genes arranged on chromosomes.

In addition to a capsid, some viruses have an outer covering called an envelope. Envelopes may have extensions, filaments, and tails made of protein. All of these spare parts help a virus attach itself to the surface of the cells of particular hosts. Some viruses attack only specific cells, such as skin, salivary glands, or nerves. Many viruses are species specific, attacking only specific organisms. Species within all five kingdoms of organisms have viruses that affect them.

12:2 Classification of Viruses

Viruses are classified according to a number of different characteristics. Shape, nucleic acid content, the presence or absence of an envelope, the type of host affected, and how they are transmitted are some of the methods used to classify viruses.

Viruses have four basic shapes. They are polyhedral or many sided, spherical, rodshaped, or many sided with a tail. The herpes virus, which causes cold sores, is a polygon with twenty sides. The tobacco mosaic virus (TMV) that causes yellow spotting on tobacco leaves is rod-shaped. The AIDS virus has a spherical envelope with extensions over its surface. Some viruses that infect bacteria have a head and a tail with leglike extensions.

Table 12–1 shows the classification of viruses according to their DNA or RNA content and some animal diseases they cause.

FIGURE 12–1.

Virus particles have a variety of shapes.

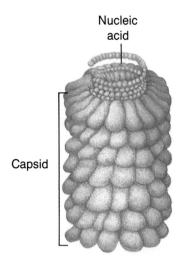

Nucleic acid

Capsid

Tobacco Mosaic Virus
(rod shaped)

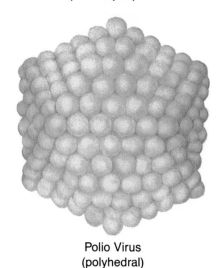

Polio Virus
(polyhedral)

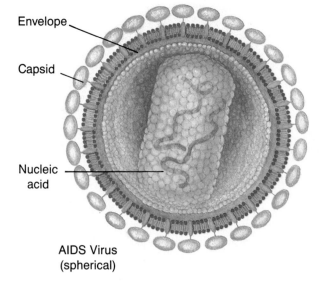

Envelope

Capsid

Nucleic acid

AIDS Virus
(spherical)

Table 12–1.

ANIMAL VIRUSES	
Virus	**Diseases Produced**
DNA Viruses:	
Adenoviruses	Pinkeye
Papovaviruses	Warts in humans, rabbits, dogs
Herpesviruses	Cold sores, chickenpox, genital herpes, mononucleosis
Poxviruses	Smallpox
RNA Viruses:	
Enteroviruses	Diarrhea, polio
Rhinoviruses	Common cold
Togaviruses	Yellow fever, German measles, equine encephalitis
Rhabdoviruses	Rabies
Retroviruses	Leukemia, AIDS

NoteWorthy

A *viroid* is a short, single strand of RNA without a capsid. Viroids are known to cause plant diseases.

Viroids are responsible for the death of more than ten million coconut palm trees in the Philippines.

Prions are small glycoprotein particles implicated with degenerative diseases in the nervous systems of mammals.

NoteWorthy

A major factor in the successful completion of the Panama Canal was the use of massive amounts of pesticide to conquer the mosquito that carries the yellow fever virus.

FIGURE 12–2.

Yellow fever is caused by an RNA virus carried by an insect vector, the mosquito, *Aedes aegypti*.

A third method of classification organizes viruses according to the vectors that transmit them. A **vector** is any organism or object that carries or transmits a disease-causing organism. Tomatoes, maple trees, and cucumbers are some of the plants affected by viruses. Vectors that transfer diseases to these plants may be machinery, fungi, worms, or insects. Even pollen and seeds transmit viruses. Viruses that infect animals are carried by vectors that include contaminated objects such as needles, body fluids, water, and food as well as insects. Animal viruses are also spread by coughing, sneezing, and physical contact.

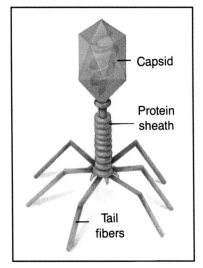

Capsid

Protein sheath

Tail fibers

a

b

FIGURE 12–3.

The complex structures of a bacterio-phage (a) can be seen with the help of the electron microscope (b).

bacteriophage:
bakterion (GK) small rod
phagein (GK) to devour

Viruses are not named in the same way as living things. They are not named according to the international rules of binomial nomen-clature. Frequently a virus is named for the disease it causes. For example, Hepatitis B virus (HBV) causes hepatitis. Rhinovirus refers to the rhinencephalon, a portion of the human nasal passage where viruses cause the common cold. A virus that infects a bacterial cell is a **bacteriophage** (bak TIHR ee uh fayj). Bacteriophages are named by a coding system that consists of a letter and a number. The T-4 bacteriophage is the virus that infects the bacterium *Escherichia coli,* a bacterium common to the human intestine.

12:3 Viral Replication

A supply of nucleic acids and proteins is needed for viruses to replicate themselves. These materials are available in living cells. During the replication process, viruses are either lytic or lysogenic. A **lytic virus** destroys its host cell during replication. A **lysogenic virus** does not kill its host cell during replication. Lysogenic viruses are also called temperate viruses. Viral replication in a lytic cycle is shown in Figure 12–4 and summarized in the following steps.

Attachment
The virus particle becomes attached to a cell at a specific site, binding to protein receptors in the cell membrane. This activity takes place much the way enzymes and substrates come together, by induced fit as described in Chapter 3.

Entry
The nucleic acid core is injected into the cell. The bacteriophage in Figure 12–4 injects its nucleic acid and leaves its capsid outside the cell. In some animal viruses, a whole virus particle is taken into the cell by the process of endocytosis.

Replication
Viral genes direct the host cell to make new viral nucleic acids

and proteins, using the materials and energy resources of the host. DNA viruses first direct the host to make new mRNA. Proteins made from this mRNA are used to make new viruses. RNA viruses work differently. Some RNA viruses move into the cell and use themselves as a template or mold on which the host cell makes new proteins. These proteins then direct the host to make new viral RNA and viral proteins needed as parts for new virus particles. Other RNA viruses, the retroviruses, behave differently. They contain an enzyme called reverse transcriptase. When a retrovirus infects a cell, it first makes viral DNA, using its RNA and reverse transcriptase. The new viral DNA makes mRNA, which in turn makes new viral proteins.

Formation

New virus particles are assembled in the cell from the newly synthesized viral nucleic acids and proteins.

Lysis and Release

The newly assembled virus particles now direct the production of enzymes that break down or lyse the host cell. The cell breaks open and releases one hundred or more new virus particles. Each new virus is capable of attacking another host cell. During the lytic process, the cell's complete metabolic activity is directed toward making new viruses. Bacteriophages that cause the lysis of their host cells are also called virulent phages.

lytic:
lyein (GK) to break down

FIGURE 12–4.

A lytic virus takes over the total metabolic activities of its host cell, replicates itself, and destroys the cell.

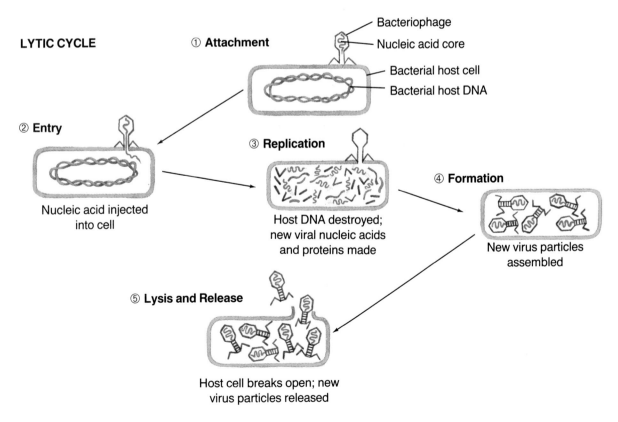

LYTIC CYCLE

① **Attachment**
- Bacteriophage
- Nucleic acid core
- Bacterial host cell
- Bacterial host DNA

② **Entry**
Nucleic acid injected into cell

③ **Replication**
Host DNA destroyed; new viral nucleic acids and proteins made

④ **Formation**
New virus particles assembled

⑤ **Lysis and Release**
Host cell breaks open; new virus particles released

LYSOGENIC CYCLE

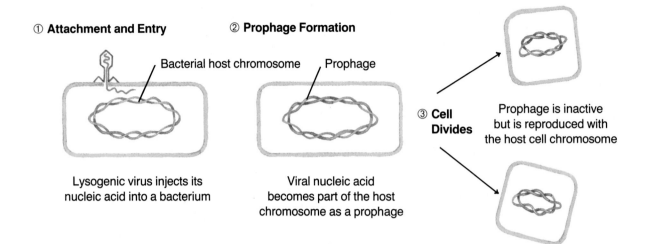

① **Attachment and Entry**

Bacterial host chromosome

Lysogenic virus injects its nucleic acid into a bacterium

② **Prophage Formation**

Prophage

Viral nucleic acid becomes part of the host chromosome as a prophage

③ **Cell Divides**

Prophage is inactive but is reproduced with the host cell chromosome

FIGURE 12–5.

Lysogenic or temperate viruses don't destroy their host. The viral nucleic acid becomes a part of the host cell chromosome and is called a pro-phage.

What is a prophage?

When a lysogenic virus infects a cell, as in Figure 12–5, the nucleic acid becomes a part of the host chromosome instead of destroying it. As the bacterial DNA is replicated, the bacteriophage nucleic acid multiplies right along with it in a process known as the lysogenic cycle. The piece of viral nucleic acid that has become part of the host cell DNA is called a **prophage.** Generations of host cells carrying prophages may form in this way with no obvious change in the way the cell functions. Scarlet fever and diphtheria are caused by bacteria that produce toxins and bring about these diseases only because they have become inhabited by specific prophages.

Some viruses remain unnoticed in the body for years without causing any disease symptoms. The herpes simplex virus that causes cold sore blisters and the hepatitis B virus, remain in the body after the initial infection. The viruses continue to replicate for years after the patient recovers from the disease. About 10 to 12 percent of people who have had hepatitis B retain the ability to spread the virus through blood transfusions.

Bacterial cells are not harmed by the prophages they carry until the viral nucleic acid becomes activated and a lytic cycle begins. Under the influence of radiation, a prophage becomes active, virus parts are produced and assembled, and the host cells lyse, releasing new viruses.

If a piece of the host cell DNA is carried away with the virus when the host cell breaks open, it may become incorporated into the DNA of the next host cell that the virus infects. This process increases the genetic variability of bacteria. As a result, some viruses cause an increase in the resistance of certain bacteria to antibiotics.

Much of the information about lytic and lysogenic viruses comes from studies of bacteriophages and how they act on bacteria. Bacteria reproduce quickly in the laboratory and bacteriophages can be produced in large numbers. Bacteriophages have become a useful tool for learning about all viruses.

12:4 Viruses and Disease

In Table 12–1, you saw many familiar diseases caused by viruses. Actually, you probably encounter numerous viruses every day. But your body is able to withstand the assault, or many of them do not cause disease in humans. Many viruses are destroyed quickly by the body's white blood cells. If the virus avoids capture, the body responds by making specific chemicals called antibodies that attack the invading virus and attach to it. The virus may be destroyed directly by the antibody or held captive by it until the virus can be surrounded and destroyed by white blood cells. These specific antibodies remain in the body of the organism after the virus has been destroyed. If the same virus attempts another invasion, it is quickly killed by the antibodies. Therefore, the organism develops an immunity to that virus. More details about how the body develops immunity are discussed in Chapter 31.

When viruses do succeed in invading an animal cell, interferon is produced. **Interferon** is a protein substance that inhibits virus replication in an animal cell that has been invaded by a virus. Your body produces interferon no matter what type of virus invades your body cells. However, interferon produced by one species of organism will not work in another organism. In other words, interferon produced by chickens will not work in humans. Much research has been done in the hope of using interferon to combat cancer, but the results have not been consistent and producing large quantities of human interferon has been a difficult process.

Viral diseases are difficult to treat because some viruses remain in the body for years without causing disease symptoms to appear. Also, viruses are not destroyed by drugs that kill bacteria. Some viral diseases are prevented with vaccines. Vaccines are solutions prepared from viral components or from inactivated viruses. The body reacts to the vaccine as if it were a real virus, and produces antibodies. The body is then immune to that particular virus. Vaccines have been developed for some specific viral diseases such as rabies, polio, and smallpox.

What is interferon?

NoteWorthy

Jonas Edward Salk, an American scientist, developed the first vaccine against polio. He destroyed the viruses' ability to reproduce but they would still cause production of antibodies in a person's body. The vaccine was first used in 1955. Albert Bruce Sabin later developed and tested a new "live" polio vaccine on himself. These polio viruses are too weak to cause serious disease.

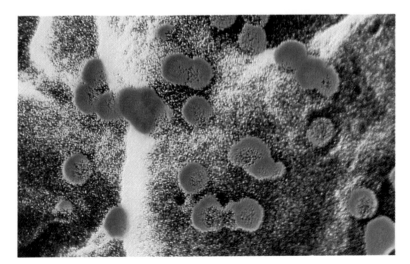

FIGURE 12–6.

The AIDS virus replicates itself by a lytic process, bringing about the destruction of its host cell.

vaccine:
vacca (L) cow

In 1798, Edward Jenner, an English country doctor, developed a vaccine for the viral disease smallpox. He administered fluid from the sores of people infected with cowpox, a similar human disease, to uninfected people with smallpox. After a mild infection developed, all symptoms disappeared. The vaccinated individuals never developed smallpox. Soon after, Louis Pasteur developed a vaccine for rabies.

Cancer is a disease characterized by cells that reproduce in an uncontrolled way. Certain viruses are thought to be involved in some human cancers, such as cancers in the lymph tissue, the uterus, and the liver. Viruses produce certain plant and animal tumors by viral transformation. Viral transformation is a process that changes normal cells to tumor cells. Tumors are solid masses that form when the reproducing cells pile up on top of one another. Research on cancer enables scientists to learn more about viruses.

12:5 History of Viruses

In the late 1880s, work on viruses helped scientists become convinced that microorganisms or microbes cause infectious disease. A young Russian botanist, Dimitri Ivanovski found that sap from a plant with tobacco mosaic virus could cause the tobacco disease even after it had passed through a filter that normally would stop the smallest known organism, a bacterium. From these results, he concluded that the cause of the disease was smaller than bacteria.

In 1935 the tobacco mosaic virus was crystallized. Living organisms cannot be crystallized. This finding was one more piece of evidence to show that viruses are not living things. Today, crystals from this original experiment still induce tobacco mosaic disease if rubbed on tobacco leaves.

More recently, the concern about the AIDS virus and its spread throughout the world, has brought the term *virus* to everyone's attention.

FIGURE 12–7.

In a classic experiment, it was discovered that the tobacco mosaic virus could be crystallized, and that these crystals could then produce the tobacco-mosaic disease in healthy tobacco plants.

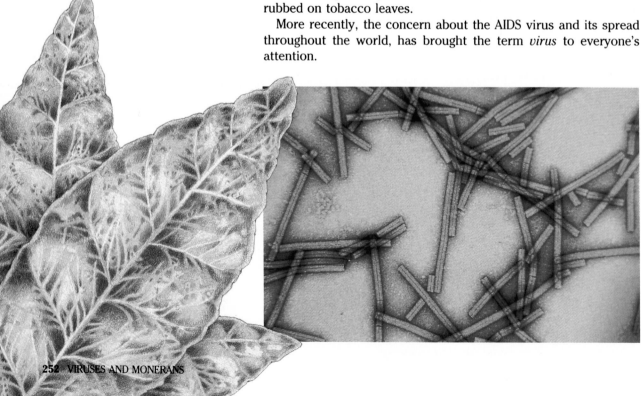

FIGURE 12–8.

Viruses have come to have significant impact on human history. Louis Pasteur developed a vaccine for rabies, and contributed information on the control of disease.

12:6 Origins of Viruses

Viruses contain DNA and RNA similar to that found in living cells. In synthesizing proteins and nucleic acids in cells, viruses step into a cell's metabolism and easily make use of the cell's normal processes. For some researchers, these activities are evidence that viruses are related to living organisms.

Where and how viruses originated is not known. Some progress has been made in understanding the makeup and activities of viruses. Scientists hypothesize that because viruses lead a parasitic existence now, they originally were genes that parasitized living things. Even though viruses pose a big question as to whether they are living or not, it has been observed that they have prokaryotic characteristics.

REVIEW

1. What are the two main components of a virus?
2. What are three ways of classifying viruses?
3. Distinguish between the lytic and lysogenic cycles.
4. **SKILL REVIEW:** A microbiologist added some viruses to a bacterial culture. Every hour, from noon to 8 P.M., he removed a sample of fluid from the culture and determined the number of viruses present in the sample. The numbers of viruses in each sample beginning at noon are 12, 14, 14, 42, 126, 379, 385, 385, and 385. Graph these results. For more help, refer to Organizing Information in the Skill Handbook, pages 810 to 813.
5. **USING CONCEPTS:** Describe the condition or state of the hepatitis B virus in a person who had the disease five years ago, but no longer shows the symptoms.

Objectives:

- list the characteristics of monerans.
- discuss how bacteria have adapted to their diverse habitats.
- recognize the distinguishing characteristics of the four phyla of Kingdom Monera.
- discuss the origins of monerans.

Several types of bacteria and some simple photosynthetic organisms make up the Kingdom Monera. They resemble some of the oldest fossils found on Earth. Four major moneran groups are the Eubacteria, Cyanobacteria, Chloroxybacteria, and the Archaebacteria. While monerans appear simple today, they play indispensable roles in ecology, health, and research.

12:7 Characteristics of Monerans

Monerans are unicellular microorganisms. Some monerans live in colonies or filaments, but each cell within the group is a separate unit. Monerans are prokaryotes and have no membrane-bound organelles. They have no mitochondria, lysosomes, endoplasmic reticulum, or nuclei. However, they do contain a large circular DNA structure and ribosomes. Additional DNA in some monerans is in the form of a smaller circle of DNA called a **plasmid.** It is these plasmids that are used in bioengineering research to change bacteria into new, but useful, forms.

bacterium:
bakterion (GK) small rod

The cell walls of monerans are made up of long chains of polysaccharides with cross links of short amino acid chains. Cell walls of most eukaryotes contain cellulose. Moneran cell walls are strong and rigid. In bacteria, this adaptation resists changes in osmotic pressure and the action of many drugs. The reason the drug penicillin is so successful in treating many bacterial diseases is that it stops the formation of these rigid walls.

Some bacteria have an additional external protective layer called a **capsule** located outside the cell wall. The capsule is made up of water and polysaccharides. The capsule protects the bacterium from being easily digested by body fluids. It also helps to maintain water balance in the bacterial cell.

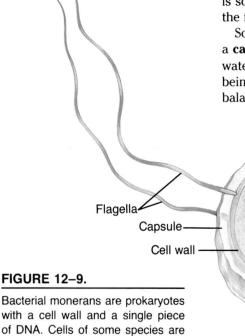
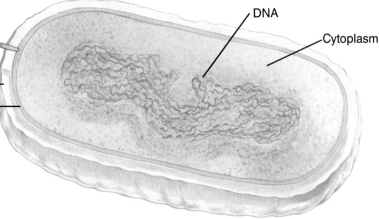

Flagella
Capsule
Cell wall
DNA
Cytoplasm

FIGURE 12–9.

Bacterial monerans are prokaryotes with a cell wall and a single piece of DNA. Cells of some species are surrounded by a protective capsule; others have flagella.

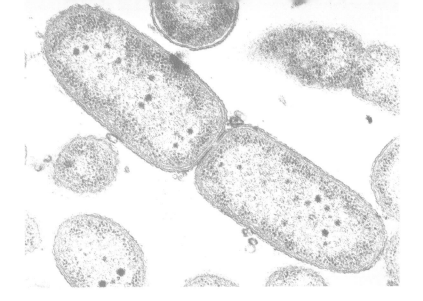

FIGURE 12–10.

Bacterial cells reproduce by binary fission, initially producing two cells approximately equal in size.

Two types of cell extensions are found in bacteria: pili (*sing.* pilus) and flagella. **Pili** are submicroscopic hairlike structures found on the surface of certain species that enable bacteria to stick to surfaces and to each other. The pili also serve as places for bacteriophages to attach to host cells. One type of pilus acts as a channel for the exchange of DNA between bacterial cells. Flagella enable some bacteria to move. Bacterial flagella are long protein extensions of the cell. Some flagella are located at one or both ends of the cell. A few bacteria have their entire surface covered with flagella.

12:8 The Life of a Bacterium

Bacteria are found in every possible habitat. Their geographic distribution ranges from the Antarctic ice fields to the hot springs of Yellowstone National Park, and from the tops of the world's highest mountains to thermal ocean vents. In spite of their simple structure, or maybe because of this simplicity, monerans survive.

Where are bacteria found?

The success of bacteria is probably due to several evolutionary adaptations. First, bacteria reproduce rapidly. Second, some bacteria can utilize substances that are poisonous to other organisms. There are bacteria that use DDT, a deadly pesticide, as their food source. Third, bacteria can exist under extreme conditions. Some live in acidic conditions with a pH less than 2.0 where no other organism can live. Everyday bacteria survive doses of enzymes and hydrochloric acid in your digestive system in a mutualistic relationship. **Mutualism** is a relationship between two species with both deriving some benefit. Fourth, bacteria have a high rate of mutation. It is a frustration to medical science that bacteria mutate easily, making some drugs ineffective.

Bacteria reproduce by dividing into two equal cells in a process known as **binary fission.** DNA is duplicated and is divided equally into the two new cells. The single bacterial DNA molecule attaches to the cell membrane and is pulled apart as the membrane grows. The cell membrane and cell wall then pinch inward from the outside and two new cells form.

Bacterial Streak Plate

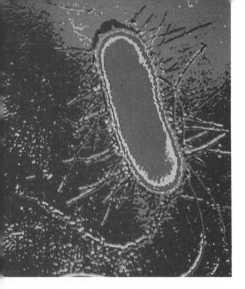

FIGURE 12–11.

Pili are thin strands through which genetic material passes from one cell to another.

What is an endospore?

Genetic information can be exchanged between bacteria as a result of conjugation. **Conjugation** is a process in which genetic recombination occurs when DNA from one bacterium moves through a pilus into another bacterium. Traits favorable to bacteria, such as drug resistance, are spread in a bacterial population this way.

Bacteria do not make their own food. They are consumers. A consumer is an organism that depends on other organisms for a source of energy. The energy sources monerans use are as varied as the organisms themselves. Most monerans satisfy their energy requirements with organic molecules such as sugars, starches, fatty materials, and proteins. Some bacteria use inorganic materials such as iron or sulfur in the process of chemosynthesis.

Bacteria are a vital link in the series of events that recycles materials in nature. They are saprobes. A **saprobe** is an organism that derives its energy from dead or dying organisms. Bacterial saprobes decompose organic matter. A **decomposer** is an organism that breaks down organic matter.

Bacteria vary from those that cannot live without free oxygen to those that cannot live with it. A bacterium that must have free oxygen to live is **obligate aerobe.** The bacteria causing tuberculosis is of this type. If bacteria cannot live in the presence of free oxygen, they are known as obligate anaerobes. An **obligate anaerobe** is an organism that does not use oxygen during respiration. Botulism, a deadly form of food poisoning, is caused by an obligate anaerobe. The most dangerous bacteria are those that are most flexible in their oxygen requirements. A bacterium capable of growing in the presence or absence of free oxygen is a facultative anaerobe.

Certain bacteria have evolved a unique way of dealing with conditions unfavorable to growth. They produce resistant structures called spores. A particular spore, called an **endospore** is resistant to adverse environmental factors. Endospores survive extremes of temperature, dehydration, chemicals, and radiation. Endospores are not reproductive structures. The bacterium that becomes an endospore is the same one that develops into a functional bacterial cell when conditions again improve.

FIGURE 12–12.

The large, circular structure in this cell is an endospore. Endospores can survive harsh conditions. The bacteria that develop from endospores in preserved foods produce toxins. This is one reason for strict controls in the processed food industry.

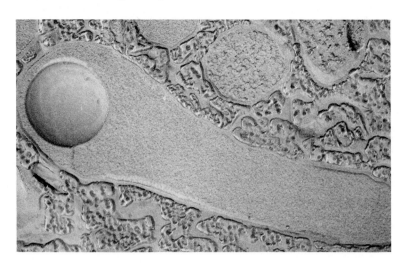

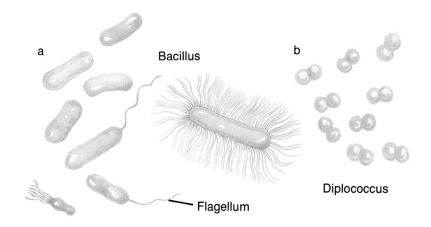

Bacillus

Flagellum

Diplococcus

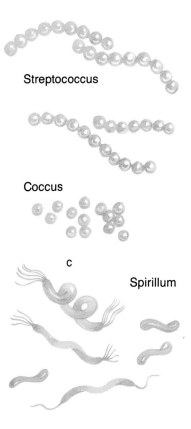

Streptococcus

Coccus

Spirillum

FIGURE 12–13.

The rod-shaped bacillus (a), the round coccus (b), and the spiral-shaped spirillum (c), are common shapes of bacteria.

12:9 Eubacteria

Scientists place many common bacteria into the Eubacteria. Within this group are the Omnibacteria, the Actinobacteria, the Rickettsias, and the Spirochaetes phyla.

The Omnibacteria is the phylum on which general descriptions of most bacteria are based. These bacteria vary in size from 0.1 μm to about 500 μm. More than 250 000 bacteria could fit on the tip of a pencil. There are three basic bacterial shapes—rod shaped, round, and spiral shaped. A rod-shaped bacterium is a **bacillus** (*pl.* bacilli). A bacterium that is round is a **coccus** (*pl.* cocci). A spiral or curved-shaped bacterium is a **spirillum** (*pl.* spirilla). These common forms are illustrated in Figure 12–13. Bacteria may be found as individuals or in groups. The arrangement or number of bacterial cells in a group is described by a prefix to its name. The prefix *strepto-* means twisted chain. Therefore, the description *streptococcus* would tell you that you have a long chain of round bacterial cells. Streptococcus is the cause of a common throat infection and scarlet fever. Other coccal bacteria stick together like clusters of grapes. Grape-like clusters of coccal bacteria are called staphylococci. Staphylococci are responsible for staph infections, such as boils, although these bacteria normally live on your skin and in your nasal passages without causing illness.

Bacillus forms may occur as single cells or in filaments of cells attached end to end. Diphtheria and tuberculosis are caused by a bacillus bacterium. Most species of Omnibacteria are decomposers that do not cause disease.

The Actinobacteria have some characteristics of fungi that you will study in Chapter 14. However, because they have no nuclear membrane, they are classed with bacteria. Many antibiotic drugs are derived from bacteria in this group.

Rickettsias are obligate parasites. To remain alive, they must live on a host. Most are found in insects. Rocky Mountain spotted fever and typhus are diseases transmitted by insects that carry rickettsiae.

The Spirochaetes have flexible cell walls and a spiral-shaped form. *Treponema pallidum* is a spirochete that causes the disease syphilis in humans.

NoteWorthy

One μm is equal to one millionth of a meter. See Appendix E on page 796 for SI units.

streptococcus:
streptos (GK) twisted chain
kokkus (GK) berry

BIOLAB

Classifying Bacteria

12

Problem: How is a key used to classify bacteria?

Materials
paper

Procedures
1. Look at the drawings of bacteria in the data table. Copy the table and diagrams.
2. Follow the directions in the key to identify each bacterium.
3. Look at the shape of each bacterium in the table. Read the directions under A of the key. Select the choice that best describes the bacterium. Move to the end of the line. If there is a name, you have identified the bacterium. If not, follow the direction given. Repeat the procedure until you arrive at a number and scientific name. Write the number next to the correct bacterium on your paper. Repeat the procedure for each bacterium.

Questions and Conclusion
1. What scientific term is used to denote the round shape?
2. Identify by scientific name the bacteria associated with the following:
   a. pneumonia   c. tetanus
   b. botulism poisoning d. anthrax
3. Looking at section B of the key, what prefix denotes that the bacteria are in clumps?

Data and Observations

Bacterium	Number	Bacterium	Number
		/////////	/////////

4. What term is used to denote the rod shape?
5. What prefix is used to denote pairs?

Conclusion: Explain how a key helps to classify bacteria.

Key

A	shape is round	go to B
AA	shape is rodlike	go to C
AAA	shape is spiral	1. *Treponema pallidum*
B	bacteria are in pairs	go to D
BB	bacteria are in chains	go to E
BBB	bacteria are in clumps ...	2. *Staphylococcus aureus*
C	bacteria are in pairs	3. *Bacillus anthracis*
CC	bacteria are in chains	4. *Bacillus lactis*
CCC	bacteria are single..........	go to F

D	bacteria have a .... heavy covering	5. *Diplococcus pneumoniae*
DD	bacteria lack a................ heavy covering	6. *Diplococcus meningitidis*
E	bacterium is .... large in size	7. *Streptococcus pyogenes*
EE	bacterium is .... small in size	8. *Streptococcus lactis*
F	bacterium has flagella ...	9. *Bacillus typhosa*
FF	bacterium has a .... spore in its center	10. *Bacillus botulinum*
FFF	bacterium has a .... spore at its end	11. *Bacillus tetani*

BIOTECHNOLOGY

WORKING BACTERIA

Archeological evidence suggests that the Romans recovered copper from Mediterranean mines with the help of bacteria. The first recorded mining operation that intentionally involved bacteria was around 1700 at copper mines in Spain. Now, isolated bacterial strains are being genetically engineered to separate metals from mineral deposits.

Microbes are being used to extract lead, zinc, gold, copper, mercury, and uranium from mineral deposits. Microbial operations require less energy than conventional mining methods. The method is pollution free and mining costs are low.

High-sulfur coal is the form responsible for much of the acid precipitation in the world. *Thiobacillus thiooxidans* and species of *Sulfolobus* are two types of bacteria that can metabolize sulfur. When introduced into piles of high-sulfur coal, these bacteria leave behind a cleaner-burning fuel.

Other researchers are working with organisms that break down phenol. Phenols are byproducts of wood treatment in pulp plants. By splicing the genes of this organism into *Escherichia coli,* large amounts of phenol-destroying bacteria can be grown rapidly. *E. coli* could turn the phenol into harmless salts. If bacteria could be tailor-made to metabolize each factory's waste, chemical companies might be able to detoxify their wastes without treatment plants.

Researchers have concentrated much of their current effort in finding naturally occurring organisms to perform cleanup duties, but the 'superbugs' are coming. They will be able to live in and make use of materials containing toxic chemicals such as arsenic and PCB's.

Bacteria have important functions in purifying coal.

12:10 Cyanobacteria

Some monerans with chlorophyll are in the phylum Cyanobacteria. They are bluish green in color and contain chlorophyll *a,* a photosynthetic pigment found in plants. Chlorophyll in cyanobacteria is free in the cytoplasm and not contained in chloroplasts as it is in plants. Cyanobacteria are autotrophs. An **autotroph** is an organism that is capable of making its own food supply. Autotrophic organisms are also called producers. A producer is an organism capable of making food that is a source of energy for itself and any organisms that feed on the producer. Cyanobacteria and plants produce carbohydrates and oxygen on which the rest of the living world depends. Many cyanobacteria are responsible for fixing nitrogen, the important process whereby atmospheric nitrogen is converted into forms that can be used by plants to make amino acids from which proteins are constructed.

Many cyanobacteria are found in ponds. Normally cyanobacteria in ponds are sources of energy and oxygen for other organisms.

cyanobacterium:
  kyanos (GK) blue
  bakterion (GK) small rod

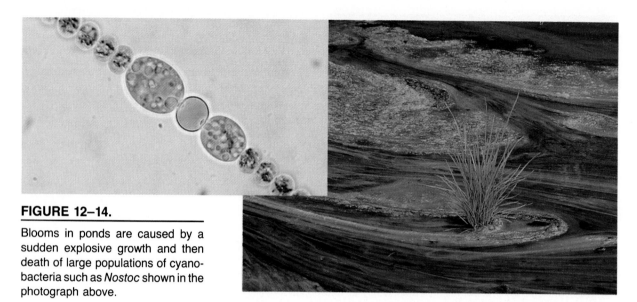

FIGURE 12–14.

Blooms in ponds are caused by a sudden explosive growth and then death of large populations of cyanobacteria such as *Nostoc* shown in the photograph above.

Periodically these areas become choked with large growths of monerans in the form of green scum. This huge growth, called a bloom, comes about when large amounts of nutrients become suddenly available, sometimes from runoffs of fertilizers in nearby fields. The cyanobacteria then die in great numbers and begin to decay. The oxygen supply in the pond becomes depleted and other organisms in the pond, such as fish, die off.

12:11 Other Monerans

A third phylum of monerans, Chloroxybacteria, is made up of photosynthetic bacteria that live in an association with marine animals called tunicates. These bacteria contain chlorophylls *a* and *b*, the main photosynthetic pigments in plants. This group may be a link to the green algae, which you will study in Chapter 13.

The Archaebacteria are a group of monerans that may give clues about the early conditions of Earth. The conditions under which they exist now may be similar to the conditions existing billions of years ago. The Archaebacteria are found in some unusual habitats, usually places with temperature extremes. Three types of archaebacteria are known. Halophiles are monerans that live in extremely salty environments, such as the Great Salt Lake in Utah. They carry on photosynthesis by using a purple pigment embedded in their cell membranes instead of chlorophyll. Methanogens produce methane gas or marsh gas as a byproduct of metabolism. These bacteria are found in anaerobic environments such as swamps, lake mud, or cows' intestines. They produce about two billion tons of methane gas each year. The methane reacts with oxygen in the air and produces carbon dioxide, affecting the concentration of carbon dioxide in the atmosphere. Thermoacidophiles live in hot, acidic conditions such as those near volcano vents, hot sulfur springs, and smoldering waste piles of coal.

NoteWorthy

Photorhizobium thompsonum is the first known bacterium that derives energy from the sun and converts nitrogen to a form usable by plants. It produces nodules on the roots of plants that supply its host with nitrogen. This relationship decreases the plant's need for chemical fertilizers.

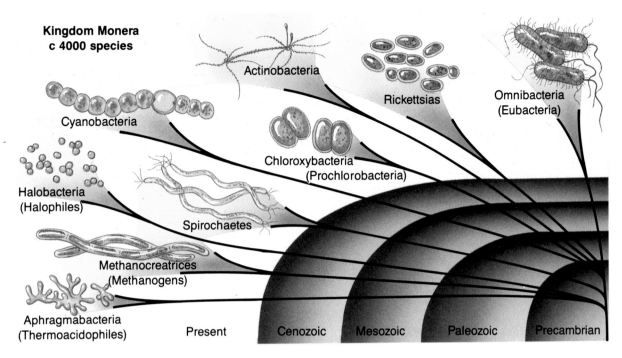

Kingdom Monera
c 4000 species

Actinobacteria

Rickettsias

Omnibacteria
(Eubacteria)

Cyanobacteria

Chloroxybacteria
(Prochlorobacteria)

Halobacteria
(Halophiles)

Spirochaetes

Methanocreatrices
(Methanogens)

Aphragmabacteria
(Thermoacidophiles)

Present   Cenozoic   Mesozoic   Paleozoic   Precambrian

12:12 Origins of Monerans

The origins of bacteria and cyanobacteria are difficult to trace because of limited fossil evidence. However, what few fossil specimens of bacteria there are have been determined to be about 3.5 billion years old, close to the age of Earth itself.

No one can deny the importance of ancestral cyanobacteria as they probably contributed a great deal to the development of an oxygenated atmosphere, which enabled other organisms to live.

Finally, present-day Archaebacteria illustrate the wide variety of environments in which ancestral moneran forms may have existed. Figure 12–15 shows bacterial relationships on a geologic time scale.

FIGURE 12–15.

The radiation of the phyla of monerans on the geologic time scale shows their relationships.

REVIEW

6. What is mutualism?
7. How do endospores and pili help bacteria survive?
8. How do cyanobacteria contribute to pollution?
9. **SKILL REVIEW:** Make a table of the four phyla in the Kingdom Monera, list their features, and give an example of each. For more help, refer to Organizing Information in the Skill Handbook, pages 810 to 813.
10. **USING CONCEPTS:** A culture of bacteria was grown in a test tube in the laboratory. Samples were taken at regular intervals. After several hours the population of bacteria in the culture began to level off and eventually began to decrease. Give some reasons to explain what took place.

DEVELOPING A VIEWPOINT

RECOMBINANT DNA

The use of the term *recombinant DNA* began when Paul Berg, an American biochemist, split DNA strands with enzymes and then recombined the DNA strands in different ways. As a result, molecules of recombinant DNA were formed. Berg shared the 1980 Nobel Prize for chemistry for his efforts. What are some of the benefits of recombinant DNA?

BACKGROUND

An important example of the use of recombinant DNA in medicine involves the production of insulin, the hormone that regulates blood sugar in humans. The gene for producing insulin has been spliced into the DNA of bacteria. When these bacteria grow and reproduce, they produce insulin. This insulin can then be recovered for use by diabetics. The same procedure has been used for human growth hormone, or hGH.

Recombinant DNA techniques are also used in agriculture. A strain of genetically altered bacteria has been found to lower the temperature at which damaging ice crystals form in plant tissues. In 1987, a crop of strawberries was sprayed with these bacteria to see if they would prevent the formation of ice crystals as they had in the laboratory. The data from the experiment suggest that the bacteria prevent frost damage and do not harm the environment. The experiment was controversial because it was the first time that an organism containing recombinant DNA was released in nature.

Some people feel that the use of recombinant DNA could be harmful. There is concern that organisms created with recombinant DNA would have no natural enemies and could spread unchecked in nature.

CASE STUDIES

1. A great deal of recombinant-DNA research has been done with soil microbes, particularly the rhizobacteria that can live in and on plant roots. Five questions must be answered for each genetically engineered microbe: Will it survive? Will it multiply? Will it spread beyond the area of application? Can it transfer its genetic material to other organisms? Will the organism be harmful?

A risk assessment for each altered organism has to be made. In general, many of these bacteria have short life spans. Also, tests seem to indicate that most of them show very little tendency to spread throughout the soil. However, the need for risk assessments will continue until scientists are sure that these microbes are safe.

2. Legumes and grains provide us with proteins, but individually they do not provide a complete set of amino acids that people need. For example, beans are low in the essential amino acids methionine and cysteine. Recombinant-DNA techniques could change that deficiency. Scientists have now been able to insert the gene for the amino acid methionine in tobacco plants. It may soon be possible to insert it into food sources such as soybeans, one kind of legume.

3. Genetic engineers have had a difficult time transferring genes into the cells of cereal crops. They have used microinjection needles, lasers, and electric shocks to try to get pieces of desirable DNA into plant cells. Sometimes the DNA fails to enter the cells. Sometimes even after it enters the cell it does not become a part of the cell's DNA. Now genetic engineers are using an "electrical-discharge particle accelerator" to blast tiny DNA-coated gold particles into plant cells. This technique has been successful with corn, soybeans, and cotton.

4. At the present time, industry is not pursuing genetically altered soil microbes as alternatives to chemical pesticides. There are political and regulatory problems that would have to be resolved.

The Environmental Protection Agency may consider classifying a pesticide product that has been made by a modified plant gene as a chemical pesticide. As such, it would be subject to the requirements listed under the pesticide laws. This means that it might be five to ten years before the product is approved.

5. Congress has held hearings on the existing regulations for organisms that have been changed by recombinant-DNA techniques. The Ecological Society of America prepared a report for Congress as a guideline for regulating genetically engineered organisms. The report states that there would be minimum ecological risk from genetically engineered organisms if there is proper planning and supervision. But the ESA also encourages small-scale field tests to develop such organisms.

6. Scientists have found a gene that controls a plant's ability to take up nutrients from the soil. The gene codes for a protein that crosses the outer membrane of cells and transports hydrogen from one side of the membrane to the other. It does this by creating an electrical difference between the inside of the cell and the outside of the cell. If scientists can get plants to produce a large number of these electrical differences, called "proton pumps," nutrient intake may be improved in all kinds of plants.

DEVELOPING YOUR VIEWPOINT

1. In your opinion, what is the most important question in assessing the risks of using genetically engineered microbes?
2. How might world populations benefit from having grains with complete sets of amino acids?
3. Discuss whether it is worth the time, expense, and technical effort to find new ways to incorporate recombinant DNA in grains.

4. Should it take so long for the approval or the disapproval of a new plant gene?
5. Why should the Ecological Society of America be interested in governmental regulations concerning organisms that have been changed by recombinant-DNA techniques?
6. Hypothesize the results of increasing nutrient uptake in plants.

SUGGESTED READINGS

1. "Genetic Flip for Firmer Tomato." *BioScience,* Dec. 1988, p. 811.
2. Grossman, Yaffa. "Toward a Science-Based Policy on the Release of Genetically Engineered Organisms." *BioScience,* Apr. 1989, p. 229.
3. Weiss, Rick. "The Revolution Will Not Be Fertilized." *Science News,* Jan. 28, 1989, p. 59.
4. Wickelgren, Ingrid. "Plant Ion-Pump Gene Cloned, Sequenced." *Science News,* Mar. 4, 1989, p. 135.

Frost-free strawberries

CHAPTER REVIEW

SUMMARY

1. A virus is a nonliving particle made up of a nucleic acid core and a protein capsid. **12:1**
2. Viruses are classified by shape, nucleic acid, type of host infected, or method of transmission. **12:2**
3. Viruses replicate and produce disease by a lytic cycle. In a lysogenic cycle, viruses are dormant and are reproduced with the host DNA. **12:3**
4. Viruses cause diseases. Viruses may be destroyed directly by the body, or prevented by vaccination. **12:4**
5. Current understanding of viruses is based on centuries of observation. Viruses may be genes that have parasitized cells. **12:5, 12:6**
6. Monerans are prokaryotic cells found in every possible habitat. All bacteria are microscopic. They are round, rod shaped, or spiral shaped. Pili and flagella are cell extensions. Bacteria reproduce by binary fission and can exchange genetic information through conjugation. Endospores are resistant structures. **12:7, 12:8**
7. Monerans are grouped into the Schizophyta, Cyanobacteria, Prochloron, and the Archaebacteria. **12:9, 12:10, 12:11**
8. The origin of monerans is obscure. Ancient cyanobacteria probably produced the oxygen in the early atmosphere. Archaebacteria give evidence of bacterial origins. **12:12**

LANGUAGE OF BIOLOGY

autotroph	endospore
bacillus	interferon
bacteriophage	lysogenic virus
binary fission	lytic virus
capsule	mutualism
coccus	obligate aerobe
conjugation	obligate anaerobe
decomposer	pili
plasmid	spirillum
prophage	vector
saprobe	

Choose the word or phrase from the list above that completes the sentence.

1. An organism or object that transmits viruses or monerans is a(n) ____.
2. A virus that infects bacteria is called a(n) ____.
3. ____ is a protein produced by a cell that inhibits virus replication.
4. An organism that breaks down organic matter is a saprobe or a(n) ____.
5. A virus that destroys its host cell is a(n) ____.
6. A(n) ____ is a spiral or curved bacterium.
7. Genetic material moves from one bacterium to another through ____ in conjugation.
8. A small, circular extra piece of DNA in a bacterium is a(n) ____.
9. A structure produced in certain bacteria when conditions become unfavorable is a(n) ____.
10. Bacteria reproduce by ____.

REVIEWING CONCEPTS

Choose the word or phrase that completes the sentence or answers the question.

11. Viruses contain ____.
    a. nuclei
    b. nucleic acids
    c. mitochondria
    d. plastids
12. A ____ is a piece of viral DNA that has become part of its host DNA.
    a. plasmid
    b. prophage
    c. pilus
    d. producer
13. An organism that produces its own source of energy is a(n) ____.
    a. decomposer
    b. saprobe
    c. autotroph
    d. heterotroph
14. Multiplication of viruses takes place by ____.
    a. replication
    b. conjugation
    c. fission
    d. budding

15. Bacteriophages are viruses that infect ___.
    a. humans   c. plants
    b. animals   d. bacteria
16. Monerans are ___.
    a. prokaryotes
    b. eukaryotes
    c. all rod shaped
    d. viruses with nuclei
17. The outer protein covering of a virus is a ___.
    a. capsule   c. consumer
    b. coccus   d. capsid
18. Bacterial endospores are ___.
    a. reproductive cells   c. new cells
    b. resistant   d. never toxic
19. A ___ can prevent a viral disease.
    a. red blood cell   c. prophage
    b. vaccine   d. lysogenic virus
20. In ___, no organism in the relationship is harmed.
    a. transformation   c. lysis
    b. decomposition   d. mutualism

UNDERSTANDING CONCEPTS

Answer the following questions using complete sentences.

21. Describe the structure of a typical virus.
22. How do Cyanobacteria and Prochlorons obtain food?
23. What happens when a lytic virus infects a cell?
24. Why are viruses described as nonliving?
25. List the major groups of the Kingdom Monera. Give one characteristic for each phyla.
26. What adaptations help bacteria survive?
27. What do monerans use for energy?
28. Compare prophages and plasmids.
29. How are viruses thought to have originated?
30. Describe how lysogenic viruses replicate.

APPLYING CONCEPTS

Answer the following questions using complete sentences.

31. How do blooms affect animal life in ponds?
32. What would happen if all bacterial saprobes were killed?
33. How can a healthy person transmit viruses.
34. Defend the statement: Not all monerans cause disease.
35. How might Archaebacteria lead to an understanding of conditions on ancient Earth?

EXTENSIONS

1. Write a report that explains how the drugs acyclovir and AZT act on viruses.
2. Research how bacteria become resistant to antibiotics. What is the significance of drug-resistant bacteria to public health?
3. Use nutrient agar to check for bacterial growth in a soil sample and air in your classroom. How could you determine if a soil sample contained fungi or bacteria that produced antibiotic chemicals?

READINGS

Fincher, J. "America's Deadly Rendezvous with the 'Spanish Lady'." *Smithsonian,* Jan. 1989, pp. 130–132.

McEvedy, C. "The Bubonic Plague." *Scientific American,* Feb. 1988, pp. 118–123.

Sagan, Dorian, and Lynn Margulis. *Garden of Microbial Delights: A Practical Guide to the Subvisible World.* New York: Harcourt, Brace, Jovanovich, 1988.

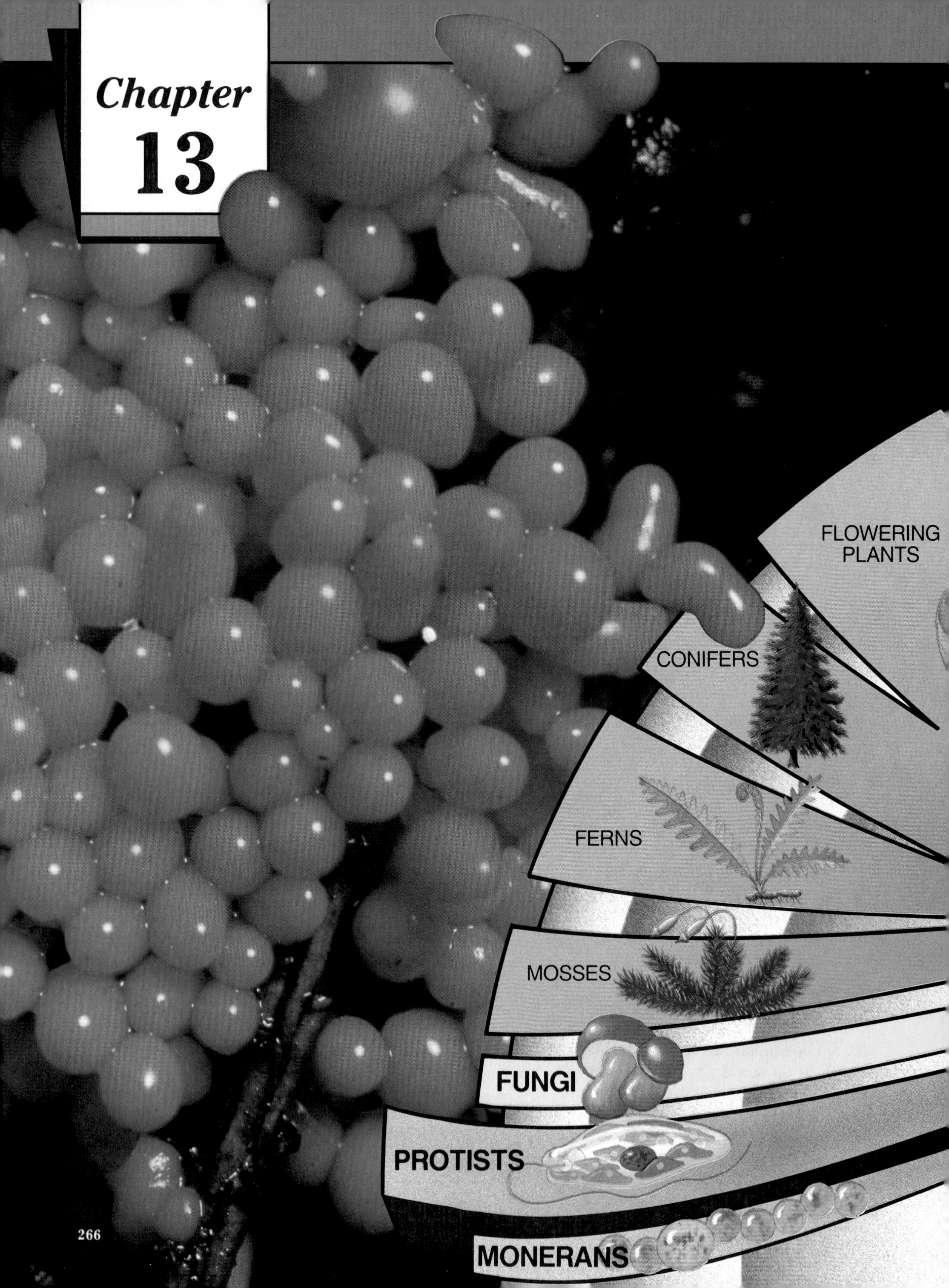

FLOWERING
PLANTS

CONIFERS

FERNS

MOSSES

FUNGI

PROTISTS

MONERANS

PROTISTS

In 1675, when Anton van Leeuwenhoek used a simple lens to look at a drop of water, he saw tiny organisms swimming and whirling around. He called the creatures "animalcules," or "little animals." In his diary Leeuwenhoek wrote: "This was for me, among all the marvels that I have discovered in nature, the most marvelous of all." It is three centuries since Leeuwenhoek's discovery, but with an ordinary light microscope, you too can see some of the same variety of protists that caught his eye and imagination. *Vorticella* on the right is classified as a protist along with the slime mold in the large photo to your left.

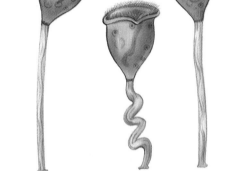

Vorticella

THE LIFE OF PROTISTS

It has been estimated that there are more than 200 000 species in the Kingdom Protista. Incredible as it may seem, some of these species have not changed in the last 1.5 billion years. Protists range from tiny unicellular amoebas found in puddles to the giant seaweeds of the ocean, to slime molds, and water molds.

13:1 Phylogeny of Protists

Although the protists are looked at as simple organisms, they are much more complex than monerans. All protists are eukaryotes. They utilize food, excrete wastes, carry out respiration, reproduce, and respond to stimuli as monerans do, but in protists, most of these processes take place in membrane-bound organelles. Protists are grouped according to their overall characteristics into animal-like, plantlike, and funguslike organisms.

Animal-like protists are known as **protozoans.** Protozoans are grouped into phyla according to the way they move or don't move. Most protozoans move by means of pseudopods, cilia, or flagella. Nonmotile protozoans have no way of pursuing and actively capturing food. They live as parasites. A **parasite** is an organism that lives in or on a host organism and may or may not harm the host. Parasite protozoans live within a ready food supply, such as a host's bloodstream or intestine.

Objectives:
- classify the Kingdom Protista into protozoans, algae, and funguslike protists.
- identify some of the characteristics of protists.
- discuss the relationship of protists to other living things.

Fruiting bodies of a cellular slime mold

Algae are plantlike protists. All algae contain at least one of four kinds of chlorophyll, but all contain other photosynthetic pigments as well. These pigments give some algae their characteristic red, brown, or yellow color. Algae are classified into phyla according to the type of pigments they contain. They are not classified in the plant kingdom because they have no roots, stems, or leaves.

Funguslike protists make up the three remaining protist phyla. Two of these phyla are referred to as the slime molds. **Slime molds** have characteristics of both protozoans and fungi and are classified by the way they reproduce. The third funguslike phylum, the water molds and mildews, contains some disease-causing organisms of historical and economic significance.

FIGURE 13–1.

The radiation of phyla of protists on the geologic time scale shows their relationships.

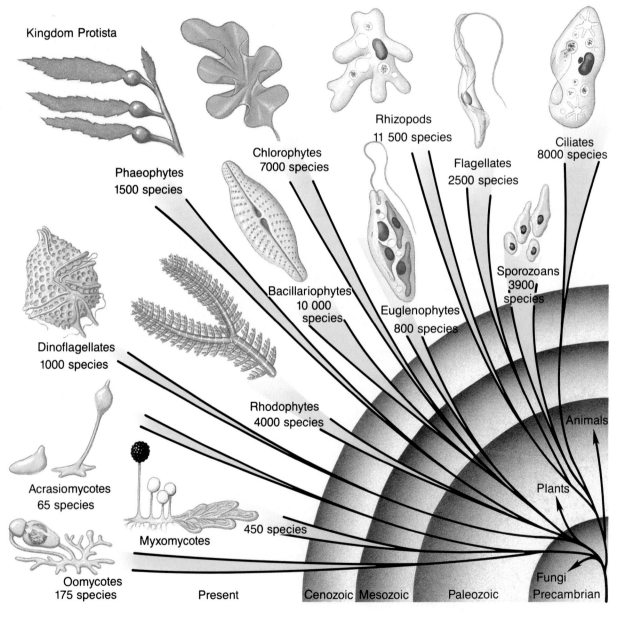

Kingdom Protista

Phaeophytes
1500 species

Chlorophytes
7000 species

Rhizopods
11 500 species

Flagellates
2500 species

Ciliates
8000 species

Bacillariophytes
10 000
species

Euglenophytes
800 species

Sporozoans
3900
species

Dinoflagellates
1000 species

Rhodophytes
4000 species

Animals

Plants

Acrasiomycotes
65 species

450 species

Myxomycotes

Oomycotes
175 species

Present

Cenozoic Mesozoic   Paleozoic

Fungi
Precambrian

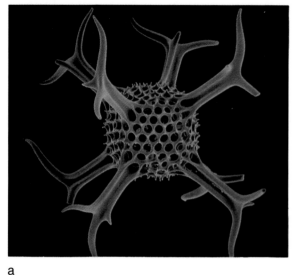

a

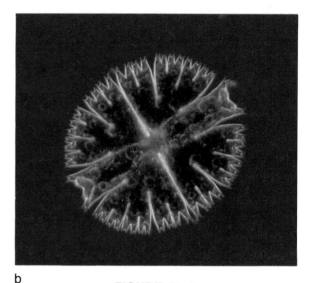

b

FIGURE 13–2.

Radiolarians (a) and a green alga called a desmid (b) illustrate some of the variety in the Kingdom Protista.

13:2 Origins of Protists

The change from prokaryotes to eukaryotes was a major step in evolution. The oldest organisms in the fossil record are over 3.5 billion years old. The first eukaryotes, however, don't even appear in the fossil record until about 1.5 billion years later. What happened during that 1.5 billion year gap? Scientists are still hypothesizing how this giant leap came about.

Recall the discussion in Chapter 11 that describes how eukaryotes evolved from prokaryotes and that green algae were probably the ancestors of modern plants. Photosynthetic prokaryotes may have been the origin of the many different kinds of chlorophyll found in algae living today. These early protists and cyanobacteria are thought to be responsible for the production of oxygen in Earth's developing atmosphere that made it possible for so many organisms to survive on land.

The variety in the Kingdom Protista gives a basis for the origin of the numerous kinds of fungi, higher plants, and animals that we have today. Such variety may have come from many different ancestors. Were they photosynthetic protists? Exactly what the ancestors of modern life forms were is still the subject of many hypotheses.

What is the importance of green algae to all other organisms?

13:3 The Importance of Protists

There is no "typical" protist. Protists come in many different shapes and sizes. Most are microscopic, but some brown seaweeds may be more than 100 m long. Some protists are jellylike blobs that constantly change shape. Others are rigid with hard shells.

Protists are found in many different places. Most are unicellular organisms living in moist environments. They populate Earth's oceans, freshwater lakes, and streams. They are also numerous in soil. Some protists live in the body tissues of plants and animals.

Whales gulp or skim quantities of plankton.

TO SINK OR NOT TO SINK?

Phytoplankton is found in seawater but has a density greater than seawater. Some of the organisms eventually tend to sink out of the lighted, or photic zone. Unicellular algae lack the means to swim actively upward to counter this tendency to sink. They must rely on adaptations to slow their sinking rate. One of the most effective adaptations they have evolved is to increase their frictional resistance with the water by increasing the surface area: volume ratio. Smaller cells accomplish this with cellular projections such as flagella or cilia. Other cells, in the form of twisted chains, allow the organism to spiral or zig-zag through the water. The shape of the cell determines the way it sinks. Some diatoms have thinner and lighter cell parts, thus reducing their density, by excluding high density ions (e.g., calcium, magnesium, and sulfate) from their cell fluid and replacing them with less dense ions. A final adaptation is the production and storage of low-density fats and oils. These fats and oils tend to promote floating rather than sinking. Why is it critical for organisms in phytoplankton to decrease their sinking rates?

Protists have evolved a variety of ways of meeting their energy requirements. Protozoans obtain nutrients by feeding on other organisms or dead organic matter. Algae are all autotrophs, making their own food by photosynthesis or chemosynthesis. Many species live at depths to which light can penetrate easily. As a result, they produce about 75 percent of Earth's oxygen. Parasitic forms obtain energy from their hosts.

What are plankton?

Many protists in the form of plankton are the food source of aquatic animals such as whales. **Plankton** are unicellular aquatic protists. Protozoans in plankton are called **zooplankton.** Unicellular algae of plankton are called **phytoplankton.** Both zooplankton and phytoplankton are constantly moved about by the motion of water.

REVIEW

1. What are the three groups of protists?
2. How are algae classified?
3. How do protists obtain energy?
4. **SKILL REVIEW:** Compare the general characteristics of algae, protozoans, and funguslike protists by making a table. For more help, refer to Organizing Information in the Skill Handbook, pages 810 to 813.
5. **USING CONCEPTS:** If whales feed on plankton, what can you infer about the amount of plankton in the world's oceans?

PROTOZOANS: ANIMAL-LIKE PROTISTS

Hollywood has magnified the prowling, slithering, and devouring habits of protozoans to unreal proportions. Knowing their microscopic size, you will be amazed at how complex these very small protists are.

13:4 Amoebas

The phylum Rhizopoda includes hundreds of species of **amoebas,** shapeless, aquatic protozoans. Amoebas move by forming **pseudopods,** cytoplasmic extensions that allow the organism to move from one place to another. The shape of the cell constantly changes as new pseudopods form. An amoeba captures large pieces of food by flowing around and over them, enclosing them in food vacuoles. Digestive enzymes are secreted into the vacuoles to break down the food. Because amoebas live in water, they are surrounded by a sea of dissolved nutrients. Therefore, some substances will diffuse directly through their cell membranes. Amoebas contain contractile vacuoles that collect and pump out excess water. This is especially necessary since freshwater amoebas live in a hypotonic environment. Amoebas are responsive. They move away from light and toward chemicals that are sources of food.

Two genera of amoebas have shells. *Foraminifera* are marine amoebas that secrete hard outer shells made of calcium carbonate. Fossil forms are used as "markers" to locate potential oil deposits. *Radiolaria* are amoebas that produce shells made of silica.

Reproduction in amoebas is asexual. **Asexual reproduction** is reproduction in which a single parent produces one or more identical offspring by fragmentation, fission, or mitotic cell division. If environmental conditions are unfavorable, an amoeba forms a cyst. Certain cyst-forming species cause dysentery, an intestinal illness known for its sharp pains and diarrhea.

Objectives:
- describe the characteristics of amoebas, flagellates, and ciliates.
- describe conjugation in *Paramecium* and its importance.
- explain how malaria is caused by a sporozoan.
- discuss the importance of the protozoans.

FIGURE 13–3.

The shape of an amoeba changes constantly as pseudopods form.

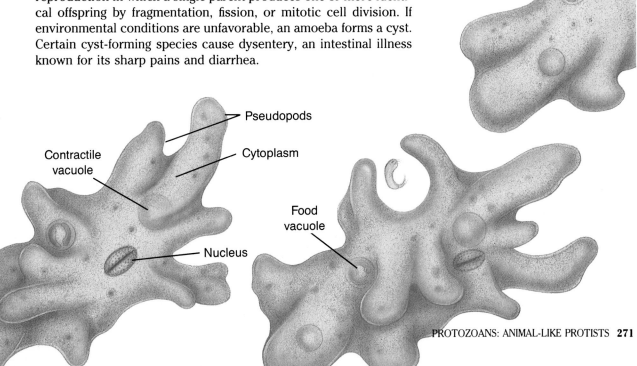

Pseudopods

Cytoplasm

Contractile vacuole

Food vacuole

Nucleus

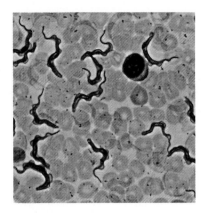

FIGURE 13–4.

Trypanosoma, a parasitic flagellate protist, causes sleeping sickness, which may be fatal to humans.

FIGURE 13–5.

The cilia on a paramecium beat in a synchronized fashion.

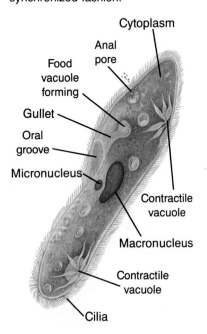

13:5 Flagellates

The phylum Zoomastigina is made up of protists that move by whipping one or more flagella from side to side. Organisms with flagella are known as **flagellates.**

Most flagellates are parasites that cause diseases in animals. *Trypanosoma* is a genus of flagellate that causes sleeping sickness in humans and cattle. Sleeping sickness results in an inflammation of the brain. These flagellates begin their life cycle by reproducing in the tsetse fly. When the fly bites a human or cow, the flagellate is transferred in the fly's saliva to the new host, where it causes the disease. Sleeping sickness is spread when another tsetse fly bites an infected host and picks up the flagellate.

Another important flagellate lives in a mutualistic relationship in the intestine of termites. It is well known that termites feed on wood, but they actually have no way to digest the cellulose in wood. The flagellate ingests pieces of wood and that converts cellulose in the wood to a carbohydrate that both the termite and the flagellate can use.

13:6 Ciliates

Members of the phylum Ciliophora move by the synchronized beating of cilia on their bodies. A **ciliate** is a protozoan that moves by means of cilia. Ciliates are the most complex of the protozoans. There are about 8000 species of ciliates. They are found in every kind of aquatic habitat, from ponds and streams, to oceans and sulfur springs.

Paramecium is a typical ciliate genus commonly found in fresh water. Its slipper-like shape is maintained by a protein sheath called a pellicle found outside the cell membrane. Cilia stick out through the pellicle. As the cilia beat, the whole animal moves forward through water in a spiral motion. Paramecia contain two nuclei. The smaller nucleus, the **micronucleus,** is active in sexual reproduction. The larger nucleus, the **macronucleus,** controls the everyday functions of the cell. The macronucleus is necessary for asexual reproduction, the usual method by which paramecia reproduce.

Paramecia usually feed on bacteria that are swept into the body through an oral groove as shown in Figure 13–5. The oral groove is lined with cilia that beat and create the sweeping effect. Once in the cell, a food vacuole forms and food is digested. Wastes are removed from the cell through an anal pore. Excess water is also removed through a pair of contractile vacuoles.

Paramecia reproduce asexually and sexually. In asexual reproduction, the micronucleus divides by mitosis. The macronucleus lengthens and breaks into two equal parts, and the cell divides crosswise into two identical cells. Paramecia also undergo a form of sexual reproduction called conjugation, in which two cells come together and exchange genetic material through their oral grooves. Conjugation, as in Figure 13–6, takes place when environmental factors, including food supplies, become less ideal. After two cells join at the

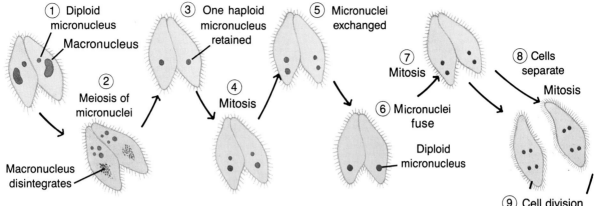

① Diploid micronucleus
Macronucleus
② Meiosis of micronuclei
③ One haploid micronucleus retained
④ Mitosis
⑤ Micronuclei exchanged
⑥ Micronuclei fuse
Diploid micronucleus
⑦ Mitosis
⑧ Cells separate
Mitosis
Macronucleus disintegrates
⑨ Cell division
Micronuclei fuse to become macronuclei

oral grooves, the macronuclei and all but one of the micronuclei disintegrate. The remaining micronucleus divides by meiosis to form four haploid micronuclei. Three of the four micronuclei disintegrate (1, 2). The remaining one then undergoes mitosis (3, 4). The nuclei produced are not the same size. The smaller of the two micronuclei is exchanged between the paramecia (5). Once into the neighboring cell, the micronucleus fuses with the larger micronucleus in the other cell (6). Each paramecium now contains one diploid micronucleus with genes from both paramecia. Mitosis takes place (7), the paramecia separate, and several nuclear divisions result in the formation of new macronuclei and micronuclei (8, 9). Each of the conjugating individuals has been genetically altered. Both go on to reproduce asexually.

FIGURE 13–6.

Conjugation in *Paramecium* introduces genetic variation.

13:7 Sporozoans

Protists belonging to the phylum Sporozoa are all parasitic, non-motile protozoans. **Sporozoans** are protists that reproduce by spores. A **spore** is a reproductive cell that can produce a new organism without fertilization. Sporozoans have complex life cycles within the blood of one or more hosts.

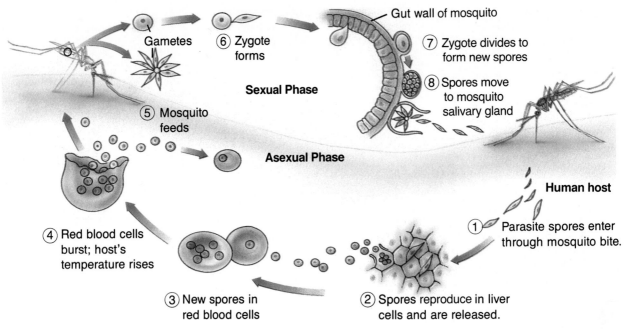

FIGURE 13–7.

Different species of *Plasmodium* cause malaria in humans, birds, and other mammals. The life cycle of *Plasmodium vivax* in humans is shown above.

Sporozoans of the genus *Plasmodium* cause malaria, a disease common in tropical climates. The life cycle depicted in Figure 13–7 begins when a female *Anopheles* mosquito bites a person who already has malaria. The mosquito takes in *Plasmodium* gametes, or reproductive cells, from the infected person's blood. The gametes move to the mosquito's digestive tract. There they fuse forming a zygote. The *Plasmodium* zygote divides many times to form numerous spores and then breaks open. The spores move to the mosquito's salivary gland. The spores are carried in the saliva of the mosquito into a new host when the mosquito bites again. Spores reproduce asexually in the liver of the host. They then move into the host's blood where they destroy red blood cells and release toxic substances that cause periodic chills and fever. Some spores develop into male and female gametes but they do not fuse. Others enter new red blood cells and destroy them. When a mosquito bites an infected host, the cycle begins again.

REVIEW

6. How do amoebas move?
7. How do ciliates differ from flagellates?
8. What makes the sporozoans different from the other protozoan groups?
9. **SKILL REVIEW:** Sequence the steps that occur during conjugation in *Paramecium.* For more help, refer to Reading Science in the Skill Handbook, pages 798 to 799.
10. **USING CONCEPTS:** Why are contractile vacuoles present in freshwater protozoa?

ALGAE: PLANTLIKE PROTISTS

It may be a surprise to you to find out that every breath you take depends on algae! Their photosynthetic activities generate three-fourths of the molecular oxygen on Earth. Just about every animal on land and in water depends either directly or indirectly on these plantlike protists. Algae support life as you know it by providing a hospitable planet on which to live. These eukaryotic autotrophs hold a very important position in the varied world of living organisms. They are the beginning of all food chains, upon which all other organisms depend.

13:8 Euglenoids

The **euglenoids,** members of phylum Euglenophyta, are protists that have traits of both plants and animals. They are like plants because they contain chlorophyll and undergo photosynthesis. However, euglenoids have no cell walls. Instead of a cell wall, euglenoids have a layer of flexible, interlocking protein fibers inside the cell membrane. Euglenoids are similar to animals because they are responsive and move by using one or two flagella for locomotion. Euglenoids have a contractile vacuole that expels excess water from the cell through an opening. They reproduce asexually by mitosis.

A typical euglenoid in Figure 13–8 has an eyespot, a red, light-sensitive structure, which assists *Euglena* in moving to areas where light stimulates photosynthesis in their chloroplasts.

If a euglenoid is placed in darkness for a long period of time, its chloroplasts disintegrate. It then begins to take in nutrients through its cell membrane much like a protozoan. For reasons like this, you can see why there are several opinions as to how to classify these protists.

Objectives:

- distinguish between plantlike and animal-like characteristics of euglenoids.
- describe the characteristics of diatoms and dinoflagellates.
- compare the variety of forms that occur in green algae.
- describe conjugation in *Spirogyra* and its importance.
- describe the concept of alternating sporophyte and gametophyte generations in algae.

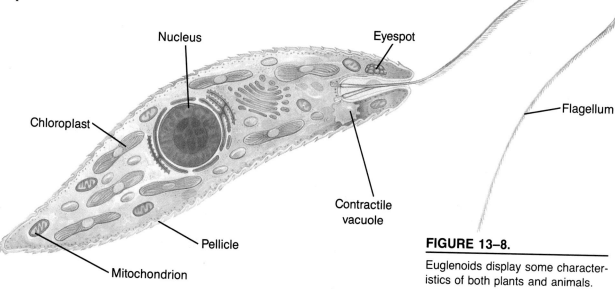

Nucleus

Eyespot

Chloroplast

Flagellum

Contractile vacuole

Pellicle

Mitochondrion

FIGURE 13–8.

Euglenoids display some characteristics of both plants and animals.

13:9 Diatoms

Diatoms, members of phylum Bacillariophyta, are photosynthetic, unicellular organisms with shells made of silica. They live in marine and fresh waters. The shells of diatoms are like small boxes with lids. One half of the shell fits inside the other half as illustrated in Figure 13–9. Diatoms are divided into two major groups according to shape. Some have radial symmetry. Others are long and have distinct right and left sides. When diatoms reproduce asexually, the two halves of the box separate. Each half produces a new half shell to fit inside itself. Each new generation is smaller than its parent cell. When diatoms reach the point of being only about one quarter of their original size, sexual reproduction may take place. Gametes form and fuse to form new diatoms. These new individuals then divide asexually.

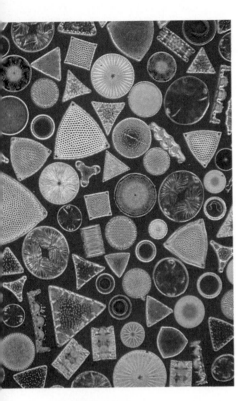

FIGURE 13–9.

As a result of asexual reproduction, diatoms become smaller in size.

How do diatoms store food?

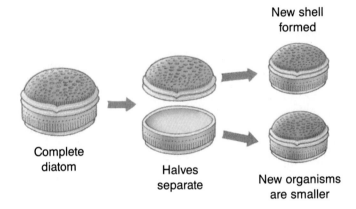

New shell formed

Complete diatom

Halves separate

New organisms are smaller

Diatoms contain chlorophyll and are autotrophs. Food is stored in the form of oils instead of starch. Fish that feed on diatoms often have an unpleasant oily taste. Cod liver oil, once given on a daily basis to children because of its vitamin A content, is made from liver oils of codfish that have eaten diatoms.

When huge populations of marine diatoms die, their silica cell walls accumulate on the ocean floor in such large quantities that they can be mined by power shovels. This diatomaceous (di ut uh MAY shus) earth is used to polish metal and is added to road paint to produce the sparkle that makes pavement lines visible at night.

13:10 Dinoflagellates

Some unicellular algae called **dinoflagellates** have cell walls made up of thick cellulose plates. They belong to the phylum Dinoflagellata. Dinoflagellates have two flagella located in grooves at right angles to each other. When these flagella beat, the cell spins slowly giving them the common name of sea whirlers. Most species are marine, but a few are found in fresh water.

Dinoflagellates are autotrophs. They contain both chlorophyll and red pigments. Many dinoflagellates live symbiotically with corals,

FIGURE 13–10.

Red tides are caused by dinoflagellates that may be as dense as 40 million organisms per cubic meter of seawater.

jellyfish, and mollusks. Some species are luminescent and give off a spooky green glow. Other species produce poisonous toxins. In the summer, dinoflagellates may undergo population explosions that turn the sea red. Toxins produced by these "red tides" cause respiratory failure in birds and fish. Humans who eat mollusks that have fed on these algae may also be poisoned. During periods of uncontrolled dinoflagellate growth, harvesting of shellfish is banned.

13:11 Green Algae

The phylum Chlorophyta is the most diverse of all the algae. More than 7000 species of green algae have been identified. The major pigment in green algae is chlorophyll, but some species also produce yellow pigments, giving the organisms a yellow-green color. The simplest alga is *Chlamydomonas,* a unicellular, flagellated organism. Others, such as *Spirogyra,* form multicellular filaments. Colonial species form groups of cells that live together. A *Volvox* colony is a hollow ball composed of 500 to 600 unicellular flagellated organisms arranged in a single layer. The cells are held together by strands of cytoplasm and their flagella face outward. When the flagella beat, the colony spins through the water.

Most species of green algae live in fresh water, but some live in moist soil, on the surface of tree trunks, and even on snow. In Chapter 14, you will learn about lichens, a mutualistic relationship of fungi and algae. Other species of green algae live in the cells and body cavities of marine invertebrates, such as hydra, clams, and anemones. Green hydra owe their color to the green algae that live inside them. The hydra provides the photosynthetic residents with protection and carbon dioxide for photosynthesis. The algae provide the hydra with food and oxygen.

FIGURE 13–11.

Chlamydomonas is the simplest of unicellular green algae. It is easily recognized by its single cup-shaped chloroplast.

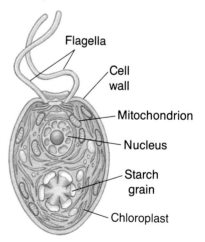

Flagella

Cell wall

Mitochondrion

Nucleus

Starch grain

Chloroplast

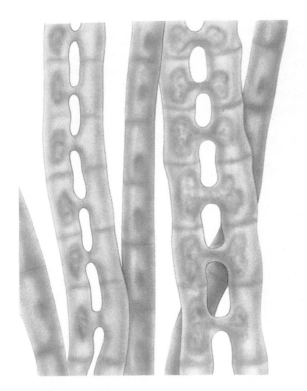
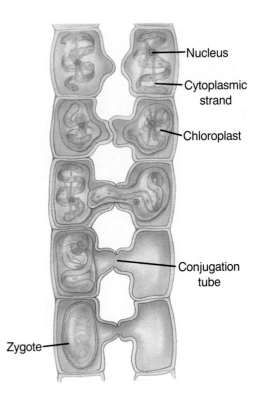

Nucleus

Cytoplasmic strand

Chloroplast

Conjugation tube

Zygote

FIGURE 13–12.

Conjugation in protists such as *Spirogyra,* serves to introduce genetic variety, and enables the organism to survive unfavorable conditions.

Green algae reproduce asexually and sexually. *Spirogyra* reproduces asexually either by mitosis or by fragmentation. In **fragmentation,** the filament breaks up into pieces, each of which grows into a new filament by mitosis. Sexual reproduction in *Spirogyra* occurs by a form of conjugation. Two filaments line up next to each other and tubes form between them. The contents of one cell flows through the tube into the adjacent cell. This material fuses and a diploid zygote results. A thick wall then forms around the zygote. This thick-walled, diploid structure is called a **zygospore.** Zygospores survive unfavorable conditions. When conditions improve, a zygospore undergoes meiosis and a new haploid *Spirogyra* filament develops.

13:12 Red and Brown Algae

phaeophyta:
phaios (GK) dusky
phyton (GK) plant

Members of the phyla Rhodophyta and Phaeophyta are the red and brown seaweeds, multicellular marine organisms. Red seaweeds grow in tropical waters or along rocky coasts in colder water. They attach to rocks by specialized structures called holdfasts. Chlorophyll allows red algae to photosynthesize in shallow waters. Other pigments in red algae enable them to photosynthesize in deeper water. These pigments absorb blue light waves, the only part of the light spectrum that penetrates depths of water over 100 m.

The largest and most complex of the protists are the brown algae, or kelp. Kelp are commonly found in cold water coastal areas. Kelp have adaptations in the form of air bladders that keep the organism near the surface where it can absorb light needed for photosynthesis. Holdfasts anchor the kelp at the bottom.

Many algae have complex life cycles that alternate haploid and diploid generations. The haploid form of the organism is the **gametophyte** because it produces gametes. Gametes from two organisms fuse to form a diploid zygote. All cells that form when the zygote divides by mitosis are diploid. The diploid form of the organism, called the **sporophyte,** then undergoes meiosis and produces haploid spores. Each haploid spore then develops into a haploid alga gametophyte and the cycle repeats. In some organisms, the gametophyte and sporophyte forms look alike. In other organisms, the two forms look very different. Many algae, fungi, and all plants go through life cycles that alternate haploid and diploid generations.

NoteWorthy

In 1985 off the Bahamas, a red alga was reported growing attached to rocks 268 meters below the surface of the water. This was a record depth for a photosynthetic organism.

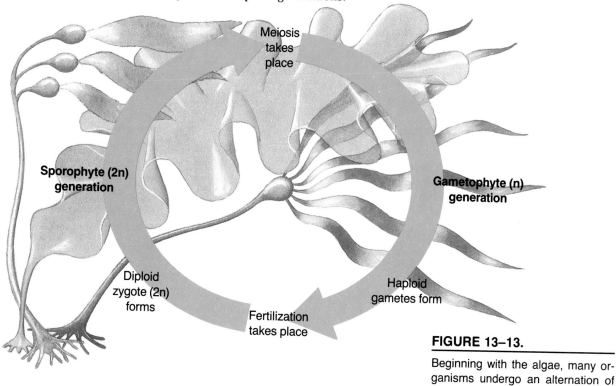

Meiosis takes place

Sporophyte (2n) generation

Gametophyte (n) generation

Diploid zygote (2n) forms

Haploid gametes form

Fertilization takes place

FIGURE 13–13.

Beginning with the algae, many organisms undergo an alternation of generations in their life cycles.

REVIEW

11. Why are algae important to living things?
12. How do the sporophyte and gametophyte phases of an organism differ from each other?
13. Why are green algae the most diverse of the alga phyla?
14. **SKILL REVIEW:** Construct a table listing the different phyla of algae. Indicate if they have one or more cells, their color, and give an example of each. For more help, refer to Organizing Information in the Skill Handbook, pages 810 to 813.
15. **USING CONCEPTS:** Do you think euglenoids should be classified with protozoans or algae? Defend your answer.

BIOLAB

Protist Responses

Problem: How do *Paramecium* and *Euglena* respond to light?

Materials
Euglena culture
Paramecium culture
microscope slides (2)
dropper
metric ruler
microscope

index card
scissors
coverslips (2)
toothpick
methyl cellulose

Procedures
1. Prepare a data table like the one shown.
2. With a toothpick place a small ring of methyl cellulose on a clean microscope slide. Place a drop of *Paramecium* culture within the ring of methyl cellulose. Place a coverslip over the ring and culture. Methyl cellulose is a thick, syrupy material that slows movement of organisms for easy observation.
3. Mount the slide on the microscope and focus under low power, locating several paramecia. Observe their body structures.
4. Cut a strip of an index card the same size as your slide. Then cut a slit 1.5 mm long and 0.2 mm wide. Place this slitted strip under the slide on the microscope stage with the slit under the area where the protists are located.
5. Formulate a **hypothesis** about how *Paramecium* and *Euglena* respond to light.
6. After several minutes, carefully remove the strip and focus on the paramecia. Record your observations.

7. Repeat steps using a *Euglena* culture.

Data and Observations

Organism	Response to light
Paramecium	
Euglena	

Questions and Conclusion
1. Where did you find most of the *Euglena* and *Paramecium* organisms after removing the index card strip? Explain their locations.
2. From the tendency of the organisms to concentrate in one area rather than another, were you able to conclude whether there was a positive (toward) or negative (away) response to light?
3. Was your **hypothesis** supported? Explain.
4. What other factors might account for a concentration of organisms in one area rather than another?
5. What other variables might you check to determine if the organisms would show a negative or positive response?
Conclusion: What can you conclude about the response of *Paramecium* and *Euglena* to light?

Fungi are classified in a distinct kingdom that you will study in Chapter 14. However, certain groups of both the slime molds and water molds show some features of fungi and protists. Slime molds are more attractive than their name implies. Many are brilliantly colored. They form delicate netlike structures on the surfaces of their food supplies. These organisms obtain energy by decomposing organic materials.

Objectives:
- contrast the two slime mold phyla in respect to cellular differences and life cycles.
- discuss the economic importance of the downy mildews and water molds.

13:13 The Slime Molds

There are two phyla of slime molds, Myxomycota, the acellular slime molds, and Acrasiomycota, the cellular slime molds. At some point in their lives, they are amoebalike or have flagella but then produce spores like fungi. Slime molds live in cool, shady areas. They grow on damp, organic matter such as rotting leaves or tree stumps.

The acellular slime molds are also known as plasmodial slime molds because they form a plasmodium. A **plasmodium** is a mass of cytoplasm in slime molds that contains many diploid nuclei but no cell walls or membranes. This slimy amoeboid mass is the feeding stage of the organism. It creeps by amoeboid movement over the ground, engulfing microscopic organisms and digesting them in food vacuoles. A plasmodium continues growing as long as conditions are favorable. It may become more than a meter in diameter and contain thousands of nuclei. When conditions become unfavorable, as in a shortage of food or water, the plasmodium forms many reproductive structures on stalks. Meiosis takes place within these

How do slime molds capture food?

FIGURE 13–14.

The feeding stage or plasmodium of an acellular slime mold is a mass of protoplasm that is amoeba-like in its movement.

reproductive structures. Haploid spores form and are released. If spores land where conditions are favorable for growth, they germinate into either flagellated cells or amoeboid cells that serve as gametes. Both of these types of cells closely resemble protozoan cells. Both kinds of cells fuse with their own kind to form diploid zygotes, which then grow into new plasmodia.

Cellular slime molds exist as individual haploid cells during their feeding stage. When food becomes scarce, amoeboid cells come together to form a multicellular mass very much like a plasmodium. However, this mass is made up of individual cells with cell membranes. The slime-covered "slug" creeps around until it finds a suitable location. Then its cells become rearranged to form a stalk with a spore-filled structure on top. When the spores mature, the structure ruptures and releases the haploid spores into the air. Each spore develops into a new individual cell that begins the life cycle again. The spores are asexual and the entire life cycle of the cellular slime molds is haploid.

FIGURE 13–15.

Cellular slime molds contain masses of individual cells, each with a cell membrane.

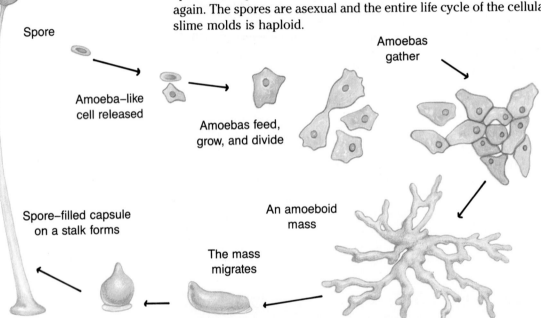

Spore

Amoeba–like cell released

Amoebas feed, grow, and divide

Amoebas gather

An amoeboid mass

Spore–filled capsule on a stalk forms

The mass migrates

13:14 Mildew and Water Molds

Organisms such as water molds, downy mildew, and white rusts are members of phylum Oomycota. This phylum is a large and varied group consisting mainly of forms that parasitize plants and others that feed on dead organisms. A few water molds are parasites of fish and fish eggs. Oomycotes usually live in water and have cell walls that are composed of cellulose. They appear as fuzzy white growths on decaying matter. Water molds produce male and female gametes. Each kind of gamete is produced by meiosis. Since oomycotes have cell walls and produce gametes, they have some characteristics of both plants and animals.

FIGURE 13–16.

Biology confronted history when a water mold infestation of potatoes resulted in a massive emigration of Irish people in the mid to late 1800s.

The water molds are important because they can cause several economically disastrous diseases in plants. In 1846 and 1847, the entire potato crop of Ireland became infected with a type of water mold. Potatoes were Ireland's main crop. The resulting famine caused the death of more than 2 million people. The course of history changed when many others left Ireland and emigrated to other countries, including the United States.

Another oomycote, a mildew, causes a serious disease in grape vines. The French wine industry was threatened in the 1870s when this organism infected French grape vines.

Cellular slime molds are of interest to biologists because of the different forms that appear during their life cycle. Biologists study these organisms to learn more about differentiation, the process by which cells develop specialized functions.

REVIEW

16. Why are the plasmodial slime molds referred to as acellular?
17. What important economic events were caused by oomycotes?
18. Why are slime molds difficult to classify?
19. **SKILL REVIEW:** If you know that a plasmodium consists of many nuclei within a single cell, what can you infer about the process that formed the plasmodium? For more help, refer to Observing and Inferring in the Skill Handbook, page 809.
20. **USING CONCEPTS:** What kinds of environments would be considered favorable for the growth of slime molds? Why?

CHAPTER REVIEW

SUMMARY

1. The Kingdom Protista contains plantlike, animal-like, and funguslike protists. **13:1**
2. Protists are eukaryotes. Higher plants evolved from green algae. **13:2**
3. Protists obtain energy in a variety of ways. Some species make up plankton. **13:3**
4. Amoebas move by pseudopods. Some have shells. **13:4**
5. Flagellates move by flagella. Many are parasites. **13:5**
6. Ciliates move by cilia. They may undergo conjugation. **13:6**
7. Sporozoans are parasites. Malaria is caused by a sporozoan. **13:7**
8. Euglenoids are algae with characteristics of both plants and animals. **13:8**
9. Diatoms are algae with silica shells. **13:9**
10. Dinoflagellates cause red tides. **13:10**
11. Green algae are diverse and have unicellular and multicellular forms. **13:11**
12. Red and brown algae show sporophyte and gametophyte stages. **13:12**
13. Slime molds are acellular and cellular. **13:13**
14. Water molds have separate gametes and are economically important. **13:14**

LANGUAGE OF BIOLOGY

algae	parasite
amoebas	phytoplankton
asexual reproduction	plankton
ciliate	plasmodium
diatoms	protozoans
dinoflagellates	pseudopods
euglenoids	slime molds
flagellates	spore
fragmentation	sporophyte
gametophyte	sporozoans
macronucleus	zooplankton
micronucleus	zygospore

Choose the word or phrase from the list above that completes the sentence.

1. ____ is a group of floating unicellular algae found in Earth's bodies of water.
2. A(n) ____ is a diploid organism that undergoes meiosis to produce haploid spores.
3. Amoebas move by means of ____.
4. A(n) ____ is a reproductive cell that produces a new organism without fertilization.
5. A mass of cytoplasm called a(n) ____ enables an acellular slime mold to move and engulf its food.
6. Sexual reproduction in ciliates is controlled by the ____.
7. Most of the oxygen in our atmosphere is generated by the ____.
8. Protists that can change their mode of nutrition depending on light availability are ____.
9. Algae shaped like interlocking lids are ____.
10. A species of ____ causes red tides.

REVIEWING CONCEPTS

Choose the word or phrase that completes the sentence or answers the question.

11. Most protozoans are similar in some ways to ____.
    a. plants   c. fungi
    b. animals   d. bacteria
12. Protists are thought to be ancestors of ____.
    a. plants   c. fungi
    b. animals   d. all of the above
13. Algae obtain their food from ____.
    a. phagocytosis   c. decomposition
    b. photosynthesis d. parasitism
14. Ancestral cyanobacteria probably evolved into ____.
    a. nuclei   c. mitochondria
    b. algae   d. chloroplasts
15. Ciliates use cilia for motion and for ____.
    a. reproduction   c. secretion
    b. excretion   d. ingestion

16. ____ must be present for malaria to spread.
    a. *Anopheles*
    b. Organisms with the disease
    c. *Plasmodium*
    d. All of the above
17. Sporozoans move by means of ____.
    a. cilia   c. pseudopodia
    b. flagella   d. none of the
                               above
18. Algae produce oxygen by the process of ____.
    a. respiration   c. photosynthesis
    b. secretion   d. excretion
19. The presence of chlorophyll allows a euglenoid to ____.
    a. make food   c. avoid enemies
    b. sense light   d. take in water
20. Diatoms store food in the form of ____.
    a. glycogen   c. starch
    b. cellulose   d. oils

UNDERSTANDING CONCEPTS

Answer the following questions using complete sentences.

21. What are the three means of locomotion used by the protozoans?
22. What is the commercial importance of diatoms?
23. What is the advantage of cyst formation in amoebas and zygospores in *Spirogyra?*
24. Describe the way paramecia take in food.
25. What main characteristic of plants is lacking in euglenoids?
26. What is the importance of foraminiferans in oil exploration?
27. How are dinoflagellates important ecologically and economically?
28. Describe conjugation in *Spirogyra.*
29. Describe the development of malaria in a host organism.
30. Compare sporophytes and gametophytes.

APPLYING CONCEPTS

Answer the following questions using complete sentences.

31. What would be an advantage of prokaryotes establishing symbiotic relationships with other prokaryotes?
32. Under what conditions would a protist reproduce asexually? Sexually?
33. What are the disadvantages of a protist such as a sporozoan being totally parasitic?
34. Why is light important to phytoplankton?
35. Contrast conjugation in *Spirogyra* with conjugation in *Paramecium.* What is the importance of the end result in each case?

EXTENSIONS

1. Compile a list of food products that contain substances derived from red and brown algae. Find out why these additives are used.
2. Termites have flagellated protozoans in their intestines that digest wood. Investigate the symbiotic relationships that aid plant-eating animals, such as cattle, in digesting cellulose.
3. Contrast the inhabitants of a plankton sample taken from a freshwater pond and one taken from temperate ocean waters.

READINGS

El-Sayed, S.Z. "Fragile Life Under the Ozone Hole." *Natural History,* Oct. 1988, pp. 72–80.
Hendricks, M. "Strike the Parasite and Spare the Host." *Science News,* Aug. 27, 1988, p. 134.
Nuzzi, R. "New York's Brown Tide." *The Conservationist,* Sept./Oct. 1988, pp. 30–35.

FLOWERING
PLANTS

CONIFERS

FERNS

MOSSES

FUNGI

PROTISTS

FUNGI

In an effort to help clean up the environment, many communities have recycling centers. Careful reuse of materials means that valuable resources are not wasted. But few people want to take time to separate bottles and cans, so very little waste winds up being recycled.

In contrast, nature has a very efficient recycling system in the form of organisms called fungi. Think about it. Sometimes before you have a chance to eat all the oranges you bought at the grocery store, one of them becomes soft and covered with a blue-green moldy growth like the one to the right. Your reaction is "Yuck!", and into the trash it goes without another thought. But stop and think. While that moldy orange is no longer useful to you as food, it still contains chemicals that are useful to other organisms. By decomposing the tissues of the orange, the fungus feeds itself and acts as an agent that recycles nutrients. The bright fungi to the left recycle nutrients in a forest.

Penicillium mold
on an orange

THE LIFE OF A FUNGUS

Fungi, along with the monerans that you studied in Chapter 12, are organisms that decompose substances containing organic compounds. Food, clothing, film, a dead mouse in a corn field, and fallen tree branches are all made up of organic materials. Therefore, they are all subject to attack by fungi. It isn't desirable to have food and clothing destroyed. But by bringing about the decay of dead organisms, fungi release nutrients trapped in these materials. In the soil, these nutrients are used by plants for growth. As a result, fungi keep Earth from becoming buried under mountains of dead organisms, dried leaves, and wastes.

14:1 General Characteristics

Various organisms are classified as fungi. Some fungi have peculiar names, such as stinkhorn, yeast, blight, rust, truffle, and puffball. Each of these fungi has certain distinctive characteristics. Most fungi need moisture, oxygen, and a supply of organic material to live and

Objectives:
- list differences between fungi and plants.
- describe the structure of fungi.
- discuss the feeding relationships of fungi and list the materials needed for growth.
- describe the ways fungi reproduce.
- discuss the importance of spores.

Fungi on a forest floor

a

b

FIGURE 14–1.

Fungi are characterized by a variety of forms. Earth stars (a) and mushrooms (b) are both classified as fungi.

FIGURE 14–2.

Hyphae form the basic structure of fungi.

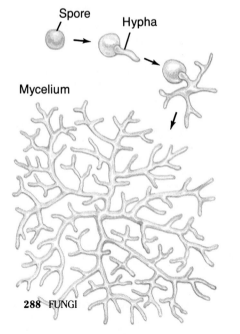

reproduce. These fungi are aerobic. Other fungi that are used in the production of beer and wine are anaerobic. Fungi are found everywhere in soil, air, fresh water, and salt water. Most species grow best at temperatures from 20 to 30°C. Others grow at cooler temperatures such as in a refrigerator container, where thick furry masses of pink, white, or black mold grow on things that are no longer recognizable as food.

Fungi used to be described as members of the plant kingdom. This conclusion was logical at the time because many fungi grow anchored in soil and have cell walls as plants have, and both plants and fungi are eukaryotes. However, enough differences have been found between plants and fungi so that scientists now classify fungi in a kingdom of their own. Members of the Kingdom Fungi are not held in the ground by roots as are plants, and they do not contain chlorophyll. Cell walls in plants are made up of a complex carbohydrate called cellulose. Cell walls of most fungi contain chitin (KITE un). **Chitin** is a complex carbohydrate and the same material that makes the outer body parts of insects hard. A few species of fungi have cell walls that are made up of cellulose or a combination of chitin and cellulose. Most fungi are multicellular. Only yeasts are unicellular among the fungi.

The basic structure of a fungus is formed from threadlike filaments called **hyphae** (*sing.* hypha). Hyphae grow and branch extensively to form a mat of filaments called a **mycelium** (*pl.* mycelia). The mushrooms that you order on pizza are masses of mycelia. Most hyphae are divided into cells by cross walls called septa. The septa usually have small holes called pores. Cytoplasm and cell organelles flow from one cell to the next through the pores. Some hyphae, therefore, have several nuclei within each cell. Some species of fungi have hyphae with no septa. Consequently, when looked at under a microscope, hundreds of nuclei can be seen streaming through these hyphae.

14:2 Nutrition

Fungi do not contain chlorophyll. Organisms without chlorophyll can't make food. They are heterotrophs. A **heterotroph** is an organism that depends on sources other than itself for its supply of energy. Most heterotrophs, such as owls, cats, and coyotes, hunt for their food. People are heterotrophs. You go to the kitchen, a grocery store, the garden, or the local fast-food restaurant for food that you need. Fungi are heterotrophs that obtain nutrients through a process called extracellular digestion. Food is digested outside the cells of the fungus. The hyphae of the fungus growing on an orange give off enzymes into the cells of the orange. The enzymes break down large organic molecules in the orange into smaller molecules. These small molecules then diffuse through the hyphal wall into the fungus cell, where they are used to synthesize materials for growth and repair. Hyphae spread throughout the orange, forming a mycelial network. More and more parts of the orange are digested and become decomposed. The more extensive the mycelial network becomes, the greater the amount of nutrients available to the fungus.

Extracellular digestion takes place whether the fungus species is a saprobe, a parasite, or a mutualist. Fungi that decompose wastes and dead organisms such as a dead bird or a tree trunk are saprobes. Parasitic fungi absorb nutrients from the cells of living hosts. The host is harmed and usually dies. The fungus that causes Dutch elm disease is a parasite. When it attacks a living elm tree, one type of hypha called haustoria (haw STOH ree uh) invades the cells of the tree, causing them to die. **Haustoria** are hyphae of parasitic fungi that absorb nutrients. Mutualistic fungi absorb nutrients from living hosts, but also perform jobs that help the host survive in some way. Mutualistic fungi help a host retain water or make minerals available. The host makes a carbohydrate such as starch available to the fungus. Most trees exist in a mutualistic relationship with fungi.

haustorium:
haurire (L) to drink

How do fungi digest food?

FIGURE 14–3.

Parasitic fungi form haustoria that penetrate host cells and promote the death of the host. The American elm in the photograph has been attacked by the fungal Dutch Elm disease.

Fungal hypha

Haustoria

Plant cells

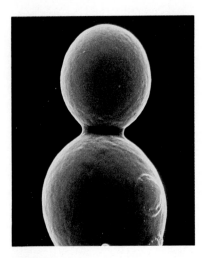

FIGURE 14–4.

Budding is the form of asexual reproduction in yeast.

FIGURE 14–5.

Sporangia cover the underside of this bracket fungus.

14:3 Reproduction

Fungi reproduce both asexually and sexually. Asexually, fungal species reproduce by fragmentation, budding, or by spores. When a fungus reproduces by fragmentation, hyphae broken from a mycelial network continue to grow and produce new hyphae. If you move a wheelbarrowful of soil from the frontyard to the backyard, numerous fungal hyphae are carried along. Many of the broken fragments at the edge of the load will continue to grow. **Budding** is a form of asexual reproduction in which mitosis takes place and a new organism forms from an outgrowth of a parent cell. Yeasts reproduce most frequently by budding.

As you learned in Chapter 12, a spore is a reproductive cell that germinates and develops into a new organism. Most fungi reproduce by spores. When a fungal spore falls on a place that has all the conditions necessary for growth, it germinates. The hyphae that are produced spread over and into the matter or substrate on which the spore has landed. Eventually some hyphae grow upward out of the substrate and produce a structure called a sporangium (spuh RAN jee um). A **sporangium** (*pl.* sporangia) is a sack or case in which spores are produced. Mushroom caps contain sporangia. The black spots or knobs on bread mold are sporangia. A sporangium is like the tip of an iceberg. A sporangium represents only a small portion of the fungus. Beneath every sporangium is an extensive network of mycelium. When you see a patch or ring of mushrooms growing in a lawn, there is always far more mycelial growth underground than you see above ground.

Spores are also formed when a fungal species undergoes sexual reproduction. The method by which sexual spores are formed is the basis on which fungi are classified into four different groups.

14:4 Adapted for Survival

Fungi have adaptations that have contributed to their widespread distribution and survival. Most of these adaptations involve sporangia and spores. First, sporangia are adapted to keep spores from drying out until they are ready to be released. A second adaptation is that spores are light enough in mass to be moved easily by a variety of carriers. Spores are usually swept along on air currents as they are released from upright sporangia. Spores released in one part of the world may be carried many kilometers in the atmosphere before landing somewhere where they can germinate. They may also be moved by splashing water, or by birds or insects. Spores of Dutch elm disease stick to the body of the European elm beetle as it feeds on infected trees. The spore-covered beetle then moves on to deposit its eggs in healthy elms, transferring spores in the process. In this way, the disease is spread.

A third adaptation for survival is that spores are produced in large numbers within sporangia. A single puffball that measures 25 cm in circumference produces close to a trillion spores. Production of large numbers ensures that at least some will survive. As you have learned, evolution occurs only when enough organisms of a species survive to reproduce.

The adaptations described above contribute to the worldwide distribution of fungi. Fungi are most abundant in tropical regions because all the conditions needed for growth are present. The warm, humid atmosphere and diverse plant and animal populations provide the temperature, moisture, and organic matter for the growth of numerous species of fungi. Fungi, in turn, contribute to the rapid decomposition of any organic matter that falls to the tropical forest floor.

Fungi are not so abundant in drier areas of the world where supplies of water and organic materials are limited. However, spores and mycelia have been found to survive extended periods of drying in both cold and hot deserts. In the Arctic, some fungi are adapted to extremely low temperatures by living in mutualism with organisms that can make their own food, such as photosynthetic algae. They provide a source of vegetation for grazing herds of nomadic animals, such as caribou.

FIGURE 14–6.

Spores released by puffballs are easily dispersed by air currents.

sporangium:
sporos (GK) seed
anggeion (GK) vessel

REVIEW

1. Distinguish between hyphae and mycelia.
2. Explain how fungi use extracellular digestion.
3. What three adaptations of fungi contribute to their survival?
4. **SKILL REVIEW:** How would you estimate the number of spores from a puffball fungus that is 10 cm in circumference? For more help, refer to Measuring in SI in the Skill Handbook, pages 806 to 808.
5. **USING CONCEPTS:** Explain why a bird's nest is a place where several types of fungi may be found.

Objectives:
- compare the four divisions of fungi.
- list fungi in each division that are helpful or harmful.
- discuss the origins of fungi.

To date, more than 100 000 fungus species have been described by mycologists, scientists who study fungi. Fungi are classified into divisions according to the way in which spores are produced during sexual reproduction cycles. The name of each division is derived from the sexual structures in each group.

14:5 Zygote Fungi

Fungi that belong to the division Zygomycota (zi goh mi KOH tuh) are saprobes. They reproduce asexually by spores and sexually by forming zygospores. Hyphae of these fungi do not have septa. The most familiar example of the Zygomycota is black bread mold, *Rhizopus stolonifer*. You may have seen this species as a black fuzzy growth on bread left forgotten in a plastic bag on the shelf. Figure 14–7 shows the patterns of asexual and sexual reproduction in *Rhizopus* on bread.

Asexual reproduction in *Rhizopus* takes place when spores germinate on the surface of a piece of bread. Hyphae form stolons and rhizoids. A **stolon** is a type of hypha that grows over the surface of

FIGURE 14–7.

The black bread mold *Rhizopus stolonifer* reproduces both asexually (a) and sexually (b).

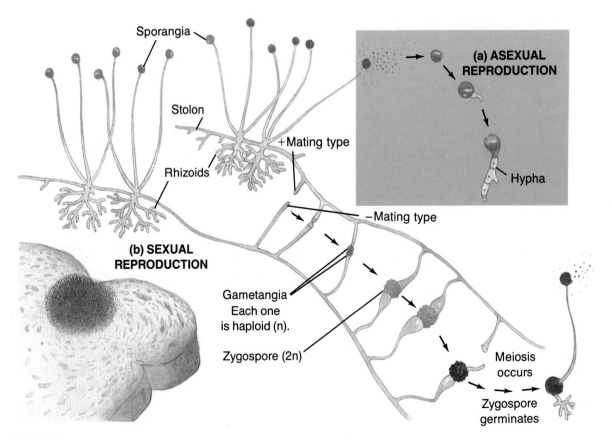

Sporangia

Stolon

+Mating type

(a) ASEXUAL REPRODUCTION

Hypha

Rhizoids

−Mating type

(b) SEXUAL REPRODUCTION

Gametangia
Each one
is haploid (n).

Zygospore (2n)

Meiosis
occurs

Zygospore
germinates

food producing a mass of mycelium. A **rhizoid** is a type of hypha that penetrates food, anchors the fungus, and absorbs nutrients. As growth continues, some of the hyphae on the surface develop into sporangia. The sporangia mature and become round black structures loaded with asexual spores that give the fungus its characteristic color. When each sporangium splits open, hundreds of spores are shot into the air. Spores that land on a moist food supply germinate and form new hyphae that continue the cycle.

When materials needed for the fungus to reproduce asexually are not available, a sexual reproduction cycle begins. For instance, if a piece of moldy bread falls down behind the refrigerator and dries out, not enough moisture remains for mold growth. In that event, structures form in the bread that enable the fungus to reproduce sexually. Sexual reproduction occurs when the tips of hyphae of two different mycelial masses within the bread come close enough together to fuse. The two different hyphae, called mating types, are labeled plus and minus. There are no female or male structures. A nucleus from each of the hyphae forms a gametangium (gam eet AN gee um). A **gametangium** is a structure that produces gametes. When the contents of the two gametangia fuse, a diploid zygote forms. This diploid cell develops into a thick-walled zygospore.

Zygospores survive periods that are unfavorable to growth. When conditions improve, zygospores absorb water, undergo meiosis, and produce haploid spores. These spores produce hyphae that are capable of producing more spores asexually. *Rhizopus* molds also decompose foods other than bread. Any food that provides a source of starch or sugar, along with moisture, can support fungal growth. Fruits are excellent hosts to fungi.

Other species of *Rhizopus* are commonly found in soil and dung. Dung is frequently used as a fertilizer. It is rich in cellulose, nitrogen, and water, compounds used by fungi for growth and reproduction.

On what does *Rhizopus* grow?

FIGURE 14–8.

A stained preparation of *Rhizopus* shows dark zygospores forming in a mycelium (a). A scanning electron micrograph (b) shows a sporangium of *Rhizopus*.

a

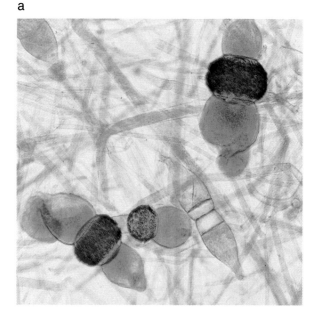

b

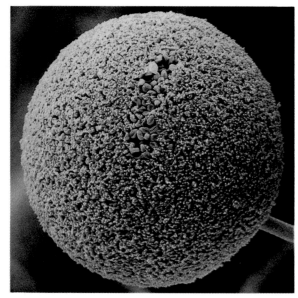

FIGURE 14–9.

Members of the Ascomycota have a variety of forms. The fungus on the left is an orange peel fungus. The morel on the right is an edible form.

FIGURE 14–10.

Most ascomycotes reproduce asexually by spores called conidia.

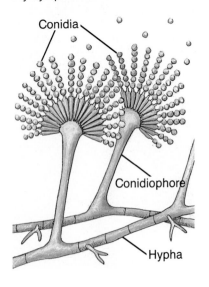

14:6 Sac Fungi

The division Ascomycota (AS coh mi koh tuh) forms the largest group of fungi. It is named for the sac-like case in which spores form during sexual reproduction. The sac-like case of the Ascomycota is called an **ascus.** Spores produced in an ascus are called **ascospores.** Ascospores are formed in cup-shaped fruiting bodies called ascocarps. Figure 14–9 shows several examples of sac fungi.

During asexual reproduction, the hyphae of the sac fungi form a structure called a conidiophore, which produces huge numbers of spores. Asexual spores produced by a conidiophore are called **conidia.** Conidia are dispersed by wind, water, or animals.

The sac fungi include many colorful molds that decorate decaying food with a blue-green, red, or brown color. Others are well known by farmers because they attack and destroy crop plants. These fungi include Dutch elm disease, apple scab, and ergot on rye. Some species live on decaying forest vegetation. Edible members of this division include truffles and morels.

The most economically important Ascomycote is yeast. Yeasts are unicellular sac fungi that usually do not produce hyphae. Yeasts occur on the surface of many fruits. They reproduce sexually by forming ascospores. More commonly, yeasts reproduce asexually by budding. Yeasts are important in the baking and fermentation industries where carbon dioxide and ethyl alcohol, formed as products of the yeast's metabolism, are used. Yeasts are becoming important tools for research in genetics because they have large chromosomes. A vaccine for the disease hepatitis B is produced by splicing human genes with those of yeast cells. Because yeasts can be produced quickly, they are an important source of the vaccine.

BIOLAB

Metabolizing Yeast

Problem: At what temperature is yeast most active?

Materials

bromthymol blue
  solution (BTB)
straw
small test tubes (4)
large test tubes (3)
one-hole stoppers for
  large test tubes with
  glass tube inserts (3)
yeast/molasses
  mixture

test-tube rack
250-mL beakers (3)
ice cubes
Celsius thermometer
hot plate
50-mL graduated
  cylinder
glass-marking pencil
10 cm rubber tubing (3)
aluminum foil

Procedures

1. Make a data table like the one shown.
2. Yeasts produce carbon dioxide during metabolism. **Hypothesize** at what temperature yeast will be most active in CO_2 production.
3. Pour 5 mL BTB into a small test tube labeled X. Using the straw, blow gently into the tube until you see a series of color changes. Cover with foil, and set it aside in a test-tube rack. Record your observation.
4. Label 3 beakers: A, B, and C. Leave beaker A empty, put ice water in beaker B, and hot water in beaker C. Place beaker C on a hot plate and adjust the temperature in beaker C to 37°C using the thermometer.
5. Label the 3 large test tubes: A, B, and C. Fill each tube with 30 mL of yeast/molasses mixture. Stopper each test tube with the one-hole stopper. Attach a piece of rubber tubing to the short glass tube in each stopper.
6. Label the 3 small test tubes: A, B, and C. Pour 5 mL BTB into each tube.
7. Place both large and small test tubes marked A in the beaker marked A. Do the same for test tubes and beakers marked B and C. Place rubber tubing from each large test tube into its small test tube of BTB. Be sure the end of the tube reaches the bottom of the BTB. Record the time you do this.
8. Record any color changes that occur in a 30-minute period and the length of time it takes for the color to change.
9. Discard all solutions as directed.

Data and Observations

Test tube	Color change(s)	Time elapsed
X		
A		
B		
C		

Questions and Conclusion

1. What caused the BTB solution to change color when you exhaled into the test tube labeled X? What was the purpose of this test tube?
2. Did the yeast/molasses solution cause a change in the color of the BTB solution? If so, why?
3. At what temperature did the first color change in the BTB tube occur?
4. Did the results of your experiment support your **hypothesis**? Explain.

Conclusion: At what temperature is yeast most active?

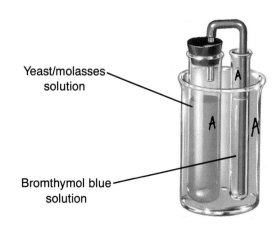

Yeast/molasses
  solution

Bromthymol blue
  solution

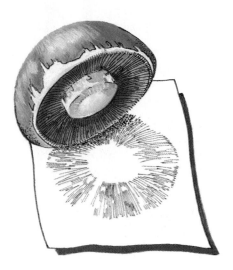

FIGURE 14–11.

Spore prints show how gills are arranged in different species of Basidiomycotes.

14:7 Club Fungi

Of all fungi, the division Basidiomycota (buh SIHD ee uh mi koht uh) is probably most familiar to you. Mushrooms, puffballs, and bracket fungi are members of the club fungi. Rusts and smuts are basidiomycotes that cause billions of dollars worth of damage to grain crops every year. Members of this division produce spores on structures called basidia during sexual reproduction. **Basidia** are club-shaped structures that produce spores by meiosis. Spores produced by basidia are called **basidiospores.** Under a mushroom cap are thin sheets of tissue called gills. The tiny club-shaped basidia are found between the gills.

The reproductive cycle of mushrooms and other fungi of this group includes several phases. Basidiospores are produced in the cap of a mushroom. When the cap opens, the gills are exposed to the air and spores are released. Figure 14–11 shows the pattern of spores from a mushroom. The basidiospores germinate to produce mycelia in the soil. As in the zygomycota, different mating types exist. When mycelia from two different mating types come in contact, two hyphae join. More mycelia develop and a new mushroom is produced. There is no asexual spore stage in the life cycle of mushrooms.

Many basidiomycotes are poisonous. Members of the genus *Amanita* are fatal. A common name for this genus is *Death Cap.*

FIGURE 14–12.

The life cycle of a mushroom shows the formation of basidiospores.

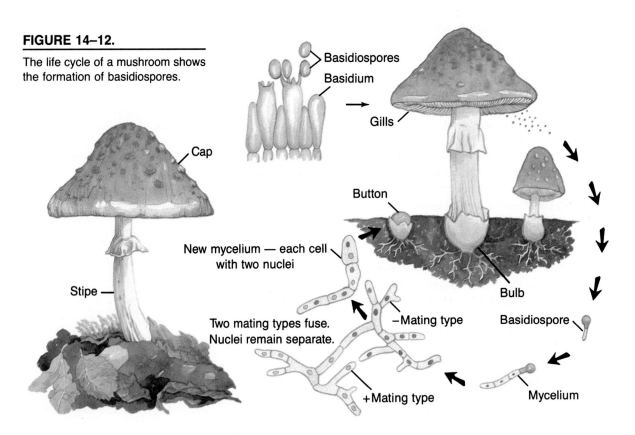

a

b

c

14:8 Imperfect Fungi

You have studied how each fungus division is named for its charac-teristic sexual reproductive structure. Almost all of the fungus divi-sions have both sexual and asexual cycles. However, there are thou-sands of fungal species that have no known sexual reproductive cycle. These fungi either reproduce only asexually or their sexual phase has not yet been observed by mycologists. All fungi with this characteristic have been grouped in the division Deuteromycota, which means "other" fungi. They are also commonly known as the Imperfect Fungi because they lack a known sexual reproductive cycle. Because conidia are formed during asexual reproduction in some species of this group, it is thought that many imperfect fungi are probably related to the Ascomycota.

Certain members of the Deuteromycota are important in the man-ufacture of cheese and drugs. Roquefort and Camembert cheeses owe their distinctive flavors to different species of the genus *Penicil-lium.* Another species of the same genus produces the drug penicil-lin. Remember the fuzzy orange? The blue-green mold growing on the orange is caused by a member of the *Penicillium* genus. Some species of imperfect fungi are used in the production of soy sauce.

Some deuteromycotes are parasites. Athlete's foot is a highly contagious disease caused by a fungal parasite that is easily spread around swimming pools and in gymnasium locker rooms. The fungus reproduces easily in the humid, dark atmosphere of gym shoes. Hyphae invade the skin and lift the cells of the surface layer. Rapid production of skin cells results in peeling skin.

Among the more unusual deuteromycotes is a group that captures insects and spiders. The life cycle of one of these predators begins when a spore falls on an insect. The spore germinates and haustoria penetrate the insect's body. The growth of the haustoria within the insect's body soon affects the animal's nervous system. The animal

FIGURE 14–13.

Smuts (a), mushrooms (b), and bracket fungi (c) are all club fungi.

FIGURE 14–14.

The drug penicillin is derived from an Imperfect Fungus.

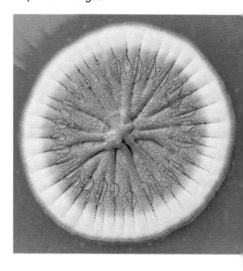

FIGURE 14–15.

Several species of the Imperfect Fungi are predatory on insects and soil organisms.

dies and small sporangia appear on its body. Spores are produced and released, and the life cycle of the fungus begins again on other insects. Other types of predatory fungi produce microscopic knobs or loops that trap and strangle microscopic soil roundworms called nematodes. The cells of the loops are sticky. When the nematode tries to move through a loop, the cells swell, trapping the worm. Haustoria invade the body of the worm, and the contents are digested and absorbed by the fungus.

In 1970, a new imperfect fungus was found that produces a substance called cyclosporine. **Cyclosporine** is a drug that suppresses the body's immune system and prevents the rejection of transplanted organs in humans. The drug does not damage bone marrow cells as happens with some other immune suppressants. Since its discovery, cyclosporine has increased the success of kidney and liver transplants. A person with a transplanted organ must take the drug for life. Cyclosporine is being investigated for use in treatment of other diseases, including some human parasitic diseases.

NoteWorthy

In 1928, Sir Alexander Fleming discovered penicillin, the first antibiotic drug. As he studied bacteria, he noticed some were dying. When he examined his cultures, he found a mold, *Penicillium notatum* growing where the bacteria died. The mold produced a substance, which he called penicillin, that killed bacteria.

FIGURE 14–16.

The lives of many people have been extended through the discovery of the drug cyclosporine.

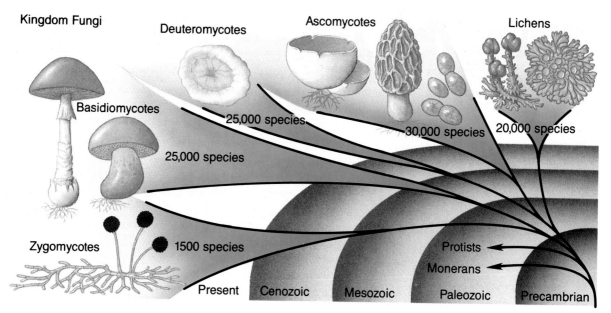

FIGURE 14-17.

Kingdom Fungi
Deuteromycotes
Ascomycotes
Lichens
Basidiomycotes
25,000 species
25,000 species
30,000 species
20,000 species
Zygomycotes
1500 species
Protists
Monerans
Present   Cenozoic   Mesozoic   Paleozoic   Precambrian

The radiation of divisions of fungi on the geologic time scale shows their relationships.

14:9 Origins

The origins of fungi are difficult to track. While fossils usually provide useful evidence of how an organism evolved, fossils of fungi are rare. Some fossil fungi have been discovered in close contact with fossil plants. Present day fungi form important and helpful feeding relationships with plants. Therefore, it might be concluded that fungi existed before and may even have been important in the movement of plants onto land in the Paleozoic Era.

Within existing fungi divisions, it is thought that species of the Basidiomycota are derived from the Ascomycota. This is because of similarities in the way nuclei are formed in both a basidium and an ascus. In Figure 14–17, which division of fungi has the most recent origin?

REVIEW

6. What characteristics are used to classify fungi?
7. Why are Basidiomycota thought to be derived from Ascomycota?
8. What are some helpful and harmful fungi and the divisions to which they belong?
9. **SKILL REVIEW:** Construct a table to compare the asexual and sexual reproductive features of Zygomycota, Ascomycota, and Basidiomycota. For more help, refer to Organizing Information in the Skill Handbook, pages 810 to 813.
10. **USING CONCEPTS:** You have found a fungus growing on a plant in the park. You take some affected leaves to school to examine them with a microscope. What characteristics will you use to determine the division to which the fungus belongs?

Immunologist

Aquatic microbiologist

Do you have allergies or know someone who does? Microbiologists are scientists who study the cause, prevention, and treatment of allergies and disease. Many microbiologists work in the areas of clinical and medical microbiology. Others are agricultural researchers or scientists employed by industry.

An **immunologist** is a microbiologist who studies how the body combats disease through the immune system. Immunologists try to determine how and why the body responds or why it doesn't respond when exposed to various disease-causing agents. These agents include monerans, protists, viruses, and fungi, or chemicals produced by these organisms when they enter the environment of the body. Immunologists develop tests to determine the presence of disease-causing organisms and develop vaccines to combat these diseases. An immunologist may also test organs to determine compatibility between donors and potential organ recipients. Organs that are not compatible will be rejected by the recipient's immune system. The cause, treatment, and prevention of acquired immune deficiency syndrome, AIDS, is one of the many challenges facing immunologists.

How did the *Valdez* oil spill off the coast of Alaska in 1989 affect the environment? **Aquatic microbiologists** were sent to Prince William Sound to investigate the extent of the damage to plants and animals in the area, and to determine how this petroleum spill affected these organisms and their aquatic environment. Fish and other wildlife are dependent on plankton in the ocean and rivers for food and breeding sites. The oil spill severely affected many interconnecting food chains and breeding grounds. Aquatic microbiologists also study how other forms of pollution, including the dumping of municipal and industrial wastes, pesticide runoff, and sewage, affect water supplies. An interesting area of research in aquatic microbiology is the study of the use of certain monerans and fungi for the breakdown of these same pollutants. It may be that genetically engineered bacteria will solve major water pollution problems.

What do mushrooms, athlete's foot, and bread mold have in common? All are fungi. A **mycologist** is a scientist who studies fungi. Mycologists work in clinical laboratories, fields and forests, industries, hospitals, and breweries. The mushroom industry employs mycologists. Industrial mycologists study how molds are used to flavor cheeses or to make drugs such as penicillin and vitamins. Fungi are a leading cause of plant diseases and indirectly contribute to the increased cost of food in the grocery store. Since many fresh foods are picked and stored far in advance of being sold, they are subject to destruction by fungi while in storage. Agricultural mycologists study plant diseases caused by fungi and research ways to control and prevent these diseases.

Mycologist

THE IMPORTANCE OF FUNGI

No species lives, survives, or adapts completely on its own. Fungi participate in symbiotic relationships. You have seen how some are saprobes, some are parasites, and some are mutualists. Many of the fungi described thus far appear to be destructive. However, they are only destructive from a human point of view. In nature, all the processes of fungi, even those that humans consider harmful, are essential to other organisms.

Objectives:
- describe the importance of fungi as decomposers.
- explain how both fungi and plants benefit in mycorrhiza.
- describe lichens and their role in the environment.

14:10 Decomposers

Recall that a decomposer is an organism that causes decay. Fungi perform an indispensable function in their role as decomposers. Fungi are members of a large food chain. Their constant activity in breaking down materials helps the biological world to continue to exist. Fungi and monerans interact to transform complex organic substances found in dead and decaying substances to raw materials that plants use, whether in a pile of leaves or a landfill. Fungi extract a portion of the energy contained in these molecules. Other decomposers, such as the monerans, continue the breakdown process and gain energy to maintain their own lives. Thus, one decomposer interacts with another for its supply of food. In nature, such an arrangement is like an assembly line in reverse. At the end of the line, simple, energy-poor substances such as carbon dioxide, water, and minerals are the end products of the work of fungi. Fungi use these raw materials for growth and development. Plants also use these recycled raw materials to assemble new supplies of energy-rich organic compounds.

In their role as decomposers, some fungal species are put to use to decompose harmful pollutants. They may be used at some time to break down hazardous chemicals found at waste-water treatment plants.

What benefits do fungi derive from their role as decomposers?

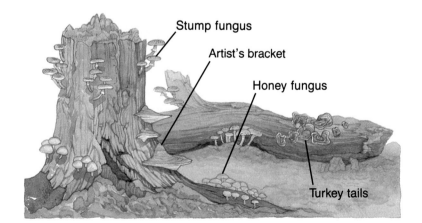

Stump fungus

Artist's bracket

Honey fungus

Turkey tails

FIGURE 14–18.

As decomposers, fungi are indispensable in the redistribution of Earth's raw materials.

14:11 Mycorrhizae

Earlier you read that most trees in the world rely on fungi that live in and on their roots to maintain a supply of minerals. The mutual association of plant roots and fungi is called **mycorrhiza** (mi koh RI zuh). This term describes a symbiotic relationship. The fungal hyphae increase the amount of nutrients moving into the plant by increasing the absorptive surface of the plant's roots. Fine, threadlike hyphae surround and often grow into the roots without harming them. Phosphorus, copper, and other minerals that are produced by decomposition of molecules in the soil enter the roots by way of the hyphae. Hyphae may also help to retain water around the roots of the tree. Organic nutrients, such as sugars and amino acids that have been synthesized by the plant, are available to the fungus.

It has been estimated that about 90 percent of tree species have mycorrhizae associated with their roots, as do a majority of agricultural plants. Almost all of the fungi of tree mycorrhizae are club fungi. The underground mycelial network of about half the species of mushrooms is associated with the roots of trees. It has been suggested that the evolution of trees has been dependent on the presence of mycorrhizae.

Mycorrhizae are extremely important in agriculture. Plants generally do not grow well if they are deprived of mycorrhizae. When transplanting a plant from one area to another, remember to carry some soil from the first area to the second. In doing so, you will improve the plant's chances of adjusting and growing in the new area. Some plants would not survive without mycorrhizae. Orchids are the most highly evolved flowering plants. But they cannot grow without fungi. Orchid seeds rely on mycorrhizae for both nutrients and a supply of water while germinating.

mycorrhiza:
mykes (GK) fungus
rhiza (GK) root

FIGURE 14–19.

Mycorrhizae are the means by which vital nutrients are supplied to most of the world's trees.

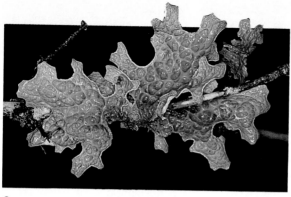
a

b

FIGURE 14–20.
Some lichens are leaflike (a). Others form crustlike growths (b) on rocks.

14:12 Lichens

A **lichen** is a mutualistic relationship of a fungus, generally an ascomycote, and a green alga or a cyanobacterium. Lichens form yellow, red, orange, or black blotches on rocks, on stone walls, and on the sides of trees. The photosynthetic cells live tangled up within the mycelia to form what appears to be one complex organism. The photosynthetic organism provides the fungus with food. Researchers have proposed that the fungal mycelium helps retain moisture and provides the alga with water and minerals absorbed from the air. The merger of fungus and alga is so complete that lichens are given a genus and species name, as though they were a single organism.

Lichens are found worldwide. In the Arctic, where plant life is sparse, lichens are the dominant form of vegetation. Reindeer and caribou graze on reindeer moss, a lichen found in the Arctic, much as cattle graze on grass elsewhere.

Lichens have been called pioneer organisms. A **pioneer** is an organism that is one of the first to move into and survive in a barren area. Because they are extremely sensitive to changes in the environment, lichens can die out quickly, especially if light becomes less available. They also are recognized as indicators of pollution. Increased air pollution causes lichens to die. As the pollutants are absorbed by the lichen, the chlorophyll-containing algae die. As a result, the fungus dies.

NoteWorthy

Litmus, a color pigment used as a chemical indicator, is produced by a lichen.

When lichens on rocks absorb water, portions swell, exerting pressure on the rock. In time, this pressure contributes to the wearing away of the rock.

REVIEW

11. Explain why the role of decomposer in fungi is important for all living things.
12. What are mycorrhizae and what is their major function?
13. Why are lichens called pioneer organisms?
14. **SKILL REVIEW:** Describe how lichens may be used as indicators of the condition of the environment. For more help, refer to Observing and Inferring in the Skill Handbook, page 809.
15. **USING CONCEPTS:** How might symbiotic relationships have helped fungi evolve?

CHAPTER REVIEW

SUMMARY

1. The body of a fungus consists of hyphae that form mycelia. Most fungal cell walls contain chitin. Cells may or may not have septa. **14:1**
2. Fungi are heterotrophs. They may be saprobes, parasites, or mutualists. **14:2**
3. Fungi reproduce asexually by spore formation, fragmentation, and budding, and sexually by spores. **14:3**
4. Fungal spores are produced in large numbers in sporangia. They are moved by air, water, and animals. **14:4**
5. Zygote fungi are saprobes that reproduce sexually by zygospores. **14:5**
6. Sac fungi reproduce sexually through ascospores and asexually by conidia. **14:6**
7. Club fungi reproduce sexually by basidiospores. Mushrooms have no asexual spores. **14:7**
8. Imperfect fungi reproduce asexually. **14:8**
9. The Basidiomycota probably evolved from the Ascomycota. **14:9**
10. Fungi decompose organic materials and recycle nutrients. **14:10**
11. Mycorrhizae supply most trees and many other plants with minerals. **14:11**
12. A lichen is a combination of an alga or cyanobacteria and a fungus. **14:12**

LANGUAGE OF BIOLOGY

ascospore	heterotroph
ascus	hyphae
basidia	lichen
basidiospore	mycelium
budding	mycorrhiza
chitin	pioneer
conidia	rhizoid
cyclosporine	sporangium
gametangium	stolon
haustoria	

Choose the word or phase from the list above that completes the sentence.

1. A(n) ____ is an organism that cannot make its own food.
2. A mass of fungal filaments is a(n) ____.
3. A(n) ____ is a structure that produces spores.
4. A(n) ____ is a horizontal hypha that grows over the surface of a substrate.
5. ____ are hyphae of parasitic fungi.
6. The sexually reproduced cells of a sac fungus are ____.
7. Yeasts reproduce asexually by ____.
8. A mushroom reproduces sexually by producing ____ on basidia.
9. A(n) ____ is a mutualistic combination of an alga and a fungus.
10. The fungi in ____ live in a symbiotic relationship with trees.

REVIEWING CONCEPTS

Choose the word or phrase that completes the sentence or answers the question.

11. Fungi differ from plants in that fungi are ____.
    a. all saprobes   c. autotrophs
    b. heterotrophs   d. all parasites
12. Fungi obtain nutrients through ____.
    a. extracellular   c. stolons
       digestion
    b. lichens   d. sporangia
13. Fungi reproduce asexually and sexually by ____.
    a. haustoria   c. spores
    b. mycorrhizae   d. budding
14. Spores of bread mold are produced asexually in a(n) ____.
    a. sporangium   c. ascus
    b. conidium   d. basidium
15. Sac fungi reproduce asexually by ____.
    a. ascospores   c. conidia
    b. basidiospores   d. zygospores

16. Cell walls of fungi are made up of ____.
a. cellulose
b. chitin and cellulose
c. chitin
d. all of these

17. Imperfect fungi lack ____ reproduction.
a. complete
b. asexual
c. any
d. sexual

18. The sexual spores of a club fungus are formed in ____.
a. basidia
b. conidiophores
c. mycelia
d. sporangia

19. ____ provide agricultural crops with nutrients.
a. Pioneers
b. Mycorrhizae
c. Sporangia
d. Lichens

20. Fungi are classified on the basis of ____.
a. color
b. sexual spores
c. taste
d. location

UNDERSTANDING CONCEPTS

Answer the following questions using complete sentences.

21. Compare the digestion by a fungus with that of an amoeba.

22. What is a mycelium and what is its relationship to mushrooms that grow in a lawn?

23. Describe the adaptations of fungi.

24. Compare sexual reproduction in *Rhizopus* with that of a mushroom.

25. What are the differences in the formation of zygospores, ascospores, and basidiospores?

26. How are lichens indicators of pollution?

27. A fungus that has cells with septa, dark blue sporangia and mycelia, but no sexual cycle would be classified in what division? Explain.

28. Discuss the statement: "Life on earth could not continue without decomposers." Relate your discussion to the functions of fungi.

29. In terms of fungi, why might it be difficult to transplant a tree from the woods to your yard?

30. Describe how, and with what structures, parasitic fungi damage their hosts.

APPLYING CONCEPTS

Answer the following questions using complete sentences.

31. How are fungi adapted to survive unfavorable conditions?

32. If all the lichens in an area of the tundra were killed, what effect would there be on the grazing animal populations of the area?

33. Discuss why it is difficult to trace the origin of fungi. Why are fossils of fungi rare?

34. Identify the algal and fungal portions of a model lichen called *Photosynthetus ascocarpus*. To which fungal division does the fungus portion of this lichen belong? Explain.

35. Discuss how fungi can contribute to the success or failure of agricultural crops.

EXTENSIONS

1. Research the fungus ergot. What division does it belong to? Describe its life cycle. Describe the role of this fungus in an outbreak of St. Anthony's fire in France in 1951.

2. Research the ingredients that retard the growth of fungi in prepackaged foods to find out what antifungal agents are used as food additives.

3. What is a fungicide? Find out how fresh fruits and vegetables are kept from molding once picked. Why is produce treated with fungicides?

READINGS

Flam, F. "Semiconductor Studies Get a Rise from Yeast." *Science News,* Apr. 15, 1989, p. 131.

Raloff, Janet. "Helping Plastics Waste Away." *Science News,* May 20, 1989, pp. 282–283.

Vogel, S. "Taming the Wild Morel." *Discover,* May 1988, pp. 58–60.

PLANTS

What is a weed?
A plant whose virtues have
  not yet been discovered.

Ralph Waldo Emerson
"Fortune of the Republic"

PLANT STRUCTURE

P icture a time when Earth looked very different from what
you see now. During the Ordovician period, over 438
million years ago, most land was covered with water. The
land that did exist above water was barren and exposed to
damaging ultraviolet radiation, pounding rains, scorching heat,
and freezing cold. Organisms existed only in the seas and
freshwater ponds where water protected them from Earth's harsh
atmosphere. Yet by the Silurian period, there were tall land
plants. Today you live on an Earth with many varieties of simple
and complex plants. In this chapter, you will study some of the
adaptations that make life on land possible for plants.

Water lily—adapted to
life in fresh water

THE EVOLUTION OF PLANTS

When the environment changes, populations of organisms will
not survive unless they are adapted. The evolution of plants from
plantlike protists took millions of years of continual environmental
changes. Over time, plants changed the appearance of Earth itself.
What were some of the adaptations that evolved and allowed plants
to survive and helped form the various ecosystems of Earth?

15:1 The Vascular System

Water is vital for life. Many marine organisms die quickly when
they wash up onto land. Likewise, freshwater organisms usually
perish when lakes and ponds evaporate during a period of drought.
Before organisms could adapt to a life on land, structures and mechanisms for the transport of water had to evolve. In plants, these
structures are the cells and tissues that make up the vascular system.
A plant's vascular system is composed of two kinds of vascular
tissues. **Vascular tissue** is plant tissue through which water and
nutrients are carried to and from the roots and aerial parts of the
plant. Those plants that developed these transport mechanisms
could grow out of water. The vascular tissues are often surrounded
by long, thick-walled cells called fibers. Fibers also help to support
a plant on land.

Objectives:
- describe the functions of vascular tissue.
- distinguish between xylem and phloem.
- explain adaptations of plants for life on land.

What structures enabled plants to survive on land?

Giant redwoods—adapted to life on land

Vascular tissues are either xylem (ZI lum) or phloem (FLOH em). **Xylem** is the vascular tissue in plants that transports water and minerals from the roots to the leaves in a plant. **Phloem** is the vascular tissue that carries sugar made in the leaves to all other parts of a plant. Both xylem and phloem are composed of tubular cells that are joined end to end. The xylem is made up of either tracheids or vessels. Both kinds of cells are dead; they do not contain cytoplasm. A **tracheid** is an elongated cell with closed, tapered ends. Water moves from tracheid to tracheid by passing through pits in the tracheid walls. A **vessel cell** is an elongated cell with open ends. Because there are no barriers to water movement, vessels transport water more efficiently than do tracheids. Plants such as ferns and pines have only tracheids. Others, such as oaks and lilies, have only vessels.

Food produced by photosynthesis is transported throughout the plant in phloem tissue. Phloem is made of **sieve cells,** which are thin-walled conductive cells with sievelike plates on their end walls. Sieve cells lack nuclei. Each phloem cell has a companion cell that does have a nucleus. Companion cells help control movement of food in the sieve cells. Also in vascular tissue are fibers for strength and parenchyma for storage. **Parenchyma** is a plant tissue that consists of simple, thin-walled cells.

FIGURE 15–1.

Longitudinal sections of stems in a flowering plant, such as wild carrot, and a fern show cells and tissues that make up the vascular system. Most of these cells are found in all plants.

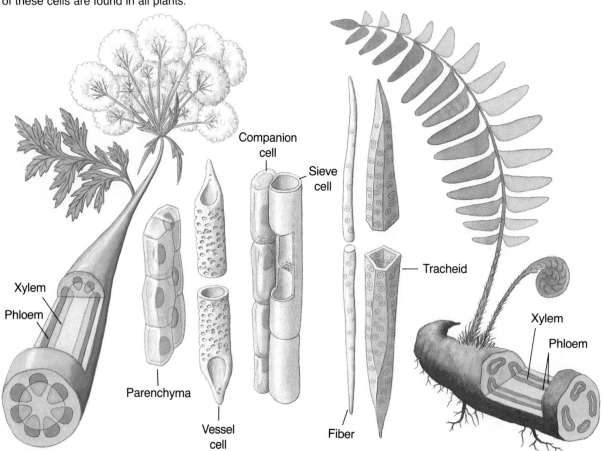

Xylem

Phloem

Parenchyma

Vessel cell

Companion cell

Sieve cell

Fiber

Tracheid

Xylem

Phloem

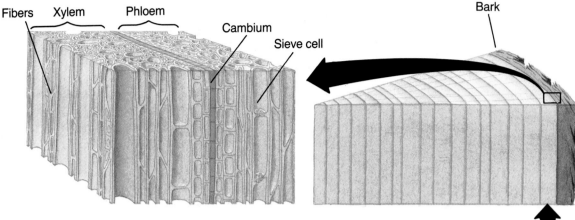

Fibers Xylem Phloem Cambium Sieve cell Bark

15:2 Other Adaptations to Land

As plants evolved, new organs such as roots, stems, and leaves evolved that helped them become more successful on land. Roots anchor plants in the ground and supply them with water and nutrients. Leaves became the primary organ for photosynthesis, allowing plants to synthesize food more efficiently. As the plants evolved more and more vascular tissue, the supply of water and minerals from the soil to the rest of the plant provided an opportunity for independence from a life surrounded by water. Stems became stronger with fibers and at last were able to support themselves in the air. As you study plants from simple to complex, you will notice that there are differences in their ability to transport water.

Recall that gametes of protists are protected from drying out because they are released into a watery environment. Plants had to evolve a new method of reproduction that did not require water for dispersal of gametes. As you learn about the different divisions of plants, notice how the methods of reproduction become less and less dependent on water when you compare the simple plants with more complex plants. By comparing levels of adaptation in plants, scientists have developed a phylogeny of the plant kingdom.

FIGURE 15–2.

A section through a woody plant stem shows the relative shapes of different cells in the vascular system.

REVIEW

1. Describe the cells of a plant's vascular system.
2. List three adaptations necessary for plants to live on land.
3. Name two functions of the vascular system.
4. **SKILL REVIEW:** Suppose you had plant specimens you wished to classify as either land plants or water plants. What characteristics would you look for to determine their correct classification? For more help, refer to Organizing Information in the Skill Handbook, pages 810 to 813.
5. **USING CONCEPTS:** Dutch elm disease is the growth of fungus in the xylem and phloem of American elm trees. Why does this disease kill the trees?

Objectives:
- name the structures of roots, and describe their forms and functions.
- name the structures of stems, and describe their forms and functions.
- name the structures of leaves, and describe their forms and functions.
- list some leaf adaptations that reduce water loss.

What types of tissue are produced by vascular cambium?

You are probably familiar with an enormous variety of leaf shapes of plants in your community. There are also many kinds of stems. Stems may be very short or tall, creeping, branched, thorny, woody, or climbing. Roots, although less variable than leaves or stems, also have different forms and functions.

15:3 Roots

Roots have two important functions. First, roots anchor the plant in the ground. Second, roots absorb water and minerals from the soil. Observe the cross section of a typical root in Figure 15–4. Notice the three tissue layers: the epidermis, cortex, and vascular cylinder of xylem and phloem. The **epidermis** is the outermost layer of cells in a plant. It has a protective function. In roots, some cells of the epidermis are modified into **root hairs,** single cells that extend from the epidermis and absorb water and minerals directly from the soil. Root hairs increase the surface area of the root system, and thus extend the volume of soil from which a plant can extract water.

Just inside the epidermis is the cortex. The **cortex** consists of parenchyma cells and is the storage tissue between the epidermis and vascular cylinder of a stem or root. The innermost layer of the cortex is called the **endodermis.** The cells of the endodermis contain suberin. Suberin is a waxy, waterproof substance that prevents water and minerals from moving out of the vascular cylinder. Just inside the endodermis and surrounding the vascular cylinder of the root is the **pericycle,** a tissue from which lateral roots arise.

In roots, xylem is often arranged in a starlike pattern in cross section. Phloem tissue lies between the rays of the "star." Xylem and phloem are separated by a layer of cells called vascular cambium. **Cambium** is growth tissue that adds only to the girth of a plant. In plants, growth in girth is called **secondary growth.** When vascular cambium divides, it produces phloem cells to the outside and xylem cells to the inside. All growth tissue in plants is called **meristem.** The cells of meristem tissue are capable of dividing indefinitely. A plant's growth occurs only in areas where meristem is present.

Many roots grow continuously, except during periods of drought or extreme cold. The **root cap** is a thimble-like mass of cells surrounding the tip of the root. As the root grows, the root cap is pushed through the soil. Root-cap cells are shed as the young root passes through the soil. Behind the root cap is a region of meristem. Since the meristem occurs at the tip, or apex of the root, it is called **apical meristem.** Cell division in apical meristem results in increase in length, known as **primary growth.** The region of elongation is behind the apical meristem. Behind the region of elongation, the root hairs form in the region of maturation. Also in this region, vascular tissues begin to develop.

FIGURE 15–3.

Root hairs are single modified cells of the root tip epidermis.

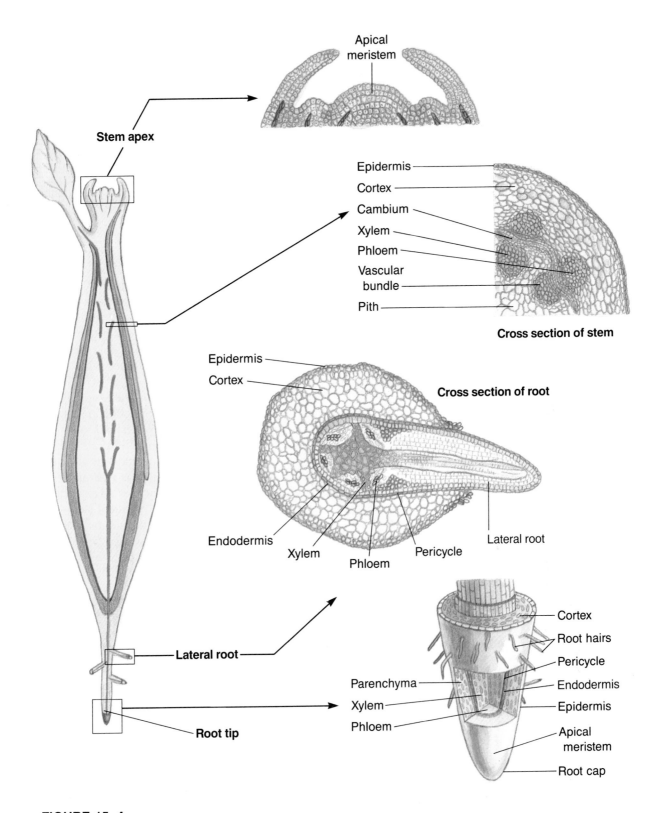

Apical meristem

Stem apex

Epidermis
Cortex
Cambium
Xylem
Phloem
Vascular bundle
Pith

Cross section of stem

Epidermis
Cortex

Cross section of root

Endodermis
Xylem
Phloem
Pericycle
Lateral root

Lateral root

Parenchyma
Xylem
Phloem

Cortex
Root hairs
Pericycle
Endodermis
Epidermis
Apical meristem
Root cap

Root tip

FIGURE 15–4.

Follow the vascular system throughout a plant.

FIGURE 15–5.

Types of roots include aerial roots (a) and taproots (b). Stems include runners (c) and rhizomes (d).

a

b

Roots show many adaptations for different functions. Sometimes roots are adapted as food storage organs and become quite large and swollen. Roots that store food are called taproots. Carrots and beets are taproots. Trees, all grasses, and many weeds have fibrous root systems that have many branches. Fibrous roots help prevent soil erosion by holding soil in place. The fibrous roots at the base of corn plants are called prop roots because they prop the plant up in the soil. Many flowering plants have a mutualistic relationship between their roots and fungi. The fungus helps the root take up water and minerals. In return, the root provides sugars and nitrogen compounds for the fungus. The roots of some plants are exposed to air and may help with the absorption of oxygen.

15:4 Stems

There are two types of plant stems. Herbaceous (her BAY shus) stems are soft and green. Lilies, beans, and petunias have herbaceous stems. Trees such as oaks, and shrubs such as roses have woody stems. Woody stems are hard and rigid and contain more xylem mixed with a lot of fibers. The woodiness is mainly due to a complex carbohydrate called lignin in the walls of older xylem cells and fibers.

Stems have several important functions. They provide support for all the above-ground parts of plants. Stems also function in storage and, if green, carry out some photosynthesis. Water and minerals move through the vascular system in stems from the roots to the leaves. The stem is an important organ of food transport for all parts of the plant. Stems produce leaf and flower buds, as well as more stems. They are sometimes modified for storage or asexual reproduction. The fleshy underground tubers of the white potato are actually stems, not roots. The thickened, underground rhizome of peonies and the long, thin rhizomes of many grasses are also modified stems. Strawberry runners are above-ground, horizontal stems.

c

d

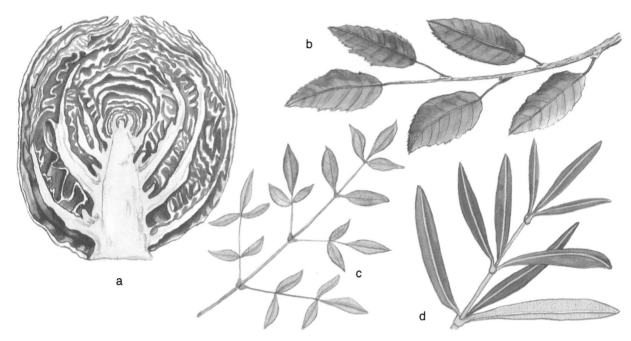

a

b

c

d

Leaves are attached to stems at nodes. The internodes of a cabbage (a) are condensed. Leaves of most plants are arranged alternately (b), opposite (c), or whorled (d).

internode:
 inter (L) between
 nodus (L) knot

Notice in Figure 15–4 that the three layers of tissues described for roots can also be seen in stems. One difference between stems and roots is the presence of loosely arranged, thin-walled parenchyma cells in the middle of some stems. Another difference between roots and stems is in the arrangement of vascular tissue. Recall that in roots, xylem is arranged in a starlike pattern with phloem between the rays of the star. In stems, three patterns of vascular tissue can be seen. In some species, the vascular tissue is in a ring of separate bundles. In other species, the pattern is a continuous ring, and in yet other species, the bundles are scattered throughout the cortex.

The cortex of stems often contains some thick-walled cells that provide support to the stem. There may also be cells that produce sticky gums or resins. You are probably familiar with the aroma in pine oil cleaners, which are extracted during the production of paper from wood pulp of pine trees.

The apical meristem in a stem is protected by young overlapping and developing leaves. Leaf buds are formed by the apical meristem. Leaf buds may develop at the apex or along the length of the stem. Where the leaves arise on the stem is called a node. An internode is the area between nodes. In some plants, the internodes are very short. For example, before a cabbage plant flowers, the internodes are very short. This is why the cabbage you buy at the grocery store is in the form of a compact head. If you examine the needles of a pine tree, you will notice they occur in bunches. The internodes are so short between these leaves that it looks as if the leaves are coming from a single node. Nodes may have one, two, or several leaves depending on the species of plant. Look at the leaf arrangements in Figure 15–6. If there is only one leaf, leaf arrangement is described as alternate. If there are two leaves, the arrangement is opposite, and if there are several, it is whorled.

FIGURE 15–7.

The history of the climate of a region can be determined from variations in a tree's annual growth rings.

Perennial stems undergo secondary growth. Perennials are plants that live from one growing season to another. As in roots, division of vascular cambium in stems produces phloem cells to the outside and xylem cells to the inside. As the vascular cambium adds cells to the xylem, the cambium is pushed toward the outside of the stem. When this happens, the vascular cambium cells divide in the other direction, making a ring of greater diameter and keeping the ring of cambium intact. In regions where growth varies according to the seasons, the vascular cambium does not divide during winter or in times of drought. Favorable growing conditions in spring trigger renewed growth. Spring xylem cells tend to be large. Xylem cells formed later in the growing season are often smaller. This annual pattern of alternating sizes of xylem produces a pattern of growth rings. The rings are used to determine the age of a tree.

Wood is secondary xylem tissue. As a tree ages, xylem toward the center of the trunk stops functioning. This xylem then fills with various substances that are often dark in color. The center wood that no longer transports water is called **heartwood**. The still functioning wood surrounding the heartwood is called **sapwood.**

FIGURE 15–8.

The sticky resin that oozes from the bark of a pine tree is produced by modified parenchyma cells within the cortex.

During secondary growth of a woody stem, cork replaces the epidermis. Cork is the name given to the cells produced toward the outside of the stem by a meristem called the cork cambium. **Bark** is the tough exterior covering of woody plants that surrounds the vascular cylinder. It includes the rings of phloem and cork cambium, but not of the xylem. Damage to the bark may kill a tree because it will cut the supply of food that is transported in the phloem tissue. As the cork cells are pushed out during growth, they become filled with waxy suberin. Suberin helps the bark protect the stem, roots, and branches from insects, disease, injury, and water loss. Also, resins as seen in Figure 15–8 are good insect repellents. The bark of a tree may be just a few centimeters thick, but huge California redwoods have bark that is up to 60 cm thick!

15:5 Leaves

Leaves are plant organs that trap light energy for photosynthesis. Most plants have leaves. The leaves of simple plants such as mosses are only one to a few cells thick. The leaves of more complex plants have a supply of vascular tissue. When you think of a leaf, you probably think only of the broad, flat, green part called the leaf blade. The stalk that joins the leaf blade to the stem is called the **petiole.** Leaves may be simple or compound. A **simple leaf** has one entire blade. The oak and dandelion have simple leaves. A **compound leaf** has a divided leaf blade. Each division of the leaf blade is called a leaflet. The honey locust and carrot have compound leaves.

If you look at a cross section of a leaf blade of a plant such as a sunflower through a microscope, it has the appearance of a sandwich. The upper and lower epidermis are the slices of bread. The epidermis of the leaf protects it by providing a barrier to infection, injury, and water loss. Sometimes the epidermis has cells with branching hairs. A thick growth of these hairs slows evaporation and provides a barrier to insects feeding on the leaf.

Describe a compound leaf.

a

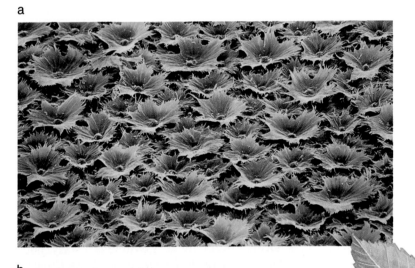

b

c

Leaf

Leaflet

Petiole

FIGURE 15–9.

Leaves are often covered with hairs or scales as in *Rhododendron* (a) for protection from cold or insects. Leaves are either simple as in *Rhododendron* (b) or compound as in hickory (c).

FIGURE 15–10.

Stomata are modified cells of a leaf epidermis (a). When water enters the guard cells, the pressure causes them to buckle causing an increase in the size of the stoma (b).

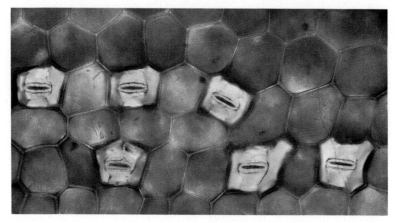

a

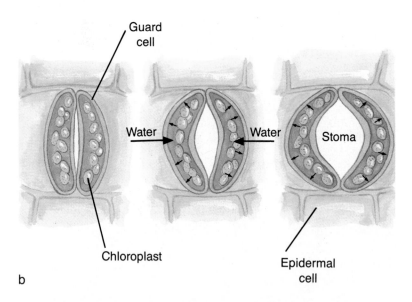

b

stoma:
stoma (GK) mouth

The epidermis is covered by a cuticle. A **cuticle** is a waxy, non-cellular layer that covers the outer surface of many plants. Cuticles prevent plant tissues from drying out. During photosynthesis and respiration, gases are exchanged through openings in the cuticle called stomata (*sing.* stoma). **Stomata** are small pores in the surfaces of leaves. Each stoma has a pair of **guard cells,** which are cells that surround and control the size of the pores of stomata.

Observe how each of the guard cells in Figure 15–10 has one thickened surface on the side next to the pore. A stoma opens when its guard cells take in water by osmosis from surrounding cells and, as a result, swell. The increase in pressure causes the cells to expand unequally on the two surfaces. Because of the thick walls next to the pore and the fact that they are joined at each end, guard cells bow, making the diameter of the stoma wider. The stoma closes when water leaves the guard cells, causing them to shrink. Plants in dry habitats usually have fewer stomata. Water lilies and other water plants have stomata only on the upper side.

The inside of the leaf sandwich is the mesophyll. **Mesophyll** is the photosynthetic layer of a leaf. Mesophyll is made of two types of parenchyma cells. Palisade parenchyma cells are column-shaped with many chloroplasts. Most of the photosynthesis takes place in the palisade layer. Spongy parenchyma is made up of loosely packed, irregular-shaped cells surrounded by air spaces. There are fewer chloroplasts in the spongy layer because they are usually on the underside of the leaf where less light is absorbed.

Bundles of vascular tissues form veins that branch throughout the mesophyll. Veins are usually surrounded by a sheath of parenchyma cells. This sheath controls the flow of materials in and out of the veins of the leaf.

mesophyll:
  mesos (GK) middle
  phyllon (GK) leaf

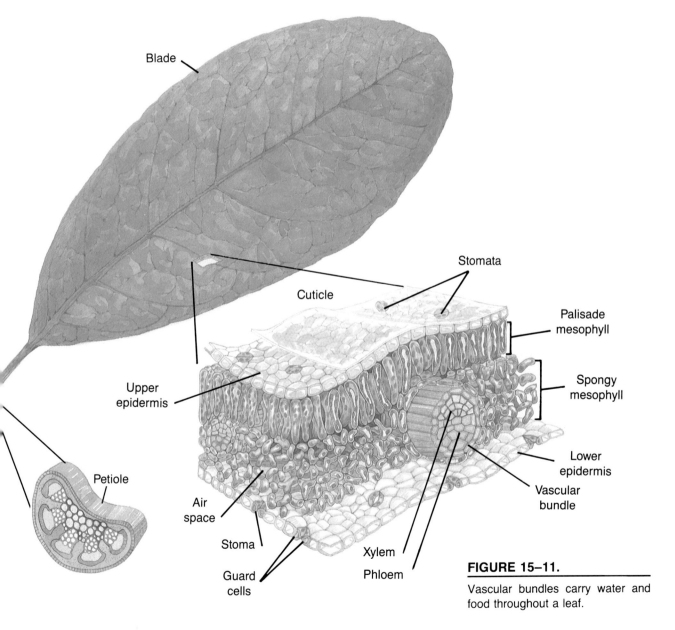

FIGURE 15–11.

Vascular bundles carry water and food throughout a leaf.

BIOLAB

Model Leaves

Problem: How do cuticles affect leaf water loss?

Materials

narrow cellophane
   tape
wax paper
thin cardboard
straight pin
graph paper
   (2 mm squares)

scissors
lamp (60-watt)
pan balance
small dish with water
paper towels
ring stand (2)
string (30 cm)

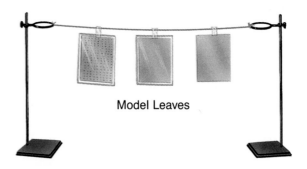

Model Leaves

Procedures

1. Make a data table like the one shown.
2. Cut three pieces of cardboard and one piece of graph paper each 10 cm × 10 cm. These will be used to make your model leaves.
3. Cut two pieces of wax paper 11 cm × 22 cm. Fold each piece of wax paper in half, making a folded piece 11 cm × 11 cm. The wax papers will be cuticles for your model leaves.
4. Put the graph paper between one folded piece of wax paper. Place this paper sandwich on a scrap of cardboard to protect the counter from scratches. Using a straight pin and the squares on the graph paper as a guide, make tiny holes through the three layers of paper, each two squares apart. Discard the graph paper.
5. Make two wax-paper envelopes by taping the full lengths of the two short sides of each folded piece of wax paper.
6. Soak each of the three cardboard pieces in the dish of water until they are saturated. Drain and blot them on paper towels.
7. Place a piece of wet cardboard into each of the two waxed paper envelopes. Tape the third side of the envelope shut. Be careful not to cover holes on the perforated envelope. The third piece of cardboard will remain uncovered.
8. Use a pan balance to determine the mass to the nearest tenth of a gram of each piece of cardboard and record in the data table.

9. Use two ring stands and a length of string to make a "clothesline" as shown, 10 cm from a light bulb. Use tape to hang the model leaves to the string so one surface of each model is toward the light.
10. **Hypothesize** which model leaves will lose the most and which will lose the least amounts of water.
11. After 30 minutes, determine and record the mass of each model leaf.
12. Calculate the mass lost for each model leaf. Record your calculations in the data table.

Data and Observations

Model Leaf	Beginning Mass	Ending Mass	Mass Lost
no cuticle	5.9	4.2	1.7
complete cuticle	6.6	6.0	0.6
cuticle with pores	6.4	5.4	1.0

Questions and Conclusion

1. What does mass lost represent?
2. What are the variables in this experiment?
3. Which model leaf lost the most mass? Explain.
4. Is your **hypothesis** supported? Explain.

Conclusion: How do cuticles affect leaf water loss?

a

b

FIGURE 15–12.

Plants such as a Venus' flytrap (a) and a Pitcher plant (b) have leaves modified for trapping insects.

Leaves have several adaptations that aid plants in surviving in very different environments. For example, leaves of plants that live in hot, arid climates often have palisade parenchyma on both the upper and lower surfaces. They may also have a layer of hairs, a thick cuticle, curled leaves, or stomata in pits that help reduce water loss. Some plants are called succulents. These plants have leaves modified to store large amounts of water. The layers of an onion or hyacinth bulb are actually the swollen bases of the previous year's leaves. The swelling is caused by stored food needed for the following year's growth. Some leaves have lost their blades and evolved into spines for protection from hungry desert animals. At the same time, these reduced leaves help conserve water. In a *Poinsettia,* the brightly colored leaves help attract insects to the petal-less flowers at the center. Some plants have become adapted to capturing insects. Their leaves have unusual modifications that include hairs that secrete a sticky substance, leaves that clamp shut when insects land on them, and tubular leaves with slippery slides that lead down into a deadly soup of digestive juices.

REVIEW

6. How does a root develop?
7. What are the tissues in a stem?
8. What are three adaptations of leaves?
9. **SKILL REVIEW:** In a cross section of a leaf, name the tissues and their functions. For more help, refer to Interpreting Scientific Illustrations in the Skill Handbook, pages 800 to 801.
10. **USING CONCEPTS:** To which kind of environment would a plant with large, broad leaves, shallow fibrous roots, and a tall woody stem be best adapted?

Objectives:

- explain how water rises in the xylem.
- list nutrients required for plant growth.
- explain how materials move in the phloem.

NoteWorthy

Ninety percent of the water taken in by plants is lost through transpiration. A single corn plant may release 200 L of water vapor in one growing season.

What molecular forces help move water up a tree?

Plants obtain materials for growth from their environment. Some of these materials are absorbed by roots. Others are absorbed by leaves and stems. Xylem brings materials together for synthesis and phloem distributes the products. What are the principles behind the movement of materials in plants?

15:6 Water

What opposing forces allow water to move against the force of gravity up through a plant from the roots to the leaves? Plants lose water vapor through their leaves by a process called **transpiration.** When water is lost to a plant's leaves, the water is replaced by osmosis from neighboring cells. The osmotic process continues from one parenchyma cell to another until xylem cells are reached. This results in a negative pressure in the column of water in the xylem. As water is pulled through the xylem tissue up the plant, other forces are involved in the movement of water from the roots.

A vacuum pump can draw water upward in a continuous column only about ten meters high. Yet plants move water much farther. How is water moved to the top of a redwood tree? Water molecules adhere strongly to the walls of the narrow xylem tubes. The highly polar structure of water molecules as described in Chapter 3, results in an attraction or cohesion between adjacent molecules. Water molecules also attract or adhere to one another. These opposing forces of cohesion and adhesion help keep the water column intact.

Stomata control water loss by closing more on hot days and at night. When stomata are closed, upward movement of water slows. The endodermis in the root keeps materials from leaking out of the xylem into surrounding root cells. Water continues to move into the xylem and causes a root pressure. Sometimes this root pressure forces water from the smaller bundles at leaf edges.

FIGURE 15–13.

Root pressure is a minor cause of water rising through plants. The moisture from transpiration condenses to form dew on a bright, cool morning.

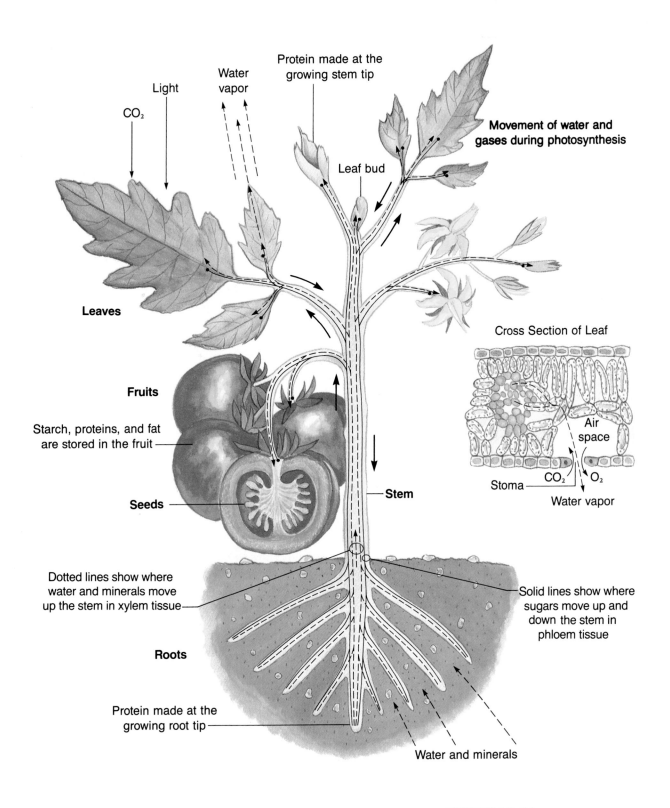

Light

CO₂

Water vapor

Protein made at the growing stem tip

Leaf bud

Movement of water and gases during photosynthesis

Leaves

Fruits

Starch, proteins, and fat are stored in the fruit

Seeds

Dotted lines show where water and minerals move up the stem in xylem tissue

Roots

Protein made at the growing root tip

Cross Section of Leaf

Air space

Stoma

CO_2

O_2

Water vapor

Stem

Solid lines show where sugars move up and down the stem in phloem tissue

Water and minerals

FIGURE 15–14.

Follow the movement of water, minerals, and sugars throughout a plant.

Hydroponic farming

GROWING PLANTS WITHOUT SOIL

Can you imagine growing plants without soil? Hydroponics is the science of growing plants in a soil-free medium. As long ago as 1860, the first formula for a nutrient solution in which plants could successfully grow without soil was developed.

Today, hydroponics is practiced in factories where vegetables are grown in controlled environments. A 1000 m^2 factory can produce as much food as a 100 000 m^2 farm. Fifty thousand seeds are planted daily. The seedlings are placed in troughs where a solution of nutrients and water flows past the roots and is recycled. The temperature, humidity, and amounts of light and carbon dioxide are kept at optimum levels for photosynthesis to occur. This results in unusually rapid growth.

Countries with hot, dry, climates and limited farm land have shown interest in this hydroponic technique. Hydroponic farms could solve the problem of food shortages in some countries where the current farming methods do not supply enough food. The problem of food shortage has grown daily with the rapid increase of world population. NASA is researching hydroponic farming for use in the space station program as a stable food source. Someday most of the vegetables you eat might be grown without soil.

15:7 Nutrients

Water isn't the only substance absorbed by plant roots. Mineral elements are also important plant nutrients taken up by roots. Minerals such as potassium enter the root by active transport.

If the absence of an element results in poor growth, disease, or death of a plant, that element is called an essential element. Essential elements required by plants in relatively large amounts include nitrogen, potassium, calcium, phosphorus, magnesium, sulfur, carbon, oxygen, and hydrogen. Elements that are required in much smaller amounts include iron, chlorine, copper, manganese, zinc, molybdenum, and boron. Calcium, iron, and manganese are not easily moved from one tissue to another. If these elements are scarce, the new leaves of a plant are affected. Potassium and magnesium are easily moved from old leaves to new leaves. Thus, if these elements are in short supply, the deficiency shows first in old leaves.

FIGURE 15–15.

These leaves are showing a lack of magnesium.

15:8 Sugars

Sugars move in two directions in the phloem. Sugars made in the leaves move from this source to a sink. A **sink** is any part of a plant that stores or uses the products of photosynthesis. Examples of sinks include meristem, developing fruits and seeds, and storage tissues such as taproots and bulbs. At the source end, sugar moves by active transport into the sieve tubes of the phloem. The phloem cells then become hypertonic to the surrounding leaf tissues. Water then enters the phloem by osmosis. Pressure builds up, forcing the solution toward the sink. At the sink, the sugars are removed by active transport. The sieve cells near the sink become hypotonic to their surroundings and water diffuses out of the phloem by osmosis. Companion cells are connected to the phloem cells by many strands of cytoplasm. They may provide the metabolic energy required to load and unload sugars. Movements upward and downward occur in different sieve tubes at the same time. In most plants, sieve tube cells are short-lived. By the end of summer, little tree phloem is still effective in transport of materials. In late winter, just before a new growing season starts, food stored in sinks travels upward to provide energy for the plant until new leaves can produce more food.

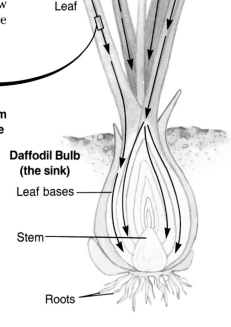

FIGURE 15–16.

In a daffodil, the source of sugars is in the leaves, and the sink is the bulb.

REVIEW

11. What mechanism allows plants to move water up tall plants?
12. Describe the movement of materials in the phloem.
13. What mineral elements are essential for plant growth?
14. **SKILL REVIEW:** Design an experiment to determine the effect of lack of a nutrient such as iron or potassium in plants. For more help, refer to Designing an Experiment in the Skill Handbook on pages 802 to 803.
15. **USING CONCEPTS:** Suppose air bubbles formed in the xylem of a plant. How might this affect water transport?

CHAPTER REVIEW

SUMMARY

1. Vascular tissue transports food, water, and minerals in plants. **15:1**
2. Roots, stems, and leaves evolved as plants became more successful on land. **15:2**
3. Roots are organized into epidermis, cortex, and a vascular cylinder. In roots, all growth occurs from meristem tissue. **15:3**
4. Stem structure is similar to that of roots. Leaf buds develop from the apical meristem. Many perennial stems undergo secondary growth. **15:4**
5. Leaves have layered structures. Adaptations such as cuticles and stomata make leaves resistant to drying. **15:5**
6. Attractive forces between water molecules and between water molecules and xylem tubes help move water from the soil and up through the plant. **15:6**
7. Lack of essential elements results in poor growth, disease, or death in plants. **15:7**
8. Sugars move by osmosis in both directions in the phloem, from source to sink. **15:8**

LANGUAGE OF BIOLOGY

apical meristem	phloem
bark	primary growth
cambium	root cap
compound leaf	root hairs
cortex	sapwood
cuticle	secondary growth
endodermis	sieve cells
epidermis	simple leaf
guard cells	sink
heartwood	stomata
meristem	tracheid
mesophyll	transpiration
parenchyma	vascular tissue
pericycle	vessel cell
petiole	xylem

Choose the word or phrase from the list above that completes the sentence.

1. ___ is the food-conducting tissue of plants.
2. Gas exchange in leaves occurs through small pores called ___.
3. A waxy, noncellular layer that covers the outer surface of plant tissue is a(n) ___.
4. Xylem is made up of vessel or ___ cells.
5. Tissue that causes secondary growth is ___.
6. In roots, the ___ protects the meristem behind it.
7. Xylem in the center of old trees is ___.
8. Phloem tubes are made up of ___.
9. The loss of water vapor through plant leaves is called ___.
10. Lateral roots form out of the ___.

REVIEWING CONCEPTS

Choose the word or phrase that completes the sentence or answers the question.

11. An adaptation to survival on land is ___.
    - a. stomata
    - b. cuticle
    - c. vascular tissue
    - d. all of the above
12. Sieve cells lack ___.
    - a. nuclei
    - b. cell walls
    - c. mitochondria
    - d. all of the above
13. ___ reduce water loss in leaves.
    - a. Guard cells
    - b. Cuticles
    - c. Hairs
    - d. All of these
14. Plant growth takes place only in ___ tissue.
    - a. xylem
    - b. phloem
    - c. cortex
    - d. meristem
15. Water moves around the plant in ___.
    - a. phloem
    - b. xylem
    - c. sieve cells
    - d. companion cells
16. Materials in the phloem move ___.
    - a. from sink to source
    - b. from source to sink
    - c. by transpiration
    - d. both a and b

17. An essential element required for healthy plant growth is ___.
   a. aluminum
   c. cobalt
   b. calcium
   d. silver

18. Veins of leaves contain ___.
   a. xylem and phloem
   c. mesophyll
   b. parenchyma
   d. cortex

19. Vascular tissue transports ___.
   a. water
   c. oxygen
   b. minerals
   d. both a and b

20. A(n) ___ plant stem is green and soft.
   a. woody
   c. underground
   b. secondary
   d. herbaceous

UNDERSTANDING CONCEPTS

Answer the following questions using complete sentences.

21. What leaf arrangements occur when there is one leaf, two leaves, and many leaves at each node of a stem?

22. Why do many desert plants have few stomata?

23. What is the difference between palisade parenchyma and spongy parenchyma in the mesophyll of a leaf?

24. What is the primary function of parenchyma cells in a stem?

25. How do guard cells regulate the movement of gases through stomata?

26. Many plants have enough energy to survive through late winter before new leaves are formed to produce food. From where does this energy come?

27. What cells make up the cortex and where is this tissue located?

28. Compare the arrangements of xylem in roots and stems.

29. Compare the stems of a herbaceous and woody plant.

30. What type of cells form the annual rings in a cross section of a tree's trunk?

APPLYING CONCEPTS

Answer the following questions using complete sentences.

31. Why is it important to keep soil around a plant's roots when transplanting the plant?

32. Compare the expected rates of water movement in the xylem during the day and at night.

33. What gas used by a plant enters through stomata? What gas produced by a plant exits?

34. Suppose you examine the annual rings in the cross section of a tree's trunk. How can you infer which rings were produced during years of drought?

35. A young child carved her initials in a tree's trunk. When returning to the tree as an adult, would she need to use a ladder to reach her initials? Explain.

EXTENSIONS

1. Observe transpiration in plants. Place plastic bags over the leaves of several different plants, securing them with twist ties. Observe the bags at one-hour intervals. Which plant lost the most water through transpiration?

2. Make a poster-sized illustration showing the movement of materials in plants.

3. Examine a head of cabbage. Study the nodes and internodes of the stem.

READINGS

Bender, Lionel. *Plants.* New York: Franklin Watts, 1988.

Carey, J. "Brave New World of Super Plants." *International Wildlife,* Nov.–Dec., 1986, pp. 16–18.

Feldman, L.J. "The Habits of Roots." *BioScience,* Oct. 1988, pp. 612–18.

FLOWERIN
PLANTS

CONIFERS

FERNS

MOSSES

FUNGI

PROTISTS

SIMPLE PLANTS

W here can you find simple plants? You know that as plants evolved, they became more and more adapted to life on land. Therefore, do we look for simple plants on the edge of the sea, on a river bank as you see on the facing page, or by a freshwater pond? These places are certainly close to the water, but you must remember that all the present-day plants, such as the fern shown here, evolved millions of years ago and the surface of Earth has changed in many ways since then. Areas that were swamps in the Silurian period have since passed through many periods of drying out and land movements. The simple plants of today are those that survived for millions of years in consistently moist places such as tropical forests. Since the Silurian, they have spread to all ecosystems where there is adequate moisture for their survival.

Walking fern

FROM PROTIST TO PLANT

Taxonomists have frequently changed their definitions of a plant. The most up-to-date classification recognizes plants as distinct from unicellular plantlike protists and seaweeds. This is the system of classification used in this textbook. However, because of comparative studies, it is generally accepted that at one time, plants evolved from the green algae. These sections will explain how plants differ from green algae and also show relationships among the different categories of simple plants.

16:1 The Life of a Plant

One distinguishing characteristic of a plant is that it has a life cycle with alternating diploid and haploid stages. Recall from Chapter 8 that the body cells of most organisms are diploid. That is, they contain two sets (2n) of chromosomes, one from each parent. By the process of meiosis in sex cells, this diploid condition is reduced to the haploid (n) number of chromosomes. In all plants, these two stages alternate.

Objectives:
- list the distinguishing characteristics of a plant.
- sequence the alternation of generations in a plant.
- list five divisions of simple plants and give an example of each.

A mossy river bank

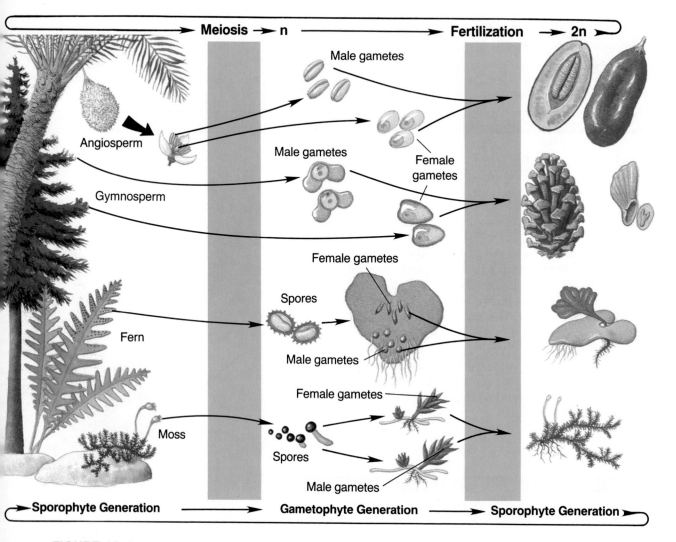

Meiosis → n ──── Fertilization → 2n

Male gametes

Angiosperm

Male gametes

Gymnosperm

Female gametes

Female gametes

Spores

Fern

Male gametes

Female gametes

Moss

Spores

Male gametes

Sporophyte Generation ────── Gametophyte Generation ────── Sporophyte Generation

FIGURE 16–1.

Every plant shows an alternation between a diploid and a haploid generation in its life cycle.

What five structures distinguish a plant?

The stage of a plant that produces the gametes is called the gametophyte. The stage that produces spores is called the sporophyte. In simple plants, such as mosses, the sporophyte is dependent on the gametophyte for a supply of water and nutrients. In the more complex plants, such as ferns and dicots, this role is reversed so that the sporophyte becomes the dominant stage of the life cycle. Follow the sequence of events in the lives of typical plants in Figure 16–1. Notice the times of meiosis and fertilization for each plant.

You have studied in Chapter 13 how plantlike protists also have alternating gametophyte and sporophyte stages. Some scientists place the brown, red, and green algae with the plant kingdom. Recall from Chapter 2 that at one time any living thing that was green was called a plant. So what distinguishes a plant? A plant might have a cuticle to protect the body tissues from drying out, leaves to absorb light, stems to support the leaves, roots to provide anchorage in the soil and for absorption of water, and some means of reproduction that doesn't require water for the transport of male and female gametes.

The gametophyte of simple plants has structures that protect the developing gametes. An **antheridium** is a male sex organ in the gametophyte of a plant. An **archegonium** is a female sex organ in the gametophyte of a plant. In simple plants, each antheridium produces a large number of sperm with flagella. The sperm leave the antheridium when mature and swim through a thin layer of water that covers the plant to a nearby archegonium. Each archegonium has one egg. When one sperm fertilizes the egg, a new diploid sporophyte develops from the resulting zygote.

FIGURE 16–2.

In plants, sperm are produced in antheridia (a), and eggs are formed in archegonia (b).

a

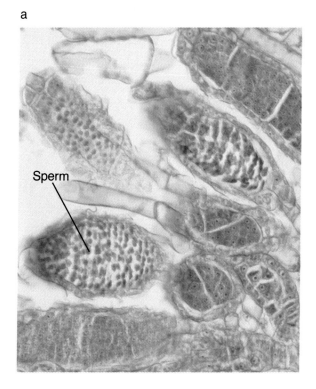

Sperm

b

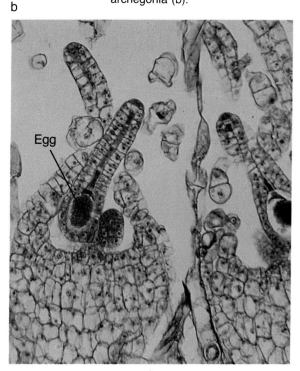

Egg

16:2 The Phylogeny of Simple Plants

In your studies of plantlike protists, you learned that there are three phyla of multicellular algae; the red, the brown, and the green algae. Using evidence that includes comparative studies of RNA, taxonomists have suggested that the green algae are probably the ancestral group of complex plants. The first plants were probably like the whisk ferns that make up the division Psilophyta.

The mosses and liverworts are two classes of division Bryophyta that are thought to have evolved over millions of years by reduction from a larger and more complex fernlike plant. Bryophytes are nonvascular plants that produce spores as a means of asexual reproduction. Vascular plants that produce spores are members of the divisions Lycophyta, the club mosses; Sphenophyta, the horsetails; and Pterophyta (teh roh FITE uh), the ferns. In Figure 16–3, you can examine how the relative sizes of these five divisions of plants have changed over their evolutionary history.

NoteWorthy

The five divisions of lower vascular plants account for less than 3 percent of all modern-day plant species.

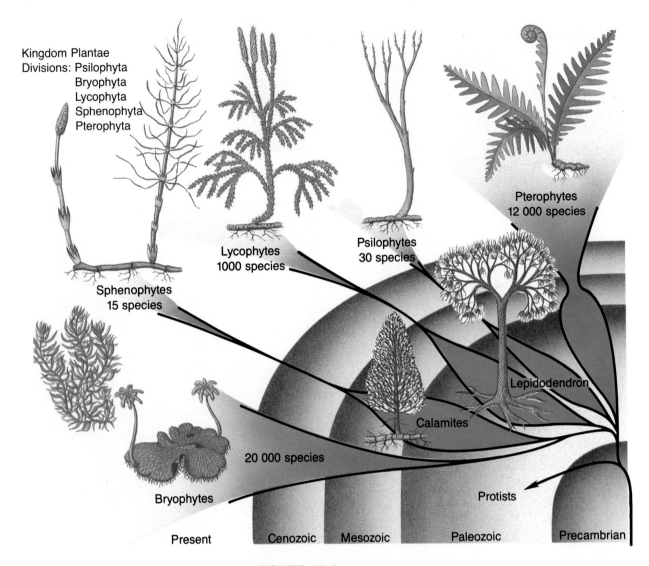

Kingdom Plantae
Divisions: Psilophyta
   Bryophyta
   Lycophyta
   Sphenophyta
   Pterophyta

Pterophytes
12 000 species

Lycophytes
1000 species

Psilophytes
30 species

Sphenophytes
15 species

Lepidodendron

Calamites

20 000 species

Protists

Bryophytes

Present   Cenozoic   Mesozoic   Paleozoic   Precambrian

FIGURE 16–3.

The radiation of divisions of simple plants on the geologic time scale shows their relationships.

REVIEW

1. What are the distinguishing characteristics of a plant?
2. How is a new sporophyte formed?
3. Name five divisions of spore-producing plants and give an example of each.
4. **SKILL REVIEW:** Make a key to distinguish simple, nonvascular plants from plantlike protists. For more help, refer to Organizing Information in the Skill Handbook, pages 810 to 813.
5. **USING CONCEPTS:** Why did only a few species of simple, spore-producing plants survive from the Silurian period?

NONVASCULAR PLANTS

Some present-day simple plants are small, grow close to the ground, and resemble in some ways the green algae found in the oceans. Like seaweeds, these plants don't have vascular tissues that would allow them the advantage of a life away from a watery environment. Nonvascular plants may not have an enormous variety of forms but they are very successful in surviving wherever there is a constant supply of fresh water. What are some of the adaptations of nonvascular plants that make them so successful?

16:3 The Life of a Bryophyte

If you have ever walked through a forest, you couldn't help but notice the velvety mats of mosses on decaying logs or even the shiny, slimy appearance of liverworts on moist rocks by a stream. Mosses and liverworts are nonvascular plants and make up the division Bryophyta. Mosses are small, low-growing plants with leafy stems. They grow on almost any cool, moist surface. The leaves are only one or two cells thick. Water moves from cell to cell within the stems and leaves of mosses by the slow process of diffusion. Nonvascular plants do not have roots to absorb water from the soil. Mosses are held on the ground by rhizoids. A **rhizoid** is a hairlike structure of one or two cells that absorbs water by osmosis.

Objectives:
- identify the characteristics of bryophytes.
- describe the life cycle of a moss.
- name several ways bryophytes are important.

rhizoid:
rhiza (GK) root

FIGURE 16–4.

Mosses are adapted to a life close to water.

What is a protonema?

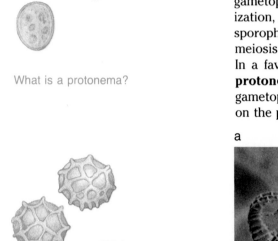

Moss
spores

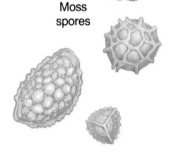

The carpet of moss you are probably most familiar with is a collection of the gametophytes of this simple, nonvascular plant. Follow the sequence of stages in Figure 16–6 that shows the alternation of generations in the life cycle of a moss. Separate male and female gametophyte plants develop from different spores. Male gametophyte plants develop antheridia that produce sperm. Female gametophytes develop archegonia containing eggs. Following fertilization, the sporophyte plant grows from the gametophyte. The sporophyte develops a capsule on top of a stalk. In the capsule, meiosis produces haploid spores that are released when mature. In a favorable environment, the spores will germinate to form a **protonema,** which is a small, green filament of cells. A new leafy gametophyte plant consisting of haploid cells develops from a bud on the protonema. From this point, the life cycle continues.

a

b

FIGURE 16–5.

The opening of a moss capsule (a) is surrounded by teethlike structures that control the release of spores. In a population of mosses (b), spore release often happens at one time.

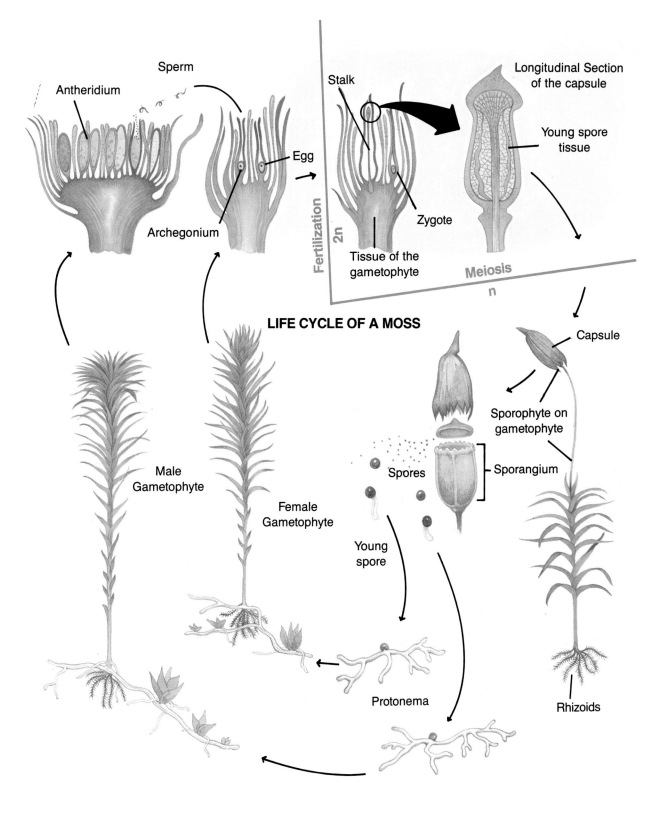

LIFE CYCLE OF A MOSS

Sperm

Antheridium

Archegonium

Egg

Fertilization

Stalk

Zygote

2n

Tissue of the gametophyte

Longitudinal Section of the capsule

Young spore tissue

Meiosis

n

Capsule

Sporophyte on gametophyte

Sporangium

Spores

Young spore

Protonema

Rhizoids

Male Gametophyte

Female Gametophyte

FIGURE 16–6.

The life cycle of a moss shows how the sporophyte is dependent on the gametophyte.

a

c

FIGURE 16–7.

Gemmae (a) form mainly on thallose liverworts (b). Leafy liverworts (c) are often difficult to distinguish from mosses.

b

Liverworts are also bryophytes. Their name was derived from an ancient use of the plant. Liverworts were believed to be herbs that cured problems with the liver. *Wort* is an old word meaning "herb." *Liver* refers to the liver-shaped plants once used in medicines. Liverworts grow on stream banks, moist limestone rocks, or soil. Sexual reproduction in liverworts is similar to that in mosses. The liverwort gametophyte has one of two forms. There are leafy liverworts that are hard to distinguish from mosses, and there are thallose liverworts. A **thallus** is a simple, flat structure that has no stems or leaves. It is anchored to the ground by rhizoids. Archegonia and antheridia are formed on upright structures that develop from the gametophyte.

The gametophytes of liverworts also reproduce asexually. One method of asexual reproduction, the development of gemmae, can be seen in Figure 16–7. **Gemmae** are asexual reproductive structures containing balls of cells that can be dispersed by rain splashes. They develop in cup-shaped structures on the top surface of the thallus.

16:4 The Importance of Bryophytes

Some bryophytes have an important role in soil formation. Mosses and liverworts that are pioneers on freshly exposed rock or soil surfaces rapidly carpet the soil with protonema filaments. As these plants die off, their organic matter is added to the soil in which larger plants can then grow. In this way, mosses play a role in the build up of organic matter that eventually becomes soil.

How do mosses aid in soil formation?

The most economically important moss is peat moss. The scientific name of peat moss is *Sphagnum*. Peat moss forms in bogs in cold and temperate regions around the world. Peat is a combination of compressed, dead *Sphagnum* and other bog plants. In Ireland, parts of Northern Europe, and Canada, peat is cut into bricks, dried, compressed, and used for fuel. Bogs generally are very acidic and contain a low level of oxygen. Bacteria that would ordinarily cause the decomposition of organic matter can't survive. *Sphagnum* leaves are equipped with large water storage cells. The water storage cells make this moss a valuable addition to garden soil because they increase its water-holding ability. Before being cut, the moss contains up to 95 percent water.

Because it appeared to possess tremendous absorption and antiseptic properties, peat moss was used in surgical dressings for wounds during World War I. These *Sphagnum* dressings helped prevent the growth of bacteria in the wounds.

FIGURE 16–8.

Decay of organic matter proceeds very slowly in *Sphagnum* bogs (a). Looking at a *Sphagnum* leaf under high power shows two kinds of cells (b). The broader cells can absorb and retain large amounts of water.

a

b

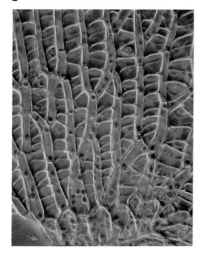

REVIEW

6. How is a protonema formed?
7. How is *Sphagnum* economically useful?
8. How is the sporophyte generation of a moss dependent on the gametophyte generation?
9. **SKILL REVIEW:** Sequence the events in the life cycle of a moss beginning with a protonema. For more help, refer to Reading Science in the Skill Handbook, pages 798 to 799.
10. **USING CONCEPTS:** What is the advantage to mosses of living in dense populations?

BIOLAB
Soil Improvement
16

Problem: How does *Sphagnum* moss affect the water-retention properties of soil?

Materials

soil	masking tape
Sphagnum moss	spoon
250-mL beaker (2)	funnel
pan balance	filter paper (2)
100-mL graduated cylinder	

Procedures

1. Copy the data table.
2. Mass 20 g of soil and place it in a beaker. Label the beaker "soil."
3. Mass 10 g of soil and place it in a second beaker. Weigh 10 g of *Sphagnum* moss and add it to the soil. Mix thoroughly with a spoon. Label the beaker, "soil-moss."
4. Measure 100 mL of water in a graduated cylinder. Pour the water into the first beaker. Refill the graduated cylinder with 100 mL of water and pour into the second beaker.
5. Write a **hypothesis** to describe the amount of water that will be absorbed by the soil in each beaker.
6. Wait five minutes. During this time, insert a funnel containing a piece of filter paper into the graduated cylinder.
7. Carefully pour the water that was not absorbed by the soil in the first beaker back into the graduated cylinder. Try to prevent soil from falling onto the filter paper. Measure the volume of water not absorbed and record the amount in your data table. Discard the water.
8. Replace the filter paper with a clean piece. Repeat step 7 using the second beaker.
9. Calculate the amount of water absorbed for each beaker.
10. Determine the absorption capacity of each type of soil, using the following formula:

$$\text{Absorption capacity} = \frac{\text{Volume of water absorbed (in mL)}}{\text{Mass of soil or mixture (in g)}}$$

Data and Observations

Material used	Volume of water not absorbed	Volume of water absorbed	Absorption capacity (mL/g)
soil			
soil and moss			

Questions and Conclusion

1. Which absorbed more water, soil or soil mixed with *Sphagnum* moss?
2. What is the value to a home gardener of adding *Sphagnum* to the garden soil?
3. Was your **hypothesis** supported by your data?

Conclusion: How does the addition of *Sphagnum* moss affect the water-retention properties of soil?

SIMPLE VASCULAR PLANTS

Vascular plants differ from bryophytes in three important ways. First, they have vascular tissue. Second, the sporophyte generation is dominant. Third, the sporophyte generation becomes independent of the gametophyte. Club mosses, spike mosses, horsetails, and ferns are simple vascular plants.

16:5 Club Mosses, Spike Mosses, and Horsetails

The club mosses, all species of *Lycopodium,* and spike mosses, all species of *Selaginella,* are members of the division Lycophyta. The leafy stems of club mosses look similar to the gametophytes of mosses. A clublike cluster of spore-bearing leaves at the end of each stem is a **strobilus** (*pl.* strobili). These clublike structures contain spores and give this group its common name. Some species of *Lycopodium* are called ground pine because they resemble miniature pine trees. Species of club mosses are endangered in some areas because they are collected for holiday decorations.

The spike mosses also produce spores in a strobilus. One species of *Selaginella* lives in the desert and is dormant during the driest part of the year. A spike moss produces two kinds of spores that develop into male and female gametophytes. Most spike mosses of the United States are very small, finely branched, and grow close to the ground in moist places. Many species of *Selaginella* are tropical.

Objectives:
- describe characteristics of club mosses, spike mosses, and horsetails.
- list the characteristics of a fern.
- summarize the life cycle of a fern.
- describe the evolution and importance of vascular spore plants.

FIGURE 16–9.

Simple vascular plants such as a club moss (a) and a spike moss (b) produce spores in strobili.

a

b

THE FORMATION OF COAL BEDS

In the Paleozoic, the climate was moist and warm, and great stretches of land were covered with forests of giant tree ferns, horsetails, and club mosses. Horsetails were up to 15 meters tall while the tree ferns were much larger than today's tropical tree ferns that can reach heights of up to 25 meters. The fronds of these ancient tree ferns reached almost two meters in length. Monstrous dragonflies with wingspans more than half a meter flew within these great forests. Under the moist and perpetual summer of the swamps, shades of green must have been dominant, since flowers had not yet evolved. As the climate gradually grew colder and drier in the early Mesozoic, all these giants became extinct, leaving behind the more diminutive horsetails and ferns that we see today on the shady forest floor.

In today's tropical forests, little material accumulates. It is broken down rapidly by decomposers and the nutrients are taken back in by the trees. However, in the Paleozoic, as the bodies of all these gigantic plants fell into swamps, they became waterlogged and sank beneath the mud. This plant material, building up on the floor of the swamp, became peat. As more and more plant material accumulated, the peat became compacted to less than one twenty-fifth of its original thickness. Lignite coal, a porous fossil fuel, was produced first from the pressure and heat process. With further compaction, the lignite became bituminous coal, and finally anthracite. For the production of a reasonably pure coal, little other sediment could be accumulating in the swamp at the same time. These Paleozoic swamp forests became the coal sediments we mine today. Why do you think these ancient plants became extinct except for a few diminutive relatives? Are there coal beds still being formed today?

Present-day tree fern

All horsetails are classified in the division Sphenophyta and all members belong to the genus *Equisetum*. Their stem structure is unlike any other among vascular plants. Sections of ribbed, hollow stem appear jointed. At each joint or node there is a whorl of scalelike leaves. Sporangia are located in a conelike strobilus at each branch tip. In some species, there are separate spore-bearing and sterile shoots.

FIGURE 16–10.

Horsetail stems contain silicon.

16:6 The Life of a Fern

The simple vascular plants you are probably most familiar with belong to the division Pterophyta (teh ruh FITE uh), the ferns. Most of the 11 000 species of ferns are tropical.

Follow the sequence of events in the life cycle of a fern as shown in Figure 16–11. A spore germinates to form a protonema that develops into a prothallus. A **prothallus** is the heart-shaped gametophyte stage of a fern. Antheridia and archegonia form on the prothallus. The antheridia usually form on the lower surface among the rhizoids, and the archegonia form near the notch of the heart-shaped prothallus. Sperm swim from the antheridia to the eggs in the archegonia.

Where do the antheridia and archegonia form on ferns?

FIGURE 16–11.

The life cycle of a fern shows how the sporophyte is independent of the gametophyte.

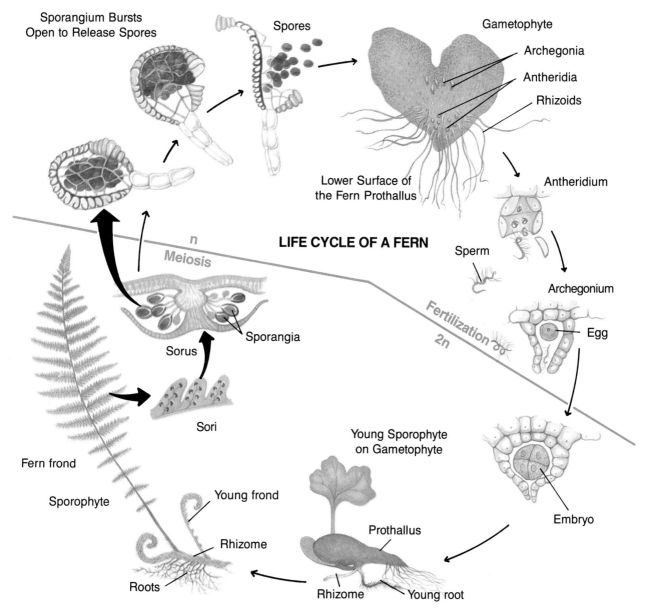

Sporangium Bursts Open to Release Spores

Spores

Gametophyte

Archegonia

Antheridia

Rhizoids

Lower Surface of the Fern Prothallus

Antheridium

Sperm

Archegonium

LIFE CYCLE OF A FERN

n

Meiosis

Fertilization ♀♂

2n

Egg

Sorus

Sporangia

Sori

Young Sporophyte on Gametophyte

Embryo

Fern frond

Sporophyte

Young frond

Rhizome

Prothallus

Roots

Rhizome

Young root

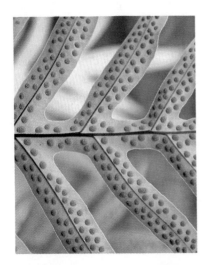

FIGURE 16–12.

Spores of a fern are produced within clusters of Sporangia on the pinnae.

In what ways did the first plants resemble whisk ferns?

The embryo that results from the fertilization of the egg in the archegonium is the start of the new sporophyte plant. At first, the sporophyte depends on the gametophyte for nutrients. The gametophyte dies when the young sporophyte develops roots and begins to make its own food by photosynthesis. The leaves of a fern are called **fronds.** Fronds often consist of many leaflets called **pinnae.** Brown spots called sori (*sing.* sorus) form on the undersides of fern pinnae. A **sorus** is a compact group of sporangia in which spores are produced by meiosis. The cycle begins again when the sporangia burst and release the spores.

16:7 The Origin and Importance of Vascular Spore Plants

Scientists hypothesize that the evolutionary paths taken by bryophytes and vascular plants separated after plants became adapted to land. Some mosses are observed to contain reduced vascular tissue. The dominant gametophyte and the general lack of vascular tissue are a combination of characteristics only found in bryophytes.

Fossils from the Devonian period provide evidence of the origin and structure of the first land plants. Plants of this period were bare upright structures with simple, branching patterns and sporangia at the ends of the branches. They resembled the present-day whisk ferns as shown in Figure 16–13. Evidence from comparative RNA studies supports this view.

Club mosses, spike mosses, and horsetails first appeared in the Devonian period about 400 million years ago and increased in abundance and diversity over the next 100 million years. Fossils of giant horsetails have been found with stems that measure 20 cm in diameter and leaves that are 10 cm long. In contrast, these structures of modern horsetails are measured in millimeters. Fossils of club mosses are also much larger than present-day mosses. Ferns appear in the fossil record shortly after the club mosses and horsetails. Club mosses, horsetails, and ferns once made up the dominant vegetation on Earth and they all contributed to the formation of fossil fuels.

FIGURE 16–13.

The oldest plant fossils are those of *Rhynia* (a) from the early Devonian period. They resemble the whisk ferns of today (b).

a

Sporangia

b

In Asia, young fern fronds are grown for food. The rhizomes of one fern have also been used to treat tapeworm infestations. Ferns are used extensively in floral decorations, as well as indoor and outdoor decorative plants.

Although horsetails are no longer used to clean pans, they are important to prospectors of precious metals. *Equisetum* plants accumulate metals such as gold from the environment.

FIGURE 16–14.

Plants of the Carboniferous period were the source of Earth's non-renewable supply of fossil fuels.

REVIEW

11. How do bryophytes differ from simple vascular plants?
12. What is the role of the prothallus in the fern life cycle?
13. Name two spore-bearing vascular plants that contributed to coal formation.
14. **SKILL REVIEW:** Make a simple key to identify mosses, liverworts, ferns, horsetails, and club mosses. For more help, refer to Organizing Information in the Skill Handbook, pages 810 to 813.
15. **USING CONCEPTS:** Compare and contrast the life cycles of a fern and a moss.

DEVELOPING A VIEWPOINT

DESTRUCTION OF TROPICAL RAIN FORESTS

Tropical rain forests are found in South America, Central America, central Asia, parts of Australia and Africa, and on some large islands. It usually rains daily in a tropical rain forest. The temperature is about 25°C all year long.

The growth in a tropical forest is dense. In fact, it is so dense that the forest floor does not get much light. Smaller shrubs and trees have a difficult time competing with larger plants for light. Not only are there many large trees, but there are also many different kinds of trees. For example, there are more kinds of trees in 0.5 km² of forest area in Malaysia than in the whole United States and Canada.

BACKGROUND

About 7 percent of Earth's surface is covered by tropical rain forests. These forests receive at least 250 cm of rain during the year. All this rain causes plants to grow rapidly. The branches of trees form a thick canopy that is usually 30 to 50 meters above the forest floor. Many kinds of animals live in the trees. In fact, many of these animals stay in the trees all the time.

In most of the countries where there are tropical rain forests, the human population is large and the people are poor. The forests are being cut down rapidly in many parts of the world. They are being felled for wood or to clear the land for farming or ranching. Many people are settling in the newly cleared areas in a move to ensure economic survival. Many are inexperienced in farming and lack knowledge of the needs of the cleared forest land.

CASE STUDIES

1. In September 1988, the astronauts on the space shuttle *Discovery* photographed the area over the Amazon River Basin. The photographs showed a large cloud that was the result of burning taking place in the tropical rain forest. The cloud covered an area equal to about one third of the United States.

2. The Pacific island of Java in Indonesia is over-populated. Some of its people were given the chance to migrate to some of the other islands in Indonesia. These ecologically fragile islands had large areas of tropical rain forest. The forests were cleared for farms. In so doing, large areas of rain forest were destroyed. Then the settlers soon discovered that the soils were too poor for sustained farming.

3. Nearly 25 million acres of rain forest are cleared every year. About half of this clearing takes place in the Amazon River Basin. If the destruction continues at this rate, all the world's rain forests could be destroyed in less than 50 years. Most of this destruction is done to create farmland. But the nutrient-poor soils of rain forests support crops for only a few years and then new forest has to be cleared.

4. Plants, especially large trees, take in carbon dioxide from the air and use it in the process of photosynthesis. But the amount of carbon dioxide in the air has been steadily increasing as a result of the burning of wood and fossil fuels. This increase has led some people to propose that Earth's climate will get warmer. The burning of tropical rain forests and their loss as "carbon-dioxide fixers" are believed to be contributing to the warming problem.

Environmentalists feel that planting new trees is necessary to slow down the global warming. In Guatemala, for example, 4000 farmers will plant 52 million tree seedlings in the next ten years. The planting was arranged to offset a coal-burning power plant in Connecticut. It is estimated that for each megawatt produced at the power plant, 5 km^2 of rain forest are needed to fix the carbon dioxide produced by the plants.

5. There are 11 million people on the island of Madagascar. Slash-and-burn clearing of rain forests to grow crops is common. Conservation is a problem for Madagascar because the people need food and other necessities now. At the turn of the century, about a quarter of the island was forested. Now, half of that is gone.

6. Studies have shown that very few nutrients wash away in the streams and rivers of undisturbed rain forests. However, the cycle of using and reusing nutrients is broken by slash- and-burn clearing or by heavy logging. Most rain forest soils are quickly degraded by torrential rains after the soils have become exposed. The layer of topsoil is quickly lost. If the land is fed with costly fertilizers, it becomes useless in about five years.

DEVELOPING YOUR VIEWPOINT

1. Why might it be a good idea to use satellites to monitor the forests of the world?

2. What can be done with stripped rain forest land that cannot sustain farming?

3. Research how the destruction of the tropical rain forest of Central and South America would affect the Panama Canal.

4. Research to find out what the greenhouse effect is and its global implications.

5. Should the farmers of Madagascar be allowed to continue to clear the rain forests? How can developing nations help their people survive and still maintain their vital resources? Is it possible to do this?

SUGGESTED READINGS

1. Booth, William. "Monitoring the Fate of the Forests from Space." *Science,* March 17, 1989, pp. 1428–1429.

2. Knox, Margaret L. "No Nation An Island." *Sierra,* May/June, 1989, pp. 78–84.

3. Linden, Eugene. "The Death of Birth." *Time,* January 2, 1989, pp. 78–84.

4. Schell, Johnathan. "Our Fragile Earth." *Discover,* October, 1989, pp. 44–50.

CHAPTER REVIEW

SUMMARY

1. The life cycles of plants have an alternation of sporophyte and gametophyte stages. **16:1**
2. Plants probably evolved from green algae. Simple plants include psilophytes, bryophytes, lycophytes, sphenophytes, and pterophytes. **16:2**
3. The sporophytes of bryophytes are dependent on the gametophyte for nutrients. Mosses are leafy. Liverworts are leafy or thallose. Bryophytes reproduce sexually by gametes and spores, and asexually by gemmae. **16:3**
4. Bryophytes provide a protective layer to soil and help in soil formation. *Sphagnum* moss is an economically important bryophyte. **16:4**
5. Lycophytes are simple vascular plants with leafy stems and spores in a strobilus. The sporophyte is independent of the gametophyte. **16:5**
6. Pterophytes have a leafy sporophyte that produces spores within a sorus. **16:6**
7. Early records of land plants are found in the Devonian period. They resembled psilophytes. The fossil record shows that club mosses, horsetails, and ferns were once the dominant plants on Earth. **16:7**

LANGUAGE OF BIOLOGY

antheridium	protonema
archegonium	rhizoid
fronds	sorus
gemmae	strobilus
pinnae	thallus
prothallus	

Choose the word or phrase from the list above that completes the sentence.

1. In nonvascular plants, a(n) ____ absorbs soil water.

2. The body of a liverwort with a flat structure that has no stems or leaves is a(n) ____.
3. The heart-shaped gametophyte stage of a fern is a(n) ____.
4. A small haploid green filament in the life cycle of a bryophyte is a(n) ____.
5. An organ in which eggs are produced and stored is a(n) ____.
6. The leaves of a fern are called ____.
7. A(n) ____ is a clublike structure with clusters of spores.
8. ____ are asexual reproductive bodies on a liverwort gametophyte.
9. A plant sperm-producing organ is a(n) ____.
10. Small leaflets on a fern frond are ____.

REVIEWING CONCEPTS

Choose the word or phrase that completes the sentence or answers the question.

11. A characteristic of all plants is a ____.
    a. rhizoid
    b. green color
    c. cuticle
    d. dominant sporophyte generation
12. Following fertilization in bryophytes, the sporophyte plant grows from the ____.
    a. protonema   c. capsule
    b. gametophyte   d. gemmae
13. The gametophyte is dominant in the ____.
    a. ferns   c. horsetails
    b. mosses   d. club mosses
14. Vascular tissue is found in the ____.
    a. mosses   c. liverworts
    b. bryophytes   d. ferns
15. The strobilus is NOT found in ____.
    a. ferns   c. club mosses
    b. horsetails   d. spike mosses
16. Liverworts reproduce asexually by ____.
    a. spores   c. gemmae
    b. rhizoids   d. antheridia

17. Horsetails are rough because of ____.
   a. silicon   c. magnesium
   b. boron   d. manganese
18. Some bryophytes are useful as ____.
   a. food   c. fuel
   b. housing   d. clothing
19. Ferns appear in the fossil record ____.
   a. before horsetails
   b. at the same time as horsetails
   c. not at all
   d. after horsetails
20. Spores are produced in ferns within ____.
   a. fronds   c. pinnae
   b. archegonia   d. sori

UNDERSTANDING CONCEPTS

Answer the following questions using complete sentences.

21. Why do all simple plants require a moist environment?
22. How does a sporophyte differ from a gametophyte?
23. Starting with meiosis, sequence the stages in the life cycle of a plant.
24. What characteristic of *Sphagnum* makes these mosses useful in packing living plant materials for transport?
25. How is the stem structure of horsetails different from that of other simple vascular plants?
26. Where would you expect to find mosses and liverworts?
27. What combination of five characteristics can be used to distinguish plants from other organisms?
28. Starting with the process of meiosis, list the stages in the life cycle of a fern.
29. What characteristics do bryophytes and vascular plants share to indicate that they evolved from a common ancestor?
30. What are the three major differences between bryophytes and pterophytes?

APPLYING CONCEPTS

Answer the following questions using complete sentences.

31. What is the evidence that many simple plants became extinct?
32. Compare the characteristics of plantlike protists, fungi, bryophytes, and simple vascular plants.
33. Many species of ferns are used as ornamental houseplants. If you were to give a fern as a gift to a friend, what sort of instructions would you list in order for your friend to keep the fern healthy?
34. Suggest an explanation for the scarcity of bryophyte fossils.
35. How is a dominant and independent sporophyte stage an adaptive advantage for complex plants such as ferns?

EXTENSIONS

1. Make a study to test the hypothesis that moss grows only on the north side of trees.
2. Examine sori of several different types of ferns under a stereomicroscope. Make a key to identify these ferns based upon characteristics of their sori.
3. Construct a terrarium containing mosses, ferns, and liverworts.

READINGS

Gensel, P.G. and H.N. Andrews. "The Evolution of Early Land Plants." *American Scientist,* Sept.–Oct. 1987, pp. 478–489.
Levathes, L.E. "Mysteries of the Bog." *National Geographic,* Mar. 1987, pp. 396–420.
Ricciuti, E.R. "Don't Look Down on the Humble Moss." *Audubon,* Sept. 1988, pp. 46–55.

CONIFERS

FLOWERING
PLANTS

FERNS

MOSSES

FUNGI

PROTISTS

SEED PLANTS: GYMNOSPERMS

Y ou may have seen a science fiction movie in which crew members on a space flight lie in suspended animation in sealed capsules. They require no food during a trip that lasts for years. As their spacecraft approaches a distant planet, they revive and resume their normal activities.

Plants acquired the ability for a type of suspended animation about 360 million years ago when the first seeds evolved. The juniper tree shown on the facing page and the yew shown here are plants that produce seeds. In this chapter, you will learn how seeds are adaptive, and about one large group of seed plants, the gymnosperms.

Yew

SEED PLANTS

Seed plants have several adaptive advantages for life on land. The fertilized egg develops within a seed, and the sperm of seed plants is enclosed in a waterproof coat. The sperm doesn't need free water to swim to the egg. These protected structures provide environments in which a plant embryo and sperm can survive for several days or even hundreds of years. The ability of seeds to survive for long periods and germinate when conditions become favorable for growth is a major competitive advantage for seed-bearing plants. Other adaptations of seed plants have enabled them to occupy many environments that are unfavorable to seedless plants.

17:1 Classifying Seed Plants

Most of the plants you can think of are probably seed plants, as they number about 270 000 species. A **seed** is a plant structure that protects the plant embryo. Seed plants have roots, stems, and leaves. Pine trees, maple trees, cacti, grasses, roses, and daffodils are all seed plants. Several systems of classification exist for plants. Some botanists group seed plants into two divisions—gymnosperms (JIHM nuh spurmz) and angiosperms (AN jee uh spurmz).

Objectives:
- differentiate between gymnosperms and angiosperms.
- describe the life cycle of a seed plant.
- name the parts of a seed and describe their functions.
- list the conditions necessary for germination.

What are the two traditional divisions of seed plants?

Juniper

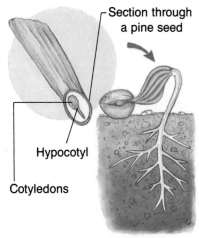

Section through a pine seed

Hypocotyl

Cotyledons

FIGURE 17–1.

The cotyledons are the last structures to emerge when a pine seed germinates.

angiosperm:
   angaion (GK) flask
   sperma (GK) seed

Angiosperms, also known as flowering plants, produce seeds inside a **fruit,** a ripened ovary. For example, when you eat an orange you first peel away a thick, outer layer, then you eat through a mass of juicy tissues, and finally you come to the seeds buried deep in the center of this fruit. Angiosperms include apples, bananas, green peppers, raspberries, and squash. Some angiosperms are monocots; others are dicots. These terms refer to the number of seed leaves, or **cotyledons,** contained in their seeds. Monocots have one cotyledon; dicots have two.

Another system of classifying plants recognizes the distinct nature of groups of gymnosperms, and this is the system presented in this textbook. There are, therefore, five divisions of seed plants: Coniferophyta, Cycadophyta, Ginkgophyta, Gnetophyta, all gymnosperms; and Anthophyta, sometimes known as the angiosperms.

The developing seeds of **gymnosperms** are not surrounded by a protective wall. Seeds of gymnosperms do not have the protection provided by a fruit. Many gymnosperms such as pine trees produce seeds in cones. These plants are often called conifers. The seeds of gymnosperms usually have more than one or two cotyledons.

FIGURE 17–2.

The fruit of an orange tree shows that it is an angiosperm because of its protected seeds. A pine tree is classified as a gymnosperm because its seeds are entirely exposed.

17:2 The Life of a Seed Plant

You have studied how, among the vascular plants, the ferns, club mosses, and horsetails all produce spores that are shed from the parent sporophyte. Recall from Chapter 16 that the spores are dispersed and germinate into gametophytes in moist environments. Seed-bearing plants don't shed spores. Instead, the spore that develops into the female gametophyte develops in an **ovule,** the egg-producing organ of a seed plant, and remains on the sporophyte plant. The male gametophyte develops inside the **pollen grain,** the sperm-producing organ of a seed plant. Development of the male and female gametophytes, and sperm and egg production all take place on the plant sporophyte in cones or flowers. Seeds result from the fertilization of the egg inside the ovule.

a

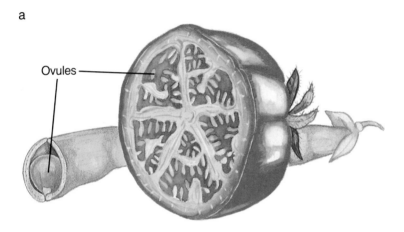

Ovules

b

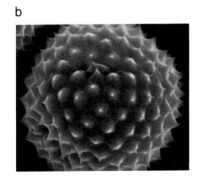

c

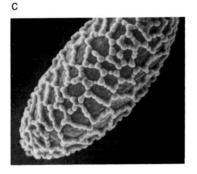

FIGURE 17–3.

In seed plants, the female gametophytes are in ovules, which later develop into seeds (a). The male gametophytes are in pollen grains (b and c).

17:3 Seed Structure

All seeds are made up of the same three parts, although the parts are not always formed from the same tissues. These parts are the plant embryo, a source of stored food, and a protective seed coat. The seed coat is a part of the old sporophyte generation. The source of stored food develops from the gametophyte. In dicots and gymnosperms, the food is stored in cotyledons. In monocot seeds, the food is stored in the **endosperm.** In the life cycle of a seed plant, the embryo is the beginning of a new sporophyte generation.

What are the three parts of a seed?

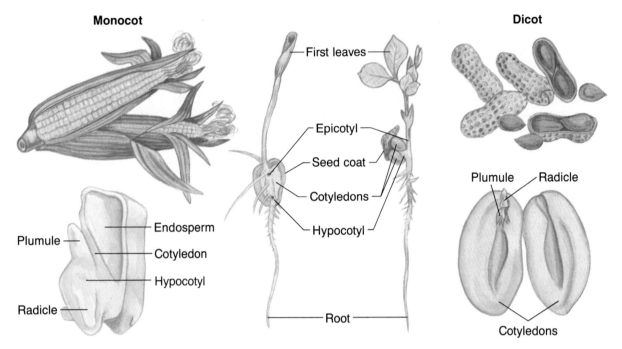

Monocot

Dicot

First leaves

Epicotyl
Seed coat
Cotyledons
Hypocotyl

Root

Plumule
Endosperm
Cotyledon
Hypocotyl
Radicle

Plumule   Radicle

Cotyledons

FIGURE 17–4.

The structures of seeds are basically the same in both monocots and dicots.

FIGURE 17–5.

The first roots of a mangrove are green until they become buried in the mud below.

The structure of all plant embryos is similar as shown in Figure 17–4. A peanut is a dicot. Above the node where the two cotyledons join and below the first true leaves is the epicotyl. The **epicotyl** is a region of the embryo that lengthens and pushes the new stem and leaves above the surface of the soil. The cotyledons are attached to the rest of the embryo at the **hypocotyl.** Just below the hypocotyl is the **radicle,** the primary root of the new plant. The primary or first shoot of the plant is the **plumule.** In a monocot, such as corn, the single cotyledon is joined to the endosperm.

Stored food is an important part of a seed. When the embryo begins to grow, it uses this food until the new leaves are exposed to the light and can produce chlorophyll for photosynthesis. When you eat corn-on-the-cob, you are eating mainly monocot endosperm. When you eat beans, you are eating mostly the stored food in the cotyledons.

17:4 Germination

When the seed is fully formed and sufficient nutrients have been stored, the seed separates from the ovary. As the seed loses water, it dries and the seed coat hardens. At this point, the seed is mature and often is able to survive conditions, such as extreme cold or drought, unfavorable to the parent plant. Once a seed is mature, it may undergo a period of inactivity called **dormancy.** Metabolic activity slows during dormancy, which may last for a few months or for several years. Some seeds, such as oak, germinate almost as soon as they land near the parent plant. Others, such as the mangrove, germinate even while still attached to the parent plant. Many desert and prairie wildflowers have long periods of dormancy.

Dormancy ends when **germination,** the beginning of the development of the seed into a new plant, begins. The absorption of enough water and the presence of oxygen and favorable temperatures usually end dormancy, but there may be other requirements. Water is important because it activates the embryo's metabolic systems. Once its metabolism has been activated, a seed must continue to receive water, or it will die. Just before the seed coat breaks open, a plant embryo begins to respire rapidly. Many seeds germinate best at temperatures between 25°C and 30°C. Arctic species have lower germinating temperatures than tropical species. When the temperature is below 0°C or above 45°C, many seeds won't germinate at all.

Some seeds have particular requirements for germination including freezing temperatures, certain lengths of daylight, fire, or extensive soaking. These adaptations to certain conditions help reduce competition for the germinating seed, and thus increase the embryo's odds of surviving. You may have seen pictures of Yellowstone National Park after fires burned much of it in 1988. Pictures taken

NoteWorthy

Germination can occur after dormancy only if the embryo is viable, meaning still alive. Lotus seeds, *Nelumbo nucifera,* have been found to be viable after lying dormant for more than 700 years.

FIGURE 17–6.

Some seeds can withstand burning, as we have seen in the new growth of plants, including lupines as seen on the left, and gentians shown below, in Yellowstone Park since the great fires of 1988.

only a year later show many plants growing in areas that had been burnt to the ground. The heating of seeds by fire with the removal of mature plants that would have competed with the seedlings provided a favorable environment for seed germination of some species. A requirement for light is common for small seeds. If a small seed is planted too deeply, it may run out of stored food before reaching the surface. Without light, a plant will die.

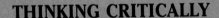

REVIEW

1. What are the two major groups of seed plants?
2. Why is stored food necessary for the survival of a seed?
3. What adaptive advantages do seeds have over spores?
4. **SKILL REVIEW:** Explain why it might be an advantage for seeds to require light for germination. For more help, refer to Reading Science in the Skill Handbook, pages 798 to 799.
5. **USING CONCEPTS:** Discuss why the plants of an area after a fire differ from those before the fire.

THINKING CRITICALLY

SLEEPING SEEDS

You may think of an experiment as a procedure that you can complete in one class period or maybe during a week or month. In 1879, Dr. W.J. Beal, a botany professor from Michigan State University, began a seed-germination experiment that has lasted more than 100 years!

Dr. Beal was interested in testing the ability of wildflower seeds to germinate after remaining dormant for long periods of time. Since seeds will germinate only when they have the right combination of oxygen, water, light, and proper temperatures, Dr. Beal had to deprive his seeds of these things. To do this, he prepared 20 jars of moist sand. In each jar he placed 50 seeds, each from 23 different species of plants. To prevent water and light from reaching the seeds, he buried the jar uncorked and mouth down in a sandy mound. For 35 years, Dr. Beal exhumed a jar every five years and tested the ability of the seeds to germinate. After his death, others continued the experiment, testing a jar of seeds every ten years. In 1980, the date of the last testing, only three species of the original 23 germinated. Germination occurred in almost half of the remaining seeds of *Verbascum blattaria,* a common European weed called moth mullein. Only a few of the other two species began to grow.

What advantages might moth mullein have over a plant species that doesn't have a period of dormancy? Dr. Beal's experiment did not test the fertility of the plants that germinated. How could this be tested?

Moth mullein

GYMNOSPERMS

The biggest, tallest, and oldest trees are gymnosperms. The largest tree known is a giant sequoia that is large enough to make 5000 million matches. Some redwoods can grow as tall as a 30-story skyscraper. A 4800-year-old bristlecone pine from the White Mountains of California is the oldest living tree known. You are probably most familiar with pines because of their cones and the fact that they grow in most regions of the United States.

Objectives:
- describe the major characteristics of the four divisions of gymnosperms.
- describe the life cycle of a conifer.
- discuss the importance of gymnosperms.
- discuss the origins of gymnosperms.

17:5 The Phylogeny of Gymnosperms

The characteristic that sets gymnosperms apart from angiosperms is the production of seeds without fruits. In fact, the word *gymnosperm* means "naked seed." During the Mesozoic era, the ability to produce seeds was probably the major factor that enabled gymnosperms to become the dominant plant life. After the evolution of angiosperms in the Cretaceous period, gymnosperms lost their world dominance. Four divisions of gymnosperms exist. Look at their phylogenetic relationships in Figure 17–7.

FIGURE 17–7.

The radiation of divisions of gymnosperms on the geologic time scale shows their relationships.

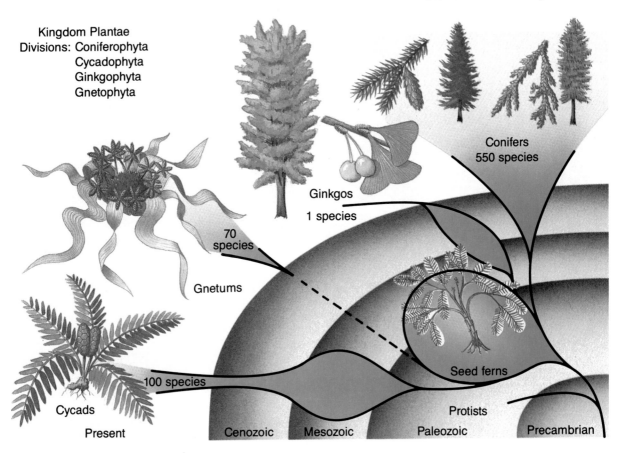

Kingdom Plantae
Divisions: Coniferophyta
Cycadophyta
Ginkgophyta
Gnetophyta

Conifers
550 species

Ginkgos
1 species

70 species

Gnetums

Seed ferns

Cycads

100 species

Protists

Present   Cenozoic   Mesozoic   Paleozoic   Precambrian

FIGURE 17–8.

The scales of the juniper cones become fleshy and give them an appearance of angiosperm fruits.

FIGURE 17–9.

Deciduous conifers include the bald cypress (a) and the larch (b). The pine (c) and the spruce (d) are evergreen conifers.

Coniferophyta

Most gymnosperms belong to division Coniferophyta. Conifers include pines, spruces, larches, cedars, yews, and junipers. Most of these plants produce seeds in woody cones. The seeds of yews and junipers are surrounded by fleshy tissues that resemble fruits of angiosperms. However, their seeds are naked when first formed and the tissues of these so-called berries are not derived from the ovary wall as are the tissues of fruits. Many conifers produce male and female cones on separate plants. In some species, the male and female cones are borne on the same plant, but the male cones may be on side branches while the female cones are at the tips of branches. In some species, the female cones are high in the tree and the male cones are on low branches. This arrangement prevents the pollen from fertilizing the same tree's own eggs.

Conifers form large forests in the northern and southern hemispheres and have many adaptations that enable them to grow in dry habitats. Most conifers are **evergreen plants,** which retain their leaves all year round. Leaves may drop off from time to time, but not all at once. Leaves of evergreens have thick cuticles and sunken stomata that prevent water loss. Some conifers such as larches and bald cypress trees are **deciduous plants,** which lose all their leaves at the same time. Loss of leaves is another plant adaptation to reducing water loss during times when water is unavailable to the plant. Think of the long, cold winters of Alaska and Siberia. The ground is frozen for many months. The roots can't take up enough water to supply the plant. In Siberia, larches drop their leaves. In Alaska, spruces are protected by their thick, needlelike leaves.

a

b

c

d

Cycadophyta

The division Cycadophyta has 100 species in ten genera. In the United States, the only present-day cycad is native to Florida. However, you may have seen cycads in greenhouses of botanical gardens. Both the trunk and leaves of a cycad resemble those of a palm tree, but the new leaves unroll in the same way as in fern fronds.

As in some conifers, cycads produce large male and female cones on separate trees. Cycads are intermediate in some structures between ancient and modern seed plants. Their sperm have flagella that allow them to swim, and yet they don't require free water to reach the egg. The sperm swim in the protection provided by a chamber within the ovule.

How are cycads like ancient seed plants?

a

b

FIGURE 17–10.

Cycads have a terminal rosette of leaves (a). All cycads have separate female (b) and male plants.

a

b

FIGURE 17–11.

The female (a) and male (b) structures of a ginkgo are on separate plants. As the ovules of a ginkgo ripen, the outer layer of the seeds becomes fleshy.

FIGURE 17–12.

Gnetum is a genus of tropical climbing plants with cones arranged around the stem.

Ginkgophyta

The division Ginkgophyta has only one living species, *Ginkgo biloba.* There are no known wild ginkgo trees. This species, considered sacred in China and Japan, has been cultivated, and thus preserved, in temple gardens for thousands of years. The name *Ginkgo* is Chinese and means "silver apricot."

Ginkgos share some characteristics with cycads. Male and female cones are produced on separate trees, and *Ginkgo* sperm have flagella. Unlike cycads and most conifers, ginkgos are deciduous. They usually lose all of their fanlike leaves within a three-hour period in the autumn. Because of their beauty and resistance to air pollution, ginkgo trees have been planted in many urban parks and gardens. The male trees are often preferred because the fleshy outer covering of the ginkgo seed on female trees has a rancid smell.

Gnetophyta

The division Gnetophyta has three genera. *Gnetum* is a genus of trees and climbing vines found in tropical and subtropical forests. The leaves of *Gnetum* are large and leathery. *Ephedra,* the only gnetophyte genus native to the United States, is a broomlike shrub with branches and small leaves that resemble those of horsetails. The third gnetophyte genus is *Welwitschia,* which has only one species that grows in South Africa. The plants have a bizarre appearance as shown in Figure 17–19 at the end of the chapter. The stem looks like a large disk lying on the ground, and two long, strap-shaped leaves grow from the stem. These leaves continue to grow for the life of the plant and may reach 180 cm in length. The leaves may split lengthwise, so that one plant seems to have many leaves, but no more than the original two are ever formed during the plant's 100-year lifetime.

17:6 The Life Cycle of a Gymnosperm

All gymnosperms produce seeds in similar ways. The life cycle of a pine can be used as a model for the seed production process of all gymnosperms. Follow the sequence of events in Figure 17–13 as you read about pine seed development.

FIGURE 17–13.

The life cycle of a pine is typical for all gymnosperms.

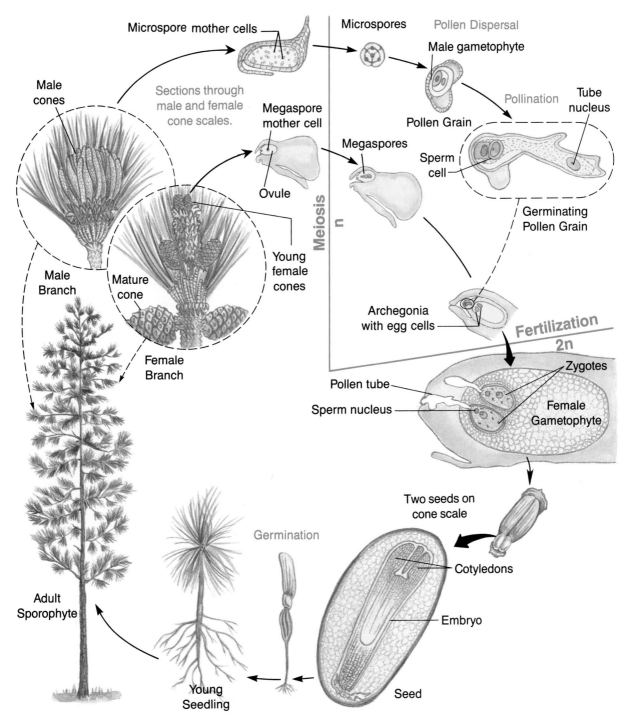

Pines produce seeds from two types of spores. The **microspore** is a reproductive cell in plants that gives rise to the sperm. The **megaspore** is a reproductive cell in plants that gives rise to the egg. Microspores and megaspores are produced in different kinds of cones. Male cones are made up of small, papery leaves called scales. In early spring, each scale of a male cone contains two sporangia that each produce haploid microspores by meiosis. Each microspore develops into a winged pollen grain. Each pollen grain contains four haploid cells.

Female pine cones are larger and more woody than male cones. The female cones of sugar pines in California and Oregon may be up to 45 cm long. Female cones are modified branch systems. Two ovules, made up of the female gametophyte with egg-containing structures, develop in sporangia on the upper surface of each scale. Each ovule produces four haploid cells by meiosis. Only one of these cells develops into a megaspore. Each ovule is covered by a thick protective layer of cells that develops into the seed coat. Notice in Figure 17–15 that there is an opening in this layer. This opening in the seed coat is called the **micropyle,** and it first allows entry of pollen and later allows entry of water for germination.

b

a

FIGURE 17–4.

Each woody scale of a female pine cone (a) has two seeds. The papery scales of male cones (b) open to release pollen.

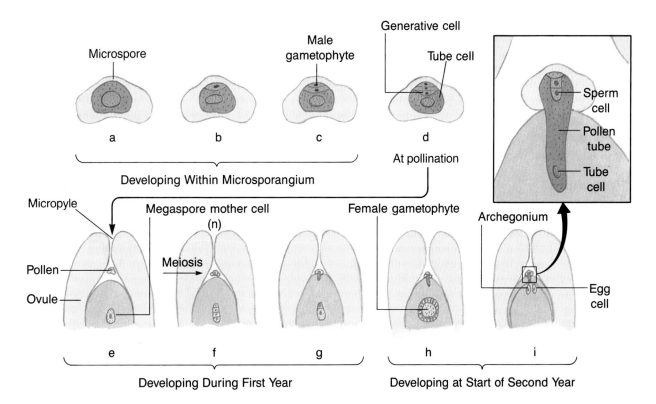

Microspore — a — b — c — d

Male gametophyte (c)

Generative cell, **Tube cell** (d)

At pollination

Developing Within Microsporangium

Sperm cell, **Pollen tube**, **Tube cell**

Micropyle, **Megaspore mother cell (n)**, **Female gametophyte**, **Archegonium**

Pollen, **Meiosis**

Ovule

e — f — g — h — i

Egg cell

Developing During First Year — Developing at Start of Second Year

For the development of a seed, pollination must first occur. **Pollination** is the transferring of pollen grains from a male to a female plant reproductive structure. In gymnosperms, pollination occurs in the spring when wind-blown pollen grains fall on the open scales of a female cone. The pollen becomes trapped in a sticky fluid near the micropyle. After pollination occurs, the scales of the female cone close, and pollen grains are drawn into the micropyle. At this point in time, two to six archegonia develop from the mature megaspore within the megasporangium. A single large egg forms in each archegonium.

Meanwhile, another process is occurring in the pollen grains at the micropyle. Two of the four haploid cells in each pollen grain degenerate. A tube cell and a generative cell remain. The tube cell causes development of a pollen tube that slowly penetrates the megasporangium. The generative cell enters the pollen tube and, a year after pollination, divides to form two sperm cells. Each pollen grain with its pollen tube cell and sperm cells makes up a mature male gametophyte. One of the sperm fertilizes the egg in the archegonium, producing an embryo. Only one embryo develops in each female gametophyte.

In pines, it takes over two years from the time the cones first appear until seeds are dispersed. In most pines, scales of mature cones separate, releasing the seeds. However, in some species of pine, cones may stay closed on the forest floor for years. For example, cones of the jack pine will open only after a fire. As a result, these trees are among the first to reappear after a fire.

FIGURE 17–15.

In seed plants, the male and female gametophytes are reduced to microscopic structures. Follow the changes that take place in the pollen and ovules of a pine before and at pollination.

What is pollination?

What is required for jack pine cones to open?

BIOLAB *Gymnosperms* 17

Problem: How do pine trees differ from one another?

Materials
cones and needles from species of pine trees
metric ruler

Procedures
1. Examine the available specimens of needles.
2. Notice that the needles are in clusters, surrounded by a sheath. For each specimen, count how many needles are in each sheath and record in the data table.
3. Measure and record the length of the needles of each specimen.
4. Examine the available cones.
5. Notice the structure of the cones. Some cones have sharp spines on their scales.
6. Examine each cone and record the absence or presence of spines. Use terms like slender, small, short, straight, and curved for your descriptions.
7. Measure and record the length of each cone.

Eastern White Pine

Longleaf Pine

Red Pine

Pitch Pine

Ponderosa Pine

Data and Observations

Pine specimen	NEEDLES		CONES	
	Number per sheath	Length (cm)	Spines	Length (cm)
Red				
Longleaf				
Pitch				
Ponderosa				
White				

Questions and Conclusion
1. Describe how the needles of the different species differ.
2. What was the most common number of needles in a sheath?
3. What is the purpose of the scales of a cone?
Conclusion: How do pine trees differ?

17:7 The Importance of Gymnosperms

Gymnosperms grow in many diverse habitats. Conifers are of great economic importance, since they produce much of the lumber used for building materials and pulp used to produce paper. Conifers are also used for making furniture and musical instruments. Although they often grow back quickly after forest fires or after a timber harvest, some conifers, such as the California redwoods, have been used to the point of endangering the species. Many substances, including disinfectants, turpentine, and pitch, are manufactured from resins of conifer trees; and the fleshy coverings of juniper seeds are used as a flavoring.

Pollen grains of conifers have been used as indicators of ancient ecosystems. Although the pollen grains themselves are short-lived, their walls are resistant to decay. Thus, they may accumulate in soils, lake sediments, and bogs and still be identified as to their species thousands of years later. Information from a pollen profile, which identifies pollen from different levels of soil, can indicate changes in vegetation in a given area over time.

a

b

FIGURE 17–16.

Pines are a source of timber for many purposes including furniture making (a) and building construction. They are also the source of pitch used by baseball players (b) to increase their grip on the bat.

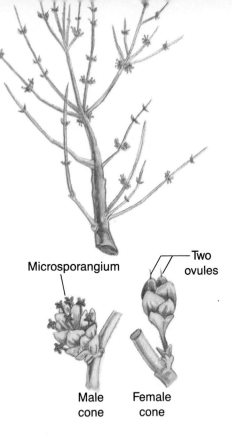

Microsporangium

Two ovules

Male cone   Female cone

FIGURE 17–17.

The value of ephedrine, an alkaloid extracted from *Ephedra* plants, was discovered in 1923 by two American scientists.

Some gymnosperms are used in medicines. The alkaloid ephedrine, extracted from *Ephedra* leaves, is commonly used to ease breathing or to counteract low blood pressure. The same plant extract has also been used in an ointment to speed up the healing process by constricting the size of blood vessels beneath the skin. Probably the greatest importance of gymnosperms is in their exchange of gases in the atmosphere through the process of photosynthesis. The felling of large regions of coniferous forests may seriously change the balance of carbon dioxide and oxygen in Earth's atmosphere.

17:8 Origins

The oldest known seed plants were a group of fern-like gymnosperms called seed ferns that grew approximately 350 million years ago. They were adapted to the warm, tropical climate that existed during that period on Earth. However, as continents moved and climates changed, these seed ferns became extinct. Conifers radiated into many areas, probably during the cool, dry Permian period.

The cycads were a dominant part of the landscape during the entire Mesozoic era. Many species of ginkgos were widespread in northern forests 270 million years ago. Because the fossil record shows that ginkgos have remained largely unchanged for well over 150 million years, it has been called a living fossil.

FIGURE 17–18.

The increasing human population demands so much from the forests of the world that they are in danger of becoming lost.

FIGURE 17–19.

Welwitschia is an unusual and ancient gymnosperm that grows only in deserts of southwest Africa. It has separate male (left) and female (right) plants.

A few gnetophytes have some characteristics in common with flowering plants, indicating that flowering plants may be descended from them. For example, the xylem of flowering plants and gnetophytes both have vessel cells. Most gymnosperms conduct water only through tracheids. The leaves of monocotyledons grow from meristems at their bases, as you probably know from the way grass continues to grow even when mowed close to the ground. *Welwitschia* is the only gymnosperm with leaves that grow in this way.

REVIEW

6. What characteristic do cycads share with simple plants?
7. Explain three ways that conifers are important.
8. To which ancestral group of plants are gymnosperms most closely related?
9. **SKILL REVIEW:** Sequence the events in the life cycle of a conifer. For more help, refer to Reading Science in the Skill Handbook, pages 798 to 799.
10. **USING CONCEPTS:** How do evergreen and deciduous plants differ? What is the adaptive value of both lifestyles?

CHAPTER REVIEW

SUMMARY

1. Seed plants are either gymnosperms or angiosperms. Only angiosperms produce flowers and fruits. **17:1**
2. Sperm and eggs are produced on the sporophyte plant, in cones or in flowers. The gametophyte is greatly reduced in seed plants. **17:2**
3. All seeds have an embryo, stored food, and a seed coat. Many seeds have adaptations that help the embryo survive. **17:3, 17:4**
4. There are four divisions of gymnosperms. **17:5**
5. In gymnosperms, seeds are formed within cones. **17:6**
6. Gymnosperms are important sources of lumber, paper pulp, and chemicals. They are also vital in maintaining a balance of carbon dioxide and oxygen in Earth's atmosphere. **17:7**
7. The earliest known seed plants were fernlike and are now extinct. Flowering plants probably evolved from gymnosperms. **17:8**

LANGUAGE OF BIOLOGY

angiosperms	hypocotyl
cotyledons	megaspore
deciduous plants	micropyle
dormancy	microspore
endosperm	ovule
epicotyl	plumule
evergreen plants	pollen grain
fruit	pollination
germination	radicle
gymnosperms	seed

Choose the word or phrase from the list above that completes the sentence.

1. A(n) ____ is a plant structure that protects the embryo.
2. Flowering plants are also called ____.
3. The sperm-producing structure of a seed plant is a(n) ____.
4. Monocots store food for the developing embryo in the ____ of the seed.
5. The ____ is the first shoot of a new plant.
6. Seeds may undergo a period of inactivity called ____.
7. ____ is the beginning of development of a seed into a new plant.
8. Plants that retain their leaves all year round are ____.
9. The transfer of pollen grains from male to female structures of a plant is called ____.
10. The ____ gives rise to the egg in plants.

REVIEWING CONCEPTS

Choose the word or phrase that completes the sentence or answers the question.

11. The radicle develops into a ____.
    a. root   c. leaf
    b. stem   d. seed
12. Pine trees belong to the division ____.
    a. Gnetophyta   c. Cycadophyta
    b. Coniferophyta   d. Ginkgophyta
13. ____ trees are deciduous conifers.
    a. Pine and cedar   c. Larch and bald cypress
    b. Pine and larch   d. Yew and cedar
14. Fruits are produced by ____.
    a. gymnosperms   c. yews
    b. angiosperms   d. junipers
15. The dominant stage of a seed plant is the ____.
    a. seed   c. gametophyte
    b. pollen grain   d. sporophyte
16. The seeds of dicots have food stored in the ____.
    a. hypocotyl   c. endosperm
    b. cotyledons   d. plumule
17. A requirement for seed germination is the presence of ____.
    a. soil   c. carbon dioxide
    b. water   d. air

18. The existence of ancient ecosystems and the type of climate at that time can be determined by the presence of fossil ____.

   a. leaves   c. pollen grains
   b. stems   d. seeds

19. The sperm in pollen grains enters the ovule through the ____.

   a. archegonium   c. tube nucleus
   b. microspore   d. micropyle

20. The gymnosperm *Ginkgo biloba* has been on Earth at least ____ years.

   a. 350 million   c. 250 million
   b. 270 million   d. 150 million

UNDERSTANDING CONCEPTS

Answer the following questions using complete sentences.

21. Distinguish between pollination and fertilization in seed plants.

22. Discuss why gymnosperms are considered economically, scientifically, and medically important.

23. Compare the functions of epicotyl, hypocotyl, radicle, and plumule.

24. What advantage does a seed coat provide an embryo?

25. Describe and name the structures in which stored food is located in the seeds of monocots and dicots.

26. What are some requirements for seed germination?

27. How are deciduous plants adapted to cold climates?

28. What structures are formed from the microspore and the megaspore?

29. In the life cycle of a pine, what is the stage that follows the production of archegonia from megaspores within the very reduced female gametophyte?

30. What are two characteristics shared by ginkgos and cycads?

APPLYING CONCEPTS

Answer the following questions using complete sentences.

31. What advantage is there to a conifer in having male cones in the lower branches?

32. How does dormancy help in the survival of a seed in a desert ecosystem?

33. In what type of climate are gymnosperms better able to survive than mosses? Why?

34. How are gymnosperm seeds protected from the environment?

35. You eat beans, peas, corn, peanuts, and cereals. Why are seeds a good source of food?

EXTENSIONS

1. Make a collection of different gymnosperm cones. Determine how they are different. Make a classification by grouping cones with similar characteristics.

2. Conduct a survey of a supermarket produce section to determine the kinds of fruits and seeds available.

3. Research how a coniferous forest and a broadleaf deciduous forest are different in their soil types.

4. Obtain seed catalogs for color photographs and make a poster that shows groups of fruits and seeds by families of plants.

READINGS

Huntley, B. and I.C. Prentice. "July Temperatures in Europe from Pollen Data, 6000 Years Before Present." *Science,* Aug. 1988, pp. 687–90.

McKee, R. "Tombstones of a Lost Forest." *Audubon,* Mar. 1988, pp. 62–73.

Mohlenbrock, R.H. "Clayton Pass, New Mexico." *Natural History,* Feb. 1988, pp. 14–16.

FLOWERING
PLANTS

CONIFERS

FERNS

MOSSES

FUNGI

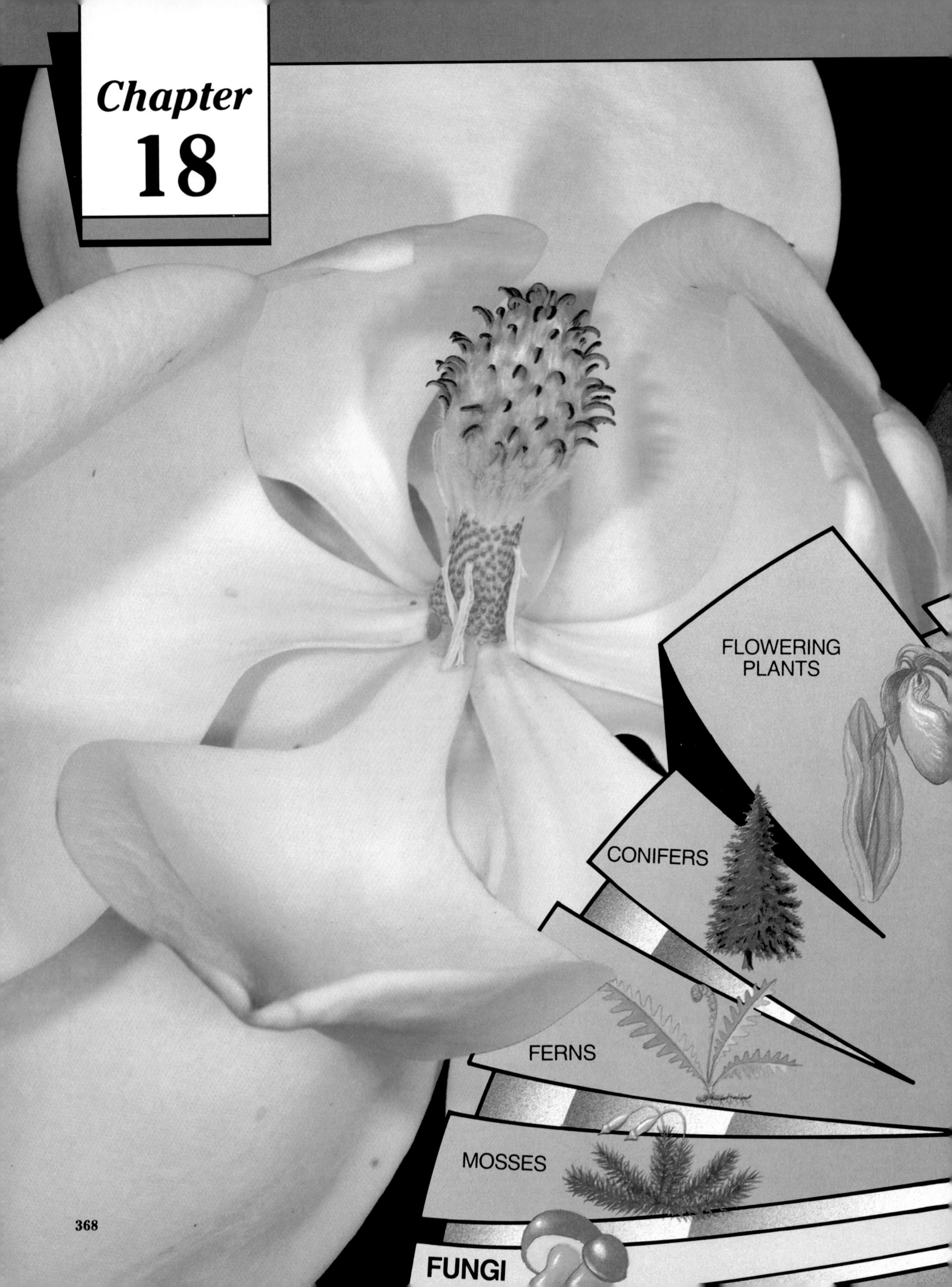

THE FLOWERING PLANTS

F our hundred million years ago, land plants began to diversify. Until the Cretaceous period, 120 million years ago, there were no flowering plants. The vegetation of Earth must have appeared as all greens and browns. The present success of flowering plants may have been due to the evolution of insects. The development of a flower, such as the magnolia shown on the facing page, attractive to insects that transport the pollen, led to greater success in reproduction than that found in gymnosperms. Pollination by animals, such as the hummingbird seen here, led to the great diversity of flowering plant species that surround us today. There are now over 250 000 species of flowering plants. It would be difficult to imagine a world without them.

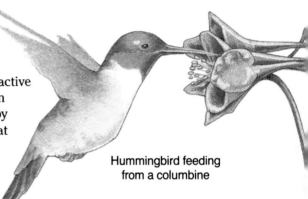

Hummingbird feeding from a columbine

ANTHOPHYTES

You learned in Chapter 17 that the two important adaptations to living on land made by gymnosperms were protection from drying out of sperm and the gametophyte. These adaptations are also found in angiosperms, the flowering plants. Today's flowering plants are well-adapted, complex organisms that have evolved along with many kinds of animals that are important in pollination and dispersal of fruits and seeds. In the following sections you will study the classification, structure, and reproduction of flowering plants, all of which are classified in the division Anthophyta.

18:1 The Flower

Recall from Chapter 17 that the seeds of anthophytes are protected by the wall of the ovary, which completely encloses the seeds and forms the fruit when mature. The process of sexual reproduction in flowering plants takes place in the flower. Although an almost limitless variation can be seen in the shapes and colors of flowers, there is a simple, basic structure.

Objectives:
- describe the structure and function of parts of a flower.
- discuss the adaptations that anthophytes have for pollination.
- classify types of fruits and their function in seed dispersal.
- discuss the origin of flowering plants.
- compare monocots and dicots.
- list several ways that flowering plants are important to humans.

Magnolia flower

a

b

c

d

FIGURE 18–1.

Flowers of anthophytes have a wide range of diversity. The catkin of a hazel (a) is a cluster of petalless, male flowers. The petals of a locust flower (b) are fused, but in a crocus (c), the petals are free. In a squash flower (d), the petals form a tube above the ovary.

What are the four major organs of a flower?

Just as the leaves of a plant are arranged around a stem, so are the parts of a flower arranged. A flower has four major organs: sepals, petals, stamens, and a pistil. Find the parts of a flower in Figure 18–2 as you study its structure. Beginning at the center of a flower and at the tip of a flower-stem axis, a **pistil** is the female structure of a flower. The pistil consists of three parts: the stigma, the style, and the ovary. The **stigma** is a sticky or feathery surface on which pollen grains will land and grow. The **style** is a slender stalk through which the pollen tube grows down to the **ovary,** where the ovules form. There may be one pistil as in a squash flower or several pistils as in a clematis flower.

A ring of stamens surrounds the pistil. A **stamen** is the male reproductive structure of a flower. At the top of a stamen is the **anther,** in which pollen is formed. A thin stalk called the filament attaches an anther to the apex of the flower stem.

Petals surround the pistil and stamens. A **petal** is the leaflike, often colorful part of a flower that is attractive to pollinators. Petals often have a perfume or sacs of sweet nectar at their bases. All of the petals together form the **corolla.** A corolla may be composed of separate petals as in a rose, or petals that are joined in various ways as in clover or orchids. The tubes, platforms, and other shapes formed by the fusion of petals are important adaptations to different methods of pollination.

FIGURE 18–2.

The petals and sepals of most flowers are modified to attract pollinators. *Delphinium* is a popular garden flower with colored sepals. The inner petals are fused to form a spur that holds nectar. Only long-tongued insects, such as bumble bees, can collect nectar from this tube.

Delphinium Flower

Petal

Sepal

Spur

Stamen

Pistil

Petals

Stigma

Anther — Style — Pistil

Stamen

Filament — Ovary

Sepals

Typical Parts of a Flower

The outermost structures of a flower are sepals. A **sepal** is the leaflike, outer flower part that protects the flower while it is a young bud. The circle of sepals is called the **calyx.** Although sepals are usually green they sometimes are as colorful as most petals.

A flower that has a pistil, stamens, petals, and sepals is called a **complete flower.** Crocuses, lilies, and tomatoes have complete flowers. An **incomplete flower** lacks one or more of these parts. Some flowers, such as those of oaks, willows, and garden beets, do not have petals and have only male and female reproductive structures. The reproductive structures may be together in one flower, in separate flowers, or even on separate plants.

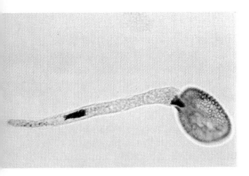

FIGURE 18–3.

A pollen grain germinates and grows into the stigma.

FIGURE 18–4.

The life cycle of a flowering plant.

18:2 The Life of a Flowering Plant

Recall from Chapter 16 that a diploid sporophyte alternates with a haploid gametophyte in a plant's life cycle. Flowering plants resemble gymnosperms in that they have small gametophytes that are retained within the body of the sporophyte. Pollen grains and ovules are formed in the same way as in gymnosperms. The tube cell and the generative cell make up the male gametophyte. The female gametophyte develops within an ovule. However, in anthophytes the ovules are completely surrounded by a protective wall of the ovary in the development of the fruit.

Inside an ovule, a cell divides twice by mitosis to form four haploid cells. As in gymnosperms, only one cell survives to produce an embryo sac containing eight nuclei. Four of the nuclei in the embryo sac are located close to the micropyle, as shown in Figure 18–4. The other four are at the opposite end of the embryo sac. One nucleus from each end moves to the middle of the embryo sac in preparation for fertilization.

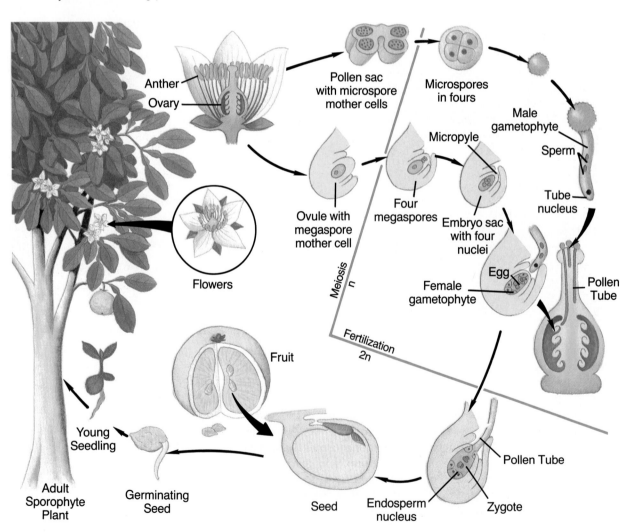

In the process of reproduction, pollen must first land on the stigma and germinate. The pollen tube grows down through the style and into the ovule where the sperm cells pass from the pollen tube into the embryo sac. One of the sperm fertilizes the central egg cell that sits near the micropyle. This union produces a zygote that develops into the embryo. A second sperm fuses with the two nuclei in the middle of the embryo sac to form endosperm. This **double fertilization,** the two events of fusion in the embryo sac, is unique to the flowering plants.

After fertilization, the zygote develops into a seed. Just as in gymnosperms, the protective layers around the embryo sac form a seed coat that protects the young plant embryo. As the ovary ripens, it develops into a fruit. Upon germination of the seed and the later production of flowers, the life cycle of a flowering plant is complete.

Bumblebee

18:3 Adaptations for Pollination

Many species of flowering plants rely on agents to carry pollen to the stigma of a flower. If you or someone you know has hay fever, you may be aware that some plants, such as grasses, have their pollen dispersed by the wind. A few species, such as duckweed and water lilies, are pollinated by water. However, in many flowering plants, relationships have evolved with animals that ensure pollination. These relationships have helped make flowering plants the most successful plant group on Earth.

For example, as shown in Figure 18–5, bees are guided to nectar by the bright markings on the landing field provided by the broad lower petals of the flower. The bee brushes against small bristles on the anthers, and pollen is released from the anther onto the bee's back. Later, the bee might visit another flower of the same species that has the same markings. The pollen carried by the bee is transferred to the stigma of the second flower. In this way, pollination is guaranteed.

NoteWorthy

Bees can see patterns on flowers that are invisible to us. These patterns are produced by reflection of ultraviolet light.

FIGURE 18–5.

As a bee enters this insect-pollinated flower, the anther is triggered to deposit pollen on the bee's body. When the bee visits another flower for nectar, the pollen is brushed onto the stigma.

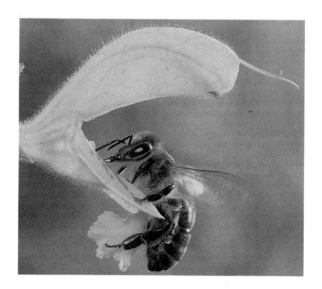

FIGURE 18–6.

Plants pollinated by the wind, such as grasses, (top left) usually have no petals. Bats (top right) visit flowers that open at night. A fly is drawn to a flower, such as the water lily shown here, that smells like rotting meat (lower left), while plants, such as in a thistle, with long, tubular flowers are most adapted to bird or moth pollination (bottom right).

After millions of years of evolution, many plants and animals have come to be completely interdependent and one species could probably not survive without the other. These pollinators seek specific types of pollen and nectar. Moths are active at night. The plants pollinated by moths have flowers with a distinctive, heavy scent that makes them easy to find in the dark. In some flowers, such as *Impatiens,* the nectar is produced in very long, tubular extensions of the petals. Since moths have long, hollow tongues, they have no problem reaching the nectar in these tubes. You may have seen a hummingbird hovering over a flower while sipping nectar with its long tongue. Flowers pollinated by hummingbirds are usually red, tubular, and contain a large amount of nectar. The characteristics of these flowers tend to attract hummingbirds. Although bees, moths, and butterflies are the most commonly known pollinators of flowering plants, some flowers depend on bats or flies for pollination. Bat-pollinated flowers have many anthers with very long filaments. Flowers pollinated by flies often smell like rotting meat.

BIOLAB *Pollination* 18

Problem: How are flowers adapted to different methods of pollination?

Materials
specimens of flowers   slides
microscope   coverslips

Procedures
1. Observe the flower specimens provided.
2. In your data table, record the name of each flower and describe its appearance. Describe colors, odors, and numbers and shapes of structures such as pistils, stamens, petals, and sepals.
3. Prepare wet mount slides of the pollen of each flower. Observe the pollen under the microscope.
4. Draw the pollen grains and record the magnification used for each drawing.
5. Draw each flower.
6. Make a **hypothesis** as to whether the pollen of each flower is dispersed mainly by the wind or by animals.

Data and Observations

Description				
Flower	Pistil	Stamens	Petals	Sepals
1				
2				
3				

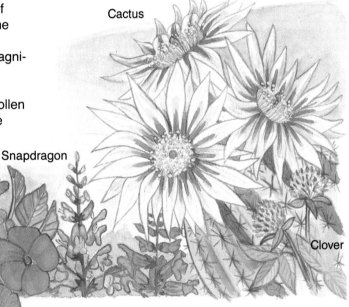

Cactus

Snapdragon

Impatiens

Grass

Marigold

Clover

Questions and Conclusion
1. Using your **hypothesis,** predict what might be some common features shared by wind-pollinated flowers?
2. What might be some common features shared by animal-pollinated flowers?
3. If a bat is a nectar-eater, to what type(s) of flowers would it be attracted?
4. What insect-attracting characteristics or structures might wind-pollinated flowers lack?

Conclusion: What are some adaptations in flowers for pollination?

18:4 Fruits and Seed Dispersal

A botanist's definition of a fruit is not always the same as the one your local grocery store clerk uses. However, you know from Chapter 17 that a fruit is a ripened ovary. Therefore, you also know that a string bean or a bell pepper is as much a fruit as a peach or a blueberry.

Fruits are of major importance in the dispersal of seeds. Seeds that are not dispersed far enough away from the parent plant must share all light and space resources with the parent and probably with many of its "siblings" also. Thus, the efficient dispersal of seeds helps reduce competition. In some cases, seeds are dispersed directly by the fruit that stays attached to the plant. In other cases the seeds are dispersed along with the fruit.

There are two categories of fruits. Some fruits such as oranges, blueberries, mangoes, tomatoes, and avocados are fleshy fruits. Tissues in the ovary wall become filled with water and sugars that make the fruit fleshy and juicy. At the same time, these fruits are often brightly colored, which is an effective adaptation for attracting animals that feed on the fruits, resulting in the dispersal of the seeds. Animals eat the fruit and either spit out the seeds or disperse them in their feces, often after they have traveled a great distance from the parent plant.

Other fruits are dry fruits. The ovary wall may start out with a fleshy green appearance as in hickory nuts or bean pods but when the fruit is fully matured, the fruit wall is dry. Sometimes, as in some beans, *Impatiens,* and some squash, the fruit wall bursts open to release the seeds with great force. Seeds may be shot several meters away from the parent plant.

FIGURE 18–7.

The two major categories of fruits are fleshy and dry. Each kind of fruit has a technical name. How is each of these fruits adapted for seed dispersal?

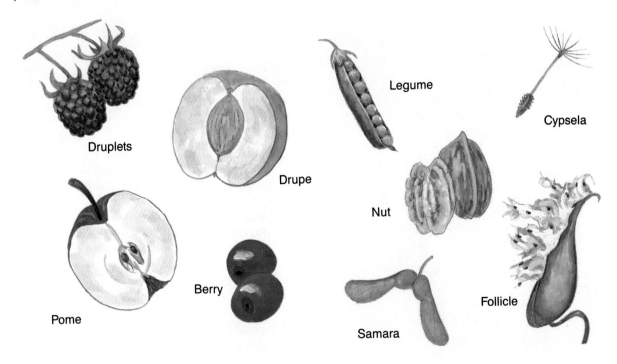

Druplets

Drupe

Legume

Cypsela

Nut

Pome

Berry

Samara

Follicle

Wind is not only an important pollen dispersal agent, but it is also a major seed dispersal agent. Some seeds, such as the dust-like seeds of orchids, are tiny enough to be carried by wind. These seeds are as light as some moss spores, and they are usually produced in such vast quantities that there will always be some that will land in favorable environments and survive. Poppy seeds are sprinkled into the air like pepper from a pepper shaker when the capsule that is the poppy fruit is blown about by the wind. Tumbleweed seeds are scattered by the wind as the whole plant rolls along the ground. The wind is the major agent of dispersal for the winged and plumed fruits of plants such as maples and dandelions.

Many seeds and fruits have air trapped in their tissues, which enables them to float. For seeds like those of coconuts and water lilies, water is the main dispersal agent. Every newly formed island quickly gets its own coconut palms because the single-seeded fruits float on ocean currents and are washed up on the beaches.

FIGURE 18–8.

Many plants have adaptations for seed dispersal by water or by explosive propulsion. Coco de mer (left) is a rare palm nut containing the largest of all seeds that germinate on the beaches of the Seychelles. *Impatiens* (above) is a common garden and houseplant with explosive fruits.

NoteWorthy

Coconut seeds have been observed to germinate after floating in water for up to 12 months.

FIGURE 18–9.

Seeds can be dispersed over great distances by animals.

Animals are another important agent of seed dispersal. Small seeds may mix with mud and stick to the feet of birds, which carry the seeds across continents. Hooked seeds and fruits cling well to fur and feathers. Even if you live in the city, you probably have had to pull beggar's ticks, burs, and cleavers from your socks in late summer.

18:5 Origins

As you learned in Chapter 17, the first seed-bearing plants resembled ferns. Seed ferns are now extinct, but they are probably a link to the ancestors of modern seed plants.

Evidence from fossils and comparisons of structures indicates that the first flowering plants may have evolved from some now-extinct group of gymnosperms in the late Jurassic. It isn't likely that scientists will find fossils of an embryo sac that shows evidence of double fertilization. But, 120 million-year-old fossil flowers have been found from the early Cretaceous period. There are still large gaps in the fossil record for the delicate structures of plants. The first flowers were probably similar to those of *Magnolia.* The many large, fleshy sepals, petals, stamens, and pistils of these first flowers would have provided plenty of food for beetles and other animals of that time.

anthophyte:
anthos (GK) flower
phyton (GK) plant
epiphyte:
epi (GK) upon
phyton (GK) plant

18:6 Phylogeny of Flowering Plants

Flowering plants may be trees, shrubs, herbs, vines, floating plants, epiphytes, or non-green parasites. **Epiphytes** (EP uh fites) are plants that attach to larger plants for support, but obtain their water and nutrients from the air. They are common in tropical forests of the world. Flowering plants also live in deserts, temperate forests, and freshwater ponds and lakes. Some are deciduous, while others are evergreen.

The life span of a flowering plant may be less than a year, two years, or many years. This diversity of lifestyles is found in each of the two classes of the division Anthophyta: Monocotyledones, known as monocots, and Dicotyledones, called dicots. Recall that one difference between monocots and dicots is in their seed structure. There are also differences in the arrangements of flower parts and in the patterns of vascular bundles in the plants roots, stems, and leaves. Examples of monocots are grasses, irises, palms, and orchids. An easy way to recognize a monocot is to count the number of stamens, petals, or sepals. These occur in threes or multiples of threes in monocots. If a plant isn't in flower, you can look for other clues to determine its class. Monocots usually have scattered bundles of vascular tissue in their stem. Also, if the veins in the leaves are parallel, such as in a daffodil, the plant is probably a monocot. There are about 60 families of monocots.

NoteWorthy

Bread wheat is a monocot. Endosperm makes up 80 percent of the kernel. White flour is made from the starchy endosperm. Wheat germ is made from the embryo.

Dicots include many herbs and nearly all the familiar large trees and shrubs except, of course, the conifers. You can recognize a dicot by counting the number of stamens, petals, and sepals the same as you do with monocots. In dicots, these parts are usually arranged in fours, fives, or multiples of these numbers. The vascular bundles of a dicot stem form a ring around a central pith. Many dicots are woody. The veins of dicot leaves are usually arranged in a network pattern. Almost three-fourths of all flowering plants are dicots. There are about 250 families of dicots. Examine some of the representatives of monocots and dicots in Figure 18–11.

NoteWorthy

Mistletoe is only one of nearly 3000 parasitic dicots.

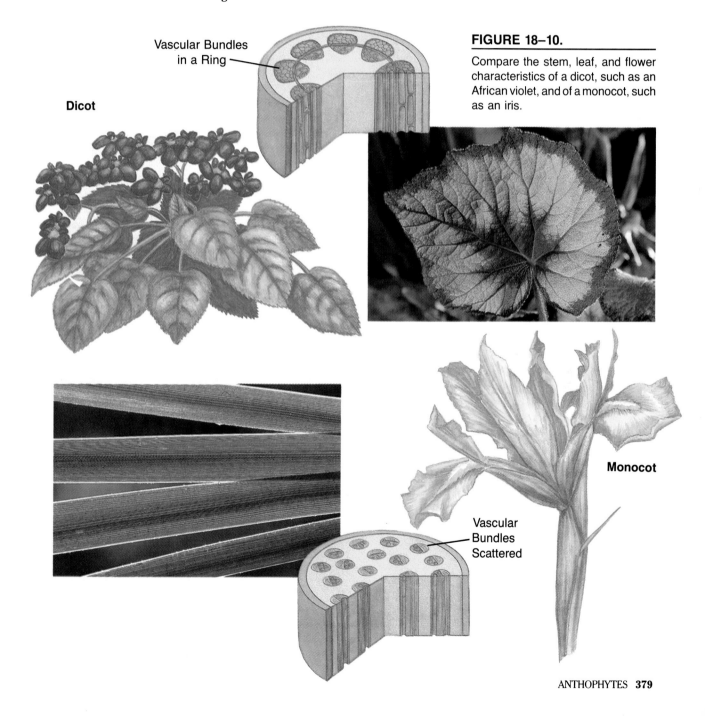

Dicot

Vascular Bundles in a Ring

FIGURE 18–10.

Compare the stem, leaf, and flower characteristics of a dicot, such as an African violet, and of a monocot, such as an iris.

Monocot

Vascular Bundles Scattered

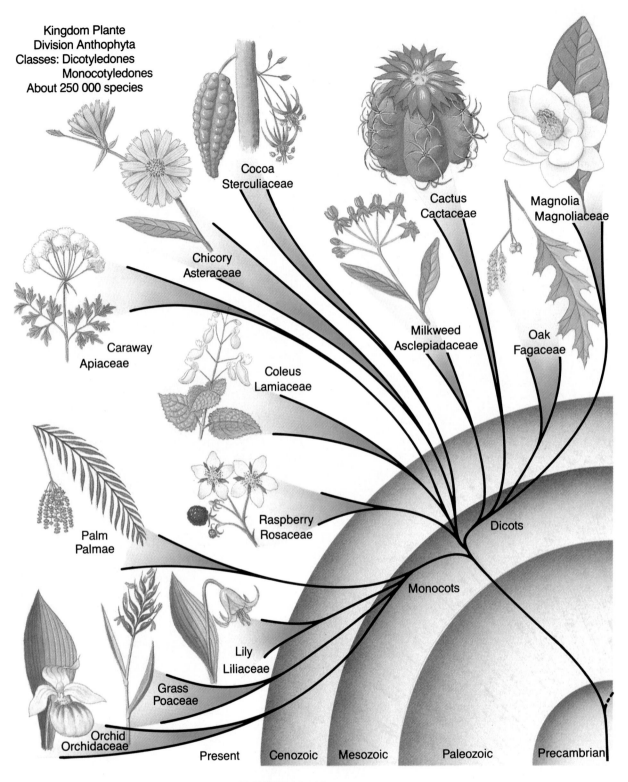

Kingdom Plante
Division Anthophyta
Classes: Dicotyledones
Monocotyledones
About 250 000 species

Cocoa
Sterculiaceae

Cactus
Cactaceae

Magnolia
Magnoliaceae

Chicory
Asteraceae

Milkweed
Asclepiadaceae

Oak
Fagaceae

Caraway
Apiaceae

Coleus
Lamiaceae

Palm
Palmae

Raspberry
Rosaceae

Dicots

Monocots

Lily
Liliaceae

Grass
Poaceae

Orchid
Orchidaceae

Present   Cenozoic   Mesozoic   Paleozoic   Precambrian

FIGURE 18–11.

The radiation of some families of flowering plants on the geologic time scale
shows their relationships.

18:7 The Importance of Flowering Plants

Flowering plants have played an important role in the development of human civilization. Agriculture probably began as an accident when seeds of weedy grains collected for food were dropped near campsites and people realized they could grow their own food. Cultivation of plants began about 11 000 years ago. Eventually, purposeful planting of seeds led to planned harvests. The practice of cultivating plants has changed the way people live. The knowledge for other uses of plants became important to the survival of humans.

The fruits of flowering plants are a major part of the diets of many animals and humans. Among the monocots, grasses produce wheat, sorghum, barley, rice, corn, and oats—all important food crops. Dates, coconuts, bananas, onions, and garlic are other important monocots that humans cultivate. Many dicots, such as peas, beans, potatoes, carrots, and cabbages, are also important food plants.

Grains such as barley and wheat, and legumes such as peas and lentils were among the first plant species cultivated by humans. Other ancient crops include olives, dates, and grapes. Rice, millet, and soybeans were grown as crops in China at about the same time wheat and barley were raised in the Near East. In the Americas, corn and beans were early crops grown by the native Americans.

FIGURE 18–12.

Three grasses—wheat, rice, and maize—are the leading staple foods of the world. Other cereals are important in different climates.

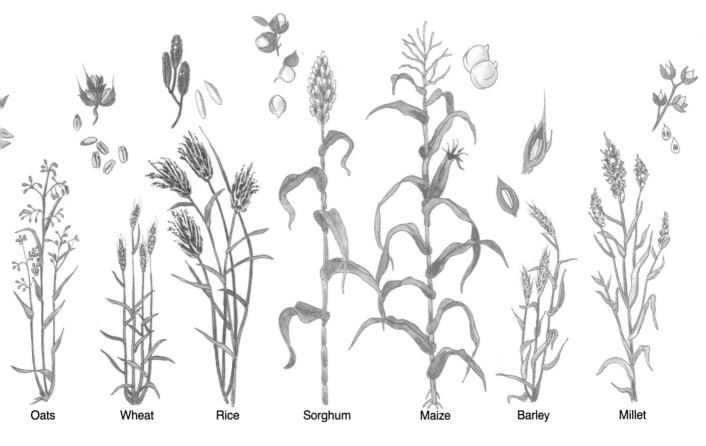

Oats   Wheat   Rice   Sorghum   Maize   Barley   Millet

FIGURE 18–13.

The oil of jojoba is used in shampoos, cosmetics, and as an engine lubricant.

What are two reasons for saving wild varieties of plants?

Other economically important products are made from flowering plants. Many fibers are derived from flowering plants such as flax for linen, cotton and rayon for clothing, and palms for rope. Perfumes, medicines, rubber, oils, pesticides, and some industrial chemicals are also products of flowering plants. Most furniture is made from the wood of flowering plants such as oak and cherry. Many flowering plants are used for ornamental purposes, such as decorating and landscaping. Flowering plants are the main source of the foods you eat. There are hundreds of known varieties of crops like corn and wheat. Many of the varieties are not cultivated, but grow wild. In some cases, crossing cultivated plants with wild varieties makes a cultivated hybrid that is more resistant to certain diseases. Seed banks are storehouses of all kinds of seeds set up in order to conserve plant genetic resources.

Valuable crops are still being developed today. For example, the shrub jojoba has been cultivated during the last two decades for the liquid wax it forms in its seeds. The liquid can be treated chemically to produce an oil that is an alternative to the sperm whale oil commonly used in industry. Many other wild species of flowering plants have potentially useful products. Scientists are concerned that many of them will be made extinct before their value to civilization will be discovered.

FIGURE 18–14.

Many cultures depend upon the products of palms for food and shelter.

REVIEW

1. What are the two main types of fruits?
2. What are the parts of a flower and what are their functions?
3. How can dicots be distinguished from monocots?
4. **SKILL REVIEW:** Diagram the stages of a pollen grain from its formation in the anther through its role in double fertilization. For more help, refer to Reading Science in the Skill Handbook, pages 798 to 799.
5. **USING CONCEPTS:** How is wind an effective agent of seed dispersal?

GROWTH REGULATION

If anyone ever said to you "look at that plant move," you would probably turn sharply to get a good look at this unexpected phenomenon. Movement is not a characteristic that we usually associate with plants. However, plants do move, even though their movement is not easily observed. Like you and all other organisms, plants grow and respond to external stimuli. Plant growth is more than just cell division. Plant growth and development is regulated by plant growth substances. How are these substances produced and what are their effects?

18:8 Plant Growth Hormones

Plant hormones regulate plant growth. A **hormone** is a chemical that is produced in one part of an organism and transported to another part where it causes a physiological change. Only a small amount of a hormone is required to cause this change.

The first plant hormone to be recognized was an **auxin,** a plant hormone that causes cell elongation. In the 1880s, Charles Darwin studied the action of a growth-regulating substance in grass seedlings. He found that light acting on the tip of an oat seedling caused the seedling to bend in an area below the tip. It was another 45 years before the chemical nature of this substance was identified by Fritz Went. Look at Went's 1926 experiment in Figure 18–15. It is now known that the bending of the grass seedlings is caused by growth of individual cells. However, the actions of plant hormones are still not yet clearly understood. The auxin indole-acetic acid, commonly abbreviated to IAA, promotes growth at the tip of a stem. Normally,

Define hormone.

Shoot tips on agar   Auxin diffused into agar block

Tips discarded
Agar cut into blocks

Agar block placed on one side of top of cut shoot

Shoot tip bent while in total darkness

FIGURE 18–15.

The first isolation of a plant hormone was made from the growing tips of oat seedlings.

auxins act to stimulate fruit development as seeds are formed. Auxins also can be used to stimulate fruit development without seed formation. As a result, seedless tomatoes and cucumbers can be produced.

Auxins are now produced synthetically. The first practical use of synthetic auxins was to aid in root growth from stem cuttings. The auxin stimulates cell growth. Many woody plants are cultivated from cuttings that are dipped into an auxin before planting. Synthetic auxins also are used to control weeds. Above a certain concentration, auxins slow down rather than stimulate growth. The herbicide 2,4-D is an auxin that kills only broad-leaved dicots, so it is commonly used in lawn weed killers. The high concentration of 2,4-D disorganizes the homeostatic balance of the cells.

About ten years after the discovery of auxins, another group of growth hormones was isolated. These hormones, called **gibberellins,** stimulate cell elongation and division. Recall from Chapter 1 that gibberellin was discovered in 1926 by two Japanese scientists, Yabuta and Sumiki, who studied the foolish seedling disease of rice. Gibberellin was isolated from a fungus that caused rice seedlings to grow so tall and thin that they fell over. Gibberellins also speed seed germination, even when light and temperature requirements have not been met. Commercially, it is used to produce uniform growth in seedlings. Gibberellins are also used to produce early seeds from plants such as cabbage and carrots that normally require two years to set seeds.

In 1955, Carlos Miller isolated a hormone called cytokinin from DNA that was broken down by heating. This material, used in small amounts, causes plant cell division. Cytokinins have been found in actively dividing tissues of many species of seed plants and in horsetails and ferns. Cytokinins are used in tissue cultures and are likely to become more important as biotechnology continues to develop.

What are the main effects of gibberellins?

FIGURE 18–16.

Cytokinins cause plant cells to reproduce into masses of more or less spherical cells that can then be used for genetic engineering.

FIGURE 18–17.

Just as your skin heals after a scratch, abscisic acid in a plant's epidermal cells help in the formation of leaf scars after leaf fall.

18:9 Hormones of Aging

In the late 1800s, Russian scientists noticed that trees next to gas street lamps lost their leaves abnormally. The leaf loss was found to be caused by ethylene leaking from the gas street lamps. **Ethylene** is a plant hormone that causes ripening of fruit followed by fruit and leaf fall.

Ethylene was used commercially before it was recognized as a plant hormone. In the early 1900s, fruit growers improved ripening of their harvested fruits by lighting a kerosene stove in the storage room. The fruit growers thought that heat from the stove was responsible for the ripening. Growers who later installed more modern heating equipment that didn't use kerosene, however, learned an expensive lesson. Ethylene is a product of burning kerosene. It was not the heat, but ethylene that sped the ripening. Walnuts, grapes, and tomatoes are commercially ripened with ethylene.

Another hormone that promotes aging in plants is abscisic acid. Abscisic acid is a plant hormone found mainly in mature green leaves and fruits, structures that separate from the plant. Applications of abscisic acid stimulate aging and the fall of plant parts.

What plant processes are affected by ethylene?

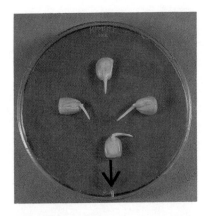

FIGURE 18–18.

The root of a germinating seed must quickly find a source of water and nutrients for the new plant to survive. The response to the force of gravity helps a root find these essential resources.

phototropism:
   photos (GK) light
   trope (GK) turn
gravitropism:
   gravis (L) heavy
   trope (GK) turn
photoperiodism:
   photos (GK) light
   peridos (GK) a cycle

18:10 Responsive Movements

Plants adjust to environmental changes by growth changes. A **tropism** is a response to a directional, external stimulus. If the tropism is positive, the plant grows toward the stimulus. If the tropism is negative, the plant grows away from the stimulus.

If you have houseplants growing in a sunny spot, you know that you need to turn the plants to keep them growing upright. Phototropism is growth toward a light source. In a stem, auxins move away from the side of the stem exposed to light. This concentration of auxins causes the cells on the "dark" side to elongate. The longer cells on one side of a stem make the stem seem to bend toward the light.

Gravitropism is a response to the force of gravity. Roots of seedlings always grow downward, even if the seed is lying on its side. Roots show positive gravitropism. Negative gravitropism is shown in the response of stems to gravity. Stems grow away from the direction of the force of gravity as shown in Figure 18–18.

A responsive movement of a plant that is independent of the direction of the stimulus is called a **nastic movement.** Leaves of the mimosa plant droop suddenly when they are touched. The folding response to touch may provide some protection from insect damage. It might also reduce water loss in drying winds. Nastic movements, since they do not involve growth or cell division, are reversible.

FIGURE 18–19.

Mimosa is commonly known as the sensitive plant because when touched its leaflets will fold up in less than one-tenth of a second.

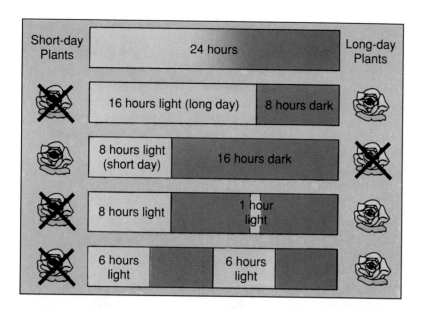

FIGURE 18–20.

Flowering depends on the length of the night. The effects of long, dark periods is opposite in short-day and long-day plants. The short-day plants, such as pansies and goldenrods, flower in the summer as nights get longer.

18:11 Photoperiodism

The U.S. Department of Agriculture was once faced with a problem. Soybeans weren't behaving the way growers wanted them to. The growers wanted soybeans to flower at specific times so they could harvest the beans at different times in the fall. Even though the growers planted the beans at different times in the spring, the beans all flowered at the same time. In 1920, W. Garner and H. Allard, two American plant breeders, experimented with the soybeans and discovered that they flowered only when days became short. They called this phenomenon **photoperiodism,** a response to a change in the lengths of light and dark in a day.

Chrysanthemums, strawberries, violets, and primroses have a flowering pattern like the soybeans. A plant that flowers only when nights are longer than a certain critical dark period is called a **short-day plant.** Short-day plants normally flower in late summer or in early spring or fall. The length of the dark period is critical for triggering flowering of short-day plants. An interruption of the dark period will delay flowering. Greenhouse-raised flowering plants are produced outside their normal flowering season by interrupting the dark period with a flash of light.

NoteWorthy

Spinach can't be grown in the tropics because it needs at least 14 hours of light per day for at least two weeks to flower. These conditions never occur in the tropics.

A **long-day plant** flowers only if nights are shorter than some critical dark period. Long-day plants flower mostly in the summer when days are long. Interrupting the dark period with a flash of light does not substitute for a long day. Spinach, lettuce, dill, oats, and red clover are examples of long-day plants. Have you noticed how different plants flower at different times during the year?

Most plants are not affected by day length. **Day-neutral plants** flower without regard to day length. Cucumbers and corn are day-neutral plants. If the warm season is long, it is possible to have the spaced harvests with these plants that the soybean growers wanted with their crops.

FIGURE 18–21.

Long-day plants are typical of the temperate regions where lengths of days and nights vary with the seasons. They include many common cultivated plants such as lettuce, spinach, and beets.

REVIEW

6. What is the commercial use of each of these plant hormones: auxin, gibberellins, cytokinins, and ethylene?
7. A Venus flytrap closes when an insect lands on it. Is this a tropism? Explain.
8. How does 2,4-D kill broadleaf plants?
9. **SKILL REVIEW:** Make a table showing plant responses to five plant hormones. For more help, refer to Organizing Information in the Skill Handbook, pages 810 to 813.
10. **USING CONCEPTS:** Are plants in the tropics more likely to be long-day, short-day, or day-neutral plants? Explain.

CAREER CHOICES

Horticulture is the development, growth, improvement, distribution, and use of fruits, vegetables, and other types of plants. Horticulturists are biologists who work for the government, in industry, or in universities. Many horticulturists work in nurseries, garden centers, arboreta, and botanical gardens to improve the quality of plants, to study their relationships, and to determine their resistance to disease. Some travel to different parts of the world in search of new and attractive species of flowers for both home and garden. They try to determine the best growing conditions for plants, including types of soil, fertilizers, and methods of cultivation. Horticulturists in research and plant breeding have helped farmers produce high quality food more economically. Some crops that once were native to warm climates can now be grown in the colder north temperate regions.

Production Nursery Manager

As a **production nursery manager,** you would coordinate the operation of a production nursery that grows woody plants to sell wholesale. Many cities make contracts with nurseries to be supplied with street trees as the city is developed. In addition to maintaining the budget of the nursery, you would be responsible for its personnel. You would train and direct assistants in the propagation of new plants. Field crews who inspected conditions of cultivating tree crops would report to you whether or not plant production was in accordance with the specifications of the various buyers. Sales representatives would inform you of the needs of your customers and any trends present in the market place.

Floriculture involves the propagation, distribution, and sales of cut flowers and potted plants. In a small shop, a **retail florist** not only manages the store, but often designs the floral arrangements for weddings, funerals, and other occasions for which cut flowers are needed. The shop also commonly sells foliage plants, flowering plants, and terraria. In larger shops, there is often a need for buyers, sales people, store managers, and designers. All of these people would work together in filling large orders. As you gained experience, you would help in the training of other sales people.

Retail Florist

As a **plant geneticist,** your research might involve the development of a less disease-prone species of plant. You might work with amino acids in cereals to make them more nutritious as food for people or as feed for animals. The improvement of cotton fibers to make them more useful and versatile to textile industries might interest you. A plant geneticist might also study the effects of sunlight, water, and certain kinds of soils on various kinds of plants grown as crops. As a plant geneticist, you might work with a plant inspector who works to prevent the spread of pests among plants. A plant geneticist could also work with a plant taxonomist to search for, name, classify, and research genetic relationships among various species of plants.

Plant Geneticist

CHAPTER REVIEW

SUMMARY

1. Complete flowers have pistils, stamens, petals, and sepals. Incomplete flowers are missing at least one of these parts. Flowering plants have enclosed ovules and double fertilization. **18:1, 18:2**
2. Many flowers are pollinated by a particular animal. Fruits and seeds are adapted for dispersal by particular agents. **18:3, 18:4**
3. Flowering plants probably evolved from a now extinct group of gymnosperms. **18:5**
4. Monocots have one cotyledon, flower parts in threes, scattered vascular bundles, and parallel leaf venation. Dicots have two cotyledons, flower parts in fours or fives, a ring of vascular bundles, and net-like leaf venation. **18:6**
5. Flowering plants are important for food, building materials, clothing, and drugs. **18:7**
6. Auxins, gibberellins, and cytokinins promote cell division and enlargement. The hormones ethylene and abscisic acid promote fruit maturation and fruit and leaf fall. **18:8, 18:9**
7. Tropisms and nastic movements are plant responses to external stimuli. Short-day plants and long-day plants flower when nights are a certain critical length. **18:10, 18:11**

LANGUAGE OF BIOLOGY

anther	long-day plant
auxin	nastic movement
calyx	ovary
complete flower	petal
corolla	photoperiodism
day-neutral plants	pistil
double fertilization	sepal
epiphytes	short-day plant
ethylene	stamen
gibberellins	stigma
hormone	style
incomplete flower	tropism

Choose the word or phrase from the list above that completes the sentence.

1. ____ are plants that live attached to larger plants and take water and nutrients from the atmosphere.
2. A response to a directional external stimulus is a(n) ____.
3. A reversible responsive movement of a plant is a(n) ____.
4. The part of a pistil that develops into a fruit is the ____.
5. The part of the pistil where pollen lands and germinates is the ____.
6. The flower structure that protects the young flower bud is a(n) ____.
7. A(n) ____ flowers only if nights are shorter than a critical value.
8. The pollen-producing part of a stamen is the ____.
9. A(n) ____ is the male structure in a flower.
10. A flower that has pistils, stamens, petals, and sepals is a(n) ____.

REVIEWING CONCEPTS

Choose the word or phrase that completes the sentence or answers the question.

11. Most flowering plants are ____.
    a. monocots   c. grasses
    b. dicots   d. hardwoods
12. An incomplete flower may be missing ____.
    a. stems   c. roots
    b. leaves   d. petals
13. Plant fibers are used for ____.
    a. fabrics   c. oils
    b. food   d. perfumes
14. Adaptations in fruits aid in ____.
    a. fertilization   c. seed dispersal
    b. pollination   d. all of the above

15. Bird-pollinated flowers are usually ____.
  a. flat   c. green
  b. tubular   d. blue

16. An early cultivated crop was ____.
  a. wheat   c. oranges
  b. corn   d. olives

17. Anthophytes evolved from ____.
  a. fungi   c. angiosperms
  b. flowering plants d. gymnosperms

18. The earliest fossils of flowering plants indicate they evolved about ____ years ago.
  a. 360 million   c. 360 000
  b. 120 million   d. less than 6000

19. ____ stimulate cell elongation.
  a. Cytokinin   c. Abscisic acid
  b. Ethylene   d. Gibberellins

20. Monocots usually have ____.
  a. 4-5 stamens   c. net-like leaf veins
  b. 3 petals   d. woody stems

UNDERSTANDING CONCEPTS

Answer the following questions using complete sentences.

21. What are five uses of plants?
22. List four differences between monocots and dicots.
23. Compare phototropism and photoperiodism.
24. Explain the process of double fertilization.
25. List five products made from flowering plants.
26. What role do flower petals play in the reproduction of flowering plants?
27. Compare hummingbird- and bee-pollinated flowers.
28. What is the difference between pollination and fertilization?
29. How are fruits important to seed dispersal?
30. Why do plant breeders hybridize different varieties of a cultivated plant species?

APPLYING CONCEPTS

Answer the following questions using complete sentences.

31. What would a florist do with a long-day plant to obtain flowers in winter?
32. Explain why it is important to maintain a diversity of plants even if they don't produce something we now use.
33. Ragweed is a short-day plant that is not found in the northern-most states. Propose an explanation based on photoperiodism for the absence of ragweed from northern Maine.
34. How might a fruit that is swallowed by an animal be different from one that attaches to the outside of an animal?
35. What is the adaptive value of a moth-pollinated plant having flower opening controlled by phototropism?

EXTENSIONS

1. Research the color perception of bees and humans. Present your information graphically.
2. Visit the produce section of a local supermarket. Identify the fruits and vegetables as monocots or dicots.
3. Design, conduct, and report on an experiment demonstrating the growth-enhancing property of gibberellins.

READINGS

Heacox, Kim. "Fatal Attraction." *International Wildlife,* May/June 1989, pp. 38–43.

Weiss, Rick. "Blazing Blossoms." *Science News,* June 24, 1989, pp. 392–394.

Wilkins, Malcolm B. *Plantwatching: How Plants Remember, Tell Time, Form Relationships and More.* New York: Facts on File, 1988.

INVERTEBRATES

In the calm world of the deeper rock pools,
now undisturbed by the tumult of incoming waves,
crabs sidle along the walls, their claws busily
touching, feeling, exploring for bits of food.
The pools are gardens of color composed of the
delicate green and ocher-yellow of encrusting
sponge, the pale pink of hydroids that stand
like clusters of fragile spring flowers . . .

Rachel Carson
The Edge of the Sea

Chapter 19

IBIANS
FISH

STARFISH

ARTHROPODS

MOLLUSKS
AND
WORMS

JELLYFISH
AND SPONGES

SIMPLE ANIMALS

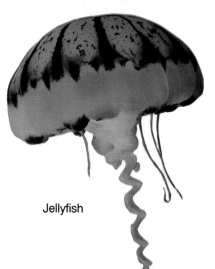

Jellyfish

An actor turns angrily on someone who has just betrayed him and snarls, "You dirty rat!" From the expression on his face and the sound of his voice, you know he thinks that his adversary is less well adapted than he is. However, rats have backbones and so do both of the actors. All three are vertebrates. Other uncomplimentary remarks that people use refer to spineless animals. So when you have the urge to call someone an insect or a spineless jellyfish, you open the door to the world of animals without backbones, namely the invertebrates. In this unit you will study the general characteristics of animals, including those invertebrates that creep, fly, or float, and a few that ooze their way through life.

INTRODUCTION TO ANIMAL LIFE

Recall from Chapter 2 that members of the animal kingdom are organisms that are multicellular, eukaryotic, and have groups of cells organized for specific jobs. These organisms are heterotrophic. They are capable of moving and responding to stimuli. Based on characteristics of body structure, animals are classified into phyla. Ninety-five percent of all animal species in the world that have been identified are invertebrates, animals without backbones.

19:1 Basic Body Plans

Each living organism, no matter how small or large, has a body plan. How these parts are arranged is called symmetry. Organisms may either show bilateral symmetry, radial symmetry, or asymmetry. **Bilateral symmetry** is a body plan in which an organism can be divided down its length into similar right and left halves that form mirror images. If you look in a mirror you see a mirror image of yourself. If you put both hands side by side, flat on a table, you can see that your right hand is almost a mirror image of your left hand. If a plane were to be drawn through your body from top to bottom, you would see that the halves of your body are mirror images. You are a bilaterally symmetrical organism with complex body organs and systems.

Objectives:

- distinguish among radial symmetry, bilateral symmetry, and asymmetry.
- name the embryonic cell layers, and describe how they form.
- describe the advantages and disadvantages of saltwater, freshwater, and land environments in which animals live.
- describe some adaptations animals have made to a land environment.

Bright members of a Cnidarian coral colony

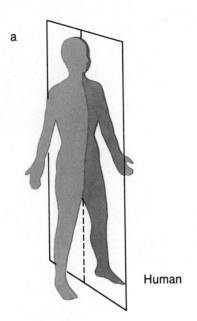

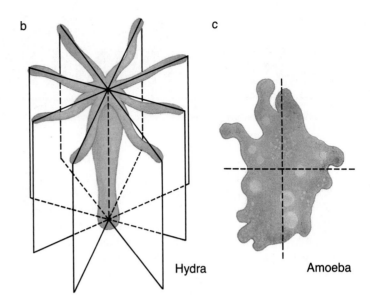

a — Human

b — Hydra

c — Amoeba

Organisms have body parts arranged so that they have bilateral symmetry (a), radial symmetry (b), or they are asymmetrical (c).

Some animals appear the same from every side. Organisms that appear to be the same from any angle show **radial symmetry.** In radial symmetry, the organization of the animal is circular, like a wheel, and it is possible to obtain two identical halves no matter how the animal is divided. A pie has radial symmetry. No matter where you cut the pie in half, the two halves will always be just about the same. In general, animals with radial symmetry have simpler body structures and no tissues, organs, or organ systems.

The simplest organisms have no symmetry. An organism without a body plan shows **asymmetry.** Amoebas are asymmetrical. Their bodies are ever changing and indefinite in shape.

19:2 Body Development

All multicellular organisms pass through an embryonic stage. During this time, genes control how an organism will look and function. This happened to you—and it happens in the life of every sponge, earthworm, and beetle as well. As you study the different animal phyla in this text, you will discover that the body plan of each successive group shows increasing complexity in tissues, organs, and systems.

From the time an animal begins to change from a zygote to an embryo, certain cells form germ layers from which specific organs will develop. Some simple animals form only two germ layers in their bodies: an outer body layer called the **ectoderm,** and an inner body layer called the **endoderm.** In more complex animals, a third cell layer develops between the endoderm and ectoderm. This middle body layer of germ cells is the **mesoderm.** It is from these three germ layers in an embryo that all body tissues and organs form. For example, your skin, hair, nails, and nervous system developed from the cells of your embryonic ectoderm. Your muscles, blood, kidneys,

What are the three embryonic cell layers of animal bodies?

ectoderm:
ektos (GK) outside
derma (GK) skin

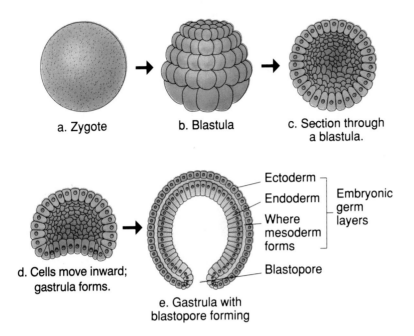

a. Zygote   b. Blastula   c. Section through a blastula.

Ectoderm
Endoderm
Where mesoderm forms
} Embryonic germ layers

Blastopore

d. Cells move inward; gastrula forms.

e. Gastrula with blastopore forming

FIGURE 19–2.

In multicellular animals, a blastula develops from a zygote (a through c). As cells move inward to form the gastrula, germ layers develop (d, e).

and reproductive organs developed from cells of the mesoderm, and the lining of your digestive tract developed from cells of the endoderm.

The germ layers are the result of a specific pattern of cell divisions in the embryo. Initially, a zygote divides to become a blastula. A **blastula** is a hollow ball of cells. As development continues, the organism remains about the same size as the ever-increasing numbers of cells move inward to form a gastrula. A **gastrula** is a two-layered structure from which the three germ cell layers develop.

In animals that have a mesoderm, a body cavity called a coelom (SEE lum) forms between the inner organs and the body wall. A **coelom** is a true body cavity completely surrounded by tissues that develop from the embryonic mesoderm. Humans have a coelom. Some other animals have a pseudocoelom. A **pseudocoelom** is a body cavity that is only partly lined with mesoderm. Some worms are pseudocoelomates. Animals that have no body cavity are **acoelomates.** Sponges and jellyfish are acoelomates.

pseudocoelum:
pseudes (GK) false
koilos (GK) hollow

FIGURE 19–3.

Simple organisms have no body cavity (a). More complex animals show development of a true body cavity (b and c).

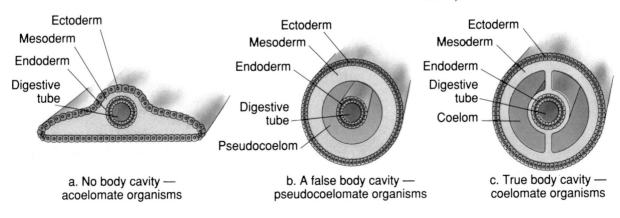

Ectoderm
Mesoderm
Endoderm
Digestive tube

a. No body cavity — acoelomate organisms

Ectoderm
Mesoderm
Endoderm
Digestive tube
Pseudocoelom

b. A false body cavity — pseudocoelomate organisms

Ectoderm
Mesoderm
Endoderm
Digestive tube
Coelom

c. True body cavity — coelomate organisms

19:3 Where Do Animals Live?

Symmetry and patterns of development are factors that determine whether an animal is classified as simple or complex. These factors are adaptations that allow organisms to survive in a variety of ecosystems.

Animals live in all types of ecosystems. Most invertebrates live in oceans. Others inhabit fresh water, and many species live on land. Many invertebrates are parasites living on plants or in the bodies of other animals. Of all of these environments, salt water is the most hospitable to animals. One advantage of a saltwater environment is that it is very buoyant. Animals in the ocean can grow very large and not face the problem of sinking. Seawater also changes very little in temperature and chemical composition from place to place and from one time to another when compared with fresh water or land. Seawater has a salt concentration similar to that in the cytoplasm of the cells of animals. Animals that live in seawater maintain homeostasis without danger of losing or gaining excess water.

Freshwater organisms have adapted to many different conditions. Freshwater ecosystems change more than saltwater ecosystems. Small ponds dry out. Streams vary in the speed at which water moves at different times of the year, causing a change in the amount of oxygen available to organisms. In addition, while fresh water keeps animals afloat, its low salt concentration results in diffusion of water into the cells of these animals. As a result, freshwater animals have adaptations to maintain water balance within their cells.

Land animals, such as insects, are not supported by water. Systems of internal and external support have evolved in the form of endoskeletons and exoskeletons. An **endoskeleton** is a supporting framework within a body. You have an endoskeleton made of bones. An **exoskeleton** is a supporting framework on the outside of a body. Although an exoskeleton of an insect may limit the animal's size, it helps withstand the force of gravity and keeps the animal from drying out.

endoskeleton:
endon (GK) within
skeletos (GK) dried up

FIGURE 19–4.

Animals such as turtles and frogs have evolved adaptations that allow them to live in different environments, yet they are still closely tied to water.

Another problem associated with life on land is the availability of water for developing offspring. Water is required for dividing cells to remain alive. Some land organisms return to water to lay eggs. Others secrete protective shells or retain developing eggs within their bodies.

The animal kingdom is classified into two major groups based on the presence or absence of a backbone. Animals with backbones are called **vertebrates.** Vertebrates include bony fish, amphibians, reptiles, birds, and mammals. **Invertebrates** are animals without backbones. There are almost two million species of invertebrates. Body shapes, structures, and life patterns are diverse. In this chapter you will study sponges and cnidarians (nid AR ee unz), two groups of simple invertebrates.

What main characteristic distinguishes invertebrates from vertebrates?

REVIEW

1. Distinguish among the different kinds of symmetry and give an example of each.
2. What are the three embryonic germ layers in animals? Name one human body organ derived from each.
3. What are two adaptations made by land animals?
4. **SKILL REVIEW:** Develop a table showing the advantages and disadvantages of living in salt water, fresh water, and on land. For more help, refer to Organizing Information in the Skill Handbook, pages 810 to 813.
5. **USING CONCEPTS:** Make a list of five household items that are asymmetrical, five that have radial symmetry, and five that have bilateral symmetry.

SPONGES

When you think of a sponge, you may think of the green or blue household sponge used for soaking up spills, washing cars, or washing dishes. Most of the sponges sold for these purposes are synthetic. If you use a real or natural sponge, you are using the remains of a simple animal that has been harvested from the ocean.

19:4 The Life of a Sponge

A natural sponge is an aquatic invertebrate belonging to the Phylum Porifera. Most sponges are found in oceans, but a few live in fresh water. They can be found in shallow ocean waters and at depths of over 1000 m. Sponges vary in size from about 1 cm in diameter to over 4 m tall. You may think of sponges as being drab in color, but many are bright shades of red, orange, yellow, and green. It has been

Objectives:
• describe the life of a sponge.
• describe the structure of a sponge.
• give functions for the four types of cells that make up a sponge body.
• compare asexual and sexual reproduction in sponges.
• discuss the uses and origins of sponges.

suggested that color may protect the sponge from the rays of the sun that penetrate the water. Sponges show great variety in body shape. Some are ball-shaped. Other species are finger-shaped or branched. A few grow like a crust over a surface, much the way a lichen grows on a rock. Some sponges have radial symmetry, but most are asymmetrical.

Adult and developing sponges are sessile animals. A **sessile** organism is one that remains permanently attached to a surface for all its adult life. Sponges live in colonies on rocks, corals, and shells. Because a sponge cannot move, it can't search for food or a mate, or swim away from predators. Freshwater sponges have no place to go as a pond or stream dries out. Sponges obtain oxygen and food from the water in which they live. They are heterotrophs. Bacteria, algae, and protozoans are their main sources of nutrients.

sessile:
  sedere (L) to sit

19:5 Characteristics of Sponges

A sponge has no tissues, organs, or organ systems. However, a sponge is equipped with adaptations that enable it to survive successfully in its sessile existence. The body plan of a sponge is simple. It is made up of two cell layers with no coelom. The two layers of cells contain four types of cells that perform all the functions that keep the sponge alive. These four cell types are pinacocytes, pore cells, collar cells, and amoebocytes.

Pinacocytes are thin, flat cells that make up the outer layer of a sponge. Pinacocytes contract to regulate the surface area of a sponge. Water is drawn into a sponge through pores or openings found all over its body. Each opening is surrounded by a single **pore cell.** The interior of the sponge is lined with collar cells. A **collar cell** is a cell with flagella that beat, causing water to be drawn through the sponge. These cells also trap and ingest food that is transported to other cells in the body by versatile cells called amoebocytes. An **amoebocyte** is an amoeba-shaped cell that moves around between the two layers of body cells. Many species of sponges have more complex body plans. The wall of the sponge may be folded in and out so that the sponge is full of channels.

How does a sponge obtain food?

FIGURE 19–5.

Sponges show variety in color, size, and shape. However, the tubelike yellow sponge (a) contains the same types of cells as the purple crustlike species (b).

a

b

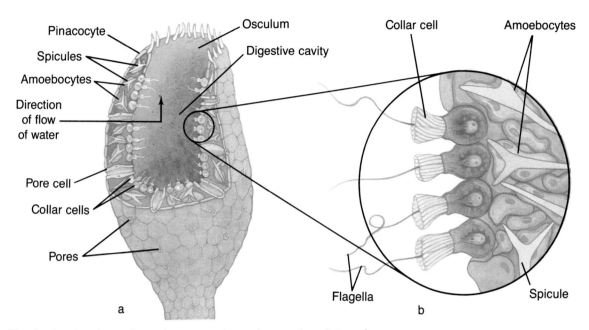

The basic structure of most sponges is made up of an internal support system in the form of spicules. Spicules are small, needlelike structures located between the body layers of a sponge. In some species, spicules are made of calcium carbonate and in others, silica. Species that contain silica spicules are delicate. They are found at great depths in the ocean where there is very little movement of currents. The shape and composition of spicules are used in the classification of sponges. A variety of spicules is shown in Figure 19–7. Some sponges are supported by an elastic protein material called spongin. Other sponges have both spicules and spongin.

Like any other living organism, a sponge gives off wastes. Water, metabolic wastes, and unused food are expelled forcefully through the osculum (AHS kyuh lum). An **osculum** is the large opening at the top of a sponge. Sponges can move enormous amounts of water. A complex sponge that is 10 cm high and 1 cm in diameter can move over 22 L of water through its body per day. The rate of water flow through the sponge is controlled by changing the size of the osculum.

A sponge does not have a nervous system. Responses are based on the diffusion of chemicals between the inner and outer layers of the body. When touched, the sponge responds slowly and only in the area touched.

19:6 Reproduction in Sponges

Sponges reproduce both asexually and sexually. Some sponges reproduce asexually by forming buds. Freshwater sponges and a few marine sponges make structures called gemmules (JEM yewlz). **Gemmules** are packets of food-filled amoebocytes surrounded by a covering of spicules. Gemmules form in the fall. They resist freezing and drying in the winter. In the spring, the cells in the gemmule are released and develop into a new sponge.

FIGURE 19–6.

Sponges are made up of four types of specialized cells (a). Spicules provide a body structure (b).

FIGURE 19–7.

The shape of spicules is used to classify sponges.

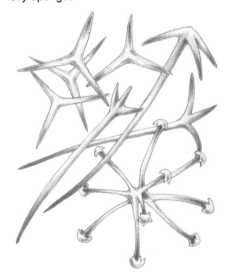

New sponges can be produced from tiny pieces of the parent sponge. A sponge can be separated into single cells. Should the cells be close to each other, they will reassemble into new sponges.

Most sponges that reproduce sexually are hermaphrodites (hur MAF ruh ditz). A **hermaphrodite** is an animal that produces both eggs and sperm. But they do not fertilize their own eggs. Sponges do not form sperm and eggs at the same time. Eggs and sperm form from enlarged amoebocytes. Sperm released into the water are carried by currents to other sponges where they fertilize eggs located between the cell layers. Development occurs within the wall of the sponge until a larva with cilia develops. The larva is released, swims, attaches to a surface, and develops into an adult. This is the only time in the life of a sponge when it does any swimming.

19:7 The Importance and Origin of Sponges

It's hard to imagine any organism feeding on food that contains glasslike spicules. However, sponges are an important source of food for some species of snails, sea stars, and fish. Their bodies also provide food and shelter for smaller invertebrates that live in the channels of the sponge's body. One species of sponge bores holes into the shell to which it has become attached. This is probably the means by which a sponge supplies itself with a source of calcium for forming its spicules. It may also recycle calcium in the ocean.

Based on observations of how well sponges adhere to seashells, researchers have genetically engineered bacteria to produce a super gluelike chemical similar to that produced by sponges.

The use of natural sponges by humans has decreased with the increased availability of synthetic sponges. Natural sponges, however, are still preferred by some people. Artists, leatherworkers, and potters use natural sponges because these sponges hold more water than synthetic ones. Natural sponges are also used in some hospitals for bathing patients because they will not cause an allergic reaction.

NoteWorthy

Extracts of sponges and corals are tested to see if they have properties that inhibit growth of viruses.

FIGURE 19–8.

Natural sponges are commonly used in pottery making.

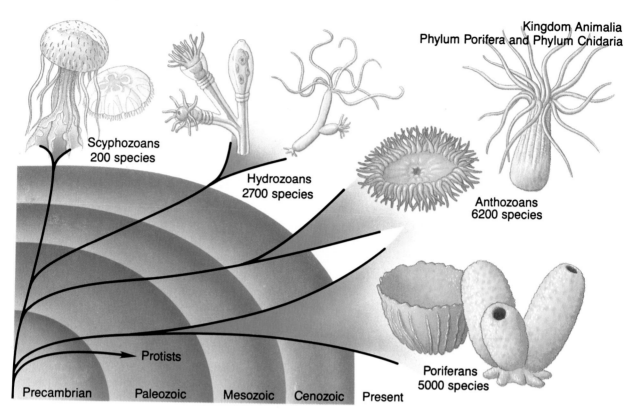

Kingdom Animalia
Phylum Porifera and Phylum Cnidaria

Scyphozoans
200 species

Hydrozoans
2700 species

Anthozoans
6200 species

Poriferans
5000 species

Protists

Precambrian   Paleozoic   Mesozoic   Cenozoic   Present

FIGURE 19–9.

The radiation of classes of sponges and cnidarians on the geologic time scale shows their relationships.

Fossils of sponges appear from early in the Paleozoic Era, about 600 million years ago. Collar cells in sponges resemble protozoans called choanoflagellates (ko AHN uh FLAJ uh laytz). Ancestral forms of these protozoans are thought to have given rise to sponges. No other groups of organisms appear to have evolved from sponges.

The body plan of sponges became more complex over time. Simple sponges with a central cavity, flat walls, and radial symmetry probably evolved first. Sponges with folded walls are considered to be more complex and probably evolved more recently. Figure 19–9 shows the phylogeny of sponges and cnidarians on the geologic time scale.

REVIEW

6. How are sponges adapted to a sessile existence?
7. Describe the functions of the four kinds of cells in a sponge.
8. Compare sexual and asexual reproduction in sponges.
9. **SKILL REVIEW:** If sponges had only one cell type, which type would make up the sponge body? For more help, refer to Reading Science in the Skill Handbook, pages 798 to 799.
10. **USING CONCEPTS:** What evolutionary advantage does the free-swimming larval form have for sponges?

Objectives:

- describe the life and characteristics of cnidarians.
- discuss the function of nematocysts.
- distinguish between a polyp and a medusa.
- compare the three classes of cnidarians.
- describe the origins and importance of cnidarians.

Jellyfish, with their trailing tentacles, often wash up on ocean beaches after storms. Jellyfish belong to the Phylum Cnidaria. These organisms are named for the stinging cells that are characteristic of the group. Cnidarians include not only jellyfish, but also tiny hydras, sea anemones, and a colorful array of corals.

19:8 The Life of Cnidarians

Cnidarians are all aquatic and most species live in the ocean. They have radial symmetry and their bodies are made up of two cell layers. In contrast to sponges, these cell layers are organized into tissues with specific functions. Cnidarians have only one body opening, a mouth.

Cnidarians have two different body plans—a polyp and a medusa. The **polyp** is a sessile, tubelike body with tentacles. A **medusa** is umbrella-shaped with tentacles, and is free-swimming. **Tentacles** are long structures surrounding the mouth that are used in obtaining food. Some cnidarians have both body forms at some stages in their life cycles. Other species maintain only one form throughout life.

The body wall of a cnidarian surrounds a cavity called a **gastrovascular cavity,** where digestion takes place. Stinging cells called nematocysts are located along the lengths of the tentacles and sometimes on the outside of the body. A **nematocyst** is a capsule that contains a wound-up thread equipped with sharp spines. Nematocysts discharge when the tentacles touch a source of food. Paralyzing poison is injected into the object along with the nematocysts.

FIGURE 19–10.

The polyp form (a) and medusa forms (b) show characteristics common to many cnidarians.

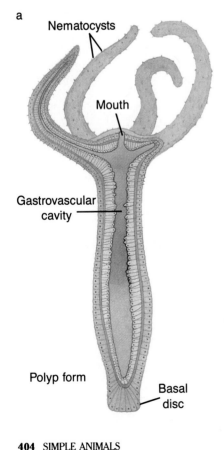

a

Nematocysts

Mouth

Gastrovascular cavity

Polyp form

Basal disc

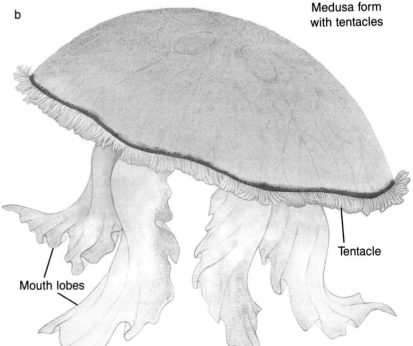

b

Medusa form with tentacles

Tentacle

Mouth lobes

FIGURE 19–11.

The typical hydra is a polyp form.

The typical action of tentacles is shown in Figure 19–11 with a polyp form cnidarian called a hydra. Hydras that live in fresh water are usually smaller than 10 mm long. They feed on other small invertebrates such as young aquatic insects, worms, and tiny shellfish. Without a microscope, a hydra looks like a piece of thread, frayed at one end. They may be colorless, white, brown, or green. Their color may be due to the food that they consume or a mutualistic relationship with algae.

When a hydra feeds, it attaches itself to a rock or leaf and stretches out with tentacles writhing above its mouth. When prey, such as a small water insect or worm, touches the tentacles of the hydra, the hydra discharges its venomous nematocysts, paralyzing the animal instantly. Since the hydra is not able to pursue injured prey, the poison must be toxic enough to subdue it instantly. After the food is brought into the hydra's mouth by the tentacles, it is digested by enzymes in the gastrovascular cavity. Undigested materials are ejected through the mouth.

Because of the cnidarian's simple two cell layer body plan, no cell is ever very far from water. Oxygen diffuses directly into the body cells from water, and carbon dioxide and nitrogen wastes diffuse out of the cells directly into the surrounding water.

Cnidarians do not have a nervous system. They are equipped with a **nerve net** that conducts impulses throughout the body of the animal. This nerve net is considered to be the simplest form of a nervous system. All parts of the body are connected by the net, but there is no center of control, such as a brain as in more complex animals. The impulses bring about contraction of musclelike cells. When touched, a hydra contracts into a tiny blob. If conditions become unfavorable, hydras become detached and somersault to a new location. Medusa forms move by contracting musclelike cells. Swimming movements of a medusa are also controlled by a nerve net.

How does a hydra obtain food?

FIGURE 19–12.

The nerve net of cnidarians is a very simple nervous system.

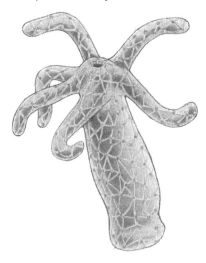

FIGURE 19–13.

Hydra respond to some stimuli by moving in a somersaulting fashion.

How does a hydra reproduce asexually?

Hydras reproduce asexually and sexually. Asexually, they form buds that grow as extensions from the body wall. Buds enlarge, develop tentacles, and break away from the parent.

Some hydras are hermaphrodites and some species have separate sexes. Sexual reproduction occurs in the fall when fertilized eggs are shed into the water. Before the fertilized egg is released by the parent hydra, a shell-like cyst forms around the developing embryo. This cyst allows the embryo to survive the winter. Young hydra hatch out in the spring when the water becomes warmer. Sexual reproduction in some other cnidarians includes both medusa and polyp forms and follows alternating sexual and asexual phases.

19:9 Phylogeny of Cnidarians

Cnidarians are divided into three main classes—the hydrozoans (hi druh ZOH unz), the scyphozoans (SKIHF uh zoh unz), and the anthozoans (AN thuh zoh unz). Hydrozoans have both polyp and medusa forms. Scyphozoans are composed of species that are mainly medusa in form, and include jellyfish. Anthozoans have only polyp forms and include the colorful sea anemones and reef-building corals.

FIGURE 19–14.

Sea anemones belong to the Anthozoan group. They are attractive but carnivorous.

Physalia, the Portuguese man-of-war, has a large, blue, gas-filled float and is an example of a hydrozoan colony. Regulation of the gas in the float allows the colony to sink down in the water or rise to the surface. A crest on the float is acted on by wind, and the colony is pushed through the water. Strands of polyps hang from the float and trail in the water. Some strands are made of feeding and reproductive polyps. Other strands, armed with nematocysts, are the food-gathering polyps. The nematocysts on these strands are larger than in most cnidarians, and they are densely arranged. *Physalia* can capture fairly large food sources. Once food, such as a fish, has been captured, the feeding polyps secrete digestive enzymes over the capture. Food-gathering strands may be over 10 m long. The venom in a large colony is powerful enough to kill a human being. Even when tentacles have become separated from the colony or are dried on the beach, the nematocysts can still inflict a painful, if not dangerous, sting.

Within the hydrozoans, the genus *Hydra* has most of the characteristics typical of cnidarians and the polyp body form. Another hydrozoan species, *Obelia,* is a colony of polyps. The colony forms from a single polyp and develops other polyps asexually in a stemlike arrangement by budding. In a mature *Obelia* colony, all of the polyps are connected. There are two types of polyps, feeding polyps with tentacles, and reproductive polyps that produce medusae. Tiny medusae are released into water, and produce egg and sperm that fuse to form a zygote. The zygote develops into a free-swimming structure called a planula that is covered with hairlike cilia. The planula attaches itself to a surface and eventually develops into a polyp form from which a new *Obelia* colony develops. *Obelia* colonies are small and delicate. They grow under piers, and on seaweed and shells.

FIGURE 19–15.

Obelia is a colony of polyps. Medusae are produced in the sexual reproduction of new colonies.

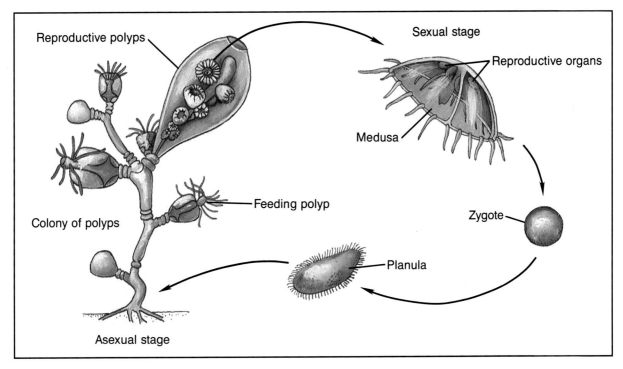

Reproductive polyps

Sexual stage

Reproductive organs

Medusa

Feeding polyp

Colony of polyps

Zygote

Planula

Asexual stage

BIOLAB *Feeding Hydra* 19

Problem: What happens when *Hydra* feed?

Materials

petri dish
eyedroppers (2)
dissecting microscope
tape
scissors

Hydra culture
Brine shrimp culture
stop watch
graph paper

Procedures

1. Make a data table like the one shown.
2. Cut a piece of graph paper the same diameter as the petri dish. Tape it to the outside of the bottom of the dish.
3. Place several drops of water in the petri dish. Using an eyedropper, transfer 3 to 4 live *Hydra* to the petri dish. Allow the *Hydra* to relax and extend their tentacles.
4. Observe the *Hydra* under low power on a dissecting microscope. Draw the animal and label the tentacles, mouth, gastrovascular cavity, and nematocysts.
5. Formulate a **hypothesis** as to which size of *Hydra* will capture and consume more food.
6. In the data table, record the length of the relaxed *Hydra,* using the grid of the graph paper to measure.
7. Using another eyedropper, transfer a few brine shrimp to the petri dish containing the *Hydra.* Observe and record the time it takes the *Hydra* to begin to feed, the number of brine shrimp it consumes in 30 minutes, and the length of the *Hydra* after this period. Record class figures on the chalkboard.
8. At the end of the class period, return the *Hydra* and any brine shrimp to their original containers. **CAUTION:** *To prevent dehydration, keep these animals in water and away from strong light.*

Questions and Conclusion

1. How do *Hydra* capture and eat their prey?
2. Was your **hypothesis** supported? Explain.
3. Is size a factor in *Hydra* feeding? Explain.

Data and Observations

Characteristics	Individual data
Length of relaxed *Hydra* (in cm)	
Time it takes for *Hydra* to begin to feed	
Time it takes for *Hydra* to eat one brine shrimp	
Number of brine shrimp eaten in 30 minutes	
Length of *Hydra* at end of 30-minute period	

4. Does class data support your individual results? Explain.
5. What stimuli cause *Hydra* to feed?
6. What is the symmetry of the *Hydra?*
7. How could you modify this experiment to test for other factors about feeding?

Conclusion: How does the size of *Hydra* relate to the number of prey eaten and the speed at which they are eaten?

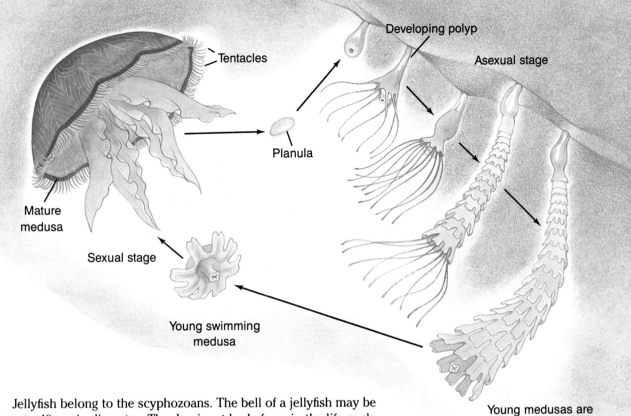

Tentacles

Developing polyp

Asexual stage

Planula

Mature
medusa

Sexual stage

Young swimming
medusa

Young medusas are
produced from the polyp

Jellyfish belong to the scyphozoans. The bell of a jellyfish may be two to 40 cm in diameter. The dominant body form in the life cycle of a jellyfish is the medusa. The medusa swims freely in ocean water because this organism is equipped with true muscle cells. The life cycle of the jellyfish *Aurelia* is illustrated in Figure 19–16. Sperm and eggs form in separate medusae. A planula develops from a fertilized egg. The planula develops into a polyp. As a polyp develops, it forms many medusae. Other members of the scyphozoans are sea wasps and box jellies. These animals are notorious for their dangerous stings. Some species found along the north coast of Australia are so toxic that a human can die in less than 20 minutes after being stung.

Anthozoans, the third group of cnidarians, have no medusa phase. Anthozoans include sea anemones and corals. You may have seen sea anemones in an aquarium. They have a colorful, flowerlike appearance, with tentacles surrounding a mouth. They spend their adult lives as single polyps attached to rocks or other solid surfaces. Some live in holes in coral reefs with only their tentacles showing above the surface of the coral. They tend to be large when compared with other cnidarians. They are also more complex than other cnidarians, some having three cell layers instead of only two.

Coral anthozoans live in colonies of polyps. Corals secrete a skeleton of calcium carbonate around their bodies. These rocklike skeletons remain for years after the polyps have died. Areas of built up coral skeleton are called coral reefs. The largest coral reefs can reach 150 km in length and reach depths of 4000-6000 m. Corals are strictly tropical and live in warm, clear water. There are many different forms and colors. Some are fingerlike; some are branched; and some are shaped like domes and flat discs. Coral reefs are one of the most diverse ocean environments. They provide habitats in which many other saltwater organisms feed and reproduce.

FIGURE 19–16.

The medusa form of jellyfish is frequently found on beaches or in shallow waters.

19:10 The Origin and Importance of Cnidarians

Cnidarians were present on Earth in the Precambrian Era, over 600 million years ago. It is known that they became abundant in the early Paleozoic Era because many are found in the explosion of marine life that appears in the fossil record.

Many scientists studying cnidarians have suggested that the medusa form evolved before the polyp form. Larvae of medusae may have formed polyps by becoming permanently attached to a surface. Colonial forms such as *Obelia* may have evolved when buds forming on single polyps did not detach. Scyphozoans probably evolved later than hydrozoans. Anthozoans may have evolved from the polyp larvae of the scyphozoans. Anthozoans are probably the most recent group to evolve because individuals such as sea anemones have a more complex body plan. Refer to the phylogeny of cnidarians in Figure 19–9.

anthozoan:
antho (GK) flower
zoan (GK) animal

Corals respond to changes in their environment.

THINKING CRITICALLY

CORAL REEF BLEACHING

Polyps of reef-building corals contain unicellular algae called zooxanthellae. These algae contain chloroplasts and carry out photosynthesis. Zooxanthellae and their chloroplasts give the coral polyps their green, yellow, and brown colors. In addition, through photosynthesis, they provide some of the oxygen and carbohydrates needed by the coral polyps. The coral polyps, in turn, give off carbon dioxide and nitrogen used by zooxanthellae in their metabolic processes. During the daylight hours zooxanthellae supply the polyps with food. At night coral polyps extend their tentacles and snare tiny organisms for food.

Occasionally coral reefs suffer from a mysterious ailment called bleaching. Bleachings have been linked to change in water temperature, lowered salt content of the water due to rains or runoff, or high waves due to hurricanes. When bleaching occurs, corals lose their zooxanthellae and become white. If bleaching lasts for weeks or months, the corals die. If zooxanthellae again begin to live in the tissues of the polyps soon after the bleaching, the polyps survive. Many polyps continue to extend their tentacles at night even while bleaching takes place. But some polyps stop extending their tentacles while bleaching takes place. The corals that cease to extend their tentacles at night are at a much greater risk of dying during bleaching than ones that continue to extend their tentacles at night during bleaching.

Why are corals that don't extend their tentacles during bleaching at a greater risk of dying than corals that do extend their tentacles during this time? What relationship exists between these organisms?

FIGURE 19–17.

FIGURE 19–17.

The Great Barrier Reef is a coral reef providing a habitat for numerous species of sponges and cnidarians.

Like sponges, cnidarians are important in ocean ecology. Cnidarians provide food and shelter for other organisms. Some turtles, immune to the venom, feed exclusively on jellyfish. Many fish live in the protection of coral reefs. Coral reefs also protect beaches and shorelines from the wearing action of ocean waves. However, corals are sensitive to pollution and can die within 24 hours of exposure to low levels of certain pollutants. Jewelry, mining for cement-making minerals, and "fishing" with explosives also contribute to the destruction of coral reefs. Cnidarians add to the great diversity of life and hold an important place in the ecology of the oceans.

How are these tiny, sometimes deadly organisms important to humans? Some cnidarians produce chemicals that are useful to humans. For example, one kind of jellyfish contains a protein that glows in the presence of calcium. Using these chemicals, chemists can follow the path of calcium in chemical reactions. Another cnidarian, the sea whip, produces a chemical that may be useful in treating arthritis.

REVIEW

11. Compare the medusa and polyp forms of cnidarians.
12. Describe how a hydra uses its nematocysts to feed.
13. How does the life of *Aurelia* differ from that of *Hydra?*
14. **SKILL REVIEW:** In a table, distinguish the three main groups of cnidarians, list their characteristics, and give an example of a member from each group. For more help, refer to Organizing Information in the Skill Handbook, pages 810 to 813.
15. **USING CONCEPTS:** Coral reefs are being destroyed at a rapid rate for many decorative items. What effect would you expect the destruction of a large coral reef to have on other ocean life?

CHAPTER REVIEW

SUMMARY

1. Animals have radial or bilateral symmetry, or they are asymmetrical. **19:1**
2. Animal tissues develop from embryonic endoderm, ectoderm, and mesoderm layers. **19:2**
3. Animals have adaptations for marine, freshwater, and land environments. **19:3**
4. Sponges are sessile aquatic animals. **19:4**
5. Sponges have one body opening and four types of specialized cells, but no tissues. **19:5**
6. Sponges can reproduce asexually. Sexually, sponges are hermaphrodites. **19:6**
7. Sponges are useful in some occupations. Sponges probably evolved from a flagellated protozoan. **19:7**
8. Cnidarians have tissues, tentacles, and nematocysts. They show polyp and/or medusa body forms. **19:8**
9. Cnidarians are classified as hydrozoans, scyphozoans, or anthozoans. **19:9**
10. Many cnidarians appear in the fossil record. Corals are colonial cnidarians, vulnerable to environmental pressures. **19:10**

LANGUAGE OF BIOLOGY

acoelomates	invertebrate
amoebocyte	medusa
asymmetry	mesoderm
bilateral symmetry	nematocyst
blastula	nerve net
coelom	osculum
collar cell	pinacocyte
ectoderm	polyp
endoderm	pore cell
endoskeleton	pseudocoelom
exoskeleton	radial symmetry
gastrovascular cavity	sessile
gastrula	tentacles
gemmule	vertebrate
hermaphrodite	

Choose the word or phrase from the list above that completes the sentence.

1. The body wall of a cnidarian surrounds a cavity called the ___.
2. A stinging cell of a cnidarian is a(n) ___.
3. An internal skeleton is a(n) ___.
4. The ___ is the outer tissue layer in animals from which the nervous system develops.
5. An animal without a backbone is a(n) ___.
6. The simplest form of nervous system is a(n) ___.
7. A(n) ___ animal such as a sponge remains attached to a surface all its adult life.
8. The umbrella-shaped, free-swimming form of cnidarians is a(n) ___.
9. In sponges, a(n) ___ has flagella and ingests food.
10. The ___ is a large opening at the top of a sponge.

REVIEWING CONCEPTS

Choose the word or phrase that completes the sentence or answers the question.

11. The shape and composition of ___ are used in classifying sponges.
    - a. amoebocytes
    - b. pores
    - c. spicules
    - d. collar cells
12. In the life cycle of the jellyfish ___.
    - a. planula develop into polyps
    - b. polyps never form
    - c. medusae never form
    - d. larvae never form
13. The Portuguese man-of-war is a colonial ___.
    - a. sponge
    - b. hydrozoan
    - c. anthozoan
    - d. scyphozoan
14. Organisms adapted to land need ___ for developing offspring.
    - a. water
    - b. protection
    - c. food
    - d. buoyancy
15. Most cnidarians have ___ symmetry.
    - a. no b. bilateral c. radial d. spherical

16. The ____ is a hollow ball of cells from which germ layers develop.
    a. gastrula   c. blastula
    b. blastopore   d. germ layer

17. Cnidarians are adapted with nematocysts on tentacles for ____.
    a. snaring a mate c. filtering water
    b. respiration   d. obtaining food

18. Packets of cells called ____ form asexually in sponges for winter survival.
    a. buds   c. gemmules
    b. larvae   d. eggs

19. Protozoans called ____ resemble collar cells.
    a. choanoflagellates c. pinacocytes
    b. amoebocytes   d. cnidarians

20. A(n) ____ is an animal that produces egg and sperm but does not fertilize itself.
    a. heterotroph   c. gemmule
    b. pinacocyte   d. hermaphrodite

UNDERSTANDING CONCEPTS

Answer the following questions using complete sentences.

21. What are the differences between hydrozoans and anthozoans? Give examples of each.
22. What are the embryonic germ layers and where and how do they form?
23. What is the difference between a vertebrate and an invertebrate?
24. Compare the functions of pinacocytes and collar cells in a sponge.
25. Describe the cnidarian nervous system.
26. What is the purpose of spicules and spongin in sponges? In what two ways are spicules used to classify sponges?
27. What are some problems animals have to adapt to on land?
28. How do nematocysts benefit cnidarians?
29. Compare reproduction in cnidarians.
30. Compare cnidarian polyp and medusa forms.

APPLYING CONCEPTS

Answer the following questions using complete sentences.

31. In what ways are cnidarians more complex than sponges?
32. How does a Portuguese man-of-war compare with a typical jellyfish?
33. Why were sponges classified as plants at one time?
34. What advantages does the hydra show over the sponge both structurally and functionally?
35. What effect would the melting of polar icecaps have on cnidarians?

EXTENSIONS

1. Describe an atoll and explain how one is formed. Where are atolls located?
2. Research methods used by commercial sponge farmers. Relate these methods to what you know about the various types of cells in sponges. Where does most sponge farming take place?
3. Use library resources to find out how precious corals differ from other corals and describe the effects of coral harvesting on coral reefs.

READINGS

Brownlee, Shannon. "Jellyfish Aren't Out to Get Us." *Discover,* Aug. 1987, pp. 42–54.
Lewis, Ricki. "Twenty Thousand Drugs Under the Sea." *Discover,* May 1988, pp. 62–69.
Roessler, Carl. *Coral Kingdoms.* New York: Abrams, 1986.

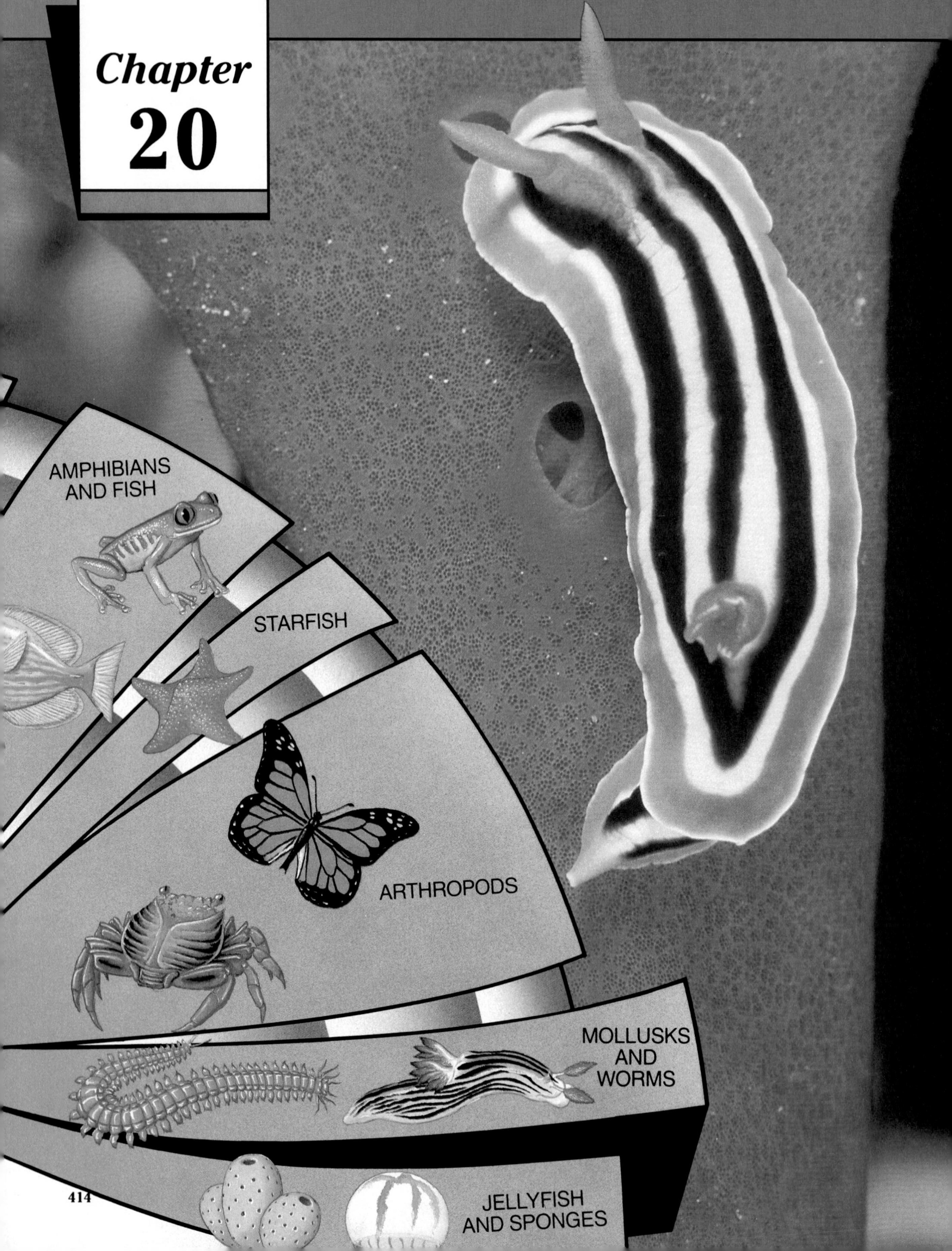

Chapter 20

AMPHIBIANS
AND FISH

STARFISH

ARTHROPODS

MOLLUSKS
AND
WORMS

JELLYFISH
AND SPONGES

WORMS AND MOLLUSKS

H ave you ever hunted with a flashlight for nightcrawlers on the night before a fishing trip? To you, the word *worm* may bring images of slimy creatures writhing around in moist soil in an old baked bean can. The earthworm is only one kind of worm. Other worms can be seen only with a microscope. Worms live inside the human body, in other animals, on plants, in water, and in soil. Whatever you may think of them, worms are essential to life. In this chapter, you will study three phyla of worms and the mollusk phylum. Mollusks are soft-bodied organisms such as clams or squid. They certainly look different from worms. However, they do have some things in common with worms. The giant triton snail on the right and the colorful sea slug to the left are both mollusks.

Giant triton snail

BILATERAL ANIMALS

Worms and mollusks are classified into phyla according to how their germ cell layers and body cavities developed as embryos. They are the first bilaterally symmetrical organisms in the animal kingdom that you will study.

In Chapter 19 you learned that an animal has bilateral symmetry when its external features and many of its internal parts are arranged in a mirror image. Animals with a complex body plan have bilateral symmetry, tissues, and organs. In this chapter, you will study a range of organisms that include some with no body cavity, some with a pseudocoelom, and some with a coelom.

Objectives:
- describe the characteristics of simple bilateral animals.
- discuss the origins and relationships of worms and mollusks.
- describe the characteristics and lifestyles of flatworms and roundworms.
- list the three classes of flatworms and their importance.
- describe roundworms important to humans.

20:1 Phylogeny of Worms and Mollusks

Worms and mollusks are all bilateral invertebrates. Their bodies usually have a definite **anterior,** or head end, with simple sense organs. They also have a **posterior,** or tail end. These animals have tissues that are organized into organs and organ systems. They also show development in the number of body openings.

A nudibranch or sea slug

Among worm groups, you will study flatworms, roundworms, and segmented worms. Flatworms develop three germ cell layers with no coelom. Some flatworms have only one body opening. Food and wastes move in and out the same opening. Roundworms have three germ cell layers with a pseudocoelom. Roundworms have two body openings, a mouth and an anus. Segmented worms, such as earthworms, develop three germ cell layers and a coelom, and have two body openings.

Worms are thought to be very old organisms. But because their bodies are soft and without any kind of hard skeletal parts, worms have left almost no fossil evidence. Only the fossilized trails and burrows of some segmented worms have been found in the floors of Pre-Cambrian seas. In addition, hard mouth parts of these worms have been found in limestone deposits from the Silurian Period.

Mollusks, such as oysters, develop three germ cell layers and a coelom. Like segmented worms, they have two body openings. In contrast to the worm phyla, there are many fossil remains of mollusks because of their hard shells. These fossils show that mollusks lived in great numbers as long as 500 million years ago. Some, like the chambered nautilus, are about the same today as they were then. Others, such as snails, have radiated into a variety of forms that include slugs and exotic nudibranchs. Figure 20–1 shows the radiation of worms and mollusks.

Why is there so little fossil evidence of worms?

FIGURE 20–1.

The radiation of classes of worms and mollusks on the geologic time scale shows their relationships.

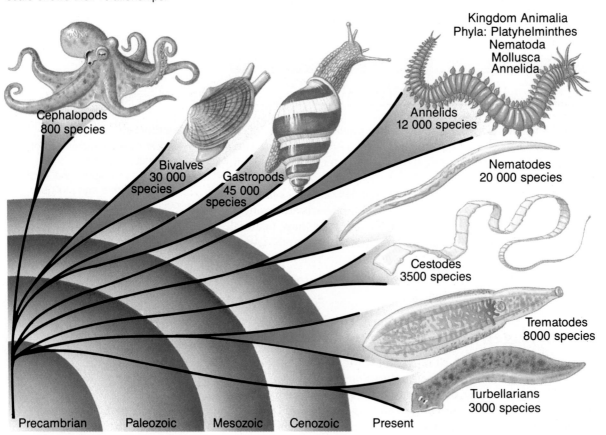

Kingdom Animalia
Phyla: Platyhelminthes
Nematoda
Mollusca
Annelida

Cephalopods
800 species

Bivalves
30 000
species

Gastropods
45 000
species

Annelids
12 000 species

Nematodes
20 000 species

Cestodes
3500 species

Trematodes
8000 species

Turbellarians
3000 species

Precambrian   Paleozoic   Mesozoic   Cenozoic   Present

20:2 Lifestyles of Worms

Worms have two basic lifestyles. They are either free-living, or they are parasites. A **free-living organism** is an organism that is not dependent on a specific feeding relationship with another organism. Free-living species are found in fresh and salt water, and in soil. Parasitic worms are either external or internal. The parasites attach themselves to their hosts with adaptations such as hooks and suckers. Parasites have little development of nervous or muscular systems. These systems are reduced because the organisms are adapted to being carried around in the bloodstream or intestine of their hosts. The parasites don't move except to feed and reproduce. Worm parasites produce hundreds of thousands of eggs, an adaptation that ensures the survival of the species. The flatworm and roundworm phyla that you will study have many examples of both free-living and parasitic species.

20:3 The Life of a Flatworm

The phylum Platyhelminthes (plat ih hel MIHN theez) includes flatworms such as planarians (pluh NER ee unz), flukes, and tapeworms. These animals are acoelomates. There are three classes of flatworms: the Turbellaria, the Trematoda, and the Cestoda.

Planarians are flatworms that belong to the class Turbellaria. Most turbellarians live in fresh water or on rocks and leaves. Planarians such as the freshwater flatworm in Figure 20–3, have many characteristics that are common to all flatworms. The body is flat with two definite surfaces. The **dorsal** surface is the upper surface of the animal. The lower surface is the **ventral** surface. A planarian moves on its ventral surface. Adaptations that assist locomotion are a streamlined body and cilia. A planarian glides over rocks or gravel in the water on a slippery slide of mucus that it makes for itself. Cilia

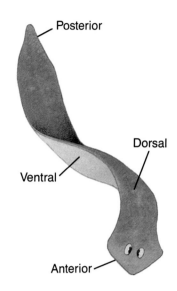

FIGURE 20–2.

Animals with bilateral symmetry have definite body regions.

FIGURE 20–3.

Flatworms have cells organized into tissues that perform specific functions.

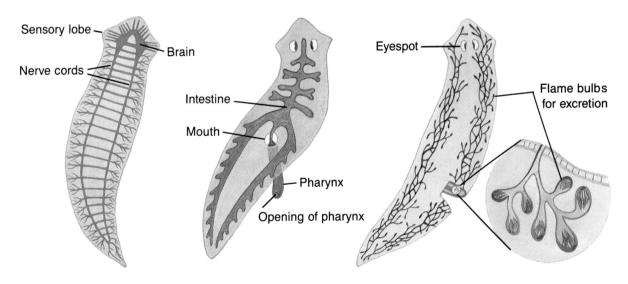

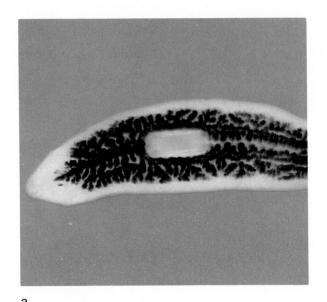

a   b

FIGURE 20–4.

Planarians show great variety in color. Contrast the simple-looking *Dugesia* (a) with its more colorful marine relative (b).

FIGURE 20–5.

Planaria are capable of producing and repairing body parts through regeneration.

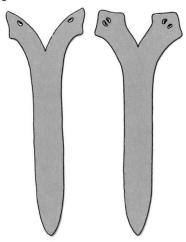

on the ventral surface push down into the mucus and the worm pulls itself along. As the worm explores its surroundings, muscles and a nervous system with a simple brain enable the worm to move and react to stimuli such as touch, water currents, and chemicals.

A planarian has two eyespots on the dorsal surface of its head. The eyespots are sensitive to light and allow the animal to react to light and dark. Eyespots detect only light; they don't form images as your eyes do. A lobe on each side of the head appears to help the animal with a sense of direction.

Planarians are free-living organisms that feed on small, live animals or the dead bodies of larger animals. They have only one body opening, a mouth, and a simple digestive system. The worm's mouth is in the middle of the ventral surface. When the planarian feeds, it extends a muscular feeding tube, the **pharynx,** through the mouth and into the food. Food is sucked into the pharynx. Any undigested food is passed back out through the pharynx.

Planarians have no respiratory or circulatory systems. Because the animal is only a few cell layers thick, oxygen and carbon dioxide diffuse easily in and out of the body. Excess water is removed from body cells by simple excretory structures called **flame bulbs.** The excess water from the flame bulbs collects in tubules and leaves the body through pores on the body surface.

Individual planaria may be isolated from potential mates. Hermaphroditism increases the probability that they will reproduce. Sperm are exchanged between two planarians. Eggs are fertilized and dropped in capsules on rocks or leaves in the water. In two or three weeks, miniature planarians hatch.

Planarians also reproduce asexually. The body can be divided almost anywhere into pieces and each piece will develop into a complete worm. **Regeneration** is the ability of an organism to replace whole body parts. Figure 20–5 shows regeneration of a planarian with two complete heads.

20:4 The Life of a Fluke

Flukes are flatworms that belong to the class Trematoda. Flukes are internal parasites. They embed themselves in tissues that line intestines. The fluke has a tough outer covering called a cuticle that protects it from the digestive juices of its host. A fluke attaches to its host by two suckers. One sucker, located at the anterior end, has a mouth for feeding. The other sucker, on the ventral surface, is for attachment. A fluke feeds on cells, blood, and other fluids of a host's body. Flukes don't have a complex digestive system because most of their diet consists of materials that have already been digested by the host.

The survival of many species of flukes depends on a life cycle that includes two or more hosts. The fluke *Schistosoma* causes the disease schistosomiasis (shihst uh soh MY uhz us) in humans. What are the hosts of *Schistosoma* shown in Figure 20–6?

The *Schistosoma* fluke is found in water in Africa, the Middle East, South America, and Asia. Many people in countries where sanitation systems have not been developed contract the parasite each year from swimming and wading in contaminated water. Although this species of fluke is not found in North America, other species of the same genus are found in the Great Lakes in North America. The normal hosts for these flukes are ducks, but the flukes do cause a minor skin irritation in humans called swimmer's itch.

What protects a fluke from being digested by its host?

a

Male — Female

Adult male and female live in veins of intestine

Eggs pass into intestine

Eggs leave body in wastes

Free-swimming larva stage

Infection through skin

Snail host eats larva

Free-swimming infective stage leaves snail host

b

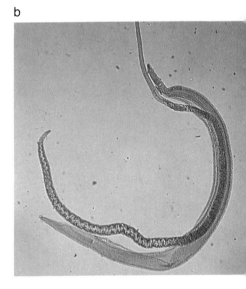

FIGURE 20–6.

The life cycle of the *Schistosoma* fluke (a), and the mature male and female stages that infect humans (b) are shown.

BILATERAL ANIMALS **419**

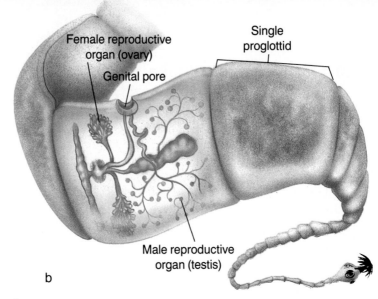

Female reproductive organ (ovary)

Genital pore

Single proglottid

Male reproductive organ (testis)

a   b

How does a tapeworm survive without a digestive system?

nematology:

nema (GK) thread
logos (GK) discourse
The study of nematodes.

20:5 The Life of a Tapeworm

The third class of flatworms are the tapeworms, which belong to the class Cestoda. Tapeworms are long, ribbon-like internal parasites. More than 1500 species of tapeworms live in the intestines of various vertebrates, including humans, dogs, cats, rats, sheep, pigs, cattle, and monkeys. The body of the tapeworm is made up of a head and individual repeating sections called proglottids. A **proglottid** is a section of a tapeworm containing muscles, nerves, flame bulbs, and male and female reproductive organs. The knob-shaped head of a tapeworm is called a **scolex.** The scolex is adapted with hooks and suckers for grasping the lining of the host's intestine. Tapeworms can grow to a length of 12 m. They have neither a digestive system nor a mouth. Food is absorbed already digested directly from the host into the proglottids. Enzymes on the surface of the proglottids break down food before it is absorbed.

The life cycle of a tapeworm usually requires several hosts. In the pork tapeworm, *Taenia solium,* pigs serve as an intermediate host. The head attaches to the host's intestinal wall. Proglottids, containing fertilized eggs, separate from the tapeworm's body and are excreted daily in the wastes of the host. When a proglottid reaches the ground, it falls apart and eggs are released. If a pig eats the eggs, they hatch into larvae in the pig's intestine. The larvae burrow into lymph or blood vessels and are carried to muscles, where cysts form. If pork meat containing the cysts is eaten raw or after insufficient cooking, the cysts are passed to a human host. In the human host, the cysts break open and develop into new tapeworms in the unlucky human's intestine.

20:6 The Life of a Roundworm

Roundworms belong to the phylum Nematoda. It is estimated that there are about a half a million species of roundworms, most of which have not yet been classified. These microscopic organisms are found in soil, animals, and fresh and salt water. One cubic meter of soil contains millions of roundworms.

Many roundworms have a parasitic lifestyle, but most species are free-living. Virtually every plant or animal species on Earth has a roundworm parasite that could inhabit it.

Roundworms have a simple body plan. The body is a tube within a tube—two cylinders with fluid in between. The body cavity is a pseudocoelom. On a flat surface, roundworms look like tiny bits of sewing thread wriggling along. They have one set of muscles, which is arranged along the length of the body but not around the body. This arrangement causes them to move in a thrashing fashion. There are two body openings, a mouth and an anus. Roundworms have a variety of reproductive habits, from species that lay eggs to species that give birth to live young.

20:7 Roundworms Important to Humans

Three common roundworm parasites of humans are *Ascaris*, hookworm, and *Trichinella*. All three parasites are most frequently found in tropical ecosystems. *Ascaris* is contracted by consuming contaminated food and water. People infected with *Ascaris* generally recover with treatment or when the worms die naturally. Prevention includes use of proper sanitation facilities. Hookworm is contracted when the young worms bore into skin, usually through bare feet. Keeping feet covered is an obvious means of preventing the spread of the disease. *Trichinella* is contracted by eating young trichina worms in improperly cooked pork. The disease is now rare in the United States because of years of strict meat inspection. Trichina worms do still exist in areas of the world where infected, uncooked meat scraps are fed to hogs, which in turn are eaten by humans.

Pinworms are the most common roundworm parasite in the United States. It is a disease that affects about 500 million people worldwide at any time. The parasite is found most often in small children who do not wash their hands before eating. The worms thrive in the host's intestines. At night, eggs are laid outside the anus, causing an irritating itch. Contaminated hands and bed clothes become a source of infection.

Heartworm is a roundworm disease in dogs. Larvae of these roundworms enter a dog's bloodstream by way of a mosquito bite. The larvae move to the heart, where they reproduce and grow, sometimes reaching lengths of 35 cm. Worms block the valves of the heart leading to and from the lungs. An infected dog can live for years, but its activity becomes gradually reduced. Preventive medicine can be given by a veterinarian.

Thousands of other species of roundworms are found in soil. Most of them are free-living species that recycle soil nutrients. These organisms feed on soil bacteria, fungi, algae, animals, and other roundworms. Some species are plant parasites. Plant parasitic roundworms have a small, hollow, arrow-like structure, called a stylet, at the anterior end of the body. The stylet is jabbed at a root cell until the cell is penetrated. Cell contents are digested by enzymes and then sucked through the stylet.

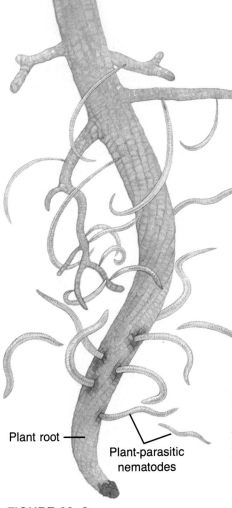

Plant root

Plant-parasitic nematodes

FIGURE 20–8.

Some species of roundworms are parasites of plant roots and cause major crop damage.

NoteWorthy

A single female trichina worm can give birth to 1500 living young.

1. What are three characteristics of bilateral animals?
2. How do flatworms differ from roundworms?
3. What is the purpose of flame bulbs?
4. **SKILL REVIEW:** What can you infer about the lifestyle of an organism that has no mouth or digestive system, but is equipped with a sucker? For more help, refer to Observing and Inferring in the Skill Handbook, page 809.
5. **USING CONCEPTS:** A farmer has a field of corn infested with a roundworm that damages corn. What can be done next year to prevent crops from being damaged?

MOLLUSKS

Objectives:

- describe the characteristics of mollusks.
- compare the lifestyles of gastropod, bivalve, and cephalopod mollusks.
- list ways mollusks are important to humans and other animals.

FIGURE 20–9.

The shell of a mollusk is specific for its species.

The Mollusk phylum is one of the most diverse groups in the animal kingdom. A walk on a beach frequently results in pocketsfull of shells of all sizes, shapes, and colors that have been homes for members of this group.

20:8 The Life of a Mollusk

If you were a biologist, how would you classify snails, clams, slugs, or a squid? All of these animals are mollusks. All are soft-bodied animals. Some have shells, while others, like the slug and squid, are adapted to life without a hard outer covering. All mollusks are bilateral and have a coelom. They also have two body openings. During embryonic development, a small opening in the gastrula called the blastopore becomes the mouth.

Many mollusks have a ventral foot for locomotion, a head with mouth, sense organs, and a simple brain, and a thin sheet of tissue called the mantle. The **mantle** is a thin membrane that surrounds the digestive, excretory, and reproductive organs of a mollusk. In many mollusks, the mantle also secretes one or more shells. Mollusks respire through gills located between the mantle and the body organs. A **gill** is a respiratory structure that removes oxygen from water. Mollusks also have complex organs such as a heart, stomach, and sense organs.

Mollusks are usually free-living. They live in marine, freshwater, and land ecosystems. Some, such as oysters and mussels, live firmly attached to surfaces. Others, like the octopus, move about freely.

The phylum Mollusca contains several classes, including Gastropoda, the belly-footed mollusks; Bivalvia, the two-shelled mollusks; and Cephalopoda, the head-footed mollusks.

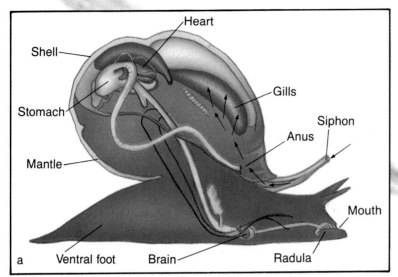

FIGURE 20–10.

The shell of a gastropod protects complex body organs (a). Snails appear comical but are well adapted for their lifestyle (b).

Labels in figure a: Heart, Shell, Gills, Stomach, Siphon, Anus, Mantle, Mouth, Ventral foot, Brain, Radula

20:9 Gastropods

One-shelled mollusks such as snails, abalones, and conches are members of the class Gastropoda, the belly-footed mollusks. Gastropods live in fresh water, salt water, or on land. These mollusks are parasites, predators, or creeping grazers. Various species float, swim, or remain more or less in one place during a lifetime. Gastropods move at what you could call a snail's pace—very slowly. Wavelike contractions of the muscular foot enable the animal to slide along on a trail of slippery mucus which it secretes as it moves. When you look at most gastropods, the most obvious part of the body is the shell. The shell is made of calcium carbonate secreted by the mantle.

If you've ever set up an aquarium, you've probably been advised to put a snail in the tank. Snails clean algae from the sides of an aquarium with a rasping structure called a radula. A **radula** is a tongue-like organ with rows of teeth used for scraping food. As the snail feeds, the radula moves back and forth, scraping food from rocks, seaweed, or the aquarium glass.

Nutrients absorbed into the blood of a mollusk are circulated within the body in an open circulatory system. An **open circulatory system** is a system in which blood moves through vessels and then into open spaces around body organs. This adaptation exposes body organs directly to blood that contains nutrients and oxygen, and removes metabolic wastes such as carbon dioxide.

Snails have some simple sensory adaptations. They have simple eyes and a pair of tentacles. The tentacles are sensitive to touch and help in the search for food.

Many gastropods that live on land are hermaphrodites, an adaptation commonly found in animals that move slowly. Most aquatic gastropods, however, have separate males and females with internal fertilization. **Internal fertilization** is the fusion of eggs with sperm inside the body of an organism.

What structure does a snail use to obtain food?

FIGURE 20–11.

Marine nudibranchs or sea slugs are gastropods without shells. They are capable of moving at 500 cm/hr.

Slugs are gastropods without shells. Slugs have adapted other means of protection. Land slugs are protected by a layer of mucus. Because of this mucous layer, a slug can survive long periods of dry conditions. Colorful sea slugs, such as the nudibranch in Figure 20–11, look like underwater porcupines. Nudibranchs feed on jellyfish. They consume the poisonous nematocysts without discharging them. The nematocysts then become incorporated in the body tissues of the sea slug and are used for defense. Fish biting into a nudibranch are repelled by a mouthful of stinging nematocysts.

20:10 Bivalve Mollusks

Two-shelled mollusks such as clams, oysters, and scallops belong to the class Bivalvia. Most bivalves are marine, but a few live in fresh water. They range in size from less than 1 mm in length to the tropical giant clam, which may be 1.5 m long. Bivalves have no distinct head. They do not have a radula. Bivalves are hinged by a strong ligament and open and close their shells by means of muscles.

Bivalves are silent filter feeders. A **filter feeder** is an organism that filters water and small organisms over gills. Water enters the gill area through one siphon and leaves through a second siphon. Refer to Figure 20–12. A thin mucous covering on the gills traps plankton and other particles. Cilia along the edge of the gills move food toward the mouth. Oxygen and carbon dioxide are also exchanged in the gills.

Most bivalves have separate males and females with external fertilization. In **external fertilization,** eggs and sperm are released into the water. In species that live in the open sea, many sperm and eggs are released to ensure fertilization.

bivalvia:
bis (L) twice
valvae (L) folding doors

What is a filter feeder?

FIGURE 20–12.

Clams are bivalves that dig in swiftly with a ventral foot (a). The internal organs of a bivalves are similar to those of gastropods (b).

a

b

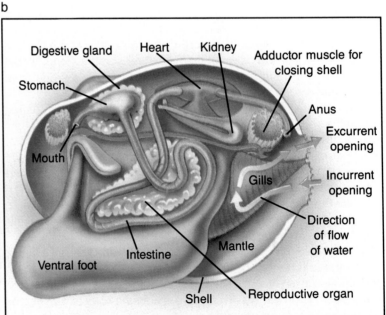

Bivalves have a variety of adaptations for survival. Clams speedily escape predators by closing their shells tightly and burrowing deep into the sand with a muscular foot. In other words, they "clam up." Oysters have no foot. They are sessile and remain permanently cemented to a hard surface. Muscles that hold oyster shells together are very strong and resist opening. Scallops spend most of their time on the sea bottom. They escape predators or unfavorable conditions by clapping their shells together rapidly and ejecting a forceful stream of water. This action propels them away with jerky, but quick movements.

NoteWorthy

It takes about 24 newtons of force to open a closed oyster shell.

20:11 Cephalopods

The head-footed mollusks are in the class Cephalopoda. This class includes octopus, squid, and chambered nautilus. All species are marine organisms. They are the most complex mollusks. The only cephalopod with a shell is the chambered nautilus, although squids have a hard, internal structure called a pen. Rather than a singular muscular foot, cephalopods have tentacles with suckers for captur-

cephalopoda:
  kephale (GK) head
  pous (GK) foot

BIOTECHNOLOGY

MARINE SUPER GLUES

One goal of biotechnology is to duplicate naturally-occurring substances. When potentially useful products are found in marine organisms, the products are extracted and tested. Often, large numbers of marine organisms are needed to produce a new product. It is costly and difficult to collect the necessary number of naturally-occuring organisms. To cut down on the need for harvesting large numbers of marine organisms, scientists turn to genetic engineering.

One product that has attracted the attention of researchers is a sticky protein made in the foot of a mussel. Using this protein, a mussel attaches itself firmly to wet surfaces such as rocks and the bottoms of ships. This adhesive is ideal for doing repair work in the mouth, in fractured bones, and in the eye—places that are impossible to keep dry. It takes several thousand mussels to produce a single gram of the glue, so scientists have turned to bioengineering. Researchers have isolated the gene that codes for a protein in the glue and have transferred the gene to bacteria and yeasts. Modification of the glue's amino acid sequence has produced a glue that sets faster and bonds more strongly, and can be broken down rapidly if necessary. Bacteria and yeasts bearing these modified genes produce the glue in a relatively short time. With bacteria and yeast doing all the work, mussels can lead their sessile lives in peace.

Glue-producing mussels

FIGURE 20–13.

Nautilus is the only remaining genus of cephalopod that still has a shell.

ing food. They have a well-developed head with a radula and sharp, beaklike jaws for capturing and tearing food. They are free-swimming predators of fish, crabs, and bivalves. They have a more complex respiratory system and a closed circulatory system. In a **closed circulatory system,** blood moves through the body in a series of blood vessels.

Octopuses have eyes similar to human eyes. The eyes and a complex brain give them the ability to distinguish sizes and shapes. Research has shown that octopuses apparently also have the capacity to learn and remember.

Although cephalopods don't have a hard shell, they have evolved other protective mechanisms. Octopuses, in spite of their fierce appearance, flee from threat, attacking as a last resort. They slither gracefully along the ocean floor on eight snakelike tentacles and hide in crevices or caves in the daytime. At night, they creep about in search of prey. When threatened, an octopus shoots out an inky screen that temporarily blinds and dulls the sense of smell of potential predators. Octopuses also change color to blend in with their surroundings.

All cephalopods have separate sexes. One tentacle of a male octopus is adapted for transferring sperm into the female. Fertilization is internal, but eggs are laid outside the body. After laying eggs, the female stays with them for anywhere from one to six months, depending on the species, until they hatch into small octopuses.

Squids have many of the same characteristics as octopuses. They have large eyes, a well-developed nervous system, arms, and tentacles. They move about by jet propulsion. With this system, squids attain speeds of 20 meters per second!

The chambered nautilus is the only cephalopod with a shell. It lives in its outer chamber and uses the other chambers to regulate buoyancy. By regulating gas movement in or out of the other chambers, the nautilus moves up or down in the water.

FIGURE 20–14.

The squid has a soft body, a mantle, and gills, characteristics common to all mollusks.

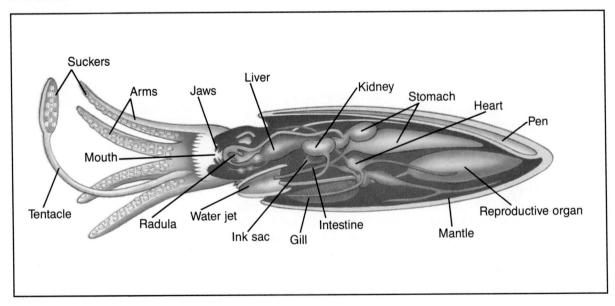

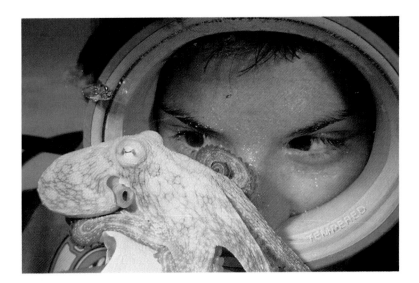

FIGURE 20–15.

The gentle octopus uses its tentacles to explore, but is capable of latching onto rocks and food with tremendous force.

20:12 The Importance of Mollusks

Mollusks are food for fish, starfish, birds, and mammals. Empty shells provide shelters for other invertebrates. Bivalves recycle huge amounts of sediment. Mussels are bivalves that live in salt marshes along the sea coast. They take in phosphorus-rich particles left by decomposing marsh grasses. Mussels recycle this phosphorus back into mud. Mud-feeding organisms then release phosphorus into the water in a form that can be used again by marsh grass and algae. These plants are food for fish and other animals. Without the mussel, the marsh environment would be altered.

Mollusks are useful in many ways. Studies of the nervous system and behavior of the octopus are being used to understand how learning takes place and how memory is retained.

Many shelled mollusks produce pearls, but only a particular species of oyster makes valuable ones. Pearls develop when a foreign body, such as a grain of sand or a parasitic worm, gets inside a mollusk shell. The mantle of the mollusk secretes a coating around the object to protect the mollusk and a pearl develops.

How are mussels important to other organisms?

REVIEW

6. What is the purpose of a radula?
7. How do cephalopods differ from other classes of mollusks?
8. How does a filter feeder obtain food?
9. **SKILL REVIEW:** Construct a key to identify the three classes of mollusks discussed. For more help, refer to Organizing Information in the Skill Handbook, pages 810 to 813.
10. **USING CONCEPTS:** What might you infer about the body structures of a clam in your aquarium that has lost its ability to make a protective shell?

Have you ever turned over a shovelful of moist soil and watched earthworms quickly disappear back into the ground? Their shiny, purple-brown bodies twist and wriggle if you try to pick them up. Earthworms, along with leeches and bristle worms, are segmented worms belonging to the phylum Annelida.

20:13 Characteristics of Segmented Worms

Members of the phylum Annelida are segmented worms. Segmented worms, like mollusks, are bilateral and have a coelom and two body openings. In this sense, they are similar to mollusks.

Annelid bodies are cylindrical and appear ringed on the outside. Each ring is a segment or section. The segments are evident inside the animal as well. Most of the body is made up of individual sections, each with some repeating body features, such as excretory organs. Many internal organs of annelids have more complex development than other worms, especially structures associated with the nervous, circulatory, and digestive functions.

20:14 The Life of a Segmented Worm

Three major classes of the phylum Annelida are the Polychetes, the Oligochetes, and the Hirudineans. Polychete worms, or bristle worms, are the largest group of segmented worms. These worms show great variety in body structures and habitats. Some of the more interesting members of this group are the tube worms that leave squiggly castings of sand as they feed. Some species push up through the surface with elaborate fanlike structures as shown in Figure 20–16.

polychaeta:
polys (GK) many
chaete (GK) bristle

oligochaeta:
oligos (GK) few
chaete (GK) bristle

FIGURE 20–16.

Serpulid worms are segmented polychete worms.

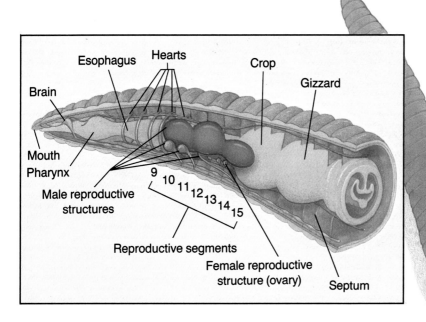

Reproductive segments 9 10 11 12 13 14 15

Labels: Brain, Esophagus, Hearts, Crop, Gizzard, Mouth, Pharynx, Male reproductive structures, Reproductive segments, Female reproductive structure (ovary), Septum

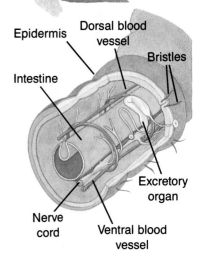

Labels: Clitellum, Epidermis, Dorsal blood vessel, Bristles, Intestine, Excretory organ, Nerve cord, Ventral blood vessel

FIGURE 20–17.

Earthworms have internal as well as external segmentation.

The Oligochete class contains the familiar earthworms. Earthworms are nocturnal animals that live in burrows. A **nocturnal** animal is one that moves about only at night. At night, earthworms come to the surface but stay close to the burrow. During the day, earthworms push through soil by swallowing it. Earthworms are adapted with a slippery mucus, bristles called setae (SEE tee), and two sets of muscles for movement. Mucus lubricates the outside of the body. The bristles from a few segments grab into the soil. When the circular muscles in front of this anchor point contract, the worm moves forward. The longitudinal muscles behind the anchor point then pull the greased worm along. While living underground, earthworms get oxygen by diffusion through their skin from water that seeps through the soil.

A diet of soil particles is pretty gritty and requires some adaptations in the digestive system. Figure 20–17 shows the body systems of an earthworm. The crop is a sac that holds soil temporarily before it is passed into the gizzard. The **gizzard** is a sac with muscular walls and hard particles that grind soil before it passes into the intestine. The remainder of the soil is eliminated through the anus as castings, often seen on the soil surface. A well-developed excretory system gets rid of metabolic wastes from each segment. The circulatory system consists of blood, blood vessels, and five pairs of enlarged blood vessels that serve as hearts. Earthworms have a system of nerve fibers in each segment, all of which are coordinated by a simple brain above the mouth.

Earthworms are hermaphrodites. From spring to fall, they reproduce sexually. During mating, two worms exchange sperm. Each worm forms a capsule for the eggs and sperm. The eggs are fertilized in the capsule, and the capsule is slipped off the worm into the soil. Eggs develop into young earthworms.

FIGURE 20–18.

Leeches have anterior (left) and posterior (right) suckers.

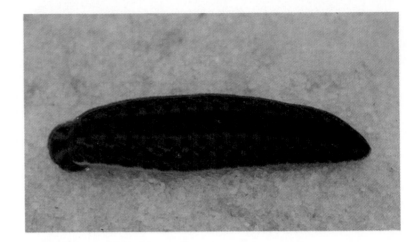

Earthworms help increase the fertility of soil. Open spaces that result from the burrowing of these natural cultivators increase soil fertility by improving drainage of water through the soil and by allowing the soil to mix with air. Burrows also enable plant roots to push through soil more easily.

Leeches are segmented worms belonging to the class Hirudinea. They lack bristles and are more flattened than earthworms. Most leeches are aquatic, but some live on land. Leeches are external parasites with many adaptations for their lifestyle. Front and rear suckers allow them to attach firmly to their hosts. Ducks, turtles, and fish are common hosts. Once a suitable host is found, the leech bites and injects an anesthetic so its victim feels no pain. A leech can ingest two to five times its own weight in one meal. Once fed, it may not eat again for a year. Bacteria in the gut of the leech digest the blood. The leech-bacteria relationship is an example of mutualism.

Today, physicians use leeches after microsurgery procedures. In this delicate surgery, not all blood vessels can be reconnected. Blood leaks into surrounding tissues and hinders other vessels that have been reconnected from growing back together. Leeches ingest this extra blood, allowing circulation to be restored to the reattached body part.

NoteWorthy

In extremely hot weather, an earthworm may burrow as far as 3 m below the soil surface. Heavy rains flood burrows and force earthworms to the surface where they die from water loss.

REVIEW

11. What are three classes of segmented worms?
12. How is the gizzard an important adaptation for the lifestyle of earthworms?
13. How do earthworms improve soil fertility?
14. **SKILL REVIEW:** Using Figure 20–17, describe the location of the brain, the excretory pores, mouth, and blood vessels of the earthworm. For more help, refer to Interpreting Scientific Illustrations in the Skill Handbook, pages 800 to 801.
15. **USING CONCEPTS:** Medicinal leeches are applied without an anesthetic after microsurgery. Explain how this is possible.

BIOLAB *Planaria Characteristics* 20

Problem: What are some characteristics of planaria?

Materials

planaria culture
dissecting needle
scalpel
small pieces of gravel
  (3)
pieces of leaves

petri dishes (2)
dissecting microscope
pond water
minced, uncooked liver
black construction
  paper

Procedures
1. Make a data table like the one shown.
2. Fill a petri dish about one-half full with pond water.
3. Using a dissecting needle, carefully transfer a living planarian to the petri dish.
4. Observe the planarian under low, and then high power on a dissecting microscope as the flatworm moves through the water. Draw the animal and label the dorsal and ventral surfaces, the anterior and posterior ends, eyespots, lateral lobes, the mouth, and the pharynx. Use the probe to gently turn the animal over to see all these structures.
5. Touch the worm gently at the anterior and posterior ends, and on the dorsal and ventral surfaces of the body with the dissecting needle.
6. Place several pieces of minced, uncooked liver in the petri dish. Observe how long it takes the planarian to begin to feed.
7. Transfer the planarian to clean pond water in a second petri dish that contains 3 small pieces of gravel and small pieces of leaves. Observe the behavior of the animal as it encounters these objects in the water.
8. Carefully slide a piece of black construction paper under the bottom of one half of the petri dish. Based on your observations, **hypothesize** whether the planarian will move into the darkened portion of the dish or not.

Questions and Conclusion
1. What color is the dorsal surface of the planarian? The ventral surface?

Data and Observations

Stimulus	Flatworm response
Touch of dissecting needle	
Presence of food	
Speed of response to food	
Presence of leaves and gravel	
Presence of darkened area in dish	

2. How did the planarian respond to the touch of the dissecting needle on the anterior and posterior ends? The dorsal and ventral surfaces? How is the animal able to respond?
3. Describe how the planarian feeds.
4. How long did it take the planarian to respond to the minced liver?
5. How did the planarian respond to the pieces of gravel and leaves?
6. What was the response of the planarian to the black construction paper? What can you infer about the response of the planarian to dark and light environments? Was your hypothesis supported? Explain.

Conclusion: What are some characteristics of planaria?

CHAPTER REVIEW

SUMMARY

1. Bilateral animals have more complex body plans and share some common origins and patterns of development. **20:1**
2. Worms are either free-living or parasitic. Parasitic forms have specific adaptions for this lifestyle. **20:2**
3. Planarians have characteristics common to all flatworms. **20:3**
4. Flukes and tapeworms are parasitic flatworms. **20:4, 20:5**
5. Roundworms have a pseudocoelom and are free-living or parasitic. **20:6, 20:7**
6. Mollusks are coelomate, soft-bodied, bilateral animals. Two of three classes of mollusks have shells. **20:8, 20:9, 20:10, 20:11**
7. Mollusks are useful as recyclers and as food. **20:12**
8. Segmented worms are coelomate and are sectioned externally and internally. **20:13**
9. There are three major classes of segmented worms. **20:14**

LANGUAGE OF BIOLOGY

anterior
closed circulatory system
dorsal
external fertilization
filter feeder
flame bulb
free-living organism
gill
gizzard
internal fertilization
mantle
nocturnal
open circulatory system
pharynx
posterior
proglottid
radula
regeneration
scolex
ventral

Choose the word or phrase from the list above that completes the sentence.

1. The ____ is a thin membrane that produces a shell in some mollusks.

2. A(n) ____ is a system in which blood moves within vessels in an animal body.
3. ____ enables an organism to replace a missing body part or repair injured parts.
4. A section of a tapeworm that contains simple muscles, nerves, flame bulbs and reproductive structures is a(n) ____.
5. In ____, eggs are fertilized outside the body of an animal, usually in water.
6. The muscular feeding tube of a planarian is called the ____.
7. A(n) ____ is the functional unit of the excretory system of planarians.
8. ____ organisms move about at night.
9. A(n) ____ moves water and food over a series of gills.
10. Gastropods and cephalopods have a rasping, toothlike ____ for scraping food from surfaces.

REVIEWING CONCEPTS

Choose the word or phrase that completes the sentence or answers the question.

11. The three classes of flatworms include flukes, tapeworms, and ____.
    a. nematodes   c. planarians
    b. cephalopods   d. gastropods
12. ____ are an important food source for humans.
    a. Flukes   c. Clams
    b. Planarians   d. Slugs
13. Worms and mollusks are all ____.
    a. acoelomate
    b. segmented
    c. bilaterally symmetrical
    d. asymmetrical
14. All flatworms are ____.
    a. parasites   c. acoelomates
    b. pseudocoelomates   d. free-living
15. Plant parasitic roundworms differ from other roundworms because they have a ____.

a. stylet   c. mantle
b. scolex   d. radula

16. Segmented worms and mollusks both have a(n) ___.

    a. coelom   c. acoelom
    b. pseudocoelom   d. radula

17. Three common human roundworm parasites are *Ascaris, Trichinella,* and ___.

    a. hookworms   c. flukes
    b. tapeworms   d. gastropods

18. Mollusks lived as long as ___ years ago.

    a. 50 million   c. 1 million
    b. 500 million   d. 50 thousand

19. A(n) ___ is a gastropod that does not have a shell.

    a. octopus   c. slug
    b. squid   d. clam

20. The ___ is the head of a tapeworm.

    a. pharynx   c. scolex
    b. proglottid   d. radula

UNDERSTANDING CONCEPTS

Answer the following questions using complete sentences.

21. How are flatworms different from mollusks?
22. In what way are segmented worms similar to mollusks?
23. Why have mollusks left a large fossil record in comparison to worms?
24. In what ways are annelids important to soil ecology?
25. How do tapeworms exist without mouths?
26. What adaptations do many intestinal worm parasites have for their lifestyle?
27. What factors distinguish the species within the three classes of mollusks?
28. How do leeches differ from other annelids?
29. What are the functions of gills in mollusks?
30. Compare movement in roundworms and segmented worms.

APPLYING CONCEPTS

Answer the following questions using complete sentences.

31. At what point could the life cycle of the pork tapeworm be interrupted so that the disease would be stopped?
32. Compare the tentacles of a cnidarian with the tentacles of an octopus.
33. If a fluke hatched with no cuticle, what would happen to it in the intestine of its host?
34. Parasites produce large numbers of eggs. What is the survival value of this adaptation?
35. How are sponges and bivalves similar?

EXTENSIONS

1. Prepare a model of a section through a block of soil, a beach, or a freshwater pond. Include worms and mollusks that might be in these habitats.
2. Investigate the formation of natural and cultured pearls. Prepare a written report with diagrams.
3. Prepare a written report about research projects that study the learning behaviors of the octopus.

READINGS

Gordon, David. "Devilfish of the Deep." *Animal Kingdom,* July/Aug. 1987, pp. 39–42.

Lent, Charles, and Michael Dickinson. "The Neurobiology of Feeding in Leeches." *Scientific American,* June 1988, pp. 98–103.

McCredie, Scott. "From Slugfest to Slug Festival." *Smithsonian,* Feb. 1989, pp. 135–140.

AND
S

AMPHIBIANS
AND FISH

STARFISH

ARTHROPODS

MOLLUSKS
AND
WORMS

434

ARTHROPODS

H ave you ever gone on a picnic only to be invaded by ants, bees, or mosquitoes? Maybe you've caught crawdads in a stream, or eaten lobster, shrimp, or crabs. What do moths, wasps, and these popular seafoods have in common? These animals are all arthropods, members of the largest phylum of animals.

Red paper wasp

THE LIFE OF AN ARTHROPOD

Arthropods occupy nearly every habitat in which life is found. You will find them deep in the ocean and high on mountain tops. They live successfully in polar regions and in the tropics. Arthropods are adapted to living in air, on land, or in water, both freshwater and saltwater environments. They feed on everything from wood, to cloth, to flesh. They destroy, pollinate, and recycle. The phylum Arthropoda includes shrimp, lobsters, crabs, ticks, mites, spiders, scorpions, centipedes, millipedes, and numerous orders of insects. Among the smallest arthropods is the hairy winged beetle that is only 0.2 mm long. At the opposite extreme is the giant Japanese spider crab that measures 3 to 4 m across. In spite of its variety, this diverse group has many common characteristics.

21:1 Characteristics of Arthropods

The typical arthropod is an invertebrate with bilateral symmetry, a coelom, an exoskeleton, and jointed structures called appendages. An **appendage** is any major structure, such as a leg or antenna, that grows out of the main body of an animal. Appendages are modified in various groups of arthropods for specific jobs such as sensing, walking, pinching, swimming, mating, and feeding. Like the annelids you studied in Chapter 20, the typical arthropod body consists of a series of segments. Unlike the annelids, segments in arthropods are fused into two or three body sections. Insects, lobsters, and crayfish have three body sections—a head, a thorax, and an abdomen. Spiders have two—an anterior section and a posterior section. Ticks have just one body section. In some arthropods, like insects, the

Objectives:
- name three major characteristics of the arthropods.
- list the advantages and disadvantages of an exoskeleton.
- describe molting in arthropods.
- compare arthropod respiratory, circulatory, and nervous systems.
- describe complete and incomplete metamorphosis.

A Florida Pericopid moth

Stag Beetle

What happens when an arthropod molts?

arthropod:
arthron (GK) joint
pous (GK) foot
molt:
mutare (L) to change

thorax contains numerous muscles for operating appendages such as wings and legs. In lobsters and crayfish, the abdomen is the section that contains muscles that control the movement of appendages. Most segments have a pair of jointed appendages.

The success of the arthropods as a group is attributed to the presence of an exoskeleton. The exoskeleton is a hard, thick outer covering made of protein and chitin, the same substance found in fungal cell walls. The exoskeleton protects and supports internal tissues. It is found over the appendages as well. Arthropods may also have a waxy layer over the exoskeleton. This waxy layer protects the animal from water loss.

Arthropods shed their old exoskeletons in the process of growth. Shedding the old outer layers of the exoskeleton is called **molting.** Before an arthropod molts, a new exoskeleton is produced under the old one. When molting occurs, the animal contracts its abdomen and forces blood into the thorax. The thorax swells, forcing the old exoskeleton to break. Some arthropods swallow air or water, increase in size, and wiggle out of their old exoskeletons. Once free of the old structure, the animal swallows more air or water, forcing various body parts to expand. A new exoskeleton hardens in a process called tanning. An animal that has just emerged from its old exoskeleton has very little protection from its enemies and little muscle strength. Many arthropods are adapted to hide in secluded places for a few hours or days while the new exoskeleton hardens. Soft-shell crabs served in restaurants are arthropods that have molted and been harvested before the new exoskeleton hardens. Most arthropods molt four to twelve times in their lives.

FIGURE 21–1.

Arthropods molt several times in their development. The old exoskeleton is discarded and a new one forms from the epidermis.

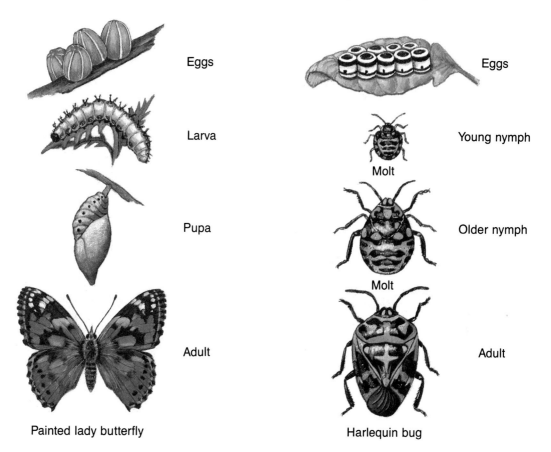

a   Complete Metamorphosis

Eggs

Larva

Pupa

Adult

Painted lady butterfly

b   Incomplete Metamorphosis

Eggs

Young nymph

Molt

Older nymph

Molt

Adult

Harlequin bug

FIGURE 21–2.

Complete metamorphosis (a) involves noticeable changes in body structure. During incomplete metamorphosis (b), intermediate stages resemble the adult form.

Molting is an important step in the development of all arthropods. However, arthropods undergo many other changes during development. Arthropods that develop from eggs laid outside the body undergo several changes in appearance before they become adults. This series of changes is called metamorphosis (met uh MOR fuh sus). Metamorphosis may be complete or incomplete. During **complete metamorphosis,** four stages occur—egg, larva, pupa, and adult. A butterfly egg hatches into a soft, wormlike **larva** (*pl.* larvae) with segments. Larvae usually have appetites that won't quit. They consume vast amounts of leaves, wood, bark, or other animals in or on which they were laid as eggs. Hungry, growing arthropod larvae are responsible for much crop damage. Larvae molt several times and develop into a pupa. The **pupa** stage in arthropods is a period of tremendous chemical and structural reorganization. Eventually an adult organism emerges from the pupa. Butterflies and bees are some of the arthropods that undergo complete metamorphosis.

During **incomplete metamorphosis,** three stages are evident— an egg, a nymph, and an adult. A **nymph** is a stage that hatches from an egg and has the appearance of a small adult, but lacks certain appendages such as wings. As a nymph develops, it undergoes several molts until it reaches adult size and form.

What are the stages of complete metamorphosis?

21:2 Body Systems of Arthropods

Arthropods have evolved complex body systems. They have a complete digestive system with a mouth, a stomach, an intestine, and an anus, together with various glands. The mouthparts of different arthropods include jaws adapted for holding, chewing, sucking, or biting. Most terrestrial arthropods excrete wastes through structures called **Malpighian tubules** found near the intestine. This is in contrast to the annelids where an excretory structure is found in each segment. Arthropods have an open circulatory system with one or more hearts and arteries, vessels that carry blood away from the heart. There are no veins, vessels that return blood to the heart. Blood returns to the heart through open body spaces.

Arthropods have a variety of ways to get oxygen into their bodies. In some arthropods, air diffuses right through the body wall. Aquatic arthropods breathe through gills. Recall that when water passes over gills, oxygen and carbon dioxide are exchanged. Land arthropods have a system of tracheal tubes or book lungs that transports oxygen directly to body tissues. A **tracheal tube** is an air duct in the animal's body lined with cuticle. Air enters and leaves the tracheal tubes through openings called **spiracles.** Spiracles are found along the thorax and abdomen. Muscle activity moves air around in the tracheal tubes. Spiders, ticks, and scorpions have book lungs. **Book lungs** are modified gills made up of blood-filled folded membranes that look like the pages of a book. Figure 21–3 illustrates tracheal tubes and book lungs in insects and spiders.

spiracle:
spirare (L) to breathe

How does air enter an insect's body?

FIGURE 21–3.

Common arthropod characteristics are shown in this insect model (a). Respiration in many arthropods takes place through tracheae (b) or book lungs (c).

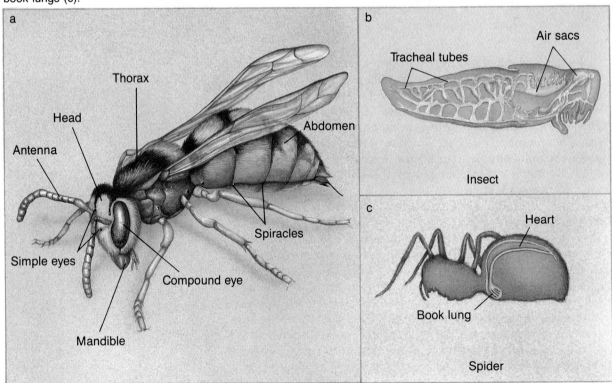

The basic arthropod nervous system consists of two ventral nerve cords, an anterior brain, and a pair of ganglia for each segment. Arthropods have organs for sight, smell, touch, and chemical sensing. The most obvious of these structures are the simple and compound eyes. Most arthropods have one pair of compound eyes and anywhere from three to eight simple eyes. A **simple eye** is a visual structure with only one lens. A **compound eye** is a visual structure with many lenses or facets. Compound eyes form as many images as there are facets. The number of facets in the compound eyes of arthropods varies with the species. Dragonflies have as many as 28 000 facets.

Most arthropod species have separate males and females and reproduce sexually. Fertilization is usually internal in land species, but is often external in aquatic species. A few species are hermaphrodites. Some species exhibit parthenogenesis. **Parthenogenesis** is a form of asexual reproduction in which an organism develops from an unfertilized egg. The female aphid in Figure 21–5 has just given birth parthenogenically.

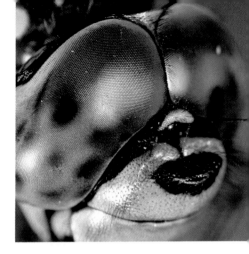

FIGURE 21–4.

The mosaic of images formed with compound eyes in insects is not very sharp, but allows the animal to be very sensitive to motion.

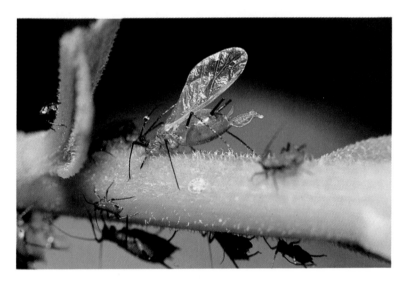

FIGURE 21–5.

Aphids give birth to female clone offspring all summer without the help of males. Males develop when food supplies and temperatures drop.

21:3 The Origins of Arthropods

Arthropods are thought to have developed from the annelids. Annelids, as you recall, have a protective cuticle and segmented bodies with some form of bristle on each segment. The exoskeleton in arthropods is harder and provides more protection than the cuticle of annelids. Most arthropods do not have the large number of segments that you see in earthworms, but their bodies do show the markings of segments. However, segments in arthropods are fused into anywhere from one to three body sections such as the head, thorax, and abdomen. These sections also show more specialization. The head of arthropods shows greater development of nerve tissue and sensory organs, such as eyes. Instead of bristles as in the annelids, a smaller number of appendages are found in arthropods. These appendages have many functions.

FIGURE 21–6.

The radiation of classes of arthropods on the geologic time scale shows their relationships.

Arthropods that exist today have been traced to fossils of the Cambrian and Paleozoic periods. In this text, you will study members of the classes summarized in Figure 21–6.

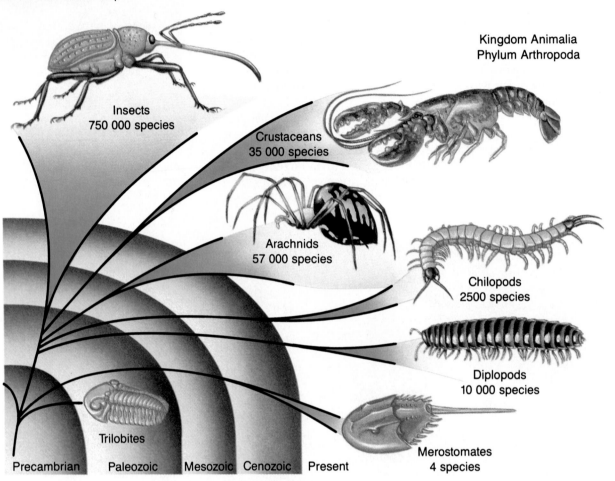

Kingdom Animalia
Phylum Arthropoda

Insects
750 000 species

Crustaceans
35 000 species

Arachnids
57 000 species

Chilopods
2500 species

Diplopods
10 000 species

Merostomates
4 species

Trilobites

Precambrian Paleozoic Mesozoic Cenozoic Present

REVIEW

1. What are three major characteristics of arthropods?
2. Describe the differences between complete and incomplete metamorphosis in arthropods.
3. What are the advantages and disadvantages of an exoskeleton?
4. **SKILL REVIEW:** What are the relationships between annelids and arthropods? For more help, refer to Reading Science in the Skill Handbook, pages 798 to 799.
5. **USING CONCEPTS:** Why might molting be a vulnerable time in the life of an arthropod?

THE DIVERSITY OF ARTHROPODS

The phylum Arthropoda contains at least one million species that have been identified. While that is an extremely large number, there are perhaps more than ten million other arthropod species yet to be discovered and identified. Arthropods are abundant in every habitat and are a source of fascination for people.

21:4 Spiders and Their Relatives

Spiders, scorpions, mites, and ticks belong to the class Arachinida. While most arthropods have three body regions, the arachnids have no distinct thorax. The mouth, sense organs, and legs are located on a fused head-thorax combination called the **cephalothorax.** In spiders, the abdomen is joined to the cephalothorax by a slender tube, or waist.

Most arachnids are terrestrial, although a few mites and spiders live in water. Arachnids breathe through tracheal tubes and book lungs. Some arachnids may have six pairs of jointed appendages. The first pair, near the mouth called **chelicerae,** are often adapted as pincers or fangs that either hold food or poison prey. The second pair of appendages, called the **pedipalps,** are adapted for holding, moving, or crushing food, or as sensory organs. The four remaining pairs of appendages are adapted as legs.

Objectives:
- describe and distinguish among the classes of arthropods.
- list members of each class of arthropods.
- discuss the adaptation of webs.
- list adaptations that contribute to the success of insects.

chelicerae:
chele (GK) claw
keros (GK) horn

FIGURE 21–7.

The wolf spider is equipped for capturing and holding prey.

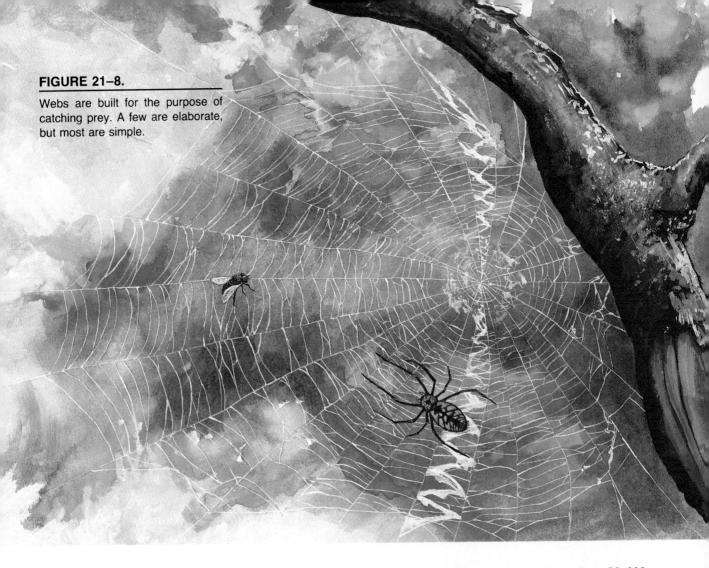

FIGURE 21–8.

Webs are built for the purpose of catching prey. A few are elaborate, but most are simple.

FIGURE 21–9.

Young spiders are carried on the back of the mother in some species.

Spiders are the largest group of arachnids. More than 30 000 species of spiders have been identified. All spiders spin silk, but not all of them make webs. Silk protein is secreted by anywhere from two to six silk glands in the abdomen. Silk is first released as a liquid from as many as one hundred small tubes. The spider then spins the silk into a thread with organs called **spinnerets.** Spiders make different kinds of silk for catching prey or making egg sacs.

Spiders have simple eyes that detect light but do not form images. Some spiders have as many as twelve simple eyes. Web-spinning spiders detect vibrations on their webs rather than see their prey.

A spider kills its prey, such as a fly, by injecting poison through its pedipalps. Using a process of extracellular digestion, digestive enzymes from the spider's mouth liquify the internal organs of the captured animal. The spider then ingests the liquified food.

Spiders reproduce sexually. In male spiders, the second pair of appendages has been adapted into a vessel that transfers sperm to the female. Females may lay large numbers of eggs or only a few. Most spiders wrap their eggs in a silken sac or cocoon, where the eggs remain until they hatch. Some spiders lay their eggs and never see their young again. Others carry the sac around with them.

Ticks and mites are the smallest arachnids. Ticks and mites differ from spiders in that they have only a single body section. The head, thorax, and abdomen are completely fused. Ticks and mites have six legs in the immature or juvenile form, but adult forms have eight legs. Mites are tiny. Many are not even visible to the naked eye. Mites such as chiggers, feed on blood, skin, plant juices, or decaying plant and animal material. House dust mites feed on discarded skin cells that collect in dust on floors, in bedding, or on clothing. Some people are allergic to mite waste products.

A walk in the woods may require a check for ticks. Ticks feed on blood from reptiles, birds, and mammals. They are very small, but capable of expanding up to 1 cm or more after a blood meal. When ticks are full, they drop off of their host to incubate eggs. A female tick may produce millions of eggs. Adult ticks may live up to three years without feeding again. Ticks are well known vectors of Lyme disease and Rocky Mountain spotted fever.

Scorpions are easily recognized by their many abdominal body segments and enlarged pincers. A scorpion also has a pointed stinger at the end of its abdominal section, which contains a poison gland. Scorpion venom, discharged in small amounts through the stinger, is toxic. Scorpions are nocturnal.

Horseshoe crabs belong to the class Merostomata. They are arthropods that are similar to the now extinct trilobites and present-day scorpions. The horseshoe crab appears today much the way it did 450 million years ago. A young horseshoe crab looks very much like a trilobite. Trilobites existed for at least 250 million years. For a while, they were the most common animal organism in the sea, but became extinct at least 300 million years ago. Sections cut through fossil horseshoe crabs have given some distinct information about the muscles and digestive system of these animals.

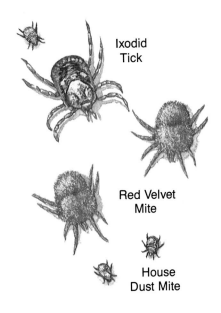

Ixodid Tick

Red Velvet Mite

House Dust Mite

FIGURE 21–10.

Scorpions sting their prey primarily as a defense mechanism.

FIGURE 21–11.

Lobsters have the heaviest exoskeleton of all the arthropods.

21:5 Crustaceans

Crustaceans are arthropods that breathe with gills. They have jaws called **mandibles,** two pairs of antennae, and two compound eyes, usually on moveable stalks.

Crabs, lobsters, shrimp, prawns, crayfish, barnacles, water fleas, and pill bugs are members of the class Crustacea. Some crustaceans have three body sections and others have only two. In lobsters, a cephalothorax is covered by a large shield called a carapace. Lobsters have no less than eleven different kinds of appendages, each with a particular job. Some internal structures of the lobster are shown in Figure 21–12. Excretory organs are called green glands. In large crustaceans, part of the stomach may be a gastric mill. The gastric mill is adapted with calcium-hardened ridges that grind up food before it passes into the intestine or gut. Because of these ridges, large crustaceans can feed on worms, insect larvae, snails, fish, tadpoles, and other crustaceans, all of which have crunchy parts.

Most crustaceans live in water and respire through gills or by diffusion through their body surface. Land crustaceans, such as pill bugs, need to live where there is moisture. They are frequently found in damp areas around foundations. Larvae of marine forms are widely dispersed in plankton.

Crustaceans are able to regenerate lost appendages. Appendages get broken off between jointed sections with a violent muscle contraction that causes them to separate from the body with very little loss of blood. Crayfish are often found with a pair of different sized appendages, because it requires several molts for a lost part to be completely replaced.

Barnacles are crustaceans that spend their lives tightly attached to objects such as boat hulls or piers, or to other creatures such as whales. In contrast to crayfish and other arthropods, a barnacle is enclosed in a hard shell. Barnacles attach themselves to objects with cement from a gland on their antennae.

FIGURE 21–12.

The internal organs of the lobster are similar to those of other crustaceans.

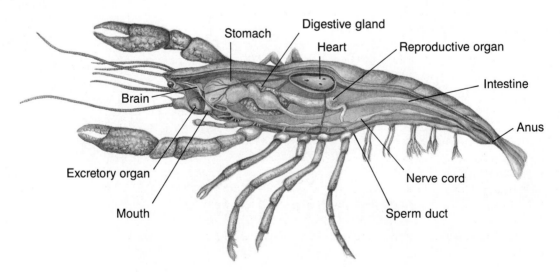

21:6 Centipedes and Millipedes

FIGURE 21–13.

Centipedes require moisture and confined spaces to survive.

Centipedes belong to the class Chilopoda and millipedes to the class Diplopoda. Centipedes and millipedes live in moist places, under rocks and logs or piles of leaves. Some centipedes feed on soft arthropods, snails, slugs, and worms. Some tropical centipedes grow to a length of 15 to 20 cm. Their bites are quite painful to humans. They are also undesirable because they can spray obnoxious smelling fluids from their "stink" glands.

A centipede may have 15 to 181 body segments. There is always an odd number of body segments, and each segment has only one pair of jointed legs. The first body segment has a pair of poison claws that secrete a toxic substance from a pair of poison glands. The last one or two segments have no appendages. Some centipedes have simple or compound eyes, but many have no eyes at all and use their antennae for sensing their surroundings.

A millipede, the so-called "thousand legger," has two simple eyes, a pair of short antennae, mandibles, and other mouthparts. The thorax has four body segments, each with only one pair of legs. The long abdomen, however, may contain over 100 body segments, each with spiracles and two pairs of legs. In contrast to its meat-eating centipede relatives, millipedes eat mostly plants and dead material. Millipedes do not bite, but some secrete disagreeable substances from pores on their bodies.

Millipede

Like spiders, millipedes and centipedes have Malpighian tubules. In contrast to spiders, however, they have no book lungs, and their spiracles are permanently open. A millipede has its reproductive organs and ducts on the third segment of the thorax. The anus is on the last body segment. Centipedes have both of these structures on the last segment.

Animals in both classes reproduce sexually. Eggs are laid in soil or in a mud nest built by the female. Young millipedes hatch with only six body segments and three pairs of legs. Other segments are added as the animal molts. Young centipedes look like small adults when they hatch.

21:7 Insects

insect:
insecare (L) to cut into

Although the animals at the bottom of the page look very different, they are all members of the class Insecta. Grasshoppers, flies, lice, butterflies, bees, beetles, and many other arthropods are classified as insects. Whether measured in terms of numbers of individuals or members of species, the class Insecta is by far the largest group of arthropods. The number of species is estimated to range from 600 000 to 3 000 000. Worldwide, there are nearly 300 000 species of beetles alone.

Numerous orders of insects have been recognized by scientists. The distinguishing features of an order usually are the type of wings, number of wings, and the growth pattern. Important orders of insects are listed in Table 21–2. You have probably met several members of each of these orders.

Most insects are small, ranging from 2 to 40 mm in length while some grasshoppers may grow to 260 mm. The largest known insects are tropical moths that have a wingspan of up to 280 mm.

Table 21–2.

CLASS INSECTA			
Order	**Example**	**Order**	**Example**
Collembola	springtails	Anoplura	sucking lice
Thysanura	silverfish	Hemiptera	true bugs
Ephemeroptera	mayflies	Neuroptera	lacewings
Odonata	dragonflies	Mecoptera	scorpion flies
Orthoptera	grasshoppers	Trichoptera	caddisflies
Phasmida	stick insects	Diptera	true flies
Dermaptera	earwigs	Siphonoptera	fleas
Dictyoptera	cockroaches	Coleoptera	beetles
Isoptera	termites	Lepidoptera	butterflies
Mallophaga	biting lice	Hymenoptera	bees, wasps, ants

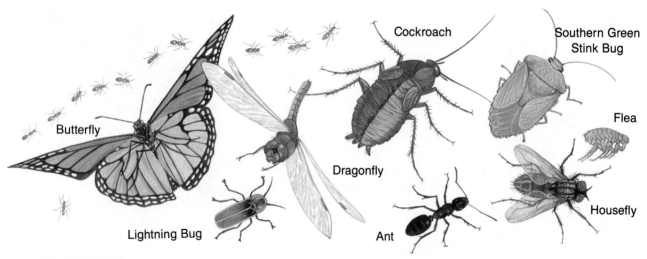

Butterfly

Lightning Bug

Dragonfly

Cockroach

Southern Green Stink Bug

Flea

Housefly

Ant

FIGURE 21–14.

The wings of most butterflies and moths are transparent. The colors and patterns are the result of a thick layer of individual colored scales.

A typical adult insect has three body sections. The head has a pair of compound eyes, a pair of antennae, and mouthparts adapted for chewing, sucking, or lapping. The thorax has three segments, each of which has a pair of jointed legs. In many insects, the second and third segments of the thorax have a pair of wings. Insects are the only invertebrates that can fly. Blood circulates through vessels in wings. Houseflies and mosquitoes have two transparent wings. Bees, wasps, butterflies, and beetles have four wings. In beetles, one pair of wings is hardened, apparently for protection. Wings of butterflies and moths have genetically controlled color patterns that are made up of thousands of individual scales. In some species, males and females have different colors and patterns.

One of the reasons insects have survived for hundreds of thousands of years is because of the large number of offspring they produce. Most insects lay eggs. Insects have a reproductive adaptation called an ovipositor for laying eggs in a variety of places. Eggs are frequently laid on the surface of leaves or twigs, but a few ovipositors are sturdy enough to penetrate bark or wood. Eggs are

NoteWorthy

The female potter wasp carries clay pellets to her building site. She fashions each pellet into a narrow-necked clay pot and then lays an egg in each pot. She then hunts and paralyzes caterpillars, pokes them into the opening of a pot, and closes the pot with a clay lid. When her larvae hatch, they have a ready supply of food.

FIGURE 21–15.

Insects such as this large moth are equipped with numerous sensory mechanisms, including hairs, antennae, and compound eyes.

protected and have an available source of food when they hatch. The extremely large numbers of eggs produced by insects also ensures that some will survive long enough to reproduce again. A few insects such as aphids produce living young.

Insects have developed nervous systems and are extremely sensitive to touch. The touch receptors are hairs or bristles. These are found on antennae, wings, and the compound eyes. Several orders of insects also have organs for hearing. A flat membrane, called the **tympanum,** is the eardrum. Tympanums may be on the thorax, abdomen, or legs. Insects without eardrums sense sound vibrations with their sensory hairs. Taste receptors, sensitive to sweet, sour, salty, and bitter, are thin-walled hairs located on or in the mouth and on the legs. Insects also respond to odors with organs on their antennae and around their mouths.

REVIEW

6. What are two differences between centipedes and millipedes?
7. Describe the functions of webs in spiders and describe how silk is produced.
8. What are two sensory adaptations of insects?
9. **SKILL REVIEW:** In table form, compare the major features of spiders, crustaceans, centipedes, millipedes, and insects. For more help, refer to Organizing Information in the Skill Handbook, pages 810 to 813.
10. **USING CONCEPTS:** How does an ovipositor, adapted for depositing eggs under tree bark, contribute to the success of an insect species?

BIOLAB

Isopod Habitat

21

Problem: Do isopods show a preference for living sites?

Materials

20-cm round cake pan
a cardboard circle, 18 cm in diameter
masking tape
large, clear plastic food storage bag (1)
glass or plastic rods about 1.0 cm diameter (2)
water
isopods of one species (20)
clock or timer
incandescent lamp (25 watt bulb)

Procedures

1. Cut cardboard in half and cover the cut edges with masking tape. Dampen but don't soak one piece of cardboard.
2. Put the glass rods in the pan with one rod centered in each half. Tape them in place. Place the damp and dry cardboard pieces on top of the glass rods so that the taped edges touch in the center of the pan.
3. Place all 20 isopods on the tape in the center of the cardboard at the same time. Put the pan inside the plastic bag, fold over the end of the bag and put it under the light with the light 20 cm from the bottom of the pan. Leave the pan undisturbed for 10 minutes.
4. Make a **hypothesis** about whether isopods show a preference for living sites when given these choices—Damp and light, Damp and dark, Dry and light, Dry and dark.

5. Prepare a data table like the one shown.
6. At the end of 10 minutes, record the number of isopods in each light treatment. Lift the cardboards and record the number of isopods in each dark treatment.

Data and Observations

Number of Isopods		
Treatments	damp	dry
dark		
light		

Questions and Conclusion

1. In what sites are your isopods usually found?
2. Which treatment most nearly matches the natural living site?
3. Was your **hypothesis** supported?
4. Are there any other factors in your experiment to which the isopods could be responding other than those being tested?
5. Why did you enclose the pan in a plastic bag before putting it under the light?
6. If an animal is not found in a particular living site, can you conclude that it does not prefer that site? Explain.

Conclusion: Do isopods show a preference for living site?

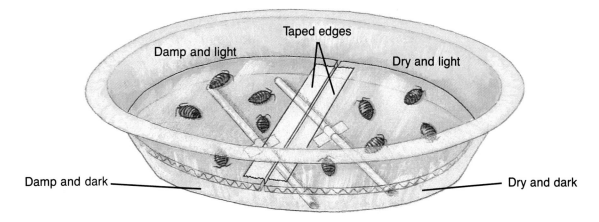

Damp and light   Taped edges   Dry and light

Damp and dark ———   ——— Dry and dark

Objectives:

- explain the features of arthropods that contribute to their diversity and survival.
- describe the relationships that exist between arthropods and humans.

Survival is the measure of biological success. The arthropods, with species such as the horseshoe crab essentially unchanged for the last 500 million years, are successful organisms. Diversity is a second measure of success. Arthropods, with the insects alone accounting for 85 percent of the described species of animals, are successful because of their variety. Large numbers of species is a third measure of success. If you were to look only at the class Insecta, you could conclude that the arthropods are successful. A square kilometer of land has 10 billion insects. What accounts for the overwhelming success of the arthropods? Why are these organisms so valuable?

21:8 Ecology of Arthropods

Nearly every source of food that exists is utilized by arthropods. As consumers, different stages of the life of arthropods are adapted to free-living, predatory, and parasitic lifestyles. They live on land, in salt water, and in fresh water. Arthropods live on the ocean floor within the tentacles of cnidarians, in your closet, and in your food.

What is biological control?

Many arthropods are parasites. Parasitic arthropods control numbers of other arthropods. Some lay their eggs in other insects. Control of arthropod pests has become a full time business, especially control of insects. Chemical control by pesticides is of questionable value. Insect species adapt quickly, causing many pesticides to become useless. The use of living organisms to control other living organisms is called biological control. Biological control mechanisms attempt to take advantage of characteristics in the life cycle or chemistry of an organism to control growing populations of that organism. The ladybird beetle is an example of biological control.

FIGURE 21–16.

Insect parasites often lay their eggs on larvae of other insects.

HONEYBEE HEATING AND COOLING

Honeybees are social insects that form large colonies consisting of one queen, a few male drones, and up to 40 000 workers, all living together in a hive. During most of the year, the temperature in the hive remains at 36°C. In hot weather, workers cool the hive by spreading water over the honeycomb and by fanning it with their wings.

Other social insects such as termites, do not survive in cold weather. In these colonies, the queen mates and then workers and drones die. In spring the queen lays eggs and builds a new colony. Honeybees are unique in that the members of the colony remain alive and actively metabolizing throughout the winter. Honeybees can't fly when temperatures fall below 10°C. For warmth in cold weather, bees cluster together in a tight ball. The colder the temperature, the more dense the ball becomes. The clustered bees produce body heat by constantly moving their legs, wings, and abdomens. In addition, the entire ball of bees moves over the honeycomb eating stored honey. The bees also shift position. Bees on the outside of the ball move toward the center, while those in the center keep moving toward the outside.

What is the adaptive advantage to a colony of honeybees surviving cold weather in an active state? How does the cold weather behavior of bees produce this advantage?

Honeybees keep their hives at a constant 36°C.

The ladybird beetle consumes large numbers of aphids, insects that damage plants. Spiders consume large numbers of insects in their daily work of staying alive. Other specific methods of biological control are discussed in Chapter 36.

Some insects are social. They live in colonies where they exhibit a variety of adaptations in body form, behavior, and function. Termites, ants, and bees are the most commonly known social arthropods. Within the colonies, particular members perform specific jobs. One or two individuals lay enormous numbers of eggs. Others provide food or fight off attackers. This separation of tasks is called division of labor.

The lifestyles of insects have an effect on the survival of the group. Nearly ninety percent of the known insects undergo complete metamorphosis. The larval forms of insects that undergo complete metamorphosis usually do not use the same food resources as the adult forms of the same species. For example, larval butterflies feed on leaves of particular plants, but adult forms of the same species may sip nectar. Therefore, adults and larvae do not compete for food resources. Different species may use only certain food sources. One kind of caterpillar feeds only on maple leaves, another only on oak, and still another only on hickory trees. This division of resources allows different kinds of arthropods to exist in the same area.

NoteWorthy

Males of the social bees develop from unfertilized eggs by parthenogenesis. Females develop from fertilized eggs.

FIGURE 21-17.

Barnacles are crustaceans that live within a shell-like apparatus. They capture food by waving their feathery legs in the water.

21:9 Arthropods and Humans

You have seen that as a group, arthropods are adapted to life on land and in water. You exist side by side with these organisms on a daily basis. You are "bugged" by them, fed by them, helped and harmed by them. The total mass of all insects on Earth is said to be more than the total mass of all other Earth's populations. Clearly, they are important.

Insects are especially important to humans. The whole process of agriculture could not exist without insect pollinators. Bees and other insects are necessary for pollination of plants. Many insects control other harmful insects. For example, ladybugs eat aphids that damage crops. A ladybug larva may consume 200-300 aphids before pupating, and another 200-500 aphids before laying eggs.

Crustaceans such as lobster and crab are harvested from the sea. Their meat is processed for food. The exoskeletons of these animals used to be dumped and had become an environmental hazard. However, research has shown that chitin can be extracted from these discarded shells and put to good use. Chitin from these sources is now being tested for use in surgical procedures, contact lenses, and artificial skin. It is also used as a fertilizer and to make feed for poultry.

Lobster, crab, crayfish, and shrimp are also food for other animals. Spiders serve an important purpose to humans. Most spiders kill harmful insects, ticks, and mites in their normal search for food. Without spiders and other predatory arthropods, Earth would be overrun with harmful insects. A few spiders have bites or stings that are harmful to humans, but most are only temporarily annoying.

Some insects make your life difficult at times. Mosquitoes, bees, wasps, and hornets cause annoying bites or painful stings. Some

FIGURE 21-18.

Ladybird beetles consume large numbers of insect pests and are a form of biological control.

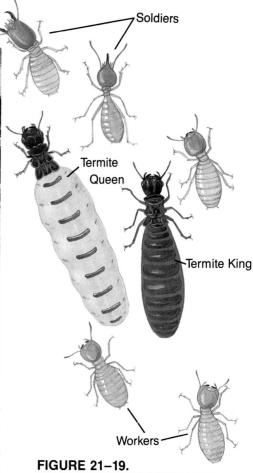

FIGURE 21–19.

Termites are social insects with queens, kings, workers, and soldiers. The photograph shows damage caused by a termite infestation in a house.

people have severe to life-threatening reactions to insect venom. Other insects, such as termites, eat you out of house and home. Insects are probably the biggest competitors humans have for food. If you grow a garden in the summer, you know that many insects harvest the crops before you get your first bite. Plant-eating insects destroy billions of dollars' worth of timber and food annually. Insects are also well known as vectors of disease. Malaria, African sleeping sickness, filariasis, typhus, yellow fever, and plague are all diseases for which insects are vectors. Some carry disease to agricultural livestock. Clearly, arthropods play important roles in the lives of all living organisms.

REVIEW

11. How can social insects show a division of labor?
12. How do arthropods compete with humans?
13. List three ways arthropods are useful to humans.
14. **SKILL REVIEW:** Without any controls, such as limited food, bad weather, or predators, a population of citrus red mites showed the following numbers of individuals: Feb. 18—20, Feb. 20—200, Feb. 25—400, Feb. 29—750, Mar. 4—2600, Mar. 9—4450. Graph the number of individuals against the time. For more help, refer to Organizing Information in the Skill Handbook, pages 810 to 813.
15. **USING CONCEPTS:** How might the release of nonfertile male insects help to control insect pest populations of a certain species?

DEVELOPING A VIEWPOINT

PESTICIDES

The changes that take place from season to season in your local park are also visible in the selection of fruits and vegetables in the produce section of the local grocery store. People have come to expect grapefruits in winter, melons and green beans in summer, and apples in the fall. They expect these foods to look perfect too. The desire for variety and perfect looking apples has, in many ways, been satisfied through the use of pesticides. Pesticides are used all over the world. They have become a regular part of the process of agriculture.

BACKGROUND

A pesticide is any chemical used to kill or control disease-causing agents. There are (1) insecticides for insect control; (2) herbicides for killing weeds we don't want to look at, or weeds that compete with food crops for nutrients; (3) fungicides for disease-causing fungi; and (4) rodenticides, used to destroy rodents that carry disease and consume stored food. Many pesticides are specific, attacking only specific plants or animals. Usually animal pesticides attack the nervous system of the organism. Some herbicides stimulate rapid growth and aging in plants. The use of pesticides has resulted in increased food supplies worldwide and better health for many people. Until DDT was first used on mosquito populations in the tropics, many people died of malaria and yellow fever. However, DDT was used in unregulated doses and its effects were not known. It was also found that this and other pesticides stayed in the environment. Eventually the use of DDT was banned in the United States, although many developing countries still use DDT. Pesticides are controlled by the Food and Drug Administration and the Environmental Protection Agency.

CASE STUDIES

1. In the fall of 1988, the United States Congress passed a bill to amend FIFRA (the Federal Insecticide, Fungicide, and Rodenticide Act). This bill is designed to protect the environment and human health from the harmful effects of pesticides. Under the amended law, the Environmental Protection Agency (EPA) will have nine years to thoroughly test about 600 ingredients currently used in pesticides. About 50 000 pesticide products are on the market that use these ingredients.

2. Much of the fruit eaten in the United States is grown in other countries. These imported products enable us to have a variety of fruits even when they are not in season in the United States. Many crops outside the United States are treated with pesticides no longer allowed in this country.

3. A two-year study of the diets of preschoolers concluded that more than half of an individual's lifetime cancer risk from pesticide residues on fruit is acquired before age six. Fruit makes up a significant part of a preschooler's diet. Parents have been advised that they can reduce these risks by scrubbing all fruit and buying fruit grown in the United States only when it is in season.

4. Integrated pest management (IPM) is being applied in the war against insect pests and pests of other kinds. In IPM, only selected chemical pesticides are used. Application of pesticides at the moment in the pest's life cycle when it is most vulnerable is practiced. However, biological control, or the use of viruses, bacteria, fungi, or parasites to produce a disease in a particular pest, is the preferred method of pest control. Use of sterilized male insects has successfully stopped the spread of some pest species.

5. Ever since they were brought to Massachusetts from Europe in 1889, gypsy moths have defoliated oaks and other hardwood trees in various areas of the United States. Some conservationists believe that the wilderness areas should be left untreated even if the oaks are reduced in numbers.

But foresters fear the loss of valuable oak timber if the moths are untreated. The pesticide used against the moths is sprayed from low-flying planes. It is not supposed to affect birds or other vertebrates, but does affect aquatic insects if it washes into rivers and streams. Recently, the larval stage has been attacked by an insect-eating fungus that seemed effective because of excessive rainfall in the area this year. No method of control has been completely effective.

6. Microbial technology may be used to control insect damage to crops. Genetically engineered bacteria that live inside the crop plants would release materials toxic to insect pests. Seeds could be vaccinated with bacteria before planting. The bacteria would die when the plant dies. At the present time, 30 million pounds of insecticides are used in the United States to fight the insect pest known as the corn borer. Only 30 pounds of the genetically engineered bacteria would be needed to treat all the corn grown in the United States.

DEVELOPING YOUR VIEWPOINT

1. What is FIFRA designed to do, and why are procedures like pesticide testing necessary?
2. Do we need to have the same variety of fruits and vegetables throughout the year?
3. Can countries keep increasing populations supplied with fruits and vegetables all year long?
4. Is biological control practical?
5. Are we making more problems for ourselves by widespread use of pesticides?
6. What might be the advantages and disadvantages of genetic engineering in controlling insects that damage crops?

SUGGESTED READINGS

1. Abrams, Isabel S. "Chemical Weapons for Plants." *Current* Health, Apr. 1989, pp. 28–29.
2. "Microbes to Aid Plants from Within." *BioScience,* Apr. 1989, pp. 227–228.
3. "Protecting Children from Toxic Foods." *U.S. News & World Report,* Mar. 13, 1989, p. 74.
4. Raloff, Janet. "Pesticide/Food Risk Greatest Under Age 6." *Science News,* Mar. 4, 1989, p. 133.
5. Schmidt, Wayne A. "Are Great Lakes Fish Safe to Eat?" *National Wildlife,* Aug./Sept. 1989, pp. 16–18.
6. Sun, Marjorie. "Congress Passes Reforms in Pesticide Law." *Science,* Oct. 7, 1988, p. 27.

Pest-free apple

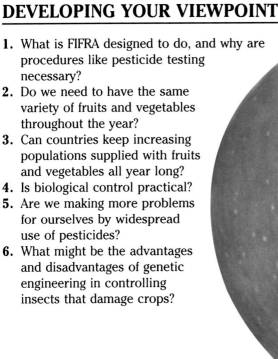

CHAPTER REVIEW

SUMMARY

1. Arthropods have segmented bodies, jointed appendages, and protective exoskeletons. They grow by molting and develop by metamorphosis. **21:1**
2. Arthropods have complex body systems with gills, tracheae, or book lungs, and compound and simple eyes. **21:2**
3. Arthropods are thought to have evolved from annelids due to the presence of body segments. **21:3**
4. Arachnids include spiders and scorpions with two body sections. Ticks and mites have one body section. **21:4**
5. Crustaceans include crayfish, barnacles, and pill bugs. **21:5**
6. Centipedes have one pair of legs per segment. Millipedes have two pairs of legs per segment. **21:6**
7. Insects have three body sections and three pairs of legs. Some insects have wings. **21:7**
8. Arthropods are both helpful and harmful. Social insects live in colonies and show division of labor. **21:8, 21:9**

LANGUAGE OF BIOLOGY

appendage	mandible
book lungs	molting
cephalothorax	nymph
chelicerae	parthenogenesis
complete	pedipalps
metamorphosis	pupa
compound eye	simple eye
incomplete	spinnerets
metamorphosis	spiracles
larva	tracheal tubes
Malpighian tubules	tympanum

Choose the word or phrase from the list above that completes the sentence.

1. A(n) ____ is a chitinous jaw.
2. In arthropods, a(n) ____ may be adapted for chewing, sensing, or walking.
3. The process of casting off an outer covering is called ____.
4. Modified gills made up of folded membranes in spiders are called ____.
5. A fused head-thorax combination is a(n) ____.
6. During ____, a pupa forms.
7. A membrane that is the hearing organ of insects is the ____.
8. Air passes into the tracheal tubes of an arthropod through ____.
9. A(n) ____ is an immature form of an insect that undergoes incomplete metamorphosis.
10. A(n) ____ is made up of many separate facets.

REVIEWING CONCEPTS

Choose the word or phrase that completes the sentence or answers the question.

11. Arthropods are thought to have developed from ____ ancestors.
    a. annelid   c. horseshoe crab
    b. mollusk   d. roundworm
12. A ____ is a fused head and thorax.
    a. chelicera   c. cephalothorax
    b. compound eye d. carapace
13. During complete metamorphosis, the egg stage is followed by the ____ stage.
    a. nymph   c. pupa
    b. larva   d. adult
14. Spiders and insects are alike in having ____.
    a. one pair of   c. jointed
       antennae   appendages
    b. wings on the   d. two body
       thorax   sections

15. Oxygen is distributed to the tissues of insects by ____.
   a. book lungs
   c. tracheal tubes
   b. gills
   d. appendages

16. ____ are appendages on spiders that can poison prey.
   a. Pedipalps
   c. Cephalothoraxes
   b. Chelicerae
   d. Spinnerets

17. Ticks and mites have only one ____.
   a. spinneret
   c. spiracle
   b. body section
   d. tympanum

18. The largest group of arthropods is the ____.
   a. Arachnids
   c. Diplopoda
   b. Crustaceans
   d. Insects

19. An insect with incomplete metamorphosis would have a form called ____.
   a. larva
   c. nymph
   b. pupa
   d. metaphor

20. Spider silk is spun with organs called ____.
   a. gills
   c. spinnerets
   b. tracheae
   d. pedipalps

UNDERSTANDING CONCEPTS

Answer the following questions using complete sentences.

21. What distinguishes a spider from a crustacean?
22. Compare complete and incomplete metamorphosis.
23. Compare the breathing systems of spiders, crustaceans, and insects.
24. Compare compound and simple eyes.
25. Why are arthropods thought to have evolved from annelids?
26. What is the purpose of a web?
27. In what ways are ticks similar to insects?
28. How do arthropods molt?
29. How is an exoskeleton protective?
30. How do millipedes and centipedes differ?

APPLYING CONCEPTS

Answer the following questions using complete sentences.

31. How might metamorphosis help an arthropod survive?
32. How does the large population of an insect species contribute to its ability to survive?
33. What can be used to control aphids?
34. Barnacles are hermaphrodites while other crustaceans, such as lobsters and crayfish, have separate sexes. Suggest why barnacles show this form of reproduction.
35. Compare the exoskeleton of arthropods with the shell of mollusks.

EXTENSIONS

1. Find out characteristics of webs made by at least two different species of spiders. Summarize your research in an illustrated report.
2. Research the history of the Japanese beetle in the United States, and methods used in an attempt to control it.
3. Investigate the research being done to find uses for chitin.

READINGS

Brandon, Heather. "The Snack that Crawls," *International Wildlife,* Mar./Apr. 1987, pp. 12–17.

Peters, T. Michael. *Insects and Human Society,* New York: Van Nostrand Reinhold Co., 1988.

Underwood, Anne. "The Witness was a Maggot." *International Wildlife,* May/June 1989, pp. 34–37.

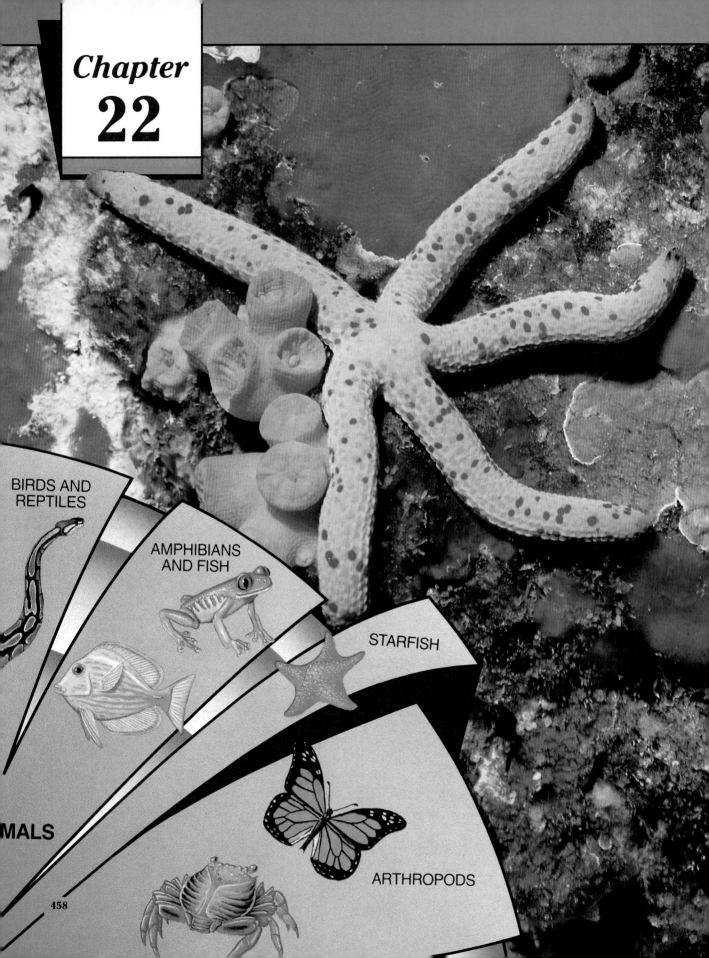

Chapter

22

BIRDS AND
REPTILES

AMPHIBIANS
AND FISH

STARFISH

MALS

ARTHROPODS

458

ECHINODERMS

Imagine swimming in the ocean near a coral reef. All around you is an incredible array of organisms. As you watch, a starfish attaches itself to a clam. The bivalve immediately clamps its shell tightly shut. But the clam is no match for the starfish, and the battle of the phyla is on. Slowly the starfish separates the clam shells, overcoming the powerful muscles of the mollusk. Once a small opening is made, the starfish dramatically pushes its stomach between the shells to feed on the mollusk that lives inside. What sounds like the plot of a horror film is really just a few moments in the life of a member of the phylum Echinodermata (ih ki nuh dur MAH tuh).

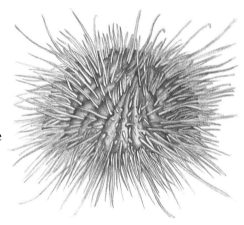

Sea urchin

THE LIFE OF AN ECHINODERM

The dried out, old starfish that is often used in classroom demonstrations is pretty drab when compared with some of its relatives. Some species of the echinoderm phylum are red, yellow, purple, black, or a combination of colors such as the starfish on the left. They also have fantastic names such as sea cucumber, sea lily, and sea urchin that hint at their appearance or behavior.

22:1 Characteristics of Echinoderms

The most striking feature of the body of an adult echinoderm is that it has radial symmetry. Many of the features that are common to all echinoderms are easily seen in starfish. Starfish will be used as a model of the phylum characteristics. Most echinoderms have five or more long tapering arms called **rays** that are joined to a central disc. Some species may have as many as twenty rays. Echinoderms have endoskeletons in the form of calcium carbonate plates. These plates are located just under the animal's epidermis. The plates are connected by short bands of soft tissue and muscle, so that the animal is fairly flexible and can even turn over. Many of these plates have spines and bumps called tubercles that stick out through the epidermis on the dorsal surface of the body. Some spines are jointed so that they can be pointed in various directions. In

Objectives:
- describe the structure of a typical echinoderm.
- list the unique adaptations shared by all echinoderms.
- describe characteristics of reproduction and development in echinoderms.
- describe the features of the five different classes of echinoderms.

A spotted starfish on the ocean floor near Hawaii

FIGURE 22–1.

Echinoderms are found in all the oceans of the world. The three starfish to the right are found in the Indian Ocean off the east coast of Mombasa in Africa.

FIGURE 22–2.

Tube feet are a characteristic of echinoderms.

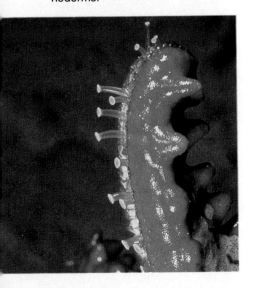

many starfish, the spines have been modified into pincers called **pedicellarias** (ped uh sehl AH ree uhz). An organism trying to crawl over the top of the starfish will be unpleasantly surprised by these tiny, powerful grabbers. In some echinoderms, the pedicellarias break off and remain attached to the unfortunate visitor.

Echinoderms have definite dorsal and ventral surfaces. On the dorsal surface of the central disc is an opening called the madreporite (muh DREH puh rite). The **madreporite** is a sieve-like disc through which water flows in and out of an echinoderm's body. Because it is like a strainer, small particles are kept from passing into the body. The starfish has a mouth on its ventral surface. Grooves run along the bottom of each ray from the mouth to the tip of the ray. In these grooves, hundreds of tiny extensions called tube feet are located. **Tube feet** are hollow, thin-walled tubes or tentacles each with a sucker on the end. Each tube foot is also connected to a round muscular structure called an **ampulla** (*pl.* ampullae). The suction action of the tube feet can produce enough force to open a clam or oyster shell. Some tube feet are used for sensory purposes and respiration.

Figure 22–3 shows details of the water vascular system, a system unique to echinoderms. The **water vascular system** is a hydraulic or water pressure system that regulates locomotion, respiration, and food capture for an echinoderm. Water enters an echinoderm's body through the madreporite and passes into the ring canal, a circular structure in the central disc. From there, water moves down a radial canal inside each ray. Ampullae and tube feet extend from the radial canal. When ampullae muscles contract, water is forced into the tube feet and they get longer. They will attach to any surface with sticky mucus produced by the tips. The muscles in the tube feet contract and force water back into the ampullae and out of the madreporite. The tube feet are released when the ampullae muscles contract again. The starfish is pulled along by the alternate extending and contracting of thousands of tube feet working separately.

Echinoderms have no head or brain, but they do have a nerve ring and a simple nerve net. At the tip of each ray on the ventral surface are sensory adaptations called **eyespots.** These eyespots consist of light-detecting cells. When walking, starfish curve up the tips of their rays so that the eyespots are turned up and outward. Echinoderms only distinguish between light and dark with their eyespots. They do not form images as you do.

Like most animals, echinoderms are heterotrophs. Their digestive system consists of a mouth, stomach, and intestine. The anus is located in the middle of the dorsal surface of the central disc in most

madreporite:
  mater (L) mother
  poros (GK) stone

FIGURE 22–3.

Starfish (a) are uniquely adapted with a water vascular system (b) and tube feet (c). Pedicellaria (d) are adaptations that discourage predators.

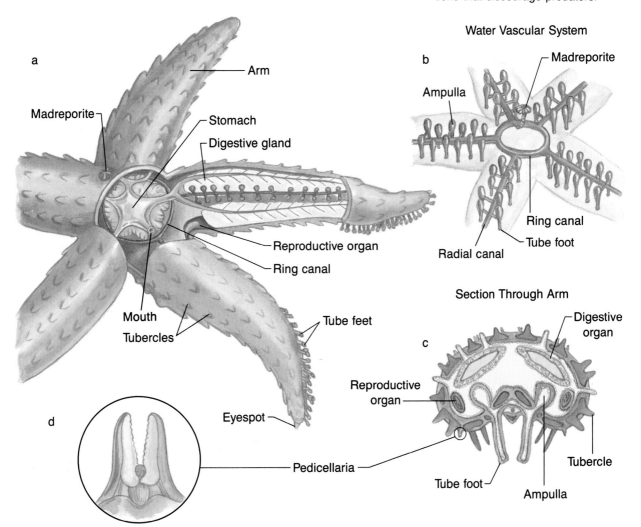

a
Arm
Madreporite
Stomach
Digestive gland
Reproductive organ
Ring canal
Mouth
Tubercles
Tube feet
Eyespot
d
Pedicellaria

Water Vascular System
b
Madreporite
Ampulla
Ring canal
Tube foot
Radial canal

Section Through Arm
Digestive organ
c
Reproductive organ
Tubercle
Tube foot
Ampulla

FIGURE 22–4.

Tremendous force is exerted when tube feet are used to open mollusk shells. In this photograph, a starfish has wrapped itself firmly around a mollusk bivalve and is prying it open.

species. The mouth on the ventral surface opens directly into the stomach. Food passes from the stomach into a small intestine that ends at the anus. Depending on the class of echinoderm, the anus is located on either the dorsal or ventral surface. To eat, an echinoderm pushes its stomach out of its mouth and spreads the stomach over the food. Powerful enzymes secreted by the stomach turn solid food into a soupy liquid that the animal can easily take in. Then the stomach is pulled back into the echinoderm's body.

Starfish have a simple circulatory system composed of vessels filled with a fluid very much like seawater. This fluid contains digested food and is moved through the system by the action of cilia that line the vessels. Respiration takes place in tiny gills that extend from the tube feet.

22:2 Reproduction and Development

Echinoderms, especially starfish, are well known for their ability to replace body parts by regeneration. New rays form to replace those lost to predators. Echinoderms also reproduce sexually with separate sexes. Sexual reproduction results when hundreds of thousands of eggs and millions of sperm are released into the water at the same time from many echinoderms in the same area. The ciliated larva that develops from the fertilized egg of an echinoderm is a **dipleurula** (di PLOOR uh luh). Dipleurulae are unique. In echinoderms, this form is bilateral even though the adult form that develops from it is radial. Through metamorphosis, a drastic change both in

dipleurula:
   dis (GK) twice, double
   pleuron (GK) side

body parts and in symmetry takes place among echinoderms. Several stages in the development of echinoderm dipleurula are shown in Figure 22–5. Adults of other echinoderm species, such as sea urchins and sea cucumbers, develop biradial symmetry. **Biradial symmetry** is a combination of radial and bilateral symmetry.

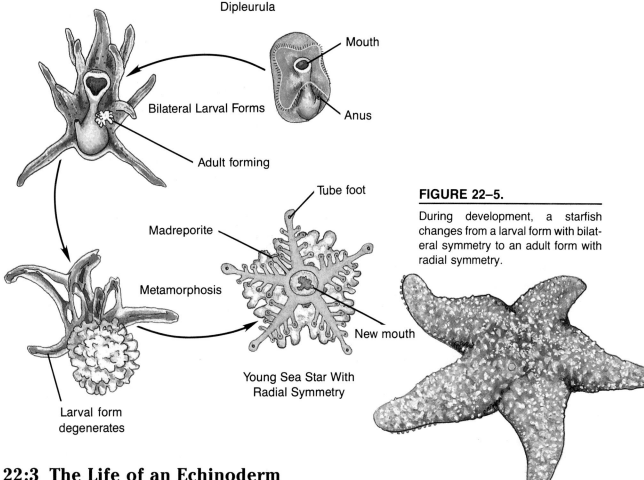

Dipleurula

Mouth

Bilateral Larval Forms

Anus

Adult forming

Tube foot

Madreporite

Metamorphosis

New mouth

Young Sea Star With
Radial Symmetry

Larval form
degenerates

FIGURE 22–5.

During development, a starfish changes from a larval form with bilateral symmetry to an adult form with radial symmetry.

22:3 The Life of an Echinoderm

Echinoderms are marine organisms that live in several levels of the ocean at different times of their lives. They are generally sluggish. Their spines and endoskeletons make them unappetizing as food for other animals. Echinoderms themselves have a varied diet. Most species feed on corals, worms, and mollusks. Others eat plankton. A few feed on **detritus,** the dead and decaying matter found on the ocean floor.

Some echinoderms live under the sand at the bottom of the ocean, but most live on the ocean floor. The ciliated larval forms are free-swimming and move around in various ocean depths. This freedom of movement means that echinoderms have an opportunity to move to areas they might not ordinarily inhabit if they had to depend on the slower moving adults. This adaptation increases the ability of the species to survive.

Where do echinoderms live?

echinoderm:
echinos (GK) spine, prickle
derma (GK) skin

NoteWorthy

When inverted, a starfish bends its rays until some of the tubes reach the ground and attach as an anchor; then it slowly rolls over.

22:4 Classification of Echinoderms

More than one-third of all echinoderm species are in the class Asteroidea to which starfish belong. Four other classes of living echinoderms are Ophiuroidea, the brittle stars; Echinoidea, the sea urchins and sand dollars; Holothuroidea, the sea cucumbers; and Crinoidea, the sea lilies and feather stars.

Brittle stars, a member of the class Ophiuroidea, are similar to starfish, but brittle stars have very long, slender rays. A brittle star moves by pushing and pulling on objects in the water and by slithering like a snake. Their tube feet are poorly developed, and they are not adapted with suckers. In spite of these factors, brittle stars move fairly rapidly across the ocean bottom. Some members of this class are called basket stars because their rays branch and intertwine, forming a basketlike structure. Brittle stars and basket stars feed on mud and debris, but a few capture prey with their rays and bring it to their mouths. Brittle stars, however, have no digestive organs other than a mouth. They are scavengers, feeding on dead and decaying material. Brittle stars are also seen moving over the surface of other organisms such as corals and sponges. If you try to pick up a brittle star, parts of it will break off in your hand. However, brittle stars have an amazing capacity for regeneration. Broken rays grow back very quickly. In addition to this form of body part replacement, brittle stars reproduce sexually and have a free-swimming larval stage.

FIGURE 22–6.

Brittle stars feed on organisms that collect on sponges, corals, and rocks.

Sand dollars and sea urchins are members of the class Echinoidea. They do not have rays as do starfish and brittle stars. Sand dollars are round and flat. Their abandoned white exoskeletons are popular items to collect. In contrast, living sand dollars bristle with short, movable spines, each made of a single crystal of calcium carbonate. Interestingly, the tube feet of sand dollars are longer than those of starfish.

Sea urchins like the one in Figure 22–7 look much like living pincushions. All sea urchins have spherical bodies formed by tightly joined plates of the endoskeleton. Sea urchins have pedicellarias that contain poison sacs. Potential predators get a stinging pinch when they try to attack. Some sea urchin species have long, movable, pointed spines. Others have fat, blunt spines. Some of these spines aid the tube feet in walking. Sea urchins move slowly over the ocean floor, feeding with the help of five sharp teeth that are adapted for scraping and chewing. The structure that contains the teeth has the curious name of Aristotle's lantern. Some sea urchins live in shallow water on the edge of coral reefs where the action of waves threatens to wash them out to sea. These sea urchins are adapted with thick spines that hold them tightly in rocky crevices. They feed on a continuous supply of plankton brought to them in ocean waves.

pedicellaria:
pediculus (L) little foot

What structure in mollusks is similar in function to Aristotle's lantern?

Sand Dollar

What is a sea cucumber likely to do if the water temperature gets too high?

NoteWorthy

The most abundant species of echinoderm—found in the Philippine Trench at a depth of 10 540 m—is a sea cucumber.

Members of the class Holothuroidea are fat, pickle-shaped animals called sea cucumbers. Sea cucumbers, like the one in Figure 22–8, have a body with a circle of tentacles around a mouth. Rows of tube feet are found down the length of the body from the mouth to the anus. Instead of hard plates, they are adapted with a leathery covering that allows them greater motion than other echinoderms. Sea cucumbers pull themselves along the ocean floor using their tentacles and tube feet. Rows of tube feet on the ventral surface are used for movement. Those on the upper surface may be used for respiration. Sea cucumbers live their lives on the sea bottom, burrowing into the surface ooze or sand.

When sea cucumbers are threatened or find themselves in an unfavorable environment or in warmer waters, they display some curious behaviors. They may expel a tangled, sticky, stringy mass of tubes through the anus, or they may actually rupture, releasing some internal organs. A new set of internal organs is regenerated in about six weeks. Another adaptation is found in the larval stage. Sea cucumber larvae develop five pairs of tube feet around their mouths and a sixth pair near the anus. The larvae move about by walking on this pair of posterior tube feet.

FIGURE 22–8.

The body of a sea cucumber is leathery in comparison with the calcium carbonate plates of other echinoderms.

a

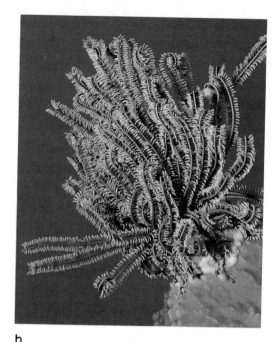

b

The class Crinoidea contains feather stars and sea lilies. There are about 630 species of crinoids living today. Crinoids are echinoderms that look like flowers. In contrast to starfish, both sea lilies and feather stars have both mouth and anus on the dorsal surface. The digestive and nervous systems are greatly reduced. Sea lilies have small, cupshaped bodies. Five flexible arms form narrow appendages attached to a central disc. Sea lilies are the only echinoderms that are sessile. They are attached to the ocean floor by a stalk. Feather stars attach to the ocean floor by a short stalk in the larval form, but as adults they are free-swimming. Feather stars are similar in appearance to sea lilies. They have flexible, rootlike appendages called **cirri** that grip the ocean floor. Feather stars can crawl through vegetation or move in a swimming fashion.

FIGURE 22–9.

The arms of feather stars divide many times, resulting in a feathered appearance (a). Sea lilies resemble fossil stalked echinoderms (b).

REVIEW

1. How does a starfish move?
2. Describe the difference in symmetry between larval and adult echinoderms.
3. What distinguishes sea cucumbers from other echinoderms?
4. **SKILL REVIEW:** Prepare a key that distinguishes between classes of echinoderms. Include information on number of rays, presence of spines, body shape, and other features you may find significant. For more help, refer to Organizing Information in the Skill Handbook, pages 810 to 813.
5. **USING CONCEPTS:** What are some adaptations of echinoderms that have resulted in their having few predators?

BIOLAB

Sea Urchin Development

22

Problem: What are the stages of sea urchin development?

Materials
microscope   colored pencils
prepared slides of sea urchin development

Procedures
1. Review the methods used for observing with a microscope. For more help, refer to Using a Microscope in the Skill Handbook, pages 804 to 805.
2. Make a copy of the data table shown.
3. Obtain a prepared slide of sea urchin development.
4. Observe each of the stages of sea urchin development. Pay particular attention to the arrangement of cells in each stage.
5. Draw and label as many stages of sea urchin development listed in the data table as you can see.
6. Return the slides to their proper place when you have completed the assignment.

Zygote	2–Cell Stage
8–Cell Stage	Blastula
Gastrula	Dipleurula

Data and Observations

Developmental Stage	Description of Stage
1-cell (Zygote)	
2-cell	
4-cell	
8-cell	
16-cell	
32-cell	
64-cell	
Hollow Ball (Blastula)	
3-cell layers (Gastrula)	
Larva (Dipleurula)	

Questions and Conclusion
1. During the first few cell divisions of the developing sea urchin, do the cells appear to grow in size or do they become smaller?
2. What is the shape of individual cells during the first few cell divisions?
3. Describe the cell positions in the hollow-ball stage.
4. Immediately after the hollow-ball stage, what appears to happen to the cells before the development of the larva?
5. What name is given to the larval stage of the sea urchin?
6. Describe the symmetry present in the larval stage of the sea urchin.

Conclusion: What stages of development does a sea urchin go through?

468 ECHINODERMS

ORIGINS AND IMPORTANCE OF ECHINODERMS

Echinoderms, as a group, date from the Paleozoic era. More than 13 000 fossil species have been identified. Of these extinct species, 5000 species were crinoids. There are approximately 6000 species of existing echinoderms.

22:5 The Phylogeny and Origins of Echinoderms

Zoologists hypothesize that echinoderms are the most advanced invertebrates because they have radial symmetry, a characteristic of simple animals, but also have complex organ systems. These features put the echinoderms in a separate position on the evolutionary scale from all the other animal phyla. The endoskeletons of echinoderms were easily fossilized. As a result, there is a good fossil record of this phylum. The underwater garden of extinct species illustrated in Figure 22–10 shows a sample of the varieties of forms that ancient members of this group apparently had. Some show shapes similar to the modern species. Others have shapes that are no longer represented.

The most primitive echinoderms were members of a class of organisms that had bilateral symmetry in their adult forms. This class is extinct. Like the modern crinoids, its members lived attached to the ocean floor by a stalk. Fossils of this group give the impression that they held their bodies parallel to the ocean floor. At least three other classes of echinoderms from the early Paleozoic era had stalks,

Objectives:
- discuss the evidence for the evolutionary position of echinoderms.
- describe how echinoderms may change the ecology of their environments.
- name two ways echinoderms are important to humans.

FIGURE 22–10.

Extinct echinoderm groups were probably all marine sea floor dwellers. Many were stalked.

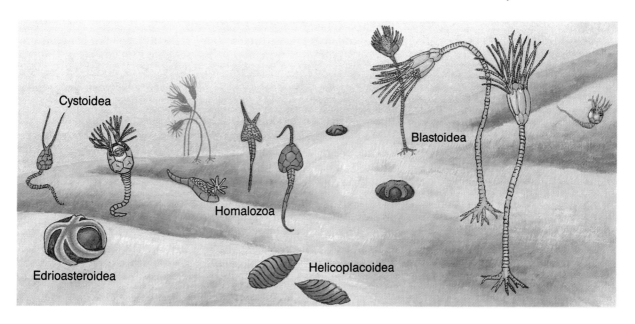

Cystoidea

Homalozoa

Edrioasteroidea

Helicoplacoidea

Blastoidea

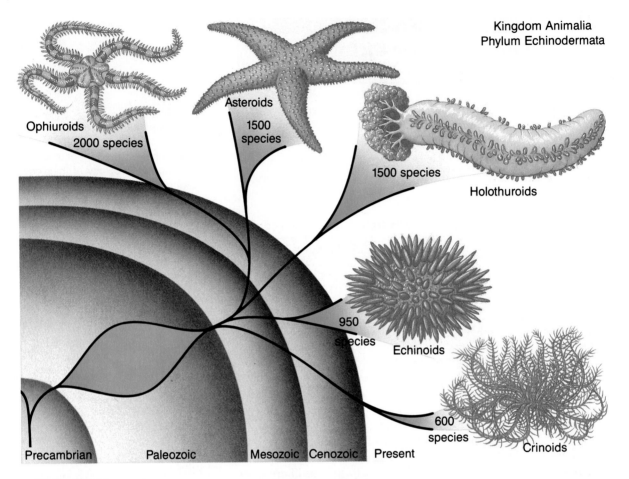

Kingdom Animalia
Phylum Echinodermata

Ophiuroids
2000 species

Asteroids
1500
species

1500 species
Holothuroids

950
species
Echinoids

600
species
Crinoids

Precambrian Paleozoic Mesozoic Cenozoic Present

FIGURE 22–11.

The radiation of classes of echinoderms on the geologic time scale
shows their relationships.

but these animals had radial symmetry. Today, all echinoderms have
radial symmetry in the adult form, but nearly all dipleurula have
bilateral symmetry. The development of a bilateral larva is the best
evidence scientists have for placing echinoderms where they are in
the evolutionary record.

Sea cucumbers, sea urchins, and starfish have all been found as
fossils from the early Paleozoic era. Fossils of brittle stars, on the
other hand, are found starting at a later period, about 275 million
years ago. During the span of 75 million years between the earliest
recorded starfish and the earliest recorded brittle stars, there are so
many fossils of echinoderms that a progression can be seen between
these two classes. Fossil records that show detailed progressive
change are rare. These fossils have led scientists to hypothesize that
brittle stars are an offshoot of starfish.

The evolutionary relationships among the classes of living echinoderms are complex. Crinoids include the primitive looking, free-
living feather stars. Crinoids do not seem to be closely related to the
other living classes of echinoderms. Of the other four classes, the
starfish and brittle stars appear to be near relatives because they all
have rays. The sea urchins and sea cucumbers are only distant
relatives of the other classes of echinoderms because their body
plans are different from starfish and brittle stars.

22:6 The Importance of Echinoderms

Echinoderms are of interest to scientists in medical research, studies of embryology, and for their vital roles within the environments they inhabit.

Echinoderms have played a role in medical research. Regeneration of rays in echinoderms has been studied extensively to help scientists learn how cells replace themselves. In echinoderms, cells and tissues near a damaged area rearrange themselves. New cells are produced that begin to function like the ones that were lost or damaged. Scientists look to this ability to regenerate lost tissue for clues on how to treat human patients with damage to tissues that can't be replaced, such as nerves.

Studies of sea urchins have provided new information about development of animal embryos in general. Messenger RNA may determine what proteins are made in the early sea urchin embryo. By studying sea urchin embryos, scientists may find clues that help in understanding embryo development in other animals, including humans.

In line with the lifestyle of many other marine inhabitants, echinoderms recycle nutrients in the ecosystem by feeding on dead and decaying materials. However, if starfish populations increase too rapidly, they can wipe out entire oyster beds in a short time. A single starfish can eat a dozen oysters or clams in a day. Oystermen used to cut up any starfish they caught while harvesting oysters. However because of the echinoderm's ability to regenerate, whole new populations of starfish were inadvertently started with this method, and the oyster farmer had a bigger problem. Millions of dollars worth of shellfish are destroyed annually by starfish and other echinoderms. In addition to this economic loss, echinoderms also disrupt the food web that depends upon oysters, clams, and other shellfish for food.

How does the ability of echinoderms to regenerate help medical scientists?

FIGURE 22–12.

A starfish can replace portions of its body by regeneration.

FIGURE 22–13.

The crown-of-thorns has been implicated in the extensive destruction of corals.

An echinoderm called the crown-of-thorns starfish is thought to be the cause of a great deal of damage to coral reefs in the Pacific Ocean. This species has been implicated in the death of more than 40 kilometers of coral along the coastline of Guam in a span of only two and a half years. It stands accused of even greater damage to the Great Barrier Reef of Australia. Where did all of these starfish come from? You may recall from Section 22:3 that starfish have few natural enemies, but in the Pacific there is a mollusk, the giant triton, which is known to eat the crown-of-thorns. The giant triton has a beautiful shell that is prized by collectors. Many giant tritons have been harvested in the Pacific by shell collectors. Scientists hypothesize that removal of this predator may be indirectly responsible for the destruction of the coral reef.

REVIEW

6. Why is there an excellent fossil record of echinoderms?
7. What is the evidence that echinoderms once had bilateral symmetry?
8. Name three ways in which echinoderms are important.
9. **SKILL REVIEW:** What is the suggested cause for the over-population of the crown-of-thorns starfish on Pacific reefs? What was the effect? For more help, refer to Reading Science in the Skill Handbook, pages 798 to 799.
10. **USING CONCEPTS:** If you were an oyster farmer, why would you be advised not to break apart and throw back any starfish that had moved into the oyster beds?

CAREER CHOICES

In this unit, you have learned about numerous invertebrates. The number of invertebrate organisms in the world presents scientists and others with a variety of occupations, from marine biologists who study the tiniest marine sponges, to beekeepers who daily work with an insect on whom the world's food resources depend.

Over 400 000 animal species inhabit Earth's oceans and are studied by **marine biologists.** The interests of marine biologists are almost as great as the number of organisms. As a marine biologist, you might study the evolutionary relationships among certain organisms to determine when and how life began. Others are interested in the ecological relationships among phyla, such as the problem between the crown-of-thorns starfish and the corals of the Great Barrier Reef that you read about in Chapter 22. Ecological marine biologists work to reduce the effects of pollution that occurs as a result of the dumping of garbage or chemical wastes in the world's oceans. Some marine biologists specialize in the physics and chemistry of ocean water and determine how tides, currents, waves, temperature, pressure, and salinity affect ocean life. Contrary to popular belief, very few marine biologists operate research vessels that embark on long oceanographic cruises. Much of the work of a marine biologist is done in the laboratory where research can be conducted under controlled conditions.

Marine Biologist

Oceans cover over 75 percent of Earth's surface. It is not surprising, then, that nearly 100 million metric tons of food is taken from the oceans each year. **Fishers** harvest food from water. Fishers catch much more than just fish. As a marine fisher, your catch might include lobsters, shrimp, and crabs, all of which are arthropods. Mollusks, such as clams and oysters, are collected by licensed clam diggers and oystermen from beds along seacoasts. Some countries practice mariculture, the farming of the ocean. Through careful selection of known breeding grounds, invertebrate food sources are harvested without exhausting the supply of organisms. To increase the supply of seafood, fishers may build artificial reefs made up of old building frameworks and even rubber tires, to give these organisms new places to breed in the ocean. Mariculture has successfully added to the world's food supply.

Fisher

Invertebrate zoologists who study the culture and breeding of bees are called **apiculturists.** Apiculturists maintain beehives from which honey and beeswax are harvested and sold. When working around the hives, an apiculturist wears protective clothing and a mask to keep from being stung. Many crops can be pollinated only by bees. Some apiculturists rent hives to farmers or orchard owners. Hundreds of thousands of bees are used each year to pollinate orchard crops. Apiculturists are also sometimes called to remove nests from buildings. Often the bees from these nests are taken back to the apiculturist's own hives. Many people keep a small number of hives as a hobby.

Apiculturist

CHAPTER REVIEW

SUMMARY

1. An echinoderm is a radially symmetrical invertebrate with a spiny outer covering, an endoskeleton, and a water vascular system. **22:1**
2. Starfish reproduce easily by regeneration. Free-swimming larvae are produced by sexual reproduction. **22:2**
3. Echinoderms are marine animals that feed on plankton, detritus, or mollusks. **22:3**
4. There are five classes of echinoderms with variations in structure and movement. **22:4**
5. Echinoderm fossils have left a rare, step-by-step record of adaptations. Echinoderms were once bilaterally symmetrical. **22:5**
6. Echinoderms are used in medical research and embryological studies. They are important marine inhabitants but become a hazard if populations go unchecked. **22:6**

LANGUAGE OF BIOLOGY

ampulla
biradial symmetry
cirri
detritus
dipleurula
eyespots

madreporite
pedicellarias
rays
tube feet
water vascular system

Choose the word or phrase from the list above that completes the sentence.

1. A(n) ____ is a ciliated larva of an echinoderm.
2. Small, pincerlike ____ are a protective adaptation for many echinoderms.
3. Some brittle stars feed on ____, the decaying material that accumulates on the bottom of the ocean.
4. A(n) ____ is a simple sensory structure located at the tip of a ray.
5. The flexible, rootlike appendages of feather stars are ____.

6. The hydraulic pressure control system that regulates movement of an echinoderm is the ____.
7. When muscles in a(n) ____ contract, water is forced into a tube foot.
8. The sieve-like opening of the water vascular system that prevents material from entering the animal is the ____.
9. Most echinoderms have body parts arranged in five or more ____.
10. ____ are hollow, thin-walled tubes with suckers that enable an echinoderm to move.

REVIEWING CONCEPTS

Choose the word or phrase that completes the sentence or answers the question.

11. Most echinoderms are equipped with ____.
    a. nematocysts   c. spines
    b. brains   d. radulas
12. The ____ of many echinoderms are made of calcium carbonate plates.
    a. endoskeletons   c. ampullae
    b. tube feet   d. cirri
13. A typical echinoderm is a(n) ____.
    a. hermaphrodite   c. heterotroph
    b. producer   d. autotroph
14. The ____ is the most primitive class of echinoderms.
    a. Asteroidea   c. Echinoidea
    b. Ophiuroidea   d. Crinoidea
15. All echinoderms move by ____.
    a. swimming
    b. water propulsion
    c. using tube feet
    d. using rays
16. In a water vascular system, water flows out through the ____.
    a. tubercles   c. madreporite
    b. pedicellarias   d. tube feet

17. Echinoderms are important in research because of their ____.
    a. feeding habits
    b. ability to regenerate
    c. tube feet
    d. eyespots
18. ____ expel their internal organs in unfavorable conditions.
    a. Starfish   c. Sea urchins
    b. Sea cucumbers   d. Sea lilies
19. You would expect to find an echinoderm in a(n) ____ habitat.
    a. lake   c. stream
    b. river   d. ocean
20. Feather stars move about on their ____.
    a. stalks   c. crinoids
    b. cirri   d. ampullae

UNDERSTANDING CONCEPTS

Answer the following questions using complete sentences.

21. How do starfish feed?
22. How is a dipleurula different from an adult echinoderm?
23. What is the advantage of a spiny outer covering in echinoderms?
24. Why are fossils of echinoderms more common than worm fossils?
25. Explain how the water vascular system works in a starfish.
26. Explain why sea cucumbers are not typical echinoderms.
27. Explain the function of the madreporite.
28. Why are echinoderms important in the ecology of coral reefs?
29. What do echinoderms feed on?
30. What feature gives evidence that echinoderms were once bilaterally symmetrical?

APPLYING CONCEPTS

Answer the following questions using complete sentences.

31. Compare the pedicellarias of echinoderms with the nematocysts in cnidarians.
32. If echinoderms were related to annelids or arthropods, what adaptation might be made in the echinoderm endoskeletal plates and body plan?
33. Explain why an oyster farmer would be concerned about starfish populations.
34. What advantages might an asteroid species have over a crinoid species?
35. How has the excessive harvesting of the giant triton mollusk affected the Great Barrier Reef?

EXTENSIONS

1. Prepare a report on one kind of echinoderm. Include important lifestyle and ecological considerations as they affect human activity.
2. Write a paragraph describing a day in the life of a particular echinoderm from the point of view of the echinoderm.
3. Set up a saltwater aquarium with one or two starfish and sea urchins. Observe the behavior of the starfish when you drop some live oysters into the tank.

READINGS

Brower, Kenneth. "State of the Reef." *Audubon,* Mar. 1989, pp. 56–80.

Rush, Elizabeth. "Diving for Gold: The Saga of the Sea Urchin." *Outdoor California,* Sept.–Oct. 1988, pp. 1–5.

Sugar, James A., "Starfish Threaten Pacific Reefs." *National Geographic,* Mar. 1970, pp. 340–353.

VERTEBRATES

He clasps the crag with crooked hands;
Close to the sun in lonely lands,
Ringed with the azure world he stands.

The wrinkled sea beneath him crawls;
He watches from his mountain walls,
And like a thunderbolt he falls.

Alfred, Lord Tennyson
"The Eagle"

Chapter 23

BIRDS AND
REPTILES

AMPHIBIANS
AND FISH

STARFISH

ANIMALS

478

ARTHROPODS

FISH AND AMPHIBIANS

I magine you lived in a vast, watery world. How would you get oxygen and food? How would you keep from sinking? You would need certain adaptations in structure and behavior to survive and reproduce. What about organisms that live on land? What kinds of problems do they face? Obtaining oxygen may be easier than in water, but support and movement are more difficult. Without moist surroundings, an organism is at risk for drying out. Amphibians, such as the one shown here, have solved some of the problems of living on land, while fish, shown left, are adapted to life in water. In this chapter, you will learn about the adaptations of fish to their watery realm and the evolutionary changes that allowed amphibians to move onto land.

Salamander

VERTEBRATES AND THEIR RELATIVES

You are a vertebrate, an animal with a backbone. There are many kinds of vertebrates, some of which directly affect your life. Perhaps you are wearing a wool sweater. Wool is a vertebrate product. If you hear birds singing as you walk home, you are listening to vertebrate music. Do you have a pet? Your pet is likely to be a vertebrate, whether it lives in water, has wings, barks, or purrs.

23:1 Chordates

All vertebrates are members of the phylum Chordata. Chordates are grouped into three subphyla. Two of these, Urochordata (YUR uh kord AH tuh) and Cephalochordata (SEF uh luh kord AH tuh), contain only small, marine animals. Subphylum Vertebrata includes fish, amphibians, reptiles, birds, and mammals.

Animals in Subphylum Urochordata are called tunicates or sea squirts. Tunicates are small, tubular animals that are microscopic to several centimeters long. Most adult tunicates live attached to objects on the sea floor. Tunicates take in water through one tube and force it out through another. Food and oxygen are filtered from the water as it passes through the animal's body. This lifestyle, called filter-feeding, is similar to that of many invertebrates, such as clams.

Objectives:
- list the characteristics of chordates.
- name and describe the three chordate subphyla.
- analyze evolutionary trends and adaptations in vertebrates.

Schooling fish

cephalochordata:
cephale (GK) head
chorda (L) cord
urochordata:
oura (GK) tail
chorda (L) cord
notochord:
noton (GK) back

What are three characteristics of chordates?

Animals in subphylum Cephalochordata are called lancelets. Lancelets are small, marine creatures, 5 to 7 cm long. Notice in Figure 23–1 that lancelets are shaped somewhat like fish. They can swim freely in the water, but they spend most of their time buried in the sand with only their heads sticking out. Like tunicates, lancelets are filter-feeders.

The third chordate subphylum, Vertebrata, is considered more complex than the tunicates and lancelets. The vertebrates show an amazing variety of adaptations to many different environments. In particular, they are well adapted to life on land. They have more complicated homeostatic mechanisms, which are necessary for varied adaptations, than any other animal group.

You may be asking yourself, "What could I possibly have in common with a sea squirt? Why are we both considered chordates?" You, the sea squirt, and all other chordates have three traits in common—a notochord, a dorsal nerve cord, and paired gill slits. A **notochord** is a tough, flexible, rodlike structure that runs along the back of an animal. In most vertebrates, the notochord exists only in the embryo. A backbone develops and replaces the notochord, which then disappears. A **dorsal nerve cord** is a bundle of nerves that lies above the notochord. In most adult chordates, the dorsal nerve cord has developed into the spinal cord. The front end of the spinal cord develops into the brain. **Gill slits** are paired openings located in the throat behind the mouth. Adult lancelets and tunicates retain the gill slits, while in fish, the gill slits develop into gills. In most land-living chordates, the gill slits disappear during embryonic development. Figure 23–2 shows the three characteristics of chordates.

b

a

FIGURE 23–1.

Lancelets (a) and tunicates (b) are small marine chordates.

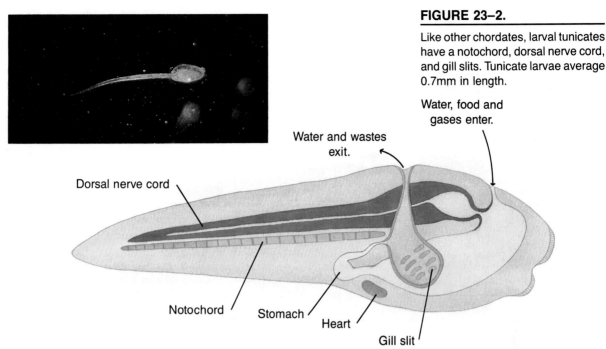

FIGURE 23–2.

Like other chordates, larval tunicates have a notochord, dorsal nerve cord, and gill slits. Tunicate larvae average 0.7mm in length.

Water, food and gases enter.

Water and wastes exit.

Dorsal nerve cord

Notochord

Stomach

Heart

Gill slit

23:2 Adaptations of Vertebrates

Sharks, frogs, snakes, robins, horses, and whales are all vertebrates. Vertebrates live nearly everywhere—in the ocean, in freshwater lakes and streams, on land, and in the air. Fish are the most common vertebrates in watery habitats. Many frogs live in and around ponds. Most snakes live on land. Birds, of course, are experts in flight, although they do nest on land. Most mammals, such as horses, are land-dwelling. Whales, however, live in the sea.

What characteristics do all vertebrates have in common that allow them to inhabit nearly every environment on Earth? All vertebrates have endoskeletons. The endoskeleton of most vertebrates includes a skull, backbone, and jointed appendages or limbs. The endoskeleton provides vertebrates with a distinct advantage over organisms with exoskeletons. Unlike an exoskeleton, an endoskeleton does not have to be shed to allow growth. Consequently, vertebrates can be enormous. Whales and elephants are the largest animals in the world. An endoskeleton also provides a large amount of surface for muscle attachment. The muscles attached to the endoskeleton allow a variety of movements.

All vertebrates have a closed circulatory system and a heart subdivided into chambers for more efficient pumping of the blood. Gas exchange takes place across gills or lungs. Although many invertebrates have gills, their gills are not very efficient at removing oxygen from the water. Fish are capable of removing 85 percent of the oxygen from water that passes over their gills. The chambered heart and efficient respiratory system allow for an active lifestyle.

Vertebrates have highly evolved nervous systems with complex brains and sense receptors. Many vertebrates have eyes, ears, taste receptors, and a highly developed sense of smell.

What is the function of the endoskeleton?

FIGURE 23–3.

Vertebrates have a variety of adaptations for locomotion.

23:3 Evolutionary Trends in Vertebrates

An important change in the evolution of vertebrates was the development of a more complex heart. Fish have a two-chambered heart, most reptiles and all amphibians have three-chambered hearts, and birds and mammals have four-chambered hearts. The difference between a four-chambered heart and a two- or three-chambered heart is that a four-chambered heart keeps oxygen-rich blood separate from oxygen-poor blood. This separation allows for a higher level of oxygen in the blood and more efficient delivery of oxygen to cells. The more oxygen cells receive, the more energy they produce during cellular respiration. This higher level of energy allows birds and mammals to be more active than fish, reptiles, or amphibians.

Adaptations for locomotion in vertebrates evolved in response to changing habitat requirements. Fish and some mammals evolved body shapes and muscles adapted for swimming. Land dwellers evolved limbs and muscles adapted for walking or flying.

An important adaptation in birds and mammals is the ability to maintain a high, constant body temperature. The high body temperature, resulting from a high rate of metabolism, permits birds and mammals to inhabit areas of the world where reptiles and amphibians can't live. Some scientists believe that the dinosaurs were driven to extinction by the cooling of Earth. Mammals, on the other hand, were equipped to handle the colder climate and, thus, survived.

REVIEW

1. List three characteristics of chordates.
2. What are the characteristics of a tunicate?
3. List three adaptations that allowed vertebrates to become successful.
4. **SKILL REVIEW:** Sequence the changes in anatomy that took place in vertebrates as they evolved. For more help, refer to Reading Science in the Skill Handbook, pages 798 to 799.
5. **USING CONCEPTS:** How is the ability to maintain a high body temperature an advantage to birds and mammals?

FISH

Objectives:
- recognize the traits of fish.
- name several adaptations in fish.
- compare the lifestyles of the three classes of fish.
- summarize how fish evolved.
- state why fish are important.

Have you ever been fishing? Do you remember the excitement you felt as a sudden tug on your line meant the bait was taken? Have you ever visited an aquarium to see strange, silent fish gliding through the water? You probably have heard stories of schools of piranhas with sawlike teeth that can reduce a horse to a skeleton in minutes. There are more than 30 000 kinds of fish. In fact, there are more kinds of fish than all other kinds of vertebrates added together!

23:4 The Life of a Fish

All fish live in water. Fish have three characteristics that allow them to live successfully in a watery habitat. First, all fish breathe with gills, Figure 23–4. Gills are structures located in the throat region that remove oxygen from water as it passes over them. Carbon dioxide is given off to the water surrounding the gills. Second, fish have fins. **Fins** are fan-shaped membranes, supported by rays or spines, that are used for steering and locomotion during swimming. In some cases, fins are used for defense. Finally, fish have scales. **Scales** are thin, round disks that cover and protect the body. The ages of some fish can be estimated by counting annual growth rings in their scales and bones. The longest-lived fish are lake sturgeons, which may reach 80 years of age. The fish with the shortest life cycles are gobies, which live for a single year. Fish are gracefully streamlined, with a body consisting of a head, trunk, and tail.

Fish are adapted to their environments in a variety of ways. For example, freshwater fish have a tendency to absorb water. Their kidneys are capable of excreting the excess water. Saltwater fish tend to lose water and have kidneys that are adapted to retaining water.

Fish have a variety of adaptations for getting food. The archerfish swims to the surface of the water and shoots a drop of water from its mouth toward an unsuspecting insect. The drop of water knocks the insect into the water and it becomes a meal. Swordfish swim into schools of fish and lash their swordlike snouts back and forth to kill their prey. The anglerfish has a lure projecting from its head and suspended just above its mouth. You can guess how it works!

What are three main characteristics of fish?

FIGURE 23–4.

Fish have gills for taking in oxygen and scales for protection. They also are streamlined, as evidenced by the photo of a garden eel.

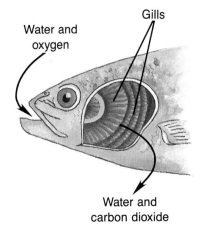

Water and oxygen

Gills

Water and carbon dioxide

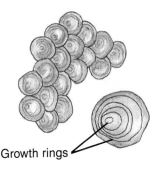

Growth rings

Other adaptations in fish are related to a variety of activities. Marine catfish carry their eggs in their mouths to protect them until they hatch. Fish that live in the Antarctic have a chemical in their blood similar to antifreeze to protect them from freezing. When threatened, pufferfish inflate themselves to several times their normal size. How is this an adaptation for defense?

23:5 Phylogeny of Fish

Jawless Fish

The simplest fish belong to the class Agnatha (ag NAYTH uh), the jawless fish. Figure 23–5 shows the two types of jawless fish, lampreys and hagfish. Both of these fish have long, tubular bodies and lack scales. Their skeletons are made of a tough, flexible material called **cartilage.** The skeleton contains no bone.

Even though lampreys and hagfish resemble one another, they are believed to be only distantly related because of differences in feeding behavior, metabolism, and reproduction. Many lampreys are parasites of other fish. A lamprey attaches itself to a fish with its round, sucker-like mouth. It then cuts into its host with sharp, toothlike structures and feeds on the host's blood and body fluids. Hagfish are scavengers, feeding on dead marine organisms. Hagfish spend their days hiding in the mud at the bottom of the ocean. When touched, their skin gives off tremendous amounts of mucus, thus allowing the fish to slither away without becoming a meal.

Hagfish are unlike other marine vertebrates in that their bodies are osmotically balanced with the surrounding water. Thus, they do not tend to lose water. Also unlike other fish, hagfish don't have separate sexes; they are hermaphrodites. A hagfish can produce either egg or sperm, although not in the same breeding season.

Agnatha:
  a (GK) not
  gnathos (GK) jaw

FIGURE 23–5.

The round, jawless mouth of a lamprey is lined with sharp, toothlike structures. Hagfish feed on the ocean bottom, as shown in this illustration. Both are jawless fish.

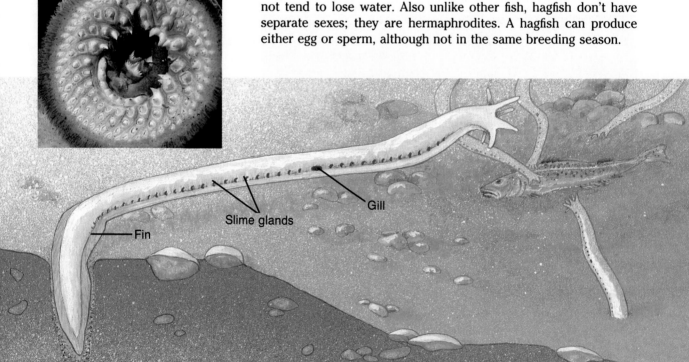

Fin

Slime glands

Gill

Enamel–like
surface

Dentin

Epidermis

Dermis

Pulp cavity

FIGURE 23–6.

Sharks have streamlined bodies and rows of sharp teeth. Their scales, shown lower right, are similar in structure to teeth.

Cartilaginous Fish

Sharks and rays belong to the class Chondrichthyes (kahn DRIK theez), the cartilaginous fish. As in jawless fish, the skeleton is formed of cartilage rather than bone. Sharks and rays are covered with scales that have toothlike spines. These spines are similar in structure and composition to teeth. Sharks and rays have well-developed jaws.

When you think of sharks, you may think of gaping jaws with rows of razor-sharp teeth. As you can see in Figure 23–6, some sharks are well-equipped to be predators. A **predator** is an animal that captures and eats other organisms. A shark's streamlined body is geared for fast movement. The pectoral fins in front and pelvic fins in back control turning movements. The powerful tail fin moves from side to side, propelling the shark forward. Movable jaws allow for grasping and crushing prey. **Prey** are organisms eaten by predators. The six to twenty rows of teeth are continually replaced and point backward to prevent prey from escaping once caught.

Success as a predator is also the result of the shark's highly developed sensory system. Like cats, sharks are well adapted to seeing in dim light. Sharks have an incredibly sensitive sense of smell and can detect extremely small amounts of chemicals in the water. Sharks can follow a trail of blood through the water for several kilometers. This ability helps them to locate prey. Sharks also can detect movement and vibrations in the water by means of their lateral line systems. The **lateral line system** is a network of fluid-filled canals running from the head down the sides of a fish. The lateral line system responds to changes in water pressure and currents.

What makes a shark such a good predator?

Chondrichthyes:
  chondros (GK) cartilage
  ichthys (GK) fish

a

b

FIGURE 23–7.

Rays have flat bodies with broad fins (a). Numerous bony fish species live on coral reefs (b).

Osteichthyes:
  osteon (GK) bone
  ichthys (GK) fish

To breathe, a shark takes in water through its mouth as it swims. The water flows out through the gills. Sharks are unable to move their gills in and out to move water across them. Therefore, most sharks must continue to swim to get oxygen. Unlike most fish, fertilization in sharks is internal. In some kinds of sharks, the fertilized eggs develop inside the body of the female. The young are then born alive. Development of the eggs inside the female's body prevents them from being eaten by predators. As a result, more offspring survive until birth.

Most rays are predators that feed on or near the ocean floor. As shown in Figure 23–7a, rays have flat bodies and broad pectoral fins. By slowly flapping its fins up and down, a ray can glide over the ocean bottom, searching for mollusks and crustaceans. A ray takes in water through openings on its head. The ray then closes the openings, forcing water over the gills where gas exchange takes place. Some rays have sharp spines with poison glands on their long tails for defense. Others have organs that can generate electricity. These organs are used to kill prey or predators.

Bony Fish

Bony fish make up the largest group of fish, class Osteichthyes (ahs tee IK theez). Figure 23–7b shows the enormous variety in this class. All bony fish have gills and highly developed sense organs, including lateral lines, and fins. Unlike sharks, the cartilage in the skeleton of a bony fish is replaced by bone during growth. Bone is harder than cartilage and provides a more supportive framework. Scales of bony fish are round disks that overlap, like shingles on a roof. While the scales of sharks are made of the same materials that form teeth, the scales of bony fish are made primarily of bone. Scales, with their slippery mucus covering, allow fish to move through water with minimal friction. Many bony fish have a swim bladder. A **swim bladder** is a thin-walled internal sac that can be filled with air. By letting air in or out of the swim bladder, a bony fish can control its depth in the water. Locate the swim bladder in Figure 23–8.

Bony fish vary in appearance, behavior, and lifestyle. Predatory fish usually have sleek bodies with powerful muscles and tail fins for fast swimming. Eels are long and snakelike and can wriggle through mud and crevices in search of food. Some bony fish have flat bodies and creep sluggishly along the ocean bottom searching for food. Such fish blend with their surroundings as a means of protection. Some bony fish live solitary lives, while others live together in large groups called schools. A large school of fish may look like one large fish to a predator, thus discouraging an attack.

In most kinds of bony fish, the sexes are separate and fertilization is external. Breeding in fish is called **spawning.** Some fish, such as eels and salmon, migrate thousands of miles to reproduce. Pacific and Atlantic salmon follow chemical signals in the water back to the freshwater streams where they hatched. Freshwater European eels swim to the Atlantic to spawn.

Bony fish are divided into three groups: the lobe-finned fish, the lungfish, and the ray-finned fish. Coelacanths (SEE luh kanths) have lobelike, fleshy fins and live at very great depths where they are difficult to find. Until 1938, coelacanths were thought to have become extinct 70 million years ago. However, since that time several of these lobe-finned oddities have been caught and studied, Figure 23–9. Coelacanths are similar to the lobe-finned fish thought to be the ancient ancestors of amphibians. As far as scientists know, coelacanths are the only living lobe-finned fish. They are sometimes referred to as "living fossils" because they have changed very little since they first appeared 400 million years ago.

What is the function of the swim bladder?

FIGURE 23–8.

Bony fish are characterized by overlapping scales, a lateral line, and a swim bladder.

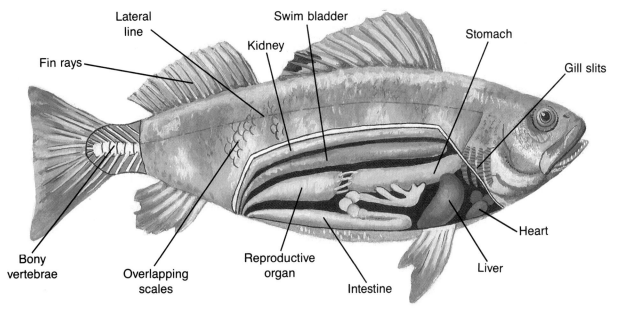

Lateral line

Kidney

Swim bladder

Stomach

Fin rays

Gill slits

Bony vertebrae

Overlapping scales

Reproductive organ

Intestine

Liver

Heart

FIGURE 23–9.

Coelacanths are lobe-finned fish that evolved 400 million years ago.

Lungfish have both lungs and gills for breathing. One type of lungfish burrows in the mud in streams and breathes through lungs when the streams dry out. Another lungfish survives in oxygen-poor water by gulping air at the surface.

Ray-finned fish have fins supported by stiff, narrow rods called **rays.** These fish are probably the most familiar to you because they are the most numerous. Ray-finned fish live in tropical waters, temperate waters, and Arctic and Antarctic waters. Some live near the water's surface, others on the bottom.

23:6 Origins of Fish

The fossil record for fish is very incomplete. However, it is suspected that the jawless ostracoderms (uh STRAK uh durmz), the first vertebrates, were the direct ancestors of present-day jawless fish, the agnathans. Ostracoderms first appeared about 500 million years ago. The cartilaginous and bony fish possibly evolved from ancient armored fish called placoderms (PLAK uh durmz). Placoderms were the first vertebrates with jaws and first appeared 440 million years ago. Having jaws gave placoderms a tremendous advantage over ostracoderms because it allowed them to be predators and feed on a large variety of food items. Placoderms also had well-developed paired fins. Thus, they were highly mobile and able to chase their prey.

Because the ostracoderms lacked jaws, they were limited to sifting through the bottom mud for small organisms. Unfortunately for the ostracoderms, they were not as well adapted as the jawed fish and they became extinct during the Paleozoic era.

Why did ostracoderms become extinct?

ostracoderm:
ostrakon (GK) shell
derma (GK) skin
placoderm:
plax (GK) plate
derma (GK) skin

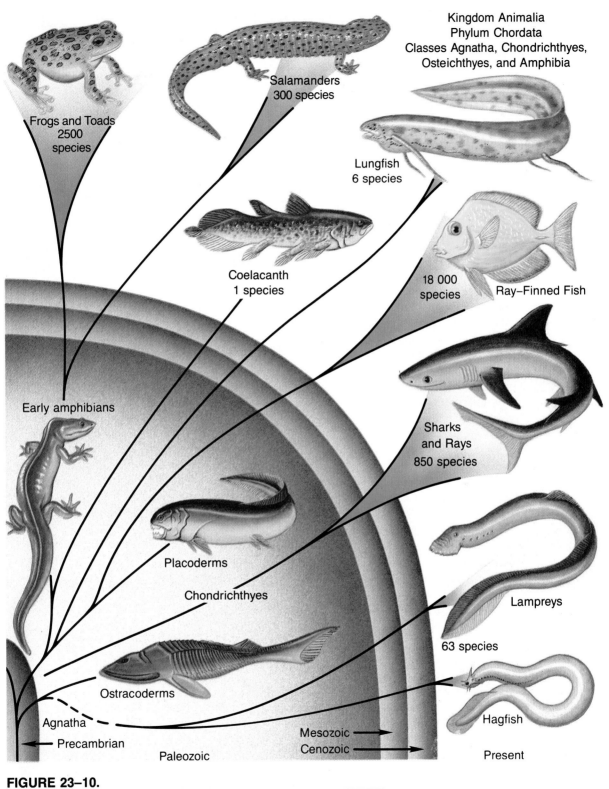

Kingdom Animalia
Phylum Chordata
Classes Agnatha, Chondrichthyes,
Osteichthyes, and Amphibia

Frogs and Toads
2500
species

Salamanders
300 species

Lungfish
6 species

Coelacanth
1 species

18 000
species

Ray–Finned Fish

Early amphibians

Sharks
and Rays
850 species

Placoderms

Chondrichthyes

Lampreys

63 species

Ostracoderms

Hagfish

Agnatha

Precambrian

Mesozoic

Cenozoic

Present

Paleozoic

FIGURE 23–10.

The radiation of classes of fish and orders of amphibians on the geologic
time scale shows their relationships.

BIOLAB

Fish Habitats

Problem: Do tropical fish prefer specific types of habitat?

Materials

aquarium setup
tropical fish (zebra, catfish, gourami)
timer
stopwatch (2)
black construction paper
masking tape
fish net

Procedures

1. Copy the data table.
2. Your teacher will assign you one of the tropical fish to test. Place the fish into the aquarium as shown in the diagram. **CAUTION:** *Always use care when handling live animals.* Wait three minutes for the animal to become accustomed to the surroundings. Develop a **hypothesis** about which part of the tank the fish will spend most of its time in.
3. Set the timer for two minutes and start one of the stopwatches. Note whether the fish is over the black gravel or the white gravel. When the fish swims over the center line, stop the first watch and start the second watch. When the fish swims over the center line again, stop the second watch. Continue to time the fish until two minutes is up.
4. Add up and record the total time spent over each color gravel in your table.
5. Note the horizontal line drawn on the side of the tank. Develop a **hypothesis** as in step 2. Using the same timing procedure as in step 3, time how long the fish spends in the top half and the bottom half of the tank. Add up and record the times in your table.
6. Cover the half of the aquarium that has black gravel with black construction paper on the sides and top of the tank. Develop a **hypothesis** as in step 2. Time the fish to see how long it spends in the light half and the dark half of the tank. Add up and record the times in your table.
7. Put your data on the chalkboard and compare it with that for the other two fish.

Data and Observations

Time in Seconds		
white gravel	black gravel	top of tank
light side	dark side	bottom of tank

Questions and Conclusion

1. Which fish preferred dark gravel? What colors were these fish?
2. Which fish preferred the dark half of the tank? What colors were these fish?
3. Which fish preferred the top of the aquarium? Which preferred the bottom?
4. Do your data for each habitat type support your **hypotheses?** Explain.

Conclusion: What types of habitats do different species of tropical fish prefer?

POPULATION GROWTH IN FISH

Scientists have developed mathematical equations for growth of natural populations. Two types of population growth can be described. The two types of populations are called r-selected populations and K-selected populations.

R-selected animals are small, have short lives, large numbers of young, and give little or no care to their young. They are well adapted to environments that are changeable. Examples of r-selected organisms include insects, crustaceans, and bacteria. In good conditions, their numbers multiply rapidly; in poor conditions, only a few survivors develop from the large numbers of eggs that are produced.

K-selected organisms are large, slow-growing, and long-lived. They produce few young, and generally provide care for them. Humans, whales, and crocodiles are examples of K-selected organisms. K-selected species do best in stable, unchanging environments, where their smaller numbers of offspring tend to survive.

The fishing industry finds that in the sea, catches of bony fish are often highly variable from year to year. One year, bony fish may be great in number and the next year, very few in number. Catches of sharks also vary, but in a different way. The catch will be good for several years, then begins to decline. Suddenly, sharks will disappear. It takes several years before they reappear.

Based on the observations of the fishing industry, are bony fish r-selected or K-selected? Explain. Are sharks r-selected or K-selected? Explain.

What kinds of population growth can be seen in sharks and bony fish?

23:7 The Importance of Fish

Many fish have relationships with other fish or marine organisms in which both benefit. Angelfish clean parasites off other fish. The brilliant colors of angelfish serve to advertise the cleaning stations they set up and guard. The angelfish benefits by having a readily available food source. Sharks and remoras also share a relationship that is beneficial to both. A remora has suckers with which it attaches to a shark and removes parasites from the shark's skin. In return, the remora receives a free ride and protection from the shark. Bitterling fish lay their eggs inside mussel shells. When the young fish leave the shell, young mussels attach to them and are thus transported to a new habitat. Shrimp construct burrows in which they and the goby both live. The goby, with its better eyesight, warns the shrimp when predators approach so the shrimp can retreat to the burrow. In the sea, sharks fulfill the same role as do lions and tigers on land. As predators, sharks keep prey populations healthy by limiting the sizes of the populations. Without sharks, prey species would increase in number and be subject to starvation and disease.

List three ways in which fish are important to other animals.

a

b

FIGURE 23–11.

A remora (a) is a fish that attaches to sharks and eats parasites on the shark's skin. The pufferfish (b) produces a poison that may have anesthetic properties.

In what two ways are fish important to humans in the field of biomedicine?

Fish are an important food source to large numbers of aquatic animals, including many sea mammals. Fish are also one of the most important sources of protein for humans. Important commercial fish include herring, tuna, swordfish, red snapper, flounder, and salmon. Recreational fishing has millions of enthusiasts. Many people raise tropical fish as a hobby. Fish products are also important. For example, fish oil is used in the manufacture of soap, paint, and glue.

In addition to being a valuable food source, fish are important in the biomedical field. Studies of dogfish cells are leading to an understanding of how the nucleus communicates with the outside of the cell. Poison from the pufferfish is being studied as a possible anesthetic. Recent studies have shown that consumption of fish oils may protect blood vessels against fat deposits that lead to heart disease.

REVIEW

6. List three characteristics of fish.
7. Compare the lifestyles of jawless fish with the lifestyles of cartilaginous fish.
8. Name three ways fish are ecologically beneficial.
9. **SKILL REVIEW:** Using Figure 23–10, sequence the evolutionary development of the different groups of fish. For more help, refer to Reading Science in the Skill Handbook, pages 798 to 799.
10. **USING CONCEPTS:** What homeostatic mechanisms do fish have that show they are more complex than mollusks and worms?

AMPHIBIANS

If an alien visitor to our planet were to watch our television programs and read our children's literature, it might return home with wondrous stories of how frogs on Earth can "talk" and change into princes with a kiss. Frogs and toads don't talk, but they do change—from fishlike tadpoles to four-legged animals with bulging eyes, loud songs, and remarkable jumping ability. In this section you will study frogs, toads, and salamanders—the amphibians.

23:8 The Life of an Amphibian

Most amphibians live a double life—one in water and one on land. Frogs and toads hatch from eggs laid in the water and grow into fishlike tadpoles. Tadpoles have fins, gills, and a two-chambered heart. As tadpoles grow into adult frogs and toads, they develop legs, lungs, and a three-chambered heart. Salamanders also hatch in the water. Young salamanders resemble the adults, but they have gills and, usually, a tail fin. Most adult salamanders lack gills and fins. Instead, they breathe with lungs and have four legs for moving about.

The skin of most amphibians is moist and smooth and lacks scales. The moistness of the skin allows for gas exchange. In addition, gas exchange takes place at the skin lining the mouth and in the lungs. Many amphibian species have webbed feet for swimming.

Objectives:
- recognize the characteristics that all amphibians have in common.
- describe and compare the life-styles of frogs, toads, and salamanders.
- summarize the evolutionary history of amphibians.
- state why amphibians are important to the ecology and to humans.

FIGURE 23–12.

The amphibian life cycle includes an aquatic tadpole stage and a terrestrial adult stage.

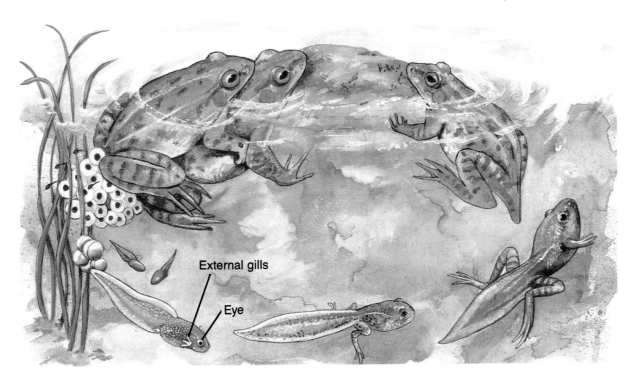

External gills

Eye

a   b

FIGURE 23–13.

The American toad (a) and the bull-frog (b) are tailless amphibians. Note the large tympanum behind the eye of the bullfrog.

Although most adult amphibians are capable of a terrestrial existence, nearly all of them rely on water for breeding. Their eggs lack protective membranes and shells and must be laid in water to keep them moist. Fertilization in most amphibians is external. Therefore, water is needed as a medium for transporting sperm.

Amphibians are ectotherms. An **ectotherm** is an animal in which the body temperature changes with the temperature of the surroundings. As a result of being ectotherms, amphibians are more numerous in regions that have warm temperatures all year. Amphibians are also more numerous where moisture is abundant. In regions that are periodically dry and in places that become cold for part of the year, amphibians become dormant. During such times, they burrow into the mud and stay there until suitable environmental conditions return. In the drier regions of Africa and Australia, some amphibians may remain dormant for years during times of drought.

23:9 Phylogeny of Amphibians

Frogs and Toads

The order Anura includes frogs and toads. Frogs are short and broad with bulging eyes, no distinct neck, long hind legs, and no tail. You may live in a part of the country where spring evenings are filled with the sounds of chorusing frogs. Frogs and toads have vocal cords that are capable of producing a wide range of sounds. **Vocal cords** are sound-producing bands of tissue in the throat. If you stretch a rubber band between two fingers and then draw another finger across it, the resulting vibration will make a sound. Vocal cords work in a similar way. As air passes over the vocal cords, they vibrate and cause the air to vibrate. Most male frogs have inflatable throat pouches that increase the volume of the sounds they make. In the spring, males call or sing to attract females. The male grasps the female and fertilizes her eggs as she lays them in the water.

anura:

   a (GK) not
   oura (GK) tail

NoteWorthy

Certain frogs protect their eggs and developing tadpoles in their vocal sacs.

Frogs have extremely sticky tongues for catching insects and worms. The tongue is fastened to the front of the mouth, instead of the back. A frog hunts by sitting partially submerged in the water with only its bulging eyes and nostrils visible. When an insect flies within range, the frog flicks out its tongue and, with unerring accuracy, snares its prey.

Frogs lack the lateral lines used by fish as sense organs. Instead, an adult frog relies on its senses of vision and hearing and on its strong hind legs for protection. You may have tried to capture a frog with your bare hands and discovered just how effective its defense mechanisms are. A frog senses vibrations by means of tympanic membranes. A **tympanic membrane** is a circular structure located on each side of the head just behind the eyes. A tympanic membrane works like a drum. It picks up vibrations from the air or water and transmits them to the frog's inner ear and then to the brain.

How does the tympanic membrane function?

Toads are very much like frogs, except they are adapted to drier environments. Toads have thick, bumpy skin that keeps them from drying out. The bumps are poison glands that serve as protection against predators. Toads have shorter legs than frogs and hop rather than jump as frogs do. Even though they are protected from drying out better than frogs are, toads still need water to breed. Their eggs, like frog eggs, do not have shells or membranes.

Salamanders

The order Urodela (yoor uh DEHL uh) includes the salamanders. Unlike a frog, a salamander has a long, slender body with a neck and tail. As you can see in Figure 23–14a, salamanders resemble lizards. However, salamanders have smooth, moist skin and lack claws. The legs of a salamander are short and attached to the sides of the body. Thus, salamanders walk with a kind of shuffle.

a

FIGURE 23–14.

Salamander traits can be seen in this spotted salamander (a). Mud puppies (b) retain their gills as adults.

b

Salamanders have more varied habits and habitats than frogs do. Some salamanders are totally aquatic, while others live in damp places on land. Some salamanders, such as the mud puppy, retain their gills throughout adulthood, Figure 23–14b. Some species of salamanders have no lungs or gills and exchange gas through their skins. Salamanders eat worms and small arthropods, the same diet preferred by frogs.

23:10 Origins of Amphibians

You have seen a variety of ways in which amphibians are a link between life in water and life on land. The fossil record shows that amphibians first appeared about 350 million years ago. Early amphibians evolved from lobe-finned fish and resembled salamanders, Figure 23–15. Early amphibians had jointed limbs for crawling about on land, sense organs for detecting sound, a fishlike tail, and gills. Some of the early amphibians grew as long as two meters. Around the middle of the Paleozoic era, the climate on Earth became warm and wet and was ideally suited for amphibians. The amphibians flourished and underwent adaptive radiation. Many new species evolved. For a time, amphibians were the dominant vertebrates on the land. However, reptiles reproduced more successfully on land than did amphibians and eventually became more numerous.

23:11 The Importance of Amphibians

Amphibians are important to the ecology of wetlands and play a vital role in insect control. They have voracious appetites and help to keep insect populations in check. Amphibians themselves are a source of food for snakes, turtles, fish, birds, and mammals.

FIGURE 23–15.

Ancient amphibians had tails and resembled present-day salamanders.

FIGURE 23–16.

Poison-dart frogs live in the forests of South America. They have very poisonous skin.

Amphibians serve as environmental monitors. Healthy populations of amphibians are an indication that the environment is in balance. Tadpoles and salamanders help to keep the environment clean by eating dead plants that can fill up ponds and streams.

Amphibians are important in the field of biomedical research. Some species of South American frogs have extremely poisonous skin. Research is underway to determine the usefulness of these poisons as anesthetics, muscle relaxants, and heart medications.

Studies of salamanders are offering clues about why animals are certain colors. Knowledge about the genetic basis of coloration in salamanders may lead to ideas regarding coloration in more complex animals. Other studies of salamanders are helping scientists to learn how limbs regenerate in animals.

REVIEW

11. List three characteristics of amphibians.
12. Describe the structure of a typical frog.
13. Name two ways amphibians are important ecologically.
14. **SKILL REVIEW:** Using Figure 23–10, sequence the evolutionary development of the different types of amphibians. For more help, refer to Reading Science in the Skill Handbook, pages 798 to 799.
15. **USING CONCEPTS:** What homeostatic mechanisms do amphibians have that show they are more complex than fish?

CHAPTER REVIEW

SUMMARY

1. Phylum Chordata is characterized by a notochord, a dorsal nerve cord, and gill slits at some time during the life cycle. Examples of chordates are tunicates, lancelets, and vertebrates. **23:1**
2. All vertebrates have an endoskeleton, a highly-evolved nervous system, and a closed circulatory system. **23:2**
3. Evolutionary changes in vertebrates as they moved from water to land included development of a more complex heart, adaptations for locomotion, and ability to maintain a constant body temperature. **23:3**
4. Traits of fish include gills for breathing, fins for movement, and scales for protection. **23:4**
5. Jawless fish lack jaws, have skeletons of cartilage, and include lampreys and hagfish. Cartilaginous fish have skeletons of cartilage, are predators, and include sharks. Bony fish have bony skeletons and are divided into three groups—lobe-finned fish, lungfish, and ray-finned fish. **23:5**
6. Jawless fish evolved from ostracoderms, the first vertebrates. Cartilaginous and bony fish evolved from placoderms, the first vertebrates with jaws. **23:6**
7. Fish are important ecologically, as a source of protein for humans, and in studies in the field of biomedicine. **23:7**
8. Amphibians hatch and develop in the water and later change to adults that spend time on land. **23:8**
9. Frogs and toads begin life in water as tadpoles and grow to adults with legs and lungs. Salamanders are long and slender and live on land and in water. **23:9**
10. Amphibians evolved from lobe-finned fish. **23:10**
11. Amphibians are important to the ecology of aquatic habitats and are used in biomedical studies. **23:11**

LANGUAGE OF BIOLOGY

cartilage
dorsal nerve cord
ectotherm
fins
gill slits
lateral line system
notochord
predator

prey
rays
scales
spawning
swim bladder
tympanic membrane
vocal cords

Choose the word or phrase from the list above that completes the sentence.

1. A(n) ____ enables bony fish to control their depth in the water.
2. A frog senses vibrations through its ____.
3. Jawless fish and sharks have ____ skeletons.
4. ____ are structures that help to support the fins of some fish.
5. Breeding in fish is called ____.
6. The ____ is a network of canals that is used to detect movement.
7. ____ are thin, round disks that cover and protect a fish's body.
8. The ____ is a bundle of nerves in vertebrates.
9. The ____ is a flexible, rodlike structure that runs along the back of a chordate.
10. A(n) ____ is an animal with body temperature that varies with the surroundings.

REVIEWING CONCEPTS

Choose the word or phrase that completes the sentence or answers the question.

11. All chordates have a notochord, dorsal nerve cord, and ____.
    a. gills   c. endoskeleton
    b. gill slits   d. scales
12. All vertebrates have ____.
    a. limbs   c. endoskeletons
    b. bony skeletons   d. gills

13. The earliest vertebrates were ____.
    a. fish
    b. birds
    c. mammals
    d. amphibians

14. Fins are used for ____.
    a. breathing
    b. gas exchange
    c. reproduction
    d. locomotion

15. Fish with cartilage skeletons and jaws are ____.
    a. lampreys
    b. eels
    c. salmon
    d. sharks

16. ____ allowed fish to move into new habitats.
    a. Jaws
    b. Gills
    c. Fins
    d. Armored plates

17. Fish are ecologically important ____.
    a. as prey
    b. as food sources
    c. as predators
    d. all of the above

18. All adult amphibians have ____.
    a. shelled eggs
    b. 3-chambered hearts
    c. gills
    d. scales

19. Salamanders are different from frogs in that salamanders have ____.
    a. 2-chambered hearts
    b. moist skin
    c. clawed toes
    d. slender bodies

20. Amphibians most likely evolved from ____.
    a. reptiles
    b. lobe-finned fish
    c. jawless fish
    d. cartilaginous fish

UNDERSTANDING CONCEPTS

Answer the following questions using complete sentences.

21. Why are tunicates considered chordates?
22. What features are common to all vertebrates?
23. Compare how jawless and bony fish feed.
24. How are fish important to humans?
25. Describe adaptations for defense in bony fish.
26. Describe the evolutionary link between fish and amphibians.
27. Compare how frogs and salamanders move.

28. How do frogs, toads, and salamanders differ?
29. How are amphibians ecologically important?
30. Why are birds more active than fish?

APPLYING CONCEPTS

Answer the following questions using complete sentences.

31. In what ways are fish and amphibians alike?
32. Compare how bivalves and tunicates feed.
33. In which sports would a frog be best? Why?
34. What kind of environment would have allowed ostracoderms to survive?
35. The male seahorse incubates its eggs in a brood pouch. The codfish lays its eggs in the open sea. Which fish would lay more eggs? Why?

EXTENSIONS

1. The Devil's Hole pupfish lives in a small pool in the Nevada desert. If this pool were to disappear, the fish would become extinct. Write a report in which you debate this issue.
2. Design an experiment to test the hypothesis that sculpins come to the surface after feeding because warm surface water aids digestion.
3. Find out how parasitic sea lampreys from the Atlantic Ocean invaded the Great Lakes.

READINGS

Bushnell, Peter G. and Kim N. Holland. "Tunas: Athletes in a Can." *Sea Frontiers,* Jan./Feb. 1989, pp. 43–48.

Doubilet, David. "Scorpionfish: Danger in Disguise." *National Geographic,* Nov. 1987, pp. 634–643.

Mattison, Chris. *Frogs and Toads of the World.* New York: Facts on File, Inc., 1987.

BIRDS AND
REPTILES

MMALS

AMPHIBIANS
AND FISH

STARFISH

ANTS

500

ANIMALS

REPTILES AND BIRDS

B irds and reptiles make up two classes of vertebrates that have very diverse characteristics. You probably can list some of the characteristics that help to distinguish the two groups. For instance, you know that snakes don't fly—birds do, and birds don't slither along the ground—snakes do. It may surprise you, however, to learn that birds and reptiles have quite a lot in common. The Indian green tree snake, shown on the left, and the Canada goose on this page both have scales and lay eggs. In this chapter, you will study the characteristics of reptiles and birds and how they are adaptive.

Canada goose

REPTILES

Fire-breathing dragons are mythical animals depicted as ferocious, lizardlike creatures. Yet, most lizards are small and timid. Certainly, none of them breathe fire! Snakes inspire more fear than almost any other type of animal. Such reactions are rooted in legends rather than based on experience. Some of our fear of reptiles may be due, in part, to our primate ancestry. Most primates show an instinctive fear of snakes. Although some reptiles are aggressive predators, most are harmless to humans.

24:1 The Life of a Reptile

The class Reptilia includes turtles, alligators, crocodiles, snakes, and lizards. This may seem like an extremely varied group, but all reptiles share certain traits. Reptiles were the first group of vertebrates capable of reproducing entirely on land. How were they able to do this? Reptiles developed two new features that enabled them to be less dependent on water for survival. The first adaptation is internal fertilization. When fertilization is internal, a body of water is not required for transporting sperm to egg. After fertilization, the female secretes a protective covering onto the egg and lays it in a nest dug in the soil. The egg covering is leathery and keeps the egg from drying out.

Objectives:
- list the adaptations of reptiles that enable them to live on land and compare these adaptations with those of amphibians.
- describe the amniotic egg and discuss its importance.
- compare the characteristics and lifestyles of turtles, tortoises, crocodiles, alligators, lizards, and snakes.
- list evolutionary trends in reptiles.
- give reasons why reptiles are important.

Indian green tree snake

FIGURE 24–1.

Birds, reptiles, and mammals are able to live on land because they have amniotic eggs. Notice in the photo of the alligator, a reptile, how the body is covered with scales.

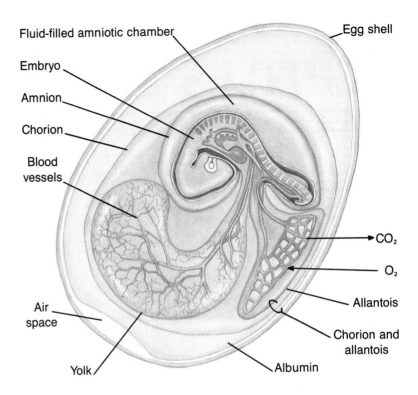

Fluid-filled amniotic chamber

Embryo

Amnion

Chorion

Blood vessels

Air space

Yolk

Egg shell

CO_2

O_2

Allantois

Chorion and allantois

Albumin

The second feature that enables reptiles to reproduce on land is an amniotic egg. An **amniotic egg** contains membranes that protect the embryo and provide it with nourishment. The **amnion** is the innermost membrane of the egg. The amnion is filled with a fluid in which the embryo floats. The fluid-filled amnion cushions the embryo. The **allantois** (uh LANT uh wus) is a membrane that grows from the embryo's gut for the collection of wastes. When a reptile hatches, it leaves behind the allantois and collected wastes. The **chorion** (KOR ee ahn) is the outermost membrane and provides for gas exchange. The chorion contains numerous blood vessels that are connected to the circulatory system of the embryo. Oxygen diffuses across the shell and into the vessels of the chorion and is then transported to the embryo. Carbon dioxide is transported from the embryo to the chorion and then diffuses across the shell into the surrounding environment.

Several other adaptations of reptiles have enabled them to live successfully on land. Look at the scales on the crocodile's body in Figure 24–1. The skin is thick and dry, not moist like the skin of an amphibian. The evolution of a thick, scaly skin protects the animal from water loss and injury. Also, a reptile's limbs are positioned under the body, rather than to the side as in amphibians. This position allows more efficient movement on land.

Reptiles breathe with lungs and have no gilled larval stage, as amphibians do. The three-chambered heart of a reptile keeps oxygen-rich blood separate from oxygen-poor blood. The heart pumps more efficiently, thus allowing for a higher level of energy production than in amphibians.

Like amphibians, reptiles are ectotherms. Their body temperature depends on the temperature of the environment. Because reptiles are dependent on the temperature of the surroundings, they do not inhabit extremely cold regions. Reptiles are numerous in both temperate and tropical regions, where climates are warm. In addition, they use behavioral adaptations to adjust their body temperature. For example, turtles sun themselves on logs to warm up, and dive into the water to cool down.

24:2 Phylogeny of Reptiles

Turtles

You may think of turtles as clumsy and slow. However, turtles belong to the order Chelonia, which is a successful group of animals. The fossil record shows that this group has been on Earth for about 200 million years.

Turtles may live primarily on land or in the water. Turtles that live on land are often called tortoises. The body of a turtle includes a top shell and a bottom shell, Figure 24–2. Most turtles can draw the limbs, tail, and head into the shell for protection against predators. Turtles have no teeth. They do have powerful jaws with a beaklike structure that is used to crush food.

Most turtles spend much of their lives in the water, feeding on aquatic insects, crustaceans, worms, small fish, and water plants. Turtles return to land to lay their eggs. The female uses her claws to dig a hole in the sand in which she lays her eggs. Turtles do not protect their eggs. Marine turtles may swim long distances from their

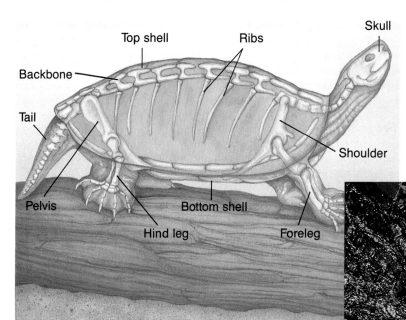

Top shell — Ribs — Skull

Backbone

Tail

Pelvis — Hind leg — Bottom shell — Foreleg — Shoulder

FIGURE 24–2.

Turtles, such as the red-eared turtle in the photo, have external shells and internal skeletons.

feeding grounds back to the beaches where they hatched to lay their eggs. For example, green turtles travel from the coast of Brazil to Ascension Island in the Atlantic Ocean, a distance of over 2000 km. Scientists are unsure how they find their way. The turtles may be using the sun and stars to navigate, or they may be following the odors of chemicals in the water.

Tortoises live on land, foraging for fruit, berries, and insects. The largest tortoises in the world are found on the Galapagos Islands off the coast of Ecuador. A Galapagos tortoise can travel a distance of 300 m plodding steadily along for one hour. In the past, sailors killed these tortoises for food. As a result, their numbers declined rapidly. Today the Galapagos tortoises are protected by law.

Crocodiles and Alligators

Crocodiles and alligators make up the order Crocodilia and are among the largest living reptiles. Crocodiles up to eight meters in length have been reported. Crocodilians of today are very similar to those that lived 160 million years ago. Alligators and crocodiles live in and near water in tropical and subtropical regions. Compare the heads of the crocodile and alligator in Figure 24–3. Crocodiles have long, slender snouts, while alligators have short, broad snouts. Both animals have powerful jaws with sharp teeth. What can you conclude about the feeding habits of alligators and crocodiles?

Crocodiles hunt by remaining motionless in the water, with only the eyes and nostrils above the surface. They are quick and aggressive, attacking animals as large as cattle. Prey are caught both in the water and on the shore. Swimming prey is dragged underwater and held there until drowned. Crocodiles build dens along the banks of rivers and lakes and use them for nesting, protection, and feeding.

FIGURE 24–3.

Crocodiles (a) and alligators (b) can be distinguished by their snouts.

a

b

Alligators are less aggressive than crocodiles. They feed on fish, turtles, waterbirds, and frogs and usually capture their prey in the water. The largest species of alligator lives in the southeastern United States and grows up to 5 m long.

Alligators and crocodiles use their powerful tails to swim, moving so rapidly that few swimming animals can escape pursuit. On land, the tail is a formidable weapon, able to knock most opponents to the ground. Even though these animals have short, stubby legs, they can move very fast over short distances.

Snakes and Lizards

Snakes and lizards belong to the order Squamata. Lizards are found in many types of habitats in all parts of the world, except in the polar regions. Some live on the ground, some burrow, some live in trees, and some are aquatic. Many are adapted to hot, dry climates. Notice the variety of lizards in Figure 24–4. Lizards have many adaptations that allow a variety of lifestyles. Geckos are small, nocturnal lizards that live in warm climates, such as that in the southern United States. The toe pads of some geckos allow them to walk across ceilings. Iguanas are often brightly-colored, with crests and frills. Skinks have long bodies and small limbs. Chameleons are tree-dwelling lizards that can change color. How might this ability be adaptive? Most lizards eat insects, although some, including the marine iguana, are plant-eaters.

Lizards are different from snakes in that lizards have moveable eyelids and ear openings. Most lizards have legs, but there are some legless lizards. Only two species of lizards are venomous—the Gila monster of the southwestern United States and Mexico and the beaded lizard of Mexico.

FIGURE 24–4.

Geckos (top left), skinks (top right), Gila monsters (bottom left), and beaded lizards (bottom right) are among the enormous variety of lizards.

NoteWorthy

Horned toads of North America are flat lizards that look very much like toads with large spines on their heads. When threatened, they inflate themselves, jump forward, hiss, and squirt blood from their eyes.

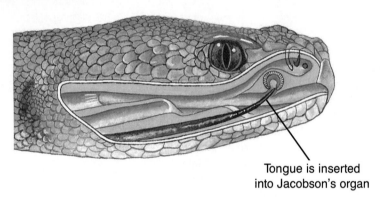

FIGURE 24–5.

Snakes sense events in their surroundings in several ways. Pit vipers, such as the pope's pit viper in the photograph, have heat-sensitive pits in the sides of their heads. Snakes also have structures called Jacobson's organs in the roofs of their mouths for sensing chemicals.

How do snakes smell?

Snakes have several adaptations for sensing events in their environment. Their best developed sense is their sense of smell. Snakes have sense organs that detect airborne chemicals, thus helping them to detect prey. You may have seen a snake flicking its tongue in and out as it picks up chemicals in the air. The snake then draws its tongue back into its mouth and inserts it into a structure called Jacobson's organ, Figure 24–5. **Jacobson's organ** is a pitlike sense organ in the roof of a snake's mouth that picks up airborne chemicals. Except for the tree-dwelling snakes, snakes have poor vision. Tree-dwelling snakes have excellent vision and are able to follow prey through thick foliage. Although snakes have no ear openings, they do have internal ears and can detect low-frequency sounds.

One group of snakes, the **pit vipers,** can detect heat by means of heat-sensitive pits in the head. Pit vipers include the rattlesnake, water moccasin, and copperhead. On what type of vertebrates would such snakes most likely prey?

Snakes kill their prey in one of three main ways. Many snakes wrap themselves around their prey. As the prey breathes out, the snake squeezes more tightly. The prey eventually dies of suffocation. A snake that kills by wrapping around its prey until it cannot breathe is called a **constrictor.** Common constrictors include boas, pythons, and anacondas.

A second way that snakes kill their prey is by injecting venom as they bite into the prey. Most poisonous snakes have hollow fangs through which the venom is injected, Figure 24–6. The venom either paralyzes the nervous system or destroys red blood cells and blood vessels.

The third and most common way snakes capture their prey is by grabbing the prey with their mouths and swallowing it whole. The snake's lower jaw unhinges from the skull, allowing the snake to consume an animal much larger than itself.

24:3 Origins

Reptiles arose from ancient amphibians about 300 million years ago. These first reptiles were called **cotylosaurs** and were the ancestors of present-day reptiles. Several reptile groups, many of which are now extinct, evolved from the cotylosaurs. These groups were the ruling reptiles, including dinosaurs and the ancestral crocodilians; and the ancient scaly reptiles. Dinosaurs became extinct during the late Mesozoic era and did not give rise to any other reptile groups. The scaly reptiles were the ancestors of snakes and lizards. Lizards evolved during the early Mesozoic. Snakes first appeared in the late Mesozoic. The evolutionary history of turtles is incomplete, but crocodilians evolved from the ruling reptile group.

cotylosaur:
 kotyl (GK) cup
 sauros (GK) lizard

FIGURE 24–6.

Constrictors, such as the boa (a) and python (b), capture their prey by wrapping themselves around it. Poisonous snakes have venom glands and hollow fangs for injecting venom into prey.

a

b

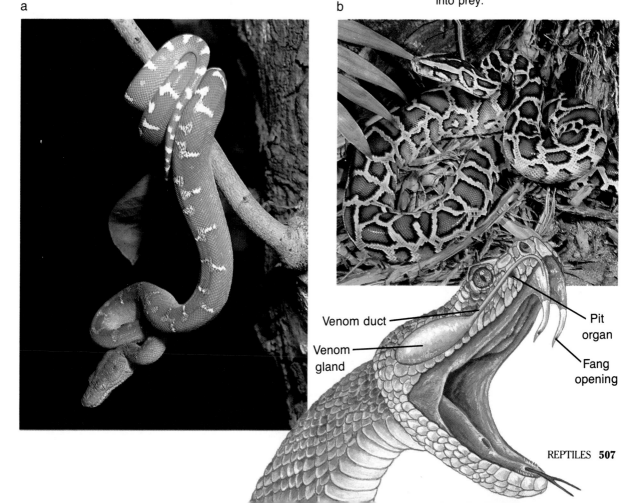

Venom duct

Venom gland

Pit organ

Fang opening

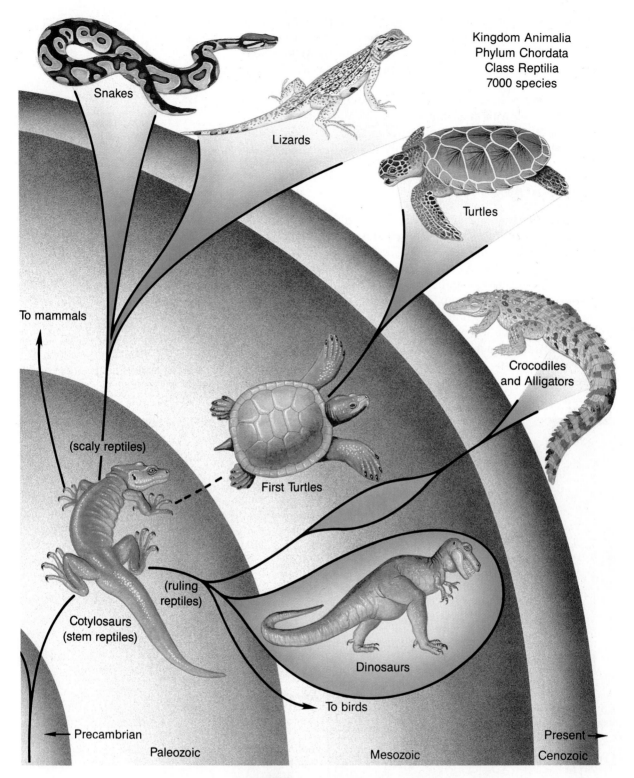

Kingdom Animalia
Phylum Chordata
Class Reptilia
7000 species

Snakes

Lizards

Turtles

Crocodiles
and Alligators

To mammals

(scaly reptiles)

First Turtles

Cotylosaurs
(stem reptiles)

(ruling
reptiles)

Dinosaurs

To birds

Precambrian

Paleozoic

Mesozoic

Present

Cenozoic

FIGURE 24–7.

The radiation of orders of reptiles on the geologic time scale shows their relationships.

TAKING THE BITE OUT OF PAIN

Pain is part of the body's response to injury. The body's most powerful pain-producing chemical is a substance known as bradykinin (BRAY dee KI nun). Dr. John Stewart of the University of Colorado has spent more than 20 years trying to find a way to neutralize the effects of bradykinin.

In 1949, a Brazilian pharmacologist discovered that bradykinin was responsible for the pain associated with the bite of the Brazilian pit viper, *Bothrops jararaca,* more commonly called jararaca. The venom itself does not contain bradykinin, but instead causes molecules in the blood of the bite victim to release bradykinin. Since this discovery, chemicals that cause the release of bradykinins have been detected in the venom of other snakes, including the diamondback rattlesnake.

Bradykinin causes pain when it binds to receptors on nerve cell membranes. The nerve cell sends a message to the brain and pain is felt. Research on pain control has focused on a way to block bradykinin. Dr. Stewart has been successful in synthesizing molecules that can bind to bradykinin, thus keeping it from binding to nerve cells. Bradykinin blockers are being tested in the form of ointments for cuts and burns, nose sprays, and remedies for toothaches and sore throats.

A rattlesnake is milked for its venom.

Although dinosaurs are no longer living, there were at one time such great numbers of them that they are considered important to our understanding of the history of life on Earth. Dinosaurs were the most numerous land animals during the Mesozoic era. Some dinosaurs were the size of chickens. Others were the largest land-dwellers that have ever lived. Some were predatory, while others were plant-eaters.

Until recently, most people thought of dinosaurs as stupid, slow, cold-blooded creatures. Scientists hypothesized that the larger dinosaurs lived in swamps and marshes because water was required to buoy their weight. Recent discoveries suggest that dinosaurs may have been warm-blooded, agile, and speedy. Many lived only on land. Some, such as *Maiasaurus,* built nests and may have cared for their young after birth.

Dinosaurs were the dominant land animals for about 160 million years. Recall from Chapter 2 that there were several periods during which mass extinction occurred. The extinction of the dinosaurs was one of those periods. There are many hypotheses about why the dinosaurs disappeared. Some scientists hypothesize that dinosaurs could not adapt to major climatic changes. Others believe that a giant meteor may have crashed into Earth, creating a storm of dust that blocked out all sunlight. As a result, the climate on Earth cooled. The dinosaurs' food sources died and they starved.

Why did dinosaurs disappear?

24:4 The Importance of Reptiles

How do reptiles keep pests in check?

You may not realize it, but reptiles have important roles in the environment and in people's lives. Reptiles help keep a variety of potential pests in check. Some snakes feed on rats and mice and are extremely beneficial to farmers. Other snakes, some turtles, and some lizards feed on slugs, centipedes, and insects, such as cockroaches and flies. Reptiles also provide food for other animals.

Snakes, lizards, and crocodilians provide food for people in many tropical countries. In South and Central America, where the iguana has been hunted nearly to extinction, research is underway to develop methods of ranching iguanas. Raising captive iguanas for food would help to save the species in the wild.

To understand how gravity affects human circulation, scientists are studying how the circulatory system of a snake works when the snake crawls uphill against the force of gravity. This information may be useful to space travelers.

Some reptiles have become endangered as a result of careless human activity. An **endangered species** is a species with numbers so low that it is in danger of becoming extinct. All species of sea turtles are classified as threatened or endangered. A species is considered to be a **threatened species** when its numbers are declining very rapidly and it may become endangered. Some turtles and their eggs are poached for food. Turtles also suffer from the effects of pollution. The main source of food for the leatherback turtle is jellyfish. The leatherback mistakes plastic trash floating in the water for jellyfish and eats it. The turtle starves because its stomach becomes full of plastic and can't digest food normally. The hawksbill turtle is hunted illegally for its shell, which is used for decoration. The green turtle is killed for its meat. Even though there are international laws protecting these species, illegal poaching often occurs. When one pound of turtle shell will bring up to $100, poaching becomes a great temptation.

FIGURE 24–8.

Iguanas are a source of food for people in South and Central America.

The American alligator is a conservation success story. Because it was hunted relentlessly for its meat and hide, the American alligator dwindled in number. Alligators are now protected by law and are becoming numerous again. In fact, the Florida Game and Freshwater Fish Commission receives regular complaints about alligators wandering onto golf courses, backyard patios, and into neighborhood pools. Some people think that the survival of the species is worth the danger and inconvenience of alligators being in places where they aren't welcome. What do you think?

FIGURE 24–9.

The leatherback turtle (left) and hawksbill turtle (right) are threatened by human activities.

REVIEW

1. What adaptations do reptiles have for living and reproducing on land?
2. Compare the ways in which turtles and alligators protect themselves.
3. How are reptiles important to the environment?
4. **SKILL REVIEW:** Look at Figure 24–7. Develop an evolutionary sequence for the groups of reptiles you studied. For more help, refer to Reading Science in the Skill Handbook, pages 798 to 799.
5. **USING CONCEPTS:** What homeostatic mechanisms do reptiles have that show that they are evolutionarily more advanced than amphibians?

BIOLAB

Reptile Adaptations

24

Problem: How is body color adaptive?

Materials
thermometers (2)
black paper
white paper
tape
goosenecked lamp

metric ruler
empty frozen juice
   cans with holes in
   one end (2)
clay

Procedures
1. Copy the data table.
2. Cover a juice can with black paper. Tape the paper in place.
3. Place a thermometer into the hole in the top of the can and secure it with clay. Make sure the hole is tightly sealed with clay. Use the diagram as a guide.
4. Prepare a second can in the same manner, using white paper instead of black.
5. Place both cans in front of a goosenecked lamp. The lamp should be 5 cm from both cans. DO NOT turn on the lamp.
6. Record the starting temperature of both cans in your data table.
7. Develop a **hypothesis** as to which can will show a higher temperature at the end of 10 minutes.
8. Turn on the lamp and allow it to shine on the cans for 10 minutes.
9. At the end of this time, record the final temperature of both cans in your data table. Calculate the total change in temperature for each can and record it in your data table.

Questions and Conclusion
1. Which color, black or white, had the greater temperature change after being heated for ten minutes?
2. Which color, black or white, absorbs light better and, therefore, warms up faster?
3. Which color reflects light better and, therefore, warms up more slowly?
4. Did you accept your **hypothesis?** Use your data to support your answer.
5. Which should absorb more light from the sun, a dark animal or a light animal? Why?
6. The ability to change skin color is an adaptation in many reptiles. Explain how this kind of adaptation may help a reptile to survive.
7. Adaptations are inherited. What may happen over many years to dark animals living in hot environments?

Conclusion: How is body color adaptive?

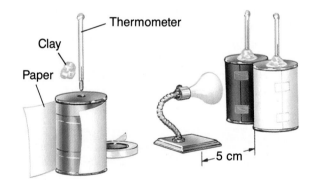

Data and Observations

Temperature readings for black and white cans			
	Starting temperature	Final temperature	Total temperature change in 10 minutes
Black can			
White can			

BIRDS

Of all animals, birds are probably the most admired by people. Birds have been envied since ancient times for their ability to soar through the air with no apparent effort. In temperate regions, the arrival of birds in the spring and their departure in the autumn mark the seasons more dramatically than a calendar. Bird-watchers number in the millions worldwide. The brilliant blue flash of a blue jay's wings, the sparkling bird song that fills the woods on a spring morning, the amusing antics of a chickadee hanging upside down on a snow-covered branch have always fascinated and delighted their earthbound human neighbors.

Objectives:
- describe the adaptations of birds.
- compare the characteristics of various bird orders.
- list evolutionary trends in birds.
- give reasons why birds are important.

24:5 The Life of a Bird

Birds are members of the class Aves. They have several traits that show their evolutionary relationship to reptiles. The skeleton of a typical bird is similar to that of some small, two-legged dinosaurs. Both birds and reptiles have scales on their feet and clawed toes. In both groups, fertilization is internal and shelled, amniotic eggs are produced. Birds, however, have evolved other features that are unique to their class. The most distinctive characteristic of birds is feathers. A **feather** is a modified scale that provides insulation and allows flight.

Feathers streamline a bird's body, making it easier for the bird to move through the air. Muscles in the skin can move groups of feathers, thereby allowing the bird to make precise maneuvers while in flight. Birds care for their feathers by using their beaks to rub oil

Flight feather

Vane

Shaft

Down feather

Quill

FIGURE 24–10.

Birds, such as this blue jay, are the only organisms with feathers.

BIRDS **513**

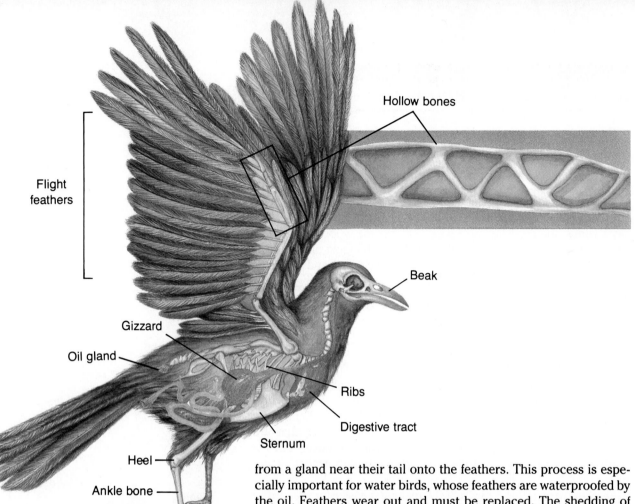

Flight feathers

Hollow bones

Beak

Gizzard

Oil gland

Ribs

Digestive tract

Sternum

Heel

Ankle bone

Toes

FIGURE 24–11.

Birds have several characteristics that enable them to fly. These characteristics include wings, a lightweight beak, a large sternum for the attachment of breast muscles, and hollow bones (inset).

sternum:
  sternon (GK) chest
endotherm:
  endon (GK) within
  therme (GK) heat

from a gland near their tail onto the feathers. This process is especially important for water birds, whose feathers are waterproofed by the oil. Feathers wear out and must be replaced. The shedding of old feathers with the growth of new ones is called **molting.** Most birds molt in the late summer. However, most birds do not lose their feathers all at once and are able to fly while they are molting.

In addition to feathers, birds have front limbs that are modified into wings. The powerful flight muscles that move the wings are attached to a large breast bone called the **sternum.** A bird's hind limbs are adapted for perching, swimming, walking, or catching prey. Many of a bird's adaptations help to reduce its weight, thus making flight easier. Bones are thin and hollow. Air sacs are located throughout the body. The jaws lack teeth. Instead, birds have horny beaks. This adaptation helps to reduce weight as there is no heavy jawbone. Like reptiles, birds lay amniotic eggs for reproduction. Because young birds do not develop inside the mother's body, the mother does not have to lift this additional weight.

Flight requires high energy levels. Several factors are involved in maintaining high energy levels in birds. First, a bird's four-chambered, rapidly beating heart moves oxygenated blood quickly throughout the body. This efficient circulation supplies the cells with the oxygen needed to produce energy. Second, birds are able to maintain high energy levels because they are endotherms. An **endotherm** is an animal that maintains a constant body temperature independently of the environmental temperature. How does temperature regulation in birds compare with that in reptiles?

Third, birds eat large amounts of food to sustain the energy needed for flight. The beaks of birds are clues to what they eat. Study the birds in Figure 24–12. Hummingbirds have evolved long beaks that are used for dipping into flowers to obtain nectar. Hawks have evolved large, curved beaks that are adapted for pulling apart prey. Pelicans have huge beaks with pouches that they use as nets for capturing fish. The anhinga spears fish with its long, pointed bill. The short, stout beak of the goldfinch is adapted for eating seeds.

Since birds have no teeth, they must grind their food in some other way. The **gizzard** is a part of the digestive tract of a bird in which food is crushed by muscular action. Crushing of food is aided by small pebbles that the bird swallows and retains in the gizzard.

What is the function of the gizzard?

Although a few birds, such as ostriches and penguins, cannot fly, most birds do fly. You probably have noticed that birds do not all fly in exactly the same way. Some birds soar, hardly flapping their wings. Others flap constantly, turning and twisting across the sky.

Modifications in basic wing structure have allowed birds to adapt to various lifestyles. Birds that move around in forests, such as sparrows, warblers, and doves, must have wings adapted for quick movement. Notice the elliptical shape of the wings of the tiny chickadee in Figure 24–13. A chickadee can change direction in 0.03 seconds, or as quickly as you can blink an eye.

FIGURE 24–12.

The beaks of hummingbirds, hawks, pelicans, anhingas, and goldfinches are adapted to different food types.

Hummingbird

Goldfinch

Pelican

Hawk

Anhinga

FIGURE 24–13.

The wings of chickadees (top left), sandpipers (top right), albatrosses (bottom left), and vultures (bottom right) are shaped differently and allow different kinds of aerial maneuvers.

Wings adapted for high speed are important to birds that fly long distances or feed on flying insects. Wings of swallows, terns, and gulls have shapes that sweep back and taper to a slender tip, promoting high speed. Fast birds, such as sandpipers, can fly at speeds up to 175 km per hour. Compare the wings of the sandpiper with those of the chickadee in Figure 24–13.

Soaring birds, such as oceanic albatrosses and frigate birds, have large wings like those of sailplanes. Such birds flap their wings only occasionally and soar on the wind currents. The albatross has a wingspan of up to 3.6 m, the largest of any bird. High-lift wings provide strong lift at low speeds. This trait enables predators, such as hawks, vultures, eagles, and owls, to carry prey while in flight.

24:6 Phylogeny and Origins of Birds

What characteristics are used to divide birds into different orders?

Birds are divided into orders based on differences in their beaks, feet, eating habits, and other characteristics. For example, ostriches, pelicans, and penguins have distinctive characteristics that set them apart. Ostriches are large, flightless birds; pelicans have throat pouches and eat fish; penguins have webbed feet and swim in the ocean. These birds belong to three of the 27 orders of birds. Representatives of some of the major bird orders are shown in Figure 24–14. Notice the characteristics of these birds and how they differ from one another.

The complete evolutionary history of birds is not clear. The fossil record is incomplete due to the fact that bird skeletons are light and delicate and, therefore, decompose easily. However, there is fossil evidence to indicate that birds evolved from small, ground-dwelling, two-legged reptiles more than 150 million years ago. The earliest bird in the fossil record is *Archaeopteryx* (ar kee AHP tuh riks). *Archaeopteryx* probably did not give rise to any other bird groups, and so is not considered the ancestor to modern birds. *Archaeopteryx* was about the size of a crow. It had feathers and wings like a modern bird. But, it also had teeth, a long tail, and clawed front toes, much like a reptile. Its skeleton was very similar to that of certain small dinosaurs. In fact, birds and dinosaurs are both thought to have a common reptilian ancestor called a thecodont.

Figure 24–15 shows that birds underwent adaptive radiation toward the end of the Mesozoic era. Most of the present-day bird orders evolved at that time.

FIGURE 24–14.

The eastern meadowlark (a), pileated woodpecker (b), snowy owl (c), puffin (d), pelican (e), and emperor penguin (f) represent six of the 27 bird orders.

a
b
c
d
e
f

FIGURE 24–15.

The radiation of orders of birds on the geologic time scale shows their relationships.

Hummingbirds

Perching
Songbirds

Woodpeckers

Archaeopteryx

Thecodont

Precambrian   Paleozoic   Mesozoic   Cenozoic   Present   Flightless
Birds

Kingdom Animalia
Phylum Chordata
Class Aves
8600 species

Owls

Quails, Turkeys,
and Chickens

Parrots

Pigeons

Gulls, Sandpipers,
and Puffins

Penguins

Swans, Geese,
and Ducks

Pelicans

Hawks, Eagles,
and Falcons

The swifts of southeast Asia make their nests entirely of their own saliva. People collect these nests and make them into a delicacy called bird's nest soup.

24:7 The Importance of Birds

Birds have many roles in the environments in which they are found. Birds help to maintain balance in the environment. Some birds eat insects that would otherwise increase in number so much that they would overwhelm natural habitats. Predatory birds feed on rats and mice and keep them in check.

Birds are agents of seed dispersal in many areas. Undigested seeds that pass out of a bird's excretory system may germinate when they land on soil. When an area has been disturbed by fire or human activity, the kinds of plants that begin to grow will be determined, in part, by the kinds of seeds carried to that area by birds. In addition, many kinds of seeds can't germinate until they are eaten by birds and their hard coverings crushed up in the gizzard.

Introduced bird species can disrupt the balance of a community. The mute swan, Figure 24–16, is a graceful, majestic bird admired by all who watch it glide across the water. Mute swans were brought to the United States in the early 1900s. They have increased in number so much that they are driving native ducks and geese out of many ponds near the east coast. One swan may eat 10 kg of water plants per day and leave several kilograms of droppings.

Approximately 1000 of the 9000 species of birds in the world are in danger of extinction due to loss of habitat and pesticide use. In the United States, progress has been made toward increasing the numbers of endangered whooping cranes and peregrine falcons, Figure 24–17. Peregrine falcons have been bred successfully in captivity and returned to the wild. Peregrines are also being trained to survive in city environments. The peregrines nest on the roofs of skyscrapers and feed on pigeons.

FIGURE 24–16.

Mute swans are the familiar swans seen in many city parks.

a

b

FIGURE 24–17.

Efforts are being made to increase the numbers of whooping cranes (a) and peregrine falcons (b).

Besides having important roles in the environment, birds are of extreme interest to people. Many people enjoy birds. Each year, bird lovers spend over $500 million on birdseed, $100 million on bird feeders, boxes, and baths, and $18 million on field guides. Many governments have birds as national symbols. You are familiar with the national symbol of the United States, the bald eagle.

Biomedical research on quails indicates that cells in the inner ear can regrow when damaged by loud sounds. Until this fact was discovered, scientists thought that these cells could not regrow when damaged. Other research with birds is providing information about what happens to damaged brain cells.

REVIEW

6. Describe three adaptations in birds.
7. What is the evolutionary significance of *Archaeopteryx?*
8. Name two ways birds are important to the environment.
9. **SKILL REVIEW:** Make a table that summarizes the adaptations birds have that enable them to fly. For more help, refer to Organizing Information in the Skill Handbook, pages 810 to 813.
10. **USING CONCEPTS:** Large, flightless birds are most common on islands that do not have large, carnivorous mammals. What hypothesis can you suggest for the evolution of large, flightless birds?

CHAPTER REVIEW

SUMMARY

1. Reptiles are vertebrates with scaly skin, lungs, and eggs with a leathery covering. **24:1**
2. The orders of reptiles include turtles, alligators and crocodiles, and lizards and snakes. **24:2**
3. Reptiles evolved from amphibians. Dinosaurs were the dominant animals on Earth during the Mesozoic era. **24:3**
4. Reptiles eat pests, are used in medical research, and are eaten for food. **24:4**
5. Birds are adapted for flight. They have feathers, wings, hollow bones, a four-chambered heart, and toothless beaks. **24:5**
6. Birds are divided into orders based on their beaks, feet, and eating habits. *Archaeopteryx* is the earliest known bird. **24:6**
7. Birds help to keep insect populations in check and are important in seed dispersal. Birds are a source of enjoyment for humans. Birds also are studied in biomedical research. **24:7**

LANGUAGE OF BIOLOGY

allantois	feather
amnion	gizzard
amniotic egg	Jacobson's organ
chorion	molting
constrictor	pit vipers
cotylosaurs	sternum
endangered species	threatened species
endotherm	

Choose the word or phrase from the list above that completes the sentence.

1. The shedding of old feathers and the growth of new ones is called ____.
2. The ____ is the innermost membrane of a reptile's egg.
3. The earliest reptiles are called ____.
4. The ____ is a structure that grinds up food.

5. Snakes with heat-sensitive pits in their heads for locating prey are called ____.
6. The ____ is a membrane that collects wastes in an amniotic egg.
7. The sense organ in the roof of a snake's mouth is called ____.
8. A snake that wraps around its prey is called a(n) ____.
9. A bird's flight muscles are attached to the ____.
10. A(n) ____ is a modified scale.

REVIEWING CONCEPTS

Choose the word or phrase that completes the sentence or answers the question.

11. Unlike most amphibians, reptiles ____.
    a. have moist skin   c. have feathers
    b. reproduce on land   d. migrate
12. A turtle's shell is an adaptation for ____.
    a. swimming   c. protection
    b. food storage   d. reproduction
13. Lizards differ from snakes by having ____.
    a. moveable eyelids   c. tongues
    b. scales   d. internal fertilization
14. Reptiles are important because they ____.
    a. disperse seeds   c. are legless
    b. eat pest species d. are poisonous
15. The dominant land animals during the Mesozoic era were reptiles called ____.
    a. cotylosaurs   c. skinks
    b. chameleons   d. dinosaurs
16. Only birds have ____.
    a. feathers   c. endothermy
    b. wings   d. amniotic eggs
17. Birds that have large wings and do not flap their wings often are adapted for ____.
    a. living in forests   c. catching insects
    b. speed   d. soaring

18. The beak of a bird is a clue to the bird's ____.
- a. flying ability
- b. feeding habits
- c. body size
- d. songs

19. Birds evolved from ____.
- a. mammals
- b. reptiles
- c. *Archaeopteryx*
- d. amphibians

20. Birds are important environmentally because they ____.
- a. are endotherms
- b. have wings
- c. disperse seeds
- d. fly

UNDERSTANDING CONCEPTS

Answer the following questions using complete sentences.

21. How is the amniotic egg an adaptation for reproducing on land?

22. How are snakes adapted to eating prey larger than themselves?

23. What characteristic of reptiles enables them to be more active than amphibians?

24. Describe one hypothesis concerning how dinosaurs became extinct.

25. Describe two ways in which birds are similar to reptiles.

26. Describe two adaptations in birds that enable them to maintain high energy levels.

27. What types of information can be obtained from studying the shapes of birds' wings?

28. How can so many different species of birds survive in each type of environment?

29. How do birds aid in seed dispersal?

30. Describe ways in which birds and reptiles are used in biomedical research.

APPLYING CONCEPTS

Answer the following questions using complete sentences.

31. Can a reptile egg drown? Explain.

32. What might happen to a snake if its poison glands stopped producing venom?

33. How are birds able to inhabit more diverse environments than reptiles?

34. How would environments be affected if there were no birds?

35. How might the fact that there are no snakes in Ireland affect the environment there?

EXTENSIONS

1. You are a playwright casting a play. Your only actors will be reptiles. Explain what your play will be about and what roles your actors will play.

2. Sea birds called ancient murrelets lay their eggs on shore. Newly hatched chicks must find their way to the sea even when it is not visible from where they hatch. The murrelets may use light, which is brightest over the water, or the sound of the waves to find their way to the sea. Design an experiment that would tell which clues the chicks use.

3. You are a genetic engineer with all the genes from all reptiles past and present available to you. You are charged with the task of creating a new reptile that will be useful in the environment into which it will be introduced, and will be useful to humans as well. Describe this reptile.

READINGS

Conniff, Richard. "Superchicken, Whose Life is it Anyway?" *Discover,* June 1988, pp. 32–36.

McIntyre, Judith W. "The Common Loon Cries for Help." *National Geographic,* Apr. 1989, pp. 514–524.

Mehrtens, John M. *Living Snakes of the World in Color.* New York: Sterling, 1987.

MAMMALS

BIRDS AND
REPTILES

FLOWERING
PLANTS

RS

AM

524

MAMMALS

I magine a creature with veins so large you could crawl through them. Imagine a creature so large it has a heart the size of a subcompact car. Now imagine a creature so small it weighs less than a penny. Imagine that same creature having a metabolic rate so high it must have a heart rate of 800 beats per minute to survive. Last of all, imagine that you have more in common with these creatures—the whale and the shrew—than almost any other organism on Earth. You, the whale, and the shrew are all mammals.

In this chapter, you will study characteristics shared by mammals and characteristics that set them apart from all other groups of living things. You also will study the differences among the different kinds of mammals.

Shrew

THE LIFE OF A MAMMAL

Mammals have several unique characteristics. They have hair, glands that secrete milk, and a specialized muscle that helps in breathing. The unique characteristics of mammals contribute to their success in being one of the most widely distributed organisms in the world.

Objectives:
- identify and describe the major characteristics of mammals.
- describe how mammals are adapted to heat and cold.

25:1 Characteristics of Mammals

Hair is a distinguishing trait of mammals and is probably the easiest trait to observe. Its main function is to provide insulation and thereby conserve body heat. Thus, a mammal is able to maintain a constant body temperature. For example, the thick coat of a polar bear is an adaptation to living in a cold climate.

Mammals are a highly successful group of animals in part because of the care they provide to their young after they are born. Part of that care involves nourishing the offspring with milk from the female's mammary glands. **Mammary glands** are glands in the female that secrete milk. The number of glands varies among mammal species. A mouse opossum has 19 mammary glands. Most primates have only two.

What is the main function of hair?

Blue whale

All mammals have diaphragms (DI uh framz). A **diaphragm** is a sheet of muscle beneath the lungs that assists with breathing. When the diaphragm contracts, the chest cavity enlarges and air moves into the lungs. When the diaphragm relaxes, the chest cavity becomes smaller and air moves out of the lungs.

Most mammals are born after a period of development within the uterus of the female. The **uterus** is a hollow, muscular organ in which development of offspring takes place. Development inside the mother's body ensures that the offspring are protected during the early stages of growth.

In addition to mammary glands, most mammals have sweat, oil, and scent glands. Sweat glands help regulate body temperature by secreting water onto the skin. As the water evaporates, it transfers excess heat from the body to the surrounding air. Oil glands lubricate hair and skin. Some mammals have scent glands that spray foul-smelling substances as a method of defense. Other scent glands release chemicals that attract mates.

Mammals can perform complex behaviors, such as learning and remembering what they have learned. Like parental care, this trait has contributed to the success of the group. The mammalian nervous system is quite complex, with a well-developed brain. The mammalian brain is folded, thus forming ridges and grooves that allow more brain tissue to fit into a small space. Compared with the brains of fish, amphibians, reptiles, and birds, the brain of a mammal is more complex. Sections of the brain that control mental processes and motor functions are larger and have more nerve tissue.

FIGURE 25–1a.

Mammals have several characteristics that set them apart from other organisms. These characteristics include a muscular diaphragm, hair, mammary glands, and a uterus in the female.

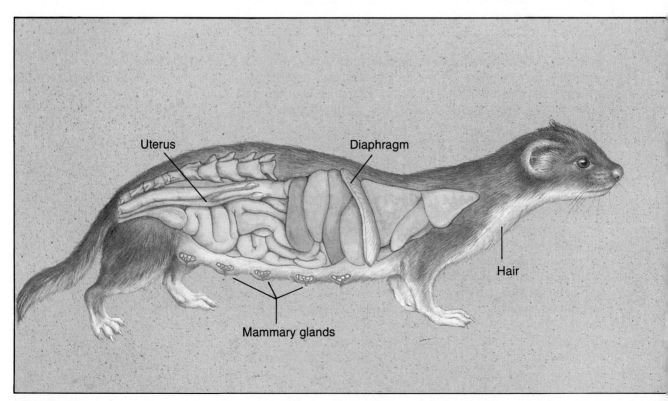

Uterus

Diaphragm

Hair

Mammary glands

Mammals in different groups have teeth adapted for eating different foods. Think of how a carpenter uses different tools, such as a chisel for scraping or a saw for cutting. Like a carpenter's tools, teeth are shaped according to the types of jobs they do. The pointed incisors of moles and shrews can hold small prey. The chisel-like incisors of beavers and mice are perfect for gnawing. Wolves and lions have canines that puncture and tear. Premolars and molars are used for tearing and grinding. Figure 25–1b shows the various types of teeth in different mammals. Most mammals have two sets of teeth in their lifetimes: milk teeth and permanent teeth. Molars often grow later and are not replaced.

Mammals have several characteristics in common with birds and reptiles. Like crocodiles and birds, mammals have a four-chambered heart. The four-chambered heart is more efficient in supplying oxygen to cells than the more primitive three-chambered heart. This efficiency allows for a higher rate of metabolism, which is necessary for nerve function and control of body temperature.

Like birds, mammals are endotherms—they maintain a fairly constant body temperature. Some reptiles maintain stable body temperatures by moving to areas with temperatures they prefer. For example, turtles sun themselves on logs to raise their body temperature and dive into the water to lower it. In contrast, endotherms have internal processes that maintain a constant body temperature. Just as a thermostat controls the temperature of your home, internal processes cool mammals if they are too warm and warm them if they are too cool, thus maintaining homeostasis.

FIGURE 25–1b.

Mammal groups are distinguished by the number and types of teeth they have (left). An advancement seen in mammals is a four-chambered heart, which is more efficient than the three-chambered heart of amphibians.

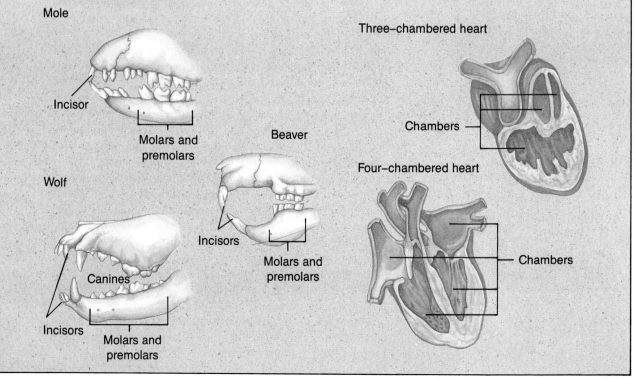

a

b

c

FIGURE 25–2.

Mammals are adapted to their environments. The cheetah can sprint up to 110 km per hour as it pursues its prey (a). The fennec is a desert mammal with large ears that aid heat loss (b). The wolverine has thick fur and is adapted to cold climates (c).

What happens to a mammal when it estivates or hibernates?

25:2 Adaptations in Mammals

Mammals have extraordinary ranges in sizes and body structures. For example, a tiny shrew weighs less than 2 g, while a blue whale can weigh 190 metric tons. Ocean-dwelling mammals are streamlined like fish. Bats, like birds, have wings and are adapted for flight. Armadillos have thick, armorlike plates similar to the scales in reptiles.

The diversity among mammals has allowed them to occupy nearly every environment on Earth. Mammals such as otters and whales live in rivers, lakes, or oceans. Others, such as bats, fly in air. Cheetahs can be found sprinting through grasslands while moles tunnel below the ground.

Climatic changes have had a great influence over mammalian adaptations. Mammals are adapted in many ways to surviving in hot or cold climates. For example, humans keep cool in hot weather by sweating. Cooling results when sweat evaporates from the skin. Adaptations to heat and cold have resulted in variations such as the amount of fur a mammal has, the ability to increase and decrease the flow of blood to the skin, and the ability to find shelter.

In desert environments, where water is limited, some small rodents survive without drinking. They obtain enough water from the foods they eat. Other desert mammals have large ears that aid heat loss. Figure 25–2b shows a mammal that is adapted to desert conditions. What are some of its adaptations to a hot climate?

Desert mammals generally are inactive during the heat of the day and feed at night when it is cooler. Some animals go into a state of estivation. **Estivation** is a state of reduced metabolism during periods of intense heat. As a result, the animal's body temperature lowers and energy is conserved. Mammals that estivate usually dig burrows below ground where it is cooler. Many bats and other small mammals partially estivate. They have lower metabolism and body temperatures during hot days and become active at night.

Many rodents and insectivores hibernate. **Hibernation** is a reduced state of metabolism in response to cold. During hibernation, the body temperature lowers. For example, the golden-mantled ground squirrel has a body temperature of around 37°C during normal activity. When the surrounding temperature drops to about 0°C, the ground squirrel's temperature drops to 2°C and it goes into hibernation. Hibernation conserves the animal's energy.

Other adaptations for cold include thick fur, small ears, and the accumulation of body fat under the skin prior to cold weather. Thick fur and body fat insulate the body and prevent heat loss. Small ears have less surface area than large ears from which body heat can escape.

Based on how they reproduce, mammals have been classified into three major groups. Some mammals, such as the duck-billed platypus, lay eggs. Some, such as kangaroos, carry the young internally until the young are able to move to the pouch and continue development there. In the third and largest group of mammals, the young complete their development inside the mother's body. Examples of this group include dogs, horses, and monkeys.

How are mammals classified into major groups?

REVIEW

1. Name four features of all mammals.
2. Describe three kinds of teeth in mammals.
3. Name three adaptations in mammals to a hot climate.
4. **SKILL REVIEW:** Make a table of the characteristics of mammals. In it, indicate the traits of mammals, their functions, and how they help mammals survive. For more help, refer to Organizing Information in the Skill Handbook, pages 810 to 813.
5. **USING CONCEPTS:** A pronghorn is a mammal that eats grain and wild grasses in fields. Describe the kind of teeth it has.

Objectives:

- compare reproduction in egg-laying, pouched, and placental mammals and give examples of each group.
- distinguish among the major groups of placental mammals and give examples of members of each group.
- trace the evolution of mammals from mammal-like reptiles.

You know that present-day mammals are classified into three major groups based on their methods of reproduction. Other traits used to classify mammals include feeding habits and structural adaptations for locomotion. As you read about the different groups of mammals and their origins, refer to Figure 25–4.

25:3 Monotremes

The smallest group of mammals are the monotremes (MAWN uh treemz). A **monotreme** is a mammal that lays eggs. Modern-day monotremes include the duck-billed platypus, which lives in Australia, and the echidna, a spiny anteater that lives in Australia, Tasmania, and New Guinea. These animals are shown in Figure 25–3.

After monotremes hatch, they lick milk from the skin and hair surrounding the mother's milk glands. Unlike other mammals, mammary glands of monotremes do not have nipples to which young can attach and suckle.

Monotremes are about the size of rabbits and are adapted to different environments. Duck-billed platypuses live in rivers and lakes. They have streamlined bodies, webbed feet, and waterproof fur, all adaptations for swimming. As adults, duck-billed platypuses dig through the mud with their bills, searching for insects and other invertebrates. The spiny anteater lives in dry, brushy areas. Spiny anteaters have strong feet and claws suited for burrowing quickly for protection or food. When threatened, spiny anteaters burrow into the ground until only their spines show. Spiny anteaters have long, sticky tongues for probing rotting wood for termites and ants.

FIGURE 25–3.

The duck-billed platypus (a) and the echidna (b) are monotremes.

a
b

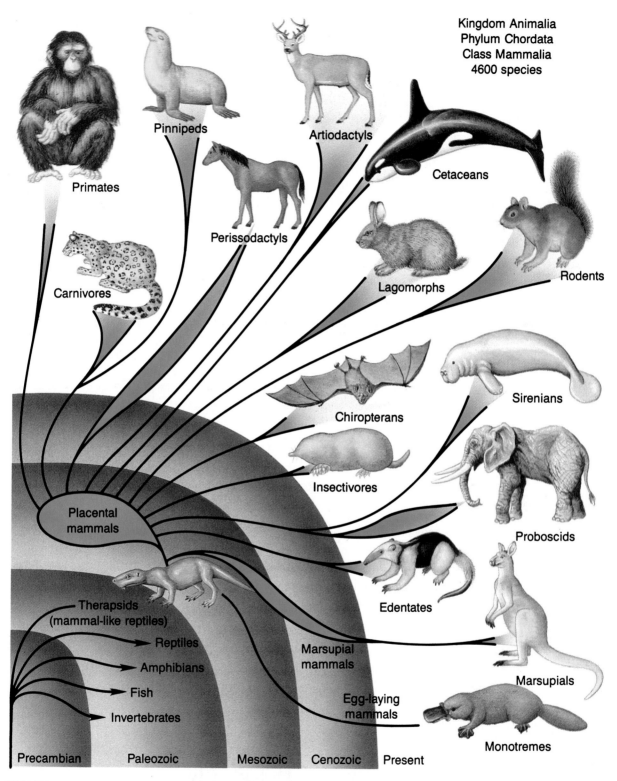

Kingdom Animalia
Phylum Chordata
Class Mammalia
4600 species

Primates

Pinnipeds

Artiodactyls

Cetaceans

Perissodactyls

Carnivores

Lagomorphs

Rodents

Chiropterans

Sirenians

Insectivores

Proboscids

Placental
mammals

Edentates

Therapsids
(mammal-like reptiles)

Reptiles

Amphibians

Marsupial
mammals

Marsupials

Fish

Egg-laying
mammals

Invertebrates

Precambian   Paleozoic   Mesozoic   Cenozoic   Present

Monotremes

FIGURE 25–4.

The radiation of orders of mammals on the geologic time scale shows their
relationships.

FIGURE 25–5.

Marsupials complete development in the mother's pouch. This young joey (baby kangaroo) is old enough to survive outside the pouch, but seeks protection there when danger threatens.

FIGURE 25–6.

At one time, the continents were a solid land mass. By the time the continents separated, marsupials had moved from South America into Australia. Today, most of the world's marsupials, such as the wombat shown here, still live in Australia.

25:4 Marsupials

A **marsupial** is a mammal that has a short period of development in the mother's body followed by a period of development in a pouch outside the mother's body. Marsupials are not developed well enough at birth to survive on their own and must complete development in the pouch. At birth, they use their tiny limbs to wriggle into the pouch. There they attach to the mother's nipples and obtain nourishment. Once they are able to leave the pouch, young marsupials still stay near their mothers and will climb into the pouch for protection.

The marsupials with which you are probably most familiar are the opossum, the only North American marsupial, and the kangaroo from Australia. Other examples of marsupials are the wombat shown in Figure 25–6, the koala, Tasmanian devil, and wallaby. Marsupials live primarily in Australia, Tasmania, and New Guinea. Some are found in South America.

Continental drift is the best explanation for why most of the world's marsupials live in Australia and why most of the placental mammals live in places *other* than Australia. The continents, once connected, have drifted apart over millions of years. The marsupials probably first appeared about 100 million years ago in South America, which was connected to Australia through Antarctica at the time. The marsupials migrated into Australia and attempted to migrate into North America. However, they were unable to compete with the placental mammals already established in North America. Placental mammals followed marsupials into South America, but they were not successful in following them into Australia. Marsupials did become established in Australia, and as Australia drifted away from the other continents, marsupials underwent adaptive radiation.

Marsupials are adapted to several different environments. Most marsupials live on land at ground level, and in tunnels below ground. Some marsupials live in trees. Kangaroos live in brushy areas and feed on grasses. Koalas live in eucalyptus trees, the leaves of which are their primary food source. Others, such as Tasmanian devils, prey on birds, mice, and snakes.

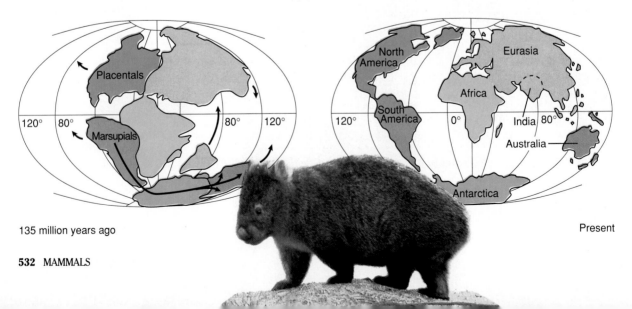

135 million years ago

Present

a

b

FIGURE 25–7.

The star mole (a) has shovel-like feet for tunneling its way through soil. The hedgehog (b) is an insectivore that lives in Europe.

How does a placental mammal get oxygen and nutrients before birth?

25:5 Placental Mammals

About 95 percent of mammals on Earth are placental mammals. A **placental mammal** is a mammal that carries its young inside the uterus until birth. Nourishment of the young inside the uterus occurs through an organ called the **placenta.**

The time during which young placental mammals develop inside the uterus is called **gestation** (jeh STAY shun). The length of gestation varies from species to species. For example, gestation in mice is 21 days, whereas gestation for an elephant is nearly two years. Table 25–1 shows the length of gestation for various mammals. Notice that larger mammals tend to have longer gestation periods.

A great deal of variation exists among placental mammals. Several orders have been identified. Some of the major orders of placental mammals are described on the following pages.

Insectivores

Mammals that eat insects are called insectivores. Members of this order are found worldwide except for Australia, most of South America, and some polar regions. Shrews and moles are insectivores found in the United States. Insectivores found in other parts of the world include golden moles and hedgehogs.

Most insectivores are small animals with long, narrow snouts and sensitive facial whiskers. Some insectivores, such as moles, are adapted for underground life. What adaptations does the mole in Figure 25–7 have for underground life? Most other insectivores are suited for life on land or in trees.

Table 25–1.

GESTATION OF MAMMALS			
Mammal	**Days**	**Mammal**	**Days**
Mouse	21	Human	266
Rabbit	30	Cow	280
Dog and cat	60	Horse	336
Sheep	145	Elephant	660

The shrew is the smallest placental mammal. It spends most of its time obtaining food. Like other insectivores, it has an extremely high metabolic rate. Metabolic rate is a measure of how quickly chemical processes occur in the body. At the beginning of this chapter, you read that a shrew has a pulse rate of 800 beats per minute. A shrew also breathes an astonishing 850 times per minute. In contrast, your heart beats 72 to 75 times per minute at rest, and you breathe 11 to 15 times per minute.

Rodents

The largest group of mammals is the rodents. Porcupines, squirrels, beavers, mice, and guinea pigs are all rodents. They are nearly worldwide in distribution and live in a wide variety of environments. Beavers build their lodges in water, mole rats tunnel underground, and squirrels nest in trees. Specializations for movement in rodents vary from those for leaping in jumping mice and climbing in porcupines to gliding in squirrels and swimming in muskrats.

The main characteristic that distinguishes rodents is a pair of greatly enlarged incisors on both the upper and lower jaws. The incisors are sharp and shaped like a chisel, Figure 25–8c. Rodents have a diet typically consisting of hard seeds, twigs, roots, and bark. The incisors, which continue to grow throughout the life of a rodent, are worn down as the animal chews. The back surface of the incisors wears away, while the front surface, which is quite hard, does not. Therefore, the teeth maintain their sharp edges.

What feature do all rodents have in common?

FIGURE 25–8.

Flying squirrels (a) and muskrats (b) are rodents. Rodents, such as the mole rat (c), have sharp, chisel-like incisors that are well suited to their diet of seeds and roots.

a

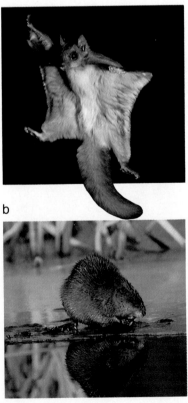

b

c

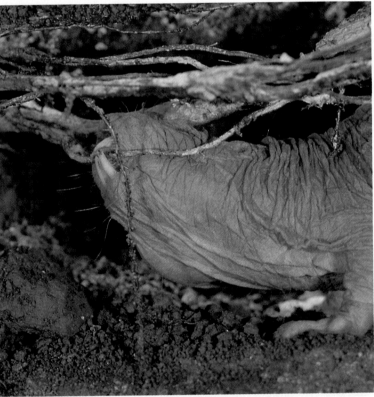

Problem: What objects cause defensive burying behavior in rodents?

Materials
mouse
aquarium with 3 to 5 cm of sawdust or sand
objects for burying
timer
stopwatches (2)

Procedures
When mice are confronted by potential predators, such as snakes, they sometimes spray sand or soil at the predator. This behavior is called defensive burying. Defensive burying can be elicited by objects that resemble predators as well as predators themselves.

1. Copy the data table.
2. Develop a **hypothesis** as to which objects a mouse will spend the most time burying.
3. Place one of the objects on the floor of the aquarium at the end farthest from the animal. **CAUTION:** *Always use care when handling live animals.*
4. Set the timer for eight minutes and start the stop watch at the same time.
5. When the animal starts burying, stop the first stop watch and start the second stop watch. Record the time it took for the animal to start burying.
6. When the animal stops burying, stop the second stopwatch. Record the time spent burying.
7. Reset the second stopwatch. Start it again each time the animal begins burying and

stop it when it stops burying. Record the amount of time spent burying each time. Continue to record burying times until eight minutes have passed.
8. Repeat steps 3 through 7 with the other objects.
9. After filling out the data chart, make a bar graph to illustrate the total amount of time spent burying each object. Refer to the figure if you need help.
10. Put your data on the chalkboard.

Questions and Conclusion
1. Which objects did your mouse spend the most time burying? The least time?
2. How do your results compare with those of the class as a whole?
3. Did any of your objects resemble predators more closely than any others? Which ones?
4. Did the objects that resembled potential predators cause more burying behavior?
5. Does your data support your **hypothesis?** Explain.

Conclusion: What objects cause defensive burying behavior in rodents?

Data and Observations

	Time to Start Burying	Time Spent Burying
Object 1:		
Object 2:		
Object 3:		
Object 4:		

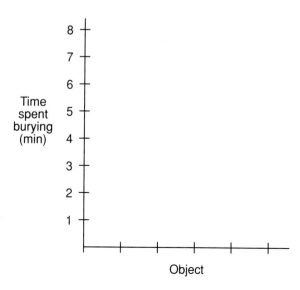

a

b

FIGURE 25–9.

The pika (a) is a lagomorph. The armadillo (b) is an edentate and has a protective covering of bony plates.

lagomorph:
  lagos (GK) hare
  morphe (GK) form
edentate:
  ex (L) without
  dens (L) tooth

NoteWorthy

Sloth hair has small pits in which green algae grow. The algae make the sloth appear green and allow it to blend in with its surroundings.

Lagomorphs

Lagomorphs resemble rodents, though blood studies show the two groups to have no close phylogenetic relationship to one another. Lagomorphs include hares, rabbits, and pikas, Figure 25–9a. These mammals differ from rodents in that they have two pairs of upper incisors. They also have vestigial tails and long legs that are adaptations for jumping and running.

Lagomorphs inhabit many different environments, including the arctic, deserts, mountains, and forests. They feed mainly at dusk or nighttime and eat bark, buds, and grasses. As in rodents, the incisors of these herbivores continue to grow throughout their lives and are worn down as the animals chew. Lagomorphs often spend the daytime hidden in burrows or in vegetation.

Edentates

Anteaters, armadillos, and tree sloths are grouped together in an order known as edentates. These mammals inhabit southern regions of the United States and Central and South America. Edentates lack teeth or have reduced teeth. Anteaters have no teeth at all. They feed on insects. Armadillos and tree sloths lack incisors and canines. Instead, they have peglike molars. Armadillos feed on plant roots; sloths eat leaves.

Anteaters have strong forelegs and large claws suited for digging in termite mounds. They have long snouts and sticky tongues for catching insects. Armadillos, Figure 25–9b, can burrow into hard soil using their strong front feet. When armadillos are disturbed, they curl up into a ball so that their heads and bellies are protected by the bony plates that cover their bodies. Tree sloths have long limbs specialized for hanging and moving in trees. In fact, a tree sloth is so adapted to living in trees that when placed on the ground, it falls over. It cannot support its own weight.

Chiropterans

The chiropterans (kih RAHP tuh runz) are bats, the only flying mammals. Bats have skin that stretches from the body, legs, and tail to the arms and fingers to form thin, membranous wings. The finger bones are greatly elongated. Hooked claws on the thumbs of the forelimbs and on the toes of the hind limbs help a bat to anchor itself when not in flight.

Most bats are active at night. They use a highly developed system of sound detection to guide themselves. You may be familiar with how workers in an airport control tower locate airplanes in flight. The air controllers send out high-frequency radar waves that bounce off the airplanes. When the signals return, they are detected by the control tower antennae. Bats have a similar system of navigation. Instead of using radio waves, as in radar detection, bats use high-frequency sound waves. The use of sound waves to locate objects in the environment is called **echolocation.** Bats emit high-pitched vocalizations that bounce off objects around them, as shown in Figure 25–10. They have very large, sensitive ears for detecting returning sound waves. A bat can determine precisely the size, distance, and rate of movement of objects in its environment. Contrary to popular belief, bats are not blind and do not attempt to fly into people's hair. In fact, some bat species have excellent vision.

There are six main groups of bats. Although all bats fly and use echolocation, each group is structurally adapted according to its particular feeding habits. Most kinds of bats eat insects. Others eat fruit, flowers, fish, or blood. Each is well adapted for its particular lifestyle and environment.

chiropteran:
cheir (GK) hand
pteron (GK) wing

FIGURE 25–10.

Bats, the only members of the chiropteran order, locate prey by means of echolocation.

Sound waves

FIGURE 25–11.

The manatee belongs to the sirenian order.

NoteWorthy

In Greek mythology, sirens were mermaids that lured ships toward shore where they would run aground. Sailors long ago thought the sea cows resembled mermaids.

Water-Dwelling Mammals

Three orders of mammals are adapted for life in water. These mammals have extraordinary diving capabilities and can stay underwater for long periods of time. A layer of fat, called blubber, serves as insulation and provides energy. The three orders of water-dwelling mammals are the cetaceans (sih TAY shunz), pinnipeds, and sirenians.

The cetaceans include whales, dolphins, and porpoises. Cetaceans have streamlined bodies, forelimbs modified into flippers, powerful tails, and no hind limbs. They have very little or no body hair. Cetaceans breathe through blowholes in the tops of their heads and can echolocate as a means of navigation. This order is divided into two main groups—those with teeth that eat prey and those with comblike filters that filter plankton from the water. The blue whale, the largest animal ever to inhabit Earth, is a filter feeder. Sperm whales have teeth and hunt their prey.

The pinnipeds include seals, elephant seals, and sea lions. These mammals spend long periods of time in the water, but move onto land to mate, give birth, or rest. Pinnipeds have hind limbs modified into flippers. In general, they have more hair than whales or sirenians. Certain species have been hunted to extinction for their furs.

The sirenians include the manatees, or sea cows. These animals have very short necks and flattened faces. They are plant-eaters.

Carnivores

Members of this order inhabit a variety of environments worldwide. Most of these animals eat flesh although some, like bears, eat plants as well. Examples of carnivores include dogs, cats, weasels, and hyenas.

Carnivores have long, pointed canines and incisors. Most also have strong jaws and long claws that aid in catching and holding prey. Carnivores usually have a keen sense of smell and good hearing. Many are extremely fast runners. All of these traits are adaptations for catching prey.

FIGURE 25–12.

Carnivores have large canines for grasping and killing prey.

a

b

FIGURE 25–13.

Hoofed mammals with an odd number of toes include the zebra (a). Hoofed mammals with an even number of toes include the moose (b).

What distinguishes the two main groups of hoofed mammals?

Hoofed Mammals

Two orders of mammals have toenails that have become modified as hooves. Hoofed mammals are placed into one of two groups based on the number of toes they have. Animals with an odd number of toes belong to the perissodactyls (puh RIHS uh DAK tulz) and include horses, zebras, and rhinoceroses. Animals with an even number of toes belong to the artiodactyls (ART ee oh DAK tulz) and include deer, moose, camels, hippos, pigs, and cows. Hoofed mammals exist on most continents.

Most hoofed mammals are large and have skeletons adapted for running. Hooves are adaptations that help to increase speed. Speed is an advantage when an animal needs to escape from predators.

Hoofed mammals have teeth with flat grinding surfaces. The teeth are ideal for eating vegetation. Many hoofed mammals chew cud. **Cud chewing** is an adaptation in which swallowed food, particularly grasses, is brought up later and chewed again. When grass is swallowed, cellulose in the cell walls is broken down by bacteria in one of several stomach pouches. The food, called cud, is then brought up. After more chewing, the cud is swallowed again and passed to three other stomach areas where digestion continues. In this way, more nutrients from the plant material are made available to the animal.

Proboscideans

The Asian and African elephants, the largest land mammals alive, make up the order of proboscideans (pruh bahs IHD ee uhnz). The main characteristic of animals in this group is an elongated nose in the form of a flexible muscular trunk. The trunk is used to gather vegetation for eating and to suck up water for drinking.

"Well, there it goes again . . . And we just sit here without opposable thumbs."

An elephant's head is large and has one pair of incisors modified into large tusks. The tusks are used for digging up roots and stripping bark from trees. Elephants have leathery, thick skin that is nearly hairless in the adult. The elephant's skin protects it against dehydration and from the sun's rays.

Primates

Primates are mammals that include monkeys, apes, and humans. Most primates live in warm regions of Africa, Asia, North America and South America. Humans are the only primates that live in nearly all areas on Earth.

Many primates are adapted for life in trees. They have long arms and clasping hands. Notice on your hand how your thumb can touch each of your fingers. A thumb that moves opposite the fingers and can touch each one is called an **opposable thumb.** An opposable thumb is important for grasping. Most species of primates have opposable thumbs and opposable large toes. Many primates have prehensile tails that enable them to swing from limb to limb in trees. A **prehensile tail** is one that can wrap around and hold onto objects. Acute vision with well-developed depth perception also aids movement in trees.

One of the most significant features of primates is a large brain compared with that of other mammals of comparable size. Primates also have a high level of intelligence. Many are capable of performing complex tasks and using tools. Chimpanzees, for example, obtain termites by poking carefully trimmed sticks into the tunnels of termite mounds. Most primates, such as chimpanzees and gorillas, have complex social lives and communication. How many of these characteristics are shared by humans?

FIGURE 25–14.

Primates have opposable thumbs (a), used for grasping objects. Some primates have prehensile tails (b) that can curl around objects for support.

a

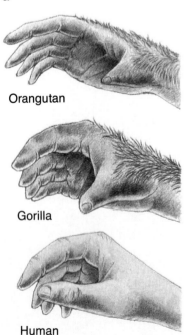

Orangutan

Gorilla

Human

b

25:6 Origins

The fossil record indicates that several groups of mammals could have evolved from therapsids. **Therapsids** were mammal-like reptiles that lived during the Paleozoic Era. These animals lived on Earth between 180 and 270 million years ago and possessed traits of both reptiles and mammals. The lower jaw and middle ear bones of therapsids were like those of reptiles. However, therapsids had straighter legs than reptiles and held them closer to the body, which enabled them to run faster. Therapsids probably were endotherms, as are present-day mammals. Monotremes, marsupials, and placentals are thought to have evolved from therapsids. Due to the unusual method of reproduction in monotremes, however, they are thought to have evolved from a different therapsid ancestor than marsupials and placentals.

The first mammals appeared about 160 to 200 million years ago. They were probably about the size of rats and were insectivores. Rodents were the next mammals to appear in the fossil record. When dinosaurs became extinct at the end of the Mesozoic Era, mammals were able to move into new environments and use food no longer being used by dinosaurs. The appearance of flowering plants at the end of the Mesozoic also supplied new living areas, food, and shelter for mammals. As a result, the numbers and kinds of mammals increased.

The Cenozoic Era is sometimes called the golden age of mammals because of the dramatic increase of mammals in the fossil record. Many of the changes in mammals may have resulted from climatic changes. For example, early in the Cenozoic, Earth became drier. North American grasslands increased and forests grew smaller. Fast-running mammals with adaptations to life in grasslands evolved at this time.

FIGURE 25–15.

Therapsids, the mammal-like reptiles, are the ancestors of present-day mammals.

What events allowed mammals to dominate Earth?

REVIEW

6. How does reproduction differ among monotremes, marsupials, and placentals?
7. Name three groups of placental mammals and describe their characteristics.
8. What are therapsids and what is their relationship to mammals?
9. **SKILL REVIEW:** You discover four new species of mammals. The traits of each species is as follows: Mammal 1—swims, eats plants; Mammal 2—burrows, eats insects; Mammal 3—flies, eats plants; Mammal 4—swims, eats insects. Classify these mammals into two groups. For more help, refer to Organizing Information in the Skill Handbook, pages 810 to 813.
10. **USING CONCEPTS:** Suppose you are a mammal that feeds on pine cone seeds and lives in a forest in a cold region. Describe the adaptations that would help you survive.

HERD SIZE IN MAMMALS

The wildebeest is a large hoofed mammal that may live in migratory herds. Migratory herds of wildebeests reach enormous sizes compared with herds that do not migrate. Migratory animals outnumber nonmigratory animals by a ratio of ten to one. Scientists wondered why the herds that migrated were so much larger than herds that didn't migrate. Was it possible that there was a difference between the amount of food available? Was predation a factor?

In the wet season, migratory herds feed on the open plain and use temporary water holes. In the dry season, these herds migrate to wooded grassland where permanent water holes are found. Resident herds live in the wooded grasslands year-round. Lions and hyenas, the main predators of wildebeest, are stationary. They make their dens and raise their young near resident herds. These predators rarely move onto the open plain.

Scientists found that migratory herds have more food available than resident herds during the wet season. During the dry season, however, both compete for the same food sources. The difference in feeding patterns may account for a difference in herd size of two to one, but not ten to one. How could scientists explain the difference in size between migratory and resident herds?

Herds of wildebeest migrate across the plains in Africa.

IMPORTANCE OF MAMMALS

Why should humans be concerned about other mammals? Mammals are vital for maintaining homeostasis in the environment. Mammals also are beneficial to humans as companions and as food sources. Think about ways you and the environment around you benefit from mammals as you read the next sections.

Objectives:
- describe ways that mammals change the environment.
- explain the importance of preserving mammal species.
- give evidence of how mammals are important in your life.

25:7 Ecology of Mammals

You already realize that mammals are a source of food and clothing for humans. Mammals are also useful in ways you may not be aware of. Burrowing animals, like moles and ground squirrels, alter soil structure and allow for soil aeration. This activity helps plants grow and thrive. Beavers change the environment dramatically when they build dams and ponds. Some mammals pick up plant seeds on their fur and disperse them. Bats pollinate flowers when they feed on nectar. Tropical bats, for example, pollinate crops of avocados, bananas, cashews, dates, and figs. Whales and walruses stir up the ocean floor in search of food and in doing so, increase the productivity of sea life.

Mammals can be problems also. Wild hog populations are increasing rapidly and they are eating and trampling forest vegetation. A

South American rodent similar to the North American muskrat devours acres of rice and sugarcane. Mice and rats carry the organisms that transmit bubonic plague and typhus.

You probably have heard about problems with endangered species. Recall that an endangered species is a species with numbers so low that it is in danger of becoming extinct. This problem is due primarily to destruction of habitat. Successful breeding programs and habitat preservation make the future of the cheetah, panda, and grizzly bear appear hopeful. The red wolf, previously extinct in the wild, has been successfully released in its native habitat.

Why is it important to preserve species? The ecology of an area can be disrupted by the disappearance of a single species. For example, extinction of the mountain lion could cause the number of deer, one of their food sources, to increase. The increase in numbers of deer leads to overgrazing and destruction of habitat. Thus, the homeostatic balance of the ecosystem is upset.

FIGURE 25–16.

Endangered species include the panda, whose numbers are declining due to loss of habitat.

25:8 Usefulness of Mammals

Perhaps you have a dog or a cat as a pet. No one needs to tell you the value of companionship provided by one of these animals. Mammals benefit humans in many ways. Mammals take part in sports such as dogsled racing and rodeo. Guide dogs assist blind people, and monkeys fetch things for people confined to wheelchairs.

Mammals are helpful to humans in medical research and patient treatment. Armadillos are studied in leprosy research because they are the only mammals other than humans to get the disease. Sometimes a patient benefits by having a pet. Holding, stroking, and caring for a pet has been shown to lower blood pressure.

What two new mammalian food sources are being explored?

Biologists are exploring the possibilities of domesticating a South American rodent called a paca in order to use it as a food source. It weighs about 11 kg, is served like turkey, and is quite nutritious. Another rodent, the squirrel, is the second most important game animal in the United States, so there are many people in the United States already eating rodents.

REVIEW

11. Name two ways mammals change the environment.
12. How does the extinction of a species affect an ecosystem?
13. Name two ways mammals are useful to humans.
14. **SKILL REVIEW:** You find a mammal fossil and observe the following traits: hooves, flattened teeth, the size of a large dog. What can you infer about its lifestyle? For more help, refer to Observing and Inferring in the Skill Handbook, page 809.
15. **USING CONCEPTS:** Scientists say that Earth is warming and will be considerably warmer 100 years from now. If you could choose to be any mammal other than a human, which would you want to be 100 years from now if the average daily temperature were 37°C? Explain.

DEVELOPING A VIEWPOINT

HARVESTING THE WILD

Human activities that affect wildlife directly are hunting, whaling, trapping, and fishing. Whenever people harvest wildlife, there is always the potential for upsetting the balance of nature. Are those who harvest wildlife motivated by sport, profit, or by the need to provide food for the human population?

BACKGROUND

Many different species of animals are hunted for a variety of reasons. Whales have been hunted for many years as a business by many nations. Today's whaling ships are fast and efficient. Whales cannot evade them and certain species of whales are approaching extinction.

In Africa, vast herds of animals are dwindling at the hands of sportsmen, zoos, and poachers. Wolves have been largely eliminated from all states except Alaska and Minnesota. Game birds are fewer in number now than they used to be. Deer, on the other hand, have increased in numbers. A possible reason is that many predators of deer are gone.

The efficient methods used by commercial fisheries today bring in enormous catches of fish for food. Methods used to catch fish inadvertently snare other animals as well. Dolphins drown when trapped in nets that catch tuna. How should fishing, whaling, and hunting be regulated?

CASE STUDIES

1. According to the Wildlife Legislative Fund of America, sport hunting, trapping, and fishing do not endanger any wildlife species. Seventy-three million sports enthusiasts in the United States support programs that preserve habitats and protect wildlife through taxes on equipment and license fees. One organization, Ducks Unlimited, has spent more than $280 million to reserve 3.5 million hectares of wetlands for waterfowl and other wildlife.

Under hunter-supported management and regulations, many species are greater in number now than during the last century. Examples are the Canada goose, whitetail deer, beaver, wild turkey, and pronghorn antelope.

2. Since 1900 more than two million whales have been harvested for oil, cosmetics, food, and other products. Gray whales were harvested in such numbers that they became threatened. In 1949, the whaling nations agreed not to hunt this whale anymore. The gray whale has made a comeback and may now be as abundant as it was before large-scale whaling.

3. At one time, many predators were regarded as dangerous animals to be eliminated. Bounties were paid for killing wolves, mountain lions, and coyotes. However, these animals are a necessary part of nature. Predators keep deer and other prey species from overpopulating their habitats and, in many cases, from dying of starvation during the winter. Predators have been reintroduced into some areas to help control the numbers of prey species.

4. The methods used by fisheries to catch large numbers of fish are so efficient that many other organisms are caught as well. Drift nets up to 60 km wide and 15 m deep catch squid, sea turtles, dolphins, seals, birds, and various kinds of fish. These nets are sometimes called "killer nets" because they catch nearly every living thing within their periphery. As fish become scarce from over harvesting, the price of fish goes up. The price increase is an incentive to catch even more fish.

5. Deer are becoming so numerous in some places that they enter residential areas in search of food. They are often seen feeding in corn fields. Deer are so abundant that many of them are hit by cars. Hundreds of deer starve to death during winter. In spite of their abundance, there are strict deer hunting laws in most states. Many conservationists believe it is far more humane to control deer populations by hunting them than by letting them starve. In some states, hunting regulations are being relaxed, and hunters are being allowed to hunt female deer as well as males.

6. Perhaps the greatest danger to some animal species is poaching, or illegal hunting. In Africa, numerous black rhinos have been killed for their horns. Namibian officials are cutting off the rhinos' horns to discourage poachers. In 1970, there were so many African elephants that some biologists were worried about overpopulation. However, the current poaching rate will cause these animals to be extinct by the year 2000. A successful poacher can collect the equivalent of ten years income with one pair of tusks.

DEVELOPING YOUR VIEWPOINT

1. Are hunting fees and taxes the best ways to generate funds for conservation programs?
2. What might be some problems associated with setting up and regulating international whaling bans?
3. Research to find out how coyotes are controlled.
4. Find out how drift nets affect the ocean areas in which they are used.
5. Does overpopulation of an animal species justify hunting it? What are some other ways to control animal populations?

6. Should regulations that allow the harvesting of elephants for their tusks be set up so that elephant hunters can make a living and operate within the law?

SUGGESTED READINGS

1. "Deconstructivist Rhinos." *Discover,* October, 1989, p. 12.
2. Linden, Eugene. "Last Stand for Africa's Elephants." *Time,* Feb. 20, 1989, pp. 76–77.
3. Starr, Douglas. "Civilizing the Hunt." *International Wildlife,* Nov./Dec. 1989, pp. 16–19.
4. Steinhart, Peter. "Taming Our Fear of Predators." *National Wildlife,* Feb./Mar. 1989, pp. 4–13.
5. Watson, Paul. *Sea Shepherd: My Fight for Whales and Seals.* New York: W.W. Norton & Company, Inc., 1982.

Black rhinoceros

CHAPTER REVIEW

SUMMARY

1. Mammals have hair, a four-chambered heart, and a diaphragm. They are endotherms and have mammary glands, different kinds of teeth, well-developed brains, and many have complex behaviors. **25:1**
2. Mammals also have several adaptations to heat and cold. They are classified into three main groups by their methods of reproduction. **25:2**
3. Duck-billed platypuses and spiny anteaters are monotremes, which are egg-laying mammals. **25:3**
4. In marsupials, the young move into the mother's pouch at birth, where they continue to develop. **25:4**
5. Placental mammals are divided into different orders based on their characteristics. Among the major orders are insectivores, rodents, lagomorphs, edentates, chiropterans, cetaceans, pinnipeds, sirenians, carnivores, hoofed mammals, proboscideans, and primates. **25:5**
6. Therapsids gave rise to mammals. The numbers of mammals increased dramatically during the Cenozoic Era. **25:6**
7. Mammals alter the environment in ways that are beneficial and harmful. **25:7**
8. Humans have benefited in many ways from other mammals. **25:8**

LANGUAGE OF BIOLOGY

cud chewing
diaphragm
echolocation
estivation
gestation
hibernation
mammary glands
marsupial

monotreme
opposable thumb
placenta
placental mammal
prehensile tail
therapsids
uterus

Choose the word or phrase from the list above that completes the sentence.

1. A bat finds its way by ____.
2. In general, the larger a mammal is, the longer its ____ period.
3. All mammals have ____.
4. A(n) ____ is an adaptation in humans for grasping.
5. The kangaroo is an example of a(n) ____.
6. ____ were mammal-like reptiles.
7. Desert mammals may undergo ____ to conserve energy.
8. A(n) ____ is an egg-laying mammal.
9. The ____ helps a mammal get oxygen to its cells.
10. ____ is an adaptation that helps hoofed mammals get more nutrients from their food.

REVIEWING CONCEPTS

Choose the word or phrase that completes the sentence or answers the question.

11. An adaptation in mammals that helps maintain body temperature is ____.
    a. a diaphragm   c. hair
    b. a prehensile tail   d. mammary glands
12. Most marsupials live in ____.
    a. South America   c. Australia
    b. North America   d. Africa
13. The young of a placental mammal develop ____.
    a. within a pouch   c. within the uterus
    b. within an egg   d. externally
14. A rodent's teeth are ____.
    a. flattened   c. reduced
    b. always growing   d. like tusks
15. Anteaters, armadillos, and sloths are classified in the same mammal group because ____.
    a. they have reduced teeth or no teeth
    b. they are burrowing animals
    c. they have blubber
    d. they graze

16. An adaptation for flight in bats is ____.
 a. being active at night
 b. hooked claws
 c. large ears
 d. elongated finger bones

17. An adaptation in carnivores for food getting is ____.
 a. toe nails modified as hooves
 b. a keen sense of smell
 c. cud chewing
 d. chisel-like teeth

18. An adaptation in hoofed animals to a diet of plants is ____.
 a. toenails modified as hooves
 b. a keen sense of smell
 c. cud chewing
 d. chisel-like teeth

19. An adaptation in mammals to a cold climate is ____.
 a. hibernation   c. body fat
 b. small ears   d. all of the above

20. Mammals became the dominant animals on Earth ____.
 a. when dinosaurs became extinct
 b. at the end of the Mesozoic Era
 c. when flowering plants appeared
 d. all of the above

UNDERSTANDING CONCEPTS

Answer the following questions using complete sentences.

21. Compare the adaptations of an ocean-dwelling mammal with those of a fish.
22. How are monotremes unlike other mammals?
23. Why must rodents gnaw and chew continually?
24. Which mammals are nearly hairless?
25. How do bats echolocate?
26. Why do most marsupials live in Australia?
27. What adaptations do mammals have to heat and cold?

28. What characteristics make you a primate?
29. What advances in research on mammals might change what you eat?
30. Describe a therapsid.

APPLYING CONCEPTS

Answer the following questions using complete sentences.

31. What is the advantage of bearing live young over laying eggs?
32. Name a mammal group that probably doesn't have sweat glands and explain why it doesn't.
33. What evidence is there that monotremes have a different ancestor than marsupials do?
34. How might the lifestyle of a mammal be different if it were not an endotherm?
35. Put the following groups in order from shortest gestation period to longest: rodents, proboscideans, edentates.

EXTENSIONS

1. Compare the characteristics of cartoon mammals with the adaptations of real mammals.
2. Suppose you are a genetic engineer in the year 3000 A.D. Create the ideal mammal pet.
3. Suppose you are a zookeeper and find that deer eat more in winter than in summer. Propose a hypothesis to explain this observation.

READINGS

Griffiths, M. "The Platypus." *Scientific American,* May 1988, pp. 84–91.

Jolly, A. "Madagascar's Lemurs: On the Edge of Survival." *National Geographic,* Aug. 1988, pp. 132–161.

Vietmeyer, N. "Roast Rodent?" *International Wildlife,* Nov.–Dec. 1988, pp. 14–16.

ANIMAL BEHAVIOR

A female sea turtle returns to the beach on which she hatched. She slowly pulls herself up on the beach and crawls above the high tide line. Using her back flippers, she begins to dig a hole in the sand. When the hole is a certain depth, she lays her eggs. The turtle then carefully covers the eggs with sand. Her task completed, she returns to the sea.

You awaken in the morning to the sound of the alarm clock. Your hand automatically hits the "off" button and you arise from bed. You then get dressed, buttoning all the right buttons, zipping zippers, and tying shoes. After eating breakfast, you walk to your bus stop and catch the correct bus to school.

Both of these stories are examples of animal behavior. Studying and understanding non-human animal behavior can help you understand the roots of your own behavior and allow you to live in harmony with the many other species of animals on Earth.

INNATE BEHAVIOR

Inheritance plays an important role in the way animals behave. You wouldn't expect a duck to tunnel underground or a mouse to fly. Yet, how does a mouse know that it must run when a cat appears? How does a mallard duck know that it must fly south for the winter?

These behaviors are genetically programmed. An animal's genetic information determines how that animal reacts to certain stimuli. Natural selection has shaped the behavior of animals just as it has shaped their body features.

26:1 Genes and Behavior

Behavior is the response of an animal to stimuli in its environment. Behavior evolves as physical characteristics do. For example, dogs demonstrate a large variety of behavior patterns that can be identified with particular breeds. Irish setters have been bred for pointing at hunted game and collies for herding domestic animals. These behaviors have a genetic basis and have been artificially selected by humans.

Objectives:
- give evidence for the genetic basis of behavior.
- recognize and explain the survival value of instinct.

Male (right) and
female (left) crickets

Changes in behavior are also the result of natural selection. The variability of behavior among individuals affects their ability to survive and reproduce. Individuals with behaviors that make them more successful at surviving and reproducing will produce more offspring. The offspring of these individuals will inherit the genetic basis for the successful behaviors or learn the behaviors, while those without the behaviors will die or fail to reproduce. Behavior that's inherited is called **innate behavior.** Let's consider an example of how innate behavior aids reproduction in lizards. In one genus of lizard, there are seven different species living in the same habitat. To attract females, male lizards bob their heads in a pattern that is distinct for their own species. This behavior is genetically controlled and aids mate recognition. Clearly, individuals won't be very successful at reproducing if they don't recognize the proper mate.

Genetically controlled behavior often can be distinguished from learned behavior by performing crossing experiments. For example, the songs produced by crickets are distinct for each species. Crossing two species that have different songs produces a hybrid cricket with a song unlike either of the original two cricket species. This new song isn't recognized by females of either species. Thus, song recognition in crickets is genetically programmed.

Behavior also can be used to show the evolutionary relatedness of species. If two species are closely related, their behavior, as well as their body forms, will be more alike than if they are not closely related. In Figure 26–1, you can see that the two snakes not only look similar, they also share behavior patterns.

Natural selection shapes a variety of behaviors that help individuals survive. Finding food, escaping predators, finding a mate, preparing a nest site, caring for young, and determining which environmental stimuli are important are examples of behaviors that are affected by natural selection.

FIGURE 26–1.

Cobras share behavioral patterns, including flattening of the neck when aroused.

FIGURE 26–2.

Wood ducklings instinctively jump into the water after hatching to search for food.

26:2 Reflexes and Instinct

The simplest form of innate behavior is a reflex. A **reflex** is a simple, automatic response that involves no conscious control. You automatically blink your eyes when an object is thrown in your face. Reflexes are important to simple animals also. A mollusk withdraws into its shell when touched. The touch stimulus may be that of a mollusk predator. These examples show that reflexes have survival value in protecting animals from danger.

An **instinct** is a complex pattern of innate behavior. A reflex can happen in less than a second. Instinctive behaviors may have several parts and take weeks to complete. Instinctive behavior begins when the animal recognizes a stimulus and continues until all parts of the behavior have been performed. Greylag geese instinctively retrieve eggs that have rolled from the nest and will go through the motions of egg retrieval even when the eggs are taken away. Instinctive behavior allows animals to survive on their own with little parental care. Wood ducks build their nests high in hollow trees. Wood ducklings instinctively jump into the water to hunt for food. They can't go back to the nest and are not fed by their parents. Without this instinctive behavior, the wood duckling wouldn't survive.

How is instinctive behavior adaptive?

REVIEW

1. How can inherited and learned behaviors be distinguished?
2. How is a reflex different from an instinct?
3. What is innate behavior?
4. **SKILL REVIEW:** Design an experiment to test whether the red belly of a male stickleback fish is the stimulus that elicits fighting behavior in other males. For more help, refer to Designing an Experiment in the Skill Handbook, pages 802 to 803.
5. **USING CONCEPTS:** How is innate behavior an advantage to an animal that hatches from an egg after its mother dies?

Objectives:
- recognize and explain the survival value of learning and imprinting.
- recognize the conditions that must occur before learning can take place.
- describe how trial and error learning and conditioning occur.
- explain how learning by insight takes place and explain what language is.

Incubation of eggs is usually an instinctive behavior in birds. However, some birds need to learn what to incubate. In an experiment with albatrosses that had little experience with nesting, scientists found that these birds would incubate a grapefruit just as if it were an egg! Albatrosses, it was discovered, must learn what an egg looks like. Sometimes behavior is innate, sometimes learned, but often it is a combination of both.

26:3 Learning

Learning is behavior that can be changed through practice or experience. The more complex an animal's brain, the more elaborate are the patterns of its learned behavior. In humans, many behaviors are learned. Speaking, reading, writing, and playing a sport are all learned. Remember when you learned to tie your shoes, ride a bike, or swim? Even these simple behaviors are learned.

Although you have learned thousands of behaviors since you were born, some animals learn things that you could never do. For example, Pacific salmon learn the precise chemical makeup of the water where they hatched. They return a distance of around 1400 km to the same stream four years later to lay their eggs. Some birds learn, after hearing it only once, a song with notes so rapid and complicated that you couldn't follow it.

Learning has survival value in a changing environment because it permits behavior to change in response to varied conditions. Learning allows an animal to adapt to change, an ability that is especially important in animals with longer life spans. The longer an animal lives, the more chance there is that its environment will change and that it will encounter unfamiliar situations. Therefore, it is important that the animal be able to modify its behavior.

FIGURE 26–3.

Salmon are able to return to the streams in which they hatched because they have learned the chemical makeup of the water.

26:4 Imprinting

Imprinting is a form of learning in which an animal forms a social attachment to another organism soon after hatching or birth. Imprinting can take place only during a specific period of time during an animal's life. This specific period of time is sometimes referred to as the sensitive time period. Even though imprinting is learned, it usually is irreversible. For example, birds that leave the nest immediately after hatching, such as geese, imprint on their mother. They learn to recognize and follow her within a day of hatching. This behavior has important survival value because goslings must follow their mother to find food and protection. However, goslings will imprint on other objects or animals if the mother is absent during the sensitive time period. In fact, if you were present during hatching, the goslings could imprint on you. Even if the real mother were to return after the sensitive time period, the goslings would continue to follow you. This preference can remain throughout the bird's life. Figure 26–4 shows the results of imprinting in goslings.

26:5 Trial and Error

The first time a young jackdaw starts to build a nest, it will use grass, bits of glass, stones, empty cans, old light bulbs, and anything else it can find. With experience, the bird finds that grasses and twigs make a better nest than light bulbs do. In this example, the jackdaw is learning by **trial and error,** a type of learning in which an animal receives a reward for making a particular response. When an animal tries one solution and then another in the course of obtaining a reward, in this case a suitable nest, it is learning by trial and error.

FIGURE 26–4.

Konrad Lorenz, a renowned ethologist (scientist who studies animal behavior), studied imprinting in ducks and geese. He found that young goslings can imprint on any object or organism that is present during hatching. Usually, that organism is the mother.

How does an animal learn by trial and error?

Some animals learn what food is suitable for eating by trial and error. When rats are confronted with a new food source, they sample a very small amount of it. In this way, they learn which food is unsuitable. Mice learn by trial and error to go through a maze for a food reward. The first time through the maze, the mouse takes many wrong turns. After several trials, the mouse has learned the correct route and reaches the food sooner. The ability to learn about its surroundings has survival value for an animal. It enables the animal to find food, water, or nesting spots.

Motivation, an internal need that causes an animal to act, is necessary for learning to take place. Motivation often involves satisfying a physical need, such as hunger or thirst. If an animal isn't motivated, it won't learn. Animals that aren't hungry won't respond to a food reward.

Punishment also influences learning. If a dog is consistently punished for chewing shoes, the dog will learn to resist the temptation to chew shoes. However, since motivation speeds up learning, a reward usually results in faster learning than punishment does.

26:6 Conditioning

When you first got a new kitten it would meow and rub against your ankles as soon as it could smell the aroma of cat food in the can or bag you were opening. After a couple of weeks, the sound of the electric can opener or the rustle of paper would attract your kitten, causing it to meow and rub against your ankles. Your kitten had become conditioned to respond to a stimulus other than the smell of food. **Conditioning** is learning by association. Your kitten learned to associate the sound of the can opener or the opening of the bag with a meal. Soon, your cat conditions you. You associate ankle-rubbing and meowing with an empty food dish.

What is a conditioned response?

FIGURE 26–5.

Many pets become conditioned to respond to the sound of a can opener. A typical response to this type of conditioning is shown here.

| Dog smells food and salivates. | Dog smells food while a bell is rung. Dog salivates. | Bell is rung and dog salivates. |

A well-known example of an early experiment in conditioning is illustrated in Figure 26–6. In 1900, Ivan Pavlov, a Russian biologist, first demonstrated conditioning in dogs. He knew that dogs salivated when they smelled food. Responding to the smell of food is a reflex, an example of innate behavior. By ringing a bell each time he presented food to a dog, Pavlov established an association between the food and the ringing bell. Eventually, the dog began to salivate at the sound of the bell alone. The dog had been conditioned to respond to a stimulus that it did not normally associate with food.

Conditioning is important for the survival of many animals. If they learn to associate certain signals with potential predators and other signals with potential food sources, they will be more likely to survive.

FIGURE 26–6.

Pavlov demonstrated conditioning in dogs by ringing a bell whenever he presented food.

26:7 Insight

In a classic study of animal behavior, a chimpanzee was given two bamboo poles, neither of which was long enough to reach some fruit placed outside its cage. The chimpanzee tried to reach the fruit with the poles. When that didn't work, it gave up and began playing with the poles. By accident, it managed to join the poles by pushing the end of the narrower pole into the hollow end of the other pole. It then used the long pole it had created to retrieve the fruit. This is an example of reasoning with insight. **Insight** is learning in which an animal uses previous experience to respond to a new situation. The animal forms a concept, or idea. The concept formed by the chimpanzee was that the added length of the pole would allow it to reach the fruit. Insight is different from trial and error learning. Both involve experience, but insight enables the animal to use previous experience to solve new problems.

NoteWorthy

In an experiment, students agreed (unknown to the teacher) to smile only when their teacher placed his hand accidently on his chest, and later when he placed his hand inside his shirt. In a remarkably short time, the professor spent the entire class period imitating Napoleon.

FIGURE 26–7.

Gorillas and chimpanzees can be taught to recognize symbols that represent objects. Here, Koko the gorilla is being taught to use a keyboard to communicate.

Much of human learning is based on insight. When you were a baby, you learned a great deal by trial and error. As you grew older, you relied more on insight. When you learned mathematics, you first learned to count. Based on your concept of numbers, you then learned to add and subtract. You continued to solve problems in mathematics based on your past experience with the subject.

Language, the use of symbols to represent ideas, is present primarily in animals with complex nervous systems, memory, and insight. Humans, with the help of spoken and written language, can benefit by what others have learned and don't have to experience everything for themselves. Humans can use accumulated knowledge as a basis on which to build new knowledge. Chimpanzees aren't physically able to talk in the same way as humans do, but they are capable of learning simple sign language. Chimpanzees can recognize symbols and words that represent objects and events. They can put words together to make simple sentences.

What is language?

REVIEW

6. What are four types of learned behavior?
7. What is the main difference between imprinting and other types of learned behavior?
8. How does learning have survival value in a changing environment?
9. **SKILL REVIEW:** Two dog trainers teach dogs to do tricks. One trainer gives her dog a biscuit whenever the dog correctly performs the trick. The other trainer does not. Which trainer will be more successful at dog training? Why? For more help, refer to Observing and Inferring in the Skill Handbook, page 809.
10. **USING CONCEPTS:** How would a mouse respond if the position of food in a maze were changed?

BIOLAB

Innate and Learned Behavior

Problem: How do innate and learned behavior differ?

Materials
mirror   stopwatch

Procedures

Part A
1. Copy the data table.
2. Look at your eyes in a mirror and note the size of your pupils with the lights on and then off.
3. Develop a **hypothesis** about whether the length of time it takes your pupils to change size will increase, decrease, or stay the same with successive trials.
4. The teacher will turn off the classroom lights. When the teacher turns on the lights and announces, "Begin!" start the stopwatch. Time how long it takes your pupils to change size. Record your data in your table.
5. Repeat step 4 four more times.

Part B
1. Note the diagram of the star.
2. Position a mirror as shown in the diagram.
3. While looking *only* into the mirror, try to trace the star.

4. Develop a **hypothesis** about whether the amount of time it takes you to trace the star will increase, decrease, or stay the same with successive trials.
5. Repeat steps 2 and 3 four more times. Have a partner use a stopwatch to time how long it takes you to draw the star. Record the data in your table.
6. Switch jobs with your lab partner and repeat steps 2 through 5.

Data and Observations

Time in seconds		
Trial	Pupil change	Trace star
1		
2		
3		
4		
5		

Questions and Conclusion
1. Was the behavior in Part A innate or learned? Why?
2. Was the behavior in Part B innate or learned? Why?
3. Did you accept your **hypotheses?** Explain.

Conclusion: How do innate and learned behavior differ?

Objectives:

- recognize and explain the survival value of territorial behavior, aggression, biological rhythms, and social hierarchies.
- explain why courtship behavior helps to ensure reproductive success.
- explain how and why animals communicate with each other.

Why do animals set up territories?

You have studied how behavior is inherited and how some behaviors can be modified by learning. Many of the behaviors animals exhibit are neither strictly learned nor strictly inherited. Regardless of whether they are innate or learned, however, appropriate behaviors help animals survive and are, therefore, adaptive. Defending resources, finding suitable mates, and maintaining relationships with other members of a group are activities that require animals to behave in certain ways if they are to survive and reproduce.

26:8 Territorial Behavior and Aggression

Many animals set up territories. A **territory** is an area that is defended against others of the same species. For animals such as gibbons, a territory represents a food supply. The establishment of territories results in more gibbons surviving and rearing young successfully. Territories allow the gibbons to spread out and use food from a wide area, rather than being crowded together and competing for the same resources.

A territory is often set up by a male as a place for a female to lay eggs or care for young. For example, the male stickleback fish defends a place on a stream bed for this purpose. The male bowerbird builds an elaborate structure called a bower and decorates it with bright objects, such as pieces of broken glass, plastic, and bottlecaps. The bowerbird defends this territory and uses the bright objects to attract females.

FIGURE 26–8.

Male bowerbirds attract females by building a bower and decorating it with bright objects.

FIGURE 26–9.

Bighorn sheep and Hercules beetles engage in aggressive behaviors to defend territories and resources such as mates or food.

Many animals produce chemicals that are used for marking territorial boundaries and locating mates. A **pheromone** is a chemical given off by an animal in order to cause a specific behavior in another animal of the same species. For example, hyenas mark the boundaries of their territories with a strong smelling pheromone given off by glands near the base of the tail. Members of one clan of hyenas rarely come into the territory of another clan. Wolves mark their territories by urinating at the boundaries. Wolf urine contains pheromones that warn other wolves to stay away. Marking territories results in the spacing out of animals so they don't compete for the same food supply in a small space.

Animals occasionally engage in aggression. **Aggression** is behavior that is used to intimidate or damage another organism. For example, animals fight or threaten each other to defend their young, their territory, or a resource such as food. Other aggressive behaviors, such as bird song, deliver the message to others of the same species to keep away.

Animals rarely fight to the death. Aggression in animals is not usually in the form of direct combat, but a series of symbolic aggressive displays. Animals with sharp teeth, beaks, claws, or horns could kill each other, but they seldom use these structures as weapons against members of their own species. In many species, these structures are reserved for killing prey or defending against attack from another species. For example, poisonous snakes don't bite each other. Instead they wind around each other and butt heads. A defeated animal either leaves the area or shows a submissive posture that keeps the winner from killing it.

NoteWorthy

In prides of lions, closely related females cooperatively defend a territory and live within it their entire lives. Males are ejected from the pride at maturity. They then take over a pride of unrelated females. This behavior prevents inbreeding.

Different species of
fireflies can be recognized
by their flash patterns

26:9 Courtship Behavior

Courtship behavior is a behavior that males and females of a species carry out before mating. Like other behaviors, courtship has evolved by natural selection. In species where females choose their mates, behavior of the male during courtship helps females select the best mates. Many courtship behaviors demonstrate the ability of an animal to be a successful parent. For example, a male bird may present a female with a twig, indicating his willingness to participate in nest building.

Some courtship behaviors are necessary to prevent females from killing males before they have had the opportunity to mate. In some spiders, the male is smaller than the female and risks the chance of being eaten if he approaches her. Before mating, the male presents the female with a "nuptial gift," an insect wrapped in a silk web. While the female is unwrapping and eating the insect, the male is able to mate with her without being attacked. After mating, however, the male may be eaten by the female anyway. Death is the price the male pays for successful reproduction.

Some courtship behaviors allow potential mates to find each other over long distances. The female silkworm moth releases a phero-mone that can attract males over a distance of several kilometers. Many frogs make sounds that can be heard for hundreds of meters.

Courtship behavior can aid in species recognition. Courtship be-haviors and songs are different for each species. For example, grass-hoppers rub their legs together, while crickets rub their wings to-gether to make distinctive calls that are recognized by potential mates. Males of different species of fireflies produce different flash patterns when they are flying around in search of mates. A female of the same species on the ground flashes back a signal that is recog-nized by the male. He then flies down to mate with her.

FIGURE 26–10.

Courtship behavior in western grebes involves an elaborate ritual that includes a walk across water.

Courtship also can synchronize male and female reproductive activity. In ring doves, the female undergoes hormonal changes during courtship that are stimulated by the male's behavior. These changes prepare her body for egg production.

26:10 Internal Clocks

A **biological rhythm** is a cyclic or repeated pattern of behavior. Many animals change their behavior in response to a day/night cycle. For example, many animals sleep at night and are awake during the day. A 24-hour cycle of behavior is called a **circadian** (suhr KAYD ee uhn) **rhythm.** In addition to a circadian rhythm, some animals change their activity in response to changes in the tides, the moon, or day length. The feeding behavior of mosquitoes follows a circadian rhythm. They feed mostly at dawn and dusk each day. Many oysters open their shells with a rhythm that corresponds to the rise and fall of the tide. Their shells are open when the tide is high and they are covered with water. When the tide goes out and the oysters are exposed to air, their shells close.

Rhythms can also occur yearly. Migration is a yearly rhythm. **Migration** is the instinctive, seasonal movement of animals. In the United States, about two-thirds of bird species fly south in the fall to feeding areas. The birds fly north again in the spring to their breeding areas. Change in day length is thought to stimulate the onset of migration. Animals navigate in a variety of ways. Some use the positions of the sun and the stars to navigate. They may use geographic clues, such as mountain ranges. Many bird species are guided by Earth's magnetic field. Migration takes remarkable strength and endurance. The Arctic tern migrates between the Arctic Circle and the Antarctic, a one-way flight of almost 18 000 km.

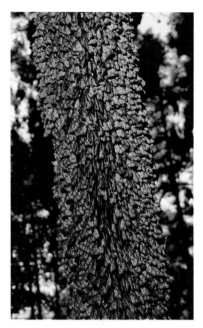

FIGURE 26–11.

Each year, thousands of monarch butterflies migrate from all over the United States and Canada to the southern United States and Mexico to breed.

What is a biological rhythm?

circadian:
circa (L) about
dies (L) day

Other yearly rhythms are hibernation and estivation. In Chapter 25, you studied that hibernation, a period of dormancy characterized by deep sleep, low metabolism, and low body temperature, allows mammals such as woodchucks and marmots to survive the winter with minimal output of energy. You also learned in Chapter 25 that estivation, a condition of dormancy similar to hibernation, is common in conditions of extreme heat. Some desert rodents cope with the harsh desert summer by estivating.

26:11 Social Behavior

Some animals spend almost their entire lives alone. Many large carnivores, such as polar bears, interact with other individuals of their species only to mate. Other animals, however, live together in groups. Examples are herds of deer, colonies of bees, and cities of humans. A **society** is a group of animals of a single species living together in an organized way.

Social behavior evolves when animals survive and reproduce better in a group than when alone. Often, animals are safer in a group than alone. A group may also act together to hunt prey. A lone wolf may not be able to kill large prey, such as an adult moose, but a group of wolves easily can. Wolves cooperate with one another during an attack, with each wolf attacking a different part of the prey's body. Other advantages of societies may be the communal rearing of young among closely related animals, such as lions, or the division of labor, such as in human and termite societies.

Why might animals hunt cooperatively?

FIGURE 26–12.

Wolves live together socially in packs and cooperate in hunting and raising their young. Strong bonds form among the members of the pack.

Animal groups are sometimes organized into different authority levels called a **dominance hierarchy.** A dominance hierarchy is like the chain of command in an army or in any business. Hierarchies often result in reduced aggression and competition because once the hierarchy is established, the members of the group know their places and can exist in harmony. Usually, one animal is the top-ranking individual. This animal often gets first access to food, water, mates, and sleeping areas. There might be several levels of individuals, each subordinate to the one above. The "pecking order" of chickens is a dominance hierarchy that is formed by chickens. The top-ranking chicken can peck any other chicken. The chicken lowest in the hierarchy is pecked at by all other chickens in the group. Two chickens approaching each other may fight, or one may give way peacefully to the other. A social hierarchy often prevents energy being wasted on continuous fighting. This energy may then be invested in reproduction. A dominance hierarchy also may be adaptive in providing a way for females to choose the best males for mating. Choosing a high-ranking male may allow a female to have better food sources or better protection for her young.

FIGURE 26–13.

Chickens form a pecking order, a dominance hierarchy in which more dominant individuals peck at less dominant individuals.

NoteWorthy

Animal groups often have colorful common names, such as a cloud of gnats, a murder of crows, a leap of lizards, a knot of toads, a gam of whales, a clowder of cats, and an exaltation of larks.

26:12 Communication

Animals communicate with each other in order to locate food, reproduce, and defend themselves. **Communication** is an exchange of information. Animals have three channels of communication open to them. They signal each other by sounds, sights, or smells. Sounds have the advantage of radiating out in all directions and being heard a long way off. The sounds of the humpback whale can be heard 1200 km away. Sounds such as songs, roars, and calls are best for communicating a lot of information quickly. For example, the song of a male cricket tells his sex, his location, and his social status.

Green tree frog

FIGURE 26–14.

Ants follow chemical trails left by other ants to find food sources.

Visual signals cannot be seen from far away, but are effective for communicating at short distances. You have already read about courtship behavior, a form of communication that uses visual displays. Visual displays might also indicate aggression or defense. For example, male bull's eye fish are silver when threatened and orange when aggressive. Visual displays also can convey important information to group members. When honeybees return to the hive from a food source, they dance in specific ways to indicate the distance and direction to the food.

Signals that use odors are broadcast widely and carry a general message. You know what the smell of a skunk means: Stay away! Other odor signals carry other messages. For example, an aroused honeybee releases an alarm pheromone that alerts other bees to assume aggressive postures and to be ready for attack. Ants leave odor trails that are used by other group members to find food. As you know, pheromones also may be used to attract mates.

REVIEW

11. Why do animals defend territories?
12. How is courtship behavior adaptive?
13. What is a dominance hierarchy and how is it adaptive?
14. **SKILL REVIEW:** Design an experiment to show that ants leave chemical trails to show other ants where food can be found. For more help, refer to Designing an Experiment in the Skill Handbook, pages 802 to 803.
15. **USING CONCEPTS:** In experiments, penguins were able to navigate to their breeding grounds when the sky was overcast. What cues did they probably use to find their way?

CAREER CHOICES

If you are interested in animals, there are a variety of careers that might appeal to you. Specialists in fish, mammals, reptiles, and other animals work in a variety of occupations in laboratories, offices, zoos, and on wildlife refuges.

As a **wildlife specialist,** you might concentrate on studying birds, mammals, or endangered species. If your job were to study endangered species, you might be involved in analyzing computer records of captive endangered species all over the world. Your job might be to decide which mammals, based on their genetic relationship to each other, would be suitable mates. If you were employed as a bird specialist you might work on a wildlife refuge. In the spring you might paddle a canoe in ponds where you had set up nesting boxes in hollow trees. These structures provide nesting places for wood ducks, a species that requires hollow trees for nesting. From your canoe, you would count the eggs in the nests to determine if the ducks found these structures attractive for nesting. If you were a mammal specialist, you might study the behavior of gorillas in a zoo and compare this behavior to that of primates in the wild. You might be involved in determining the possible effect of a proposed power plant on a deer population. To do this, you might spend a couple of months on cross-country skis examining the daily movement patterns of wild deer herds. You might be employed by a state wildlife agency to take a census of a beaver population. You could spend your days riding in a helicopter and scanning the ground with binoculars for beaver ponds, lodges, and dams.

A **fishery biologist** is a scientist involved in managing fishery resources. If you were a fishery biologist, you might have to come up with a plan to deal with a problem of overpopulation of certain fish species in a particular body of water. You might also supervise habitat improvements. Or, you might raise eggs and young fish in a hatchery for later release into the wild. A fishery biologist conducts inventories of fish and is responsible for protecting rare and endangered fish species. As a fishery biologist, you might work closely with state wildlife agencies and the United States Fish and Wildlife Service to manage aquatic ecosystems in the National Forests.

Say cheese! As a **wildlife photographer,** you might spend much of your time focusing on a frog, mingling with monkeys, eyeing an elephant, or following a fish to get the perfect shot. Many wildlife photographers are self-employed and sell their photographs to magazine, textbook, and tradebook publishers. A wildlife photographer may travel all over the world to capture pictures of animals in their natural habitats. Wildlife photography might include spending many hours perched in trees, wading through swamps, or swimming around a coral reef to get the picture worth a thousand words. A wildlife photographer might also work with a museum exhibitor to plan, design, and set up wildlife exhibits in a museum.

Wildlife specialist

Fishery biologist

Wildlife photographer

565

CHAPTER REVIEW

SUMMARY

1. Behavior is controlled by genes and modified by natural selection. **26:1**
2. Reflexes are simple forms of innate behavior. Instincts are complex patterns of innate behavior. **26:2**
3. Learning has survival value because it allows behavior to be modified. **26:3**
4. Imprinting, trial and error, conditioning, and insight are types of learned behavior with important survival value to animals. **26:4, 26:5, 26:6, 26:7**
5. Aggression toward members of the same species rarely causes injury or death. **26:8**
6. Courtship behavior helps to ensure successful reproduction. **26:9**
7. Biological rhythms are behavior patterns repeated at regular intervals. **26:10**
8. Animals living in groups may form dominance hierarchies that result in reduced aggression. **26:11**
9. Animals communicate by sound, visual signals, and smells. They communicate to find food and mates, to defend themselves, and to indicate aggression. **26:12**

LANGUAGE OF BIOLOGY

aggression
behavior
biological rhythm
circadian rhythm
communication
conditioning
courtship behavior
dominance hierarchy
imprinting
innate behavior
insight
instinct
language
learning
migration
motivation
pheromone
reflex
society
territory
trial and error

Choose the word or phrase from the list above that completes the sentence.

1. Behavior that is inherited is called ____.
2. A(n) ____ is a complex pattern of innate behavior.
3. Fighting behavior is called ____.
4. A 24-hour cycle of behavior is called a(n) ____.
5. An animal group organized into different authority levels is a(n) ____.
6. ____ is an exchange of information.
7. An area that is defended against others of the same species is a(n) ____.
8. ____ is a form of learning in which an animal forms a social attachment soon after birth.
9. ____ is the yearly movement of animals.
10. ____ is an internal need that causes an animal to act.

REVIEWING CONCEPTS

Choose the word or phrase that completes the sentence or answers the question.

11. Behavior is shaped by ____.
    a. natural selection   c. migration
    b. territories   d. aggression
12. Courtship behavior may include ____.
    a. sounds   c. pheromones
    b. flashes of light   d. all of the above
13. Annual rhythms include ____.
    a. hibernation   c. migration
    b. estivation   d. all of the above
14. Learning cannot take place without ____.
    a. instinct   c. motivation
    b. imprinting   d. insight
15. Animals communicate in order to ____.
    a. locate food   c. defend themselves
    b. reproduce   d. all of the above
16. ____ involves the formation of a concept.
    a. instinct   c. imprinting
    b. insight   d. innate

17. Complex language is found mainly in animals with ____.
    a. pheromones   c. reflexes
    b. insight   d. territories
18. A duckling following its mother after it hatches is an example of ____.
    a. trial and error   c. imprinting
    b. insight   d. migration
19. ____ involves learning by making mistakes.
    a. Imprinting   c. Trial and error
    b. Conditioning   d. Insight
20. Pulling your hand away from a hot object is an example of a(n) ____.
    a. reflex   c. punishment
    b. instinct   d. biological rhythm

UNDERSTANDING CONCEPTS

Answer the following questions using complete sentences.

21. What is the survival value of variable behavior?
22. Which type of learning is more complex, trial and error or insight? Why?
23. Compare the advantages and disadvantages of innate behavior and learned behavior.
24. Name a behavior you learned by trial and error, by conditioning, and by insight.
25. By accident, a gull drops a snail on the road. The snail's shell breaks and the gull eats the snail. The gull continues to drop mollusks on the road. What type of behavior is this?
26. Chameleons can catch insects on the first try. Is this behavior innate or learned?
27. Explain how courtship could aid in species recognition.
28. Bighorn rams are rarely injured or killed when they fight. Why?
29. When a dog gives up a fight, it exposes its neck. What type of behavior is this?
30. During the mating season, male deer roar. For what purpose?

APPLYING CONCEPTS

Answer the following questions using complete sentences.

31. Why do large grazing animals, such as zebras, live in herds?
32. When Charles Darwin visited the Galapagos Islands in 1835, he was amazed that the animals would allow him to touch them. Why were they not afraid?
33. Can you suggest any advantages of a dominance hierarchy in a nonterritorial species?
34. You want your dog to bring your slippers when the alarm clock rings in the morning. How would you train it to do this?
35. Sheep and monkeys recognize the faces of their own species in photographs. Sheep cannot identify upside-down faces, but monkeys can. Why?

EXTENSIONS

1. Write a report on Karl von Frisch's research on honeybee communication.
2. Set up a feeding station for squirrels or birds. Record the time the animals spend feeding, watching, chasing, and vocalizing.
3. Design a maze to compare the length of time it takes rats and gerbils to learn the maze.

READINGS

Blaustein, Andrew R. and Richard O'Hara. "Kin Recognition in Tadpoles." *Scientific American,* Jan. 1986, pp. 108–116.

Heinrich, Bernd. "The Raven's Feast." *Natural History,* Feb. 1989, pp. 44–50.

Slater, Peter J.B. (Editor). *The Encyclopedia of Animal Behavior.* New York: Facts on File Publications, 1987.

HUMAN BIOLOGY

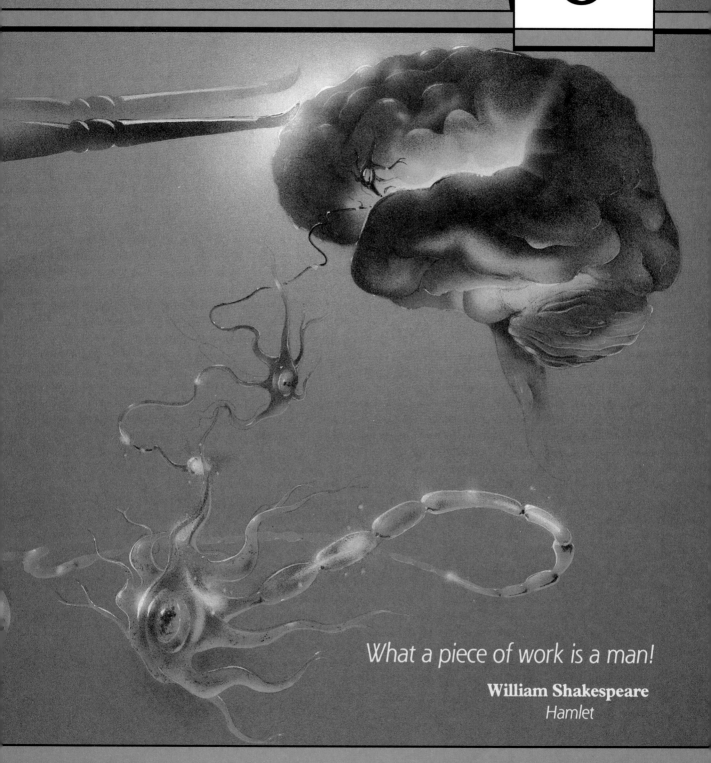

What a piece of work is a man!

William Shakespeare
Hamlet

Chapter 27

NERVOUS AND CHEMICAL CONTROL

There you are, seated next to your best friend, in the front car of a roller coaster. Right now you are wondering why you said you'd take this ride. Calm is hardly the word for what you are feeling. Your hands are sweating, and you are trying to swallow normally. In your body, molecules are splitting, and cells are dividing. Impulses are bolting through your nervous system. Your heartbeat begins to increase. Periodically, you take great gulps of air. The activities of your body accelerate with anticipation of what you are about to experience. How does your body maintain control in situations like this? In this chapter you will study two systems that control and regulate human body activities under all conditions—the nervous system and the endocrine system.

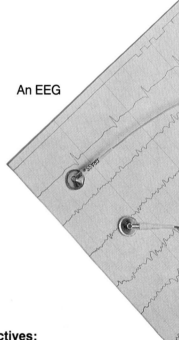

An EEG

BODY ORGANIZATION

Your body contains about 100 trillion cells. The body systems that control and monitor reactions to your internal and external environment depend on these cells operating together. These systems keep body activity in check by processing information and by enabling you to make adjustments to changes that take place from minute to minute in your environment.

Objectives:
- describe the four types of body tissues.
- identify major body organs and systems.

27:1 Body Tissues

In Chapter 1, a tissue is described as a group of cells that function together to perform an activity. The cells of the body are organized into four basic tissues. These four tissues are epithelial tissue, connective tissue, muscle tissue, and nerve tissue. Each type of tissue is adapted to perform specific functions.

Epithelial tissue is a tissue that covers the body and lines organs and body cavities. It is made up of one or more layers of tightly packed cells. Epithelial tissue protects, absorbs, and secretes. Everything that passes into or out of your body moves through epithelial tissue at some point. The most common example of epithelial tissue is the outer layer of your skin, called the epidermis. In addition,

NoteWorthy

An EEG or electroencephalogram is a tracing of brain waves.

A nerve-activating experience in progress

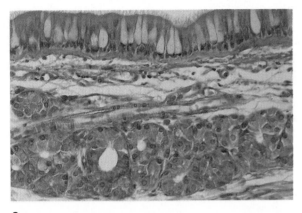

a

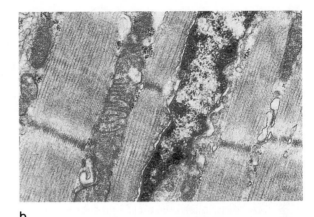

b

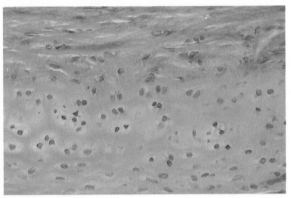

c

d

FIGURE 27–1.

Epithelial tissue (a), muscle tissue (b), connective tissue (c), and nerve tissue (d), make up the organs and systems of the body.

epithelium:
epi (GK) on
thele (GK) cover a surface

glands, such as salivary glands, mammary glands that produce milk, oil or sebaceous glands that get blocked and result in acne, and sweat glands are all made of epithelial tissue. It also lines your breathing passages and your digestive tract.

Connective tissue is tissue that supports and joins various parts of the body. Cartilage, bone, ligaments, tendons, blood, and the membranes that bind internal organs together are all connective tissue. The cells of connective tissue appear scattered and separated by different substances. Blood has fluid between the cells. Bone cells are separated by hard deposits of calcium compounds. Tendons and ligaments contain elastic protein fibers between their cells.

Cells that contract make up **muscle tissue.** In Chapter 28 you will study the details of skeletal, smooth, and cardiac muscle. Skeletal muscle, a tissue most obvious in body builders, is attached to bones and moves the body. Smooth muscle makes up the walls of many of your internal organs. It is found in the walls of your stomach and blood vessels, and moves food through your intestines. Cardiac muscle is found only in the heart. It pumps blood through kilometers of large and small vessels in your body.

The fourth tissue, **nerve tissue,** is made of cells that have the ability to transmit impulses. Nerve tissue is found in the brain, the spinal cord, and in all the nerves of the body. This tissue enables the body to respond to stimuli.

27:2 Body Organs and Systems

Groups of two or more tissues that function together make up organs. Your stomach is an organ. It has all four types of tissues. Layers of muscle contract to churn food you have eaten. Tissues made up of epithelial cells produce enzymes that act on chemicals in food while it is being churned. Nerve tissue stimulates muscles to contract. A thin layer of connective tissue over the outside of the stomach keeps the organ in place. Other examples of organs are your skin, bones, heart, and brain.

Organs work together in systems to accomplish specific functions. Your respiratory system is made up of air passages, muscles, a diaphragm, and a pair of lungs. Its overall function is to move a supply of oxygen from inhaled air to the circulatory system. The respiratory system is also a vehicle for transporting carbon dioxide wastes away from the blood. Neither the air passages nor the lungs

BIOTECHNOLOGY

DEVELOPMENTAL GENES—MASTER BUILDERS

Scientists are beginning to understand how genetic information is translated from a single cell into a three-dimensional organism. It has been discovered that genes may map out the entire body while the embryo is still only a small mass of seemingly unspecialized cells. Genes determine what cells will become muscle or epithelial tissue, and at what stage these tissues will begin to form. Interestingly, multicellular animals, from flies to humans, appear to possess almost identical sets of these developmental genes.

During embryonic development, genes in some cells become active, and others are turned off. Many of the genes that influence embryonic development contain a long stretch of nearly identical DNA. This segment of DNA is called the "homeobox" and seems to be part of a master control system of developmental chemicals. A small change in a homeobox gene could cause significant changes later in development.

Some of these genes chemically mark the location of body segments within the developing embryo. Being sure that genes are switched on at the right time is as important as being sure that the correct genes are turned on at the proper position. One of the mechanisms involves changes in the ratio of cytoplasm to genetic material in dividing cells. In rapidly dividing cells, the amount of cytoplasm per cell decreases. When the amount of cytoplasm reaches a critically low level compared with the amount of genetic information, a series of genes become activated, and the organism begins to take shape. The similarity of homeobox genes among multicellular organisms gives some evidence that these animals share a common origin in their evolutionary history.

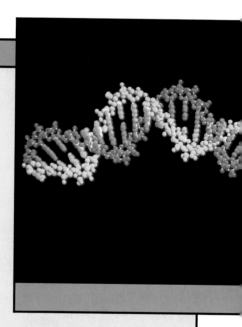

DNA in genes control embryonic development.

could accomplish this job alone. Each organ system plays a role in maintaining the body's homeostasis. If one system breaks down, other systems are affected. If you break a leg, the skeletal system is primarily affected. However, muscles in the immediate area are stretched or torn, and blood tissues in the broken bone are also affected. The systems of the human body, their organs, and their functions are listed in Table 27–1.

Table 27–1.

BODY SYSTEMS		
System	**Organs**	**Function**
Nervous	Brain, spinal cord, nerves, sense organs	Regulates most body systems with impulses transmitted on neurons
Endocrine	Ductless glands	Secretes hormones
Integument	Skin, hair, nails, sweat glands, oil glands	Protects body from infection and water loss; contains sensory receptors
Skeletal	Bones, cartilage, and ligaments	Support, protection; attachment of muscles, body store of calcium and phosphorus
Muscular	Skeletal, smooth, and cardiac muscle	Body movement
Digestive	Mouth, stomach, intestines	Makes food soluble, and passes nutrients to the blood
Respiratory	Lungs and air passageways	Delivers oxygen to and removes carbon dioxide from blood
Circulatory	Heart, blood vessels, blood	Transports oxygen, CO_2; brings functions and products of all body systems together
Urinary	Kidney, bladder, ureter, urethra	Filters waste from blood
Lymphatic	Lymph vessels, nodes, lymph glands	Defends body against disease
Reproductive	Testes, ovaries, and associated structures	Produces sperm and eggs; site of fertilization of egg and of fetal development

FIGURE 27–2.

Blood is a connective tissue of the circulatory system.

Human Blood Cells

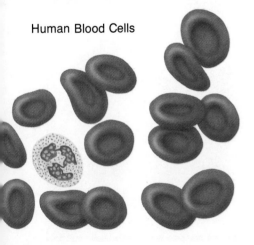

1. What are the four types of body tissue?
2. Distinguish between an organ and a system, using two examples of each.
3. What are the three kinds of muscles?
4. **SKILL REVIEW:** Refer to Table 27–1 to determine what three systems are involved in protection of the body. For more help, refer to Organizing Information in the Skill Handbook, pages 810 to 813.
5. **USING CONCEPTS:** How does the body maintain homeostasis if you break your right leg and need crutches and a cast for several months?

NERVOUS SYSTEM

Every complex machine has a set of regulatory controls to start it, stop it, speed it up, and slow it down. One of the control mechanisms in the human body is the nervous system. The nervous system is like a vast electronic switchboard. Messages about your internal and external environments are received and processed, and the body responds. For example, on a cold day you find yourself shivering. Receptors in your skin respond to lower temperatures. Shivering is an adaptation of the nervous system that helps maintain normal body temperature by causing muscles to contract rapidly and uncontrollably, thereby releasing heat. The nervous system relays messages, monitors changes in body systems, and responds to internal and external stimuli. As a result, homeostasis is maintained.

Objectives:
- identify and describe the two parts of the nervous system.
- diagram and describe how impulses travel in the nervous system.
- describe the parts of the brain.
- describe the function of the major parts of the central nervous system.
- state the parts and functions of the peripheral nervous system.

27:3 Anatomy and Function

The human nervous system is usually described in two basic parts: the central nervous system (CNS) and the peripheral nervous system (PNS). The **central nervous system** is made up of the brain and spinal cord. It acts as a control center, coordinating body activities. The **peripheral nervous system** is made of nerves that carry messages to and from the central nervous system. The nervous system makes rapid changes in the body to maintain homeostasis. A stimulus, such as cold air, is picked up by receptors in your skin. The stimulus initiates an impulse in a nerve. The impulse is carried to the CNS. Here, the impulse transfers to a second type of nerve that carries the impulse away from the CNS to a muscle and causes the muscle to contract. The contraction of the muscle is an effect. The muscle is an effector. In summary, the activity of the nervous system is a relationship between receptors and effectors.

What is the difference between a receptor and an effector?

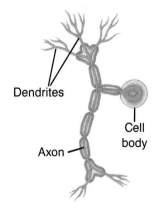

a   Sensory Neuron

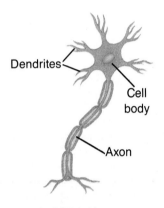

b   Motor Neuron

FIGURE 27–3.

Sensory neurons transmit impulses from receptors to the CNS (a). Motor neurons (b) transmit impulses from the CNS to effectors such as muscles and glands.

The basic unit of structure and function in the nervous system is the **neuron.** Neurons are cells that conduct impulses. Neurons in Figure 27–3 are made up of a cell body, dendrites, and an axon. Dendrites and axons branch out from the cell body. Dendrites receive impulses and carry them toward the cell body. An axon carries impulses away from the cell body. Neurons are classified as sensory, motor, or interneurons. A sensory neuron carries impulses to the brain and spinal cord. A motor neuron carries impulses away from the brain and spinal cord. Interneurons relay impulses from sensory to motor neurons.

27:4 How Neurons Work

When someone smashes into you in the hallway at school, the sensory receptors in your arm become stimulated. If the stimulus is strong enough, an impulse is started in these neurons. The impulse is carried to the spinal cord and then to your brain. In your brain, the impulse is switched over to motor neurons. Motor neurons then transmit the impulse back to muscles in your arm and you are able to move your arm out of the way. How does this take place?

A resting neuron is one that is not transmitting an impulse. For an impulse to move along a neuron, several things must happen. Look at Figure 27–4. Sodium ions exist outside the cell in large concentration because the membrane blocks sodium from entering the cell. At the same time, potassium ions inside the cell tend to move freely out of the cell through the membrane. These two factors increase concentration of positive charges on the outside of a membrane. As a result, the inside of the membrane is more negative by comparison. Under these conditions, the membrane is said to be polarized. A polarized

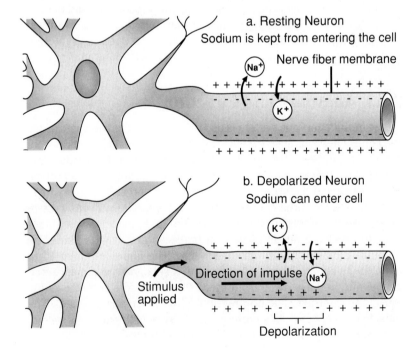

a. Resting Neuron
Sodium is kept from entering the cell

Nerve fiber membrane

b. Depolarized Neuron
Sodium can enter cell

Direction of impulse

Stimulus applied

Depolarization

FIGURE 27–4.

An impulse moves along a neuron by way of a wave of depolarization.

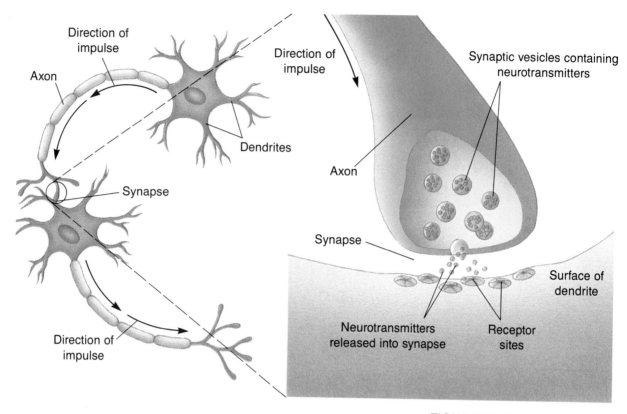

FIGURE 27–5.

At a synapse, neurotransmitters pour into specific sites on nearby dendrites.

membrane has the potential to do work. In this case, work is the transmission of an impulse.

When a stimulus excites a neuron, pores or gates in the membrane open up and sodium ions rush into the cell. As the positive sodium ions build up inside the membrane, the outside of the membrane now is negatively charged by comparison. This alteration in charge is called **depolarization.** An impulse moves along a nerve as a wave of depolarization moves down the axon. The membrane repolarizes immediately behind it. Sodium ions move back out through the membrane and the charges are as they were in the resting neuron. Neurons work on an **all-or-none law,** meaning that the neuron either transmits an impulse or it doesn't.

Impulses moving to the brain and back move across small spaces between neurons. The space between neurons is called a **synapse** or synaptic cleft. As an impulse reaches the end of an axon, small, membrane-bound packages containing chemicals burst out into the synapse. A chemical that crosses a synapse is a **neurotransmitter.** Neurotransmitters diffuse across the synapse and stimulate a depolarization in the next dendrite. Nerve impulses move through the nervous system by this method, much the way each runner in a relay race begins to run only when the baton has been received. A synapse is a one-way valve, allowing a nerve impulse to pass from axons to dendrites. Neurotransmitters are quickly broken down by enzymes in the synapse to prevent the continuous relay of impulses. Synapses also occur where nerves make contact with muscle fibers.

What is a synapse?

NoteWorthy

The speed of an impulse averages between 1 m/s and 120 m/s. Large nerves with myelin coverings transmit impulses even more quickly.

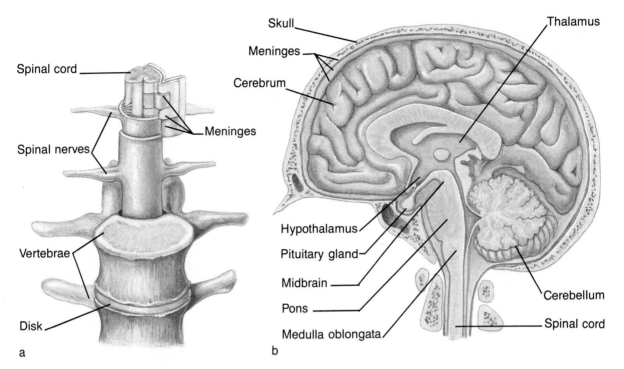

Spinal cord
Spinal nerves
Vertebrae
Disk
Meninges

a

Skull
Meninges
Cerebrum
Thalamus
Hypothalamus
Pituitary gland
Midbrain
Pons
Medulla oblongata
Cerebellum
Spinal cord

b

FIGURE 27–6.

The spinal cord (a) is protected by vertebrae and discs made of cartilage. The brain has lobes that control specific body functions (b).

27:5 Central Nervous System

Recall that the central nervous system is made up of the brain and spinal cord. The brain is the main control center of the nervous system. It receives and transmits impulses by way of the spinal cord, which connects the brain to the rest of the nervous system. The brain and spinal cord are protected by bone, fluid, and three layers of connective tissue called meninges. Spinal fluid between these membranes allows the brain to float and cushions it from injury. Figure 27–6 depicts the brain and its structures. The spinal cord is about 45 cm long and protected by vertebrae.

The three main portions of the brain are the cerebrum, the cerebellum, and the brain stem. The **cerebrum** is divided into two halves called hemispheres. Conscious activities, memory, language, and the senses are controlled in the cerebrum. The outside of the cerebrum is gray and wrinkled with folds and grooves. The inside is white because of myelin-covered axons.

The portion of the brain that receives and sends sensory signals to the cerebrum is called the **thalamus.** It receives all sensory information except smell. The **hypothalamus** is a small area of the brain below the thalamus that controls activities related to homeostasis, such as body temperature, hunger, thirst, and sleep. It is also the main connection between the nervous system and the endocrine system. The **cerebellum** controls balance, posture, and coordination. If the cerebellum is injured, movements become jerky.

The brain stem is made up of the medulla oblongata, the pons, and the midbrain. The **medulla oblongata** controls involuntary activities such as breathing, heartbeat rate, swallowing, and sneezing. The pons and midbrain are pathways to the brain.

27:6 Peripheral Nervous System

The peripheral nervous system carries impulses between the body and the central nervous system. The peripheral nervous system consists of two subsystems—the somatic nervous system and the autonomic nervous system.

The **somatic nervous system** is made up of 12 pairs of cranial nerves from the brain and 31 pairs of spinal nerves from the spinal cord. These nerves are actually bundles of neurons bound together by connective tissue. Some contain only sensory neurons and some contain only motor neurons, but most nerves of the body are mixed. Mixed nerves contain bundles of sensory neurons bound together with bundles of motor neurons. These nerves relay information between the CNS, skeletal muscles, and your skin. This pathway is voluntary and under conscious control, meaning that you can decide to move or not to move body parts under the control of this system. The **autonomic nervous system** carries impulses from the CNS to internal organs. These impulses produce responses that are involuntary. They are not under conscious control. For example, glands in your stomach pour out hydrochloric acid without any decision on your part.

A **reflex** is an automatic response to a stimulus. Reflexes such as shivering and vomiting take place for the most part in the peripheral nervous system. For example, if your doctor strikes a tendon below your knee cap, your lower leg swings out involuntarily. Nerve impulses that cause reflexes don't have to travel to the brain. Instead, the impulse travels directly to the spinal cord from the affected body part. Within the spinal cord, the impulse synapses with a small neuron called an interneuron. The impulse is then moved to a motor neuron that transmits the impulse to an effector in the knee. A knee jerk results. The brain becomes aware of the reflex after it occurs. Reflexes are the shortest nerve pathways in the body.

reflex:
reflectere (L) to turn back

FIGURE 27–7.

Reflexes operate with such speed that you may have already pulled your hand away before you are aware that it has been burned.

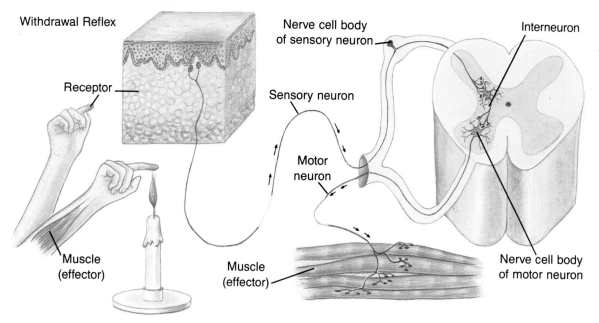

Withdrawal Reflex

Receptor

Muscle (effector)

Nerve cell body of sensory neuron

Sensory neuron

Motor neuron

Muscle (effector)

Interneuron

Nerve cell body of motor neuron

FIGURE 27–8.

Frightening situations require the interaction of the sympathetic and parasympathetic nervous systems to maintain homeostasis.

What are two subdivisions of the autonomic nervous system?

Imagine that you are spending the night alone in a big, old, deserted house. Suddenly, a creaking sound comes from the basement. You are convinced that you hear footsteps. Your heart begins to pound. You want to yell for help, but can't force the sound out of your throat. Your breathing becomes rapid. You're in a clutch. Your thoughts race wildly as you try to figure out what to do—stay and confront the unknown—or run fast to get out! The reactions that make up your responses in this situation are controlled by the autonomic nervous system.

There are two divisions to the autonomic nervous system—the sympathetic nervous system and the parasympathetic nervous system. The sympathetic nervous system controls many internal functions during times of stress. Without a conscious decision on your part, the body sends glucose to muscles and nerve tissue where extra energy is required. Under stressful conditions, the sympathetic system increases heartbeat rate. Blood flow is directed to arms and legs and away from the digestive system.

The parasympathetic nervous system controls many internal functions of the body at rest. The neurons in this system produce effects opposite to those of the sympathetic nervous system. The parasympathetic nervous system is in control when you are relaxed.

REVIEW

6. What are the charges inside and outside a resting neuron?
7. What are the parts of the brain?
8. List the divisions of the autonomic nervous system and their functions.
9. **SKILL REVIEW:** Sequence the events as a nerve impulse moves from one neuron to another. For more help, refer to Reading Science in the Skill Handbook, pages 798 to 799.
10. **USING CONCEPTS:** Why is it impossible to stop a reflex from taking place?

BIOLAB

Reaction Time

Problem: Do distractions affect reactions?

Materials
meter stick

Procedures
1. Make a data table like the one shown.
2. Work in pairs. Sit comfortably facing your partner. Your partner should stand.
3. Have your partner hold the top of a meter stick between thumb and index finger.
4. Hold your thumb and index finger about 2.5 cm on either side of the lower end of the meter stick without touching the meter stick.
5. Tell your partner to drop the meter stick straight down between your fingers.
6. Catch the meter stick between your thumb and index finger as soon as it begins to fall. Measure how far it falls before you catch it.
7. Practice several times before you begin to collect data.
8. Run Trials 1 to 10, recording the number of cm the meter stick drops each time. Average the results of the 10 trials.
9. **Hypothesize** whether a distraction will affect your ability to respond and catch the ruler.
10. Repeat the experiment using the distraction of counting backwards in units of fives (100, 95, 90, . . .), and tell your partner to drop the meter stick.
11. Run the distraction experiment for 10 trials and calculate an average.
12. You and your partner should then switch roles and repeat steps 2 through 11.

Questions and Conclusion
1. In terms of your data, how was your reaction time affected by a distraction?
2. Did your reaction time improve with practice? Explain.
3. Name two activities where quick reaction time is important.
4. Name two factors that would decrease reaction time.
5. Was your **hypothesis** supported as to whether a distraction affected your ability to respond? Explain.

Conclusion: Do distractions affect reactions? Explain.

Data and Observations

Distance on meter stick in cm										
Trials	1	2	3	4	5	6	7	8	9	10
Without Distraction										
With Distraction										

Objectives:

- outline how chemoreception makes smell and taste possible.
- outline the process of photoreception.
- summarize the principles of mechanoreception and sequence the pathway of sound through the ear.
- describe the functions of skin in sensory reception.
- describe the effect of drugs on the nervous system.

Picture yourself in a park on a beautiful summer day. You stretch out on the grass and look up at the sky. Puffy white clouds float by against a background of brilliant blue. You feel a breeze blowing against your skin, and grass tickles your toes. You hear birds and feel the bite of a mosquito, and you smell the sweet fragrance of honeysuckle. You open up your picnic basket and take out a container of lemonade. As you drink it, you enjoy its sweet and sour taste. Your awareness of sensations is made possible by your senses: sight, touch, smell, taste, and hearing. Senses enable you to detect and respond to conditions in your environment.

27:7 Chemoreception

The senses of smell and taste depend on receptors that detect molecules in a gas form. They operate by a process called chemoreception. Chemoreception is the response of a neuron to a chemical stimulus which initiates a nerve impulse that travels to the brain. The receptors for smell are hairlike nerve endings located in the upper portion of your nose that respond to molecules in the air. Chemicals acting on the hairs initiate impulses in a cranial nerve called the olfactory nerve. In the cerebrum, the signal is interpreted and a particular odor is noticed.

The senses of taste and smell are closely linked. In fact, much of what you taste is due to your sense of smell. The sensation of taste occurs when chemicals dissolved in saliva make contact with sensory receptors on your tongue. The receptors for taste are called **taste buds.** Signals from the taste buds travel along a nerve to the medulla, then to the thalamus, and finally to the cerebrum. Tastes that you experience can be divided into four basic categories: sour, salt, bitter, and sweet. Certain regions of your tongue react more strongly to particular tastes. Where on the tongue in Figure 27–9 are you most likely to taste a sour lemon? The saltiness of a potato chip? Food may taste different to different people.

FIGURE 27–9.

Areas on the tongue respond to chemicals in food with different intensities (a). A nerve ending at the base of a taste bud (b) transmits impulses to the cerebrum (c).

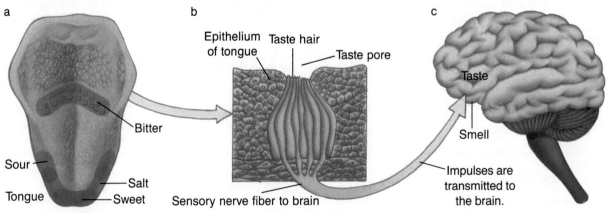

a

Bitter

Sour

Tongue

Salt

Sweet

b

Epithelium of tongue Taste hair

Taste pore

Sensory nerve fiber to brain

c

Taste

Smell

Impulses are transmitted to the brain.

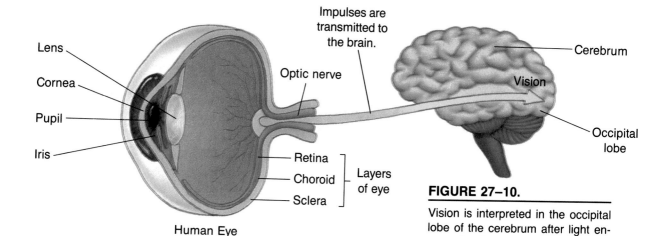

Lens

Cornea

Pupil

Iris

Impulses are transmitted to the brain.

Optic nerve

Retina

Choroid

Sclera

} Layers of eye

Human Eye

Cerebrum

Vision

Occipital lobe

FIGURE 27–10.

Vision is interpreted in the occipital lobe of the cerebrum after light energy stimulates the retina.

27:8 Photoreception

Sensory receptors in the eye are responsive to light energy. Photoreception is the response of a neuron to energy in the form of a light stimulus. Look at Figure 27–10 above to follow the pathway of light. First, light enters the cornea and moves through the pupil, an opening in the iris muscle. The colored iris muscle regulates the amount of light entering the eye in much the same way as the diaphragm of a camera regulates the amount of light that eventually strikes the film. You have probably noticed that your pupils constrict when light is bright, and dilate or become larger when there isn't enough light. After light passes through the pupil, it passes through a lens, a solid structure that focuses light on the back of the eye, where it strikes the retina. The **retina** is a layer of nerve tissue made up of cells that respond to light energy. Two types of cells—rods and cones—are found in the retina. Rods are adapted for vision in dim light. They help you detect shape and movement. Cones are adapted for detecting color and for sharp vision. These cells are stimulated by bright light. Cones are most concentrated in a small area of the retina called the fovea. At the back of the eye, retinal tissue comes together to form the optic nerve. This nerve leads to the thalamus and then to the cerebrum.

What does the retina respond to?

27:9 Mechanoreception

Every sound, from the softest whisper to the loudest cymbal crash, causes the air around the source of the sound to vibrate. These vibrations are known as sound waves. Sound waves are compressional waves. When sound waves enter your ear, a process called mechanoreception takes place. Mechanoreception is the response of a neuron to a physical movement. Deep in the ear, the vibrations stimulate a nerve impulse. This takes place when the ear converts sound waves into a nerve impulse that moves along the auditory nerve to the brain. Hearing results.

NoteWorthy

The human ear can distinguish more than 10 000 different tones. Humans distinguish three characteristics of sound: pitch, tone, and volume.

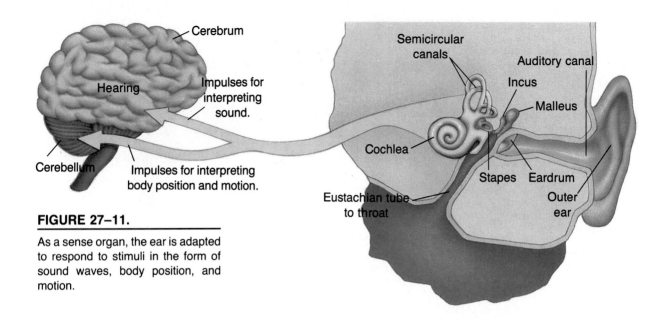

Cerebrum

Hearing

Impulses for
interpreting
sound.

Cerebellum

Impulses for interpreting
body position and motion.

Semicircular
canals

Auditory canal

Incus

Malleus

Cochlea

Stapes   Eardrum

Eustachian tube
to throat

Outer
ear

FIGURE 27–11.

As a sense organ, the ear is adapted
to respond to stimuli in the form of
sound waves, body position, and
motion.

What is the function of the cochlea?

Hearing begins when sound waves enter the outer ear and travel
down the ear canal. At the end of the ear canal, the sound waves
strike a membrane called the eardrum, and cause it to vibrate. The
vibrations then pass to three bones in the middle ear—the malleus,
the incus, and the stapes—causing them to vibrate. The stapes is
connected to a membranous oval window on a snail-shaped structure called the **cochlea** in the inner ear. The cochlea is filled with
fluid and lined with hair cells. As the stapes vibrates, it causes the
membrane in the window to vibrate. The fluid in the cochlea picks
up the vibrations, moves against the hair cells, and causes them to
bend. The movement of the hairs starts a depolarization in the
auditory nerve. High pitched sounds act on hairs at the base of the
cochlea. Low pitched sounds stimulate hairs at the tip of the cochlea
to vibrate. Impulses travel to the temporal lobe of the cerebrum.

The ear also converts the physical signal of head position to nerve
impulses that inform the brain about body equilibrium. Maintaining
equilibrium is the function of the semicircular canals of the inner
ear. Like the cochlea, the semicircular canals are filled with a thick
fluid and hairs. When you tilt your head, the fluid and hairs move.
The mechanical movements of the hairs stimulate the neurons to
carry a impulse to the cerebellum and the cerebrum. There, impulses
from motor neurons stimulate muscles in the head and neck to
readjust the position of the head. Perhaps you have had the experience of feeling dizzy after a carnival ride that spins you around and
around. When you stop, your brain receives conflicting signals. The
fluid in your semicircular canals is still moving, sending impulses to
your brain indicating that you are still spinning.

Sacs below the semicircular canals also contain fluid and receptor
hair cells. These cells provide information about static equilibrium
or the orientation of your head, and are essential for maintaining
posture.

Skin is something most people hardly pay attention to until it is itchy or broken by a cut. However, the body responds to various stimuli that act on receptors in the skin. Figure 27–12 shows the variety of receptors in the skin. Skin contains receptors that detect changes in temperature, touch, pressure, and pain. It is through these receptors that your body meets and responds to its environment.

27:10 Drugs and the Body

A drug is any substance that causes a change in body functions. Drugs affect the nervous system in several ways. They may cause increased or decreased neurotransmitter activity at a synapse, or alter the way an individual views him or herself and the environment.

Use of drugs to relieve pain, alter mood, or cure illness is an ancient practice. Drugs that are prescribed for these purposes have saved many lives. Excessive use of these products for the sake of stimulating an effect, however, disrupts the body's normal functions.

Usually, drugs are prescribed in a particular dosage—"Penicillin, 250 mg to be taken every four hours." This means that in the space of four hours, your body can metabolize 250 mg of that drug. In particular, the cells of your liver process this dosage.

Penicillin is an antibiotic drug used to combat bacterial diseases in the body. Other drugs that have become the center of concern are those that have traditionally been prescribed to relieve pain and either elevate or depress moods. These drugs act on the nervous system. If a person were to abuse a drug like penicillin, his or her digestive system would eventually be affected. However, abuse of drugs that alter the functions of the nervous system or products made from them, such as crack and methamphetamine, leads to addiction and permanent changes in the body. Tolerance of addictive drugs occurs when the liver processes the dosage faster, and more of the drug is needed to achieve a desired effect. Physical dependence on a drug occurs when the body responds in such a way as

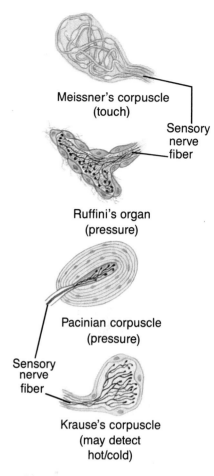

Meissner's corpuscle (touch)

Sensory nerve fiber

Ruffini's organ (pressure)

Pacinian corpuscle (pressure)

Sensory nerve fiber

Krause's corpuscle (may detect hot/cold)

FIGURE 27–12.

Receptors in the skin are often your first contact with the environment.

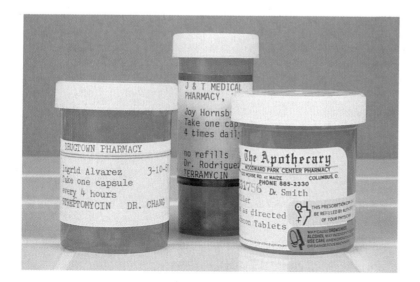

FIGURE 27–13.

A dose of a drug is given at a rate the body can metabolize.

How do stimulants work at a synapse?

to "need" the drug for normal day to day functioning. The body responds to withdrawal from the drug on which it is physically dependent by becoming physically ill.

Any drug that speeds up the activities of the nervous system is a **stimulant.** Amphetamines are stimulants that prevent the breakdown of neurotransmitters at a synapse. As a result, neurons on the receiving side of the synapse are kept continually stimulated. Abuse of amphetamines can cause convulsions, hallucinations, and sometimes death.

The stimulants cocaine and crack cause elevated blood pressure and an increase in the breathing rate. Large doses can have the opposite effect. Cocaine at first stimulates and then depresses the CNS. Inhaling cocaine or crack damages sensory neurons and bone in nasal passages. Cocaine is a powerful vasoconstrictor. A vasoconstrictor decreases the diameter of a blood vessel, cutting down on the amount of blood that can move to an organ. Blood pressure increases. Death from heart attack has resulted when blood to the heart became restricted.

Caffeine is a colorless stimulant normally present in coffee, tea, and chocolate. It is added to many diet and aspirin products and to soft drinks. Caffeine increases heartbeat rate and urination, and causes wakefulness in some people.

Nicotine is a mild stimulant derived from tobacco, and is found in cigars, cigarettes, pipe tobacco, and smokeless tobacco products. The effects of nicotine have been well documented. You are probably familiar with the warnings printed on cigarette packages. The most common problems associated with nicotine are lung cancer and circulatory problems, especially heart attack. Nicotine can enter the bloodstream from exposed tissues in the mouth and through the lungs. Nerve tissues in the mouth, taste buds, and nasal tissues are affected and loss of taste can occur. At the very least, these senses decrease with the use of these products.

Pain killers such as codeine, morphine, and opium are classified as depressants. A **depressant** inhibits transmission of sensory im-

FIGURE 27–14.

Plants are a common source of drugs. Caffeine is derived from coffee beans (a), cocaine is extracted from the leaves of the coca plant (b), and tobacco plants produce nicotine (c).

a

b

c

pulses at a synapse. Anesthetics affect sensory nerves and motor nerves. If, for example, the dentist administers a local anesthetic, your lips, cheeks, and gums become numb and you will have difficulty speaking clearly because muscles that control your tongue are not receiving impulses from motor neurons.

Ethyl alcohol is the depressant found in alcoholic beverages. Ethyl alcohol slows breathing and decreases muscle control. The effects of alcohol are modified by the age and weight of an individual, by how much alcohol is consumed, the rate of consumption, and how fast it is absorbed into the bloodstream. Overall, the greater the amount consumed, the greater the effects. The rate of absorption increases when little or no food is eaten. Alcohol is absorbed directly into the bloodstream from the stomach and small intestine. Food slows down the rate of absorption. The liver metabolizes 95 percent of alcohol that is consumed. The remaining five percent is excreted through the lungs and in urine. Table 27–2 shows the effects of blood alcohol levels on body functions.

Table 27–2.

EFFECTS OF ALCOHOL ON BODY FUNCTIONS	
Percent	Effect
0.02	Unnaturally relaxed; false exhilaration
0.06	Coordination poor; speech slurred
0.10	legal limit of intoxication tolerated
0.12	Senses distorted; vomiting occurs
0.50	Deep coma; danger of death

Hallucinogens cause distortions of reality. Mind-altering drugs include LSD, mescaline, and PCP, sometimes called "angel dust." These drugs affect the nervous system by altering the amount of neurotransmitter at the synapse, resulting in a distorted perception of ordinary events.

hallucinate:
allucinari (L) to dream

REVIEW

11. What is chemoreception and what senses does it involve?
12. List three sense organs and the form of energy that stimulates each one.
13. Explain the effects of stimulants on neurotransmitters at a synapse.
14. **SKILL REVIEW:** List the sequence of structures through which sound passes to reach the auditory nerve. For more help, refer to Reading Science in the Skill Handbook, pages 798 to 799.
15. **USING CONCEPTS:** How does a depressant work on the nervous system so that one becomes unable to judge distances when stepping off a curb or driving?

Objectives:

- describe the structures and functions of the endocrine system.
- summarize the four functions of hormones and how they are regulated.
- explain the role of the endocrine system in human growth.
- describe the role of the endocrine system in dealing with stress and nutrient absorption.

hormone:
hormaein (GK) to excite

FIGURE 27–15.

The pituitary gland secretes many hormones that affect other endocrine glands.

You have learned that the nervous system acts as a control mechanism for the human body. The endocrine system is a system of chemical control that works somewhat like a thermostat. Many machines, such as automobiles and furnaces, have thermostats to regulate temperature. When the machine becomes too hot, a signal from the thermostat activates a fan or other cooling system. Once the temperature has returned to normal, the lowered temperature signals the thermostat to turn off the cooling system.

27:11 Structure and Function

In the human body, the endocrine system, in response to signals from the nervous system, produces chemicals that act to turn on, speed up, slow down, or turn off the activities of various tissues and organs. This regulatory action helps the body maintain homeostasis.

The endocrine system is made up of endocrine glands. An **endocrine gland** is a gland without a duct. These glands secrete chemicals called hormones directly into the bloodstream. A **hormone** is the chemical secreted by an endocrine gland that brings about an effect in a specific tissue or organ. Most hormones are proteins or lipids called steroids. The specific tissue affected by a hormone is called a **target tissue.** The bloodstream enables all tissues of the body to come in contact with all hormones, but only specific target tissues react to a specific hormone. Hormones work in very small amounts.

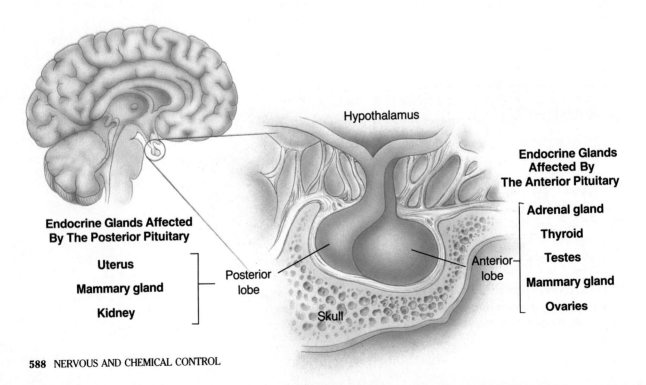

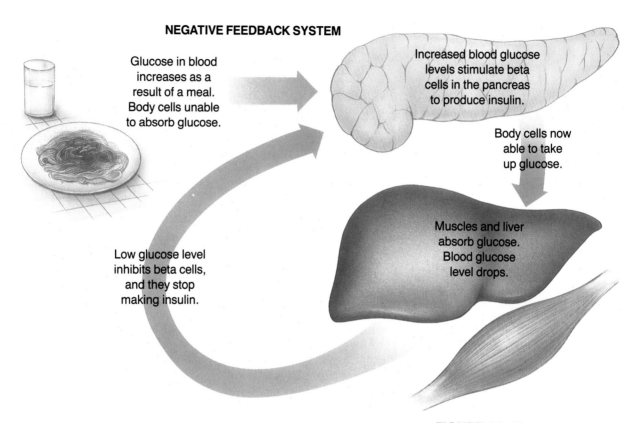

NEGATIVE FEEDBACK SYSTEM

Glucose in blood increases as a result of a meal. Body cells unable to absorb glucose.

Increased blood glucose levels stimulate beta cells in the pancreas to produce insulin.

Body cells now able to take up glucose.

Low glucose level inhibits beta cells, and they stop making insulin.

Muscles and liver absorb glucose. Blood glucose level drops.

FIGURE 27–16.

Endocrine glands of the body function on a negative-feedback system.

Hormones are carried to their target tissues by proteins in the blood. Target tissues "recognize" their hormones chemically. Hormone molecules fit into sites in their target tissues the way a specific key fits into only one lock. Hormones may bring about permanent changes in target tissues. Reproductive hormones stimulate the development of secondary sex characteristics in adolescence. The activity of reproductive hormones is described in Chapter 32.

The nervous system and the endocrine system are linked by the activities of the hypothalamus. The hypothalamus makes releasing factors that stimulate or inhibit the pituitary gland, which is the master endocrine gland. The pituitary gland produces hormones that stimulate other endocrine glands to produce their hormones.

In comparison to the nervous system, hormones bring about change slowly in the body. However, the effect of hormones lasts much longer than those of the nervous system.

As stated earlier, hormones control body processes in much the same way that temperatures are controlled by a thermostat. The **negative-feedback system** is the basis of hormone regulation. If too much hormone builds up in the bloodstream, the gland is signaled to stop production of the hormone. When the amount of hormone drops to a certain low level in the blood, the gland begins producing hormone again. This constant interaction is a major feature of the body's homeostatic mechanism. Since there is at least a small amount of all hormones present in the blood at any time, the body is always engaged in this homeostatic negative-feedback activity.

What is a negative-feedback system?

FIGURE 27–17.

Too much or too little growth hormone at key development periods in the human body may result in a giant or a midget.

27:12 Human Growth

Two endocrine glands are involved in controlling growth—the anterior pituitary gland and the thyroid gland. The anterior pituitary gland is located at the base of the brain and secretes human growth hormone (HGH). Growth hormone activates bones and skeletal muscle cells to grow and multiply. Growth hormone also stimulates cells to metabolize fat for energy. The growth function of the anterior pituitary is regulated by the hypothalamus.

The thyroid gland is located in the throat just below the larynx, or voice box. Cells within the thyroid produce hormones that regulate growth, development, and the activities of the nervous system. These hormones work with growth hormone to accelerate body growth, particularly of nervous tissue, during the growing years.

Sometimes the pituitary gland does not produce the right amount of growth hormone. When this happens, a midget or giant results. In midgets, too little growth hormone is produced. Bone growth stops before normal height is reached. This condition has been treated by administering growth hormone during childhood. In giants, too much growth hormone during the developing years causes an abnormal increase in the length of bones, and a person grows very large.

NoteWorthy

Acromegaly is giantism resulting from excessive pituitary secretion. The bones of the face, hands, and feet become enlarged.

27:13 Stress

Another important function of the endocrine system allows the body to deal with stress. Homeostatic mechanisms are designed to counteract the stresses of everyday life. Some of these stresses are external, such as running to catch a bus or staying up late to finish homework. Other stresses are internal, such as stage fright.

If stress is extreme or prolonged, normal homeostatic mechanisms may not be sufficient to counteract it. The hypothalamus is the body's watchdog against stress. The hypothalamus monitors the internal body situations that change the homeostatic balance like a dog reacts to an intruder. When stress first appears, the hypothalamus stimulates the sympathetic nervous system and the adrenal gland. The adrenal gland secretes the hormones, epinephrine and norepinephrine. The sympathetic nervous system and these hormones set into motion the fight-or-flight mechanism. Think about the last time you had to give a report in front of a class. Your heart rate increased, blood was sent to the skeletal muscles, sweat increased, and your breathing was hard to control. Some of this is counteracted by the parasympathetic system.

Some stressful situations do not go away quickly. If the stress continues over many days, the hypothalamus stimulates the anterior pituitary. The anterior pituitary in turn stimulates the adrenal gland to secrete the hormones that cause the body to start using proteins as sources of energy instead of carbohydrates. Blood vessels also become constricted. Unless this condition is rapidly reversed, body organs can be damaged.

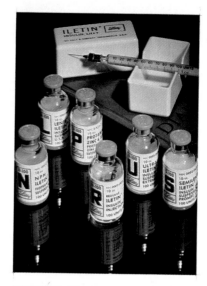

FIGURE 27–18.

Products are available for diabetics to test blood glucose levels each day.

27:14 Absorption of Nutrients

The pancreas is an organ located near the stomach. The pancreas is usually associated with digestion since it produces digestive enzymes. However, embedded in the tissues of the pancreas are cells that perform an endocrine function. The islets of Langerhans are endocrine cells within the pancreas that produce insulin. **Insulin** is a hormone that enables glucose to move into a cell by making the cell membrane permeable to glucose. Glucose is primarily used in cells as the source of ATP. Refer to the diagram in Figure 27–16.

Some individuals cannot make insulin or enough insulin. They have diabetes mellitus. Glucose can't enter the cells. Instead, it accumulates in the bloodstream. This results in proteins and fats within cells being broken down for sources of energy.

To counteract the diabetic condition, a combination of diet and medication is used. Some diabetic conditions are controlled strictly by diet. Other diabetics are referred to as being insulin-dependent. These individuals take a daily glucose reading from a simple urine test. They then take a specified amount of insulin.

insulin:
  insula (L) island

REVIEW

16. What is the relationship between a hormone and a target tissue?
17. What is the link between the nervous and endocrine systems?
18. Which glands and hormones are involved in human growth?
19. **SKILL REVIEW:** Make a model to show how negative-feedback control works. For more help, refer to Reading Science in the Skill Handbook, pages 798 to 799.
20. **USING CONCEPTS:** Where does the negative-feedback system appear to fail in the case of giantism?

CHAPTER REVIEW

SUMMARY

1. Human body cells are organized into tissues, organs, and organ systems. **27:1, 27:2**
2. The nervous system is a system of receptors and effectors made up of the central and peripheral nervous systems. The neuron is the function unit of the nervous system. **27:3**
3. Impulses move along a neuron in a wave of depolarization and move to other neurons by chemicals at synapses. **27:4**
4. The central nervous system consists of the brain and spinal cord. **27:5**
5. The peripheral nervous system consists of the somatic and autonomic systems. A reflex is involuntary. **27:6**
6. The senses respond to chemical, light, and mechanical stimuli. **27:7, 27:8, 27:9**
7. Stimulants and depressants affect all body systems. **27:10**
8. The endocrine glands secrete hormones and regulate body functions by a negative feedback system. **27:11**
9. Human growth, stress, and glucose absorption are affected by hormone secretions. **27:12, 27:13, 27:14**

LANGUAGE OF BIOLOGY

all-or-none law
autonomic nervous
   system
central nervous
   system
cerebellum
cerebrum
cochlea
connective tissue
depolarization
depressant
endocrine gland
epithelial tissue

hormone
hypothalamus
insulin
medulla oblongata
muscle tissue
negative-feedback
   system
nerve tissue
neuron
neurotransmitter
peripheral nervous
   system
reflex

retina
somatic nervous
   system
stimulant

synapse
target tissue
taste buds
thalamus

Choose the word or phrase from the list above that completes the sentence.

1. The ___ is the shortest nerve pathway in the body.
2. ___ is a group of cells that contract.
3. A portion of the brain involved in producing coordinated movements is the ___.
4. The ___ is a part of the brain that links the endocrine system and the nervous system.
5. A(n) ___ is the basic unit of the nervous system.
6. An impulse moves along a neuron in a wave of ___.
7. A(n) ___ is a chemical released into a synapse.
8. A drug that speeds up the activity of the nervous system is called a(n) ___.
9. The brain and spinal cord make up the ___.
10. A chemical produced by an endocrine gland that stimulates a target tissue is a(n) ___.

REVIEWING CONCEPTS

Choose the word or phrase that completes the sentence or answers the question.

11. The three organizational levels of cells in the body are ___.
    a. epithelial, muscle, and nerve
    b. nerve, neuron, and brain
    c. cell, dendrite, and axon
    d. tissue, organ, organ system
12. The function of connective tissue is to ___.
    a. contract   c. transmit
    b. support   d. protect
13. The medulla oblongata controls ___.
    a. coordination   c. hearing
    b. sight   d. breathing

14. A synapse is a ____.
a. sensory impulse
b. space in the brain
c. space between neurons
d. motor impulse

15. ____ is an example of a stimulant.
a. Alcohol   c. Barbiturates
b. Cocaine   d. LSD

16. Conscious activities are controlled by the ____.
a. cerebrum   c. hypothalamus
b. cerebellum   d. thalamus

17. The retina is the part of the eye that ____.
a. forms an image   c. admits light
b. responds to light d. focuses light

18. Sound waves stimulate nerves in the ____.
a. outer ear   c. cochlea
b. eardrum   d. middle ear

19. Negative-feedback controls regulate ____.
a. neurons   c. neurotransmitters
b. hormones   d. reflexes

20. A reflex travels to the ____.
a. cerebrum first   c. endocrine system
b. spinal cord   d. hypothalamus

UNDERSTANDING CONCEPTS

Answer the following questions using complete sentences.

21. Name five systems of the body, their organs, and their functions.
22. How is the hypothalamus a regulator of homeostasis?
23. How do the nervous and endocrine systems work together in response to stress.
24. What is the condition of charges on the membrane of a resting neuron?
25. Contrast the two divisions of the autonomic nervous system.
26. What are the functions of the fluid and hair cells in the cochlea?

27. What is the all-or-none law?
28. Explain the difference between sensory neurons and motor neurons.
29. How does a reflex work?
30. Construct a diagram showing the glands and hormones that control growth.

APPLYING CONCEPTS

Answer the following questions using complete sentences.

31. What might cause seasickness?
32. Nerve cells act as transformers of energy, changing one type of energy into another. Describe how this occurs in the mouth.
33. Certain chemicals prevent the breakdown of enzymes that remove neurotransmitters at a synapse. How does this affect the body?
34. Describe the route an impulse travels from a stimulus to a muscle contraction.
35. What might take place if the liver were damaged and unable to metabolize a stimulant?

EXTENSIONS

1. Research the causes of nearsightedness.
2. Research the cranial nerves. Diagram their positions and state their functions.
3. Prepare a short report on Charles Stratton, alias "General Tom Thumb." Relate your discussion to the endocrine system.

READINGS

Alpher, Joseph. "Our Dual Memory." *Science 86,* July/Aug. 1986, pp. 44–49.

Bylinsky, Gene. "Breakthrough in the Brain." *Fortune,* Mar. 28, 1988 , pp. 116–124.

Vogel, Shawna. "In the Blink of an Eye." *Discover,* Feb. 1989, pp. 62–64.

PROTECTION, SUPPORT, AND LOCOMOTION

How long do you suppose it took the athlete on the left to get into shape for competition? Many athletes train to condition their bodies. What does this conditioning involve? It may involve running to increase muscle tone and strengthen parts of the skeletal system. It may involve lifting weights to increase muscle mass and tighten the skin. The combination of a strong skeleton, dense muscles, and taut skin means that the athlete has reached peak physical condition. Even if you are not an athlete, your bones provide a framework for your muscles, much as the frame of a building provides support for the walls and roof. Your skin protects your bones, muscles, and other body systems. It is like the coat of paint that protects the structure of the building against the effects of the elements—rain, blistering sun, and extreme temperatures. In this chapter, you will study the human body systems that protect the body, provide the body's framework, and aid movement.

SKIN: THE BODY'S PROTECTION

Do you have oily or dry skin? Do you protect your skin from the sun's harmful rays? Many products are sold that help people care for their skin. Perhaps you have used creams, lotions, and antiseptics on your skin. Why does the skin need this help? Constant exposure to solar radiation and friction expose the skin to burning, drying, and abrasion. Although this vast body covering may seem like just a wrapping on the surface of the body, it is a complex organ.

Objectives:
- identify and describe the parts and functions of skin.
- outline the healing process that takes place when skin is injured.
- summarize the effects that environmental factors and aging have on skin.

28:1 Anatomy of the Skin

Skin is composed of many layers of cells that are classified into two major components. The outer, thinner layer of the skin is the **epidermis.** The epidermis is composed of both dead and living cells. Flattened, dead cells make up the outermost layers of the epidermis. These dead cells are shed continually. The epidermal cells contain a protein called **keratin** (KER ut un) that helps waterproof and protect the cell layers beneath.

epidermis:
  epi (GK) on
  derma (GK) skin
follicle:
  follis (L) bag

The inner layers of the epidermis contain living cells that divide mitotically and cells that contain melanin (MEL uh nun). **Melanin** is a cell pigment that colors the skin and protects the cells from damage by solar radiation. The amount and distribution of melanin in your skin is determined by your genotype. People with dark skin produce more melanin. The cells that produce more melanin are found in lower layers of the epidermis. Epidermal cells take up melanin by phagocytosis and are pushed toward the surface and shed. Another pigment, carotene, is found in the skin layers of Oriental people. The combination of carotene and melanin gives the skin a yellowish hue. Exposure to sunlight causes melanin to increase in production and darken. Thus, the skin becomes tanner. Limited tanning further protects the body against radiation.

The epidermis on the fingers and palms of the hands, and on the toes and soles of the feet contains ridges and grooves. These ridges and grooves are arranged in patterns that are specific for each individual and are formed before birth. Prints of these patterns are used to distinguish individuals. Often, babies have their footprints recorded at birth to establish an identification record, Figure 28–1.

The second major component of the skin is the dermis. The **dermis** is the inner, thicker portion of the skin. The thickness of the dermis varies in different parts of the body. For example, dermis is three to four millimeters thick on the palms of the hands and soles of the feet, but only 0.5 mm on the surface of the eye. The dermis has a lot of connective tissue that contains elastic fibers that allow the skin to stretch. For example, the elastic fibers in the dermis allow the skin to stretch when tissues swell due to injury. The skin's elasticity is most obvious during the later stages of pregnancy, when the skin stretches to accommodate the pregnant mother's expanding abdomen. Although this ability to stretch allows the skin to conform to changes in body shape, it can become a problem for people who lose large amounts of weight. During the weight-gaining stage, the skin stretches to accommodate fat deposits. When weight is lost rapidly, the extra skin remains and sags.

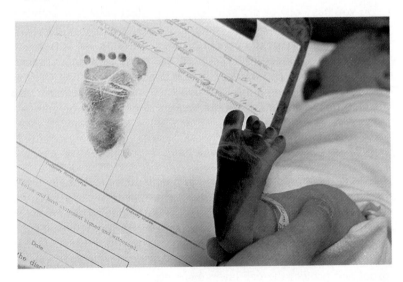

FIGURE 28–1.

A baby's footprint is unique and can be used to identify an individual.

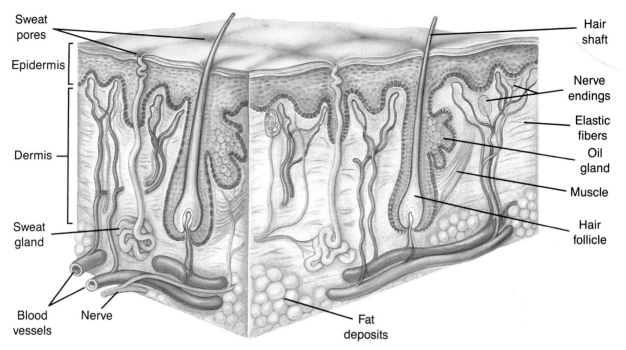

Sweat pores

Epidermis

Dermis

Sweat gland

Blood vessels   Nerve

Hair shaft

Nerve endings

Elastic fibers

Oil gland

Muscle

Hair follicle

Fat deposits

FIGURE 28–2.

A cross section of human skin shows many structures, including vessels, nerves, and glands.

The dermis also contains many other structures, such as blood vessels, nerves, nerve endings, sweat glands, and oil glands. Underneath the dermis there are varying amounts of fat deposits. These deposits function to retain body heat and to store food for long periods of time. Locate the structures of the dermis in Figure 28–2.

Hairs grow in narrow cavities of the dermis called **hair follicles.** As hair follicles develop, they become supplied with blood vessels and nerves and become attached to muscle tissue. Muscle contraction causes the hairs to stand up, thus providing an insulating layer of air on the surface of the skin. This air layer helps to reduce heat loss. "Goose bumps" are a result of the skin being raised by muscle contractions at the hair follicle.

28:2 Functions of the Skin

Skin is one of the largest organs in your body and, as such, has four vital roles in maintaining homeostasis. First, the skin helps to regulate your body temperature. Think about how your body warms up as you exercise. The skin contains blood vessels that dilate when the body becomes hot. The amount of blood that flows through the blood vessels increases and heat is given off. If you are cold, the blood vessels in the skin constrict and heat is conserved.

One noticeable thing that happens to your skin as you warm up during strenuous exercise is that it becomes wet. Glands in the dermis produce sweat in response to the increase in body temperature. Heat from the body is transferred to sweat on the surface of the skin. As the sweat evaporates, the body cools. A person usually loses about 900 mL of sweat each day depending on the type of activity and the temperature and humidity of the environment.

NoteWorthy

Mosquitoes are attracted to lactic acid in human sweat. Some people produce more lactic acid and are more attractive to mosquitoes.

BIOLAB *Fingerprint Patterns* **28**

Problem: Do each of your fingers have a unique fingerprint?

Materials
black ink pad
5 × 7 index card
magnifying glass

Procedures
1. Copy the data table.
2. Develop a **hypothesis** about whether or not each of your fingers has a unique fingerprint.
3. Draw five squares 3 × 3 cm each on an index card. Label the squares 1 through 5.
4. Press the tip of your thumb onto the surface of the ink pad. Check to make sure that ink transferred onto your thumb.
5. Roll your thumb from left to right across square 1 on the index card. Immediately lift your thumb straight up from the paper.
6. Repeat steps 4 and 5 with each of your other four fingers. Use squares 2 through 5 on your index card.
7. Wash and dry your fingers.
8. With a magnifying glass, observe the prints. Identify the patterns of each fingerprint by comparing it with the diagrams. Write the pattern names on the index card and in your data table.
9. Compare your fingerprints with those of three other people in the class.

Data and Observations

Finger	Pattern name	Ridge patterns
1		
2		
3		
4		
5		

Questions and Conclusion
1. Are any of your fingerprint patterns the same on your five fingers? If so, which ones are repeated and which fingers are they on?
2. Do any of your fingerprints have the same patterns as those of your three classmates?
3. Why is a fingerprint a good way to identify a person?
4. Where else on your body might you have the kinds of skin patterns seen on your fingertips?
5. Do your data support your **hypothesis?**
Conclusion: Does each of your fingers have a unique fingerprint?

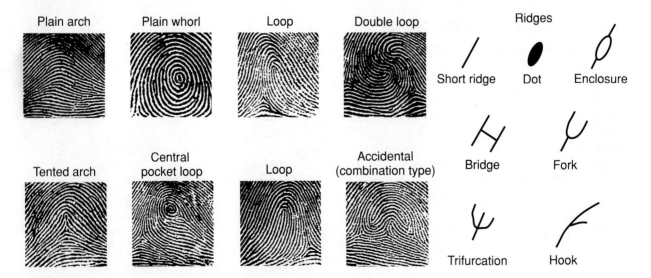

Plain arch   Plain whorl   Loop   Double loop

Ridges
Short ridge   Dot   Enclosure

Bridge   Fork

Tented arch   Central pocket loop   Loop   Accidental (combination type)

Trifurcation   Hook

Sweating not only helps control body temperature, but also functions in excretion. Water, salts, and various organic wastes are excreted from the body through sweat glands. One result of excessive sweating may be the loss of too much salt from the body.

A second important function of skin is to serve as a protective layer. It protects the body from physical and chemical damage and from the invasion of microbes. The skin also protects against water loss and from ultraviolet damage by the sun. Even though the skin protects the body from infection, it is far from sterile. Each square centimeter of the skin has about five million bacteria living on it. Helpful bacteria on the skin surface keep harmful bacteria from growing on the skin. The bacteria digest the organic compounds in sweat. The waste products of these bacteria cause body odor.

What causes body odor?

Third, the skin functions as a sense organ. The nerve cells in the dermis receive stimuli from the environment and relay information about pressure, pain, and temperature. The nerves in the dermis send this information to the central nervous system. The central nervous system then processes the information so you can feel the heat of the sun's rays, the cold of an ice cube, the pain of a bee sting, or the pleasant pressure of a handshake.

A fourth vital function of the skin is to produce Vitamin D when exposed to ultraviolet light from the sun. Vitamin D is the only vitamin the human body can make. Vitamin D aids the absorption of calcium from the digestive tract into the bloodstream. In the winter in northern climates, the skin receives lower levels of sunlight and makes less Vitamin D. In the United States, milk often has Vitamin D added to it to compensate for this lower vitamin production.

28:3 Damage to the Skin

When the skin is injured by breaks or tears that extend into the dermis, bleeding can occur. Figure 28–3 shows the stages involved in skin repair. The first reaction of the body is to restore the integrity of the skin. A clot is formed over the wound and the wound is closed

FIGURE 28–3.

Skin repairs itself in several stages.

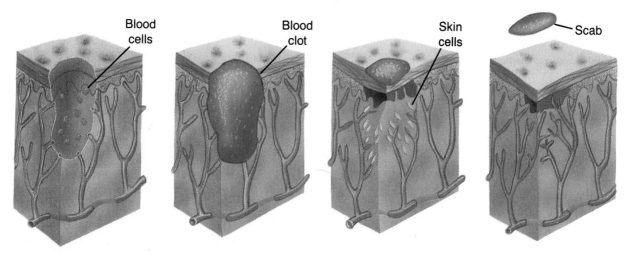

Blood cells

Blood clot

Skin cells

Scab

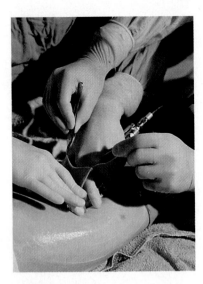

FIGURE 28–4.

Severe burns may be covered with artificial skin (the thin, transparent rectangle) until the burn patient is able to grow new skin.

What changes happen to skin as it ages?

by the formation of a scab. Blood vessels dilate and white blood cells speed to the wound site to fight infection. During the healing process, skin cells beneath the scab move to the wound. Skin cells begin to multiply and fill in the gap. Eventually, the scab falls off to expose new skin. If a wound is large, a scar may form.

Have you ever suffered a painful sunburn? The pain and redness is an indication of damage to the skin cells. Exposure to the sun causes skin to age more rapidly and can result in sunburns. The rays that cause the most damage to skin cells are ultraviolet rays. Other burns can result from contact with chemicals or hot objects.

Burns are rated according to their severity. First-degree burns involve the death of epidermal cells. First-degree burns are characterized by redness and mild pain. A second-degree burn damages skin cells down to the dermis and can result in blistering and scarring. Third-degree burns destroy the epidermis and dermis. Skin function is lost and regrowth of the skin is slow, with much scarring. Skin grafts may be required to replace the lost skin. Skin can be removed from another area of the patient's body and transplanted to a burned area. Artificial skin, like that shown in Figure 28–4, can be used to help cover burned areas and prevent infection and loss of body fluids while the burn victim is growing new skin.

Skin cancers can result from exposure to the ultraviolet rays of the sun. A **melanoma** (mel uh NOH muh) is a cancer of the pigmented cells of the skin and is one of the most dangerous kinds of cancer. It is most common in people between the ages of 35 and 50 and is more common in people with lighter colored skin. Sun blocks can be applied to the skin to decrease the risk of harm.

Did you notice a change in your skin as you entered your teens? Your oil glands increased in size and oil production increased when you began developing into an adult. As oil production increases, bacterial infections of the oil glands increase. These infections are commonly called acne.

Aging of the skin is evidenced by an increase in wrinkles and sagging. Wrinkles appear because the skin becomes less elastic with age. As aging progresses, the oil glands produce less oil. The skin becomes drier. Sagging and loss of elasticity are caused by increased deposition of calcium in the underlying layers of the skin.

REVIEW

1. What structures are found in the dermis?
2. How does the skin control body temperature?
3. What environmental factors does the skin protect the underlying tissue layers from?
4. **SKILL REVIEW:** List the steps that occur when a cut in the skin heals. For more help, refer to Reading Science in the Skill Handbook, pages 798 to 799.
5. **USING CONCEPTS:** Why is it dangerous to run a 26-mile marathon and not drink enough liquids during the race?

BONES: THE BODY'S SUPPORT

You had more bones when you were born than you have now. Some bones of your skeleton have grown together since you were born. Your head, for example, had soft spots before your birth. Soft spots are regions where the bones of the skull have not grown together yet. The flexibility of a baby's skull allows it to pass more easily through the birth canal of its mother. By age 20, your skull bones will have completely grown together.

28:4 Anatomy of the Skeletal System

The adult human skeleton has 206 bones and two main parts. The **axial skeleton** includes the bones that support the head and is centrally located in the body. The **appendicular** (ap uhn DIK yuh ler) **skeleton** includes the bones associated with the upper and lower extremities.

Objectives:
- name the two divisions of the skeleton and list the functions of the skeleton.
- describe the types of moveable joints.
- describe how the skeleton forms and how it functions.
- describe the structure and functions of bone.
- summarize ways in which the skeleton can be damaged.

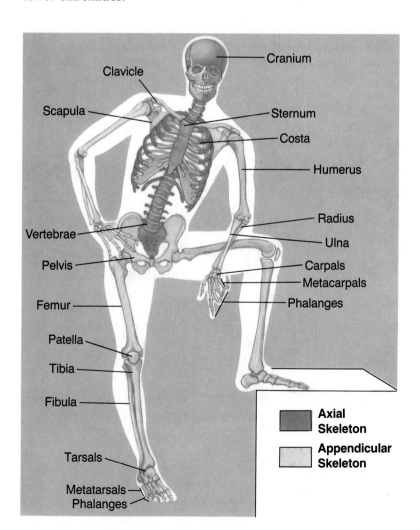

FIGURE 28–5.

The skeleton consists of axial and appendicular regions. The axial skeleton is shown in a darker color.

bursa:
 bursa (L) purse, bag
osteocyte:
 osteon (GK) bone
 kytos (GK) hollow vessel

What is marrow?

FIGURE 28–6.

Joints move in several different ways and are enclosed by ligaments.

A **joint** is the site where two or more bones meet. Most joints allow movement but some, such as the joints in the skull, are fixed. Fixed joints are joints that do not move. There are several types of moveable joints that allow for different kinds of movement. Ball-and-socket joints allow rotational movements. The joints of the hips and shoulders are ball-and-socket joints. Gliding joints occur in the wrists and ankles and allow bones to slide against each other. Hinge joints are present in the elbows, knees, fingers, and toes, and allow back-and-forth movement like a door hinge. Pivot joints allow bones to twist against each other. The joint where the first two vertebrae of the neck meet is a pivot joint. Figure 28–6 shows the kinds of joints in the skeleton.

Joints are enclosed by ligaments, Figure 28–6. A **ligament** is a tough band of tissue that connects bones to bones. The ends of the bones are covered with a layer of cartilage. Between the cartilage ends of the bones is a cell-lined bag of fluid called a **bursa.** The bursa acts as a cushion to keep the bones from rubbing against each other.

The structure of bone is shown in Figure 28–7. Compact bone, or hard bone, is surrounded by a membrane. The membrane supplies blood vessels and nerves to the bone and contains cells involved in bone growth and repair. Inside the compact bone is less dense bone called spongy bone. The center cavity of a bone is filled with a soft tissue called **marrow.** Notice that in cross section the compact bone in Figure 28–7 looks like a series of rings. The rings, along with the

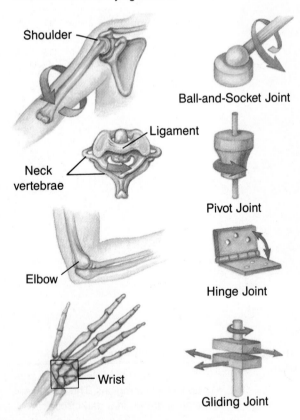

Shoulder

Ligament

Neck
vertebrae

Elbow

Wrist

Ball-and-Socket Joint

Pivot Joint

Hinge Joint

Gliding Joint

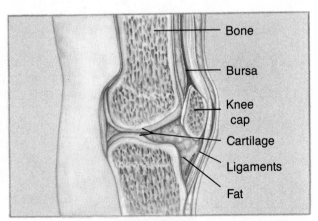

Bone

Bursa

Knee
cap

Cartilage

Ligaments

Fat

Knee Joint

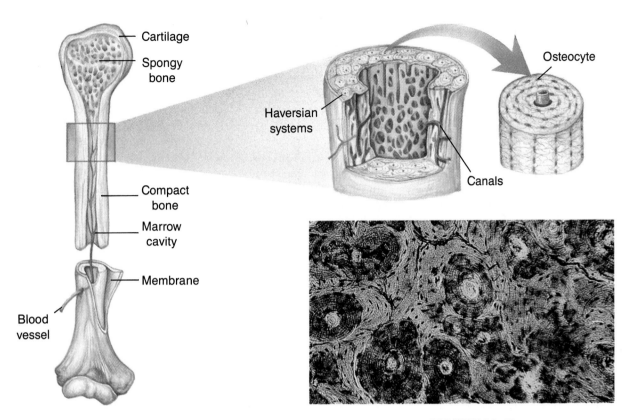

Cartilage

Spongy bone

Haversian systems

Osteocyte

Canals

Compact bone

Marrow cavity

Membrane

Blood vessel

FIGURE 28–7.

Bone has several components, including compact bone, spongy bone, and a surrounding membrane. The photograph shows a cross section of compact bone.

canals they surround, make up what are called Haversian (huh VUR zhun) systems. The rings contain **osteocytes** (AHS tee uh sites), the bone cells. These bone cells produce the system of canals. Calcium salts in the canal system help give the bone strength. Each canal contains blood vessels and a nerve that supplies nutrients and nerve impulses to the living cells of the bone.

28:5 Function of the Skeletal System

The skeletal system is the framework that gives support to the body. Imagine yourself without that framework. You might resemble a human-sized earthworm if you had no supporting structure. In addition to support, the skeleton protects the internal organs.

Besides support and protection, the skeleton is designed to allow for efficient movement. Muscles are attached to the skeleton by **tendons.** As muscles contract, they pull against the end of the bone that does not move. By having a firm point of attachment to pull against, the muscles can work efficiently.

The bones of the skeleton also serve as a storehouse for minerals. Bones store several minerals, including calcium and phosphorus. Calcium is a critical part of the diet for healthy, strong bones. Calcium is also needed in other parts of the body, such as in the nerves for transmission of nerve impulses and in the muscles for muscle contraction. Minerals are removed from bones when needed elsewhere in the body. When calcium is needed by the body for nerve

What are the functions of the skeleton?

action or muscle contraction, parathyroid hormone from the para-thyroid gland causes calcium to be taken out of the bones and to increase in the blood. When the calcium level in the blood becomes too high, calcitonin from the thyroid gland causes calcium to move from the blood into the bones. The body depends on such regulatory systems to keep life systems functioning and maintain homeostasis.

Another function of bones is to produce blood cells and store fat. Red marrow, found in the humerus, femur, sternum, ribs, vertebrae and pelvis, produces red blood cells, some white blood cells, and cell fragments that are involved in blood clotting. Yellow marrow found in many other bones stores fat and aids in producing red blood cells when there is a massive blood loss due to severe injury.

28:6 How the Skeleton Forms

How does the human skeleton form?

The skeleton of an embryo is made of cartilage. By the ninth week of development, bone begins to replace cartilage. Cells that produce calcium salts are formed. The deposition of calcium salts and other ions helps to harden the cartilage, thus transforming it to bone. The adult skeleton is almost all bone, with cartilage found in regions such as the nose tip, external ears, and discs between the vertebrae.

Bones grow both in length and diameter. Growth in length occurs at the end of bones in cartilage plates. Growth in diameter occurs between the cartilage plates, at the center of the bone shaft, Figure 28–8. By age twenty, 98 percent of the growth of the skeleton is completed. The sex hormones produced at sexual maturity cause the bone-forming cells to divide more rapidly. This rapid division causes a growth spurt in teenagers. However, these same hormones also cause the cartilage cells at the ends of the bones to degenerate. As these cells die, growth slows. After growth stops, bone-forming cells are involved mainly in repair and replacement of cells.

NoteWorthy

X rays of Egyptian mummies show that the ancient Egyptians suffered from arthritis.

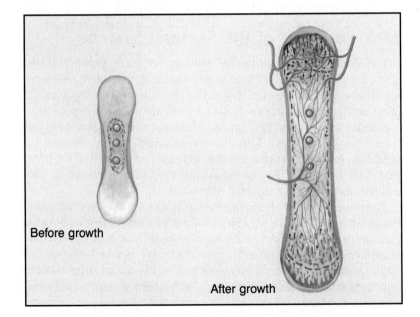

Before growth

After growth

FIGURE 28–8.

Notice in the figure that as the bone grew, the pins did not change positions. Where do bones grow in length?

28:7 Damage to the Skeletal System

Perhaps you have fractured a bone and had the injured area set. When bones are broken, a doctor moves them back into place and then they are kept immobile until the bone tissue regrows and fills in the break. Sometimes an injury results in torn cartilage. For example, if the knee is hit hard in athletic play, small pieces of cartilage can break off. The pieces cause pain and swelling in the joint. They are usually removed surgically.

A forcible twisting of a joint, called a sprain, can result in injury to ligaments and tendons. Such an injury most often occurs at joints with a large range of motion, such as the wrist, ankle, or knee.

You may remember having your back checked by the school nurse when you were younger. The nurse was looking for an abnormal curvature of the spine, a condition known as scoliosis (skoh lee OH sus). Scoliosis is shown in the X ray in Figure 28–9. If this condition goes untreated, it can result in severe back problems in adulthood. Treatment involves exercise, use of a back brace, or sometimes surgery, depending on the severity of the condition.

Arthritis is an inflammation of the joints. It can be caused by infections or injury to the joints. One kind of arthritis results in large bone spurs in the joints. Arthritis is painful and movement may become limited. Exercise helps prevent total loss of movement. The causes of arthritis are not completely known.

The composition of bones changes as a person ages. Throughout life, minerals are deposited in the bones. These minerals, such as calcium and phosphorus, make the bones hard. A child's bones have more collagen protein and fewer minerals than the bones of an adult and as a result, are more flexible. Bones tend to become more brittle as their composition changes with aging. Osteoporosis (ahs tee oh pur ROH sus) is a condition in which there is loss of bone mass, with bones becoming more porous. Osteoporosis is most common in older women because they produce smaller amounts of a hormone that aids in bone formation. Osteoporosis results in a hunched back, weak bones, and an increased susceptibility to fractures. Exercise and eating dairy products help strengthen bones.

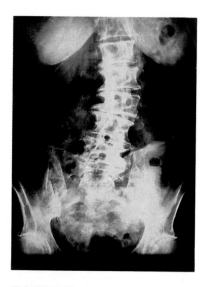

FIGURE 28–9.

In scoliosis, the spine curves abnormally.

What is osteoporosis?

REVIEW

6. Distinguish between the appendicular skeleton and the axial skeleton.
7. List the five main kinds of joints and how each moves.
8. How do bones help regulate mineral levels in the body?
9. **SKILL REVIEW:** List the steps involved in skeleton formation. For more help, refer to Reading Science in the Skill Handbook, pages 798 to 799.
10. **USING CONCEPTS:** If a person reached sexual maturity earlier than the normal age of 12 to 14 years, what effect would you expect this early maturity to have on bone growth?

Objectives:

- distinguish among the three types of muscles.
- describe the structure of a myofibril and summarize the sliding filament theory.
- summarize the factors involved in muscle strength.

Perhaps you have seen the Olympic games on television. Think about the different athletes involved in the games. You may be able to tell what sports some of them participate in just by looking at their body shapes. Weight lifters have body shapes different from downhill skiers. Swimmers and ice skaters have different shapes, too. An ice skater has tremendous leg muscle development. A swimmer has larger shoulder muscles. Athletes exercise to build muscle strength and size. What muscles are well developed in other athletes?

28:8 Types of Muscles

Distinguish between the three types of muscles.

Nearly half of your body mass is muscle. The muscles in the body are of three main kinds, as shown in Figure 28–10. **Smooth muscle** is a type of muscle that is found in internal organs. The cells of smooth muscle are spindle shaped and have a single nucleus. The trachea, digestive tract, and reproductive tract are lined with smooth muscle. Smooth muscle does not contract under conscious control and is therefore called **involuntary muscle.** Contractions of smooth muscle are slow and prolonged compared with the other two kinds of muscle contractions.

Cardiac muscle is a type of muscle that makes up the heart. Cells in cardiac muscle are striated. Striated describes the cells' microscopic appearance. When magnified, cardiac muscle cells appear striped. This striped pattern is due to the arrangement of protein microfilaments within the cell. Cardiac muscle cells are interconnected and form a network that helps the heart muscle contract more efficiently. Contraction in cardiac muscle is involuntary and rhythmic.

Skeletal muscle is a kind of muscle that is attached to bones and moves the skeleton. Skeletal muscle is also striated. Each skeletal muscle cell has more than one nucleus and may be up to 30 cm long.

FIGURE 28–10.

Smooth muscle (a) has long, tapered cells. Cardiac muscle (b) and skeletal muscle (c) are both striated.

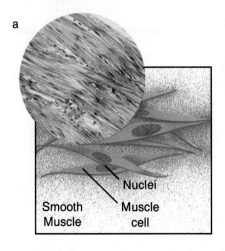

a

Smooth Muscle   Nuclei   Muscle cell

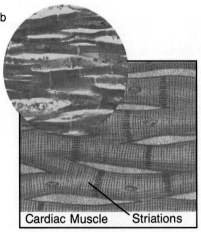

b

Cardiac Muscle   Striations

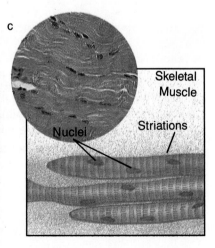

c

Skeletal Muscle

Nuclei   Striations

The contractions of skeletal muscles can be consciously controlled. A muscle that contracts under conscious control is called **voluntary muscle.** Skeletal muscle contractions are short and strong. The majority of the muscles in your body are skeletal muscles.

28:9 Movement and Muscle Contraction

Body movement would not occur without muscle contraction. Whether you are playing tennis or pushing a lawn mower, your muscles are contracting as they do work. Recall that muscles are attached to bones by tendons. When the muscle contracts, the bones are pulled by the tendons. Figure 28–11 shows the movement of the lower arm. When the biceps muscle contracts, the lower arm is moved upward. When the triceps muscle on the back of the upper arm contracts, the lower arm moves downward. Muscles work in pairs, like the biceps-triceps pair, to move bones.

How muscles contract is related to their structure. Figure 28–11 shows that muscle tissue is made up of muscle cells or fibers. Muscle fibers are made up of smaller fibers called **myofibrils** (mi oh FI brulz). Each myofibril is composed of even smaller protein filaments. The filaments consist of two main kinds: thick filaments and thin filaments. The thick filaments of myofibrils are made of the protein **myosin** (MI uh sun). The thin filaments of myofibrils are made of the protein **actin.** The arrangement of myosin and actin gives skeletal muscle its striated appearance. Notice in Figure 28–11 that each myofibril appears to be divided into sections. Each section of a myofibril is called a **sarcomere** (SAR kuh mer) and is the functional unit of muscle.

The sliding filament theory is currently the best explanation for how muscle contraction occurs. The **sliding filament theory** states that the actin filaments within the sarcomere slide toward one another during contraction. When a nerve signals a skeletal muscle to

myofibril:
  mys (GK) muscle
  fibrilla (L) small fiber
myosin:
  mys (GK) muscle
actin:
  aktis (GK) ray
sarcomere:
  sarx (GK) flesh
  meros (GK) part

FIGURE 28–11.

Muscles act in pairs and consist of bundles of fibers that are made up of smaller myofibrils.

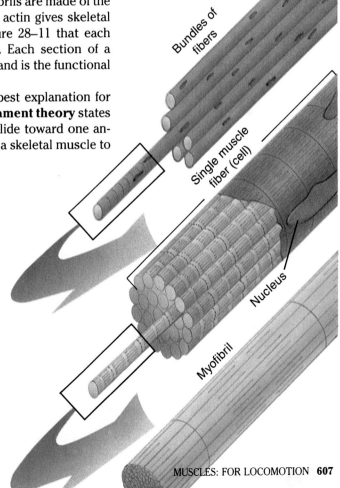

Bundles of fibers

Single muscle fiber (cell)

Nucleus

Myofibril

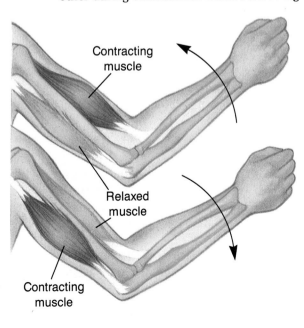

Contracting muscle

Relaxed muscle

Contracting muscle

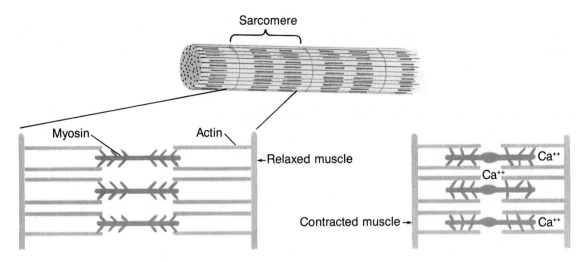

FIGURE 28–12.

As myofibrils contract, each sarcomere shortens.

contract, calcium is released inside the muscle fiber. The presence of calcium causes attachments to form between the myosin and actin filaments. The actin filaments are pulled inward toward the center of each sarcomere, shortening the sarcomere as shown in Figure 28–12. When the muscle relaxes, the filaments return to their original positions.

Recall from Chapter 6 that ATP is produced during cellular respiration, which can be either aerobic or anaerobic. Muscle activity generally uses ATP formed during aerobic respiration, but also can use ATP that is formed during anaerobic respiration. Think about what happens when you are running. When you run to get to class on time, your muscles may not be getting oxygen fast enough to sustain aerobic respiration. Thus, the amount of ATP available becomes limited. For your muscle cells to get the energy they need, they must rely on anaerobic respiration as well. Lactic acid, a byproduct of anaerobic respiration, builds up in muscle cells. When high levels of lactic acid build up in the muscle tissue, fatigue and pain can result. As the excess lactic acid is passed into the bloodstream, the blood becomes more acid, and rapid breathing is stimulated. As you "catch your breath," oxygen is supplied to your muscles and the lactic acid is broken down. Leftover lactic acid in the muscles causes muscle soreness. As your muscles contract, they also produce large amounts of heat. This heat is used to maintain body temperature.

How do muscles function anaerobically?

28:10 Muscle Strength

What factors affect muscle strength?

The number of muscle fibers you have is fixed before you are born. Muscle strength does not depend on the number of fibers, but rather on their thickness and on how many of them contract at one time. Thicker fibers are stronger and contribute to muscle mass. Exercise stresses muscles slightly; as a result, the fibers increase in size.

Regular exercise can result in overall body fitness and endurance that can affect muscle strength. Body fitness is related to the condition of the heart and the number of capillaries in body tissue. One component of physical fitness is the efficiency of the heart in pumping blood to the tissues. Increased physical fitness results in a greater number of capillaries in the muscle tissue. Endurance is a measure of how long you can continue to exercise and depends on how much fuel your muscles can store. A muscle that is continually exercised is stronger and can store more fuel.

Anabolic steroids (an uh BAHL ik • STER oydz) are drugs used to increase muscle mass. You may have seen well-known sports people disqualified from competition for abusing these drugs. Steroids can be dangerous and may cause liver, heart, or kidney damage.

REVIEW

11. What are the three main types of muscle and where are they found?
12. Describe the sliding filament theory of muscle contraction.
13. How does exercise improve muscle strength?
14. **SKILL REVIEW:** Study Figure 28–11. Describe the composition of muscle fibers. For more help, refer to Interpreting Scientific Illustrations in the Skill Handbook, pages 800 to 801.
15. **USING CONCEPTS:** Why would a disease that caused paralysis of smooth muscles be life threatening?

THINKING CRITICALLY

RIGOR MORTIS

When a person dies, the respiratory and circulatory systems that obtain and deliver oxygen to the muscles stop functioning. For an hour or two, anaerobic cellular respiration produces energy in the form of ATP. However, the amount of ATP produced is not enough to cause the muscles to contract fully.

Rigor mortis is the stiffening of both voluntary and involuntary muscles after death. The muscle fibers are frozen in position. Rigor mortis generally develops about an hour or two after death, and usually proceeds from the upper body to the lower body. Full rigor takes ten to twelve hours. The order in which the muscles stiffen is believed to be related to fiber length. Rigor mortis affects smaller fibers in the jaw area first, medium length fibers in the neck area next, and longer fibers in the legs last.

Rigor mortis gradually subsides and within 24 to 36 hours after death has disappeared completely. Rigor mortis subsides in the same order as it develops. The muscles loosen due to tissue decay caused by the release of enzymes. What is happening at the cellular level during rigor mortis? How can rigor mortis be used to estimate time of death?

A coroner determines time of death based on the degree of rigor mortis.

CHAPTER REVIEW

SUMMARY

1. Skin is composed of the outer epidermis and inner dermis. **28:1**
2. Skin regulates body temperature, protects the body, aids excretion, functions as a sense organ, and produces Vitamin D. **28:2**
3. The skin responds to injury and aging and can be affected by infections, sunburn, burns, and cancer. **28:3**
4. The skeleton is subdivided into the axial and appendicular skeletons. The point where two bones meet is called a joint. **28:4**
5. The skeleton supports the body, provides a place for muscle attachment, protects vital organs, manufactures blood cells, and serves as a storehouse for minerals. **28:5**
6. The skeleton forms by replacing cartilage with bone. Bones grow in length at the ends and in diameter at the center of the bone shaft. **28:6**
7. Disorders and damage such as fractures, torn cartilage, sprains, scoliosis, arthritis, and osteoporosis can affect the skeleton. **28:7**
8. There are three types of muscles: smooth, cardiac, and skeletal. **28:8**
9. Skeletal muscles contract due to sliding myofibrils made of actin and myosin. **28:9**
10. Muscle strength is due to fiber thickness, number of fibers contracting, fitness, and endurance. **28:10**

LANGUAGE OF BIOLOGY

actin
appendicular skeleton
arthritis
axial skeleton
bursa
cardiac muscle
dermis
epidermis

hair follicles
involuntary muscle
joint
keratin
ligament
marrow
melanin
melanoma

myofibrils
myosin
osteocytes
sarcomere
skeletal muscle

sliding filament theory
smooth muscle
tendons
voluntary muscle

Choose the word or phrase from the list above that completes the sentence.

1. The ___ contains blood vessels, nerves, sweat glands, and oil glands.
2. ___ are found at the bases of hairs.
3. ___ is the pigment found in skin cells.
4. A(n) ___ is the bag of fluid that is found in a moveable joint.
5. A(n) ___ is a tough band of connective tissue that connects bones to bones.
6. ___ is the inflammation of a joint.
7. ___ is the type of muscle that lines your digestive system.
8. ___ are the tiny cylinders that make up a muscle fiber.
9. ___ is the protein that makes up the thick myofilaments.
10. A(n) ___ is the unit of muscle contraction.

REVIEWING CONCEPTS

Choose the word or phrase that completes the sentence or answers the question.

11. What part of the skin has cells that respond to sunlight to color the skin?
    a. epidermis   c. connective tissue
    b. dermis   d. keratin
12. The skin is waterproofed by ___.
    a. melanin   c. actin
    b. keratin   d. calcitonin
13. Which of the following is a function of skin?
    a. support   c. filter the blood
    b. protection   d. produce Vitamin C
14. Where are red blood cells made?
    a. in the dermis   c. in yellow marrow
    b. in red marrow   d. in cardiac muscle

15. Which of the following is a hormone that controls calcium level in the blood?
    - a. melanin
    - b. keratin
    - c. actin
    - d. calcitonin

16. Which of the following bones is a part of the axial skeleton?
    - a. vertebrae
    - b. radius
    - c. humerus
    - d. tibia

17. What type of joint is in the elbow?
    - a. hinge
    - b. ball-and-socket
    - c. pivot
    - d. fixed

18. Which of the following is voluntary muscle?
    - a. smooth
    - b. cardiac
    - c. skeletal
    - d. all of the above

19. Which of the following is consistent with the sliding filament theory?
    - a. The myosin filament is pulled inward.
    - b. The sarcomere shortens during contraction.
    - c. The filaments slide in the presence of calcitonin.
    - d. During relaxation, the filaments are pulled inward.

20. Muscle strength is due to each of the following EXCEPT ____.
    - a. the number of fibers that contract at one time
    - b. the number of fibers in a muscle
    - c. the thickness of the fibers
    - d. body fitness and endurance

UNDERSTANDING CONCEPTS

Answer the following questions using complete sentences.

21. Refute the idea that the skin is just an outer wrapping for an animal.
22. How is skin color determined?
23. Why do blood vessels dilate at a wound site?
24. What are the functions of bone marrow?
25. How does bone composition change with age?

26. Explain how the muscles and bones function together in locomotion.
27. How do muscles work in pairs?
28. What happens to muscle filaments when the muscle relaxes?
29. What causes lactic acid to build up in muscles?
30. How is fitness related to muscle condition?

APPLYING CONCEPTS

Answer the following questions using complete sentences.

31. Why is recovery from third-degree burns slower than from first-degree burns?
32. What part of a bone may be bruised?
33. What would happen if the red marrow were destroyed by radiation?
34. What would happen if you injected calcium into a muscle fiber?
35. How could you use the skeleton to determine the age of a person?

EXTENSIONS

1. Interview a doctor of sports medicine and prepare a report on common sports injuries.
2. Construct a model to show how bones and muscles work together to move appendages.
3. Find out how changes in the weather may affect people who have arthritis.

READINGS

Moser, Penny Ward. "An Anti-Ageing (sic) Cream with a New Wrinkle: It May Work." *Discover,* Aug. 1987, pp. 72–79.

"Muscling in Madness." *Discover,* Sept. 1988, p. 8.

Williams III, Gurney. "Hair-Raising Science." *Omni,* Nov. 1988, pp. 58–63, 112–116.

DIGESTION AND NUTRITION

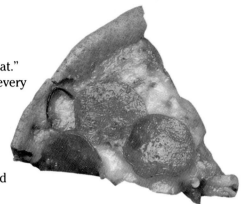

You may have heard someone say, "You are what you eat." What does this mean? You know that if you eat pizza every day for a week, you will not turn into a pizza! But this saying is true in another way. The chemical makeup of your body is similar to the chemical makeup of food. Your body contains protein, carbohydrates, fat, and water. These same nutrients are in the food you eat. In this chapter, you will learn about the nutrients in foods and how they are processed by your body.

FOLLOWING A MEAL

As in many animals you have studied, the human digestive system is a tube that developed from endoderm cells in the embryo. Different parts of the tube form different digestive organs. As you read about the digestive system, you will follow a meal through the organs of digestion. The structure and function of each part of the digestive system will be described together.

29:1 Chewing and Swallowing

The digestive system has five functions. The first is ingestion, another way of saying the taking in of food. The next two functions take place at the same time: they are the digestion of food and the movement of food along the digestive tract. The remaining two functions are the absorption of digested foods into the cells of the body and the elimination of indigestible materials from the body.

Digestion begins in the mouth. Suppose you are having pizza for lunch. The first thing you do is bite off a piece and chew it for a few seconds. As you know, your teeth are important for this activity.

Teeth are located in sockets in the jaw bones and have three regions: the crown, the root, and the neck. Notice in Figure 29-1 that the crown is the portion of the tooth above the gums. The root is the part of the tooth that is embedded in the socket. The neck of the tooth is the region between the crown and the root.

Objectives:
- describe the anatomy and functions of the mouth, esophagus, stomach, small intestine, and large intestine.
- describe the functions of the enzymes that play a role in digestion.
- outline the pathway food follows through the digestive tract and summarize what happens at each step along the pathway.
- summarize how the nervous and endocrine systems control the digestive process.

FIGURE 29–1.

Teeth are composed of a crown, a root, and a neck and are involved in mechanical digestion.

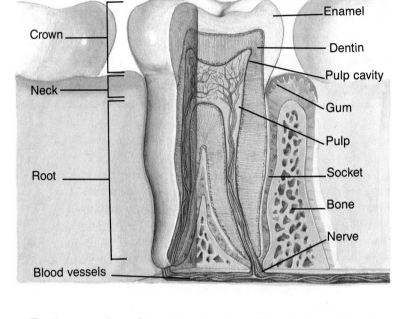

epiglottis:
epi (GK) upon
glotta (GK) tongue

peristalsis:
peri (GK) around
stellein (GK) to draw in

esophagus:
oisein (GK) to carry
phagein (GK) to eat

What is the function of amylase?

Teeth are made mainly of dentin, a bonelike substance that gives a tooth its shape and strength. The dentin encloses a cavity filled with pulp. Pulp is a connective tissue that contains blood vessels and nerves. The dentin of the crown is covered with enamel that consists mostly of calcium salts. Tooth enamel is the hardest substance in the body.

Think about what happens as you chew. Your tongue moves food around in your mouth and helps position the food between the teeth as you chew. Chewing is part of mechanical digestion. **Mechanical digestion** is the physical process of breaking food into smaller pieces. Mechanical digestion increases the surface area of food particles and prepares them for chemical digestion. **Chemical digestion** is a structural change in food in which large molecules are broken down into smaller ones and results from the action of enzymes. Table 29–1 lists the enzymes secreted by the digestive system.

Chemical digestion of starches begins in the mouth. Recall from Chapter 3 that starches are large polysaccharides. As you chew on the piece of pizza, six salivary glands secrete saliva into your mouth, Figure 29–2. Saliva is a slightly alkaline solution that adds water and the enzyme amylase (AM uh lays) to the food. **Amylase** is a digestive enzyme that breaks down starch into smaller sugar molecules, disaccharides, and monosaccharides. Some of the starches in the pizza are broken down by the amylase in the mouth.

When the bite of pizza is thoroughly chewed, the tongue shapes it into a ball, and moves it to the back of the mouth to be swallowed. Swallowing forces the food from the mouth to the esophagus. The **esophagus** is the muscular tube that connects the mouth to the stomach. It takes about 10 to 15 seconds for the food to move through the esophagus to the stomach. Food is moved along within the esophagus by peristalsis (per uh STAHL sus). **Peristalsis** is a series of involuntary muscular contractions along the digestive tract.

Table 29–1.

DIGESTIVE ENZYMES			
Organ	**Enzyme**	**Acts on**	**Product**
Salivary glands	Salivary amylase	Starch	Disaccharide
Stomach	Pepsin	Proteins	Peptides
Pancreas	Pancreatic amylase	Starch	Disaccharide
	Trypsin	Proteins	Peptides
	Pancreatic lipase	Fats	Fatty acids and glycerol
	Nucleases	Nucleic acids	Sugar and nitrogen bases
Small intestine	Maltase, sucrase, lactase	Disaccharide	Monosaccharide
	Peptidase	Peptides	Amino acids
	Nuclease	Nucleic acids	Sugar and nitrogen bases

Have you ever had food "go down the wrong way?" When you swallow, the food passes over the windpipe, the tube that leads to the lungs. Usually when you swallow, a flap of skin called the **epiglottis** (ep uh GLAHT us) covers the opening to the windpipe. Thus, breathing is temporarily interrupted. After the food passes into the esophagus, the epiglottis opens again. If you talk or laugh as you swallow, the epiglottis opens, and the food may enter the windpipe. Your response, a reflex, is to choke and cough, forcing the food out of the windpipe.

FIGURE 29–2.

There are six salivary glands that aid chemical digestion, three on each side of the jaw (a). Food is moved along the esophagus by peristalsis (b).

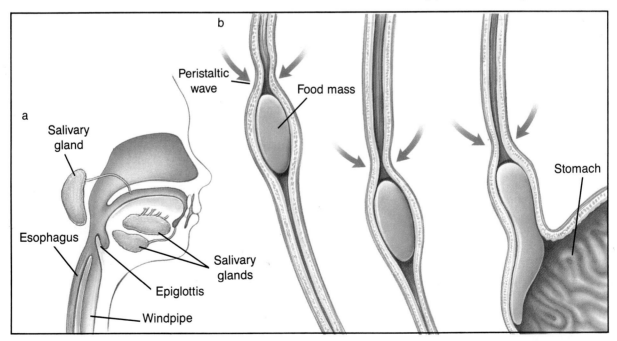

29:2 Food in the Stomach

When food reaches the bottom of the esophagus, a valve at the top of the stomach lets the food enter the stomach. The **stomach** is a muscular pouch-like enlargement of the digestive tract that is shaped like the letter *J*. Three layers of muscles make up the wall of the stomach. When these muscles contract, they mix the food in the stomach. This action is another part of mechanical digestion. Figure 29–3 shows how food is mixed in the stomach.

The lining of the stomach contains about 35 million glands that secrete a mixture of chemicals called gastric juices. Gastric juices contain hydrochloric acid and pepsin. **Pepsin** is a digestive enzyme that begins the chemical digestion of proteins in food. The enzyme pepsin works only in an acid environment. Hydrochloric acid provides the necessary acid environment for pepsin to function by lowering the stomach contents to a pH of 2. Thus, pepsin is able to digest the proteins in the cheese and pepperoni on your pizza.

Perhaps you know someone who has had an ulcer. An ulcer is a sore in the wall of the digestive system. Ulcers can occur in the esophagus, stomach, or intestine. Increased secretion of hydrochloric acid is associated with most ulcers. Emotions, especially stress, and certain foods can stimulate increased acid secretion in some people. It is thought that this increased acid may make a person more susceptible to ulcers. Ulcers can be treated by changes in diet or by medication. In extreme cases, surgery may be required to repair the damage to the digestive system.

Knowing that the stomach secretes acids and enzymes, you may be wondering why the stomach doesn't digest itself. There are two reasons. First, the stomach lining secretes mucus. This mucus forms a protective layer on the inside of the stomach. Second, the cells lining the stomach replace themselves constantly. You have a new stomach lining about every three days.

Food remains in the stomach for two to five hours. By the time the food is ready to leave the stomach, it is in the form of a thin liquid.

FIGURE 29–3.

Food enters the stomach and is kept there by a valve. Muscular contractions of the stomach mix the food, and another valve opens to release the stomach contents to the intestine.

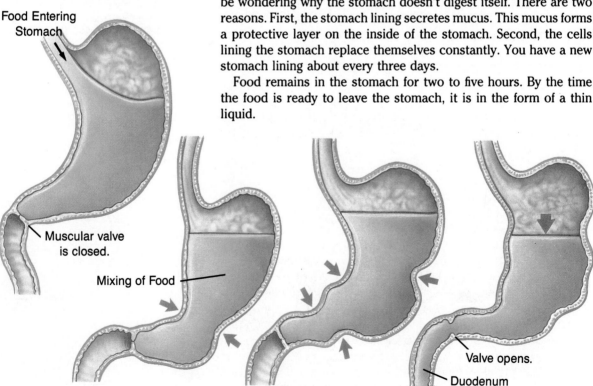

Food Entering Stomach

Muscular valve is closed.

Mixing of Food

Valve opens.

Duodenum

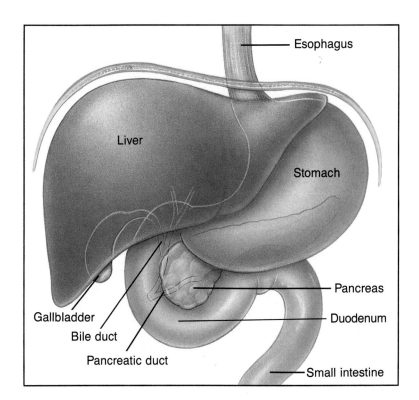

FIGURE 29–4.

Both the liver and the pancreas produce substances necessary for digestion in the small intestine.

29:3 Digestion and Absorption

From the stomach, the liquid that was your bite of pizza moves into the small intestine. A muscular valve at the lower end of the stomach opens, and food passes from the stomach into the small intestine. The **small intestine** is a muscular tube about six meters long. This may not sound small to you. However, the small intestine is only 2.5 cm in diameter. It is this small diameter that gives the small intestine its name. The small intestine is where the rest of your pizza meal is broken down. Carbohydrates and proteins undergo further chemical digestion. In fact, most chemical digestion takes place in the small intestine. Both mechanical and chemical digestion of fats take place in the small intestine as well.

The first 25 cm of the small intestine is called the **duodenum** (doo AHD un um). Although the inner walls of the duodenum secrete enzymes, most of the enzymes and chemicals that function in the duodenum enter it through a duct from the pancreas and the liver.

The **pancreas** (PAN kree us) is a soft, flattened gland that lies beneath the stomach. It secretes both digestive enzymes and hormones. The pancreas secretes a mixture of enzymes called pancreatic juices. These enzymes break down carbohydrates, proteins, and fats. The pancreas also secretes sodium bicarbonate. Sodium bicarbonate makes pancreatic juice alkaline. Recall that the mixture leaving the stomach is acidic. The alkalinity of the pancreatic juice neutralizes the acidity and stops any further action of pepsin.

The **liver** is a complex gland located below the lung cavity. A chemical called bile is made in the liver, then stored in the gallblad-

duodenum:
duodecim (L) twelve
The length of the duodenum is about 12 finger widths.

What is the function of the pancreas?

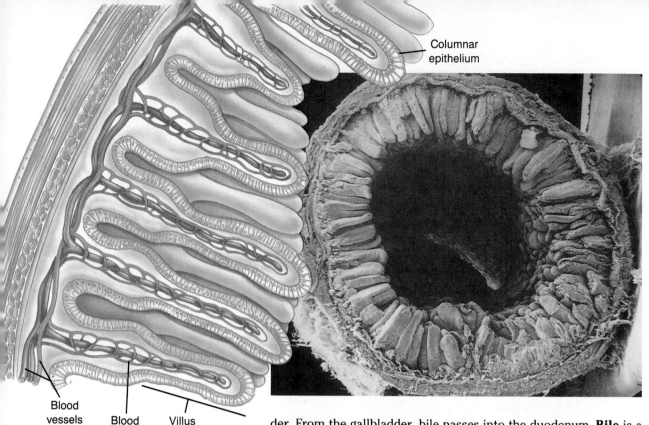

Columnar
epithelium

Blood
vessels

Blood
vessel
network

Villus

FIGURE 29–5.

The small intestine is lined by finger-like projections called villi. The photograph shows a cross section of the small intestine magnified 30 times.

villus:
villus (L) tuft of shaggy hair
appendix:
ad (L) to
pendere (L) to hang

der. From the gallbladder, bile passes into the duodenum. **Bile** is a chemical that breaks fats into small droplets. Although bile is a chemical, this step is part of mechanical digestion. Large drops of fat are broken apart into smaller droplets, but the fat molecules are not changed chemically by bile. Although the liver and pancreas have important roles in digestion, food does not pass through them.

The pizza stays in the small intestine for three to eight hours and is slowly moved along by peristalsis. As the food moves through the small intestine, it passes over many fingerlike structures, called villi. A **villus** is a projection on the lining of the small intestine that absorbs digested food. The shape of the villi greatly increases the surface area of the small intestine. Notice in Figure 29–5 that a network of blood vessels goes into and out of each villus. The digested food is absorbed into these vessels from the intestinal cavity. As food comes to the end of its passage through the small intestine, only the materials from your pizza that could not be digested remain in the digestive tract.

29:4 Wastes

After digested food has been absorbed by the small intestine, the indigestible materials pass into the large intestine, also called the colon. The **large intestine** is a muscular tube about 1.5 m long. The large intestine is much shorter than the small intestine. However, it is much wider than the small intestine. The diameter of the large intestine is about 6.5 cm. The **appendix** is an extension of the first part of the large intestine. Although the appendix does not function in digestion, it contains lymph tissue and may have a role in immunity, which is discussed in Chapter 31.

The large intestine absorbs water from the mixture of indigestible materials. As water is absorbed, the mixture becomes less liquid. Bacteria in the large intestine digest some of the remaining material, resulting in the production of methane gas. Intestinal bacteria also synthesize some B vitamins and vitamin K, which are absorbed by the body. After three to ten hours in the large intestine, the remaining indigestible material, now called feces, reaches the rectum. The **rectum** is the last section of the digestive system. Feces are eliminated from the body through the anus.

A common digestive disorder is diarrhea. Diarrhea occurs when food moves too rapidly through the large intestine. Food is not in the large intestine long enough to have the correct amount of water removed from it and absorbed into the body and as a result, the body can dehydrate. Diarrhea can be caused by stress or by bacterial or viral infections.

Constipation is caused by food moving too slowly through the large intestine. If feces remain in the large intestine too long, too much water will be absorbed into the body, making the feces hard and dry. Constipation can result from too little bulk in the diet, or from lack of exercise.

FIGURE 29–6.

All the digestive organs work together to make the nutrients in the food you eat available to your body.

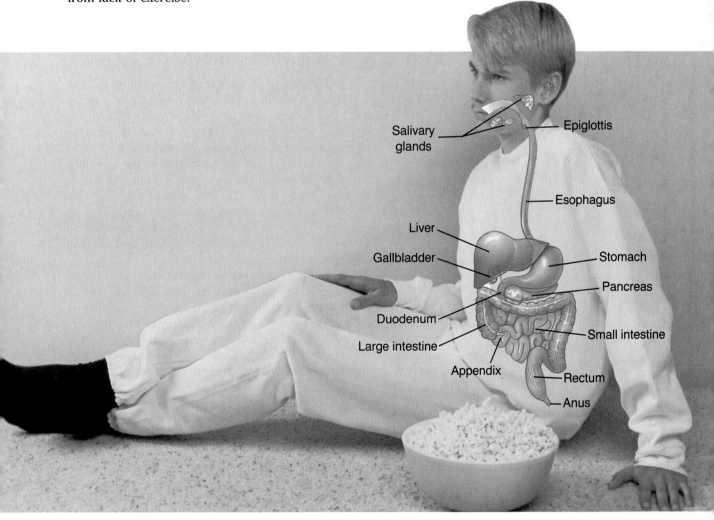

Salivary glands

Epiglottis

Esophagus

Liver

Gallbladder

Stomach

Pancreas

Duodenum

Small intestine

Large intestine

Appendix

Rectum

Anus

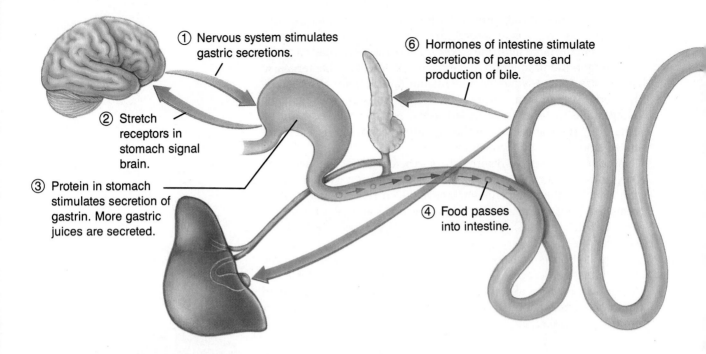

① Nervous system stimulates gastric secretions.

② Stretch receptors in stomach signal brain.

③ Protein in stomach stimulates secretion of gastrin. More gastric juices are secreted.

④ Food passes into intestine.

⑥ Hormones of intestine stimulate secretions of pancreas and production of bile.

FIGURE 29–7.

Digestion is controlled by signals from the nervous system and by hormones.

What is the role of gastrin?

29:5 How Is Digestion Controlled?

Digestion is controlled by interactions among the nervous system, the endocrine system, and the digestive system itself. Let's consider how these interactions take place as food passes through the digestive system, beginning at the mouth. Secretion of saliva is under the control of the nervous system. Small amounts of saliva are normally secreted to keep the mouth moist. When food is in the mouth, it stimulates the salivary glands to increase the secretion of saliva, which helps to dissolve the food. The smell or sight of food also increases the secretion of saliva in preparation for eating. This response involves the cerebrum and the memories that are associated with food. When you look at a picture of your favorite food or smell it cooking, you may notice that your mouth waters.

The secretion of gastric juice in the stomach is under the control of both the nervous and endocrine systems. The sight or smell of food stimulates the secretion of gastric juices. This response is controlled by the nervous system. Once food is in the stomach, nerve receptors respond to the stretching of the stomach and signal the medulla of the brain. The medulla then stimulates the stomach glands to continue the secretion of gastric juices. Recall that these gastric juices are responsible for beginning the digestion of proteins. Protein in the stomach stimulates the stomach lining to secrete gastrin. **Gastrin** is a hormone that is absorbed into the blood and further stimulates the glands in the stomach to secrete gastric juices.

As food passes into the intestine, hormones are secreted by the intestine. These hormones inhibit the secretion of gastric juices in the stomach, thus slowing its action, and stimulate pancreatic secretions. They also stimulate the production and release of bile.

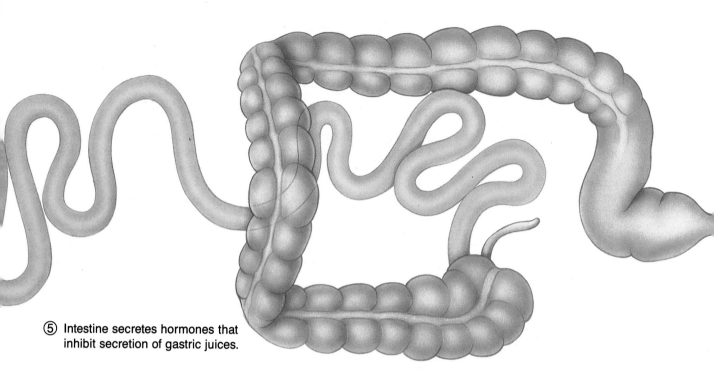

⑤ Intestine secretes hormones that inhibit secretion of gastric juices.

The parts of your digestive system "know" when to begin digesting food because of nervous and chemical signals. But, how do you "know" when to eat? Your food intake is monitored by two nervous centers in the hypothalamus of the brain working together. The **hunger center** is the part of the hypothalamus that stimulates you to eat. The hunger center itself is stimulated by a drop in the level of glucose in the blood. As a result, you feel hungry and want to eat to satisfy that hunger. As you eat, food fills your stomach and it begins to stretch. This stretching stimulates nerves in the stomach, and a signal is sent to the satiety (suh TI ut ee) center of the brain. The **satiety center** is the part of the hypothalamus that signals you to stop eating. It "tells" you when you are full. The hunger center and satiety center work together to maintain a constant level of glucose in the blood and, thus, maintain homeostasis.

What is the role of the hypothalamus in food intake?

REVIEW

1. List, in order from mouth to anus, the organs through which food passes.
2. In which two parts of the digestive system are starches digested?
3. How does the brain function in digestion?
4. **SKILL REVIEW:** Prepare a graph representing the time food remains in each part of the digestive tract. For more help, refer to Organizing Information in the Skill Handbook, pages 810 to 813.
5. **USING CONCEPTS:** How do antacids help as a treatment for ulcers?

Objectives:

- list the six classes of nutrients and summarize their role in body nutrition.
- summarize how body heat is produced and regulated.
- summarize how the level of sugar in the blood is controlled.

To be considered a food, a substance must provide energy or building materials, or it must assist in some body process. There are six kinds of nutrients in foods. They are carbohydrates, fats, proteins, minerals, vitamins, and water. These substances take part in the chemical reactions of the body and help to maintain homeostasis. You supply these nutrients when you eat foods from the five main food groups, Figure 29–8.

29:6 Carbohydrates

Recall from Chapter 3 that carbohydrates are starches and sugars. These nutrients are important as sources of energy for your body. Sugars are simple carbohydrates. Sources of sugars in the diet include fruit, table sugar, syrups, jellies, and sweets. Starches are more complex carbohydrates. They are found in bread, cereal, potatoes, rice, corn, beans, and pasta.

During digestion, complex carbohydrates are broken down into simple sugars such as glucose, fructose, and galactose. These simple sugars are absorbed into the bloodstream and are carried to the liver. In the liver, simple sugars are converted to glycogen. Glycogen is a polysaccharide and is the form in which sugars are stored in the liver as well as in skeletal muscle. When the body needs energy, glycogen is broken down again into simple sugars that are used to fuel cell processes.

FIGURE 29–8.

The five food groups are the milk group, meat group, fruit-vegetable group, grain group, and combination group. The combination group includes foods that come from more than one group, such as spaghetti.

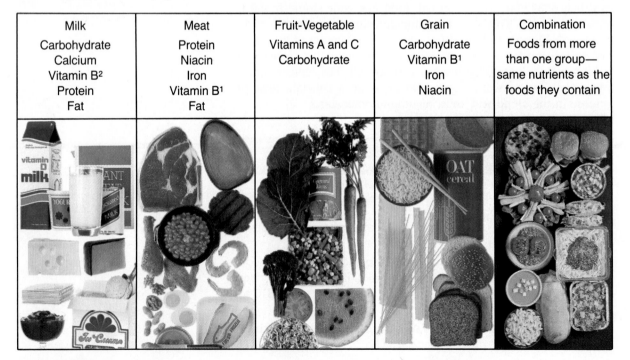

Milk	Meat	Fruit-Vegetable	Grain	Combination
Carbohydrate	Protein	Vitamins A and C	Carbohydrate	Foods from more
Calcium	Niacin	Carbohydrate	Vitamin B^1	than one group—
Vitamin B^2	Iron		Iron	same nutrients as the
Protein	Vitamin B^1		Niacin	foods they contain
Fat	Fat			

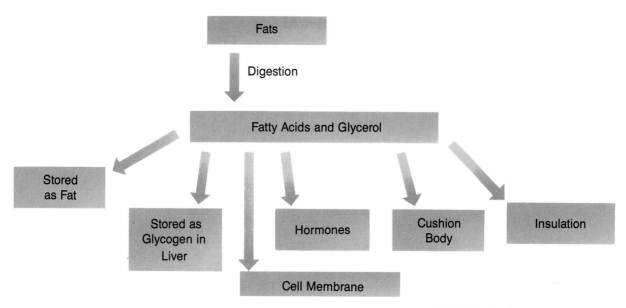

29:7 Fats

Fats are an energy source for your body and are also used as building materials. Recall from Chapter 5 that fats are the building blocks of the cell membrane. Fats are also used in the production of some hormones, cushion the body organs against injury, and insulate the body from cold. Sources of fat in the diet include meats, dairy products, cooking oils, and nuts.

In the digestive system, fats are broken down into fatty acids and glycerol. These products are absorbed in the small intestine and then carried to the liver. The liver absorbs fats, which are then converted to glycogen or stored as fat. Unused fats are stored in fat deposits throughout your body.

29:8 Proteins

Proteins have many uses in your body. Enzymes are proteins. So are antibodies, many hormones, and chemicals that help the blood to clot. Proteins make up the functional units of muscles and are part of many cell structures, including the cell membrane. Sources of protein include meat, eggs, dairy products, rice, and beans.

During digestion, proteins are broken down into amino acids. The amino acids are absorbed into the bloodstream and then carried to the liver. The liver can convert amino acids to fats or glucose, both of which can be used for energy. The body uses amino acids for energy only if other energy sources are used up. Most amino acids are absorbed by cells and used for protein synthesis. The human body needs 20 different amino acids to carry out protein synthesis, but it can make only 12 of them. The rest must be consumed in the diet in the form of proteins. Amino acids that must be consumed in the diet are called essential amino acids. Sources of essential amino acids include meats, dried beans, whole grains, and cheese.

FIGURE 29–9.

In the digestive system, fats are broken down to fatty acids and glycerol, which are used by the body for a variety of functions.

Eggs, peanuts, beans, and peas are among the foods rich in protein.

29:9 Minerals and Vitamins

A **mineral** is an inorganic substance that serves as a building material or takes part in chemical reactions in the body. Minerals make up about four percent of total body weight. Most of the mineral content of the body is in the skeleton. Calcium and phosphorus form much of the structure of bone. Table 29–2 lists the functions of some of the minerals that are needed by humans. Notice that the body does not use minerals as energy sources, but does rely on them for many other body functions.

A **vitamin** is an organic nutrient required in a tiny amount to maintain growth and metabolism. Vitamins do not provide energy or building materials in the body; rather their function is to regulate processes in the body. There are two main groups of vitamins: fat-soluble vitamins and water-soluble vitamins. Fat-soluble vitamins must be dissolved in fat before they are absorbed into the small intestine. Now you can see one reason fat is necessary in your diet. Fat-soluble vitamins can be stored in the body, usually in the liver. Excess amounts of fat-soluble vitamins in the diet can be toxic. Water-soluble vitamins dissolve readily in water. Water-soluble vitamins are not stored in the body. Excess amounts are excreted in the urine.

Some vitamins are synthesized by the body. For example, vitamin D, a fat-soluble vitamin, is synthesized in the skin. Vitamin K and some B vitamins are made by bacteria in the large intestine. However, many vitamins cannot be made by the body. They must be consumed in the diet. Table 29–3 summarizes the roles of vitamins. Some food sources of vitamins are also listed. You can see that without vitamins, the body can't maintain homeostasis.

What is the role of vitamins in the body?

NoteWorthy

In the eighteenth century, British sailors on long voyages discovered that eating limes prevented scurvy, a disease caused by lack of vitamin C in the diet. For this reason, British sailors were called "limeys."

Table 29–2.

VITAL MINERALS		
Mineral	**Function**	**Source**
Calcium	formation of bones and teeth, blood clotting, normal muscle and nerve activity	milk, cheese, nuts, whole-grain cereals, meats
Phosphorus	formation of bones and teeth, regulation of blood pH, muscle contraction and nerve activity, component of enzymes, DNA, RNA, and ATP	milk, whole-grain cereals, meats, vegetables
Iron	component of hemoglobin (carries oxygen to body cells) and cytochromes (ATP formation)	liver, egg yolk, peas, enriched cereals, whole grains, meat, raisins, leafy vegetables
Iodine	part of thyroid hormone, required by thyroid gland	seafood, egg, milk, iodized table salt
Sodium	regulation of body fluid pH, transmission of nerve impulses	bacon, butter, table salt, vegetables
Potassium	transmission of nerve impulses, muscle contraction	vegetables, bananas, ketchup
Magnesium	muscle and nerve function, bone formation, enzyme function	potatoes, fruits, whole-grain cereals, vegetables
Fluorine	teeth structure	fluoridated water

Table 29–3.

VITAMINS		
Vitamin	**Function**	**Source**
Fat-soluble		
A	maintain health of epithelial cells; formation of light-absorbing pigment; growth of bones and teeth	liver, broccoli, green and yellow vegetables, tomatoes, butter, egg yolk
D	absorption of calcium and phosphorus in digestive tract	egg yolk, shrimp, yeast, liver, fortified milk
E	formation of DNA, RNA, and red blood cells	leafy vegetables, milk, butter
K	blood clotting	green vegetables, tomatoes
Water-soluble		
B_1	sugar metabolism; synthesis of neurotransmitters	ham, eggs, green vegetables, chicken, raisins, seafood, soybeans, milk
B_2 (riboflavin)	sugar and protein metabolism in cells of eye, skin, intestine, blood	green vegetables, meats, yeast, eggs
Niacin	energy-releasing reactions; fat metabolism	yeast, meats, liver, fish, whole-grain cereals, nuts
B_6	fat metabolism	salmon, yeast, tomatoes, corn, spinach, liver, yogurt
B_{12}	red blood cell formation; metabolism of amino acids	liver, milk, cheese, eggs, meats
Pantothenic acid	aerobic respiration; synthesis of hormones	liver, yeast, green vegetables, cereal
Folic acid	synthesis of DNA and RNA; production of red and white blood cells	liver, leafy green vegetables
Biotin	aerobic respiration; fat metabolism	yeast, liver, egg yolk
C	protein metabolism; wound healing	citrus fruits, tomatoes, leafy green vegetables

BIOLAB *Nutrients*  29

Problem: Which foods contain starch and which contain glucose?

Materials

glass slides (10)
iodine solution
sugar test paper
food samples for
    starch test
food samples for
    sugar test
droppers (6)
forceps
water
paper towels

Procedures

1. Copy the data table.
2. Develop a **hypothesis** about which of the foods listed in the table contain starch and which contain glucose.
3. Using clean forceps, put 10 grains of cooked rice on a glass slide. Rice is a food known to contain starch. Rinse and dry the forceps.
4. Add 3 drops of iodine to the rice. The iodine will turn purple in the presence of starch. **CAUTION:** *Iodine is poisonous and will burn the skin.*
5. Using clean forceps, put a small piece of bread on a glass slide. Add 3 drops of iodine. Rinse and dry the forceps.
6. Record in your table whether or not starch is present in bread.

7. Repeat steps 5 and 6 with each of the remaining food samples.
8. Using a dropper, put a drop of honey on a glass slide. Honey is a food known to contain glucose.
9. Touch a piece of sugar test paper to the honey. The green color that appears on the test paper shows that glucose is present.
10. Using a clean dropper, put a drop of raw egg white on a glass slide and touch a piece of sugar test paper to the egg white.
11. Record in your data table whether a green color appears and whether glucose is present.
12. Repeat steps 10 and 11 with the remaining food samples. Use a different dropper and test paper for each food tested.

Data and Observations

Food	Starch present?	Food	Glucose present?
Rice	yes	Honey	yes
Bread		Egg white	
Potato		Maple syrup	
Egg white		Milk	
Spaghetti		Molasses	

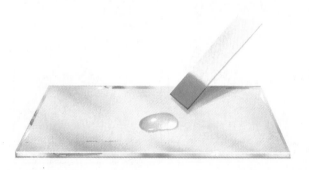

Questions and Conclusion

1. Which of the foods tested contained starch? Which contained glucose?
2. What was the purpose of using the rice and honey?
3. Is your **hypothesis** supported by your data? Explain.
4. Starch and glucose are what type of nutrient?
5. Why was it important to rinse and dry the forceps after each test?
Conclusion: Which foods contain starch and which contain glucose?

DIETARY FIBER

Cellulose is a complex carbohydrate that is found in the cell walls of plants. Most organisms are unable to break down cellulose into glucose. However, a few microorganisms are able to produce cellulase, an enzyme that accomplishes this job. These microorganisms are found in the intestines of ruminant animals such as cows and sheep and are responsible for the digestion of the grasses these animals eat.

Indigestible material in our diet is called dietary fiber, or bulk. Fruits, vegetables, and whole grains are the main sources of the fiber we eat. Although fiber does not supply energy, it is needed in the diet. Fiber provides roughage that stimulates peristalsis in the digestive tract. This stimulation helps prevent constipation. Scientists have shown that fiber reduces the risk of colon cancer and other intestinal problems. There is also evidence that some sources of fiber, such as oat and rice bran, lower the amount of cholesterol in the blood.

Why can't humans digest cellulose? How would our dietary needs be affected if we could digest cellulose?

These foods are rich in dietary fiber.

29:10 Water

Water is the most abundant substance in the body. Water makes up 60 percent of red blood cells and 75 percent of muscle cells. It plays a role in many chemical reactions in the body and is necessary for the breakdown of foods in digestion. Recall from Chapter 3 the role that water plays in the hydrolysis of large molecules. Water is an excellent solvent and will dissolve many substances. Oxygen and food could not enter your cells without water. Moisture on the surfaces of the respiratory and digestive systems make absorption of oxygen and food possible.

Water absorbs and releases heat very slowly. It is this characteristic that helps to regulate body temperature. A large amount of heat is needed to raise the temperature of water. Because the body contains so much water, this property helps keep the body temperature nearly constant.

You can see from its functions in the body that water is an important nutrient for maintaining homeostasis. A person can live several weeks without food, but can live only a few days without water. The body loses about 2.5 L of water per day through sweat and urine and, therefore, water must be replaced constantly.

List the functions of water in the body.

29:11 Metabolism and Body Heat

In Chapter 1, you learned that all of the chemical reactions of the body taken together are called metabolism. Some of these chemical reactions break down materials. The digestion of a slice of pizza involves many chemical reactions. The proteins in the cheese and pepperoni are broken down into amino acids. Once in your cells, the amino acids from the pizza are put together to form your own particular proteins.

You may have heard that someone has a fast or a slow metabolism. Each person's metabolic reactions take place at a certain rate. If these reactions are rapid, a person will use the energy in food quickly. The energy content of food is measured in units of heat called Calories. The number of Calories needed each day varies from person to person and depends on body mass, age, sex, and level of activity. In general, males need more Calories per day than females. Teenagers need more Calories than adults because they are experiencing growth spurts. Active people need more Calories than inactive people, and larger people need more Calories than smaller people. Most adults need between 1700 and 2500 Calories per day. If you eat more Calories than your body can metabolize, you will store the extra energy as body fat and gain weight. If you eat fewer Calories than your body can metabolize, you will use some of the energy stored in body fat and lose weight.

The breakdown of food in the body generates heat. The higher the metabolic rate, the faster foods are broken down, and the more heat is produced. Exercise and nervous system stimulation affect metabolic rate and heat production. During exercise, metabolic rate and heat production can increase by as much as 40 times. What happens to you when you have to take an exam? Do you get nervous and begin to perspire? Nervousness increases metabolic rate, which makes you feel warm. Heat produced by the body must be continuously removed or the body will become dangerously hot. The hypothalamus of the brain monitors body temperature and thereby maintains homeostasis. If you are too warm, the hypothalamus responds by allowing you to perspire. As the perspiration evaporates, heat is removed from your body. If you lose too much heat, your hypothalamus will stimulate an increase in metabolism. You also may shiver. This muscular action generates heat.

FIGURE 29–10.

When too much internal body heat is generated, the body cools itself by perspiring.

29:12 Nutrients and Homeostasis

Your body needs a constant supply of energy, yet you do not need to eat constantly. As a meal is digested and the nutrients are absorbed, your blood has more than enough nutrients in it. As blood passes from the intestine to the liver, the liver absorbs extra nutrients from the blood. This action keeps the levels of nutrients in the blood fairly constant. For example, when carbohydrates are broken down into glucose and absorbed in the intestine, the blood entering the liver will be high in glucose. The liver reacts to the high level of glucose in the blood by converting some of the glucose to glycogen. When glucose is no longer being absorbed in the intestine, the liver will receive blood that is low in glucose. When this happens, the liver converts some of the stored glycogen back to glucose.

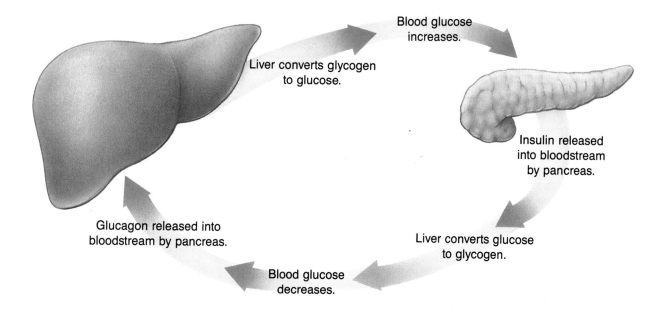

Blood glucose increases.

Liver converts glycogen to glucose.

Insulin released into bloodstream by pancreas.

Glucagon released into bloodstream by pancreas.

Liver converts glucose to glycogen.

Blood glucose decreases.

Hormones also control the level of glucose in the blood. Recall that the pancreas has two sets of functions, digestive and hormonal. The hormones produced by the pancreas are insulin and glucagon. They have opposite effects and work together to control the level of glucose in the blood. **Insulin** is a hormone that causes a decrease in blood glucose. Insulin reduces the level of glucose in the blood in four different ways. One, insulin causes body cells to absorb more glucose from the blood. Two, insulin increases the rate at which glucose undergoes cellular respiration. Three, insulin stimulates the liver to absorb glucose and convert it to glycogen. Finally, insulin stimulates fat cells to take in glucose and convert it to fat. When blood glucose levels fall below a certain level, insulin production slows.

Glucagon is a hormone that causes an increase in blood glucose levels. This hormone stimulates the liver to convert glycogen to glucose and release it into the blood when blood glucose levels are low. Insulin and glucagon both help the body maintain homeostasis by keeping the level of glucose in the blood constant.

FIGURE 29–11.

The level of glucose in the blood is kept constant by interactions between the activities of the liver and glucagon and insulin production.

What is the function of glucagon?

REVIEW

6. What role does protein have in the body?
7. Summarize the role of vitamins in the body.
8. How does water help keep body temperature constant?
9. **SKILL REVIEW:** Prepare a chart of food groups high in each of the six nutrients. For more help, refer to Organizing Information in the Skill Handbook, pages 810 to 813.
10. **USING CONCEPTS:** Why is the liver important in maintaining homeostasis?

DEVELOPING A VIEWPOINT

BODY IMAGE

Almost everyone thinks about how he or she looks. People usually want to look their best. This attitude is healthy most of the time. Sometimes, however, people develop a distorted perception of themselves and resort to drastic measures to change their body image. Dieting, fitness, fashion, and body building have become preoccupations.

BACKGROUND

If you were to take a poll of teenagers and ask them what concerns them most, you would find that they are very concerned about what others think about them. Part of this concern involves body image. A person's body image may include how he or she feels about his or her height, build, figure, posture, complexion, and clothing. Other topics such as hair color and style, earrings, glasses or contact lenses, eye color and shape, and nose shape are also included under the category of body image. Your body image, then, is the total of all the physical factors that other people can observe about you and that you can observe about yourself.

CASE STUDIES

1. Concern about body weight has become a national obsession in the United States. Dozens of fad diets written by self-proclaimed diet experts have flooded the market. There are grapefruit diets, liquid protein diets, and low-carbohydrate diets. Many people have gone on these diets and claim remarkable weight loss. Because these diets can achieve such dramatic results, many people view them as a valuable tool in the battle against being overweight. Most fad diets eliminate specific food groups from the diet. Many doctors maintain that eliminating food groups can be hazardous to health. In addition, weight lost rapidly during a fad diet is usually put back on just as quickly.

2. According to a recent study, today's teenagers have about 20 percent more body fat than teenagers of 20 years ago. The cause is a lack of exercise or physical activity. In previous generations, people focused on physical activity in their leisure time. Today, however, the television set is on for seven hours a day in the average home in the United States.

3. A popular notion about vitamins is that more is better. Some people who take huge doses of vitamin C claim they have not had colds for years. Others report feeling more energetic and healthy after taking vitamins for several weeks or months. However, there is no scientific evidence that taking vitamins will improve health in an already healthy person who eats a balanced diet. Moreover, huge doses of some vitamins can be toxic. Too much vitamin A can cause enlargement of the liver and swelling in the bones. Overdoses of vitamin D can lead to mineral loss from bones and hardening of blood vessels. At best, many doctors maintain that taking vitamin supplements has no effect on health. Nonetheless, millions of dollars worth of vitamins are sold over-the-counter each year.

4. Many people are so concerned about obesity that they develop eating disorders. Bulimia is an eating disorder characterized by overeating followed by forced vomiting and the use of laxatives. Bulimia can affect the salt balance of the body. Frequent vomiting can damage the esophagus, and frequent use of laxatives causes damage to the intestine. Most bulimics, however, are normal weight with little reason to be worried about excess weight. Anorexia nervosa is a disorder that involves self-imposed starvation and results in an extreme loss of weight. Body weight may drop by 25 percent below normal. Metabolism slows and menstruation may stop. The bones become weak. The individual may eventually die of starvation or heart failure. Individuals with anorexia or bulimia are usually single, young females. More women than men are affected by these disorders. Both disorders often indicate emotional problems and feelings of lack of control over one's life.

5. Flip through any magazine and take a look at the advertisements. All the people in the ads are young, attractive, and perfectly proportioned. How did they achieve their looks—were they all born that way? Do they represent a cross section of the general population? Many people feel compelled to manipulate their bodies in an attempt to achieve an "ideal" look. Tanning parlors have sprung up all across the United States, in spite of doctors' warnings that excessive tanning is unhealthy. People spend thousands of dollars on cosmetic surgery to have body parts tucked, enlarged, reduced, or reshaped. People have their teeth bonded for the sake of appearance. Bonding involves the application of synthetic material to the tooth to achieve a more pleasing shape or color.

6. Body building is a popular sport, with thousands of enthusiasts. Body builders may spend several hours a day lifting weights when training for competitive events. Body builders take pride in achieving large, well-defined muscles. Some people, however, believe body builders go too far in trying to achieve muscular bodies and that bulky muscles are unattractive.

Jim was in middle school when he decided to join the wrestling team. Impatient to develop strength, he resorted to using anabolic steroids, illegally obtained from a friend. By the time he was a high school junior, his health and personality had deteriorated and he was hospitalized. Use of anabolic steroids is illegal and harmful to body organs, especially to someone as young as Jim whose organs were undergoing rapid development.

DEVELOPING YOUR VIEWPOINT

1. Should fad diets be taken off the market?
2. Would you say that television can be detrimental to human health? Explain.
3. Should vitamins be available only by prescription?
4. What would you do if you suspected a friend of yours had anorexia nervosa or bulimia?
5. Under what circumstances would manipulating the body by means of cosmetic surgery or tanning parlors be acceptable?
6. Discuss the health aspects of body building.

SUGGESTED READINGS

1. Brownell, Kelly D. "When and How to Diet." *Psychology Today,* June 1989, pp. 40–42, 44, 46.
2. Findlay, Steven. "Buying the Perfect Body." *U.S. News & World Report,* May 1, 1989, pp. 68–75.
3. Haukebo, Kirsten. "Are You a Fashion Victim?" *Current Health,* Apr. 1989, pp. 26–27.

CHAPTER REVIEW

SUMMARY

1. Digestion begins in the mouth with both mechanical and chemical action on food. The esophagus transports food to the stomach where mechanical and chemical digestion continue. **29:1, 29:2**
2. In the small intestine, digestion is completed and food is absorbed. The liver and pancreas have roles in digestion. **29:3**
3. The large intestine absorbs water before indigestible materials are eliminated. **29:4**
4. Digestion is controlled by the cerebrum, hypothalamus, medulla, and by hormones. **29:5**
5. Carbohydrates are the main source of energy for the body. **29:6**
6. Fats are used as a source of energy and as building blocks. **29:7**
7. Proteins are used as building materials, enzymes, hormones, and antibodies. **29:8**
8. Minerals serve as structural materials or take part in chemical reactions. Vitamins are needed for growth and metabolism. **29:9**
9. Water serves many vital functions in the body. **29:10**
10. Metabolic rate determines how quickly energy is burned and how much body heat is generated. **29:11**
11. Insulin and glucagon are two hormones that help to regulate blood sugar levels. **29:12**

LANGUAGE OF BIOLOGY

amylase	glucagon
appendix	hunger center
bile	insulin
chemical digestion	large intestine
duodenum	liver
epiglottis	mechanical digestion
esophagus	mineral
gastrin	pancreas

pepsin	small intestine
peristalsis	stomach
rectum	villus
satiety center	vitamin

Choose the word or phrase from the list above that completes the sentence.

1. ____ is the physical process of breaking food into smaller pieces.
2. The enzyme ____ breaks down starch.
3. The ____ connects the mouth and stomach.
4. ____ are involuntary muscle contractions that move food through the digestive tract.
5. The ____ is the first portion of the small intestine.
6. A(n) ____ is a structure in the small intestine that absorbs digested food.
7. The part of the hypothalamus that stimulates you to eat is called the ____.
8. ____ is a hormone that stimulates glands in the stomach to secrete gastric juices.
9. A(n) ____ is an organic nutrient required to maintain growth and metabolism.
10. ____ is a hormone that decreases blood sugar level.

REVIEWING CONCEPTS

Choose the word or phrase that completes the sentence or answers the question.

11. Chewing is an example of ____.
    a. mechanical digestion
    b. chemical digestion
    c. peristalsis
    d. metabolism
12. The ____ monitors body temperature.
    a. medulla
    b. hypothalamus
    c. cerebrum
    d. satiety center
13. The digestive enzyme ____ works only in an acid environment.
    a. amylase
    b. pepsin
    c. glucagon
    d. gastrin

14. Water is absorbed in the ____.
  a. mouth c. small intestine
  b. stomach d. large intestine

15. Which structure does not digest any food?
  a. mouth c. stomach
  b. esophagus d. small intestine

16. Bile is produced by the ____.
  a. duodenum c. gallbladder
  b. liver d. pancreas

17. Hunger is controlled by the ____.
  a. medulla c. stomach
  b. hypothalamus d. hormones

18. The ____ converts excess glucose to glycogen.
  a. liver c. small intestine
  b. pancreas d. large intestine

19. The final products of the digestion of fats are ____.
  a. glucose
  b. amino acids
  c. fatty acids and glycerol
  d. disaccharides

20. The final products of the digestion of proteins are ____.
  a. sucrose c. glucose
  b. amino acids d. polysaccharides

UNDERSTANDING CONCEPTS

Answer the following questions using complete sentences.

21. Why is it important to chew food thoroughly?
22. What keeps the stomach from digesting itself?
23. Why is the pancreas considered part of the digestive system?
24. How does gastrin help control digestion?
25. What is the function of nuclease in the pancreas?
26. What happens if peristalsis is too rapid? Too slow?
27. How is body temperature regulated?

28. Why does the body need a diet high in carbohydrates?
29. Why is fat an important part of the diet?
30. Describe the relationship between insulin and glucagon.

APPLYING CONCEPTS

Answer the following questions using complete sentences.

31. Achlorhydria is a condition in which the stomach fails to secrete hydrochloric acid. How would this condition affect digestion?
32. Evaluate the nutritional value of a hamburger, french fries, and soda pop.
33. Compare the digestion of regular soda pop with sugar-free soda pop.
34. How is the body like a furnace?
35. What would happen to a person if the numbers of bacteria in the intestine were lowered due to chronic diarrhea?

EXTENSIONS

1. Keep track of everything you eat for one day and analyze your nutrient intake.
2. Interview a nutritionist. Find out which foods are considered good for the heart.
3. Investigate the causes of high blood cholesterol. Is there a genetic factor in having high cholesterol?

READINGS

Bennett, W.I. "Overactive Machinery." *The New York Times Magazine,* May 7, 1989, pp. 59–60.
Brand, David. "Searching for Life's Elixir." *Time,* Dec. 29, 1988, pp. 62–66.
Fox, M. "Fast (low-fat) Foods." *Health,* May 1988, pp. 45–47.

Chapter 30

RESPIRATION, CIRCULATION, EXCRETION

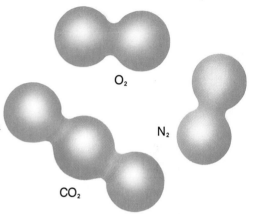

T ake a deep breath. You just took in a mixture of nitrogen, oxygen, carbon dioxide, and a few other gases. A portion of the air you inhaled, in the form of oxygen, was picked up by your bloodstream and carried to cells throughout your body. The swimmer on the left is dependent on this occurring in order to get across the pool. Blood also transports nutrients such as glucose. In body cells, oxygen and glucose are used for respiration. Wastes are produced as by-products of this activity. In this chapter, you will study how oxygen is taken in and used by the body and the role of the circulatory system as it relates to many other body systems. All cells in the body communicate chemically with each other by way of the circulatory system. Blood and wastes are chemical fingerprints that reflect the condition of your health.

THE RESPIRATORY SYSTEM

When most people hear the word *respiration,* they think of breathing. However, you are an oxygen-dependent organism and breathing is only a part of the respiration process. Respiration includes all the processes involved in getting oxygen to the cells of your body and getting rid of carbon dioxide. Respiration also involves the formation of ATP, as you studied in Chapter 6.

30:1 Structures of the Respiratory System

Your respiratory system is made up of a pair of lungs, a series of passageways that includes the trachea (TRAY kee uh) and bronchial tubes, and a thin sheet of muscle, the diaphragm. Air enters your body either through your mouth or your nose. Air that enters through your nose gets warmed, moistened, and filtered by mucous membranes as it moves down to your lungs. If you are a mouth-breather, inhaled air frequently feels cold, and has a drying effect on your mouth and throat. Once air has entered the body, it passes to the pharynx at the back of the throat, moves past the epiglottis, and passes through the larynx, or voice box. The epiglottis is a flap of

Objectives:
- list the structures involved in external respiration.
- describe the mechanics of breathing.
- describe mechanisms for keeping lungs clear.
- explain how breathing is controlled.
- contrast external respiration and internal respiration.

tissue at the upper end of the larynx that closes when you swallow food. This prevents food and other large materials from getting into the air passages. Air then travels down the **trachea,** the passageway that leads to the lungs. Figure 30–1 shows that the trachea then divides into two narrower tubes called bronchi. These branch many times into numerous microscopic tubules that eventually expand into thousands of thin-walled sacs called alveoli (*sing.* alveolus). **Alveoli** are the sacs of the lungs where oxygen and carbon dioxide are exchanged by diffusion between air and blood. Diffusion takes place easily because the wall of each alveolus is only one cell thick. The exchange of oxygen and carbon dioxide within the alveoli is called **external respiration.**

Clusters of alveoli are surrounded by networks of tiny blood vessels. Blood in these vessels has come from the cells of the body and contains wastes from cellular respiration. This blood is high in carbon dioxide and low in oxygen. The exchange of carbon dioxide for oxygen in the lungs is like a shuttle bus station. Passengers arrive and get off buses as new passengers push to get on. As carbon dioxide from the body diffuses from the blood into the air in the alveoli, oxygen diffuses from the air in the alveoli into the blood, making the blood rich in oxygen. Oxygen-rich blood then leaves the lungs and is pumped by the heart to the cells throughout the body.

FIGURE 30–1.

The respiratory system is the means by which oxygen enters the human body.

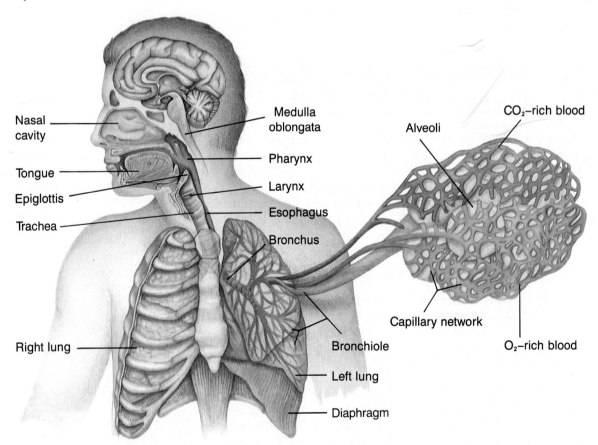

Nasal cavity

Tongue

Epiglottis

Trachea

Right lung

Medulla oblongata

Pharynx

Larynx

Esophagus

Bronchus

Bronchiole

Left lung

Diaphragm

Alveoli

CO_2–rich blood

Capillary network

O_2–rich blood

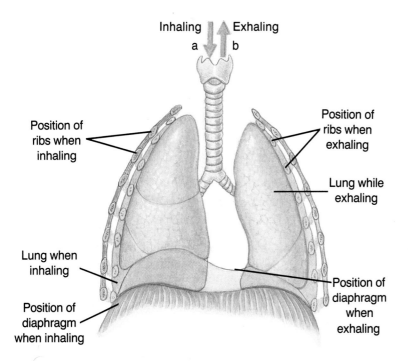

Inhaling   Exhaling
  a   b

Position of ribs when inhaling

Position of ribs when exhaling

Lung while exhaling

Lung when inhaling

Position of diaphragm when exhaling

Position of diaphragm when inhaling

FIGURE 30–2.

As the diaphragm moves down, air rushes into the alveoli (a). When the diaphragm relaxes, it pushes up against the lungs, forcing air out (b).

30:2 The Mechanics of Breathing

At rest, your diaphragm is relaxed in a dome-shape under your lungs. When you inhale, the muscles between your ribs contract, and your rib cage rises as illustrated in Figure 30–2 above. Your diaphragm contracts, becomes flattened, and moves lower in the chest cavity. As a result, the size of the space in the chest cavity is now larger. These two muscle actions increase the total volume of the cavity surrounding your lungs. Along with this increased volume, a partial vacuum is also produced around your lungs. Air outside the body exerts pressure. Therefore, air now rushes into your lungs because the air outside your body is under a higher pressure than the air in your lungs.

When you exhale, the muscles over the ribs relax and your ribs drop down in the chest cavity. Your diaphragm relaxes and returns to its resting, dome-shaped position. The relaxation of these muscles decreases the volume of the chest cavity, putting pressure on the air forcing it out of the alveoli. Healthy alveoli are elastic. They stretch as you inhale and return to normal as you exhale.

30:3 The Control of Breathing

Once oxygen is transported to the cells of the body, it is used for cellular respiration. In Chapter 6, you learned that cellular respiration is the process that uses oxygen to break down glucose within cells, resulting in the production of energy in the form of ATP. Carbon dioxide and water are waste products that result from cellular respiration. The carbon dioxide diffuses into the blood. When the carbon dioxide reaches the lungs, it diffuses into the alveoli.

FIGURE 30–3.

Speech and song result from the movement of air through the vocal cords as they are stretched and contracted.

How does the medulla control breathing?

hyperventilation:
hyper (GK) above
ventus (L) a wind

Breathing is an involuntary process controlled by the chemistry of your blood as it interacts with the medulla oblongata. It is a homeostatic process. The medulla oblongata is sensitive to the amount of carbon dioxide in the blood and sends signals to the rib muscles and diaphragm. As a result, these muscles contract and you inhale. If you exercise, the medulla responds to the higher levels of carbon dioxide by sending more frequent nerve signals to the rib muscles and diaphragm. Breathing becomes more rapid.

Under some conditions, a person may breathe too rapidly or hyperventilate. When hyperventilation occurs, most of the carbon dioxide in the blood is forced out and the oxygen level of the blood is extremely high. The level of carbon dioxide becomes so low that the medulla is not stimulated to start the inhalation process. However, cellular respiration is still taking place in body cells. Oxygen is being used up and increasing amounts of carbon dioxide are being released into the blood. Eventually, the level of carbon dioxide in the blood reaches the point where the medulla is stimulated.

FIGURE 30–4.

Oxygen is given to relieve respiratory problems.

30:4 Clearing the Way

The air you breathe is far from clean. In your lifetime you will inhale enough particulate matter to fill a large cereal box. This matter includes particles of dust, pollen, molds, and soil, other people's cigarette smoke, numerous environmental pollutants in the air, and millions of bacteria. Your respiratory passages are equipped with adaptations in the form of mucus, cilia, and the cough and sneeze reflexes to prevent most of this material from reaching your alveoli. The trachea and bronchi are lined with cilia and cells that secrete mucus, a thick protein mixture that traps most solid particles. The cilia constantly beat in the direction of your throat. Mucus is moved up to a point where you feel the urge to clear your throat. You swallow the rubbery gob and it breaks down in your digestive system.

FIGURE 30–5.

Air pollutants significantly decrease the amount of oxygen in the atmosphere.

If a large particle works its way into your trachea or onto your epiglottis, a cough reflex is initiated. The vocal cords are first shut tight and air pressure builds up behind them. Then a blast of air forces them open suddenly. Mucus and the unwanted matter are blown out of the air passages at a tremendous rate.

Sometimes bacteria are successful in establishing themselves in the moist atmosphere of the lungs and a disease like pneumonia occurs. Prolonged exposure to cigarette smoke is a well-known cause of lung cancer and other diseases such as chronic bronchitis. **Emphysema** is a lung condition in which the walls of the alveoli lose their elasticity. When a person with emphysema exhales, the alveoli remain expanded and full of air. Emphysema is usually caused by irritation of the lung tissue over a long period of time. Cigarette smoke, air pollution, and industrial dust are the most common lung irritants. These conditions may cause permanent changes in the tissues or their destruction. As a result, oxygen and carbon dioxide are not exchanged properly and less oxygen reaches body cells.

NoteWorthy

Cigarette smokers carry almost 5 percent less oxygen in their blood than nonsmokers.

Approximately eight microbes enter the lungs with every breath (200 000 per day).

REVIEW

1. Trace the path of an oxygen molecule from your nose to a cell.
2. How is external respiration different from cellular respiration?
3. How is breathing a homeostatic activity?
4. **SKILL REVIEW:** What is the sequence of muscle actions during inhaling and exhaling. For more help, refer to Reading Science in the Skill Handbook, pages 798 to 799.
5. **USING CONCEPTS:** During temper tantrums, four-year-old Jimmy often threatens to hold his breath. Many parents are afraid that a child might be harmed by this behavior. What will happen to Jimmy if he does hold his breath?

BIO LAB

Exercise and CO₂

Problem: How does exercise affect the amount of carbon dioxide exhaled?

Materials
distilled water
250-mL flask
dropper bottle of phenolphthalein indicator
dropper bottle of 0.04% NaOH
plastic straw

Procedures
1. Make a data table like the one shown.
2. **CAUTION:** *Put on goggles. NaOH can cause burns. Always place the dropper back in the bottle. Flush all spills with excess water.*
3. Form a **hypothesis** as to whether exercise will increase or decrease the amount of carbon dioxide that you exhale.
4. Place 200 mL of distilled water in a 250-mL flask and add 4 or 5 drops of phenolphthalein indicator. Phenolphthalein indicator is clear in the presence of an acid and pink in the presence of a base.
5. Add 0.04% NaOH drop by drop to the flask while gently swirling until a faint pink color remains in the solution for one minute. Place the dropper back in the 0.04% NaOH.
6. Exhale through the straw into the flask. **CAUTION:** *Do not inhale through the straw.*
7. Continue to exhale through the straw just until the pink color disappears and the solution remains clear.
8. Again add 0.04% NaOH drop by drop, swirling the flask until the solution again remains pink for one minute. In your data table, record the number of drops of 0.04% NaOH needed to produce the pink color while at rest. NaOH is used to neutralize the carbonic acid. Record class data.
9. Rinse out the flask as directed by your teacher. Repeat steps 3 through 8 immediately after jogging in place for one minute. Record the number of drops of 0.04% NaOH needed after jogging. Record class data on the chalkboard. Average the class results for both conditions.

Data and Observations

Numbers of drops NaOH		
Condition	**Individual**	**Class Average**
At rest		
After jogging		

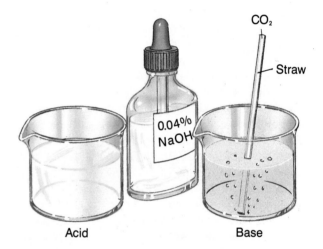

CO₂

Straw

0.04% NaOH

Acid

Base

Questions and Conclusion
1. Did the number of drops of NaOH needed increase or decrease after exercise?
2. Did your results support your **hypothesis?** Explain.
3. How do your individual results compare with your class averages?
4. Explain why the breathing rate of an individual increases during exercise.
5. What factors, other than exercise, could affect carbon dioxide production?

Conclusion: How does exercise affect the amount of carbon dioxide exhaled?

THE CIRCULATORY SYSTEM

Your body contains a closed circulatory system with several major parts: a fluid with cells, a pathway for the fluid, and a pumping structure to move the fluid. The fluid is blood. The pathway is made up of kilometers of blood vessels that extend to the trillions of cells in your body. The pumping structure is your heart.

30:5 Blood

Blood is a mixture of fluid, cells, and fragments of cells. Table 30–1 summarizes information about human blood components. The fluid portion of the blood in which blood cells move is called **plasma.** Plasma is straw-colored colloid that makes up about 55 percent of the total volume of blood. Blood cells and platelets are suspended in plasma.

Objectives:
- describe the composition and functions of blood.
- explain the importance of blood types.
- trace the route blood takes through the body.
- trace the pathway blood takes through the heart.
- explain how heartbeat rate is controlled.
- compare systolic and diastolic pressures.

Table 30–1.

Blood Components	
Component	**Characteristics**
Red blood cells	Transport oxygen and some carbon dioxide; lack a nucleus; contain hemoglobin
White blood cells	Large; several different types; all contain nuclei; defend the body against disease
Platelets	Cell fragments needed for blood clotting
Plasma	Liquid; contains proteins; carries red and white blood cells, platelets, nutrients, enzymes, hormones, gases, and inorganic salts

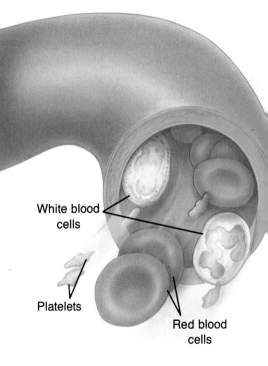

White blood cells

Platelets

Red blood cells

The cellular part of blood is made up of red blood cells, several kinds of white blood cells, and cell fragments called platelets. **Red blood cells** are cells that carry oxygen. They make up 44 percent of blood. Red blood cells are round and disk-shaped. They are produced at the incredible rate of about 2.3 million per second in the red bone marrow of the ribs, humerus, femur, sternum, and other long bones. At the same time, about an equal number of old red blood cells are being destroyed in the liver and the spleen, an organ of the lymphatic system. Red blood cells in humans do not have nuclei. At a very early stage in its development, a red blood cell has a nucleus. However, the nucleus is lost as the cell enters the bloodstream. Perhaps as a result, red blood cells have a limited life span. They remain active in the bloodstream only for about 120 days after which they are destroyed.

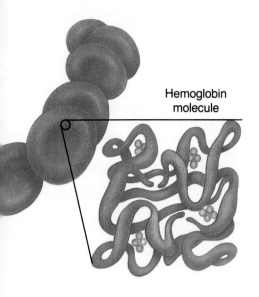

Hemoglobin
molecule

Red blood cells are equipped with hemoglobin that picks up oxygen that enters the body. **Hemoglobin** is an iron-containing protein molecule by which oxygen and some carbon dioxide are transported. Hemoglobin is also the pigment that gives red blood cells their color. In the lungs, oxygen entering the body becomes loosely attached to hemoglobin and is carried to the body cells. As blood passes tissues where oxygen concentration is low, the oxygen attached to hemoglobin diffuses from the red blood cells into the tissues.

Once work has been done in a cell, wastes in the form of carbon dioxide diffuse into the blood and are carried in the bloodstream to the lungs. About 70 percent of the carbon dioxide combines with water and sodium ions in the plasma to form sodium bicarbonate. The remaining 30 percent travels back to the lungs dissolved in the plasma and attached to hemoglobin.

White blood cells make up only one percent of your blood. **White blood cells** are cells that play a major role in protecting the body from foreign substances and from organisms that cause disease. The role of white blood cells and their function in immunity will be discussed in detail in Chapter 31. White blood cells are very different in appearance from red blood cells. White blood cells are larger, have a nucleus, and are fewer in number than red blood cells.

Your blood also contains some cell fragments. **Platelets** are pieces of cells that are involved in blood clotting in response to injury. They are produced from large cells in red bone marrow. They have a short life span, remaining in the blood for only about one week. At the time of an injury, platelets release a substance that starts a series of reactions that results in the formation of a blood clot. A sticky network of protein fibers called fibrin forms a web over the wound, trapping escaping blood components. Eventually a dry, leathery scab forms. The steps in the process of scab formation are illustrated in Chapter 28.

NoteWorthy

Hemoglobin carries oxygen and carbon dioxide at the same time, but on different parts of the molecule. Carbon monoxide binds more easily and more firmly to hemoglobin than does oxygen.

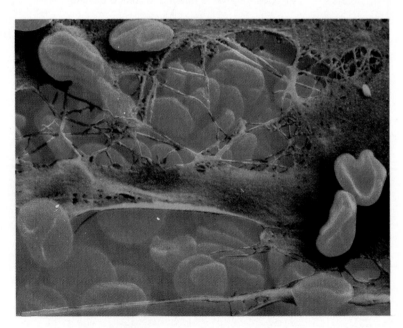

FIGURE 30–6.

Fibrin, formed as a result of broken platelets, traps red blood cells at the site of a break in the skin.

30:6 Blood Types

Red blood cell membranes contain proteins called antigens. Antigens are molecules that bring about the formation of large protein molecules called antibodies, and then react with them. An antibody is a substance produced by the body that will react with a specific antigen. There are many blood antigen systems, or blood groups, on the surface of red blood cells.

Knowing blood groups becomes important whenever blood is transfused from one person to another. Most people's blood contains both antigens and antibodies. For each antigen on a red blood cell, there is an antibody that will react with it. However, your blood contains antibodies for proteins that are *not* found on your own red blood cells. In Chapter 9, you learned that there are four blood types—A, B, AB, and O. You have inherited one of these blood types from your parents. The letters stand for the type of antigen found on the red blood cells in your body. Your plasma also contains specific antibodies that do not react with the antigen that is on your red blood cells. For example, if you have type A blood, you have the A antigen on your red blood cells and the anti-B antibody in your plasma. You do *not* have anti-A antibodies, because they would react with your red blood cells. If the wrong kind of blood is given during a transfusion, the antigens in the donated blood will react with antibodies in the recipient's plasma. A person with type A blood can only receive type A blood. If you tried to transfuse type B blood into this person, the antibodies in the plasma of the type A blood would attack the antigens on type B blood cells. The incoming red blood cells would be destroyed. Moreover, the materials released from the destroyed cells can cause kidney damage that can lead to death. Table 30-2 shows blood antigens and their antibodies.

Table 30–2.

Human Blood Types	
Antigens, Cells	**Antibodies, Plasma**
A	Anti-B
B	Anti-A
A and B	None
None (O)	Anti-A and B

FIGURE 30–7.

Human blood antigens and antibodies are inherited.

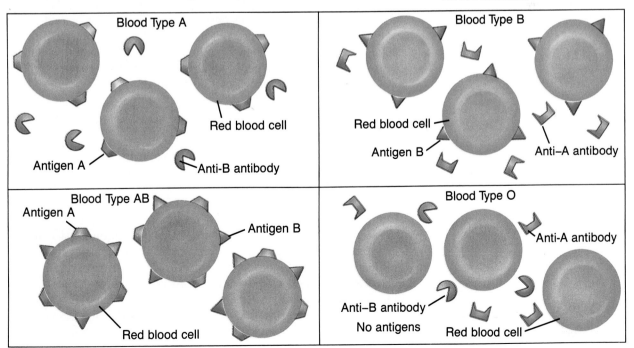

THE CIRCULATORY SYSTEM **643**

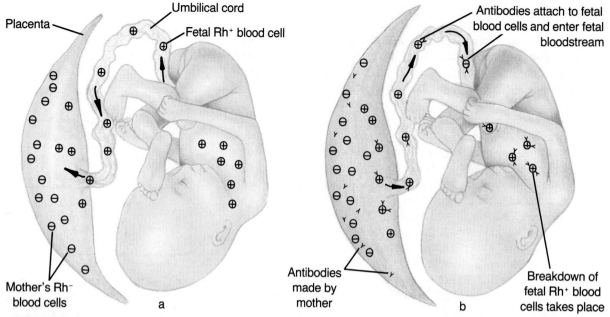

Placenta

Umbilical cord

Fetal Rh⁺ blood cell

Antibodies attach to fetal
blood cells and enter fetal
bloodstream

Mother's Rh⁻
blood cells

a

Antibodies
made by
mother

Breakdown of
fetal Rh⁺ blood
cells takes place

b

FIGURE 30–8.

Red blood cells of an Rh⁺ fetus cross the placenta to mix with the mother's Rh⁻ blood (a). The mother makes antibodies against the Rh⁺ fetal blood. These antibodies may then attack and destroy red blood cells in the fetus (b).

Why is a knowledge of blood antigens important in a transfusion?

Another blood group complication occurs in some pregnancies. This problem involves the antigen called Rh or Rhesus factor, also an inherited characteristic. People are Rh positive (Rh⁺) if they have the Rh antigen factor. They are Rh negative (Rh⁻) if they don't have this factor. During pregnancy and the birth process, a small amount of the baby's blood may mix with the mother's blood. If the baby is Rh⁺, and the mother is Rh⁻, the mother will develop anti-Rh⁺ antibodies in her bloodstream. If she becomes pregnant a second time, these antibodies will cross the placenta. If the new fetus is Rh⁺, the anti-Rh⁺ antibodies from the mother will destroy red blood cells in the fetus. This problem has become less common since researchers have discovered a way to prevent it. At 28 weeks and shortly after each Rh⁺ baby is born, the Rh⁻ mother is given a substance, which binds to the antibodies in her bloodstream so that they are removed. As a result, the next fetus will not be in danger.

30:7 Blood Vessels

The main structures of the circulatory system are the heart, which acts as a pump, and the blood vessels, through which blood flows. The heart will be discussed in Section 30:8. There are three types of blood vessels—arteries, capillaries, and veins. Each is different in structure and function. **Arteries** are large, muscular, elastic vessels that carry blood away from the heart. Arteries have thick walls and carry blood that is under great pressure. After branching off from the heart, they divide into smaller arteries that in turn divide into even smaller vessels called arterioles. Arterioles enter tissues and branch many times into the smallest vessels called capillaries. **Capillaries** are microscopic blood vessels with walls that are only one cell thick. This feature enables nutrients and gases to diffuse easily between the blood and tissues. Capillaries are extensive in active tissues such as muscle, but are lacking in the lens of the eye.

As blood leaves the tissues, the capillaries join to form slightly larger vessels called venules. The venules merge to form **veins,** which are large blood vessels that carry blood from the tissues back toward the heart. Blood in veins is not under pressure as great as that in arteries. Therefore, the walls of veins are thinner than the walls of arteries. In some veins, especially those in your arms and legs, blood travels uphill against gravity. These veins are equipped with valves that prevent blood from flowing backwards.

Blood flow can be slowed or blocked. If fats build up in arteries, a condition called **atherosclerosis** occurs. Fatty substances, such as cholesterol, are deposited on the inner walls of arteries. Vessels become blocked with fatty deposits called plaque. Plaque blocks the flow of blood and can lead to strokes or heart attacks.

Arteries that supply blood to the heart muscle itself are called coronary arteries. When plaque forms in coronary arteries, blood supply to the heart muscle becomes blocked. This blockage is the cause of one kind of heart attack. Blood, and the oxygen it carries, are prevented from reaching the heart muscle and tissue damage results. Some heart conditions can be treated surgically. Coronary bypass surgery is a treatment for blockage of coronary arteries. A part of a blood vessel from another part of the body is used to replace or bypass the clogged artery and restore a normal blood supply to the heart muscle.

How does plaque affect blood flow in arteries?

FIGURE 30–9.

An artery carries blood away from the heart (a). Veins carry blood toward the heart (b). Capillaries form an extensive web in tissues (c).

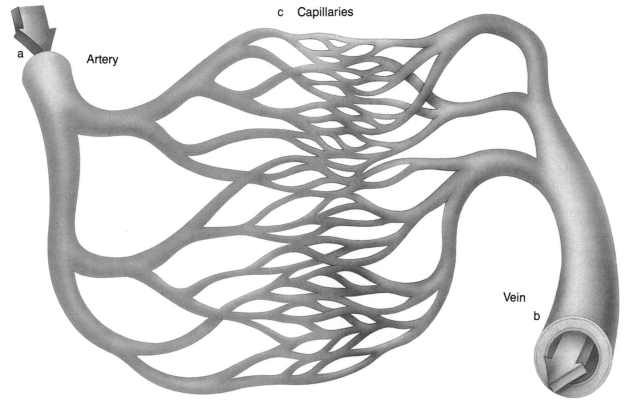

c Capillaries

a Artery

Vein

b

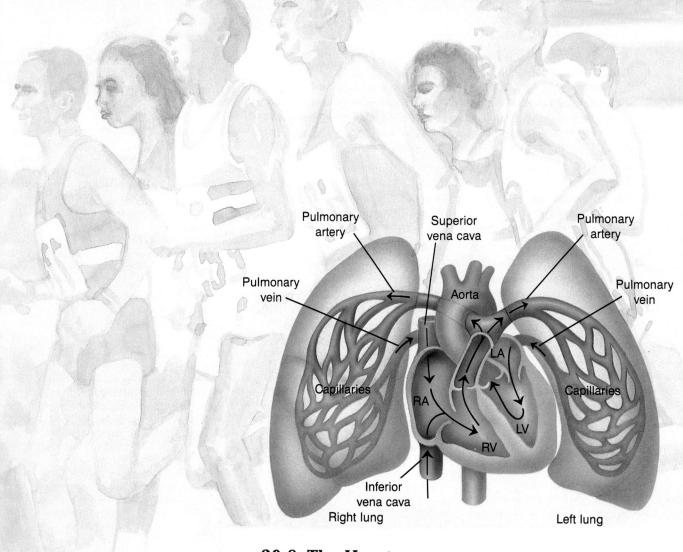

Pulmonary artery

Superior vena cava

Pulmonary artery

Pulmonary vein

Aorta

Pulmonary vein

Capillaries

LA

Capillaries

RA

LV

RV

Inferior vena cava

Right lung

Left lung

30:8 The Heart

The vessels in the body are of little value unless there is a way to move blood through them. The main purpose of the heart is to constantly move blood throughout the body. Your heart is a large organ made of cardiac muscle cells that have a rich supply of mitochondria. The human heart has four chambers. The two anterior chambers of the heart are the **atria** (*sing.* atrium). The two posterior chambers of the heart are the **ventricles.** The walls of the atria are thinner and less muscular than those of the ventricles. As you will see, the ventricles perform more work than the atria, a factor that contributes to the thickness of the muscle. In addition, the left ventricle is larger than the one on the right, so the heart is somewhat lopsided. Blood enters the heart through the atria and leaves the heart through the ventricles. Both atria fill up at the same time. The right atrium receives oxygen-poor blood from the head and body through two large vessels called the vena cavae. The left atrium receives oxygen-rich blood from the lungs through two pulmonary veins. The two atria contract, pushing blood down into the two ventricles. Then the ventricles both contract.

FIGURE 30–10.

Blood is pumped throughout the body by the heart.

The right ventricle contracts, pushing the oxygen-poor blood against gravity, out of the heart, toward the lungs through the pulmonary arteries. At the same time, the left ventricle forcefully pushes oxygen-rich blood out to the arteries of the body through the aorta. The aorta is the largest blood vessel in the body. If you were to trace a drop of blood through the entire system, you could begin with blood coming back from the body through the vena cava to the heart. Blood travels first into the right atrium, then the right ventricle, and through the pulmonary arteries to the lungs. In the lungs it drops off its carbon dioxide and picks up oxygen. Now it moves through the pulmonary veins to the left atrium, into the left ventricle, and then out to the body through the aorta. Between the atria and the ventricles are one-way valves that keep blood from flowing back into the atria. Valves in the arteries leaving the heart prevent back flow.

When your heart beats, it also makes sounds, which are described as "lubb" and "dupp." The sounds are caused by the closing of the valves. The closing of the valves between the atria and ventricles causes the "lubb" sound. The closing of the valves between the ventricles and arteries causes the "dupp" sound. A device called a stethoscope is used to listen to these sounds.

What is the purpose of valves in the heart?

FIGURE 30–11.

The heart is made up of cardiac muscle (a). Valves in the heart help control the amount of blood that enters and leaves the heart (b).

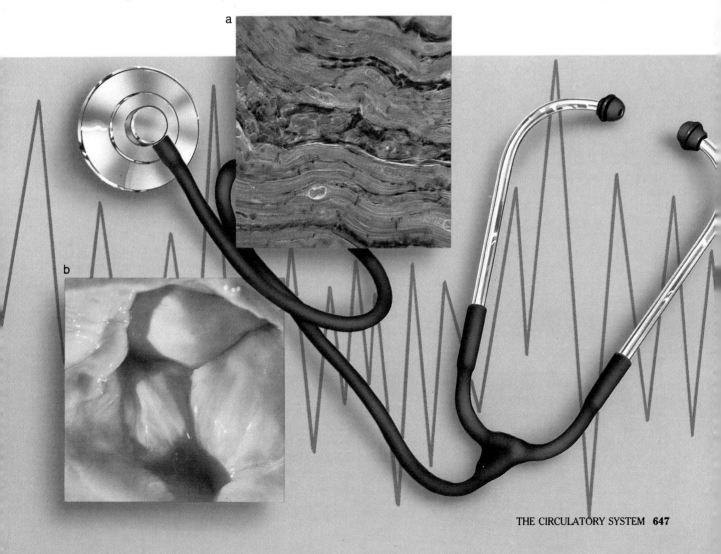

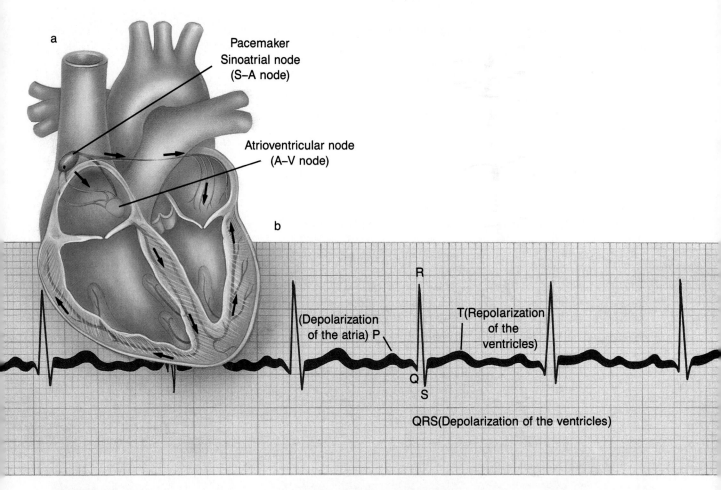

a

Pacemaker
Sinoatrial node
(S–A node)

Atrioventricular node
(A–V node)

b

R

(Depolarization
of the atria) P

T(Repolarization
of the
ventricles)

Q

S

QRS(Depolarization of the ventricles)

FIGURE 30–12.

The pacemaker is a mass of muscle tissue that controls the heart's rhythm (a). This activity can be recorded as an electrocardiogram (b).

NoteWorthy

The advantage of a four-chambered heart, as in birds and mammals, is the complete separation of oxygenated from deoxygenated blood. Only oxygenated blood goes to the body tissues for cellular respiration.

A healthy adult human heart beats at about 72 beats per minute at rest. The heartbeat rate is set by an area in the heart called the pacemaker. The **pacemaker** is a group of cells at the top of the right atrium that generates an electrical impulse that spreads over the atria. The impulse signals both atria to contract at almost the same time. The pacemaker also triggers a second set of cells at the base of the right atrium to send the same electrical impulse over the ventricles, causing them to contract. The pattern of a heartbeat can be drawn or traced by an electrocardiograph. An **electrocardiogram,** or EKG, is a record of the electrical changes in the heart. The EKG is an important tool in diagnosing abnormal heart rhythms or patterns. In Figure 30–12 you can see a normal EKG pattern. Each peak or valley in the diagram represents a particular activity during a heartbeat.

Exercise, stimulants, increased body temperature, or strong emotions increase heartbeat rate. The medulla oblongata regulates the rate of the pacemaker, speeding or slowing its activity. This is another example of homeostasis. If the heart beats too fast, sensory nerves in arteries near the heart become stretched. A signal is sent to the medulla. The medulla then slows the pacemaker. If the heart slows down too much, pressure drops in the arteries and the medulla signals the pacemaker to speed up.

ON THE LEVEL

Under normal conditions, blood flows at a consistent rate into the thin-walled right and left atria. About 70 percent of this blood then flows from the atria into the ventricles, even before the atria contract. When the atria contract, the remaining 30 percent is forced into the ventricles.

The volume of blood ejected from the left ventricle into the aorta per minute is called the cardiac output. Cardiac output is figured by measuring the amount of blood pumped out by the left ventricle during each heartbeat and the number of beats per minute. Actual cardiac output depends on how much blood enters the ventricle during the diastolic phase. As the heartbeat rate increases, the length of time the ventricle spends in the diastolic phase becomes shorter and shorter.

During exercise, cardiac output may increase to as much as four to six times normal. You would think that it would just continue to increase, but in actual measurements, the heartbeat rate rises and then levels off. Why do you think your heartbeat rate levels off? Why does it not continue to get higher and higher as you exercise?

Exercise influences cardiac output.

30:9 Blood Pressure

Each time the heart beats, a surge of blood flows from the left ventricle into the aorta. In some parts of the body, arteries are fairly close to the body surface. The surge of blood can be felt as it moves through the artery. This surge of blood through an artery is called a **pulse.** There is one pulse beat for every heartbeat. You can feel a pulse in the radial artery in your wrist or in the carotid artery in your neck.

A pulse beat represents the pressure that blood exerts as it pushes against the walls of an artery. **Blood pressure** is the force that the blood exerts on the vessels of the body. This pressure rises and falls as the heart contracts and then relaxes. Pressure is exerted on all vessels throughout the body, but it is most common to talk about blood pressure in arteries. Blood pressure rises sharply when the ventricles contract. The high pressure, caused by the contraction of the ventricles, is called systolic (sihs TAHL ihk) pressure. Blood pressure then drops dramatically as the ventricles relax. The lowest pressure occurs just before the ventricles contract again, and is called diastolic (di uh STAHL ihk) pressure.

How do systolic and diastolic pressures differ?

Blood pressure is usually measured in the brachial artery of the upper arm. A pressure cuff is wrapped around the arm and inflated until it blocks circulation in the artery. The pressure cuff is connected to a measuring device. A stethoscope is used to listen to the blood in the artery. As the pressure in the cuff is released, blood first begins to move through the artery in spurts that can be heard

FIGURE 30–13.

Certain lifestyle choices can aggravate problems in the circulatory system.

through the stethoscope. The pressure measured at this point is systolic pressure. As the cuff pressure is released further, the blood flows through the artery more smoothly and the sound of the spurts can no longer be heard. The pressure at this point is the diastolic pressure. The difference between the two pressures is called pulse pressure.

High blood pressure is the most common disorder affecting the heart and blood vessels and is a result of heredity and lifestyle. High blood pressure can harm the brain and kidneys, as well as the heart. Fortunately, high blood pressure can be controlled in a number of ways. Persons with high blood pressure are encouraged to lose weight, stop smoking, restrict their intake of sodium, and get more exercise. Relaxation techniques help some people lower their blood pressure. Medication is prescribed for others.

REVIEW

6. List the four main components of blood.
7. Distinguish between an artery and a vein.
8. Trace the path taken by a red blood cell as it passes from the left atrium to the right ventricle.
9. **SKILL REVIEW:** Make a pie graph showing the relative proportions of the components of blood. For more help, refer to Organizing Information in the Skill Handbook, pages 810 to 813.
10. **USING CONCEPTS:** The level of carbon dioxide in the blood affects breathing rate. It also affects the heartbeat rate. How would you expect high levels of carbon dioxide to affect the heartbeat rate?

THE URINARY SYSTEM

Excretion is a process that involves many systems of the body. In Chapter 28, you learned about sweat as a waste product, and in Chapter 29, you studied the elimination of digestive wastes. Carbon dioxide, as you have seen, is eliminated through the lungs. Organic wastes, excess salts, and water produced by cells are removed from the blood and excreted through the urinary system. All of these processes are maintained for the homeostasis of the body.

Objectives:
- describe the structure and functions of the excretory system.
- explain the hormonal control of the kidneys.

30:10 Structures of the Urinary System

The urinary system is made up of two kidneys, a pair of ureters, a smooth muscle bag called the bladder, and a urethra. One kidney is located on each side of your spine, at about waist level. The job of the **kidneys** is to filter blood that has collected wastes from cells throughout the body and to maintain the homeostasis of body fluids. Each kidney is connected to a tube called a ureter that leads to the urinary bladder. The urinary bladder stores a solution of protein wastes, called urine.

Each kidney is made up of about one million tiny filtering units. Each filtering unit in a kidney is called a **nephron.** Figure 30–14 shows the parts of a typical nephron. A nephron is made up of a capsule and a collecting duct. Blood entering the kidney carries cell wastes. Blood leaving the kidney has had these wastes removed and the body's water balance has been maintained. Blood that enters a nephron is under high pressure. As a result of this pressure, water, glucose, vitamins, amino acids, small proteins, protein wastes, and ions from the blood pass into the Bowman's capsule. Blood cells

What are two functions of the kidneys?

FIGURE 30–14.

The human urinary system (a) is made up of a pair of kidneys, ureters, and a urinary bladder. The kidney (b) contains filtering units called nephrons (c).

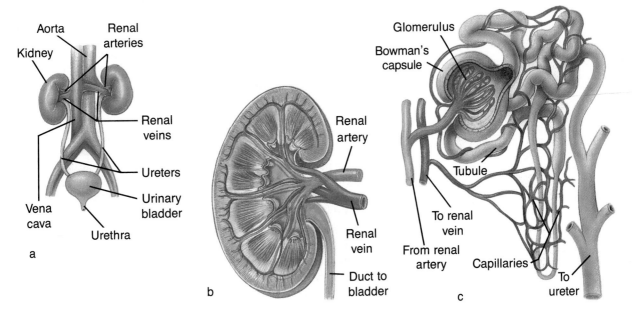

a — Aorta, Renal arteries, Kidney, Renal veins, Ureters, Urinary bladder, Vena cava, Urethra

b — Renal artery, Renal vein, Duct to bladder

c — Glomerulus, Bowman's capsule, Tubule, To renal vein, From renal artery, Capillaries, To ureter

and most proteins are too large to pass through the wall of the blood vessel and so these components stay within the blood vessel. The liquid squeezed into the nephron capsule passes through a narrow tubule. Normally, as the liquid moves through the tubule, most of the ions and water, and all of the glucose and amino acids are reabsorbed into the bloodstream. This second phase is the process by which the body's water balance is maintained. Small molecules such as water, diffuse back into the blood. Other molecules, such as ions, are moved back into the capillaries by active transport. The liquid remaining in the tubule—composed of excess water, waste molecules, and excess ions—is **urine,** the waste that flows through the ureter to the urinary bladder. Urine passes from the urinary bladder out of the body through a tube called the urethra. You produce about two liters of urine a day.

FIGURE 30–15.

In the nephron, filtration and reabsorption take place.

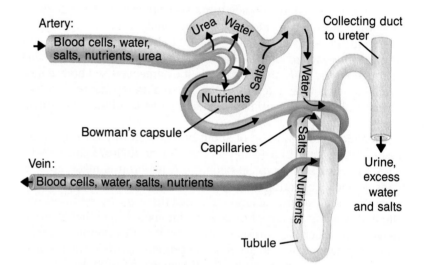

30:11 The Excretory System's Role in Homeostasis

The major waste products of the cells are nitrogenous wastes, which come from the breakdown of proteins. These wastes include ammonia and urea. Both compounds are toxic and have to be removed from the blood regularly. In addition to removing these wastes, the kidneys control sodium levels in the blood by removing and reabsorbing ions from the blood. This helps control the osmotic pressure of the blood. The kidneys regulate the pH of blood by excreting hydrogen ions and reabsorbing sodium bicarbonate.

The kidneys regulate chemical balances in the body by controlling which materials are eliminated. Much of this control involves the important step of reabsorption in the tubules of the nephron. This activity is controlled by hormones. Recall from Chapter 27 that hormones work on a feedback system. **Antidiuretic hormone** (ADH) is a hormone produced by the hypothalamus that stimulates the reabsorption of water in a nephron. This keeps both the fluid level of the body and blood pressure from decreasing. If you drink a large amount of water, the fluid level of the body increases. This

How does ADH work?

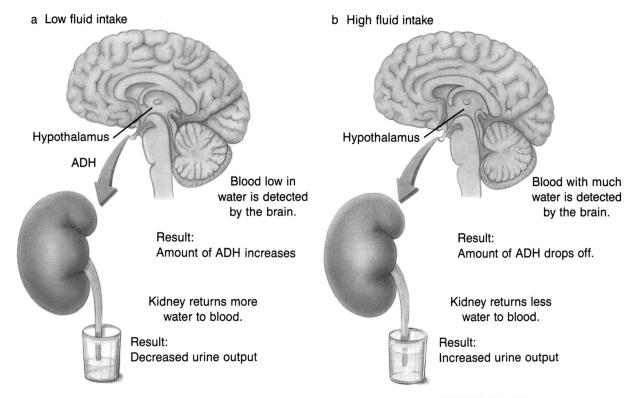

a Low fluid intake

Hypothalamus

ADH

Blood low in
water is detected
by the brain.

Result:
Amount of ADH increases

Kidney returns more
water to blood.

Result:
Decreased urine output

b High fluid intake

Hypothalamus

Blood with much
water is detected
by the brain.

Result:
Amount of ADH drops off.

Kidney returns less
water to blood.

Result:
Increased urine output

FIGURE 30–16.

The amount of urine produced by the kidneys is the result of an interaction between body fluid levels and ADH (a and b).

nephron:
nephros (GK) kidney

increase in water triggers the hypothalamus to slow up production of ADH. As a result, more water is eliminated. When the water level in the blood drops too low, the hypothalamus will again produce more ADH.

The adrenal glands are endocrine glands that lie on top of each kidney. **Aldosterone** is an adrenal gland hormone that stimulates reabsorption of sodium and chloride ions. Reabsorption of these ions also causes some reabsorption of water. A person on a high sodium diet takes in large amounts of sodium and chloride ions. As a result, aldosterone production decreases and more sodium is eliminated. The body depends on a normal functioning of a feedback system in the kidneys.

REVIEW

11. What does the kidney nephron do?
12. What are the major components of urine?
13. How does ADH help maintain homeostasis?
14. **SKILL REVIEW:** Trace the sequence of urinary waste from a cell to the outside of the body. For more help, refer to Organizing Information in the Skill Handbook, pages 810 to 813.
15. **USING CONCEPTS:** It is a very hot day. You are sweating and you feel thirsty. When you drink, you replace water. What other substance might you need to replace? Explain.

CHAPTER REVIEW

LANGUAGE OF BIOLOGY

aldosterone	kidneys
alveoli	nephron
antidiuretic hormone	pacemaker
atherosclerosis	plasma
arteries	platelets
atria	pulse
blood pressure	red blood cells
capillaries	trachea
electrocardiogram	urine
emphysema	veins
external respiration	ventricles
hemoglobin	white blood cells

Choose the word or phrase from the list above that completes the sentence.

1. The small air sacs in the lungs where oxygen and carbon dioxide are exchanged are ____.

2. ____ is the exchange of oxygen and carbon dioxide within the alveoli.
3. The ____ stimulates electrical impulses that cause atria to contract.
4. ____ is a protein molecule bound to a pigment that contains iron.
5. ____ are cell fragments in blood that are involved in blood clotting.
6. Microscopic blood vessels whose walls are only one cell thick are ____.
7. The two more muscular chambers of the heart are the ____.
8. The force that blood exerts on the vessels of the body is ____.
9. The filtering unit of the kidney is the ____.
10. ____ is a hormone that stimulates reabsorption of water in the nephron.

REVIEWING CONCEPTS

Choose the word or phrase that completes the sentence or answers the question.

11. Gas exchange occurs in the ____.
    - a. alveoli
    - b. bronchi
    - c. nasal cavity
    - d. trachea
12. When you inhale, ____.
    - a. alveoli return to their normal shape
    - b. the diaphragm contracts
    - c. rib muscles relax
    - d. none of these
13. Breathing is controlled by the ____.
    - a. lungs
    - b. alveoli
    - c. cerebellum
    - d. medulla
14. Oxygen is carried by ____.
    - a. plasma
    - b. platelets
    - c. red blood cells
    - d. white blood cells
15. In emphysema, ____ lose their elasticity.
    - a. arteries
    - b. capillaries
    - c. veins
    - d. alveoli

16. Blood returning from the lungs enters the ___ of the heart.
    a. left atrium   c. right atrium
    b. left ventricle   d. right ventricle
17. A condition in which fatty substances build up in the blood vessels is ___.
    a. anemia   c. leukemia
    b. atherosclerosis d. none of these
18. Urine leaves the kidney through the ___.
    a. capsule   c. ureter
    b. nephron   d. urethra
19. The kidneys regulate ___ of blood.
    a. osmotic pressure c. sodium level
    b. pH   d. all of these
20. Pressure caused by the contraction of the ventricles is ___.
    a. venous   c. atrial
    b. diastolic   d. systolic

UNDERSTANDING CONCEPTS

Answer the following questions using complete sentences.

21. Compare external respiration and cellular respiration.
22. Describe the steps in inhalation and exhalation.
23. Explain how breathing is controlled.
24. How are red blood cells different from other body cells?
25. Why must blood types be known before a transfusion?
26. Describe how capillaries are structurally adapted for exchanging materials with body cells.
27. What is the role of the pacemaker?
28. What is the function of heart valves?
29. Compare the liquid in the capsule of the nephron with the urine that leaves the kidney.
30. How does the adrenal gland affect the function of the kidneys?

APPLYING CONCEPTS

Answer the following questions using complete sentences.

31. Explain why all blood in all arteries is not oxygen rich. Where in the circulatory system do arteries carry oxygen-poor blood?
32. Carbon monoxide combines with hemoglobin more strongly than oxygen does. How does this explain why someone with carbon monoxide poisoning looks blue?
33. Think about the structure of the nephron, and suggest a reason why high blood pressure can damage the kidneys.
34. Alcohol inhibits the hypothalamus from secreting antidiuretic hormone. What is the effect on the body when this occurs?
35. What systems and waste products make up the body's excretory function?

EXTENSIONS

1. Research what takes place when a lung collapses. Find out the technique used to reinflate a collapsed lung.
2. Do a library research paper on the portable kidney machine.
3. Research the role of the American Red Cross and the American Lung Association. Report on your findings to the class.

READINGS

Carey, Joseph. "The Little Pebble that Hurts." *U.S. News & World Report,* May 2, 1988, pp. 68–70.

Clark, Matt. "Inside the Artificial Heart: Why It Failed—and Why New Ones May Work." *Newsweek,* Feb. 22, 1988, pp. 74–76.

Langone, John. "Leapin' Lizards! This Doc Zaps Hearts." *Discover,* Aug. 1987, pp. 56–61.

Chapter 31

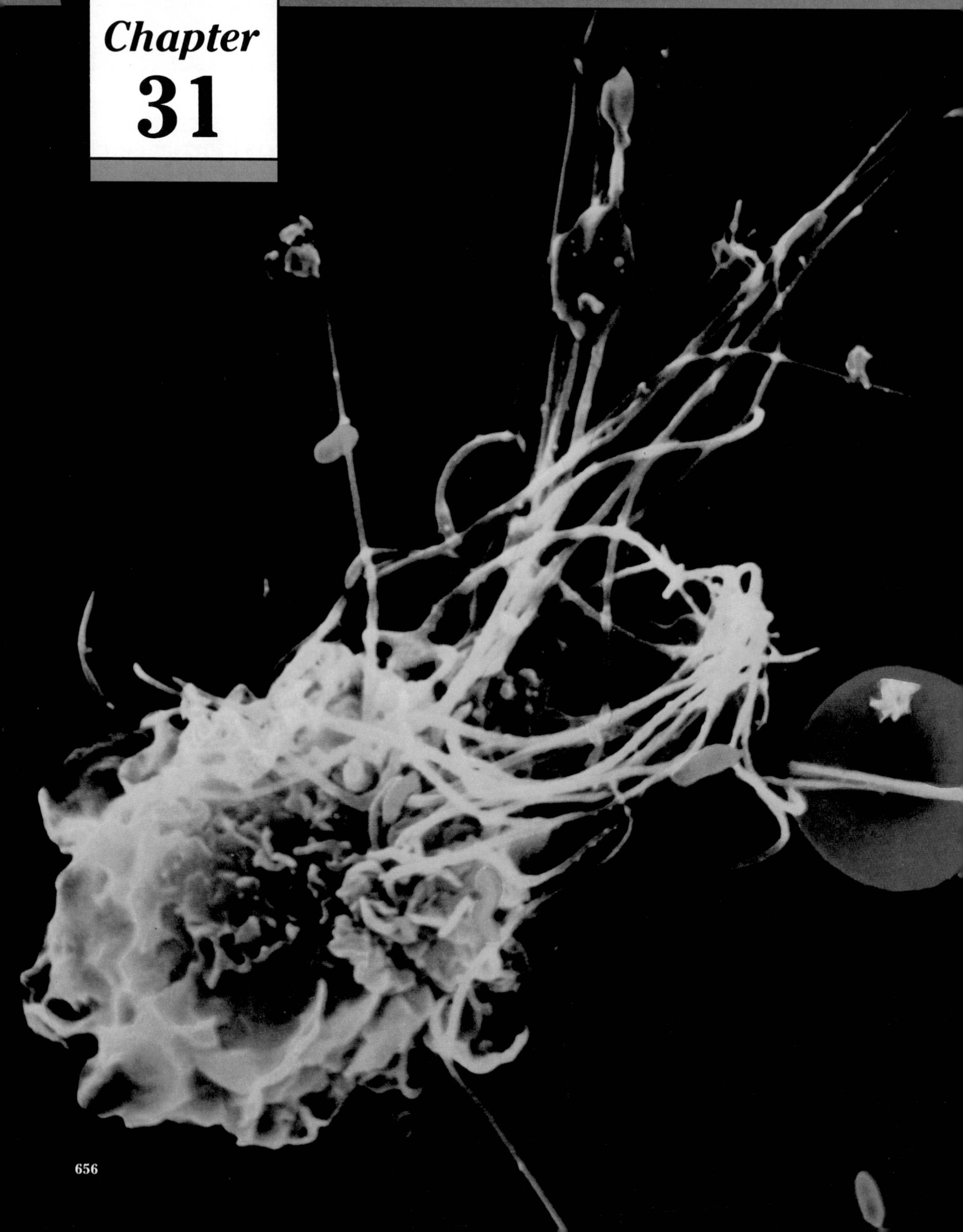

IMMUNITY

A war is constantly going on day after day and your body is the battleground. There are hordes of unseen enemies. They cluster around you on every surface, from your school desk to the doorknob. The soldiers in this war are too tiny to be seen with your eyes. How does your body prevent these invaders from gaining a stronghold? Once inside your body, the invaders are encountered by cells in the body fluids. These fluids are filtered by the lymphatic system. In this chapter you will study the lymphatic system and the ways the body mounts a defense against disease-causing organisms.

THE LYMPHATIC SYSTEM

The lymphatic system has two important functions. One function is to maintain homeostasis by keeping body fluids at a constant level. The second function is to help the body defend itself against disease.

31:1 Lymphatic Pathways

Your body cells are constantly bathed with fluid. This fluid keeps the cells moist, nourishes them, and collects cellular wastes. The fluid surrounding your cells is called tissue fluid. **Tissue fluid** is the fluid that forms when water and dissolved substances diffuse from the bloodstream and into the surrounding tissues. In order to maintain homeostasis, the body must have a way of removing tissue fluid from the intercellular spaces so that it doesn't build up. The lymphatic system maintains fluid balance by collecting the tissue fluid and returning it to the bloodstream. Tissue fluid is collected by lymph capillaries. After tissue fluid enters the lymphatic vessels, it is called **lymph.** Lymph also contains white blood cells that play a role in the body's defense system.

The lymph capillaries converge to form larger vessels called lymph veins. There are no lymph arteries because flow of lymph is in one direction only, toward the heart. Lymph veins from all over the body converge to form two lymph ducts. Lymph is collected by these two ducts and returned to the bloodstream in the shoulder area.

Objectives:
- describe the anatomy of the lymphatic system.
- explain the functions of the lymphatic system and organs.

A macrophage (yellow) ingests and destroys bacteria (green).

31:2 Lymph Tissues

The lymphatic system includes tissues and organs that have closely related functions. At certain locations along the lymphatic pathways, the lymph veins pass through lymph nodes as shown in Figure 31–1. **Lymph nodes** are small masses of tissue that filter the lymph. They are packed with **lymphocytes,** white blood cells that function in the body's defense system. As lymph is filtered through the lymph nodes, invading organisms such as bacteria are destroyed by the lymphocytes.

The spleen is the largest lymphatic organ in your body. The spleen contains a large number of lymphocytes that destroy waste particles. It also filters worn-out or damaged red blood cells and platelets from the blood. Unlike the lymph nodes, the spleen doesn't filter lymph.

The tonsils are collections of lymphatic tissue in the throat. They protect against microbes entering the mouth or nose.

The thymus gland is another lymphatic organ, located above the heart. The thymus gland is prominent in infants and young children, and functions in the development of the defense system. You will study the relationship between the thymus and the body's defense system later in this chapter.

lymphocyte:
   lympha (L) water
   kytos (GK) hollow

FIGURE 31–1.

The lymphatic system collects tissue fluid, filters it, and returns it to the bloodstream.

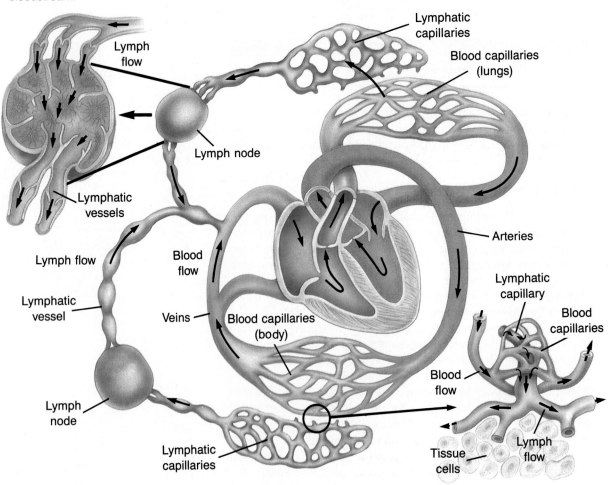

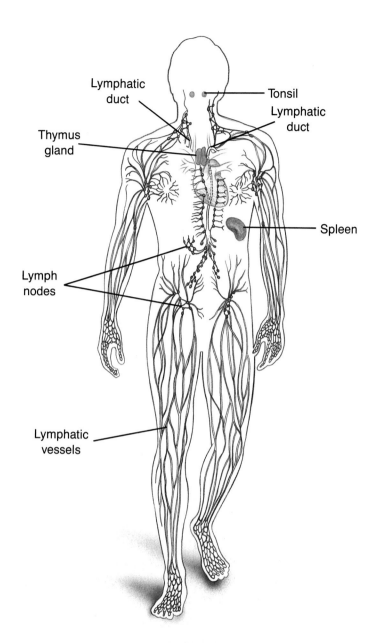

Lymphatic duct

Tonsil

Lymphatic duct

Thymus gland

Spleen

Lymph nodes

Lymphatic vessels

FIGURE 31–2.

Organs of the lymphatic system include the spleen, tonsils, and thymus gland.

REVIEW

1. Name three organs that are part of the lymphatic system.
2. Describe the composition of lymph.
3. How is tissue fluid produced?
4. **SKILL REVIEW:** Sequence the pathway tissue fluid follows back to the heart. For more help, refer to Organizing Information in the Skill Handbook, pages 810 to 813.
5. **USING CONCEPTS:** What advantages might there be in removing the tonsils of a child who gets numerous colds and sore throats? What might be a disadvantage?

Objectives:

- identify sources of infection and outline the steps of Koch's postulates.
- describe how infections are transmitted.

Remember the last time you had a cold? Even though your defenses may have responded quickly, the cold virus was able to invade your body. Your homeostatic mechanisms were upset and cold symptoms developed.

31:3 Sources of Infection

Recall from Chapter 12 that any disease-producing microbe is called a pathogen. The main sources of pathogens are soil, infected people, and other animals. The infectious organisms must first gain entry to your body. The primary entrances are the mouth, nose, eyes, and ears. Pathogens also can enter the urinary-reproductive tract or open wounds on the skin.

Once in the body, pathogens use the host's cells for shelter and food, sometimes causing harm. Pathogens vary in their ability to start and maintain an infection in a host. Some pathogens have the ability to evade or even overcome local host defenses. Other pathogens can only establish an infection if the host's defenses are already lowered. Many pathogens injure the host by producing toxins. Toxins are chemical substances that are harmful to the normal functioning of cells. Tetanus is a disease caused by a bacterial toxin. Other pathogens cause disease by destroying the host's cells. The virus that causes polio destroys nerve cells. Pathogens also vary in their ability to harm the host once an infection is established. A cold virus causes less harm than the AIDS virus.

In 1876, Robert Koch, a German physician, established a technique that is still used today to determine whether a certain organism is the source of a particular infection. Koch's procedures, which follow

FIGURE 31–3.

Koch's postulates are steps used to identify infectious pathogens.

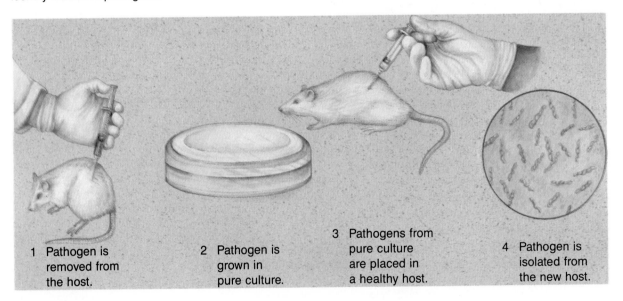

1 Pathogen is removed from the host.

2 Pathogen is grown in pure culture.

3 Pathogens from pure culture are placed in a healthy host.

4 Pathogen is isolated from the new host.

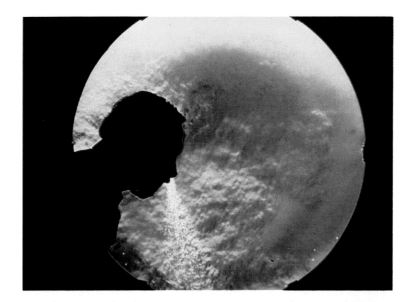

FIGURE 31–4.

The water droplets produced by a sneeze can be seen as a red and yellow cloud in this photo.

well-developed scientific methods, are called Koch's postulates and are stated as follows: (1) The pathogen must be found in the host and isolated from it. (2) The pathogen must be grown in a pure culture. (3) When pathogens from the pure culture are placed in a healthy host, they must produce symptoms of the disease. (4) The pathogen must be isolated from the new host. Study the four steps of Koch's postulates in Figure 31–3. Unfortunately, Koch's postulates can't always be carried out. Some pathogens can't be grown in a pure culture. For example, the pathogen that causes leprosy will not grow on an artificial surface in the laboratory. It requires living tissue to grow. Scientists were able to fulfill Koch's postulates only after they discovered that the leprosy pathogen would grow in armadillos.

How are Koch's postulates used to identify sources of infection?

31:4 Transmission of Infections

For a disease to be infectious, pathogens must pass from one host to another. Pathogens can be transferred by direct contact from one human host to another. Sexually transmitted diseases, such as syphilis, AIDS, and gonorrhea, are spread by sexual contact.

Many diseases are spread by indirect contact. The pathogen may be transmitted by objects or by organisms, in which case the organism transmitting the pathogen is called a vector. Food, water, and objects such as toys, dishes, or needles are objects that may harbor pathogens. When pathogens are released, such as in a cough or sneeze, they land on all nearby surfaces. Figure 31–4 shows the cloud of droplets produced by a sneeze. These droplets can remain in the air or land on food, hands, dishes, or any other material. Frequent hand washing helps to prevent the spread of pathogens contained in the droplet because most people frequently touch their faces without thinking about it. Pathogens on the hands are then transferred to the eyes, nose, or mouth and are thus able to invade the body.

In order to prevent transmission of diseases in public eating places, most restaurants have equipment that cleans and disinfects the dishes and utensils. Home dishwashers also help prevent the transmission of diseases. Today, laws require food handlers to wash their hands thoroughly before preparing food.

Pathogens also can be transmitted by infected water. Raw sewage seeping into a water supply contains microbes that can spread diseases. A leaky septic tank can infect an entire community if it leaks into the community water supply.

How do vectors transmit diseases?

Many human diseases are transmitted by the bites of arthropod vectors, such as fleas, lice, ticks, flies, and mosquitoes. Table 31–1 lists diseases that can be passed to humans by arthropods. The arthropod first bites an infected person, then transmits the pathogen to an uninfected person when it feeds again. Houseflies also transmit diseases by landing on infected material, such as animal wastes, and then landing on fresh food eaten by humans.

NoteWorthy

"Typhoid Mary" was a carrier of the bacterium that causes typhoid fever. Although she had no symptoms of the disease, she transmitted it to many people through her work as a restaurant cook in the early 1900s.

Table 31–1.

DISEASES TRANSMITTED BY ARTHROPODS	
Disease	**Vector**
Malaria	Mosquitoes
Lyme disease	Ticks
Bubonic plague	Fleas, ticks
African sleeping sickness	Tsetse flies

When an infectious disease spreads rapidly and uncontrollably, an **epidemic** occurs. The job of public health agencies is to try to see that diseases are contained so they do not reach epidemic proportions. Public health organizations in the United States work closely with the World Health Organization (WHO), which monitors diseases worldwide. Because of the efforts of WHO, no naturally occurring cases of smallpox have been reported since 1977.

REVIEW

6. What are two major sources of pathogens?
7. How do bacterial toxins harm the body?
8. By what routes do infectious organisms gain access to the body?
9. **SKILL REVIEW:** Design an experiment to prove that a newly identified bacterium causes a type of pneumonia. For more help, refer to Designing an Experiment in the Skill Handbook, pages 802 to 803.
10. **USING CONCEPTS:** Explain why a disease might be common during hot weather but rare during cold weather.

Your body constantly works to maintain homeostasis by fighting harmful substances in the environment. Pathogens bombard the body all the time. All animals have defense mechanisms that provide protection against pathogens. Some defense mechanisms are non-specific. They are effective against a wide variety of pathogens. Other mechanisms are highly specific and are effective against only one particular kind of disease-causing organism.

31:5 Nonspecific Defense Mechanisms

Nonspecific defense mechanisms are of two general types: physical defenses and chemical defenses. Physical defenses prevent pathogens from entering the body. If pathogens do enter the body, chemical defenses help to destroy them.

Skin is often called the body's first line of defense because most pathogens can't pass through unbroken skin. The multiple layers that make up the skin form an impermeable physical barrier. Skin is populated by millions of relatively harmless organisms that inhibit the multiplication of pathogens that also land on the skin.

Besides the skin, pathogens encounter physical defenses in the form of mucus, saliva, and tears. Mucus is a fluid secreted by membranes lining body cavities. Mucus is slightly sticky and traps many microbes as they enter the body. It also prevents body tissues from drying out. The mucous membranes of the respiratory tract contain cilia that move trapped bacteria and mucus toward the pharynx where they are continually swallowed and passed to the stomach. In the stomach, microbes are unable to survive due to the acidity of the stomach contents. Thus, the stomach provides a chemical defense against invasion of the body by pathogens. The mucous membranes of the nose contain hairs that trap and filter microbes, dust, and pollutants from the air.

Objectives:
- define and give examples of non-specific defense mechanisms.
- define and give examples of specific defense mechanisms.
- summarize and compare cellular and antibody immunity.
- explain how AIDS disables the immune system.
- describe four types of immunity.

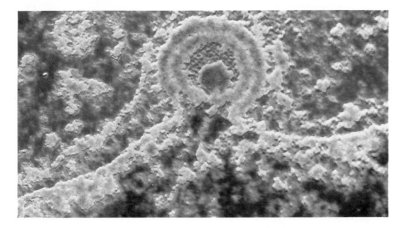

FIGURE 31–5.

Sometimes, physical and chemical defenses aren't enough to prevent pathogens from invading the body. This herpes virus (magnified 75 500 times) is invading the host cell's cytoplasm (blue).

Tears provide a physical defense by constantly washing the surface of your eyes. Saliva washes microbes from the surfaces of your teeth. Both of these fluids also provide chemical defenses because they contain lysozyme, an enzyme that destroys many bacteria.

Once pathogens enter the body, several other reactions occur that help to destroy the pathogens and restore homeostasis. Cells infected with viruses produce a protein called interferon that interferes with viral reproduction. Infected cells release interferon, which is then taken up by noninfected cells. The noninfected cells are thus protected against infection by the virus.

A second type of nonspecific body reaction that takes place when pathogens invade the body is the formation of complement. **Complement** is a group of proteins found in blood that attach to the surfaces of pathogens and help destroy them. Complement is so-named because it also complements substances made by the body as part of the body's specific defense mechanism. You will study the role of complement in specific defense later in this chapter.

A third type of nonspecific body reaction that helps to protect the body against pathogens that have entered body cells is phagocytosis. Recall from Chapter 5 that phagocytosis is the engulfing of foreign particles by cells. Phagocytosis is usually carried out by phagocytes. **Phagocytes** are white blood cells that ingest and destroy pathogens by surrounding and engulfing them. Phagocytes migrate out of the capillaries to the infected area, Figure 31–6. These cells will attack anything they recognize as foreign. For example, in the lungs phagocytes engulf dust particles that are breathed in from the air.

A fourth type of nonspecific body reaction is inflammation. **Inflammation** is a reaction by tissues to any type of injury, including that caused by physical force, chemical substances, extreme temperatures, radiation, and pathogens. Inflammation produces swelling, pain, heat, and redness in the damaged area. Inflammation begins

phagocyte:
phagein (GK) to eat
kytos (GK) hollow

FIGURE 31–6.

Phagocytes migrate out of capillaries by squeezing through the spaces between the cells of the capillary. The photo shows a scanning micrograph of a phagocyte.

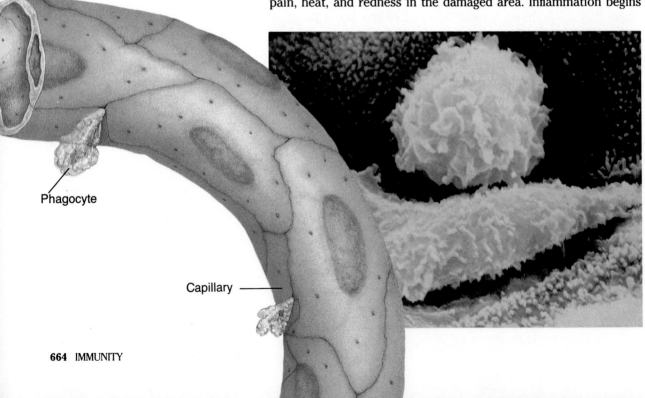

Phagocyte

Capillary

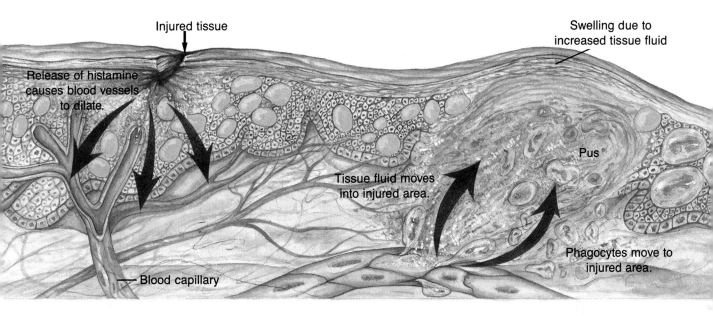

Injured tissue

Release of histamine causes blood vessels to dilate.

Blood capillary

Swelling due to increased tissue fluid

Tissue fluid moves into injured area.

Pus

Phagocytes move to injured area.

FIGURE 31–7.

Inflammation is the body's response to injury.

What happens during inflammation?

when damaged cells release histamine, Figure 31–7. Histamine is a chemical that causes blood vessels in the injured area to dilate. The blood vessels thus become more permeable to tissue fluid. This increase in tissue fluid in the injured area is an attempt by the body to destroy toxic agents and restore homeostasis. Dilation of blood vessels is responsible for the redness, while the increase in tissue fluid at the damaged area is responsible for the swelling experienced during inflammation. As inflammation proceeds, phagocytes migrate into the injured area and begin to ingest pathogens. Phagocytes also release proteins that cause body temperature to rise, resulting in fever. The increase in temperature inhibits the growth of pathogens and speeds up body reactions that aid tissue repair.

In all but mild infections, pus will form at the injured area. **Pus** is a thick fluid that contains living and nonliving white blood cells, pathogens, and tissue debris. As the injured area heals, dead cells and tissue debris are removed by the phagocytes and new cells form by mitosis.

31:6 Specific Defense Mechanisms

Despite the formidable action of the nonspecific defense mechanisms, they are not aimed at a single enemy. They serve as a general defense while the specific defense mechanisms are being mobilized, a process that takes several days. Specific defense is the job of the lymphatic system.

Specific defense mechanisms are collectively called immune responses. Immune responses depend on the ability of the body to recognize the differences between itself and foreign matter. Many cells of the human body have molecules on their surface that are unique to an individual. The body is able to recognize these molecules as *self.* Anything that is not *self* is considered by the body to

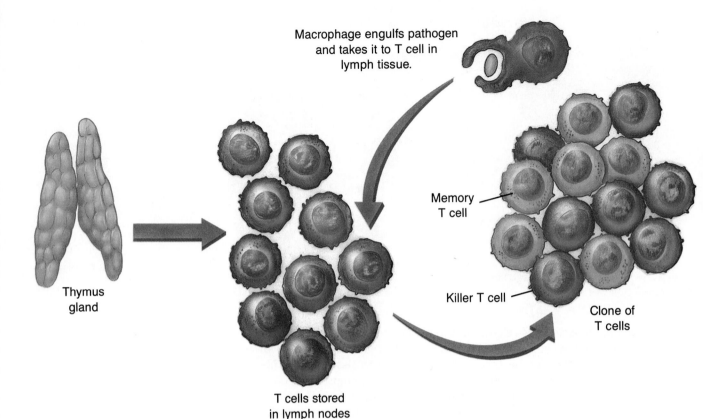

Macrophage engulfs pathogen
and takes it to T cell in
lymph tissue.

Thymus
gland

Memory
T cell

Killer T cell

Clone of
T cells

T cells stored
in lymph nodes

antigen:
anti (GK) against
genos (GK) birth

Compare an antigen and an antibody.

be *nonself.* Substances recognized by the body as *nonself* are said to be antigens. An **antigen** is a substance capable of stimulating a specific immune response. Antigens may be proteins, carbohydrates, or a combination of the two. Antigens are present on the surface of whole organisms, such as bacteria, or found on parts of organisms, such as the pollen grains of plants. When an antigen is introduced into your body, it causes the production of antibodies. An **antibody** is a protein produced in response to an antigen.

31:7 Cellular Immunity

Resistance to a specific pathogen by means of an immune response is called **immunity.** There are two types of immunity—cellular immunity and antibody immunity. Cellular immunity develops more slowly than antibody immunity and is the type of immune response seen when a body is invaded by pathogens such as the mumps virus.

Cellular immunity involves direct contact with cells bearing antigens on their surfaces. The cells that make contact are T cells and macrophages. A **macrophage** is a large white blood cell that can engulf foreign matter. **T cells** are lymphocytes that are involved in cellular immunity. Immature T cells are produced by the bone marrow and then transported to the thymus gland. T cells acquired their name because they are processed in the thymus gland. Processing causes the immature T cells to differentiate into mature cells. After

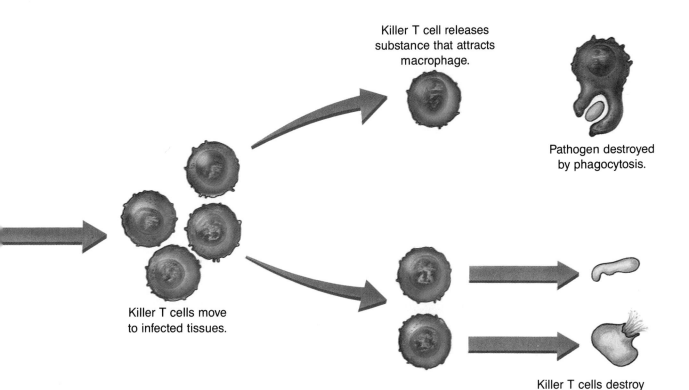

Killer T cell releases substance that attracts macrophage.

Pathogen destroyed by phagocytosis.

Killer T cells move to infected tissues.

Killer T cells destroy pathogen directly by causing it to burst or releasing toxin.

T cells are processed, they leave the thymus and enter the lymphatic system where they are stored in the lymph nodes. Thousands of different kinds of T cells are processed by the thymus gland, each capable of recognizing a specific antigen.

The process of cellular immunity takes place in several stages, Figure 31–8. When a certain type of pathogen invades the body, macrophages engulf the pathogen and bring it to T cells in the lymph tissue. The pathogen stimulates the T cells to reproduce. Each T cell that reproduces forms a clone of T cells. Some of the T cells from the clone, killer T cells, go out to infected tissues to destroy the pathogen. At the infection site, killer T cells may destroy the pathogen directly, or they may release a substance that attracts macrophages to the site. The macrophages then destroy the pathogen by phagocytosis.

Some of the T cells remain behind in the lymph organs after they are formed. These T cells are called memory T cells. If the same type of pathogen ever invades the body again, the memory T cells respond rapidly to destroy it. In a response involving memory T cells, invading pathogens are destroyed before they can cause disease. For this reason, there are many diseases you will not suffer from more than once. You can, however, get a disease more than once if it is caused by more than one pathogen or if the response of memory T cells is not permanent. For example, you know that you can get colds and the flu repeatedly. That is because there are hundreds of varieties of cold and influenza viruses, each one with unique antigens.

FIGURE 31–8.

Cellular immunity involves direct contact with antigen-bearing cells by T cells and takes place in several stages.

31:8 Antibody Immunity

Antibody immunity involves indirect contact with cells bearing antigens on their surfaces. In this type of immunity, antigens are destroyed by antibodies. Several types of cells are involved in antibody immunity. **B cells** are lymphocytes involved in antibody production. B cells are produced in the bone marrow and released to the lymphatic tissue. Unlike T cells, B cells are not processed by the thymus gland. There are thousands of different kinds of B cells, each one capable of reacting with a specific antigen and producing a specific antibody. Note the shape of an antibody molecule in Figure 31–9.

As in cellular immunity, several stages are involved in antibody immunity. When a pathogen invades your body, it is brought to a B cell in the lymph organs by a macrophage. Before the B cell can react, however, it must be activated by a helper T cell. Once the B cell has been activated, it begins to reproduce rapidly. Soon, a clone of B cells is formed, each B cell exactly like the first B cell. The B cells begin to secrete large numbers of antibody molecules. Although the B cells never leave the lymph nodes, the antibodies are carried throughout the body by the blood and tissue fluid. Antibodies destroy antigens directly by causing pathogens to clump together. The clumps are then destroyed by macrophages. Antibodies also destroy antigens by activating the group of proteins called complement. Complement is activated by a series of reactions, beginning with the binding of antibodies to antigens. The antigen-antibody complex

What are the roles of B cells and helper and suppressor T cells?

FIGURE 31–9.

Antibody immunity involves production of antibodies by B cells. The presence of antibodies sets off a series of reactions that end with destruction of the pathogen.

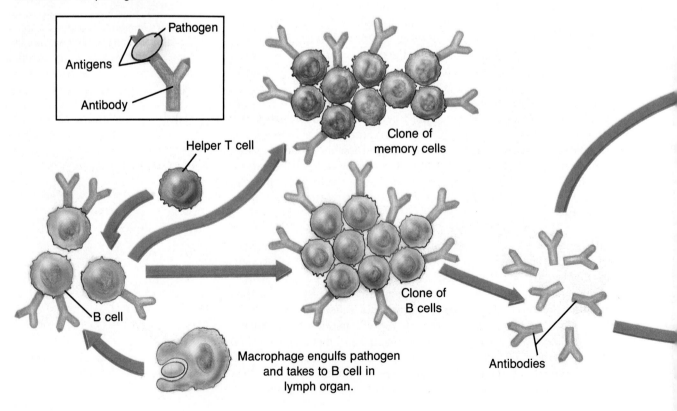

Pathogen

Antigens

Antibody

Helper T cell

Clone of memory cells

B cell

Clone of B cells

Macrophage engulfs pathogen and takes to B cell in lymph organ.

Antibodies

then binds to the complement. Activated complement helps to destroy antigens by attracting macrophages to the infected area and making the antigen-bearing cell more susceptible to phagocytosis, or by causing the antigen-bearing cell to rupture. Once the antigen has been destroyed, suppressor T cells direct the B cells to cease making antibodies. As with T cells, some of the B cells become memory cells in case of another attack by the same pathogen.

When tissues or organs are transplanted to replace injured or diseased ones, the immune system of the person receiving the transplant often causes the transplanted material to be rejected. The mechanism by which the transplant is destroyed may be the result of cellular immunity or antibody immunity. In order to make transplants successful, physicians try to closely match the donor and recipient tissue proteins. The most successful transplants occur when a person's own tissues are used in another part of the body. For example, in treating burn patients, skin grafts are frequently transplanted from one area of the patient's body to the burned area.

Usually, the body's immune response helps to keep the body healthy and maintain homeostasis. Sometimes, however, the immune response malfunctions, resulting in an autoimmune disease. Autoimmune diseases sometimes involve a malfunction of suppressor T cells, so that they fail to suppress antibody production. Thus, the body produces antibodies against itself. An example of an autoimmune disease is rheumatic fever, in which antibodies are formed against the heart. Another example is juvenile diabetes, in which antibodies are formed against the pancreas.

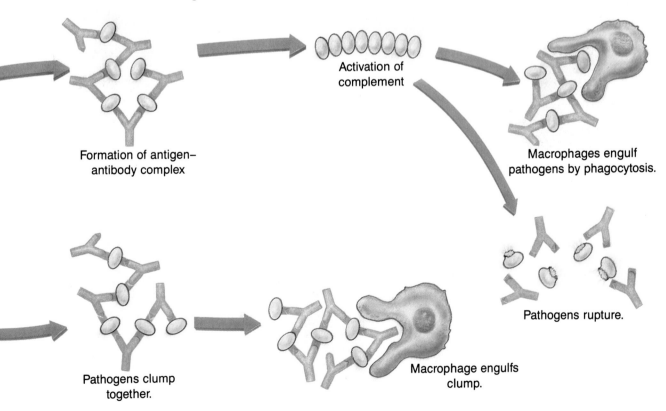

Formation of antigen–antibody complex

Activation of complement

Macrophages engulf pathogens by phagocytosis.

Pathogens rupture.

Pathogens clump together.

Macrophage engulfs clump.

BIOLAB

White Blood Cells

Problem: What are the percentages of different kinds of white blood cells?

Materials
prepared slide of human blood
microscope

Procedures
1. Copy the data table.
2. Mount the slide on the microscope and focus on low power. Turn the slide to high power and move the slide around to examine the red blood cells and the white blood cells, which contain nuclei.
3. Locate a neutrophil. This cell will have a nucleus with several lobes, usually three. Neutrophils are phagocytic cells. They leave the capillaries and arrive first at a wound site. Diagram a neutrophil.
4. Locate a lymphocyte. Lymphocytes have nuclei that nearly fill the cell. Diagram a lymphocyte.
5. Locate a monocyte. Monocytes are the largest cells. They will be two to three times the size of the other cells. A monocyte contains a round nucleus that fills about half the cell. Monocytes are phagocytic cells and are called macrophages when they leave the bloodstream. Diagram a monocyte.
6. There are two other types of white blood cells that are low in number. Basophils are white blood cells covered with granules that are stained purple. Basophils release histamine. Eosinophils are white blood cells covered with granules that are stained pink. Eosinophils are phagocytic and are believed to be important in fighting infections. Diagram a basophil and an eosinophil.
7. Develop a **hypothesis** as to the percentage of each type of white blood cell.
8. Count a total of 50 white blood cells and keep track in your table of how many of each type you see.
9. To calculate the percent of each type of white blood cell, multiply the number of each cell type by two. Record the percent of each cell type in your data table.

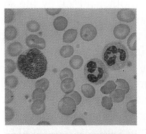
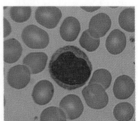
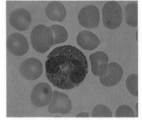
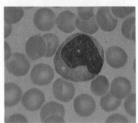

Data and Observations

Type of white blood cell	Number Counted	%	Diagram
Neutrophil			
Lymphocyte			
Monocyte			
Basophil			
Eosinophil			
Total			

Questions and Conclusion
1. Which type of white blood cell was most common? Second most common?
2. What major difference did you notice between red and white blood cells?
3. Why would you expect the white blood cell count to go up during an infection?
4. Do your data support your **hypothesis?** Explain.

Conclusion: What are the percentages of different kinds of white blood cells?

31:9 AIDS and the Immune System

Acquired immune deficiency syndrome, commonly called **AIDS,** is a disease of the immune system caused by a retrovirus. Recall from Chapter 12 that viral infections occur when viral nucleic acids, usually DNA, enter the host cell and become incorporated into the host DNA. The AIDS retrovirus has RNA as its nucleic acid, so an extra step is required before its nucleic acid can be incorporated into host DNA. Follow the sequence of an invasion by the AIDS virus in Figure 31–10. The viral RNA is used as a template to make viral DNA. This viral DNA then becomes part of the host DNA, where it can remain dormant for many years.

The AIDS retrovirus attacks helper T cells. Since helper T cells regulate and activate other cells involved in the immune response, the entire system is affected when the helper T cells are invaded. The AIDS host becomes unable to fight off secondary infections such as pneumonia and usually dies of these infections or rare forms of cancer.

AIDS is transmitted in body fluids such as blood, semen, or vaginal secretions. The virus can be passed from person to person in one of four ways. First, AIDS is primarily a sexually-transmitted disease. The ability of this virus to remain dormant for many years means that individuals can infect others during the period when they appear to be healthy. Usually, these people are unaware that they carry the retrovirus. The second way in which the retrovirus can be spread is through infected blood products. There have been a few cases in which blood used during blood transfusions has been contaminated with the AIDS virus. For this reason, blood banks test all blood for the presence of AIDS. A third way AIDS can be transmitted is by the sharing of contaminated needles and syringes, which is common among people who abuse drugs. A fourth way AIDS can be transmitted is from an infected mother to her unborn child.

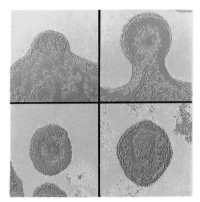

AIDS virus being released from the host cell

FIGURE 31–10.

Retroviruses replicate by synthesizing DNA from their own RNA within the host cell. The viral DNA is then incorporated into the host's DNA.

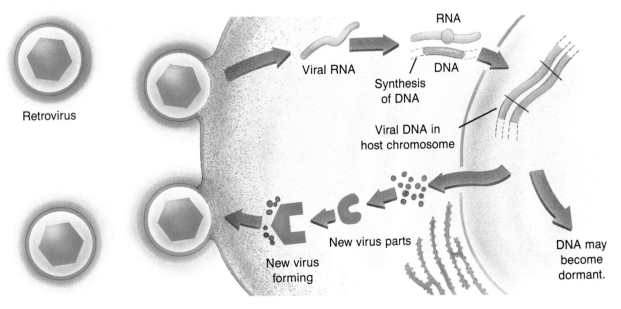

Retrovirus · Viral RNA · RNA · DNA · Synthesis of DNA · Viral DNA in host chromosome · New virus parts · New virus forming · DNA may become dormant.

SHINGLES

Chicken pox is a common childhood disease that is caused by a virus. Chicken pox is highly infectious; approximately 75 percent of all children under the age of 15 have been infected by the virus. You may remember having to stay home as you recovered from chicken pox. The disease is usually not serious and patients recover without complications.

Shingles is a disease similar to chicken pox that affects adults. At one time, these two diseases were thought to be caused by two different viruses. However, scientists now know that a shingles infection is a reactivated chicken pox infection.

In some kinds of viral infections, virus particles become "hidden" in the host nucleus and remain inactive for an extended period of time. During this period, the virus particles are replicated. If a change in the well-being of the host occurs and the immune system is weakened, the virus may shift into the lytic cycle. Recall that in the lytic cycle of a virus, the virus destroys the host cell. Following the lytic cycle, the virus infects healthy cells and causes an infection: shingles.

Why is the immune system unable to destroy all the virus particles during a chicken pox infection? Why are memory cells unable to prevent an attack of shingles?

Chicken pox and shingles are caused by the same virus.

AIDS cannot be spread by casual contact. Hugging, touching, and handshakes do not spread AIDS. People who work with AIDS patients will not be infected, as long as they are careful to avoid contact between their bloodstream and the patient's body fluids.

31:10 Treating Infectious Disease

You have studied how immunity develops in response to antigens. Immunity may be either passive or active. Passive immunity develops as a result of the introduction of antibodies. Active immunity develops as a result of exposure to pathogens. There are two ways in which passive immunity may develop, and two ways in which active immunity may develop.

Natural passive immunity develops when antibodies are passed from a mother to her unborn baby. The baby also receives antibodies through the mother's milk. Immunity lasts for several months until the baby's own immune system begins to function.

Artificial passive immunity develops as a result of the introduction of antibodies that are produced by other humans or by animals. For example, antibodies from the blood of horses are given to people to prevent tetanus, a bacterial disease. Artificial passive immunity is usually short-term. If you come in contact with the tetanus bacterium more than once, you will need an additional shot of antibodies.

| Natural passive: mother's antibodies | Artificial passive: animal antibodies | Natural active: disease pathogens | Artificial active: vaccine |

FIGURE 31–11.

Immunity may be passive or active.

Natural active immunity develops when a person is exposed to live pathogens. The person develops symptoms of the disease and will be immune to the disease if exposed to the pathogen again. A person may have diseases such as mumps or smallpox, and never experience them again due to natural active immunity.

Artificial active immunity results when a vaccine is given. A **vaccine** is a substance that consists of weakened or dead pathogens and causes immunity. In 1798, Edward Jenner, an English country doctor, demonstrated the first safe vaccination procedure. Jenner knew that dairy workers who acquired cowpox from infected cows were spared from smallpox during epidemics. Cowpox is a disease similar to but milder than smallpox. To test whether immunity to cowpox also caused immunity to smallpox, Jenner infected a boy with cowpox. The boy developed a mild cowpox infection. Six weeks later, Jenner infected the boy with smallpox. The boy did not become ill with smallpox. The viruses for cowpox and smallpox are so similar that the immune system cannot tell them apart.

How does a vaccine provide immunity?

REVIEW

11. Name five nonspecific defense mechanisms.
12. What is the difference between artificial passive immunity and artificial active immunity?
13. How does the immune system recognize an invader as *nonself*?
14. **SKILL REVIEW:** Sequence the events that occur in an inflammation reaction. For more help, refer to Reading Science in the Skill Handbook, pages 798 to 799.
15. **USING CONCEPTS:** Why is it adaptive for memory cells to remain in the immune system after an invasion by pathogens?

CHAPTER REVIEW

SUMMARY

1. The lymphatic system is composed of one-way vessels that carry lymph; tissues such as lymph nodes, spleen, and thymus; and lymphocytes. **31:1, 31:2**
2. The source of an infection can be established by following Koch's postulates. **31:3**
3. Infections are transmitted directly, or indirectly by vectors. **31:4**
4. Nonspecific defenses provide general protection to the body against pathogens. **31:5**
5. Immunity provides a way of fighting specific pathogens by recognizing invaders as *nonself.* **31:6**
6. Cellular immunity involves T cells that directly attack invading pathogens. **31:7**
7. B-cell immunity involves the production of specific antibodies. **31:8**
8. AIDS is a disease that disables the immune system. **31:9**
9. Immunity may be active or passive. Passive immunity involves the introduction of antibodies. Active immunity develops as a result of the introduction of pathogens. **31:10**

LANGUAGE OF BIOLOGY

AIDS	lymph nodes
antibody	lymphocytes
antigen	macrophage
B cells	phagocytes
complement	pus
epidemic	T cells
immunity	tissue fluid
inflammation	vaccine
lymph	

Choose the word or phrase from the list above that completes the sentence.

1. _____ is a fluid that has passed out of the small blood vessels to bathe the body tissues.

2. _____ is a fluid that has been collected from the body tissues.
3. _____ is a fluid that contains white blood cells, pathogens, and tissue debris.
4. _____ is specific resistance to a disease.
5. A(n) _____ is a foreign substance that causes an organism to produce antibodies.
6. A(n) _____ is a phagocytic white blood cell that entraps foreign substances and takes them to the lymphocytes.
7. A(n) _____ is a protein produced in response to the presence of an antigen.
8. When an infectious disease spreads uncontrollably, the disease has become a(n) _____.
9. _____ are lymphocytes that produce antibodies.
10. A(n) _____ consists of dead or live, weakened pathogens that are introduced into your body.

REVIEWING CONCEPTS

Choose the word or phrase that completes the sentence or answers the question.

11. A _____ is a mass of lymph tissue that filters lymph.
    - a. thymus gland
    - b. spleen
    - c. lymph node
    - d. lymphocyte
12. A poison that is produced by a pathogen and damages the host is a(n) _____.
    - a. toxin
    - b. antigen
    - c. allergen
    - d. vaccine
13. _____ is a nonspecific defense mechanism.
    - a. Skin
    - b. Fever
    - c. Inflammation
    - d. All of the above
14. _____ is a vector that transmits disease.
    - a. Mucus
    - b. An insect
    - c. Water
    - d. All of the above
15. _____ is an immune response to a pathogen.
    - a. Inflammation
    - b. Antibody formation
    - c. Disease
    - d. Pus formation

16. A _____ attacks a pathogen directly.
    a. B cell
    b. memory cell
    c. lymph node
    d. T cell

17. Memory cells are formed by _____.
    a. antigens of infecting agents
    b. T cells
    c. pus
    d. bacterial pathogens

18. _____ immunity develops when antibodies are introduced into a body.
    a. Passive
    b. Active
    c. Acquired active
    d. Localized

19. Which of the following filters lymph?
    a. migrating phagocytes
    b. spleen
    c. thymus
    d. lymph nodes

20. The AIDS virus attacks _____.
    a. B cells that secrete antibodies
    b. macrophages
    c. helper T cells
    d. killer T cells

UNDERSTANDING CONCEPTS

Answer the following questions using complete sentences.

21. Tears and saliva contain lysozyme. What is it and what does it do?
22. What role do phagocytes play in defending the body against disease?
23. What role does complement play in antibody immunity?
24. In what ways are diseases transmitted?
25. In what two ways is active immunity produced?
26. How is immunity different from nonspecific defense mechanisms?
27. Describe the relationship between an antigen and an antibody.
28. When you have had a disease, why do you normally not get it again?
29. Why are there no lymph arteries?
30. How did Jenner discover a safe smallpox vaccine?

APPLYING CONCEPTS

Answer the following questions using complete sentences.

31. Cholera, a waterborne disease, often reaches epidemic proportions after a flood. Explain.
32. Immunosuppressive drugs that are given to a recipient of a transplant must be taken for the rest of the recipient's life. Explain.
33. Why must burn patients be kept in pathogen-free isolation?
34. Why might it be a good idea to allow a fever to continue untreated?
35. Why would it be difficult to apply Koch's postulates to prove that the AIDS virus causes AIDS?

EXTENSIONS

1. Find out about your own vaccination history. Find out what diseases you have been vaccinated against and when these vaccinations were given.
2. Scientists have developed a technique in the lab to produce antibodies against cancer cells. Find out about monoclonal antibody techniques.
3. Some magazines carry monthly columns on AIDS like "AIDS Watch" in *Discover.* Prepare a report on knowledge gained concerning AIDS in the last six months.

READINGS

Jaret, Peter. "The War Within." *National Geographic,* June 1986, pp. 702–735.

Jaroff, Leon. "Stop That Germ!" *Time,* May 23, 1988, pp. 56–64.

Kolata, Gina. "Immune Boosters." *Discover,* Sept. 1987, pp. 68–74.

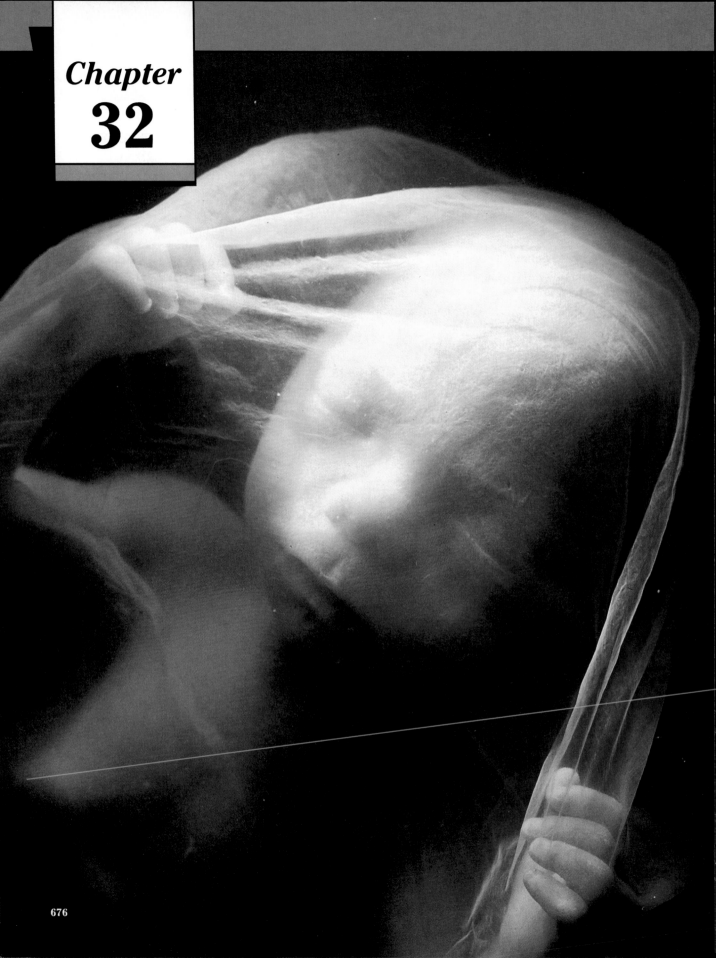

REPRODUCTION AND DEVELOPMENT

Reproduction is the process by which life on Earth is sustained. Humans and other sexually reproducing organisms form eggs and sperm as a means of carrying genetic information from one generation to the next. The egg and sperm unite and the result is the development of a new organism. The photo on the left shows a four-month-old fetus surrounded by the membrane that protects it during development. What led to the stage of development seen in the photo? In this chapter, you will learn about structures and processes in humans that function to continue the species.

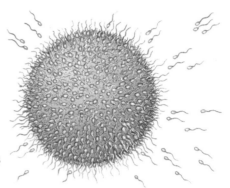

Of the hundreds of sperm that surround this egg, only one will fertilize it.

REPRODUCTIVE SYSTEMS

In previous chapters, you have read that most human body systems are alike in males and females. Human male and female reproductive systems are also similar in that each is well adapted for production of sex cells. However, these systems are different in structure and function, particularly in the methods of sperm and egg production. The roles of males and females in fertilization and production of offspring also differ greatly.

32:1 Human Male Anatomy

As males mature, their bodies change. One of those changes is the beginning of sperm production. Recall from Chapter 19 that sperm are produced in organs called testes. A male has two testes, each of which contains about 1000 tubes that produce sperm. The testes begin to develop inside the body cavity before birth. At birth, the testes move down into the scrotum (SKROHT um). The **scrotum** is a muscular sac located outside the male's body cavity. The temperature inside the scrotum is about 3°C cooler than inside the body cavity. The cooler temperature is important for sperm development because sperm cannot survive long at normal body temperatures.

Sperm are produced through meiosis by cells lining the tubes inside the testes. Recall from Chapter 8 that meiosis is a type of cell division that produces haploid cells. Each of the four haploid cells

Objectives:
- identify and describe the parts of the male and female reproductive systems.
- compare egg and sperm production.
- list the changes that occur in males and females at puberty.
- summarize the stages of the menstrual cycle.
- describe common diseases and disorders of the male and female reproductive systems.

The amnion appears as a thin veil surrounding this four-month-old fetus.

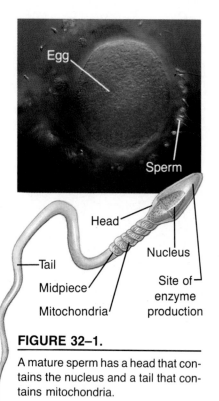

FIGURE 32–1.

A mature sperm has a head that contains the nucleus and a tail that contains mitochondria.

FIGURE 32–2.

The male reproductive system is shown from the front (left) and the side (right).

produced by one cell within a testis develops into a mature sperm. The process takes about ten weeks. Each cell loses much of its cytoplasm and becomes streamlined and lightened for movement. A long tail develops. The tail is packed with mitochondria, which provide energy in the form of ATP. Enzymes that will help the sperm penetrate the egg are produced. Once a male has reached sexual maturity, he produces sperm for the rest of his life.

After sperm are produced, they move from the testis into the epididymis (ep uh DIHD uh mus). The **epididymis** is a coiled tube within the scrotum in which sperm mature. When sperm are released from the epididymis, they enter the vas deferens (VAS • DEF uh runz). The **vas deferens** is a tube connected to the urethra just below the urinary bladder. The **urethra** is a tube that transports urine out of the body. The urethra also transports sperm out of the male's body. Urine and sperm, however, do not mix. A muscle located at the base of the bladder contracts to prevent urine from entering the urethra as sperm are ejected from the penis.

As sperm are released from the epididymis, fluid is added to them by five glands. Locate these glands in Figure 32–2. The **seminal vesicles** are two glands located beneath the bladder that empty a sugary fluid into the vas deferens. The fluid provides energy for sperm. Located below the seminal vesicles is the prostate gland. The **prostate gland** adds a basic fluid that helps protect the sperm from the acid environment of the female reproductive system. The two tiny **bulbourethral** (bul boh yoo REE thrul) **glands** located beneath the prostate add mucus to the sperm mixture. The mucus acts as a lubricant. The combination of sperm and fluids from the glands is called **semen.**

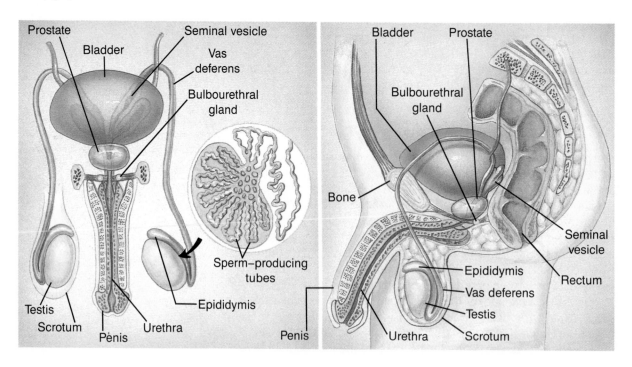

32:2 Human Female Anatomy

As in males, maturation in females is highlighted by changes in the reproductive system. One of those changes is the development of eggs. You studied in Chapter 19 that eggs are produced in organs called ovaries. Each of a female's two ovaries is about the size and shape of an almond. The ovaries are located in the lower part of the body cavity. Each ovary is partly surrounded by the opening of the oviduct. The **oviduct,** or fallopian tube, is the tube through which an egg passes from the ovary to the uterus. Recall from Chapter 25 that the uterus is a hollow, muscular organ in which development takes place. The lower opening or neck of the uterus is called the **cervix** (SUR vihks). The uterus connects to a muscular tube, the **vagina,** at the cervix. The vagina opens to the outside of the female's body.

A female begins producing eggs even before she is born. The cells in the ovaries divide until the first stage of meiosis, Prophase I. At birth, a female has all the potential eggs she will ever have. After she becomes sexually mature, the Prophase I cells continue to divide, usually one at a time. The meiotic divisions are uneven, so that one of the four resulting cells, the egg, receives most of the cytoplasm. The cytoplasm contains nutrients for the mature egg. The other three cells, called polar bodies, die.

About once a month, an egg ruptures from the surface of the ovary, a process called **ovulation.** The egg is swept down the oviduct toward the uterus by movement of cilia that line the oviduct. Muscular contractions of the tube also help propel the egg down the tube. Trace the pathway of an egg in Figure 32–3.

When do eggs complete meiosis?

FIGURE 32–3.

The female reproductive system is shown from the front (left) and the side (right).

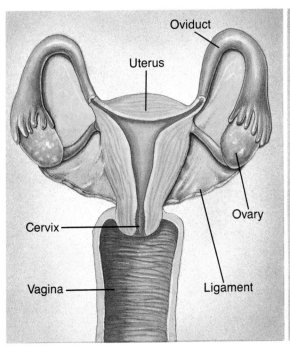

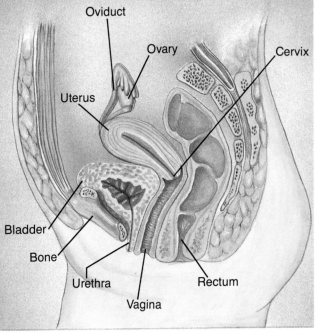

32:3 Puberty

You have studied how changes occur in males and females as they become sexually mature. These changes are controlled by sex hormones. The time during which changes occur in the human body in response to sex hormones is called **puberty.** Puberty usually begins between the ages of 10 and 16. The hypothalamus, which is a structure located near the center of the brain and just above the pituitary gland, sends a chemical signal to the pituitary. The pituitary begins producing follicle-stimulating hormone and luteinizing hormone. This event is shown in Figure 32–4. **Follicle-stimulating hormone** (FSH) is a hormone produced by the pituitary gland that stimulates the production of sex cells. **Luteinizing** (LEWT ee uh nize ing) **hormone** (LH) is a hormone produced by the pituitary gland that stimulates ovulation in females and sex hormone production in both males and females.

In males, FSH causes the testes to begin sperm production. LH causes the cells surrounding the tubes in the testes to begin secreting testosterone (teh STAHS tuh rohn). **Testosterone** is the sex hormone responsible for secondary sex characteristics in males. These characteristics include: increase in body hair, especially on the face, under the arms, and in the pubic area; increase in muscle mass; deepening of the voice; and development of the reproductive glands and organs.

In females, FSH stimulates the development of a follicle in the ovary. A **follicle** is a group of cells that contain an egg. FSH causes the release of estrogen (ES truh jun) from the ovary. **Estrogen** is the hormone responsible for secondary sex characteristics in females. Secondary sex characteristics in females include: increase in body hair, especially under the arms and in the pubic area; broadening of the hips; increase in fat deposits in the breasts, buttocks, and thighs; and the onset of the menstrual cycle.

In both males and females, the growth rates of the long bones of the arms and legs increase during puberty. The lengthening of these bones usually stops before a person is in his or her early twenties.

FIGURE 32–4.

The production of FSH and LH by the pituitary causes sex cell development and sex hormone production.

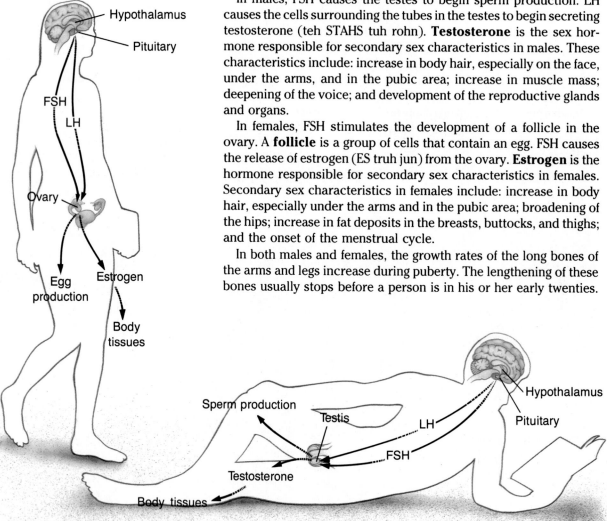

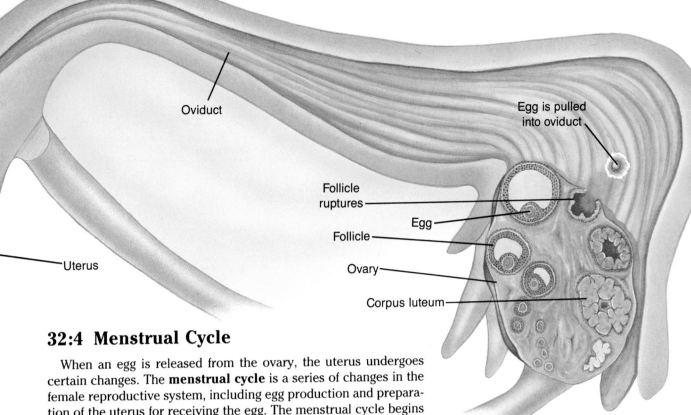

Oviduct

Egg is pulled
into oviduct

Follicle
ruptures

Egg

Follicle

Ovary

Uterus

Corpus luteum

32:4 Menstrual Cycle

When an egg is released from the ovary, the uterus undergoes certain changes. The **menstrual cycle** is a series of changes in the female reproductive system, including egg production and preparation of the uterus for receiving the egg. The menstrual cycle begins at puberty. It continues for about 30 to 40 years until menopause, the end of the menstrual cycle.

The length of the menstrual cycle varies from person to person. The average length is 28 days. The cycle has three main stages: (1) flow stage, (2) follicular stage, and (3) luteal stage.

Flow Stage. Day one of the menstrual cycle is the day menstrual flow begins. Menstrual flow is the loss of the blood-rich lining of the uterus through the vagina. The flow stage usually lasts about five days.

Follicular Stage. Days 6 to 14 of the menstrual cycle make up the follicular stage. During this stage, FSH released by the pituitary gland stimulates the maturation of a follicle in the ovary. The growing follicle begins secreting estrogen. The release of estrogen slows down the release of FSH. This type of response is called negative feedback. In negative feedback, one event inhibits another. A familiar example of negative feedback is the thermostat on your furnace. When the temperature in your house rises to a certain point, the thermostat signals the furnace to shut off. Thus, the temperature does not become too warm. In a female, the slowing of FSH release in response to estrogen is a negative feedback response. This response prevents the maturation of more follicles at this time.

The presence of estrogen stimulates cell division in the lining of the uterus. The result is an increase in the thickness of the uterine lining. The presence of estrogen also stimulates the release of LH. On about Day 14, the level of LH increases sharply. The increase in LH causes the follicle to rupture, releasing the egg. Recall that this process is called ovulation. For most women, ovulation takes place unnoticed. The beating of cilia at the opening to the oviduct causes a suction that pulls the egg into the oviduct.

FIGURE 32–5.

An egg develops within a follicle as the follicle matures. After the egg is released, the corpus luteum develops from the follicle.

What are the main events of the flow stage and follicular stage of the menstrual cycle?

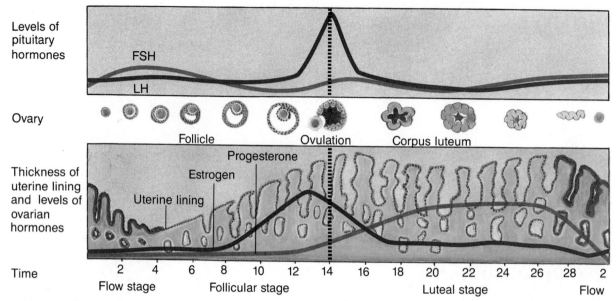

Levels of pituitary hormones

FSH

LH

Ovary

Follicle   Ovulation   Corpus luteum

Thickness of uterine lining and levels of ovarian hormones

Progesterone

Estrogen

Uterine lining

Time

| 2 | 4 | 6 | 8 | 10 | 12 | 14 | 16 | 18 | 20 | 22 | 24 | 26 | 28 | 2 |

Flow stage   Follicular stage   Luteal stage   Flow

FIGURE 32–6.

The levels of hormones vary during the menstrual cycle. Note that estrogen increases during the follicular stage and progesterone increases during the luteal stage. LH increases sharply during ovulation.

progesterone:
  pro (L) before
  gestare (L) to bear
corpus luteum:
  corpus (L) body
  luteus (L) orange-yellow
The corpus luteum is a yellowish structure that develops after the egg is released.

Luteal Stage. Days 15 to 28 of the menstrual cycle are the luteal stage. The luteal stage is named for a structure on the ovary called the corpus luteum (KOR pus • LEWT ee um). The **corpus luteum** is the structure that develops from the follicle after the egg is released. The corpus luteum produces **progesterone** (proh JES tuh rahn), a hormone that prepares the uterus for receiving the egg. Progesterone causes the uterine lining to continue to thicken and accumulate fat and glycogen. Through negative feedback, progesterone prevents production of LH. Without LH, ovulation will not occur again if the egg is fertilized.

If fertilization of an egg does not occur, the corpus luteum degenerates and the progesterone level drops. The thick uterine lining flows out of the female's body through the vagina. With the shedding of the uterine lining, the flow stage begins again. Figure 32–6 shows the events in the stages of the menstrual cycle. Notice the changes that take place in the hormone levels and lining of the uterus.

32:5 Diseases of the Reproductive System

The human reproductive system is subject to diseases and disorders that upset the body's homeostasis. Certain diseases affect men more than women and vice versa. Some diseases, such as sexually transmitted diseases, do not discriminate between males and females.

Prostate disorders and diseases are common problems in the male reproductive system. The prostate gland is susceptible to infection, enlargement, or cancerous tumors, especially in older men. Because the prostate surrounds the urethra, these disorders can obstruct urine flow and cause severe pain. About one-third of males over age 60 experience an enlarged prostate. Treatment can involve removal of part or all of the gland.

BIOLAB *Menstrual Cycle* 32

Problem: What are the hormone patterns during the menstrual cycle?

Materials
graph paper
colored pencils (red, yellow, blue, green)

Procedures
1. Study the table and develop a **hypothesis** as to how the data would appear in a graph. In your hypothesis, state on which days you think the levels of the four hormones are rising and on which days they are falling.
2. On the top half of a piece of graph paper, draw and label the axes of a graph as shown in the top diagram. Number this graph, Graph 1.
3. Plot the LH and FSH data from the table using a yellow pencil for LH and a blue pencil for FSH on Graph 1.
4. On the bottom half of the same piece of graph paper, draw and label another set of axes as shown in the bottom diagram. Number this graph, Graph 2.
5. Plot the estrogen and progesterone data from the table using a red pencil for estrogen and a green pencil for progesterone on Graph 2.
6. On graphs 1 and 2, indicate the days on which the three stages (flow, follicular, and luteal) of the menstrual cycle start and end.

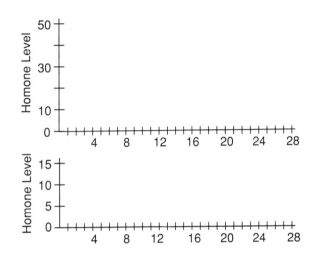

Questions and Conclusion
1. What happens to the levels of the four hormones on days 1 through 14 of the menstrual cycle? On days 15 through 28?
2. On Graph 2, use a green pencil to make a dashed line to indicate how the progesterone level would look if pregnancy occurred.
3. Did you accept your original **hypothesis**? Use your data to support your answer.

Conclusion: Summarize the patterns of each of the four hormones of the menstrual cycle.

Data and Observations

Day	1	2	3	4	5	6	7	8	9	10	11	12	13	14
LH	16	17	17	17	17	17	17	17	17	17	21	46	50	35
FSH	13	14	14	14	15	14	14	13	11	10	9	8	22	15
Estrogen	5	4	4	4	4	5	5	6	8	10	12	13	14	13
Progesterone	1	1	1	1	1	1	1	1	1	1	1	1	1	2

Day	15	16	17	18	19	20	21	22	23	24	25	26	27	28
LH	22	20	20	19	19	18	17	17	16	16	15	14	13	13
FSH	10	8	7	7	7	7	7	6	6	6	5	6	7	7
Estrogen	11	10	9	9	9	10	10	11	11	11	12	11	9	8
Progesterone	3	4	6	7	10	12	13	14	15	14	13	9	5	3

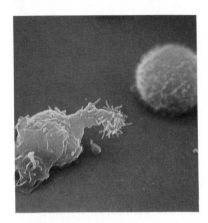

FIGURE 32–7.

A Pap test detects the presence of cancer cells like the ones shown in this photo.

How can microbes affect the reproductive system?

Many women are affected by premenstrual syndrome (PMS) during the luteal stage and sometimes into the flow stage of the menstrual cycle. Symptoms of PMS include swelling and tenderness of the breasts, headache, fatigue, irritability, and depression or anxiety.

Cancer of the cervix is a common disease of the female reproductive system. Fortunately, this cancer can be detected in its early stages by means of a Pap test. In a Pap test, cells from the vagina and cervix are removed with a swab and examined with a microscope. Abnormal cells are thus detected. If detected in its early stages, cancer of the cervix is curable.

Toxic shock syndrome (TSS) is a disease caused by a bacterial infection. Females who use tampons incorrectly are at greater risk for this disease because tampons provide a favorable environment for growth of the bacterium. Symptoms of TSS include fever, vomiting, diarrhea, and skin rash. If the disease continues unchecked, a drop in blood pressure and shock may occur. Antibiotics are an effective form of treatment for TSS when it is caught early.

A large group of microbial diseases that affect the reproductive systems of both males and females are the sexually transmitted diseases. Gonorrhea is a bacterial infection that primarily affects the membranes lining the reproductive tract. In males, the urethra may become inflamed, making urination painful. Gonorrhea in females may cause infection of the cervix or oviducts. If untreated, gonorrhea can cause sterility. Syphilis is a bacterial infection that progresses through several stages, starting with an open sore and progressing to the infection of body organs, including the brain. If the infection spreads to the nervous system, blindness, hearing loss, or insanity may result. Although gonorrhea and syphilis are widespread diseases, both are curable. Antibiotics, such as penicillin, administered in the early stages are effective in treating these diseases. Genital herpes, on the other hand, is an incurable viral infection. This infection causes painful blisters that disappear and reappear in the genital area.

REVIEW

1. List the structures of the female reproductive system.
2. Explain why meiosis in a female results in one-fourth as many cells as meiosis in a male.
3. List the events in each stage of the menstrual cycle.
4. **SKILL REVIEW:** Study Figure 32–2. Using the terms dorsal, ventral, anterior, posterior, superior, and inferior, describe where the epididymis is in relation to the vas deferens. Describe where the prostate is in relation to the testes. For more help, refer to Interpreting Scientific Illustrations in the Skill Handbook, pages 800 to 801.
5. **USING CONCEPTS:** The testes are enclosed within the scrotum, which is located outside the body cavity. The ovaries, however, are within the body cavity. Explain this difference.

DEVELOPMENT BEFORE BIRTH

You started out life as a single, fertilized cell no larger than the period at the end of this sentence. You grew from that one cell, called a zygote, and now you have trillions of cells. How did you survive before you were born? What kinds of changes took place as you developed?

32:6 Fertilization and Implantation

For an egg to become fertilized, the egg and sperm must be present in the oviduct at the same time. Figure 32–8 shows where fertilization takes place. You have read that an egg travels from one ovary to the uterus once a month. It takes about three days for the egg to reach the uterus. Sperm must be present during the first two days in order for fertilization to occur. During ejaculation, strong muscular contractions within the male reproductive system force semen from the body. Several hundred million sperm are forced out of the penis and into the female's reproductive system.

How is it possible that of the millions of sperm released into the vagina during ejaculation, only one fertilizes the mature egg? The fluids secreted by the vagina are acidic and destroy thousands of the delicate sperm. Some sperm survive because of the buffering effect of semen. The surviving sperm swim up the vagina into the uterus. Their movement is aided by muscular contractions of the female reproductive tract.

Objectives:
- describe fertilization and implantation.
- describe the embryonic membranes and explain how the placenta functions.
- list the events during each trimester of pregnancy.
- explain what can cause problems during fetal development.
- describe ways problems can be detected before birth.

FIGURE 32–8.

An egg is fertilized within the oviduct. The photo shows an egg on its journey to the uterus.

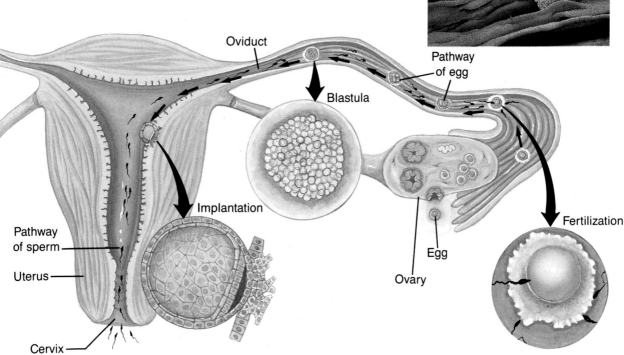

Of the sperm that enter the uterus, only a few hundred pass into the oviducts. Once a sperm penetrates the egg, the egg develops a protective membrane that prevents other sperm from entering it. Only one sperm penetrates the egg, and its nucleus combines with the egg nucleus to form a zygote.

As the fertilized egg passes down the oviduct, it begins to divide by mitosis. Within 36 hours after fertilization, there are two cells. The fertilized egg is now an embryo. The cells continue to divide. By the sixth day after fertilization, a hollow ball of cells called a blastula has formed. The blastula attaches to the uterine lining 8 to 10 days after fertilization. The attaching of the embryo to the lining of the uterus is called **implantation.** Fertilization with implantation marks the beginning of pregnancy.

How does a zygote change before it is implanted?

32:7 Embryonic Membranes and the Placenta

As an embryo divides, protective membranes form around it. The membranes are like the ones in a bird's egg, which you studied in Chapter 24. The amnion is the inner membrane and is filled with a clear, watery fluid called amniotic fluid. The amniotic fluid moistens and protects the embryo. The allantois is a membrane that is an outgrowth of the digestive tract of the embryo. Blood vessels of the allantois form the umbilical cord. The **umbilical cord** is a structure that attaches the embryo to the wall of the uterus. The chorion is the outermost membrane of the embryo. About 14 days after fertilization, fingerlike projections of the chorion, called chorionic villi, begin to grow into the uterine wall. Together, the chorion and the part of the uterus to which it is attached form the placenta. The vessels within the umbilical cord connect the circulatory system of the embryo to the placenta.

FIGURE 32–9.

Protective membranes surround the developing embryo.

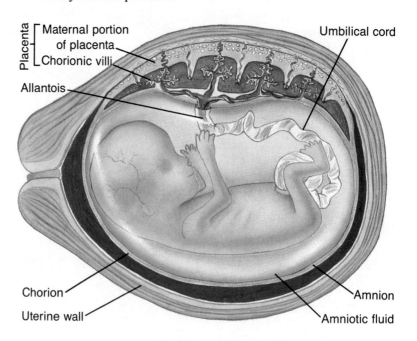

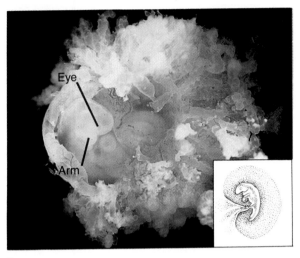

Eye

Arm

a

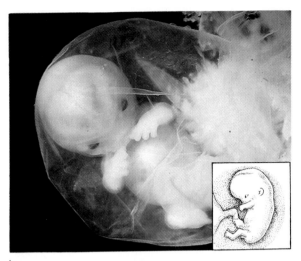

b

FIGURE 32–10.

A one-month embryo (a) and a two-month embryo (b) are shown enlarged and actual size.

Both the chorionic villi and the uterine wall have rich supplies of blood vessels that bring oxygen and nutrients to the embryo and carry away wastes. The blood vessels of the two structures, however, do not connect to one another. Therefore, the blood of the embryo and that of the mother do not mix. Notice in Figure 32–9 where the embryonic membranes and placenta are located in relation to the embryo.

How are nutrients and wastes passed between mother and embryo? Substances such as digested food, oxygen, and antibodies diffuse from the mother's blood vessels into the embryo's blood vessels at the placenta. The substances are carried by the blood in the umbilical cord to the embryo. Waste products from the embryo travel through the umbilical blood vessels and then diffuse into the blood of the mother at the placenta. These waste products are then removed by the mother's excretory system.

What is exchanged at the placenta?

You have studied how progesterone causes the uterine lining to thicken in preparation for receiving a fertilized egg. Chorionic gonadotropin, a hormone secreted by the chorion, maintains the corpus luteum so that it continues to secrete progesterone after an egg is fertilized. Thus, the uterine lining is maintained. At about the fifth week of pregnancy, the placenta takes over the secretion of progesterone.

32:8 Fetal Development

Pregnancy in humans usually lasts about 266 days, or about nine months. This time span is divided into three trimesters, each equal to three months. Each trimester represents a significant stage in the development of the embryo.

During the first trimester, all the body systems of the embryo begin to form. The heart, brain and lungs begin to form in the first month. The heart begins to beat around the twenty-fifth day of development. During the second month, the embryo's hands, fingers, feet, and toes begin to take shape. By the eighth week, all systems are present and the embryo is referred to as a **fetus.** By the ninth week, the eyelids

NoteWorthy

Chorionic gonadotropin can be detected in the urine of a pregnant woman. Early pregnancy tests detect the presence of this hormone.

In the 17th century, scientists believed the sperm was like a miniature adult, with all systems and features completely developed.

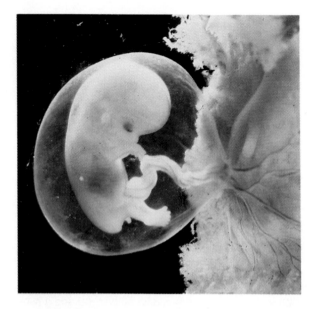
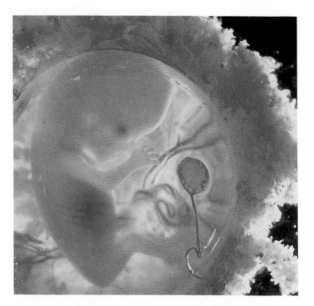

a   b

FIGURE 32–11.

A three-month fetus (a) is shown actual size. A fetus grows to about 34 cm in the second trimester (b).

During which trimester does the fetus's position change so that it becomes ready for birth?

form. As muscle development progresses, the fetus gains mobility. At the end of the first trimester, the fetus has a mass of about 28 g and is about 7.5 cm long from the top of its head to its buttocks. The sex of the fetus can be determined in the first trimester by the appearance of the external sex organs.

During the second trimester, growth and maturation of fetal tissues continues. Growth is rapid at the beginning of the second trimester, but then slows by the beginning of the fifth month. The skin is covered with a white, fatty substance that protects the skin against the wet environment of the fetus. During the second trimester, the mother can feel the fetus move. At this time, the fetus can suck its thumb, thus exercising the muscles that will allow the baby to nurse later. By the end of the second trimester, the fetus has a mass of about 650 g and is about 34 cm long. At this point, the fetus can survive outside the uterus with medical assistance, such as a respirator and intensive care.

The mass of the fetus more than triples during the third trimester. The fetus moves freely within the amniotic cavity, kicking, stretching and exercising its muscles. During the eighth month, the eyes open. During the ninth month, the fetus moves into its final position. Its head usually points downward and toward the mother's back. By the end of the third trimester, the fetus has a mass of about 3000 g and is about 50 cm long. All of its body systems have developed and it can now survive independently outside the uterus.

32:9 Problems with Fetal Development

The fetus is very sensitive to substances such as alcohol, nicotine, other drugs, and infectious microbes. These substances can pass from the mother to the embryo or fetus through the placenta. Harmful substances can cause birth defects or diseases.

Alcohol consumption during pregnancy may cause malformations in the fetus's head, heart, and nervous systems and retard fetal growth. Fetal alcohol syndrome (FAS) is a serious disorder resulting from alcohol consumption during pregnancy. A baby born with FAS is often malformed and mentally retarded. It is unclear how much alcohol a pregnant woman can drink without damaging the fetus.

Besides alcohol, other drugs pass through the placenta. Doctors often advise pregnant women not to take over-the-counter or prescription drugs. Cigarette smoking is discouraged. The nicotine in cigarette smoke retards fetal growth. Use of heroin or cocaine during pregnancy causes the fetus to be born addicted to these drugs.

Some microbes can cause harm to the fetus. If the mother contracts German measles (rubella) during the first trimester of pregnancy, the baby may be born blind, deaf, or mentally retarded. The AIDS virus is capable of passing from the infected mother to the fetus through the placenta. Most newborns infected with the AIDS virus will develop the disease and die shortly after birth.

How does alcohol affect a fetus? How can infectious microbes affect a fetus?

32:10 Detecting Problems Before Birth

Perhaps you know someone with hemophilia. Technology allows physicians to diagnose this and other genetic disorders, such as sickle-cell anemia, cystic fibrosis, and Down syndrome, before a baby is born. Amniocentesis is a method of diagnosing problems in the fetus. It involves removing some of the amniotic fluid and cells that surround the fetus. The fluid is removed through the abdomen of the pregnant woman with a syringe as shown in Figure 32–12. The cells are cultured and then examined for chromosomal and biochemical disorders.

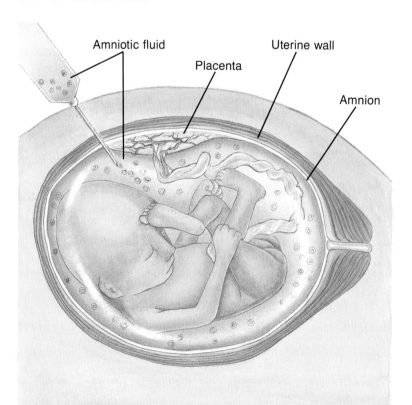

Amniotic fluid

Placenta

Uterine wall

Amnion

FIGURE 32–12.

In amniocentesis, amniotic fluid is withdrawn, and the fetal cells contained in it are studied.

DEVELOPMENT BEFORE BIRTH **689**

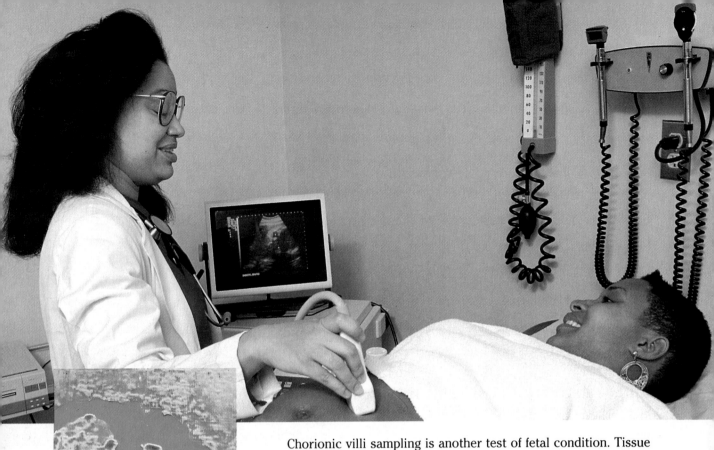

FIGURE 32–13.

Ultrasound involves the use of sound waves to create a visual image.

Chorionic villi sampling is another test of fetal condition. Tissue from the fetal chorion is removed through the mother's vagina. The tissue is then evaluated for genetic disorders. This test can be performed earlier in pregnancy than amniocentesis. There is less risk of infection to the fetus because neither the abdominal wall, the uterus, nor the amniotic cavity are penetrated.

Ultrasound is a method commonly used to determine fetal age, growth, sex, and position. This technique also can be used to detect multiple fetuses (twins, triplets). Ultrasound involves the use of sound waves to create a visual image of the developing fetus. In this procedure, sound waves are directed into the abdomen of the pregnant woman. The waves echo back to a receiver and the echo is translated into an image on a screen. An advantage of ultrasound is that it does not involve entry into the uterus. Figure 32–13 shows an ultrasound image. How many fetuses do you see in the image?

REVIEW

6. What changes occur in the zygote as it passes down the oviduct?
7. What is the function of the placenta?
8. How are problems with fetal development detected?
9. **SKILL REVIEW:** List the events in the three trimesters of pregnancy. For more help, refer to Reading Science in the Skill Handbook, pages 798 to 799.
10. **USING CONCEPTS:** Compare the functions of human embryonic membranes with those inside a bird's egg.

CAREER CHOICES

What comes to mind when someone mentions careers in human health? Physicians, nurses, and other clinic and hospital staff are common responses. Careers in human health, however, range from these typical responses to dentists, medical librarians, industrial hygienists, museum exhibitors, and sports therapists. In spite of the wide differences in what they do, all human health care professionals must have a working knowledge of the anatomy of the human body and how the body functions.

How close are we to a cure for cancer? As a **biological technician,** you might work at a cancer research laboratory or at a center for disease control. If you were to work in a lab that studies cancer and its causes, you might be responsible for investigating blood and tissue samples from cancer patients. You would be a team member involved in the ongoing research needed to control this life-threatening illness. If you worked in a disease control laboratory, you might assist other biological scientists in isolating and growing certain pathogenic microorganisms from the blood and tissue samples. Your job might involve processing the samples and cultures so that they may be examined with light and electron microscopes.

Biological Technician

Are there too many pesticides on our apples? What are the effects of background radiation on humans? How is a construction worker affected by the noise associated with the job? **Human ecologists** focus on health problems related to poor sanitation, poor working conditions, and other environmental factors. As a sanitarian, you would inspect food handlers in restaurants, cafeterias, and supermarkets for cleanliness. You also would inspect the facilities themselves to be sure they met established standards for cleanliness and operating procedures. If conditions were below accepted levels, you might work with the establishments to develop and manage programs for controlling contamination of foods. Carelessness by food handlers is often attributed to cases of food poisoning. Sanitarians often work for city or county health boards. An industrial hygienist attempts to reduce pollution, noise, and pests, such as insects in the work place. An environmental engineer might design, build, and operate sewage and water treatment plants.

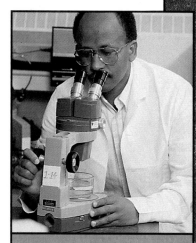
Human Ecologist

How do food additives, drugs, medicines, dyes, insecticides, and herbicides affect people who ingest them? Many industries employ **pharmacologists,** scientists who study the effects of natural and manufactured substances on plants and animals, including humans. As a pharmacologist, you might be employed in the pharmaceutical industry. Your research might involve studying the effects of new products on human body systems, such as the cardiovascular system. Pharmacologists also conduct research to discover new drugs and medicines to help prevent or treat diseases and disorders, such as heart attacks, cancer, and diabetes.

Pharmacologist

Objectives:

- describe the three stages of birth.
- summarize the developmental stages of humans after they are born.
- list ways that the homeostatic balance of the body is affected by aging.

Development within the uterus represents the most rapid stage of growth in the life cycle of a human. However, changes do not stop at the end of the third trimester. Changes continue following birth and throughout life.

32:11 Birth

What events occur during the dilation stage of birth?

Birth is the process by which a baby is pushed out of the uterus and passes out of the mother's body. What triggers the onset of birth is not fully understood. There are, however, three recognizable stages: dilation, expulsion, and afterbirth.

Dilation refers to the opening of the cervix to allow for passage of the baby. Dilation begins with mild contractions of the uterine muscles. These contractions, called labor, move the baby toward the cervix. Dilation lasts about twenty hours, with the contractions gradually increasing in strength and duration. When fully dilated, the opening of the cervix is about 10 cm, approximately the width of your hand. During the last stage of dilation, the amnion ruptures and releases the amniotic fluid through the vagina. At this time, the vagina is referred to as the birth canal.

When the cervix has dilated fully, strong contractions of the uterus move the baby through the cervix into the birth canal. At this time, expulsion, the second stage of birth, begins. Expulsion is the movement of the baby down the birth canal and out of the body. The events that take place during expulsion are shown in Figure 32–14. The mother assists with expelling the baby by contracting voluntary muscles of the abdomen in time with the uterine contractions. The expulsion stage usually lasts 20 minutes to an hour. After the baby

FIGURE 32–14.

The stages of birth are dilation, expulsion, and afterbirth.

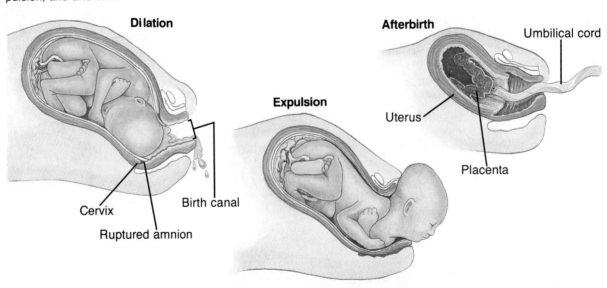

Dilation

Cervix

Ruptured amnion

Birth canal

Expulsion

Afterbirth

Umbilical cord

Uterus

Placenta

is born, the umbilical cord is clamped and cut near the baby's abdomen. The bit of cord that is left decays and falls off leaving a scar, called the naval.

Labor contractions continue for 10 to 15 minutes after the expulsion stage. These contractions push the afterbirth, which is the remains of the placenta and embryonic membranes, out of the mother's body.

32:12 Growth and Aging

After a baby is born, a period of rapid growth and learning begins. The first two years in a human's life are infancy. During infancy, the brain undergoes tremendous development as the infant learns to control its limbs, roll over, sit, crawl, and walk. Much of the second year of life is spent developing language.

During childhood, the time following infancy, dexterity and muscle coordination increase. A child develops the ability to reason and solve problems. Adolescence follows childhood. Puberty takes place during adolescence. The adolescent gradually passes into adulthood. In an adult, the organs have reached their maximum mass, and growth is complete.

As an adult ages, physical strength declines and changes in sensory abilities, especially vision and hearing, occur. Homeostatic mechanisms become less efficient. For example, body temperature is more difficult to regulate. Metabolism and digestion become slower. Some changes associated with old age—whitening of the hair and wrinkling of the skin—can be seen easily. However, many of the characteristics associated with old age, such as loss of memory, may be signs of disease. With good care, the body can remain healthy as it ages.

Research on what causes aging is ongoing. A widely accepted hypothesis suggests that cells accumulate errors in cell chemistry and eventually die. You may notice as you age that you develop more and more moles on your skin. These moles are the result of errors in cell division. Another hypothesis is that aging is a normal event controlled by genes. Genes that control aging cause certain cell events to shut down at predetermined times.

FIGURE 32–15.

Changes in physical appearance are quite apparent during growth and aging. Internal changes are not as obvious.

NoteWorthy

According to the autoimmune theory of aging, the body develops an immune response to itself as it ages. The body may destroy its own cells while letting foreign cells—such as cancer cells—survive.

REVIEW

11. What events occur during dilation?
12. How does the human body change during childhood?
13. What changes occur as a person ages?
14. **SKILL REVIEW:** Someone tells you that as a person ages, it is normal for the personality to change. Do you think this statement is valid? Why or why not? For more help, refer to Reading Science in the Skill Handbook, pages 798 to 799.
15. **USING CONCEPTS:** Compare the birth of a human baby with that of a marsupial mammal.

CHAPTER REVIEW

SUMMARY

1. The male reproductive system produces sperm, which move from the testes through tubes to the outside of the body. The female reproductive system produces eggs that move from ovaries into oviducts. **32:1, 32:2**
2. Changes in males and females at puberty are the result of production of FSH, LH, and other sex hormones. **32:3**
3. The menstrual cycle involves release of eggs from the ovaries and preparation of the uterus for receiving an egg. **32:4**
4. Diseases or disorders can affect the male and female reproductive systems. **32:5**
5. Fertilization occurs in the oviduct. The ball of cells that develops from the fertilized egg implants in the uterine wall. **32:6**
6. The embryo becomes enclosed in membranes within the uterus. Materials are exchanged between a pregnant woman and the fetus through the placenta. The embryo changes from a small ball of cells to a well-developed fetus. **32:7, 32:8**
7. Alcohol, nicotine, and microbes can pass across the placenta. Problems with a fetus can be detected using various techniques. **32:9, 32:10**
8. Birth involves dilation of the cervix, expulsion of the baby, and release of the afterbirth. **32:11**
9. Infancy, childhood, adolescence, and adulthood are stages of human development. Homeostatic balances in the body are affected by aging. **32:12**

LANGUAGE OF BIOLOGY

bulbourethral glands
cervix
corpus luteum
epididymis
estrogen
fetus
follicle
follicle-stimulating hormone
implantation
luteinizing hormone
menstrual cycle
oviduct
ovulation
progesterone
prostate gland
puberty
scrotum
semen
seminal vesicles
testosterone
umbilical cord
urethra
vagina
vas deferens

Choose the word or phrase from the list above that completes the sentence.

1. The testes are located inside the ____.
2. A tube that carries eggs is a(n) ____.
3. The time during adolescence when the body changes in response to sex hormones is ____.
4. The hormone responsible for male secondary sex characteristics is ____.
5. ____ occurs around Day 14 of the menstrual cycle.
6. A ruptured follicle forms a(n) ____.
7. The attachment of the embryo to the uterine wall is called ____.
8. The uterus opens to the outside of the body through the ____.
9. The hormone that maintains the uterine lining during pregnancy is ____.
10. After 8 weeks, the embryo is called a(n) ____.

REVIEWING CONCEPTS

Choose the word or phrase that completes the sentence or answers the question.

11. Through which tube do sperm pass as they move from the testes toward the outside of the body?
    a. oviducts
    b. vas deferens
    c. ureter
    d. fallopian tube
12. What helps move the egg into the oviduct?
    a. movement of cilia in the oviduct
    b. uterine contractions
    c. amoeboid movements of the egg
    d. none of the above

13. The fetal stage in humans is ___.
    a. the first 8 weeks after fertilization
    b. from 9 weeks until birth
    c. the entire pregnancy
    d. after birth

14. Fertilization occurs in the ___.
    a. uterus   c. ovary
    b. vagina   d. oviduct

15. Which of the following is not a disease caused by a microbe?
    a. syphilis   c. gonorrhea
    b. PMS   d. genital herpes

16. In a 28-day menstrual cycle, on what day might ovulation occur?
    a. Day 2   b. Day 8   c. Day 14   d. Day 26

17. Sex hormones are NOT produced by the ___.
    a. pituitary   c. prostate
    b. ovary   d. testis

18. Ovulation is stimulated by ___.
    a. PMS   b. TSS   c. FSH   d. LH

19. Semen is composed of ___.
    a. sperm
    b. prostate secretions
    c. seminal vesicle secretions
    d. all of the above

20. The ___ is where nutrients and wastes are exchanged between the mother and fetus.
    a. placenta   c. amnion
    b. umbilical cord   d. cervix

UNDERSTANDING CONCEPTS

Answer the following questions using complete sentences.

21. Why are the testes outside the body cavity?
22. Compare egg and sperm production.
23. Explain the general effects of FSH and LH during puberty.
24. How is the uterine lining maintained before fertilization occurs?
25. Explain how a fetus gets oxygen.

26. Compare the events of the first trimester of pregnancy with those of the third trimester.
27. Describe how the placenta forms.
28. How does ultrasound work?
29. What is the function of the umbilical cord?
30. When is human development most rapid?

APPLYING CONCEPTS

Answer the following questions using complete sentences.

31. What would be the effect of an abnormally low LH level in females?
32. Why do pregnancy tests test for chorionic gonadotropin?
33. If the navel is one end of the umbilical cord, where was the other end before birth?
34. What might happen if FSH were to increase instead of decrease in response to estrogen?
35. What problems result if the placenta detaches during pregnancy?

EXTENSIONS

1. Visit an obstetrician. Find out what procedures are followed during birth.
2. Find out why the menstrual cycles of female athletes can be disrupted during training.
3. Research some solutions to infertility.

READINGS

Barnes, Deborah M. "Orchestrating the Sperm-Egg Summit." *Science,* Mar. 4, 1988, pp. 1091–1092.

Furuhjelm, Mirjam, Axel Ingelman-Sundberg and Claes Wirsen. *A Child is Born.* New York: Dell Publishing Co., Inc., 1965.

Wechsler, Rob. "Hostile Womb." *Discover,* Mar. 1988, pp. 82–87.

ECOLOGY

The world seems likely to last a long, long time,
  and we ought to make provisions for the future . . .
We are trustees of the future.
We are not here for ourselves alone.

James Bryce
"Trustees of the Future"

Chapter
33

FUNDAMENTALS OF ECOLOGY

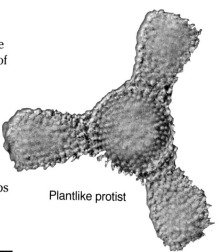

The ozone layer is a layer of gas that surrounds Earth. The ozone layer has received much attention lately because of the concern that human activity is damaging it. Even though we can't see the ozone layer, we know it protects us from certain types of radiation. All organisms—plants, animals, bacteria, fungi, and the protist pictured on this page—can be affected by excessive radiation. Thus, relationships exist between living things and the nonliving environment. Studying and understanding these relationships is what the science of ecology is all about. Understanding these relationships can further the development of useful conservation measures.

Plantlike protist

ORGANISMS AND THEIR ENVIRONMENTS

You're already aware of some relationships among organisms and their environments. You have studied that water temperature affects fish. You have also studied relationships between organisms. You know bacteria and fungi are organisms that cause diseases in other living things. Organisms interact with each other and their environments in many ways. These interactions are woven together to form a rich tapestry of life relationships.

33:1 The Biosphere

The portion of Earth that supports life and extends from several kilometers up in the atmosphere to the deepest parts of the oceans is called the biosphere. The three regions of the biosphere—air, water, and land—are interrelated. If chemicals, such as pesticides, are sprayed into the air, they eventually pass into water systems or cover the land. Fertilizers spread over the land may get into the water or air. Care must be taken to protect all parts of the biosphere so that organisms in each part survive.

Every organism in the biosphere depends on its environment for survival. The environment supplies energy and materials for growth and repair. For example, plants use sunlight, water, carbon dioxide, and inorganic nutrients for photosynthesis.

Objectives:
- identify major biotic and abiotic factors in the environment.
- distinguish between a population and a community.
- compare a species' habitat with its niche.
- list the conditions needed for an ecosystem to remain stable.

What are some ways organisms depend on the environment?

FIGURE 33–1.

This field of wildflowers is an example of a population.

What is an abiotic factor?
What is a biotic factor?

Organisms depend on both nonliving and living factors in the environment. **Ecology** is the study of relationships between organisms and the living and nonliving factors in their environments. Nonliving factors in the environment are called **abiotic** (ay bi AHT ihk) **factors.** Abiotic factors include water, soil, temperature, light, air, and minerals. Living factors in the environment are called **biotic** (bi AHT ihk) **factors.** All the living organisms in a pond represent the biotic factors for that pond. Plants, bacteria, fish, worms, and crayfish are typical pond organisms.

33:2 Populations and Communities

Think of a Vermont forest ablaze with color in the fall. All the maple trees in that forest taken together are considered a population. Recall that a population is a group of organisms of the same species that live in one area during a specific time. Another example of a population is all the mosquitoes on the surface of a quiet pond in summer.

Populations interact with each other in a variety of ways. Some populations are food sources for other populations. Some populations decompose materials to be recycled or reused by still other populations. All the populations living in an area and interacting with each other make up a **community.** The populations of maple trees, birch trees, trillium, wood frogs, red-eyed vireos, and morel mushrooms in a Vermont forest are among the organisms that make up that forest community.

Within a community, each type of organism is found in a particular habitat. A **habitat** is the environment of a particular type of organism. For example, ferns are typically found in moist, shady areas of a forest community. The habitat of some snails is the leaf litter on the forest floor. In a pond community, a frog's habitat is near the edge of the water and includes both water and land. A trout in the same community has its habitat in the deeper, cooler portion of the pond. You can think of a habitat as the home address of a species.

Each species in the community also performs particular functions. Maple trees produce organic food molecules through photosynthesis and create the shade needed by ferns. These functions of the maple tree are part of its niche (NITSH). A **niche** is the role of a species within the community. The niche includes what a species needs to survive and reproduce in its environment. What a species eats, how it obtains food, how its members attract mates, and where it lives are part of what makes up a species' niche. In other words, a niche is the lifestyle or occupation of a species.

Habitats often overlap so that different species are found in the same location. But, no two species can occupy exactly the same niche at the same time for very long. If they do, they begin to compete for the same requirements. This competition is harmful to each species. More energy may be spent on defending a resource than on using it. You may think that all the birds within a single tree have the same niche. Careful observation, however, will reveal significant differences in the roles of the different bird species. Some birds eat insects, while others eat seeds. Some feed beneath the tree, while others feed in the tree. Some birds don't feed in the tree at all. The birds also may have different reproductive habits. They have different mating behaviors and nest in different spots.

33:3 Ecosystems

The biotic community and its abiotic environment interact and function as a system. The system that results from the interaction between community and environment is called an ecosystem. The interaction involves the transfer of energy and materials among organisms. Ecosystems have no size limitations. An ecosystem may be as large as a desert or as small as the drops of water on a plant leaf. Plants, soil bacteria, soil nutrients, air spaces in the soil, light, moisture, and temperature are parts of a garden ecosystem.

FIGURE 33–2.

A desert and the drops of water on a leaf are examples of ecosystems. The plants in the desert scene are Joshua trees.

An ecosystem remains balanced as long as three conditions are met. First, it must have a relatively constant source of energy. Sunlight supplies energy to most ecosystems. Second, the energy must be converted into a type of energy usable to organisms. Third, organic matter and inorganic nutrients need to be recycled.

An ecosystem becomes unstable when any of the three conditions is affected. For example, if the flow of energy from the sun is disrupted, photosynthesis is affected. Plants die because they can no longer synthesize their own food. Without plants for food, other organisms die. If essential nutrients are unavailable or if certain species die off, the ecosystem could lose the ability to sustain itself. For an ecosystem to remain stable, there must be a dynamic balance between its biotic and abiotic factors.

What conditions might cause an ecosystem to become unstable?

REVIEW

1. What are abiotic factors and biotic factors? List three examples of each.
2. What is the difference between a population and a community? Give an example of each.
3. List three conditions required for a stable ecosystem.
4. **SKILL REVIEW:** Construct a graph to show the relationship between temperature and population size for an algal species and a fish species. The fish depend on the algae for food. As the temperature of the water increases, the number of algae begins to decrease. Use a dotted line to show the predicted change in the population size of the fish. For more help, refer to Organizing Information in the Skill Handbook, pages 810 to 813.
5. **USING CONCEPTS:** How can the application of pesticides in one part of the world affect organisms in another part of the world?

BIOTIC RELATIONSHIPS

Objectives:
- compare mutualism, parasitism, and commensalism.
- describe the roles of producers, consumers, and decomposers.
- compare food chains and webs.
- describe what happens to energy as it flows through an ecosystem.
- interpret pyramid models.
- explain how individuals compete.
- explain how predation helps to control populations.

Suppose you are going to run in a marathon tomorrow. You have heard that carbohydrate loading tonight will provide extra energy for the race. Therefore, you carefully select high-carbohydrate foods. The foods that you eat are products of other organisms. The carbohydrates you eat may come from wheat. What you are doing when you consume other life forms is establishing a biotic relationship.

In addition to consuming other organisms, you compete with other organisms for food. Every summer, insects such as beetles and grasshoppers compete with humans for produce raised in home vegetable gardens. The garden plants themselves compete with one another for light, moisture, and soil nutrients. In the next sections, the relationships that develop among organisms will be examined.

33:4 Symbiotic Relationships

The close physical contact between species leads to interactions in which a species may benefit, be harmed, or remain unaffected by its relationship with other species. The term used to describe these relationships is symbiosis. Symbiosis is usually divided into three categories—mutualism, parasitism, and commensalism.

Mutualism occurs when two organisms benefit from living together. Bees pollinate plants and at the same time receive food in the form of nectar and pollen. Termites eat wood but cannot digest the cellulose in the wood. Protozoans living in the gut of the termite digest cellulose. The termite is able to use the energy from the cellulose molecule, and the protozoan receives protection and nutrients from the termite. This relationship is of mutual benefit.

Parasitism involves the taking of nourishment by one organism from its host. All types of organisms can be parasitized. Important plant parasites include fungi that cause wheat rust and corn smut. Bacteria parasitize plants and animals and are responsible for human diseases, including gonorrhea. Viruses can parasitize all life forms, even bacteria. The most successful parasites are the ones that weaken or harm their host, but do not kill it. If the host dies, the parasite must find a new host, or it will also die.

Commensalism is a type of symbiosis in which one species benefits but the second species does not seem to benefit or be harmed by the relationship. In a sense, the host is merely providing a habitat for the commensal organism. Barnacles attach to whales and filter food from the water as the whale swims along. The host whale is not harmed. Plants called epiphytes live high above the ground on the trunks and branches of trees in tropical and subtropical forests. Epiphytes lack well-developed root systems and absorb moisture from the air through thin-celled root hairs. Water that drips down from the tree tops is collected by the leaves and flower petals of the epiphytes. Thus, the epiphyte receives support and moisture from the tree. The tree is not harmed, nor does it appear to benefit from this relationship.

FIGURE 33–3.

Oxpeckers eat insects that parasitize the water buffalo. Certain aphids suck fluids from plants and convert them to honeydew, a nutrient. When stroked by ants, the aphids secrete the honeydew. In return, the aphids receive protection. Both relationships are examples of mutualism.

How do symbiotic relationships benefit organisms?

herbivore:
    herba (L) grass
    vorare (L) to devour
carnivore:
    caro (L) flesh
    vorare (L) to devour
omnivore:
    omnis (L) all
    vorare (L) to devour

33:5 Feeding Relationships

In a stable ecosystem, very little is wasted. Grasshoppers eat the leaves of plants. Grasshoppers are eaten by snakes or bullfrogs. These animals may then be eaten by hawks. When hawks die, they are consumed by protists and fungi. The nutrients that come from the remains of the dead organisms eventually are used by green plants. Thus, matter is cycled through an ecosystem.

Feeding relationships in nature may be as simple as the one just described, or they may involve many more organisms. However, all feeding relationships have producers, consumers, and decomposers. Plants, certain protists, and some monerans are the producers in an ecosystem. Producers, in turn, become a source of food and energy for consumers, such as grasshoppers. Consumers that feed directly on producers are called primary consumers or herbivores. A **herbivore** is a plant eater. Primary consumers are eaten by secondary consumers, and so on. A consumer that gets most of its food from eating the flesh of other animals is known as a **carnivore.** An **omnivore** eats both plants and animals.

Decomposers are consumers as well. Protists and fungi, which you studied in Chapter 13 and 14, are common types of decomposers. Just as all feeding relationships begin with producers, they all end with decomposers. Decomposers break down and consume dead organisms and wastes. In the process, they recycle a large part of the broken-down substances back to the producers.

Nutrients are transferred from producers to consumers in a feeding relationship called a **food chain.** Each organism that eats, absorbs, or decomposes another is thus a link in that chain. An aquatic food chain is shown in Figure 33–4. A food chain may be fairly simple, with only one level of consumer, or it may have several levels of consumers, as this one does.

When food is eaten, what happens to the energy stored in the food molecules?

FIGURE 33–4.

This aquatic food chain has three levels of consumers.

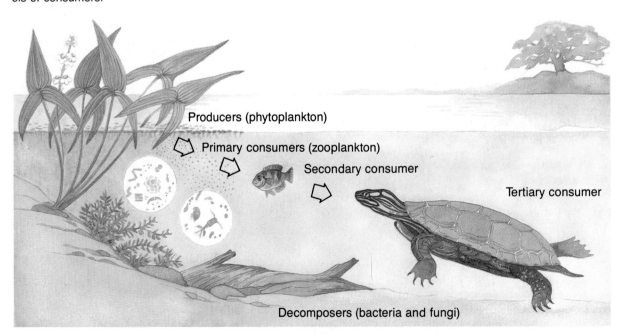

Producers (phytoplankton)

Primary consumers (zooplankton)

Secondary consumer

Tertiary consumer

Decomposers (bacteria and fungi)

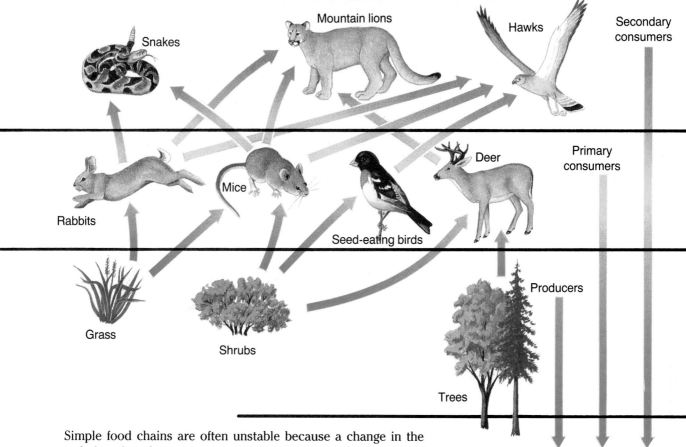

Simple food chains are often unstable because a change in the population size of any species can affect the chain. For example, if a primary consumer depends on one plant species for its food, the loss of that plant species through overgrazing, climatic changes, or habitat destruction could result in the death of the consumer. As an example, consider the giant panda. Giant pandas are close to extinction because bamboo forests, their primary food source, are being cleared for land development. Simple food chains, such as the panda example, are rare in nature. However, in ecosystems that are recovering after volcanic activity or fires, simple food chains are the first signs of community recovery. These simple food chains also are seen in newly formed areas such as volcanic islands.

The different levels of producers and consumers in a food chain are called **trophic levels.** Producers belong to the first trophic level, primary consumers the second, and secondary consumers the third. In nature, most organisms rely on many different sources of food for their nutritional needs. Animals may feed on several different types of food at the same or different trophic levels. Depending on the availability of specific foods, foxes may eat mice, rabbits, berries, or insects. Sea otters eat clams, sea urchins, mussels, and abalone. Bears eat berries as well as fish. At which levels do humans feed?

Complex feeding relationships begin to develop when a consumer eats foods from different trophic levels. Food chains interconnect in a feeding sequence known as a **food web.** Food webs represent a network of food chains and, thus, provide stability to the ecosystem. Each species can choose from a variety of food sources. Examine the food web shown in Figure 33–5. Try to determine the number of different food chains within it. It's difficult, isn't it?

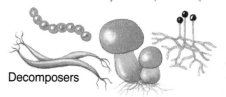

FIGURE 33–5.

This simplified food web has several levels of consumers, many of which feed on several different items.

trophic:
trophe (GK) nourishment

33:6 Energy Flow Through an Ecosystem

In an ecosystem, matter is recycled but energy is not. Solar energy from the sun is collected and converted into chemical energy by producers. As organisms at each succeeding trophic level break down their food, some of the chemical energy is converted to thermal energy, which is given off as heat. This process of energy transfer is not 100 percent efficient. It is governed by the Second Law of Thermodynamics. This law states that each time energy is transferred in a system, there is a reduction in the amount of usable energy. Let's look at how this principle holds true in ecosystems.

At each trophic level of a food chain, some energy is used by organisms for growth and metabolism, some energy is given off in the form of metabolic wastes, some energy is bound up in molecules that the consumer cannot digest, and some is given off as heat. Energy used by organisms for metabolism and energy given off as wastes or heat is not available to the next consumer. Therefore, the amount of usable energy in the ecosystem decreases with higher trophic levels, Figure 33–6. Ecosystems cannot remain stable without a constant input of solar energy. Organisms within the ecosystem require a constant supply of food to maintain their life processes.

The amount of energy available varies from one trophic level to the next. Most scientists, however, agree to a ten percent rule. That is, ten percent of the total energy at one level is stored in the tissues of organisms and thus available to consumers at the next level. Ninety percent of the energy is used for metabolism or given off as wastes or heat. Thus, if 10 000 units of energy are available to a first-level consumer, the second-level consumer has about 1000 units of energy available to it. The ten percent rule helps to explain why there are relatively few large carnivores in a given ecosystem and why there are rarely more than five trophic levels in a food chain. At the fifth level, the amount of available energy is one ten-thousandth the amount of energy available at the first level.

Why is only a small percentage of energy converted into new organic matter?

NoteWorthy

Even though the ten percent rule does not appear very efficient, it is more efficient than the three to five percent efficiency of many mechanical devices.

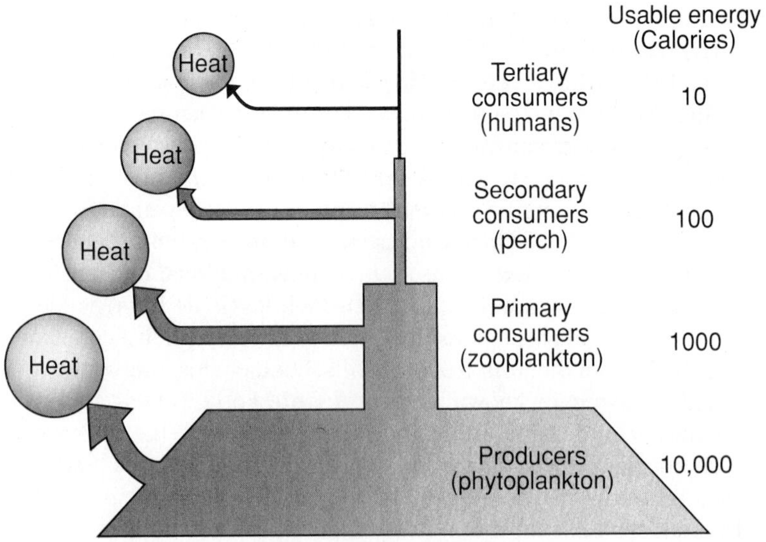

	Usable energy (Calories)
Tertiary consumers (humans)	10
Secondary consumers (perch)	100
Primary consumers (zooplankton)	1000
Producers (phytoplankton)	10,000

FIGURE 33–6.

At each trophic level of a food chain, energy is lost as heat.

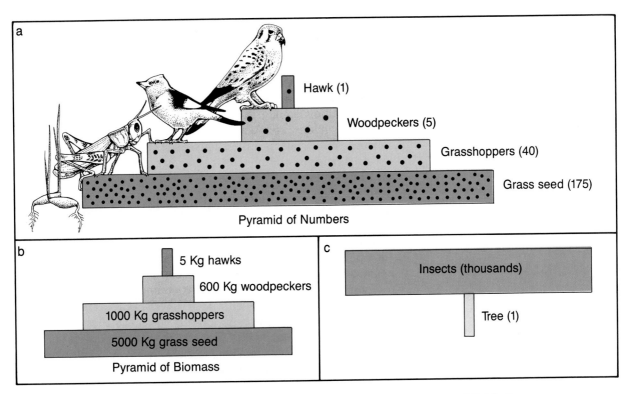

a

Hawk (1)

Woodpeckers (5)

Grasshoppers (40)

Grass seed (175)

Pyramid of Numbers

b

5 Kg hawks

600 Kg woodpeckers

1000 Kg grasshoppers

5000 Kg grass seed

Pyramid of Biomass

c

Insects (thousands)

Tree (1)

Three pyramid models aid in predicting the outcomes of feeding relationships. First, a pyramid of energy shows that the amount of available energy decreases with successively higher trophic levels. Second, a pyramid of numbers shows that at successively higher trophic levels, there are fewer organisms. Note in Figure 33–7 that our sample ecosystem can support only one hawk, while it can support five woodpeckers. Third, a pyramid of biomass is a model that shows that an ecosystem can support less living matter at successively higher trophic levels. Biomass is a measure of the total amount of living matter in an ecosystem.

Energy pyramids are always wider at the base than they are at the top. If you look more closely at pyramids of numbers or biomass, you sometimes see something different. A pyramid of numbers, for example, is affected by the sizes of organisms. One tree might provide food for thousands of insects. Thus, there are more consumers than producers. This kind of inverted pyramid also exists for biomass, especially in the oceans. Consider whales. The biomass of a whale is several times greater than the total biomass of the plankton it consumes. The whale is able to survive because plankton reproduce very rapidly and maintain their population size.

Pyramid models emphasize four important principles.

(1) All food chains begin with producers.

(2) Consumers depend, directly or indirectly, on producers for their energy.

(3) The amount of energy available at each trophic level is directly related to the number of links in a food chain.

(4) Solar energy is required as an energy source.

FIGURE 33–7.

Pyramids of numbers (a) show how many individuals an ecosystem can support. Pyramids of biomass (b) show how much living matter an ecosystem can support. The inverted pyramid (c) shows that one tree (producer) can support thousands of insects (primary consumers).

NoteWorthy

A tuna must consume about one ton of phytoplankton to produce the meat in one can of tuna fish.

33:7 Population Regulation

Competition among organisms affects the size and distribution of populations. Organisms compete for resources, including food, water, light, space, mates, and nutrients. Competition occurs among members of the same species or among different species. Let's look at competition among bullfrogs. In the spring, bullfrogs emerge from their underwater burrows to breed. Male bullfrogs establish territories and call to attract females. The number of males that secure territories is limited by the number of breeding males and by the total area of the pond. Some male bullfrogs are successful in securing territories; many are not. Males that are not successful must use different strategies if they are to breed. Typically, these males try to intercept females on their way to males holding territories. If competition becomes too severe, males will migrate to new ponds in search of territories. Competition among bullfrogs regulates the distribution of bullfrog populations.

The second kind of competition is competition that takes place between two species. Recall that no two species can occupy the same niche at the same time for very long. If niches do overlap, species will tend to compete. The more the niches overlap, the more competition there will be. The outcome of such competition is that one species will lose, and may be driven to extinction.

In nature, when the range of two species overlaps, the species tend to have different niche requirements. The result is that competition is minimized. Let's return to our bird example from Section 33:2. In it, the different bird species used different food sources even though they inhabited the same type of tree. In fact, this example is similar to one that occurs in nature. Several species of warblers feed in the same type of spruce tree. Careful observation reveals that the bay-breasted warbler, Cape May warbler, and myrtle warbler feed in different parts of the tree, Figure 33–8. Therefore, competition among these species is reduced and they are able to live together.

What happens when the members of one species compete for the same resources?

FIGURE 33–8.

The Cape May warbler, bay-breasted warbler, and myrtle warbler feed in different parts of the same type of spruce tree.

Bay–breasted warbler   Cape May warbler   Myrtle warbler

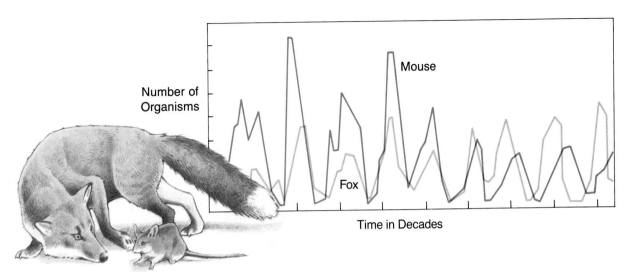

Number of Organisms

Mouse

Fox

Time in Decades

Predation is another factor that controls populations. Predation limits the sizes of both predator and prey populations. Recall from Chapter 23 that a predator is an organism that captures and eats another. The organism the predator captures is the prey. Notice in Figure 33–9 that when the number of prey increases, the number of predators also increases. With the increase in predators, more prey are captured and eaten. The prey population decreases. With a decrease in the prey population, less food is available for the predator. The predator population decreases. The rise and fall of numbers of predators and prey may be observed when species are restricted to a small area with few additional food sources. However, it may not be observed when organisms rely on several food sources, as in a food web. A population of barred owls that preys on mice, rats, rabbits, or birds can remain relatively stable. In turn, the populations of mice, rats, rabbits, and birds will remain relatively stable due in part to the feeding behavior of the barred owl.

FIGURE 33–9.

In some predator-prey relationships, the numbers of predators and prey rise and fall in a repeated cycle.

How does predation help to control population size?

REVIEW

6. Explain the difference between mutualism and commensalism.
7. What three things do food chains and food webs have in common?
8. What is meant by the ten percent rule?
9. **SKILL REVIEW:** Calculate the amount of energy available to a person in the following food chain. The producers are algae in a lake and contain 1000 units of energy. The algae are eaten by a small fish. The small fish is eaten by another larger fish that in turn is eaten by trout. A trout is caught by a person fishing, who takes it home and eats it. For more help, refer to Measuring in SI in the Skill Handbook, pages 806 to 808.
10. **USING CONCEPTS:** Why don't food chains have ten or twelve trophic levels?

White Mountain National Forest was the site of the Hubbard Brook Experiment.

THINKING CRITICALLY

CHEMICAL CYCLING

The Hubbard Brook Experiment is a well-documented study of biochemical cycling in a forest ecosystem. The study took place in White Mountain National Forest in New Hampshire in the 1960s. Researchers calculated the amount of nitrogen going into and coming out of the ecosystem. To calculate the amount of nitrogen going into the system, they measured the amount of this substance in precipitation that fell in the area. To calculate nitrogen output, they constructed channels that collected the water flowing out of different areas. In this way, they were able to measure the amount of nitrogen leaving the system in the water. They found that the level of nitrogen entering the ecosystem was about the same as the level of nitrogen leaving it. Thus, the system was maintaining a homeostatic balance.

As part of the experiment, a 15-hectare area of the forest was cleared during the winter of 1965–1966. Researchers wanted to find out what effect clearing would have on the cycling of nitrogen. They cut all of the trees and shrubs. Nothing was removed from the area, and regrowth was prevented by spraying with herbicides for nine months. The following summer, they calculated the amount of nitrogen going into and coming out of the altered system. What do you think the scientists discovered when they did their calculations? Describe the changes that may have occurred in the ecosystem.

Objectives:
- describe the relationship between living and nonliving components in biogeochemical cycles.
- describe the flow of carbon through the biosphere.
- explain how nitrogen from the atmosphere becomes available to plants.
- distinguish between the two phosphorus cycles.
- discuss the importance of the water cycle.

ABIOTIC FACTORS

Organisms require many chemical elements for growth and maintenance. Carbon, hydrogen, oxygen, nitrogen, phosphorus, and sulfur make up about 95 percent of the mass of all living things. Earth contains fixed amounts of chemical elements. Thus, it is important that they be recycled quickly and efficiently.

33:8 Chemical Cycling in Ecosystems

Elements move from the abiotic environment to organisms and back again to the environment. This regular exchange of elements between the living and nonliving parts of an ecosystem is called a **biogeochemical cycle.** Recall from Section 33:6 that energy is not recycled and that a constant supply of energy is needed for an ecosystem to continue functioning.

Elements such as carbon, oxygen, and nitrogen are found free or in compounds in the oceans and atmosphere. Biogeochemical cycles may be classified by the part of the biosphere that contains a large amount of an element. Carbon, oxygen, and nitrogen are found in gaseous form in the atmosphere. The elements phosphorus, sulfur, calcium, magnesium, and copper usually are found in solid form in rock. Movement of elements between air, land, and water is slower than movement of elements between organisms.

33:9 The Carbon Cycle

Carbon, the backbone of organic compounds, is essential to all living things. Study Figure 33–10 as you read about the cycling of this important element through the ecosystem. Carbon dioxide moves from the atmosphere to aquatic and terrestrial producers, which use it to make organic compounds. Consumers take in carbon from the producers. Thus, carbon is passed through the food chain. During respiration, organisms in the food chain release carbon dioxide back into the atmosphere or water. When organisms die, the carbon compounds in their remains are first broken down by decomposers and then carbon is released to the atmosphere or water as carbon dioxide.

Carbon in ocean water may be dissolved in the form of carbon dioxide or stored in the form of calcium carbonate in rocks and animal shells. Carbon dioxide in the oceans enters the atmosphere by diffusion and returns to the water dissolved in precipitation.

In an ecosystem, organisms that die but fail to decompose may be converted to fossil fuels—coal, oil, or gas. Left undisturbed, fossil fuels will not break down, and the carbon they contain can remain stored for millions of years. However, when fossil fuels are burned, carbon reenters the atmosphere in great amounts. It is estimated that carbon dioxide in the atmosphere has increased by 15 percent during the last 100 years. This increase is due, in part, to fossil fuel combustion. Carbon dioxide is being put into the atmosphere faster than it can cycle through the biosphere.

What are sources of carbon in the atmosphere and oceans?

FIGURE 33–10.

Carbon is cycled between the biotic and abiotic parts of the environment.

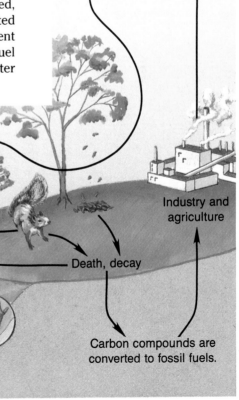

33:10 The Nitrogen Cycle

Nitrogen, like carbon, is an essential element for organisms. Recall from Chapter 3 that nitrogen is a component of nucleic acids and proteins, the building blocks of living matter. As you read about the nitrogen cycle, refer to Figure 33–11. Nitrogen gas makes up nearly 78 percent of the atmosphere. Plants, animals, fungi, and protists can't use nitrogen in this form. A small amount of atmospheric nitrogen is converted to usable nitrogen compounds by lightning. However, most nitrogen gas is converted into usable nitrogen compounds by bacteria living in nodules on the roots of legumes. Legumes are members of the pea family and include beans and clover. Nitrogen compounds in root nodules are used by plants to synthesize proteins and other compounds needed by the plant.

Nitrogen compounds within plants are passed through the food chain or used by the plants themselves. When plants and animals die, the proteins in their remains are broken down in a series of steps. First, the proteins are broken down into amino acids by microscopic decomposers. Amino acids are broken down further into ammonia. Ammonia is converted into nitrite ions, and nitrite ions are converted into nitrate ions by two different groups of bacteria. The energy released during these conversions is used by the bacteria as an energy source. Nitrogen is not necessarily cycled back to the atmosphere before entering the biotic portion of the cycle again. Nitrates dissolved in soil water may be taken up by the roots of plants and used as a food source. Other nitrates are converted back to gaseous nitrogen by bacteria and released back to the atmosphere.

FIGURE 33–11.

In the nitrogen cycle, different nitrogen compounds are formed.

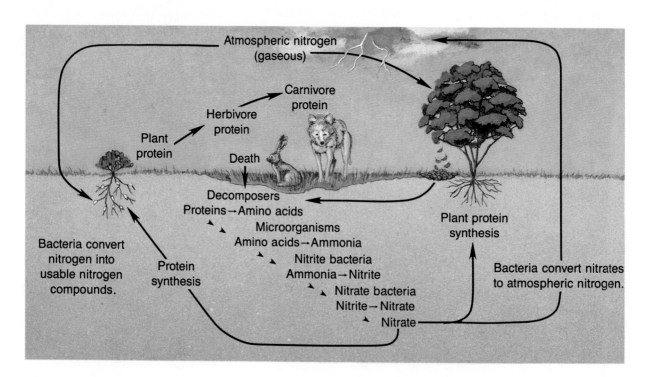

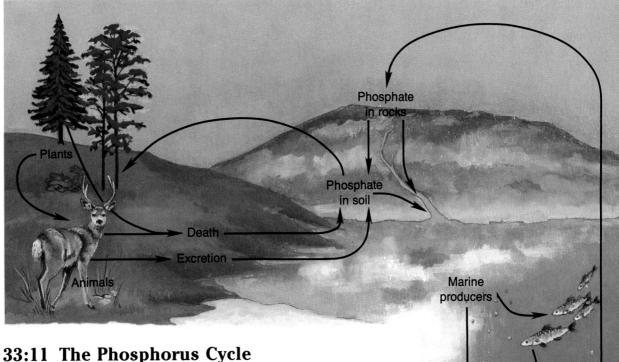

33:11 The Phosphorus Cycle

The cycling of phosphorus is important because, like nitrogen, phosphorus is a component of nucleic acids. As you read about the phosphorus cycle, look at Figure 33–12. The phosphorus cycle consists of two interconnecting cycles. First, phosphates in rock and soil are taken up by plants. Plants are eaten by herbivores, and phosphorus passes through the food chain. Phosphates reenter the soil in the form of plant and animal wastes. This portion of the cycle is rapid and is usually confined to small areas.

In the second cycle, large amounts of phosphates enter water systems through erosion or runoff from farmland and sewage and end up in the oceans. Phosphates are used by marine producers and pass through the food chain. When marine organisms decompose, phosphorus binds with ocean sediments. Over long periods of time, a shifting of Earth's crust may cause mountains and islands to develop. The sea floor rises up and is no longer covered by water. As phosphorus in mountain rock or island soil is weathered or eroded, it returns to the oceans or is passed through the food chain. The cycling of phosphorus between land and oceans may take as long as a million years.

33:12 The Water Cycle

Water is the most abundant resource on Earth's surface. As you read about the cycling of this vital substance, refer to Figure 33–13. Water moves from the atmosphere to the surface of Earth in the form of rain or snow. Once it falls to Earth, water follows several routes. It may evaporate and return to the atmosphere. Evaporation

FIGURE 33–12.

The phosphorus cycle includes a rapid cycle and a slow cycle that involves movement of phosphorus between land and sea.

FIGURE 33-13.

Water moves in a cycle between organisms on land, the land itself, and the atmosphere.

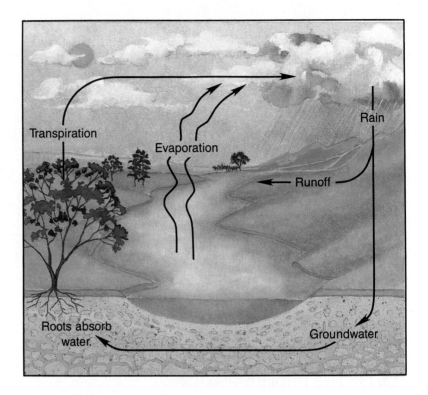

Transpiration

Evaporation

Rain

Runoff

Roots absorb water.

Groundwater

helps to regulate temperature and concentrate minerals in the soil. Plants absorb some water through their roots and return it to the atmosphere through transpiration. Some water runs off the land into rivers, lakes, or oceans, and some water seeps into the ground. Water seeping into the ground becomes part of the groundwater supply. **Groundwater** is water beneath the ground that supplies wells and springs. Storage sites for groundwater include aquifers. **Aquifers** are large, lakelike bodies of water underground.

The continual cycling of water through an ecosystem maintains freshwater lakes and streams. As you have seen in Sections 33:9–33:11, the cycling of chemical nutrients depends on water. All organisms depend on water for cellular respiration, and producers also use it for photosynthesis. Clearly, the most abundant resource on Earth is also one of the most precious.

Why is the cycling of water so important?

REVIEW

11. What happens to carbon when fossil fuels are burned?
12. How is atmospheric nitrogen made available to plants?
13. How do plants function in the water cycle?
14. **SKILL REVIEW:** List the sequence of events in a nitrogen cycle. For more help, refer to Reading Science in the Skill Handbook, pages 798 to 799.
15. **USING CONCEPTS:** How might the water cycle be affected if the plants in an area were completely destroyed?

BIOLAB *Abiotic Factors* 33

Problem: How do brine shrimp respond to an abiotic factor, such as light intensity?

Materials
brine shrimp mixture (100 mL)
100-cm blackened tygon tube
100-cm clear tygon tube
1-mL pipette   tube clamp (3)
cork (2)   test-tube rack
test tube (8)   tape
meter stick   stereomicroscope
methyl cellulose   wax pencil
50-mL graduate cylinder   flood lamp
petri dish (4)

Procedures
Brine shrimp live in shallow coastal waters where light penetrates.
1. Copy the data table.
2. Stopper one end of a blackened tygon tube with a cork. Measure 50 mL of brine shrimp mixture into a graduated cylinder. Fill the tygon tube with the 50 mL of brine shrimp mixture. Stopper the other end. Place three loosened tube clamps 25 cm apart along the tube as shown in the figure. Tape the tube to the table top.
3. Wait 20 minutes and tighten the middle clamp first, then the end clamps. Hold the corks so that they do not pop out. This procedure divides the tube into four sections.
4. Pour the contents of each section into a clean test tube. Label the test tubes 1 through 4 with a wax marking pencil.
5. Using a pipette, remove a 1-mL sample of brine shrimp from test tube 1 and pour it into a petri dish. Add a few drops of methyl cellulose and count all the live shrimp. Count five 1-mL samples from the first test tube. Calculate and record the average number of brine shrimp per mL for the five samples.
6. Repeat step 5 with test tubes 2 through 4.
7. Repeat step 2 with a clear tygon tube.
8. Place a flood lamp 30 cm from one end of the clear tygon tube and shine it directly toward the tube as shown in the figure.

9. Develop a **hypothesis** as to which section of the clear tube will contain the most live brine shrimp after 20 minutes.
10. Repeat steps 3 through 6.

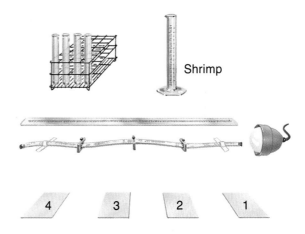
Shrimp

4   3   2   1

Data and Observations

Average number of live brine shrimp per mL		
Test tube	No flood lamp	Flood lamp
1		
2		
3		
4		

Questions and Conclusion
1. Based on your results, which light intensity is most favorable to brine shrimp? Explain.
2. Which light intensity is least favorable? Explain.
3. What is the purpose of the black tube?
4. Do your data support your **hypothesis?** Explain.
Conclusion: How do brine shrimp respond to light intensity?

CHAPTER REVIEW

SUMMARY

1. Organisms in the biosphere depend on living and nonliving factors in their environments for energy and materials. **33:1**
2. Organisms can be grouped into populations and communities. Each species has a certain habitat and niche. **33:2**
3. An ecosystem results from the interaction between community and environment. **33:3**
4. Symbiotic relationships include mutualism, parasitism, and commensalism. **33:4**
5. Nutrients are transferred from producers to consumers in food chains and food webs. **33:5**
6. As energy passes through an ecosystem, some energy is used for growth and some is released as heat. **33:6**
7. Competition and predation regulate population size and distribution. **33:7**
8. Chemicals move through the environment in biogeochemical cycles that often are interconnected. **33:8**
9. Carbon, nitrogen, phosphorus, and water are cycled from abiotic parts of the environment to biotic parts and back again. **33:9, 33:10, 33:11, 33:12**

LANGUAGE OF BIOLOGY

abiotic factors	food chain
aquifers	food web
biogeochemical cycle	groundwater
biotic factors	habitat
carnivore	herbivore
commensalism	niche
community	omnivore
ecology	trophic levels

Choose the word or phrase from the list above that completes the sentence.

1. ____ include light, temperature, and water.

2. A species' ____ is its role.
3. A type of symbiosis in which one species benefits and the other is unaffected is ____.
4. ____ include all the organisms in a community.
5. The feeding sequence through which energy passes from the eaten to the eater is a(n) ____.
6. Feeding levels within a food chain are ____.
7. Interlocking food chains form a(n) ____.
8. ____ supplies water to wells and springs.
9. A(n) ____ is the cyclic movement of chemicals within an ecosystem.
10. A(n) ____ eats both plants and animals.

REVIEWING CONCEPTS

Choose the word or phrase that completes the sentence or answers the question.

11. An organism's environment consists of ____.
    a. abiotic factors   c. its habitat
    b. biotic factors   d. all the above
12. A species' role in the ecosystem is its ____.
    a. community   c. population
    b. habitat   d. niche
13. Which is NOT required for a stable ecosystem?
    a. producers   c. decomposers
    b. herbivores   d. an energy source
14. Examples of producers are ____.
    a. carnivores   c. herbivores
    b. green plants   d. animals
15. Which of the following is a food chain?
    a. grasshoppers → grass
    b. leaves → fungi → hawks → snake
    c. grain → mice → cat
    d. mushroom → tree → owl → mosquito
16. The ten percent rule applies to ____.
    a. pyramids of   c. pyramids of
       biomass   numbers
    b. energy pyramids d. biotic factors

17. Bees pollinating plants while receiving food is an example of ____.
   a. parasitism
   c. commensalism
   b. mutualism
   d. competition
18. Competition between different species does NOT involve competition for ____.
   a. food sources
   c. light
   b. mates
   d. all of the above
19. Which of the following statements is true?
   a. Consumers depend on producers for energy.
   b. Producers depend on omnivores for energy.
   c. Energy is recycled.
   d. Food chains begin with carnivores.
20. Formation of fossil fuels is part of the ____.
   a. water cycle
   c. carbon cycle
   b. nitrogen cycle
   d. phosphorus cycle

UNDERSTANDING CONCEPTS

Answer the following questions using complete sentences.

21. Explain why the cycling of phosphorus may take as long as a million years.
22. Name two ways in which all organisms depend on water.
23. How is the Second Law of Thermodynamics related to the ten percent rule?
24. Why are decomposers also consumers?
25. How is competition reduced between species that live in the same area?
26. In an ecosystem, what happens to energy not available for metabolism?
27. Why can't we refer to the transfer of energy in an ecosystem as a cycle?
28. How do food webs help to maintain a homeostatic balance in an ecosystem?
29. How are pyramids of numbers and pyramids of energy alike?
30. Explain why the giant panda is part of a simple food chain.

APPLYING CONCEPTS

Answer the following questions using complete sentences.

31. How would you describe the niche occupied by humans?
32. What effect can humans have on predator-prey relationships?
33. Predict what would happen to the size of a population over time if a species had no competition from other species and resources were limited.
34. What would happen in an ecosystem if all the decomposers were to die?
35. For what resources do humans compete?

EXTENSIONS

1. Find an area near your school that can be observed on a daily basis. You might choose a vacant lot, part of the school grounds, or a section of a bush. Identify biotic and abiotic components in the area you select.
2. Set up a small ecosystem in a glass jar. See what happens as you vary different abiotic factors such as light and moisture. What happens if you use sterilized soil? What happens when you introduce a new plant or animal species into the enclosed system?
3. Research how introduction of the starling to the United States affected the environment.

READINGS

Grove, Noel. "Quietly Conserving Nature." *National Geographic,* Dec. 1988, pp. 818–845.
Steinhart, Peter. "Taming Our Fear of Predators." *National Wildlife,* Feb./Mar. 1989, pp. 4–13.
Stephens, Sharon. "Lapp Life after Chernobyl." *Natural History,* Dec. 1987, pp. 32–40.

DISTRIBUTION OF COMMUNITIES

Organisms, populations, and communities are all limited by many factors in their environments. Competition and predator-prey relationships are two of the biotic, or living, factors that limit the sizes of populations. You read about the effects of these biotic factors in Chapter 33. Abiotic, or nonliving, factors that limit organisms include temperature, sunlight, water, currents, wind, and elevation. How do abiotic factors help to determine the structure of communities, such as the grasslands in Africa? What kinds of adaptations do organisms, such as the zebras and the gazelle shown on this page, have for surviving in this environment? In this chapter, you will study how environmental conditions influence the development of communities of organisms and their distribution.

Gazelle

HOW ORGANISMS ARE LIMITED

Have you ever returned from a trip to find that your potted plants had wilted and died? They died because no one watered them. What happens to grass if you cover it with a board for a few days? The grass underneath the board turns yellow. Both the potted plants and the grass were limited in their functions by environmental conditions. What factors limited their growth? Water and sunlight are two environmental factors that affect how organisms function in their environment. What other limits can the environment place on organisms?

34:1 Limits of Tolerance

Each species of organism has some set of environmental conditions that are just right, or optimum, for its growth, maintenance, and reproduction. The common carp is found in freshwater ponds and lakes that are warm and full of plankton suspended in the water. Cacti are most plentiful in hot, dry deserts, where there is a lot of sunshine and very little rain. Polar bears thrive in the frigid, snowy environment of the Arctic.

Objectives:
- describe what is meant by an organism's limits of tolerance.
- explain what happens when organisms encounter conditions outside their limits of tolerance.
- explain what a limiting factor is and how it affects the distribution of organisms.
- give examples of abiotic factors that are limiting for plants.

African savannah

FIGURE 34–1.

The saguaro thrives under conditions of low annual rainfall.

Organisms don't always live under optimum conditions. Most organisms can tolerate or adapt to a range of environmental conditions. The range of conditions under which an organism is able to function and survive are its **limits of tolerance.** For carp, the optimum water temperature is 20°C, but they can continue to function at a temperature range of 10°C to 32°C. The giant saguaro cactus, Figure 34–1, is found in deserts where rainfall ranges from 0 mm to 10 mm yearly. The limits of tolerance vary with each individual and each species. An organism's physical condition and its stage in its life cycle affect its limits of tolerance. In general, however, more individuals of a species will be able to survive under optimum conditions, Figure 34–2.

What happens when a condition is outside the limits of tolerance for an organism? Think about trout. Trout require high concentrations of oxygen dissolved in water to survive. Cold water can hold more dissolved oxygen than warm water. Trout, therefore, function best in cold-water streams. As water temperature rises, trout become stressed. If the water temperature continues to rise, the trout will die. For trout, its limits of tolerance for water temperature are affected by its limits of tolerance for oxygen. In nature, organisms must deal with many different limiting conditions at one time.

34:2 Limiting Factors

The presence and success of an organism or population of organisms depend upon a complex system of biotic and abiotic conditions. Any one of these conditions that approaches or exceeds the limits of tolerance for an organism is called a limiting factor. A **limiting factor** is a condition that determines the survival of an organism or species in its environment. For trout, oxygen is a limiting factor. Any factor that restricts the existence, numbers, reproduction, or distribution of organisms is a limiting factor.

FIGURE 34–2.

The largest number of individuals of a species will survive when conditions are optimal. As conditions become less favorable, fewer and fewer individuals survive until none are present.

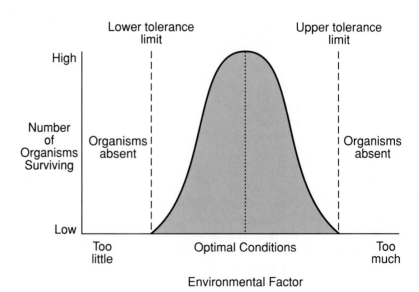

BIOLAB

Limits of Tolerance

Problem: What are the limits of tolerance for hormone concentration in tomato plants?

Materials

tomato seedlings (6)　corks with holes
metric ruler　aluminum foil
test tubes (6)　wax pencil
test-tube rack　labels
plant hormone solutions (five concentrations)

Procedures

1. Copy the data table.
2. Develop a **hypothesis** about the effects of hormone concentration on the growth and development of tomato roots. In your hypothesis, state which concentration will cause the most growth and which will cause the least.
3. Label the test tubes 1 through 6. Fill five of the tubes with the following concentrations of hormone solution.
   - tube 1—0.01 mg/L
   - tube 2—0.10 mg/L
   - tube 3—1.0 mg/L
   - tube 4—10.0 mg/L
   - tube 5—100.0 mg/L
4. Choose six healthy tomato seedlings and carefully remove each plant from the soil. Gently wash the root systems with tap water.
5. Measure the length of the roots of each seedling. Record the lengths in your data chart.
6. Thread the wet root system of each plant through the hole in a cork stopper. Place each plant in a separate tube. Be sure to cover the entire root with solution.
7. Place aluminum foil around each tube.
8. Fill the sixth tube with tap water. Repeat steps 6 and 7 with the sixth plant.
9. Place the test tubes in a test-tube rack and label it with your name. Place the rack in an undisturbed corner of the room.
10. At the end of three weeks, measure and record the length of the roots.
11. Prepare a bar graph to show the changes in root length for each plant.

Data and Observations

	Length of roots in cm		
Tube	Hormone concentration	Start of experiment	End of experiment
1	0.01 mg/L		
2	0.10 mg/L		
3	1.0 mg/L		
4	10.0 mg/L		
5	100.0 mg/L		
6	0 mg/L		

Questions and Conclusion

1. At which hormone concentration did the tomato roots grow the most? The least?
2. What happened to the tomato plants in tubes 4 and 5? Explain.
3. How does plant hormone concentration affect root growth?
4. Was your original **hypothesis** supported by your data? Why or why not?

Conclusion: What are the limits of tolerance for hormone concentration in tomato plants?

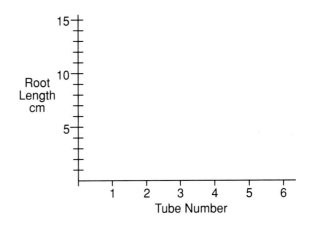

a

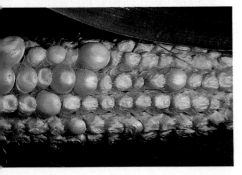

b

FIGURE 34–3.

A limiting factor for growth of crops is rainfall. Corn survives when rainfall is adequate (a), but cannot survive under drought conditions (b).

A limiting factor may be lacking or too abundant. For example, when a potted plant wilts, too little water is the limiting factor in the plant's survival. Think of what would happen if you watered this plant every day. Too much water is just as harmful to plants as not enough.

Abiotic conditions that are limiting factors for plants are temperature, sunlight, water, and chemical nutrients. The amounts of these factors available to plants determine plant growth and survival. Many limiting factors work together to affect plants. For example, soil temperature influences the rate of absorption of water and nutrients by the plant's roots.

The intensity and duration of sunlight affect plant growth and survival. Some plants require full sunlight to grow properly. Other plants cannot survive in direct sunlight. Orchids depend on trees for support and receive indirect sunlight filtered through the tree's leaves. What would happen to an orchid placed in direct sunlight? For orchids, direct sunlight is a limiting factor.

Water is another limiting factor for plant survival. Periodic droughts throughout the world are quite common. During drought conditions, water is a limiting factor for grass and many other plants, Figure 34–3. If these plants include food crops, human populations may also be affected by the drought.

Plants require chemical nutrients such as nitrogen and phosphorus for growth and survival. Chemical nutrients are dissolved in water and taken up by the plant's roots. Different nutrients are soluble in water at different pH levels. Recall that pH is a measure of the acidity or alkalinity of a substance. As the pH of the soil becomes more alkaline, certain essential nutrients may no longer be available to plants, and the plants will die.

All of the factors that limit plant growth—temperature, sunlight, water, and nutrients—are factors that limit other kinds of organisms that make up a community. Because most animals depend on plants for food, the types of plants able to grow in an environment affect the types of animals that survive there as well.

REVIEW

1. What are an organism's limits of tolerance for any one factor?
2. What is a limiting factor?
3. Name four abiotic factors that may become limiting for plants.
4. **SKILL REVIEW:** Using the following data, graph the limits of tolerance for temperature for bass. The first number in each pair is temperature in °C; the second number is number of bass surviving at that temperature: 5, 20; 10, 30; 15, 40; 20, 60; 25, 60; 30, 50; 35, 50; 40, 40. For more help, refer to Organizing Information in the Skill Handbook, pages 810 to 813.
5. **USING CONCEPTS:** Design an experiment using potted plants to test if water, sunlight, temperature, or chemical nutrients is the most limiting factor for plant growth.

ECOLOGICAL SUCCESSION

The presence of different populations of plants and animals in an area can change the environment. Sometimes these changes make it difficult for certain species to continue to survive in the area. The seedlings of pine trees require full sunlight to germinate and grow. As more pine trees grow, fewer pine seedlings can survive in the shade the trees provide. This same increase in shade makes it possible for the seedlings of other trees, such as elms, oaks, or hickories, to develop. Over time, organisms in the environment are followed by whole new sets of organisms, and the result is a complete change in the community.

34:3 Primary Succession

A gradual change in the structure of a community over time is called **succession.** Succession is an orderly process of community development that occurs in predictable stages. Ecologists have studied the organisms associated with each stage to try to understand how succession works. The two types of succession are primary succession and secondary succession.

Primary succession is the formation of new communities in areas that started out as bare land, Figure 34–4. When a coral reef is exposed to the air as a result of earthquake activity on the ocean floor, the organisms living on the reef die and the coral skeletons remain. Gradually, soil particles and plant seeds and spores carried by the wind are deposited on the coral. Over time, soil develops and plant communities form. New volcanic islands, newly formed ponds or reservoirs, sand dunes, and land that has been strip mined all may undergo primary succession.

Objectives:
- explain what is meant by succession.
- give examples of situations under which primary succession might occur.
- explain the difference between primary and secondary succession.
- identify the major characteristics of climax communities.

Where does primary succession occur?

FIGURE 34–4.

Primary succession may take place on a volcanic island.

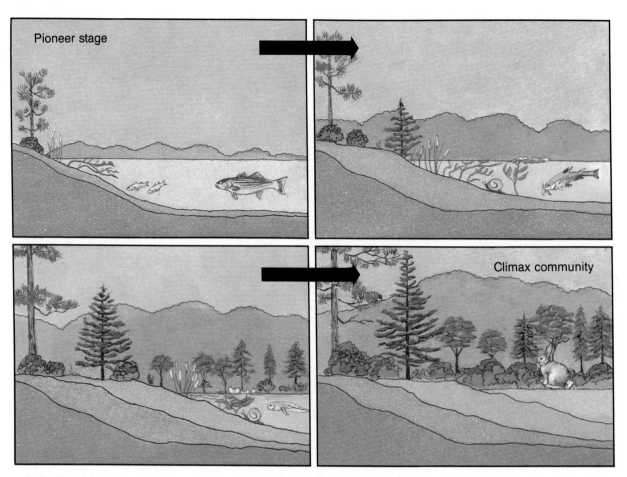

Pioneer stage

Climax community

FIGURE 34–5.

As a pond undergoes primary succession, it fills with soil and plant material, and the pond organisms change.

NoteWorthy

The eruption of Mount St. Helens provided a unique opportunity for scientists to study primary succession. Virtually all life forms in the area were destroyed when the volcano erupted.

The first organisms to colonize a region are known as pioneer species. To survive, pioneer species must have extremely wide limits of tolerance. Pioneers may have to withstand extremes of temperature and water availability. The ground may be subject to periodic flooding and rapid water loss in the heat of the day. Some organisms capable of surviving these conditions are protozoans, cyanobacteria, algae, and lichens. They usually arrive in the form of spores that are tolerant of extreme environmental factors. In aquatic environments, dust and soil particles are blown into the water and settle to the bottom of the pond or lake. They provide anchorage and nutrients for underwater plants. Monerans and spores of algae and lichens also are blown into the water. As the submerged organisms die, they are broken down by bacteria, and their nutrients are released into the water. The presence of one kind of organism has changed the environment in such a way that conditions become favorable for other kinds of organisms. This sequence of life, growth, and death of organisms is repeated constantly. Each time the environment is changed, new populations move into the area. Primary succession may take hundreds to thousands of years to reach a point where the community remains balanced, or stable. Some of the stages of primary succession in a pond are shown in Figure 34–5.

34:4 Secondary Succession

Succession is often disturbed by fire, floods, earthquakes, or human activities. Grasslands or forests are cleared for agricultural purposes or for lumbering. If these areas are abandoned or left undisturbed, succession begins once again. An abandoned pasture or orchard eventually will be invaded by various grasses, shrubs, and trees in a type of succession known as secondary succession. **Secondary succession** is the return of an area to its previous condition after it has been disturbed, Figure 34–6.

In the summer of 1988, fire swept through Yellowstone National Park. Thousands of acres of trees, shrubs, and grasses burned to the ground. Many animals died from the smoke and the flames. Many others moved out of the area. People are now able to observe Yellowstone undergoing secondary succession. Ash from the dead plants and animals is providing nutrients for plant seedlings. As new plants move into the area, animal populations will return. These animals will contribute organic matter to the soil and more plants will then move into the area. More plants mean more food sources for herbivores. More herbivores mean more food for carnivores. In succession, populations change and communities continually develop.

34:5 Climax Communities

In any area, ecological succession eventually reaches a stage in which the biotic and abiotic factors are balanced. A community in which such a balance is achieved is called a climax community. A **climax community** is one that has reached the end of succession. The type of climax community that develops is determined by the limiting factors of the environment. In areas where water is a limiting factor, the climax community may be a desert. On a mountain, the climax community may include lichens and mosses, but no trees because of the limiting factors of temperature, water, and wind. As long as the environmental conditions remain constant, the climax community will endure.

How might the normal sequence of succession be disturbed?

FIGURE 34–6.

Secondary succession may take place in a forest disturbed by fire, such as this forest in Yellowstone National Park.

The early stages of succession usually involve few species. Many of these species are involved in symbiotic relationships such as mutualism and commensalism. The major feeding patterns in these early stages are simple food chains. Minor changes in environmental conditions may interrupt the food chain and disturb succession. Succession may restart several times until a greater variety of organisms are present.

A climax community contains many species. Food webs instead of food chains predominate. The large number of associations among species gives stability to the climax community. It is capable of withstanding minor changes in the environment without being destroyed. For example, a colder than usual winter would not necessarily upset the balance of a forest in Oregon, even though many plants and animals would die. You may recall from Chapter 1 that the ability to withstand environmental change is also one of the characteristics of living organisms.

REVIEW

6. What is ecological succession?
7. Distinguish between primary and secondary succession.
8. What is a climax community?
9. **SKILL REVIEW:** List the kinds of organisms and the order in which they might appear in the succession of a coral island. For more help, refer to Reading Science in the Skill Handbook, pages 798 to 799.
10. **USING CONCEPTS:** Describe succession in a river valley recovering from flooding.

TERRESTRIAL BIOMES

Objectives:
- identify the seven major terrestrial biomes.
- identify the major limiting factors governing the distribution of biomes.
- describe the characteristics of each biome.
- give examples of organisms found in each biome.

If you were to begin at the Equator and travel north or south, you would notice a gradual change in the temperature and amount of sunlight. Weather in the tropics is hot and humid, but the weather gets colder and drier as you move toward the poles. The gradual changes in temperature and sunlight result in changes in the species that can survive in a particular environment. As the limits of tolerance for each species are reached, fewer and fewer individuals of that species survive. Eventually that species will disappear and another species with different limits of tolerance will take over the niche vacated by the original species. For example, forests near the Equator have palm trees and banyans. Forests farther from the Equator may have beeches, maples, or oaks. Still farther from the Equator, firs and pines become predominant. If you continue toward the poles, environmental conditions change so much that no trees survive!

34:6 Deserts

In each hemisphere, there are large geographic areas with similar weather patterns and climax communities. These large geographic areas with similar climax communities are called **biomes.** The distribution of biomes over Earth is influenced by three main limiting factors—precipitation, temperature, and light intensity. As you study the different biomes, refer to Figure 34–7 as a reminder of how they are distributed.

Desert biomes are found on most continents. Deserts are found most often between the Tropic of Cancer and the Tropic of Capricorn. In the deserts of the world, evaporation rates are high, and the differences between daytime and nighttime temperatures may be extreme. The soil may be alkaline with little organic matter, or it may be mostly sand. Plants are few and often widely scattered. Without protective cover, the land gains heat rapidly during the day and loses it rapidly at night. Precipitation in the desert averages less than 25 cm a year, making water the major limiting factor.

When you think of a desert, do you automatically think of a bare landscape that is hot year-round? The Sahara desert of Africa, the Mohave desert in Nevada, and the Sonoran desert in the southwestern United States and northwestern Mexico are examples of hot deserts. But deserts also may be relatively cool due to high altitudes. Examples of cool deserts are the Gobi and Tibetan deserts of Asia, deserts in Bolivia, and the Great Basin region of the United States.

FIGURE 34–7.

The distribution of the world's major terrestrial biomes is shown on this map.

- Ice
- Tundra
- Taiga
- Temperate forest
- Tropical rain forest
- Temperate grassland
- Desert
- Tropical grassland

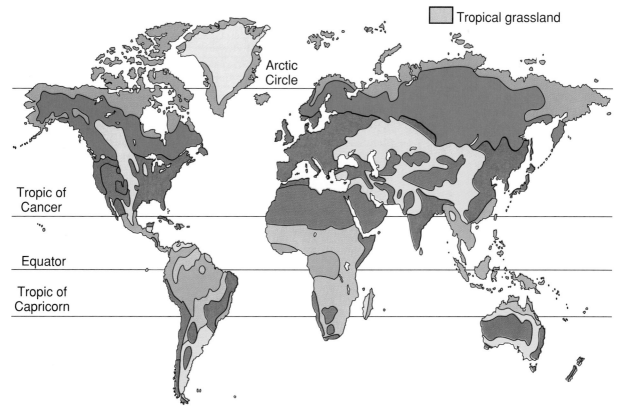

Arctic Circle

Tropic of Cancer

Equator

Tropic of Capricorn

FIGURE 34–8.

Desert organisms, such as lizards and cacti, are adapted to hot, dry conditions.

What are some adaptations of desert plants?

Desert organisms have developed a variety of adaptations to cope with their environmental limits. Some desert plants avoid drought by growing only when there is enough moisture. Desert annuals, such as the desert dandelion, grow from seeds to flowering plants in one short rainy season. They survive as seeds until the next favorable period. Other plants store water in their tissues during the rains, then use the water in later dry periods. The saguaro cactus, a plant of the Sonoran desert, is one example of this type of plant. Plants in the desert usually have small leaves or leaves that are modified into spines to reduce water loss. Ecologists have found that some desert plants release chemical inhibitors from their roots. These chemicals prevent other plants from growing nearby. The wide spacing of desert plants reduces competition among the plants for water.

Reptiles, insects, birds, and mammals are common in all deserts. Many desert animals are nocturnal, sleeping during the day and becoming active at night. Desert animals that sleep during the day in burrows or shaded areas include rattlesnakes, scorpions, and lizards. Birds often have nesting and breeding cycles that coincide with the scarce desert rains. Some animals are adapted to the lack of water by having the ability to reduce the loss of water from their own bodies. The kangaroo rat can obtain enough water from the seeds it eats and does not require drinking water.

34:7 Tropical Rain Forests

In most tropical rain forest biomes, water is in ample supply. Tropical rain forests may receive as much as 500 cm of rain a year. Located near the Equator, tropical rain forests contain more species than any other biome. Plant species are numerous, but few species are dominant.

Rain forests consist of several layers of vegetation as you move from the forest floor to the top of the tallest trees. The topmost layer of the forest is the canopy, which forms an unbroken layer of green about 45 m above the forest floor. A few very tall trees project above the canopy. Between the canopy and the forest floor there is an understory layer consisting of smaller trees, ferns, and climbing plants. Nutrients are abundant in rain forests, but they are found mostly in the vegetation rather than the soil. When leaves and other plant materials fall to the forest floor, they decompose and the released nutrients are quickly taken up by plant roots. If the forest cover is removed by logging or farmers clearing land for agriculture, the soil is exposed to the tropical rainstorms and is washed away.

Animal species are abundant in tropical rain forests. Birds are common and include parrots, toucans, and birds-of-paradise. There are many reptiles in the rain forest, such as chameleons, iguanas, and tree-dwelling snakes. There are thousands of insect species as well. Mammals such as monkeys and sloths are found in the trees, while animals such as the jaguar seek prey along the forest floor.

Tropical rain forests are found all over the world. The three main areas where rain forests exist are in the Amazon-Orinoco river basins in South America; the Congo, Niger, and Zambezi river basins of central and western Africa; and in the Malaysia-Indonesia-New Guinea areas of Asia. The rain forests of these three areas differ from each other in the exact species of plants and animals present, but they are remarkably similar in forest structure and ecology.

Why is soil in the tropical rain forests poor in nutrients?

FIGURE 34–9.

The toucan lives in the tropical rain forests of Brazil.

34:8 Tropical Savannas

What limiting factor is responsible for the development of a savanna?

When the rainfall in the tropics is divided into wet and dry seasons, a tropical grassland or **savanna** develops. In tropical savannas, the rainfall pattern prevents the growth of forests. Instead, there are large areas of grassland with scattered small trees and shrubs. During the dry season, savannas are subject to periodic fires. Trees and grass must be resistant to both drought and fire to survive. Therefore, the number of species found in tropical savannas is not large. Three or four genera of grasses are dominant, and the few tree species in the savannas are entirely different from the trees of the rain forest. Baobabs, euphorbias, acacia, and palms are the trees of the savanna.

The most extensive savannas are in Africa, but savannas are also found in South America and Australia. The Serengeti Plain extends over vast areas of Tanzania and Kenya in East Africa. You may have seen photographs of herds of wildebeest, zebra, and gazelle on the Serengeti. Lions and cheetahs are carnivores that feed on these herds. Other large herbivores found in savannas include elephants, giraffes, and rhinoceroses. Kangaroos and wallabies are common in the Australian savanna.

34:9 Temperate Forests

Temperate forests are found in areas where rainfall averages between 50 cm and 150 cm annually and is distributed evenly throughout the year. Temperate forests have four seasons, with warm summers and cold winters. The soil in temperate forests is rich and deep, with active microbial populations.

FIGURE 34–10.

Large termite mounds (a) and families of elephants (b) are common in the African savanna.

a

b

FIGURE 34–11.

Raccoons are common in temperate forests.

Most temperate forest trees are deciduous. Recall from Chapter 16 that deciduous trees lose their leaves all at once each year, usually in the fall. This loss of leaves allows the trees to conserve water in the colder months. In the summer, deciduous plants have thick foliage that enables them to produce large amounts of food. This food is stored for use in the other seasons.

At one time, temperate deciduous forests covered eastern North America, all of Europe, parts of Japan and Australia, and the tip of South America. Over time, human populations have changed much of this original forest by cutting trees for lumber and clearing land for agriculture.

How have the temperate forests been reduced in size?

As you change latitude, the community structure of temperate forests also changes. Beech, birch, and maple trees are common in central regions of North America, while oaks and hickories are more abundant in western and southern regions. Shrubs and grasses are found throughout temperate forest ecosystems, and many animal groups are represented here. Squirrels, foxes, raccoons, and deer are common. Many bird species migrate to warmer climates as winter approaches.

34:10 Temperate Grasslands

Grasslands are found in temperate zones where rainfall is too low to support forest ecosystems but higher than that of most desert regions. Rainfall is not evenly distributed over the year. The root systems of grasses in temperate grasslands sometimes extend 1 to 2 m deep, forming areas of thick sod. The prairies of North America, the pampas of South America, and the steppes of Central Asia are all temperate grasslands.

Running, leaping, and burrowing for protection are adaptations that have helped animals of temperate grasslands survive the lack of trees. In North America, coyotes, prairie dogs, and bison are common grassland animals. Many kinds of rodents are found in temperate grasslands, as are different species of hawks that feed on them.

FIGURE 34–12.

Herds of bison are native to the North American grasslands.

How can a grassland become a desert?

Temperate grasslands cover about 25 percent of Earth's land surface and are North America's largest biome. Grasslands worldwide have been altered a great deal as a result of human activities, such as grazing of domestic animals. When grasses are consumed by overgrazing and the roots are trampled by herds of animals, the grass cannot recover. Without roots to hold soil, the soil may be washed away by rainfall or blown away by wind, resulting in desert conditions.

34:11 The Taiga

Circling the northern hemisphere between 50°N and 60°N latitude is a vast forest region known as the northern forest or the taiga (TI guh). In the taiga, winters are long and cold, with temperatures occasionally dropping to −70°C. Most of the precipitation in the taiga is in the form of snow. In northern Europe and North America, spruce trees are the dominant species in the taiga. In Siberia, pine, cedar, and larch are common. These thick stands of trees permit little light to penetrate to the forest floor. As a result, there are few species of grass or shrubs. Mosses and lichens cover the forest floor.

Plants in the taiga have needle-like leaves that reduce water loss and conserve heat. Most coniferous trees are shaped like cones, with a point at the top and broadening toward the base. When snow falls on these trees, it tends to roll down the tree, reducing damage to the branches.

Summers in the taiga are short, lasting only two to four months. Insects such as mosquitoes, black flies, gnats, and horseflies abound in the summer. These insects make the taiga inhospitable to humans and very difficult for migrating herds of caribou and reindeer.

FIGURE 34–13.

The taiga is home to birds such as the crossbill.

Animals in the taiga often have thick layers of fat beneath their skin. Many taiga animals change color in the winter and blend in with the snow. Broad footpads are another adaptation to the snowy conditions. Musk ox and black bears are common in the taiga. Birds, such as the crossbill and the nutcracker, typically have bills adapted to removing seeds from the cones of the trees. Numerous insects live in or on the trees. Weevils, leaf beetles, and bark beetles feed on the needles, leaves, and wood.

34:12 The Tundra

Nearly 20 percent of Earth's land surface is covered by an icy plain known as the arctic tundra. The tundra is located in the extreme northern part of the northern hemisphere near the North Pole. Arctic tundra extends northward from North America, Europe, and Asia.

The primary limiting factors in the tundra are very low temperatures and a short growing season. The ground remains frozen except for a few centimeters on the surface during the growing season. The permanently frozen lower layer of soil in the tundra is called **permafrost.** Vegetation in the tundra consists mostly of lichens, grasses, and dwarf woody plants such as cranberry bushes. Many of these plants have small, hairy, leathery leaves that conserve water. Small size and a rapid life cycle are common adaptations of plants to the short summers.

A few mammals are found year-round in the tundra, despite such poor conditions. Caribou in North America and reindeer in northern Europe travel across the tundra in search of food. Musk ox, arctic hares, and arctic foxes all live in the tundra.

NoteWorthy

The word *tundra* is from the Russian language and means "north of the timberline." The word *taiga* is Russian for "subarctic evergreen forest." Both types of biomes cover large expanses of Soviet Siberia.

FIGURE 34–14.

Caribou move across the tundra seaching for food.

Some mountainous areas have tundra-like conditions at high elevations above the treeline. These areas are called alpine tundra after the European Alps, where such conditions exist. Alpine tundra conditions are also found on a few peaks in the Adirondack Mountains of New York State, in the Rockies, and in the Himalayas of Asia. Alpine tundra differs from Arctic tundra in that the soil is not permanently frozen, there is more snow, and the amount of sunlight each day is greater.

Both tundra and alpine tundra biomes are very fragile ecosystems. Small alterations to the environment of the tundra can destroy it. Once the tundra has been altered, it may take hundreds of years to recover.

REVIEW

11. Name seven terrestrial biomes.
12. List three factors that limit the distribution of biomes.
13. Name three differences between the tundra and the taiga.
14. **SKILL REVIEW:** Make a table to show climate, plant types, plant adaptations, animal types, and animal adaptations for the different biomes. For more help, refer to Organizing Information in the Skill Handbook, pages 810 to 813.
15. **USING CONCEPTS:** Compare the Amazon jungle, a tropical rain forest, with the northern Mississippi River valley, a temperate forest.

MISSION TO PLANET EARTH

The decade of the 1990s promises to be filled with spacecraft exploring the stars, the solar system, and our biosphere. One exciting space project is a joint mission by NASA, the European Space Agency (ESA), and Japan. The project is called the Earth Observing System (EOS). Five giant orbiting platforms will be launched beginning in 1996. NASA and ESA will launch two and Japan will launch one. The space platforms will weigh about 15 metric tons each and will be designed to operate for at least 15 years. The platforms will provide the first comprehensive look at how the world's environment changes over time.

These satellites will monitor Earth with instruments that will measure temperature, wind velocity and direction, and atmospheric chemistry. The sensitive eyes of EOS will monitor the shrinking of tropical rain forests and polar ice caps. Instruments that can detect and measure photosynthetic pigments will help determine the role of ocean organisms in absorbing carbon dioxide. Infrared sensors will measure chemical reactions in the atmosphere that lead to ozone depletion.

The data collected by EOS will be enough to fill the equivalent of 10 000 Washington, D.C., phone books every day. Analysis of this data will enable researchers to produce computer simulations that can predict and assess the long-term effects of human activities.

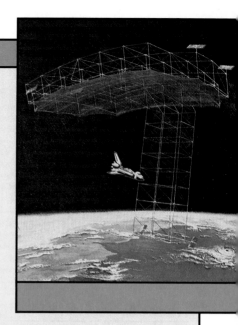

The EOS will monitor environmental conditions on Earth.

AQUATIC BIOMES

Over 70 percent of Earth's surface is covered with water. Of that total, over 95 percent is found in the oceans. The remaining 5 percent is fresh water.

Aquatic biomes are divided into two groups depending upon salinity, or the concentration of dissolved salts in the water. Saltwater communities include oceans, coral reefs, and coastal wetlands. Freshwater communities may be flowing water systems such as rivers and streams, or standing water systems, such as lakes, ponds, some wetland areas, and artificial reservoirs. Temperature, light, dissolved salts, and dissolved oxygen are limiting factors in aquatic biomes.

Objectives:
- identify the different zones found in a marine ecosystem and characterize the types of organisms found in each zone.
- explain the differences between oligotrophic and eutrophic lakes.
- describe the process of eutrophication.

34:13 Marine Ecosystems

Ecologists generally describe the ocean in terms of zones, with many habitats within each zone. If you stood on the shore at the edge of the ocean and were able to walk on the ocean floor, you

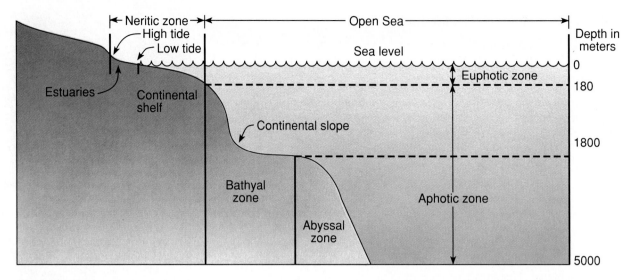

FIGURE 34–15.

The ocean is divided into zones based on depth and amount of sunlight penetration.

What are three zones in the ocean based on depth?

aphotic:
  a (GK) without
  phos (GK) light
euphotic:
  eu (GK) well
  phos (GK) light

would soon come to the end of the continental shelf. The area from the shore to the end of the continental shelf is the **neritic** (nuh RIHT ihk) **zone,** or the zone near to the shore. From the edge of the neritic zone, there is a continental slope, and then the ocean floor levels off. This area is called the **bathyal** (BATH ee ul) **zone,** or deep ocean zone. The bathyal zone extends from 180 m to about 1800 m in depth. Finally you would arrive at the **abyssal** (uh BIS ul) **zone,** or the very bottom of the ocean, which goes down to about 5000 m.

Another system of zones in the ocean can be described by the depth of sunlight penetration. The upper layer of the ocean, where light penetrates, is the **euphotic** (yoo FOHT ik) **zone.** In this area, phytoplankton produce food through photosynthesis. Zooplankton eat the phytoplankton and are in turn eaten by small fish such as herring. The neritic zone generally falls within the euphotic zone and is very productive. Below the euphotic zone is the **aphotic** (ay FOHT ik) **zone,** an area where little light is able to penetrate. Organisms in the aphotic zone depend on food that filters down from the euphotic zone. Study the zones of the ocean shown in Figure 34–15.

Animals in the ocean have adapted to the zone in which they live. In the bathyal zone, which is dark and murky, fish that are capable of producing their own light are found. Animals in the abyssal zone are subject to tremendous water pressure. Fish in the abyssal zone have large jaws and teeth, small skeletons, and slow metabolisms. These adaptations allow the fish to survive in the deep, cold waters.

In areas where ocean waters mix with freshwater rivers and streams, an **estuary** (ES chuh wer ee) is formed. Salt marshes and tropical mangrove swamps are examples of estuarine environments. These areas serve as breeding grounds for many species of birds, fish, and marine invertebrates. Clams, crabs, and small fish like the minnow are common in estuaries. Many species, including humans, rely on these areas for food. The unique combination of fresh and saltwater environments found in estuaries supports a rich diversity of species.

34:14 Freshwater Environments

Lakes, reservoirs, ponds, bogs, swamps, and marshes are considered inland standing water habitats. Springs, brooks, streams, and rivers are known as running water habitats. Both types of communities have low salinity and are associated with land.

Lakes and ponds occur in areas where depressions in the land are filled with fresh water. Both may have layers or zones similar to those found in the open sea. Lakes tend to cover larger surface areas than ponds and may be quite deep. **Oligotrophic** (AHL ih goh TROH fihk) lakes are those that are cold and deep, with few nutrients, but large amounts of dissolved oxygen. Shallow, warm lakes with a large supply of nutrients but limited dissolved oxygen are **eutrophic** lakes. In lakes and ponds, succession occurs just as on land. New lakes are oligotrophic, but as they age, they gradually change until they become eutrophic. The natural aging of a lake is called **eutrophication** (yoo troh fuh KAY shun). Sediment fills the lake and the depth decreases. Nutrients accumulate and water temperature rises. As water temperature rises, the amount of dissolved oxygen in the water decreases, and the species of organisms change.

The natural aging of lakes causes a change in the number and types of populations in the lake. Oligotrophic lakes have low plankton populations but may contain fish species such as trout. Eutrophic lakes support large plankton populations that use large amounts of oxygen. Species adapted to warmer waters and low oxygen may live in these nutrient-rich lakes. Catfish and carp are common in eutrophic lakes. Human activity often causes an increase in nutrient levels in lakes and ponds and speeds up eutrophication. For example, fertilizers that contain large amounts of nitrates run off the land and into streams and ponds.

Water from rivers and streams flows downhill toward the oceans. Organisms have adapted to the swift currents and cling to rock surfaces along the stream bottom. Insect larvae attach themselves to rocks by suckers that develop from their gills or other body parts. Rapid stream movement adds oxygen to the water and stirs up nutrients. In the slow-moving areas of rivers and streams, nutrients accumulate in the warm water and species are more diverse.

FIGURE 34–16.

Rapid eutrophication is causing this pond to become covered with algae.

What are some differences between oligotrophic and eutrophic lakes?

REVIEW

16. Name three zones found in the ocean.
17. Explain the difference between the euphotic and aphotic zones.
18. What happens during eutrophication?
19. **SKILL REVIEW:** You believe that a lake near your home is undergoing rapid eutrophication. Describe how you would test your hypothesis. For more help, refer to Designing an Experiment in the Skill Handbook, pages 802 to 803.
20. **USING CONCEPTS:** Explain what might happen to marine fish if salt marshes are filled in for housing developments.

CHAPTER REVIEW

SUMMARY

1. Each species has its own limits of tolerance to environmental conditions. Limiting factors may restrict the abundance, growth, or distribution of organisms. **34:1, 34:2**
2. Succession is a change in the structure of a community. Primary succession occurs on bare land. When succession is interrupted and begins again, it is called secondary succession. The final stage of succession is the climax community. **34:3, 34:4, 34:5**
3. There are seven major terrestrial biomes. The distribution of biomes is determined by precipitation, temperature, and light intensity. Each biome is characterized by its types of climax communities. **34:6, 34:7, 34:8, 34:9, 34:10, 34:11, 34:12**
4. Oceans are divided into several zones. Estuaries are formed when freshwater rivers mix with ocean waters. **34:13**
5. Freshwater environments include standing water and running water habitats. **34:14**

LANGUAGE OF BIOLOGY

abyssal zone	limiting factor
aphotic zone	limits of tolerance
bathyal zone	neritic zone
biomes	oligotrophic
climax community	permafrost
estuary	primary succession
euphotic zone	savanna
eutrophic	secondary succession
eutrophication	succession

Choose the word or phrase from the list above that completes the sentence.

1. A factor that determines the survival of an organism in its environment is a(n) ____.
2. The area of the ocean that light penetrates is the ____.
3. A gradual change in the structure of a community over time is called ____.
4. The permanently frozen layer of soil in the tundra is called ____.
5. The type of succession that takes place in an abandoned orchard is ____.
6. The final stage of succession is the ____.
7. Large geographic units with climax communities similar to those in other parts of the world are known as ____.
8. A young, cold, nutrient-poor lake is called a(n) ____ lake.
9. A grassland in the tropics is called a(n) ____.
10. An area in which ocean water mixes with freshwater rivers is a(n) ____.

REVIEWING CONCEPTS

Choose the word or phrase that completes the sentence or answers the question.

11. Ecological succession ____.
    a. does not depend on abiotic factors
    b. is the gradual change in a community
    c. begins with a climax community
    d. is not observed in desert communities
12. Primary succession occurs on ____.
    a. cleared fields   c. sand dunes
    b. orchards   d. burned forests
13. An organism's limits of tolerance ____.
    a. are its ability to reproduce
    b. are the conditions it survives under
    c. are controlled by its diet
    d. are always controlled by rainfall
14. The bathyal zone is ____.
    a. the middle zone   c. 5000 m deep
    b. near the shore   d. the deepest zone
15. Excess nitrates in a lake ____.
    a. cause the water temperature to drop
    b. increase the rate of eutrophication
    c. cause the oxygen level to rise
    d. interrupt succession

16. The differences between forests and grass-lands are the result of different ____.
   a. amounts of rainfall
   b. temperatures
   c. amounts of light
   d. all of these

17. If the young and mature trees in a forest are the same species, the forest is ____.
   a. a climax community
   b. not stable
   c. a pioneer community
   d. dying

18. Which is NOT associated with deserts?
   a. sandy soil
   b. plants with spines
   c. nocturnal animals
   d. numerous lichens

19. Tundra conditions above the treeline are called ____ zones.
   a. Alpine
   b. European
   c. Adirondack
   d. Arctic

20. Secondary succession occurs on ____.
   a. land exposed by retreating glaciers
   b. newly formed volcanic islands
   c. abandoned farmlands
   d. coral reefs exposed to air

UNDERSTANDING CONCEPTS

Answer the following questions using complete sentences.

21. What is the relationship between an organism's limits of tolerance and limiting factors?
22. Describe the sequence of events that might occur in an area if a volcano erupted.
23. What are the traits of a pioneer species?
24. What determines the type of climax community that will develop in an area?
25. How are adaptations of desert plants and tundra plants similar?
26. Explain why the soil in tropical rain forests is poor in nutrients.
27. Describe ways in which temperate forests differ from forests of the taiga.

28. What limiting factors shape the tundra?
29. Compare oligotrophic and eutrophic lakes.
30. Why do trout survive better in oligotrophic lakes than eutrophic lakes?

APPLYING CONCEPTS

Answer the following questions using complete sentences.

31. Why does a tropical rain forest that has been cleared make poor farmland?
32. During succession, species bring about their own destruction by changing their environment. Explain this statement.
33. Why are oceans important to sustaining life on this planet?
34. Flies live in almost every biome. Describe their limits of tolerance for temperature.
35. How would succession in Yellowstone National Park be affected if animals did not return after the fire of 1988?

EXTENSIONS

1. Design the ideal desert garden.
2. Design an experiment for comparing the types of soil organisms in grassy and forest areas.
3. Try to determine the type of succession taking place in a crack in a sidewalk.

READINGS

Allen, William H. "Biocultural Restoration of a Tropical Forest." *Bioscience,* Mar. 1988, pp. 156–161.

Milne, Brian. "Warming to an Arctic Spring." *International Wildlife,* May–June 1987, pp. 30–34.

Ripper, Chuck. "Sketchbook: Secret Life of a Forest." *National Wildlife,* June–July 1987, pp. 30–31.

Chapter 35

HUMAN DEMANDS ON THE BIOSPHERE

Coconuts

What things would you need if you were marooned on an island like the one shown in the photograph? What would you eat? You could probably fish in the lagoon and eat coconuts from the coconut tree. What would you drink? You can't drink seawater, so you would need a source of fresh water. Coconuts are full of water when they are fresh and are a rich source of nutrients as well. Would coconuts and fish provide all the nutrients you needed? How about clothing? Your clothes would last for a while, but constant exposure to salt water and sun would destroy them. Where would you sleep? How would you cook? These are just a few problems you would have on an island where the resources are limited.

RESOURCES AND HUMAN ACTIVITIES

Our planet Earth is like an island floating in space. Earth's resources are limited, too, although they are much greater than those of an island in the ocean. Some of Earth's resources can be used only once. In this section, you will learn about Earth's resources and how humans have used or overused them.

35:1 Resources Are Limited

On an island, you can see what resources are available at a glance. Sunlight, salt water, sand, palm trees, and a few land and sea animals are the primary natural resources found there. A **natural resource** is any part of the natural environment used by humans for their benefit. Soil, water, forests, wildlife, minerals, and even human populations may be natural resources. On Earth, natural resources are not distributed evenly. Some areas have large amounts of a few important resources. For example, Malaysia contains more than one-third of the world's tin. Can you imagine life in the United States without tin cans? Other areas have large amounts of many resources. Rain forests have ample supplies of wood, fruits, and rubber. Some areas, of course, have very few resources. In fact, deserts may be made up almost entirely of sand!

Objectives:
- distinguish between renewable and nonrenewable resources and list examples of each.
- describe how population size changes with different birth and death rates, and identify the factors that affect population growth rate.
- distinguish between density-dependent factors and density-independent factors.
- describe problems caused by human overpopulation.

FIGURE 35–1.

The dodo became extinct over 300 years ago.

What is a fossil fuel?

Oil rig

Natural resources can be grouped into two categories depending upon their ability to be recycled. When a material is recyclable, it can be used more than once. A **renewable resource** is a natural resource that can be recycled by natural processes. Natural recycling involves the decomposing of a substance by bacteria and fungi in the soil. It also involves the production of new resources by biological means, such as the reproducing of plants. Examples of renewable or potentially renewable resources are soils, air, water, plants, animals, and some minerals. A **nonrenewable resource** is a natural resource that is available in limited amounts and is not replaced or recycled by natural processes. Can you think of a nonrenewable resource that you depend on every day?

The next time you stop at a gas station, think about the resource you are using to power your car. Is gasoline a renewable or nonrenewable resource? Gasoline, kerosene, plastics, and even petroleum jelly are all products made from petroleum, a nonrenewable resource. Petroleum, coal, and natural gas are fossil fuels. A **fossil fuel** is the remains of organisms that lived millions of years ago. All of these fossil fuels are considered nonrenewable because of the great span of time required to convert organic organisms into petroleum. Other nonrenewable resources that humans depend on are metals such as copper, iron, tin, silver, uranium, and gold. Also, minerals that are recycled very slowly, such as phosphorus, are considered nonrenewable. It takes 500 to 1000 years for a 2.5 cm deep layer of topsoil to form. Should topsoil be considered a nonrenewable resource?

Could animals or plants ever be nonrenewable? In most cases, plants and animals can continue to reproduce and replace themselves as long as the environment remains stable. However, some plant and animal species have become extinct. You could say these organisms are nonrenewable. Have you ever called anyone a dodo? You know that dodo means silly or stupid. But did you know that this term comes from the extinct dodo bird? This bird, once found on the island of Mauritius, was unable to fly. It was so unafraid of humans that when Europeans landed on the island, the dodo birds walked right up to them and were promptly killed for food. In a few short years, all the dodos were dead. Humans were responsible for making a nonrenewable resource out of a previously renewable one.

35:2 Human Population Growth

No matter where you live, you probably have seen changes in your community over the last few years. Perhaps new roads have been built, new buildings and houses have been constructed, or dirt roads have been replaced by asphalt roads. There may be new schools or new shopping centers. Why do you think new schools and roads are needed? There probably are more people living in your community than there were when you were born. The human population in your community has grown.

Recall from Chapter 34 that temperature, water, oxygen, food availability, and space are factors that limit the growth and distribution of populations. A population might expand indefinitely if these limiting factors are in abundant supply. The rate at which a population grows is determined by the difference between its birth rate and its death rate. If the birth rate remains the same and the death rate falls, the total population size will increase. The population also will increase if the death rate stays the same and the birth rate increases. Factors that limit human populations specifically include too little food, lack of safe drinking water, poor medical care, and contagious diseases.

The populations of different countries grow at different rates. In 1988, the world's annual growth rate was 1.7 percent. In many developing countries the rate was nearly 3 percent, while in Western Europe the rate was 0.3 percent. The growth rate in the United States

FIGURE 35–2.

World human population growth has risen dramatically since the middle of the nineteenth century (a). The age structure of a population is the number of individuals of each sex and age in a population (b).

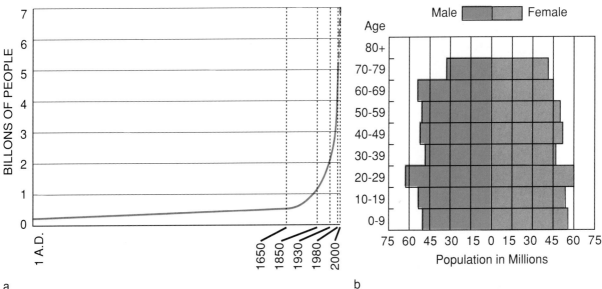

a

b

What major factor determines population growth rate?

in 1988 was 0.7 percent. The age structure of a population is a big factor in determining its growth potential. The **age structure** of a population is the percentage of each sex at each age in a population. Birth rates in less developed countries may be higher than in more technologically advanced countries because people in developing countries have many children to be sure a few will survive. Additional reasons for large families might include lack of family planning or lack of resources such as contraceptives.

As more food and better medical care are developed, death rates often decline. In more developed countries like the United States, birth rates are low, but not as low as in Western Europe. The population continues to increase in the United States because the death rate is decreasing faster than the birth rate. If the birth rate and death rate become equal, the population eventually will stabilize. The length of time needed to stabilize population size is affected by its age structure, movement of individuals into the area, and birth and death rates.

Certain factors, known as **density-independent factors,** affect populations no matter what their size. The density of a population is the number of individuals in a particular area. Temperature changes, precipitation, earthquakes, natural fires, and floods are density-independent factors. For example, all the plants and animals in a forest, no matter how many plants and animals there are, will be affected if there is a forest fire. Many of the animals will escape and leave the forest; many of the animals and plants will die. Factors that affect populations and that are related to population size are **density-dependent factors.** Density-dependent factors are most obvious in large populations. Space, waste materials, and soil nutrients are examples of density-dependent factors. For example, as the population density increases, space and nutrients become limiting, and waste products accumulate and must be broken down or stored.

In 1988, the world's human population exceeded five billion individuals. About 87 million people are added annually. This growth of the human population has become a limiting factor for other species.

FIGURE 35–3.

Human populations are affected by density-independent factors, such as earthquakes.

More humans require more goods and services and more land to grow food and build houses. Many plant and animal species are being destroyed as a result of the human need for more food, shelter, waste storage, and space. Because of human need, the tropical rain forests of the world are being cut down at an extremely rapid rate. These forests hold 40 to 50 percent of all the species of plants and animals on Earth. By 1988, 80 percent of the African rain forests, 60 percent of the Asian rain forests, and 40 percent of the South American rain forests had been destroyed.

REVIEW

1. Explain the difference between renewable resources and nonrenewable resources.
2. Name three factors that limit the growth rate of the human population.
3. Distinguish between density-independent factors and density-dependent factors.
4. **SKILL REVIEW:** Draw a graph to show the changes in a population when the birth rate increases but the death rate remains stable. For more help, refer to Organizing Information in the Skill Handbook, pages 810 to 813.
5. **USING CONCEPTS:** What limiting factors might affect a population of monkeys in a tropical rain forest?

HUMAN INTERACTIONS WITH THE ENVIRONMENT

Science and technology are helping people to live longer in all types of environments. But, technology also has many harmful side effects. Fossil fuels provide humans with a source of electricity and energy to operate vehicles. The disadvantage of burning fossil fuels is that they release dangerous gases into the air. Chemical fertilizers allow us to produce more food on smaller amounts of land. The disadvantage of using fertilizers is that these chemicals become pollutants when they enter the water supply. In this section, you will learn about four problems resulting from technology—air pollution, water pollution, land pollution, and endangered species.

35:3 Air Pollution

What does the term air pollution mean to you? You may think of factory smokestacks belching thick, gray smoke into the sky or car exhaust. Pollution occurs when any part of the environment is contaminated or becomes unclean from waste products. A factory

Objectives:
- identify the major sources of air pollution.
- describe the causes of acid precipitation, the greenhouse effect, and the depletion of the ozone layer.
- identify different types of problems associated with water pollution.
- list some types of land pollution.
- identify the differences between biodegradable and non-biodegradable pollutants.
- identify ways in which humans place wildlife in danger.
- distinguish between threatened and endangered species.

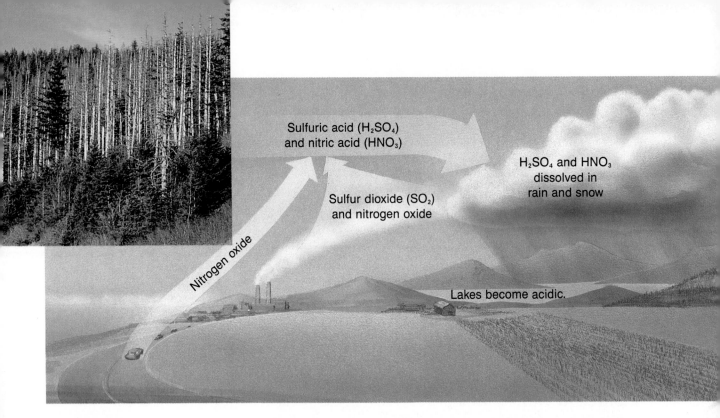

Sulfuric acid (H₂SO₄) and nitric acid (HNO₃)

H₂SO₄ and HNO₃ dissolved in rain and snow

Sulfur dioxide (SO₂) and nitrogen oxide

Nitrogen oxide

Lakes become acidic.

FIGURE 35–4.

Acid precipitation forms when sulfur dioxides and nitrogen oxides from the burning of fossil fuels combine with water vapor in the air. The forest in this photo is suffering the effects of acid precipitation.

may produce large quantities of sulfur dioxide, nitrogen dioxide, or small particles of ash and dust called **particulates.** Cars release large amounts of carbon monoxide, nitrogen oxides, hydrocarbons, and heavy metals such as lead into the air. These pollutants contaminate the air. A **pollutant** is a waste product that makes the environment unclean or impure.

Some air pollution is produced naturally. Volcanoes erupt and spew tons of rocks, dust, ash, and poisonous gases into the air. In 1988, millions of hectares of forest land in the western United States burned, creating air pollution problems for humans and forest organisms. However, most air pollution is the result of human activity. The primary source of air pollution is the burning of fossil fuels for energy. Coal-burning power plants are a major source of sulfur dioxide. In the United States, over 25 million metric tons of sulfur dioxide gas are put into the air each year. Sulfur dioxide is responsible for two-thirds of the acidity in acid precipitation. **Acid precipitation** is rain, snow, or fog in which sulfur dioxide and nitrogen oxides are dissolved to form weak acid solutions, Figure 35–4. Nitrogen oxides are pollutants that form as a result of the combustion of petroleum in car and truck engines and furnaces. In addition to causing acid precipitation, sulfur dioxide can irritate lung tissue and lower the body's resistance to respiratory infections.

In areas subject to acid precipitation, the acidified rain or snow falls onto surface water. The acids in the precipitation reduce the pH of surface water, thus killing many organisms that cannot tolerate low pH levels. Many lakes in New York and Canada have pH levels between 4.2 and 5.0. This high acidity has had serious results. All the fish populations in 300 lakes in the Adirondack Mountains have been wiped out as a result of acid precipitation.

In many developing countries, forests and grasslands are completely cleared for farming by burning. This slash-and-burn agriculture is responsible for destroying millions of hectares of tropical forests. When large areas are burned on purpose or by accident, two effects are seen. First, the burning itself releases large quantities of carbon dioxide into the atmosphere. Second, the forest is gone and can no longer remove carbon dioxide from the atmosphere. Concentrations of carbon dioxide, water vapor, nitrogen oxides, and other pollutants in the atmosphere influence the temperature near the ground. Together, these gases form a layer around Earth and act like the panes of glass in a greenhouse. They allow sunlight to pass through and warm the surface of Earth. This heat from Earth radiates up and some escapes into space. The rest is trapped by the layer of gases. As the layer of gases builds up, more and more heat is trapped near Earth's surface. This process of heat retention by atmospheric gases is known as the **greenhouse effect.**

In the upper atmosphere, oxygen is transformed into ozone in a photochemical reaction with ultraviolet solar radiation. Ozone is a molecule composed of three oxygen atoms. The ozone layer prevents excessive ultraviolet radiation from reaching Earth's surface. Large quantities of ultraviolet radiation can cause skin cancer and eye problems. Ultraviolet radiation may affect marine and freshwater food webs by destroying phytoplankton populations. Phytoplankton are important because they are the primary producers in aquatic ecosystems. They also produce oxygen and absorb carbon dioxide through photosynthesis.

What activities add carbon dioxide to the atmosphere?

FIGURE 35–5.

The greenhouse effect results when large amounts of carbon dioxide and other gases trap heat near the surface of Earth.

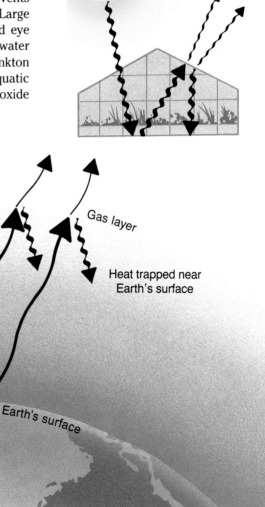

Solar radiation

Gas layer

Heat trapped near Earth's surface

Earth's surface

FIGURE 35–6.

Smog forms when nitrogen oxides and hydrocarbons combine with water vapor in the air.

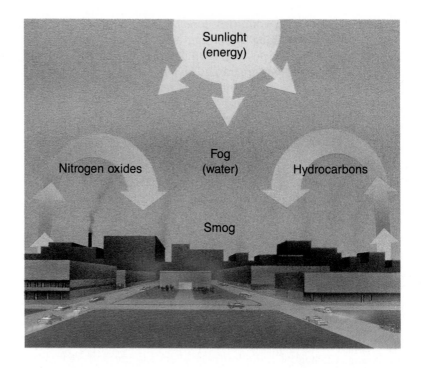

The destruction of the ozone layer could cause serious problems for life on Earth. Chemicals called chlorofluorocarbons (CFCs) play a major role in ozone destruction. These chemicals are used as insulators, coolants, and in spray can propellants. Major sources of CFCs in the United States are the manufacture of plastic foam food containers and freon, a gas used as a coolant in air conditioners. When CFCs absorb ultraviolet light, they release chlorine atoms that react with and destroy the ozone layer. Even if CFCs were banned today, their effects would continue for about 100 years because they move slowly into the upper atmosphere.

Smog is the result of ultraviolet radiation reacting with nitrogen oxides and hydrocarbons from automobile exhausts in the lower atmosphere, Figure 35–6. **Smog** is a fog made heavier and darker by smoke and chemical fumes. The word *smog* is a combination of the words *smoke* and *fog*. Smog is irritating to the eyes, nose, and lungs, and can be particularly dangerous for those who already have respiratory difficulties.

Some air pollution problems can be found inside your own home. You may have heard of radon, a radioactive gas that occurs naturally in the ground. Radon can build up to dangerous levels in poorly ventilated buildings. Another type of indoor air pollution comes from insulation that contains formaldehyde, a colorless gas used as a preservative. Formaldehyde leaks into the air and causes chronic headaches and intestinal problems. Homes constructed today are often airtight for energy conservation. However, reduced air flow may increase temperatures and trap pollutants within a house. Installing additional fans and ducts to carry polluted air outside the building can reduce indoor pollution.

What is smog?

35:4 Water Pollution

In the spring of 1989, an oil tanker ran aground off the shore of Alaska and spilled tonnes of crude oil into the sea. Sea birds, otters, fish, and other sea organisms died. Thousands of volunteers and officials helped in the cleanup. However, there was so much oil that it was impossible for the workers to restore the beaches to their original state, to clean the oil off all the wildlife that became coated with it, or to remove all the oil that floated in the ocean.

Water is the most abundant resource on Earth. If all the water on Earth were equal to 100 L of water, nearly 97 L of it would be salt water. Fresh water would account for 3 L out of the total. Of those 3 L, only 0.003 L would be usable. Fresh water is found in lakes, rivers, and streams, or as groundwater stored in aquifers.

Water pollutants are grouped into five basic categories: organic substances, inorganic substances, sediments, heat, and radioactive substances. Organic sources of water pollution include sewage, animal manure, disease-causing microbes, oil, gasoline, fertilizers, pesticides, and plastics. Inorganic pollutants include plant nutrients such as nitrates and phosphates, and chemicals such as acids, salts, toxic metals, and their compounds. Sediment pollutants are particulates that have been mixed with water. Sediments include soil, silt, or small particles of organic and inorganic substances. Heat pollution results when power plants use water from lakes or reservoirs for cooling purposes. The water may be returned to its source several degrees warmer than it was originally. Warmer water holds less oxygen than cool water, and so organisms die due to lack of oxygen.

NoteWorthy

Lake Baikal in the Soviet Union is over 1.5 km deep and is estimated to hold one-fourth of the world's fresh water.

0.003% usable water

3% fresh water

97% salt water

FIGURE 35–7.

Only a small fraction of the water covering Earth is usable fresh water. Spilling oil in our water supplies disrupts ecosystems and destroys wildlife.

BIOLAB *Pollution* 35

Problem: What are the effects of pollutants on living organisms?

Materials

Euglena culture
stereomicroscope
microscope slides (7)
coverslips (7)
methyl cellulose
medicine droppers (8)
paper towels

sodium chloride (NaCl)
  (1%, 3%, 5%)
copper sulfate
  (CuSO₄)
  (0.5, 1.0, 5.0 mg/L)
water
wax pencil

Procedures

1. Copy the data table.
2. Develop a **hypothesis** about how each of the chemical pollutants will affect *Euglena*.
3. Label a microscope slide "water." Add a drop of *Euglena* culture. Add a drop of methyl cellulose and a coverslip.
4. Observe the slide for three minutes using the stereomicroscope. Note size, shape, color, and type of movement. Record this information in your data table.
5. At the edge of the coverslip, add one drop of water to the slide. Place a small piece of paper towel at the opposite edge of the coverslip. Carefully observe the reactions of the *Euglena* as the water moves under the coverslip. Notice any changes in shape and movement.
6. Label six slides with the names and concentrations of the test solutions.

7. Repeat step 3 using one of the slides prepared in step 6. Repeat step 5 using a test solution. Be sure to use the same test solution as marked on the slide.
8. Note the time. To determine recovery time, replace the test solution with water using the same procedure as in step 5. Observe the *Euglena*'s reaction. If the organism recovers, record the length of time required to bring about recovery. If it does not recover, write "no recovery" in your table.
9. Repeat steps 7 and 8 with the other test solutions.
10. Put your data on the chalkboard. Compare your data with the rest of the class.
11. Wash your hands after handling microbes. Give the microbes to your teacher for proper disposal.

Questions and Conclusion

1. Did your organism show any difference in recovery time for the different test solutions?
2. Was your **hypothesis** correct? Explain.
3. Since *Euglena* are important food sources to organisms that live in water, what kinds of effects would be caused by their death?
Conclusion: What can you say about the effects of various pollutants on living organisms?

Data and Observations

Appearance of Organism:			
Solution	**Concentration**	**Reaction**	**Recovery Time**
NaCl	1%		
	3%		
	5%		
CuSO₄	0.5 mg/L		
	1.0 mg/L		
	5.0 mg/L		

a

FIGURE 35–8.

Using water for irrigation can lower water levels underground, leading to the formation of sinkholes (a). What to do with solid wastes is an ever-increasing problem (b).

b

The use of water to irrigate farmland causes unique problems. Water pumped from underground often contains dissolved mineral salts. When this water is used on the surface for irrigation, some of the water evaporates, leaving the salts behind. Over time, the soil becomes saltier and saltier. The result is that the soil can produce fewer and fewer crops. Another problem caused by irrigation is that water is removed from underground aquifers faster than it can be replaced. The level of the water goes down and the soil above it collapses to create a giant sinkhole. When water supplies in one area decrease, humans often use up the water from adjacent areas. As a result, there may not be enough water left to move into rivers or lakes. Again, the water level goes down and breeding grounds for birds and fish and food webs in the area are affected.

What are some of the problems associated with water used for irrigation?

35:5 Land Pollution

Did you stop at a fast-food restaurant for lunch this week? You probably ate the food—but what did you do with the plastic foam container, the plastic straw, and the paper cup? You probably threw them away in a trash container. What happens to your trash after that? Where is it stored? Does it ever decompose? The trash from your lunch becomes part of the billions of metric tons of solid wastes that are dumped, burned, and buried each year all over the world.

NoteWorthy

Each year, residents of the United States throw away 1.6 billion disposable diapers, 1.6 billion ink pens, 2 billion razors and blades, and 220 million tires.

FIGURE 35–9.

Toxic wastes are put into huge drums and buried in landfills.

Unfortunately, Larry had always approached from the side that wasn't posted, and a natural phenomenon was destroyed before anyone could react.

When you think of land pollution, you probably think about garbage. The solid wastes that make up garbage are the cans, bottles, paper, plastic, metals, dirt, and spoiled food that people throw away every day. Each American produces about 1.8 kg of solid waste per day, or about 657 kg of waste each year. However, the largest amount of solid waste is produced as a result of agricultural and mining activities. More than half the solid waste in the United States consists of animal manure and by-products of agriculture. Another 30 percent of the total consists of piles of rock, sand, dirt, and wastes left over from mining processes. By law, much of these mining wastes must be put back into the area when mining is completed. Before that happens, however, these wastes pollute both air and water resources. Industrial wastes make up the remaining 15 percent of solid waste and consist of scrap metal, plastics, paper, and ash.

Where does this solid waste go when it is thrown away? In the past, wastes have been thrown into canyons, dumped into wetlands, and buried in landfills. Cities along the coast frequently sent barges out into the oceans to dump their garbage. But, these activities are just moving the wastes to different locations. They are not getting rid of them.

Natural ecosystems have built-in mechanisms for recycling matter. Decomposers break down wastes and make the compounds in them available to other organisms in the ecosystem. Technological advances have allowed humans to convert natural materials into new products. Many of these products are in forms that bacteria and fungi cannot easily decompose.

Some solid wastes, such as wood products or food, can be broken down easily by natural processes. Animal wastes, newspapers, and dead leaves are also broken down into their chemical nutrients by decomposers in the soil. Wastes or pollutants that can be broken down into chemical nutrients by decomposers are called **biodegradable.** Waste products that cannot be broken down by decomposers are called **non-biodegradable.** Non-biodegradable wastes create pollution that remains for hundreds of years.

A sanitary landfill is supposed to be free of toxic substances. However, many sanitary landfills are contaminated with toxic or radioactive wastes. There is currently much debate over where and how to store toxic and radioactive wastes. A major problem is the storage of plutonium, a radioactive waste. Plutonium remains radioactive for nearly 240 000 years. It is difficult to find a container that can hold plutonium for that length of time without breaking down. Radioactive and toxic wastes stored in landfills may seep into the groundwater supply and contaminate drinking water, causing cancer and birth defects in humans living near the landfills.

Why are radioactive and toxic wastes in landfills dangerous?

As you travel through your city or town, take notice of the many types of solid waste you see. Waste paper, cans, and bottles can be found at home or in your school. Abandoned cars, tires, and plastic containers often litter the roadsides. Think about ways you could reduce the amount of waste you throw away each day.

THINKING CRITICALLY

BIODEGRADABLE PLASTICS

Landfills contain millions of objects made of plastic. Only 0.5 percent of the plastic used in the United States is recycled. The rest ends up in landfills. Mountains of plastic cups, utensils, wrappers, and bags are added to the piles of plastic each day. In addition, garbage is put into plastic bags and added to the growing mounds of plastic. This garbage can't decompose because the plastic bags seal out the air that bacteria need to break down organic wastes. Samples taken from landfills, in fact, have turned up food items that appeared perfectly preserved—carrots were still orange!

Research on solutions to the solid waste problem has focused on the development of plastics that can be broken down by bacteria and fungi. Plastics of the future may be made of plant materials such as cornstarch, cellulose, or soy protein. By combining these materials with polyethylene, a petroleum-based plastic that can't decompose, scientists hope to develop a plastic that is strong and can be attacked by microbes. The new plastics currently available are about six percent cornstarch. One goal of the research is to develop plastics that are 50 to 60 percent starch. Plastics with this much starch in them, however, are not strong. Starch absorbs water and the plastic begins to break down even before it is discarded. Progress is being made in plastic research, however, and scientists are optimistic that they will be able to develop a cheap, strong product that can be decomposed by microbes.

How is the addition of starch to plastic important to the environment? Why are microbes able to decompose starch-containing plastics, but not pure polyethylene? What effect will this new technology have on farmers?

Corn starch is combined with polyethylene to create plastics that are biodegradable.

rthy

ecies becomes extinct ev-
In contrast, dinosaurs went
at the rate of one species ev-
j00 years.

35:6 Endangered Species

Have you ever seen a Carolina parakeet or a Bali tiger? Unless you have seen one of these animals stuffed in a museum, the answer is no. Both the Carolina parakeet and the Bali tiger are extinct. These animals became extinct because they were hunted and killed by people and their habitats were destroyed.

Wildlife is the term used for any wild plant or animal. Over the last few years, the total populations of many wild species have been decreasing. This decrease is due primarily to changes in wildlife habitats. People have drained wetlands for housing developments, cleared forests for logging and cattle grazing, plowed grasslands for farming, and filled in swamps with garbage. Sometimes wildlife is able to adapt to these changes, or move on to areas that are not yet occupied by people. Many times, however, these changes are so abrupt that the wildlife is unable to adapt. As a result, the number of individuals of a species begins to decline. Recall from Chapter 24 that a species is considered to be a threatened species when its numbers are declining rapidly. A species is considered to be an endangered species when its numbers are so low that extinction is possible. The California condor is an endangered species because of the small number of individuals that exist.

In some cases, wildlife is endangered by hunting rather than habitat destruction. The black rhinoceros of Africa is endangered because it is being hunted by poachers who kill it for its horns. Rhinoceros horns are used to make the handles of daggers carried by men in North Yemen. Rhino horns are also used to make medicines in many parts of Asia. Eighty-five percent of Africa's black rhinoceroses were killed for their horns between 1970 and 1985. Elephants may soon become endangered as well. They are killed for their ivory tusks, which are used to make jewelry and ornamental carvings. Many spotted cat species, such as cheetahs and leopards, are also in danger. Their beautiful spotted pelts are made into fur coats.

What two practices threaten wildlife?

FIGURE 35–10.

Many species living in the Everglades are at risk due to land development.

FIGURE 35–11.

Human activities are threatening desert ecosystems.

Human activity affects plants as well as animals. In the southwestern United States, people have been stealing huge saguaro cactus plants from protected deserts. These plants are sold as ornamental plants for gardens. Plant life in the desert is also in danger because of the use of recreational vehicles. These vehicles can destroy fragile plant life in seconds. Sometimes the destruction is so complete that the area will never recover.

How do humans endanger plants?

Many plant species are important to humans as sources of medicines and potential food. One-half of all drugs used to treat human diseases originally came from plants. Quinine, a drug used to treat the disease malaria, comes from the bark of the cinchona (sihn KOH nuh) tree. Seventy-five major drugs are obtained from plants. There are perhaps thousands of plant and animal species in the tropical rain forests that remain to be studied. Some of these plants or animals might provide cures for diseases that have not even been described yet.

REVIEW

6. Describe two major sources of pollution and the types of pollution they cause.
7. Explain why carbon dioxide and water vapor, two harmless gases, contribute to the greenhouse effect.
8. How do humans endanger plant and animal species?
9. **SKILL REVIEW:** Draw a pie graph showing the makeup of solid wastes in the United States. For more help, refer to Organizing Information in the Skill Handbook, pages 810 to 813.
10. **USING CONCEPTS:** Explain how an average family could reduce the amount of solid waste it produces weekly.

TOXIC WASTE

Toxic wastes are wastes that poison living organisms. These wastes may be released into the air, the water, or the soil as a result of some industrial process or by carelessness. As a result of past problems, such as the high incidence of cancer in some communities, many toxic substances are now evaluated for harmful effects.

BACKGROUND

Pollution is an ongoing problem in air, water, and soil of industrial and nonindustrial nations.

Products used in the home, such as paint thinners, insect sprays, solvents, polishes, and cleaners, may be toxic. When you throw the containers away or flush the materials down the drain, these chemicals frequently end up in landfills or in the groundwater. You have contributed to the problem of toxic wastes.

Toxic wastes that contaminate the soil are taken up by plants along with nutrients. Eventually, the wastes may get back to people in their food or water.

What kinds of toxic wastes have been found in the environment? Pesticides, PCBs, dioxin, mercury, benzene, arsenic, lead, asbestos, vinyl chloride, chromium, ethylene oxide, urethane, and formaldehyde are among the chemical pollutants now in nature. Nuclear wastes are perhaps the most dangerous toxic waste. Careless disposal of nuclear wastes has occurred everywhere nuclear products have been used.

CASE STUDIES

1. Greenpeace, an organization dedicated to preserving the environment through confrontation, promotes the idea that toxic pollution starts in the home. Members of this organization believe that many of the cleaners, polishes, and sprays used in the home are hazardous to family health. The organization has worked to inform the public about the proper disposal of toxic wastes. However, Greenpeace also has individuals who boldly confront companies that dump toxic wastes. They confront the problem of toxic waste at its source in order to attract media attention and raise the consciousness of the public about pollution.

2. Proposition 65 was approved by California voters in 1986. This law is known as the Safe Drinking Water and Toxic Enforcement Act. The law states that the public must be warned if industry knowingly exposes people to a substance that poses a significant risk of cancer or birth defects. Industry is concerned that other states will pass similar laws because it would be costly to the industries. One of the law's critics says that Proposition 65 has nothing to do with public health. This critic feels that pollution is not a significant cancer risk and that we must focus on poor diet, exposure to ultraviolet radiation, and tobacco as the most significant risks to health.

3. More than half of the people in the United States get their drinking water from wells that tap into groundwater supplies. Hydrocarbons that have leaked from underground storage tanks have polluted groundwater supplies more than any other class of chemicals. Most of these hydrocarbons are in the form of crude oil, gasoline, and creosote. Bacteria that live in aquifers are able to convert some hydrocarbons to carbon dioxide. However, these bacteria can break down only one percent of the hydrocarbons in the water. When liquids that contain oxygen or nutrients are pumped into the aquifers, bacteria in the groundwater can consume larger volumes of pollutants.

4. The standard way to dispose of toxic wastes has been to bury them in landfills that are lined with compacted clay. The clay is designed to keep toxic wastes and water from escaping. However, landfills have been leaking because water containing dissolved toxins flows from areas of high pressure within the landfill to dry areas of low pressure outside the landfill. Another way to deal with toxic wastes is to cement them in place. In this process, contaminated soil, cement, clay, and neutralizing chemicals are blended together. The clay surrounds the toxins, thus encasing them.

5. There are nearly 1000 toxic waste sites on the Environmental Protection Agency's Superfund priority list. It is suspected that thousands of others have yet to be identified. The Superfund priority list contains sites that are hazardous because they are leaking toxic wastes. Many abandoned factory dumps, gulleys filled with toxic garbage, and rotting drums of toxins along roadsides are still unlisted.

6. According to the Pentagon's toxic cleanup program at military bases, "there are islands of pollution that will become national sacrifice sites." In other words, some sites are never going to be cleaned up. It costs too much. It is estimated that it would cost up to $130 billion dollars to clean up the nation's existing toxic waste sites. At the same time, some states collect significant revenues by burying wastes not wanted by other states.

DEVELOPING YOUR VIEWPOINT

1. Research the activities of Greenpeace. How can you be sure that public action groups are acting in your interest?
2. Should Proposition 65 or a similar ordinance be the law of the entire United States?
3. Where does your community get its drinking water? Is pumping oxygen and nutrients into groundwater so that bacteria can break down pollutants a practical solution to polluted groundwater? Why or why not?
4. Are all landfills constructed in the same way? What regulations cover landfills in your area?

Toxic waste warning

Is there anyplace in your community where you can dispose of aging household toxic substances safely?
5. Why are there so many sites that need to be cleaned up?
6. If a toxic waste dump near your home were declared a "national sacrifice site" what action, if any, might you take?

SUGGESTED READINGS

1. Raloff, Janet. "Unexpected Leakage Through Landfill Liners." *Science News,* Mar. 18, 1989, p. 164.
2. Revkin, Michael. "Uncle Sam's Toxic Folly." *U.S. News & World Report,* Mar. 27, 1989, pp. 20–22.
3. Steinhart, Peter. "Down in the Dumps." *Audubon,* May 1986, pp. 102–109.
4. St. Onge, Julie. "Runoff Runs Amok." *Sierra,* Nov./Dec. 1988, pp. 28, 30, 32.

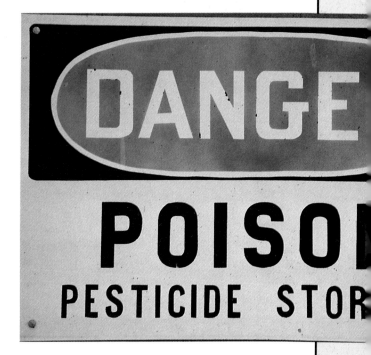

SUMMARY

1. Renewable resources may be replaced if managed properly. Nonrenewable resources cannot be replaced by natural processes. **35:1**
2. Population growth depends on birth and death rates. Population size and growth rate are affected by the age structure of a population and the availability of food, medical services, and sanitary facilities. Density-dependent and density-independent factors may limit population growth. **35:2**
3. Air pollution causes acid precipitation, the greenhouse effect, ozone destruction, destruction of wildlife, and health problems in humans. **35:3**
4. Water pollution is caused by organic and inorganic substances, sediments, heat, and radioactive substances. **35:4**
5. Land pollution occurs when solid wastes are disposed. Solid wastes may be biodegradable or non-biodegradable and include cans, bottles, paper, and plastic. Solid wastes are burned or placed in landfills. **35:5**
6. Some human activity destroys wildlife habitats. Some wildlife may become extinct. **35:6**

LANGUAGE OF BIOLOGY

acid precipitation
age structure
biodegradable
density-dependent
  factors
density-independent
  factors
fossil fuel

greenhouse effect
natural resource
non-biodegradable
nonrenewable resource
particulates
pollutant
renewable resource
smog

Choose the word or phrase from the list above that completes the sentence.

1. A pollutant capable of being broken down by natural processes is ___.

2. A resource with limited amounts that can't be replaced is a(n) ___.
3. A waste product that makes the environment impure or unclean is a(n) ___.
4. A(n) ___ is a nonrenewable resource that is burned to produce energy.
5. Any part of the environment that humans can use for their own purposes is a(n) ___.
6. The warming of Earth is due to the ___.
7. ___ are related to the number of individuals in a population.
8. ___ is made up of chemical fumes and smoke.
9. The percentage of each sex at each age in a population is its ___.
10. ___ affect populations no matter what their size.

REVIEWING CONCEPTS

Choose the word or phrase that completes the sentence or answers the question.

11. Which of the following is renewable?
    a. petroleum   c. coal
    b. paper   d. natural gas
12. Which of the following is a major factor in population growth?
    a. construction   c. energy
    b. natural resources   d. age structure
13. A population will begin to increase if the birth rate remains the same and the death rate ___.
    a. increases   c. remains the same
    b. decreases   d. none of the above
14. Acid precipitation comes largely from ___.
    a. burning fossil fuels   c. ozone
    b. fertilizer runoff   d. radon
15. Non-biodegradable wastes may include ___.
    a. plant materials   c. plastics
    b. food   d. newspapers

16. As the human population increases, ____.
   a. space becomes limiting
   b. wastes accumulate
   c. plants and animals are destroyed
   d. all of the above

17. Ozone in the upper atmosphere ____.
   a. blocks ultraviolet radiation
   b. breaks down pollutants in the air
   c. prevents the greenhouse effect
   d. prevents species extinction

18. Organic water pollutants include ____.
   a. heat   c. sewage
   b. salts   d. phosphorus

19. Irrigation is a problem because it ____.
   a. uses electricity   c. doesn't work
   b. creates aquifers   d. makes soil salty

20. Species become extinct because of ____.
   a. ozone depletion   c. greenhouse effect
   b. loss of habitat   d. CFCs

UNDERSTANDING CONCEPTS

Answer the following questions using complete sentences.

21. How do density-dependent and density-independent factors affect population growth?

22. How does the age structure of the human population affect its growth rate?

23. What are two major sources of air pollution?

24. How can nonrenewable resources be made to last longer?

25. How does destruction of tropical rain forests affect the search for cures for diseases?

26. Why is heat pollution of water dangerous to wildlife?

27. How does acid precipitation affect species?

28. How have agricultural and manufacturing processes added to the greenhouse effect?

29. Why is disposal of radioactive wastes difficult?

30. What is the role of bacteria and fungi in solid waste disposal?

APPLYING CONCEPTS

Answer the following questions using complete sentences.

31. What effect will destruction of the ozone layer in polar regions have on populations in the temperate zone?

32. Explain how the removal of CFCs from spray cans has improved the ozone layer.

33. If humans delay having children until age 30, what effect would it have on world population?

34. What would be the effect on the environment if all milk were packaged in cardboard containers?

35. Why should a city dweller be concerned about the environmental impact of surface mining?

EXTENSIONS

1. What technologies do you believe should be eliminated in order to protect the environment? Why? Make a chart to show how you would replace these technologies.

2. Make a list of the major environmental problems in your city or state. What actions can be taken to eliminate or reduce the problems?

3. Find out how your local water supply is treated.

READINGS

El-Sayed, S.Z. "Fragile Life Under the Ozone Hole." *Natural History,* Oct. 1988, pp. 72–80.

Livermore, B. "Very Personal Pollution." *Health,* Mar. 1989, pp. 42–47, 94.

Revkin, A.C. "Endless Summer: Living with the Greenhouse Effect." *Discover,* Oct. 1988, pp. 50–61.

Chapter 36

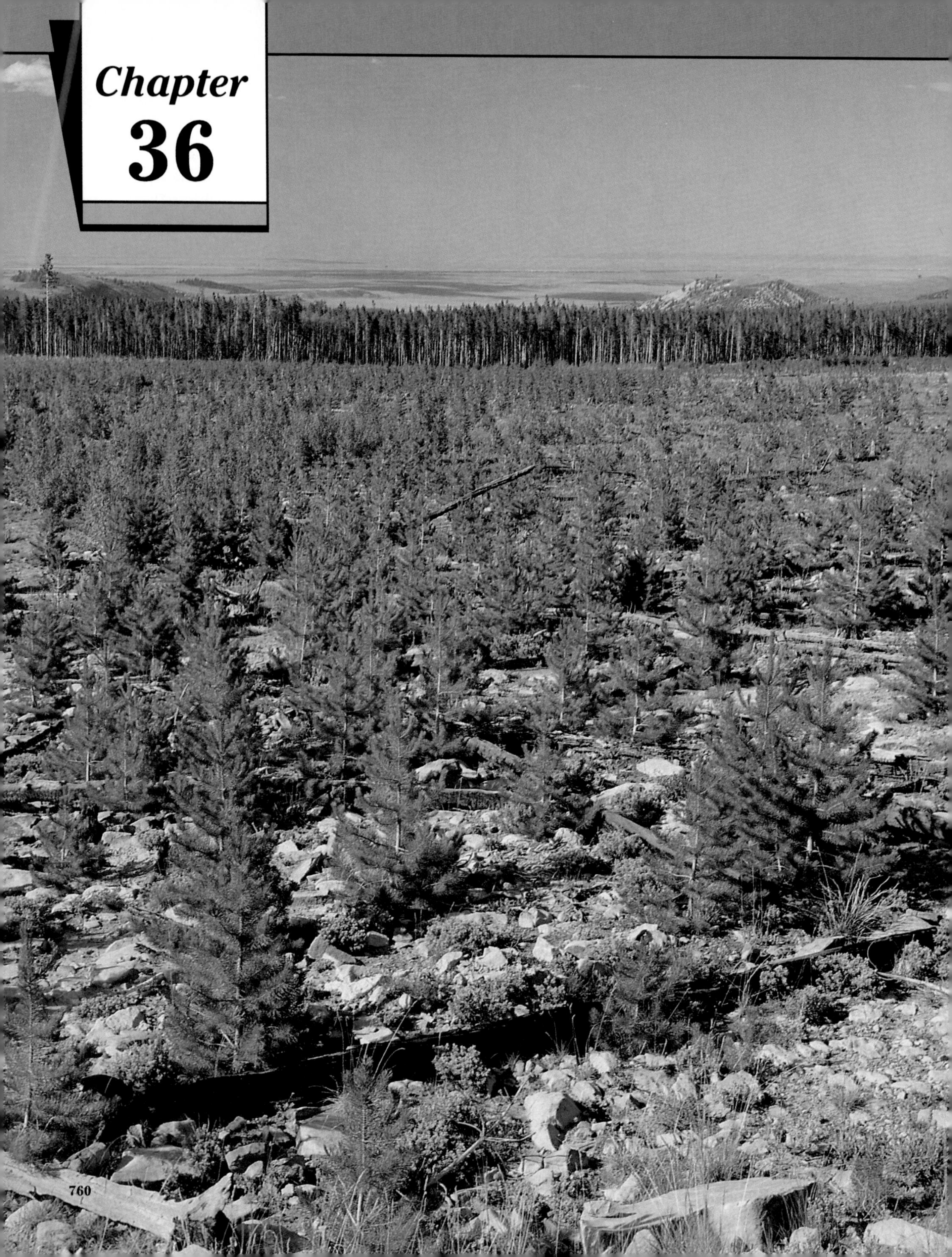

MAINTAINING A BALANCE

Do you read the newspaper each morning? Perhaps you carry your lunch to school in a paper bag. What about reading magazines? All these activities have one thing in common: each involves the use of paper. You know that paper is made from wood, a renewable resource. But what happens to the newspaper, the bag, and the magazine when you are finished with them? They usually end up in the trash. Where will society put the trash when there's no more space for it in landfills? What can be done to reduce the amount of waste that humans produce?

USING RESOURCES WISELY

Look at the photographs on these two pages. The entire side of the mountain has been planted with tree seedlings to produce lumber 20 years from now. The newspapers are tied into a bundle for recycling. Both of these photos show ways that humans can use limited resources wisely. In this chapter, you will learn how governments and individuals are responding to environmental challenges.

36:1 Cleaning Up the Air

Have you ever driven behind a smoke-belching city bus or a poorly-maintained diesel truck? Perhaps you tried to breathe through your mouth to avoid the nasty smell, only to find your throat irritated by fumes you couldn't see. Air pollution from vehicles and power-generating plants is a major problem.

In the United States, cleaning up the air began in 1970 with the passage of the Clean Air Act. Even though this act required some control of emissions from power plants, dozens of huge coal-fired power plants were covered by a "grandfather clause." This means that these plants weren't required to abide by the law because they existed before the law was passed. Proposed legislation before Congress would require industry to reduce sulfur dioxide emissions by up to 40 percent over the next ten years. Technologies now available are able to reduce sulfur dioxide by 95 percent or more, so this goal is within reach.

Objectives:
- describe ways of cleaning up air and water pollution.
- explain how wastes can be recycled.
- list reasons to protect soil and forest resources.
- identify ways humans are protecting endangered species.

Land undergoing reforestation

What are sources of carbon dioxide in the atmosphere?

High levels of carbon dioxide are another major source of air pollution. This gas is produced by the burning of fossil fuels, particularly in cars and other vehicles. Over half of the world's carbon dioxide pollution is produced by the three largest industrial nations—the United States, the Soviet Union, and China. If these three nations switched to cleaner, more fuel-efficient cars, this type of pollution could be reduced greatly. Some companies have already produced car engines that can get 63 miles to the gallon. In the United States, an increase of just one mile per gallon in average fuel efficiency would improve air quality as much as the closing of six coal-fired power plants!

Other air pollutants that can be reduced are chlorofluorocarbons, or CFCs. These gases destroy ozone in the upper atmosphere. CFCs are used as propellants in aerosol cans and in the manufacturing of plastics. Most of these products can be made without CFCs. In fact, the use of CFCs for aerosol sprays was banned ten years ago by the United States, Canada, and Sweden. If the rest of the world banned the use of CFCs in aerosols, the world's production of CFCs could be reduced by 25 percent.

Much of today's air pollution could be eliminated if countries worked together. Plans for this type of cooperation on air pollution are underway. Thirty-four nations have agreed to work on global solutions to the air pollution problem. How can this be done? First, automobile manufacturers may be required to produce more fuel-efficient cars at a cost people can afford. Second, all power plants may be required to install scrubbers on their smokestacks to remove harmful pollutants. A **scrubber** is a device that sprays a fine mist of

FIGURE 36–1.

Scrubbers help to remove particulates from smoke and gases passing through them.

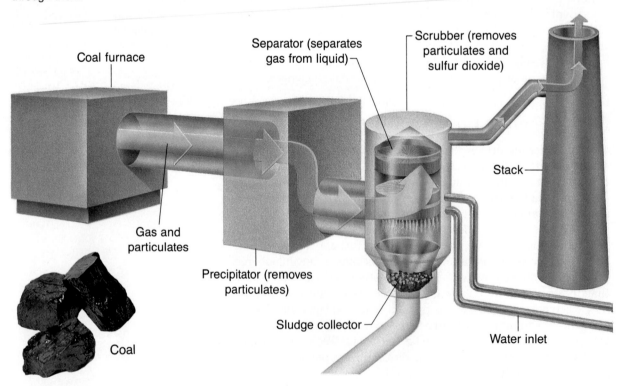

Coal furnace

Separator (separates gas from liquid)

Scrubber (removes particulates and sulfur dioxide)

Stack

Gas and particulates

Precipitator (removes particulates)

Sludge collector

Water inlet

Coal

FIGURE 36–2.

Hydroelectric power plants and windmills generate electricity with minimal impact on the environment.

water that removes particulates and sulfur dioxide from polluted air, Figure 36–1. Third, power plants might switch from coal and other fossil fuels to cleaner fuels, including solar energy, nuclear energy, hydroelectric power, wind energy, and low-sulfur coal. If the countries of Earth commit themselves to controlling air pollution, most of it will be eliminated in the future.

36:2 Cleaning Up the Water

Because water is Earth's most abundant resource, humans haven't been very concerned with its protection or conservation in the past. **Conservation** is the wise and careful use of Earth's resources. Throughout human history, water has been used for domestic, municipal, and industrial purposes, with little thought given to the effect such uses had on the cleanliness or abundance of water. This is no longer true.

Many communities are now aware of how precious water is, and they are beginning to promote cleaner water, water conservation, and recycling. Many communities have water treatment plants that filter out sediments, kill bacteria, and produce water that is clean and safe to drink. Some communities reuse water that already has been used for another purpose. For example, water used in washing machines can be used to wash cars, clean streets, and water lawns. There are programs designed to encourage people to conserve water by reducing the amount of water used in flushing the toilet, or to bathe by taking showers instead of baths. Dams and canals prevent flooding, while reservoirs and water tanks store excess water so that it is available when water supplies are low.

BIOLAB *Water Pollution* 36

Problem: What might be the effect of increased nutrients on bodies of water?

Materials
Euglena culture
test tubes with screw caps (4)
wax pencil
0.3% phosphate solution (100 mL)
0.3% nitrate solution (100 mL)
medicine dropper
graduated cylinder
distilled water

Procedures
1. Copy the data table.
2. Using a wax pencil, label each test tube with your name and one of the following solutions:
   Tube 1—water
   Tube 2—phosphate
   Tube 3—nitrate
   Tube 4—phosphate and nitrate
3. Using a graduated cylinder and plain water, determine the total volume of each tube. Then, calculate the volume of solution required to fill each tube 80 percent full. Fill each tube 80 percent full with the appropriate solution. For tube 4, put in equal amounts of phosphate and nitrate to total 80 percent.
4. Gently swirl the *Euglena* culture to be sure it is thoroughly mixed. Place 5 drops of culture into each of the four tubes.
5. Tightly screw a cap onto each tube and place the tubes on their sides in a window or under a light source.
6. Develop a **hypothesis** about which tubes will show the most growth of *Euglena* after two weeks. Growth will be judged by changes in color and density of *Euglena*. The cultures will become darker and denser as the number of *Euglena* increases.
7. Examine the tubes at the ends of one and two weeks. To record your observations, make one to five plus marks in your data table to indicate the relative amounts of growth in each tube.

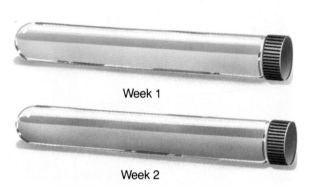

Week 1

Week 2

Data and Observations

Growth of *Euglena*		
Tube	Week 1	Week 2
1		
2		
3		
4		

Questions and Conclusion
1. Which tube showed the most growth? The least?
2. Compare the growth of *Euglena* in tubes 3 and 4.
3. What was the purpose of tube 1?
4. Did your data support your **hypothesis?** Explain.
5. This investigation is a qualitative study. Qualitative studies show relative changes among different test groups. Changes among test groups are observed rather than measured. In a quantitative study, changes among test groups are measured. What steps could you take to make this investigation quantitative?
6. What do the results of this investigation suggest regarding the treatment of water?
Conclusion: What might be the effect of increasing nutrient levels in bodies of water?

Industry also is learning to protect water sources. Water used for cooling purposes picks up heat from whatever it is cooling. Some industries now hold this water in outdoor ponds until it releases some of the heat it has absorbed. Some industries reuse this water, and never return it to the source. To take advantage of the warm water, some companies are raising fish in the outdoor ponds. Many countries now have laws that prohibit industry from disposing of wastes in water sources. For example, Lake Erie was too polluted for swimming or fishing in the 1960s. Today, however, people can swim and fish in Lake Erie because the industries on the lake's shores were required to reduce their polluting actions.

New technologies are being developed to help eliminate water pollution that develops as a result of agricultural practices. A more efficient method of irrigation called the **trickle system** slowly releases water and nutrients near the roots of crop plants, Figure 36–3. This type of system reduces water runoff and soil erosion. Computer-controlled sprinkler systems adjust the amount of water released by monitoring soil moisture and weather conditions. These systems can thus conserve water resources.

One way you can help conserve water is by using less of it on a daily basis. Humans need about 15 to 20 L a day to fulfill basic needs such as drinking and cooking. In the United States, however, each individual uses about 800 L each day. How can you conserve water? First, turn the water off while you brush your teeth or wash dishes. Put bricks in the toilet tank to reduce the amount of water used per flush. Steaming foods when you cook uses less water than boiling. Reusing water that was used to cook vegetables or pasta also saves water. How does your community conserve or protect water resources? How have you, as an individual, conserved water?

FIGURE 36–3.

A trickle system conserves water by slowly releasing it to the soil.

What are some ways of conserving water?

36:3 Disposing of Wastes

Do you take out the garbage each night? If you do, then you know that your household produces lots of solid wastes. Cans, papers, bottles, plastic cartons, and leftover foods make up most of the garbage a household produces. But did you realize that in many parts of the world your garbage would be considered a resource? Most of what you throw away can be reused or recycled. You know that aluminum cans, glass bottles, and newspaper can be recycled. **Recycling** is the reusing of resources. Some communities have recycling centers for these materials. Aluminum and glass can be melted down and reused, while newspaper can be chopped up and bleached to make new paper.

Recycling materials such as cans, bottles, and paper is one way that individuals can reduce the amount of waste they produce each day. One reused soft drink can means one less can that must be made from new materials. The aluminum from which the can is made is a metal and a nonrenewable resource. Eventually, we may run out of aluminum deposits. It makes good sense to use aluminum over and over. Another benefit from recycling aluminum is that it costs far less to recycle aluminum than it does to dig it out of the ground. Plastic is another material that can be recycled. Some companies harvest plastic bottles and bags from city garbage dumps to make other plastic products. In some communities, individuals are required to separate the solid wastes in their garbage. Plastics, glass, and aluminum are put into separate containers, thus making recycling more efficient.

What materials are collected by recycling centers?

FIGURE 36–4.

Recycling helps to reduce solid waste and conserve resources.

FIGURE 36–5.

Used nuclear fuel rods are stored in huge vats of water.

A solid waste that concerns people very much is nuclear waste. Some types of nuclear waste can remain radioactive for 240 000 years. Much of the nuclear waste is in the form of nuclear fuel rods that have been used to generate nuclear energy for electricity. How can nuclear waste be stored in a way to prevent it from affecting the soil, water, or air? In the United States, used nuclear fuel rods are stored in vats of water at the nuclear power plant, Figure 36–5. However, the power plants are running out of space to store used fuel rods. New containers are being designed to hold nuclear waste. In Sweden, used nuclear fuel is encased in copper cylinders that are supposed to last up to a million years without corroding.

A major source of waste in today's landfills is disposable diapers. Disposable diapers have created a tremendous waste disposal problem. Diapers contain feces that should be dealt with in sewage treatment plants where bacteria are killed by adding chemicals to the water. When these wastes are left in landfills, bacterial populations increase rapidly. Eventually, these bacteria enter water supplies and cause health problems for people. A second problem with disposable diapers is that they aren't biodegradable. One company has begun to produce disposable diapers that break down with exposure to sunlight. Unfortunately, most diapers are disposed of in plastic bags. No sunlight ever reaches them. Scientists have also developed a partially biodegradable plastic bag made with cornstarch.

There are a few communities around the world that are taking a more aggressive stand on their solid waste problems. Some cities have built trash-burning power plants that use city-produced trash for production of electricity. Unfortunately, some solutions may lead to other problems. Many trash-burning plants release air pollutants.

NoteWorthy

In the United States, less than one percent of the estimated 15 to 20 billion pounds of plastic that is discarded annually is recycled.

36:4 Protecting Soil and Forest Resources

Earth's resources are limited in several different ways. You studied in Chapter 35 that it takes 500 to 1000 years for a 2.5 cm layer of topsoil to form. What happens to that topsoil when land is used for farming? Plowing and harvesting expose the topsoil to erosion. **Erosion** is the washing away of exposed soil by wind or water. Erosion may occur naturally, as in a community undergoing primary succession. Recall from Chapter 34 that when primary succession begins, there are no plants to hold the soil in place. On land that has been cleared for farming, the process of erosion is accelerated. Erosion can be reduced in one of several ways. Plowing along the contour of the land, known as **contour plowing,** helps to reduce water runoff, and therefore, erosion, Figure 36–6. Terracing also helps to reduce runoff. **Terracing** is the practice of creating level strips of land on a slope. Plowing at right angles to the prevailing winds and planting trees for windbreaks also help to reduce erosion.

The raising of crops requires enormous amounts of nutrients, many of which are obtained from the soil. If the same crop is planted on a piece of land year after year, it will deplete the nutrients contained in the soil. **Soil depletion** is the reduction of soil fertility by the removal of organic materials and nutrients from the soil. Soil depletion can be reduced by careful farming practices, such as crop rotation. **Crop rotation** is the alternating of crops on a piece of land. For example, if a nutrient-depleting crop such as corn is grown one year, a soil-enriching crop such as beans may be grown the next. Recall that beans are legumes and have nitrogen-fixing bacteria in their roots. The nitrogen-fixing bacteria convert nitrogen to nitrates and thus increase the levels of nutrients in the soil.

erosion:
erodere (L) to wear away

FIGURE 36–6.

Terracing (left) and contour plowing (right) are farming methods that help to reduce soil erosion.

FIGURE 36–7.

In clear-cutting, whole areas are lumbered.

You know that resources are classified as renewable or nonrenewable, but even renewable resources may become limited. For example, paper is made from trees, and trees are normally considered renewable resources. What if the forests that are cut down for paper are not replanted? Eventually, wood would become a limited resource. In the United States and Canada, wood producers and lumber companies often clear-cut forests, Figure 36–7. **Clear-cutting** is the practice of cutting down all the trees in measured plots. After clear-cutting, the lumber companies may replant the forests in a process called reforestation. **Reforestation** is the restoring of a forest after a harvest by means of planting seedling trees. Even though it takes from five to twenty years for these trees to reach a size suitable for harvesting, reforestation helps to ensure that trees and forests remain a renewable resource.

The harvesting of large stands of trees causes other problems. Tree roots take up water quickly and keep soil in place. Trees provide food and shelter for many different organisms. When all the trees are harvested from an area, the soil surface is left unprotected for a period of time. As a result, wind and water erode the soil and expose less fertile subsoils. Even when trees are replanted soon after a forest has been clear-cut, soil erosion continues because the seedlings are unable to hold down the soil. The nature of the forest also changes. Forests that have never been cleared before are often climax forests. Climax forests are able to withstand changes because they are relatively stable. After climax forests are cleared, the new plantings usually consist of only one species, a species best suited for lumber or papermaking. The resulting forest often can't support the same

How could wood become a nonrenewable resource?

FIGURE 36–8.

Slash-and-burn agriculture is used in the tropics to clear forested land for farming. After a few years, however, the soil can no longer support crops and ends up like that in the left-hand photo.

How does slash-and-burn agriculture contribute to soil erosion?

organisms that the climax forest supported, and the number of species decreases. What do you think happens in such a forest if a tree disease specific to the one tree species enters the ecosystem?

Recall from Chapter 34 that in tropical forests the nutrients are held in the trees rather than in the soil. When tropical rain forests are cleared by slash-and-burn agriculture, heavy tropical rains wash away what little fertile soil there is. **Slash-and-burn agriculture** is the cutting down and burning of large stands of trees so that the land can be used for agriculture, Figure 36–8. Farmers clear the land to grow crops, but after two or three harvests, the soils are exhausted of nutrients. The farmers have no choice but to clear more forested land to plant crops. Some countries are having success with reforestation programs, but these programs will not restore the diversity of the original forest for thousands of years.

Several actions can be taken to help protect resources. Many countries have conservation groups working to protect forests by developing parks in which no one is allowed to collect plants or other organisms. Some governments are teaching people how to plant trees for use as firewood and lumber in order to protect nearby forests. In countries where slash-and-burn agriculture has been practiced, many old fields have become forests again. Farmers in Peru are encouraged to clear these forests for agriculture rather than clearing new forests. In countries where forests are cut for firewood, many private and government agencies are providing improved stoves that burn firewood more efficiently. All of these efforts can help to protect forest resources and ensure that trees remain renewable resources for future generations.

36:5 Protecting Species

Governments are becoming more and more involved with the protection of species. Consider what has taken place in China with the giant panda. The giant panda is an endangered species found only in a small area of China. Giant pandas eat mostly bamboo plants and live in bamboo forests. They once were found all over southern China. As the bamboo forests were cleared for farming, however, the number of pandas dwindled. To ensure the panda's survival, the government of China has designated wildlife preserves in the remaining bamboo forests. A **wildlife preserve** is an area set aside for the protection of wildlife species. Hunting and fishing are prohibited on wildlife preserves. The Chinese are also replanting bamboo forests to increase the panda's habitat. Scientists have developed breeding programs to find ways to help captive pandas reproduce more successfully. The hope is that zoo-bred pandas can be reintroduced into the wild once a suitable habitat is made available.

You may think that once an animal or plant species becomes endangered its fate is sealed and extinction is certain to occur. Since 1900, however, several species in the United States have recovered and are no longer considered endangered. The American alligator, once near extinction, is now quite numerous and is found in many waterways throughout the southeastern United States. The pronghorn antelope population, Figure 36–9, has increased from 13 000 to one million animals. Wild turkeys have shown a similar recovery. Their numbers have increased from 30 000 to 3.8 million. Even the trumpeter swan population, Figure 36–10, down to only 73 individuals in 1900, has increased in size to 900. Although the trumpeter

NoteWorthy

Of the 1035 species that are endangered worldwide, 529 are in the United States. They include the desert pupfish, the black-footed ferret, and the Florida Key deer.

FIGURE 36–9.

Pronghorn antelopes (left) and wild turkeys (right) are two species that have recovered from near-extinction.

FIGURE 36–10.

Although whooping cranes (left) and trumpeter swans (right) are increasing in number, both are still endangered.

swan is still endangered, its numbers are continuing to increase. The whooping crane and the American bison are two other species that have come back from the edge of extinction due to human efforts.

How have these animal species been able to recover? Laws protecting species and their habitats have contributed to the recovery of some species. For example, in 1970 the United States government banned the shipping of alligator hides. In addition, over 40 wildlife preserves covering 45 million hectares have been established in the United States to provide a relatively safe haven for wildlife.

REVIEW

1. How can sulfur dioxide, CFCs, and carbon dioxide be cleared from the air?
2. How can water pollution from agricultural sources be reduced?
3. Explain what happens when a forest is cleared for lumber and not replanted.
4. **SKILL REVIEW:** Make a table to show five major sources of solid waste and ways they can be dealt with. For more help, refer to Organizing Information in the Skill Handbook, pages 810 to 813.
5. **USING CONCEPTS:** Explain how planting bamboo forests in China and captive breeding programs in zoos may help giant pandas survive as a species.

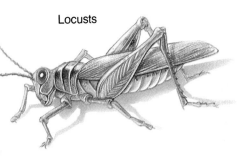

A LOOK TO THE FUTURE

Science and technology have helped humans lead more comfortable lives, but using new technology often causes new problems. In Chapter 35, you studied some of the disadvantages of misusing technology. Air and water pollution, habitat destruction, and endangered species are the result, in part, of human activities. In this chapter you have seen some of the ways humans are solving these problems. But what about the future? The development of new technologies may help prevent further damage to our planet. Can biology play a role in helping to develop new and better technologies? The answer is yes. Can you as an individual help solve environmental problems today as well as in the future? This section will help you answer that question for yourself.

36:6 The Role of Biotechnology

Have you ever seen a swarm of locusts like the one in Figure 36–11? In many parts of the world, locusts swarm over farmlands and devour everything in sight within a few hours. For many farmers, this means the loss of their entire income for a season. What if there were some way to predict when locusts were going to swarm? Farmers could plan for this event and not plant crops until the locusts were gone. Perhaps scientists could find a way to prevent locusts from reproducing by introducing sterile males into the population. It's possible that farmers could release locust predators on

Objectives:

- summarize the role of biotechnology in solving environmental problems.
- describe ways each individual can solve environmental problems.

Locusts

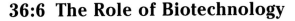

FIGURE 36–11.

Locust swarms can be controlled by introducing sterile males into the population.

their farms to keep down the numbers of locusts and thereby reduce damage to crops. All of these possible solutions to the locust problem are a result of biotechnology. **Biotechnology** is the use of biology and technology to solve problems.

Look at Figure 36–12. The organisms devouring the plant's leaves are gypsy moth caterpillars. Gypsy moth caterpillars eat the leaves of many kinds of plants, thus robbing the plant of its means of carrying out photosynthesis. How can you get rid of gypsy moth caterpillars? In the past you might have sprayed your garden or trees with a pesticide. However, many pesticides are harmful to the environment. Use of biotechnology makes chemical pesticides unnecessary. Gypsy moth caterpillars, as well as many other insect species, can be controlled by the use of pheromones. Pheromones produced by female gypsy moths and used to attract males can be synthesized in the lab. The synthetic pheromones are then placed in a trap and used to lure males. Once trapped, the males are no longer available to mate, thus reducing the number of caterpillar offspring. This technique is an example of biological control. A **biological control** is a process in which biological relationships among organisms are used by humans to control populations of pest organisms. In the example just described, the biological relationship is the reproductive behavior of gypsy moths. A second type of biological control is the use of genetic engineering to control plant diseases. Through genetic engineering, scientists have developed tomato plants that are resistant to tomato mosaic virus. A third type of biological control being explored is integrated pest management. **Integrated pest management** is the use of biological, chemical, cultural, and mechanical pest control techniques to control pests on agricultural land. For example, to control certain insects in corn, a biological control might be allowing chickens to eat bugs in the

What is integrated pest management?

Adult gypsy moth

FIGURE 36–12.

Gypsy moth caterpillars can be prevented from mating by using pheromones to lure the males into traps.

FIGURE 36–13.

Hoeing to prevent the spread of weeds (left) is a mechanical control technique that does not pollute the environment. Plants such as chrysanthemums (right) can serve as natural pesticides.

soil around corn plants. A chemical control might be spraying the young corn plants with a pesticide that kills only the corn pest. A cultural control method might be to plant other crops in alternate rows with the corn plants. Plants such as marigolds and chrysanthemums contain chemicals that are natural pesticides. Planting these species between corn rows can help to reduce insect infestations. Mechanical control techniques include weeding, mulching, and plowing. Integrated pest management may use all of these techniques at different times or only two of them at the same time. With integrated pest management, the need for chemical pesticides is reduced. As a result, there is less runoff of pesticides into water resources and, therefore, less water pollution.

36:7 Individual Responsibility

What do you think would happen in your community if the sanitation workers suddenly decided not to pick up trash for a week? It wouldn't take long for the town officials to do something about it, because trash is a health hazard for everyone. Sanitation workers perform a function that is very important to the well-being of all the individuals in a community.

Just as sanitation workers have a responsibility to the community, each person in the community has responsibilities, too. Some of your responsibilities include going to school, doing your homework, and helping with chores at home. Your parents have responsibilities to provide for your needs, go to work, and abide by society's laws. Regardless of their jobs, all people have the responsibility to pay taxes and support their government. Beyond these responsibilities, you and the people in your community are becoming more aware of your responsibilities to the environment in which you live.

FIGURE 36–14.

Land used for strip mines or sanitary landfills can be restored to its former beauty and enjoyed by all.

You know that power plants and chemical companies are required to clean up their emissions in order to reduce air and water pollution. But do you know what you can do to help? If you change the oil in your car, you can dispose of it by taking it to service stations that collect old oil in proper containers. If you go to a ball game, you can clean up all the litter you brought with you—and maybe someone else's litter, too. If there is a recycling center nearby, you can encourage your family, neighbors, and friends to recycle aluminum cans, newspapers, and glass bottles. If you have a garden, you can use biological controls instead of chemical pesticides. Don't throw away dead leaves and grass cuttings—make a compost pile instead. When you buy groceries, take along a shopping bag or cardboard box to bring them home and say no to a paper or plastic bag. You also can make a difference by saving electricity. If you leave the room, turn off the lights. All of these actions are ways you can improve the environment, save energy, and use resources wisely. Earth is your home and you will spend your life here.

REVIEW

6. How does biotechnology help solve the pollution problem?
7. Explain how you can reduce pests in your garden without using chemical pesticides.
8. Name three things an individual can do to conserve resources.
9. **SKILL REVIEW:** Design an experiment to compare the relative effectiveness of biological, chemical, cultural, and mechanical pest control techniques on controlling an outbreak of aphids. For more help, refer to Designing an Experiment in the Skill Handbook, pages 802 to 803.
10. **USING CONCEPTS:** What could you do if you discovered that a local field was being used to dump cans of old paint?

CAREER CHOICES

To a farmer or a gardener, soil is material in which plants grow. An engineer defines soil as unconsolidated materials. To a biologist, soil is a mixture of weathered rocks, air, organic matter, and water. Soil is one of Earth's most important resources. It takes hundreds or even thousands of years for soil to form. Yet, soil erodes away at the rate of billions of metric tons per year. How can soil and land be protected and conserved?

Were the fires that destroyed hundreds of thousands of hectares of forests in Yellowstone National Park in 1988 due to natural causes? A **criminal investigator** with the United States Forest Service works to protect this country's national forests. As a criminal investigator, you would be responsible for investigating the causes of fires, timber theft, looting, the destruction of archeological sights, and other crimes that occur in federally-owned forests. You would work closely with other federal agencies and local law enforcers to detect and eliminate illegal activities in national forests.

Criminal investigator

Forestry aides and technicians assist professional foresters in all phases of forestry work. Some aides and technicians serve on firefighting crews or act as fire lookouts. Others collect and record data on tree heights and diameters. This information is then used to determine whether or not an area will be thinned to increase timber productivity. Forestry aides and technicians also assist foresters in eliminating sick or dead trees, pruning trees, and planting seedlings.

In the 1930s, soil left exposed on farmlands in the Great Plains was blown away by high winds, thus creating huge dust storms and resulting in the loss of fertile topsoil. In recent years, poor agricultural practices have contributed to the loss of over six billion metric tons of topsoil per year in the United States. A **soil conservationist** is a scientist who provides technical assistance to homeowners, farmers, and ranchers to help protect their soil from deterioration and erosion. Many soil conservationists work with the American Soil Conservation Service. As a soil conservationist, you would work closely with homeowners or farmers to develop programs that provide the most beneficial use of the land. Most of your time would be spent outdoors visiting areas with soil problems, determining the sources of the problems, and helping the landowners eliminate the problems. If you were working with a homeowner, you might help develop solutions for soil drainage problems. Correct placement of drainage lines or septic tanks would depend on your expert advice. As a soil conservationist, you would be expected to know how to make and read topographical maps. These maps show the contours of the land and are instrumental in helping to identify areas that may be susceptible to erosion. Working with farmers could involve developing maps that would tell the farmer where the land contours were. Thus, the farmer would know where to plow to minimize soil erosion.

Forestry technician

Soil conservationist

CHAPTER REVIEW

SUMMARY

1. Building fuel-efficient cars, requiring power plants to install scrubbers, and switching to cleaner fuels can reduce air pollution. **36:1**
2. Water pollution can be reduced by water treatment plants, reusing and recycling water, and enforcing laws that prohibit waste disposal in water sources. **36:2**
3. Many solid wastes are resources that can be reused, recycled, or burned to produce energy. **36:3**
4. Soils can be protected in a variety of ways. Forests are important to the environment and are a source of food. **36:4**
5. Reconstruction of habitat may help save many endangered species. **36:5**
6. Many pollution problems can be solved with wise use of biotechnology. **36:6**
7. Each person can become involved in environmental protection. **36:7**

LANGUAGE OF BIOLOGY

biological control
biotechnology
clear-cutting
conservation
contour plowing
crop rotation
erosion
integrated pest
  management
recycling
reforestation
scrubber
slash-and-burn
  agriculture
soil depletion
terracing
trickle system
wildlife preserve

Choose the word or phrase from the list above that completes the sentence.

1. A more efficient irrigation method that releases water and nutrients directly to plant roots is the ____.
2. A process in which biological relationships among organisms are used to control pests is a(n) ____.
3. The use of biology and technology to solve environmental problems is ____.
4. The use of biological, chemical, cultural, and mechanical pest control techniques is called ____.
5. ____ is the restoring of a forest by planting seedlings.
6. ____ is the practice of cutting down all the trees in a measured plot.
7. ____ is the wise use of Earth's resources.
8. ____ is the practice of creating level strips of land to reduce soil erosion.
9. ____ exposes the soil of tropical rain forests to heavy tropical rains.
10. An area set aside for the protection of wildlife species is a(n) ____.

REVIEWING CONCEPTS

Choose the word or phrase that completes the sentence or answers the question.

11. Carbon dioxide gas is produced by ____.
    a. sunlight
    b. burning fossil fuels
    c. CFCs
    d. smog
12. Ozone is destroyed by ____.
    a. chlorofluorocarbons
    b. sulfur dioxide
    c. nitrogen dioxide
    d. clouds
13. Water pollution in communities can be controlled by ____.
    a. rain
    b. landfills
    c. heating the water
    d. water treatment plants
14. Individuals can conserve water by ____.
    a. using the trickle system to water lawns
    b. installing solar panels
    c. putting bricks in the toilet tank
    d. drinking milk
15. Which of the following cannot be recycled?
    a. glass bottles
    b. coal
    c. aluminum cans
    d. newspaper

16. Why is nuclear waste a problem?
    a. It catches fire.   c. It can explode.
    b. It dissolves.   d. It is radioactive.

17. Why can't a replanted forest support the same organisms the climax forest supported?
    a. All the animals left.
    b. There is not enough shade.
    c. It often consists of only one tree species.
    d. Insects destroy the new tree seedlings.

18. Species on the brink of extinction ____.
    a. can't be saved
    b. may be helped with breeding programs
    c. are all in zoos
    d. are not found in the United States

19. An example of a biological control is ____.
    a. chemical pesticides
    b. plowing
    c. introducing predators
    d. weeding

20. Individuals can help the environment by ____.
    a. listening to radio instead of watching TV
    b. writing letters instead of phoning
    c. refusing shopping bags
    d. driving instead of taking a bus

UNDERSTANDING CONCEPTS

Answer the following questions using complete sentences.

21. Name three ways to clean up air pollution.
22. How is industry learning to protect water resources?
23. How are communities promoting cleaner water and conservation of water?
24. How does recycling solid materials protect the environment?
25. Why must lumbering be controlled?
26. How do improved agricultural practices help to control erosion?
27. How have governments helped to protect wildlife species?
28. How does integrated pest management help to preserve a clean environment?

29. How does genetic engineering contribute to the solving of pollution problems?
30. How can individuals reduce pollution and conserve resources?

APPLYING CONCEPTS

Answer the following questions using complete sentences.

31. Besides the activities mentioned in this chapter, what could an individual do to conserve resources and reduce pollution?
32. How would you go about organizing a recycling center in your community?
33. What could a person do to get rid of tent caterpillars in a birch tree without polluting the environment?
34. How might biodegradable plastics help solve the solid waste problem?
35. How can producing more fuel-efficient cars help reduce air pollution?

EXTENSIONS

1. Find out what methods are being used in your area to conserve soil and water.
2. Find out what local utility companies are doing to encourage energy conservation.
3. Visit a local recycling center. Find out what materials are recycled and how they are reused.

READINGS

Canine, C. "Generating Megawatts." *Harrowsmith,* Mar./Apr. 1989, pp. 42–51.

Gillette, B. "Controlling Mosquitoes Biologically." *BioScience,* Feb. 1988, pp. 80–83.

Starr, D. "How to Protect the Ozone Layer." *National Wildlife,* Dec./Jan. 1988, pp. 26–28.

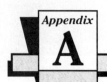

Classification of Organisms

The system of classification used in this textbook is explained in Chapter 2. There are five kingdoms of life. The system recognizes one kingdom of organisms that are prokaryotes: Kingdom Monera; and four kingdoms of eukaryotes: Kingdom Protista, Kingdom Fungi, Kingdom Plantae, and Kingdom Animalia. There are many systems of classification due to the fact that taxonomists disagree as to the relatedness of some groups, such as the seaweeds, the slime molds, and water molds. These groups have intermediate characteristics between two different Kingdoms. They are placed in one Kingdom by some taxonomists and in other groups by other taxonomists. In the system of classification used in this textbook, the Kingdom Protista is made diverse by the inclusion of seaweeds, slime molds, and water molds. It is, however, a popular system that reflects the phylogeny of organisms as accepted by most scientists today.

All of the phyla, divisions, and classes of organisms as discussed in this textbook are outlined in this appendix. Viruses are not classified here as living organisms, but are described in Chapter 12.

KINGDOM MONERA

Prokaryotes; the bacteria. Unicellular organisms, sometimes forming filaments or colonies. Organisms that lack a nucleus or other membrane-bound structures. When flagella are present they are simple with a single fiber of protein. Reproduction is mainly asexual.

ARCHAEBACTERIA (ancient bacteria)

Phylum Methanocreatrices (methanogens)
Methane-producing; anaerobic; either nonmotile or with flagella; found in sewage, swamps, and intestines of animals including humans. Examples: *Methanogenium, Methanobacterium.*

Phylum Halobacteria (halophiles)
Rod-shaped; aerobic; live in salt flats and salt solutions; produce pinkish-orange pigments. Example: *Halococcus.*

Phylum Aphragmabacteria (Thermoacidophiles)
Wall-less; found on leaves of citrus plants, in scorching springs of yellowstone, and in humans as a cause of pneumonia. Examples: *Mycoplasma, Thermoplasma.*

Mycoplasma

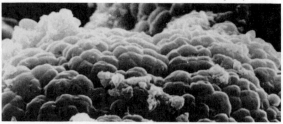

EUBACTERIA (true bacteria)

Phylum Omnibacteria
Rod-shaped or comma-shaped; anaerobic; one flagellum. Examples: *Escherichia, Salmonella.*

Phylum Actinobacteria
Filamentous; pathogenic, causing diseases such as leprosy and tuberculosis; some form nitrogen-fixing nodules on plant roots; many are a source of antibiotics. Examples: *Frankia, Streptomyces.*

Phylum Spirochaetae (spirochetes)
Tightly-coiled; anaerobic; spirilla with two to more than 100 flagella; commonly found in tooth plaque, in clams, and in the stomachs of cattle. Examples: *Spirochaeta, Treponema.*

Spirochaeta

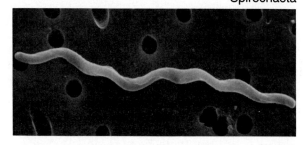

Phylum Chloroxybacteria (grass-green bacteria)
Photosynthetic autotrophs; marine; cocci; nonmotile. Example: *Prochloron.*

Phylum Cyanobacteria (blue-green bacteria)
Photosynthetic autotrophs; many fix atmospheric nitrogen; some form filaments or colonies. Examples: *Nostoc, Anabaena.*

KINGDOM PROTISTA

Mainly unicellular eukaryotes but also includes the multicellular seaweeds. Eukaryotes have a nucleus and other membrane-bound cell structures. Flagella, when present, are complex with an internal 9 + 2 arrangement of protein fibers. They are either heterotrophs or autotrophs: some capture their prey; some absorb food; and some make their own food. Some protists are animal-like, some are plant-like, and some are funguslike.

ANIMAL-LIKE PROTISTS

Phylum Rhizopoda (amoebas)
Unicellular heterotrophs; move by pseudopodia; reproduce by fission. Examples: *Amoeba, Foraminifera.*

Amoeba

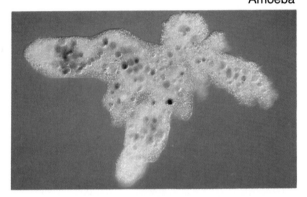

Phylum Ciliophora (ciliates)
Unicellular heterotrophs with large numbers of cilia; reproduce by conjugation. Example: *Paramecium.*

Phylum Sporozoa (sporozoans)
Unicellular heterotrophs; nonmotile; parasites of animals; form spores. Example: *Plasmodium.*

Phylum Zoomastigina (flagellates)
A diverse group of unicellular, flagellated, free-living or parasitic heterotrophs; from one to a thousand whiplike flagella; swim rapidly. Examples: *Giardia, Trypanosoma.*

PLANTLIKE PROTISTS

Phylum Euglenophyta (euglenoids)
Unicellular; photosynthetic autotrophs with two unequal flagella; reproduce by fission. Example: *Euglena.*

Phylum Bacillariophyta (diatoms)
Unicellular; photosynthetic autotrophs with a double shell of tan or brown silica resembling a petri dish with its lid; flagella absent; live in both salt and fresh water. Example: *Diatoma.*

Phylum Dinoflagellata (dinoflagellates)
Unicellular; photosynthetic autotrophs with stiff cellulose plates and two unequal flagella at right angles on the body; many are symbiotic in animals, form colorful tides, or are bioluminescent at regular intervals. Examples: *Gongaulax, Gymnodinium.*

Phylum Rhodophyta (red algae)
Mostly marine and multicellular autotrophs; with green and red pigments; no flagella. Example: *Gracilaria.*

Phylum Phaeophyta (brown algae)
Mostly marine and multicellular autotrophs; with green and brown pigments; keep afloat by bladders of carbon monoxide. Examples: *Sargassum, Laminaria.*

Phylum Chlorophyta (green algae)
Unicellular or multicellular autotrophs; with cellulose cell walls; live in salt or fresh water; have green and orange pigments; some with two equal flagella; others with no flagella. Examples: *Spirogyra, Chlamydomonas.*

FUNGUSLIKE PROTISTS

Phylum Acrasiomycota (cellular slime molds)
Unicellular, amoebalike; heterotrophs; aggregate in masses to form sporangia that release new amoeba-like forms. Examples: *Dictyostelium, Acrasia.*

Phylum Myxomycota (plasmodial slime molds)
Multicellular, slimy masses that can move from place to place; heterotrophs; sporangia form spores with new amoebalike forms. Examples: *Physarum, Ceratiomyxa.*

Slime mold

Phylum Oomycota (water molds, mildews)
Aquatic or terrestrial; unicellular or multicellular parasites, or saprobes that absorb dead organic matter; with cellulose cell walls; cause diseases of plants and animals. Examples: *Phytophthora, Saprolegnia.*

KINGDOM FUNGI

Filamentous eukaryotes with many nuclei. The nuclei are haploid. The zygote is the only diploid stage in the life cycle. Cell walls rich in chitin. No flagella. Filaments of fungi grow into a food source, secrete enzymes, and absorb the digested products.

Phylum Zygomycota (bread molds)
Hyphae aseptate except when forming sporangia; zygotes formed within a zygospore. Examples: *Mucor, Rhizopus.*

Phylum Ascomycota (yeasts and cup fungi)
Many cause plant diseases; hyphae divided by incomplete septas; spores formed in asci; syngamy within each ascus produces the zygote that divides to form ascospores. Examples: *Aleuria, Morchella.*

Scarlet cup fungus

Phylum Basidiomycota (mushrooms and rusts)
Hyphae divided by incomplete septas; basidiospores develop on stalks that project from the basidium; most form fruiting bodies outside their food source. Examples: *Amanita, Agaricus.*

Phylum Deuteromycota (imperfect fungi)
An artificial group made up mostly of ascomycotes for which the reproductive structures are unknown. Examples: *Fusarium, Monilia.*

Lichens (symbiosis between fungus and alga)
Symbiotic associations between an ascomycote or a basidiomycote and either a green alga or a cyanobacterium; fungus provides protection; the autotrophic organism produces a source of food. Examples: *Parmelia, Cladonia.*

KINGDOM PLANTAE

Multicellular eukaryotes. Cells contain chloroplasts with chlorophylls a and b, and that store starch. The cell walls have cellulose and sometimes lignin. They are protected by a waxy cuticle. All plants have an alternation of generations.

SPORE PLANTS

Division Bryophyta (bryophytes)
Nonvascular plants with dominant gametophyte stage; spores formed in capsules; sperm with two flagella; sporophyte dependent on gametophyte for water and nutrient supply.

Class Mucopsida (mosses)
Small, leafy plants with spores in capsules on stalks at tips of leafy stems; either upright or creeping stems; each rhizoid is several cells long. Examples: *Bryum, Polytrichum.*

Class Hepaticopsida (liverworts)
Some leafy and some thallose creeping gametophytes; green sporophytes enclosed within gametophyte; each rhizoid is just one long cell. Examples: *Porella, Pellia.*

Pellia

Division Psilophyta (whisk ferns)
Leafless, vascular plants with no distinction between root and stem; gametophytes with motile sperm; meiosis results in formation of spores. Example: *Psilotum.*

Division Lycophyta (club mosses)
Vascular plants with leafy sporophyte and spores in strobili; gametophytes with motile sperm. Examples: *Lycopodium, Selaginella.*

Division Sphenophyta (horsetails)
Vascular plants with ribbed and jointed stems; scalelike leaves; spores produced in conelike strobili; gametophytes with motile sperm. Example: *Equisetum.*

Division Pterophyta (ferns)
Vascular plants with rhizomes; sporophyte often with finely divided fronds; spores produced in clusters of sporangia called sori; gametophytes with motile sperm. Examples: *Polypodium, Asplenium.*

SEED PLANTS
Division Ginkgophyta (ginkgos)
Deciduous gymnosperms, in which ovules are naked at fertilization; one species living called the maidenhair tree; fan-shaped leaves with branching veins; ovules fleshy; sperm with flagella inside the pollen; gametophytes reduced and held within the ovule or pollen grain. Example: *Ginkgo.*

Division Cycadophyta (cycads)
Palmlike gymnosperms; large compound leaves; cones at the stem apex; sperm with flagella inside the pollen. Examples: *Cycas, Encephalartos.*

Division Coniferophyta (conifers)
Deciduous or evergreen gymnosperms; mostly trees, some shrubs; leaves needlelike or scalelike, hard and leathery; sperm nonmotile and transferred to ovule by the pollen tube. Examples: *Pinus, Picea.*

Division Gnetophyta (gnetum)
A diverse group of three genera of gymnosperms; lack antheridia; sperm nonmotile. Examples: *Welwitschia, Ephedra.*

Division Anthophyta (flowering plants)
The dominant group of plants; angiosperms in which ovules are protected at fertilization by an ovary; antheridia and archegonia lacking gametophytes reduced to a few cells; sperm carried to ovules by the pollen tube: have flowers and fruits; fertilization is double, forming the zygote and the endosperm of the embryo.

Class Dicotyledones (dicots)
Flowering plants with two cotyledons; leaves with netlike veins; flower parts in fours or fives; vascular bundles form a ring in the stem. Examples: *Acer, Chrysanthemum.*

Class Monocotyledones (monocots)
Flowering plants with one cotyledon; leaves with parallel veins; flower parts in threes; vascular bundles are scattered in the stems. Examples: *Allium, Phoenix.*

Cattleya orchid

KINGDOM ANIMALIA
Multicellular eukaryotes that ingest their food. Most animals have cells organized into tissues, organs, and organ systems. Eggs are nonmotile and much larger than the motile sperm.

INVERTEBRATES
Phylum Porifera (sponges)
Different types of cells are grouped together forming a network of chambers; amoebalike cells secrete spicules; collar cells with beating flagella that draw food in through pores; both marine and freshwater species. Examples: *Euspongia, Euplectella.*

Phylum Cnidaria (corals, jellyfish, hydras)
Radially symmetrical with two layers of cells surrounding a body cavity with one opening at the mouth; mouth is fringed by tentacles that sting and paralyze prey; two types of body structures in the life cycle are sessile polyps and free-swimming medusas; polyps often reproduce by budding; medusas reproduce sexually; nearly all marine.

Class Hydrozoa (hydroids)
Typical hydroids pass through both polyp and medusa phases in their life cycles, but some live only as polyps; most are colonial. Examples: *Obelia, Hydra.*

Class Scyphozoa (jellyfish)
The medusa phase is the dominant form of the life cycle; most jellyfish are found in coastal waters. Examples: *Aurelia, Cassiopea.*

Class Anthozoa (corals, sea anemones)
Only polyp stages occur; either solitary or colonial. Example: *Madrepora.*

Jellyfish

Phylum Platyhelminthes (flatworms)
Bilaterally symmetrical with no coelom or circulatory system; the simplest animals that have organs; the gut has only one opening; hermaphrodites.

Class Turbellaria (free-living flatworms)
Move by means of cilia; have eyespots; marine or freshwater species. Example: *Planaria.*

Class Trematoda (flukes)
Parasitic worms with a life cycle that involves two or more hosts. Examples: *Schistosoma, Fasciola.*

Class Cestoda (tapeworms)
Parasitic worm with no digestive tract; absorb food through their body walls. Examples: *Taenia, Echinococcus.*

Phylum Nematoda (roundworms)
Bilaterally symmetrical; cylindrical; with a pseudocoelom; many parasites of plants and animals; occur almost everywhere. Example: *Ascaris.*

Phylum Mollusca (mollusks)
Bilaterally symmetrical; coelomate; both terrestrial and aquatic; locomotion by a muscular foot; many have a head, shells, and a radula for obtaining food; the circulatory system is open.

Class Gastropoda (snails and slugs)
Most have a spiral shell, a head, and one or two pairs of tentacles; slugs have lost their external shells over time. Examples: *Helix, Littorina.*

Slug

Class Bivalvia (bivalves)
Have two hinged shells and a wedge-shaped foot; no distinct head or radula; filter feeders; disperse by free-swimming larvae. Examples: *Mytilus, Pecten.*

Class Cephalopoda (octopuses, squids)
They evolved into a series of tentacles; the shell is internal, external, or absent; have highly developed eyes; a complex nervous system. Examples: *Octopus, Loligo.*

Phylum Annelida (annelids)
Segmented worms; bilaterally symmetrical; have a coelom; a brain; a closed circulatory system; digestive tract with two openings.

Class Polychaeta (polychaetes)
Mainly marine; distinct head; eyes; movement by parapodia on most segments; free- swimming larvae. Examples: *Nereis, Bispira.*

Class Oligochaete (earthworms)
Terrestrial or aquatic; no distinct head; poorly developed sense organs. Example: *Lumbricus.*

Class Hirudinea (leeches)
External parasites; dorsiventrally flattened; predators or scavengers; suckers at one or both ends of body. Example: *Hirudo.*

Phylum Arthropoda (arthropods)
Bilaterally symmetrical; a coelom; segmented body; chitinous exoskeleton; complete digestive tract; jointed appendages; the largest phylum of animals.

Class Arachnida (spiders, mites, scorpions)
Mainly terrestrial; carnivorous; have chelicerae and pedipalps for catching prey; four pairs of walking legs. Examples: *Araneus, Trombicula.*

Class Merostomata (horseshoe crabs)
Marine; have chelicerae, five pairs of walking legs, and book gills. Example: *Limulus.*

Class Crustacea (lobsters, crayfish, crabs)
Mainly aquatic; have mandibles and two-branched appendages; many with free-swimming larvae; two pairs of antennae. Examples: *Balanus, Homarus.*

Class Chilopoda (centipedes)
Carnivores; a head with mandibles; 15 to 177 body segments, each with one pair of legs. Examples: *Scolopendra, Scutigera.*

Class Diplopoda (millipedes)
Mostly herbivores; head with mandibles; 20 to 200 segments, each with two pairs of legs. Example: *Cylindroiulus.*

Class Insecta (insects)
Mostly terrestrial; body with a head, a thorax, and abdomen; mouthparts different in each order; compound eyes; one pair of antennae on the head; six legs on the thorax; wings either absent or one or two pairs on the thorax; many have complex metamorphosis; about 28 orders.

Butterfly

Phylum Echinodermata (echinoderms)
Marine invertebrates with a coelom; more or less radially symmetrical adults; calcareous plates in the epidermis; water vascular system extends as tube feet through pores in the plates.

Class Crinoidea (sea lilies, feather stars)
Filter feeders; mouth and anus in a disc on upper surface; 5 to 200 feathery arms around margin of this disc. Example: *Antedon.*

Sea star

Class Asteroidea (sea stars)
Star-shaped; five to many arms from a central disc; mouth and anus on lower surface; move by rows of tube feet. Example: *Asterias.*

Class Ophiuroidea (brittle stars)
Star-shaped; arms long, slender, spiny, and flexible. Example: *Ophiothrix.*

Class Echinoidea (sea urchins and sand dollars)
No distinct arms; a rigid external covering; move by tube feet or jointed spines. Example: *Echinus.*

Class Holothuroidea (sea cucumbers)
Sluglike; lie on their sides. Example: *Cucumaria.*

VERTEBRATES

Phylum Chordata (chordates)
Bilaterally symmetrical; coelom; have a notochord, hollow nerve cord, gill slits, and a tail at some stage of their development.

Subphylum Urochordata (tunicates)
Free-swimming larvae with a notochord; adults saclike and no body cavity; obtain food by movement of cilia. Example: *Ciona.*

Subphylum Cephalochordata (lancelets)
Marine; fishlike; a permanent notochord; no internal skeleton; filter feeders by movement of cilia at gill slits. Example: *Branchiostoma.*

Subphylum Vertebrata (vertebrates)
Notochord replaced by cartilage or bone forming a segmented vertebral column called the backbone; a distinct head with a skull and brain; nerve chord protected by the vertebral column.

Class Agnatha (lampreys and hagfish)
Aquatic; no scales; eel-like; jawless fish; cartilaginous skeleton; no fins; parasites or scavengers. Example: *Petromyzon.*

Class Chondrichthyes (sharks, skates, rays)
Mostly marine; skeleton of cartilage; fins; scales pointed; no air bladders. Example: *Manta.*

Class Osteichthyes (bony fish)
Abundant in both marine and fresh water; bony skeletons; fins; scales; air bladders. Examples: *Salmo, Anguilla, Hippocampus, Gadus.*

Damsel fish

Class Amphibia (salamanders, frogs, and toads)
Ectothermic; egg-laying; lack scales; larvae respire with gills; adults respire with lungs; depend on a moist environment for at least one part of their life cycles; have incomplete double circulation; three orders.

Class Reptilia (reptiles)
Ectothermic; amniotic eggs; scales; respire with lungs; most are terrestrial; have incomplete double circulation; legs absent in snakes and some lizards; four orders.

Class Aves (birds)
Endothermic; feathers; forelimbs are modified into wings; most can fly; all lay amniotic eggs; respire with lungs; terrestrial; have complete double circulation; about 30 orders.

Cheetahs

Class Mammalia (mammals)
Endothermic; complete double circulation; hairy epidermis; forelimbs modified into wings in bats, and flippers in aquatic mammals; females have mammary glands that secrete milk to nourish the young.

This list of Greek and Latin roots will help you interpret the meaning of biological terms. The column headed *Root* gives many of the actual Greek (GK) or Latin (L) root words used in science. If more than one word is given, the first is the full word in Greek or Latin. The letter groups that follow are forms in which the root word is most often found combined in science words. In the second column is the meaning of the root as it is used in science. The third column shows a typical science word containing the root from the first column. Most of these words can be found in your textbook.

Root	Meaning	Example	Root	Meaning	Example
a, an (GK)	not, without	anaerobic	binarius (L)	pair	binary fission
abilis (L)	able to	biodegradable	bios (GK)	life	biology
ad (L)	to, attached to	appendix	blastos (GK)	bud	blastula
aequus (L)	equal	equilibrium	bryon (GK)	moss	bryophyte
aeros (GK)	air	anaerobic	bursa (L)	purse, bag	bursa
agon (GK)	assembly	glucagon			
aktis (GK)	ray	actin	caedere, cide (L)	kill	insecticide
allas (GK)	sausage	allantois	capillus (L)	hair	capillary
allelon (GK)	of each other	allele	carn (L)	flesh	carnivore
allucinari (L)	to dream	hallucinate	carno (L)	flesh	carnivore
alveolus (L)	small pit	alveolus	cella, cellula (L)	small room	protocells
amnos (GK)	lamb	amnion	cervix (L)	neck	cervix
amoibe (GK)	change	amoebocyte	cetus (L)	whale	cetacean
amphi (GK)	both, about, around	amphibian	chaite, chaet (GK)	bristle	oligochaeta
			cheir (GK)	hand	chiropteran
amylum (L)	starch	amylase	chele (GK)	claw	chelicerae
ana (L)	away, onward	anaphase	chloros (GK)	pale green	chlorophyll
andro (GK)	male	androgens	chondros (GK)	cartilage	Chondrichthyes
anggeion, angio (GK)	vessel, container	angiosperm	chondros (GK)	grain	mitochondrion
anthos (GK)	flower	anthophyte	chorda (L)	cord	urochordata
anti (GK)	against, away, opposite	antibody	chorion (GK)	skin	chorion
			chroma, chrom (GK)	colored	chromosome
aqua (L)	water	aquatic	chronos (GK)	time	chronometer
archaios, archeo (GK)	ancient, primitive	archaebacteria	circa (L)	about	circadian
			cirrus (L)	curl	cirri
arthron (GK)	joint, jointed	arthropod	codex (L)	tablet for writing	codon
artios (GK)	even	artiodactyl	corpus (L)	body	corpus luteum
askos (GK)	bag	ascospore	cum, col, com, con (L)	with, together	convergent
aster (GK)	star	Asteroidea			
autos (GK)	self	autoimmune	cuticula (L)	thin skin	cuticle
bakterion (GK)	small rod	bacterium			
bi, bis (L)	two, twice	bipedal	daktylos (GK)	finger	perissodactyl

Root	Meaning	Example	Root	Meaning	Example
de (L)	away, from	decompose	gestare (L)	to bear	progesterone
decidere (L)	to fall down	deciduous	glene (GK)	eyeball	euglenoid
degradare (L)	to reduce in rank	biodegradable	globus (L)	sphere	hemoglobin
dendron (GK)	tree	dendrite	glotta (GK)	tongue	epiglottis
dens (L)	tooth	edentate	glykys, glu (GK)	sweet	glycolysis
derma (GK)	skin	epidermis	gnathos (GK)	jaw	Agnatha
deterere (L)	loose material	detritus	gonos, gon (GK)	reproductive, sexual	gonorrhea
dia, di (GK)	through, apart	diastolic	gradus (L)	a step	gradualism
dies (L)	day	circadian	graphos (GK)	written	chromatograph
diploos (GK)	twofold, double	diploid	gravis (L)	heavy	gravitropism
dis, di (GK)	twice, two	disaccharide	gymnos (GK)	naked, bare	gymnosperm
dis, di (L)	apart, away	disruptive	gyne (GK)	female, woman	gynoecium
dormire (L)	to sleep	dormancy			
drom, drome (GK)	running, racing	dromedary	haima, emia (GK)	blood	hemoglobin
ducere (L)	to lead	oviduct	halo (GK)	salt	halophile
			haploos (GK)	simple	haploid
echinos (GK)	spine	echinoderm	haurire (L)	to drink	haustorium
eidos, oid (GK)	form, appearance	rhizoid	helix (L)	spiral	helix
ella (GK)	small	organelle	hemi (GK)	half	hemisphere
endon, en, endo (GK)	within	endosperm	herba (L)	grass	herbivore
			hermaphroditos (GK)	combining both sexes	hermaphrodite
engchyma (GK)	infusion	parenchyma	heteros (GK)	other	heterotrophic
enteron (GK)	intestine, gut	enterocolitis	hierarches (GK)	rank	hierarchy
entomon (GK)	insect	entomology	hippos (GK)	horse	hippopotamus
epi (GK)	upon, above	epidermis	histos (GK)	tissue	histology
equus (L)	horse	Equisetum	holos (GK)	whole	Holothuroidea
erythros (GK)	red	erythrocyte	homo (L)	man	hominid
eu (GK)	well, true, good	eukaryote	homos (GK)	same, alike	homologous
evolutus (L)	rolled out	evolution	hormaein (GK)	to excite	hormone
ex, e (L)	out	extinction	hydor, hydro (GK)	water	hydrolysis
exo (GK)	out, outside	exoskeleton	hyper (GK)	over, above	hyperventilation
extra (L)	outside, beyond	extracellular	hyphe (GK)	web	hypha
			hypo (GK)	under, below	hypotonic
ferre (L)	to bear	porifera			
fibrilla (L)	small fiber	myofibril	ichthys (GK)	fish	Osteichthyes
fissus (L)	a split	binary fission	instinctus (L)	impulse	instinct
flagellum (L)	whip	flagellum	insula (L)	island	insulin
follis (L)	bag	follicle	inter (L)	between	internode
fossilis (L)	dug up	microfossils	intra (L)	within, inside	intracellular
fungus (L)	mushroom	fungus	isos (GK)	equal	isotonic
			itis (GK)	inflammation, disease	arthritis
gamo, gam (GK)	marriage	gamete			
gaster (GK)	stomach	gastropoda	jugare (L)	join together	conjugate
ge, geo (GK)	earth	geology			
gemmula (L)	little bud	gemmule	kardia, cardia (GK)	heart	cardiac
genesis (L)	origin, birth	parthenogenesis	karyon (GK)	nut	prokaryote
genos, gen, geny (GK)	race	genotype	kata, cata (GK)	break down	catabolism

Root	Meaning	Example	Root	Meaning	Example
kephale, ceph (GK)	head	cephalopoda	nema (GK)	thread	nematology
keras (GK)	horn	chelicerae	nemato (GK)	thread, threadlike	nematode
kinein (GK)	to move	kinetic	neos (GK)	new	Neolithic
koilos, coel (GK)	hollow cavity, belly	coelom	nephros (GK)	kidney	nephron
			neuro (GK)	nerve	neurology
kokkus (GK)	berry	streptococcus	nodus (L)	knot, knob	internode
kolla (GK)	glue	colloid	nomos, nomy (GK)	ordered knowledge, law	taxonomy
kotyl, cotyl (GK)	cup	cotylosaur			
kreas (GK)	flesh	pancreas	noton (GK)	back	notochord
krinoeides (GK)	lilylike	Crinoidea			
kyanos, cyano (GK)	blue	cyanobacterium	oikos, eco (GK)	household	ecosystem
			oisein, eso (GK)	to carry	esophagus
kystis, cyst (GK)	bladder, sac	cystitis	oligos (GK)	few, little	oligochaeta
kytos, cyt (GK)	hollow, cell	lymphocyte	omnis (L)	all	omnivore
			ophis (GK)	serpent	Ophiuroidea
lagos (GK)	hare	lagomorph	ophthalmos (GK)	referring to the eye	ophthalmologist
leukos (GK)	white	leukocyte			
libra (L)	balance	equilibrium	organon (GK)	tool, implement	organelle
logos, logy (GK)	study, word	biology	ornis (GK)	bird	ornithology
luminescere (L)	to grow light	bioluminescence	orthos (GK)	straight	orthodontist
luteus (L)	orange-yellow	corpus luteum	osculum (L)	small mouth	osculum
lyein, lysis (GK)	to split, loosen	lysosome	osteon (GK)	bone	osteocyte
lympha (L)	water	lymphocyte	ostrakon (GK)	shell	ostracoderm
			oura, ura (GK)	tail	anura
makros (GK)	large	macrophage	ous, oto (GK)	ear	otology
marsupium (L)	pouch	marsupial	ovum (L)	egg	oviduct
meare (L)	to glide	permeable			
megas (GK)	large	megaspore	palaios, paleo (GK)	ancient	paleontology
melas (GK)	black, dark	melanin	pan (GK)	all	pancreas
meristos (GK)	divided	meristem	para (GK)	beside	parenchyma
meros (GK)	part	polymer	parthenos (GK)	virgin	parthenogenesis
mesos (GK)	middle	mesophyll	pathos (GK)	disease, suffering	pathogenic
meta (GK)	after, following	metaphase	pausere (L)	to rest	decompose
metabole (GK)	change	metabolism	pendere (L)	to hang	appendix
meter (GK)	a measurement	diameter	per (L)	through	permeable
mikros, micro (GK)	small	microscope	peri (GK)	around	peristalsis
			periodos (GK)	a cycle	photoperiodism
mimos (GK)	a mime	mimicry	pes, pedis (L)	foot	bipedal
mitos (GK)	thread	mitochondrion	phagein (GK)	to eat	phagocyte
molluscus (L)	soft	mollusk	phainein (GK)	to show	phenotype
monos (GK)	single	monotreme	phaios (GK)	dusky	phaeophyta
morphe (GK)	form	lagomorph	phase (GK)	stage, appearance	metaphase
mors, mort (L)	death	mortality			
mucus (L)	mucus, slime	mucosa	pherein, phor (GK)	to carry	pheromone
multus (L)	many	multicellular	phloios (GK)	inner bark	phloem
mutare (L)	to change	mutation	phos, photos (GK)	light	phototropism
mykes, myc (GK)	fungus	mycorrhiza	phyllon (GK)	leaf	chlorophyll
mys (GK)	muscle	myosin	phylon (GK)	related group	phylogeny

Root	Meaning	Example	Root	Meaning	Example
phyton (GK)	plant	epiphyte	stasis (GK)	standing, staying	homeostasis
pinax (GK)	tablet	pinacocytes	stellein, stol (GK)	to draw in	peristalsis
pinein (GK)	to drink	pinocytosis	sternon (GK)	chest	sternum
pinna (L)	feather	pinniped	stinguere (L)	to quench	extinction
plasma (GK)	mold, form	plasmodium	stolo (L)	shoot	stolon
plastos (GK)	formed object	chloroplast	stoma (GK)	mouth	stoma
platys (GK)	flat	platyhelminthes	streptos (GK)	twisted chain	streptococcus
plax (GK)	plate	placoderm	syn (GK)	together	systolic
pleuron (GK)	side	dipleurula	synapsis (GK)	union	synapse
plicare (L)	to fold	replication	systema (GK)	composite whole	ecosystem
polys, poly (GK)	many	polymer			
poros (GK)	channel	porifera	taxis, taxo (GK)	to arrange	taxonomy
post (L)	after	posterior	telos (GK)	end	telophase
pous, pod (GK)	foot	gastropoda	terra (L)	land, Earth	terrestrial
prae, pre (L)	before	Precambrian	thele (GK)	cover a surface	epithelium
primus (L)	first	primary	therme (GK)	heat	endotherm
pro (GK and L)	before, for	prokaryote	thrix, trich (GK)	hair	trichocyst
proboskis (GK)	trunk	proboscidean	tome (GK)	cutting	anatomy
producere (L)	to bring forth	reproduction	trachia (GK)	windpipe	tracheid
protos (GK)	first	protocells	trans (L)	across	transpiration
pseudes (GK)	false	pseudopod	trematodes (GK)	having holes	monotreme
pteron (GK)	wing	chiropteran	trope (GK)	turn	gravitropism
punctus (L)	a point	punctuated	trophe (GK)	nourishment	heterotrophic
pupa (L)	doll	pupa	turbo (L)	whirl	turbellaria
			tympanon (GK)	drum	tympanum
radius (L)	ray	radial	typos (GK)	model	genotype
re (L)	again	reproduction			
reflectere (L)	to turn back	reflex	uni (L)	one	unicellular
rhiza (GK)	root	mycorrhiza	uterus (L)	womb	uterus
rhodon (GK)	rose	rhodophyte			
rota (L)	wheel	rotifer	vacca (L)	cow	vaccine
rumpere (L)	to break	disruptive	vagina (L)	sheath	vagina
			valvae (L)	folding doors	bivalvia
saeta (L)	bristle	Equisetum	vasculum (L)	small vessel	vascular
sapros (GK)	rotten	saprobe	venter (L)	belly	ventricle
sarx (GK)	flesh	sarcomere	ventus (L)	a wind	hyperventilation
sauros (GK)	lizard	cotylosaur	vergere (L)	to slant, incline	convergent
scire (L)	to know	science	villus (L)	shaggy hair	villus
scribere, script (L)	to write	transcription	virus (L)	poisonous liquid	virus
sedere, ses (L)	to sit	sessile			
semi (L)	half	semicircle	vorare (L)	to devour	carnivore
skopein, scop (GK)	to look	microscope			
soma (GK)	body	lysosome	xeros (GK)	dry	xerophyte
sperma (GK)	seed	angiosperm	xylon (GK)	wood	xylem
spirare (L)	to breathe	spiracle			
sporos (GK)	seed	microspore	zoon, zo (GK)	animal	zoology
staphylo (GK)	bunch of grapes	staphylococcus	zygotos (GK)	joined together	zygote

Biochemistry

THE CITRIC ACID CYCLE

In Chapter 6, you learned that the citric acid cycle is an important feature of aerobic respiration. The citric acid cycle is also called the Krebs cycle in honor of Sir Hans Krebs (1900–1981), a British biochemist who worked out its reactions. Chapter 6 gave a simple presentation of the citric acid cycle. Here, you can examine the cycle more closely and observe the changes in chemical structure that occur. In this way, you can see how the cycle releases energy efficiently and in a stepwise manner. Keep in mind that all the reactions are carried out by enzymes.

Follow the diagram of the cycle on the next page, beginning with the entry of acetyl coenzyme A. Besides glycolysis of glucose, acetyl CoA can come from the breakdown of fats, proteins, and other carbohydrates. Acetyl CoA attaches its two carbon atoms to a 4-carbon molecule of oxaloacetic acid to produce a 6-carbon compound, citric acid. This is the acid that gives a sour taste to lemons, oranges, and other citrus fruit. An enzyme causes citric acid to lose a water molecule to form *cis*-aconitic acid. The next reaction takes in a water molecule, but the atoms go to different positions to produce isocitric acid.

In the next reaction, an enzyme removes two hydrogen atoms which are added to NAD^+ to form $NADH + H^+$. The product, oxalosuccinic acid, loses a molecule of carbon dioxide to form α-ketoglutaric acid. This compound combines with coenzyme A and loses two hydrogen atoms to form another unit of $NADH + H^+$. It then gives off another molecule of carbon dioxide to produce succinyl CoA. Notice that the cycle has now returned to a 4-carbon unit. However, several more events take place before the cycle is ready to take in another acetyl group.

Succinyl CoA loses coenzyme A and releases enough energy to form a molecule of ATP from ADP and a phosphate group (P_i). This leaves succinic acid, which loses two hydrogen atoms to FAD, a carrier molecule similar to NAD^+. The resulting fumaric acid reacts with water to form malic acid. Malic acid loses two hydrogen atoms to form NADH $+ H^+$ and oxaloacetic acid, which can now react

with a new acetyl CoA to start the citric acid cycle again.

From Chapter 6, recall that during glycolysis, each 6-carbon glucose has been split into two pyruvic acid molecules having three carbon atoms each. In forming acetyl CoA, each pyruvic acid loses a carbon atom as carbon dioxide. Therefore, each glucose contributes two acetyl groups, resulting in two turns of the cycle.

So far, you have seen little energy released by the citric acid cycle—only one ATP is produced during each turn of the cycle. Remember, though, that several pairs of hydrogen atoms have been attached to the carrier molecules NAD^+ and FAD. These carriers deliver their hydrogen electrons to the electron transport chain where the major energy payoff occurs. Recall that the hydrogens end up combining with an oxygen atom at the end of the chain. Without oxygen, the chain cannot process the hydrogen removed during the citric acid cycle.

The following account shows the energy yield from one glucose molecule going through aerobic respiration. Review in Chapter 6 the processes leading up to the citric acid cycle. In general, the electron transport chain produces three ATP for each pair of electrons it receives from $NADH + H^+$ and two ATP for every $FADH_2$.

Step	ATP	NADPH + H^+	FADH$_2$
Glycolysis	2	2	0
Acetyl CoA formation	0	2	0
Citric Acid Cycle (2 turns)	2	6	2
Totals	4	10	2
ATP Produced	4	30	4
Total ATP output = 4 + 30 + 4 = 38 molecules			

Because of inefficiency and other factors, the ATP yield is seldom 38 molecules but more often between 32 and 36.

Citric Acid Cycle

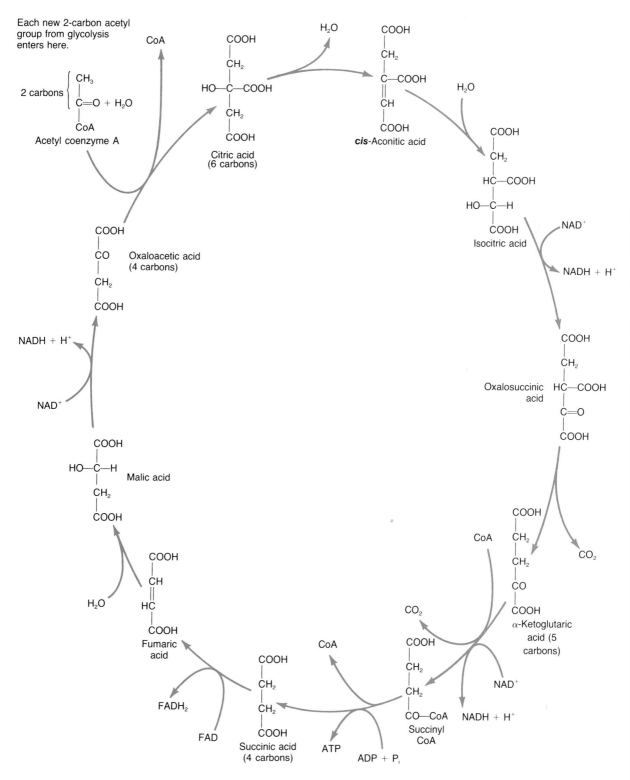

Each new 2-carbon acetyl group from glycolysis enters here.

2 carbons $\{$ Acetyl coenzyme A

Citric acid (6 carbons)

H_2O

cis-Aconitic acid

H_2O

Isocitric acid

NAD^+

$NADH + H^+$

Oxalosuccinic acid

CO_2

α-Ketoglutaric acid (5 carbons)

NAD^+

$NADH + H^+$

CO_2

Succinyl CoA

CoA

CoA

ATP

$ADP + P_i$

Succinic acid (4 carbons)

FAD

$FADH_2$

Fumaric acid

H_2O

Malic acid

NAD^+

$NADH + H^+$

Oxaloacetic acid (4 carbons)

CoA

THE CALVIN CYCLE

The Calvin cycle was previously called the dark reactions of photosynthesis, and this term may still be found in some books. The Calvin cycle was called the dark reactions to differentiate it from the light reactions and to emphasize the fact that light was not required for the reactions to take place. Most scientists now think the term "dark reactions" is misleading because the cycle cannot take place without energy and raw materials furnished by the light reactions. In addition, the term led many students to believe that the Calvin cycle occurred only in the dark.

As you learned in Chapter 6, the Calvin cycle takes place in the stroma of chloroplasts. The overall function of the Calvin cycle is to fix carbon dioxide from the atmosphere, and use it to build organic molecules that store energy. Examples of products of the Calvin cycle include simple sugars such as glucose, disaccharides such as sucrose, and polysaccharides such as starch and cellulose. Molecules produced by the Calvin cycle also produce fats and oils as well as amino acids for proteins. It is the Calvin cycle and its suppliers, the light reactions, that enable green plants to be called producers.

On the following page is a more detailed version of the Calvin cycle than was presented in Chapter 6. All the reactions shown are carried out by enzymes. In the following diagram, six carbon dioxide molecules are shown going through the cycle. The purpose is to show the fixation of enough carbon molecules to form a typical 6-carbon sugar.

To begin, six carbon dioxide molecules are combined by an enzyme with six molecules of ribulose bisphosphate. This reaction changes the 5-carbon molecules of ribulose bisphosphate to 6-carbon molecules. The unstable 6-carbon molecules formed break down into twelve 3-carbon molecules of phosphoglyceric acid (PGA). Notice that at this point, there are 36 carbon atoms in the cycle.

In the next step, materials and energy provided by the light reactions are first used in the Calvin cycle. With the energy and the phosphate groups from twelve ATPs, the twelve PGAs are transformed into twelve molecules of diphosphoglyceric acid. Then, twelve NADPH + twelve H^+ from the light reactions contribute hydrogen atoms, and twelve phosphate groups are removed. This process leaves twelve phosphoglyceraldehyde (PGAL) molecules. Still, there are 36 carbon atoms in the cycle.

PGAL is the substance that leaves the cycle to be used in making sugar, starch, cellulose, and other products. Two PGALs would be removed from the cycle to form a 6-carbon sugar such as glucose. The two PGALs that are removed contain six carbon atoms. This leaves ten PGALs in the cycle for a total of 30 carbon atoms. However, the 30 carbon atoms are in the form of 3-carbon molecules. To complete the cycle, six new 5-carbon ribulose diphosphate molecules must be formed from ten 3-carbon units. To accomplish this transformation, several reactions take place. These reactions combine, rearrange, break apart, and recombine molecules, finally to yield six molecules of ribulose phosphate. If you would like to see what the intermediate reactions are, consult any modern biochemistry reference. Ribulose phosphate reacts with six more ATPs produced by light reactions. This yields six molecules of ribulose diphosphate ready to fix another six CO_2 molecules.

The Calvin Cycle

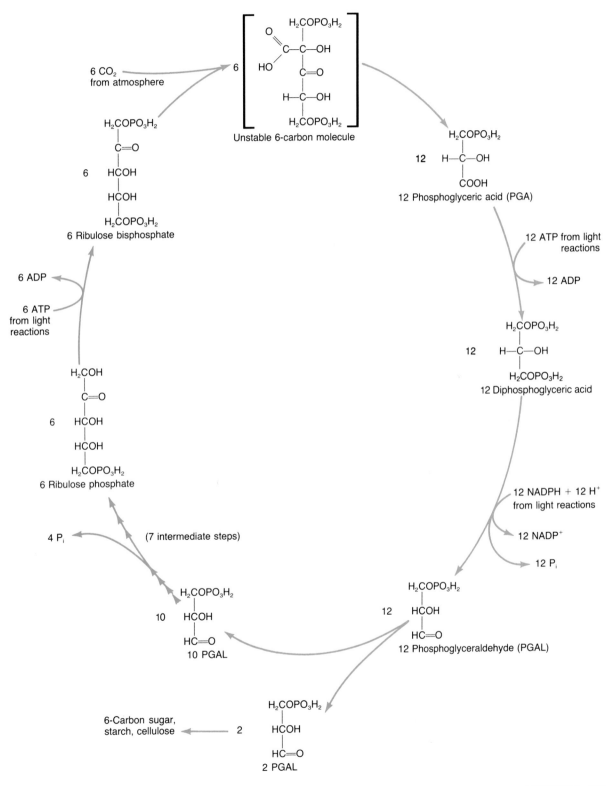

6 CO₂ from atmosphere

6 [Unstable 6-carbon molecule]

12 Phosphoglyceric acid (PGA)

12 ATP from light reactions

12 ADP

6 Ribulose bisphosphate

6 ADP

6 ATP from light reactions

12 Diphosphoglyceric acid

6 Ribulose phosphate

12 NADPH + 12 H⁺ from light reactions

12 NADP⁺

12 Pᵢ

4 Pᵢ

(7 intermediate steps)

10 PGAL

12 Phosphoglyceraldehyde (PGAL)

6-Carbon sugar, starch, cellulose

2 PGAL

Appendix D

Safety in the Laboratory

The biology laboratory is a safe place to work if you are aware of important safety rules and if you are careful. You must be responsible for your own safety and for the safety of others. The safety rules given here will protect you and others from harm in the lab. While carrying out procedures in any of the **Biolabs,** notice the safety symbols and caution statements. The safety symbols are explained in the chart on the next page.

1. Always obtain your teacher's permission to begin a lab.
2. Study the procedure. If you have questions, ask your teacher. Be sure you understand all safety symbols shown.
3. Use the safety equipment provided for you. Goggles and a safety apron should be worn when any lab calls for using chemicals.
4. When you are heating a test tube, always slant it so the mouth points away from you and others.
5. Never eat or drink in the lab. Never inhale chemicals. Do not taste any substance or draw any material into your mouth.
6. If you spill any chemical, wash it off immediately with water. Report the spill immediately to your teacher.

7. Know the location and proper use of the fire extinguisher, safety shower, fire blanket, first aid kit, and fire alarm.
8. Keep all materials away from open flames. Tie back long hair.
9. If a fire should break out in the classroom, or if your clothing should catch fire, smother it with the fire blanket or a coat, or get under a safety shower. **NEVER RUN.**
10. Report any accident or injury, no matter how small, to your teacher.

Follow these procedures as you clean up your work area.

1. Turn off the water and gas. Disconnect electrical devices.
2. Return materials to their places.
3. Dispose of chemicals and other materials as directed by your teacher. Place broken glass and solid substances in the proper containers. Never discard materials in the sink.
4. Clean your work area.
5. Wash your hands thoroughly after working in the laboratory.

Injury	Safe response
FIRST AID IN THE LABORATORY	
Burns	Apply cold water. Call your teacher immediately.
Cuts and bruises	Stop any bleeding by applying direct pressure. Cover cuts with a clean dressing. Apply cold compresses to bruises. Call your teacher immediately.
Fainting	Leave the person lying down. Loosen any tight clothing and keep crowds away. Call your teacher immediately.
Foreign matter in eye	Flush with plenty of water. Use eyewash bottle or fountain.
Poisoning	Note the suspected poisoning agent and call your teacher immediately.
Any spills on skin	Flush with large amounts of water or use safety shower. Call your teacher immediately.

Safety Symbols

DISPOSAL ALERT
This symbol appears when care must be taken to dispose of materials properly.

ANIMAL SAFETY
This symbol appears whenever live animals are studied and the safety of the animals and the students must be ensured.

BIOLOGICAL HAZARD
This symbol appears when there is danger involving bacteria, fungi, or protists.

RADIOACTIVE SAFETY
This symbol appears when radioactive materials are used.

OPEN FLAME ALERT
This symbol appears when use of an open flame could cause a fire or an explosion.

CLOTHING PROTECTION SAFETY
This symbol appears when substances used could stain or burn clothing.

THERMAL SAFETY
This symbol appears as a reminder to use caution when handling hot objects.

FIRE SAFETY
This symbol appears when care should be taken around open flames.

SHARP OBJECT SAFETY
This symbol appears when a danger of cuts or punctures caused by the use of sharp objects exists.

EXPLOSION SAFETY
This symbol appears when the misuse of chemicals could cause an explosion.

FUME SAFETY
This symbol appears when chemicals or chemical reactions could cause dangerous fumes.

EYE SAFETY
This symbol appears when a danger to the eyes exists. Safety goggles should be worn when this symbol appears.

ELECTRICAL SAFETY
This symbol appears when care should be taken when using electrical equipment.

POISON SAFETY
This symbol appears when poisonous substances are used.

PLANT SAFETY
This symbol appears when poisonous plants or plants with thorns are handled.

CHEMICAL SAFETY
This symbol appears when chemicals used can cause burns or are poisonous if absorbed through the skin.

Appendix E

SI Measurement

The International System (SI) of Measurement is accepted as the standard for measurement throughout most of the world. Four of the base units in SI are the meter, liter, kilogram, and second. Other frequently used SI units are degrees, joules, newtons, watts, and pascals. The size of a unit can be determined from the prefix used with the base unit name. For example: *kilo* means a thousand; *milli* means a thousandth; *micro* means a millionth; and *centi* means a hundredth. The tables below give the standard symbols for these SI units and some of their equivalents.

Larger and smaller units of measurement in SI are obtained by multiplying or dividing the base unit by some multiple of ten. Multiply to change from larger units to smaller units. Divide to change from smaller units to larger units. For example, to change 1 km to m, you would multiply 1 km by 1000 to obtain 1000 m. To change 10 g to kg, you would divide 10 g by 1000 to obtain 0.01 kg.

Table E–1

COMMON SI UNITS			
Measurement	**Unit**	**Symbol**	**Equivalents**
Length	1 millimeter	mm	1000 micrometers (μm)
	1 centimeter	cm	10 millimeters (mm)
	1 meter	m	100 centimeters (cm)
	1 kilometer	km	1000 meters (m)
Volume	1 milliliter	mL	1 cubic centimeter (cm^3 or cc)
	1 liter	L	1000 milliliters (mL)
Mass	1 gram	g	1000 milligrams (mg)
	1 kilogram	kg	1000 grams (g)
	1 tonne	t	1000 kilograms (kg) = 1 metric ton
Time	1 second	s	
Area	1 square meter	m^2	10 000 square centimeters (cm^2)
	1 square kilometer	km^2	1 000 000 square meters (m^2)
	1 hectare	ha	10 000 square meters (m^2)
Temperature	1 Kelvin	K	1 degree Celsius (°C)

Table E–2

OTHER SI UNITS			
Measurement	**Unit**	**Symbol**	**Units of Expression**
Energy	Joule	J	$kg \times m^2/s^2$
Force	Newton	N	$kg \times m/s^2$
Power	Watt	W	$kg \times m^2/s^3$ (J/s)
Pressure	Pascal	Pa	$kg/(m \times s^2)$ (N/m^2)

Appendix F — Periodic Table

Periodic Table

Based on Carbon 12 = 12.0000

Metals — **Transition Elements** — **Nonmetals**

Key:
- Atomic number: 1
- Symbol: H
- Element name: Hydrogen
- Atomic mass: 1.00794

† Metalloids lie along this heavy stairstep line.

* mass of isotope with longest half-life, that is, the most stable isotope of the element

Group	1	2	3	4	5	6	7	8	9	10	11	12	13	14	15	16	17	18
1	1 H Hydrogen 1.00794																	2 He Helium 4.002602
2	3 Li Lithium 6.941	4 Be Beryllium 9.01218											5 B Boron 10.811	6 C Carbon 12.011	7 N Nitrogen 14.0067	8 O Oxygen 15.9994	9 F Fluorine 18.998403	10 Ne Neon 20.179
3	11 Na Sodium 22.98977	12 Mg Magnesium 24.305											13 Al Aluminum 26.98154	14 Si Silicon 28.0855	15 P Phosphorus 30.97376	16 S Sulfur 32.06	17 Cl Chlorine 35.453	18 Ar Argon 39.948
4	19 K Potassium 39.0983	20 Ca Calcium 40.078	21 Sc Scandium 44.95591	22 Ti Titanium 47.88	23 V Vanadium 50.9415	24 Cr Chromium 51.9961	25 Mn Manganese 54.9380	26 Fe Iron 55.847	27 Co Cobalt 58.9332	28 Ni Nickel 58.69	29 Cu Copper 63.546	30 Zn Zinc 65.39	31 Ga Gallium 69.723	32 Ge Germanium 72.59	33 As Arsenic 74.9216	34 Se Selenium 78.96	35 Br Bromine 79.904	36 Kr Krypton 83.80
5	37 Rb Rubidium 85.4678	38 Sr Strontium 87.62	39 Y Yttrium 88.9059	40 Zr Zirconium 91.224	41 Nb Niobium 92.9064	42 Mo Molybdenum 95.94	43 Tc Technetium 97.9072*	44 Ru Ruthenium 101.07	45 Rh Rhodium 102.9055	46 Pd Palladium 106.42	47 Ag Silver 107.8682	48 Cd Cadmium 112.41	49 In Indium 114.82	50 Sn Tin 118.710	51 Sb Antimony 121.75	52 Te Tellurium 127.60	53 I Iodine 126.9045	54 Xe Xenon 131.29
6	55 Cs Cesium 132.9054	56 Ba Barium 137.33	57 La Lanthanum 138.9055	72 Hf Hafnium 178.49	73 Ta Tantalum 180.9479	74 W Tungsten 183.85	75 Re Rhenium 186.207	76 Os Osmium 190.2	77 Ir Iridium 192.22	78 Pt Platinum 195.08	79 Au Gold 196.9665	80 Hg Mercury 200.59	81 Tl Thallium 204.383	82 Pb Lead 207.2	83 Bi Bismuth 208.9804	84 Po Polonium 208.9824*	85 At Astatine 209.9872*	86 Rn Radon 222.017*
7	87 Fr Francium 223.0197*	88 Ra Radium 226.0254	89 Ac Actinium 227.0278*	104 Unq Unnilquadium 261*	105 Unp Unnilpentium 262*	106 Unh Unnilhexium 263*	107 Uns Unnilseptium 262*	108 Uno Unniloctium 265*	109 Une Unnilennium 266*									

Lanthanoid Series

58 Ce Cerium 140.12	59 Pr Praseodymium 140.9077	60 Nd Neodymium 144.24	61 Pm Promethium 144.9128*	62 Sm Samarium 150.36	63 Eu Europium 151.96	64 Gd Gadolinium 157.25	65 Tb Terbium 158.9254	66 Dy Dysprosium 162.50	67 Ho Holmium 164.9304	68 Er Erbium 167.26	69 Tm Thulium 168.9342	70 Yb Ytterbium 173.04	71 Lu Lutetium 174.967

Actinoid Series

90 Th Thorium 232.0381	91 Pa Protactinium 231.0359*	92 U Uranium 238.0289	93 Np Neptunium 237.0482	94 Pu Plutonium 244.0642*	95 Am Americium 243.0614*	96 Cm Curium 247.0703*	97 Bk Berkelium 247.0703*	98 Cf Californium 251.0796*	99 Es Einsteinium 252.0828*	100 Fm Fermium 257.0951*	101 Md Mendelevium 258.986*	102 No Nobelium 259.1009*	103 Lr Lawrencium 260.1054*

SKILL HANDBOOK

1 READING SCIENCE

Reading a science text is different from reading other types of printed material. If you read a short story or a novel, you follow the actions of the characters as they interact within a plot. Magazine articles are usually read for light entertainment, or to find out more information about such things as motorcycles or famous people. The purpose of reading science is different. You read science to understand and remember new ideas.

Throughout this course, your teacher will give you reading assignments from the science text. At times, you may also be asked to look up related information in reference books, encyclopedias, and magazines. How can you read these materials so that you understand and remember what you have read?

One useful technique utilizes three steps: previewing, reading carefully, and reviewing. First, preview the assignment to get a general idea of the topic. Read all the words in boldfaced print. Then, read any questions or notes in the margins and at the end of a section. Be sure to look at photographs, captions, and tables.

The second step is to read carefully. Look for the main idea in each paragraph. Focus on vocabulary words and science words unfamiliar to you. After each paragraph, paraphrase the main idea and define each vocabulary or unfamiliar word in your own words on paper. Outline any major processes that have been described. Answer questions that are in the margins and at the end of a section.

The last step is to review the reading assignment. Reread each section. In your own words, summarize the main ideas in that section. Look at each boldfaced word and define it in your own words. Finally, be sure you can answer all questions in the section from memory. If you have trouble stating main ideas, defining vocabulary, or answering questions, reread the appropriate paragraphs until you can answer them from memory.

FACT OR OPINION?

When reading science, you may sometimes have to distinguish fact from opinion. A fact is a piece of information that is based on evidence in the form of data. The same results will occur again and again when facts are tested, measured, or observed no matter who studies the material. Is it a fact that wearing seatbelts saves lives? Yes, this is a fact because it is based on the data provided by crash tests and by the review of serious accidents.

An opinion is a view or judgment about a particular subject or event. An opinion may be held by one person or shared by several people. Opinions may or may not be based on facts. Even when based on facts, there is not specific data from testing, measuring, or observing. A view held by some students is that studying while listening to the radio will result in higher grades. Because this is true for some students but not others, this statement is an opinion.

Being able to tell the difference between facts and opinions is important for you in order to make decisions in everyday life. Distinguishing fact from opinion is also important in science because facts are used in the development of scientific laws and underlie scientific theories.

SCIENTIFIC TERMINOLOGY

Science is a language with technical vocabulary. Knowing the etymology of words can help you interpret their meanings. Etymology is the study of the origins of words. For example, the word biology comes from the Greek words *bios* and *logos*. *Bios* is the Greek word for life, and the Greek word *logos* means "the study." Biology, then, is a study of life. Here is a list of several Greek words.

Greek Word	Meaning
botanikos	of herbs
gene	kind
heteros	different
logos	study
mikros	small
skopos	to look at
zoion	animals

How do the Greek words help you understand the meaning of the words microscope, botany, heterogeneous, and zoology?

Many scientific terms are built from prefixes, suffixes, and root words that have been derived from Latin or Greek words. Familiarity with these terms will help you decode many of the science words you encounter. Look at the following list of prefixes, suffixes, and root words.

Word part	Meaning
arthro-	jointed
chlor-	green
gymno-	naked
-ism	state or condition
-phyll	leaf
photo-	light
pseud-	fake; false
-pod	foot
sperm	seed
trop-	turning

Using the list of words, can you identify a characteristic of arthropods or explain what a phototropism might be? What other words can you make from the table? Compare each word you make with its meaning in the glossary or a dictionary.

You won't always have a dictionary with you, so when you encounter an unfamiliar word in science, break it into prefixes, suffixes, and root words. Use the parts of the word that you know to help you get a general idea of the meaning of the word.

SEQUENCING

Much of your everyday life follows a pattern or sequence. You follow a certain sequence as you prepare for school each morning. When you arrive at school, you attend classes in a specific sequence. Sequencing is the arranging or ordering of ideas or events.

Suppose you bought a stereo with an AM/FM radio, compact disk player, and dual cassette deck. How should you hook up the components? You would probably find it best to follow the sequence of steps in the instruction manual. Steps in the manual are arranged to allow you to hook up the components safely. Events are often arranged in chronological order. When the basketball team wins enough local games, it is able to go to the playoffs. After winning the playoffs, the team can play the championship game.

When reading science you will notice sequences. For example, both the circulation of blood through the heart and the process of photosynthesis are sequences. The steps in the activities in this book are written in sequence. Each step must be performed in its given order or sequence to obtain meaningful results.

Being able to sequence in science tests your understanding. When you are asked to sequence, carefully list the steps necessary to complete the sequence. After listing the steps, review them to make sure the steps are complete and in a logical order.

2 INTERPRETING SCIENTIFIC ILLUSTRATIONS

As you read this textbook you will see drawings, diagrams, photographs, and tables. These illustrations have been included to help you understand, interpret, and remember what you have read. Illustrations provide examples that clarify something you have read or provide additional information about the topic you're studying.

Most illustrations have captions. Others are there to stimulate your curiosity. A caption is a brief comment that identifies or explains. Diagrams and tables often have labels. Examine all illustrations and tables in this textbook carefully and read all captions and labels.

ORIENTATION

It is helpful to know several technical terms that are often used when referring to an organism. Look at the illustration of the planarian.

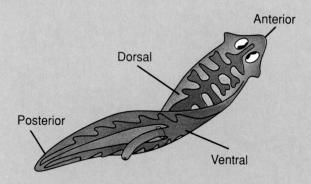

Notice that the figure illustrates the upper and lower sides of the planarian. The word *dorsal* refers to the upper side or back of an animal. The word *ventral* is the lower side or belly of the animal.

You'll also notice the terms *anterior* and *posterior*. Note that anterior refers to the front or head end of the planaria, and posterior is the rear or tail end.

These terms will be used several times in the text, especially in chapters that describe the features of different animal phyla.

SYMMETRY

Symmetry is a term used in reference to the arrangement of the parts of an organism. Throughout this textbook, you will read descriptions of organisms. Frequently, the symmetry of the organism is a part of that description. While symmetry may not seem as important as how an organism feeds, this characteristic plays an important role in where the organism is placed phylogenetically and helps to show its relationship to other organisms. It appears that those organisms with less complicated symmetry lead simpler, but no less important lifestyles than those with more complex symmetry.

Many organisms have *bilateral symmetry*. An organism is bilaterally symmetrical if it can be divided by a plane from top to bottom and front to back to produce two similar halves. The bee and the human form in the illustration have bilateral symmetry. There is only one way to divide the bee

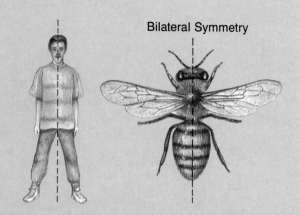

Bilateral Symmetry

and the human so both halves are similar and reflect one another.

Other organisms have *radial symmetry*. Radial symmetry is the arrangement of similar parts around a central point or axis. Organisms with radial symmetry have body structures in a circle around an axis running from top to bottom or from front to back. The hydra and the daisy flower have radial symmetry. The dotted lines in the illustrations indicate several possible planes that divide the daisy and the hydra into symmetrical parts. Notice that no matter how they are cut through the center, two similar parts are produced. Other familiar examples of radial symmetry might include an automobile tire and objects like a plate or a pie.

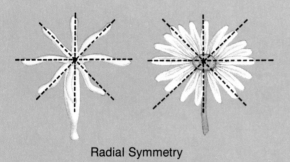

Radial Symmetry

Some organisms, like amoebas, are *asymmetrical.* An asymmetrical organism can't be divided into two similar halves. No matter how you try to divide them, no two parts ever look alike. Examine the following diagrams and determine whether the organisms are bilaterally or radially symmetrical, or asymmetrical.

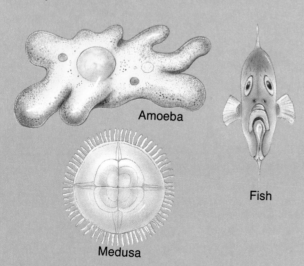

Amoeba

Medusa

Fish

SECTIONS

When you look at a bone or a carrot, there is no way that you can tell what they look like inside. Both the bone and the carrot appear simple from the outside, but in fact have many complex structures within.

A sectional illustration of a structure shows its internal parts and their arrangement, which you cannot otherwise see. Two common sections used in biology are cross sections and longitudinal sections. Look at the illustration of the carrot. When you cut a carrot into coin shaped pieces, you make cross sections that enable you to see the radial arrangement of tissues in the carrot. To do this, you cut at right angles to the carrot's lengthwise axis. If you cut the carrot lengthwise in half, you make longitudinal sections and you can see the lengthwise arrangement of tissues.

You will find many illustrations of sections of organisms and organs in this textbook. You will find that sections contain valuable visual information that is useful in understanding and interpreting text descriptions.

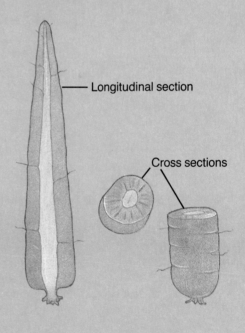

Longitudinal section

Cross sections

3 DESIGNING AN EXPERIMENT

Have you ever had a bike chain that kept falling off? Did you ever have to try to fix a broken lawn mower? How did you solve these problems? Without realizing it, you probably used some of the same methods scientists use.

Much of the work of scientists involves solving problems. Scientists ask questions and propose hypotheses to explain and interpret things and events in the world. To solve problems, scientists make observations, perform tests, and gather data.

In biology, many questions are investigated by observing organisms in their natural environment. However, scientists often design experiments to answer questions that come from their observations. An experiment is a method of problem-solving in which a scientist uses an organized procedure and controls various factors in an attempt to answer a question.

When designing an experiment, the first step is to state the problem clearly. Then, based on what has been observed, a hypothesis, or proposed solution, is stated. The hypothesis is tested in an experiment during which observations are made and data are collected. After the data are interpreted, a conclusion, or logical answer to the problem is stated. Then a determination is made as to whether the results support or don't support the hypothesis.

HYPOTHESIZING

Imagine you are preparing for school. You plug the hair dryer into the electric outlet and turn on the switch. Nothing happens. You have a problem; the hair dryer does not work. Why? Two possibilities are (1) the hair dryer is broken, or (2) the electricity is off. Regardless of your answer, you are hypothesizing. You are forming hypotheses, or suggested explanations for the problem. A hypothesis is neither right nor wrong. It is only either supported by the results of the tests or not supported.

Stating a hypothesis is not enough. To be useful, a hypothesis needs to be based on available infor-

mation and needs to be tested. Observing the electric light was working or noticing the hair dryer had a strange rattle might be information you would use in hypothesizing that the hair dryer didn't work because it was broken. This seems to be a very logical explanation, but you still do not know if it is supported. The hypothesis needs to be tested. You will know if the hypothesis is supported after you perform a test and examine the results.

Suppose you tested the hair dryer in an electric outlet in another room and it worked. The hypothesis that the hair dryer was broken wouldn't be supported. You would then use this information to revise and refine your hypothesis. Remember that the revised hypothesis is only a proposed explanation until you have tested it and examined the results.

VARIABLES, CONSTANTS, AND CONTROLS

When scientists design experiments, they manipulate a single condition to determine its effect on what happens while all other conditions are kept the same. The condition that is manipulated is called the independent variable. The dependent variable is any change that results from the manipulation of the independent variable. The conditions that are kept the same during the experiment are called constants.

To be certain the observed changes were only the result of manipulation of the independent variable, scientists use what is called a control as a standard of comparison. A control is a sample that is treated exactly the same way as the experimental sample, but the independent variable is either not applied or held at a fixed level so no changes take place. By comparing the change in the dependent variable to the control, the effect of the independent variable can be seen.

Suppose that while reading a magazine you notice an advertisement for a new skin medication. You wonder how skin medications affect the growth of skin bacteria. How would you design a controlled experiment to find out? Think about what would be the independent and dependent variables, constants, and control as you read about the description of the experiment.

This is how you might set up the experiment. Label each dish with a letter to indicate a particular skin medication. Stroke a cotton swab across your forehead and rub it once over sterile nutrient agar in a petri dish. You then moisten another cotton ball with one skin medication, rub the cotton ball once over the nutrient agar, and replace the cover. You repeat the process for the other skin medications being tested. In the last petri dish, you do not apply any skin medication. You seal the petri dishes with tape and place them in a warm, dark location for five days. After five days, you examine the dishes, record and interpret your data and observations, and form a conclusion.

What are the independent and dependent variables in the experiment? Because you are applying skin medications to the bacteria-infected petri dishes, the independent variable is the application of skin medication. Since the dependent variable is any change that results from the independent variable, the dependent variable is the amount of growth of skin bacteria in each dish. What factors must be kept the same during the experiment? The constants are the size and shape of the petri dishes, the type and amount of nutrient agar, identical applications of skin bacteria and skin medications, the placement in the same location, and the same observation time. Why wasn't skin medication applied to the last dish? The last dish is the control. The growth of skin bacteria in the control will be used as a standard to compare with the amount of growth in the other dishes.

Every time you read about, perform, or design a controlled experiment, you should be able to identify the independent and dependent variables, list all of the factors that must be held constant, and have a control against which to compare your experimental results.

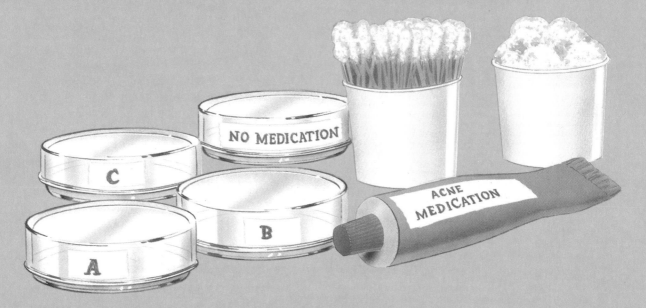

4 USING A MICROSCOPE

A microscope is an optical instrument that enlarges images of very small objects. Since many organisms are too small to be seen by the unaided eye, you will find the microscope valuable in studying biology.

Most high school biology classes use compound light microscopes. A compound light microscope is an instrument in which two or more lenses enlarge the image of an object. Each lens further enlarges the image of the object.

Although there are many types of compound microscopes, their parts are similar. Learn the names of the parts labeled in the illustration.

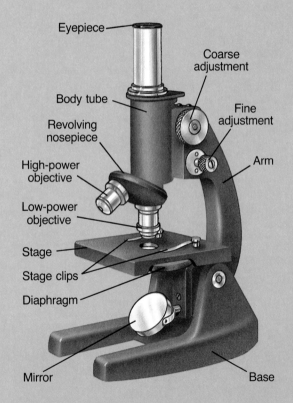

Eyepiece
Coarse adjustment
Body tube
Fine adjustment
Revolving nosepiece
High-power objective
Arm
Low-power objective
Stage
Stage clips
Diaphragm
Mirror
Base

Here are several precautions you should take when using any microscope.

1. Always carry the microscope holding the arm with one hand and supporting the base with the other hand.

2. Never use direct sunlight as a light source. Turn off any substage illuminator unless you are viewing an object.
3. Don't touch the lens with your finger. Use lens paper to clean lenses.
4. Never lower the coarse adjustment knob when looking through the eyepiece lens.
5. Always focus first with the low-power objective.
6. Don't use the coarse adjustment knob when the high-power objective is in position.
7. Store the microscope covered.

To use a microscope, follow these rules.

1. Place the microscope on a flat surface that has been cleared of objects. The arm should be toward you.
2. Make sure the low-power objective is positioned above the stage. Look at the microscope from the side and use the coarse adjustment knob to raise the objective about four centimeters above the stage.
3. Place a slide on the stage making sure the object to be viewed is over the opening. Secure the slide with stage clips.
4. Looking through the eyepiece, adjust the diaphragm so that you see a bright field.
5. As you watch from the side, use the coarse adjustment knob to lower the objective lens until it is close to the cover slip of the slide.
6. Look through the eyepiece again. Slowly turn the coarse adjustment knob to raise the objective lens until the object comes into view.
7. Bring the object into sharp focus with the fine adjustment knob.
8. Turn the nosepiece until the high-power objective clicks into place. Use the fine adjustment knob to bring the object into sharp focus. **DO NOT** use the coarse adjustment knob when a high-power objective is in position.
9. When you are ready to put the microscope away, click the low-power objective into position over the stage, and remove the slide before storing the microscope.

MAKING A WET MOUNT SLIDE

A wet mount slide is a temporary preparation of living organisms or tissues. It is made with water or a stain.

Preparing a wet mount slide is a simple procedure. Look at the illustrations as you follow the steps.

1. Carefully place the item that you want to look at in the center of a clean glass slide. Make sure your sample is thin enough for light to pass through.
2. Use a medicine dropper to place one drop of water on the sample.
3. Hold a clean coverslip by the edges, and place it at one side of the drop of water. The water will flow along the edge of the coverslip.
4. Gently lower the coverslip on to the drop of water until the coverslip lies flat. If you have too much water or a lot of air bubbles, touch the edge of a paper towel to the edge of the coverslip and the towel will draw off excess water and force air out.
5. To stain a sample, place a small drop of stain at one edge of the coverslip. Draw the stain under the coverslip by touching a piece of paper towel to the opposite side of the cover slip. The paper towel will slowly absorb the water and pull the stain across the specimen.

CALCULATING MAGNIFICATION

You can calculate magnification of objects seen under a microscope if you know its "power" or magnifying ability. Magnification is simply a comparison of the image size with the actual size of the object being viewed. Suppose a lens has a magnifying power of 5X. Then the image of the object when viewed through the lens would be magnified five times actual size.

The total magnification of lenses on a compound microscope can be found by multiplying the magnifying power of the eyepiece lens by the magnifying power of the objective lens. For example, if the magnifying power of the eyepiece lens is 10X and the magnifying power of the low-power objective lens is 5X, then the total magnification of the microscope is 5×10 or 50X.

power of eyepiece lens	$\times$	power of objective lens	=	magnification
10X	$\times$	5X	=	50X

What would be the total magnification of this microscope using the high-power objective with a magnifying power of 43X? The total magnification would be 10×43 or 430X.

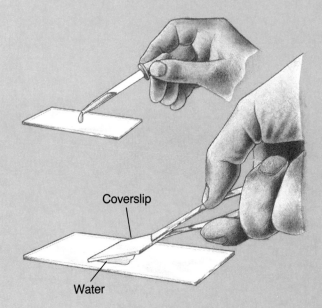

Coverslip

Water

Scientific experiments and investigations often involve making accurate measurements of observations. For these measurements to be meaningful, other scientists must be able to use the same measurements.

To avoid problems with different units of measurement, a uniform standard of measurement was developed providing an international standard of comparison for measurements in science and everyday living. You are probably familiar with the metric system of measurement. The metric system was developed in 1795 by a group of scientists to provide a uniform system of measurement. Then, in 1960, a modern form of the metric system called the International System (SI) of units was adopted for worldwide use. Your text uses metric units in all its measurements. In this text, you will make measurements in investigations and experiments using the metric system.

The metric units meter, gram, and liter are units used to measure length, mass, and volume respectively. You may recall that in the metric system unit sizes vary by multiples of ten. When changing from larger units to smaller, multiply by ten. When changing from smaller units to larger, divide by ten. Prefixes are used to name larger and smaller units. For example, the prefix *centi-* attached to the unit *meter* is centimeter or one hundredth (0.01) of a meter. The following table has some common metric prefixes and their meanings.

Metric Prefixes			
Prefix	**Symbol**	**Meaning**	
kilo-	k	1 000	thousand
hecto-	h	100	hundred
deka-	da	10	ten
deci-	d	0.1	tenth
centi-	c	0.01	hundredth
milli-	m	0.001	thousandth

LENGTH, VOLUME, AND MASS

A meter is the SI unit used to measure distance. Common distances you will measure are length, width, and height. To get an idea of the length of a meter, look at the knob on the door. The distance from the door knob to the floor is about one meter. For measuring smaller distances, a meter is divided into 100 equal parts called centimeters (cm). When still smaller units are needed, each centimeter is divided into ten equal units called millimeters (mm). A millimeter is one thousandth of a meter. Look at the illustration. Most meter sticks and metric rulers have similar lines indicating centimeters and millimeters. Centimeter lines are usually numbered. The shorter lines between each centimeter are millimeter marks.

To use the metric ruler or meter stick, first decide on a unit of measurement. Then, line up the end of the ruler with one edge of the object to be measured, and read the number of the unit where the object ends. To measure the length of the microscope slide in the illustration, you would line up one end with the 0 centimeter mark. Next, you would read the number of millimeters where the other edge of the slide ends. What is the length of the slide in the illustration? The length of the slide is 75 mm.

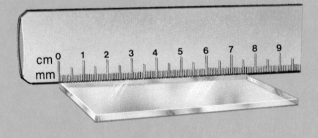

At times, you will also need to measure the surface area of objects. The standard SI unit for area is the square meter (m^2). A square meter is a surface that is one meter long and one meter wide. Similarly, a square centimeter (cm^2) would be a square one centimeter long on each side. The surface area of rectangular areas can be determined by multiplying length times width. For example, if the length of a book cover measures 25 cm and its width is 20 cm, the area would be 25×20 or 500 cm^2. That means that it would take 500 one by one centimeter squares of paper to cover the surface of the book.

Units of length are also used to determine the volume of rectangular solids. Volume is the amount of space occupied by an object. The cubic meter (m^3) is the standard SI unit for volume. A cubic meter would be a box measuring 1 meter in length, width, and height. The volume of rectangular objects can be determined by multiplying length times width times height. If the dimensions of a book are 25 cm by 20 cm by 2 cm, the volume would be 25 cm $\times$ 20 cm $\times$ 2 cm or 1000 cm^3. It would take 1000 cubes one centimeter on each side to take up the same amount of space.

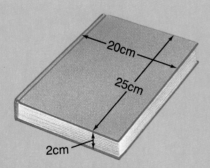

Liquid volume is usually measured in a unit called a liter. A liter has the same volume as 1000 cm^3. When a liter is divided into one thousand equal parts, each part is a milliliter (mL). A milliliter, then, takes up a volume of one cubic centimeter. To get an idea of the size of a milliliter think of a cube measuring one centimeter on each side. The amount of a liquid needed to fill the cube equals one milliliter.

Scientists generally measure the volume of liquids in glass graduated cylinders. The cylinders are graduated or marked with lines from bottom to top. Each graduation represents one milliliter.

To read the volume of liquid in a graduated cylinder, place the cylinder on a smooth flat surface. Liquids in a glass cylinder have a curved surface, or meniscus, similar to that in the illustration. Looking at the graduations from a horizontal line of sight, read the volume of the liquid from the bottom of the meniscus. If you use a plastic graduated cylinder, liquids will not form a meniscus.

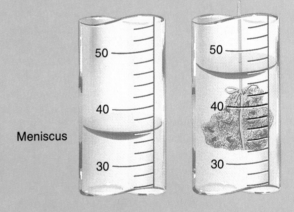

You can use a graduated cylinder to determine the volume of an irregularly shaped object such as a ring or a pebble. Partially fill a graduated cylinder with water. Read and record the level of the water. Tie a string around the ring or pebble to be measured and carefully lower it into the graduated cylinder. Read and record the new level of the water. The volume of the object will be the difference between the first reading and the second reading. Look at the illustration. Subtracting the first reading from the second reading, the volume of the object is 10 mL.

In a laboratory, a balance is used to find the mass of an object in grams. A beam balance has a pan on one side and a set of beams on the other. The beams hold objects of known mass called riders. Here are some directions on how to use a balance. Always carry a balance by holding the beam support with one hand and placing the other hand under the balance. Never place a hot object directly on the pan. Also, never pour chemicals directly on the balance pan. Place dry chemicals on paper or in a glass container after you have massed the paper or container. Mass liquid chemicals in glass containers.

Although there are many types of balances, similar steps are used to find the mass of an object. The illustration shows a balance similar to one you might use in science class.

Before massing an object, set the balance to zero by sliding all riders back to the zero point. Release the locking mechanism if your balance has one. Check the pointer to make sure it swings an equal distance above and below the zero point of the scale. If necessary, turn the adjusting screw until you have an equal swing.

To mass an object, place the object on the pan. Starting with the rider with the largest mass, slide the riders along the beams. Move the rider along the beam until the pointer drops below the zero point. Then move it back one notch. Repeat the process with each beam. When the pointer swings an equal distance above and below the zero point, take a reading of the riders. The mass of the object will be the sum of the masses indicated on the beams.

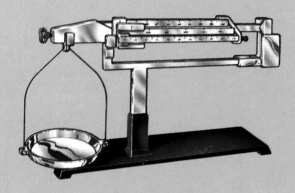

SAMPLING AND ESTIMATING

When working with large populations of organisms, scientists usually cannot observe or study every organism. Instead, they use a sample of the population. Sampling is taking a small portion of organisms of a population for research. By making careful observations or manipulating variables with a portion of a group, information is discovered and conclusions are drawn about the population as a whole.

Suppose you are trying to determine the effect of an inorganic chemical on the growth of water lilies. It would be impossible to test the entire population of water lilies, so you would select part of the population for your experiment. Through careful experimentation and observation on a sample of the population, you could generalize the effect of the chemical on the entire population.

Scientific work also involves estimating. Estimating is making a judgment of size or number without actually measuring or counting every member of a population.

Have you ever tried to guess how many beans were in a sealed jar? If you did, you were estimating. What if you knew the jar of beans held one liter (1000 mL)? If you knew that 30 beans would fit in a 100 milliliter jar, how many jelly beans would you estimate to be in the one liter jar? If you said about 300 beans, your estimate would be close to the actual number of beans.

Scientists use a similar process to estimate populations of organisms. Scientists count the actual number of organisms in a sample and estimate the number of organisms in a larger area. For example, if a scientist wanted to count the number of microorganisms in a petri dish, a microscope could be used to count the number of organisms in a one square millimeter sample. To determine the total population of the culture, the number of organisms in the square millimeter sample is multiplied by the total number of millimeters in the culture.

6 OBSERVING AND INFERRING

One of the most important attributes of a scientist is the ability to make accurate and detailed observations of objects and events. Just as scientists must be skilled at observing, you must also be skilled at using your senses. You must be able to see, hear, smell, feel, and sometimes taste in scientific work.

Imagine it's the weekend and you are attending a track meet. What do you see? You would probably first notice the crowd or the runners racing around the course. If you observe more carefully, you might notice the number of the lead runner. Now, what do you hear? It might be the crowd cheering on the runners.

When you use your senses alone to make observations, as in a track race, they are called qualitative observations. Another type of observation scientists use is quantitative observation. These observations form data. They involve measurements. Quantitative observations provide a concrete basis of comparison. For example, scientists would report the amount of food eaten by an organism in grams and the increase of height in a plant in millimeters.

What qualitative and quantitative observations might you make about a french fry in a fast food restaurant? Qualitative observations might include looking golden brown, smelling greasy, tasting salty, feeling hot, and sounding crunchy. Quantitative observations about the same fry might include a mass of 2 grams, a temperature of 55 degrees Celsius, and a length of 8 centimeters. These are your data.

Once scientists have made observations, they use the data to make an inference. For example, after observing that 85 of one hundred isopods prefer moist humus rather than moist sand, a scientist might infer the isopod would be found on the forest floor rather than along the sandy shore of a stream. Or, after observing an unknown liquid boil at 78°C, a scientist might infer the liquid is not water, which boils at 100°C, but some other solution.

In your biology class you will also make inferences. You will be asked to propose interpretations, explanations, or causes from data collected in your observations. Let's try it. If you observe that your class has a substitute teacher, what might you infer? You might infer that your regular teacher is sick. What might you infer from the observations of the french fry in the example? You might infer that the fries will taste good. Making inferences helps you explain and interpret events around you.

7 | ORGANIZING INFORMATION

Like a library, much of the world has been organized. To understand the world, people have ordered and categorized many objects and events and placed them into groups by observing their similarities, differences, and interrelationships.

CLASSIFYING

One way to organize objects or events is to classify them. Classifying is systematically arranging objects or events into groups based on common properties. Grocery stores contain sections or aisles containing dairy products, meats, bread, or produce. Each section is then divided into smaller groups. For example, the produce section is usually divided into vegetable and fruit sections. The fruit section may be subdivided into bins that separate apples and pears.

When classifying, first observe the similarities and differences among the objects and determine a property or set of properties that will be useful. You sort the objects by each property. Then examine each group and determine another property or set of properties shared by some members of the group but not by others. Divide the group into subgroups based on these properties. Then divide the subgroups into yet smaller groups. What properties could you use to classify the hats below?

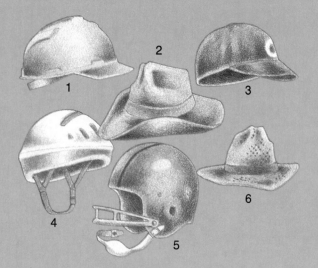

Properties that could be used to group the hats might include whether the hats are hard or soft, whether they have a bill or do not have a bill, and whether the hats have a chin strap or not, and so on. Once the initial property is decided on, then choose another property to further subdivide each group. The process continues until each hat has been separated into its own subgroup as follows.

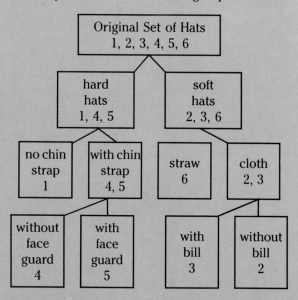

MAKING AND USING KEYS

Keys are used to classify and identify unknown organisms. A key is an arrangement of characteristics designed to identify similarities and differences among organisms. Characteristics of an unknown organism are compared with the characteristics listed in a series of numbered steps.

A key usually consists of two or more statements listing first general characteristics and then progressing to more and more specific characteristics. Only one of the statements in each set of numbered steps can be true for a single organism.

To use the following key, select one of the birds in the illustration. Read the first pair of statements, and choose the one that best describes a charac-

Egret

Cardinal

Woodpecker

Owl

Duck

teristic of the bird. The statement you choose will direct you to another pair of statements. Continue reading and choosing statements until your choice names the bird. To practice using keys, select a guide book from your library and identify organisms in your environment.

Bird Identification Key
1A Long bill..(go to 2)
1B Short bill......................................(go to 3)
2A Sharp, pointed bill..........................(egret)
2B Rounded flat bill..............................(duck)
3A Top bill hooked................................(owl)
3B Top bill not hooked....................(go to 4)
4A Thin, pointed bill..............(woodpecker)
4B Thick, pointed bill....................(cardinal)

MAKING AND USING TABLES

In your text, tables have been included to organize and summarize information to help you understand it.

Tables usually have a title telling you what information is being presented. Look at the table entitled "Compatible Blood Types." Notice that the table is organized into columns and rows. The first column in the table lists items that are to be compared. In this table, donor blood types are being compared. Across the top of the table is a list of characteristics. This table lists the blood types of different receivers that are being compared with the blood types of the donors listed in the first column.

Compatible Blood Types				
Donor Blood Type	Receiver Blood Type			
	A	B	AB	O
A	yes	no	yes	no
B	no	yes	yes	no
AB	no	no	yes	no
O	yes	yes	yes	yes

Could a receiver with blood type B safely receive blood type AB from a donor? To find the answer, find receiver type B in the top row of the table and the donor type AB in the first column of the table. The space where the row and column meet contains the answer as to whether the blood types are compatible. The answer to this question is no. Could a receiver with blood type A safely receive blood type O? You should have answered yes because that is the reply located in the space where the column and row intersect.

MAKING AND USING GRAPHS

Graphing

Often information can be communicated more easily with a picture instead of words. Graphs show data in picture form and make the analysis of data easier. Three basic types of graphs are used in science to organize information. These are the line graph, the bar graph, and the pie graph.

Making a Line Graph

Line graphs are used to show the relationship between two variables.

A line graph is made of two axes. The variables tested by the experimenter are written along the axes. The independent variable always goes along the horizontal, or x-axis. The dependent variable always goes along the vertical, or y-axis.

Suppose you wanted to make a line graph of the daily high temperatures for a school week.

Daily High Temperatures	
Day	Temperature °C
M	15
T	16
W	18
T	13
F	10

How would you set up the axes? Day is the independent variable and should be on the x-axis. Temperature is the dependent variable and should be on the y-axis.

Next, label each axis with a scale. On the x-axis, simply list the days. To make a scale of the temperatures for the y-axis, determine the range of the data. Subtract the smallest value in your list of data from the largest value. The difference between 18 and 10 is 8 degrees. You need a spread of at least 8 units along the y-axis. After examining the data, you might decide to start numbering the y-axis at 5 and number by fives to 20.

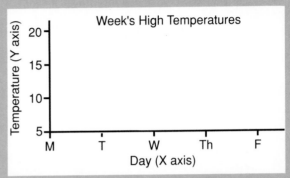

The first pair of data you want to plot is Monday, 15. Locate Monday on the x-axis and 15 on the y-axis. Sight straight up from Monday and straight across from 15. The point where these two imaginary lines cross is where the data point should be plotted. After all the points are plotted, connect them with straight lines.

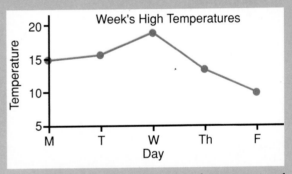

Sometimes you may want to plot two sets of data on the same graph. Suppose you want to compare the week's low temperatures with the highs. The graph would show both high and low temperatures. A key is included to tell you which set of data is which.

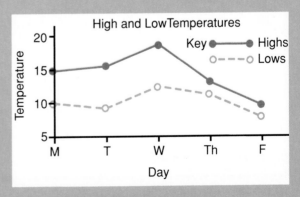

Making a Bar Graph

A bar graph is similar to a line graph, but a bar graph has thick bars instead of data points. Bar graphs are often used to show comparisons. To make a bar graph, set up your axes in the same way as for a line graph. Plot your data by drawing bars that extend from the *x*-axis to the point where your imaginary extensions of the *x*-axis and *y*-axis intersect. Look at the bar graph below. The activity performed by a male or female is the independent variable. The number of calories used per hour is being compared.

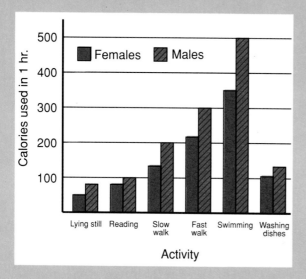

Making a Pie Graph

A pie graph uses parts of a circle to display data. A pie graph shows how each part is related to the whole. Each part of a pie graph is called a section. When all the sections of the pie are added together, they equal 100 percent or the total of whatever you are working with.

To make a pie graph, you need to calculate how much of the pie each section should take. As a living organism, you are very dependent on water. As a resident of planet Earth, you also need to be aware of your responsibility toward valuable resources such as water. Suppose you wanted to make a pie graph that shows where Earth's water

supply is found. Earth's total supply is 1398 million cubic kilometers. Therefore, the whole pie will represent this amount. The volume of water in Earth's oceans is 1356 million km^3. Glacial ice contains 28 million km^3. Freshwater contains 14 million km^3. Each of these three locations will be represented by a section of the pie graph. To find how much of the pie each section should take, follow this rule. Divide the amount of water in each location by the total amount of water. Multiply your answer by 360, which is the number of degrees in a circle. Round your answer to the nearest whole number. The ocean section would be determined using the following calculation.

$$\frac{1356}{1398} \times 360 = 349.18 \text{ or } 349°$$

Use the following procedure to plot this section on the graph. Use a compass to draw a circle. Use a ruler to draw a line from the edge of the circle to its center. Put your protractor on this line and use it to mark a point on the edge of the circle at 349°. Connect this point with a straight line to the center of the circle. Repeat this procedure starting from the line you just drew for each section of the circle. Label all the sections of your graph.

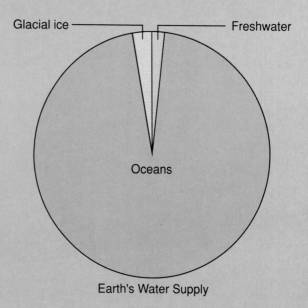

GLOSSARY-INDEX

An index is a place where you can look to find page references for structures, vocabulary terms, or organisms described in your textbook. A glossary is the place where you look for the meaning of terms. Both an index and a glossary list terms in alphabetical order. In **_Biology: The Dynamics of Life,_** the glossary has been incorporated into the index to save you time in your search for the meaning of a word and its location in your textbook. At the same time, the Glossary-Index gives you extra references to related topics and gives you a better opportunity for understanding a term in context.

Each vocabulary term that is boldfaced in the chapters of this textbook is listed in the Glossary-Index in boldface type, followed by its definition. The page number on which the definition is located is also printed in boldface type. Some terms are followed in parentheses by a guide to pronunciation. Other important terms such as names of organisms, famous scientists, or basic biological concepts and structures make up the remainder of the Glossary-Index.

Abbreviations follow many of the page number references. These include: _illus._ if the term is illustrated on that page; _nw._ when the term is mentioned in a NoteWorthy; _t.crit._ for Thinking Critically; _tech._ for BioTechnology; _lab._ for Biolab; _car._ for Career Choices; _dav._ for Developing a Viewpoint; _sk.hbk._ for skills in the Skill Handbook. Below is a pronunciation key to help you read the terms used in this textbook.

PRONUNCIATION KEY

a . . . back (BAK)	i (i + con + e) . . . idea, life (i DEE uh, LIFE)	sh . . . shelf (SHELF)
er . . . care, fair (KER, FER)	oh . . . go (GOH)	ch . . . nature (NAY chur)
ay . . . day (DAY)	aw . . . soft (SAWFT)	g . . . gift (GIHFT)
ah . . . father (FAHTH ur)	or . . . orbit (OR but)	j . . . gem, edge (JEM, EJ)
ar . . . car (KAR)	oy . . . coin (KOYN)	ing . . . sing (SING)
ow . . . flower, loud (FLOW ur, LOWD)	oo . . . foot (FOOT)	zh . . . vision (VIHZH un)
e . . . less (LES)	yoo . . . pure (PYOOR)	k . . . cake (KAYK)
ee . . . leaf (LEEF)	ew . . . food (FEWD)	s . . . seed, cent (SEED, SENT)
ih . . . trip (TRIHP)	yew . . . few (FYEW)	z . . . zone, raise (SOHN, RAYZ)
	uh (u + con) . . . comma, mother (KAHM uh, MUTH ur)	

A

abiotic factor: (ay bi AHT ihk) factor in an environment not having life but that supports the living factors **700,** 710, 711 *illus.,* 715 *lab.,* 719, 725

absolute dating: 31

abyssal zone: (uh BIS ul) the depth of the ocean that begins at the bathyal zone **736,** 736 *illus.*

Acetabularia: 86 *t.crit.*

acetic acid: 117 *illus.*

acetyl-CoA: 117 *illus.*

acid: a substance yielding hydrogen ions in water **61,** 61 *illus.*

acid precipitation: precipitation abnormally high in sulfuric and nitric acid content caused by industrial pollution **746,** 746 *illus.* and *nw.*

acoelomate: simple multicellular organism that has no body cavity **397,** 397 *illus.,* 417

acquired characteristic: a characteristic of an organism caused by a response to the environment and passed on to its offspring **205**

acquired immune deficiency syndrome (AIDS): a disease of the immune system 6 *nw.,* 69 *tech.,* 300, **671,** 671 *illus.,* 689

acromegaly: 590 *illus.* and *nw.*

actin: a protein that comprises the thin filaments of myofibrils **607**

active transport: the transport of materials across a membrane and against a gradient **102,** 102 *illus.,* 103 *illus.,* 105 *t.crit.*

adaptation: a variation in an organism that makes it better able to cope with its environment **22,** 22 *illus.* and *nw.,* 23 *illus.,* 94 *illus.,* 105 *t.crit.,* 107 *illus.* and *nw.,* 209, 209 *illus.,* 210 *illus.,* 231 *illus.,* 451 *t.crit.,* 461 *illus.*

adaptations to land: 311

adaptive radiation: the evolution of a species in an area into several related species having different survival characteristics 216 *illus.,* **217,** 217 *illus.*

adenosine diphosphate (ADP): a molecule that contains two energy phosphate groups and is capable of bonding a third group to form stored energy for a cell **112,** 113, 113 *illus.*

adenosine triphosphate (ATP): a molecule that stores useable energy, on which the cell is dependent for life 103 *illus.,* 111, **112,** 112 *illus.,* 113, 113 *illus.,* 114 *illus.,* 115, 115 *illus.,* 119 *nw.,* 608, 609 *t.crit.,* 678

adolescence: 695

ADP: *See* adenosine diphosphate

aerobic process: (uh ROH bihk) respiratory process that requires oxygen **115**

aerobic respiration: 117, 122, 126, 126 *illus.*

age structure: the percentage of each sex at each age in a population **744**

aging: 695

aggression: behavior of an organism that is used to intimidate or damage another organism **559,** 559 *illus.* and *nw.*

Agnatha: 484

agriculture: 381, 381 *illus.*

AIDS: *See* acquired immune deficiency syndrome

albatross: 516 *illus.*

albinism: 186 *illus.,* 190 *illus.*

alcohol effects: 587 *table*

alcoholic fermentation: the process by which certain yeasts decompose sugars in the absence of oxygen **116,** 116 *illus.*

aldosterone: a steroid adrenal hormone 652 *illus.,* **653,** 653 *illus.*

algae: unicellular or multicellular protists that have chlorophyll 86 *t.crit.,* 126, **268,** 269 *illus.,* 270 *t.crit.,* 275, 277, 277 *illus.,* 278, 278 *illus.,* 279 *illus.* and *nw.,* 280 *lab.,* 423, 536 *nw.,* 724, 737 *illus.*

allantois: (uh LANT uh wus) a fluid-filled, saclike, extraembryonic membrane lying between the chorion and amnion of embryos **502**

all-or-none law: the principle that a neuron either transmits an impulse or it does not **577**

Allard, Harry Ardell (1880–1963): 387

allele: (uh LEEL) two or more different genes that occupy the same position on homologous chromosomes **174,** 174 *illus.,* 185 *illus.,* 186, 186 *illus.* and *table,* 188 *illus.,* 190 *illus.,* 213 *illus.*

allele frequency: the proportion of each allele in the gene pool **212,** 212 *illus.,* 213 *illus.* and *nw.*

alligator: 511

alternation of generations: 279 *illus.,* 329, 330 *illus.,* 334 *illus.,* 341 *illus.*

alveoli: sacs of the lungs where gas is exchanged by diffusion between air and blood **636,** 636 *illus.,* 637 *illus.*

amino acid: organic compound that contains one or more basic amino groups and one or more acidic carboxyl groups **67,** 67 *illus.,* 69 *tech.,* 137 *illus.,* 140 *illus.,* 239 *car.,* 389 *car.,* 712

amniocentesis: 689, 689 *illus.*

amniotic fluid **502**

amnion: the innermost of the membranes enveloping the embryo in the uterus and filled with amniotic fluid **502,** 686, 689 *illus.*

amniotic egg: an egg that contains protective membranes and provides the embryo with nourishment **502,** 502 *illus.*

amoeba: unicellular protist found in water and soil; shapeless aquatic protozoan that forms pseudopods 104 *illus.*, **271,** 271 *illus.*, 281 *illus.*

amoebocyte: an amoeba-shaped cell that moves around between the two layers of body cells in a sponge **400**

amphibian: 489 *illus.*, 492–497, 493 *illus.*, 494, 494 *illus.*, 495 *nw.*, 496, 496 *illus.*, 526 *illus.*

ampulla: the sac at the base of a tube foot in certain echinoderms **460,** 460 *illus.*

amylase: (AM uh lays) one of a group of enzymes that split apart starch, glycogen, and related polysaccharide molecules in digestion **614,** 615 *illus.*

anaconda: 506

anaerobic process: respiratory process that takes place in the absence of oxygen 43 *t. crit.*, **115,** 608, 609 *t. crit.*

analogous structures: body parts such as wings that are similar in function in different organisms, but which have different origins of development **202,** 202 *illus.*

anaphase: the stage of mitosis in which the sister chromatids or homologous chromosomes move apart and toward the poles of the nucleus 146 *illus.*, **147,** 149 *lab.*

angiosperm: a flowering plant in the division Anthophyta **350,** 350 *illus.*, 356 *illus.*

anglerfish: 443

Anhinga: 515 *illus.*

Animal Kingdom: 38 *illus.*, 45

annelid worms: 428, 429 *illus.*, 439

ant: 112 *illus.*

anterior: toward the front or head end of an animal's body **415,** 430 *illus.*

anther: pollen-producing structure of a flower **370,** 370 *illus.*, 371 *illus.*, 372 *illus.*, 373 *illus.*, *nw.*

antheridium: a male sex organ in simple plants **331,** 331 *illus.*

anthophyte: 369–382, 370 *illus.*, 373 *illus.* and *nw.*

anthropologist: 239 *car.*

antibiotic: 298 *nw.*

antibody: a protein produced in response to an antigen **666,** 668, 668 *illus.*, 669 *illus.*

anticodon: the sequence of three nucleotides of transfer RNA **140,** 140 *illus.*

antidiuretic hormone (ADH): a hormone that stimulates reabsorption of water in a nephron **652,** 652 *illus.*, 653 *illus.*

antigen: a substance capable of stimulating a specific immune response **666,** 667 *illus.*

aorta: 646 *illus.*, 647

apes: 234, 235

aphids: 435, 439 *illus.*, 452, 703 *illus.*

aphotic zone: (ay FOHT ik) the layer of a body of water below the euphotic zone where little or no light penetrates **736,** 736 *illus.*

apical meristem: a growth region of plant tissues located at the tips of roots and stems **312**

apiculturist: 473 *car.*

appendage: any major structure growing out of the body of an organism, such as antennae, bristles, legs **435**

appendicular skeleton: (ap uhn DIK yuh ler) the bones associated with the upper and lower extremities **601,** 601 *illus.*

appendix: an intestinal diverticulum extending from the blind end of the cecum **618**

aquatic food chain: 704 *illus.*

aquatic microbiologist: 300 *car.*

aquifer: an underground water-bearing rock; a group of rock formations that acts as a storage site for water **714**

Arachnida: 441

archaebacteria: prokaryotes that resemble bacteria 43 *t. crit.*, **230,** 231 *illus.*, 260, 261

archegonium: a female sex organ in simple plants **331,** 331 *illus.*

Archeopteryx: 517 *illus.*, 518–519

Aristotle (384–322 B.C.): 35

armadillo: 543

artery: blood vessel that carries blood away from the heart **644,** 645 *illus.*

arthritis: a painful inflammation of the joints caused by infection or injury 604 *nw.*, **605**

arthropod: 435–455, 436 *illus.*, 438, 438 *illus.*, 439, 440 *illus.*, 441, 444 *illus.*, 450, 452, 452 *illus.* and *nw.*, 473 *car.*, 662 *table*

artificial classification: 35, 35 *illus.*

artificial skin: 600 *illus.*

Ascomycota: 294 *illus.*

ascospore: a spore formed in globular or cup-shaped structure called an ascocarp **294**

ascus: a membranous sac in ascomycote fungi inside which spores form during sexual reproduction **294,** 294 *illus.*

asexual reproduction: reproduction without

C

carbon dioxide: 127 *t.crit.*, 324 *tech.*, 747 *illus.*

carbon–14 dating: 31 *nw.*

carbon monoxide: 642 *nw.*

carbonate compounds: 127 *t.crit.*

Carboniferous: 343 *illus.*

cardiac muscle: muscle that makes up the heart **606,** 606 *illus.*

cardiac output: 649 *t.crit.*

caribou: 94, 94 *illus.*

carnivore: a consumer that gets its nutrition from the flesh of other organisms 406 *illus.*, 538, 538 *illus.*, **704,** 704 *illus.*, 706, 725

carrier: an organism that is heterozygous for a recessive gene that may be inherited by its offspring **190,** 190 *illus.*, 191 *illus.*, 194 *illus.*

cartilage: a tough, flexible material that contains no bone; found in some fish **484,** 484 *illus.*, 605

cartilaginous fish: 485–488

cell: the basic living unit of an organism 14 *tech.*, **17,** 17 *illus.*, 18 *illus.* and *nw.*, 22 *nw.*, 92 *illus.*, 94 *illus.*, 98 *illus.*, 99 *illus.*, 101 *illus.* and *nw.*, 104 *illus.*, 106, 106 *illus.* and *nw.*, 107 *illus.* and *nw.*

cell controller: 86 *t.crit.*

cell cycle: the complete sequence of events of cell division **146,** 146 *illus.* and *nw.*, 147 *nw.*, 148 *illus.*, 149 *lab.*

cell respiration: 117 *nw.*

cell theory: the theory that describes the cell, its relationship to organisms, and its origin 75, 75 *nw.*, 76 *illus.*, **77,** 80 *illus.*, 81 *illus.*

cell wall: a rigid structure that surrounds the plasma membrane in certain organisms such as plants, bacteria, and fungi **81,** 81 *illus.* and *nw.*, 627 *t.crit.*

cellular immunity: 666, 667 *illus.*

cellulose: a polysaccharide in living plants, fungi, monerans, and protists that forms cell wall structure 65 *nw.*, **81,** 81 *illus.*, 123 *illus.*, 627 *t.crit.*, 753 *t.crit.*

Cenozoic: 201, 541

centipede: 445, 445 *illus.*

central nervous system (CNS): one of two basic parts of the human nervous system, composed of the brain and spinal cord **575,** 576 *illus.*

centrioles: microtubule bundles in a cell with a structure like that of cilia **146**

centromere: the point at which sister chromatids are held together **146**

Cephalochordata: 479–480

cephalopod mollusks: 422, 425, 426 *illus.*

cephalothorax: the anterior section of arachnids composed of a fused head and thorax **441,** 441 *illus.*

cerebellum: one of three main portions of the brain that controls balance, posture, and coordination **578**

cerebrum: one of three main portions of the brain that controls conscious activities, memory, language, and the senses **578,** 582 *illus.*, 583 *illus.*

cervix: (SUR vihks) the lower opening, or neck, of the uterus **679**

Cestoda: 417

cetaceans: 538

C–4: 124 *illus.*

chelicerae: the first pair of appendages near the mouth of arachnids **441,** 441 *illus.*

Chelonia: 503

chemical cycling: 710, 710 *t.crit.*

chemical digestion: structural change in food caused by the action of enzymes on molecules **614,** 615 *illus.* and *table*

chemical reactions: 57, 57 *illus.*

chemoreception: 582, 582 *illus.*

chemosynthesis: a chemical reaction that organisms use to synthesize food **28,** 42

chicken pox: 672 *t.crit.*

Chilopoda: 445

chimpanzee: 40 *nw.*, 156 *illus.*

Chiroptera: 537, 537 *illus.*

chitin: (KITE un) a complex carbohydrate that comprises the exoskeleton of insects and the cell walls of most fungi 81 *nw.*, **288**

chlorophyll: green pigment that traps light in chloroplasts **120,** 120 *illus.*, 121 *illus.*

chloroplast: a plastid in photosynthetic plants that converts light into usable energy **84,** 84 *illus.*, 121 *illus.*, 410 *t.crit.*

cholesterol: 94, 94 *illus.*, 627 *t.crit.*

Chondrichthyes: 485

chordate: 479, 480 *illus.*, 481 *illus.*

chorion: (KOR ee ahn) the outermost membranes of amniotes, enclosing the embryo and all of its other membranes **502**

chorionic gonadotropin: 687, 687 *nw.*

Chlamydomonas: 277, 277 *illus.*

chromatin: tangles of DNA strands wound around protein molecules within the nucleus **79**

chromosome: a DNA-containing linear structure in cell nuclei **145**

chromosome map: a model showing the locations of all the known genes in a chromosome **163,** 163 *illus.*

cilia: (SIHL ee uh) short hairlike processes on the plasma membrane of certain cells of a multicellular organism or of unicellular organisms that assist in locomotion **85,** 85 *illus.*

ciliate: a protist that moves by means of cilia **272,** 272 *illus.*

circadian rhythm: (suhr KAYD ee uhn) a 24-hour cycle of behavior **561,** 561 *illus.*

circulatory system: 609 *t.crit.,* 641–650

cirri: appendages that enable some members of the class Crinoidea to walk about **467,** 467 *illus.*

citric acid cycle: a series of aerobic respiratory processes providing energy for storage in the form of high energy phosphate bonds **117,** 117 *illus.,* 118 *illus.*

class: a category ranking between the categories of order and phylum **37,** 403 *illus.,* 470 *illus.*

classification: a systematic arrangement of plants and animals into categories **34,** 34 *illus.,* 35 *illus.* and *nw.,* 36 *illus.,* 43 *t.crit.,* 389 *car.*

classifying: 34 *illus.,* 35 *illus.,* 41 *lab.,* 258 *lab.,* 401 *illus.,* 810–811 *sk.hbk.*

Clean Air Act (1970): 761

clear-cutting: the complete removal of trees in an area **769,** 769 *illus.*

climax community: a stable community in an area that will undergo no further change and represents the culmination of ecological succession **725,** 725 *nw.,* 726

clitellum: 429 *illus.*

clone: 666 *illus.,* 667

closed circulatory system: a system in which blood moves through the body in a series of blood vessels **426**

club fungi: 296, 296 *illus.*

club moss: 339, 339 *illus.*

cnidarian: 399, 403 *illus.,* 404 *illus.,* 405 *illus.,* 411

coal: 259, 260, 340 *t.crit.,* 742, 746

cocaine: 586

coccus: a bacterium of round, spherical, or oval shape; may exist singly, in clusters, or in chains **257,** 257 *illus.*

cochlea: the snail-shaped canal of the inner ear that contains hair cells receptive to vibrations that stimulate the auditory nerve for hearing 583 *nw.,* **584,** 584 *illus.*

codon: a three base unit of the genetic code **137,** 137 *illus.,* 140 *illus.,* 167 *illus.*

coelacanth: 488 *illus.*

coelom: (SEE lum) a true body cavity completely surrounded by tissues that develop from the embryonic mesoderm **397,** 397 *illus.*

collar cell: a cell with flagella that beat, causing water to be drawn through the body of a sponge **400**

colloid: an aggregate of molecules in a finely divided state, dispersed in a medium, which resists sedimentation, diffusion, and filtration **59,** 59 *illus.* and *nw.*

color blindness: 187, 187 *illus.*

commensalism: a symbiotic relationship in which one organism derives benefit and the other is unharmed but does not benefit **703,** 726

communication: the exchange of information **563,** 564 *illus.*

community: the combination of all the populations living and interacting with each other in a given area **700,** 701 *nw.,* 723, 725, 725 *nw.,* 735, 737

compact bone: 602, 603 *illus.*

competition: 701, 708, 708 *illus.,* 719, 728

complement: proteins that form in blood to combat pathogens **664**

complete flower: a flower having all four structures—sepals, petals, stamens, and pistils 370 *illus.,* **371,** 371 *illus.*

complete metamorphosis: (met uh MOR fuh sus) in arthropods, the development of an individual through four stages—egg, larva, pupa, and adult **437,** 437 *illus.*

compound: a substance formed by the union of two or more elements, generally differing entirely in physical characteristics from any of its components **54,** 54 *illus.,* 58 *illus.*

compound eye: a structure of vision having many lenses or facets **439,** 439 *illus.,* 448 *illus.*

compound leaf: a leaf having a divided leaf blade **317,** 317 *illus.*

compound light microscope: a microscope that uses light and two or more lenses to magnify an object and make it visible **76,** 77 *illus.* and *nw.*

concentration gradient: the difference in concentration of a substance across space **96,** 96 *illus.*

conclusion: 14, 15

condensation: 64 *illus.,* 65 *illus.,* 67 *illus.*

conditioning: a form of learning by association **554,** 554 *illus.,* 555 *illus.* and *nw.*

cones: 583

conidia: a structure in which a mass of spores are produced by a conidiophore in Ascomycote fungi **294,** 294 *illus.,* 297

conidiaphore: 294

conifers: 44, 356, 356 *illus.*

conjugation: the process whereby genetic recombination takes place in bacteria; in protists **256,** 256 *illus.,* 272, 273 *illus.*

connective tissue: tissue that supports and joins various parts of the body **572,** 572 *illus.,* 574 *illus.*

conservation: the wise and careful use of Earth's resources **763,** 763 *illus.,* 765 *illus.,* 766 *illus.,* 768, 768 *illus.,* 776 *illus.*

constrictor: a snake that coils around and crushes its prey **506,** 507 *illus.*

consumer: a type of organism that obtains energy from eating other organisms **28,** 202 *illus.,* 704 *illus.,* 705 *illus.,* 706 *illus.,* 707 *illus.*

contour plowing: plowing along the contour of the land to reduce water runoff and erosion **768,** 768 *illus.*

contractile vacuole: an organelle that collects excess water and then contracts to squeeze the water out of cells **98,** 272

control group: 12, 802 *sk.hbk.*

convergent evolution: the gradual process in which different taxonomic groups become similar **217,** 217 *illus.*

Copernicus, Nicolas (1473–1543): 27

coral: 402 *nw.,* 409, 410 *t.crit.,* 464 *illus.,* 472 *illus.,* 486 *illus.,* 565 *car.,* 701 *nw.*

cork: 316

corn: 14 *nw.,* 124 *illus.,* 156 *illus.,* 184 *lab.*

corolla: the whorl of petals in a flower **370,** 370 *illus.,* 371 *illus.*

coronary arteries: 645

coroner: 609 *t.crit.*

corpus luteum: (KOR pus LEWT ee um) the structure that develops from the follicle after the egg is released during the menstrual cycle 681 *illus.,* **682**

cortex: storage tissue that lies between the epidermis and vascular cylinder of a stem or root **312,** 316 *illus.*

cotyledon: the first leaf of a plant embryo **350,** 350 *illus.*

cotylosaurs: ancestral reptiles **507**

courtship behavior: behavior that males and females of a species participate in prior to mating **560,** 560 *illus.*

covalent bond: denoting an interatomic bond characterized by the sharing of electrons **55,** 55 *illus.*

crack: 586

crassulacean acid metabolism (CAM): 124 *illus.*

crayfish: 444

Cretaceous: 31, 369

Crick, Francis (1916–): 133

criminal investigator: 777 *car.*

Crinoidea: 464

crinoides: 467, 467 *illus.*

crocodiles, alligators: 504, 504 *illus.*

Cro-Magnon: an early form of *Homo sapiens* 237 *nw.,* **238,** 238 *illus.*

crop rotation: alternating of crops on a piece of land to prevent depletion of soil nutrients **768**

crossing over: the exchange of genetic material between two homologous chromosomes during meiosis **158,** 162 *illus.*

Crown-of-Thorns: 472, 472 *illus.*

crustacean: 444, 444 *illus.,* 452 *illus.*

cud chewing: the process by which hoofed mammals swallow food and later bring back up partially digested food and re-chew it **539,** 539 *illus.*

cuticle: the waxy, non-cellular layer that covers the outer surface of some plants **318,** 318 *illus.* and *nw.,* 320 *lab.*

cyanobacteria: 42, 126, 259, 260 *illus.,* 303

cycads: 357, 357 *illus.*

cyclosporine: a substance found in some imperfect fungi and used as a drug to suppress the body's immune system after transplant surgery **298,** 298 *illus.* and *nw.*

cystic fibrosis: 101 *nw.*

cytokinins: 384, 384 *illus.*

cytoplasm: the protoplasm of a cell within which the organelles are suspended 79 *illus.,* **82,** 149 *lab.,* 158, 573 *tech.,* 663 *illus.*

cytoskeleton: protein fibers composing the structural framework of a cell **85,** 85 *illus.*

cytotechnologist: 144 *car.*

D

Dart, Raymond (1893–1988): 236

Darwin, Charles Robert (1809–1882): 204, 204 *illus.,* 206, 206 *illus.* and *nw.,* 216 *illus.,* 383

Darwin's finches: 216 *illus.*

data: 13–14

da Vinci, Leonardo (1452–1519): 7, 7 *illus.*

day-neutral plants: plants that bloom regardless of day length   387 *illus.* and *nw.,* **388,** 388 *illus.*

deciduous plant: a plant that sheds its leaves at the end of a growing season   **356,** 356 *illus.*

decomposer: a heterotrophic organism that breaks down the complex compounds of dead protoplasm   **256,** 301, 301 *illus.,* 340 *t.crit.,* 711, 753 *t.crit.*

deletion: loss of a chromosome segment of any size   **168**

dendrite: 576, 577, 577 *illus.*

density-dependent factor: a factor that affects populations and is related to population size **744**

density-independent factor: a factor that affects populations no matter what the size of the population   **744,** 744 *illus.*

dentin: 614, 614 *illus.*

deoxyribonucleic acid (DNA): nucleic acid containing deoxyribose as the sugar component and found in the chromatin and chromosomes of cells   **69,** 70 *illus.,* 131, 132 *illus.* and *nw.,* 133 *illus.,* 134, 134 *illus.,* 136, 136 *illus.,* 138, 138 *illus.,* 139 *illus.,* 145 *illus.,* 155, 163 *illus.* and *nw.,* 165 *tech.,* 166, 167 *nw.,* 195 *illus.,* 203, 203 *illus.* and *nw.,* 239 *car.,* 254 *illus.,* 573 *tech.,* 671 *illus.*

dependent variable: a single factor measured in an experimental group as part of an experiment; for example, in an experiment to determine the effect of hormones on plant growth, growth is the dependent variable   **12,** 12 *illus.,* 802 *sk.hbk.*

depolarization: an alteration in the charge of a neuron in which the outside of the neuron becomes negatively charged in comparison to the inside   576 *illus.,* **577**

depressant: any substance that inhibits transmission of sensory impulses at a synapse   585 *illus.,* **586,** 586 *illus.,* 587 *table*

dermis: the thicker, inner portion of the skin **596,** 596 *nw.,* 597 *illus.*

desert: 725, 727, 728 *illus.,* 731

Designing an Experiment: 802–803 *sk.hbk.*

detritus: matter resulting from or remaining after decomposition   **463**

Deuteromycota: 297

development: the sum of changes that take place during the life of an organism   **21,** 21 *illus.,* 144 *car.,* 463 *illus.*

developmental biologist: 144 *car.*

developmental genes: 573 *tech.*

Devonian: 30 *illus.*

diabetes: 591, 669

diaphragm: (DI uh fram) a sheet of muscle beneath the lungs that assists in breathing   **526**

diatom: photosynthetic unicellular algal protist with a siliceous cell wall   **276,** 276 *illus.*

dicot: 350, 379, 379 *illus.*

dietary fiber: 627 *t.crit.*

diffusion: particle movement from an area of higher concentration to an area of lower concentration   **96,** 96 *illus.,* 97 *illus.* and *nw.*

digestion: 613–621

digestive enzymes: 615 *table,* 623 *illus.*

dihybrid cross: a cross between two individuals that differ in two characteristics   **181,** 181 *illus.,* 182 *illus.* and *table,* 184 *lab.*

dinoflagellate: unicellular alga with two flagella and a cell wall of cellulose plates; the cause of toxic red tides   **276,** 277 *illus.*

dinosaurs: 509

dipleurula: (di PLOOR uh luh) any bilaterally symmetrical, ciliated echinoderm larva   **462,** 463 *illus.,* 468 *lab.*

diploid: (DIP loyd) having two sets of chromosomes in a cell   **156,** 157 *nw.*

Diplopoda: 445

directional selection: a type of natural selection that produces a change of a population in one direction   **214,** 214 *illus.*

disaccharide: condensation product of two monosaccharides bonding together with the elimination of a water molecule   **65,** 65 *illus.*

disease: 6, 6 *nw.,* 11–12, 12 *illus.,* 14 *tech.*

disruptive selection: a type of natural selection that results in two separate and different populations   **214,** 214 *illus.*

divergent evolution: evolutionary pattern in which related species become less alike   **216,** 216 *illus.* and *nw.*

division: a group of related classes of plants; also called a phylum and ranking below a kingdom   **37**

DNA: *See* deoxyribonucleic acid

DNA fingerprinting: 192, 193

DNA sequencing machine: 203 *nw.*

dodo bird: 742 *illus.*

dog breeds: 175 *nw.,* 194 *illus.*

dominance hierarchy: in animal societies, the ranking of individuals according to levels of authority   **563,** 563 *illus.* and *nw.*

dominant trait: the condition in which only the phenotype determined by one of two genes is expressed in the heterozygous condition **176,** 176 *illus.,* 177 *illus.,* 178 *illus.,* 179 *illus.,* 181 *illus.,* 182 *illus.,* 185, 185 *illus.,* 186 *illus.,* 188 *illus.*

dormancy: a state of inactivity during plant development **352,** 352 *illus.,* 353 *illus.* and *nw.,* 354 *t.crit.*

dorsal: located near or on the back of an animal **417,** 417 *illus.*

dorsal nerve cord: a bundle of nerves that lies above the notochord; an identifying characteristic of chordates **480,** 481 *illus.*

double fertilization: in flowering plants, fertilization of the egg and the two nuclei within the embryo sac **373,** 373 *illus.* and *nw.*

double helix: the dual spiral structure of DNA **133,** 133 *illus.*

Drosophila: See fruit fly

drugs: 585, 585 *illus.,* 587 *table*

duck-billed platypus: 529, 530 *illus.*

Dugesia: 418 *illus.*

duodenum: (doo AHD un um) the part of the small intestine that extends 25 cm from the lower end of the stomach **617**

Dutch elm disease: 291, 291 *illus.*

dwarfism: 190, 191 *illus.*

dynamic equilibrium: a condition in which there is continuous movement of molecules but no overall change in concentration **96,** 96 *illus.*

ear: 584, 584 *illus.*

Earth Observing System (EOS): 735 *tech.*

earthworms: 428 *nw.,* 429 *illus.,* 430 *nw.,* 603

echidna: 530 *illus.*

echinoderms: 459–472, 460 *illus.,* 463, 464, 466 *illus.* and *nw.,* 467 *illus.,* 469, 469 *illus.,* 470 *illus.,* 471, 471 *illus.*

Echinoidea: 464

echolocation: a method by which chiropterans use sound waves to locate objects in the environment **537,** 537 *illus.*

ecology: the study of interrelationships among organisms, and between organisms and the environment 699–715, **700**

ecosystem: system that results from the interaction between all the organisms in an area and the environment 28 *illus.,* **29,** 565 *car.,* 701, 701 *illus.,* 735, 755 *illus.*

ectoderm: the outer layer of cells in the embryo from which specific organs develop **396,** 397 *illus.*

ectotherm: an animal in which the body temperature changes in response to its surrounding temperature **494**

edentates: 536, 536 *illus.*

eel: 483 *illus.,* 487 *nw.*

effectors: 576 *illus.*

egg: the female sex cell or gamete **156,** 679 *nw.,* 681 *illus.,* 685 *illus.*

ejaculation: 685

EKG: *See* electrocardiogram

electrocardiogram (EKG): a record of electrical changes in the heart muscle during heartbeat **648,** 648 *illus.* and *nw.*

electron: 52, 53 *illus.,* 55 *illus.,* 56 *illus.,* 60 *illus.,* 118 *illus.*

electron cloud: 52, 53 *illus.*

electron microscope: a microscope that provides increased levels of magnification by passing a stream of electrons over or through an object **77,** 92 *illus.,* 165 *tech.,* 248 *illus.*

electron transport chain: a series of substances along which electrons are transferred, releasing energy in the process **118,** 119 *illus.,* 126

elements: 52 *illus.* and *table*

Elodea: 87 *lab.,* 125 *lab.*

embryo: an early stage of development in any multicellular organism **202,** 202 *illus.,* 378 *nw.,* 573 *tech.,* 686 *illus.,* 687 *illus.*

emphysema: a lung condition in which the walls of the alveoli lose their elasticity **639,** 639 *illus.* and *nw.*

endangered species: a species with population numbers so low that it is in danger of becoming extinct 32, 33 *dav.,* 213 *nw.,* **510, 543,** 543 *illus.,* 565 *car.,* 754, 754 *illus.* and *nw.,* 755 *illus.,* 771 *illus.* and *nw.,* 772 *illus.*

endocrine gland: a gland having no ducts that secretes hormones directly into the bloodstream **588,** 588 *illus.,* 589 *illus.*

endocrine system: 588–591

endocytosis: the process in which a cell surrounds and takes in material from its environment **103,** 103 *illus.,* 104 *illus.*

endoderm: the inner layer of cells in the embryo from which specific organs develop **396,** 397 *illus.*

endodermis: innermost layer of the cortex; contains a waxy substance that prevents water from moving out of the vascular cylinder of a plant **312**

endoplasmic reticulum (ER): a folded membrane of the cytoplasm that functions in protein synthesis and transport of proteins **82,** 82 *illus.*

endoskeleton: a support framework within a body **398,** 398 *illus.,* 481

endosperm: tissue in which food is stored within a seed **351,** 352 *illus.*

endospore: a resistant structure formed within some bacteria during unfavorable conditions **256,** 256 *illus.*

endotherm: an animal that produces enough heat from its own metabolism to keep its body temperature higher than that of its environment **514**

energy: the capacity for action or work 20 *illus.,* 65 *illus.,* 103 *illus.,* **111,** 112 *illus.,* 113, 113 *illus.,* 114 *illus.,* 115, 122 *illus.,* 166, 260 *nw.,* 702, 706, 706 *illus.*

enzyme: a protein that speeds up the rate of a chemical reaction without being permanently changed by the reaction 6 *nw.,* **68,** 68 *illus.,* 69 *tech.,* 124 *nw.,* 140 *illus.,* 195 *illus.,* 289, 627 *t.crit.*

enzyme action: 71 *lab.*

epicotyl: the point of the embryo that grows longer and pushes a new stem and leaves above soil level **352,** 352 *illus.*

epidemic: the rapid spread of an infectious disease **662,** 673

epidermis: the outer, thin protective layer of skin; of a leaf **312,** 312 *illus.,* 317, 318 *illus.,* 436 *illus.,* 527 *nw.,* **595,** 596, 596 *illus.* and *nw.*

epididymis: (ep uh DIHD uh mus) a coiled tube within the scrotum in which sperm mature **678,** 678 *illus.*

epiglottis: (ep uh GLAHT us) a flap of elastic cartilage that protects the opening to the trachea **615,** 636 *illus.*

epiphyte: (EP uh fite) plant that grows on other plants for support, but obtains nutrition from the air **378,** 378 *nw.,* 379 *illus.* and *nw.*

epithelial tissue: tissue that covers the body and lines body cavities, organs, and ducts **571,** 572 *illus.,* 573 *tech.*

erosion: the washing away of exposed soil by wind or water **768,** 768 *illus.,* 777 *car.*

Escherichia coli: 259 *tech.,* 703 *nw.*

esophagus: the tubular portion of the alimentary canal that connects the mouth to the stomach **614,** 615 *illus.*

essential elements: 52, 52 *table*

Estimating: 808 *sk.hbk.*

estivation: a state of reduced metabolism during periods of intense heat, allowing energy conservation **528**

estrogen: (ES truh jun) the female sex hormone that influences secondary sex characteristics in females **680,** 682 *illus.*

estuary: (ES chuh wer ee) areas either upstream or offshore where fresh water and ocean water mix **736**

ethylene: plant hormone that causes fruit maturation 383 *illus.,* 384 *illus.,* **385,** 385 *illus.*

euglenoid: a protist that possesses traits of both animals and plants **275,** 275 *illus.,* 280 *lab.*

eukaryote: an organism that has cells with membrane-bound structures **37,** 37 *illus.,* 43 *t.crit.,* 94 *illus.,* 232, 232 *illus.,* 233 *illus.,* 395

euphotic zone: (yoo FOHT ik) the uppermost layer of a body of water that receives sufficient sunlight for the growth of green plants **736,** 736 *illus.*

European Space Agency (ESA): 735 *tech.*

eutrophic: a body of water in which the supply of organic nutrients is high but dissolved oxygen is low **737**

eutrophication: (yoo troh fuh KAY shun) the natural aging of a lake in which the level of nutrients and water temperature increase, thus changing the environment and the species of organisms **737,** 737 *illus.*

evergreen plants: perennially green plants **356,** 356 *illus.,* 359 *illus.,* 362 *lab.,* 363 *illus.,* 364 *illus.*

evolution: a continuing process of genetic change in a population of organisms over long periods of time **29,** 30 *illus.,* 45 *illus.,* 113, 127 *t.crit.,* 199, 201, 204, 204 *illus.,* 207, 211, 212, 222 *illus.,* 232 *illus.,* 233 *illus.,* 234 *illus.,* 239 *car.,* 482, 573 *tech.*

excretory system: 618, 619, 652

exercise and CO_2: 640 *lab.,* 649 *t.crit.*

exocytosis: the process by which waste materials are expelled from a cell **104,** 104 *illus.*

exoskeleton: a framework of support on the outside of a body **398,** 398 *illus.,* 436 *illus.,* 444 *illus.,* 452, 465 *illus.,* 481

experiment: a series of procedures performed to test a hypothesis **12–15**, 12 *illus.*

experimental group: 12

external fertilization: process involving the union of male and female sex cells outside the body of the female **424**

external respiration: the exchange of oxygen and carbon dioxide within the alveoli **636,** 636 *illus.*

extinction: the worldwide death of a species 30 *illus.*, **31**, 211 *t.crit.*, 239 *car.*, 469 *illus.*, 482, 520, 538, 543, 705, 708, 742 *illus.*, 754 *nw.*, 771 *illus.* and *nw.*

extracellular digestion: 289

eyespot: a simple organ that responds to light in many invertebrates, such as in euglenas and echinoderms 275 *illus.*, **461,** 461 *illus.*

F

facilitated diffusion: the diffusion of materials across a plasma membrane by transport proteins **101,** 101 *illus.* and *nw.*, 102 *illus.*

Fact or Opinion: 798 *sk.hbk.*

falcon: 520

family: a taxonomic category above a genus and below an order, and which is based upon the grouping of related genera **36**, 36 *illus.*

fatty acids: 66 *illus.*

feather: a modified scale that forms the plumage of a bird and provides insulation **513,** 513 *illus.*

feather stars: 467, 467 *illus.*

feeding hydra: 408 *lab.*

fermentation: 116 *illus.*, 294

ferns: 341, 341 *illus.*

fertilization: the fusion of male and female gametes **160,** 423, 424

fetal alcohol syndrome (FAS): 689

fetus: the term expressing the embryo after the eighth week of development when all systems are present **687,** 688 *illus.*, 689 *illus.*

filter feeder: an organism that feeds by filtering water and small organisms over its gills **424,** 538

fingerprints: 596, 596 *illus.* and *nw.*, 598 *lab.*

fins: fan-shaped membranes supported by spines and used by fish for steering and locomotion **483,** 486 *illus.*

firefly: 195 *illus.*

fish: 482, 482 *illus.*, 483 *illus.*, 484 *illus.*, 486 *illus.*, 487 *illus.*, 488 *illus.*, 489 *illus.*, 490 *lab.*, 491 *nw.* and *t.crit.*, 492, 492 *illus.*, 706 *nw.*

fish habitats: 490 *lab.*

fishers: 473 *car.*

fishery biologist: 565 *car.*

five kingdom classification: 38 *illus.*, 42, 126

flagella: (fluh JEL uh) threadlike structures that project out from a cell's surface and provide for locomotion **42,** 42 *illus.*, **85,** 254 *illus.*

flagellate: a protist that moves by means of whipping flagella **272,** 272 *illus.*

flame bulb: excretory structure that removes excess water from body cells of many invertebrates including flatworms 417 illus, **418**

flatworm: 417, 417 *illus.*, 418 *illus.*

Fleming, Sir Alexander (1881–1955): 298 *nw.*

flight: 447, 501, 513–516, 537, 537 *illus.*

flow stage: during the menstrual cycle, the loss of the blood-rich lining of the uterus; usually lasts five days **681**

flowering plants: 44, 369–389

fluid mosaic model: describes the ability of the phospholipid and protein molecules of a membrane to flow among one another **93,** 94 *illus.*

flukes: 419, 419 *illus.*

follicle: a group of cells within the ovary that contain an egg **680,** 681 *illus.*

follicle-stimulating hormone (FSH): a hormone made by the pituitary that stimulates production of sex cells **680,** 680 *illus.*, 681

follicular stage: 681, 682 *illus.*

F₁ generation: the offspring resulting from the crossbreeding of unrelated parents **175,** 176 *illus.*, 177 *illus.*, 181 *illus.*, 185 *illus.*

food chain: a feeding relationship in which nutrients are transferred from producers, through several levels of consumers, to decomposers 301, **704,** 704 *illus.*, 706 *illus.*, 726

food web: the interconnecting of food chains into a complex feeding sequence **705,** 705 *illus.*, 709, 726

foolish seedling disease: 11, 14 *tech.*

forestry aides and technicians: 777 *car.*

formaldehyde: 748

fossil: the remains, traces, or imprints of an organism preserved in the Earth's crust some time during the geologic past **31,** 31 *nw.*, 44, 127 *t.crit.*, 199, 200 *illus.* and *nw.*, 222 *illus.*, 239 *car.*, 467 *illus.*, 711

fossil fuel: a hydrocarbon fuel derived from living matter of a previous geologic time 340 *t.crit.*, **742,** 746 *illus.*

fossil plants: 342 *illus.*

Fox, Sidney (1912–): 230

fragmentation: a type of asexual reproduction in which an algae filament breaks off and grows into a new filament by mitosis **278,** 278 *illus.*

frameshift mutation: insertion or deletion of a nitrogen base that produces a type of gene mutation **167,** 167 *illus.*

Franklin, Rosalind (1920–1958): 132–133

free-living organism: an organism that is not dependent on a specific feeding relationship with any other organism **417**

frogs: 493 *illus.*, 494, 494 *illus.* and *nw.*, 495 *nw.*, 497 *illus.*, 708

frond: leaf of a fern **342,** 342 *illus.*

fructose: 63 *illus.*, 65 *illus.*

fruit: a ripened ovary **350,** 350 *illus.*, 356 *illus.*, 358 *illus.*, 376 *illus.*, 377

fruit and seed dispersal: 373 *illus.* and *nw.*, 374 *illus.*, 376 *illus.* and *nw.*, 377 *illus.* and *nw.*

fruit fly: 156, 160 *illus.*, 164 *illus.*, 169 *lab.*

FSH: *See* follicle-stimulating hormone

F₂ generation: the offspring produced by the inbreeding of the first filial generation **176,** 176 *illus.*, 177 *illus.*, 182 *illus.* and *table*

fungus: a unicellular or multicellular eukaryote that has cell walls and obtains food by absorption 11, 12 *illus.*, 15, 38 *illus.*, **44,** 44 *illus.* and *nw.*, 69 *tech.*, 81 *nw.*, 287, 288 *illus.*, 289 *illus.*, 290 *illus.*, 291, 292, 292 *illus.*, 294, 294 *illus.*, 296, 296 *illus.*, 297, 297 *illus.*, 298 *illus.* and *nw.*, 299 *illus.* and *nw.*, 301, 301 *illus.*, 742

G

Galapagos Islands: 215, 216, 216 *nw.*

gametangium: (gam eet AN gee um) in fungi, an organ or cell in which gametes are produced **293**

gamete: a sex cell; formed when the number of chromosomes is halved during reproduction **156,** 160 *illus.*, 177 *illus.*, 180 *illus.*

gametophyte: the form of algae or plants that contains gamete producing organs and produces gametes or sex cells **279,** 279 *illus.* and *nw.*

Garner, Wightman Wells (1875–1956): 387

gastric mill: 444

gastrin: a polypeptide hormone that stimulates the stomach to release gastric acid **620,** 620 *illus.*

gastropod: 422, 423 *illus.*, 424 *illus.*

gastrovascular cavity: cavity in which digestion takes place; seen in cnidarians **404**

gastrula: a two-layered structure from which the three germ cell layers develop during embryonic cell division **397,** 397 *illus.*

gecko: 505

gemmae: asexual reproductive structures of a liverwort **336,** 336 *illus.*

gemmule: (JEM yewl) resistant reproductive structures of sponges that consist of amoebocytes surrounded by spicules **401**

gene: a segment of DNA that controls specific hereditary traits **155,** 160 *illus.*, 161 *illus.* and *nw.*, 163 *illus.*, 167 *illus.* and *nw.*, 187 *illus.*, 189 *t.crit.*, 212 *illus.*, 239 *car.*, 259 *tech.*, 549, 573 *tech.*

gene flow: the movement of genes in and out of the gene pool by means of organisms leaving and entering a population **213,** 213 *illus.* and *nw.*

gene pool: all the genes in a population **212,** 212 *illus.*

gene splicing: the cutting of DNA by enzymes and insertion of a piece of foreign DNA **195,** 195 *illus.*

genetic drift: the random fluctuation of gene frequencies from generation to generation **213,** 213 *illus.* and *nw.*

genetic engineering: the intentional production of new genes and alteration of genomes by the substitution or addition of new genetic material **195,** 195 *illus.*, 239 *car.*, 259 *tech.*, 262, 263 *dav.*, 425 *tech.*

genetic equilibrium: the condition in which the allele frequencies in a population remain the same from one generation to the next **212,** 212 *illus.*

genetic recombination: exchange of genetic material between homologous chromosomes during meiosis I that results in variation among offspring **162,** 162 *illus.*, 195 *illus.*

genetic testing: 192, 193 *dav.*

genetic variations: 169 *lab.*

genetics: the branch of biology that deals with the study of heredity 14 *nw.*, **173,** 189 *t.crit.*, 195 *illus.*, 573 *tech.*

genotype: the genetic constitution of an organism; it determines the traits of an organism **160,** 161 *nw.,* 163 *nw.,* 164 *illus.,* 191 *illus.*

genus: group of similar species that are alike in general features, but possessing specific differences 29 *illus.,* **35,** 236 *illus.,* 296 *illus.,* 426 *illus.*

geographic isolation: a condition that occurs if a physical barrier separates a population into groups **215**

geologic time scale: 30 *illus.,* 37, 38 *illus.,* 261 *illus.,* 299 *illus.,* 380 *illus.,* 403 *illus.,* 416 *illus.,* 440 *illus.,* 470 *illus.,* 489 *illus.,* 508 *illus.,* 531 *illus.*

German measles: 689

germination: the development of a seed into a new plant 352, 352 *illus.,* **353,** 353 *illus.* and *nw.,* 354 *t.crit.*

germ layers: 397 *illus.*

gestation: (jeh STAY shun) the time during which young placental mammals develop inside the uterus **533,** 533 *table*

Gibberella fungus: 15

gibberellic acid: 9 *lab.,* 14, 14 *tech.,* 15 *nw.*

gibberellin: plant hormone that stimulates cell elongation and division 14, 15, **384,** 384 *illus.*

Gila monster: 505

gill: a respiratory structure that removes oxygen from water 105 *t.crit.,* **422,** 426 *illus.,* 483 *illus.,* 495 *illus.*

gill slits: paired openings located in the throat behind the mouth; an identifying feature of a chordate 202 *illus.,* **480,** 481 *illus.*

ginkgo: 358, 358 *illus.*

gizzard: in earthworms, a sac with muscular walls and hard particles that grinds soil before it is passed into the intestine; part of the digestive tract of a bird in which food is crushed by muscular action **429, 515,** 520

glands: 572, 588, 588 *illus.*

glucagon: a proteinaceous pancreatic hormone that increases blood sugar **629,** 629 *illus.*

glucose: 63 *illus.,* 65 *illus.,* 115 *illus.,* 119 *nw.,* 589 *illus.,* 591, 626 *lab.,* 627 *t.crit.,* 629 *illus.*

glycerol: 66 *illus.,* 623 *illus.*

glycogen: 65, 622, 629 *illus.*

glycolysis: (gli KAHL uh sus) the enzymatic breakdown of glucose with the formation of pyruvic acid and the formation of energy in the form of adenosine triphosphate energy **115,** 115 *illus.*

Golden age of mammals: 541

Golgi complex: (GAWL jee) closely stacked, flattened sacs that contain proteins within a living cell **82,** 83 *illus.*

gonorrhea: 661

gradualism: the gradual change of species over time **211**

grana: stacked arrangement of thylakoid membranes within a chloroplast **121**

Grand Canyon: 31 *illus.*

grapes: 14 *tech.*

Graphing: 812–813 *sk.hbk.*

Great Barrier Reef: 411 *illus.,* 472, 472 *illus.,* 473 *car.*

green algae: 277, 277 *illus.,* 278, 278 *illus.*

greenhouse effect: phenomenon that results from the absorption of solar radiation by Earth and a steady rise in atmospheric temperature **747,** 747 *illus.*

groundwater: water beneath Earth's surface that lies between saturated soil and rock and that supplies wells and springs **714,** 714 *illus.*

growth: an increase in the amount of living material in an organism **20,** 20 *illus.,* 22 *illus.,* 239 *car.,* 693, 693 *illus.* and *nw.*

guard cells: cells that surround and control the size of stomata in plants **318,** 318 *illus.*

gymnosperm: seed plant having a naked ovule **350,** 355, 355 *illus.,* 359, 359 *illus.,* 362 *lab.,* 363, 363 *illus.,* 364 *illus.,* 365 *illus.*

H

habitat: the environment in which an organism or biological population lives or grows 565 *car.,* **700,** 735

Haeckel, Ernst (1834–1919): 37

hagfish: 484, 484 *illus.*

hair follicle: narrow cavity in the dermis in which a hair grows **597,** 597 *illus.*

halophiles: 260

haploid: a condition whereby a cell has a single set of chromosomes or one half the number of the diploid cell **156,** 157 *nw.,* 677

haustoria: (haw STOH ree uh) hypha of a parasitic fungus; invades the cells of a host to absorb nutrients **289,** 289 *illus.,* 297

hearing: 584

heartwood: the older, inactive central wood of a tree or woody plant **316,** 316 *illus.*

heartworm: 421

hemoglobin: the iron-containing, oxygen-carrying molecule of red blood cells 52, 68, **642,** 642 *illus.* and *nw.*

hemophilia: 189, 190

Hepatitis B virus: 248

herbaceous stems: 314

herbivore: an organism that feeds on plants; a primary consumer 536, **704,** 704 *illus.* and *nw.*, 713, 725

heredity: the characteristics that are genetically transmitted to an individual organism 173

hermaphrodite: (hur MAF ruh dite) a condition in which both male and female reproductive organs are present in an individual **402,** 423, 429, 484

heterotroph: any organism that obtains its energy and nutrients from sources other than itself **289,** 395

heterozygous: condition in which two homologous chromosomes have different alleles for a trait **178,** 178 *illus.,* 180 *illus.,* 181 *illus.,* 213 *illus.*

hexaploid: 168 *illus.*

hibernation: a reduced state of metabolism in response to cold temperatures that allows energy conservation 23 *illus.,* **529,** 529 *nw.*

histamine: 665

H.M.S. Beagle: 206, 206 *nw.*

holdfast: 278

Holothuroidea: 464, 464 *illus.*

homeobox genes: 573 *tech.*

homeostasis: regulation and maintenance of a steady internal environment while responding to changes in the external environment **22,** 22 *illus.* and *nw.,* 23 *illus.,* 29, 91, 105 *t.crit.,* 527, 580 *illus.,* 604, 652, 710 *t.crit.*

hominid: a humanlike, bipedal primate **236,** 236 *illus.*

Homo erectus: an upright extinct species of human; known from fossils **237**

Homo habilis: a fossil hominid considered to be the first to use tools **236,** 236 *illus.,* 237, 237 *nw.,* 238, 238 *illus.,* 239 *car.*

Homo sapiens: the modern hominid 40 *nw.,* **237,** 237 *nw.,* 239 *car.*

homologous chromosomes: the members of a single pair of matched chromosomes **156,** 156 *illus.* and *table,* 158 *illus.,* 162 *illus.*

homologous structures: structures that are similar in form, function, and origin, yet found in different species; may indicate closeness of origin **201,** 201 *illus.*

homozygous: condition in which two homologous chromosomes have identical alleles for the same trait **178,** 213 *illus.*

honeybees: 157 *nw.,* 451 *nw.* and *t.crit.,* 564

hoofed mammals: 94, 94 *illus.,* 539, 539 *illus.,* 542 *t.crit.,* 704 *nw.*

Hooke, Robert (1635–1703): 75, 75 *nw.,* 76 *illus.*

hormone: the chemical secreted by an endocrine gland that brings about an effect in a specific tissue or organ; also produces growth and responses in plants **383,** 383 *illus.,* 385, 385 *illus.,* **588,** 588 *illus.,* 590 *illus.*

horseshoe crab: 443

horsetails: 339, 340 *illus.*

hot springs: 43 *t.crit.*

Hubbard Brook Experiment: 710 *t.crit.*

human blood groups, types: 186 *table,* 643, 643 *table*

human ecologists: 691 *car.*

human evolution: 234–238

human growth: 590, 590 *illus.*

human population growth: 743, 743 *illus.* and *nw.,* 744 *illus.*

hummingbird: 113 *illus.,* 515 *illus.*

hunger center: the part of the hypothalamus that stimulates a desire to eat **621**

hybrid: an offspring that results from a cross between closely related species of organisms **194,** 194 *illus.* and *nw.*

hydra: 405 *illus.,* 406 *illus.,* 408 *lab.*

hydrogen: 53 *illus.,* 55 *illus.,* 118 *illus.*

hydrolysis: 64 *illus.*

hydroponics: 324 *tech.*

hypertonic solution: a solution in which the concentration of dissolved substances outside the cell is higher than the concentration of those substances inside the cell, making the concentration of water lower outside the cell **98,** 99 *illus.*

hyperventilate: 638

hyphae: threadlike filaments that form the basic structure of a fungus **288,** 288 *illus.,* 297

hypocotyl: the point at which the cotyledons are attached in a seed plant **352**

hypothalamus: a small area of the brain that controls homeostatic activities such as body temperature, hunger, thirst, and sleep **578**

hypothesis: a possible solution to a problem based on all currently known facts; a prediction that must be testable **11**–13, 11 *illus.,* 14 *nw.*

Hypothesizing: 802 *sk.hbk.*

hypotonic solution: a solution in which the concentration of dissolved substances outside the cell is lower than the concentration of those substances inside the cell, making the concentration of water higher outside the cell **98,** 99 *illus.,* 105 *t.crit.*

immune system: 656–673

immunity: resistance to a particular pathogen by an immune response 657, **666,** 667 *illus.,* 668, 668 *illus.,* 673 *illus.*

immunologist: 300 *car.*

imperfect fungi: 297, 297 *illus.,* 298

implantation: the attaching of the embryo to the lining of the uterus to establish fertilization 685, **686**

imprinting: the formation of a social attachment by one organism to another soon after birth or hatching **553,** 553 *illus.*

impulse: 576 *illus.,* 577 *nw.,* 582 *illus.*

inbreeding: fertilization of gametes from the same parents or closely related parents 174 *illus.,* **175,** 175 *nw.* and *table,* 176 *illus.,* 559 *nw.*

incomplete dominance: the condition resulting when two alleles produce three phenotypes instead of two; neither allele of a pair is completely dominant **185,** 185 *illus.*

incomplete flower: flowers lacking one or more flower parts 370 *illus.,* **371,** 371 *illus.*

incomplete metamorphosis: (met uh MOR fuh sus) three stages in the development of some organisms; egg, nymph, adult; the nymph resembles the adult form **437,** 437 *illus.*

incubation: 552

independent variable: the condition being tested in an experiment **12,** 12 *illus.,* 802 *sk.hbk.*

indigestible material: 627 *t.crit.*

infectious disease: 660, 660 *illus.,* 661, 661 *illus.,* 662 *nw.* and *table,* 663, 663 *illus.,* 672, 672 *t.crit.*

inflammation: the response by body tissue to injury; produces swelling, heat, pain, redness **664,** 665 *illus.*

innate behavior: behavior that is inherited **550,** 550 *illus.,* 557 *lab.*

insect pollinators: 211 *t.crit.,* 370, 373, 373 *illus.* and *nw.,* 374

insectivores: 529, 533, 533 *illus.*

insects: 22 *illus.,* 81 *nw.,* 211 *t.crit.,* 438 *illus.,* 446, 446 *table,* 447 *illus.* and *nw.,* 448 *illus.,* 450 *illus.,* 451 *t.crit.,* 452 *illus.,* 453 *illus.,* 473 *car.,* 703 *illus.,* 704 *nw.,* 707 *illus.,* 728

insight: the use of previous experience by an animal to respond to a new situation **555,** 555 *illus.* and *nw.,* 556 *illus.*

instinct: a complex pattern of innate behavior **551,** 551 *illus.*

insulin: a protein hormone produced by the beta cells of the islet of Langerhans of the pancreas that is vital in the control of carbohydrate and fat metabolism; lacking in diabetics **591,** 591 *illus.,* **629,** 629 *illus.*

integrated pest management: use of multiple pest control techniques 454 *dav.,* **774,** 775 *illus.*

interferon: a protein produced by intact animal cells when infected with viruses **251,** 251 *nw.*

internal fertilization: the fusion of eggs with sperm inside the body of an organism **423**

interphase: the period between succeeding mitotic divisions **146,** 146 *illus.,* 148 *illus.,* 149 *lab.*

Interpreting Scientific Illustrations: 800 *sk.hbk.*

inversion: a chromosomal rearrangement in which two breaks take place in a chromosome and the fragment between the breaks rotates 180 degrees before rejoining with no genetic information loss **167,** 167 *illus.*

invertebrate: an animal without a backbone 395, 398 *illus.,* **399,** 473 *car.*

involuntary muscle: the smooth muscle of the trachea, digestive tract and reproductive tract that does not contract under conscious control **606,** 609 *t.crit.*

iodine: 52

ion: an atom or group of atoms carrying a charge of electricity by having gained or lost one or more electrons **56,** 56 *illus.,* 58 *illus.,* 60 *illus.,* 103 *illus.,* 189 *t.crit.*

ionic bond: a chemical bond formed by the complete transfer of one or more electrons from one kind of atom to another **56,** 56 *illus.*

iron: 52

Islets of Langerhans: 591

isomers: compounds that have the same simple formula as other compounds but that differ in chemical or physical properties **63,** 63 *illus.*

isopod habitat: 449 *lab.*

isotonic solution: a solution in which the concentration of dissolved substances outside the cell is the same as inside the cell; concentration of water is the same inside and outside the cell **98,** 98 *illus.,* 99 *illus.*

isotopes: atoms of the same element have different numbers of neutrons **53,** 53 *illus.*

Ivanovsky, Dimitri (1864–1920): 252

J

Jacobson's organ: an olfactory canal in the nasal mucosa that ends in a blind pouch; highly developed in reptiles but vestigial in humans **506,** 506 *illus.*

jawless fish: 484 *illus.*

jellyfish: 409 *illus.*

Jenner, Edward (1749–1823): 252, 673

Johanson, Donald (1943–): 236

joint: the site where two bones meet, normally allowing movement **602,** 602 *illus.*

Jurassic: 31, 378

juvenile diabetes: 669

K

keratin: (KER ut un) a protein in epidermal cells which help waterproof and protect the cell layers beneath **595**

kidneys: organs that filter liquid wastes from the blood **651,** 651 *illus.,* 653 *illus.*

kinetic energy: energy of motion **95,** 95 *illus.*

kingdom: a group of related phyla or divisions **37,** 38–39 *illus.*

Kingdom Animalia: 39 *illus.,* 45

Kingdom Fungi: 38 *illus.,* 44, 286–303

Kingdom Monera: 38 *illus.,* 42, 43 *t.crit.,* 254–261, 261 *illus.*

Kingdom Plantae: 38 *illus.,* 45

Kingdom Protista: 37, 38 *illus.,* 43, 267–283, 268 *illus.,* 269 *illus.*

Koch, Robert (1843–1910): 660, 660 *illus.,* 661

K-selected populations: 491 *t.crit.*

L

lactic acid: 116 *illus.,* 597 *nw.,* 608

lactic acid fermentation: the formation of lactic acid by fermentation in some bacteria, plants, and in most animals **117**

ladybird beetle: 451, 452 *illus.*

lagomorphs: 536, 536 *illus.*

Lamarck, Jean Baptiste de (1744–1829): 204, 204 *illus.,* 205

lamprey: 484

lancelets: 480 *illus.*

language: the use of symbols and voice sounds to represent ideas **556,** 556 *illus.*

large intestine: the portion of the intestine that extends from the ileum to the anus **618**

larva: the wormlike feeding stage that develops from an egg in complete metamorphosis; a stage in development **437,** 437 *illus.*

lateral line system: a network of fluid-filled canals running from the head down the sides of fish; a balancing organ **485,** 487 *illus.*

laterite: 728 *nw.*

law of dominance: only the dominant trait appears in the offspring of a cross between two pure lines for different traits **176,** 176 *illus.*

law of independent assortment: the inheritance of alleles for one trait is not affected if the genes for a second trait are located on separate chromosomes **183,** 183 *illus.*

law of segregation: during reproduction, the two factors that control each trait separate or segregate, and one factor from each pair is passed to the offspring **177,** 177 *illus.*

Leakey, Louis (1903–1972): 236

Leakey, Mary (1913–): 236

Leakey, Richard (1944–): 236

learning: behavior that can be changed through experience or practice **552,** 552 *illus.,* 557 *lab.*

leaves: 317–321

leeches: 428, 430 *illus.*

Leeuwenhoek, Anton van (1632–1723): 76

Length: 807 *sk.hbk.*

leukemia: 166

lice: 446

lichens: the mutualistic relationship of a green alga and a fungus, being so complete that a genus and species name is assigned them as though they were a single organism **303,** 303 *illus.* and *nw.*

life of a flowering plant: 372, 372 *illus.*

ligament: a tough band of tissue that connects bones to bones **602,** 602 *illus.*

light reactions: reactions in which light excites electrons and water splits into hydrogen and oxygen during photosynthesis **122**

limiting factor: a condition that determines the survival of an organism in its environment **720,** 720 *illus.,* 722 *illus.,* 727

limits of tolerance: an organism's range of living conditions within an environment that allows it to survive 719, **720,** 720 *illus.,* 721 *lab.,* 722, 722 *illus.*

linkage group: genes located on a single chromosome that are usually inherited together **162**

Linnaeus, Carolus (1707–1778): 35

Linnean Society: 207

lipid: an organic compound made by cells for long-term energy storage **66,** 66 *illus.* and *nw.*

liver: an organ that secretes bile and acts in formation of blood and metabolism; breaks down substances such as alcohol and drugs **617,** 617 *illus.,* 629 *illus.*

liverworts: 336, 336 *illus.*

lizards: 505, 505 *illus.* and *nw.*

lobe-finned fish: 488 *illus.,* 496

lobster: 435, 444 *illus.*

locomotion: 482 *illus.,* 606

long-day plant: a plant that flowers in response to a long photoperiod 387 *illus.* and *nw.,* **388,** 388 *illus.*

Lucy: 236, 236 *illus.*

lungfish: 448, 449 *illus.*

luteal stage: days 15 to 28 of the menstrual cycle **682,** 682 *illus.*

luteinizing hormone (LH): (LEWT ee uh nize ing) a hormone that stimulates ovulation in females and sex hormone production in both males and females **680,** 680 *illus.,* 681, 682 *illus.*

Lyme disease: 443

lymph: colorless tissue fluid that circulates through the lymphatic system **657**

lymphatic system: 657, 658, 658 *illus.,* 659 *illus.*

lymph node: a small mass of tissue that filters lymph **658,** 658 *illus.*

lymphocyte: white blood cell found in lymph nodes that function in the body's defense system **658,** 658 *illus.*

lysogenic virus: a virus that does not kill its host

cell during replication **248,** 249 *illus.,* 250 *illus.,* 251 *illus.*

lysosome: (LI suh sohm) a cell organelle that contains digestive enzymes used for digestion **83,** 83 *nw.*

lytic virus: a virus that destroys its host cell during the process of replicating itself **248,** 249 *illus.,* 251 *illus.,* 672 *t.crit.*

M

macromolecules: 63

macronucleus: large nucleus in the cells of ciliated protozoans **272,** 272 *illus.,* 273 *illus.*

macrophage: a large white blood cell capable of engulfing pathogens and foreign matter **666,** 670 *lab.*

madreporite: (muh DREH puh rite) a delicately perforated sieve plate at the distal end of the stone canal in echinoderms **460,** 461 *illus.*

maggots: 224 *illus.,* 452 *nw.*

magnesium: 52

Magnification: 805 *sk.hbk.*

Making a Wet Mount Slide: 805 *sk.hbk.*

malaria: 274

Mallon, Mary (Typhoid Mary) (1868?–1938): 662 *nw.*

Malpighian tubules: excretory tubes leading from the digestive tracts in insects **438,** 438 *illus.*

Malvaceae: 36, 36 *illus.*

mammal adaptations: 528, 528 *illus.*

mammal characteristics: 525, 526 *illus.,* 527 *nw.*

mammalian heart: 526 *illus.*

mammary gland: gland in the female mammal that secretes milk to nourish offspring **525**

manatee: 538 *illus.*

mandibles: jaws on some organisms **444,** 444 *illus.*

mantle: a thin membrane that surrounds the digestive, excretory, and reproductive organs of mollusks, and secretes a shell in shelled species **422,** 426 *illus.*

maple: 10 *illus.,* 21

marine biologists: 473 *car.*

marine super glues: 425 *tech.*

marrow: a soft tissue that fills the center cavity of the bone **602,** 604

marsupial: a mammal whose offspring undergoes a short period of development in the mother's body and then an extensive period of development in a pouch outside the mother's body **532,** 532 *illus.*

Mass: 806 *sk.hbk.*

master control system: 573 *tech.*

matter: anything that occupies space and has mass **18,** 18 *illus.* and *nw.*, 20 *illus.*, 95 *illus.*

McClintock, Barbara (1902–): 14 *nw.*

Measuring in SI: 806 *sk.hbk.*

mechanical digestion: the physical process of breaking food into smaller pieces such as results from chewing **614,** 614 *illus.*, 616 *illus.*

mechanoreception: 583, 583 *nw.*, 584 *illus.*

medulla oblongata: a portion of the brain stem that controls involuntary activities **578**

medusa: any of various free-swimming cnidarians having a bell- or bowl-shaped body with tentacles **404,** 404 *illus.*

megaspore: reproductive cell in plants that gives rise to the egg **360,** 360 *illus.*, 361 *illus.*

meiosis: the process of cell division that results in the formation of haploid gametes by reducing the number of chromosomes by one half through two divisions of the nucleus **157,** 157 *illus.*, 158 *illus.* and *nw.*, 677

melanin: (MEL uh nun) a cell pigment that colors the skin and protects the cells from damage by solar radiation **596**

melanoma: (mel uh NOH muh) cancer of the pigmented cells of the skin, more common in people with lighter colored skin **600**

membrane: 82, 602, 603 *illus.*, 686 *illus.*

Mendel, Gregor (1822–1884): 15, 173, 176 *illus.*, 181, 182 *table,* 183 *illus.*

menstrual cycle: a series of changes in the female reproductive system including egg production and the preparation of the uterus for receiving the egg **681,** 682 *illus.*, 683 *lab.*

meristem: all growth tissue in plants **312**

mesoderm: the middle layer of cells in an animal embryo from which specific organs develop **396,** 397 *illus.*

mesophyll: the photosynthetic layer of a leaf made up of palisade and spongy parenchyma **319,** 319 *illus.*

Mesozoic: 30 *illus.*, 340 *t.crit.*, 507, 517, 541

messenger RNA (mRNA): the RNA copy of a DNA code for a sequence of amino acids in a specific protein chain **138,** 138 *illus.* and *nw.*

metabolism: the combination of all the chemical changes that take place in an organism **20,** 20 *illus.*, 22 *nw.*, 42, 144 *car.*, 249 *illus.*, 259 *tech.*, 451 *t.crit.*, 482, 527, 585 *illus.*, 627, 628 *illus.*, 703 *nw.*, 706, 706 *illus.*

metaphase: phase in mitosis during which sister chromatids become attached by a centromere to the spindle fibers **146** *illus.*, **147,** 149 *lab.*, 157, 158 *illus.*, 159

methane: 55, 57 *illus.*, 260

methanogens: 260

microbes: 42 *nw.*, 226 *illus.*, 259 *tech.*, 639 *nw.*, 753 *t.crit.*

microbial geneticists: 239 *car.*

microbiologists: 300 *car.*

microfilament: cytoplasmic fibrous structure made of protein and found in living cells **85,** 606

microfossil: microscopic fossil remains of the first organism on Earth; shapes are spherical or like a filament made up of short rods **230,** 231 *illus.*, 239 *car.*

micronucleus: the smaller nuclear mass in ciliated protists; active in conjugation and sexual reproduction **272,** 272 *illus.*, 273 *illus.*

microorganisms: 42 *nw.*

micropyle: the opening in a seed coat for entry of pollen and water **360,** 360 *illus.*, 361 *illus.*

microscope: 76 *illus.*, *see* compound light, scanning electron, electron

microspheres: 229 *lab.*

microspore: reproductive cell in plants that gives rise to sperm **360,** 360 *illus.*, 361 *illus.*

microtubules: hollow tube-like filaments made of protein and found in certain cell components **85**

migration: instinctive seasonal movement of animals **561,** 561 *illus.*

migratory animals: 542 *t.crit.*, 732

mildew: 282

Miller, Carlos (1923–): 384, 384 *illus.*

Miller, Stanley (1930–): 228, 228 *illus.*, 230

millipedes: 435, 445 *illus.*

mimicry: a structural adaptation that provides protection for an organism because its appearance is a copy of another organism **210,** 210 *illus.*, 211 *t.crit.*

mineral: an inorganic substance that serves as a building material or takes part in chemical reactions in an organism **102** *illus.*, **624,** 624 *table*

mitochondria: (mite uh KAHN dree un) cytoplasmic organelle in living cells containing enzymes that release energy from the chemical bonds of food molecules   18 *illus.*, **84,** 84 *illus.*, 121 *illus.*, 678 *illus.*

mitosis: the division of the nucleus of a cell into two nuclei containing identical DNA   **145,** 158 *illus.*, 159, 686

mixture: a mingling together of two or more substances without the occurrence of a reaction   **58,** 58 *illus.*

model leaves: 320 *lab.*

modifier gene: a regulatory gene that changes the expression of other genes   **164**

molecule: a particle in which atoms bond together by sharing electrons in covalent bonds   18 *illus.*, 19 *illus.*, **55,** 55 *illus.*, 57 *illus.*, 58 *illus.*, 60 *illus.*, 63 *illus.*, 81 *illus.*, 96 *illus.*, 102 *illus.*, 103 *illus.*, 112 *illus.*, 117 *illus.*, 118 *illus.*, 119 *illus.* and *nw.*, 132 *nw.*, 139 *illus.*, 187 *illus.*, 509 *tech.*, 642 *nw.*

mollusks: 422–427, 422 *illus.*, 426 *illus.*, 427, 462 *illus.*, 473 *car.*

molting: the shedding of an outer covering   **436,** 436 *illus.*, **514**

moneran: a unicellular prokaryote organism with no formed nucleus; comprising the Kingdom Monera; bacteria, cyanobacteria   38 *illus.*, **42,** 43 *t.crit.*, 254, 254 *illus.*, 260, 261, 261 *illus.*, 287

monocot: 350, 378, 378 *nw.*, 379 *illus.*

monohybrid cross: a cross that involves only a single trait with two phenotypes   178 *illus.*, **179,** 179 *illus.*

monomer: the molecular subunit of a polymer   **63,** 63 *illus.*, 64 *illus.*, 65 *illus.*, 69 *illus.*

monosaccharide: the simplest type of carbohydrate; monomer of which all carbohydrates are made   **65,** 65 *illus.*

monosomy: the condition of a zygote that has only one chromosome of a pair; usually lethal   **168**

monotreme: (MAWN uh treem) a mammal that lays eggs   **530,** 530 *illus.*

Morgan, Thomas Hunt (1866–1945): 160 *illus.*

mosquitoes: 247 *illus.* and *nw.*, 597 *nw.*, 700

mosses: 333, 333 *illus.*, 334 *illus.*, 335 *illus.*, 336, 337 *illus.*

moth mullein: 354 *t.crit.*

motivation: an internal need that causes an organism to act   **554**

motor neurons: 576 *illus.*

Mount St. Helens: 724 *nw.*

multicellular organism: an organism consisting of many cells   **17,** 17 *illus.*, 19 *illus.*, 29, 43, 44, 396, 397 *illus.*, 573 *tech.*

multiple alleles: a set of three or more alleles, only two of which can be present in a somatic cell at the same time   **186,** 186 *illus.* and *table*

muscle system: 606–609

muscle tissue: tissue composed of cells containing contractile fibers; three types are smooth, cardiac, and skeletal   21, 23, **572,** 572 *illus.*, 573 *tech.*

mushrooms: 288 *illus.*, 290, 296 *illus.*, 297 *illus.*, 299 *nw.*

mussels: 425 *tech.*

mutagen: an agent as a radioactive element or ultraviolet light that causes biological mutation   **166,** 166 *illus.*

mutation: a permanent change in the genetic material of a cell   **166,** 167 *illus.* and *nw.*

mutualism: symbiotic relationship in which both species derive benefit   **255,** 430, 703, 703 *illus.*, 726

mycelium: the mass of hyphae that comprises a fungus growth   **288,** 289, 290, 302

mycologist: 292, 297, 300 *car.*

mycorrhiza: (mi koh RI zuh) a symbiotic relationship between plant roots and fungi, which enables roots to absorb some nutrients more efficiently   **302,** 302 *illus.* and *nw.*, 314

myelin: 577 *nw.*, 578 *nw.*

myofibril: (mi oh FI brul) small protein fibers that make up muscle tissue; made up of actin and myosin   **607,** 607 *illus.*, 608 *illus.*

myosin: (MI uh sun) the protein that comprises the thick filaments of myofibrils   **607**

N

nastic movement: a reversible, responsive movement of a plant   **386,** 386 *illus.*

natural classification: 35, 37

natural resource: any part of the natural environment used by humans for their benefit; includes soil, water, plants, and animals   **741**

natural selection: the theory that a mechanism for change in populations occurs when organisms with characteristics most favorable for survival in a particular environment are able to pass these traits on to offspring **207,** 208 *lab.,* 209, 209 *illus.,* 210 *illus.,* 211 *t.crit.,* 212 *illus.,* 214 *illus.*

Nautilus: 426 *illus.*

Neanderthal: fossil form of the *H. sapiens* hominid with a short, heavy body, massive bones, a small chin, and large brow ridges; used well-made stone tools to kill large animals **237,** 237 *nw.*

Needham, John (1713–1781): 225

negative-feedback system: hormone regulation in the human body occurring when the gland is signaled to slow down production of a hormone **589,** 589 *illus.*

nematocyst: in cnidarians, a capsule containing a sharp barb that delivers a poison for obtaining food or self defense; on tentacles **404,** 424

nephron: the functional unit in the kidney through which metabolic wastes and excess water are filtered from the blood **651,** 651 *illus.,* 652 *illus.*

neritic zone: (nuh RIHT ihk) the shoreline waters from the shore to the end of the continental shelf **736,** 736 *illus.*

nerve net: the simplest form of a nervous system with no center of control such as a brain; found in simple invertebrates **405,** 405 *illus.*

nerve tissue: tissue composed of cells that have the ability to respond to stimuli and transmit impulses **572,** 572 *illus.*

nervous system: 575–587

neuron: a nerve cell, including the cell body, axon, and dendrites, that conducts impulses; the functional unit of the nervous system **576,** 576 *illus.,* 578 *nw.*

neurotransmitter: a chemical that crosses a synapse and stimulates a change in polarization in the next neuron **577,** 577 *illus.*

neutron: 52

niche: (NITSH) the role a species plays in its community **701,** 708, 726

nicotinamide dinucleotide (NAD): 116, 116 *illus.*

nitrogen: 52, 260 *nw.,* 710 *t.crit.,* 712, 712 *illus.* and *nw.*

nitrogen bases: four organic ring structures of DNA—adenine, quanine, cytosine, and thymine **131,** 132 *illus.* and *nw.,* 138 *nw.*

Nobel Prize: 14 *nw.*

nocturnal: an animal that moves about only at night **429**

non-biodegradable: a substance that cannot be chemically degraded or decomposed by natural effectors **753,** 753 *t.crit.*

nondisjunction: failure of paired chromosomes to separate during the process of mitosis **168**

nonrenewable resource: a natural resource available in limited amounts and is not replaceable by natural processes **742,** 742 *illus.*

nonspecific defense mechanisms: 663

notochord: a tough, flexible, rodlike structure that runs along the back of an animal; only in the embryo in most vertebrates **480,** 481 *illus.*

nucleic acid: a large complex macromolecule that stores information in the form of a code; DNA, RNA **69,** 69 *illus.,* 250 *illus.,* 712, 713

nucleolus: a structure within the nucleus that produces ribosomes **79**

nucleotides: the individual monomers that link together to form a nucleic acid; made up of a nitrogen base, a ribose sugar, and a phosphate group **69,** 69 *illus.,* 132 *illus.* and *nw.,* 138 *nw.,* 203 *nw.*

nucleus (atomic): the central portion of an atom; made up of tightly packed protons and neutrons 37 *illus.,* 42, **52,** 53 *illus.,* 69 *tech.*

nucleus (cell): the organelle that acts as a control center in a eukaryotic cell **79,** 79 *illus.,* 86 *t.crit.,* 107 *illus.* and *nw.,* 155, 672 *t.crit.,* 678 *illus.*

nudibranchs: 423 *illus.,* 424

nutrients: 324 *tech.,* 626 *lab.*

nutrition: 289, 289 *illus.,* 613, 622, 628

nymph: a preadult stage of incomplete metamorphosis in some arthropods; resembles the adult form closely **437,** 437 *illus.*

O

Obelia colony: 407 *illus.* and *nw.*

obligate aerobe: an organism (bacterium) that requires free oxygen to live **256**

obligate anaerobe: an organism (bacterium) that will live or grow only in the absence of free oxygen; does not use oxygen during respiration **256**

observation: 13, 13 *illus.*

Observing and Inferring: 809 *sk.hbk.*

observing the cell cycle: 149 *lab.*

occipital lobe: 583 *illus.*

octopus: 427 *illus.*

oligochete worms: 428, 428 *illus.*

oligotrophic: (AHL ih goh TROH fihk) freshwater lakes that are cold and deep, with few nutrients, but large amounts of dissolved oxygen **737**

omnivore: a consumer that gets its nourishment from plants as well as animals **704,** 704 *illus.*

On the Origin of Species By Means of Natural Selection (Darwin, 1859): 207

Oparin, Alexander (1894–1980): 227–228

open circulatory system: a system in which blood moves through vessels and then into open spaces around body organs bathing them directly with oxygen-containing blood **423**

Ophiuroidea: 464

opposable thumb: a thumb in some mammals, which moves opposite the fingers and can touch each, allowing a grasping advantage **540,** 540 *illus.*

orbiting platforms: 735 *tech.*

order: a category below a class and above a family, comprised of related families **37**

organ: a combination of tissues in the form of a structure that performs a specific function **19,** 19 *illus.,* 574 *table*

organ system: a group of organs that work together to carry out life functions **19,** 19 *illus.*

organ transplants: 298

organelle: a membrane-bound cell structure that performs one or more functions 18 *illus.,* **19,** 233 *illus.*

organic compounds: 62, 65 *nw.*

organism: an individual that carries out all life functions **17,** 17 *illus.,* 20 *illus.,* 21 *illus.,* 22 *illus.,* 104 *illus.,* 107 *illus.,* 136 *illus.,* 144 *car.,* 231 *illus.,* 239 *car.,* 464 *illus.,* 553 *illus.*

Organizing Information: 810–813 *sk.hbk.*

origins: 541, 541 *illus.,* 573–574

osculum: (AHS kyuh lum) the large opening at the top of a sponge through which water flows **401**

osmosis: the diffusion of fluid through a semipermeable membrane **97,** 97 *illus.* and *nw.,* 99 *illus.,* 105 *t.crit.*

Osteichthyes: 486

osteocytes: (AHS tee uh sites) bone cells that produce the system of canals within the Haversian system **603**

osteoporosis: 605

ostracoderms: 488

outbreeding: the fertilization of gametes from unrelated parents **175,** 176 *illus.*

ovary: the basal portion of a pistil in a seed plant; the organ in an animal that produces eggs **370,** 370 *illus.,* 679, 679 *illus.* and *nw.*

oviduct: the fallopian tube; the tube through which an egg passes from an ovary to the uterus **679,** 684, 685 *illus.*

ovulation: release of an egg from the surface of the ovary **679,** 681, 681 *illus.,* 682 *illus.*

ovule: a structure in the ovary of a seed plant **351,** 351 *illus.,* 358 *illus.,* 360 *illus.,* 361 *illus.*

oxygen: 53 *illus.,* 116 *illus.,* 127 *t.crit.*

oxytocin: 692 *nw.*

ozone layer: 28

P

pacemaker: tissue in the right atrium that regulates heartbeat rhythm **648,** 648 *illus.* and *nw.*

paleontologist: 239 *car.*

Paleozoic: 30 *illus.,* 340 *t.crit.,* 403, 440, 488, 496, 541

pancreas: (PAN kree us) a gland behind the stomach that secretes digestive enzymes and produces insulin 589 *illus.,* 591, **617,** 617 *illus.*

panda: 543

pap test: 684 *illus.*

paramecium: 272, 272 *illus.,* 273 *illus.*

parasite: an organism that lives in a host organism and may or may not harm its host **267,** 297, 301, 417, 419 *illus.,* 420 *illus.,* 421 *illus.,* 450 *illus.,* 492 *illus.*

parasitic disease: 298, 419 *illus.* and *nw.,* 420 *nw.,* 421 *illus.*

parasitize: 703 *illus.*

parasympathetic nervous system: 580

parenchyma: the plant tissue made up of thin-walled cells **310**

parthenogenesis: reproduction of an organism from an unfertilized egg **439** *illus.,* 451 *nw.*

particulates: small particles of ash and dust comprising industrial pollutants **746,** 746 *illus.* and *nw.*

passive transport: the movement of substances across plasma membranes without the use of energy **101,** 101 *illus.* and *nw.*

Pasteur, Louis (1822–1895): 11 *nw.,* 226, 226 *illus.,* 252, 253 *illus.*

patenting organisms: 142, 143 *dav.*

Pavlov, Ivan (1849–1936): 555, 555 *illus.*

pea plants: 174 *illus.*, 175 *table*, 176 *illus.*, 177 *illus.*

peanut: 352, 352 *illus.*

pecking order: 563 *illus.*

pedicellaria: (ped uh sehl AH ree uh) a small grasping structure on an echinoderm **460,** 461 *illus.*

pedigree: the ancestral line of an organism 189, **190,** 190 *illus.*

pedipalps: the second pair of appendages on arachnids **441,** 441 *illus.*

pelican: 515 *illus.*

penicillin: 297 *illus.*, 298 *nw.*, 684

peppered moth: 209, 209 *illus.*

pepsin: a digestive enzyme found in gastric juice that catalyzes the breakdown of protein **616,** 616 *illus.* and *nw.*

peptide bond: a covalent bond formed between amino acids **67,** 67 *illus.*, 140 *illus.*

perennial plant: 316

pericycle: a tissue inside the endodermis and around a vascular cylinder; gives rise to lateral roots **312**

peripheral nervous system (PNS): nerves that carry messages to and from the central nervous system **575**

perissodactyl: 539

peristalsis: (per uh STAHL sus) rhythmic progressive wave of muscular contraction in tubes, such as the intestines **614,** 615 *illus.*, 627 *t.crit.*

permafrost: permanently frozen subsoil continuous in tundra regions and occurring locally in perennially frigid areas **733**

Permian: 31

pesticides: 454, 455 *dav.*

petal: leaflike flower part **370,** 371 *illus.*, 374 *illus.*

petiole: the stalk that joins the leaf blade to the stem of a plant **317**

phagocyte: white blood cell that destroys pathogens **664,** 664 *illus.*

phagocytosis: the process by which large particles or whole cells move into a cell **104,** 104 *illus.*

pharmacologist: 509 *tech.*, 691 *car.*

pharynx: the upper expanded portion of the digestive tube between the esophagus and the mouth and nasal cavities **418**

phenol: 259 *tech.*

phenotype: the physical appearance of an organism as opposed to its genotype **160,** 178 *illus.*, 212 *illus.*

pheromone: a hormone secreted by an animal for marking territorial boundaries **559,** 559 *illus.* and *nw.*

Philippine Trench: 466 *nw.*

pH level: 61 *illus.*, 722

phloem: (FLOH em) a complex, food-conducting vascular tissue in higher plants **310,** 310 *illus.*, 311 *illus.*, 313 *illus.*, 314 *illus.*, 315 *illus.*

phospholipid: a group of lipid compounds occurring in plant and animal tissues with stored fats **93,** 93 *illus.*

phosphorus cycle: 713, 713 *illus.*

photolysis: (foh TAHL uh sus) chemical decomposition induced by light generated energy **122**

photoperiodism: responses of organisms to day or night length **387,** 387 *illus.* and *nw.*, 388 *illus.*

photoreception: 583, 583 *illus.*

photosynthesis: the building up of chemical substances under the influence of light **28,** 42, 43 *nw.*, 120, 122 *illus.*, 124, 124 *illus.*, 125 *lab.*, 126, 126 *illus.*, 127 *t.crit.*, 310, 324 *tech.*, 699, 736

phylogenetic classification: 37, 42

phylogenetic tree: 203, 203 *illus.*

phylogeny: the history of species describing its evolutionary development **37,** 38 *illus.*, 40, 203 *illus.* and *nw.*, 403 *illus.*

phylum: a category below kingdom and above a class composed of groups of related classes **37,** 217 *illus.*, 261 *illus.*, 422, 473 *car.*

phytoplankton: floating unicellular algae **270,** 270 *t.crit.*, 707 *nw.*, 736

pigment: 121 *illus.*

pili: a fine filamentous appendage that occurs on some bacteria **255,** 256 *illus.*

pill bug: 444

pinacocyte: thin flat cell that makes up the outer layer of a sponge **400,** 400 *illus.*

pine: 21, 359, 359 *illus.*

pinnae: leaflets of a frond **342,** 342 *illus.*

pinniped: 538

pinocytosis: endocytosis involving the transport of liquid droplets or small particles into a cell **104,** 104 *illus.*

pinworm: 421

pioneer: an organism, such as a lichen, that is one of the first to move into and survive in a barren environment **303,** 724

pistil: the female structure of a flower **370,** 370 *illus.*, 372 *illus.*, 373 *illus.* and *nw.*, 375 *lab.*

premenstrual syndrome (PMS): 684

prey: organisms which are captured and eaten by predators   441 *illus.*, 442 *illus.*, 443 *illus.*, **485,** 487 *nw.*, 507 *illus.*, 528 *illus.*, 537 *illus.*, 538 *illus.*, 709 *illus.*

primary growth: cell division in the apical meristem that results in increase in length   **312**

primary succession: the beginning of new communities in areas that were previously barren   **723,** 723 *illus.*, 724 *illus.* and *nw.*

primates: mammals such as humans, monkeys, and apes   **234,** 234 *illus.*, 236, 236 *illus.*, 239 *car.*, 540, 540 *illus.*, 565 *car.*, 596 *nw.*

prions: 247 *nw.*

probability: the branch of mathematics that predicts the occurrence of chance events   **180,** 180 *illus.*

proboscideans: 539

Prochlorophyta: 260

producer: an organism that generates its own food; an autotroph   **28,** 704, 707 *illus.*

production nursery manager: 389 *car.*

progesterone: (proh JES tuh rahn) a hormone that prepares the uterus for receiving the egg   **682,** 682 *illus.*

proglottid: one of numerous body segments of a tapeworm containing muscles, nerves, flame bulbs, and reproductive organs   **420,** 420 *illus.*

prokaryote: a unicellular microorganism whose cell does not have a limiting membrane around its nuclear material   **37,** 37 *illus.*, 42 *nw.*, 43 *t.crit.*, 145 *illus.*, 230, 232 *illus.*, 254 *illus.*

prophage: viral nucleic acid that reproduces with the host cell DNA without altering the host cell functions   **250,** 250 *illus.*

prophase: the initial stage of mitotic or meiotic cell division   **146,** 146 *illus.*, 149 *lab.*, 158, 159, 162 *illus.*, 679

prostate gland: a gland in the male reproductive system that secretes a basic fluid to protect sperm against the acid environment of the female reproductive tract   **678**

protein: complex nitrogen containing organic compounds of high molecular weight that have amino acids as their basic structural units   **67,** 67 *illus.*, 68 *illus.*, 69 *tech.*, 82 *illus.*, 83 *illus.*, 93 *illus.*, 102 *illus.*, 103 *illus.*, 119 *illus.*, 124 *nw.*, 132 *illus.* and *nw.*, 137 *illus.*, 140, 140 *illus.*, 144 *car.*, 706 *nw.*

prothallus: the heart-shaped gametophyte stage

of a fern; develops from a protonema   335 *illus.*, **341,** 341 *illus.*

protist: simple eukaryote having variable characteristics and comprising the Kingdom Protista   38 *illus.*, 42 *nw.*, **43,** 43 *nw.*, 85 *illus.*, 104 *illus.*, 267, 268 *illus.*, 269, 269 *illus.*, 271, 272 *illus.*, 275, 275 *illus.*, 278 *illus.*, 280 *lab.*, 281, 329

protocell: laboratory produced molecule able to simulate cell division and energy metabolism   **230,** 230 *illus.*

proton: 52, 53 *illus.*

protonema: a small green filament of cells in mosses and ferns; develops from a spore   **334,** 334 *illus.*

protozoan: protists with animal-like characteristics   **267,** 268 *illus.*, 271–274

pseudocoelom: a body cavity only partly lined with embryonic mesoderm   **397,** 397 *illus.*

pseudopod: temporary extension of the cytoplasm of a cell   **271,** 271 *illus.*

puberty: period of time in which changes occur in the human body in response to sex hormones   **680,** 680 *illus.*

puffball: 287, 291 *illus.*, 296

pufferfish: 492

pulse: rhythmic surge of blood through a blood vessel   **649,** 649 *t.crit.*

punctuated equilibrium: a theory that describes the pattern of evolution that states that species remain unchanged for long periods and then are found to change rapidly, in a short span of time, rather than gradually   **211**

Punnett square: (PUN ut) a tool used to predict the possible offspring of crosses between different genotypes   **179,** 179 *illus.*, 180 *illus.*, 187 *illus.*, 189 *t.crit.*, 191 *illus.*, 213 *illus.*

pupa: the preadult stage of change in complete metamorphosis for arthropods   **437,** 437 *illus.*

pus: a fluid that forms in infected tissue; a collection of dead white blood cells and bacteria   **665,** 665 *illus.*

pyramids: 707 *illus.*

pyruvic acid: 115, 115 *illus.*, 116 *illus.*, 117 *illus.*

python: 506

R

radial symmetry: the organization of an organism in which the body part arrangement is circular and produces two identical halves no matter how divided   395, **396,** 396 *illus.,* 463 *illus.*

radiant heat: 127 *t.crit.*

radiation: 261 *illus.,* 416 *illus.,* 440 *illus.,* 470 *illus.,* 489 *illus.,* 508 *illus.,* 518 *illus.,* 531 *illus.,* 699

radicle: the embryonic root of a flowering plant   **352,** 352 *illus.,* 353 *illus.* and *nw.*

radioactive elements: 31

radioactive isotope: 53 *illus.,* 200 *nw.*

radon radiation: 166 *nw.,* 748

radula: a snail's tongue-like organ with rows of teeth used for scrapping food   **423**

rattlesnake: 506

ray-finned fish: 448, 489 *illus.*

rays: stiff narrow rods which support fins on fish; the arms of an echinoderm   **459,** 461 *illus.,* 464 *illus.* and *nw.,* 465 *illus.,* 486 *illus.,* **488**

reaction time: 581 *lab.*

Reading Science: 798 *sk.hbk.*

receptor: 576 *illus.,* 585 *illus.*

recessive trait: a hereditary characteristic not expressed in the presence of another characteristic   **176,** 176 *illus.,* 177 *illus.,* 179 *illus.,* 181 *illus.,* 182 *illus.,* 188 *illus.,* 190 *illus.*

recombinant DNA: DNA resulting from the insertion of a sequence of genes from one organism into the DNA of another organism   **195,** 195 *illus.,* 262, 263 *dav.*

rectum: the last section of the digestive system   **619,** 619 *illus.*

recycling: the reuse of resources   **766,** 766 *illus.,* 767 *illus.* and *nw.,* 776 *illus.*

red algae: 278

red blood cell: cell in the blood that carries oxygen   106 *nw.,* **641,** 641 *table,* 642 *illus.,* 643 *table,* 644 *illus.*

red tide: 277, 277 *illus.*

Redi, Francesco (1626?–1697): 224, 224 *illus.*

reef building corals: 410 *t.crit.*

reflex: an automatic response to a stimulus   **551, 579,** 579 *illus.,* 581 *lab.*

reforestation: the replanting of a forest   **769,** 769 *illus.*

regeneration: the ability of an organism to replace body parts   **418,** 418 *illus.,* 471 *illus.*

regulatory gene: a gene that controls the expression or lack of expression of structural genes   **164**

reindeer moss: 303

relative dating: 31

remora: 492 *illus.*

renewable resource: a natural resource that can be recycled by natural processes   **742**

replication: the process by which a DNA molecule is copied   **134,** 134 *illus.,* 136 *illus.*

reproduction: process by which organisms generate others of the same kind; may be sexual or asexual   **21,** 290, 290 *illus.,* 677, 682, *see* individual phyla and divisions

reproductive isolation: previously interbreeding groups are prevented from producing fertile offspring   **216,** 216 *illus.* and *nw.*

reproductive system: 677, 678 *illus.,* 679 *illus.,* 682

reptile adaptations: 512 *lab.*

reptiles: 501–512, 502 *illus.,* 503, 505, 505 *illus.* and *nw.,* 506 *illus.,* 507 *illus.,* 508 *illus.,* 509 *tech.,* 510, 510 *illus.,* 512 *lab.,* 513, 541 *illus.,* 550 *illus.,* 565 *car.,* 728, 729

resident herds: 542 *t.crit.*

respiration: the process by which food molecules in a cell are broken down to release energy   **115,** 127 *t.crit.,* 438 *illus.,* 635, 636, 636 *illus.,* 648 *nw.*

respiratory system: 189 *t.crit.,* 609 *t.crit.,* 634–640, 635, 636 *illus.,* 638 *illus.*

response: the reaction of an organism to a stimulus   **22,** 22 *illus.* and *nw.,* 23 *illus.*

resting neuron: 576, 576 *illus.*

retail florist: 389 *car.*

retina: a photoreceptive layer of cells in the eye   **583,** 583 *illus.*

retroviruses: 247 *table,* 249, 671 *illus.*

Rh factor: 644, 644 *illus.*

rhizoid: a type of hypha that penetrates food, anchors the fungus and absorbs nutrients; a hairlike structure made up of one or two cells   **293,** 314 *illus.,* **333**

rhizome: 314, 314 *illus.*

Rhizopus: 292 *illus.,* 293 *illus.*

ribonucleic acid (RNA): 137, 137 *illus.,* 138, 138 *illus.,* 139 *illus.,* 140, 140 *illus.,* 247 *illus.* and *nw.,* 671 *illus.*

ribosomal RNA (rRNA): comprises part of the ribosomes   **138,** 138 *illus.*

ribosomes: small, complex particles composed of various proteins and ribonucleic   **82,** 82 *illus.,* 138

rice: 11–15, 14 *tech.*

rigor mortis: 609 *t.crit.*

Rocky Mountain Spotted Fever: 443

rod: 7 *nw.,* 583

rodents: 534, 535 *lab.,* 704 *nw.,* 728, 731

S

species: a group of organisms that look alike and successfully reproduce among themselves **29,** 29 *illus.,* 38 *illus.,* 40 *nw.,* 41 *lab.,* 45 *illus.,* 86 *t.crit.,* 190 *illus.,* 211 *t.crit.,* 214 *illus.,* 239 *car.,* 254 *illus.,* 259 *tech.,* 296 *illus.,* 298 *illus.,* 442 *illus.,* 466 *illus.* and *nw.,* 473 *car.,* 565 *car.,* 705, 720 *illus.,* 724, 726, 737, 754 *illus.* and *nw.,* 771 *illus.* and *nw.*

species variations: 208 *lab.*

specific defense mechanisms: 665

spectrum: 120 *illus.*

sperm: the male germ cell or gamete **156,** 677, 678 *illus.,* 687 *nw.*

sperm whales: 420 *nw.,* 538

Sphagnum moss: 337, 337 *illus.*

spicules: 401 *illus.*

spiders: 441, 441 *illus.,* 442, 442 *illus.*

spider silk and webs: 63 *illus.,* 442, 442 *illus.*

spike moss: 339, 339 *illus.*

spinal cord: 575, 578, 578 *illus.*

spinal fluid: 578

spindle fibers: fiberlike elements extending across a cell **146**

spinneret: a posterior structure in spiders through which silky filaments are secreted **442**

spiny anteater: 530

spiracles: respiratory openings in the exoskeleton of insects or arthropods **438,** 438 *illus.*

spirillum: a bacterium with a spiral form **257,** 257 *illus.*

Spirogyra: 278, 278 *illus.*

spleen: 658, 659 *illus.*

sponges: 399, 400 *illus.,* 401 *illus.,* 402 *illus.* and *nw.,* 403 *illus.,* 411 *illus.,* 464 *illus.,* 473 *car.*

spongin: 401 *illus.*

spongy bone: 602, 603 *illus.*

spontaneous generation: hypothetical development of living organisms from nonliving matter **224,** 224 *illus.,* 225 *illus.*

sporangium: (spuh RAN jee um) a cell in which asexual spores are produced **290,** 290 *illus.* and *nw.*

spore: a cell from which a new organism is produced without fertilization by another cell 272 *illus.,* **273,** 273 *illus.,* 290, 291 *illus.,* 294 *illus.,* 296 *illus.*

sporophyte: the spore-producing phase in algae and plant life cycles **279,** 279 *illus.* and *nw.,* 335 *illus.,* 341 *illus.*

sporozoans: parasitic protozoan protists that reproduce by spores **273,** 274 *illus.* and *nw.*

Squamata: 505

squid: 426 *illus.*

stabilizing selection: a type of natural selection that favors the average individuals in a population **214,** 214 *illus.*

stamen: the male reproductive structure of a flower **370,** 370 *illus.*

starfish: 459–464, 460 *illus.,* 461 *illus.,* 462 *illus.,* 470

stems: 314–316

sterility: 677 *nw.,* 684

sternum: a long flat bone articulating with the cartilages of and forming the midventral support of most of the ribs; the breast bone **514,** 514 *illus.*

stethoscope: 8 *illus.,* 647

Stewart, Dr. John (1924–): 509 *tech.*

stigma: the rough or sticky surface of the pistil to which pollen grains will stick in flowering plants **370,** 370 *illus.,* 372 *illus.,* 373 *illus.* and *nw.*

stimulant: any drug that speeds up the activities of the nervous system 585 *illus.,* **586,** 587 *table*

stimulus: the condition that provokes a reaction from an organism **22,** 22 *illus.* and *nw.,* 23 *illus.,* 583

stolon: a type of hypha that grows across the surface of food and produces a mass of mycelium **292**

stomach: a muscular pouch-like organ of the digestive system **616,** 616 *illus.* and *nw.*

stomata: small pores in the surfaces of leaves **318,** 318 *illus.*

strobilus: a clublike cluster of spore-bearing leaves in a club moss **339,** 339 *illus.,* 340 *illus.*

stroma: the supporting material that surrounds the grana in a chloroplast thylakoid **121**

structural gene: controls the production of polypeptide chains and proteins **164**

style: the usually slender part of a pistil **370,** 370 *illus.*

substrate: 68, 68 *illus.*

succession: the orderly, predictable gradual change in a community over time; primary and secondary **723,** 725 *nw.,* 737

succulents: 321

sucrose: 65 *illus.*

sugar: 65, 65 *illus.,* 324, 325, 325 *illus.*

Sumiki, Yusuke (b. 1901): 384

suspension: dispersion through a liquid of a solid in finely divided particles large enough to be detected by optical means **59**

Sutton, Walter (1877–1916): 160

swan, mute: 520

swim bladder: a thin-walled internal sac in a bony fish, filled with air, controls depth to which fish descend **487**, 487 *illus.*

swordfish: 559

symbiosis: a close association between two organisms; usually mutually beneficial **232**, 232 *illus.*

symbiosis hypothesis: theory of eukaryote cell evolution; ancestral plant and animal cells evolved as a result of a mutually helpful relationship between anaerobic prokaryotes and aerobic bacteria **232**, 232 *illus.*, 233 *illus.*

sympathetic nervous system: 580 *illus.*

synapse: the space between an axon of one neuron to the dendrite of another over which a nerve impulse is transmitted **577**, 577 *illus.*

syphilis: 661

system: *See* organ system

Tables: 811 *sk. hbk.*

tadpole stage: 493 *illus.*, 494 *nw.*, 497

taiga: 732, 733 *illus.* and *nw.*

tapeworm: 420, 420 *illus.* and *nw.*

taproots: 314, 314 *illus.*

target tissue: the specific tissue affected by a particular hormone **588**, 588 *illus.*

Tasmanian devil: 532

taste buds: sensory receptors on the tongue **582**, 582 *illus.*

Tatum, Edward (1909–1975): 164

taxonomists: 40

taxonomy: the science, laws, or principles of classification **34**, 35, 36, 37 *illus.*

T cells: lymphocytes involved in cellular immunity **666**, 667 *illus.*

technology: the practical application of science **5**

teeth: 614, 614 *illus.;* in mammals: 527, 526–527 *illus.*

telophase: the final phase of mitosis, in which the chromosomes of daughter cells are grouped in new nuclei 146 *illus.*, **147**, 149 *lab.*

temperate forests: 730, 731 *illus.*, 732 *illus.*

tendons: the material that attaches muscles to the skeleton **603**, 607

tentacle: in a cnidarian, the long structures surrounding the mouth used for obtaining food **404**, 405 *illus.*, 406 *nw.*, 410 *t.crit.*, 423, 427 *illus.*

termites: 272, 453, 453 *illus.*

terracing: farming by creating level strips of land on a slope **768**, 768 *illus.*

terrestrial adult stage: 493 *illus.*

terrestrial biomes: 726, 727 *illus.*

territory: an area that is defended against others of the same species **558**, 558 *illus.*, 559 *illus.* and *nw.*

testcross: a genetic cross between an organism showing the homozygous recessive trait to determine the genotype of the other organism 190, **191**, 191 *illus.*

testes: 677 *nw.*, 679 *nw.*

testosterone: (teh STAHS tuh rohn) the male sex hormone that influences the development of male characteristics **680**

thalamus: a portion of the brain that receives and sends all sensory signals to the cerebrum except smell **578**

thallus: a simple, flat structure in plants that has no stems or leaves **336**, 336 *illus.*, 337 *illus.*

theory: a scientific explanation in which there is a high degree of confidence **14**, 14 *nw.*

therapsids: mammal-like reptiles that lived during the Paleozoic era **541**, 541 *illus.*

thermoacidophiles: 260

thorax: 438 *illus.*

threatened species: a species with a population so small in numbers that it is in danger of becoming extinct **510**

three-dimensional image: 165 *tech.*

thylakoid membranes: (THI luh koyd) a series of membranes in a chloroplast within which solar energy is trapped **121**

thymus: 658, 659 *illus.*, 666

thyroid: 590

tick: 435, 441, 443 *illus.*

tissue: a group of functionally similar cells **19**, 19 *illus.*, 571, 572, 572 *illus.*

tissue fluid: fluid that is collected by lymph capillaries **657**, 658 *illus.*

tissue plasminogen activator: 69 *tech.*

toads: 493 *illus.*, 494, 494 *illus.* 563 *nw.*

tobacco mosaic virus: 252 *illus.*

tonsils: 658, 659 *illus.*

tortoise: 504

toxic shock syndrome (TSS): 684

toxic waste: 752 *illus.*, 756, 757

trachea: (TRAY kee uh) the main tubelike structure through which air passes to and from the lungs **636,** 636 *illus.*

tracheal tube: the internal respiratory tube of insects and some terrestrial arthropods **438,** 438 *illus.*

tracheid: one of the elongated tapering supporting and conductive cells in woody tissue **310**

transcription: formation of RNA on sections of the DNA molecule **138,** 138 *illus.* and *nw.,* 139 *illus.*

transfer RNA (tRNA): nucleotides that transfer amino acids to ribosomes for addition to the protein chain **138,** 138 *illus.* and *nw.*

translation: process by which mRNA is read and converted into a specific sequence of amino acids in a protein **140,** 140 *illus.*

translocation: the transfer of a chromosome segment from its usual position to a chromosome of a different homologous pair **167,** 167 *illus.*

transmission electron microscope (TEM): an advanced microscope that intensifies magnification by passing a beam of electrons through an object **77,** 78 *illus.*

transpiration: the process through which plants lose water vapor **322,** 322 *illus.* and *nw.,* 323 *illus.*

transport proteins: proteins embedded in lipid bilayers of plasma membranes that facilitate transport of materials through the membranes **101,** 101 *illus.* and *nw.*

trial and error: a behavior in which an organism receives a reward for making a particular response **553**

trichina: 421, 421 *nw.*

trickle system: a practical and efficient method of agricultural irrigation **765,** 765 *illus.*

trilobites: 200, 443

trimester: 687

trisomy: three of a particular chromosome instead of the normal pair of homologous chromosomes **168**

trophic levels: a feeding stratum in a food chain of an ecosystem **705,** 706 *illus.*

tropical rain forests: 340, 344, 345 *dav.,* 728, 728 *nw.,* 729, 729 *illus.,* 735 *tech.,* 770, 770 *illus.*

tropism: orientation movement of a plant **386,** 386 *illus.*

Trypanosoma: 272 *illus.*

tsetse fly: 272

tube feet: footlike extensions of the radial canals of and controlled by the water vascular system in echinoderms; capable of powerful grasping **460,** 460 *illus.,* 461 *illus.,* 462 *illus.,* 464 *nw.*

tundra: 733, 733 *nw.,* 734 *illus.*

tunicates: 479 *nw.,* 480 *illus.,* 481 *illus.*

Turbellaria: 417, 417 *illus.,* 418 *illus.*

turgor pressure: (TUR gur) the pressure that builds in a plant cell as a result of osmosis **98**

turtles: 398 *illus.,* 503, 503 *illus.* and *nw.,* 511 *illus.*

tympanic membrane: a circular structure in a frog's head that responds to air or water vibrations and transmits them to the inner ear and to the brain **494** *illus.,* **495**

tympanum: a thin membrane covering an organ of hearing in insects **448,** 448 *illus.*

types of muscles: 572, 572 *illus.,* 606, 606 *illus.,* 607, 607 *illus.,* 609 *t.crit.*

Typhoid Mary (1868?–1938): 662 *nw.*

U

ultrasound: 690, 690 *illus.*

umbilical cord: a structure that attaches the embryo to the wall of the uterus **686,** 686 *illus.*

unicellular organism: a single celled organism in which all life functions are carried out **17,** 17 *illus.,* 29, 37, 43, 44, 410 *t.crit.*

unsaturated: 66 *illus.* and *nw.,* 67 *illus.*

urethra: a tube through which urine and sperm leave the body **678**

Urey, Harold (1893–1981): 228, 228 *illus.,* 230

urinary system: 651, 651 *illus.,* 652 *illus.,* 653 *illus.*

urine: waste fluid excreted by the kidneys **652,** 652 *illus.,* 653 *illus.*

Urochordata: 479–480

Urodela: 495

usefulness of mammals: 543, 543 *nw.*

Using a Microscope: 804–805 *sk.hbk.*

uterine contractions: 692 *nw.*

uterus: a hollow, muscular organ in the female mammal in which offspring develop **526,** 685 *illus.*

V

vaccine: a material composed of weakened or dead pathogens capable of causing immunity 251 *nw.*, 252, **673,** 673 *illus.*

vacuole: (VAK yuh wohl) a membrane-bound cavity within a cell that functions in digestion, storage, secretion, or excretion **83,** 83 *illus.*

vagina: a muscular tube at the cervix that opens to the outside of the female body **679**

van Leeuwenhoek, Anton (1632–1723): 76, 76 *illus.*, 267

Variables, Constants, and Controls: 802–803 *sk.hbk.*

variation: 29

vascular tissue: the conducting tissue found in higher plants **309,** 310 *illus.*, 311 *illus.*, 313 *illus.*, 314 *illus.*, 315 *illus.*

vas deferens: (VAS DEF uh runz) a tube connected to the urethra just below the bladder **678**

vasoconstrictor: 586

vector: an organism capable of transmitting an infectious agent among vertebrates **247,** 247 *illus.* and *nw.*

vein: blood vessel that carries blood toward the heart **645,** 645 *illus.*

vena cavae: 646, 646 *illus.*

venom: 507 *illus.*, 509 *tech.*

ventral: on or near the undersurface of an animal body **417,** 417 *illus.*

ventral foot: 424 *illus.*

ventricles: the two chambers of the heart from which blood circulates to the lungs and the body **646,** 646 *illus.*, 647 *illus.*, 649 *t.crit.*

Venus flytrap: 321 *illus.*

vertebrate: an animal with a backbone 239 *car.*, 395, **399,** 479, 482 *illus.*, 502 *illus.*

vessel cell: an elongated cell with open ends in plants **310**

vestigial structures: an organism's body parts that provide evidence of evolution; body parts that are reduced in size and appear to serve no function **202**

Victoria, Queen of England (1819–1901): 188, 189

villus: projections of the mucous membrane of the small intestine that serves as sites of adsorption **618,** 618 *illus.*

vine: 14 *tech.* and *illus.*

Virchow, Rudolf (1821–1902): 77

virus: 6 *nw.*, 42 *nw.*, 69 *tech.*, 245, 246, 246 *illus.*, 247 *illus.*, *nw.* and *table*, 249 *illus.*, 250 *illus.*, 251, 251 *illus.*, 252, 252 *illus.*, 253, 253 *illus.*, 402 *nw.*, 672 *t.crit.*, 703

vital minerals: 624 *table*

vitamin: complex organic substances found in plant and animal tissue; required in small quantities for controlling metabolic processes 116, 599, **624,** 624 *nw.*, 625 *table*, 703 *nw.*

vocal cords: sound-producing bands of tissue in the throat **494,** 494 *nw.*, 635, 637 *illus.*

volcano: 127 *t.crit.*, 723 *illus.*, 724 *nw.*

Volume: 807–808 *sk.hbk.*

voluntary muscle: the type of muscle that is consciously controlled 572, 572 *illus.*, **607,** 609 *t.crit.*

Volvox: 277

vulture: 516 *illus.*

W

wallaby: 502

Wallace, Alfred Russel (1823–1913): 207

water cycle: 713, 714 *illus.*, 722, 722 *illus.*

water-dwelling mammals: 538, 538 *illus.*

water moccasin: 506

water mold: 282

water molecules: 58 *illus.*, 59, 60 *illus.*

water pollution: 764 *lab.*

water vascular system: an internal closed system of reservoirs and ducts containing a watery fluid in echinoderms that controls movement, respiration, and food capture **460,** 461 *illus.*

Watson, Dr. James (1928–): 133, 163 *nw.*

wave of depolarization: 576 *illus.*

whale: 270, 491 *nw.*

whisck ferns: 342

white and grey matter: 578 *nw.*

white blood cells: blood cells that protect the body from disease; contain nuclei 641 *table*, **642,** 670 *lab.*

wildebeest: 542 *t.crit.*, 730

wildlife harvesting: 544, 545 *dav.*

wildlife photographer: 565 *car.*

wildlife preserve: an area reserved and secured for wildlife protection **771,** 771 *illus.* and *nw.*, 772 *illus.*

wildlife specialist: 565 *car.*

wings: 438 *illus.*, 447, 447 *illus.*

wolf, red: 543
Wolffia: 44 *nw.*
wombat: 532 *illus.*
wood duck: 551 *illus.*
World Health Organization (WHO): 419 *nw.*, 662

X rays: 166, 604 *nw.*, 605
xylem: (ZI lum) the principal water-conducting tissue and the chief supporting tissue of higher plants **310,** 310 *illus.*, 311 *illus.*, 313 *illus.*, 314 *illus.*, 315 *illus.*

Yabuta, Teijiro (1888–1977): 384
yeast: 37 *illus.*, 116, 116 *illus.*, 290 *illus.*, 294
Yellowstone National Park: 353, 353 *illus.* and *nw.*, 725, 725 *illus.*, 777 *car.*

zooplankton: floating aquatic animal-like protists **270,** 270 *t. crit.*
zooxanthellae: 410 *t. crit.*
zygospore: a thick-walled resting spore formed in unfavorable conditions 277, 277 *illus.*, **278,** 278 *illus.*, 279 *illus.* and *nw.*, 292, 292 *illus.*
zygote: a single cell that is the result of fertilization 168, **177,** 396, 397 *illus.*, 407, 685, 686
zygote fungi: 292, 292 *illus.*, 293, 293 *illus.*

PHOTO CREDITS

ACKNOWLEDGMENTS

Page 153: From *The Log From the Sea of Cortez* by John Steinbeck. Copyright John Steinbeck and Edward F. Ricketts 1941, copyright John Steinbeck 1951, reproduced by permission of Curtis Brown, London, on behalf of the author's estate.

Copyright 1941 by John Steinbeck and Edward F. Ricketts, renewed © 1969 by John Steinbeck and Edward F. Ricketts, Jr. Reprinted by permission of Viking Penguin, a division of Penguin Books USA Inc.

Page 393: From *The Edge of the Sea* by Rachel Carson, illustrated by Bob Hines. Copyright © 1955 by Rachel L. Carson. Copyright © renewed 1983 by Roger Christie. Copyright © renewed 1983 by Robert W. Hines. Reprinted by permission of Houghton Mifflin Co.

Page 568: Copyright © 1933, 1961 James Thurber. From *My Life and Hard Times,* published by Harper & Row.

Every reasonable effort has been made to trace the owners of copyrighted material and to make due acknowledgment. Any errors or omissions drawn to our attention will be gladly rectified in future editions.

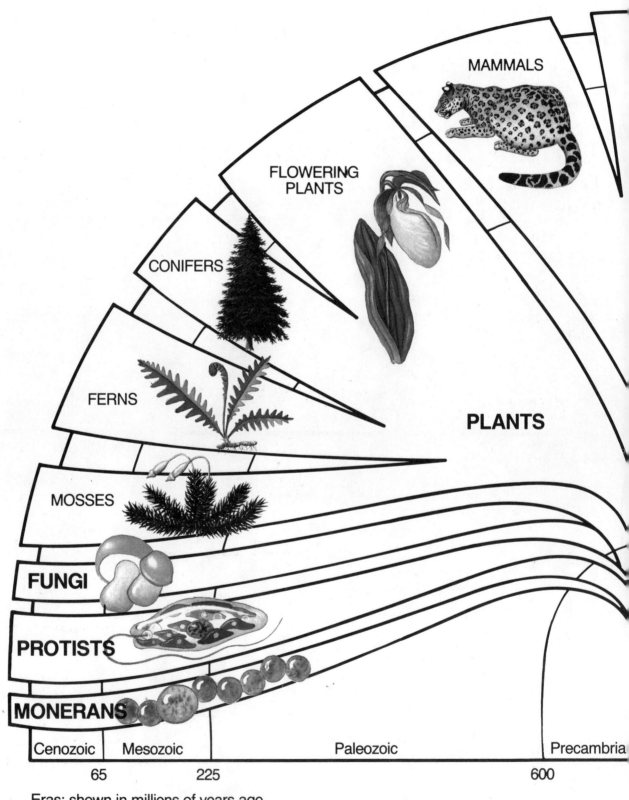

MAMMALS

FLOWERING
PLANTS

CONIFERS

FERNS

PLANTS

MOSSES

FUNGI

PROTISTS

MONERANS

Cenozoic	Mesozoic	Paleozoic	Precambria

65 225 600

Eras: shown in millions of years ago